Data Network Design

McGraw-Hill Series on Computer Communications

ISBN	AUTHOR	TITLE
0-07-005147-X	Bates	*Voice and Data Communications Handbook*
0-07-005669-2	Benner	*Fibre Channel: Gigabit Communications and I/O for Computer Networks*
0-07-005590-4	Black	*Frame Relay Networks: Specifications and Implementation*, 2/e
0-07-005560-2	Black	*TCP/IP and Related Protocols*, 2/e
0-07-011486-2	Chiong	*SNA Interconnections: Bridging and Routing SNA in Hierarchical, Peer, and High-Speed Networks*
0-07-057688-2	Dhawan	*Mobile Computing*
0-07-020359-8	Feit	*SNMP: A Guide to Network Management*
0-07-021389-5	Feit	*TCP/IP: Architecture, Protocols, and Implementation with IPv6 and IP Security*, 2/e
0-07-024043-4	Goralski	*Introduction to ATM Networking*
0-07-034249-0	Kessler	*ISDN: Concepts, Facilities, and Services*, 3/e
0-07-035968-7	Kumar	*Broadband Communications*
0-07-041051-8	Matusow	*SNA, APPN, HPR and TCP/IP Integration*
0-07-060362-6	McDysan/Spohn	*ATM: Theory and Applications*
0-07-044362-9	Muller	*Network Planning Procurement and Management*
0-07-046380-8	Nemzow	*Ethernet Management Guide*, 3/e
0-07-049663-3	Peterson	*ICP/IP Networking: A Guide to the IBM Environments*
0-07-051506-9	Ranade/Sackett	*Introduction to SNA Networking*, 2/e
0-07-054991-5	Russell	*Signaling System #7*
0-07-057199-6	Saunders	*McGraw-Hill High-Speed LANs Handbook*
0-07-057639-4	Simonds	*Network Security: Date and Voice Communications*
0-07-069416-8	Summers	*ISDN Implementor's Guide*
0-07-063301-0	Taylor	*McGraw-Hill Internetworking Command Reference*
0-07-063263-4	Taylor	*McGraw-Hill Internetworking Handbook*
0-07-063639-7	Terplan	*Effective Management of Local Area Networks*, 2/e
0-07-065766-1	Udupa	*Network Management System Essentials*

Data Network Design

Darren L. Spohn

Second Edition

McGraw-Hill

New York San Francisco Washington, D.C. Auckland Bogotá
Caracas Lisbon London Madrid Mexico City Milan
Montreal New Delhi San Juan Singapore
Sydney Tokyo Toronto

Library of Congress Cataloging-in-Publication Data

Spohn, Darren L.
Data network design / Darren L. Spohn.—2nd ed.
p. cm.—(McGraw-Hill series on computer communications)
Includes index.
ISBN 0-07-060363-4
1. Computer networks. 2. Computer network protocols. 3. Computer networks—Standards. 4. Computer network architectures. I. Title. II. Series.
TK5105.5.S66 1997
004.6—dc20 96-41060
CIP

McGraw-Hill
A Division of The McGraw-Hill Companies

4 5 6 7 8 9 0 DOC/DOC 9 0 1 0 9 8 7

ISBN 0-07-060363-4

The sponsoring editor for this book was Steven Elliot, the editing supervisor was Stephen M. Smith, and the production supervisor was Pamela A. Pelton.

Printed and bound by R. R. Donnelley & Sons Company.

The first edition of this book was dedicated to my parents, Karl and Regina, and my best friend (now wife), Becky. For this edition I add a dedication to my son, Alexander. There is nothing better in this world than family.

Contents

Preface

PURPOSE OF THIS BOOK

The primary objective of this book is to teach the principles and science of designing a data network through the presentation of a *broad scope* of data and computer communications standards, architectures, hardware, software, protocols, technologies, and services as they relate to designing data networks. The book attempts to take the reader through the entire network design process, from compiling the requirements through design and into optimization techniques. Tried and true methods are presented, augmented by new developments in the industry, thus providing a tome complete with referenced technical details and real world experience.

Emphasis is placed on the predominant technologies of the 1990s and emerging technologies of the next century, including X.25 packet switching, frame relay, SMDS, ATM, and SONET. This book is designed to walk the reader through the process of a data-network design using these technologies, paying attention to both the technical and business decisions required. It is the author's intent to provide a broad overview of these topics with insight into practical design aspects of each, allowing the reader to perform an end-to-end network design. Standards and reference pointers are provided to the reader for further detailed study.

The logical and physical design of hardware and software is not the only process in a network design. Network designs encompass many aspects including making the business case, compiling the requirements, choosing the technology, planning for capacity, vendor selection, and weighing all the issues before the actual design begins. After these efforts have produced a workable design plan, there are additional issues which must be addressed, including operations, maintenance, and management support structures. While resolution of many of these additional tasks often falls to the project manager, many other people must be involved in the many processes affecting the integrity of the design, and must assess the impact of each decision as it relates to the overall network design.

This book will concentrate on the science and art of data-network design, and will include detailed operational descriptions of:

- X.25 packet switching
- Frame relay
- SMDS
- ATM
- SONET

A detailed design book, resplendent with addressing schemes, detailed bus structures, discrete circuit operations, and protocol specifics would take volumes. In fact, one book could be published on each protocol and technology. The primary purpose of this text, however, is to provide a *global view* of these technologies and how they can play a key role in the data-network design process.

INTENDED AUDIENCE

This text is designed for data communications novices through advanced design engineers, including all levels of communications management. Some business and data communications basics are provided in the beginning chapters. The text presents design material at a high level, assuming the reader has access to resources or colleagues with a background in basic data communications and a working knowledge of transmission basics. Although this skill level is assumed, some discussion on hardware and protocol basics is provided. The book serves as professional reading as well as a desktop reference guide, and has been used in many college classrooms across the United States.

It is important to note that this entire text has been rewritten from the first edition. Thanks to everyone for their submissions, corrections, and comments over the past three years.

OVERVIEW OF THIS BOOK

Data Network Design, Second Edition, is divided into six parts.

Part 1 provides the business drivers and networking directions that have shaped data communications.

Chapter 1 defines data-network design through the evolution and history of communications along with the recent move to outsourcing and out-tasking.

Chapter 2 presents the changes in corporate infrastructures and the applications and communications technologies that have enabled us to move in new directions in computer and information networking.

Part 2 provides a broad overview of the standards and services that define data networking: organizations, architectures, circuits, hardware, and protocols.

Chapter 3 presents national and global industry standards organizations, current forums, and the processes of standardization.

Chapter 4 presents the seven-layer OSI Reference Model (OSIRM), standard computer and protocol architectures, the digital hierarchy, the history of ISDN, and the definition of network services.

Part 3 introduces the reader to the basics of transmission, networks, hardware, and switching.

Chapter 5 provides a thorough coverage of network topologies, circuit types and services, a study of private versus switched networks, asynchronous and synchronous transmission methods, and an in-depth review of the predominant types of data-networking hardware.

Chapter 6 provides the reader with a study of multiplexing and switching technologies, including circuit and packet switching.

Part 4 presents a detailed study of protocols and interfaces.

Chapter 7 starts with the first two layers of the OSIRM including the physical layer and the data-link layer, along with its Media Access Control (MAC) and Logical Link Control (LLC) sublayers. The chapter concludes with a study of switching in the LAN environment.

Chapter 8 presents a study of bridging and routing protocols, as well as network and transport layer protocols of the OSIRM. Legacy SNA protocols are presented, including a study of internetworking SNA protocols over routed and switched environments. At this point the reader should understand the basics.

Chapter 9 is devoted solely to the principles and application of packet switching.

Chapters 10 and 11 present the definition, standards, protocols, transmission theory, operation, and service provided by frame relay.

Chapter 12 then presents the theory and application behind SMDS.

Chapters 13 and 14 provide a study of ATM theory and application.

Chapter 15 presents SONET.

These technology chapters in Part 3 explain protocol structure, format, interfaces, and theory. They also contain software, hardware, and design recommendations.

Part 5 steps the reader through defining data-network design requirements, performing the traffic analysis and capacity-planning process, and comparing circuit-, packet-, frame-, and cell-switched technologies.

Chapter 16 assists the designer in analyzing the complete set of user requirements.

Chapter 17 then provides the traffic-analysis calculations that turn these requirements into a capacity plan. These two chapters lead directly into the access design.

Chapter 18 provides numerous comparisons of every aspect of each technology and service.

Chapter 19 provides guidelines for the RFI and RFP processes as well as criteria for choosing a service provider and the future relationship with that service provider.

Part 6 deals with the design and management of networks.

Chapter 20 starts with the access design – the point where the user accesses the network or public network service.

Chapter 21 continues with the backbone design. The backbone is often a switched-network service. This chapter also contains some valuable practical insights on network tuning.

Chapter 22 presents addressing, including a primer on IP and IPX address design.

Chapter 23 presents operations and maintenance issues, as well as network-management protocols and techniques including SNMP and RMON.

Chapter 24 describes design and management tool types, components, and capabilities.

Chapter 25 presents a study of international private and public data networking.

This book also contains several appendixes. *Appendix A* lists the major acronyms and abbreviations used in the book. *Appendix B* provides a reference of national and international standards sources. *Appendix C* gives a reference table for creating IP network address masks. *Appendix D* provides a summary of all IP address subnet mask types. And, finally, the *Glossary* defines common terms associated with the technologies, architectures, services, and protocols encountered throughout the book.

INTRODUCTION

Voice, data, and video – which of these three methods of communications do you use every day? The answer is probably all three. Every day we talk on a fixed or cellular phone, interface with some form of personal or mainframe computer or server (even an ATM cash machine!), or watch television and video tapes at home and at work. But how is information "networked" between those human interface devices – phones, computers, and video display or recorders? Often there are complex data communications networks that aggregate and then transmit and receive this "data" across the neighborhood or across the world. It is with these data-communications networks, or more specifically their design, that we deal with in this book.

Data-communications users are constantly demanding and using more bandwidth or network resources. Portable cellular phones, Internet access from the home, and video phones are just a few examples where the consumer requires more network resources or bandwidth. Distributed computing with client-server applications, voice-data-video integration at the desktop, huge cross-country file transfers of medical imaging files and databases, and desktop video conferencing are a few corporate applications that are driving the need for more bandwidth. And it is not just more bandwidth that consumers want, but cheaper and more flexible bandwidth, and not only dedicated, but on-demand! The data-transfer bandwidths for text, video, voice, and imaging traffic increase exponentially, as do the networks required to transport that traffic.

We are now living in a distributed data world. Everyone needs access to everyone else's data. Networks made of many meshed dedicated circuits are quickly becoming the exception as switched public and private data networks span the globe. Computers need to talk to one another the same way people pick up the phone and dial anyone in the world. Telecommuting is on the rise and mobile computing is a necessity. Because of these needs, the market for high-speed data transport is exploding. The age of gigabit-per-second data transport is here. Local and metropolitan area networks (LANs and MANs) have crossed the 100 Mbps threshold and wide area network (WAN) communication speeds in the megabits and soon gigabits per second are becoming commonplace. Technologies such as ATM are offering the key WAN platforms over which multimegabit services such as frame relay, SMDS, and IP are being offered. And IP networks continue to proliferate.

Many businesses' bandwidth requirements are exploding, such as medical institutions that transfer multimegabit imaging files, and film-making companies that store and transport video images recorded directly into a computer and digitized. The most important aspect of these style networks is their ability to store and retrieve large image files. For large networks requiring flexible addressing and transfer of data of this type, SMDS and ATM offer alternatives to dedicated private lines. And it seems that ATM-based platforms offering frame relay, IP, SMDS, circuit emulation, and LAN extension and emulation services will provide the longer term solution.

LANs and client-server applications have become an integral element of almost every major corporation. The move is toward visual-oriented end-user interfaces in computer software packages that are becoming icon-based through the use of Graphical User Interfaces (GUIs). As the number of LANs continues to grow, so do their local and wide area interconnectivity requirements. Router networks have replaced the older private line bridge network infrastructures, and they themselves are being somewhat replaced with switching hub technology. Frame relay emerged in the 1990s as the first high-speed, bandwidth-on-demand service to compete directly with private lines. But LAN-to-LAN is not the only technology best served by frame relay. Many businesses have an imbedded SNA traffic base. Much of this traffic is also ideal for frame relay transport. One thing is constant across all of these trends – the need for more bandwidth.

In the search for new technology to provide data transport bandwidths and internetworking of this scale, we often rely on versions of older packet technology. Packet switching has moved into the 1990s in the form of frame relay and cell switching. As services such as frame relay and ATM gain increasing support from equipment vendors and carriers, and IP networks continue to proliferate, the user — as usual — seems to be the driving factor as to which technology will succeed.

Virtual LAN capability is appearing in LAN switches to redefine communication flows and reduce routing requirements within the customer premises environment. Routers still play a key role, but now the user must decide not only when to bridge or route but also when to route or switch. A number of 100 Mbps technologies such as Fiber Distributed Data Interface (FDDI) and 100 Mbps Ethernet are allowing existing LAN users to increase their transfer speeds in the LAN almost tenfold. LAN segmentation down to single user LANs is also helping. Synchronous Optical NETwork (SONET) standards are now providing fiber-optic, virtually error-free MAN and WAN transport in speeds in the gigabit-per-second range for these high-bandwidth services, and ATM hubs and switches are now on the market to offer new levels of user quality of service and traffic segmentation and optimization.

Designing a data network to handle a diverse user application and technology base is a complex task. Capacity requirements begin to boggle the mind as LAN users project peak traffic periods of up to 50:1. With X.25 packet switching, the network provided many services that made the user rely on the network for error correction of data and end-to-end link-level data integrity. Frame and cell networks push this requirement to the end-user CPE and the devices running the applications, and require the end user to apply much more intelligence with higher-layer protocols when transporting data. Now, computer users who once had to worry only about how long it would take to move or access data are now faced with data-transport protocols which promise to deliver a majority of the data, while leaving the discovery of lost data and subsequent retransmission to the transport through application layers. Two very different ways of viewing data communications have merged — the computer user who looks at data transport in the view of delay, and the telecommunications user who views data transport is terms of acceptable levels of lost data, error correction, retransmission, and quality of service. Couple this with multiple protocol and architecture environments and you have quite a challenge in designing a single homogeneous network.

The data-network designer must now bridge the gap between data-transport services and user applications and services, physical and data-link layer protocols and higher-layer protocols. This means building a network which involves both local area and wide area communications. The new developments discussed will bridge the gap between these historically separate LAN and WAN domains and provide the end user with the information required to perform a design that spans both environments. Large-scale, wide-area public networks and services are available that provide connectivity that is flexible and easy to install, with a small amount of delay and high throughput, while offering pricing that is both fixed (like private line service) and usage-based (like IP service). This allows for cost efficiencies while providing higher transport speeds for larger data volumes.

After learning the technologies and services available, many users ask the classic question, "Which service or technology should I use?" This book will show that the answer to this question is based on many factors and may have several answers. There is rarely a single solution, and the decision of technology and service generally come down to what is best for the application and what is affordable — price versus performance — as well as what entails the least change for the user and best positions them for future expansion.

HOW TO USE THIS BOOK FOR COURSES

Many state universities use Data Network Design in their engineering curriculum. The book is designed similar to a textbook in that it teaches the science of data network design in a chronological order, with technology examples augmented by numerous graphics.

Chapters to be taught in a basic architectures, protocols, technologies, and services course (PT1) are Chapters 1 through 15, and 18. Chapters to be taught in an advanced protocols and technologies course (PT2) are Chapters 7 through 25. The student should have a minimum working knowledge of the material contained in Chapters 1 through 6.

Chapters to be included in a pure design course (ND1) are the entire book, with focus on Chapters 16 through 25. The student should have a minimum working knowledge of Chapters 1 through 6, and some knowledge of the material covered in Chapters 7 through 15.

The material in this book can be taught and covered in two or three semesters. Three semesters' worth of study, along with the suggested course outlines and guidelines for selecting the course material, are outlined above. There is some overlap, and the recommended progression is from the basic course PT1, to the advanced course PT2, and finally to the pure design course ND1, with both design tool and test scenario hand calculated network design labs. PT2 and ND1 should begin with the overview chapters shown to reaffirm a working knowledge of basic protocols and their operation, since the advanced protocols are modifications or perturbations of simpler or more complex protocol operations. Labs should contain design problems based on the cumulative knowledge gained from the class reading and outside reading assignments (recent technology updates). The exercises should involve multiple design tool exposure and problems. Special or final exams (all or a portion) should include at least one multiprotocol or multitechnology network design problem. Students should be encouraged to use the text as a "working document", noting any changes as the standards are revised and updated. The author plans to publish updated editions of this book as appropriate technology changes may warrant, and welcomes suggested changes or corrections from readers in writing (current address may be obtained from McGraw-Hill) or via e-mail (dspohn@netsolve.net). Supplemental documentation and instructional tools may be obtained from the author at extra charge.

AUTHOR'S DISCLAIMER

Accurate and timely information is provided up to the date of publication. While many of the standards presented in the First Edition are now final, some of the standards used in this Second Edition are recommendations at the time of writing and are assumed will become final soon after publication. At times, the author will present material that is practical in a large-scale design, but is simply not possible in the normal small-business communications environment. Also, in many cases, examples are presented on a larger scale. The presented material must be scaled down on a case-by-case basis. Many data communications networks operate, and will continue to run, quite well on dedicated private lines, but eventually the economics of switched technologies and services, even on the smallest scale, are worth investigating. Please excuse the blatant assumption that the user is ready to implement these advanced technologies – in many cases it will take some time before they can be implemented. Also, please excuse any personal biases which may have crept into the text.

ACKNOWLEDGMENTS

Many people have helped prepare this book. They have provided comments on various drafts, information on products and services, and other value-added services. In particular, I would like to thank for assistance on the First Edition, Mr. Gene Wahlberg of Bay Networks; Mr. Arthur Henley of E-net; Mr. Ed Braunston of General DataCom; Mr. Charan Khurana and Ms. Margot Peterson of IBM; Ms. Beverly Dygart of MAKE Systems; Mr. Gary Kessler of MAN Technology Corporation; Mr. Lance Boxer, Mr. Carl Geib, Dr.

David McDysan, and Mr. Paul Metzger of MCI; and Dr. James F. Mollenauer of Technical Strategy Associates. Without their help a Second Edition would not have been possible.

For assistance on the Second Edition I would like to thank Mr. Jerry Davis of 3COM; Mr. Joel Adams of Adams Capital Management; Mr. Ron Appleton and Mr. Brian Noel of AT&T; Mr. Bill Backus of Bell Laboratories; Mr. Jim Gayton and Mr. Chuck Sullivan of Cascade Communications; Mr. Doug Hantula and Mr. David O'Leary, and Mr. Dave Travis of Cisco Systems; Mr. Scott Grau of E-net; Mr. Bill Flannigan of Fastcom; Mr. Gary Kessler of MAN Technology Corporation; Mr. Curtis Brownmiller, Mr. Mike Conn, Mr. Herb Frizzell Sr., Dr. David McDysan, Mr. Paul Metzger, and Mr. Scott Thompson of MCI; Mr. Jorge Chong, Mr. Steve Davies, Mr. Mark Hofer, Mr. Penn Rabb, Mr. Michael Turner, and Mr. Craig Tysdal of NetSolve; and Mr. Dave Runnels of Sprint, along with other colleagues who over the last 14 years have shared their knowledge and expertise. They have helped me develop a greater understanding and appreciation for data network design.

This book does not reflect any policy, position, or posture of NetSolve Inc. A caveat should be added that this work was not funded or supported financially by NetSolve or by NetSolve resources. Ideas and concepts expressed are strictly those of the author. Information pertaining to specific vendor or service provider products is based upon open literature freely provided and adapted as required. My friends and associates at NetSolve did support the project in spirit, especially Craig Tysdal, and are hereby thanked.

Much of the networking and computer clip art used in this book was provided by NetDraw. The NetDraw product provides over 1600 high-quality, full color images and symbols. NetDraw is a registered trademark of Network World, Inc. and can be reached at 800-643-4668.

Special thanks go to Mr. Herb Frizzell, Sr. for both the English style and syntax review as well as select submissions, and for enduring the many edits for the Second Edition. And thanks to Senior Editing Supervisor Stephen Smith, Senior Editor Steven Elliot, Assistant Editor Donna Namarato, and all the rest of the staff at McGraw-Hill who assisted me on this project.

And to my wife Becky — her never-ending support throughout has helped me accomplish this project (again!).

The combined support and assistance of these people has made this book possible.

Darren L. Spohn

Data Network Design

Part 1

Data Communications - Business Drivers and Networking Directions

How does one determine when a data communications network is required? Or that an existing data or computer communications network requires a new technology to meet its ever-growing needs? Some may answer, "We need to perform a business case analysis". Others may say, "We know our needs – they are driving us toward one – and we need it now!" Data communications managers and engineers need to solve the questions of why, what, when, and how, and then make business decisions based on present and future data and computer communications.

Part 1 of this book will define network design and the need for data communications. History provides insight into the future. This is also true in data communications, and thus we first study the history of communications. A historical perspective can provide insight into what technologies and services may be successful, as it seems that technologies reinvent themselves in the form of analog or digital, asynchronous or synchronous communications. Outsourcing and outtasking are also important, and a discussion of factors driving the need for outsourcing of data networks will be discussed.

Part 1 next takes you through the many application, technology, and infrastructure changes; business drivers; and the decision processes that determine the actual need for a data network. The dollars and cents "business case" can be accomplished only after the network designer or manager knows and understands the requirements of the business and the users. Part 1 will provide the first step toward defining a statement of work required for a network design analysis.

Chapter

1

Data Communications - Past to Future

This chapter focuses first on defining data network design and the need for a data communications network. We first turn our attention to a discussion of the historical directions of computers and networking. After describing modern day communications, we explore the future computer and networking directions that will carry us into the twenty-first century.

A short review of recent history shows a larger percentage of resources are being dedicated to data compared to voice communications, and data traffic volumes seem to be growing faster than voice. This acceleration is precipitated by the information revolution and an increased dependence on data communications. In this process we explore the world of the data engineer and manager, in particular what to expect in the coming years. This chapter concludes with a discussion of outsourcing and out-tasking trends. Each of these alternatives is analyzed in an objective manner, allowing users to determine if outsourcing is a viable alternative. Outsourcing and out-tasking are playing a key role in communications networks as many companies find the complexities of building and managing an advanced communications network are outside their core competencies. These businesses are turning to professionals to provide full service outsourcing or out-tasking augmentation of existing internal or required skills.

1.1 WHAT IS NETWORK DESIGN?

Network design, specifically data network design, is a broad field of study. It encompasses and interacts with almost every portion of the business. Data is defined as information from which conclusions are drawn. "Data" is often used in the plural to refer to multiple collections of information. Data can reside in microcomputers, minicomputers, mainframes, routers, switches, storage devices, and even the human brain (although for some people this is sometimes questioned). Data units are grouped into bits and bytes, and these units, in multiples, form data streams. Sending data streams over a medium from one point to another is called data transport. The medium that delivers data from point A to point B or point C is called a "network". Figure 1.1 depicts a sample data communications network of three sites, where point A serves as the headquarters and points B and C as remote access sites. This example is oversimplified to demonstrate that the network extends from the output port on a user device to the input port on a remote destination user device, and often includes user premises equipment.

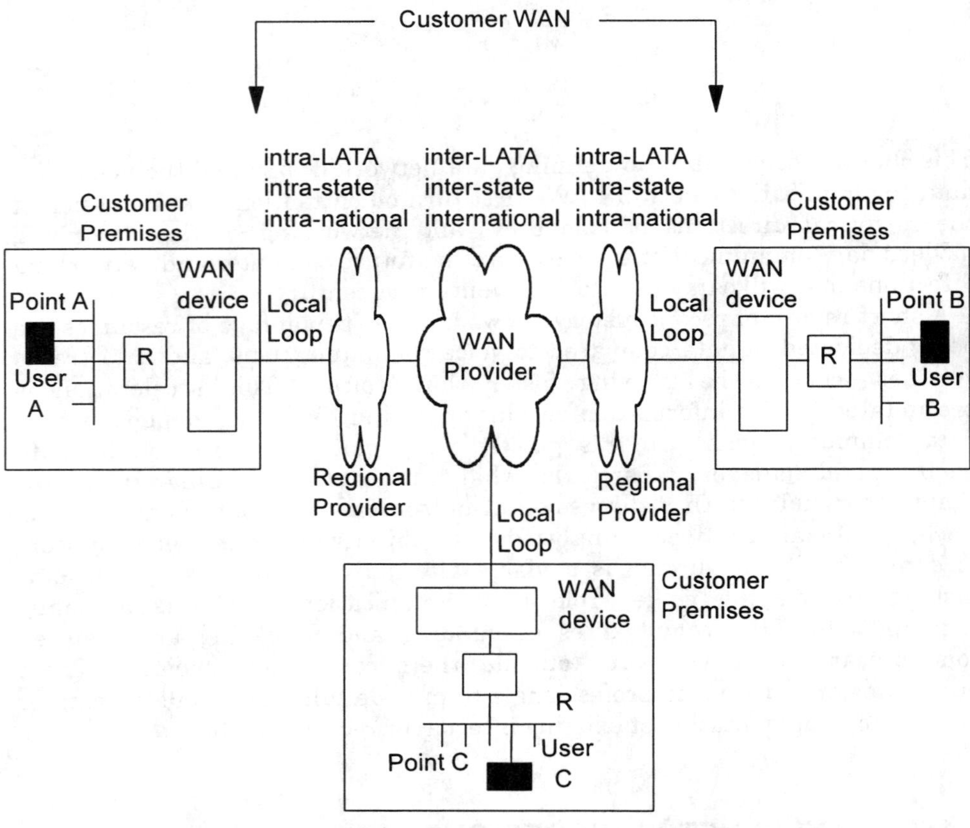

Figure 1.1 Data Communications Network

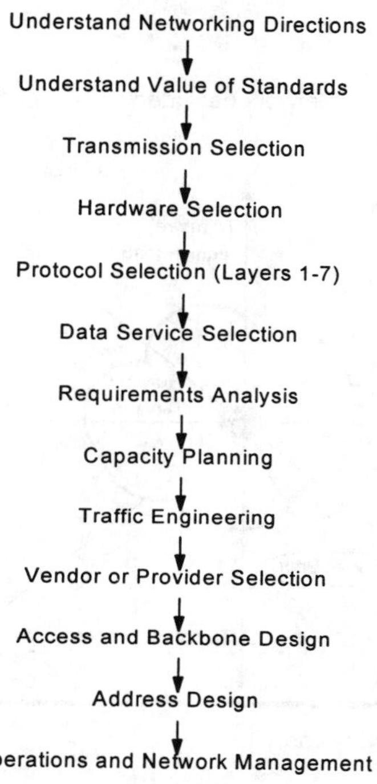

Figure 1.2 Network Design Steps

But data network design does not just focus on the transport of data. It is a broad field of study encompassing the creation of a communications infrastructure that comprehends user applications; network architectures, infrastructures and topologies; public standards, services, protocols, data transport techniques; and their analysis, planning, and implementation. It goes beyond simply understanding the technical details of protocols connecting one element of hardware or software to another to facilitate data transfer and the knowledge of standards and basic telecommunications. Specialization by engineers and managers in a single networking discipline or traffic type is no longer enough. Focus cannot be split between voice and data traffic, or the local area network (LAN) and wide area network (WAN), but instead must be directed at both as a single *system*.

The networking portion of design deals with the inter-connectivity of multiple applications, devices, and protocols into a single or multiple network infrastructures. One of the key features of a good design is that it is built to support both present and future requirements. A network is defined as a snare or catching device that, once built, attracts and "catches" many applications not originally destined to be supported. The "snare" concept will become more evident in subsequent chapters.

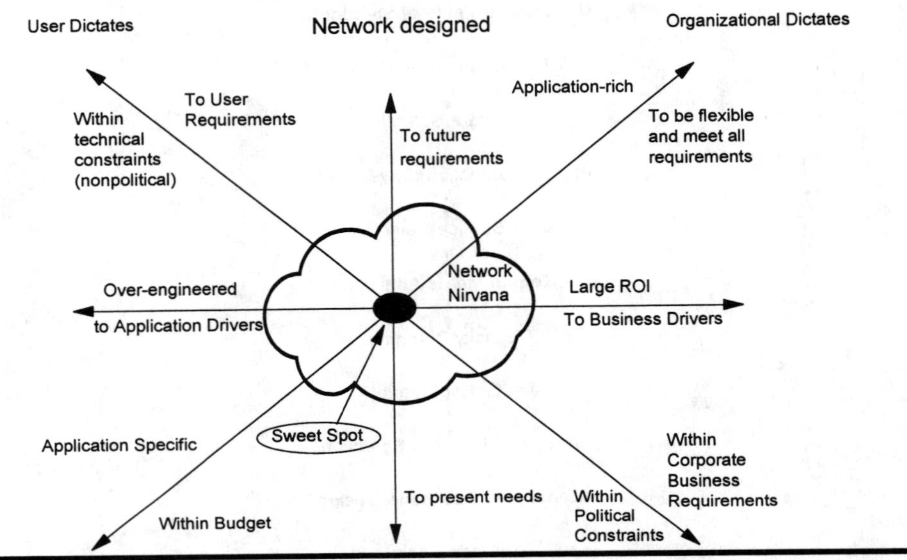

Figure 1.3 Network Design Nirvana

Network design can be viewed as a series of events from determining the basic requirements to managing the network after it is built. Figure 1.2 shows the steps taken in this text to perform a network design. These steps are presented in chronological order as they are presented in this book.

The network designer strives to achieve "network Nirvana", or the point where the network design comes as close as possible to meeting both the user and organizational dictates. These needs are often in conflict. Reaching this balance point between each end of the spectrum is the essence of network design. Figure 1.3 illustrates the many factors – business and technical, economic and political – that influence the network design. The art of network design is achieving the design that falls in the "sweet spot".

A data communications network, when designed efficiently, can and does become the lifeblood of a business organization. The new network can create many options not present under the old style of communications, such as desktop video-conferencing, e-mail, file sharing, web browsing, and many other benefits discussed in this book. It can also be extremely detrimental to the business if designed incorrectly. Figure 1.4 depicts another example of a data communications network, with more detail than the former, showing a few of the many types of user-to-network elements interfacing to the network as access devices.

Network design historically has consisted of engineering primarily for the transport of voice or low-speed data traffic over dedicated private line facilities. The entire infrastructure of communications before 1960 was based primarily on analog technology. In this era, data communications adapted to the analog world. Deployment of synchronous digital transmission began in the 1980s. This was the beginning of the categorization of voice as data. A myriad of developments in analog and digital data transport technologies has brought us into the information era, founded on digital and now fiber-optic transport. One of the most significant factors in the evolution and acceleration of the information era has been the digitization of transport networks. Digital technology has increased network, switch, and computer performance. The same digital technology has enabled the construction of huge transport networks capable of providing subscriber service for all forms of voice, video, and data traffic and even assuring specific quality-of-service parameters. Network design, which once started with just the transparent transport of voice and data, now has to comprise all protocol interactions from user applications through network protocols and LAN and WAN physical and logical connectivity.

Thus, our charter is to understand all aspects of network design in order to make comprehensive decisions when designing a network. A working understanding of solid design principles enables the design engineer or manager to successfully manage a data communications network from conception through implementation and upkeep. The engineer or manager must clearly comprehend the fundamental concepts of network design as presented in this book. Change is accelerating as we move into the twenty-first century. Data transport formats change, speeds increase at exponential rates, vendors strive to produce products to meet standards under development or create new standards, and technologies become more efficient at a rate that makes equipment seem almost obsolete by the time it is deployed into the network.

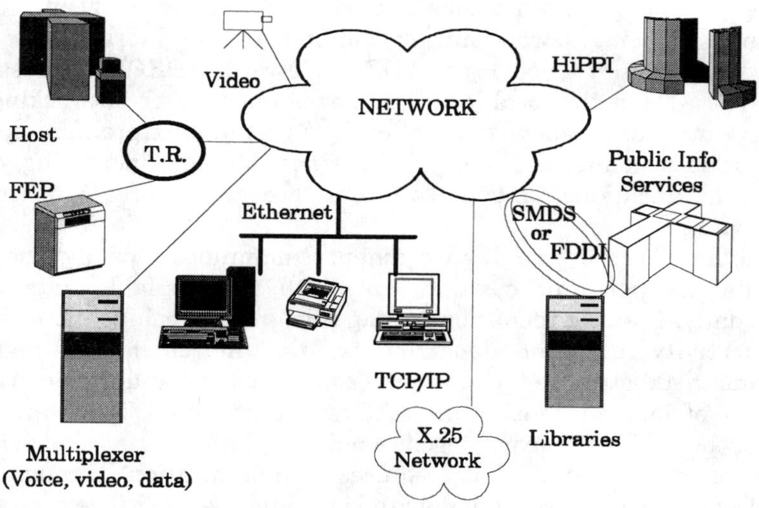

Figure 1.4 Data Communications Network with User-to-Network Interfaces

This book deals primarily with network design relating to computer and data communications networks. A data communications network design is defined as a complete communications system-level design encompassing user access (ingress and egress), the transportation medium and data transport elements, as well as all internal and external factors that affect, manage, or interact with the communications medium. A data communications network domain includes the hardware, software, management, and any other subsets of the communications network. This also includes the user interface to the network - up to and including the application level. This list is far from comprehensive, but includes the basic elements. We will focus on the network at both a micro and macro level – from detailed architecture and protocol design to high-level systems design.

1.2 DEFINING DATA COMMUNICATIONS NEEDS

The first step in the process of corporate data identity is to define the need for data communications services, which should be prioritized with respect to other needs in the organization and with the flexibility to incorporate future requirements. We start by focusing on the applications, current communications technology, and corporate infrastructure enablers driving the need.

One of the most likely scenarios is as follows: a flatter, leaner organization is emerging, driving the need for each individual to have access to more data and to communicate with more users and shared resources. Businesses are being driven to increase their reliance on less expensive, user controllable, multiple platform communications access in a multi-vendor environment. This change is being borne out by the move from hierarchical System Network Architecture (SNA) and DEC Network (DECNET) host-based networks to LANs at the local level and peer-to-peer inter-networking of the Internet or Intranet at the wide area level. As computers proliferate, so does the need for data communications. The business becomes increasingly reliant on data communications, and the "network" becomes a force which must be reckoned with.

Demand for corporate and government communications increases each year, while the per unit cost of bandwidth for available data services decreases daily. Possible scenarios fueling this growth include increased LAN inter-connectivity between departments, the movement of mainframe applications to a distributed client-server architecture, and the emergence of a new class of image-intensive interactive applications. There are a large number of possible scenarios, each leading to the same conclusion: the explosion of data traffic that requires communication throughout the business to meet ever-increasing demands for high-performance computing to every desktop.

How can these increased data requirements, phenomenal growth of user applications, processing power, and demand for connectivity and bandwidth be defined and understood? How can this parallel shift from hierarchical to flat, decentralized networks and organizations be quantified? This and the next chapter provide answers to these questions and more of an in-depth look at perspectives on past, current, and future communications architectures, changes in applications, and the protocols that provide the enabler to change.

1.3 FROM VOICE NETWORKS TO DATA NETWORKS

A dramatic shift from voice communications networks to data communications networks has occurred over the past 20 years. Data communications now affects many aspects of our lives: stock market transactions, medical research networks, electronic mail, World Wide Web (WWW) access, and even the Automatic Teller Machines (the other "ATM"!) that provide us with money on practically every street corner. What chain of events made data communications become so integral to our daily life in the last generation? How did the move occur so quickly from voice networks using analog transmission facilities to voice networks using digital transmission facilities, to all digital transmission facilities integrating voice, data, and video traffic? With these questions in mind, this chapter now begins with a review of the evolution of communications. As background, the history of voice communications is presented as the precursor to data communications.

1.3.1 A Brief History of Communications

Figure 1.5 depicts a view of the history of communication along the dimensions of analog versus digital encoding and synchronous versus asynchronous timing, or scheduling. The beginnings of spoken human communication are estimated to be over 50,000 years old. Graphic images have been found in caves over 20,000 years old. Written records over 5,000 years old have been found. Digital long-distance optical communications began when the ancient Greeks used digital, optical communications to relay information using placement of torches on towers at relay stations before the birth of Christ. The Greeks and Romans also popularized *scheduled* public announcements and speeches as early examples of broadcast communications, as well as individual, *unscheduled* communication in forums and debates.

In the seventeenth and eighteenth centuries, optical telegraphy was used extensively in Europe. Later, electrical telegraphy was invented by Samuel F. B. Morse in 1846, marking the beginning of modern digital electromagnetic communications. Radio telegraphy was invented shortly afterwards by G. Marconi. Broadcast analog radio communications of audio signals followed in the late nineteenth and early twentieth centuries. This technology was also applied to analog voice communication in the same time frame. Television signal broadcasting became commercially viable in the late 1940s. Then, in the 1950s, the conversion of analog voice to digital signals in the Plesiochronous Digital Hierarchy (PDH) began in large metropolitan areas to make better use of installed cabling. This was followed by the invention of packet switching in the 1960s as an offshoot of research into secure military communication networks. Fiber-optic transmission and the concept of synchronous digital transmission were introduced in the early 1980s. Analog transmission of voice had a brief renaissance using Single SideBand (SSB) in the 1980s. ATM moves the wheel of technology around the circle back into the domain of digital asynchronous communication.

The next major leap in emerging technology is Wavelength Division Multiplexing (WDM), which is analog and asynchronous and uses colors of light to extend the available bandwidth of a single fiber-optic fiber well into the gigabits per second. The speed of digital communication has increased geometrically over time through each of these evolving phases of technology.

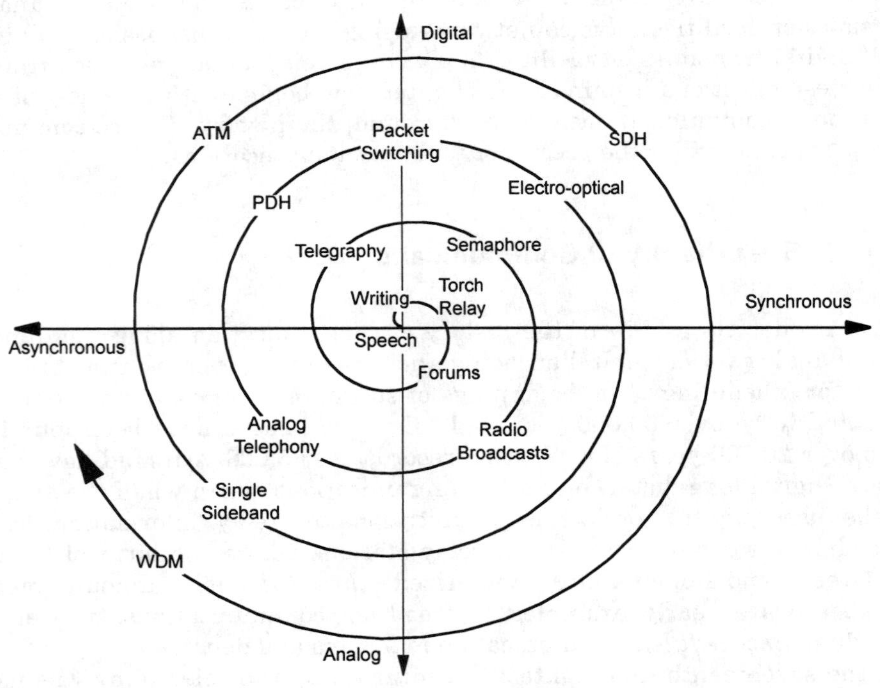

Figure 1.5 Data Communications "Wheel of Reincarnation"

This is not a perfect analogy — sometimes the wheel spins faster than at other times. For example, in the current day we move from Asynchronous Transfer Mode (ATM), an asynchronous digital technology, all the way around to Wavelength Division Multiplexing (WDM), an asynchronous, analog technology.

The military has been a key user of data communications networks throughout history. The telegraph was significant to the Union forces in the Civil War. Many data-processing and early computer systems were developed during World War II, when systems integration was driven by the necessity to reduce complexity. This trend continues even today, as is evident in system-level outsourcing and out-tasking described later in this chapter. After World War II, the command and control centers, weapons and sensor systems, and voice networks, and the computers that ran these systems needed to be centrally controlled within one interconnected communications network. This was the beginning of the U.S. Department of Defense (DoD) telecommunications architecture. Today, the U.S. DoD architecture is one of many data communications platforms in use. A government standard for protocols at DoD is the Government OSI Protocol (GOSIP) that is now a requirement in many Requests for Proposals (RFPs). So far, however, ways have been found around government requirements for GOSIP included in most government bids.

The next major advance by the DoD was the establishment of the Advanced Research Projects Agency NETwork (ARPANET). ARPANET was established in 1971 as the first packet-switched network. This data network connected military and civilian locations, as well as universities. In 1983, a majority of ARPANET users, including European and Pacific Rim contingents, were split off to form the Defense Data Network (DDN) — also referred to as MILNET. Some locations in the U.S. and Europe remained with ARPANET, and are now merged with the DARPA Internet, which provides connectivity to many universities and national telecommunications networks. The original ARPANET was decommissioned in 1990. Many of the advances in computer communications, including routing and networking, have been developed through experience on the Internet. The explosive growth of the Internet and now World Wide Web (WWW) has to some extent been fueled by the requirement to build larger, faster, and more feature-rich networks in the future. The Internet core is comprised of BBN, NETCOM, PSI, MFS/UUNET, and the U.S. government.

Host-based networks accessed by local and remote terminals evolved through the use of private networks and packet-switched services. The primary example is the IBM Systems Network Architecture (SNA). This architecture provides the platform for many dumb terminals and workstations to communicate with an intelligent host or mainframe in a hierarchical, or star, fashion. This hierarchy was developed for two reasons: collecting expensive intelligence at the host and allowing the terminals to have little resident intelligence was the most cost-effective trade-off, and transmission facilities that could be shared at the access point, as with multipoint circuits, were much more cost effective than dedicated point-to-point circuits to every site.

Local area networks (LANs) were the next major development in the computer communications networking environment, with the advent of Ethernet produced by Xerox, DEC, and Intel in 1974. Client-server architectures and distributed processing across both LANs and WANs signaled the beginning of modern data communications. This ends the short course on the History of Data 101 — now we move on to more recent data history starting after 1980.

1.3.2 A Recent History of Data Communications

The primary challenge faced by many corporations today is how to cope with the move from a single controlled application and protocol environment with structured and centralized applications to one of individual choice across multiple protocols and even architectures. Tie this to the flattening of interconnected LAN networks to support the astounding rate of personal computer proliferation and you have a paradigm shift. This network flattening and shift to client-server computing began the (r)evolution of the corporate data network, sometimes called the Information Revolution. What started as a PC for home use has now become a corporate necessity. It was a natural evolutionary choice for the visionary network design engineer to address the users in these islands of information — the distributed LAN interconnecting desktops and the centralized mainframe Management Information Systems (MIS) arena — by creating a common environment using routers and switches to achieve inter-working and inter-connectivity. This is a key reason for the tremendous success of the router industry, and now switched and virtual LAN (VLAN) devices.

Just as minicomputers invaded mainframe turf when the cost of minis fell to departmental budget approval levels, bypassing corporate MIS budget approval, so too have the falling costs of routers and the LAN switch phenomenon enabled enhanced LAN and routed protocol connectivity. Routers enabled the segmentation of the corporate LAN into user groups, which further enabled inter-departmental connectivity of diverse LAN technologies and protocols in a cost-effective manner. Many "home-grown" router networks placed cost and control more in the hands of the end user than they have ever been before. In the late 1980s, many users asked themselves the question, "why conform to corporate MIS dictates when you can build your own departmental LAN and handle 90 percent of your data processing needs?" When there was a need to interconnect these LANs, the MIS manager and entrepreneurial LAN managers had to work together in order to integrate access from the LANs to the VAX and IBM mainframes. In addition, WAN interconnectivity often went beyond the scope of a single

LAN manager and had costs that had to be shared across multiple LANs. The router also found its place here as the gateway to the WAN and continued the user-control wave into the 1990s. This role may eventually be conceded to ATM switches during the turn of the century.

ATM arrives in this era of expanding, even euphoric, expectations from users caught up in this new wave of freedom. The high-performance workstation users, for whom even Ethernet speeds of 100M bps are too slow, are leading the next data communications revolution, with many focused on ATM as the solution. The MIS manager still needs to focus attention on the design and maintenance of the host and front-end processor systems because many mission-critical applications still reside there. The LAN manager needs to focus on the needs of the high-performance workstation user and server, while continuing to enhance the support provided to the users employing legacy technology. Bringing the requirements of these two divergent realms into a single ubiquitous and seamless network is essential. One should not become caught up in the glamour of a single integration technology such as ATM until a clear path is defined for migrating mission-critical applications from an older technology to a newer one. Again, the snare concept tells us that a well-designed network that was once intended for a single application and protocol will easily snare many more applications and protocols throughout its life.

1.4 CURRENT NETWORK INFRASTRUCTURE – THE TELEPHONE NETWORK

History repeats itself, and voice and data communications history is no exception to the rule. Voice communications has a long history of competition, starting with the telegraph and box phone, through the extension of long lines business across the country, and into modern day divestiture and "open" competition. This evolution, a by-product of national policy, has been cyclic — competition, regulation, natural monopoly, deregulation, and again competition. With the advent of a digital network, data communications also has had competition in the T1 carrier business. Now for a trip through the history of the U.S. telephone network. It took many competitive efforts to achieve what we have today in the United States. AT&T, plagued by independent telephone competition at the beginning of the century, succeeded in building a government-sanctioned natural "monopoly" only to lose it again during divestiture. Now as traditional IntereXchange Carriers (IXCs) move into the local access business and Local Exchange Carriers (LECs) move into long-haul (inter-LATA) service, the lines again begin to blur.

1.4.1 The United States

The telephone was patented on March 7, 1876, by Alexander Graham Bell. The first box telephone was patented the very next year, on January 30, 1877. That same year, over 600 telephones were connected to each other via point-to-point private lines. Mr. Bell also carried his invention to Europe in 1877 and demonstrated its operation to Queen Victoria and other world dignitaries. Thus, the information era of telecommunications was born. On January 28, 1878, the first telephone exchange was opened in New Haven, Connecticut, and users were switched manually at "central" by an operator. The number of exchanges spread rapidly until the New England Telephone Company was formed on February 12, 1878. Throughout the next three years many companies changed hands. Companies like Western Union, the National Bell Telephone Company, and the American Speaking Telephone Company competed over telephone rights. In November 1879, an agreement was reached that Western Union would remain solely in the telegraph business and the National Bell Telephone Company, which became the American Bell Telephone Company, would remain solely in the "telephone" business.

The next major development was the formation of the American Telephone and Telegraph Company (AT&T) in 1885. This company was formed as a subsidiary of the American Bell Telephone Company to handle the nation's long lines business, but AT&T grew, and in 1900 absorbed the Bell Company. Later, in 1911, AT&T organized territorial divisions called Bell Associated Companies, which in turn paid licensing fees to AT&T for patents. Throughout the early part of the century, AT&T fought a hard battle against independent telephone competition, buying out those they could and refusing to connect to others. The Kingsbury commitment was made by AT&T in 1913 under government regulatory pressure, allowing independents to interconnect with AT&T. In 1921, the Graham Act was passed by Congress, legitimizing AT&T as a "natural monopoly". From this point until divestiture, AT&T enjoyed the status of a monopoly.

The AT&T monopoly comprised AT&T Headquarters, 23 Bell Associated Companies, Western Electric Company, and Bell Telephone Laboratories. This monopoly was broken up during what is called "divestiture". The Modified Final Judgment (MFJ) was issued by Judge Harold Greene of the U.S. District Court in Washington, D.C., for AT&T to divest itself of all of the Bell Operating Companies (BOCs). Figure 1.6 shows each of the post-divestiture Regional Bell Operating Companies (RBOCs) and their areas of coverage. These seven RBOCs were:

- Pacific Telesis
- US West
- SBC Communications
- Ameritech

- Bell South
- Bell Atlantic
- NYNEX

Another major decision at divestiture was to not allow RBOCs to manufacture Customer Premises Equipment (CPE). One hundred and sixty Local Area Transport Areas (LATAs) were designated for local access. Independent telephone companies could elect to come under the LATA plan or not; most larger ones did. The RBOCs could provide service within designated LATA areas only, leaving the long distance companies — AT&T, MCI, Sprint — to provide the inter-LATA connectivity. AT&T was split into AT&T Communications and AT&T Technologies and forbidden to use the "Bell" system logo. Now it seems AT&T will have a chance to reclaim the Bell territory it lost almost a decade ago with legislation allowing fair competition in local and long-distance services. The Telecommunications Bill of 1996 allows for competition in long-distance, local, cellular, and cable industries.

Data communications networks evolved in much the same way as voice networks. Dedicated private lines connected users to centralized switches, and eventually to national and worldwide switched networks with classes of access and hierarchical backbone designs.

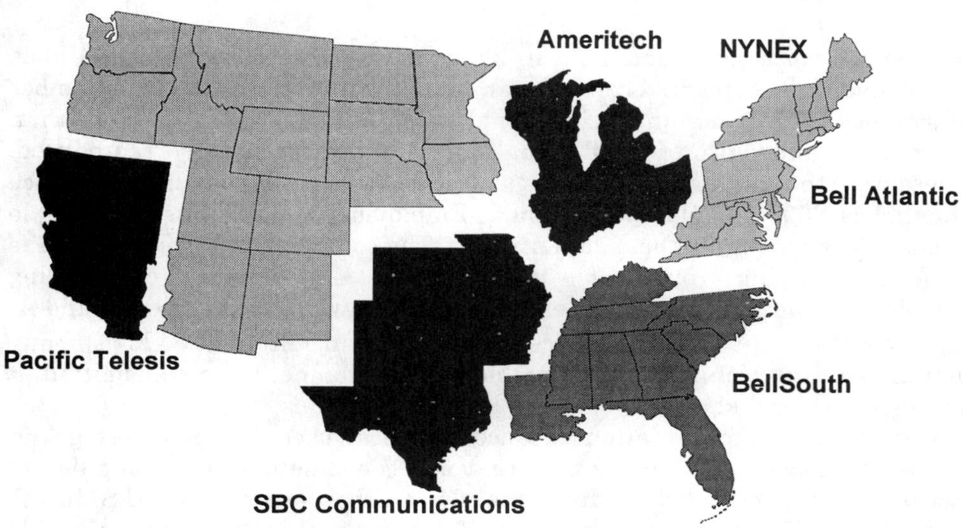

Figure 1.6 Seven Regional Bell Operating Companies – Post-Divestiture

1.4.2 Europe and the Pacific Rim

The European and Pacific Rim telephone industry is evolving in a similar manner as the U.S. industry. The historical model was for the predominant telecommunications carrier to be owned by government entities through what are called postal telegraph and telephone (PTT) agencies. Many of the more industrialized countries have moved from the PTT environment and sold off government-owned entities to public markets and owners, or allowed national and foreign competition into some or all of their telecommunications markets. In the United States, communications entities are privately owned but loosely regulated by governmental agencies. In Europe and the Pacific Rim, many countries have opened telecommunications and services to local or foreign competition. Those PTTs that remain are typically both operated *and* regulated by the government. Many of the remaining PTT monopolies are being realigned into two organizations — traditional services such as local dial tone and competitive services such as virtual private and switched network services. The multinational (trans-national) companies helped force this change. In fact, many multinational communications companies like Cable and Wireless are challenging local PTTs or the dominant carrier for access and transport services. The competitive environment that prevails in the U.S. since the AT&T breakup appears to be happening internationally.

1.4.3 Voice as Low-Speed Data

A standard voice-grade channel can be accurately represented by a 64 kbps (or 56 kbps) data stream. Nyquist's sampling theorem states that the number of samples taken from an analog signal must be taken at a rate more than *twice* the bandwidth of that signal for it to be accurately reproduced. Therefore, the minimum sampling rate for a 4000-Hz bandwidth voice channel is 8000 samples per second. Employing 8 (or 7) bits per sample yields a 64 kbps (or 56 kbps) data stream. The coding of each voice sample is performed using one of two different nonlinear companding (COMpression/exPANDING) schemes, called μ-Law in North America and A-Law elsewhere. In fact, while voice is typically transmitted at 64 kbps, many digital encoding techniques now enable a voice channel to be transmitted at speeds as low as 8 kbps.

The 64 kbps representation of voice was first used for engineering and economic reasons to multiplex more voice conversations onto bundles of twisted pairs in crowded conduits, mainly in urban areas of the U.S. in the mid-1950s. Twenty-four voice channels were multiplexed onto a single twisted pair in what was known as a T1 repeater system, using a DS1 signal format. Chapter 4 reviews the DS1 signal format in detail. The scarce resource of twisted pairs was now utilized at 2400 percent of its previous capacity, a tremendous enhancement! The fact that these multiplexing methods could be used for the purpose of data communications came later.

Voice is very sensitive to delay, and somewhat loss-sensitive. Users do not tolerate appreciable delay during a full-duplex or half-duplex conversation, because it can inhibit interaction or result in annoying echo, nor will they accept sentence-flow garbling by the loss of entire syllables. Variations in delay can cause the speaker's voice to become unrecognizable, or render the speech unintelligible. The loss of small portions of syllables or words in voice communications is usually acceptable, however. Satellite delay, which most people have experienced, is a good example of the effects of large delay (in terms of echo) and the impact on interactive conversation. Certain new technologies such as ATM can handle delay-sensitive voice traffic, while other technologies such as frame relay have difficulties providing the high quality of service required to carry this type of traffic.

1.4.4 Voice and Data over the Current Network Infrastructure

The public telephone network naturally evolved from a narrow-band to a broadband hierarchy based upon circuit economic considerations such as the aggregation of circuits into a common medium (24 DS0 circuits onto a single DS1, 28 DS1s onto a single DS3, etc.). Figure 1.7 depicts the classical five-level public telephone network hierarchy developed to minimize cost and achieve traffic engineering economies of scale, which resulted in a corresponding increase in bandwidth at higher levels in the hierarchy. Customers are connected to the telephone network by a *local loop* which is provided by narrow-band twisted pair access lines to the lowest level of the hierarchy, the Class 5 central office telephone switch. A *twisted pair* is composed of two wires that are twisted to minimize impairments in analog transmission such as crosstalk and interference. These twisted pairs are bundled into cables and then aggregated at the central office. Generally, if the distance traversed is greater than a few miles, the local loops are aggregated into larger bandwidths for transmission over microwave, copper, or, increasingly, optical fiber. Indeed, the DS1 and DS3 multiplex levels were created for this very reason, their use for data occurring by later invention and innovation rather than initial design.

Class 5 switches may be directly connected, or else connect to larger Class 4 tandem switches, which can be connected to even larger tandem switches such as the Class 3 and 2. The final route choice is via Class 1 switches, which are connected at the highest bandwidth aggregate level. In general, switches are larger at higher levels in the hierarchy, even though a Class 5 switch in a large metropolitan area can be quite large.

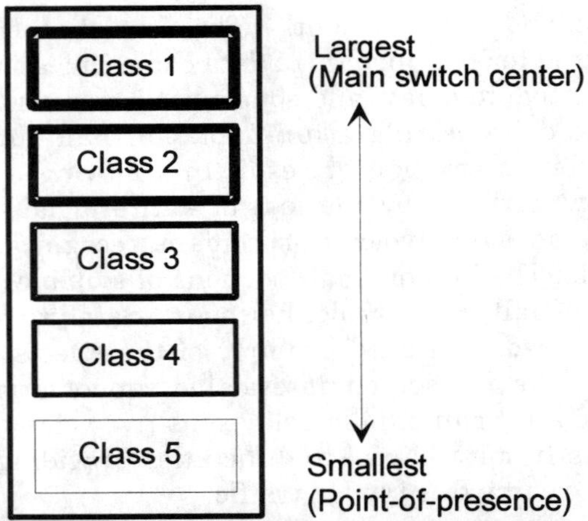

Figure 1.7 Public Telephone Network Hierarchy

There is a move toward a flatter, more distributed network of fully interconnected Class 4 or 5 switches. The number of levels has not yet been reduced to one, but in many cases there are only two or three levels in a hierarchical phone network. Again, this parallels the move of most major businesses from a hierarchical organization to a flatter, distributed organization.

Voice channels are time division multiplexed on digital transmission systems. When compared to data, the main difference is that voice calls are circuit switched, whereas data can be either message, packet, cell, or circuit switched as described in Chapter 6. Both voice and data applications require large bandwidths, but for different reasons. Data applications require large bandwidth to support the peak rate of applications, while voice requires larger aggregate bandwidth to multiplex large numbers of individual voice circuits.

One interesting point is that many personal home computer users who access the Internet, probably use their phone "voice" line for a longer daily duration than for actual voice calls. These calls are perceived by the voice network as voice calls, when in effect they are actually data calls. As telecommuting and access to the Internet from home increase, it begs the question, how much "voice" traffic is really "data" traffic in unstructured form?

1.5 THE DATA REVOLUTION

The 1990s yielded a broadband data revolution with a rallying cry of "bandwidth-on-demand!" The expectation of bandwidth-on-demand was created by the LAN where a user shared a high-speed medium with many other users, having access to the full shared medium bandwidth "on-demand." This worked well when every user required only a small portion of the shared medium, but has become a significant problem as the power of desktop technology has increased while the Ethernet capability remained at 10M bps for many years. Now there are finally emerging protocols like 100M bps Ethernet and 25M bps and 155M bps (full-duplex) ATM. Then the concept of bandwidth-on-demand moved from the LAN into the WAN. Bandwidth-on-demand expectations for the WAN were driven by users requiring near-LAN connect speeds across the WAN.

There is another interpretation of bandwidth-on-demand advocated by those with a background in circuit switching. This definition is that a user requests bandwidth, and is either granted the full request or is denied access completely (i.e., blocked); this is similar to making a phone call — the call either goes through or you get a busy signal. This is, in effect, the implementation of ISDN service. We shall see that specific applications can make use of one definition or the other, but usually not both.

This section shows how the growth in data communications has taken the lead over that of voice communications in both total volume and the introduction of new services. The discussion then moves on to cover how various services best meet application needs in terms of bandwidth, delay, and burstiness (defined as the ratio of the peak traffic rate to the average traffic rate). The section concludes with the observation that the data revolution is global, social, and economic in scope.

1.5.1 Data Communications Takes the Lead

Data growth is occurring at a factor of approximately 25 percent per year, far outpacing the average growth of voice, at only 6 to 8 percent per year. The consequence of this differential in growth is plotted in Figure 1.8, which projects the U.S. common carrier voice and data services revenues for the growth rates cited above. If these growth rates remain constant, data network revenue would exceed voice network revenue prior to the year 2000. Of course, there are many factors which may cause these growth rates to change, so this is only one possible outcome. However, it makes the point that the era of emerging data communications dominance is near. Groupware, electronic mail, file transfer, local area network interconnection, interactive applications, and emerging computer communications applications represent just a few examples of how data communications is exceeding voice communications in creating the demand for new capabilities.

For businesses that rely on their communications and information flow as the lifeblood of their business, effective and highly available data communications can not only give them a competitive edge, it can put them on a leading edge. This leading edge can create both benefits and risks. Once a business experiences effective data communications, it becomes "hooked" on its own network. The data and computer communications network quickly becomes the lifeblood of the company. Take, for example, the financial services company whose data communications network transmits information for millions of dollars in funds transfers per hour.

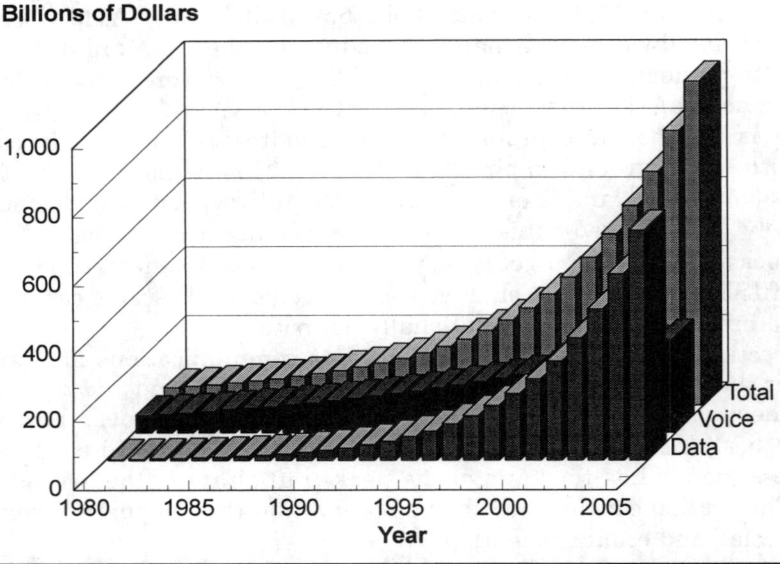

Figure 1.8 Extrapolation of U.S. Carrier Voice and Data Revenue Growth

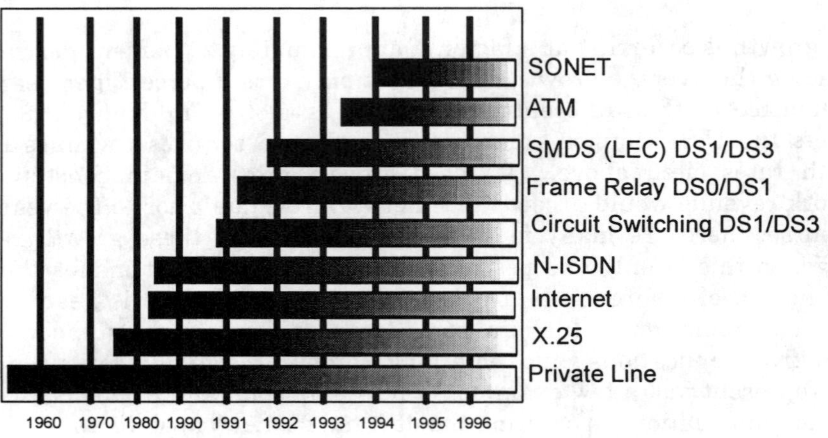

Figure 1.9 Data Services Introduction History

Another example where information transfer is critical: a shipping company that operates on a just-in-time shipping schedule. A company needs voice network communications, but a private voice network can only become so large since it is limited by the company's size. Voice communications traffic can be forecast and has predictable characteristics. On the other hand, data communications traffic characteristics can be a different ball game with new rules. Once a company uses a data network, there is no limit to its potential.

Key services and switching technologies that represent the existing and emerging data market include:

- Private lines
- X.25
- Internet
- Narrow-band ISDN
- Circuit switching
- Frame relay
- Switched Multimegabit Data Service (SMDS)
- ATM
- SONET

Figure 1.9 shows the time frame for the introduction of the major data services over roughly the past 30 years. Broadband data communication has fast become the prevalent market in the 1990s within the US and most of Europe—and at the forefront is frame relay, SONET, and ATM. The 1990s can be called the era of inter-working, simply because of the widespread use of these broadband technologies and services and the inter-networking of LANs. Not shown in this figure are the many forms of wireless communications services now emerging.

1.5.2 Business Relies on Data Communications

The level of dependence of a corporation on its data communications network is not always readily apparent. Despite limited dedicated personnel resources, studies show that a major portion of most business office budgets are still devoted to data communications. From this dedication, and the chaos that occurs when the network goes down, it is intuitively obvious that data communications networks are fundamental to the successful operation of any business. Computers, terminals, modems, facsimile machines, security systems, and even most telephone systems transmit some form of data communications. The design of a data communications network can have a direct impact on the success or failure of a business.

Cost also plays a major role in determining network needs, and more often is driven more by the cost of services provided by the carrier than by the actual equipment costs. Often services supplied by carriers or vendors are expensed, whereas the purchase of equipment is a depreciated capital expenditure. Equipment expenses often turn out to be a very small part of the total expenses of operating a network, eclipsed by both people and tools.

1.5.3 A New World Order for Data?

The drive is on for corporations to extend their data and networks internationally. Corporate global enterprise networks are proliferating at an astonishing rate as international circuit costs decline and service ubiquity increases. Does this point to a new world order for data? If so, then one must become part of this new world order of data communications to survive.

Data communications has taken on a global view in many of its facets. International standards, of course, are a prerequisite for global connectivity. There is much progress in this area. The latest generation of transmission rates is the same for the first time in history, as shown in Chapter 4. There is increasing cooperation between standards bodies on an international scale, as reviewed in Chapter 3. The entire standardization process is changing to better meet the accelerating needs of users; witness the tremendous international success of ATM with the help of the ATM Forum. ATM is being standardized on a worldwide basis independent of physical-link speed.

International private line connectivity is growing faster than transoceanic cables and fiber can be installed. International switched services are booming, with current product offerings providing a broad range of switched service speeds and technologies. The entire world is being connected by fiber optic transmission systems. Figure 1.10 illustrates the international fiber optic connectivity that is now in place. A single fiber-optic cable can carry more than 1 terahertz, or 1000 gigahertz, of capacity with a bit error rate (BER) of one bit per million.

Figure 1.10 International Fiber-Optic Cable Systems

Recent political, technological, economic, and regulatory changes worldwide have spurred international data network interoperability. New U.S. interest is occurring, for instance, in the countries of Mexico and Canada through the North American Free Trade Agreement (NAFTA). Growth has primarily been in the U.S., Europe, the Pacific Rim, and Southeast Asia. Markets in South America, New Zealand, Australia, Russia, and countries once part of the Eastern Bloc and the now-defunct Soviet Union have been slower to emerge, but are gaining momentum through the development of infrastructures based on state-of-the-art technology. Many of these countries are skipping older (intermediate) technologies and building infrastructure with newer technologies, in effect leap-frogging over intermediate technologies (but still often not building networks with leading-edge, state-of-the-art technologies). Postal, Telegraphy, and Telephony (PTT) monopolies are realigning with open market competition, making worldwide advanced data communications a reality.

The 1990s saw a surge in mergers and strategic partnerships, and the term "coopetition" (a blend of cooperation and competition) was coined in the communications industry. Every day the sun rises on a new international merger or partnership among carriers, hardware vendors, PTTs, governmental agencies, and small companies who fill niche markets, and many among old rivals. Many joint ventures have sprung up both nationally and internationally. These range from brand-name computer vendors trying to beat out smaller clone vendors to the large interexchange and international carriers who vie for entrance into foreign markets.

1.6 THE NEW WORLD DATA MANAGER OR ENGINEER—THINK DATA SERVICES!

Does the data revolution discussed above spell a new world order for data? If so, the data engineer and manager need to understand their role in this brave new world. Since this text is written primarily for network engineers and managers, it is important to look into their world and view how these changes directly affect their working environment. Many data communications "experts" are people that have made the jump from voice to data. Other talented individuals started working in the LAN as administrators or installers and expanded upon their base of expertise, while others exploited a background in traditional WAN equipment like multiplexers or packet switches. Businesses are relying more on data communications today than ever before. Each of these individuals needs to understand the data service options open to them and how data is quickly replacing voice. Today's communications engineer and manager must have a clear understanding of LAN and WAN technologies; design networks that are not just faster and larger but smarter; and able to adapt to rapid change and growth. This is especially true as data services offer high-speed bandwidth but still heavily rely on a large amount of end-user (and network designer) intelligence to truly optimize their resources. Mix all this with a little planning and philosophy of data network engineering in the next century and you have a recipe for success in dealing with these new technologies and services.

1.6.1 The Data Services Option

What are some of the recent trends and tools at the network engineer and manager's disposal? A public data service is one tool that offers opportunities to maintain cost-effective quality networking while remaining technologically current. In an age where customer service and quality reign over price, the winner is often the company or individual who provides quality network services such as good user response, well-planned operations activities, user-friendliness, and an entrepreneurial answer to customer needs. The service provider who accomplishes this through deployment of intelligent network technologies will emerge the true winner. Equipment cost variance is usually one of the last considerations, as multiple vendors are capable of providing products at close to the same price. The communications industry is now competitive in both technology and services. The five keys to providing successful data services are

- Fast and efficient user response
- Efficient and productive operations
- User-friendliness (provider and user defined) and responsiveness
- Entrepreneurial answer to customer needs
- Ease of implementation with minimal user disruption

Emerging data technologies are never at a loss for vendors or service providers. This is evident in the large number of vendors offering products before standards are published. These vendors offer versions of a current recommendation, and announce plans to upgrade to the "official standard" when indeed it becomes a published standard. Often, even users drive standards in test labs or interest groups before either the vendors or the standards committees can come to agreement and publish the officially accepted standard. Customers have real-world business problems that must be solved today. Beware of nonstandard public network service offerings, but explore standard ones as a good alternative to building your own network.

1.6.2 Not Just Faster and Larger, but Smarter Networks

Faster and larger networks are definitely within the corporate plan, but these networks are only being built to a size that will efficiently utilize the resources available and be manageable from an operations viewpoint. The engineer of the twenty-first century designs *smart, reliable, and scaleable* networks, not just faster networks. This new smart network becomes an efficient machine, run by smart data services. Network intelligence is distributed. Data transport technologies have become less intelligent yet much more reliable in availability and error rates, and count on the user to provide the end-to-end protocol intelligence or intelligent networking services. Thus, with many of the newer technologies such as frame relay, it behooves the user to have the intelligence on the premises.

LANs and routed WAN networking have experienced explosive growth. Five to ten years ago, the network engineer who built upon proprietary multiplexer solutions to support high-bandwidth traffic could not foresee the growth and change in routed and switched wide area networking. Soon after, it became quite evident that there would be a need for multi-megabit LAN data transport across the WAN. A data manager with foresight laid plans for a network that could support this transport, such as a router or cell switch solution. The manager who did not plan ahead scrambled to throw bandwidth at a proprietary multiplexer solution while quickly coming up to speed with new technologies, as network users clamored for new technologies and services. The recent trend in planning is toward hybrid networks which provide ubiquitous access for a broad range of applications and network support systems. ATM is one technology that has potential to enable this planning strategy. Networks are hybrid at various levels: voice/data; private/public; C.O.-based, Centrex-like services/premises-based PBXs, etc. This book is designed to help you understand these services and technologies and enable success in your current and future planning horizons.

1.6.3 Planning

Planning is one of the most important functions a data engineer or manager can perform. Proper planning saves money, time, and resources. As data networks continue to grow in size and complexity, so do user demands upon that network. Proactive planning becomes the key factor to network survivability, and thus job security. The data manager and engineer must plan for and anticipate change in user and technology environments. Therefore, an ongoing process of redesign and optimization is a prerequisite for an efficient and cost-effective network. One area where this is particularly true is the networking of LANs and routed WANs.

1.6.4 Psychology

Psychology plays a major role in data network design, though it is hard to quantify. When the two major disciplines of computer communications and telecommunications come together, entire departments overlap. Support structures, departmental responsibilities, and even functional group responsibilities are duplicated, while each side tries to come up to speed with the other. This can cause emotional and psychological battles which have nothing to do with technological issues. While these are management issues, they should be anticipated. There will be a need to cross these traditional boundaries. The data network manager or engineer must clearly define the roles and responsibilities for each individual on the staff. Computer operations and telephony have traditionally been separate functions. Only recently have they begun merging—often with the MIS or data computer groups absorbing the telecommunications or voice communications entities. The designer must eliminate or at least minimize the turf battles which result between telecommunications wiring closets and computer server locations, communications room patch panel and cross-connect access, and modem pool and bypass access. Since the last printing of this book, the size of data communications (LAN and WAN) departments have begun to outstrip the traditional voice network support staff, and voice in many cases has been subsumed by the data group.

At times there exists a sort of technology struggle between the old style of brute force mainframe and front-end processors against the new style of desktop workstation and server devices (such as Pentium processor-based computers) which are capable of outperforming some of the older mainframes and front-end processors in price and performance. Each has its place in the new hybrid computer-telecommunications network. The important thing to understand is the interaction between each of these interest groups and to develop the mindset of a network manager or engineer who understands both worlds.

Just as minicomputers invaded mainframe turf when the cost of minis fell to departmental budget approval levels and the department level users did not have to go to corporate MIS for budget approval, so, also, the router and LAN switching phenomenon has accelerated LAN-WAN connectivity due to falling cost. Thus cost and control are more in the hands of the end user. Why conform to corporate MIS dictates when you can build your own departmental LAN and handle 90 percent of your data-processing needs? The MIS manager is thus forced to integrate his or her VAXs and IBM mainframes into the corporate distributed data structure, which is now being run by entrepreneurial LAN managers. These LAN managers are born from change, and provide the users with the hand-holding, customized design, application development and customer service they feel they have been denied and deprived of for years.

The personal computer has driven control from the hands of the MIS executive to the user's fingertips. This has been a "power to the people" movement, with workstation expenses hidden in everything from network equipment costs to office supplies. Router and switching hub costs are diving into the few thousand dollar range. And the applications are moving from the mainframe environment to workstation-server-based client-server computing groups. Internet access requirements and usage continue to grow at an astounding rate.

MIS should focus attention on the design and maintenance of the host and front-end processor systems. Bringing these devices and their applications into the new mainstream of LAN/WAN/MAN networking is essential, and if done wrong could be fruitless and costly. While these devices still provide valuable resources and applications, they must be integrated with local and wide area networks with foresight and precision. In later chapters, the pros and cons of each approach and how to effectively design a data communications network to span both worlds will be presented.

1.6.5 The Data Manager and the Data Engineer

A distinction must be made between the voice engineer/manager and the data engineer/manager. The voice engineer deals primarily with analog communications, which include standard telephony elements such as telephones, wiring closets and punch-down blocks, phone lines, cross connects, PBXs, and other communications equipment that eventually interface to the digital portion of the communications network. The data or computer communications engineer looks at the world in terms of ones and zeros, computer interface cards, LAN hubs, bridges, routers, LAN cabling systems, and WAN communications (which sometimes includes voice and data systems integration). The data engineer deals with both analog and digital communications because all analog data is changed to digital data before it is transferred across a network, and newer technologies such as ATM merge analog and data traffic onto a common communications infrastructure. This is especially true with the broadband data services based on technologies like frame relay and ATM. Thus, a knowledge of both analog and digital is essential to the data engineer.

Analog networks can include digital communications. One example is a modem. Modulator-demodulators (modems) convert a *digital* computer or terminal signal to *analog* tones for transport across an analog network. A data network has the capability of transmitting analog signals across digital facilities by using methods of sampling, coding, and quantizing. These digitizing conversions are explained in basic books on communication theory and are not discussed here, but the principles are similar. While there is still a call for skilled voice engineers, data engineers have already dominated the communications market, as predicted in the last edition of this book. Many businesses are realizing the need for effective data communications, and are integrating their voice communications with data communications. The recent reappearance of Integrated Services Digital Network (ISDN) services is an indication of this change.

The data network manager and engineer must have at least a working knowledge of available technologies and strive to attain a broad base of knowledge to be able to provide a working solution to any networking problem. It is good if the data manager has served some time as a data engineer. There are conflicting views on this subject. However, the view to which this book subscribes is that a good engineer with proper management training and project management experience will make a better engineering manager than a general-purpose manager who is later given some technical training. This assumes that the engineer has education in general-purpose business strategies, and that the educational level is achieved through higher education. This statement is based upon two major assumptions. It is easier to train a technical mind to perform administrative management duties than it is to teach an administrative management mind the technical aspects of complex technologies. Also, network project engineers often pick up management skills early in their careers by virtue of team-oriented engineering environments.

1.7 OUTSOURCING AND OUT-TASKING TRENDS CONTINUE

The choice between outsourcing or out-tasking versus an internally designed and developed network is one that spans every aspect of the business, and is one of the most important decisions of the network manager. An internally designed and developed network involves all stages of planning, building, and maintaining a network for the business. Outsourcing of network needs involves a third party taking over some (out-tasking) or all aspects of the corporation's data network, where various elements of control range from simple monitoring to design and management of the entire network. Out-tasking can be performed on mundane tasks to mission critical functions, and can augment or replace the requirement for internal resources.

The decision of outsourcing and out-tasking key business and network functions is often one of business policy based on many factors, as we will discuss in this section. Many corporations use outsourcing as a competitive tool rather than just for cost savings and control. Since a company's computer and communications system is the lifeblood of the organization, outsourcing is one of the most important decisions an organization can make.

What is outsourcing? What issues and considerations are associated with an outsourcing contract? Can outsourcing be broken down into pieces, termed out-tasking? What are the benefits and drawbacks of outsourcing and out-tasking? This section summarizes the primary factors to consider before signing an outsourcing agreement.

1.7.1 Outsourcing and Out-tasking Defined

Outsourcing is defined as contracting one or more outside vendors to design, develop, and implement a solution for a company's communication needs. This may include, but is not limited to, planning, designing, installing, managing, owning, leasing, operating, and controlling a communications network. Full responsibility for some portion of the company's network communications assets will be transferred to, or assumed by, the outsourcing vendor. *Out-tasking* is a new term that defines the outsourcing of specific tasks, rather than the entire network. Many times a corporation does not have the skilled resources or does not want to make a significant buy decision in one area, like network management, and will contract out that specific task.

Good strategic planning and innovative techniques must prevail regardless of whether the design is performed internally or is outsourced. First, evaluate the existing available resources. Compare the pros and cons of obtaining new resources versus contracting out the service. If the analysis determines that outsourcing is not justified, then analyze the systems and technologies available that can optimize the operation in-house. If the decision is to outsource, begin by shopping among multiple vendors. Always remember that portions of the organization or network may be out-tasked, while others could be retained in-house. In fact, this is one method of retaining your key people should the out-tasking deal go sour or terminate unexpectedly.

The requirements-gathering process is a critical step before outsourcing can begin. Compare the two major scenarios — *private network* versus *virtual private network (VPN)* configurations — before making the decision to outsource. Cost factors, of course, are a major consideration. This is where the "make versus buy" step begins. During the planning stages, a balance must be maintained between designing a network to accommodate internal applications and designing the internal applications to accommodate the network. Network applications and the network itself often grow together after the network is built. The capacity-planning process is critical throughout the life cycle of the network. Applications are analyzed on an individual and aggregate basis to determine the best network solution. A network design engineer will have various levels of knowledge at his or her disposal, ranging from projected traffic bandwidths between sites to a complete traffic and protocol profile for each application.

1.7.2 Outsourcing Considerations

The decision to outsource is often one of business policy based on many factors, including:

* Allow company to focus on its business charter and core competencies
* Corporate resource availability limitations
* Sensitivity of the data
* Return on investment (ROI) analysis
* Skill set and reliability of the vendor
* Cost factors of either owning the business elements or leasing them from the outsource partner (make vs. buy)
* Retention of control
* Resource or financial constraints
* Deductible expense versus capital investment

Other factors, such as how much support is required for how long, contract stipulations between user and vendor, and the loyalty to existing company employees, also play a major role in the outsourcing decision. Many business aspects should be considered for possible impact by outsourcing, including:

⇒ Resources (staff and existing investments)
⇒ Questions on skill sets and reliability of the vendors performing the outsourcing function
⇒ Cost savings or eventual loss
⇒ Control of the hardware and software
⇒ Network monitoring
⇒ Future of the company to either continue outsourcing or to bring the business back in-house

As with any business case analysis, all expenses of an outsourcing deal should be analyzed in detail for proof of the validity of cost savings versus expenditures. This is the process of determining what would most cost effectively be outsourced. A business considering outsourcing must do the following:

- Understand what would be best to be outsourced
- Define expectations of the implementation
- Plan what to do with current resources (most importantly people, space currently being occupied, and tools currently used!)
- Fully understand the vendor-user relationship
- Compare current employee skill sets with those of outsourcing company
- Define the extent of outsourcing, for example, protocols, interfaces, and locations

- Clearly define levels of control and methods of regaining it should that be required
- Determine the duration of the outsourcing contract, ideally three to five years
- Plan for future capability and expansion
- Choose a reliable outsourcing company, preferable one with experience and a track record – ask for references
- Understand the monetary impacts before and after outsourcing
- Maintain the loyalty of the retained staff, and ensure loyalty of the new staff
- Do not announce your intentions prematurely

If ability to manage or control the network internally is lost, and the external vendor source fails to perform, how difficult is it to rebuild the internal networking department? The loss of skilled people may be difficult and costly to recover. When outsourcing is chosen as the alternative, a strategic plan must be implemented with contingencies for each of these possible scenarios. Regardless of which solution is chosen, a clear-cut plan must be in place vis-à-vis the vendor for a minimum of two years. Define the vendor's plan for updating technology and workforce. Make sure the outsourcing vendor is able to adapt to your company's business needs, as well as their own, to maintain your future growth and competitiveness. Alternate outsourcing vendors must remain an option.

Now let's take a look at a few of the key outsourcing considerations in detail.

1.7.3 Resources

When a company decides to outsource, there will be either a reduction in staff (common with outsourcing) or an avoidance of the need for new or additional network staff (common for out-tasking). If there were individuals assigned to the specific network tasks outsourced, many or all will either be subsumed by the outsourcer, reassigned, or cut. Their knowledge can be quite valuable to other areas of the business. While this can translate to cost savings for the company in head count or the ability to use these people for other job functions, it may have a detrimental effect on efficiency. Reassignment of these individuals must be optimized by moving them to an area where they can focus on the core competencies of your business.

The outsourcing vendor can also become an extension of the networking staff. In this case, the out-tasking company assumes responsibility for the more menial and time consuming tasks, allowing the network professionals within the company to change the focus of their efforts on more critical concerns for the core business. The outsourcing deal must be closely monitored for increasing vendor fees, a degradation of performance, and a loss of priority, which may cause potential problems down the road. Always look for a service level guarantee. If the outsourcing goes sour, rehiring good people who were cut in favor of the vendor could be quite expensive and difficult.

Outsourcing can also provide an increased value-added service to companies who only wish to outsource a portion of their network operations, such as monitoring, disaster recovery, or data transport. This selective outsourcing is also known as out-tasking.

1.7.4 Skill Sets and Reliability

Will the vendor you have outsourced to have the same or better skill sets and reliability than your own staff? Does your existing staff lack the efficiency and organization needed to manage the network? Measuring the tradeoffs of existing skill sets to those gained from outsourcing is a necessity. The critical cost factors in outsourcing are people, not computers. Skilled professionals are difficult to find and expensive to retrain. It takes a large investment to keep them current with constant technological updates and training. Researching the vendor's past experience with customers is a necessary task before choosing a vendor. Contact current customers for a reference and determine if the vendor has managed a network such as yours before.

One major benefit of outsourcing is that it enables your experienced staff to work on other strategic projects key to the success of your business. In fact, building and managing a data communications network is often *not* the core competency of most corporations. These otherwise routine everyday repetitive tasks are sometimes best outsourced to relieve existing staff and free up resources to focus on mission-critical applications. These freed up resources can enhance the long-term strategy of the business by avoiding the more mundane network building and management tasks. One such task discussed is the migration of applications from mainframe platforms to distributed processing platforms of mini- and microcomputers networked by LANs. Many outsourcing firms hire technology experts, which, were they to be hired as permanent staff, would be very expensive resources, yet are packaged much more cost-effectively with the outsourcing deal. Outsourcing can also be the catalyst to help combine departmental resources from both telecommunications and computer communications departments into a single department.

1.7.5 Monetary Impacts and Return on Investment (ROI)

Monetary impacts vary between corporations, but the bottom line is how outsourcing affects your departmental and corporation expenses. If you decide to build, install, and manage a network yourself, will you get a return on investment (and continued return as you constantly update network resources) better than outsourcing the entire operation? Most studies say probably not. Cost remains one of the major driving factors in the decision to outsource. Consensus is that outsourcing can save a corporation money, and that large capital expenditures can be minimized (mostly incurred by the outsourcer — but shared with other contracts), but all cost savings and additional costs incurred (including opportunity costs) must be measured in the business case. Costs associated with corporate networking must be clearly defined and compared to the portion of these costs outsourcing would eliminate or augment. An outside vendor can achieve cost savings by providing network services such as access to public, shared, frame, and cell-switched networks, which can save a considerable sum of money for the corporation currently using private lines. True savings can be achieved when the vendor supplies all network services down to the user, and the cost of outsourcing can be directly compared to the cost of existing or planned operational costs.

Some companies with financial difficulties or shortages of capital prefer outsourcing to take care of communications while they concentrate on building the core business. While the technical business case may call for a new network, the economics may paint a different picture. The network must be an economically viable investment at some point early in its life cycle. How much will the network *cost* compared with how much the network will *save* the company? Savings can take the form of *hard* or *soft* dollars. Hard dollar savings could include straight cost avoidance savings of doing it yourself, headcount decreases, or pure network cost savings from the existing technology or architecture. Soft dollar savings could include productivity increases, performance increases, and future cost avoidance. Cost should primarily be weighed against reliability and performance, with support running a close third. The network should be implemented with minimal adaptation costs, multiple uses and capabilities, with a strong return on investment (ROI) as measured in hard and soft dollars for the business.

Network operations usually constitutes a major portion of network costs, and thus out-tasking of network operations could be a viable alternative. While networks are the focus of this book, many other support systems are required to make the network design run. These systems include network management, billing, administration, order entry and tracking systems, and many other enablers to the business operations of the company. These services are used to manage and maintain the network and can constitute a considerable portion of the entire network expense. The price of procuring and installing CPE and end-user equipment, which use high-bandwidth data services, is also a consideration. The bottom line is that the network designer must consider many costs other than those associated with the procurement of data communications transmission and hardware.

1.7.6 Control

There is always the fear of losing control of the communications network to the vendor. A corporation always wants to feel that the control of its mission-critical applications, which are key to its success, are in good hands. Privacy, security, and availability become critical questions for the vendor. How do you manage the vendor's effectiveness in handling your traffic? This is part of the trust relationship which must be built between the user and the vendor. If the corporation retains its network manager, which it should, that manager now has someone focused on making sure the vendors fulfill their outsourcing objectives. The same proactive attitude within the corporation should also be shown by the vendor.

1.7.7 To What Extent?

How high on the OSI Reference Model (OSIRM) do you outsource? Outsourcing can range from private line physical layer transport of data to complete outsourcing services which include all seven layers of the model. The more layers that are outsourced, the higher the level of expertise needed, and the closer the outsource extends to the user. Typical outsourcing for switched services ranges from the physical layer (Layer 1) to the transport or inter-networking layer (Layer 4). In this scenario, almost all of the application control, Layers 5 to 7, remains with the user. Corporations that require total systems outsourcing are best advised to look at multiple vendors, as each outsourcer has its own area of expertise, such as LAN versus WAN.

1.7.8 How Long?

There is no predetermined length of time for outsourcing, but, in general, contract periods should not extend more than three to seven years before renewal. This cycle can be reduced to three to five years with reviews and cancellation clauses, depending on the shelf life of the technology. What factors drive the contract length?

- ◊ Shelf life of the technology
- ◊ Half-life of original price points
- ◊ Applications churn
- ◊ Business sizing and growth rate

There should also be a technological currency clause provided by the vendor. This prohibits locking the organization into one vendor or one technology cycle. The half-life for technology is shrinking year by year, and extended outsourcing contracts that do not contain these provisions can lock the user into an obsolete or non-cost-effective technology platform—ultimately impacting the overall business. Price structures should be renegotiated even more often, and be flexible enough to take into account industry and tariff changes. Beware of locking into and becoming dependent upon one vendor, who may use this reliance to raise the price of outsourcing accordingly. One way to avoid this time trap is to always use technologies that strictly adhere to international standards and provide a clear migration path to future technologies. Also, some corporations have divided up outsourcing into at least two parts to let competing vendors vie for their business – again the example of LAN and WAN.

The outsourcing vendor should provide network performance analysis at least once a month, and these analyses should be reviewed with the customer on a monthly, quarterly, or, at the most, semi-annual basis to ascertain if the vendor is providing the contracted network performance. Network performance guarantees are always desirable.

1.7.9 Vendor/User Relationships — The Contract

A very close relationship exists between user and vendor. This relationship is built during the vendor proposal stage. A good idea is to observe how the vendor handles methods of measurement for performance, diversity, availability, and reliability; technology revisions and upgrades; and backup plans for its other large customers. These measurements should be clear and easy to understand and, of course, quantifiable.

Always remember to treat the vendors with respect, as they will be your partners for the length of the contract. This is probably how you will be treated as well. A good idea is to create a business relationship with the outsourcing entities before engaging their legal department. Be aware, however, that some corporate resources will be required to "manage the vendor", and a lack of vendor control or understanding can easily damage this relationship. The vendor manager should be involved with the entire project, in some cases beginning as early as the contract negotiation.

1.7.10 Cost of Ownership – Make vs. Buy Analysis for Management

In most network designs the cost of managing the network is overlooked or minimized. Equipment and infrastructure (local loops, long-distance circuits, and data services like FR) costs are very tangible. Management costs, on the other hand, are much less tangible until after the network is installed – when the real requirement for management is felt. The greatest challenge to users attempting remote office connectivity solutions is management, not equipment costs and bandwidth. If network management is not in your company's core competency list, or you believe that it could be more efficiently and less expensively outsourced, then you will want to consider out-tasking some or all of your network management requirements rather than try to build these capabilities internally. In this section, we will compare the costs of outsourcing the network management portion of the network to the costs of building and performing network management internally.

To manage a network you need a combination of technical expertise, the proper tools and support systems, and a well-defined set of proactive processes. SNMP is simply (pardon the pun) a network management protocol – a method for sending data about a discrete state of the network from a network device to a network management presentation manager. The SNMP protocol and the presentation manager (like HP OpenView or SUNNet Manager) are just two tools used in a reactive management process, and these tools only monitor network layer alarms (e.g., presence or absence of an IP address or port on the network). The network typically has many other elements than just an IP address, such as the transport backbone (e.g., private line, FR, or ATM), transport switches, local loops, and DTE and DCE devices. Each of these devices requires monitoring and information to be stored and managed. This information on customers, vendors, software, hardware, logical and physical configurations, and circuit records must then be linked and correlated to be useful. Software and firmware must be constantly upgraded, as the major router and switch manufacturers come out with on average two to three major releases and 10 to 20 "dot" patches per year alone. Device configurations must be backed up and stored, and be retrievable over the network. Constant performance engineering on devices and transport must be performed on a regular basis to ensure network optimization. All these processes require more than just fault management.

Table 1.1 contains an example of the make versus buy analysis for outsourcing proactive management of a 10-site data network with 5 days, 8 hours per day coverage, and a 50-site data network with 7 days, 5 hours per day coverage. This service is purely designed for fault management only. Table 1.2 shows the same design using an outsourcing vendor that charges $200 per site to provide the total management services. This analysis assumes the customer has no management equipment or talent to start. Note that the potential savings are significant.

What are a company's options? One option is to hire a substantial staff, build the management systems, integrate the tools and information, and constantly train to maintain a level of technological currency, *or* out-task specific parts of these items to achieve the desired result.

Table 1.1 **Make vs. Buy Analysis for Network Management**

YEAR ONE	10 sites 5×8	50 Sites 7×24
Network management workstation	$12,000	$16,000
SNMP application (e.g. OpenView)	15,000	15,000
SNMP applications platform (e.g., SUN Sparc)	35,000	35,000
Vendor element modules (3 modules)	9,000	9,000
Other WAN tools (packet analyzers, sniffers)	20,000	30,000
Facilities and environmental	2,000	8,000
Training & travel	2,000	2,000
Inter-network administrators	60,000	250,000
FIRST YEAR'S TOTAL	$155,000	$371,000

YEARS 2 & 3		
Management software/hardware maintenance	$4,000	$5,000
Facilities and environmental	2,000	8,000
Internetwork administrators	60,000	250,000
YEAR 2 & 3 TOTAL (each year)	$66,000	$263,000

Table 1.2 **Make vs. Buy Outsourcing Option**

Network Management Costs	10 sites	50 sites
First year costs	$24,000	$120,000
First year savings	$131,000	$251,000
Year 2 & 3 costs	$24,000	$120,000
Year 2 & 3 savings (each year)	$42,000	$143,000

Source: NetSolve, Cost of Ownership, 1996.

1.7.11 Summary of Benefits and Drawbacks

The primary benefits of outsourcing are:

- \+ Uses vendor experience and specialists
- \+ Allows your company to focus on its core business rather than designing, installing, and managing networks
- \+ Reduces costs (improved ROI) and resources required
- \+ Augments existing work force with skilled workers

The potential drawbacks of outsourcing include:

- Loss of control
- Possible loss of in-house expertise and resources
- Possible sacrifice of technology flexibility
- Risk of impact to critical systems if vendor fails

These potential drawbacks can be countered with good planning, smart management, and proper choice of vendor.

1.7.12 The Future of Outsourcing

The market for outsourcing continues to grow rapidly. More third-party companies are providing outsourcing packages. The complexities of outsourcing grow as users move from bridged and multiplexed to routed to switched environments. Also, as LANs continue to proliferate, the number of disparate protocols increases drastically, and all of them require interconnectivity. Outsourcing and out-tasking are clearly here to stay, and are having a major impact on the computer and communications industries. There are obviously many short-term benefits from outsourcing, but what about the long-term effects? Many people who disagree with outsourcing say that the long-term expenses outweigh the short-term gains. This underscores the need to first develop an accurate business case. Outsourcing is clearly here to stay, and the markets for outsourcing and out-tasking continue to grow at a rapid rate. Ask yourself the question – is designing, installing, and managing a network part of our core competencies, and if not, should I consider outsourcing part or all of it?

1.8 REVIEW

In this chapter we previewed what constitutes a network design, the factors that influence network design, the history behind voice and data networking, and the direction in which data and computer communications is heading. We took a detailed look at the actual need for data and computer communications networks throughout industry, business, and user perspectives and perceptions. We defined data network design beginning with a history of both voice telecommunications and data computer communications, and how both have evolved and combined to set the stage for broadband networking in the twenty-first century. These new networks provide access for many types of traffic and applications, many of which require large amounts of bandwidth and an intelligent network to provide ubiquitous access through bandwidth-on-demand services and technologies. The data revolution has affected the data network design engineer and manager, from both a national and global view of data services and technologies. The importance of *planning* in network design was covered. Insight was provided into the roles and responsibilities of the new world network design manager and engineer. Finally, an objective look at outsourcing and out-tasking was presented as an alternative to designing, building, and managing part or all of your network.

Chapter

2

Computer and Information Networking Directions

What drives the business need for a data network? And what are the key enablers that make that network change and evolve, requiring a continual design effort? Data and computer communications are an integral part of any major business. As businesses continually re-engineer themselves, so too must data networks.

Since the first edition of this book, the acceleration toward multimedia, client-server applications, Intranet and Internet communications, and broadband technologies like FR and ATM has intensified. The effect that emerging broadband data networks and the Internet have had upon corporate data networking is nothing short of phenomenal. Our charter is to understand the many changes and enablers affecting the data communications landscape, including: network infrastructure, application, communications technology, and corporate infrastructure changes.

In this chapter we take principles and trends now occurring in the late 20th century and extrapolate them forward into the 21st century. The network paradigms explored in this chapter are based on the premise that the corporation is continually innovating applications, technologies, and infrastructures to win the war against technological obsolescence.

2.1 APPLICATIONS AS KEY ENABLERS

Consumer and commercial applications are changing, creating a need for more bandwidth-on-demand. Combined exponential growths in computing power and the nonlinear growth in intercommunications have created an overall demand for data communications that is greater than exponential. These factors, together referred to as the *accelerating bandwidth principle,* is further accelerated itself by the increased power of the desktop computer. Multimedia is one example of a high-speed bandwidth application requiring a high-speed communications network.

2.1.1 Consumer and Commercial Applications

Consumer service applications requiring high bandwidth are enabling technologies such as ATM. These applications require high flexibility and performance, and include:

- Entertainment imaging
- Home-shopping services employing multimedia voice, data, image, and video using on-line databases and catalogues
- Medical imaging
- Video-on-demand for popular movies
- E-mail and multimessaging systems
- Interactive multimedia applications and games

Some applications require not only broadband service but also the capability of a broadcast public service. These include:

- Distance learning
- On-line video libraries for home study
- Video desktop training courses
- Video-on-demand

There are many commercial public service applications that are pushing the envelope for high and flexible bandwidths such as:

- LAN/MAN/WAN seamless inter-connectivity and internetworking
- Telecommuting applications
- Distributed data access
- Large file transfer and real-time access to files
- Electronic publishing
- Finance industry reports
- Graphic-intensive industrial engineering applications (e.g., CAD, CAM, CAE, CIM) on-line
- Collaborative computing such as groupware
- Cooperative computing such as concurrent CAD/CAM engineering
- Integrated voice, video, data multiplexing, and switching
- Terminal-to-mainframe communications
- Video conferencing
- CD ROM servers
- Inventory control systems
- Multimedia applications to the desktop (e.g., e-mail)
- Desktop publishing
- Remote database access
- Electronic fund transfer (EFT)
- Financial modeling

- Electronic commerce
- Leading edge ATM work groups
- Collapsed backbone campus networks
- Seamless interworking with legacy systems using ATM

Many of these applications are not yet widely deployed, but each will drive the need for greater and more flexible bandwidth.

2.1.2 Application Demand for Bandwidth

The above applications range from providing cost consolidation efficiencies to changing the dynamics of the business. Many applications demonstrate that people increasingly rely on visual or image information rather than audio or text information, as predicted by the old but accurate adage that a picture is worth a thousand words. The increase in telecommuting and conducting business from the home also illustrates the trend to rely on visual or image information. The recent partnering and buyout of cable firms by information transport and telecommunications providers also portend major changes in the infrastructure for providing interactive multimedia networking to the home.

As new technologies emerge, their proponents often look for a single "killer application" for success. More often the case is that many applications or implementations working together can make a technology successful in the desktop or the local, campus, metropolitan, and wide area network.

There are two generic types of information that applications require: an object of fixed size that must be transferred and a stream of information that can be characterized by a certain data rate or bandwidth. Multimedia involves combinations of these basic information transfers. The tradeoffs in response time, throughput, and the number of simultaneous applications that can be supported by technologies such as ATM are illustrated through several simple examples.

Figure 2.1 shows the time to transfer an object of a certain size at a particular transfer rate. Along the horizontal axis a number of common information objects are listed as an illustration of the object size in millions of bytes (megabytes or Mbytes). The general trend is that the time required to transfer the information which represents the object decreases as the transfer rate is increased. A real-time service would require immediate transfer in tens of milliseconds. The utility of the service in an interactive, near-real-time mode is usually perceived as requiring a transfer time of no more than a few seconds. A non-real-time or batch application may require many seconds up to minutes, or even hours, for transfer of an object.

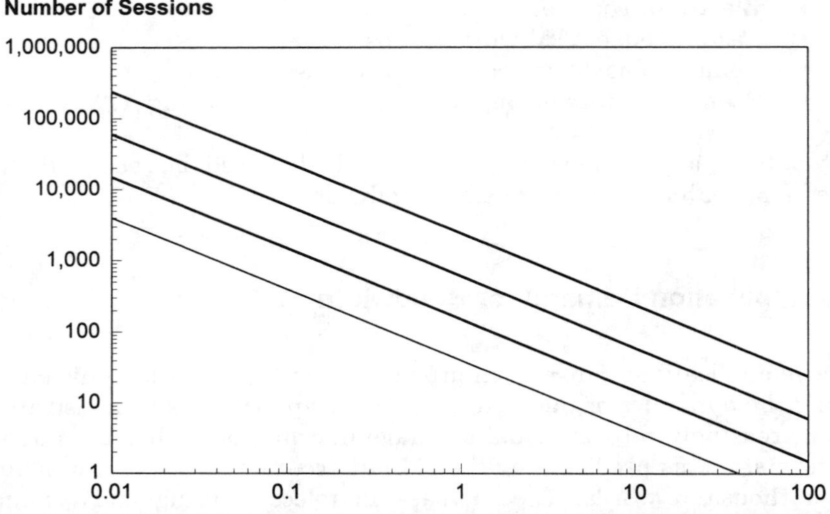

Figure 2.1 Object Transfer Time as a Function of Bandwidth

Now let's look at applications such as audio and video that use a certain amount of bandwidth. The bandwidth may be a fixed, continuous amount or an average amount.

Figure 2.2 plots the number of these applications requiring a certain fixed bandwidth that can be supported by allocated bandwidths of 50 Mbps (megabits per second) and higher. In general, as the bandwidth required by each application increases, the number of simultaneous applications supported decreases. Of course, allocating more overall bandwidth increases the number of fixed-rate applications that can be supported. A technology such as ATM is flexible enough to support many applications of different rates in the same network; however, these are not illustrated in this figure.

2.1.3 New Multimedia Applications

These application trends all point to a move toward visual reality—a dynamic, interactive visual representation of information rather than just textual or simple, static graphical representation. *Multimedia* is a term often used to represent the combination and presentation of multiple forms of data to the user.

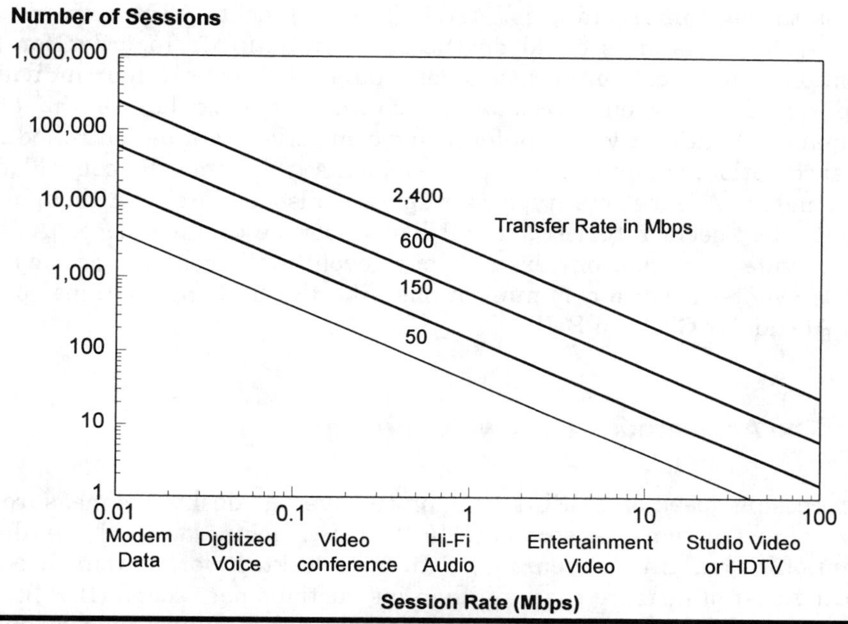

Figure 2.2 Number of Fixed Rate Application Sessions Supported

Multimedia is taking the user community by storm. Sound cards are almost commonplace in most home computers, and many users sport microphones and small cameras. Multimedia has also found its way into the commercial market with many of the applications mentioned above. Technologies such as ATM are being deployed to offer the capability to support time-sensitive traffic, typically voice or video, and offer enhanced delivery options such as point-to-multipoint and eventually broadcast. High-speed ATM multicast applications may include a broadcast of a video-conferencing application that includes text and video. Applications that can take advantage of the attributes of broadband data technologies such as ATM are now appearing – to support true voice, data, and video traffic integration with guaranteed Quality of Service (QoS) for each traffic type. These technologies allow bandwidth and connectivity to be flexibly and dynamically allocated.

Figure 2.3 shows a multimedia desktop workstation in Chicago. The person is holding a video conference with four other individuals in New York, London, Paris, and Washington, D.C. In this example, an automatic translation server could be connected for language conversion between the parties speaking different languages (not shown in the figure). Using ATM technology, an ATM interface card in the Chicago workstation could combine the video of the built-in monitor camera, the telephone, and text data into a single 25 or 155 Mbps ATM transmission stream to a local ATM switch. The ATM switch then broadcasts the voice, data, and video to switches at all four locations through intervening ATM WANs in the global ATM network. Of course, each of the sites could do the same in return. In order for this application to be effective, all attendees would need to have four individual pop-up screens on their workstations so that they could see the other participants. Multicast video-conferencing connections can be controlled by a conference option, where the choice of recipients is dynamically controlled by the originator. A "meet me" type conference is also available. Although this capability may seem futuristic, it will likely soon be commonplace. AT&T's multicast video service is one example of a revolution in communications that parallels events in voice communications, like the first international phone call by Alexander Graham Bell.

2.1.4 The Accelerating Bandwidth Principle

The processing speed of a CPU sitting on the average desktop is measured in millions of instructions per second (MIPS). This machine would have filled a medium office building 20 years ago. In fact, desktop workstations are now appearing that offer more than a billion instructions per second (BIPS). Not only are the MIPS of yesteryear centralized in the computing power on the desktop today, but the need to interconnect them is growing as well. The growth in the need to communicate data is driven by new distributed processing applications, like groupware, shared databases, desktop video conferencing, shared workspaces, multimedia, and electronic mail. These two trends in the increase in computing power and the need for any-to-any communications combine to result in the *accelerating bandwidth principle.*

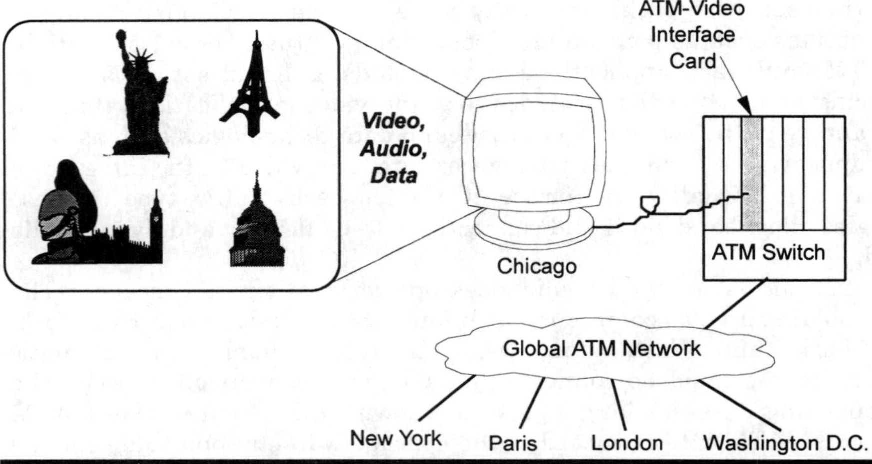

Figure 2.3 Multipoint, Multimedia ATM Application of the Future

Current LAN and WAN network bandwidths cannot handle for very long the accelerating need for bandwidth. Witness Ethernet, where initially 10 Mbps, even if utilized at only a 40 percent efficiency, initially offered a tremendous amount of bandwidth in the local area. As workstation power and application demands increased, however, Ethernet LANs "ran out of gas" and had to be segmented to increase bandwidth and resegmented until in some cases there was only one workstation per Ethernet segment. In this case Ethernet switches started to emerge as the "common bus" that Ethernet 10M bps used to provide. And Ethernet 100 Mbps is starting to proliferate. FDDI and Ethernet 100 Mbps were invented to provide 10 times more bandwidth (100 Mbps) than Ethernet 10 Mbps, but on the leading edge of workstation technology even FDDI has already become a bandwidth constraint. Furthermore, FDDI was initially designed for support of only data applications and is looking for multimedia options. As a further illustration of the explosive growth that can be caused by open interconnections, observe the tremendous growth rate of traffic on the Internet and the World Wide Web (WWW)—20 to 25 percent per month! Furthermore, with the advent of audio and video multicast, the demand outstrips Internet capacity on occasion.

Required connectivity is driven by the method in which business is performed, flow of information, and the nature of the organizational structure. In a flatter, empowered organization each individual may send, or provide access to, information that would only have been sent upwards in the preceding, hierarchical organization. There is a limit to how much interconnection can grow. There is a large amount of room for growth in an organization with a deep organizational hierarchy and even a modest number of direct reports. Networks too are getting much bigger and demanding much more bandwidth.

The following shows how the combined exponential growths in computing power and the nonlinear growth in intercommunications create an overall demand for data communications that is greater than exponential. These phenomena are collectively referred to as the *accelerating bandwidth principle*. Before exploring this concept, let's first review Amdahl's law. Amdahl's law states that the average application requires processing cycles, storage, and data communication speeds in roughly equal proportion, namely 1 MIPS, 1 Mbyte, and 1 Mbps. In the accelerating bandwidth principle the claim is that this rule no longer holds true.

Figure 2.4 illustrates the accelerating bandwidth principle. The curve labeled MIPS/desk represents the exponential growth in computing power at the desktop at a rate of approximately 175 percent growth every two years. The curve labeled Mbps/MIPS represents the nonlinear growth of the required data communication of approximately 3 percent per year, resulting in a doubling of Amdahl's law of the proportion of bandwidth to processing power over 25 years. The curve labeled Mbps/desk, which is the product of MIPS/desk and Mbps/MIPS, represents the data communications bandwidth predicted by the accelerating bandwidth principle.

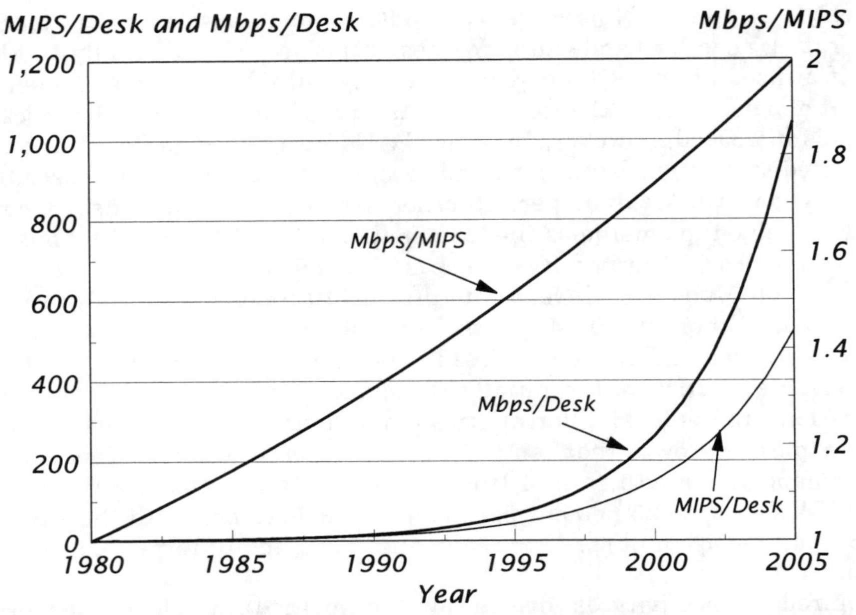

Figure 2.4 Accelerating Bandwidth Principle

The accelerating bandwidth principle points to the inadequacy of Ethernet and FDDI and illustrates the need for true Gigabit-per-second (Gbps) networking in the not too distant future. Another way to offset the increasing need for communications bandwidth is the use of improved compression, which reduces the amount of data requiring transmission. However, compression only yields improvement up to the information theoretic limits.

Applications and business needs expand to fill the opportunities that technology can provide cost-effectively. The usage of computing and communications by applications is largely driven by cost. Basic computing and communications costs have been declining dramatically for the last 20 years.

Figure 2.5 plots over time the costs of processing, storage, and communications. The decreasing $/MIPS, $/Mbyte of RAM, $/Mbyte of disk and $/Mbps/mile over time shown in this figure are all exponentially *decreasing* since they are nearly straight lines on the semilog scale. The $/MIPS and $/Mbyte are derived for microprocessor technology and semiconductor memory. The exponential increase in computing speed and accessible memory is a well-established trend, driven by integrated circuit technology, that will extend well into the next century. Recent trends in processor and memory technology may even exceed exponential growth! The $/Mbps/mile curve is for fiber optic transmission. Note that the cost of transmission is decreasing slightly faster than that of computer processing. The cost of mechanical disk storage is decreasing at the slowest rate.

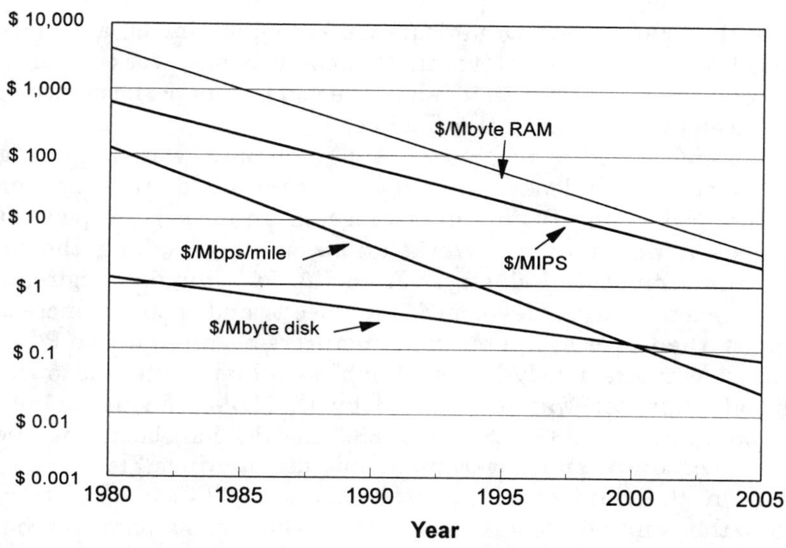

Figure 2.5 Technology Cost Trends over Time

The fact that transmission costs are decreasing more rapidly than mass memory and processing costs provides economic reinforcement for the accelerating bandwidth principle. It is becoming less expensive to have information transmitted over a data network than it is to store it locally, or perform calculations to generate it. If you believe in this principle, you may subscribe to each user having less *intelligent* personal computing devices and accessing intelligent services within the network, such as the Internet today. Why store the information on a local hard drive or CD ROM, when the network will store it and send it to you on demand for a fraction of the cost? Are we moving backwards? We spent the last 15 years evolving from the dumb VT100 terminal. When the cost or value of copyrighted or licensed information content such as distance learning, information on demand, and other interactive services is taken into account, this becomes an even greater justification for the accelerating bandwidth principle.

2.1.5 Power to the Desktop

Obviously, one of the biggest trends influencing the explosion of bandwidth requirements and the subsequent success of transport technologies like ATM is the proliferation of computing power to the desktop and its subsequent use in distributed computing. Personal computer and workstation processing power (MIPS), memory size (Mbytes), and display size (Mpixels) are increasing at an exponential rate, with distributed networks taking these workstation attributes closer to every user on the network—in fact, to the desktop and even to the application. Organizational reengineering creates a demand for increased bandwidths to interconnect these PCs and workstations. This increase is occurring at a rate faster than the computing performance metrics due to the accelerating bandwidth principle.

Personal computers (PCs) such as the Apple computer were born in "garage shops" and were initially looked at as toys for games and other amusements. That has changed as the PC matured and had an even more powerful son referred to as a workstation. Workstations are now taking the premier position in the computing industry. From the PC's humble beginnings, as software applications were developed and speeds and memory increased as costs dropped, the larger computer manufacturers began to notice PCs on the desks of users who previously had a "dumb" terminal connected to the host. The personal computer was legitimized by the IBM announcement of its personal computer in 1983. Since 1983, the PC has been the industry standard for corporate and government microcomputing. Figure 2.6 shows the growth in the number of professionals using PCs. This trend has continued to the point where virtually every desktop has a personal computer and mobile personal computing devices have gone beyond the laptop to the palmtop. In fact, some industry experts claim there is a move toward less intelligent and processor-intensive PCs for desktop access to distributed Internet-based services.

In an ironic twist of fate IBM attempted to set a proprietary *de facto* industry standard by introducing the microchannel architecture, not making it open like the initial PC Industry Standard Architecture (ISA). Soon after, several other manufacturers surpassed IBM in PC market share, including the upstart "garage shop" Apple! Now the standard PC with the Microsoft Windows operating system appears to be the worldwide standard.

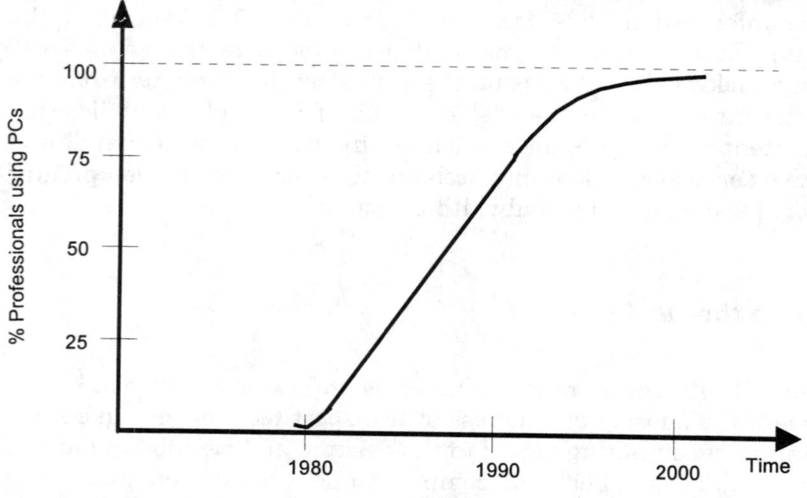

Figure 2.6 Increasing Use of Personal Computers

The PC has provided the user with the device for desktop access to the world of data. Mass storage of information has shrunk to a fraction of its original size and cost. Now the critical element is no longer hardware, but software. Indeed, the cost of software on a modern PC can easily exceed that of the hardware investment.

2.2 COMMUNICATIONS TECHNOLOGIES AS ENABLERS

The applications driving the need for high-performance data communications networks, in particular, a high-bandwidth wide area network, have been reviewed. This section now explores the technology enablers. Technology enablers take on many forms, from the need for higher speeds, increased flexibility, improved efficiency, and support for multiple traffic types to support entirely new applications. To understand where a technology is going and its short- and long-term benefit to the user, one must first understand the S curves of technological evolution and the phases by which it is accepted by users.

2.2.1 S Curves of Technological Evolution

The evolution of a technology can be viewed as an S curve on an X-Y axis, where the horizontal axis is time and the vertical axis is the maturity or market presence of the technology. Notice Figure 2.7 where frame relay and ATM are portrayed. Notice that frame relay began deployment in 1990, picked up steam with phenomenal growth rate of >200 percent per year in 1993-95, and in 1996 became a commodity market. Frame relay growth leads the charge in flexible bandwidth-on-demand services, with a five-year growth in worldwide revenues going from less than $50 million in 1992 to a $2-billion market as of 1996, representing more than 10,000 customers and 200,000 ports. Predictions for ATM service growth outstrip even these figures. ATM, while picking up steam, has tremendous growth potential even more than frame relay, because it serves more traffic types and services (including frame relay). Note that ATM maturity in the LAN is preceding the WAN. Sometimes a technology will never reach the drastic growth cycle and die out. The ISDN curve would look flat for many years and is just now picking up in parallel with ATM.

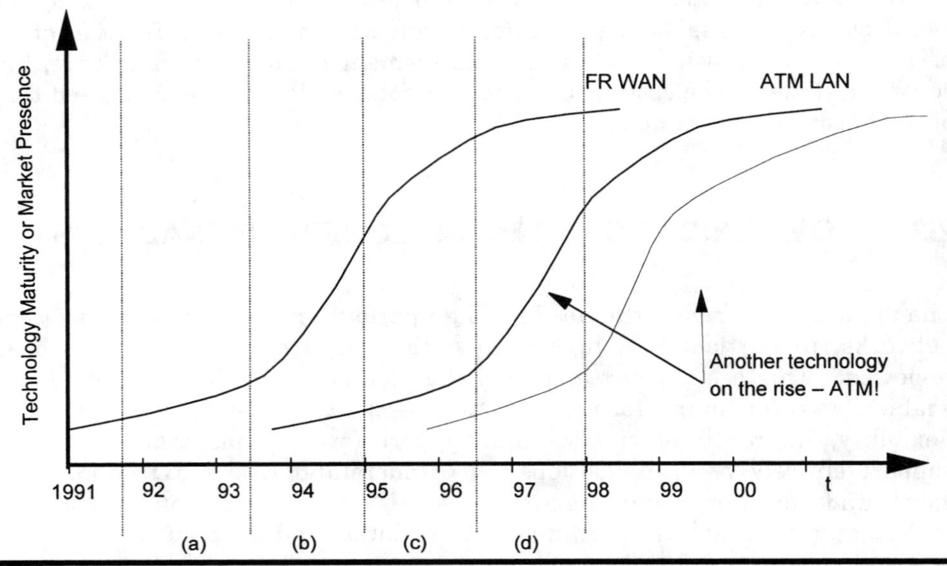

Figure 2.7 S curves of Technology

2.2.2 Technology Acceptance Phases

Another way to measure a technology's success might be in how well it is able to catch the wave of technological innovation. The bell curve of classic market or product life cycles is presented in Figure 2.8. Timing is the key. The life cycles of the technologies presented in this book are illustrated in Figure 2.9. As time evolves, a technology can only meet the needs of a portion of the overall market. In this example, the need and measure is bandwidth-related. ATM technology will eventually predominate over frame relay. One example of a possible next technology wave after ATM is the use of optical and/or wavelength switching at very high speeds. Wavelength Division Multiplexing (WDM) may offer the next generation transport service. At lower speeds, ATM may have technology competition from improved compression, modems, or variable-length IP switching. The relative values and timing of each technology are not intended to be precise, but merely to illustrate a possible future scenario. No technology will last forever, and legacy technologies generally take a long time to disappear from the scene.

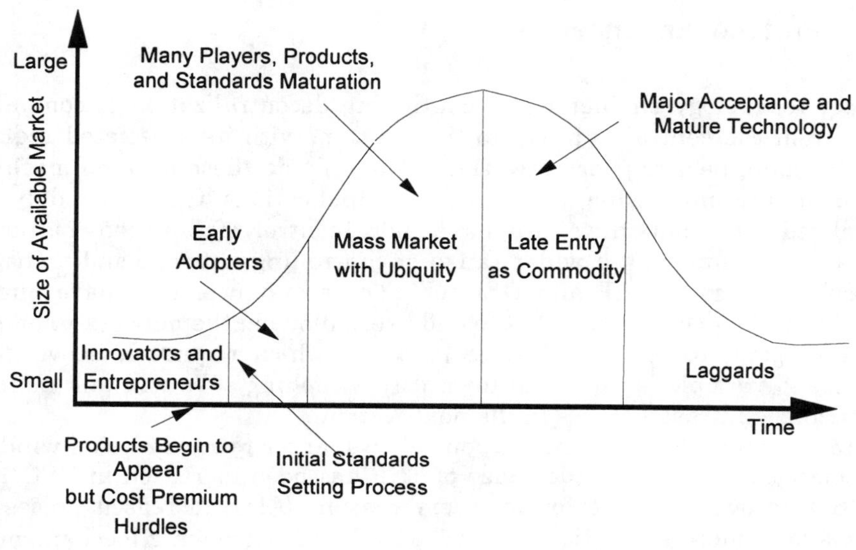

Figure 2.8 Classic Product to Market Life Cycle

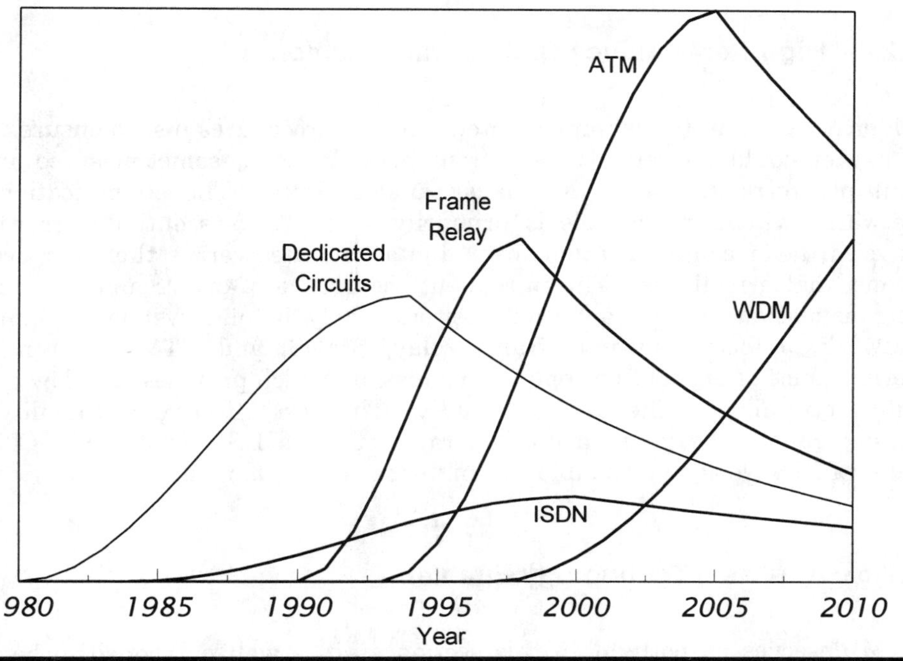

Figure 2.9 Waves of Technological Innovation over Time

2.2.3 Protocol Enhancements

Another technology enabler is the continuing decentralization of computing power from the centralized host to the desktop, with its associated requirement for more peer-to-peer networking. Not only do these desktop machines now have the processing power to run applications that once only the centralized host had, they also have more control of how information is passed, thus employing a wider range of controlling network and transport protocols such as TCP/IP and DECnet. These enhancements have pushed network intelligence outward to the end user, allowing the network to employ less intelligent, more cost effective protocols which require less overhead. One recent example is the trend toward IP switching. We will talk more on decentralized infrastructures in the next section.

Increased storage in the end stations allows larger retransmission windows to be maintained. The window size of TCP has been increased in RFC 1323 from 64k to over 1 Gbyte for this very reason. Also, increased processing power allows more sophisticated flow control and windowing mechanisms to be implemented in the end systems. One example of protocol complexity is demonstrated in the sophisticated TCP flow control algorithms in the end station versus the relatively simple Internet Protocol (IP) used in routers and switches.

2.2.4 High-Performance Digital Transmission

Older network protocols implemented complex procedures just to ensure that a packet could be reliably sent from node to node, sometimes requiring multiple retransmissions over noisy analog links. The simplification of network switching protocols is primarily a result of essentially error-free physical layer communications over digital facilities versus the older error-prone analog facilities. The infrequent occurrence of errors and associated retransmission is then achieved cost-effectively in end systems. Simpler network protocols, such as frame relay, SMDS, and ATM, rely on the performance of digital fiber-optic transmission, which provides very low error rates, typically on the order of 10^{-12}. The cost effective availability of plesiochronous digital transmission rates such as DS1, DS3, and SONET rates of STS-Nc is a key enabler for high-speed broadband services.

2.2.5 ATM as a Technology Enabler

ATM deserves a spotlight in this section as it is well positioned to be the leading technology enabler for communications by the turn of the century. ATM is a multiplexing and switching technology that is designed for flexibility at the expense of efficiency – offering multiple levels of quality of service for multimedia traffic. For any *single* application it is usually possible to find a better data communications technique, but ATM excels where it is desirable for applications with different performance, quality of service, and business requirements to be performed on the same computer, multiplexer, router, switch, and/or network. For these applications the flexibility of ATM can result in a solution that is more cost effective than several separate, individually optimized technologies. Furthermore, the flexibility of ATM can "future-proof" investments since unenvisioned, future applications may also be supported by ATM.

Let's compare the technology revolution of the 1980's multiplexer technology to late 1990 ATM technology. The widespread use of T1 multiplexers in the 1980s was predicted to be a precursor to a wave of T3 (which is the common name for DS3, as explained in Chapter 4) multiplexer deployment, which has not occurred. Understanding the reasons for the T1 multiplexer success and the lack of the adoption of T3 multiplexers is central to placing the potential benefits of ATM in perspective. T1 multiplexers allowed high-performance, relatively low-cost DS1 (colloquially called T1) facilities to be shared between a variety of applications on a quasistatic basis using Time Division Multiplexing (TDM). TDM bandwidth allocation is not well suited to high-performance, bursty data communications. The growth in demand for data communications has increased dramatically, but the demand for TDM-based service has not kept pace with the overall demand for bandwidth. DS3 speeds are over 28 times that of the DS1, but cost only 5 to 10 times more. The economics and restrictions of TDM of the T3 multiplexer were simply never justified for most users because better choices for public services were available within the planning horizon, such as frame relay, SMDS, and ATM.

ATM offers the capability to extend the LAN or MAN across the WAN at speeds comparable to the LAN or MAN (currently 10 to 100 Mbps) at less cost, because the bandwidth and switches are economically shared across many users, as shown in Figure 2.10. Instead of having to funnel the bandwidth of interconnected LANs down to the lower bandwidth provided by the static allocation of TDM connecting sites via DS1s in the DS3 access line, as shown in Figure 2.10a, ATM provides each LAN with the capability to burst at the full LAN access speed across the WAN on the DS3 access line, as shown in Figure 2.10b. This figure shows how TDM LAN interconnection takes much longer to transfer data, as shown by the time plots of actual usage on the access lines. Since all users do not burst simultaneously, and indeed are controlled so that they cannot, access to peak bandwidth on demand can be accommodated almost all of the time. Extreme economies of scale can be obtained by integrating multiple applications on the same physical network.

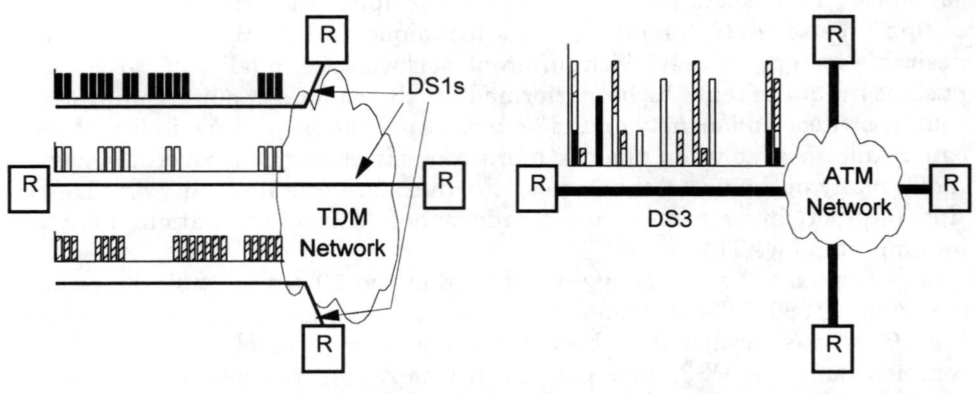

Figure 2.10 More Usable Bandwidth for Less Cost

The need for public network ATM service is growing as users quickly find that the capital cost of building a private ATM WAN is huge, compared with using a shared, partitioned, public network service. This will be even more evident as public network providers add multiple protocol feature support to their services. A financial interest can also play a part here, too, since expense dollars are paid for public services in lieu of capital dollars spent for private equipment. Within many corporations the expense-oriented approach can be more readily justified than the capital-oriented approach.

2.2.6 Technology that Future-Proofs Your Investment

Always look for a technology or service that can future-proof or protect your investment. While ATM seems to be the technology leader for the rest of this decade, standards continue to evolve and generations of equipment can be separated by only a few years or even months. When public service providers make ATM a core part of their backbone and service offerings, they achieve the benefit of flexibility and scalability. Flexibility and scalability take on many forms. Being able to increase the number and size of switches, users, and circuits is a key benefit. Support for a distributed architecture for high reliability is another benefit. The capability to upgrade network elements to faster processors, and upgrade routers, switches, hubs and workstations to the same standards-based architecture, is also a potential benefit. No technology will remain efficient and cost effective forever, but the flexibility and scalability of ATM hardware and software potentially provide a longer life cycle than other MAN and WAN technologies, which "future-proofs" the ATM investment.

2.3 CORPORATE INFRASTRUCTURES ARE CHANGING

Transmission infrastructures are evolving and changing with the proliferation of high-performance digital transmission over fiber optics – changes required for broadband networking. Networks are evolving from centralized to distributed processing, fueled by the move toward distributed computing, client-server, and Web server networking. This shift is causing traditional SNA legacy protocols to merge with inter-networking protocols like TCP/IP. LANs, MANs, and WANs are merging in the process, as LANs demand native transfer speeds across the WAN. Shared media may be meeting their death as multi-user LANs begin to run out of speed (bandwidth) and users begin to segment LANs populated by fewer users, combining single user LAN segments with LAN switches. Distributed routing with ATM technology moves to the periphery of the network, where it is more cost effective, and can connect families of LAN switches. The cost of bandwidth in the LAN and WAN decreases rapidly, and advances in fiber-optic transmission technology such as WDM will make bandwidth in the future very inexpensive. These trends have enabled new methods of creating LAN work-groups sharing multiple servers that span multiple physical locations – and hence the growth of virtual LANs (VLANs). The Internet has not escaped these trends; witness the creation of intranets within the Internet and the creation of client-server and Web server intranetworks. Will IP and ATM be the technologies that provide the infrastructure to support these trends? Let's first look at the evolution in transmission infrastructures.

2.3.1 Transmission Infrastructure Evolution

International and national transmission infrastructures in modern countries have largely replaced digital microwave facilities with fiber optics even more rapidly than analog facilities were previously displaced by digital transmission systems. Satellite communication has evolved as a high-quality digital transmission medium for connectivity to remote areas or as backup to terrestrial facilities, and there are even satellites designed specifically to handle ATM traffic. Along all major traffic routes fiber has replaced microwave, and in thinner routes fiber will soon replace the digital microwave facilities that just recently replaced analog microwave. Just about every major metropolitan area is fiber-capable, with access speeds now reaching into the gigabits. Significant deployment of fiber to the curb and to the home is now beginning. Modern digital and fiber optic transmission communications are ushering in a new baseline for the performance of digital data communications, just as digital transmission made long-distance-calling sound quality as good as local calls just 15 years ago. The impact and benefits of high-performance digital transmission over fiber optics are recurring themes throughout this book. These changes in the remoderniza-tion of the fiber infrastructure all accelerate the move toward broadband networking.

2.3.2 From Centralized to Distributed Networks

Computer communications networks have evolved from centralized main-frame computing, through the minicomputer era, and into the era in the last 30 years of the distributed personal computer and workstation processing. The first data computer communications networks resembled a hierarchical, or star, topology. Access from remote sites homed back to a central location where the mainframe computer resided (usually an IBM host or DEC VAX). Figure 2.11 shows this centralized, hierarchical computer network topology. Note that the star and hierarchy are actually different ways of drawing the same centralized network topology.

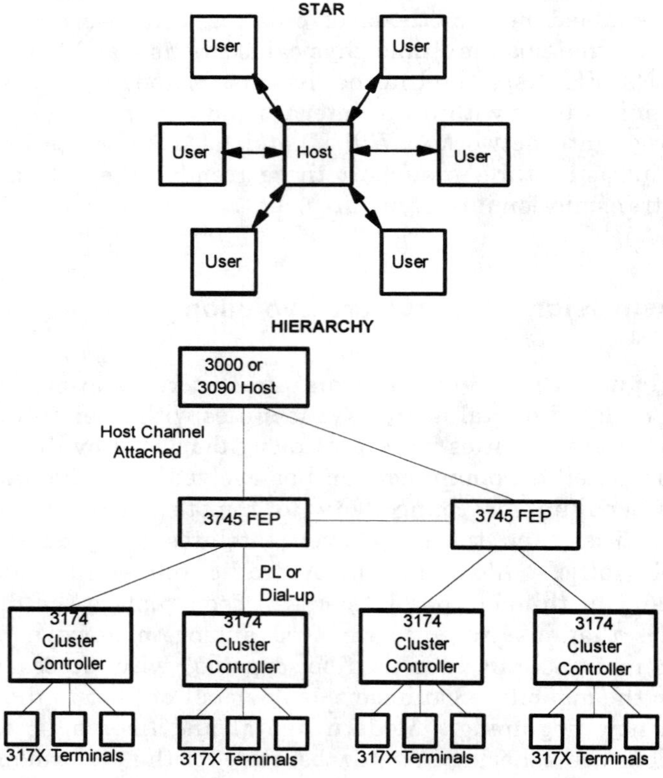

Figure 2.11 Centralized Star and Hierarchical Topology

There is a great parallel happening here between networks and organizations. Networks and entire corporate organizations are making the transition from hierarchical to distributed structures, both requiring greater interconnection and more productivity from each element or individual. This move from a hierarchical structure to a distributed structure is called *flattening*. In networks, flattening means there are fewer network elements but greater logical interconnection. In organizations, flattening is often referred to as the elimination of middle management, which requires greater horizontal communication and interaction within the organization. This trend continues as the corporation is re-engineered, which also requires re-engineering of the supporting computing and communication network infrastructure. Both scenarios create the need for increased connectivity and communications.

a. Five-Level Hierarchy

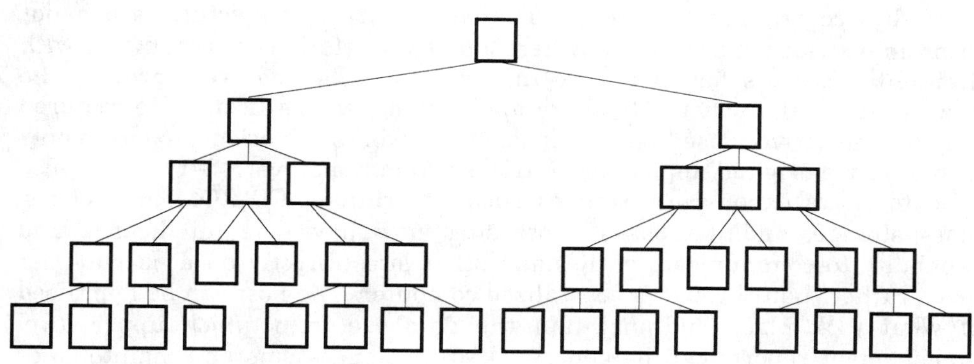

b. Three-Level Hierarchy

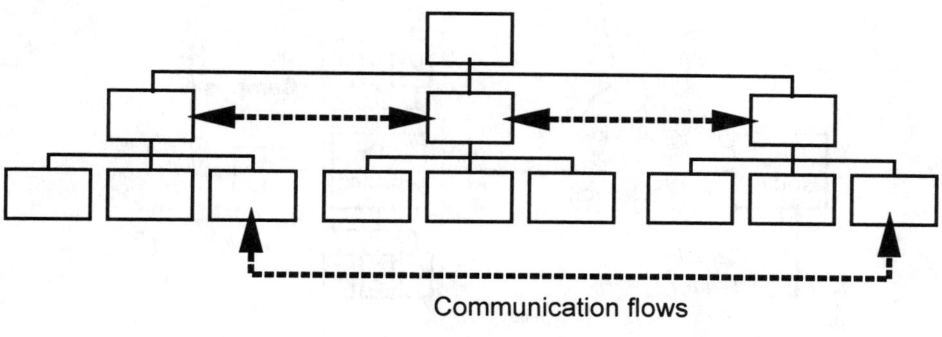

Figure 2.12 Flattening of Network and Organizational Structures

Figure 2.12 illustrates this parallel between organizational and network flattening, in this case, from a five-tier hierarchical design (a) to a more distributed three-tier network (b) which provides for fewer hierarchical interactions, as shown by the horizontal arrows. Each box represents an employee/manager or a router/switch/hub. Note the peer-to-peer communications flows.

2.3.3 Distributed Computing and Client-Server Networking

Today, more and more computing is accomplished through distributed processing and client-server relationships. *Distributed processing* is defined as the distribution of network intelligence and processing to many network sites, where each site communicates on a peer-to-peer level, rather than through a centralized hierarchy. The *client-server* architecture is a major trend in distributed processing, where client workstations communicate with distributed servers for their core information. These servers provide the means for multiple clients to share applications, with a license fee required only for the actively used applications. Client workstations then operate only a shell of the original application retrieved from the server. Servers are also used to share expensive resources such as printers, CD-ROM juke boxes, mass storage, and databases. Most sites now have the intelligence and capability to communicate with many other sites directly on a peer-to-peer level, rather than through a centralized computer. The host can be appraised of what took place and maintain the database from which upper level management reports can be generated so that operations and maintenance issues are addressed, using systems such as IBM's NetView.

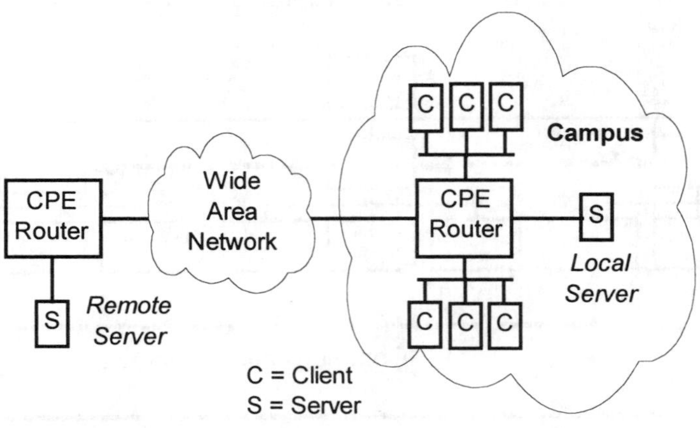

Figure 2.13 Distributed Client-Server Processing Network

Client-server computing distributes the actual storage and processing of information among many sites as opposed to storing and processing all information at a single, centralized location. This model reflects the increasingly flatter organizational structure and the need for increased connectivity and communications shown above. Figure 2.13 illustrates a computer communications network supporting the distributed client-server architecture. A server may be locally attached to a router or remotely accessed across the WAN.

2.3.4 IBM SNA and Internetwork Protocol Convergence

The architectural differences between IBM's hierarchical SNA protocol structure and newer Internet Protocol (IP)-based routed networks are complex but are also converging. Many devices explored in the following chapters allow for SNA traffic to be combined with true "routable" traffic in a routed or switched architectural environment. This is creating a groundswell of traditional SNA users moving to technologies like frame relay and ATM.

2.3.5 The Need for LAN/MAN/WAN Connectivity

Almost every major corporate location has one or multiple LANs. LAN traffic, which once was confined to WAN speeds that were significantly lower than LAN speeds, is now using broadband services capable of providing true LAN connect speeds across the WAN. There are two general scenarios found in corporations and growing businesses that drive the need for greater LAN connectivity across the wide area. The first is increased need for interconnection between distributed computing devices on LANs. The second is the logical extension of the LAN across wider geographic areas. The geographically dispersed LANs now have a range of connectivity choices — from dedicated circuits to switched wide area and metropolitan area networks and broadband data services. The choice of technology and services is based upon many factors other than cost. The paramount goal is to define the business need to connect these disparate networks. Computer networking has been defined in many ways. The following six definitions are used throughout the book:

Local Area Network (LAN): distance on the order of 0.1 km (350 ft); providing local connectivity, typically within a building, floor, or room. Some LAN segments are even dedicated to a single user.

Campus Area Network (CAN): distance on the order of 1 km (1.6 mi.); providing connectivity between buildings in the same general area.

Metropolitan Area Network (MAN): distance on the order of 10 km (30 mi.); providing regional connectivity, typically between campuses over the geographic area associated with a major population center.

Wide Area Network (WAN): distance on the order of 100 to 10,000 km (60 to 6000 mi.); providing national connectivity.

Global Area Network (GAN): distance on the order of 1000 to 20,000 km (600 to 12,000 mi.) or more; providing connectivity between nations.

Virtual Local Area Network (VLAN): distance varies from a few feet to thousands of kilometers; providing virtual LAN connectivity to geographically diverse users, appearing as if they share the same physical LAN.

Typical LAN interconnect speeds, which were once limited to thousands of bits per second (kbps), are now typically tens or hundreds of millions of bits per second (Mbps), and soon even billions of bits per second (Gbps). Once the LAN is established and operational, many factors drive the LAN to expand in physical and logical size. The amount of data traffic continues to grow at rates that average 30 percent per year, along with the bridges, routers, hubs, gateways, and switches required to transport, switch, and route. Worldwide LAN interconnection is a reality of life for many international corporations – witness the Internet. The business drivers for expanding local area networking usually fall into one or more of the following categories:

- Increased inter-LAN traffic
- Remote and mobile access
- Higher available transmission rates
- Increased application function and performance
- Cross-domain routing or cross-mainframe access capabilities
- Need to expand boundaries of the LAN
- Intra- and intercompany additional user connectivity required
- Low installation and capital costs of new technology
- Expansion of the business through growth or acquisition

The technology drivers of inter-networking LANs lead to the hybrid use of private data networks in conjunction with public WAN services in large corporations. This is occurring with a strong emphasis toward delivering bandwidth-on-demand. One interpretation of bandwidth-on-demand arose in the LAN environment, where many users shared a single high-bandwidth medium. At any instant only one user was likely to be active and hence had the entire shared medium bandwidth available for his or her use. Hence, bandwidth was not dedicated and was available to users "on demand." The realization of this concept within networks other than those on a shared medium can be seen in ATM technology and architecture. Another interpretation is analogous to the switched telephone network, where a call (demand) is placed for bandwidth. The call attempt usually succeeds, failing only with a small blocking probability, and hence is also interpreted as bandwidth-on-demand.

Users are spending much more on service and support budgets than hardware and software budgets. This statistic shows the decreasing cost of the equipment, as opposed to the increasing cost of support systems required to run the LAN. As further evidence of this trend, the use of high-bandwidth circuits and services to support these networks just about doubles each year.

Another opposite trend is the actual decrease in the need for bandwidth due to more efficient coding and compression schemes. The most common evidence is the availability of modems for communication over voice-grade lines that now exceed the capacity of ISDN using compression. Also note the decrease in the coding rates of video conferencing, North American Television Standard Coding (NTSC), and High Definition TeleVision (HDTV) over time. Acceptable video conferencing for business can be achieved at DS0 (64 kbps) rates today. NTSC coding was achieved at DS3 (45 Mbps) rates in the late 1980s, and is now approaching the DS1 (1.5 Mbps) rate for noninteractive programming. The need for 150 Mbps for HDTV transmission has also evaporated due to similar increases in coding efficiencies. Of course, the improvements in coding efficiencies are limited by the actual information content of the signal. In general, these schemes for efficient coding and compression arise when bandwidth is inordinately expensive, or a competitive niche occurs that justifies the expense of such coding or compression.

2.3.6 The Death of Shared Media – LAN Switching?

Normal LAN and MAN technologies — Ethernet (IEEE 802.3), Token Ring (IEEE 802.5), FDDI (ANSI X3.139 or ISO 9314), and the Distributed Queue Dual Bus (DQDB) (IEEE 802.6) — all connect to network devices through a shared medium, as shown in Figure 2.14a. Bandwidth is shared between all users on the shared medium with each user potentially having access to the entire bandwidth. A problem occurs when more than a few users are active on a 10 Mbps Ethernet, resulting in a usable throughput of less than 4 Mbps. Capacity begins to become the limiting factor. Token Ring, FDDI, and DQDB achieve better utilization through a more sophisticated bandwidth-sharing protocol, but when the users' desktop rate begins to approach the shared medium's speed, there is no choice but to move to the next higher-speed shared medium LAN solution or to segment the LANs with fewer users. The consequence is that the number of users per LAN segment has continually decreased, creating the market for switching hubs and bridges, as shown in Figure 2.14b. As workstation power increases, this example reduces to a single user per LAN segment connected to a LAN switch, as shown on the right-hand side of Figure 2.14c. This is where ATM comes in as a common logical interface technology that can scale in speed without requiring changes in software to support a new shared-medium solution, as shown in Figure 2.14d.

The late 1990s have seen an intelligent routing move toward the periphery of the network and more switching in the LAN. As users move toward Ethernet and Fast Ethernet as the LAN technologies of choice, and reduce the numbers on each Ethernet segment (sometimes down to a single user), the requirement emerges for a device that can provide switching of LAN traffic within the LAN at the MAC layer without complicated routing schemes. Thus, LAN switching hubs begin to dominate the LAN intra- and inter-connectivity market, solving the problems of graceful LAN segmentation and growing capacity constraints with a scalable solution.

2.3.7 The Move to Distributed Routing

As LAN switching proliferates, the requirement for routing moves toward the periphery of the LAN as the primary WAN interface. LAN switching can be performed in the work-group environment, and more expensive routing can be performed at the periphery of the network. Distributing routing of traffic is still required from the LAN to the WAN. Complex routing functions are rarely required. Distributed routing with ATM technology moves the routing and network designation function to the periphery of the network, where it is more cost effective and can connect families of LAN switches.

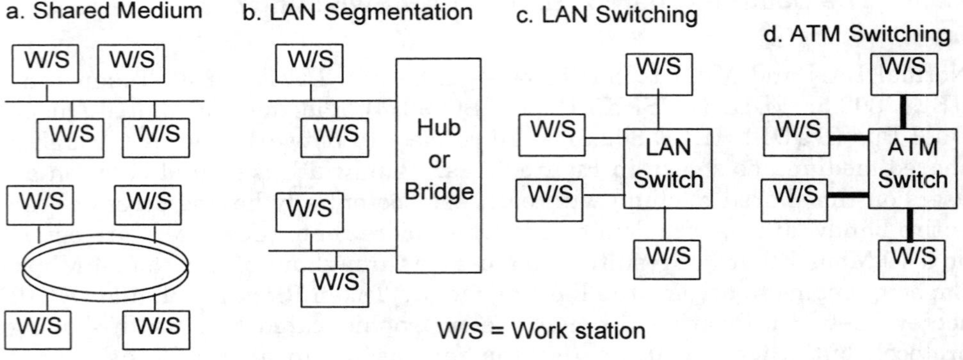

Figure 2.14 Evolution from Shared Medium to High-Performance Switching

2.3.8 Merging of LAN and WAN – Free Bandwidth?

Two complementary phenomena are occurring simultaneously. LAN and WAN speeds are merging to provide virtual LAN connectivity across the WAN. The cost of WAN and LAN bandwidth is becoming less expensive. This expense is counterbalanced somewhat by the need for higher WAN speeds. Bandwidth in the WAN and LAN is not yet free but getting very close, comparatively, to free. Evidence the advent of Wave Division Multiplexing (WDM) proving terabit speeds across a single fiber, fiber to the desktop and home at a few cents per feet, and the cost of LAN interface cards, hubs, and MAC switching getting cheaper and cheaper per user.

So where is the real cost element in data networking in the next century? Information is currency. The networking elements that will cost the most money are management, support, maintenance, and information management. The price almost always follows the value, and with intelligent networks the value is in information, configuration, and network management.

2.3.9 Virtual LAN (VLAN)

The LANs we have known and grown to love (or hate) over the last 20 years were designed so that all users of specific resources were grouped and assigned on a single physical LAN. As LAN resources are distributed, the requirement increases for many users not *physically* colocated to share the same resources. This causes many users to shed their physical bodies (shared local LAN resources) for the greater nirvana of the *logical* work-group. VLAN resources still appear local to each user, regardless of whether they share the same physical LAN and all its resources or are half a continent away. These virtual LANs can also be multiprotocol rather than using the same MAC protocol (such as Ethernet over IP). Figure 2.15 shows an example of a virtual LAN connecting user devices in three geographic locations. Note that user A and B have access to the server in location 2 as if they were on the local FDDI LAN. Many VLAN designs are being built with switching hubs that use some proprietary method of switching between VLAN user groups. The common methods of implementation at press time included the proprietary Inter-Switch Link (ISL), IEEE 802.10, and ATM LAN Emulation (LANE) standards. More information will be provided on each VLAN implementation in Chapter 7.

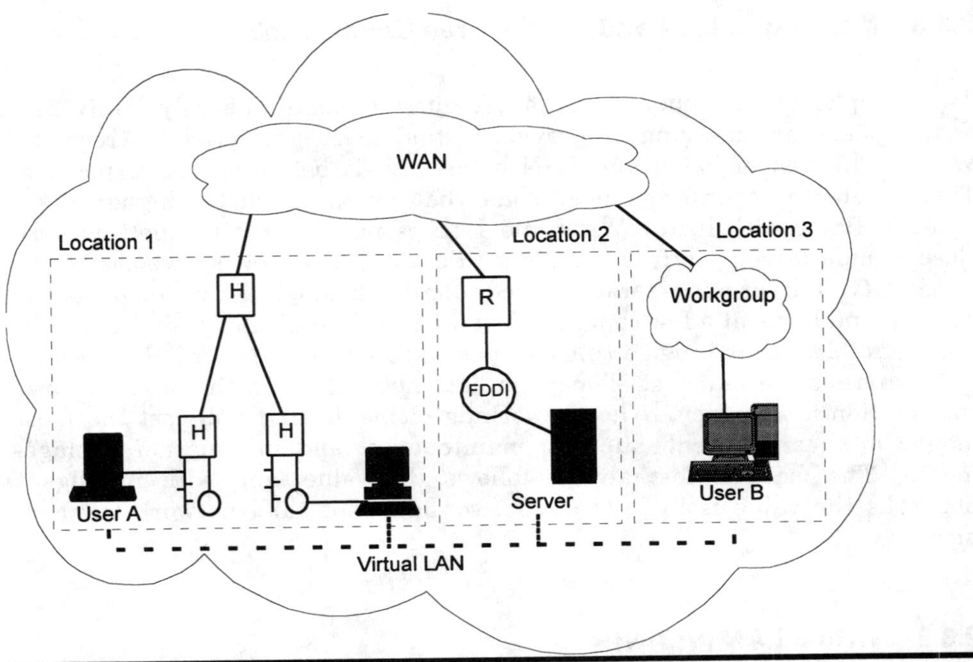

Figure 2.15 Virtual LAN Example

2.3.10 Intranet within the Internet and Client-Server Intranetworks

The Internet continues to be the most commonly used medium for computer communications. The Internet services market was estimated at $2 billion in 1996. The estimated number of Internet users is speculated at over 50 million, with a double digit growth rate each month. The Internet continues to be *the* information superhighway – the Infobahn.Curiously, internetworks are beginning to form within the Internet. Labeled "intra-net within Internet", these communities of users communicate with each other within their company by means of the public Internet. The concept is similar to Virtual Private Data Networks (VPDNs), but instead uses the Internet as the transport utility.

2.3.11 Seamless Protocol and Service Interworking – ATM?

How do all these protocols tie together over a single network infrastructure? Most enterprises have more than one location and also have more applications than just data. The original premise of Broadband ISDN (B-ISDN) was to provide the capability to serve voice, video, and data using the same technology. This concept has been dubbed "seamless inter-working" across the LAN and WAN. Figure 2.16 illustrates this vision of seamless inter-working. Voice, video, and data are converted to ATM at the user site, where they are interconnected to the WAN via ATM. Access to voice and other legacy services is shown in the WAN. It is likely that ATM will not replace the older T1 multiplexers initially, but will provide a migration path through the support of circuit emulation in the interim, as illustrated in Figure 2.16. In the longer term, ATM may even provide direct transport of voice across the WAN, most likely on transoceanic cables first. ATM may potentially integrate what currently are completely separate data and voice networks, using different carriers and services to form a single unified network. There are other advantages to this approach such as a single network management infrastructure and reduction of access and transmission costs.

Typically, only 10 to 20 percent of LAN traffic goes over the WAN. This percentage is increasing with the growth of VLANs. Current LANs can only achieve a sustained 30 to 70 percent load on the actual LAN speed in order to keep queuing delays reasonable. ATM can extend the LAN across the WAN with degradation in access time limited essentially by only the speed of light. There is a tradeoff between bandwidth and latency limits that applications encounter depending on the transport technology and media used, and ATM technology and service is no exception.

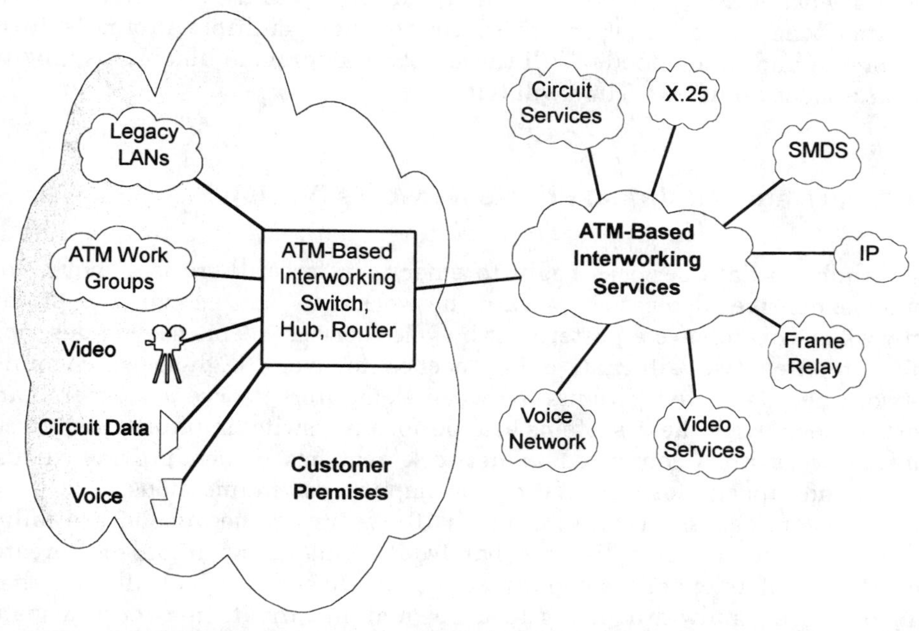

Figure 2.16 Seamless Interworking

This argument of seamless inter-working also extends to mobile computing and access via standard telephone lines to these services. Mobile communications and phone links that extend the LAN to the automobile, train, meeting room, or hotel room will become commonplace as business travelers take with them mobile-communications-equipped PCs and computing devices. Lower-speed access will perform sophisticated data compression for interconnection into the seamless inter-network.

2.4 THE DATA NETWORK OF THE 2000s

Have you ever wondered what the architecture of tomorrow's data network will look like? This section takes a look at data network progression into the 21st century. Static, predefined private communications networks are migrating to dynamic, virtual networks — networks with ubiquitous access that can inter-work past, present, and future protocols, and any-to-any communications. Virtual, public data networks are adding more and more intelligence, in essence enabling the network to become the computer. The corporation is becoming more and more dependent upon virtual data networking to run the day-to-day business, requiring both partitioning and security. The war on technical obsolescence has begun, and is taken to new heights with ATM technology. Will ATM in the LAN and WAN be the Rosetta stone for protocol interworking to allow multiple protocols to be deciphered and understood? Will these networks provide ubiquitous, any-to-any access for all users? Time will tell.

2.4.1 Private and Virtual Private Networks (VPNs)

As broadband data services begin to emerge in force, there is a move from using expensive dedicated private networks to shared virtual private networks. This follows a pattern set by voice services. This section describes and compares two alternative approaches for very high-speed computer networking: dedicated circuits between computers, servers, routers, and workstations (with these systems also performing switching functions) versus shared-access lines connected to network switches, which provide virtual, on-demand capacity for workstation-to-computer communications.

Many users choose private networks 10+ years ago because of the falling transport prices of long distance bandwidth and deregulation had created uncertainty of telephone company support. Divestiture had allowed these long-distance bandwidth prices to drop, making private networks a viable solution for voice and data. Many users built intelligent multiplexer networks to aggregate traffic and more efficiently use the carrier bandwidth (higher utilization). The monopoly carriers held back T1 offerings from customers until the new carriers offered T1 bandwidths and even AT&T was forced to provide T1 capabilities to the DoD as the first customer. Private networks provided efficient, reliable interoffice communications. Efficiencies in voice compression helped to keep costs down.

Long-distance carriers provided private virtual networks with voice services for years, allowing users to manage virtual private networks within the carriers' public voice network. This was creatively marketed as services over and above private line usage. Thus, virtual private data networks began to be offered in the same manner. The cheap voice rates offered by carrier voice VPNs made migration to carrier-based VPNs irresistible. The T1 multiplexer networks that were cost-justified a few years before saw voice bleeding off to VPNs while data remained to provide approximately 80 percent of the fill in T1 private multiplexer networks. Most private networks are now dominated by data, which has become their primary investment.

Figure 2.17 illustrates the first alternative to a private network that traditionally has been comprised of dedicated circuits. Servers are shown connected to multiplexed remote workstation clusters. Each server/router and remote workstation router/bridge has two links to two separate computers via the network Points of Presence (PoPs) to provide survivability in the event of link failures. When a workstation is not directly connected to the desired server, the intermediate routers must perform switching and routing.

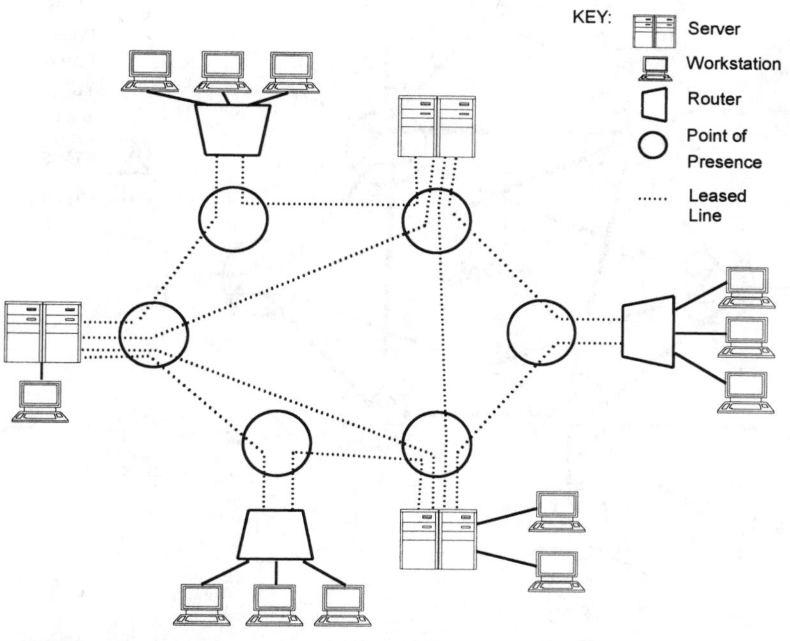

Figure 2.17 Dedicated Circuit Private Network Example

The advantages of this private network approach are full user control and simple, less expensive network technology. The disadvantages are nonproductive redundancy, dedicated link capacity, additional equipment costs to perform switching and routing, and the need to engineer the private line trunks for peak capacity.

Figure 2.18 illustrates the same set of servers, routers, remote routed/bridged workstation clusters, and network PoPs as in the private network, but as part of a shared, virtual network. A separate virtual video network shares the backbone, as shown in the figure. An ATM switch is placed at each network PoP which has access lines to each user. The ATM switches are highly interconnected by very high-speed links shared across multiple users, providing multiple services by dynamically allocating shared resources. Only a *single* access line is required for each user, thus halving the access cost when compared with the previous example. The reliability of access is identical to that of the dedicated network, assuming that the access circuits in the dedicated network take the same route to the network PoP. The ATM switches perform routing and switching, relieving the routers and servers of this task.

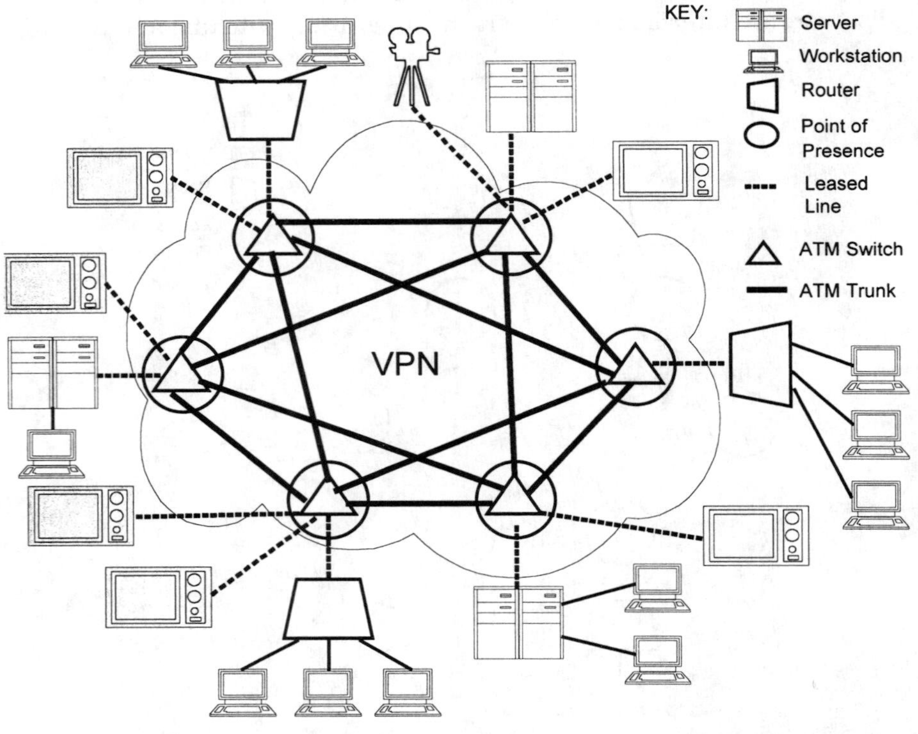

Figure 2.18 Virtual Private Network Example

In summary, the advantages of the virtual network alternative are:

- Reduced access line charges
- Capability to satisfy high peak bandwidth demands (particularly during low activity intervals for other services)
- Cost impacts proportional to usage (versus cost proportional to peak rate in the dedicated network alternative)
- Enhanced availability and reliability.

Disadvantages include:

- Less predictable peak capacity
- Less user control

A Virtual Private Network (VPN) is defined as a network partition of shared public network resources between multiple users to form a private network that *appears private to the users* but is still part of a larger public network. Carriers tout and advertise their VPN services to the user as having the benefits of a private network but also providing the economies and cost savings of switched services. The virtual network is a subset of the carriers' larger network, but provides the image of a complete data network to the user. Thus, VPNs offer multiple virtual networks within a single physical network. A corporate-wide frame relay network for client XYZ within a public frame relay service network is one example of a VPN. Shared network resources are assigned in fair proportion to the bandwidth required by customers.

In a virtual private network a single access circuit from the site to the network is usually sufficient, because multiple virtual circuits can be provided from multiple users at a site to their destination on the network. For example, each virtual circuit can be allocated a peak rate equal to the access circuit, but have a sum of average rates that is less than the access circuit. Figure 2.19 demonstrates this concept by showing how users A, B, C, and D at site 1 all have a single physical circuit into their premises FR or ATM device which converts these inputs to four FR or ATM virtual circuits (as indicated by the different line styles) and then transmits them over a *single* physical FR or ATM access circuit to the network switch. These individual user virtual circuits are logically switched across the FR or ATM network to the destination premises device where they are delivered to the physical access circuit of the end user, as illustrated in the figure. Note that while this single circuit provides good aggregation, it can also be a single point of failure for all users accessing the network.

The availability of switched broadband data services, with their bandwidth sharing capabilities through new technologies such as frame relay and cell switching, has lured users away from private point-to-point networks and onto public networks. Thus, they attain the increased reliability of very large public data network platforms and cost savings vis-à-vis private line operations due to the economies of scale of the larger backbone infrastructure and its high availability and resiliency to failure with built-in alternate routing. VPN alternatives to dedicated facilities can be provided in NxDS0, DS1 and DS3 speeds, and well into the gigabit speeds with services based on ATM and SONET architectures.

An added advantage to public networks now being used quite often is for the user to tap the knowledge of the public network engineers and managers. Customers of public network services gain access to public network assets, such as engineering personnel, experience, resources, and network management. If done correctly, data consultation can be obtained to attract additional voice and data business. This is like having an in-house consulting service. But it is a two-way street. At the same time, the provider is allowed to learn the customer's business and applications and can sell into this customer base.

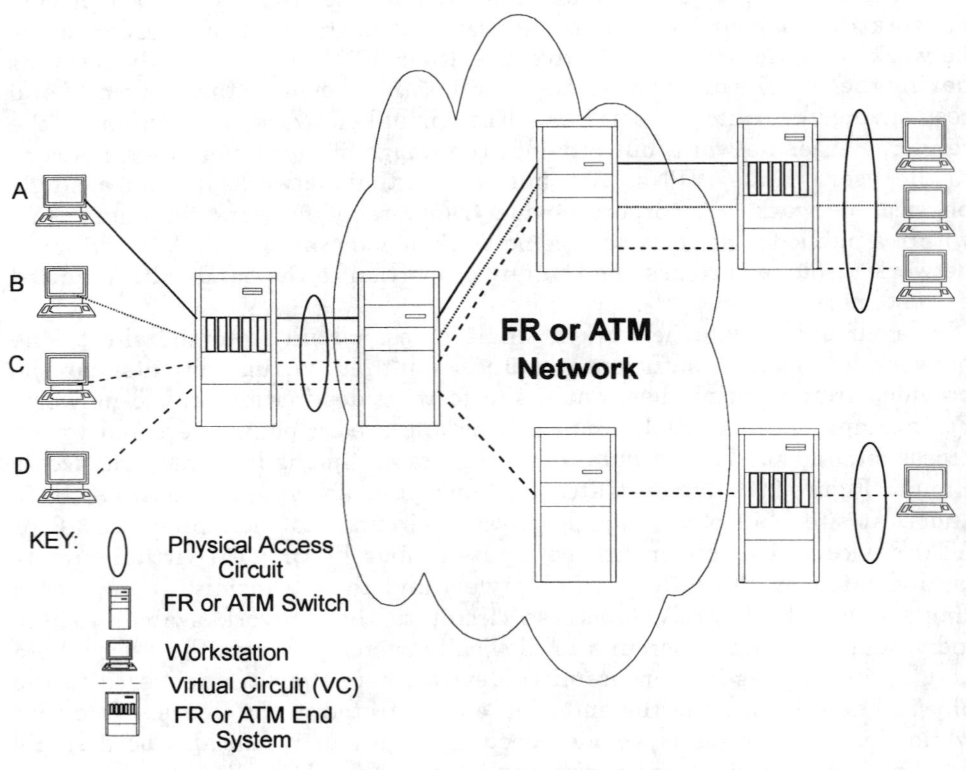

Figure 2.19 Detailed Example of a Virtual Private Network (VPN)

Virtual networking is in many ways a type of outsourcing. By providing advanced voice, data, and video services with customized network management, billing, and support systems to back these services, many data service providers offer a form of outsourcing. This outsourcing takes the form of resource reduction for systems and services which otherwise would have to be accomplished in house. Other benefits of virtual private networks which parallel outsourcing include carrier-provided network management, bandwidth management, fault tolerance, intelligent bridging and routing, security, order entry and order processing, and integration and standardization. Virtual data networks can also be used as an overflow technique or as a complete replacement for existing networks. The network manager needs to decide what portion of the network resources to retain or replace, keeping in mind the costs of access to the public network, not just end-to-end circuits as in a private network. These advantages are additional bonuses of switched services. If anything, the network provider becomes a free consultant, offering experience, knowledge, and sometimes even manpower to potential or existing customers. The rules of outsourcing previously discussed also pertain to virtual private data networking and switched public data network services.

There are many challenges facing VPN providers. Users require an increased level of control over network resources, like the ability to offer the user the capability to modify the network on the fly without long lead times. One example of this is frame relay service, where users still need to submit orders and wait days to change a Permanent Virtual Circuit (PVC). In the near future, users should have the capability to modify their own PVC routing almost instantaneously. The same is true for Virtual Paths (VPs) and Virtual Channels (VCs) in an ATM service, where not only should the user be allowed routing and adds/moves/changes but also the capability to change parameters like quality of service (QoS).

2.4.2 The Intelligent Data Network

Corporations and governments are moving towards using faster, larger, and more intelligent data communications networks — where more routing, addressing, and switching intelligence lies *within* the network, rather than outside it. They are also looking for intelligent network services, rather than simple, traditional private line or circuit switched data services. The term *intelligent network* connotes some level of *value-added* service provided by the network. Examples include address translation versus interpretation, intelligent routing decisions made within the network by route servers rather than predefined routes across the network, and protocol conversion rather than just transparent (to the user) protocol transport. Network intelligence can also mean a service offering based on centralized, intelligent, network-based devices that serve as information servers offering voice, video, and imaging interpretation, routing, and on-line service features. Prime examples are the interactive database services, such as CompuServe and America On-line.

Users want networks that are "smarter", not just faster and better interfaces. Users want access to intelligent public data services so that they can better leverage the intelligence within their own network. Current and emerging data communication services are just now slowly adding this type of intelligence to their networks — intelligence which in the 1980s resided at the premises. Now, network service providers offer alternative network intelligence that is extended to the user premises where significant intelligence may not be practical.

There is thus a tradeoff between intelligent networks and intelligent user equipment. Many factors, driven by global industry standardization and the development of technology, will influence decisions on where the network intelligence will reside. The market is both technology-driven and user-driven. For example, international providers want the network intelligence to reside in international gateway nodes. National carriers want intelligence to reside in carrier Points of Presence (PoPs). Local exchange carriers (LECs) or Postal, Telegraph & Telephone Ministry/Administrations (PTTs) want intelligence mainly in the serving Central Office (CO). Customer Premises Equipment (CPE) vendors want the intelligence to reside at the premises. The profits of the next century lie in the intelligent functions, not the connectivity function, with all of the aforementioned groups recognizing this fact. The user needs to mix and match all of the above options for the best cost and functional advantage — typically in a "hybrid" networking environment using a mixture of components to meet the needs of the intelligent data communications network of the future. However, the network users and network providers must also work together to ensure that the mix and blend of technology being used meets business goals. This is critical for continued successful business operation. Relating these responsibilities to the strategic business objectives of the company will guarantee ongoing success.

2.4.3 Meeting the Needs of the Enterprise

Large enterprise networks typically have a few large locations that serve as major traffic sources and sinks. Typical applications are large computer centers, large office complexes with many information workers, campuses requiring high-tech communication, data or image repositories, and large-volume data or image sources. These large locations have a significant community of interest among them; however, the enterprise usually also requires a relatively large number of smaller locations needing at least partial, lower performance access to this same information. The smaller locations have fewer users, and generally cannot justify the higher cost of equipment or networking facilities. Cost generally increases as performance, number of features, and flexibility needs increase.

Hybrid networks with ATM inter-working at the larger sites and frame relay or ISDN access for the many smaller locations are now beginning to appear. These lower-speed access sites require more efficient access rather than high performance, and thus frame relay access through low-end routing and bridging products is often more cost effective than ATM. This is because the cost per bit per second generally decreases as the public network access speed increases. For example, the approximate ratio of DS1/DS0 and DS3/DS1 tariffs is approximately 10:1, while the speed difference is approximately 25:1. This means that a higher-speed interface can be operated at 40 percent efficiency at the same cost per bit per second. Conversely, the lower-speed interface costs 2.5 times as much per bit per second, and therefore efficiency can be important.

What does the virtual enterprise network look like for the beginning of the next century? Figure 2.20 illustrates an ATM-based interworking network cloud connecting a few large sites to many small sites. Such a network is composed of many smaller sites and few larger sites, which is typical of large enterprises, such as corporations, governments, and other organizations. Principal needs are multiple levels of service characterized by parameters such as throughput, quality, and billing. Again, the smaller sites could use dial, switched, dedicated private line, ISDN, IP, frame relay, SMDS, or ATM access protocols. There are many other protocol options available; these just seem to be the predominant ones as of this printing.

2.4.4 Virtual Network Partitioning and Security

Data traffic often represents the most private and sensitive information of an enterprise. Therefore, the majority of data traffic is intra-enterprise. In contrast, a large amount of voice traffic is communicated between enterprises over public telephone lines. Data communications in large part still occurs on private line networks, or else uses modem communications over public telephone lines. The tremendous growth in Internet traffic is an example of the burgeoning demand for data communication over public shared facilities. Even though an increasing amount of data traffic is communicated between enterprises, it is still typically less than 10 percent of the total data traffic. If public data services provide good security and partitioning, then inter-enterprise traffic could increase in public, shared carrier services. An enterprise, however, needs to control what communication can occur within as well as outside its boundaries. Security screening, filtering, and blocking can be done in a connection-oriented environment through signaling, or in a connectionless environment through the use of screening tables or filters.

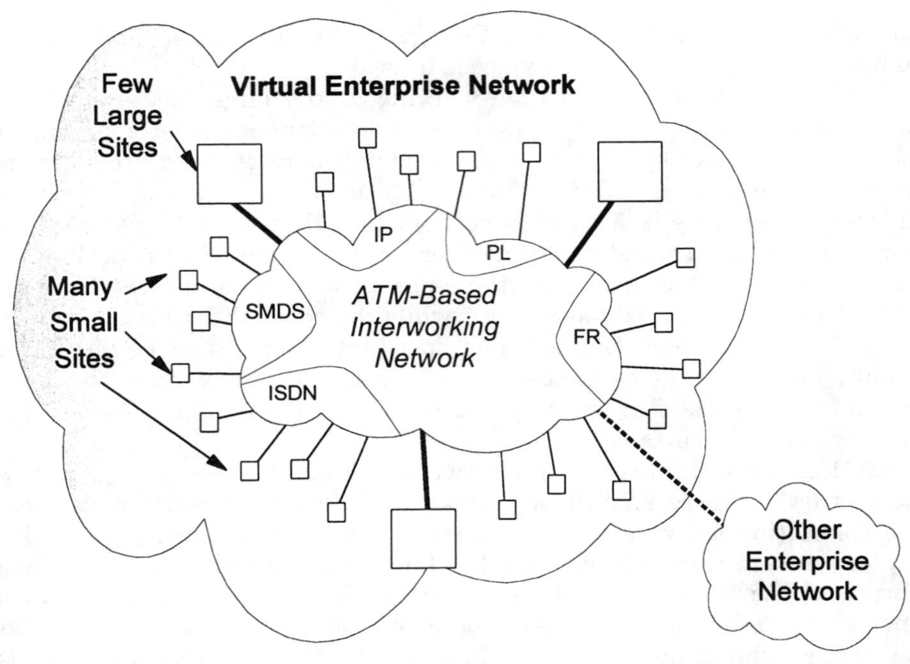

Figure 2.20 Typical Enterprise Network

Corporate, government, and university inter-networking have also exploded. When the corporate network of company A is tied to the corporate network of company B, via either private lines or switched services, inter-networking takes place as shown in Figure 2.21. This is often the case when two companies need to share vital information such as engineering CAD/CAM files, databases, group-ware, and other applications. This connectivity between two or more corporate, government, or university private networks usually occurs through the use of public network services. Inter-networking works well as long as security precautions are taken by both the service provider and the end-user networks. It is a common practice today for users to install separate "fire-wall" routers that filter packets, circuits, and application protocols to prevent intrusion from the "outside" and "inside". Another trend is to install security servers within the LAN and WAN infrastructure and use physical key-coded security devices on the remote and dial access ports to the network, but placing these "bars on the windows" is just the first step in network perimeter security.

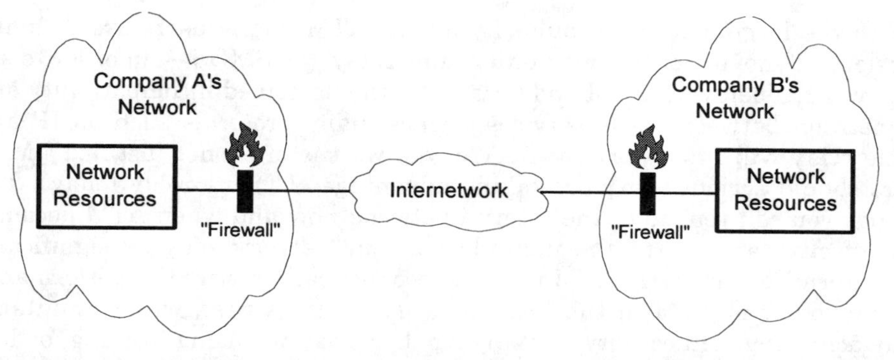

Figure 2.21 Intercorporate Internetworking

2.4.5 The War on Technological Obsolescence

Business users are concerned with maximizing their investment in computing and data communications equipment. Rapid advances in computing make a maximum productive technology lifetime of three to five years typical. Generally, the most expensive computer equipment is justified for only a small set of mission-critical applications. A similar situation exists in the area of data communications.

Currently, most intra-enterprise data communication networks are constructed from Customer Premises Equipment (CPE) interconnected by private lines at DS1/E1 speeds or less. The advent of public data network services, such as frame relay, SMDS, ATM, and their attractive cost efficiencies, has motivated some customers to migrate a portion of their bursty data from private lines to virtual private networks. *Burstiness* is defined as the ratio of the peak traffic rate to the average traffic rate. Virtual networks offer higher peak rates at affordable levels because there is normally no penalty for idle time, or equivalently, a low average rate for overusage (such as bursting above CIR with frame relay service).

Frame relay usually can be economically installed in most existing CPE with only a software upgrade. In addition to software upgrades, SMDS and ATM usually require new CPE, or an external CSU/DSU. There is a low-speed alternative to both SMDS and ATM called the Data eXchange Interface (DXI). This is an HDLC-based protocol that encapsulates and/or maps the SMDS and ATM header functionality between a DTE and a DCE. This means that most CPE can be upgraded via software, at a cost similar to that of frame relay. The DXI protocols are better suited for early, cost effective, low-speed implementation of SMDS and ATM. There is, of course, additional cost for the CSU/DSU; however, this special SMDS or ATM CSU/DSU can multiplex many lower-speed DXI interfaces onto a higher-speed ATM or SMDS cell interface cost-effectively.

With the large amount of publicity about ATM, many users are delaying decisions on moving data traffic onto frame relay and SMDS — in order to see what will happen with ATM and because of the perceived incompatibility and competition between these services. Since many protocols such as IP and frame relay will inter-work over ATM, the wait is often not justified. Most users should seriously explore taking advantage of frame relay today. The savings you can realize in the interim between now and when ATM becomes cost effective and worth the upgrade for your network may be significant. One alternative for early ATM use is to economically justify the performance and flexibility of ATM in the LAN at large locations first, while simultaneously achieving connectivity to many smaller locations using existing, or less expensive, equipment and access speeds enabled by ATM-based protocol inter-working or frame relay.

2.4.6 Ubiquitous Access and Any-to-Any Communications

Ubiquitous access to an intelligent data communications network with any day-to-day communications has become more important as corporations inter-company communications requirements increase. Users want to access the data network as a large "cloud" and thus be able to talk to any other user connected to that cloud without requiring any knowledge of the internals of the network cloud. A prerequisite to this capability is the assignment of a globally unique address to each user. The public voice network has these characteristics, with several lessons from that domain applicable to data networks. There is also the experience of the Internet, which has different addressing characteristics, a significant factor. If a user cannot reach any other user on the public data network, as is taken for granted in telephony and has become a *fait accompli* on the Internet, then the resulting data service will have little utility. Addressing will be explored in greater detail in Chapter 22.

2.4.7 As Reliable as the Phone Network

Similar to the expectation of universal connectivity from telephony, data users expect public data networks to be as reliable as the telephone network. Intelligent networks based on frame relay and ATM rely on their fiber transport to be both nearly error-free and nearly outage-free or may detect errors and faults and require retransmission. Redundancy and restoration must be observed at every step in the design, with SONET technology providing this capability in some configurations or ATM-based restoration algorithms in others. Since many applications do not provide error correction or switching to alternate paths, the capability for an ATM network to guarantee nearly error-free transmission and continuous availability is important.

Successful service providers offer services with high availability and low error rates as required by the corporations and government entities that build their enterprise networks on the virtual network. The switch from conventional private lines to broadband switched services is progressing, but there will always be a need for dedicated private lines for specialized applications. The incremental reliability of the public data network, low error rates, and the reduced price of switched data services based on the economies of scale inherent in the carrier frame and cell-based infrastructures make switched data services even more appealing in comparison to dedicated private line services as time progresses.

2.4.8 Interoperability

Interoperability in data communications is defined as the communication and intelligent interaction between dissimilar network architectures, protocols, and systems linked by some common medium. This medium can take the form of an operating system, protocol, architecture, logical connection, or physical connection. The medium may even be as simple as network interface cards which support the same protocol.

Some difficulties encountered in providing interoperable networks include the large investment, multiple standards and protocols to support and convert, changing business requirements, lack of network management and design tools, and simple network inconsistencies. Open systems become increasingly important as the number of protocols and applications interacting in the wide area network increase. The next chapter will cover the multiple industry standards through which the network designer achieves true interoperability.

2.5 REVIEW

In this chapter we introduced the key application, technology, and infrastructure changes that are the shaping forces of networking for the beginning of the 21st century. Corporate and consumer applications are demanding high-speed multimedia bandwidth to the desktop. Broadband technologies such as ATM, SONET, and Wave Division Multiplexing (WDM) are emerging that offer protocol and transmission enhancements over today's communications super-highways and enable the cost effective transport of these new applications. Finally, corporate infrastructures are shifting from legacy systems with hierarchical, centralized computing to more distributed, client-server environments that form the backbone of large communications networks to carry these broadband technologies and applications. The landscape of data networking of the next century is that of constant change and virtualization of networking resources, and constant war with technological obsolescence. It is to that environment that we turn our study.

Now that we have discussed the building blocks of networking, we will move to Part 2 of the book: standards in the industry. Standards will be the connecting link that defines the measurements and steps to making dissimilar devices conform as much as possible to a common standard.

Part

2

Standards and Services

This section begins with an overview of the primary standards organizations, committees, and forums which influence many of the technologies discussed in this book. Six major architectures dominate and shape the protocols of computer and data communications. Each major architecture will be covered and explained. The Open Systems Interconnect Reference Model (OSIRM) is introduced here, and each protocol architecture prevalent in the industry today is compared and contrasted to it. We next explore the digital hierarchy that has defined data communications for decades. Part 2 finishes with Integrated Services Digital Network (ISDN) basics, which form the root of services like Asynchronous Transfer Mode (ATM), and a look at service definitions.

Chapter

3

Understanding the Standards and Their Makers

This chapter is designed to provide an overview of the primary standards organizations, committees, and forums and how they shape today's computer and communications industry standards. How standards organizations interface is even more fascinating than how standards themselves develop. The exponential rate of technology development and technological advancement presents an ever-increasing challenge to the players, and tests the standards and specifications process. An explosion of standards forums has occurred, primarily driven by vendors, users, and service providers. A few of the most recent forums are influencing many of the high-bandwidth services such as frame relay, SMDS, and ATM.

3.1 CREATING STANDARDS—THE PLAYERS

Perhaps the single most important factor for successful standards and industry specifications is responsiveness to real user needs. Standards created for things with no real user need are rarely successful. Why are standards important? In the past, standalone systems (e.g., CPU, terminal, printer, etc.) worked well together for one application. In fact, at one time IBM had over 50 operating systems which worked just fine as standalone units. The interconnection of these systems by users created a de facto standard called Systems Network Architecture (SNA). In fact, ASCII was developed by non-IBM companies so as not to get "locked" into IBM's EBCDIC coding, for example. Then ANSI blessed ASCII. Today, the exponential rate of technology development and technological advancement seems at times to outpace even the ratification of standards, and standards no longer always lead the deployment of technology. Witness frame relay, where four companies banded together and built a de facto standard that was years later adopted by worldwide standards institutions.

Some of the most important questions a user can present to a vendor are "Does it conform to industry standards, which ones, and how?" Standards play a critical role in an age where standardized national and international interoperability is a key to successful data communications. Let's now look at the key players in the standards setting process.

3.1.1 Vendors

Standards are a two-edged sword for vendors: on the one hand they must consider the standards, while on the other hand they must consider developing something proprietary to differentiate their products. The proprietary feature may increase the cost but add value, or remove some noncritical portion of the standard to achieve lower cost. Vendors are usually very active in the standards process. In the emerging era of ATM, a very complex technology with many variations, vendors are becoming even more concerned with meeting industry standards. Vendors who remain completely proprietary, or try to dictate the standards with their offerings, are confronted by users unwilling to risk their future business plans on proprietary systems.

Vendors can also drive standards, either by de facto industry standardization, through formal standards bodies, or through industry forums. De facto standardization can occur when a vendor is either an entrepreneur or the dominant supplier in the industry who wants to associate the new technology with its name, such as IBM with SNA. De facto standards in high-technology areas, however, do not last forever. Sometimes the dominant vendor is not the only one in the market with a product, but their product quality or market share makes it the de facto standard around which other vendors must design.

3.1.2 Users

Users do better when they purchase equipment conforming to industry standards rather than non-standards-based products because they can competitively shop for products and services and be assured that there will be some level of interoperability. A certain comfort level exists in knowing that the equipment a company stakes its business communications on has the ability to interface with equipment from other vendors. Especially in the context of international inter-connectivity, standards are of paramount importance. Also, users play a key role in developing standards since the use of standard equipment (as well as vendor acceptance) determines the success or failure of the standard.

Ubiquitous deployment is often required for standards success. Vendors say: "We will provide it when customers sign up." Customers say: "We will sign up when it is universally available at the right price, *unless* we see something else better and less expensive." For example, take the ISDN standard. ISDN in North America for over a decade did not become available ubiquitously, and hence was not successful. Recently, for example, the BOCs and LECs agreed to promote a "National ISDN" – a subset of the original standard – or at least a common denominator that would be acceptable to almost everyone. Today, ISDN is more widely available and has less competition in other countries, and therefore is very successful. In fact, many RBOCs such as Pacific Bell and SBC have lowered the price of ISDN service to the point where users are willing to brave the "standards soup" for low-cost, high-speed access. Users usually do not play a very active part in the standardization and specification process. Instead they signal their approval with their purchases — they vote with their money.

3.1.3 Network Service Providers

Network service providers also actively participate in the standard-making process. In a sense they are also users. Service providers are often driven by vendors, but service providers often select vendors that adhere to industry standards but still provide some (usually nonstandard) capability for differentiation. This does not lock them into one vendor's proprietary implementation, and can allow the existence of a multiple vendor environment. Providers must not only make multiple vendor implementations interoperate within their networks, but they must also ensure the availability of industry standard interfaces to provide value-added services to users.

3.2 CREATING STANDARDS—THE PROCESS

In this section the general standards and specification process is reviewed. Figure 3.1 illustrates the generic process of standardization and specification. The process begins with a plan to work on a certain area, which is reviewed through written contributions in technical meetings. The result is usually a document which is drafted and updated by the editor in response to contributions and agreements achieved in the meetings. The group reviews the drafts of this document, often progressing through several stages of voting and approval — eventually resulting in a final standard or specification. The standards process can be hindered by business and politics, with the final measure of success being user acceptance and interoperable implementations.

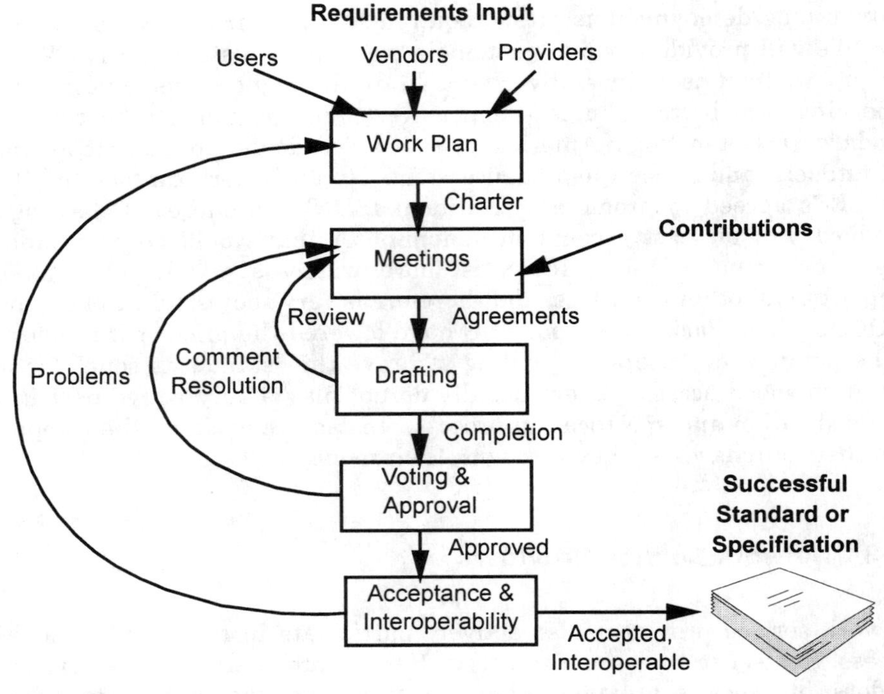

Figure 3.1 Generic Standardization and Specification Process

3.2.1 Work Plan

Most standards and specifications groups first agree on a work plan. A work plan defines the topics to be worked on, a charter for the activity, an organization for performing the work, and usually a very high-level set of objectives. User input and involvement most likely occur at this stage, either indirectly or sometimes even through direct participation. This is the time when vendors and service providers often voice their high-level requirements. The work plan for updating an existing standard almost always includes some changes resulting from user feedback or interoperability issues. Often an approximate time frame is set for completion of the standard or specification.

3.2.2 Meetings and Contributions

The majority of the work occurs at technical meetings. A meeting can last from several days to several weeks. Participants submit written contributions which propose specific text and drawings for the standard, present background information, present arguments for or against a particular approach, or serve as liaisons from other standards or specification bodies. Usually these contributions are discussed, and if the contribution proposes adding text to a baseline document, then a process is employed to determine whether the proposal is accepted, amended, or rejected. In formal standards bodies, there is usually an attempt to achieve consensus before agreeing to include a contribution's input. In some industry forums a straw vote is taken to determine whether the proposal is accepted.

If there is a large committee structure, then a meeting normally begins and ends with a plenary session where representatives from all subcommittees attend. After the plenary meeting, multiple subcommittee meetings usually occur in parallel. The subcommittees are granted some autonomy, however, since they usually must review major changes or key decisions in the plenary session. Meetings are also used to resolve issues that arise from the drafting, review, voting, or approval process described in the following section.

3.2.3 Drafting and Review

A key individual in the development of a standard or specification is the editor. The editor drafts text based upon the contributions, as amended in the meeting. The editor is often trusted to research related standards and specifications and align the document accordingly. A key part of any standards or specification technical activity is the ongoing review, correction, and improvement of the "working" document or baseline text. Working documents therefore provide a major input to meetings and become the basis for contributions for the next meeting, which will further define the requirements in the document.

3.2.4 Voting and Approval

Once a particular document has reached a "draft" status, it is usually distributed for a preliminary vote. Comments that members believe must be addressed in order to approve the document as a standard or specification are often addressed via a comment resolution process at meetings, resulting in more drafting for the editor. The voting step of the process differs in various bodies in the number of members required to approve a change. If complete concurrence is the objective, then the process can be quite lengthy; if only a majority vote is required, then progress may be more rapid, but possibly increases risk. Once the comment resolution process is completed, the standard or specification then goes to a final vote. Again, depending upon the rules governing the standards or specification body, anything from a simple majority to a certain percentage to unanimous approval is required for the body to release the document as an approved standard or specification. Often there will also be a supervisory board which will review the proposed standard for consistency with the format, style, scope, and quality required by that body in the final approval stage.

3.2.5 User Acceptance and Interoperability

Since customers have business problems today that sometimes can only be solved by proprietary implementations *prior* to formal standards, waiting until the perfect standard is designed and approved may put them out of business. Therefore, the user is caught in the dilemma of adopting an emerging standard now or waiting for it to become more mature. Users primarily determine the success of standards by creating the demand for specific capabilities and even technology, and by purchasing implementations from vendors and carriers supporting that standard.

The key technical measure of the success of a standard or specification is whether implementations from multiple vendors or carriers inter-operate according to the details of the documentation. The documents should specify a minimum subset of interfaces, function, and protocol to achieve this goal. Additional documentation, testing, and industry interoperability forums may be required, such as those established for the Internet (IETF), FDDI (ANSI), and N-ISDN (ITU-T).

If customers do not accept a standard, or if significant interoperability issues arise, then this feedback is provided back into the standards process for future consideration. Acceptance by the vendor community also plays a key role in the success or failure of standards, since if no implementation of the standard is built, no user can buy it!

3.2.6 Business and Politics

Standards organizations and industry forums have had increased participation and scope in recent years. With this increased number of people working on a plethora of problems, there comes the inevitable burden of bureaucracy. Service providers, vendors, and, to some extent users, view the chance to participate in the standard-setting process as an opportunity to express themselves and impress their views upon the industry. This is a double-edged sword: while participation is necessary, biases are brought to the committees which can tie up decision making and bog down the process of making standards. One example in ATM standards is that of Generic Flow Control (GFC), where the attempt to achieve agreement on a shared medium solution for ATM was never reached for this reason. The impact of this type of situation depends on whether the committee operates on a complete consensus basis or some form of majority rule. All too often a consensus-based approach ends up being a compromise with multiple, incompatible options stated in the standard. There is then a need to form a subset of a standard as an interoperability specification to reduce the number of choices and translate the ambiguities of the standard into specific equipment requirements.

Standards can also have omissions or "holes" that are undefined and left to vendor interpretation because they simply weren't conceived as issues. These holes may exist because no agreement could be reached on how the requirement should be standardized or because the standards committee moved on to a different area of the standard. Standards usually identify these items "for further study" (ffs) just to point out that there is an awareness of a need for a function or element that isn't standardized yet, but could be in the future.

Vendors can play the game of supporting their proprietary solution to make it a standard before their competitor's proprietary solution becomes a standard. This alone can delay and draw out a standards process for many months or even years. While standards organizations take their time to publish standards, some vendors try to take the lead and build equipment designed around a proposed standard or a partially issued standard, and then promise compliance with the standard once it is finally published. If they guess right, they can be well ahead of the pack; if they miss the mark, a significant investment could be lost.

3.3 STANDARDS AND SPECIFICATION BODIES

Industry forums provide a vehicle for driving industry standards, and the rallying points for standardization and interoperability. The actual industry standards are developed and approved by standards organizations. These standards bodies, along with users and vendors, play the most important part in deciding what actually becomes a standard. Users can also drive standards with the need for a specific technology and the desire to incorporate it as soon as possible. The standards organizations and forums provide common ground between users and vendors. They provide guidelines for the industry that define the interoperability requirements not only between computer communications, but between computer and user communications. While standards organizations are composed of both users and vendors, they attempt to remain objective about the standardization of technologies that could have a drastic impact on the businesses of both.

There are currently two classes of standardization and specification bodies that drive the technologies covered in this text: formal standards bodies and industry forums.

The leading formal international standards body is the International Telecommunications Union–Telecommunications Standardization Sector (ITU-T), formerly called the International Telegraph and Telephone Consultative Committee (CCITT). The ITU was formed in Western Europe in the late 1800s. The premier formal standards organization in the United States is the American National Standards Institute (ANSI) and its predominant communications committee the T1 Standards Committee. The premier formal standards organization in Europe is the European Telecommunications Standards Institute (ETSI).

Other key standards and specification bodies include the Institute of Electrical and Electronics Engineers (IEEE); international standards bodies include the International Organization for Standardization (ISO) and International Electrotechnical Commission (IEC). Although the Federal Communications Commission (FCC) is not a standards-setting organization, it is a major regulatory power in the United States and also deserves mention.

3.3.1 International Telecommunications Union (ITU)

The International Telecommunications Union (ITU) was founded in 1948 and dates back as far as 1865. The ITU charter is to produce telegraphy and telephone technical, operating, and tariff issue recommendations. The ITU committee formerly known as the CCITT is renamed the Telecommunications Standardization Sector now referred to as the ITU-T. The ITU-T is a United Nations sponsored treaty organization. The U.S. voting member in the ITU-T is a representative of the U.S. Department of State, and includes technical advisors through the U.S. National Committee for the ITU-T. Only members may attend meetings. The standards produced by the ITU-T are identified as ITU-T Recommendations in this book.

Up until 1988, the ITU-T published approved recommendations once every four years in the form of a set of books which were often referred to by the color of their covers — red, yellow, blue, etc. After 1988 an accelerated standards process was adopted, where all subsequent recommendations are published when completed. These are now called "white books."

During a study period, which is now typically two years instead of four, a number of questions are assigned to a study group. The study group then organizes into lower-level committees and produces working documents and draft recommendations. These study groups were once referred to by Roman numerals in the CCITT days, but in the new modernized ITU-T, the study groups are now referred to by decimal numbers. Study group 1, for example, is involved with B-ISDN services aspects; study group 11 is responsible for signaling protocols; and study group 13 is responsible for defining the ATM-related functions. The address and phone number, and Internet address to obtain further information about the ITU-T are

International Telecommunications Union–Telecommunications
Place Des Nations
Rue De Varembe
Geneve 20, Switzerland 1211
+41 22 730 5111
www.itu.ch

3.3.2 American National Standards Institute (ANSI)

The American National Standards Institute (ANSI) acts as the North American primary standards body, as well as the official interface to all international standards bodies. To ensure that standards sanctioned by ANSI are impartial to vendor, user, and service provider alike, contributions pending standardization are contributed from many voluntary nonprofit, nongovernmental organizations, including the Institute of Electrical and Electronic Engineers (IEEE), the Electronic Industries Association (EIA), and the Computer and Business Equipment Manufacturers Association (CBEMA). ANSI is also a member and active participant in the International Standards Committee, and the United Nations sits at the top of the standards bodies hierarchy.

ANSI standards define both electronic and industrial standards for the national and international communities. ANSI defines *national standards* such as American National Standards. These standards are published with the following number scheme:

ANSI/NNNN XXXX-19XX - Standard Name,

where **NNNN** is the name of the contributing organization (e.g., IEEE),

XXXX is a letter and/or number combination signifying the field of study and the reference number of the standard within that field,

19XX is the date the standard was officially published,

Standard Name is the name of the standard.

ANSI defines *international standards* sanctioned by the ISO in a similar manner:

ANSI/ISO XXXX-19XX - Standard Name,

where the fields are the same as for national standards.

3.3.3 ANSI T1 Standards Committee

The T1 Standards Committee on Telecommunications is one of the most important standards bodies dealing with data communications and telecommunications in the United States. The committee, established in 1984, is sponsored by the Alliance for Telecommunications Industry Solutions (ATIS) and accredited by ANSI. ANSI T1 committee standards are developed in close coordination with the ITU-T, and address characteristics of technology that are unique to North America. Particular ANSI T1 subcommittees are involved with different aspects of standardization.

Established in February 1984, the mission of the ANSI Accredited Standards Committee T1 is to develop technical standards and reports supporting the interconnection and interoperability of telecommunications networks at interfaces with end-user systems, carriers, information and enhanced service providers, and customer premises equipment (CPE). The Alliance for Telecommunications Industry Solutions (ATIS) sponsors and provides the secretariat support for Standards Committee T1. Membership and full participation in the ANSI Accredited Standards T1 Committee and its technical subcommittees is open to all parties with a direct interest in the T1 process and activities. Free of dominance from a single interest, this open membership and balanced participation safeguards the integrity and efficiency of the standards formulation process. ASNI due process procedures further ensure fairness.

ANSI Committee T1 develops standards and technical reports related to interfaces for U.S. telecommunications networks, some of which are associated with other North American telecommunications networks. T1 also develops positions on related subjects under consideration in various international standards bodies. Specifically, T1 focuses on those functions and characteristics associated with the interconnection and interoperability of telecommunications networks at interfaces with end-user systems, carriers, and information and enhanced service providers. These include switching, signaling, transmission, performance, operation, administration, and maintenance aspects. Committee T1 is also concerned with procedural matters at points of interconnection, such as maintenance and provisioning methods and documentation, for which standardization would benefit the telecommunications industry.

Committee T1 currently has six technical subcommittees that are advised and managed by the T1 Advisory Group (T1AG). Each recommends standards and develops technical reports in its area of expertise. The subcommittees also recommend positions on matters under consideration by other North American and international standards bodies.

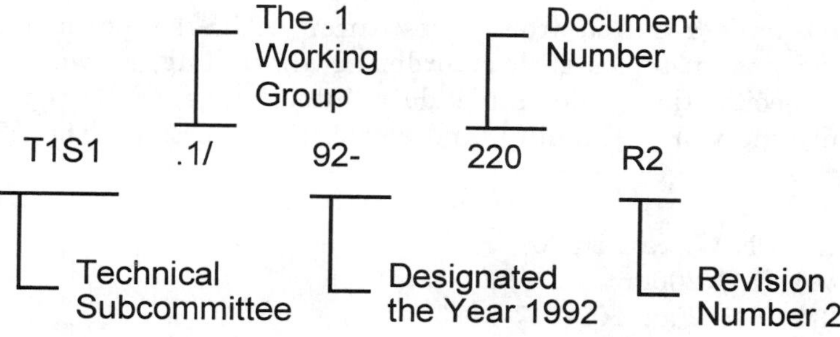

Figure 3.2 T1S1 General Numbering Plan Format

T1A1	Performance and Signal Processing
T1E1	Interfaces, Power, and Protection of Networks
T1M1	Internetwork Operations, Administration, Maintenance, and Provisioning
T1P1	System Engineering, Standards Planning, and Program Management
T1S1	Services, Architectures, and Signaling
T1X1	Digital Hierarchy and Synchronization

These technical subcommittees (TSCs), in turn, have established a number of working groups (WGs) and subworking groups (SWGs) to perform the detailed standards work associated with approved standards projects.

When reading technical recommendations published by the T1 Committee, it is useful to understand the document numbering plan. These numbering plans shown below are consistent across all ANSI technical documentation. Figure 3.2 shows the general document numbering plan format.

Two other organizations which adopt ANSI standards are the Federal Information Processing Standards (FIPS) group, where work is used for government procurement standards, and the Department of Defense (DoD), which dictates mandatory standards for governmental use such as the Government OSI Protocol (GOSIP).

3.3.4 Alliance for Telecommunications Industry Solutions (ATIS)

The Alliance for Telecommunications Industry Solutions (ATIS), formerly the Exchange Carriers Standards Association (ECSA), sponsors the T1 Standards Committee, which is also responsible for SONET standards in North America. ATIS was originally incorporated as a not-for-profit association in 1983 and was called the Exchange Carriers' Standards Association (ECSA). Renamed in 1993, ATIS comprises members of the telecommunications industry to address exchange access, interconnection, and other technical issues that have resulted from divestiture. ATIS supports a number of industry forums on topics such as ordering and billing, network operations, bar code specifications, electronic data interchange (EDI), open network architecture, network reliability, and electrical protection. The ATIS can be reached at

1200 G Street N.W., Suite 500
Washington, D.C. 20005
Ph: 202-434-8845, Fax: 202-347-7125
http://www.t1.org

3.3.5 European Telecommunications Standards Institute (ETSI)

The European Telecommunications Standards Institute (ETSI) is primarily involved in the standardization of European telecommunications. The ITU-T develops recommendations for worldwide use, while the role of regional bodies, such as ETSI in Europe and ANSI in America, is to generate, on the basis of global standards, more detailed specifications adapted to the unique historical, technical, and regulatory situation of each region. The address and phone number to obtain further information about ETSI are

European Telecommunications Standards Institute (ETSI)
Route de Lucioles
06291 Sophia Antipolis
Cedex, Valbonne
France
+33 92 944200

3.3.6 Institute for Electrical and Electronics Engineers (IEEE)

The Institute for Electrical and Electronics Engineers (IEEE) was formed in 1963 by a merger of the American Institute of Electrical Engineers (AIEE) and the Institute of Radio Engineers (IRE). It is now the world's largest professional engineering society. Standardization has always been a core activity of these two organizations. Through an international membership, the IEEE carries on that function by developing and disseminating electrotechnical standards which are recognized worldwide. Standard guides, practices, and reference manuals are developed by the IEEE to define these standards. *The IEEE is truly a member-driven standards body which represents the engineering community.* Anyone who is sponsored can become a member of the IEEE. Standards are approved through the IEEE Standards Board. Many publications, journals, and newsletters are published by members under the IEEE title, containing various proposals and outlining technology trends.

The primary IEEE standards discussed here are the IEEE 802.X standards, which include 802.1 through 802.6 and define such technologies as Ethernet (802.3), Token Bus (802.4), Token Ring (802.5), and metropolitan area networking (MAN) (802.6). The IEEE 802 standards are developed by the IEEE LAN Standards Committees.

3.3.7 Bell Communications Research (Bellcore)

Bellcore is now more of a private development center than a standards organization. The original intent of Bellcore was to act as a center for coordination and research for the Regional Holding Companies (RHCs) in the aftermath of divestiture. Over time it developed into a very powerful driving force for the Regional Bell Operating Companies (RBOCs). Historically, Bellcore centered its research on the operations and support systems (OSSs) for the BOCs. This included hardware and software research, development, and even design of these systems. Always setting its sights on the public network, Bellcore next expanded its consulting services and participation in standards recommendations. The Switched Multimegabit Data Service (SMDS) Bellcore Recommendations, which will be discussed in later chapters, is evidence of its intent to move new technologies into standards.

Bellcore technical publications were divided into Bell System pre-divestiture (before January 1, 1984) and postdivestiture documentation. The pre-divestiture documentation included compatibility bulletins (CBs), information publications (IPs), technical descriptions (TDs), and technical references (PUBs). Since many of these documents have been revised and reissued by Bellcore under the postdivestiture format, we will concentrate on those new formats.

Bellcore's postdivestiture documentation is divided into the following categories.

Framework Technical Advisories (FAs). These contain preliminary early Bellcore views with very generic requirements, and act as catalysts for the telecommunication industry. FAs are often superseded by TAs.

Technical Advisories (TAs). These contain preliminary views of proposed generic requirements for interfaces, products, and new services and technologies. TAs are often superseded by TRs.

Technical References (TRs). These contain the developed and mature views of TAs.

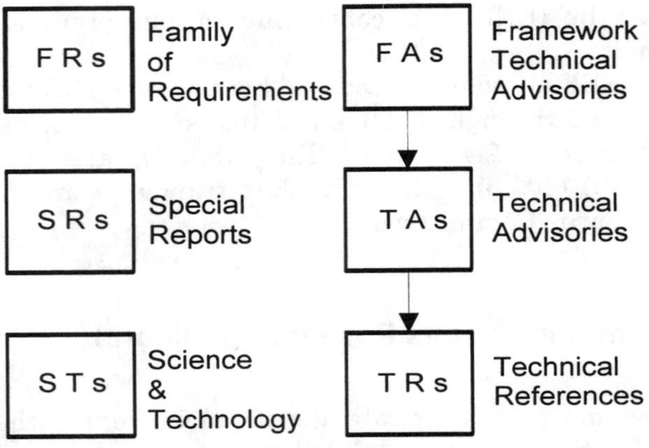

Figure 3.3 Bellcore Postdivestiture Documentation

Family of Requirements (FRs). These contain complete sets of related TRs.

Special Reports (SRs). These contain documentation of other technical interest not mentioned in previous documents.

Science and Technology (STs). These contain highly technical information that needs to be conveyed to the telecommunications industry.

Figure 3.3 shows these document types and their evolution cycle. Since Bellcore went private and is no longer a recognized standards organization, all Bellcore documents now carry the Generic Requirement (GR) label. For more information, refer to www.bellcore.com.

3.3.8 International Organization for Standardization/ International Electrotechnical Commission (ISO/IEC)

The International Organization for Standardization (ISO) is a voluntary international standards body made up of representatives of over 90 countries and chartered to cover many subjects. The organizational structure is based upon technical committees made up of subcommittees, which in turn are made up of working groups. Standards are published first as Draft Proposals (DPs) from working groups. Once approved, they become Draft International Standards (DIS) for ballot by the Technical Subcommittee. Upon approval, they become an international standard with the same DP number originally assigned by the Working Group.

Data communications standards, more commonly called information technology standards, are handled by the ISO Technical Committee 97. The

International Electrotechnical Commission (IEC) and the ISO formed the Joint Technical Committee 1 (JTC 1) to produce joint ISO/IEC standards for information processing. The ISO/IEC JTC 1 includes participants of standardization bodies from 22 countries who submit standards to the ISO. It is interesting to note that ANSI administers the secretariat of the JTC 1, as well as four of its subcommittees. Three of these four primary standards subcommittees defining the subject matter here are Telecommunications, Open Systems Interconnection, and Text and Office Systems.

3.3.9 Federal Communications Commission (FCC)

The Federal Communications Commission (FCC) is not a standards organization, but it has served as the regulatory authority for radio, television, wire, and cable communications within the United States. The FCC has the charter to retain regulatory control over interstate and international commerce concerning communications. The FCC strives for competitiveness in these markets, which relates to the public benefits of marketplace fairness, up-to-date and quality communications systems, and a broad range of communications offerings for the consumer. The FCC also has responsibilities for reviewing the rate and service change applications for telegraph and telephone companies, reviewing the technical specifications of communications hardware, and setting reasonable common carrier rates of return. These goals extend to the regional holding companies (RHCs) and the interexchange carriers (IXCs), and to any technical and regulatory policy issues by which they are affected.

3.3.10 Additional National Standards Bodies

The Computer and Business Equipment Manufacturers Association (CBEMA) sets standards for computer and business hardware. The Electronic Industries Association (EIA) and Telecommunications Industries Association (TIA) set standards on the communications, computers, and electronics fields, with an emphasis on inter-connectivity between these fields. Both represent the manufacturing community, and the EIA is active as a trade organization and as an ANSI-accredited standards organization.

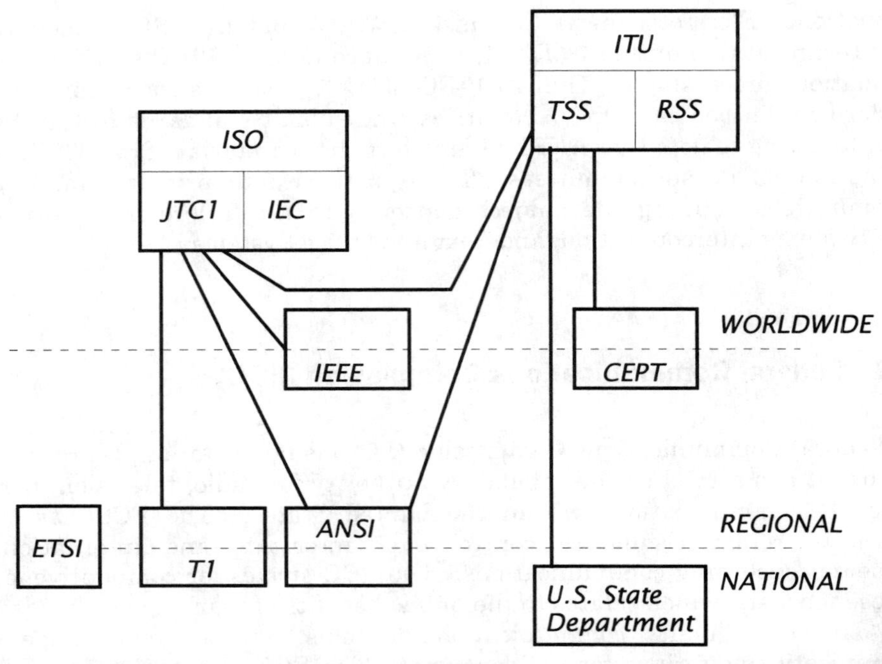

Figure 3.4 Standards Organizations

3.3.11 Additional International Standards Bodies

One additional international standards organization is the European Computer Manufacturers Association (ECMA), which establishes manufacturing computer standards. The member body of the ISO and IEC for the Netherlands is the Nederlands Normalisatie Instituut (NNI), for Saudi Arabia it is the Saudi Arabian Standards Organization (SASO), for Sweden it is the Standardiseringskommissionen i Sverige (SIS), and for Finland it is the Suomen Standardisoimisliito (SFS). The group dedicated to establishing European standards as national standards is the Comite Europeen de Normalisation (CEN). The CEN is also active in the ISO. Members of both the CEN and ISO include the Danish standards organization Dansk Standardiseringsrad (DS), the National Standards Authority of Ireland (NSAI), and the British Standards Institution (BSI). The French national Association Francaise de Normalisation (AFNOR) supports the ISO activities, as does the German Deutsches Institut fur Nromung (DIN). Canada has the Canadian Standards Association (CSA) as its primary standards association, and the primary Japanese standards body is the Japanese Industrial Standards Committee (JISC).

3.3.12 How Do They Interface?

Standards organizations and industry forums and committees interact on both a national and international level. Standards set by organizations that fail to anticipate all of the impacts can either be accepted or shunned by other rivals of nonnational organizations, causing dual standards to be implemented, thus defeating the purpose of standardization.

Figure 3.4 shows the standards organizations discussed and how they interact. The figure is layered, showing organizations which span the United States (national), a given geographic region (such as Europe) (regional), and those which span the globe (worldwide).

Table 3.1 shows a summary of the standards organizations discussed, along with their areas of participation and influence.

In an age where global connectivity and communications is becoming the keystone for international business, the existence of global communication standards is imperative. The industries of both national and international business must drive these standards bodies to develop standards that are as consistent as possible. Interfaces, protocols, regulation, network management, and many other support technologies must become inter-operable.

Heading down the road toward open systems, it is the responsibility of standards organizations to push for a global standard for telecommunications, and that standard seems to be open systems. From the music of the spheres in the “seventh” heaven, to Dante's rings of descending layers to the bottom-most depths of hell, people can relate to the degrees or "layers" that connect things together. Thus we have developed the seven-layer OSI reference model (OSIRM). The OSIRM defines the development of hardware and software, systems and media, and communications services and processes. Vendors and service providers who define hardware and systems based upon these standards will gain a larger piece of the world data communications market share. Governments, IXCs, and PTTs can also play a major role in shaping these standards. But this global standardization process does not stop at organizations such as the ITU-T and JTC1, however. On the contrary, it typically starts at user group and forum levels. Following is a discussion of the user's groups and forums helping to shape these standards both nationally and internationally.

TABLE 3.1 Standards Bodies

Standard Body	Standards Issues Covered	Sphere of Influence
ANSI	Electronics and industrial standards	Regional
T1 Standards Committee	Data communications	National
IEEE	General engineering, computer and communications, LANs and MANs	International
ISO/IEC	Data communications, NM, information technology	International
ITU-T	Telecommunications, data communications, telegraph and telephone	International
U.S. State Department	Telecommunications, data communications, telegraph and telephone	National
BELLCORE	RBOC research & development, SMDS	National
FCC	Regulatory for communications	National
CBEMA	Computer & business hardware	National
EIA/TIA	Communications, computers, electronic fields	National
ECMA	Manufacturers' computer standards	European
ATIS	Telecommunications, data communications	National
ETSI	Data communications, telecommunications issues	European
NNI, SASO, SIS, SFS, CEN, DS, NSAI, BSI, AFNOR, DIN, CSA, JISC	Varies	International

3.4 CURRENT FORUMS

A new style of "jump starting" the standards process emerged in the 1990s in the formation of industry forums. These are not formal standards committees, but independent groups formed by vendors, users, and industry experts who want to ensure standards for interoperability, but who do not want to add further implementation details to standards. Instead, specifications, or, implementation agreements, are published by selecting an inter-operable subset of requirements from standards, clarifying ambiguities, or in some cases, specifying certain aspects in advance of standards. Sometimes these forums provide valuable contributions to the formal standards organizations (often as already implemented, and hence proven and not theoretical, approaches) like the LMI Specifications developed by the Gang of Four for frame relay, speeding along the acceptance of an interface, protocol, or other aspect of a technology. Often, more than writing and publishing the standards is required for success. The multiple vendor and provider agreements developed in these industry forums are often essential to a standard's success.

One critical aspect influencing standards acceptance that is often overlooked is the development of services and applications to accompany the standards. An example of this is ISDN basic (BRI) and primary (PRI) rate interfaces, where the technology is fully developed but was still at a loss for applications for many years. ISDN was basically a PTT/telephone company standard used to upgrade, digitize, and put the latest technology into the utilities' networks for maximum efficiency — the end user was not a significant factor in the equation. Little wonder end users did not perceive its immediate value. Acceptance by the vendor community also plays a key role in the success or failure of standards. The forum which keeps both the standard and the applications for that standard in mind will likely cause the standard to "live long and prosper", or at least live longer than those that concentrate primarily on the development of standards. User trial communities and university test beds are other methods employed by these forums to help speed up the testing and acceptance of these new technologies. The Internet protocol is one of the best examples of a standards process where the protocols that are standardized are proven to work first – the "rough consensus and working code" approach to standardization.

Some recent forums have made sizable impacts on technology development and standardization. Most of these forums provide training centers, seminars, and interoperability tests in test labs, and strictly adhere to parallel standards development by national and international standards bodies. Standards development seems to take place best in this "free market" of standards just as the "free market" of ideas has stimulated Western culture.

There are four major industry forums currently active in our areas of study: the Frame Relay Forum, the SMDS Interest Group (SIG), the ATM Forum, and the Internet Engineering Task Force (IETF). A few additional national and international forums are also presented here.

3.4.1 Frame Relay Forum

The Frame Relay Forum was formed in January 1991 as a non-profit organization dedicated to promoting the acceptance and implementation of frame relay based upon national and international standards. The group originated when the "Gang of Four" (cisco Systems, Inc., Digital Equipment Corporation, Northern Telecom, Inc., and StrataCom, Inc.) developed the frame relay Local Management Interface (LMI) specification, making it voluntarily available to those who wanted to join (about 40 to date) and then saw a need to carry on this work using the vehicle of the Frame Relay Forum. The coalition continues to grow each year and includes participation from Pacific Rim and European firms. The organization is divided into three groups: technical, organizational, and marketing. The Frame Relay Forum (FRF) submits all of its standards work to the international standards organizations, ensuring worldwide interoperability.

While the FRF is not a standards body, it is a "forum" for frame relay users to discuss implementation issues and drive the standards bodies such as ANSI and ITU-T to implement what the users (and vendors whose equipment relies on the user version of the standard) really require. One example of their efforts is their assistance to ANSI in implementing the LMI specifications. The committee also drives for interoperability between implementations of frame relay, and thus between users, as well as developing testing and certification standards.

Forums often corroborated closely in the production specifications. One recent example is the work between the Frame Relay Forum and the ATM Forum in the production of Frame Relay/ATM inter-working specifications.

3.4.2 SMDS Interest Group (SIG)

The SMDS Interest Group (SIG) and SMDS User Group are chartered with developing guidelines for interoperability between SMDS hardware, services, and applications. Participation involves primarily SMDS hardware vendors, service providers including the seven RBOCs, and the major inter-exchange carriers. As with many user groups, the SIG works with the major standards bodies and other user groups to ensure compatibility among standards. One example is how the SIG is working closely with the ATM Forum to specify the inter-working of SMDS with ATM networks.

3.4.3 ATM Forum

The ATM Forum was formed in October 1991 by four companies: Northern Telecom (NorTel), Sprint, SUN Microsystems, and Digital Equipment

Corporation (DEC). In January 1992, the membership was opened to the industry. There are currently three categories of membership: principal, auditing, and user. Only principal members can participate in technical and marketing committee meetings. Auditing members receive copies of the technical and marketing committee documents, but cannot participate in the meetings. Only user members may participate in End User Roundtable (ENR) meetings.

There are three types of committees in the ATM Forum: Technical, Market Awareness, and End User. The Technical Committee produces implementation specifications and is organized into a number of technical "subject matter expert" subcommittees. The Market Awareness and Education (MA&E) Committee produces tutorials, presentations, press releases, newsletters, and other informative material. There are branches of this committee in North America, Europe, and Asia. The End User Roundtable (ENR) user group was formed in August 1993, with the goal of collecting higher-level requirements and providing these to the Technical and MA&E committees. ATM membership is broken down into principal members, auditing members, and user members, each with various voting privileges. The address, phone number, and Internet address to obtain information about the ATM Forum are

The ATM Forum
303 Vintage Park Drive
Foster City, CA 94404
+1 415 578 6860
info@atmforum.com
www.atmforum.com

3.4.4 Internet Engineering Task Force (IETF)

The Internet Activities Board (IAB) was formed in 1983 by DARPA. By 1989 the Internet had grown so large that the IAB was reorganized, and the principal work of developing specifications to achieve interoperability was assigned to an Internet Engineering Task Force (IETF), split into eight areas, each with an area director. The initial objective of the IAB/IETF was to define the necessary specifications required for inter-operable implementations using the Internet Protocol (IP) suite. Specifications are drafted in documents called Request For Comments (RFC). These RFCs pass through a draft stage and a proposed stage prior to becoming an approved standard. Another possible outcome of a draft or proposed standard is that it is archived as an experimental RFC. Out-of-date RFCs are archived as historical standards. The archival of all approved as well as historical or experimental RFCs has created a storehouse of protocol and networking knowledge that is available to the world. The address, phone number, and most importantly,

Internet address to obtain more information about the IETF and the Internet are

Internet Society
1985 Preston White Drive, Suite 100
Reston, VA 22091
+01 703 620 8990
isoc@nri.reston.va.us

One spin-off from the IETF is the Internet Society. The Internet Society is chartered with speeding the evolution and growth of the Internet communications network as an international research network. Within this group is the Internet Activities Board, comprising users of Internet; it was the old governing board for the Internet. The Internet Activities Board has established such standards as TCP/IP. The Internet Society remains the administrative body for the Internet, providing functions such as database administration, user training, and Internet interoperability among its user community. The Internet Engineering Task Force (IETF) establishes the standards for Internet engineering, while the Internet Research Task Force (IRTF) pursues ongoing research.

3.4.5 Additional National Forums

The Switched Digital Services Application Forum (SDSAF) is dedicated to promoting the use of switched services from 56K bps to DS3, including frame relay. Membership is composed of various vendors and carriers, each with a vested interest in the success of switched services. The thrust of their charter is to address the issue of vendor interoperability in the switching world. The goal of the SDSAF is for applications to be developed using switched services so that interoperability and private networking issues can be solved and more publicity may be given to switched services.

Another group focused primarily on network management standards is the Network Management Consortium. This consortium works to speed the integration and interoperability of various vendor SNMP implementations of systems and agents. The members are primarily network equipment vendors who employ products with SNMP capabilities.

The North American ISDN User's Forum is chartered with establishing a commercial infrastructure for ISDN in North America. Also, the Open Systems Interconnect Network Management (NM) Forum is composed of many vendors developing network management interfaces to the OSI architecture. The OSI NM Forum has developed the System to Management System standard which will speed interoperability between proprietary vendor hardware and software.

3.5 REVIEW

This chapter identified the organizations that are taking an active role in standardizing and specifying many of the technologies introduced in this book. The standards-making process accelerates and improves every year, especially with catalysts like the industry forums. The role of the various players in the standards process, users, vendors, and service providers, was covered. The standards process was then described in terms of how standards are developed and finalized. Comments were provided on differences in approach between the various organizations and their efforts to cooperate to develop standards for faster deployment.

Chapter

4

Protocol and Transmission Basics

Protocols are the standards by which we communicate. A *protocol* is similar to a language, conveying meaning and understanding through some form of communication. Computer communication protocols are defined as sets of rules and message exchanges. Protocol communications are modeled in a layered fashion, with lower-layer protocols providing services to the next higher layer. For one computer to talk to another, each must be able to understand the other's protocol. Protocols play an important role in data communications; without them islands of users would be unable to communicate. Protocols are defined through protocol architectures, the most well known being the seven-layer Open Systems Interconnect Reference Model (OSIRM), which is introduced in this chapter. The concept of layered protocols is largely due to the OSI reference model; however, the protocol specifics of OSIRM are not widely implemented. Non-OSI, proprietary architectures have propagated a variety of protocols, many of which are used extensively today, such as TCP/IP and SNA. Still, each of these architectures has a similar layering structure. This concept of layering has enabled the entire industry of multi-protocol routing that has dominated for over a decade.

The physical layer is the lowest-layer protocol that provides access to the transmission medium, specifying details concerning physical interface signaling, timing, and pin-level configuration. Data link layer protocols allow communications with the physical layer and provide link-by-link error detection/correction, multiplexing, and flow control. Included in the data link layer are both the Logical Link Control (LLC) and the Medium Access Control (MAC) sub-layers in Local Area Network (LAN) communications. Network layer protocols then take over by providing end-to-end addressing, flow control, and integrity checking. The transport layer provides multiplexing onto the network layer, expedited delivery, and further integrity checking. The session layer establishes a connection between end systems. Finally, the presentation layer manipulates data into different forms for the highest and most complicated layer, the application layer. This chapter also introduces the Integrated Services Digital Network (ISDN) protocol reference model, as it plays an important role in the Broadband-ISDN (B-ISDN) protocol reference model.

Transmission basics are also introduced in this chapter. Digital Time Division Multiplexing (TDM) and the standard plesiochronous digital hierarchy that forms the underlying fabric of most wide area communications are introduced. Next, a comparison of the OSI Connection-Oriented Network Services (CONS) and ConnectionLess Network Services (CLNS) is presented. This chapter concludes with a comparison of private line to switched networks.

4.1 BASIC PROTOCOL-LAYERING CONCEPTS

A protocol is defined by Webster's New World Dictionary as "a set of rules governing the communications and the transfer of data between machines, as in computer systems". Communications and data transfer between machines takes place at many "layers". These layers are defined within software or hardware, and the communications can be anything from software messages to the raising or lowering of voltage levels on the physical interface. Each layer therefore has a specific interface to the other layers, and these protocols interact either within their layer interface or between multiple layer interfaces. Figure 4.1 illustrates the basic concept of protocol layering that is relevant to the technologies discussed in this book. Let's now look at these protocol-layering concepts in detail.

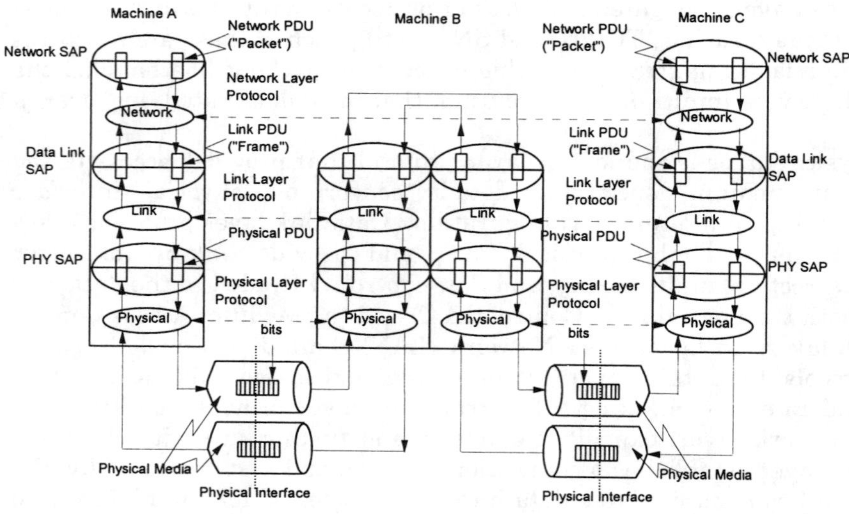

Figure 4.1 Physical, Link, and Network Layers

Interfaces can be either physical or logical in nature. The term *interface* is used in two ways in different standards bodies. First, primarily in the ITU view, physical interfaces provide the physical connection between different types of hardware, with protocols providing rules, conventions, and the intelligence to pass data over these interfaces between peer protocol layers. Normally, the view is that bits flow over physical interfaces. In the OSI view, interfaces exist between protocol layers. Normally, the view is that *Protocol Data Units* (PDUs), or *messages*, pass through protocol interfaces. These interfaces between layers are called Service Access Points (SAPs) because they are the points where the lower layer provides service to the higher layer. Stated another way, the physical interfaces provide the path for data flow between machines, while protocols manage that data flow across this path using protocol interfaces within the machines. Physical interfaces and protocols must be compatible for accurate data communications. Many network designs now incorporate multiple levels of protocols and interfaces, always starting at the physical layer.

The concepts behind the use of multiple protocol layers are important. The concepts of physical, data link, and network layer protocols can now be defined on a high level. Most technologies covered in this text have their roots in the physical, data link, and network layers of the OSI protocol model, as we will see in future chapters.

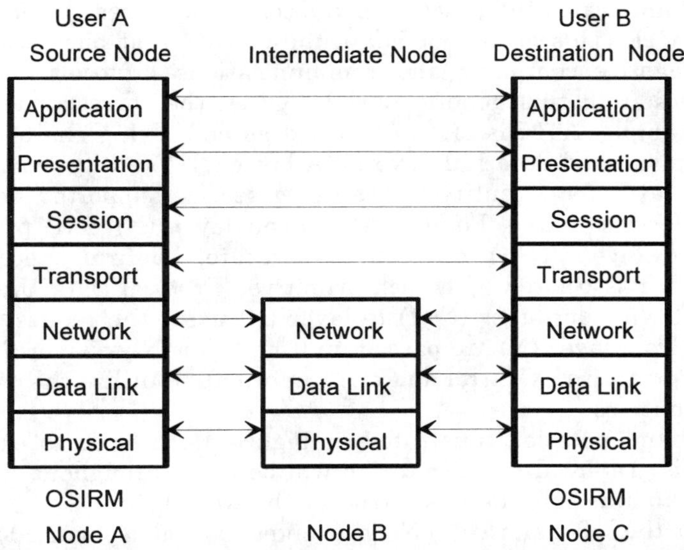

Figure 4.2 Open Systems Interconnection Reference Model (OSIRM)

4.2 LAYERED REFERENCE MODELS — THE OSIRM

The Open Systems Interconnection Reference Model (OSIRM) was intended to define the functions and protocols necessary for any computer system to connect to any other computer system, regardless of the manufacturer. This model was developed by the International Organization for Standardization (ISO), beginning in 1977 with the formation of ISO Technical Subcommittee 97 (TC97), and Subcommittee 16 (SC16), and was officially documented in 1983 in ISO standard 7498. Figure 4.2 depicts the basic OSI reference model showing a source, A intermediate, B and destination C node and the protocol stack within each. The layers are represented starting from the bottom at the first layer, which has a physical interface to the adjacent node, to the top-most seventh layer, which usually resides on the user end device (workstation) or host that interacts with user applications. Each of these seven layers represents one or more protocols that define the functional operation of communications between user and network elements. All protocol communications between layers are "peer-to-peer", depicted as horizontal arrows between the layers. Emerging standards span all seven layers of the model, as summarized below. Although OSI has standardized many of these protocols, only a few are in widespread use. The layering concept; however, has been widely adopted by every major computer and communications standards body.

Figure 4.3 illustrates the basic elements common to every layer of the OSI reference model. This is the portion of the OSIRM that has become widely used to categorize computer and communications protocols according to characteristics from this generic model. Often the correspondence is not exact; for example, ATM is often described as embodying characteristics of both the physical and data link layers. A layer (N+1) entity communicates with a peer layer (N+1) entity by way of a service supported at layer (N) through a Service Access Point (SAP). The layer (N) SAP provides the primitives to layer (N+1) of request, indicate, confirm, and response. Parameters are associated with each primitive. Protocol Data Units (PDUs) are passed down from layer (N+1) to layer (N) using the request primitive, while PDUs from layer (N) are passed up from layer (N) to layer (N+1) using the indicate primitive. Control and error information utilize the confirm and response primitives.

The shorthand notation illustrated in Figure 4.4 is used to express this concept. This graphical representation will be used throughout the technology chapters to illustrate the PDU structure between layers.

Starting at the left-hand side, Node A takes data at layer (N+1), which is connected to Node B by a layer (N–1) protocol. On the link between Nodes A and B we illustrate the resultant enveloping of the layer headers (HDR) and trailers (TRL) that are carried by the layer (N–1) protocol. Node B performs a transformation from layer (N) to the correspondingly layered, different protocols called layer (N)' and layer (N–1)'. The resultant action of these protocol entities is shown by the layer (N–1)' PDU on the link between nodes B and C.

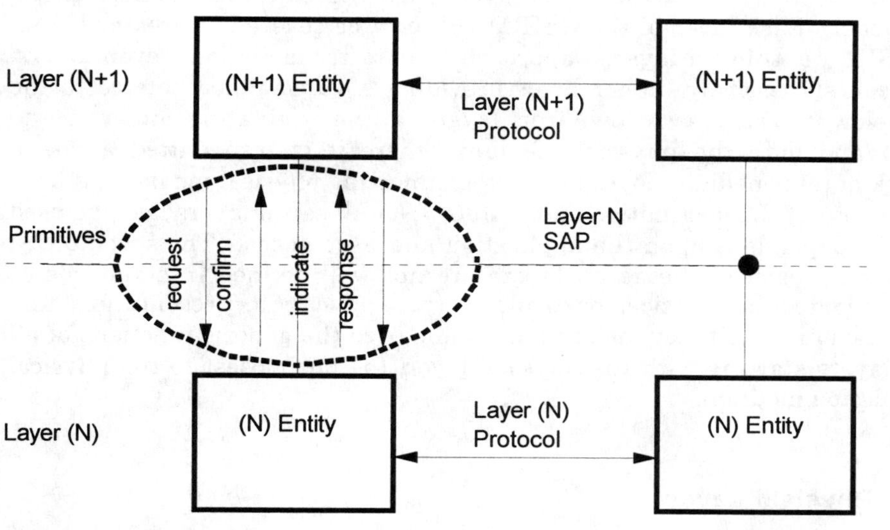

Figure 4.3 Illustration of Layered Protocol Model

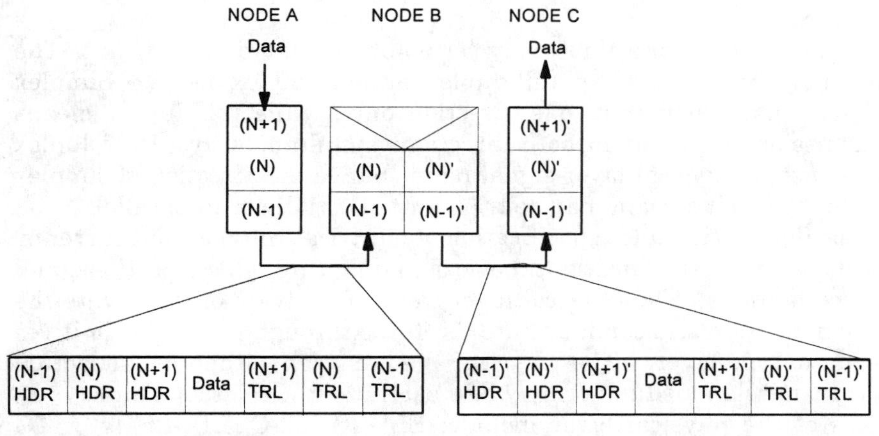

Figure 4.4 Shorthand Protocol Model Notation

4.3 LAYERS OF THE OSI REFERENCE MODEL

Many computer networking architectures can be modeled by comparing them to the basic structure of the seven-layer Open Systems Interconnect Reference Model. Each layer of the OSIRM will now be covered in greater detail. The OSIRM outlines a layered approach to data transmission: seven layers, with each successively higher layer providing a value-added service to the layer below it. Data flows down from layer 7 at the originating end system to layer 1 and onto the physical medium, where it is transmitted across a network of intermediate nodes over interconnecting physical media, and back up to layer 7 of the destination end system. Not all seven layers need be used — this is dependent upon the application and user needs. The specific OSI protocols for each of the seven layers are not well defined in standards or widely adopted in practice, particularly the application, presentation, and session layers. The following sections summarize the generic functions of all seven layers starting with the physical layer, the one closest to the physical transmission medium.

4.3.1 Physical Layer

The first layer encountered is the physical layer (L1), which provides for the transparent transmission of a bit stream across the physical interconnection of network elements. The intelligence managing the data stream and protocols residing above the physical layer are transparently conveyed by the physical layer.

The physical layer connections may be point-to-point or multipoint. The connection may be operated in full-duplex or half-duplex mode. Simplex means that transmission is in one direction only, while full-duplex means that transmission can occur in both directions simultaneously. Half-duplex involves the use of physical layer signaling to change the direction of simplex transmission. The bit stream may be transmitted serially or in parallel.

The physical layer includes specification of electrical voltages and currents, mechanical connector specifications, basic signaling through connections, and signaling conventions. The physical layer can also activate or deactivate the transmission medium and communicate its status through protocol primitives with the data link layer. The physical medium can either be an actual physical transmission medium or may be a satellite or wireless medium.

Examples of the physical layer include: EIA-RS-232-C, EIA-RS-449, ITU X.21/X.21bis, ITU V.35, IEEE 802 LAN, ISO 9314 FDDI, and the HSSI interface. One example of a wireless physical interface is a wireless LAN.

The terms *Data Termination Equipment* (DTE) and *Data Communication Equipment* (DCE) refer to the hardware on either side of a communications channel interface. DTE equipment is typically a computer or terminal which acts as an end point for transmitted and received data via a physical interface to a DCE. DCE equipment is typically a modem or communication device, which has a different physical interface than that of the DTE. One commonly used type of DCE is called a Channel Service Unit/Data Service Unit (CSU/DSU); it converts the DTE/DCE interface to a telephony-based interface. Figure 4.5 shows a common end-to-end network configuration where DTE1 talks to DCE1, which in turn formats the transmission for transfer over the network to the end DCE, which then interfaces to the end DTE. Also note that a single device can carry both a DTE and DCE designation, depending on its position and function in the network.

4.3.2 Data Link Layer

The data link layer is layer 2 (L2) in the seven-layer OSI reference model, and the second layer in most other computer architecture models as well. The primary function of the data link layer is to establish a reliable protocol interface across the physical layer (L1) on behalf of the network layer (L3). This means that the link layer performs error detection and possibly even error correction. Toward this end, the data link control functions establish a peer-to-peer relationship across each physical link between machines. The data link layer entities exchange clearly delimited protocol data units, which are commonly called *frames*. The data link layer may use a limited form of addressing such that multiple data link layer protocol interfaces can be multiplexed across a single physical layer interface. There may be a flow control function to control the flow of frames such that a fast sender does not overrun a slow receiver.

Computer communications via local area networks utilizes special functions of the data link layer called the MAC and LLC layers. The MAC layer protocols form the basis of LAN and MAN standards used by the IEEE 802.X LAN protocol suite, which includes Ethernet, Token Ring, and Token Bus.

Examples of the link layer include ISO 7776, ITU X.25 link layer, ISDN LAP-D, ISO HDLC, and MAC-layer protocols such as the ISO 9314-2 FDDI Token Ring MAC. The 802.X protocol structures will be covered later in this chapter.

Some of the new services, such as frame relay and ATM, can be viewed as using only the first two layers of the OSI reference model, and rely heavily on reducing the link layer services to increase speeds at lower costs because of the resulting protocol simplification. A key difference between frame relay and ATM is that the addresses can take on an end-to-end significance, whereas in the OSI link layer addresses are only significant between nodes. Part of the 802.6 Distributed Queue Dual Bus (DQDB) standard is also called a layer 2 protocol.

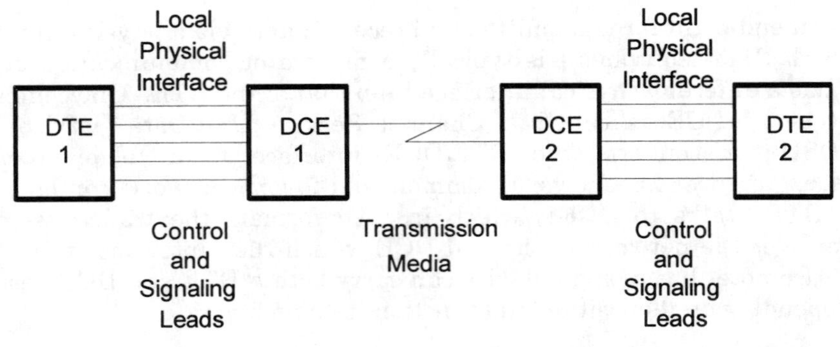

Figure 4.5 DTE to DTE Communications

4.3.3 Network Layer

The third layer (L3) encountered is the network layer. The principal function of the network layer is to provide reliable, in-sequence delivery of protocol data between transport layer entities. In order to do this, the network layer always has an end-to-end addressing capability. A unique network-layer address is assigned to each network-layer protocol entity. A network-layer protocol may communicate with its peer over a route of intermediate machines with physical, data link, and network layers. The determination of this route is called the *routing function*. Routing protocols and operation will be covered in Chapter 8. Network layer PDUs are often called *packets*.

The network layer may also perform end-to-end flow control and the segmentation and reassembly of data. The network layer is the most protocol-intensive portion of packet networks. Some examples of protocols used in the network layer are the ITU X.25 and X.75 packet level and gateway protocols, the Internet Protocol (IP), CCITT/ITU-T Q.931, Q.933, Q.2931, and the OSI CLNP.

The network layer is used to define data call establishment procedures for packet and cell-switched networks in ISDN and B-ISDN. For example, ATM signaling utilizes a layer 3 protocol for call setup and disconnection. SMDS also employs a layer 3 protocol to provide an end-to-end datagram service using E.164 (i.e., telephone numbers) for addressing. Each of these concepts will be covered in their respective protocol chapters.

4.3.4 Transport Layer

The fourth layer (L4) encountered is the transport layer. The principal function of the transport layer is to interconnect session layer entities.

Historically it has been called the host-to-host layer. Principal functions that it performs are segmentation, re-assembly, and multiplexing over a single network-layer interface. The transport layer allows a session-layer entity to request a class of service, which must be mapped onto appropriate network-layer capabilities. It is the fourth layer's responsibility to manage end-to-end flow control. The transport layer may often perform error detection and correction as well, which has become increasingly more important since it provides a higher-level error correction and retransmission protocol for new services such as frame relay, SMDS, and ATM. Often frame relay users will ask what happens when "DE" frames are discarded. It is the responsibility of the transport layer to retransmit packets lost due to discarded and lost DE-marked frames. One example of the transport layer includes the ITU X.224 OSI transport protocol TP4. Another widely used example of a transport type of protocol is the Internet Transmission Control Protocol (TCP).

4.3.5 Session Layer

The fifth layer (L5) encountered is the session layer. The session layer is essentially the user's interface to the network, which may have some data transformations performed by the presentation layer. Sessions usually provide connections between a user, such as a terminal or LAN workstation, and a central processor or host. So-called peer-to-peer session-layer protocols can directly connect user applications. Session-layer protocols are usually rather complex, involving negotiation of parameters and exchange of information about the end user applications. The session layer has addresses that are meaningful to end users. Other session-layer functions include flow control, dialog management, control over the direction of data transfer, and transaction support.

Some examples of the session layer are terminal-to-mainframe log-on procedures, transfer of user information, and the setup of information and resource allocations. The ISO standard for the session layer is the ISO 8327/ITU X.225 connection-oriented session protocol.

4.3.6 Presentation Layer

The sixth layer (L6) encountered is the presentation layer. The presentation layer determines how data is presented to the user. Official standards are now complete for this layer. Many vendors have also implemented proprietary solutions. One reason for these proprietary solutions is that the use of the presentation layer is predominantly equipment dependent. Some examples of presentation-layer protocols are video and text display formats, data code conversion between software programs, and peripheral management and control, using protocols such as ITU X.410 and ITU X.226 OSI connection-oriented protocol.

4.3.7 Application Layer

The seventh layer (L7) encountered is the application layer. This layer manages the program or device generating the data to the network. The application layer is an "equipment-dependent" protocol, and lends itself to proprietary vendor interpretation. Examples of standardized application-layer protocols include ITU X.400, X.420 X.500 – X.520 directory management, ISO 8613/ITU T.411-419 Office Document Architecture (ODA), and the ISO 10026 distributed Transaction Processing (TP).

4.4 STANDARD COMPUTER ARCHITECTURES

Seven major computer architectures have shaped and standardized the computer networking industry in the late 20th century. These include the OSIRM; the IEEE LAN, MAN, and WAN 802.X standards; the ISDN; IBM's SNA; DEC's DNA; General Motors' Manufacturing Automation Protocol (MAP); and the Boeing Computer Services' Technical and Office Products Systems (TOP). This section explains each of these seven leading architectures. The OSIRM was covered earlier in this chapter. We will also explore the non-Internet protocol architectures – Novell's Internet Packet Exchange (IPX), DECnet's Phase V, Xerox's XNS, and Apple's AppleTalk.

4.4.1 IEEE 802.X Series (LAN/MAN/WAN)

Local, metropolitan, and wide area networks (LANs, MANs, and WANs) were defined in Chapter 2. The standards body that has played the greatest role in the development of LAN standards has been the Institute of Electrical and Electronics Engineers (IEEE).

The IEEE 802.X reference model defines three layers and two sub-layers of operation. Figure 4.6 shows these three layers of the IEEE 802 model. Layer 1 is the physical layer, layer 2 is composed of the medium access control (MAC) sublayer and the logical link control (LLC) sublayer, and layer 3 is the network layer. The standards for the network layer are still under development.

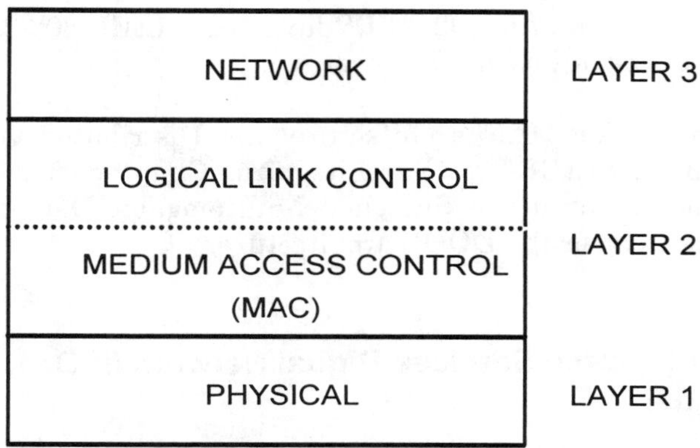

Figure 4.6 IEEE 802.X Architecture

The logical link layer 2 operates the same way for all LAN architectures, but not for the MAN architecture (a completely different beast!). The logical link control layer and physical layer operate differently for each of the local and metropolitan area network architectures. The LLC layer manages call establishment, data transfer, and call termination through three types of services: connection-oriented, unacknowledged connectionless, and acknowledged connection-oriented. All three will be covered in the next chapter.

There are three major LAN architectures defined in the 802.X standards. Ethernet and Token Ring are by far the most common, with Ethernet now the predominant protocol.

Ethernet. IEEE 802.3 and Ethernet common specifications form what is called the Ethernet standard. The first Ethernet products appeared in 1981, and now sales for Ethernet outpace the other 802 architectures. There are four Ethernet frame formats, each mutually incompatible. Ethernet works primarily in the link layer, where users contend for bus resources and send data through CMSA/CD and Token Passing. The interface is 10 Mbps. Fast Ethernet speeds are available in 100 Mbps.

Token Bus. IEEE 802.4 forms what is called the Token Bus standard. The Token Bus has never been very popular as a standard, probably because its standard specified an operating range designed to operate at what later turned out to be the peak performance that could be achieved. Token Bus defines both physical and data-rate options that use analog signaling.

Token Ring. IEEE 802.5 Token Ring architecture was developed by IBM development labs in Zurich, Switzerland. The first Token Ring products appeared in 1986. Token Ring initially gained on Ethernet as the popular LAN standard, but in the past five years has given ground to Ethernet.

Token Ring operates on the 802.2 LLC layer with IEEE 802.2 Type 1 protocol and 802.5 MAC Token Passing Protocol.

There is one major MAN architecture: the Distributed Queue Dual Bus (DQDB) (defined by IEEE 802.6) architecture. Chapter 12 is devoted entirely to this architecture and the Switched Multimegabit Data Service (SMDS) which can operate over the DQDB architecture.

4.4.2 The Integrated Services Digital Network (ISDN) Protocol Model

Integrated Services Digital Network (ISDN) standards were first developed by the ITU in 1972, with the first standards documents published in 1984. The original intent of ISDN was to provide a conversion of telecommunications transmission and switching techniques to a digital architecture, providing end-user-to-end-user digital service for voice, data, and video. But ISDN standards have been used for much more. ISDN standards are also at the root of ATM (previously B-ISDN) standards.

The primary ISDN architecture concept consists of multiple devices connecting through an ISDN network termination device (called a TE) into the central office environment where information services are provided, as shown in Figure 4.7. ISDN introduced the notion of multiple planes: the bearer service (or user plane), the control plane, and the management plane. A different OSI layer-structured protocol suite for each plane was defined in ISDN as described below.

The ISDN architectural structure is composed similar to the OSIRM, as shown in Figure 4.8. While all seven protocol layers are the same as the OSIRM, the physical, data link, and network layers define the lower-layer functions, which include the bearer services. These layers define physical connectivity and transmission as defined in ITU-T Recommendations I.430, I.431, and I.432; data link management, flow, error, and synchronization control as defined in ITU-T Q.921(LAP-D); and network addressing, congestion control, end-to-end call establishment, routing or relaying, and switching as defined in Recommendations Q.931/I.451, Q.932/I.452, and Q.933/I.453. The transport, session, presentation, and application layers define the higher-layer functions, including the teleservices which define services such as messaging, telephone, and telex. Standards for these layers are host-to-host and application specific.

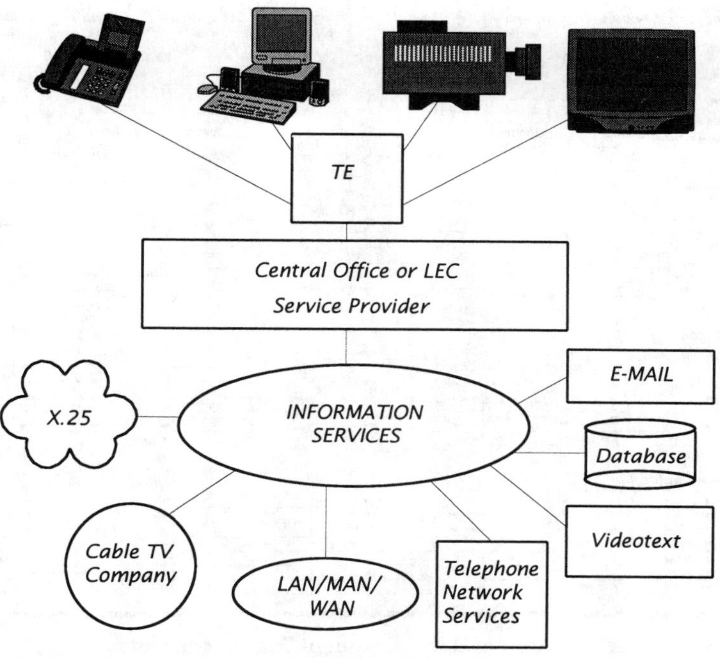

Figure 4.7 ISDN Information Services Concepts

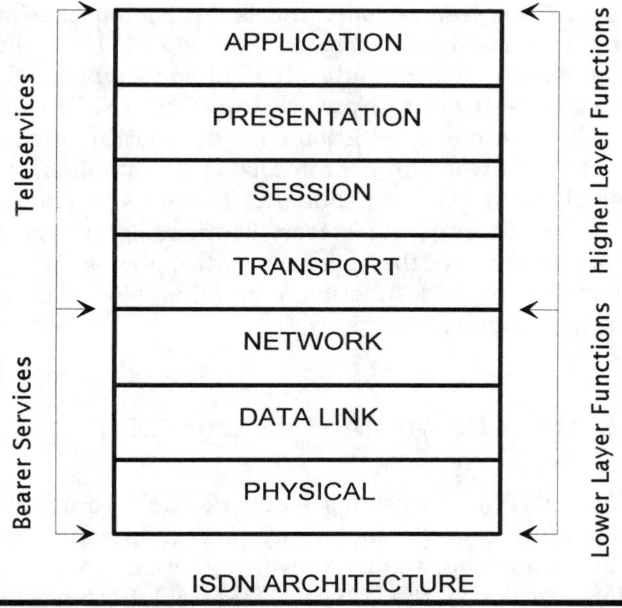

Figure 4.8 ISDN Architecture

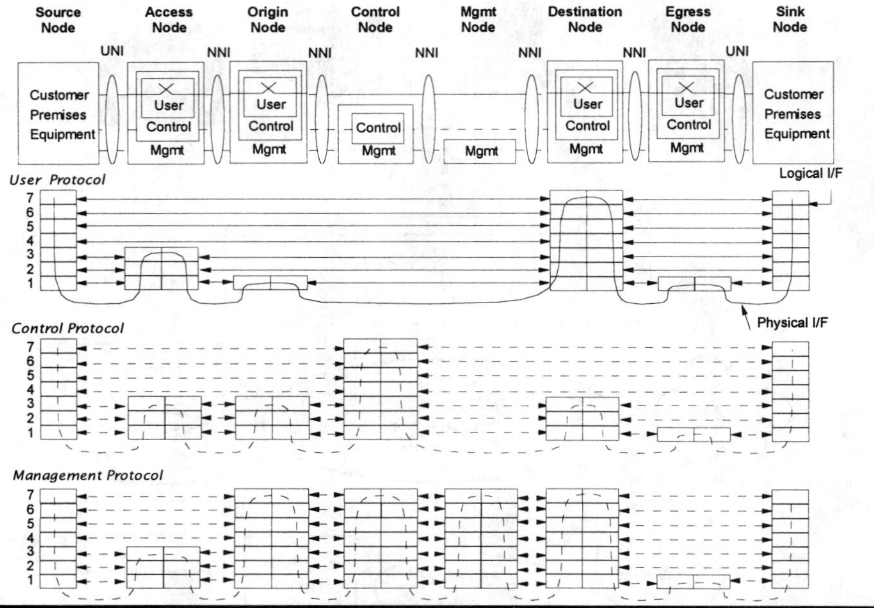

Figure 4.9 ISDN User, Control, and Management Plane Protocols

The ISDN architecture of the user, control, and management planes is shown in Figure 4.9. The user protocol (or bearer service) is layer 1 for circuit-mode, layer 2 for frame-mode, and layer 3 for packet-mode services. Teleservices and value-added services are modeled as higher layers. Intermediate nodes may provide only physical connectivity. User Network Interfaces (UNI) and Network-to-Network Interfaces (NNI) will be explained later. Conceptually, another application runs the control, or signaling, plane. The purpose of the control plane protocols is to establish, configure, and release the user plane (bearer) capabilities. Finally, the management plane is responsible for monitoring the status, configuring the parameters, and measuring the performance of the user and control planes.

The protocol structure and functional building blocks of ISDN will be covered later in this chapter.

4.4.3 IBM's Systems Network Architecture (SNA)

The introduction by IBM of Systems Network Architecture (SNA) in 1974 signaled the beginning of a vendor proprietary architecture which remains prominent in the computing industry even today. SNA has remained the dominant architecture into the 1990s. OSI and SNA architectures and protocols are still competing today, so that many users of multiprotocol environments either retain separate networks for their IP/IPX traffic and

SNA traffic, or encapsulate or translate their SNA traffic into a protocol that is more "routable". SNA was IBM's method of creating a computing empire through standardization, and revolved around the mainframe and (distributed) front-end processors. The point of IBM attempting to standardize among its own products, and not other vendors' equipment and protocols, is sometimes forgotten. By providing a hierarchy of network-access methods, IBM created a network that could accommodate a wide variety of users, protocols, and applications, while retaining ultimate control in the mainframe host and front-end processors. The move from centralized to distributed processing has had pronounced effects on SNA, and Advanced Peer-to-Peer Networking (APPN) using Advanced Peer-to-Peer Communications (APPC), otherwise labeled LU6.2, from IBM has emerged to attempt to save the homogeneous SNA networks from open standards. But most users have decided to shun APPN for less elegant (and less expensive) solutions we will discuss later in this text.

The SNA architecture layers are similar to the OSI Reference Model. Figure 4.10 shows the SNA architecture model. The network control functions reside in the physical, data link, path, transmission, and data flow control layers. The physical and data link layers define functions similar to the OSIRM, with serial data links employing the SDLC protocol and channel attachments employing the S/370 protocol. The path control layer provides the flow control and routing between point-to-point logical channels on virtual circuits through the network, establishing the logical connection between both the source and the destination nodes. The path layer provides paths without addressing, which forces OSI protocols to *bridge* SNA traffic rather than to *route* or *switch*. The transmission layer provides session management and flow control over SNA sessions which it establishes, maintains, and terminates. The transmission layer also contains some routing functions. The data flow layer provides services related to the actual user sessions, with both layers operating at times in parallel. The network services functions reside in the presentation and transaction layers. These two layers combined are also called the function management layer. The presentation layer formats and presents the data to the users, as well as performing data translation, compression and encryption. The transaction services layer provides network management and configuration services, as well as a fully functional user interface to the network operations. SNA protocol and inter-networking over IP networks will be detailed in later chapters.

IBM has recently opened up its SNA standard with APPN using APPC protocols. More will be said on these protocols in later chapters.

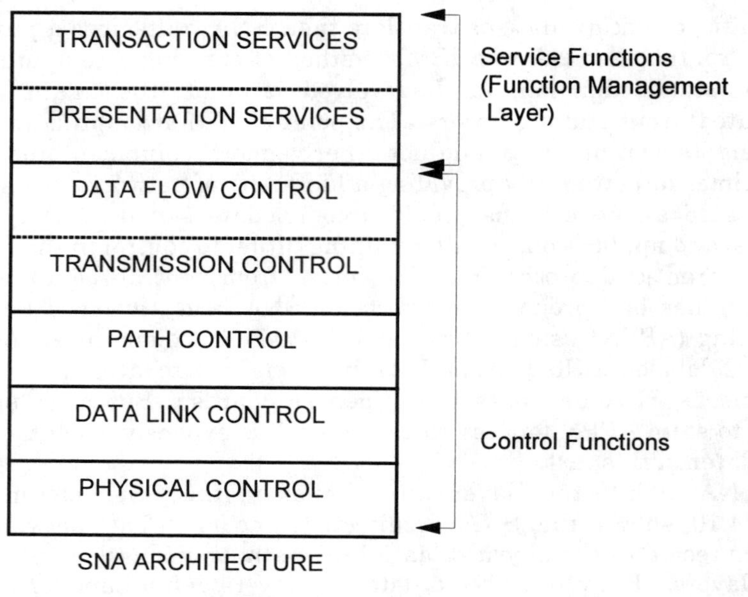

Figure 4.10 SNA Architecture

4.4.4 Digital Equipment Corporation's Digital Network Architecture (DNA) and DECnet Phases IV and V

The Digital Network Architecture (DNA), was created in 1975 by Digital Equipment Corporation (DEC). DEC's standards architecture is Digital Network Architecture (DNA), of which DECnet comprises the networking protocols. DECnet Phase IV, introduced in 1982, is by far the most popular, with support for Ethernet and large networks, and DECnet Phase V is the most recent publication of the architecture. DECnet Phase V provides a true open systems architecture. The architecture is again similar to the OSIRM, but with the addition of a network management layer.

Figure 4.11 shows the traditional DNA architecture model. The physical layer is similar to the OSIRM and uses protocols such as X.21, EIA-232-D, ISO 8802, V.24, and V.28. The data link layer is also similar to the OSIRM and uses X.25, Ethernet, ISO 8802, HDLC, and DDCMP protocols. The routing layer provides a sort of network-wide datagram service through the use of X.25, CLNP, and CLNS. The end communications layer provides the end-to-end communications service to the higher functional layers, as well as performing logical channel multiplexing. The session control layer provides the higher layers' processes with system-dependent communications functions through sessions. The network application layer provides user services to the network management and user layers. The user layer contains user-defined application programs. The network management layer provides management for all six other layers and distributed network management throughout nodes in the network.

With DECnet routing, multiple areas are established across the WAN, with each area supporting up to 1023 attached end nodes or hosts. The maximum number of areas is 63. There are two levels of routing within DECnet. Level 1 defines intra-area routing, and level 2 defines inter-area routing. DECnet assigns its own MAC address to each station on the LAN.

DECnet has announced DECnet Phase V, also called Advantage Networks. The relation of DECnet Phase V to the OSIRM can be found in Figure 4.16. Phase V contains enhancements to older versions and now uses the bottom four layers of the OSIRM, as well as being backward compatible to Phase IV. It also bundles TCP/IP functionality with the OSI protocol stack. DECnet V also supports File Transfer and Access Management (FTAM) and provides a gateway function to the TCP/IP File Transfer Protocol (FTP). It can be seen that DECnet V supports all of the older protocols (in parentheses) as well as their newer protocol stack which resembles the OSI reference model.

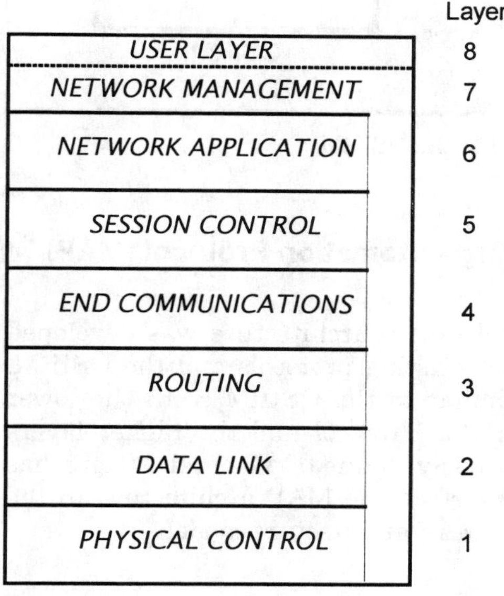

Figure 4.11 DNA Architecture

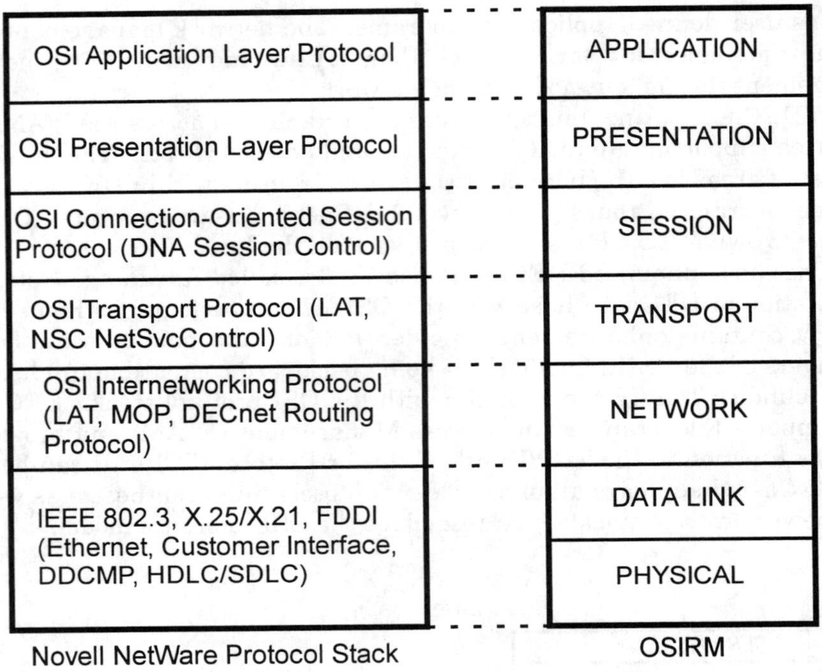

Novell NetWare Protocol Stack	OSIRM
OSI Application Layer Protocol	APPLICATION
OSI Presentation Layer Protocol	PRESENTATION
OSI Connection-Oriented Session Protocol (DNA Session Control)	SESSION
OSI Transport Protocol (LAT, NSC NetSvcControl)	TRANSPORT
OSI Internetworking Protocol (LAT, MOP, DECnet Routing Protocol)	NETWORK
IEEE 802.3, X.25/X.21, FDDI (Ethernet, Customer Interface, DDCMP, HDLC/SDLC)	DATA LINK
	PHYSICAL

Figure 4.12 DECnet Protocol Stack Compared to the OSIRM

4.4.5 General Motors' Manufacturing Automation Protocol (MAP)

The Manufacturing Automation Protocol (MAP) architecture was developed by General Motors as a conglomerate of existing protocols and the OSIRM. MAP uses an architecture structure similar to the OSIRM, with the lower layers utilizing the IEEE 802.4 Token Bus Protocol and the higher layers using the standard OSI protocols previously defined. General Motors has also built implementation profiles to interface the MAP architecture to the OSI architecture. Figure 4.12 shows the MAP architecture model.

4.4.6 Boeing Computer Services' Technical and Office Protocol (TOP)

The Technical and Office Protocol (TOP) was developed by Boeing Computer Services through a user group that needed computer communications standards for vendors serving Boeing to meet stringent architectural guidelines. The architecture structure is again similar to the OSIRM, with the lower layers using IEEE 802.3 Ethernet or 802.5 Token Ring protocols. Boeing has also built implementation profiles to interface the TOP architecture to the OSI architecture. The TOP architecture is shown in Figure 4.13.

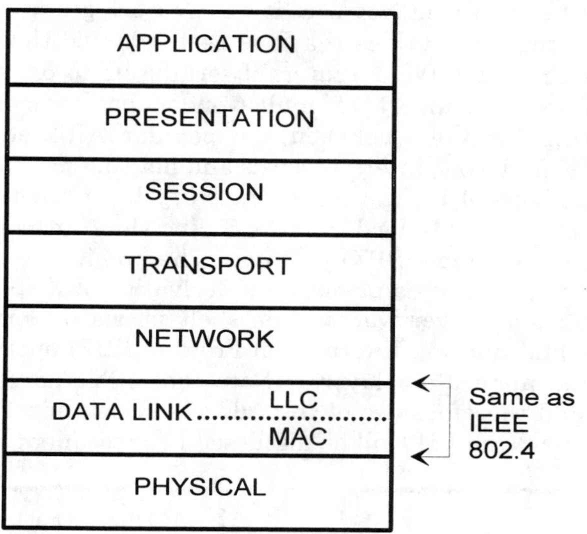

Figure 4.13 MAP Architecture

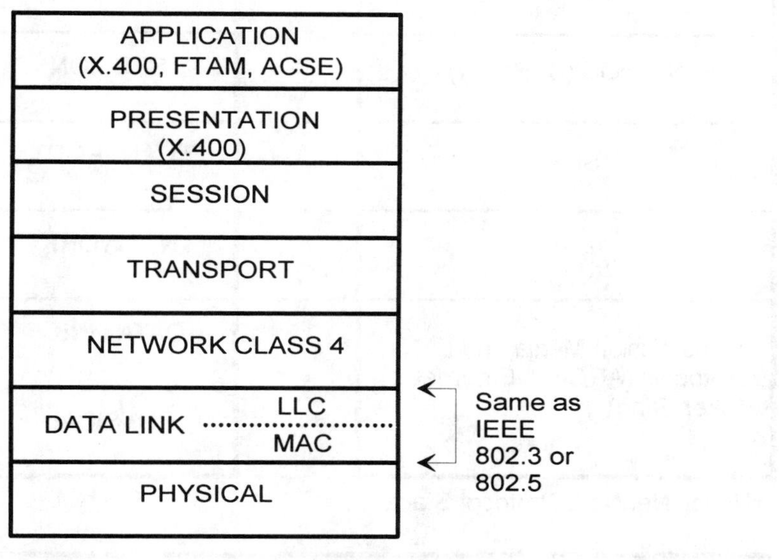

Figure 4.14 TOP Architecture

4.4.7 Novell's Internet Packet Exchange (IPX)

Novell NetWare was the most popular operating system with the leading market share in client-server implementations as of printing, with Windows NT fast approaching. Novell NetWare is a LAN work-group operating system for client-server communications that has been adapted through Novell IPX into a wide area network (WAN) internetworking protocol. Its popularity is primarily due to its support of multi-vendor environments, specifically providing routing functions between the popular ARCnet, Ethernet, and Token Ring LAN protocols, interface cards and networks.

As shown in Figure 4.14, the Novell network layer uses Internet Packet eXchange (IPX) protocol (derived from XNS) and the transport layer uses the Sequence Packet Exchange (SPX) protocol. The architecture used by Novell is very similar to XNS and is primarily a derivative of XNS. NetWare Core Protocol (NCP) client-server workstation shell software, Service Advertising Protocol (SAP), and Routing Information Protocol (RIP) operate above at the presentation and application layers. Note that IPX addresses include the MAC address and therefore use of the Address Resolution Protocol (ARP) is not necessary. SAP and RIP will be discussed in subsequent chapters.

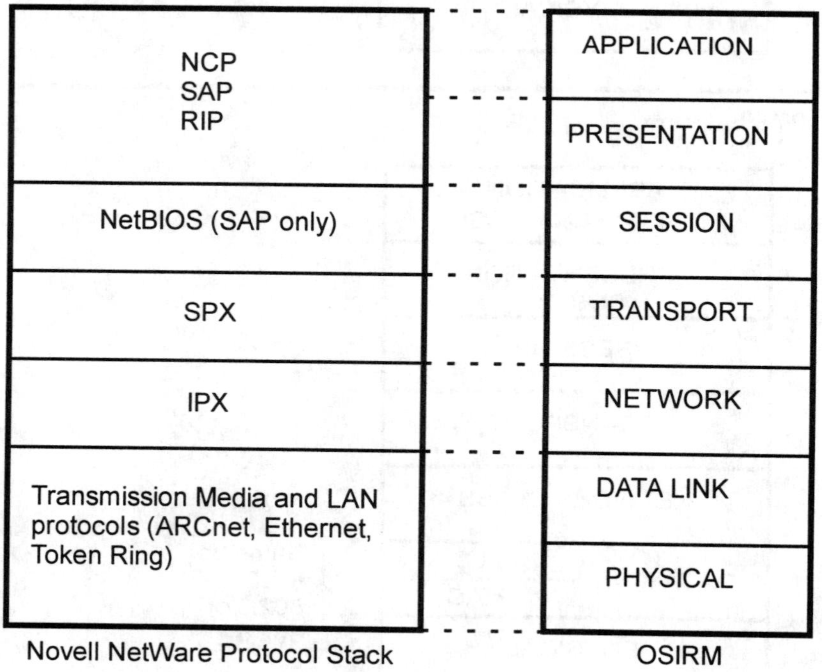

Figure 4.15 Novell NetWare Protocol Stack

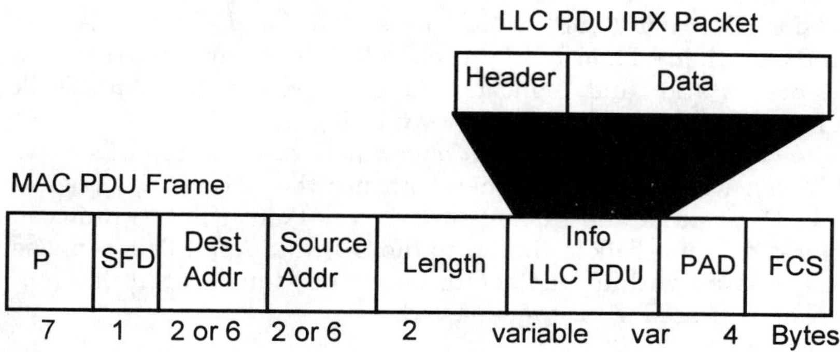

Figure 4.16 IPX and MAC Frame

The Internet Packet Exchange (IPX) protocol is a standard defined within the Novell NetWare architecture. IPX formats the NCP data for transmission over the physical media and LAN access protocols (ARCnet, Ethernet, and Token Ring). The IPX packet is then inserted into the information (data) field on the 802.3 MAC frame, as shown in Figure 4.15. Novell IPX supports encapsulation into ARCnet, Ethernet (including 802.3 with SNAP and 802.2), Token Ring, and Novell's proprietary data link protocol. IPX addressing and routing is similar to IP, and the SPX protocol performs packet sequencing similar to TCP.

4.4.8 AppleTalk

AppleTalk Phase II is another routed protocol defined by Apple Computer, Inc., supporting both data link access methods discussed. AppleTalk runs over the 802.2 LLC portion of the LAN data link control layer. The physical layer supports Ethernet, Token Ring, and LocalTalk hardware. The data link layer supports Ethertalk Link Access Protocol (ELAP), Token Talk Link Access Protocol (TLAP), or LocalTalk Link Access Protocol (LLAP). The network layer is strictly the Datagram Delivery Protocol (DDP), similar to IP. Routing Table Maintenance Protocol (RTMP), AppleTalk Echo Protocol (AEP), AppleTalk Transaction Protocol (ATP) and Name Binding Protocol (NBP) make up the transport layer end-to-end protocols. Zone Information Protocol (ZIP) and AppleTalk Data Stream Protocol (ADSP) session layer protocols can directly interface to DDP. Other session layer protocols include

AppleTalk Session Protocol (ASP) which uses ATP, and Printer Access Protocol which uses either ATP or NBP. AppleTalk Filing Protocol (AFP) and Postscript offer presentation and application layer interfaces. The AppleTalk protocol stack is similar to the OSIRM as shown in Figure 4.17.

EtherTalk and TokenTalk are applications which run on AppleTalk for Ethernet and Token Ring networks. They both use the IEEE 802.2 Logical Link Control (LLC) protocol and Subnetwork Access Point (SNAP) protocol. The protocol stack for AppleTalk is similar to the OSIRM. AppleTalk can also be carried encapsulated within DECnet through the "tunneling technique" through the use of dedicated point-to-point VAXs.

4.4.9 Xerox Network Systems (XNS)

XNS, or Xerox Network Systems architecture, was originally conceived for integrating Xerox office applications in the early 1980s. XNS standards are defined in the Xerox Gray Book of standards at two levels and its implementations are primarily vendor specific. The layer 0 transmission media manages the interaction of data between the device and the network. The XNS synchronous point-to-point protocol could be used at this layer. The layer 1 Internet datagram protocol layer defines the data flow across the network via packet addressing via the Internetwork Datagram Protocol (IDP). The layer 2 transport layer defines end-to-end connectivity through echo protocol, error protocol, and Routing Information Protocol (RIP) and is designed to primarily operate over Ethernet. The layer 3 control layer manages device resources, data structures, and data formatting for display devices. The layer 4 application layer manages the application data manipulation. Figure 4.18 shows the five layers of XNS in correspondence to the OSIRM. In normal XNS operation, each packet is routed like a datagram over the best link available.

4.4.10 Architecture Joint Ventures

Some major architectures have blended to produce cross-architecture models. One example is the Office Document Architecture (ODA), developed as a joint effort between ISO, ITU, and ECMA. This architecture provides a common format for document interchange that can be used for all word processors. Many of the major vendors mentioned previously with proprietary architectures now support the ODA architecture. Similar efforts took place in the blending of ISDN standards into the 802.X LAN standards.

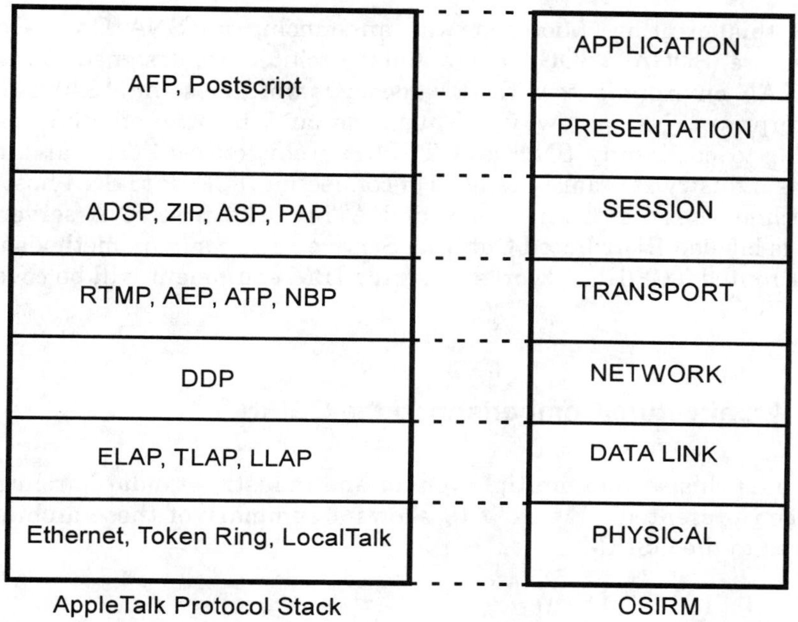

AppleTalk Protocol Stack	OSIRM
AFP, Postscript	APPLICATION
	PRESENTATION
ADSP, ZIP, ASP, PAP	SESSION
RTMP, AEP, ATP, NBP	TRANSPORT
DDP	NETWORK
ELAP, TLAP, LLAP	DATA LINK
Ethernet, Token Ring, LocalTalk	PHYSICAL

Figure 4.17 AppleTalk Protocol Stack Compared to the OSIRM

LAYER	XNS Protocol Stack	OSIRM
4	APPLICATION	APPLICATION
3	CONTROL	PRESENTATION
		SESSION
2	TRANSPORT	TRANSPORT
1	INTERNET	NETWORK
0	TRANSMISSION MEDIA	DATA LINK
		PHYSICAL

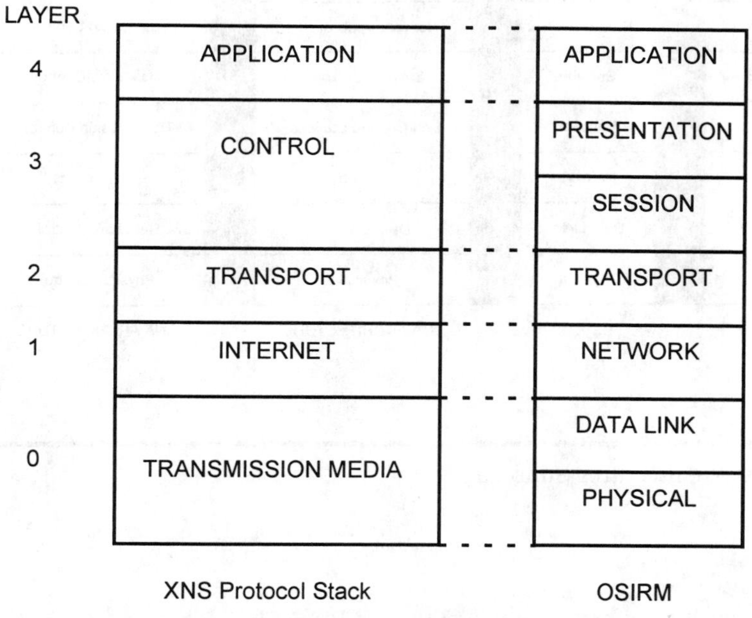

Figure 4.18 XNS Protocol Stack Compared to the OSIRM

As of this printing, Microsoft was announcing an SNA Open Gateway Architecture (SOGA). SOGA is a scalable architecture designed to integrate routed LAN environments with IBM legacy mainframes and AS400s through an enterprise SNA gateway. Thus, the architecture offers a gateway approach to combining SNA and TCP/IP architectures. The architecture supports industry standard methods of connecting TCP/IP to SNA host access over technologies like frame relay and ATM. The first SNA server-based service is labeled Distributed Gateway Service. The common methods used to connect routed TCP/IP networks to legacy IBM equipment will be covered in Chapter 8.

4.4.11 Architecture Comparison to the OSIRM

Throughout this section multiple vendor and industry standard architectures have been presented. Figure 4.19 shows a summary of these architectures compared to the OSIRM.

IEEE 802.X / TOP / MAP	OSIRM / ISDN	DNA ARCHITECTURE	SNA ARCHITECTURE
Application			
Presentation	Application	User Layer Network Management	Transaction Services
Session	Presentation	Network Application	Presentation Services
Transport	Session	Session Control	Data Flow Control
Network	Transport	End Communications	Transmission Control
Logical Link Control	Network	Routing	Path Control
Medium Access Control	Data Link	Data Link	Data Link Control
Physical	Physical	Physical	Physical Control

Figure 4.19 Architectures Summary

4.5 DIGITAL TIME DIVISION MULTIPLEXING (TDM) AND THE DIGITAL HIERARCHY

Public networks developed plesiochronous digital transmission for economic transmission of voice which was then used for data. Recently the Synchronous Optical NETwork (SONET) in North America and the Synchronous Digital Hierarchy (SDH) have been developed internationally in support of higher speed and better quality digital transmission. This section reviews some basics of these technologies.

4.5.1 Plesiochronous Digital Hierarchy

The so-called plesiochronous (which means nearly synchronous) digital hierarchy was developed nearly 40 years ago by Bell Labs to carry digitized voice over twisted wire more efficiently in major urban areas. This evolved first as the North American Digital Hierarchy, depicted in Table 4.1. Each format is called a digital stream (DS) and is assigned a level in the hierarchy. The lower-numbered digital streams are multiplexed into the higher-numbered digital streams within a certain frequency tolerance. There is no fixed relationship in the data between levels of the hierarchy, except at the lowest level called DS0 at a rate of 64k bps.

Table 4.1 North American Digital Hierarchy

Signal Name	Rate	Structure	Number of DS0s
DS0	64 kbps	Time Slot	1
DS1	1.544 Mbps	24xDS0	24
DS1c	-	2xDS1	48
DS2	-	2xDS1c	96
DS3	44.736 Mbps	7xDS2	672

A transmission repeater system over a four-wire twisted pair was defined and called T1. The term “T1” is often used colloquially to refer to a DS1 signal. There is actually no such thing as a “T3” signal, even though it is often used to colloquially refer to a DS3 signal. The actual interfaces for DS1 and DS3 are called the DSX1 and DSX3 interfaces, respectively, in ANSI standards. The DSX1 is a four-wire interface, while the DSX3 interface is a dual coaxial cable interface.

Closely related hierarchies were also developed in Europe and Japan. These hierarchies are summarized in Table 4.2. All of these hierarchies have the property that multiplexing is done in successive levels to move between successive speeds, and that the speed of each of these levels is asynchronous with respect to the others within a certain tolerance.

Table 4.2 Summary of International Plesiochronous Digital Hierarchies

Digital Multiplexing Levels	Number of Voice Channels	Bit Rate (Mbps)		
		North America	Europe	Japan
0	1	0.064	0.064	0.064
1	24	1.544		1.544
	30		2.048	
	48	3.152		3.152
2	96	6.312		6.312
	120		8.448	
3	480		34.368	32.064
	672	44.376		
	1344	91.053		
	1440			97.728
4	1920		139.264	
	4032	274.176		
	5760			397.200
5	7680		565.148	

An important consequence of these digital hierarchies on data communications is that only a discrete set of fixed rates is available, namely nxDS0 (where $1 \le n \le 24$ in North America and Japan and $1 \le n \le 30$ in Europe), and then the next levels in the respective multiplex hierarchies.

4.5.2 SONET and the Synchronous Digital Hierarchy (SDH)

The North American Synchronous Optical NETwork (SONET) and the closely related international Synchronous Digital Hierarchy (SDH) are the next step in the evolution of Time Division Multiplexing (TDM). SONET/SDH have two key benefits over Plesiochronous Digital Hierarchy (PDH): rates of higher speeds are defined, and direct multiplexing is possible without intermediate multiplexing stages. This is accomplished through the use of pointers in the multiplexing overhead that directly identify the position of the payload. Furthermore, the fiber-optic transmission signal transfers a very accurate clock rate along transmission paths all the way to end systems.

The North American SONET signal formats are designated by the term STS-N as Synchronous Transport Signals (STS) at *N* times the basic STS-1 (51.84 Mbps) building block rate. Signals at speeds less than the STS-1 rate are called Virtual Tributaries (VTs). The optical characteristics of the signal that carries SONET payloads is called the Optical Carrier (OC-N). An STS-*N* signal can be carried on any OC-*M*, as long as M ≥ N. SONET transmission rates and tributaries will be covered in Chapter 15.

The ITU has developed a similar synchronous multiplex hierarchy with the same advantages using a basic building block called the Synchronous Transfer Module (STM-1) with a rate of 155.52 Mbps that is exactly equal to the STS-3 rate. There is therefore a direct mapping between the SONET STS-3*N* rates and the ITU STM-N rates. An STM-1 frame is equivalent to an STS-3c frame in structure. However, there are still some incompatibilities between SONET and SDH in the definition and use of overhead information. A set of lower-speed signals, called Virtual Containers (VCs) is also defined in SDH.

Table 4.3 compares the mapping of the North American and ITU PDH rates to the corresponding SONET Virtual Tributary (VT) and SDH Virtual Container (VC) rates and terminology. Note that the common 1.5-, 2-, 6- and 44-Mbps rates are mapped consistently. The other common rates are at 155 and 622 Mbps.

Table 4.3 SONET/SDH Equivalent to Plesiochronous Digital Hierarchy

North American SONET VT	ITU SDH VC	SONET rate (Mbps)	SDH rate (Mbps)
VT1.5	VC-11	1.544	
VT2.0	VC-12		2.048
VT3.0		3.152	
VT6.0	VC-2	6.312	6.312
	VC-3	44.736	34.368
	VC-4		139.264
STS-1		51.84	
STS-3	STM-1	155.52	155.52
STS-12	STM-4	622.08	622.08

The framing format and details on SONET can be found in Chapter 15.

4.6 BASICS AND HISTORY OF ISDN

ISDN is the Phoenix of the late 1990s, rising out of the flames and ashes of the past 20 years to take its place as competition to the dedicated local loop, an alternate dial access protocol to services like the Internet, and a variety of other consumer and corporate uses. We now turn our attention to the original Integrated Services Digital Network (ISDN) standards, where most of the frame and cell-switched protocols discussed in this book have their roots. First, the ISDN Basic Rate Interface (BRI) and Primary Rate Interface (PRI) services are described. Next, the basic ISDN protocol and framing structure are covered. Subsequent to the definition of Broadband ISDN (B-ISDN), the ISDN standards are now referred to as the Narrowband ISDN (N-ISDN) standards. More detail on the data link layer aspects of ISDN will be covered in Chapter 7.

4.6.1 ISDN Basics

ISDN was built upon the Time Division Multiplexing (TDM) hierarchy developed for digital telephony as defined in previous sections. The CCITT/ITU-T has defined and is still defining many standards for the ISDN. Two standards are defined for the physical interface to ISDN: Basic Rate Interface (BRI), or basic access, as defined in ITU-T ISDN I.430, and the Primary Rate Interface (PRI), as defined in ITU-T ISDN I.431. Both standards define the electrical characteristics, signaling, coding, and frame formats of ISDN communications across the user access interface (S/T) reference point. The physical layer provides transmission capability, activation, and deactivation of Terminal Equipment (TE) and Network Termination (NT), Data (D)-channel access for TE, maintenance functions, and channel status indications. The basic infrastructure for these physical implementations and the definition for the S and T reference points, TE, and NT, are contained in ITU-T Recommendation I.412. ISDN functional groups and reference points (as defined in ITU-T Recommendation I.411) are shown in Figure 4.20.

The physical interface in ISDN is one part of the D-channel protocol, and defines a full-duplex, synchronous connection between the TE layer 1 terminal side of the basic access interface (TE1, TA, and NT2 functional group aspects) and the NT layer 1 terminal side of the basic access interface (NT1 and NT2 functional group aspects). Figure 4.21 shows both a point-to-point configuration with one transmitter and one receiver per interchange circuit, as well as a multipoint configuration with multiple TE, both for BRI. Note that only one TE can use the line at the same time. Both bus distances cannot exceed 1000 m, except when using a short passive bus, as opposed to an extended passive bus in multipoint mode, where the limitation is 180 m. The bit rate in both directions is 192 kbps.

4.6.2 BRI and PRI Service and Protocol Structures

BRI and PRI service configurations are defined as follows:

- **Basic Rate Interface (BRI):** provides two 64-kbps bearer (B) channels for the carriage of user data and one 16-kbps control, messaging, and network management data (D) channel. This interface is commonly referred to as 2B+D. BRI was intended for customer access devices requiring voice, data, and video communications.

- **Primary Rate Interface (PRI):** provides 23 64-kbps bearer (B) channels and one 64 kbps data (D) signaling channel referred to in North America as 23B+D. Internationally 30 B channels are provided in a 30B+D configuration. The PRI was intended for use by higher bandwidth or shared customer devices such as the Private Branch eXchange (PBX), personal computer, and LAN.

The ISDN PRI provides a single 1.544 Mbps DS1 or a 2.048 Mbps E-1 data rate channel over a full-duplex synchronous point-to-point channel using the standard Time Division Multiplexing (TDM) hierarchy introduced earlier in this chapter. ITU Recommendations G.703 and G.704 define the electrical and frame formats of the PRI interface, respectively. The 1.544 Mbps rate is accomplished by sending 8000 frames per second with each frame containing 193 bits. The DS1 stream comprises 24 DS0 channels of 64 kbps each, containing 23 B-channels at 64 kbps each and one D-channel at 64 kbps.

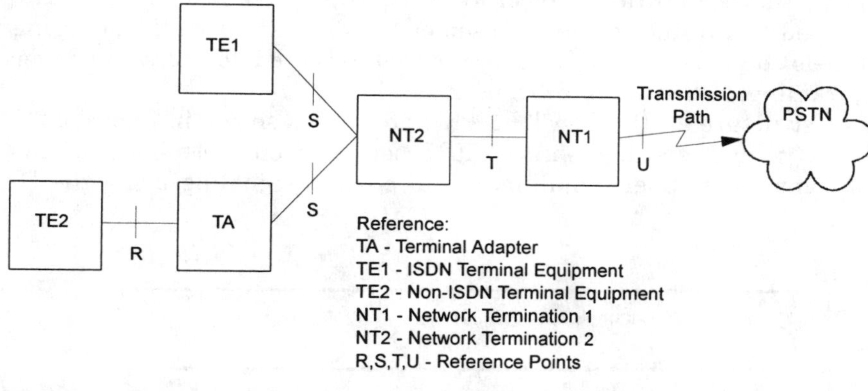

Figure 4.20 ISDN Functional Groups and Reference Points

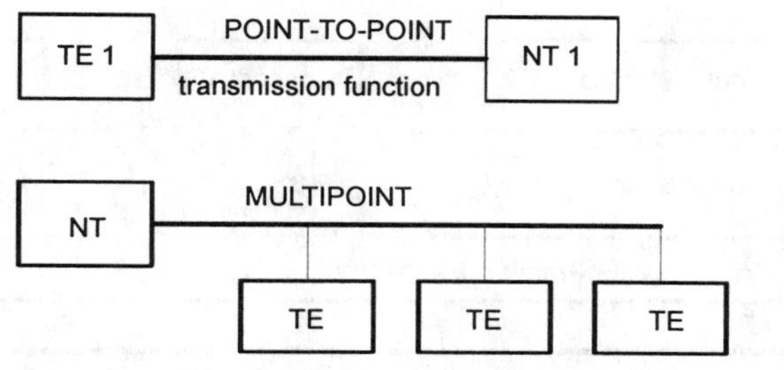

Figure 4.21 ISDN BRI Point-to-Point and Multipoint Configurations

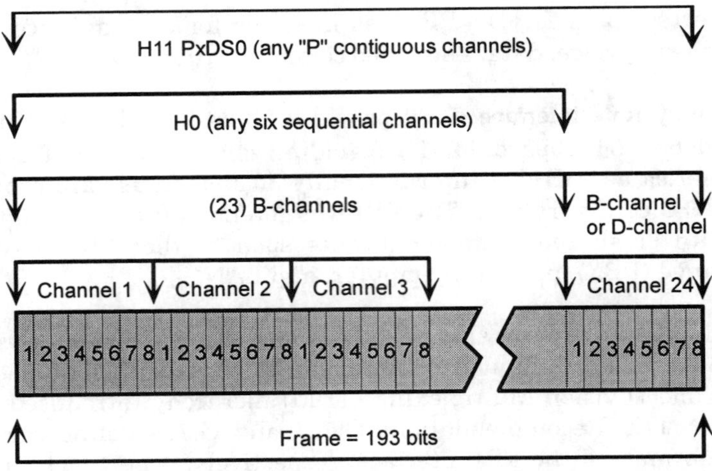

Figure 4.22 1.544 Mbps PRI Frame Structure

Figure 4.22 shows the frame structure of the DS1 1.544M bps PRI. The CEPT E1-based PRI frame structure is somewhat different from this, offering 30 B-channels, one D-channel, and a channel reserved for physical layer signaling, framing, and synchronization.

The frame structure for the CEPT E1 PRI interface is shown in Figure 4.23. A primary attribute distinguishing ISDN service from telephony is the concept of common channel signaling, or out-of-band signaling using the D-channel.

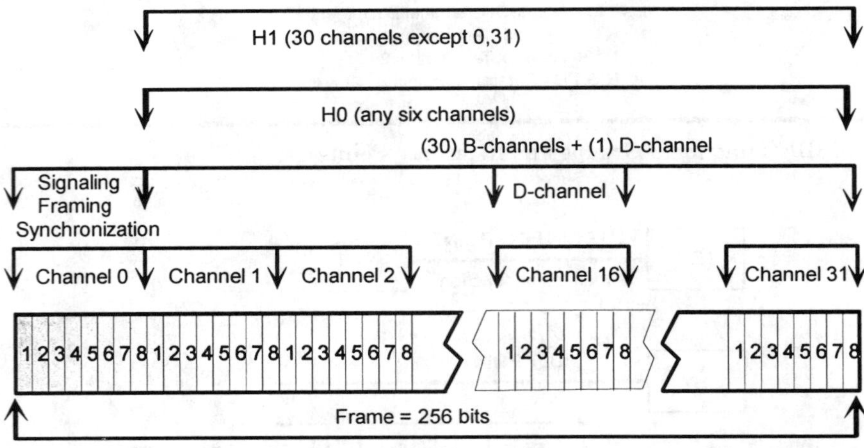

Figure 4.23 CEPT E1 PRI Frame Structure

H-channels are used in PRIs. Two types are defined: H_0-channel signals that have a bit rate of 384 kbps and H_1-channels that have a bit rate of 1536 kbps for H_{11}-channels in the U.S., and 1920 kbps for H_{12}-channels in Europe. These channels (except for the H_{12}-channel implementation) use B-channel slots on a PRI that is configured as either 24 × B or 30 × B. Note that this means that the D signaling channel is provided on a separate physical interface. The D-channel and B-channels may share the same physical interface, or the D-channel on one interface may control the B-channels on several physical interfaces.

There is also a capability to establish a *n*xDS0 bearer service, where *n* ranges from 1 to 24 (or 30 at the European channel rate) via ISDN signaling. The *n*xDS0 service uses *n* contiguous time slots or a bit-map-specified set of DS0 time slots in the DS1 or E1 frame. This is called the MultiRate Circuit Mode Bearer Service (MRCMBS). Also, ISDN signaling can establish a Frame Mode Bearer Service (FMBS) or a switched X.25 connection.

4.7 DEFINITION OF NETWORK SERVICES

Data network services are categorized in the OSIRM as being either connection oriented or connectionless. Connection oriented services involve establishing a connection between physical or logical end points prior to the transfer of data. Examples of Connection-Oriented Network Services (CONS) are frame relay and ATM.

Connectionless services, on the other hand, provide end-to-end logical connectivity and do not require the establishment of a connection prior to data transfer. Examples of Connectionless Network Services (CLNS) are IP and SMDS. Historically, connection-oriented services were generally used in WANs, while connectionless services were primarily used in LANs. ATM (and its associated adaptation layers) is one example of a protocol that provides the capability to support both connection-oriented and connectionless services.

4.7.1 Connection-Oriented Network Services (CONS)

Connection-oriented network services (CONS) require establishment of a connection between the origin and destination before transferring data. Usually the connection is established as a path of links through intermediate nodes in a network. Once established, all data travels over this same path in the network. The requirement that data must arrive at the destination in the same order as sent by the origin is fundamental to all connection-oriented services.

If the connection is established by network management or provisioning actions and is left up indefinitely, then it is called a Permanent Virtual Circuit (PVC). If control signaling of any type is used to establish and take down the connection dynamically, then it is called a Switched Virtual Circuit (SVC).

When a PVC is used, a permanent connection is made between two or more physical or logical interfaces. The connection may be established by physical wiring, equipment configuration commands, service provider provisioning procedures, or combinations of these actions. These actions may take several minutes to several weeks, depending upon exactly what is required. Once the PVC is established, data may be transferred over it. PVCs are usually established for long periods of time. Examples of physical PVCs are analog private lines, DTE-to-DCE connections, and digital (dedicated) private lines. Examples of logical PVCs are the X.25 PVC, frame relay PVC, and ATM PVC.

In the case of an SVC service, only the access line and address for the origin and each destination point need to be provisioned beforehand. The use of a control-signaling protocol plays a central role in SVC services. Via the signaling protocol, the origin requests that a connection be made by the network to one or more destinations. The network determines the physical (and logical) location of the destination(s) and attempts to establish the connection through intermediate node(s) to the destination(s). The success or failure of the attempt is indicated back to the originator. There may also be a progress indication to the originator, alerting for the destination, or other handshaking elements of the signaling protocol as well. Often the destination(s) also utilize signaling to allow them to either accept or reject the call. In the case of a failed attempt, the signaling protocol usually informs the originator of the reason the attempt failed. Once the connection is established, then data can be transferred over the connection. Usually SVCs are utilized so that resources can be shared by allowing users to dynamically connect and disconnect using the signaling protocol. The signaling protocol usually allows either the originator or destination(s) to initiate a disconnect action. Furthermore, a failure in the network or of the originator or destination(s) usually results in an automatic disconnect. Examples of SVCs are telephone calls, ISDN and X.25 calls, frame relay SVCs, and ATM SVCs.

The above description may sound complicated, but it isn't. There is a direct analogy to each of the above terms in the steps of establishing and taking down an SVC connection-oriented service and a normal telephone call, as illustrated in Table 4.4. In fact, much of the complexity of ISDN is introduced by having a more complicated signaling protocol with new names as summarized below. ISDN can support voice calls since the required signaling primitives are part of the signaling protocol.

Table 4.4 General Signaling Comparison to Voice Call

General Signaling Protocol Terminology	Voice Telephone Call Example
Provision access/address	Order service from phone company
Handshaking	Dial tone
Origin request	Dialing the number
Successful attempt indication	Ringing tone
Unsuccessful attempt indication	Busy tone
Destination acceptance	Answering the phone
Data transfer	Talking on the phone
Disconnect request	Hanging up the phone

In the case of a switched connection, data is transferred over a connection established through the network, and this same connection is then disconnected, or taken down, after it is no longer needed. The advantage of this additional complexity is that resources can be shared in time, and in some cases the charges for use of a public service can be significantly less for an SVC than they would be for a comparable set of PVCs. In the case of physical SVCs, the entire bandwidth of the connection is available to the end points. In the case of logical SVCs, the network may be doing some statistical sharing of bandwidth in the switches interior to the network. Connection-oriented services are therefore best used if the required data transfer is intermittent, but lasts quite a bit longer than the time required by the signaling protocol to establish it. Also, SVCs can be used to control bandwidth allocation or access to a shared resource, such as a dial-up database service.

Most of the OSI architecture introduced earlier in this chapter is based on connection-oriented services. Private lines and circuit switching are a few examples of connection-oriented services provided by the telephony-oriented carriers, whose primary service is based on connection-oriented services. X.25 PVC and frame relay PVC services are also offered by many carriers and service providers.

4.7.2 Connectionless Network Services (CLNS)

In connectionless network services (CLNS), no prior establishment of an end-to-end connection is required for data transmission. Thus, there is no predetermined path that data must take through the network. Therefore, in some connectionless services data may arrive at the destination in a different order than it was sent from the origin. In contrast to connection-oriented services, which may be physical and/or logical, connectionless services are always logical. Another key attribute of many connectionless services is that there is no need for provisioning; you simply plug in the end station equipment, and you are connected! This is often called "plug and play" in data communications.

In connectionless services, the originating node transmits packets to the destination via the best path from that node. As other nodes receive these packets, they interpret the address information in the packet and process it based on this node's position in the network and its selection of the best path to the destination as determined by a routing algorithm. The node then switches packets destined for other nodes onto a trunk, and delivers those packets destined for users connected to this node. In a connectionless service the delivery of the packet or cell is not guaranteed; therefore applications must rely on higher-level protocols to perform the end-to-end error detection/correction and data integrity checking. Flow control is usually minimal (if any), and the service often does not provide for error detection or correction. Bandwidth efficiency and message sequencing are sacrificed for high performance through fast switching of packets, avoiding the overhead incurred through call establishment and management. Connectionless service is sometimes referred to as datagram service.

The dynamic, automatic determination of which node to select when switching a packet in the above process is, in general, a complicated problem. The generic term for protocols that determine this next hop-selection mechanism is *routing protocols*. Chapter 8 reviews some aspects of routing protocols.

Connectionless service is the predominant mode of communications in LANs because it is well suited to the intermittent, bursty traffic found on applications that use LANs. LANs also take key advantage of the "plug-and-play" property. Low-level logical LAN connectivity is usually established automatically simply by plugging in the wiring to the LAN adapter interface on the end system. Besides the common LAN technologies such as Ethernet, Token Ring, and FDDI, there is the Internet Protocol (IP) designed for the WAN that has seen great acceptance. By virtue of the routing protocols, IP also has the plug-and-play property that simply attaching (a properly configured) computer to the Internet allows data communication to occur. This is done by the other nodes in the network discovering the added node through routing messages, and adding this to their next hop decision tables. Some connectionless data services technologies such as IP have seen widescale acceptance, whereas others, such as SMDS, have found much more limited acceptance. Both of these CLNS can operate over ATM through a specific adaptation layer.

4.8 REVIEW

This chapter introduced the seven major architectures used in the late 20th century. Also introduced was the concept of protocol layering and the notation that is used throughout the book. A brief description covered the OSIRM and its seven layers were described: physical, data link, network, transport, session, presentation, and application. The coverage then moved to digital Time Division Multiplexing (TDM), originally designed to provide more cost-effective telephone calls, and now representing the foundation for the beginnings of high-performance digital data communications. Upon this foundation, construction of the Narrowband Integrated Services Digital Network (N-ISDN) protocol model was built. The concepts of separate user, control, and management protocols from N-ISDN were then carried forward into the emerging Broadband ISDN (B-ISDN). Definitions were given of connection-oriented and connectionless services. Finally, private line and switched networks were compared.

4.9 REFERENCES

G. Kessler, *ISDN: Concepts, Facilities and Services,* McGraw-Hill, 2d ed., 1993.

G. Kessler, D. Train, *MANs*, McGraw-Hill, 1991.

J. Turner, "Design of an Integrated Services Packet Network," *IEEE Transactions on Communications*, November 1986.

R. Dayton, *Telecommunications*, McGraw-Hill, 1st ed., 1991.

Part

3

The Basics – Transmission, Networks, Hardware, and Switching

This section provides an introduction to transmission, network, hardware, multiplexing, and switching techniques and technologies. The section begins with an overview of network topologies and the circuit types that serve as the pipes between network nodal equipment. The equipment serving as the building blocks of data networks is covered in detail, including transmission equipment, bridges, routers, gateways, multiplexers, and switches. Circuit-switching and packet-switching concepts are introduced in preparation for later technology chapters. The key techniques of multiplexing and switching are given ample coverage.

Chapter

5

Transmission, Networks, and Hardware Types

This chapter provides an overview of common network topologies, circuits, connections, and transmission types, along with the fundamentals of bridging and routing. Five major network topologies are defined in this chapter and form the basis for most network designs. The presentation then covers the types of connections and circuits that interconnect these topologies. Each circuit type has characteristics, such as the direction of data flow, bit- or byte-oriented transmission, and physical characteristics. Finally, the major data communications hardware types that form the building blocks of today's data networks are discussed, including bridges, routers, hubs, switches, and gateways.

5.1 GENERAL NETWORK TOPOLOGIES

The five most commonly used network topologies for computer and data communications networks are: point-to-point, multipoint (or common bus), star, ring (or loop), and mesh. The term *node* will be used to designate a network data communications element such as a router, switch, or multiplexer. The term *link* will be used to designate a circuit connection between nodes. A link may be either logical such as with a Permanent Virtual Circuit (PVC), or physical as with a dedicated private line. Illustrated examples are provided for each network topology.

5.1.1 Point-to-Point

Point-to-point connectivity is the simplest topology, providing a single *link* between two *nodes*. This link can be composed of multiple physical and/or logical circuits. Figure 5.1 shows three examples of point-to-point links. The first example (a) shows a single link between node A and node B with a single physical and logical (or virtual) circuit. Notice that communications can flow in both directions simultaneously over the same physical and logical circuit. The second example (b) depicts a single link between node A and node B with multiple logical circuits riding over a single physical link. The third example (c) depicts a single path between node A and node B with multiple (four to be exact) physical circuits, each physical circuit carrying multiple logical circuits.

Point-to-point configurations are the most common method of connectivity. Many data communications networks and the applications that ride them use point-to-point topologies in metropolitan (MAN) and wide area network (WAN) configurations. For example, almost every user access to the many types of MAN or WAN network services (such as packet switching, frame relay, and ATM) use some form of point-to-point topology. An example of the point-to-point topology is the private line or dedicated circuit.

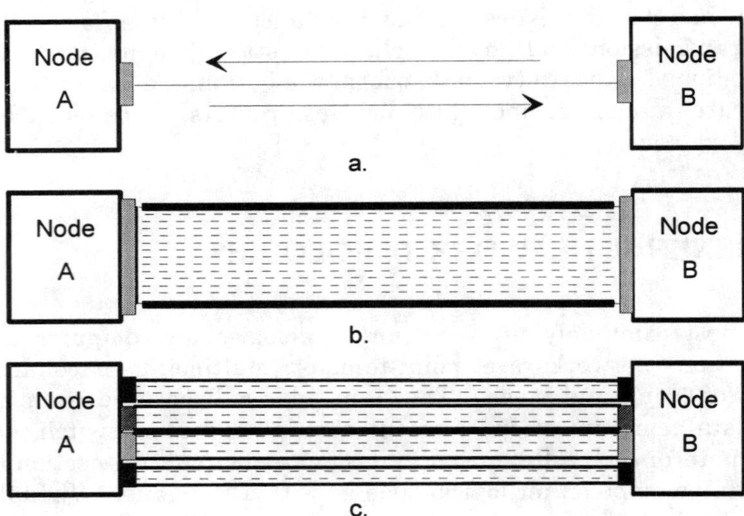

Figure 5.1 Point-to-Point Topology Examples

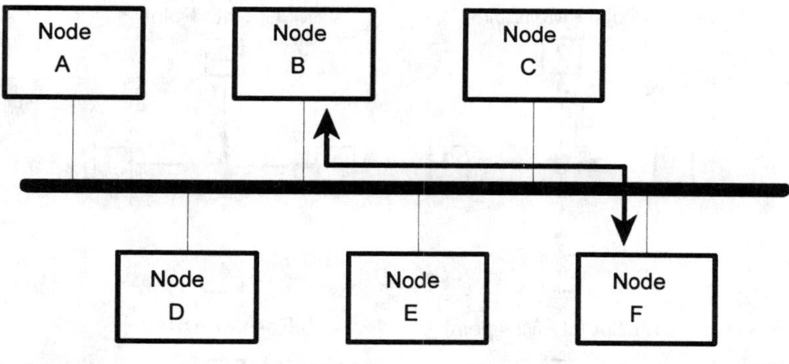

Figure 5.2 Common Bus Multipoint Topology

5.1.2 Common Bus (Multipoint)

A common realization of multipoint is the common bus topology, where all nodes are physically connected to a common bus structure. Figure 5.2 shows the multipoint common bus topology, where nodes A through F communicate via a common physical and logical bus. The IEEE 802.4 Token Bus, the IEEE 802.3 Ethernet, and the IEEE 802.6 Distributed Queue Dual Bus (DQDB) all use a common bus topology, as do many other proprietary vendor architectures. The common bus is also called a shared medium topology.

A multidrop analog line is commonly used for the SNA SDLC local loop access. In this example, an analog signal is broadcast from a master station to all slave stations. In the return direction all slave signals are added and returned to the master. The SNA SDLC protocol, which can use a multipoint circuit for access, will be defined in greater detail in Chapter 7.

Other conceptual examples of the multipoint topology are illustrated in Figure 5.3. Another commonly used multipoint topology is that of broadcast, or point-to-multipoint, which is defined in the B-ISDN standards as the case in which one sender's data is received by many other nodes. Yet another example is that of "incast," or multipoint-to-point, where multiple senders' signals are received at one destination, such as in the slave-to-master direction. In this conceptual illustration note that the multipoint-multipoint (i.e., shared medium, or multicast) topology is effectively the combination of a point-multipoint and multipoint-point topology, as the name implies. The point-to-point topology is also illustrated for comparison purposes.

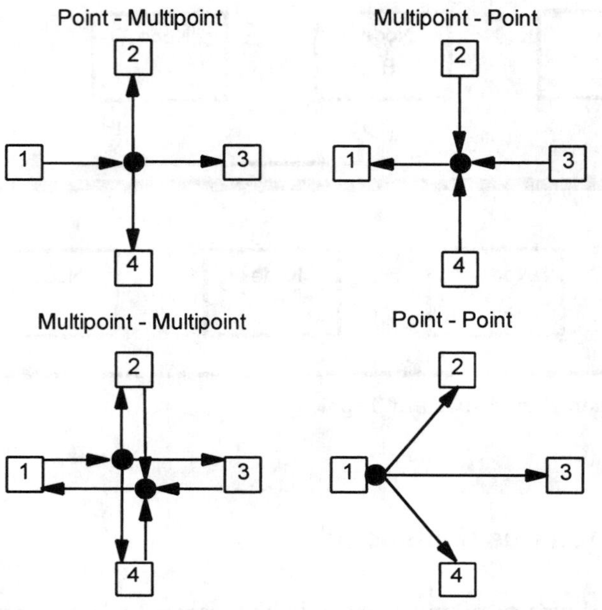

Figure 5.3 Conceptual Illustration of Multipoint Topologies

5.1.3 Star

The star topology developed during the era when most computer communications were centrally controlled by a mainframe. It also has its analogy in the voice world where one central switch is connected to multiple remote switching nodes, each serving hundreds to even thousands of telephones. This network radiates in a starlike fashion from the central switch through the remote switches to the telephones on people's desks. All devices in the network are connected to the central node, which usually performs the processing and switching. Nodes communicate with each other through point-to-point or multidrop links radiating from the central node. The difference between this topology and that of the multipoint topology is that the central node only provides point-to-point connections between any edge node on either a physical or logically switched basis.

Figure 5.4 shows a star topology, where node A serves as the center of the star and nodes B through E communicate with each other via connections switched through node A. Another example of a star topology is many remote terminal locations accessing a centralized host processor. These terminals are often called "dumb" terminals since the processing power and intelligence is resident in the host.

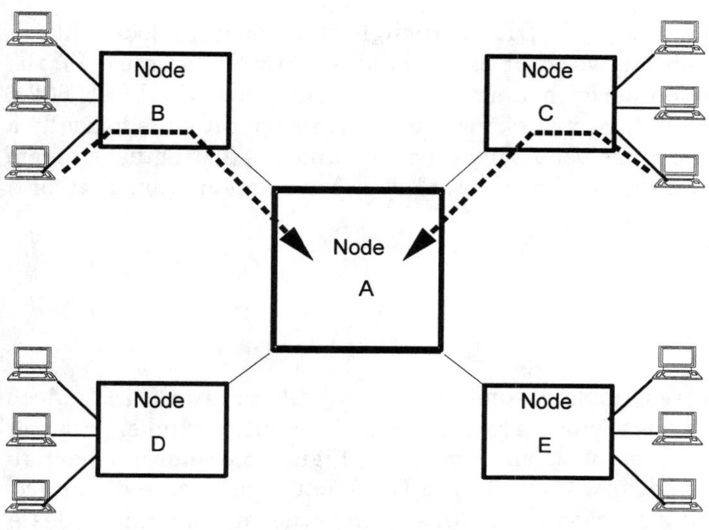

Figure 5.4 Star Topology

The physical star topology is widely used to connect devices to a central hub. The central hub may logically organize the physical star as a logical bus or ring as is commonly done in LAN wiring hubs.

In some WAN designs, the central hub site is typically a headquarters location where the main applications reside and to which all remote sites connect. Network designs based on the original SNA architecture resemble a star topology, where remote and local terminals directly communicate with communications controllers, who would then pass the information in star fashion to front-end processors, which pass the information to the host. Communications back to the remote users must follow the same hierarchy.

5.1.4 Ring

The loop, or ring, topology is used for networks in which communications data flow is unidirectional according to a particular protocol. A ring is established, and each device passes information in the direction of the ring's traffic flow, while the destination strips the information off the ring and the token, or bandwidth reservation scheme, is released to pass more data.

Figure 5.5 shows a ring network where node A passes information (frame 1) to node C via the ring and through node D (steps 1 and 2). Node C then returns a confirmation (frame 2) to node A via node B (step 3), at which point node A removes this data from the ring (step 4). There is reuse of capacity in this ring example because the destination removes the information from the ring to make better use of capacity. Examples of the ring topology are the

IEEE 802.5 Token Ring and FDDI. Although this topology looks like a special case of a mesh network, it is covered separately because of the different switching action performed at each node. Note that the IEEE 802.6 physical topology is often drawn as a ring; however, its operation is logically a bus. SONET protection rings use a ring topology, and are distinguished from a mesh topology by the difference in nodal switching action from that of a mesh of circuit switches.

5.1.5 Mesh

Many switched networks employ some form of mesh architecture. Mesh networks have many nodes which are connected by multiple links. Figures 5.6 and 5.7 show two types of mesh networks. Figure 5.6 shows a partial-mesh network where nodes A, C, F, E, and G have a high degree of connectivity by virtue of having at least three links to any other node, while nodes A and D have only two links to other nodes. Often the number of links connected to a node is called its degree (of connectivity).

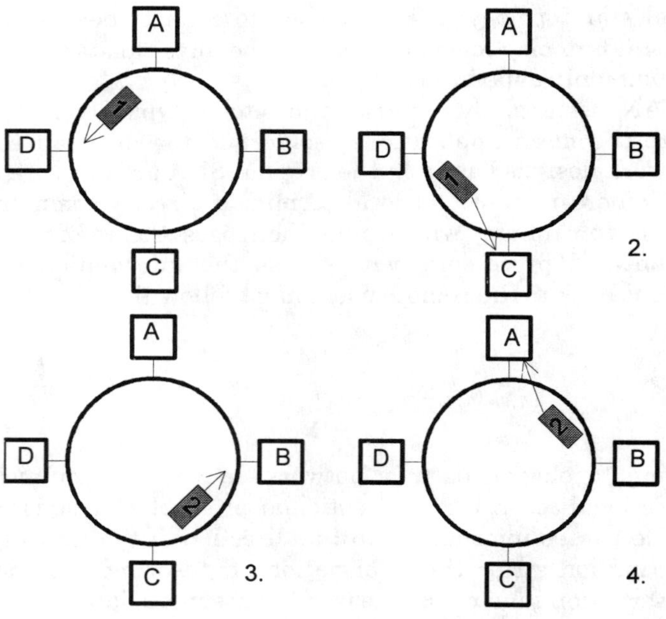

Figure 5.5 Ring or Loop Topology

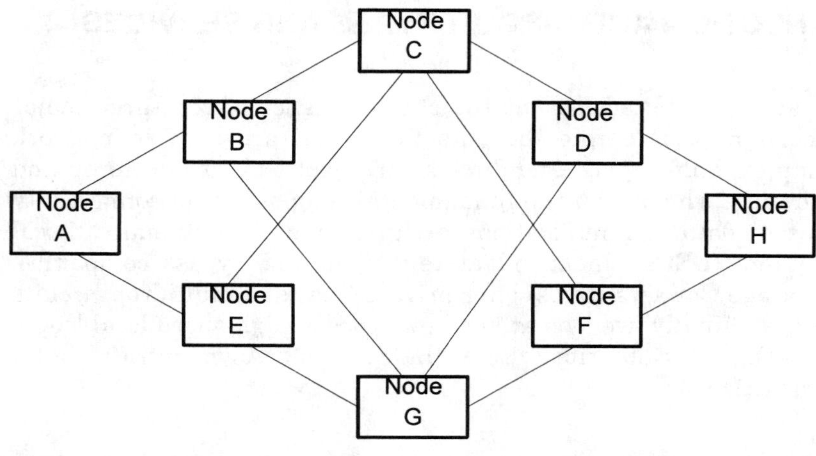

Figure 5.6 Partial-Mesh Network

Figure 5.7 shows a full-mesh network where each node has a link to every other node. Almost every major computer and data communications network uses a mesh topology to give alternate routes for backup and traffic loads, but few use a full-mesh topology primarily because of high cost factors associated with having a large number of links. This is because a full-mesh N-node network has $\frac{N(N-1)}{2}$ links, which is on the order of N^2. For networks with N greater than 4 to 8 nodes, partial-mesh networks are usually employed.

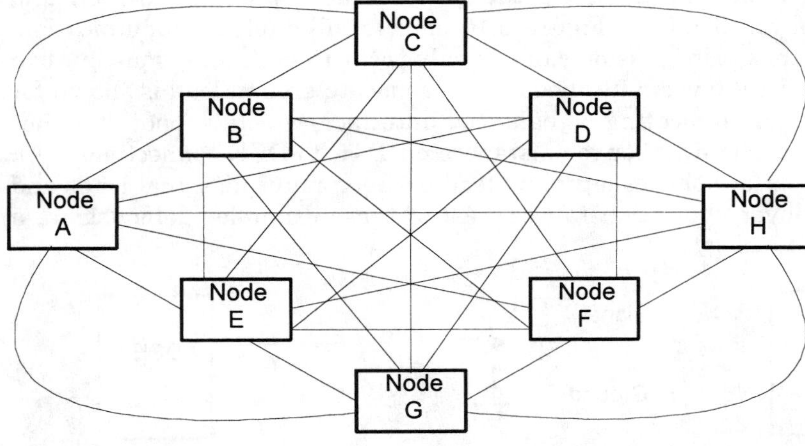

Figure 5.7 Full-Mesh Network

5.2 CONNECTION AND CIRCUIT TYPES AND SERVICES

This section takes a detailed look at the characteristics of the three major types of connections that define the data flows that are used in network topologies: simplex, half-duplex, and duplex. We next look at multidrop and private line circuits, which form the fundamental components of connectivity for most types of data communications architectures. Additionally, Local Exchange Carriers (LECs), independent telephone and bypass companies, and Inter-eXchange Carriers (IXCs) offer private lines and multidrop circuits as a tariff service. Finally, we look at two new types of high-speed local loop – the High-rate Digital Subscriber Line (HDSL) and Asymmetric Digital Subscriber Line (ADSL).

5.2.1 Connection Types: Simplex, Half-Duplex, and Duplex

DTE-to-DCE connections provide a local, limited-distance physical connection between Data Terminal Equipment (DTE) or Terminal Equipment (TE), such as a computer, and Data Communications Equipment (DCE), such as a modem. The physical medium can be two-wire, four-wire, coaxial, fiber optic, or a variety of other interfaces. Figure 5.8 depicts a connection between a DTE and a DCE running simplex communications, which means that transmission is possible only in a single direction. Figure 5.9 shows a DTE/DCE connection using half-duplex communications, which means that a transmission can occur in two directions (as illustrated by the two-headed arrow) but only one direction is allowed at a time. The change of transmission direction is accomplished via the control leads between the DTE and DCE at the physical layer. Figure 5.10 depicts full-duplex communication, which means that transmission can not only occur in both directions but can occur in both directions simultaneously. A separate ground lead is shown for each data signal, indicating a balanced interface which supports higher transmission speeds over longer distances on DTE-to-DCE connections. An unbalanced interface shares a ground lead between multiple signal leads and operates only over shorter distances. All of these examples demonstrate a point-to-point topology.

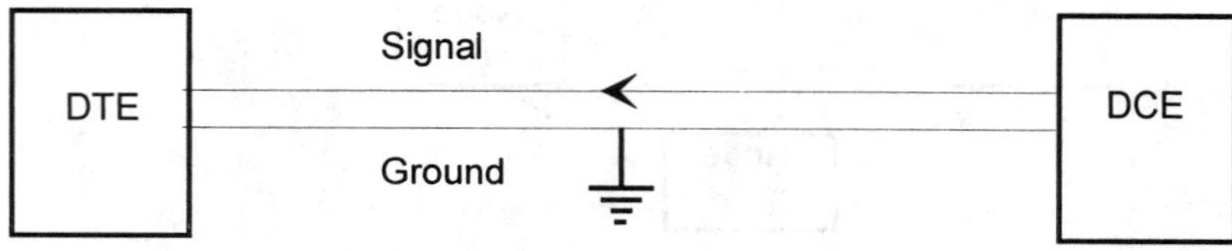

Figure 5.8 Simplex DTE/DCE Connection

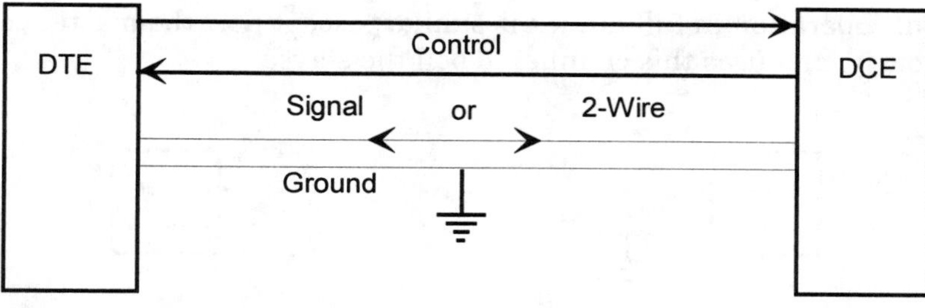

Figure 5.9 Half-Duplex DTE/DCE Connection

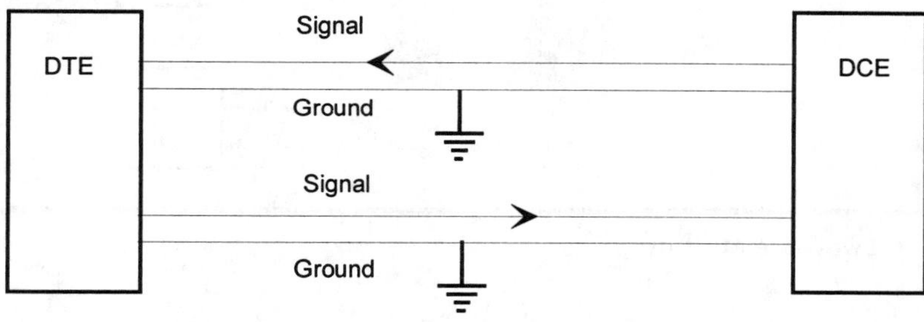

Figure 5.10 Full-Duplex DTE/DCE Connection

5.2.2 Multidrop Circuits

When one user, typically the originator of information, needs to communicate with multiple users over a shared facility, a multidrop circuit can be used. Figure 5.11 shows a two-wire multidrop circuit, and Figure 5.12 shows a four-wire multidrop circuit. In SNA multidrop networks, many remote users (B, C, and D) share a single low cost multidrop access circuit to a central site (A), Only one user (B, C, or D) may send data to the main leg of the circuit (A) at any one time. When using multidrop circuits, there is a master-slave relationship between the master A and slaves B, C, and D. A typical application is where the master A is a cluster controller and B through D are dumb terminals, connected to a host (either local or remote) to provide cost-effective access to a centralized host. Note that when dealing with an SDLC loop operating on a two-wire multidrop circuit, only a half-duplex connection protocol can be used, as indicated by the two-headed arrow, while full-duplex operation can be accommodated on a four-wire circuit, as indicated by the single-headed arrow on the path in each direction. In half-duplex operation the master sends out data to the slaves, and polls them for any response. The slave sets a "final" bit in its response, indicating the last frame to be returned. Operation in full duplex is similar, except now the master can send continuously, and uses this channel to poll the slaves.

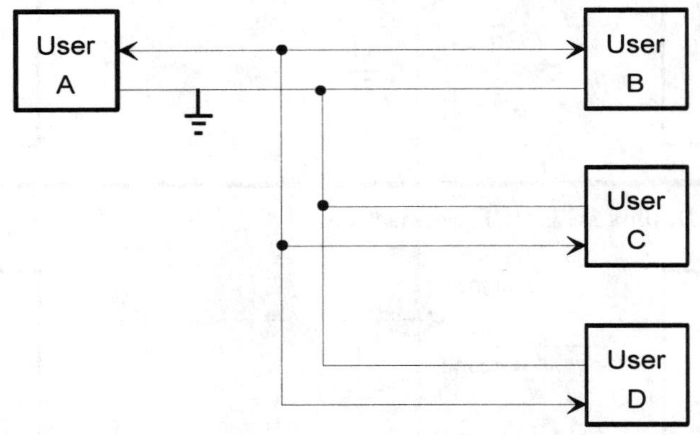

Figure 5.11 Two-Wire Multidrop

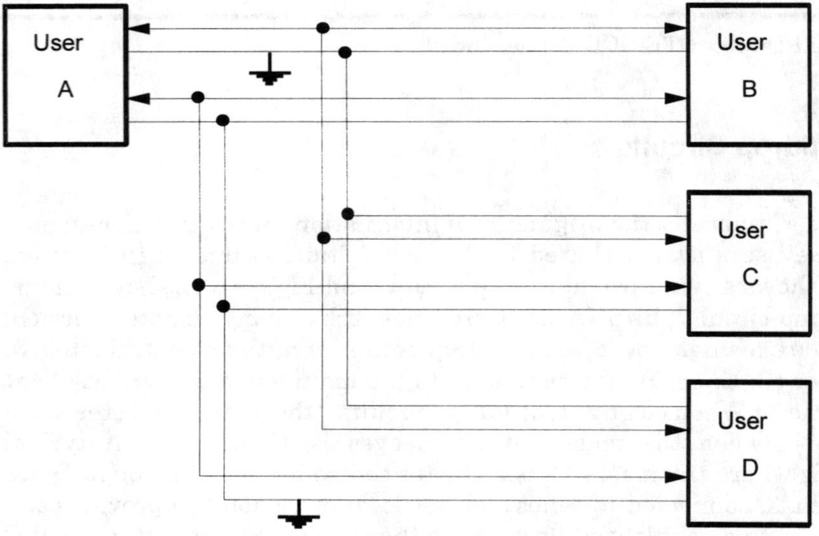

Figure 5.12 Four-Wire Multidrop

5.2.3 Private Lines and Local Loops

A private, or leased, line is a dedicated circuit leased from a LEC or carrier, leased for a predetermined period of time, usually in increments of months or years. A private line may be upgraded by paying extra for a defined quality of service, such that conditioning is performed to ensure that a better error rate is achieved, which makes a tremendous difference in data communications. As LECs and carriers install all-fiber networks, digital private lines with much lower error rates are replacing the old voice-grade analog data circuits, at the same or even lower costs. Although analog voice grade lines are still available, most communications are carried on digital facilities. In the United States, there are very few private lines left that use microwave or analog circuits. This is especially true in major metropolitan areas.

When leased lines are used to access other services, they are called *access lines* or *local loops*. Leased access lines can be purchased through LECs, through competitive access providers (CAPs), through IXCs or, alternatively, user-owned access arrangements. Access from these alternate sources is generally less expensive than the local telephone company prices. But, of course, the alternative access carrier usually “cream-skims” the lucrative traffic and leaves the “skimmed milk” of the smaller, more remote, or occasional users for the LEC to serve.

Private lines in Europe and Pacific Rim countries are still very expensive, and transoceanic fiber access is still limited. A carrier also must make an agreement with the party at the other side of a fiber to offer the transoceanic service. Prices are dropping, but they require significant investment in small amounts of bandwidth, a situation which is often taken for granted in the United States. The high cost of international private lines may justify the cost of sophisticated, statistical multiplexers, or statistical multiplexing services like frame relay, to utilize the expensive bandwidth as efficiently as possible. New fiber-optic technologies like erbium-doping techniques are enabling long trans-oceanic fiber runs that do not require repeaters, thus significantly driving down the cost of trans-continental communications. These savings will eventually reach the consumer.

5.2.4 ADSL and HDSL

Another form of DS1 rate signal, operating over four wires, is the High-rate Digital Subscriber Line (HDSL). HDSLs eliminate the cost of repeaters every 2000 ft as in a standard T1 repeater system, and are not affected by bridge taps (i.e., splices). They need to be within 12,000 ft of the serving central office, which covers over 80 percent of the DS1 customers in the United States. Asymmetric Digital Subscriber Lines (ADSLs) are also becoming available and offer higher speeds (up to 640 kbps) and better performance.

The goal of the ADSL technology is to deliver a video signal and telephone service over a majority of the existing copper, twisted pairs currently connected to homes. Fiber To The Curb (FTTC) and Fiber To The Home (FTTH) will not see widescale deployment until after the turn of the century. Both these technologies will enable services like ATM and higher rate ADSL-like technologies to proliferate to the residential consumer.

5.3 PRIVATE LEASED LINES VS. SWITCHED NETWORKS

In keeping with the discussion matter of this chapter, it is important to review the benefits and risks of private line networks vs. switched networks. There are three general options to data-transport networks today: private line or dedicated leased line networks, switched networks, and hybrid designs incorporating a mix of both. Dedicated lines, also called private or leased lines, are dedicated circuits between two or more user devices. This type of circuit represents a dedicated private portion of bandwidth between two or more ports on the network, hence the term *private line*. A private line is dedicated to one customer; the opposite is a public service shared among multiple customers. This private circuit is available for a set fee (usually an initial nonrecurring and a monthly recurring fee) to a customer 24 hours a day, 7 days a week. High volumes of traffic with frequent use justify this type of circuit. The only users of the circuit are the ports at both ends of the circuit. The bandwidth resources are in no way shared within the network. These circuits are also leased by carriers to the public, hence the term leased lines.

The second alternative is a switched network transport circuit. This can range from simple circuit switching, in which users dynamically select from a pool of multiple public service lines with fixed bandwidths, to intelligent ubiquitous switched access networks where bandwidth is only allocated and used when needed, such as frame and cell relay networks.

Corporate communications usually comprises a hybrid network employing both solutions. The circuits requiring dedicated bandwidth to accommodate predictable volumes of constant-bandwidth traffic use *dedicate*d circuits, while users requiring one-to-many connectivity, bandwidth-on-demand, and flexible or more dynamic access use *switched* network access. These decisions are also influenced by other factors such as burstiness of data, traffic patterns and bandwidth maximums, minimum delay, to name a few. The three types of network services that match the access types above include: private line services dedicated to one customer, virtual private services which look like private services but ride on a public or shared network platform, and public network switched services.

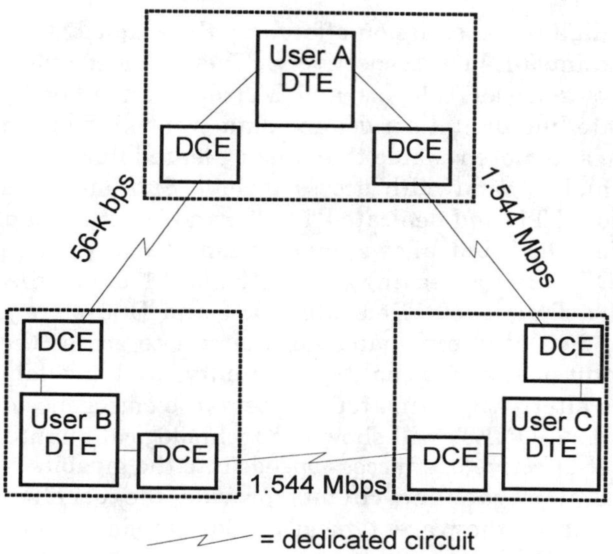

Figure 5.13 Leased Line Network

5.3.1 Private (Leased) Line Networks

Dedicated or private lines are the simplest form of point-to-point communications. Circuits leased from a carrier ("leased lines") are a form of private line. Private lines provide a dedicated circuit of fixed bandwidth between two points. Figure 5.13 shows three user devices connected via private lines. User A has a dedicated 56-kbps circuit to user B, as well as a dedicated 1.544 Mbps circuit to user C. Users B and C have a dedicated 1.544 Mbps circuit between them. Private line bandwidths will vary, but typically follow standard speed conventions of 9600 bps, 19.2-kbps, 56/64-kbps, *N*xDS0 (DS0 increments) and 1.544 Mbps. Users will generally lease a private line when the entire bandwidth will always be available between two points of choice whenever it is needed. They do not want to share this bandwidth with anyone else, nor do they want to contend with other users to establish the circuit (or wait the delay time to establish it) to receive their required bandwidth.

Leased lines come in many grades and speeds. The most basic traditional service available consists of analog and digital leased lines of DS0, fractional-T1, and DS1 speeds. These lines require a modem for data-to-voice conversion and transmission or a channel service unit (CSU) or digital service unit (DSU) for line conditioning and proper framing and formatting. This type of service ranges from economic analog circuits to higher-grade Digital Data

Service (DDS) digital transmission offered by the major IXCs and LECs both inter-LATA and intra-LATA, respectively. They are also offered by alternate access providers such as Teleport and Metropolitan Fiber Systems (MFS). DDS is a private-line digital service for data transmission, and is generally more expensive and more reliable than analog leased lines.

Options for higher bandwidth access include SubRate Data Multiplexing (SRDM), fractional T1, and dedicated T1, T2, and T3. SRDM offers the same access speeds as DDS, but allows aggregation of many low-speed channels into a single DS0 for cost savings. Fractional T1 offers the same type of service, but at a DS1 level. Dedicated DS1 and DS3 offer just what they state, a single, dedicated high-bandwidth circuit to access the carrier. If a user wants additional functionality, reliability, and availability, switched services are the alternative. In later chapters, the emergence of Synchronous Optical Networks (SONET) will show the technological quantum leap that is now moving cost-effective user access speeds into the gigabits.

While dedicated private-line circuits provide the benefit of guaranteed available bandwidth, they are typically nonredundant. Although at the network level the DXCs carrying private lines have network layer disaster recovery, so the risk is at the access level, unless LEC/CAP access redundancy is ordered and routed. If the private line of any of its associated transmission equipment should fail or be taken out of commission (e.g., a fiber cut) the users on each end cannot communicate (unless they have some method of reconnecting or dialing around the failure). Thus, the user must decide what level of availability is needed for communications between facilities. A decision for switched services backup is predicated on these tradeoffs.

Many options are available for assuring high availability in private lines. Automatic Line Protection Service (ALPS) technology is one of the simplest (yet very expensive) ways of providing a hot-swap capability between two access circuits of the same speed. When employing ALPS, two 1.544 Mbps trunks are used. If one goes down, the ALPS system automatically switches traffic to the remaining 1.544 Mbps trunk with a minimal service interruption of typically 50 milliseconds. Figure 5.14 depicts the use of an ALPS system between user A and user C. If circuit 1 were to fail, the ALPS service would switch user traffic to transport across circuit 2. Circuit 1 could be brought up and switched back into service after the problem that took the circuit out of commission was corrected. Many other methods of routing traffic around physical network failures are discussed in later chapters.

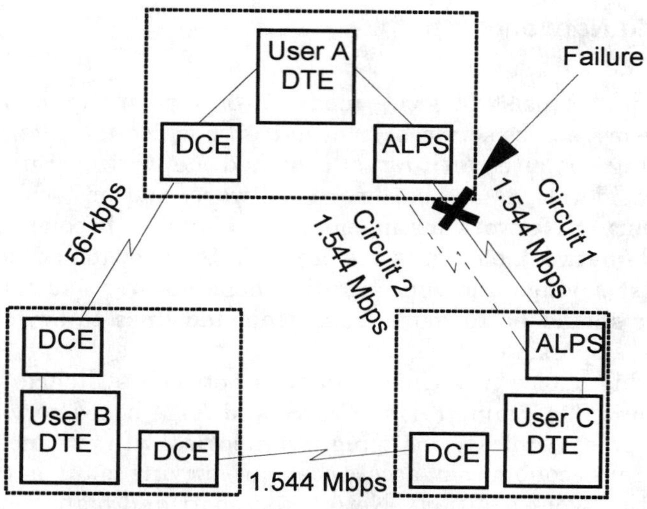

Figure 5.14 Leased Line with ALPS

5.3.2 Switched Networks

Switched networks can range from simple circuit switching to advanced packet and cell switching, and can include new technologies such as Asynchronous Transfer Mode (ATM). The main characteristics of switched networks include

- Addressing capability
- Multiple protocol and interface support
- One-to-many, many-to-one, and many-to-many connectivity
- Network intelligence above the physical transport layer

Circuit and packet (including frame and cell) switching are two major types of switched network techniques. Each of these techniques will be defined in detail later. The ultimate method of achieving high availability can be achieved by using a switched network. Three examples of switched service offerings are Frame Relay (FR), Switched Multimegabit Data Service (SMDS), and ATM. Examples of switched networks will be shown in later chapters.

5.3.3 Hybrid Networks

Hybrid networks consist of some measure or mixture of private-line and switched network access services, or even traffic which transits a private line before entering or after exiting a switched network. Either way, the important considerations are hardware, software, and protocol compatibility (or transparency). Network management and support become more difficult when multiple network elements are crossed. Since switched networks offer significant cost savings and concentration benefits over dedicated lines, the driving factor should be to move from dedicated lines to switched network access as soon as possible.

Today, the big choice in switched data is between switched services (like Switched 56 and T1), frame relay, SMDS, and ATM-based services. Ubiquitous network access, quickly changing technologies with enhanced reliability, and the apparent economics of access costs are driving many network designs to a switched network solution. Network support and management are also driving factors. Each of these decisions should be accompanied by a cost comparison of separate networks to a single network, or a private line to switched solution.

5.4 DATA TRANSMISSION METHODS

Digital data transmission methods are often characterized as being either asynchronous or synchronous. The terms *asynchronous* and *synchronous* are used in different contexts and have entirely different meanings. The most common use of these terms is in the comparison of asynchronous vs. synchronous character or message transmissions. Since this text presents a study of ATM technology, it is important to review another use of these two terms, as in Synchronous versus Asynchronous Transfer Mode (STM and ATM). These two entirely different meanings of the same term can be confusing, which is why this section presents them together so that the reader can appreciate the differences.

5.4.1 Asynchronous and Synchronous Data Transmission

Asynchronous character transmission has no clock either in or associated with the transmitted digital data stream. Characters are transmitted as a series of bits, with each character identified separately by start and stop bits, as illustrated in the example of ASCII characters in Figure 5.15. There will typically be a variable amount of time between each character transmission. Analog modem communication employs this method extensively. The baud rate defines a nominal clock rate, which is the maximum asynchronous bit rate. The stop bit can be greater than a baud interval in duration. Since at least 10-baud intervals are required to represent each character, the usable bit rate is no more than 80 percent of the baud rate.

Asynchronous character transmission usually operates at low speeds (typically 9600 bps). Asynchronous interfaces include RS232-C and D, as well as X.21.

Synchronous data transmission clocks the bits at a regular rate by a clocking signal either associated with, or derived from, the transmitted digital data stream. Therefore sender and receiver must have a means to derive a common clock within a certain frequency tolerance. On a parallel interface there is often a separate clock lead. Data flows in character streams are called message-framed data. Figure 5.16 shows a typical synchronous data stream. The message begins with two synchronization (SYNCH) characters and a Start Of Message (SOM) character. The Control (C) character(s) denote the type of user data or message following. The user data follows next. The Cyclic Redundancy Check (CRC) character checks the data for errors, and the End Of Message (EOM) character signals the end of the transmission stream. The equipment then looks for another two SYNC characters for the next piece of information.

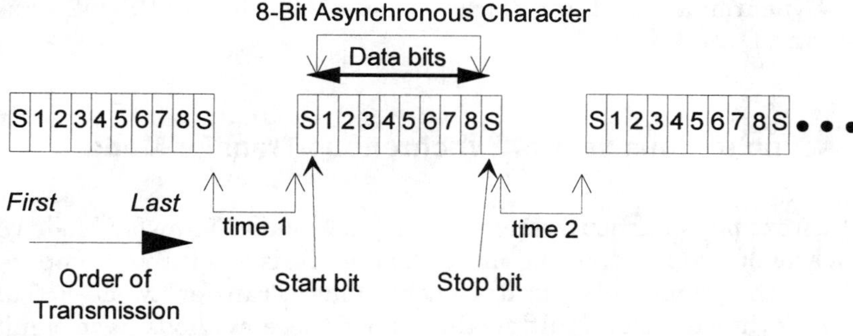

Figure 5.15 Asynchronous Modem Character Transmission

Synch	Synch	SOM	Control	Data	CRC	EOM

Synch - Synchronization
SOM - Start of Message
Control - Specifies User Message
Data - User Data Stream
CRC - Cyclic Redundancy Check
EOM - End of Message

Figure 5.16 Synchronous Framed Data Message

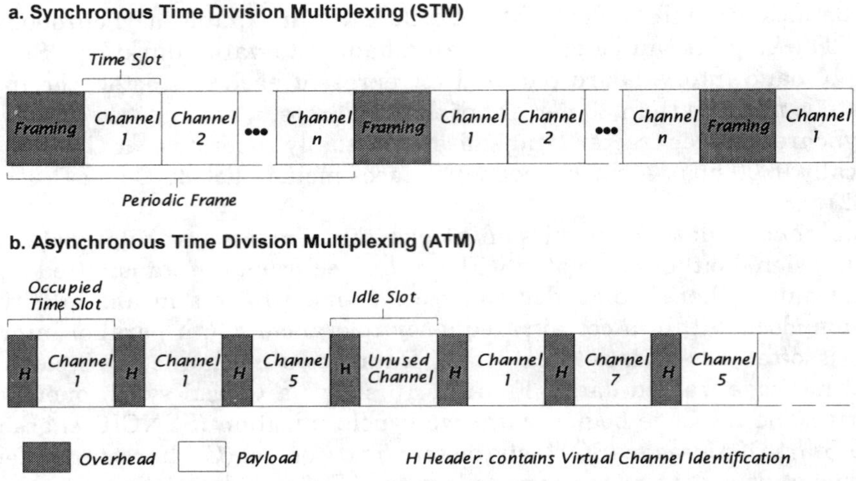

a. Synchronous Time Division Multiplexing (STM)

Time Slot

Framing | Channel 1 | Channel 2 | ••• | Channel n | Framing | Channel 1 | Channel 2 | ••• | Channel n | Framing | Channel 1

Periodic Frame

b. Asynchronous Time Division Multiplexing (ATM)

Occupied Time Slot

Idle Slot

H | Channel 1 | H | Channel 1 | H | Channel 5 | H | Unused Channel | H | Channel 1 | H | Channel 7 | H | Channel 5

Overhead   Payload   H Header: contains Virtual Channel Identification

Figure 5.17 Illustration of STM and ATM Multiplexing

Synchronous data transmission usually operates at speeds of 1200 bps and higher. Synchronous data interfaces include V.35, RS449/RS-442 balanced, RS232-C and D, and X.21.

5.4.2 Asynchronous versus Synchronous Transfer Mode

Since this text pays particular detail to Asynchronous Transfer Mode (ATM), or asynchronous time division multiplexing, it is useful to compare this method to the commonly used Synchronous Transfer Mode (STM), or synchronous time division multiplexing. Both these methods have significant differences.

Figure 5.17 shows an example of STM and ATM. Figure 5.17a illustrates an STM stream where each time slot represents a reserved piece of bandwidth dedicated to a single channel, such as a DS0 in a DS1. Each frame contains *n* dedicated time slots per frame; for example, *n* is 192 in a DS1. Overhead fields identify STM frames that often contain operations information as well, for example, the 193rd bit in a DS1 frame. Thus, if a channel is not transmitting data, the time slot remains reserved and is still transmitted, without any useful payload. In this case, if the other channels have more data to transmit, they have to wait until their reserved, assigned time slot occurs again. Frequent empty time slots result in low line utilization.

ATM uses a completely different approach. A header field prefixes each fixed length payload, as shown in Figure 5.17b. The header identifies the virtual channel. Therefore, the time slots are available to *any user* who has data ready to transmit. If no users are ready to transmit, then an empty, or idle, cell is sent. Traffic patterns that are not continuous are usually carried much more efficiently by ATM as compared with STM. The current approach is to carry ATM cells over very high-speed STM transmission networks, such as SONET and SDH. The match between high transmission speeds of SONET and SDH and the flexibility of ATM is a good one.

5.5 HARDWARE DISTINCTIONS

Data-networking topologies are the roads by which data can travel. We will now explore the wide variety of LAN and WAN access devices which utilize these roads. The various types of equipment that are available now or under development for use in the local, metropolitan, and wide area are reviewed in this section. The principal networking equipment categories in place today include switches, routers, and hubs. There are also a number of other (usually lower-level functions) that can be used in a building block manner, such as multiplexers, concentrators, CSU/DSUs, and bridging devices, that are summarized here. Multiplexer and switch access devices will be considered in the next chapter.

Here is a critical item: Before bridges and routers were available, the functions that these devices now serve were once performed in mainframes and front-end processors. The migration was from cluster controllers and front-end processors to simple routing devices and then to router-based networks. This was a major paradigm shift in the last two decades. As personal computing arrived on the scene, and as MIPS moved to the desktop during decentralization, the bridging and routing functions traditionally accomplished at the FEP/host complex migrated towards the desktop. The advent of personal computing, along with local and wide area networking, made routing and switching outside the mainframe environment a necessity.

Perhaps the greatest driving factor was the multiple MAC and network layer protocols operating within and between LANs as they moved into the WAN environment. Due to these diverse markets, technologies, and protocol suites, there evolved a need to make diverse LAN, WAN, and operating-system protocols speak one language (or at least provide a translation between similar languages on similar types of LANs). When bridges and routers first came along, they were designed to deal with lower-speed LANs. Now the functions of bridging, routing, and switching have merged in many cases into a single device. And with increased processor speeds, more advanced technologies, and concomitant reduced costs, these devices now support an extension of diverse LAN speeds over the WAN with access speeds from the kilobits per second up into the gigabits per second speeds.

Each hardware type mentioned in this chapter provides a different set of functionality, which can either be provided separately or together in one piece of equipment. Each provides protocol support for certain levels of the

OSIRM, as well as other proprietary architectures. For simplicity of discussion, and since the OSIRM seems to be the common architectural point of reference (along with the IEEE 802.X protocol model), the protocol support for each hardware device will be given in reference to the seven-layer OSIRM reference model. Repeaters and brouters have come to play a reduced role, yielding to remote-access routers and Small Office Home Office (SOHO) devices that require only a subset of their larger counterparts. Intelligent LAN hubs that provide LAN connectivity and concentration, bridging, routing, and switching will also be covered in detail. Each of these new hardware technologies offers specific advantages and disadvantages depending upon user applications, protocols, addressing, and data transport needs. The network designer must understand each of these technologies to ensure successful LAN-MAN-WAN connectivity, interoperability, and integration. Starting with the most simple devices will allow us to work toward the most complex.

5.5.1 Repeaters

Repeaters are inexpensive distance-extension devices, providing physical distance extension through signal regeneration for point-to-point circuits. This allows a network to extend the distance between network devices, similar to an extension cord for electricity, while providing electrical isolation during problem conditions. Thus, repeaters offer the capability to extend an existing LAN segment. Repeaters possess very little intelligence. They are commonly used as signal regenerators, protecting against signal attenuation while improving signal quality. Due to this lack of intelligence, repeaters add value by maintaining the integrity of all data being passed, but they are completely transparent to all data content. Drawbacks to using repeaters include possible network congestion caused by the overhead they add due to repeating and *jitter* imposed by signal delay. The effects of excessive jitter will be covered in later chapters. Repeaters form the core component of hubs. Repeaters use only the physical layer of the OSIRM. Figure 5.18 portrays user A and user B communicating via a repeater in relation to the OSIRM. Note that only the physical layer 1 is used by a repeater. Multiport Transceiver Units (MTUs) are used with thick net coaxial (10BASE5) cabling, Multiport Repeater Units (MRUs) with thin-net (10BASE2) media, and wiring concentrators are typically used with unshielded twisted pair (UTP) (10BASET), but also can be used with thick and thin net cabling.

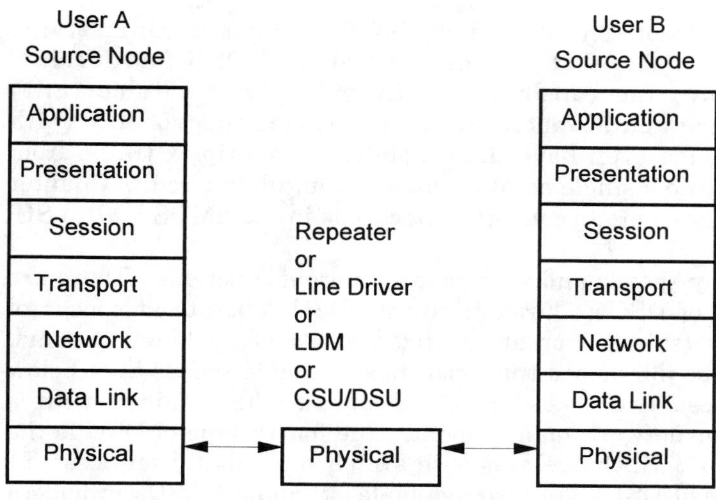

Figure 5.18 Repeater, LDM, CSU/DSU and the OSIRM

5.5.2 Line Drivers/Limited-Distance Modems

Line drivers, also called Limited-Distance Modems (LDMs), are used to extend the distance of a physical circuit. Basic telecommunications courses teach that modems provide modulation/demodulation between analog and digital data. LDMs provide the same functionality, but in the form of a repeater. Figure 5.16 showed the OSIRM layer used by line drivers and LDMs.

5.5.3 Channel Service Unit (CSU) and Data Service Unit (DSU)

The terms *Channel Service Unit* (CSU) and *Data Service Unit* (DSU) are often incorrectly used interchangeably. Originally, the CSU was developed to protect CPE from voltage surges in the access line. Additional remote testing and monitoring capability such as bipolar violation and loop-back testing was later added. The DSU was typically the lower-speed device, providing signal format and protocol translation, timing recovery, synchronous sampling, as well as acting as the termination point for digital data circuits (DDS) 56-kbps and below. The CSU was a higher-speed device, used at DS1 rates, which could also be used at lower speeds. The CSU terminates digital circuits with the same features as a DSU, but it also provides many feature functions not provided by the DSU, such as filtering, line equalization, line conditioning, signal regeneration and amplification, circuit loop-back testing capabilities, and error control protocol conversion (i.e., B8ZS) peculiar to DS1 service. Today, a device is available that has merged CSU and DSU functionality. CSUs and DSUs have the capability for Extended Super Frame (ESF) monitoring and testing and advanced SNMP monitoring functionality (with their own MIBs). Some even have the capability to multiplex traffic from multiple input ports into a single point-to-point or multidrop circuit. Chapter 12 will explain how they help to convert protocols as in the SMDS DXI-to-SIP conversion.

DSUs come in many speeds and with many different functions. There are six major categories of DSUs. First, fixed-rate DSUs operate at speeds of 19.2-kbps and below (subrate) or at the fixed speed of 56 kbps. Second, Multirate DSUs can be purchased that operate at variable speeds at or below 56-kbps. Third, these two types of DSUs can also be obtained with a secondary channel for network management. The fourth type of DSU is the switched 56-kbps DSU, which operates with switched 56 digital services. T1 dedicated and switched DSUs are also available. Standard CSUs provide a T1 circuit interface, and can have properties similar to the DSUs mentioned above. Finally, CSUs and DSUs are capable of multiplexing multiple T1, V.35, and RS-232 user ports into a single data stream for "integrated access" into a LEC or IXC switch, where they can be demultiplexed and passed to the appropriate service.

Many CSU and DSU vendors are now marketing DS-3/E-3 products, which provide the High-Speed Serial Interface (HSSI) for direct DS-3 connectivity. A few of the vendors, such as Digital Link and ADC Kentrox offer Switched MultiMegabit Data Service (SMDS) support. But let the buyer beware, *caveat emptor*, for many of these SMDS support functions are proprietary between the CSU and DSU vendors and a particular hardware vendor.

With the emergence of broadband services such as SMDS and ATM DXI, the CSU takes on an entirely new function apart from its normal functionality. Some SMDS and ATM CSUs actually perform some of the required protocol conversion and cell segmentation, going far beyond their original function as a power protector interface. For example with SMDS DXI, special SMDS CSUs actually take the high-level L3_PDU frame and segment it into L2_PDU cells, performing part of the SMDS protocol function within the CSU! The CSU then interfaces to the SMDS network through a SMDS Interface Protocol (SIP). SIP will be reviewed in detail in Chapter 12.

Also note that many times a specific CSU or DSU setting or feature works best depending on the layer 2 protocol being passed, such as with frame relay, where B8ZS is the option of choice for DS1 speeds using ESF.

DSU/CSU standard interfaces include 56-kbps, FT1 and DS1 using EIA-232-C, V.35, and HSSI (on DS-3 models). CSU and DSU operation is similar to that shown in Figure 5.18 with repeaters, and the OSIRM layer used by CSUs and DSUs is shown in this same figure. Note that only physical layer 1 is used by a CSU or DSU (except with the SMDS DSU and ATM DSU).

5.5.4 Intelligent LAN Hubs

LAN hubs, also called concentrator hubs, are devices that connect multiple LAN segments (i.e. Ethernet, Token Ring) or single workstations (or servers) and combine them on a shared back-plane. Thus, a hub can be used to combine multiple workstations or servers onto a single LAN segment, or multiple LAN segments into a single LAN segment or WAN port. The former case is the hub acting as a repeater for multiple LAN Network Interface Cards (NICs) – the workstations interface to the LAN media (i.e., 10BASE-T). Larger hubs typically have multiple repeater cards and serve many workstations. In the latter case, the hub must perform a bridging or routing function, which will be explained later. Hubs can also perform switching directly between workstations and servers, or between LAN segments.

LAN hubs have been classified into four generations. Figure 5.19 illustrates each generation of LAN hub along with its LAN protocol support at each stage. Hub configurations tend to model the star topology, with the hub as the center and each LAN device attached directly to the hub. The first-generation LAN hub started to appear in 1984 and acted as a repeater for a single type of LAN connectivity (i.e., an Ethernet homogeneous environment). These hubs provided the functionality of a LAN concentration point, supporting a single bus to provide physical connectivity for multiple ports on multiple LANs operating on the same architecture (later different LAN types could be multiplexed, such as Ethernet and Token Ring). This function was similar to that of a combination patch panel and repeater, as is shown in Figure 5.19a. One example is IBM's Multistation Access Unit (MAU) wiring concentrator used for Token Ring coaxial hubbing.

Second-generation LAN hubs provided the same bus architectures, but accommodated different LAN architectures over multiple ports, such as Ethernet and Token Ring. Additional features such as local and remote network management and configuration capability were also added, as shown in Figure 5.19b.

Third-generation LAN hubs provide multiple buses for connectivity similar to the second generation, but also add bridging and routing functions. Most hub vendors now have ATM integrated into their hubs, the range of physical media support is much wider, and often multiple multimegabit buses are in the hub architecture. Third-generation LAN hubs also have additional network management features, and are sometimes called "smart hubs". This generation also saw the appearance of ATM wide area proprietary trunk interfaces. These hubs are shown in Figure 5.19c. Support for some form of network management protocol, like the Simple Network Management Protocol (SNMP), is a must.

Fourth-generation switching hubs have appeared in the latter part of the 1990s. Switching hubs offer all the capabilities mentioned above with the addition of MAC-layer switching, transparent bridging, and standard wide area trunk interfaces. These hubs are shown in Figure 5.19d.

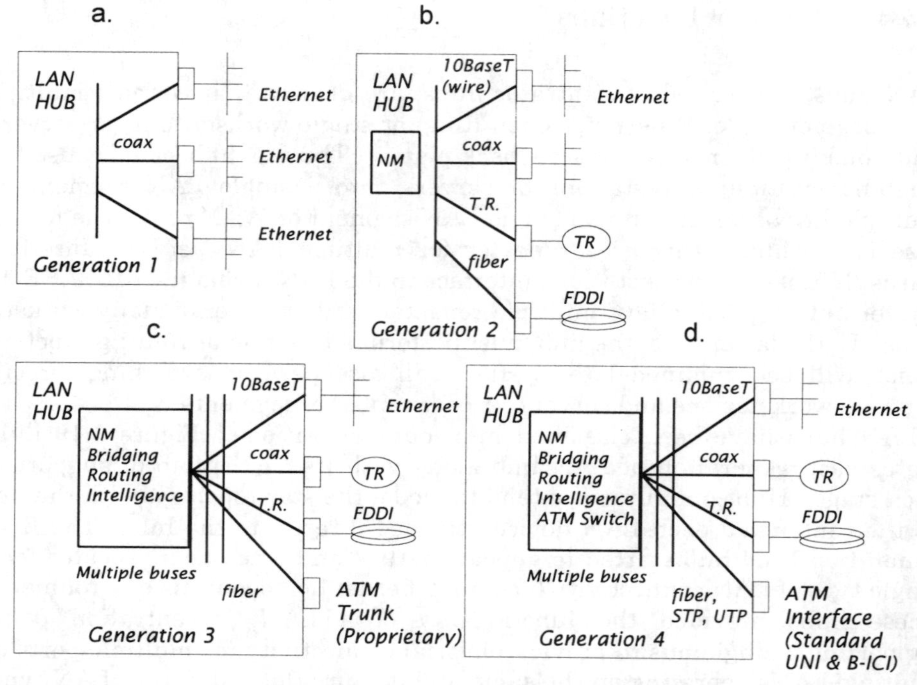

Figure 5.19 Four Generations of Wiring Hubs

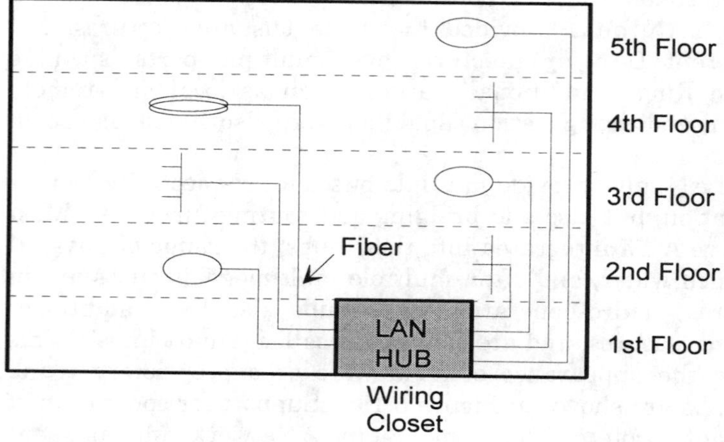

Figure 5.20 LAN Hub Building Plan

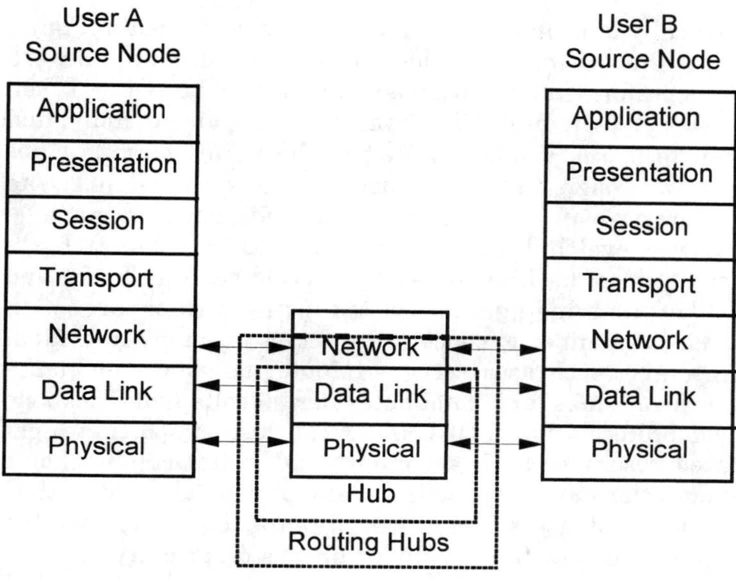

Figure 5.21 Hub Communications via the OSIRM

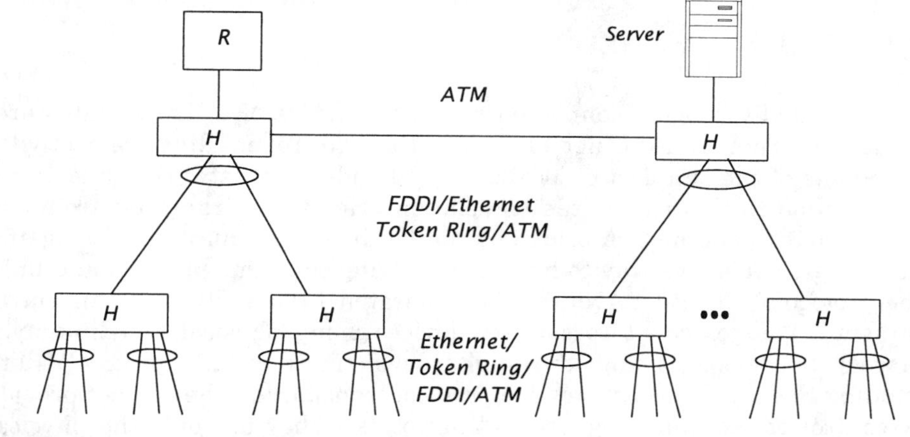

Figure 5.22 Hub Interfaces, Functions, and Architecture

Figure 5.20 shows a building using a LAN hub to connect multiple LANs of the same type or different types (Ethernet to Ethernet, Ethernet to Token Ring, Token Ring to Token Ring) between multiple floors. The following sections on bridges and routers will explain these techniques from the protocol and OSIRM point of view. Figure 5.21 shows the OSIRM layers used by LAN hubs. Notice that hubs use the physical and data link layers and routing hubs use part of the network layer.

Hub designs are typically built in a hierarchical nature, as shown in Figure 10.22. Here we see the wiring collection, segmentation, and network management functions performed by hubs. Usually many Ethernet or Token Ring twisted pair lines, FDDI, and ATM over twisted pair to individual workstations, are run to a hub usually located in the wiring closet. Hubs allow administrators to assign individual users to a resource (e.g., an Ethernet segment), shown as an ellipse in the figure, via network management commands. Lower-level hubs are often connected in a hierarchy to higher-level hubs, sometimes via higher-speed protocols such as FDDI and ATM over optical fiber and high-grade twisted pairs. Hubs are often employed in a hierarchical manner to concentrate access for many individual users to a shared resource, such as a server or router as shown in Figure 10.22. The highest level hubs are candidates for a collapsed backbone architecture based on protocols like FDDI and ATM, also supporting high-speed access to shared resources such as routers and switches. Stackable modular hub implementations are also available, and provide an easy method of upgrade as the number of users increases. Beware, however, that the interconnect bus used in stackable hubs is almost always proprietary.

5.5.5 Bridges

Bridges typically provide connectivity between LANs of a like architecture, such as Ethernet to Ethernet or Token Ring to Token Ring connectivity, forming one of the simplest of local area and wide area network connections. The exception to this rule is the translation bridge that translates from one media format to another. A bridge uses a minimal amount of processing and thus is a less expensive way to link LANs having the same physical and link-layer protocols. These LANs can be separated by a hallway or an entire continent. Bridges can also connect devices using physical and link-layer protocols to devices using the higher-level IEEE 802.X protocol suite (including FDDI). Since bridges are protocol transparent, they do not provide flow control or recognize higher-level protocols. They use only the physical and link layers of the OSI reference model and support both the logical link control (LLC) and the media access control (MAC) layers of LAN transmission.

Figure 5.23 portrays the same user A and user B now communicating via a bridge over the physical and link layers of the OSIRM. Bridges operate at the media access control (MAC) layer of the OSI data link layer (DLL). Both users are implementing the same protocol stack for layer 1 and 2, and the bridge does not modify the information flow in any way (except a required MAC-layer conversion in translation bridging, depending on whether a header is included as part of the "information flow"). The bridge supports linking at the physical and link level, but provides no addressing or switching functionality. Thus, the user provides all addressing and protocol translation. Bridges simply pass traffic from one network segment to another based on the destination MAC address of the packet being passed. If the destination address of the frame received by the bridge is not local to the bridge, the frame is obviously destined for another LAN and thus the bridge simply forwards the frame on to the next network device.

Bridges will store and forward packets between bridges as packet switches would, but the bridge cannot act as a switch. The exception to this rule is the LAN switch, which performs bridging in most cases. Bridges send each packet to a remote user based upon a destination address. Bridges can recognize either a fixed routing table scheme or, for more expensive bridges, a dynamic learning routing scheme. Bridges can "learn" the network through the use of intelligent bridging and routing protocols, and some bridges are able to dynamically update their forwarding tables. Bridging protocols will be discussed later. Another key capability of bridges is their ability to filter data. But a major drawback to bridges is that they cannot forward data if operating at their maximum filtering rate. Bridges deployed in a network do not have advance knowledge of the network to which they are attached. They are blind to devices other than those that attach to their logical path structure. The flexibility of bridge connectivity will be discussed further when we cover bridge protocols in Chapter 8.

There are four major types of bridges: transparent, translating, encapsulating, and source route bridging. Each provides different functionality for the various LAN architectures.

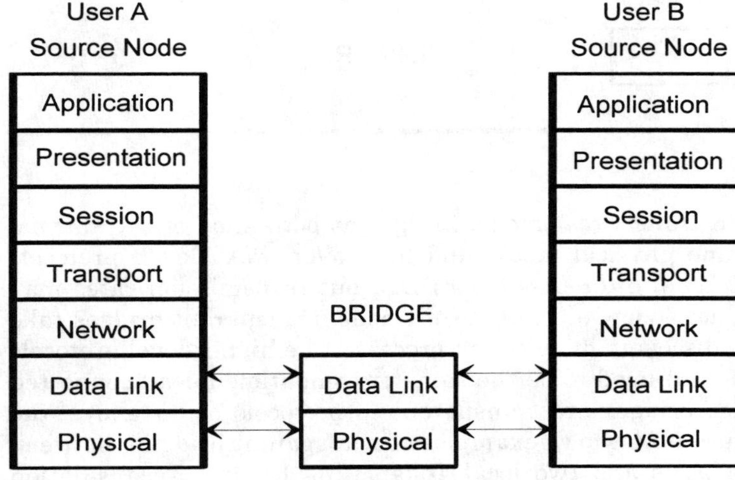

Figure 5.23 Bridge Communications via the OSIRM

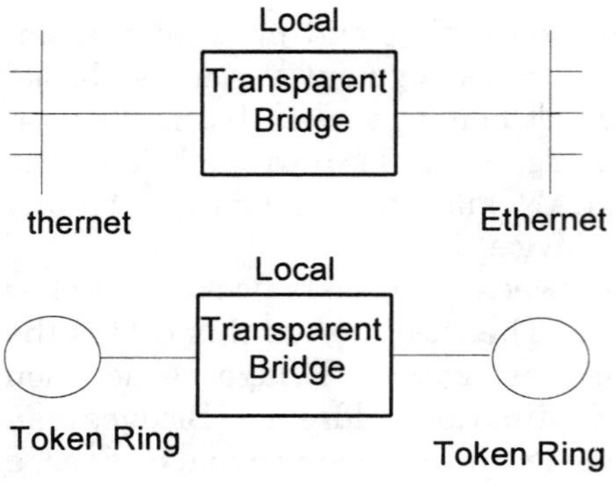

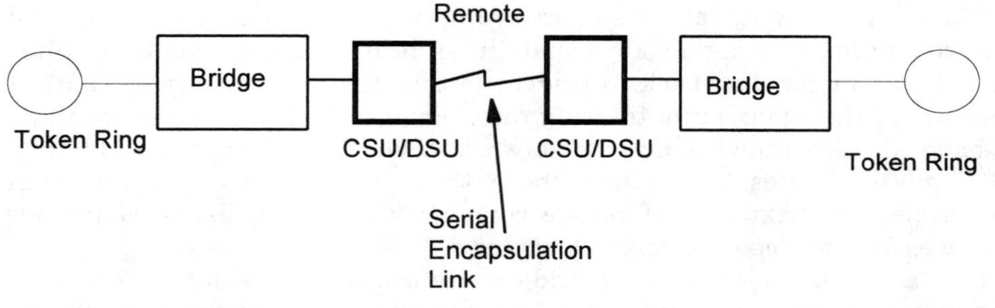

Figure 5.24 Transparent Bridging

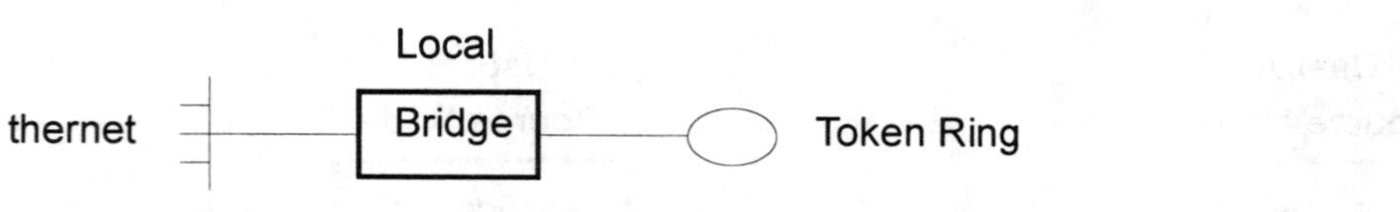

Figure 5.25 Translation Bridging

When operating in *transparent* mode, bridges at both ends of a transmission support the same physical media and link layer (MAC-level) protocols from the IEEE 802.X suite (or possibly FDDI), but transmission rates may vary. From the point of view of the network node, transparent bridges take no part in the route discovery or selection process. The higher-level protocols (OSI layer 3 and higher) need to be the same or compatible for all connected applications, because bridges are transparent to protocols at, or above, the network layer. Figure 5.24 shows examples of transparent bridging between two local Ethernet LANs and two local Token Ring LANs. Encapsulation bridging between two Token Ring LANs is also shown requiring CSUs or DSUs. In encapsulation bridging, the LAN frame is placed in an (HDLC, PPP, or proprietary) serial encapsulation over the point-to-point circuit, then de-encapsulated without modification at the other end.

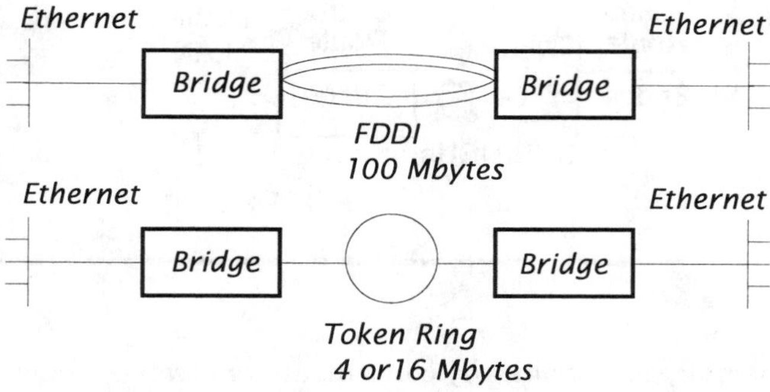

Figure 5.26 Encapsulation Bridging

Sometimes the bridge needs to send data between dissimilar LANs, for example, from an Ethernet to a Token Ring. When operating in *translation* mode, bridges at both ends of the transmission can use different physical media and link (MAC-level) protocols. Translating bridges thus translate from one media format to another — manipulating the MAC-layer frame structure associated with each media type. Protocols in the network layer and higher must still be compatible. Figure 5.25 shows an example of translation bridging between dissimilar local Ethernet and Token Ring LANs. Translation bridges do not provide segmentation services, so the frame sizes of each LAN host must be configured for the same supportable length.

When operating in *encapsulation* mode, bridges at both ends of the transmission must use the same physical and link layer (MAC-level) LAN protocols, but the "transmission network" between the bridges can provide a similar or different physical media and MAC-level protocol. Encapsulating bridges provide a network interconnection or extension by placing received frames within a media-specific "envelope" and forwarding the encapsulated frame to another bridge for delivery to the destination. This is common when multiple Ethernet segments are served by a Token Ring or FDDI backbone. The backbone then serves as the WAN protocol.

Figure 5.26 shows two examples of encapsulation bridging. The first example illustrates two remote 10 Mbps Ethernet LANs being bridged via a metropolitan 100 Mbps FDDI network. The second example shows the same two Ethernet LANs, this time bridged over a 4 or 16 Mbps Token Ring network. Pay heed when encapsulating large MAC frames into smaller frame sizes. Remember that the maximum frame size for Ethernet is 1500 bytes, whereas the Token Ring frame size can be up to 4500 bytes.

The fourth type of bridging is through *source route bridging*. Figure 5.27 shows a source route bridging scheme between two remote Token Ring LANs and three source route bridges. The third Token Ring LAN is used only for transit. Source route bridging will be discussed in detail in the next chapter.

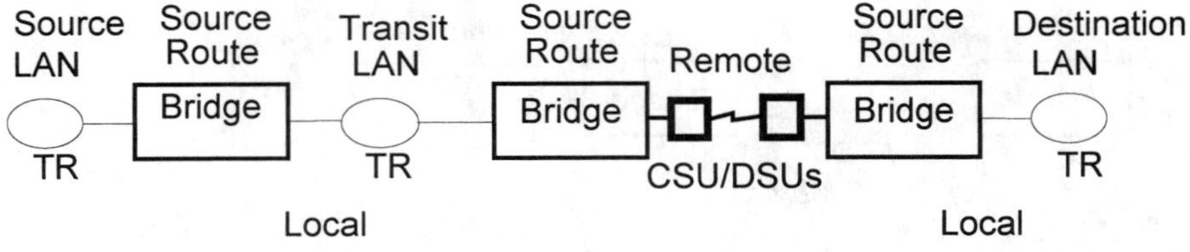

Figure 5.27 Source Route Bridging

Bridges are best used in small, geographically concentrated networks which do not require a large customer addressing base and are needed to connect a fairly static network design. Bridging speeds vary, supporting subrate DS0 through T1 to T3, and even supporting FDDIs of 100 Mbps and higher bridging speeds. These high speeds are needed to support the high-speed LANs connected to the bridge, such as 10 Mbps Ethernet and 16 Mbps Token Ring. Bridges provide either local, remote, or both local and remote support.

Careful future planning is required when deploying a bridged network solution. The manager or engineer who employs a bridge solution may find that very soon his or her bridge solution will resemble the wood and stone bridge — built in 1850 and designed to accommodate a horse and carriage. Soon there will be a need to drive not only a car but trucks over the bridge, but one year later rather than 150 years later. Thus, bridges can be good solutions for networks utilizing only one protocol and one architecture with no plans to change, or for very static network designs with multiple protocols and architectures that have close local control.

Some major disadvantages are associated with bridging. For example, bridges are susceptible to multicast or broadcast storms. These storms occur when a network bridge floods the network with repeated useless information, regenerating messages planned for one user so that many retransmissions occur to all bridges in the network. The broadcast propagates throughout the network until response time and available bandwidth become unmanageable. This problem increases with the size of the network and number of users attached.

To minimize the problem, smart bridging techniques can provide some level of traffic isolation. Some bridges cope with broadcast storms by segmenting the bridged network into domains that restrict broadcast storms to a limited area. This containment method coupled with a multicast traffic ceiling effectively controls broadcast storms. Bridges are also limited in both address retention and memory. They are designed to retain a limited amount of information and can handle only limited network changes. The more changes occurring in the network, the greater is the traffic passing between routers to update routing tables — thus an unstable network could occur.

Due to these disadvantages and limited capabilities, bridges should not be used in network designs calling for multiple protocol support, dynamic networks requiring frequent changes, or large networks of greater than 50 nodes. For networks with these requirements, more intelligent and robust devices will provide much of the bridging functionality and additional routing intelligence, as well as eliminate the disadvantages of bridging. Enter the router.

5.5.6 Routers

Routers provide inter-connectivity between like and unlike devices on the local and wide area network, as well as extending the LAN into the metropolitan and wide area networking arena. Routers are protocol sensitive, and can either bridge or route a large suite of network-layer and higher-layer protocols. Thus, they support various LAN devices that can employ a variety of networking protocols and addressing schemes. Routers understand the entire network, not just locally connected devices, and will route based on many factors to determine the best path. Routers have formed the core of the next generation of computer internetworking devices. As mentioned previously, routers have subsumed many of the legacy functions of cluster-controllers-to-FEP-to-mainframe communications. Almost all Internet traffic traverses multiple routers. Routers emerged into the marketplace over the last two decades (starting with the first-generation routers which appeared at MIT, Stamford, and CMU in 1983 and ARPANET predecessors three years earlier) as the hottest thing since multiplexers, with much more intelligence than bridges or multiplexers.

Routers use the physical, link, and network layers of the OSIRM to provide addressing and switching functionality. Figure 5.28 shows the relation of the router to the OSIRM. Both users may exercise the same protocol stack up to layer 3. A router's main functionality resides in the data-link and network-layer protocols but it also uses the physical layer. Applications at both ends of the transmission do not need to support the same LAN protocol from the IEEE 802.X suite, or protocols up to OSI level 3 within the same architecture, but they do need to have the same protocol from the fourth through seventh layers of the OSIRM (or at least the intelligence at the user end to provide the gateway functionality, if needed).

Routers use their own internetworking protocol suite. Through the use of routing tables as shown in Figure 5.29, and routing protocols such as OSPF, routers retain artificial intelligence, called "dynamic knowledge", of the entire network. These routing protocols can discover network topology changes and provide rerouting based upon dynamic routing tables. Routers can limit the number of hop counts by their intelligent routing protocols. Routers employ large addressing schemes typically up to 4 bytes worth of addresses in a logical network (or more with Novell IPX or OSI CLNP). Routers also support large packet sizes. For example, frame relay uses a maximum packet size of around 8000 bytes. Internal bus speeds are also much higher, typically in excess of a gigabit per second. The other major advantage of routers is their ability to perform these functions primarily through the use of software, which makes future revision and support for upgrades much easier.

Routers use routing protocols to route packets from node to node based on the packet-defined protocol information including least-cost routing, minimum delay, minimum distance, and least-congestion conditions. Multiprotocol routers provide support for multiple protocols simultaneously. Figure 5.30 illustrates the range of interfaces and scope of routing. Routers are often connected by real or virtual circuits. Routers have very sophisticated software, and now are being delivered with special-purpose firmware and hardware to increase packet-routing throughput. Current routers can forward in excess of 200,000 IP packets per second.

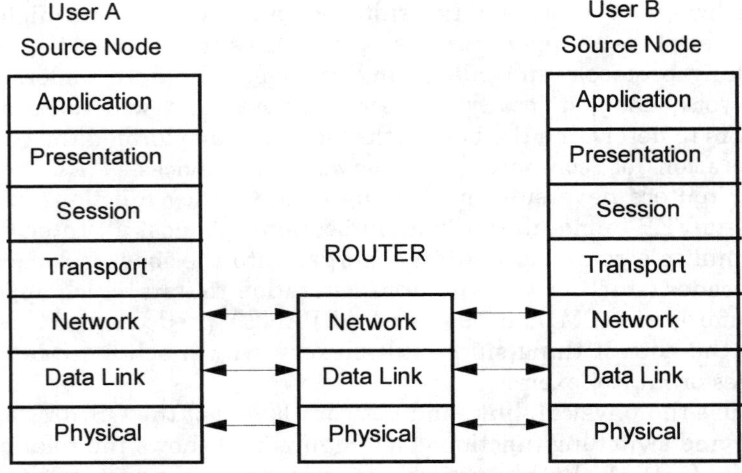

Figure 5.28 Router Communications via the OSIRM

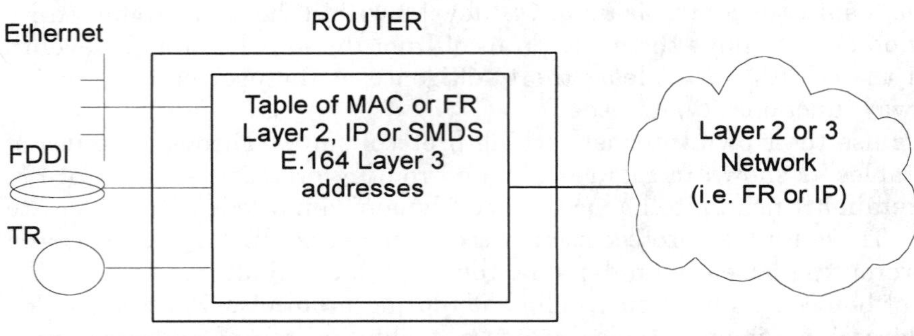

Figure 5.29 Router Functions

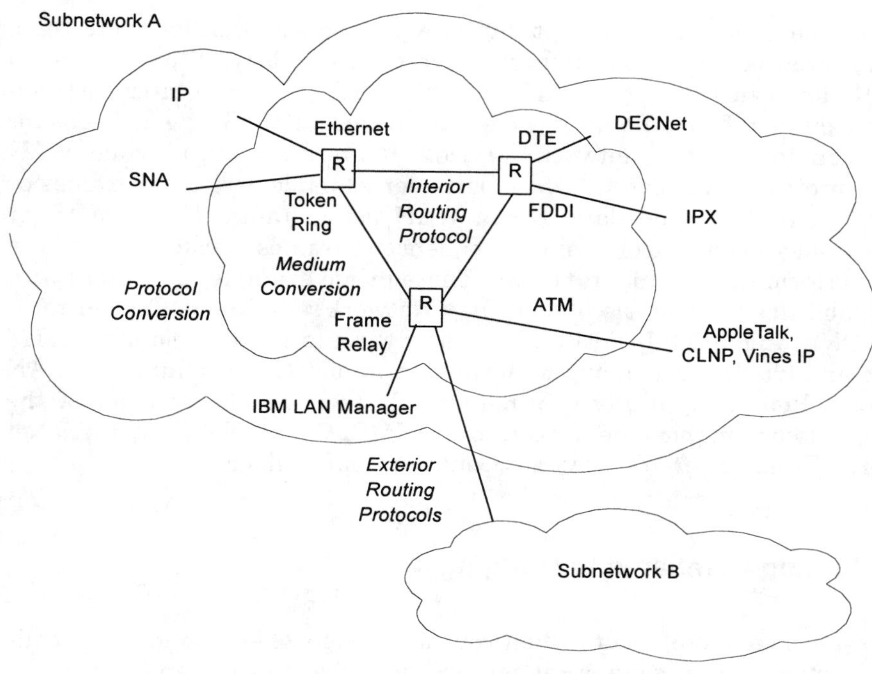

Figure 5.30 Routing Interfaces, Functions, and Architecture

Routers automatically discover the addresses of devices connected to a network of routers. They use an interior routing protocol, and to a network of networks using an exterior routing protocol. Static routing where the router is manually configured is also possible and not uncommon. Indeed, even the naming of networks as subnetworks of a larger network has proven to be a very scalable concept. Notice that the term *network* can be anything from a piece of cable that forms a LAN segment to many devices internetworked across a large geographic area that are managed by a single system and share a common addressing scheme. Packets are routed based upon the destination address, sometimes using the source address as well, or even an end-to-end route specification. Routers connect dissimilar protocols by way of routing and data protocol conversion. Routers can handle both connection-oriented and connectionless network services. Routers also interconnect dissimilar media via media conversion. Routers also continually monitor the state of the links that interconnect routers in a network, or the links with other networks through a variety of routing protocols, such as the Routing Information Protocol (RIP), the Border Gateway Protocol (BGP), or the Open Shortest Path First (OSPF) routing protocol. Each of these protocols are covered in detail later. Through these protocols, routers can discover network topology changes and provide dynamic rerouting.

As access devices, routers accept multiple protocols and either route them to another local port on the router, or convert them to a WAN protocol, such as TCP/IP, for transfer over a WAN link. When doing so, the router encapsulates, for example, IP traffic into frame relay frames, SMDS, or ATM cells for transmission to a public network service. Routers can also switch WAN transport protocols between interface ports, for example, switching frames or cells. When routers send data over a WAN using frame relay, SMDS, or ATM, they may need to look inside a sequence of frames, packets, or cells in order to perform the routing function. Three prime examples of routers with these capabilities are the Cisco 7000, Bay Network's Backbone Concentrator Node (BCN), and 3COM NetBuilder. Many routers today support ATM interface and trunk cards, along with some form of ATM switching and LAN emulation. Routers typically are manageable through one or more of the following network management protocols: SNMP, CMIP, NetView, LAN Net Manager, DEC MOP, or Windows PC Configuration Builder.

5.5.7 Routing Compared to Bridging

A great sage once wrote, "route when you can, bridge when you must". While routing is much more complex, it is also more feature-rich and has many advantages over bridging. Routers provide a level of congestion control not present in bridges, thus allowing the router to *dynamically* reroute traffic over, for example, the least-cost path. Routers reduce broadcast storm danger by providing segmentation capability within the network. Thus, the network designer can build a hierarchical addressing scheme and design smart routing tables, which operate somewhat similar to the filtering capabilities of bridges, but with the additional flexibility to define virtual network subsets within a larger network definition. Routers differ from bridges in that they provide protocol translation between users at the link level, while bridges just pass information in a store-and-forward mode between devices of similar protocol structure. Greater detail will be forthcoming when we discuss router access network design. Routers that utilize IP routing schemes can solve packet-fragmentation problems caused by technologies such as X.25 and FDDI. Packet fragmentation is necessary whenever two media types with different size packets are used. Routers have the ability to translate between MAC layers. Unlike bridges, routers can be isolated and routed around when network problems exist. Routers contain a level of investment protection over less intelligent devices.

However, there are also a few disadvantages to routers. Routing algorithms, discussed in great detail later, typically require more system memory resources than bridges and are very complex to design and manage. Modern routing algorithms and implementations (i.e., IS-IS, OSPF, and BGP) are comparable to bridging in the amount of bandwidth overhead. This is because of the additional intelligence needed in the routing protocols and the various congestion-control techniques implemented.

Many router vendors have implemented multiple processors within the network interface card and faster platforms and processors (such as RISC machines) to eliminate throughput problems caused by increased traffic loads of routing protocols. Table 5.1 shows a comparison of bridge and router uses and capabilities.

TABLE 5.1 Bridging to Routing Comparison

Functionality	Bridging	Routing
Data sources	One source and destination	Multiple sources and destinations
Network addressing	No	Yes
Packet handling	Pass packet transparently	Interpret packet
Forward packets	Out bridge	Specific destination
Global network intelligence	None	Knows status of all devices
Priority schemes	No	Yes
Security	Based on isolating	Based on routing protocol

It is a good idea to *bridge* when you need less overhead, have the same LAN media type across the entire network, have a small centralized LAN with a simple topology, or need to transport protocols that cannot be routed, such as NetBIOS and DEC LAT. Spanning trees allow for response to topology changes, but they are slower than modern routing protocols.

Routing should be performed when you want to route traffic based upon network parameters like least-cost route, have multiple MAC protocol environments, have large, dynamic networks with complex topologies, want dynamic routing around failed links over paths that run in parallel, or have network and subnetwork addressing requirements.

At present, Cisco still holds the largest share (over half) of the router market. In fact, most of the routers on the Internet backbone are Cisco. Every major router vendor supports bridging and routing capabilities. Even high-end multiplexer vendors are providing bridge and router capability in their products. Prices of routers have dropped, and many providers offer low-end remote access products that have a subset of protocol and memory resources from their larger counterparts. In fact, low end small office and home office (SOHO) routers can be purchased for less than a thousand dollars today.

Many bridging and routing functions have been built into workstations, PCs, and servers. While this offers the cost and management advantages of using only a single device, users should be aware of product support, scale, upgrade, and manageability limitations. Choose the right device that will grow with your network. Purchase a full router rather than a bridge – you may not need routing today, but as your network grows you can upgrade without having to replace the device. It may be less expensive in the long run to purchase a router with port expansion rather than taking the network down and installing a larger or more feature-rich router later. Port sizing and traffic growth patterns will typically dictate the size of the router.

5.5.8 Brouters

The term *brouter* is a conflate word formed by *bridge* and *router*. Brouters perform the functions of both bridges and routers, that is, they have the ability to route some protocols and bridge others. Some protocols need to be bridged (such as DEC LAT and IBM NetBIOS) rather than routed. Brouters were developed from the need to expand single-port bridges to multiple ports to support IBM Source Routing Protocol and Source Routing Transparent Protocol. The routing done by brouters is transparent to both the network-layer protocols and end stations, and is accomplished in the MAC address. Thus, brouters do not look at the network-level address. Rather they route based on the MAC header. Router logical functionality is similar to that of bridges and routers as shown in previous figures. The term brouter is rarely used anymore, and the more common form is in remote access routers that only require a subset of bridging and routing.

5.5.9 Switches

There are four general classes of switches. Work-group or local switches switch traffic within a work group, such as between workstations or local LANs. Enterprise switches connect multiple departments or work groups. Edge switches serve as access or entry switches to a public data service. Carrier backbone (CO) switches act as high-speed interconnects for edge switches. Figure 5.31 shows these four types of switches.

Usually a private switched network is connected to one or more public switched networks. Switches are connection-oriented devices. Users interface to switches and communicate the connection request information via a user-to-network interface (UNI) signaling protocol. Between switches an interswitch protocol may be used. Networks are interconnected via a more complex network-to-network interface (NNI) signaling protocol. Signaling functions may be emulated by network management protocols where individual cross-connects are made. These switching fundamentals are illustrated in Figure 5.32.

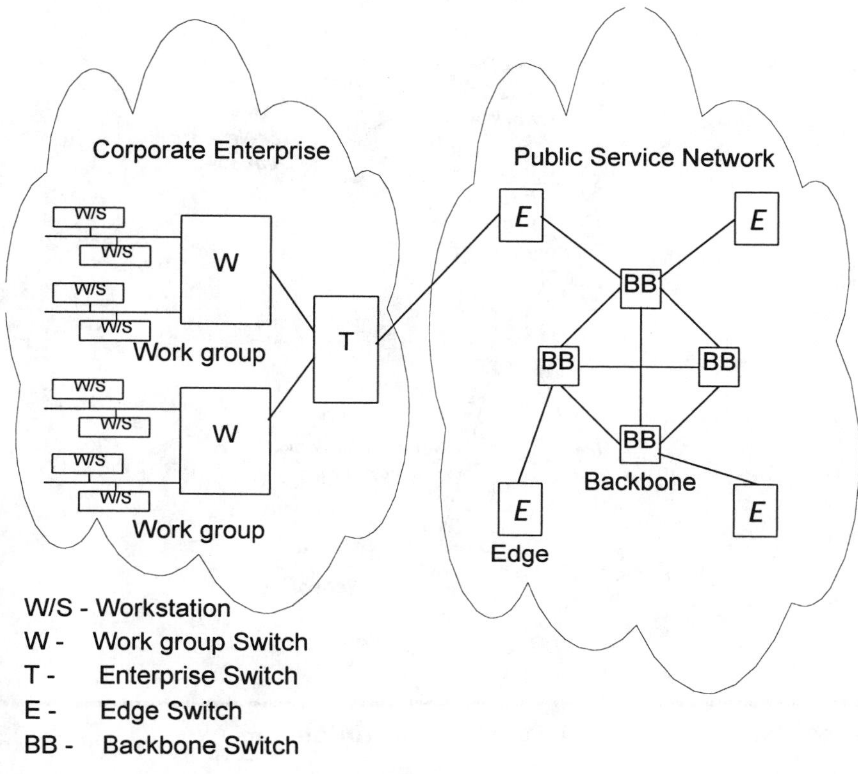

Figure 5.31 Switching Interfaces, Functions, and Architecture

There is much confusion as to what layers of the OSIRM are used when switching. There are basically two types of switches. Layer 2 switches are commonly referred to as LAN switches, and switch frames typically at the MAC layer. Hybrid layer 2-3 switches are used when some form of packet, frame, or cell switching is being used, such as when routing IP or performing true ATM switching. Sometimes the function of the switch and other devices like routing will merge. For example, there is a push to place routing within ATM switches, as they can provide a better quality of service through protocol features specific to ATM. But nothing is free and there is a trade-off – the virtual circuits (VCs) used in ATM are expensive network resources. With routing that uses quality of services, each router must maintain the state of every other switch in the network. The same is true for ATM switches that include routing and maintain quality of service. More on ATM switching will be covered in later chapters, and switching methods are covered in detail in Chapter 6. As you can see, once you have mastered the basic principles of networking, they will appear again and again – in technologies not yet invented.

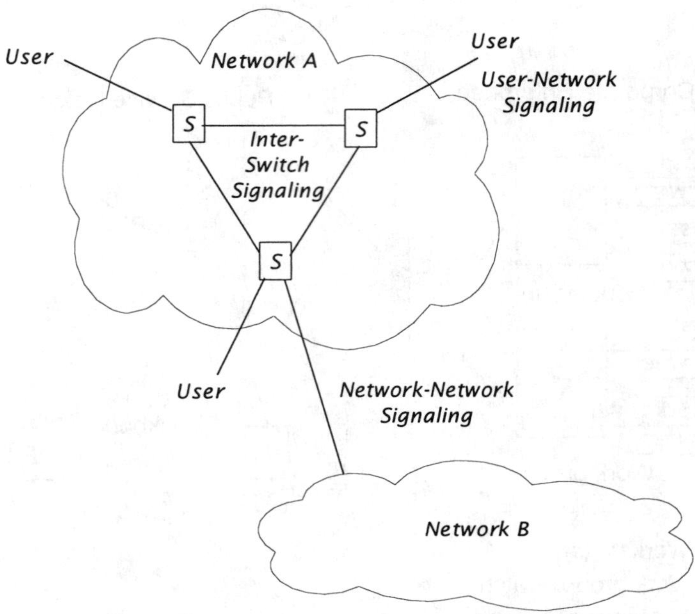

Figure 5.32 Switching Interfaces, Functions, and Architecture

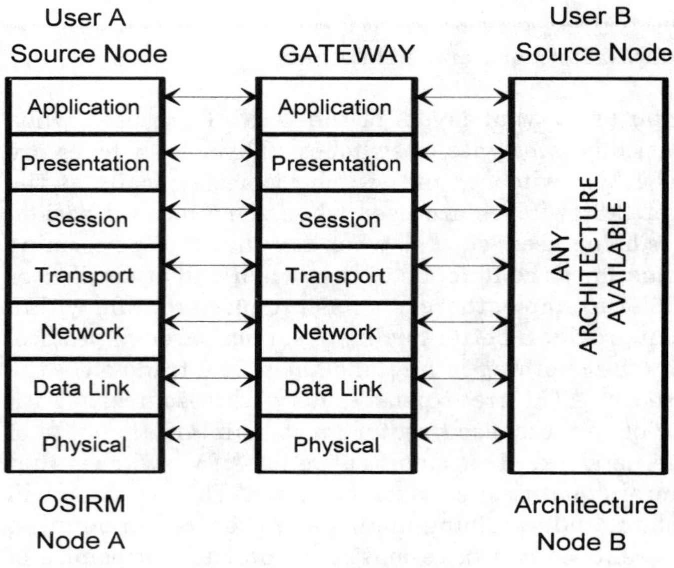

Figure 5.33 Gateway Communications via the OSIRM

5.5.10 Gateways

Gateways provide all of the inter-connectivity provided by routers and bridges; but, in addition, they furnish connectivity and conversion between the seven layers of the OSIRM as well as other proprietary protocols. Some applications use priority schemes not consistent between the OSI layers and proprietary protocol structures. Gateways are often application specific and, because of their complex protocol conversions, often slower than bridges and routers.

One example of a gateway function is interfacing a device using SNA with a device using the OSI protocol stack. The gateway will convert from SNA to an OSI protocol structure (as well as the reverse conversion from OSI to SNA). Thus, the gateway's main functionality resides in its role of protocol translator for architectures such as SNA, DECnet, Internet TCP/IP, and OSI. It can also translate between IEEE 802.X architectures such as Ethernet to Token Ring LANs and vice versa. If protocol functionality is needed in excess of that found in routers, then the gateway is the device of choice. Gateways can reside within workstations or servers, minicomputers, and mainframes, and are considerably more expensive than routers. Some routers have limited built-in gateway functionality. Figure 5.33 portrays the same two users as the last example, this time connected via a gateway. This figure also shows the relationship of gateways to the OSIRM. Both users may have different protocol stacks in any of the seven levels with both OSI and non-OSI protocol architectures.

There are three major disadvantages of gateways: low throughput during peak traffic conditions, user-to-gateway priority handling, and store-and-forward characteristics. During periods of peak traffic, a gateway may become the networks main congestion point, having to spend the majority of its time translating between many protocol suites. Gateways are often store-and-forward devices, forwarding only the information requested by the destination node. In spite of these drawbacks, and the high expense of gateways, there is a growing need for their functionality. As users transition toward the OSI industry standards, gateways will fill an important niche for many years to come in uniting disparate protocols.

5.5.11 From Bridges to Routers to Hubs

Since the last edition of this book, routers have predominated within most major data inter-networks. Bridge networks, on all but large SNA shops, are vanishing in lieu of homogeneous router-based networks. Switching hubs are also playing a key role in this shift, as they aggregate many LAN segments much more cost effectively and they provide greater flexibility. This change is pushing the routing function *further toward the WAN*. This is an important trend to understand.

Many personal computer manufacturers are building hardware and software to perform bridging and routing functions. Expansion boards plugging into the workstation bus may be less expensive than a standalone unit, but usually at the sacrifice of throughput or feature and functions. Personal computer architectures cannot compete with routers that have internal bus speeds into the gigabit ranges, and their processors cannot handle the hundreds of thousands of packets per second required by standalone models with packet-processing speeds of almost 1 million packets per second. For the ad hoc user, though, PC-based bridging or routing functionality may prove most cost-effective. Software can also be implemented on UNIX-based computers to perform bridging and routing, but the same problems and limitations are encountered. Advances in processor and back-plane bus speeds, hardware architectures, and software coding continue to push the envelope on router capabilities and speeds.

Network management for these devices is being accomplished through proprietary platforms with Simple Network Management Protocol (SNMP) support for monitoring. Most vendors provide SNMP agents in their software base, realizing that this management protocol has become the network management *de facto* standard of choice. Because of its simplicity, SNMP is one of the only standards that enables multiple vendors and hardware platforms to communicate through one network-management platform. The network design engineer must review all user network-management requirements before making a decision, because additional proprietary platform support may be required. Each vendor usually implements its own proprietary element management system.

5.5.12 The PBX

For years, the Private Branch eXchange (PBX) is the key device that has separated the voice and data world. With the advent of ATM technology, users, vendors, and carriers are adopting an ATM switching approach to PBXs. PBXs provide automatic setup of circuits between telephone sets today, which most current ATM switches do not plan to do. Traditional PBX call processing and call control are slowly being built into ATM switching architectures. The PBX vendors do not see this happening, in fact they see the opposite – ATM-ready PBX products replacing ATM LAN switches. One likely scenario will be a coexistence of ATM-ready PBXs and ATM switches with call-processing and control capability in both the campus and wide area. ATM interfaces are now available for PBXs. One example is the Siemens-ROLM product. The more probable scenario is that high-end ATM network modules with front-end PBXs to the WAN, and the feature-rich call processing software in the PBX will continue to handle the traditional voice traffic requirements.

5.6 REVIEW

In data communications, various topology, circuit types, transmission, and hardware types have evolved. The main topologies include point-to-point, multipoint, star, ring, and mesh. The three types of signal transfer are: simplex, half duplex, and duplex, as well as asynchronous and synchronous data transfer. The chapter concluded with a detailed discussion of each major type of network communications hardware and some layer 2 and 3 switching devices such as bridges, routers, and gateways, leaving a detailed discussion of multiplexers and switches to the next chapter.

Chapter

6

Multiplexing and Switching Technologies – An Overview

This chapter provides an overview of multiplexer and switching technologies. Multiplexing takes many forms and makes up the core of many advanced data networks. Multiplexing techniques based on Space Division (SDM), Frequency Division (FDM), Time Division (TDM), and Addressing are covered in detail. We will then review the major types of multiplexers on the market and assist the reader with selection. Next, point-to-point, point-to-multipoint, space division, time division, address, and frequency or wavelength switching are covered, along with the hybrid matrix switch. Each section also reviews each specific type of switch. Next, we cover circuit switching and its implementation in Digital Cross-Connect (DXC) devices. Finally, the origins and genealogy of packet switching are covered, focusing on the progressive introduction of X.25, frame relay, fast packet, and Asynchronous Transfer Mode (ATM) switching. Frame relay and ATM will be discussed in detail in subsequent chapters. This chapter serves as the reference point for comparing multiplexing and switching technologies.

6.1 MULTIPLEXING TECHNOLOGIES

There is a close relationship between multiplexing and switching. Multiplexing defines the means by which multiple streams of information from multiple users share a common physical transmission medium, all of which may require some or all of the bandwidth at any given time. This bandwidth sharing on the access reduces access costs for a user to get to the network, whether it is a dedicated digital network comprising private lines, a switched service, or a genuine switched network. Some multiplexing techniques assign fixed bandwidth to each user, while others use statistical multiplexing methods that make more efficient use of the transmission facilities that interface to the network. Multiplexing positions can be defined by space, time, frequency, or address.

Switching takes multiple instances of a physical transmission medium, each containing multiplexed information streams, and rearranges the information streams between the input and output of the switch. In other words, information from a particular physical link in a specific multiplex position is switched to another output physical link, usually in a different multiplex position.

This section first covers multiplexing methods, and then covers point-to-point and point-to-multipoint switching functions.

6.1.1 Multiplexer Defined

A *multiplexer* is essentially a very simple switch composed of a multiplexing function and a demultiplexing function, as illustrated in Figure 6.1. The multiplexing function shares many inputs to a single output. The demultiplexing function has one input which must be distributed to many outputs. The multiplexing and demultiplexing functions can be implemented by any of the generic switching functions described in the previous section. Usually a method from the same class is used for both the multiplexing and demultiplexing functions, so that the multiplexing method used on each of the interfaces is symmetric in each direction. The overall speed or capacity on the access side interfaces is generally less than that on the trunk side in most multiplexers. For example, this often corresponds to different levels in the Time Division Multiplex (TDM) hierarchy, an example that we will cover in some detail.

The geometric symbol with the small end on the side of the single output (called the trunk side) and the large end on the side with multiple interfaces (called the access side) frequently denotes a multiplexer in block diagrams. It graphically illustrates the many-to-one relationship from the large side to the small side, and the one-to-many relationship from the small side to the large side.

Multiplexing techniques can be used to share a physical medium between multiple users at two different sites over a private line with each pair of users requiring some or all of the bandwidth at any given time. Some multiplexing techniques statistically assign fixed bandwidth to each user. Other multiplexing methods statistically assign bandwidth to users based upon demand to make more efficient use of the transmission facilities that interface to the network. TDM is often used to reduce the effective cost of a private access line or international private line by combining multiple lower-speed users over a single higher-speed facility.

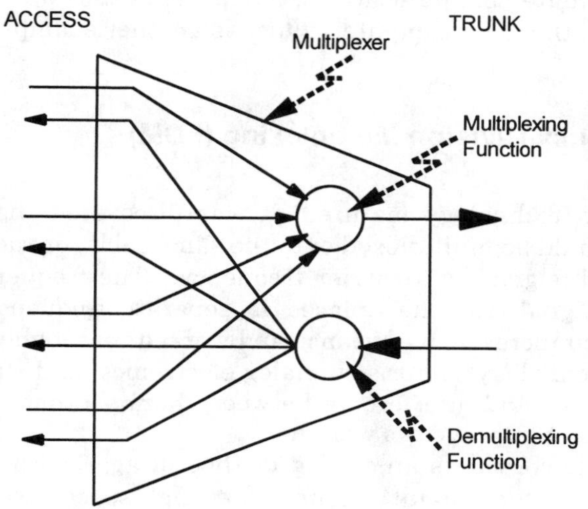

Figure 6.1 Switching Model of a Multiplexer

6.1.2 Multiplexing Methods Summarized

There are four basic multiplexing methods covered: space, frequency, time, and address. This is also the historical order in which these developed in data communications. Space, frequency, and time multiplexing all occur at the physical layer of the OSI reference model. Address switching occurs at higher layers.

6.1.3 Space Division Multiplexing (SDM)

SDM essentially reduces to the concept of cable management. This can be facilitated by mechanical patch panels, or, increasingly more so, by optical and electronic patch panels. To a large extent, SDM is falling out of favor, and is being replaced by space division switching or other types of multiplexing.

An example of SDM is seen where multiple cables interconnect equipment. In other words, *space division* means physically separate. The original telephone networks, where a pair of wires connected everyone who wished to communicate, is an example of the first use of SDM. The exclusive use of SDM quickly became impractical, as evidenced by old photographs of the sky of major metropolitan cities being blackened by the large number of wire pairs. In early data communications, a separate cable was run from every terminal back to the main computer, which is another example of SDM.

6.1.4 Frequency Division Multiplexing (FDM)

As transmission technology matured, it was discovered that many analog conversations could be multiplexed onto the same cable, or radio spectrum, by modulating each signal by a carrier frequency. The frequency spectrum of the baseband signal was then placed in separate frequency bands. This yielded a marked increase in efficiency and worked reasonably well for analog signals. The technology comprised analog electronics, and suffered problems of noise, distortion, and interference between channels that complicated data communications. Support costs were high.

FDM was widely used as an analog method of aggregating multiple voice channels into larger circuit groups for high-speed transport. FDM multiplexes 12 voice-grade, full-duplex channels into a single 48-kHz bandwidth group by translating each voiceband signal's carrier frequency. These groups are then further multiplexed into a master group comprising 24 groups. Multiple master-group analog voice signals are then transmitted over analog microwave systems. A lower-frequency analog microwave spectrum was used to frequency division multiplex a DS1 digital data stream in a technique called Data Under Voice (DUV). Figure 6.2 shows an example of a frequency division multiplexer servicing ten 2400-bps user data channels and providing a single 56-kbps network trunk.

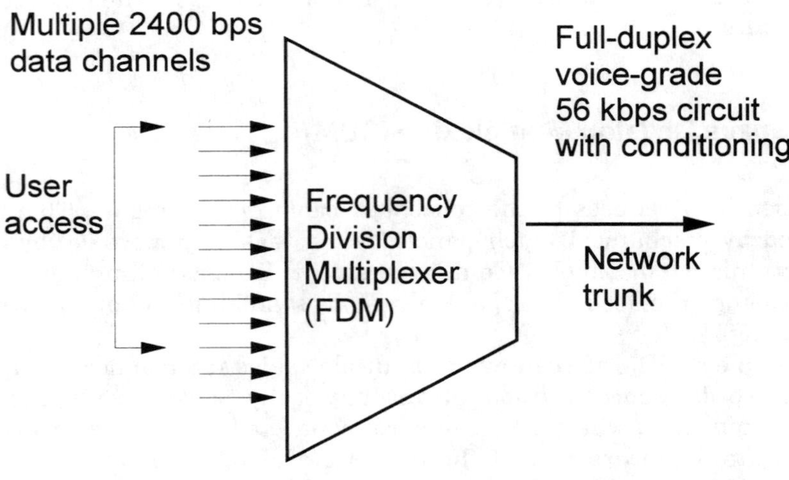

Figure 6.2 Frequency Division Multiplexer

One variation of FDM is Wavelength Division Multiplexing (WDM). WDM on optical fibers is very analogous to FDM in coaxial cable and microwave systems. Optical fiber is *transparent* in two windows centered around wavelengths of 1300 and 1550 nanometers or nm (10^{-9} m), as shown in the plot of loss versus wavelength in Figure 6.3. The total bandwidth in these two windows exceeds 30,000 GHz. One bps per hertz (Hz) would result in a bandwidth of over 30 *trillion* bps per fiber!

The carrier frequency at the center of the 1300-nm window is 180 GHz and it is 125 GHz in the 1550-nm window. The sharp attenuation at 1400 nm is due to residual amounts of water (an OH radical) still present in the glass. Continuing improvements in optical-fiber manufacturing will likely make even more optical bandwidth accessible in the future. Commercial long-haul, fiber-optic transmission is now using two wavelengths per fiber, in what is called wideband WDM, in each of these windows. Research and prototype implementations of narrowband WDM will allow a much larger number of optical carriers to share a fiber which is nearing commercial deployment.

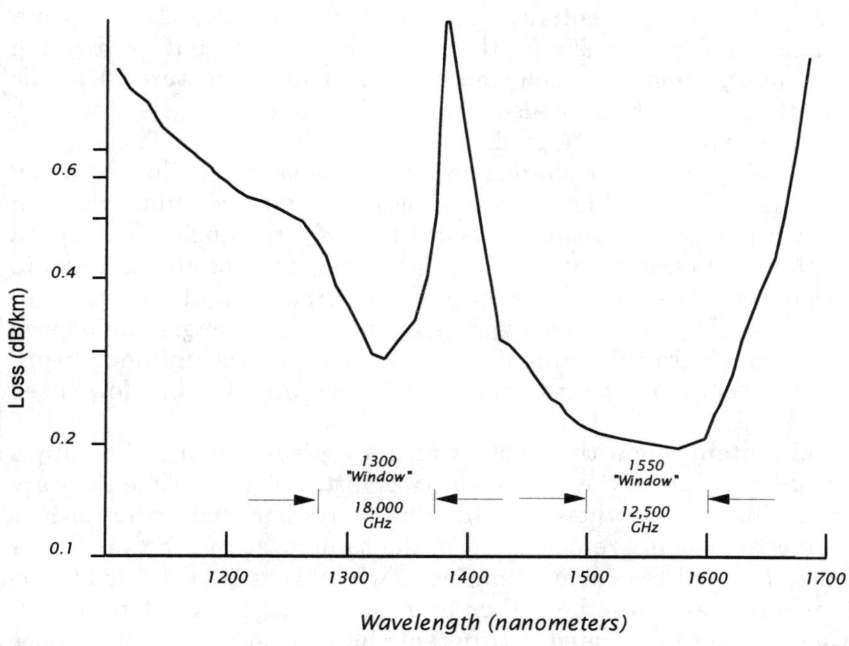

Figure 6.3 Optical Fiber Transfer Characteristic

6.1.5 Time Division Multiplexing (TDM)

TDM was originally developed in the public telephone network in the 1950s to eliminate FDM filtering and noise problems when many signals were multiplexed onto the same transmission medium. Later, there was a need to increase the multiplexing efficiency in crowded bundles of cables in large cities. This technique made use of the emerging solid-state electronics, and was entirely digital. Analog information was first converted to digital information prior to transmission. The initial cost of this technique was high, but was less than the cost of replacing existing cables or digging larger tunnels. In the early 1980s, TDM networks using smart multiplexers began to appear in some private data networks, forming the primary method to share costly data transmission facilities among multiple users.

In the last decade, TDM has matured and become the prevalent multiplexing method in most modern telecommunication networks. It is now taken for granted that every voice conversation is converted to digital data, transmitted an arbitrary distance, and then converted back to an audible signal. The consequence is that the quality of a voice call carried by digital TDM is now essentially independent of distance. Data communications is more sensitive than digitized voice, but is reaping tremendous benefits from the deployment of TDM infrastructure in public networks. In theory a TDM may also be applied to analog signals; however, this application was never widely used.

TDM allows multiple users to share a digital transmission medium by using preallocated time slots. Figure 6.4 shows a standard time division multiplexer with eight low-speed users sharing a single high-speed transmission line to a remote multiplexer. TDM assigns a specific time slot to each low-speed channel — in this case: slots one through eight. These eight synchronous time slots are then aggregated to form a single high-speed synchronous channel. In this example, five users are accessing the network with 9600 bps synchronous data circuits and three are 2400 bps low-speed users.

One channel contains eight time slots, which are preallocated and occupy a predetermined bit layout of the combined transmitted signal. Time slots are dedicated to a single user, whether data is being transmitted or the user is idle. The same time slots are dedicated to the same user in the same order for every frame transmitted. Thus, time slot 2 will always be dedicated to the same user, regardless of whether other users are transmitting data or not. Different time slots are dedicated to different channel sources, such as voice channels, data, or video. Multiplexer inputs typically include and can carry simultaneously asynchronous and synchronous data, digitized voice, and even video. After the T1 signal is transmitted across the network, it is received at the destination multiplexer node. Each channel is then demultiplexed at the receiving node. All transmissions through multiplexers are point-to-point.

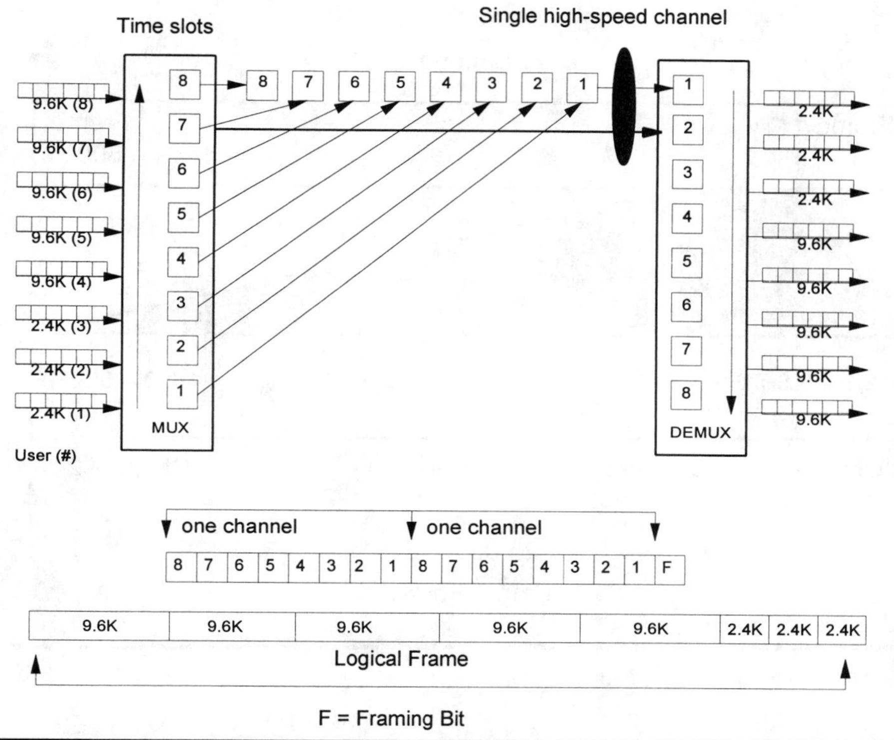

Figure 6.4 Time Division Multiplexer

A single T1 circuit can be configured for 24 to 196 allocated channels. The standard T1 1.544 Mbps data channel contains 8000 frames per second. Each frame is transmitted every 125 μs for a total of 24 multiplexed voice grade channels. Each frame contains eight bits for each of the 24 channels ($8 \times 24 = 192$) plus one framing bit (1) for a total of 193 bits per frame. Each channel uses 64,000 bps. The total T1 transmission can be seen in Figure 6.5, along with the frame format.

International circuits often use the CCITT E1 Conference on European Post and Telegraph (CEPT) standard, which supports a data transmission rate of 2.048 Mbps. Each E1 data channel contains frames with 30 or 32 multiplexed voice-grade channels. This allows 1.920M bps for voice channels and 128-kbps for framing and synchronization. Multiplexers often use the DSX-1 standard for a physical interface with D4/ESF framing, while the CEPT/G.703 physical interface standard is commonly used for the E1 interface. For a user requiring access speeds from DS0 to T1 access, the cost break-even point based upon tariff structures is typically five to seven DS0s where going to a 24-channel T1 is cost justified.

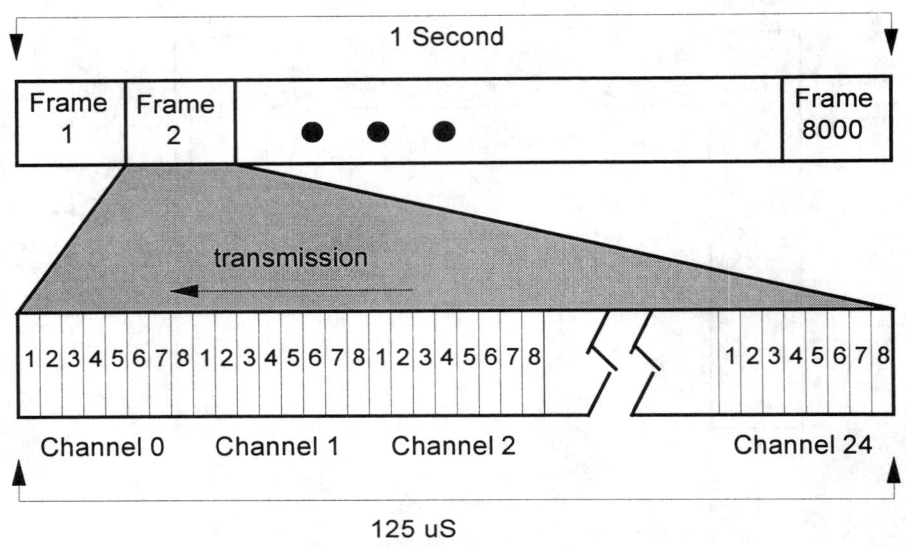

Figure 6.5 T1 Transmission Frame Format

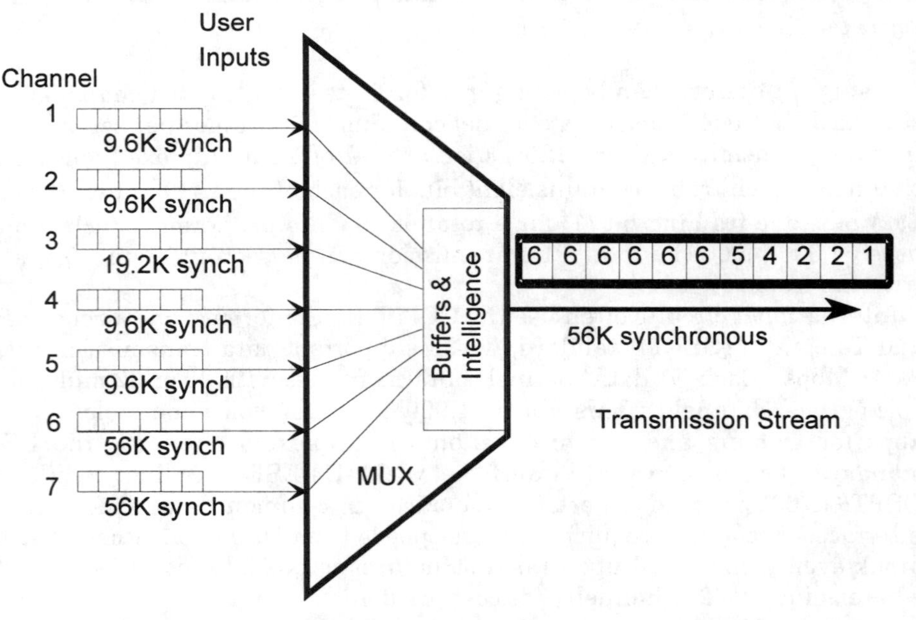

Figure 6.6 Statistical Multiplexer

6.1.6 Address or Label Multiplexing

Address, or label, multiplexing was first invented in the era of poor-quality FDM analog transmission. A more common name for address multiplexing is Asynchronous Time Division Multiplexing (ATDM). Transmission was expensive, and there was a need to share it among many data users. Each "packet" of information was prefixed by an address that each node interpreted. Each node decided whether the packet was received correctly, and if not, arranged to have it resent by the prior node until it was received correctly. SNA, DECNET, and X.25 are early examples of address multiplexing and switching. More recent examples are frame relay and ATM. The remainder of this book covers the address multiplexing method in great detail.

A widely used example of address multiplexing is found in statistical multiplexers. Statistical multiplexing, also called Statistical Time Division Multiplexing (STDM), or Asynchronous Time Division Multiplexing (ATDM), operates similarly to TDM, except that it dynamically assigns time slots only to users who need data transmission. Efficiencies of up to 4:1 are gained for voice transmission by utilizing available time slots, rather than wasting them on users who are not speaking. Higher or lower statistical multiplex gains can be obtained for data traffic depending upon the burstiness (peak-to-average statistics) of the data traffic. The net effect is an increase in overall throughput for users since time slots are not "reserved" or dedicated to individual users — thus dynamic allocation of bandwidth achieves higher throughput. Figure 6.6 shows a statistical multiplexer which takes multiple low-speed synchronous (could also be asynchronous) user inputs for aggregation into a single 56-kbps synchronous bit stream for transmission. The methods used to multiplex the various channels include: bit-, character-, block-, and message-oriented multiplexing, each requiring buffering, and more overhead and intelligence than basic time division multiplexing.

Figure 6.6 shows an excerpt from a statistical multiplexed data stream. In a statistical multiplexer, the output bandwidth is a 1:N output-to-input ratio less than the aggregate input bandwidth. This is done on purpose, assuming that not all input channels will be transmitting at the same time when each channel is sampled for transmission. Thus, the output synchronous data stream allocates bandwidth only to users who require it, and does not waste time slots by dedicating bandwidth to users who do not require it. Note in the example that channels 1, 2, 4, 5, and 6 are transmitting, and together utilizing the 128-kbps trunk bandwidth. Using the same example, if channel 3 were to also transmit data at the same instant, the total transmission requirements would exceed the available circuit transmission speed out of the multiplexer, and buffers would begin to store the information until space on the transmission circuit could become available.

One type of block-oriented multiplexer is the concentrator. Concentrators transmit blocks of information for each user as needed, adding an address to each block to identify the user and in most instances providing store-and-forward capabilities. This mode of transmission is similar to asynchronous block transmission, and multiplexers utilizing this technique are called Asynchronous Time Division Multiplexers (ATDMs). This form of statistical multiplexing is similar to packet switching but operates over a single dedicated circuit between two points, as opposed to packet switching, which has multiple paths and destinations. The primary difference between concentration and multiplexing is that concentrators have additional intelligence to understand the contents of the data being passed and can route the information streams based upon the data within them. A study of ATDM will be made when we study ATM.

Another type of statistical multiplexing is Statistical Packet Multiplexing (SPM). Statistical packet multiplexers combine the packet switching of X.25 with the statistical multiplexing of STDM. SPM operates similarly to STDM in that it still cannot effectively transmit delay-sensitive information such as voice and video. There is still the overhead delay of guaranteed delivery of packets, but efficiencies are gained in dynamic bandwidth allocation and sharing by assigning active bandwidth to the channels which need bandwidth at any given time. Each multiplexer groups the user data into packets passed through the network, multiplexer to multiplexer, similar to packet switching.

6.2 TYPES OF MULTIPLEXERS

Multiplexing is the process of aggregating multiple low-speed channels into a single high-data-rate channel. There are four major types of multiplexers used in data network designs: the access multiplexer (or channel bank), the network multiplexer, the drop-and-insert multiplexer, and the aggregator multiplexer. Capabilities and benefits of each type will be discussed. These multiplexers often contain the capability for demultiplexing. Demultiplexing is the segmenting of a single high-rate channel into multiple low-speed channels.

Most forms of multiplexing are protocol-transparent and protocol-independent. The user interface for multiplexing is at the physical layer, and all layer 2 through layer 7 protocols pass transparently to the network. Figure 6.7 shows the protocol stack operation of a multiplexer network. This provides for fast end-to-end transmission times since there is no need to interpret the data during transport. All channels on a multiplexer are either configured to take up certain time slots in the TDM channel or dynamically allocated to the available bandwidth. Either way, the bandwidth between the source and destination node is a "fixed" transmission speed. Any changes to the bandwidth allocation must be performed to both the source and destination nodes. We will see later how frame relay eliminates these restrictions.

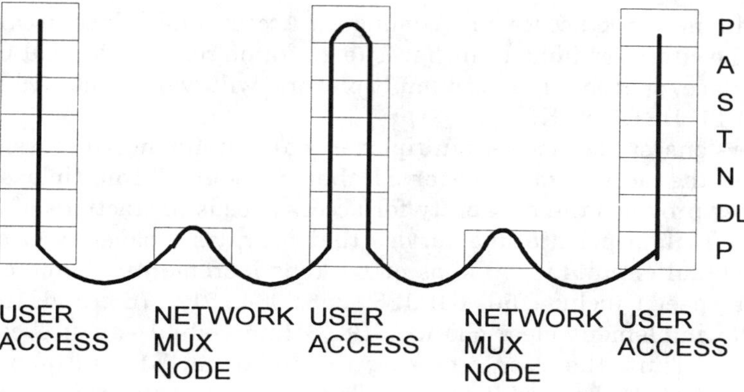

Figure 6.7 Protocol Stack Operation of the Multiplexer via the OSIRM

6.2.1 Access or Channel Bank Multiplexers

Access, or channel bank multiplexers, provide the first level of user access to the multiplexer network. These devices typically reside on the user or customer premises and are usually referred to as Customer Premises Equipment (CPE) devices. These CPE devices are locally controlled and configured. Intelligent T1 access multiplexers are often used to combine voice and data signals into one high-speed data channel. These multiplexers can provide network access for a variety of user asynchronous and synchronous, low- and high-speed inputs including:

- Terminal
- Data telephone
- Compressed voice and video
- Front-End Processor (FEP)
- Personal computer
- Host computer
- Remote peripheral
- Analog and digital Private Branch Exchange (PBX)
- Low-speed video
- Imaging applications
- Transaction-oriented device
- Local Area Network (LAN)

Access multiplexers usually provide one or more T1 trunks to the next class of larger multiplexers, the backbone multiplexer. Access multiplexers are less expensive and less growth-oriented. They are best suited for static networks where there is little change, rather than dynamic networks where changes in network access are common. Access multiplexers can handle many of the circuit-switched interfaces (e.g., frame relay, X.25, SDLC/HDLC). The interface speeds of access multiplexers will vary and include DS0, fractional T1, DS1, and E1.

Two versions of the access multiplexer warrant further discussion. One version of the access multiplexer is the fractional T1multiplexer. This multiplexer provides the capability for access speeds in fractions of a full T1. Fractional T1 is a private line service that provides a capacity of one to 23 DS0 individual circuits in 56 kbps or 64 kbps increments. Some commonly used FT1 speeds include 56, 64, 128, 256, 384, 512, 768, and 1024 kbps. Users who implement clear-channel B8ZS line coding can use contiguous bandwidth. Thus, the user accessing the fractional T1 multiplexer incurs only the cost of the bandwidth used. This was one of the first steps toward providing bandwidth-on-demand, because the user only pays for a "fraction" of the T1, not the entire T1. Figure 6.8 shows an example of an access Fractional T1 multiplexer, with multiple fractions of T1 speeds for user access into a shared-T1 1.544 Mbps network access circuit.

Another version of the access multiplexer is the SubRate Data Multiplexer (SRDM) shown in Figure 6.9. SRDMs provide multiplexing at the sub-DS0 level, aggregating multiple low-speed channels into a single DS0 channel. SRDM access speeds include 2400, 4800, 9600, and 19,200 bps. Again, the user accessing the SRDM multiplexer incurs only the cost of the bandwidth used. When we discuss frame relay access, a form of SRDM is used called the Frame Relay Access Device (FRAD). Both fractional T1 and SRDM optimize the use of access trunks for multiple low-speed users who, without these devices, would have to purchase a full DS0 or DS1 service even though they are using only a portion of its full bandwidth.

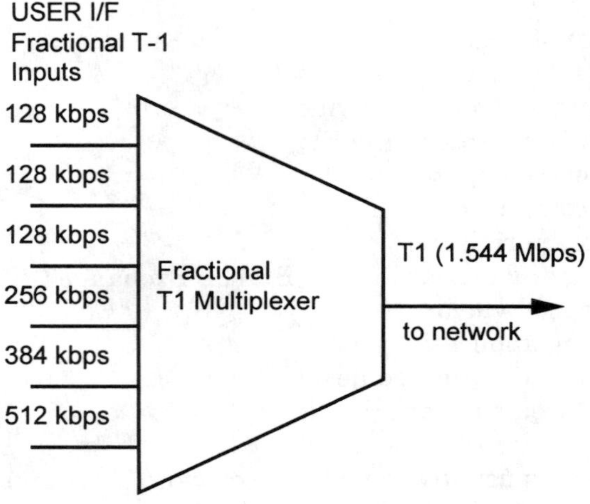

Figure 6.8 Fractional T1 Multiplexer

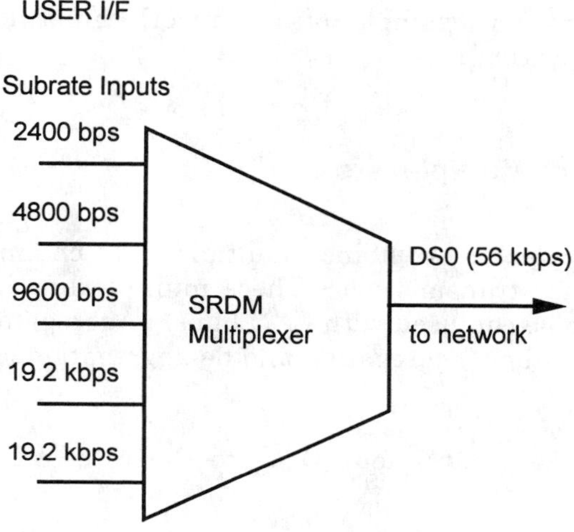

Figure 6.9 SubRate Data Multiplexer (SRDM)

6.2.2 Network Multiplexers

Network multiplexers accept the input data rates (and usually those much higher as well) of access multiplexers, typically supporting T1 on the access side and T3 or higher on the network side. Their trunk capacity is also much larger than access multiplexers, ranging from a dozen user trunks to hundreds, and supporting many more network trunks at higher speeds. Network multiplexers provide the additional functionality of network-management systems, have local and remote provisioning and configuration capability, and contain intelligent functions not found in less-expensive access multiplexers. Private and public data transport network backbones are built using network multiplexers. Network multiplexers also better position the backbone portion of the network for port growth and expansion (i.e., increased access and backbone circuit capacity).

Dynamic reroute capability is an important feature in network multiplexers. The multiplexer dynamic reroute capability can either be performed by predefined "routing tables" residing in software at each node or downloaded from the network management center, or through "routing algorithms", which update the network dynamically during changing network conditions. Algorithm control can also reside at either the individual nodes or at the network-management center. Either way, it is important to fully understand these capabilities before deciding upon a multiplexer vendor.

Figure 6.10 shows an example of a network multiplexer and various multiplexer input possibilities.

6.2.3 Aggregator Multiplexers

Aggregator multiplexers combine multiple T1 channels into higher-bandwidth pipes for transmission. These multiplexers are also sometimes called hubs (not to be confused with LAN hubs). Aggregator multiplexers are labeled based upon their aggregation and de-aggregation rates. These labels include:

M12 Multiplexers. Aggregates four DS1s to the rate of DS2 (or vice versa demultiplex).

M13 Multiplexers. Aggregates 28 DS1s to the rate of DS3 (or demultiplex). This is shown in Figure 6.11.

M23 Multiplexers. Aggregates seven DS2s to the rate of DS3 (or vice versa demultiplex).

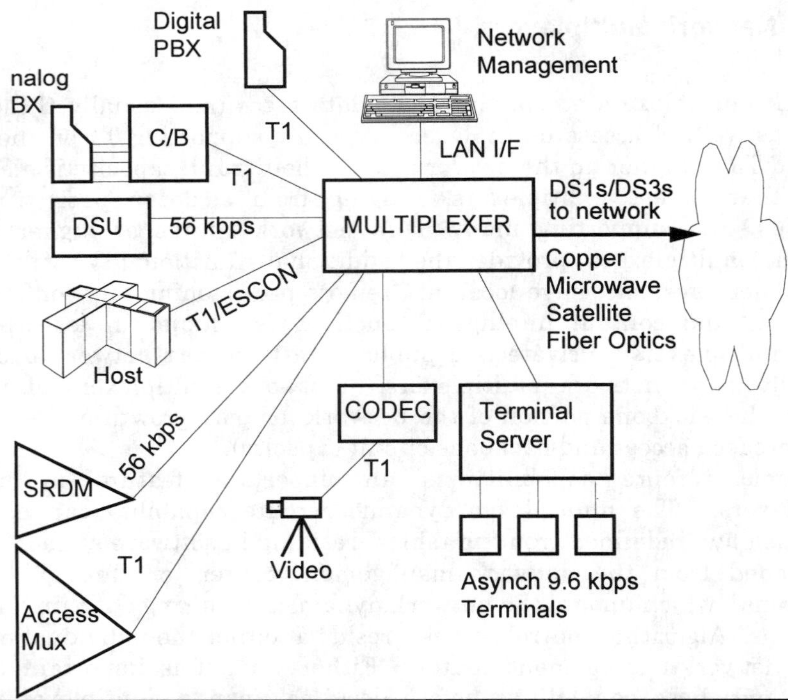

Figure 6.10 Network Multiplexer Example

Figure 6.11 M13 Multiplexer

M22 and M44 Multiplexers. Provides configuration management and rerouting capability of 22 and 44 channels, respectively.

MX3 Multiplexers. Aggregates different combinations of DS1s and DS2s to the rate of DS3 (or vice versa demultiplex).

It is also important to note that synchronization of the aggregate circuits within many of these multiplexers (even as the individual DS1s within the DS3 M13 multiplexer) is not supported by many vendors. This will have a major impact when services depending heavily on channel synchronization (such as Synchronous Optical Network, or SONET) are deployed and the multiplexer needs to be replaced.

Some aggregator multiplexers also offer the capability for switched N × 56/64- kbps services. This provides the user with multiple dial-up DS0 interfaces into a multiplexer, with the user impression of "bandwidth-on-demand" in 56/64 kbps units. Carriers offer this service through the variety of multiplexer devices mentioned above. This switched DS0 service is the most cost-effective method of bandwidth-on-demand using a multiplexer, and is quite powerful when used by a statistical multiplexer. Switched 56 will be covered in detail when circuit switching is discussed. Aggregator multiplexers are slowly being replaced by the drop-and-insert multiplexers and Digital Access Cross Connects (DXC). Both types of hardware are covered in this chapter.

6.2.4 Drop-and-Insert Multiplexers

Drop-and-insert multiplexers are special-purpose multiplexers designed to drop and insert low-speed channels in and out of a high-speed multiplexed channel like a T1. Channel speeds dropped and inserted are typically 56 or 64 kbps. Each DS0 is demultiplexed and remultiplexed for transmission.

Figure 6.12 shows a drop-and-insert multiplexer operation, where two 56-kbps channels (channels 1 and 2) are dropped out and replaced by two new user 56-kbps channels before the total 24 56-kbps channels are multiplexed and retransmitted. Some drop-and-insert multiplexers add circuit switching and network performance monitoring to their list of capabilities.

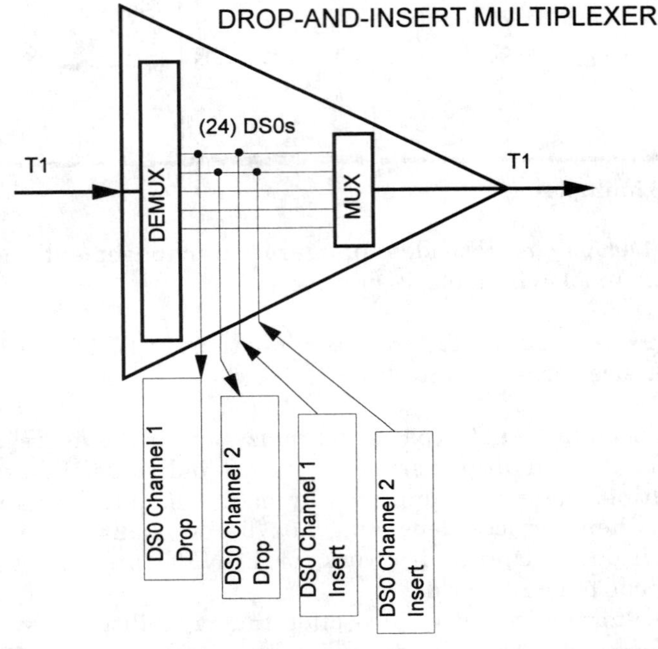

Figure 6.12 Drop-and-Insert Multiplexer Operation

6.2.5 Selection of a Multiplexer

Since many options are available in multiplexers, each requirement must be analyzed to determine which type is the best fit for current and future applications. Some of the major decision criteria for all types of multiplexers are as follows:

- Level of intelligence required
- Speed of access (typically 9600 bps to T1)
- Speed of egress (typically 56-kbps to T3, and possibly SONET)
- Capability of upgrading to LAN/WAN, T3, SONET speeds
- Number of ports or cards per node
- Maximum number of nodes in one logical network
- Compatibility with other CPE
- Virtual network partitioning capabilities
- Protocols and interfaces supported (such as frame relay or LAN)
- Nonproprietary architecture
- Voice quantization schemes supported (PCM 64-kbps, ADPCM 32-kbps)

- Network media interfaces supported (i.e., copper, fiber)
- Physical interface standards supported (RS-232, V.35, ISDN, CCITT G.703)
- Types of framing (D4, ESF, B8ZS)
- Price versus functionality (cost versus feature function)
- Topologies supported (point-to-point, drop-and-insert)
- Network-management and network-diagnostic capabilities (terminal, graphical interface, proprietary or industry standard, SNMP manageable)
- Clocking restoration
- Event reporting
- Amount of circuit bandwidth available after multiplexer proprietary overhead (1.344 Mbps of user data out of 1.544 Mbps)
- Capability of selecting the primary alternate route
- Automatic fault isolation and reroute capabilities
- Call reroute capabilities
- Degree to which the multiplexer offers dynamic bandwidth allocation of all data speeds
- Warranty available

Two major factors exert pressure on multiplex vendors to modify their traditional support of low-speed asynchronous and synchronous traffic. The importance of public network interoperability in network standards and signaling as well as the Digital Cross Connects (DXCs) will be discussed in the next section. Another important factor influencing multiplexer survival is the carrier pricing of switched services such as frame relay and SMDS. If these services are priced low enough, the TDM multiplexers will be forced into the role of local site concentrator and leave the wide area networking to routers and bridges. One example is the requirement of "network-side" frame relay interfaces on multiplexers.

6.2.6 The Future of Multiplexing

The moving target of technology is providing new methods to route and distribute data. Multiplexers have come upon hard times during this decade. Bandwidth requirements are increasing. But, as they increase, so does the demand for more intelligence to manage that bandwidth in an efficient and user-controllable manner. Users no longer just want to aggregate their traffic into a single point-to-point circuit. Distributed, client-server computing and any-to-any communication requirements are driving users to more intelligent devices, such as routers and switching hubs. Multiplexer vendors are trying to keep pace by offering interface cards, additional interface options, and cost reductions, but the intelligent switching and routing vendors are stealing much of the data-transport market from the multiplexer vendors. The only true successes seem to be in the hybrid, multiplexer-switching products market.

Many multiplexer vendors offer LAN and switching protocol access cards for their multiplexer products. Some offer completely separate router hardware that is inter-operable with their existing multiplexer lines. These interface cards and routers provide an access interface of either single or multiple LAN circuits, frame relay channels, or even ATM access. Much more efficient platforms have developed to handle LAN and WAN integration to replace the multiplexers. With LAN/WAN interface speeds increasing in leaps and bounds past the 100 Mbps range, and router vendors selling cost-effective CPE devices to transport these LAN speeds (some even natively) across the WAN, it may not make sense to purchase T1 and T3 multiplexers whose proprietary interfaces are quickly becoming obsolete. Some multiplexer vendors have formed alliances with router and switch vendors to offer integrated solutions, but the real test for the multiplex vendors is to offer this hardware at cost-effective prices compared to router and hub products.

Multiplex vendors continue to modify existing product lines and build alliances to further their aging multiplexer product base. Multiplexers still have limitations compared to their routing and switching competition: slow bus-speed architecture compared with routers, fixed circuit connections as opposed to dynamic switched connectivity, and connection-oriented as opposed to a connectionless service platform. The basic fact is that T1 multiplexers are not well suited for LAN/WAN traffic.

The user must clearly define short- and long-term requirements for varying types of traffic before deciding upon a multiplexer solution. Interface and protocol options must be determined. This decision-making process will be covered later.

6.3 SWITCHING TECHNIQUES

This section covers each of the major point-to-point switching functions and techniques: space, time, address, and frequency. Examples are provided for each, including the hybrid matrix switch. The examples chosen for this section define terminology and illustrate concepts that provide background for material in subsequent chapters.

6.3.1 Point-to-Point Switching Functions

Figure 6.13 illustrates the four basic kinds of point-to-point connection functions that can be performed by a multiplexer or switch.

Space division switching delivers a signal from one physical (i.e., spatial) interface to another physical interface. One example is a copper crosspoint switch.

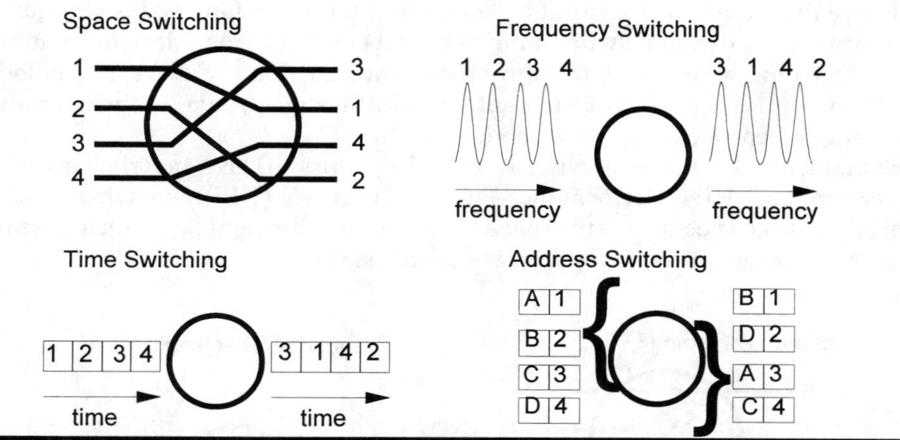

Figure 6.13 Point-to-Point Switching Function Definitions

Time division switching changes the order of time slots within a single spatial data stream, organized by the Time Division Multiplexing (TDM) method.

Address switching changes the address field in data packets, which may be further multiplexed into spatial, time, or frequency signals. This book focuses on this switching method, as applied to packet, frame, and cell switching.

Finally, *frequency* (or wavelength) switching translates signals from one carrier frequency (wavelength) to another. Wavelength Division Multiplexing (WDM) in optical fibers uses this method.

6.3.2 Point-to-Multipoint Switching Functions

The concept of switching is extended from the case of point-to-point to the broadcast, or point-to-multipoint case, as shown in Figure 6.14. A space division broadcast switch replicates a single input signal on two or more outputs. A simple example is a coaxial television signal splitter. FDM broadcast switching replicates the same signal on multiple output carrier frequencies. TDM broadcast switching fills multiple output time slots with the data from the same input. Address broadcast switching fills multiple packets with different addresses with identical information from the same input packet.

6.3.3 Space Division Switching

Figure 6.15 illustrates a simple two-input, two-output crossbar network, using the crosspoint nodal function. An example connection is shown by the boldface lines and control inputs. Notice that a total of four nodes is required. Classical space division switch fabrics have been built from electromechanical and electronic elements with the crosspoint function. Future technologies involving optical crosspoint elements with either electronic or optical control are being researched and developed.

Examples of space division switches are DTE matrix switches, supercomputer High Performance Parallel Interface (HPPI) switches, and 3/3 digital cross-connects. Many space division switches employ multiple stages of crosspoint networks to yield larger switch sizes.

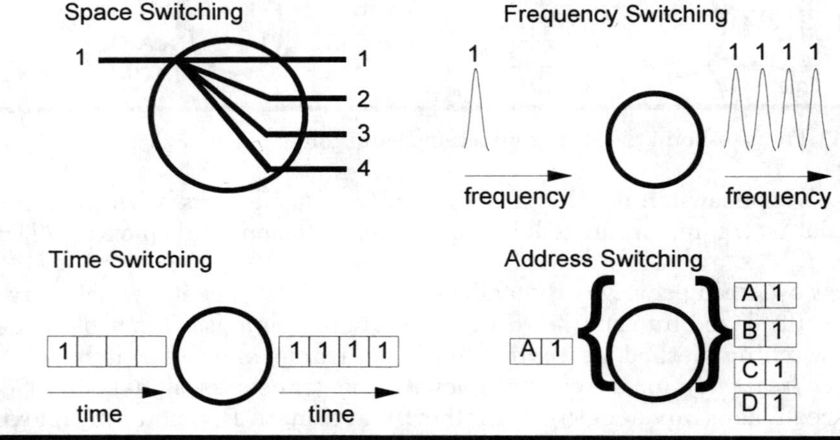

Figure 6.14 Point-to-Multipoint Switching Function Definitions

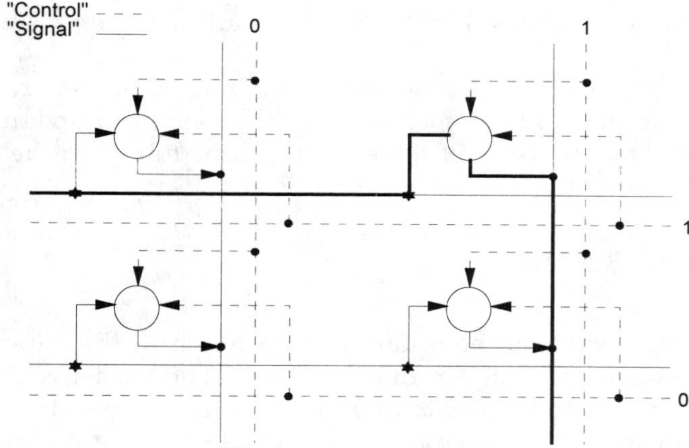

Figure 6.15 Two-Input, Two-Output Crossbar Network

6.3.4 Time Division Switching

The operation of current digital telephone switches may be viewed as being made up of an interconnected network of special-purpose computers called Time Division Switches (TDS).

TDS operation is shown in Figure 6.16. Each TDM frame has M time slots. The input time slot m, labeled $I(m)$, is stored in the input sample array $x(t)$ in position m. The output address memory $y(t)$ is scanned sequentially by increasing t from 1 to M each frame time. The contents of the address array $y(t)$ identify the index into the input time slot array x that is to be output during time slot t on the output line. In the example of Figure 6.16, $y(n)$ has the value m, which causes input time slot m to be switched to output time slot n. Note that the input sample array must be double buffered in an actual implementation so that time slot phase can be maintained for inputs and outputs with different frame clock phases.

This TDS function is performed for M time slots, that is, once every frame time. This must occur in less than $\tau = 125$ μs (1/8000) for all slots, $n = 1,\ldots,M$. The maximum TDS size is therefore determined by the TDS execution rate, I instructions per second (or equivalently I^{-1} seconds per instruction); then the TDS switch size M must satisfy the inequality $M \leq \tau I$.

The TDS is effectively a very special-purpose computer designed to operate at very high speeds. For I ranging from 100 to 1000 MIPs, the maximum TDS switch size M ranges from 12,500 to 125,000, which is the range of modern single-stage Time Division Switches (TDS). Larger TDSs can be constructed by interconnecting TDSs via multiple stage crosspoint-type networks.

Usually, some time slots are reserved in the input frame in order to be able to update the output address memory. In this way, the update rate of the switch is limited by the usage of some slots for scheduling overhead.

6.3.5 Address Switching

Address switching operates on a data stream in which the data is organized into packets, each with a header and a payload. The header contains address information that is used in switching decisions at each node. The address determines which physical port the packet is output to, along with any translation of the header address value. All possible connection topologies can be implemented within this switching architecture: point-point, point-to-multipoint, multipoint-to-point, and multipoint-to-multipoint. We illustrate these topologies in the following example.

Figure 6.17 illustrates four address switches, each with two inputs and two outputs.

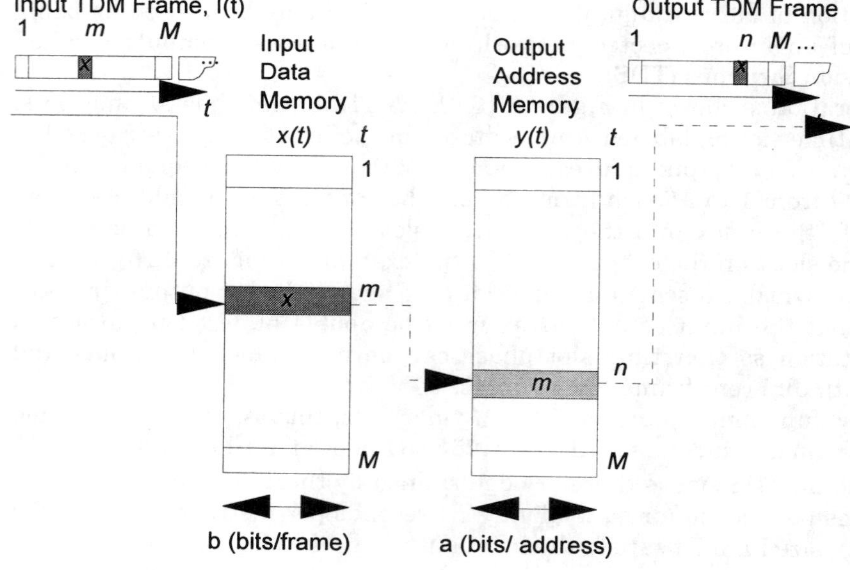

Figure 6.16 Illustration of Time Division Switch Operation

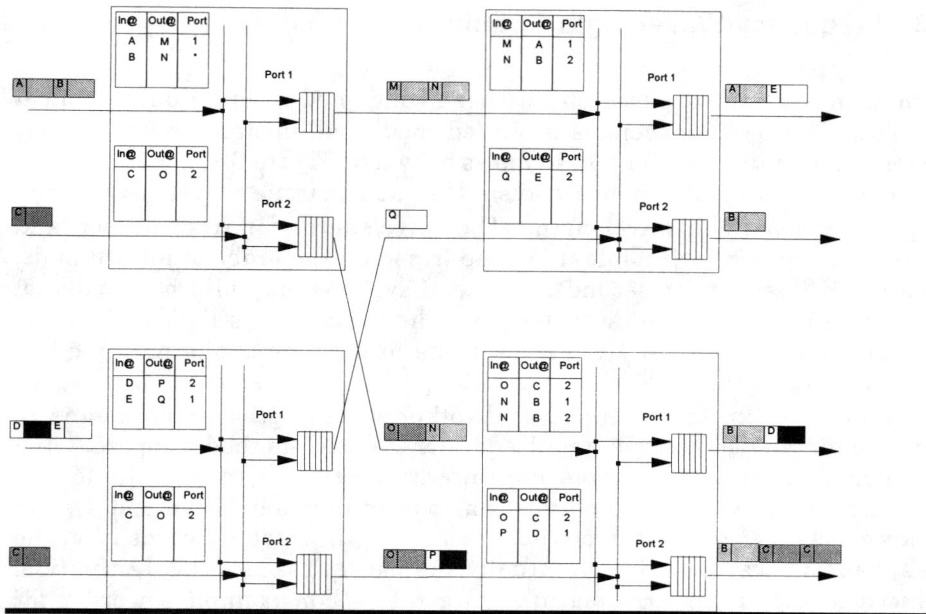

Figure 6.17 Address Switching Example

Packets (either fixed or variable in length) arrive at the inputs as shown on the left-hand side of the figure with addresses indicated by letters in the header symbolized by the square to the left of each shaded payload. The payload shading is carried through the switching operations from left to right to allow the switching result of the address switches to be traced visually. The input address indexes into a table using the column labeled In@, which identifies the address for use on output in the column Out@, and the physical output port on which the packet is sent in the column labeled Port. For example, the input packet addressed as *A* is output on port 1 using address *M*. Conceptually, each switch functions as a pair of busses which connect to the output port buffers. Packets destined for a particular output port are queued for transmission. Buffering is required because contention may occur for the same output port. At the next switch the same process occurs until the packets are output on the right-hand side of the figure.

The packets labeled A, D, and E form point-to-point connections. The packets labeled B form point-to-multipoint connections. The packets labeled C form multipoint-to-point connections. Address switching and multiplexing are at the heart of ATM, which later chapters will cover in great detail.

6.3.6 Frequency/Wavelength Switching

A significant amount of research has been conducted recently on all-optical networks. The basic concept is a shared media, all-photonic network that interconnects a number of end systems as shown in Figure 6.18.

The optical end system nodes transmit on at least one wavelength λ and receive on at least one wavelength. The wavelengths for transmission and reception are currently tunable in a time frame on the order of milliseconds, with an objective of microseconds. The end systems may also be capable of receiving on more than one wavelength. The wavelengths indicated by the subscripts on the character λ are used in the next example of a multiple hop optical network.

If the end system cannot receive all other wavelengths, some means to provide inter-connectivity is required. One early method proposed and implemented is that of multiple hop interconnections. In a multiple hop system, each end system also performs a routing function. If an end system node receives a packet that is not destined for it, the node forwards it on the node's transmit wavelength. Eventually the packet reaches the destination, as shown in the trellis drawing of Figure 6.19. For example, in order for station 1 to transmit to station 4, it first sends on wavelength λ_1, which is received by node 2. Node 2 examines the packet header and determines that it is not the destination, and retransmits the packet on wavelength λ_2. Node 3 receives the packet, examines the packet header, and forwards it on λ_3, which is received by the destination, Node 4.

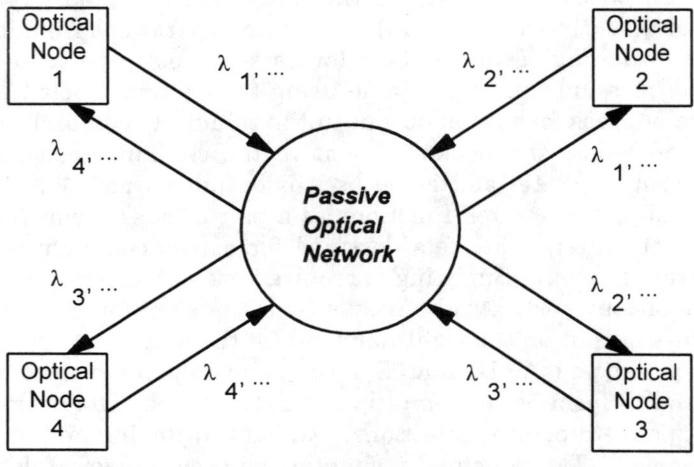

Figure 6.18 Illustration of Optical WDM Network

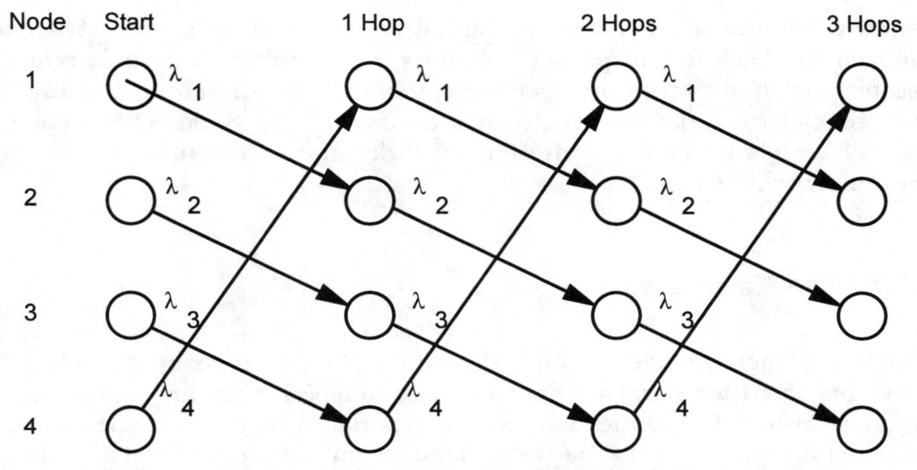

Figure 6.19 Illustration of Multiple Hop WDM Network Trellis

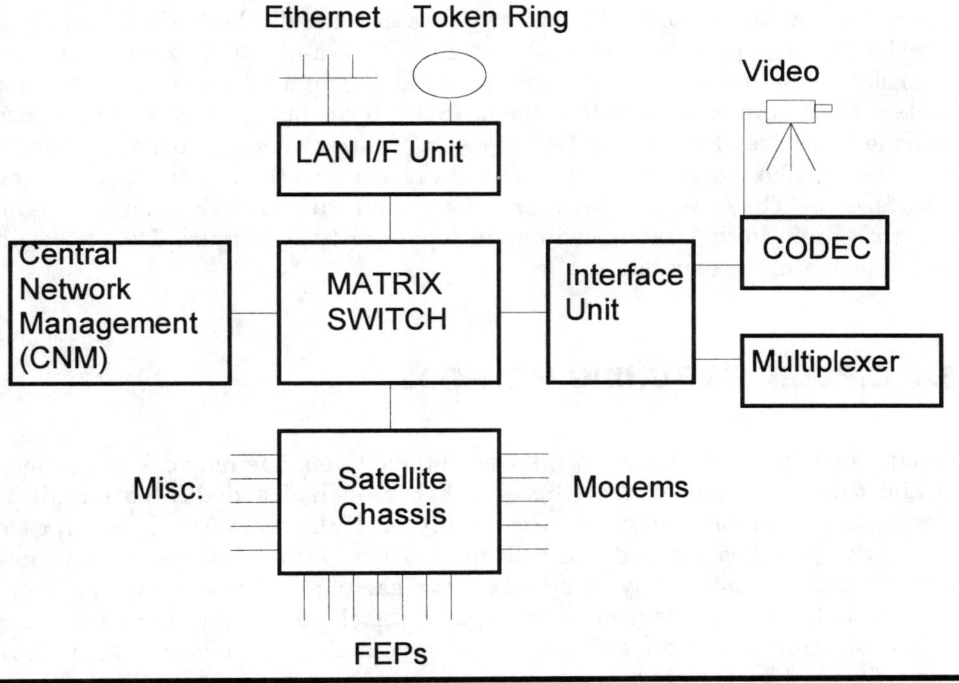

Figure 6.20 Matrix Switch

This multiple hop process makes inefficient use of the processing power of each node as the number of nodes grows large, so recent research has focused on single-hop designs. In these designs the tunable transmitter and receiver are often employed. There is a need for some means to allocate and share the bandwidth in the optical network. Circuit-based signaling has been tried, but the user feedback is that packet switching, not circuit switching, is required because the circuit setup time is unacceptable. Fixed allocation of bandwidth in a time-slotted manner is also not desirable. Dynamic scheduling and collision avoidance hold promise for a solution to the demands of very high-speed networking.

6.3.7 The Matrix Switch

Matrix switches provide a simplistic form of T1 multiplexing and offer the capability to switch ports similar to a cross-connect. They are composed of a high-speed bus for connection between ports. They are controlled and switched through a central network-management center, and can manage the entire network from a single point. This allows for centralized control and diagnostics, as well as quick network restoration in case of failure. The major drawback is the possibility of a matrix switch failure, which would bring down the entire network. Matrix switches can handle both DTE and DCE interfaces, and provide conversion from DTE and DCE to a four-wire interface. Matrix switches can be accessed through gateways or interface units. Most interfaces are low speed (9600 bps), but matrix switches also provide interfaces for T1 and LAN speeds. Matrix switches usually support in excess of 4096 ports. A satellite chassis forms a method of distributing line interfaces. They aggregate many low- and high-speed interfaces and transmit them to the matrix switch via copper or fiber. Figure 6.20 shows an example of a matrix switch.

6.4 CIRCUIT SWITCHING METHODS

Circuit switching originated in the voice public telephone network. Let's look at the first telephone usage where each person had a dedicated circuit to every other person, which is essentially a PVC service. This type of connectivity makes sense if you talk to very few people and very few people talk to you. Historically this was how early telephone networks were constructed until the maze of wires began to block out the sun in urban areas before electromechanical switching was invented by Strowger. Now, let's move forward to the modern day, where the typical person makes calls to hundreds of different destinations, for business and pleasure. It is unrealistic to think that in this modern age each of these call origination and destination points would have its own dedicated circuit, since it would be much too expensive. Yet a person picks up the phone in one city and calls a person in another city. When this call goes through and both ends begin communicating, they are doing so over a Switched Virtual Circuit (SVC).

That circuit is dedicated to the two people until they terminate the call. If they hang up and call back, another circuit is established in the same manner, but not necessarily over the exact same path as before. In this manner, common network resources (circuits) are shared among many users.

6.4.1 Circuit Switching Illustrated

Figure 6.21 shows a simplified comparison of two communications networks connecting eight users, labeled user A through user H, which could be LANs, MANs, PBXs or hosts. Network a shows dedicated private line circuits connecting each user, while network b shows circuit-switched access to a common, shared network with a single access line for each user. In network a each user has seven access lines into the network for dedicated circuits connecting to a distant access line for each possible destination. Data or voice is transmitted only via the physical layer. The data is not processed, but instead just passed across the network regardless of the content. The example in the circuit-switched network b shows user A talking with user H, and user D talking with user E. Any user can communicate with any other user, although not simultaneously, just as in the telephone network.

Today, computers need to "talk" to each other in the same manner. Computers can only talk over the telephone network if a modem is used to convert data signals to signals that can be carried over the circuit-switched voice network. *Modem* is a contraction for modulator-demodulator. The modem presents a DCE interface to the computer equipment, and outputs a signal that is compatible with a standard phone line.

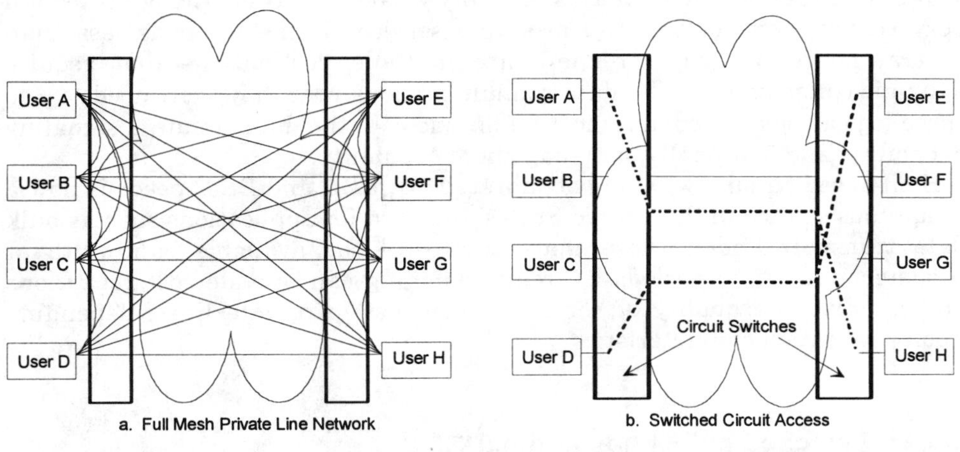

Figure 6.21 Dedicated (Private Line) versus Switched-Circuit Access

Data calls that use circuit switching operate in the same manner, but the transmission is not restricted to voice. A point-to-point telephone call is established by a computer whenever data communication is required and remains up. Either the application or the end user disconnects the circuit when it is done. Since circuit switching is a form of connection-oriented service, the same factors apply. The entire circuit bandwidth is dedicated for the duration of the call. Circuit switching is an ideal technology for traffic that needs constant bandwidth but can tolerate relatively long call establishment and disconnection times.

Figure 6.22 illustrates this process between two users, A and B. Call setup delay associated with the call setup and confirmation is a major consideration with circuit switching for data communications. The call setup time and modem training time can often be as long as 10 to 30 seconds. Telephone switch routing usually does not minimize the propagation delay; however, this is usually not a critical factor for data applications operating at the lower speeds of the telephone network.

Circuit switching still remains the most common type of public switched data service. Data circuit switching was much slower to emerge on the market than voice circuit switching, primarily because of the need to digitize switches initially, but is now widely available. Also, the additional complexity of ISDN signaling requires software updates in switches as well as end-user equipment.

Circuit switching has been used historically as a backup for private line services. It remains the most cost-viable option for private network users, with most switched 56-kbps data services selling at less than 20 cents per minute to less than 5 cents per minute depending on time of day, usage, speed, error-free rate, and other factors. This price is getting very close to that of voice service, since that is basically what it is! This pricing makes it a very cost-effective option to leased-line services if the usage is less than several hours per day, or there are multiple destinations that require dynamic connectivity. The data communications user, however, needs up to three logical types of communication for one call: the data circuit, a signaling capability, and, optionally, a management capability.

High-speed circuit switching of subrate DS1, DS1, and DS3 speeds is now a ubiquitous service in the United States and used for applications such as bulk data transport and/or those that require all the available bandwidth at predetermined time periods. Circuit switching can provide cost reductions and improve the quality of service in contrast to private lines, depending upon application characteristics.

6.4.2 Switched nx56 kbps and nxDS0

Since Time Division Multiplexing (TDM) uses 8000 samples per second per DS0 channel, a difference arises from the fact that 56-kbps uses only seven bits per sample, while 64 kbps uses all eight. The 56 kbps rate resulted from the historical use by the telephone network of one bit per sample in what is called *robbed bit signaling* in digital transmissions.

Switched 56 kbps, or simply switched 56, is a service offered in both the private and public networking environments. Often a Channel Service Unit/Data Service Unit (CSU/DSU) device is used via dedicated 56 kbps or DS0 lines on the CSU side to access a switched 56 kbps service. On the DSU side, a standard DCE interface is presented to the computer equipment, as was discussed at the beginning of this chapter.

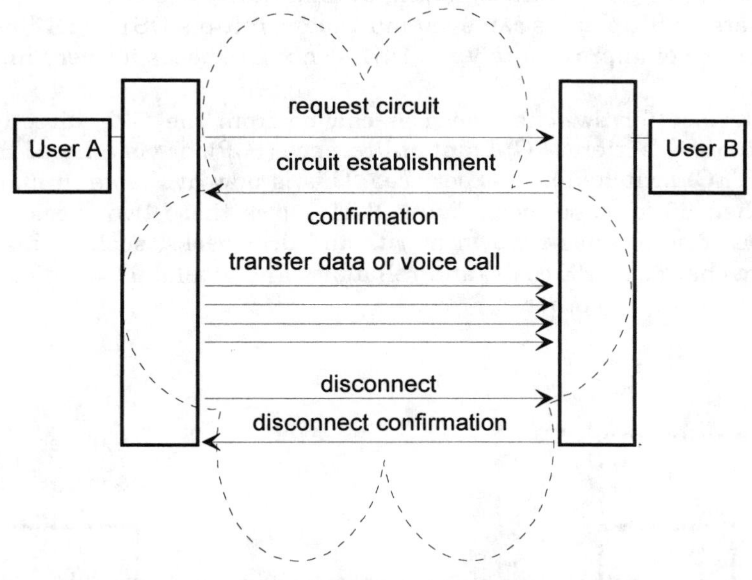

Figure 6.22 Call Establishment and Disconnect

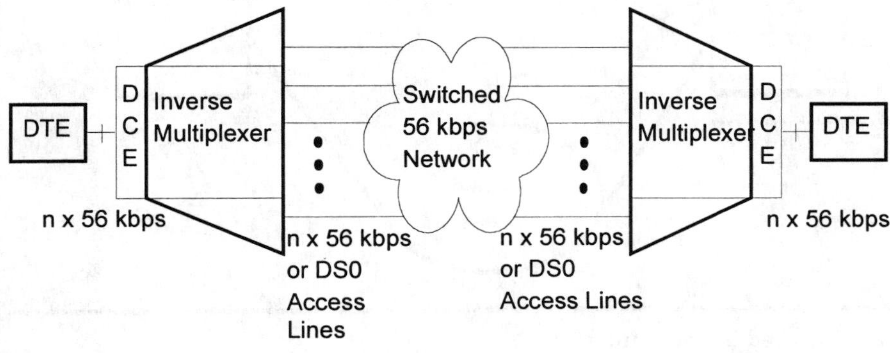

Figure 6.23 Illustration of Inverse Multiplexer Operation

Another important class of equipment comprises inverse multiplexers, which offer the capability to interface to multiple 56-kbps or DS0 interfaces, as illustrated in Figure 6.23. The inverse multiplexer provides a DCE interface to the computer that aggregates the bandwidth available to the DTE in approximately 56/64 kbps increments. The actual bandwidth provided to the DTE is slightly less than n × 56/64 kbps because the inverse multiplexer consumes some bandwidth in its operation. Many of these devices allow 56/64 kbps channels to be dialed up or disconnected on demand, offering a form of bandwidth-on-demand. Some router equipment has the intelligence to generate this signaling automatically based upon traffic load. Some inverse multiplexers can even multiplex multiple DS1 or E1 lines into a DCE interface of approximately n × DS1 or n × E1 speeds for very high-speed connectivity.

The interface for switched services can be from the CPE directly to the IntereXchange Carrier (IXC) Point of Presence (PoP), or via a Local Exchange Carrier (LEC) switched access service. This is now available in many areas for switched 56 kbps service. Figure 6.24 shows these two types of access. Each type of access has its own merits and drawbacks, such as installation and usage charges, CPE costs, and reliability and availability, which must be weighed against each other.

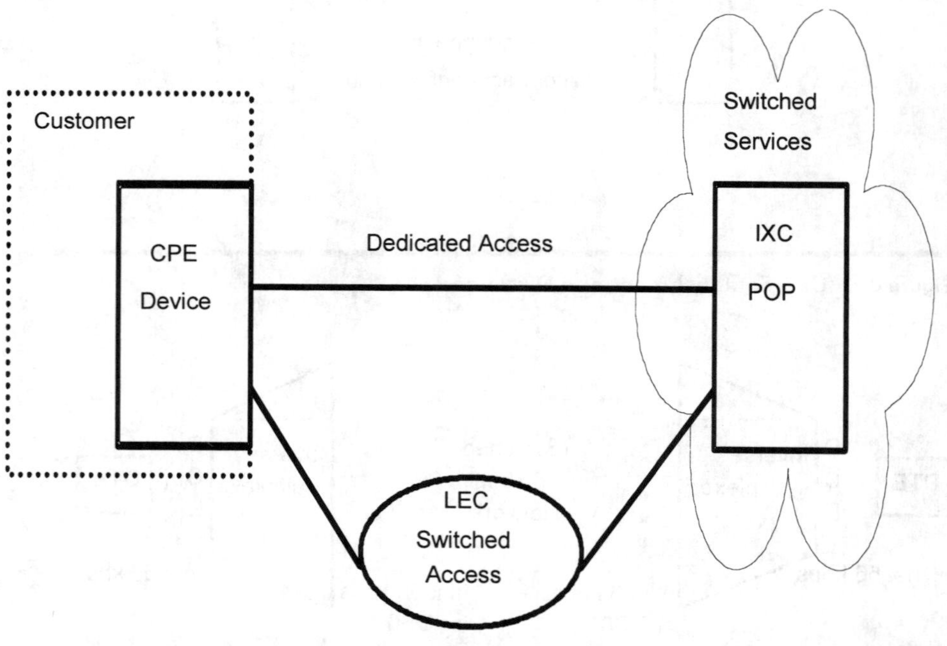

Figure 6.24 Switched Services Interfaces

Many users implement switched 56/64 kbps services as a backup for private lines and to transport non-mission-critical data traffic. Others use it for infrequent high-data-rate, constant bandwidth data transfers. The typical traffic is long-duration, relatively constant bandwidth data transfers, such as batch file transfers, database backups, and highly aggregated, predictable data traffic.

Most switched services are at the 56/64 kbps level, but new services offering higher bandwidth multiples of 56 kbps are now becoming popular, such as switched 384 kbps, DS1, and even DS3. Some carriers offer noncontiguous and contiguous fractional DS1 or n × DS0 reconfigurable or switched services. Reconfigurable services often utilize a computer terminal to rearrange digital cross-connects to provide a slower version of n × DS0 switching. The ISDN-based version of this service is called the MultiRate Circuit Mode Bearer Service (MRCMBS) which supports switched n × DS0.

Video conferencing is one example where multiple 56-kbps circuits are combined to form a single high-speed video conference channel at speeds such as 112 kbps or 224 kbps. Imaging and CAD/CAM file transfer are also good examples of high-bandwidth switched traffic. Some examples of switched DS1 service traffic include video, imaging, and data center disaster recovery. MCI was the first carrier to offer all of these switched services, but now all the major IXCs offer them.

6.4.3 Digital Access Cross-Connects (DXC)

Digital access cross-connects (DXC) are central office devices capable of grooming multiple DS0 channels within a T1 and, in some cases, multiple DS1 channels within a T3. This provides a patch panel effect, where individual DS0s and DS1s can be mixed and matched between higher bandwidth aggregates. Digital access cross-connects also perform reconfiguration, restoration and disaster recovery, circuit reroute, testing, and monitoring.

Figure 6.25 shows an example of a DXC 1/0, where 24 DS0 channels are groomed within one of the 28 T1s which terminate at the DXC. DXCs also have the capability for network disaster recovery.

The major types of DXCs include:

DXC1/0. Supports subrate DS0s reroute capability within a DS1.

DXC3/1. Supports subrate DS1s reroute capability within a DS3.

DXC3/3. Supports multiple DS3s reroute capability.

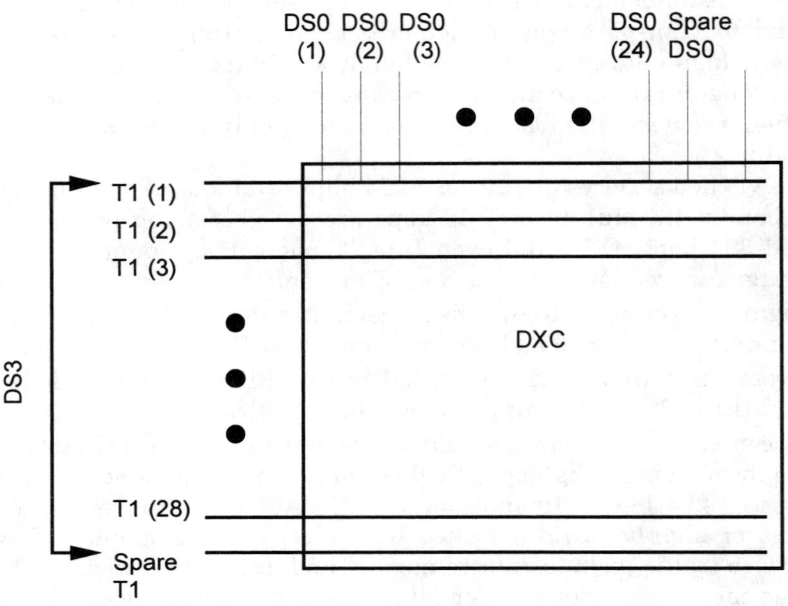

Figure 6.25 DXC 1/0

Figure 6.26 shows a network where both DXC 3/1 and DXC 3/3s are deployed.

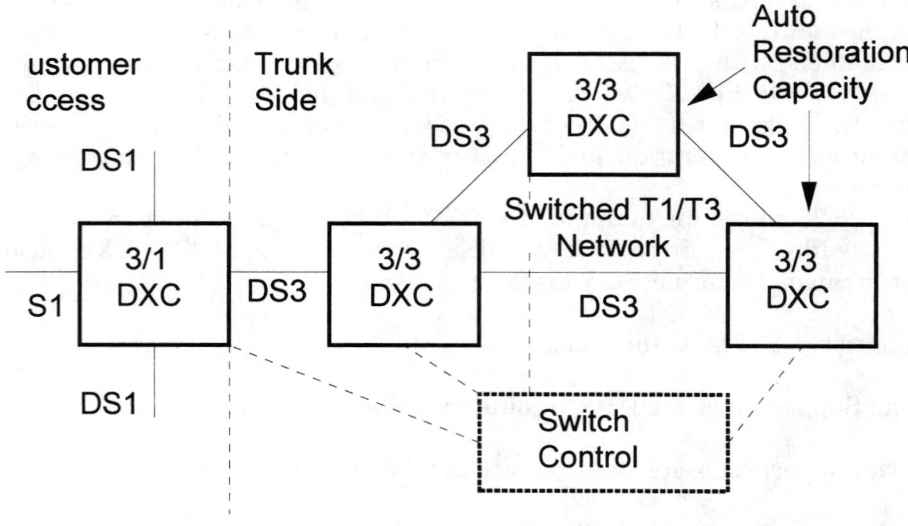

Figure 6.26 DXC 3/1 and DXC 3/3 Network Example

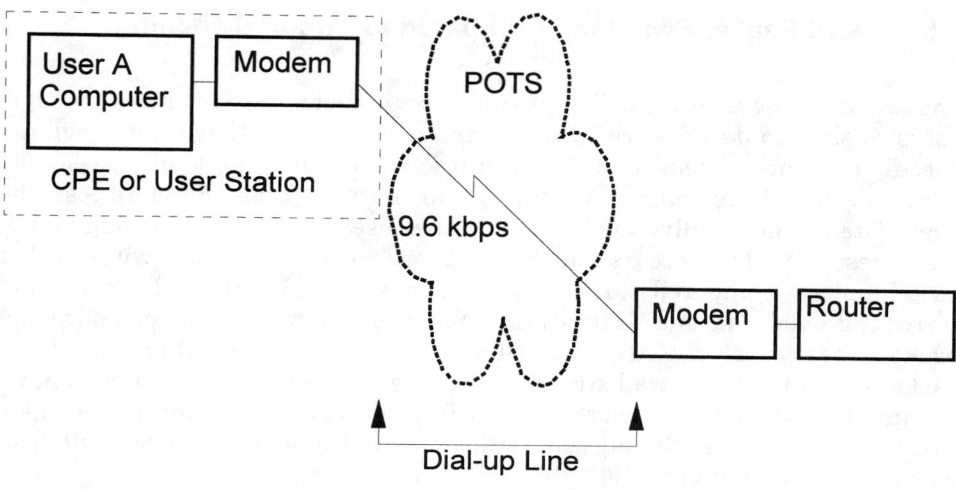

Figure 6.27 Remote Access Configuration

6.4.4 Dial-Up Lines

Dial-up lines represent low-speed dedicated point-to-point circuits that are established for a fixed period of time and then disconnected, similar to making a phone call. This type of circuit uses the Plain Old Telephone Service (POTS) for access, with access speeds typically at 9600 bps but up to and including 56 kbps. Figure 6.27 shows a user who accesses a remote router via a 9600-bps dial-up line. A dial-up modem is used to access the telephone network. High-speed circuit switching can be compared to dial-up lines, where bandwidth is "dialed up" as needed. ISDN dial-up access offers a 16-kbps (D-channel), 64-kbps (B-channel), or a 128-kbps (2B) circuit.

6.5 PACKET-SWITCHING TECHNOLOGIES

This section has been added to provide a brief overview of packet-switching technology before delving into detail in subsequent chapters. *Packet switching* is a broad term which began with X.25 packet-switching services. It is now used in one form or another to represent frame relay, SMDS, and ATM services. It is important to clear up the confusion with associating these diverse technologies with packet switching. First we look at packet switching vs. circuit switching, then move to the history of packet switching, and conclude with a brief introduction to the major packet-switched protocols and technologies discussed in this text.

6.5.1 X.25 Packet Switching Compared to Circuit Switching

Packet switching is much different from circuit switching. It allows multiple users to share data-network facilities and bandwidth, rather than providing specific amounts of dedicated bandwidth to each user. The traffic passed by packet-switched networks is "bursty" in nature, and therefore can be aggregated statistically to maximize the use of on-demand bandwidth resources. While there is much more overhead associated with packet switching as compared to circuit switching, X.25 error checking and correcting overhead guarantees error-free delivery by the use of addressed packets that transit the network. Due to the connectionless characteristic of packet switching in contradistinction to connection-oriented circuit switching, the intelligence of the network nodes will route packets around failed links, whereas in circuit switching the entire circuit would need to be switched, leading to service interruption.

6.5.2 Darwin's Theory and Packet Switching Evolution

Charles Darwin took nearly as much time to arrive at his theory of evolution as it has taken for packet switching to be conceived and sweep the world of data communications. The basic tenets of Darwin's theory of evolution are natural selection, survival of the fittest, and the need to adapt to a changing environment.

This section takes the reader through a brief summary of the history of packet switching which references the genealogy shown in Figure 6.28. The genesis of packet switching began with the proprietary computer communication architectures by IBM called Systems Network Architecture (SNA) and DEC's Digital Network Architecture (DNA). The Synchronous Data Link Control (SDLC) protocol from SNA was refined upon and standardized as the High-level Data Link Control (HDLC) protocol, which begat X.25 and Link Access Procedure D (LAP-D) within ISDN. Frame relay evolved as basically a leaner, meaner LAP-D protocol. OSI adopted the X.25 protocol as the first link and packet layer standard.

Around the same time that OSI was being developed, the United States Advanced Research Projects Agency (ARPA) was working on a network with universities, think tanks, and industry that resulted in the suite of applications and high-level protocols based upon the Internet Protocol (IP). Ethernet also sprung up about this time as a result of experiments on packet radio communication in Hawaii. Ethernet has now evolved into Fast Ethernet or 100 Mbps Ethernet. Token Ring was also developed by IBM shortly after Ethernet, and has evolved into the higher-speed FDDI. Within the past 10 to 15 years the concepts of Fast Packet Switching (FPS) and the Distributed Queue Dual Bus (DQDB) have resulted in the Switched

Multimegabit Data Service (SMDS) and Asynchronous Transfer Mode (ATM) technologies.

Packet switching played an increasingly important role in the rapidly changing environment of distributed processing in the 1990s. Several environmental factors drove the direction of data communications evolution. There emerged an accelerating need for more bandwidth driven by increasing computing power, increasing need for interconnectivity, and the need to support larger networks where any user or application can communicate with any other (ubiquity of communications). The low error rate of modern fiber-optic, satellite, and radio communications enabled more cost-effective implementation of higher-speed data communications. The same technology that increases computer power was used to increase packet switching performance.

This changing environment has created new opportunities for new species of data communications protocols. The improved quality of transmission facilities alone was a major force in the evolution of frame relay, SMDS, and ATM. These newer protocols are streamlined in that they do not perform error correction by retransmission within the network, thus relying on higher layer protocols to perform this function more efficiently. The fixed slot and cell size of SMDS and ATM have also enabled cost-effective implementation of switching machines. The increasing capabilities of high-speed electronics have been an essential ingredient in SMDS and ATM devices.

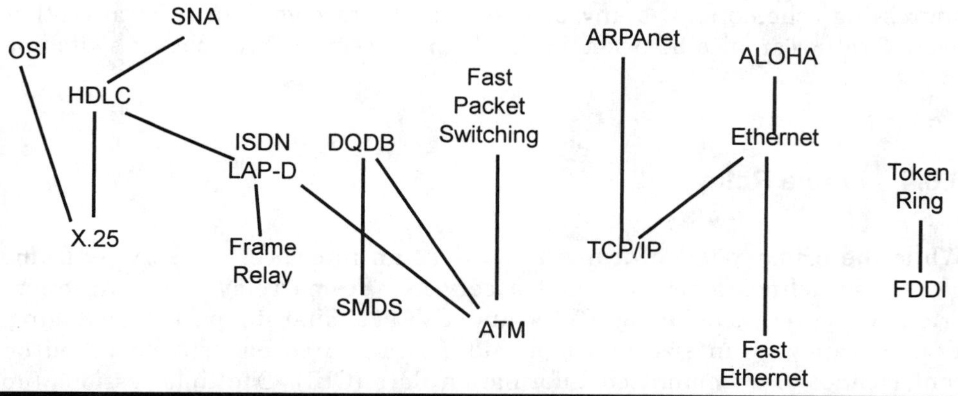

Figure 6.28 Genealogy of Packet Switching

6.5.3 X.25

X.25 was the first protocol issued defining packet switching. Access speeds range up to 56 kbps. Trunks between network nodes are limited to 56/64 kbps (with the capability for fractional and full T1 speeds under proprietary implementations). X.25 contains the error detection and correction and flow control needed for the older analog transport networks of the 1980s. But much of this overhead and the processor-intensive operations are not needed in today's fiber-optic networks environment. X.25 Packet switching is solely a connectionless service using connection-oriented virtual circuits, and is good for time-insensitive data transmission but poor for connection-oriented and time-sensitive voice and video. Packet switches pass data through the network, node to node, employing a queuing scheme for buffering and transmitting data. Data is received and passed if bandwidth is available. If it is not, data is stored in the queue until bandwidth is available (and to the extent of the memory buffer). The end nodes are responsible for error detection and correction and to initiate error recovery. The newer fast packet services do not perform this queuing function, rather they drop the extra traffic that cannot be transmitted over a congested network and force the application to do the error checking at higher layers. Congestion is one parameter that has not yet been effectively solved in these new services.

X.25 allows numerous virtual circuits on the same physical path, and can transport packet sizes up to 4,096 bytes. Both Permanent Virtual Circuits (PVCs) and Switched Virtual Circuits (SVCs) are supported in X.25, and the addressing scheme allows any user to send or receive data from any other user. Traffic can also be prioritized. Chapter 9 covers X.25 packet switching in detail.

6.5.4 Frame Relay

While the primary use of frame relay is as an interface to a service, frame relay also defines a protocol and a service. Frame relay is a connection-oriented service employing PVCs and SVCs similar to packet switching. Frames can vary in size and bandwidth is allocated on demand based on conformance to a Committed Information Rate (CIR). Multiple sessions (up to 1000 PVCs) can take place over a single physical circuit, and these access circuits can range from DS0, through fractional T1 speeds, and up to a T1 (minus the overhead). Thus, it exhibits a similar statistical multiplexing feature as X.25. Frame relay is only a transport service, and does not employ the packet processing of X.25, which guarantees end-to-end error and flow control. Instead, frame relay relies on the user to implement higher-level protocols in the upper layer of the OSIRM for flow control and error correction (such as Transmission Control Protocol (TCP). Frame relay must be transmitted over reliable fiber-optic transmission media with low bit-error ratios, because errored or excess (blocked) data is simply discarded, since error detection and correction is not built into frame relay because of the assumption of the reliability of the fiber-optics. Chapters 10 and 11 provide a detailed explanation of frame relay. Later, frame relay design using frame relay circuits and routers is considered.

There are seven functions provided by frame relay that are also provided by X.25. These include address translation, discard of incorrect frames, fill of interframe time, FCS checking and generation, flag recognition and generation, recognition of invalid frames, and transparency. The concept of PVCs and SVCs is also similar. This together constitutes about one-fourth the services provided by X.25, and frame relay can be viewed as a subset of X.25 packet-switching technology and functions. It can be seen that while the scaling down of services contributes to a less intelligent network, the benefit is a reduction in overhead if clean transmission media are used. It also provides much higher transmission speeds. Still, frame relay is not a replacement for X.25 packet switching, especially if poor transmission facilities are inescapable and guaranteed delivery is a must.

6.5.5 Fast Packet

Fast packet is a term for a data transmission technique, trademarked by Stratacom. It is not a defined standard, protocol, or service. Fast packet is a *backbone* technology (as opposed to frame relay *access* technology) which combines attributes of both circuit switching and packet switching. Fast packet can accommodate both (time) delay-sensitive traffic (e.g., voice and video) as well as data traffic not affected by variable delay. It also offers low network delay and high network resource efficiency. Fast packet resembles a circuit switch for constant-bandwidth traffic such as voice and video (isosynchronous) and a packet switch for "bursty" data traffic such as local and wide area network traffic, dynamically increasing the bandwidth for high-bandwidth requirements and decreasing it for low-bandwidth requirements.

Fast packet switching speeds up packet transfer and delivery through reduction of overhead since error detection and correction is not done in the intermediate nodes. The packets or cells passing through the network use the data link layer instead of the network layer. These packet or cell sizes can either be *fixed* (cell switching and ATM) or *variable* (frame relay). Fast packet can also provide protocol transparency. This causes minimal node delay, while providing addressing and routing capabilities. Fast packet technologies typically use advanced fiber-optic transport media, such as T3 and SONET.

Fast Packet Multiplexing (FPM) is a general term for providing the capabilities of fast packet switching through multiplexing various types of traffic onto the transmission medium. FPM is characterized by a combination of both TDM and SPM, where packets of fixed or variable size, of fixed or variable delay-sensitive traffic, are statistically multiplexed over a network high-bandwidth circuit. Packets pass *through* network devices rather than into and out of them, thus providing minimal nodal delay. FPM can also dynamically reallocate bandwidth on any packet, regardless of whether it is within the multiplexer or partially in transit. This leads to variable or fixed packet or cell sizes based upon the transmission medium being used. The most common form of FPM is the new ATM technology, which uses a fixed cell switching form of fast packet multiplexing. We will discuss this technology in great detail in Chapters 13 and 14.

The IEEE 802.6 DQDB architecture provides the platform for a form of fast packet switching called Switched Multimegabit Data Service (SMDS). SMDS uses the IEEE 802.6 MAN technology discussed in Chapter 12.

6.5.6 Asynchronous Transfer Mode (ATM)

ATM is another form of fast packet switching. ATM packetizes voice, data, and video and then "statistically multiplexes" the packets onto the same high-speed data channel. ATM provides two types of connection: virtual *channel*, which provides logical packet connection between two users, and virtual *path*, which defines a source to destination route for users.

ATM is a technology which allows for the transmission of data, voice, and video traffic simultaneously over high-bandwidth circuits, typically on the order of hundreds of Megabits per second (Mbps) to Gigabits per second (Gbps) in the foreseeable future. ATM hardware and software platforms form a communications architecture based on the switching and relaying of small units of data called *cells.* The primary difference between ATM-based services and other existing data communications services, such as frame relay, SMDS, and FDDI, is that ATM is the first technology and protocol structure to effectively integrate voice, data, and video over the same communications channel at speeds in excess of DS3 (45 Mbps) and E4 (140 Mbps).

ATM transmission services include:

- Full-duplex 155.52 Mbps
- Asymmetrical transmission from subscriber to network at 155.52 Mbps in one direction and 622.08 Mbps in the other
- Full-duplex 622.08 Mbps service

Chapters 13 and 14 cover ATM, and a discussion on SONET can be found in Chapter 15. These are some of the more exciting technologies being used today.

6.5.7 Integrated Circuit / Packet Switches

Switches are available that combine both circuit- and packet-switching capabilities within the same unit. These devices combine X.25, frame relay, or ATM packet/frame/cell switching with TDM techniques, and can even include DXC and channel bank functions. Thus, a large variety of traffic — from bursty LAN to dedicated DS1 and DS3 data streams — can be handled in the most efficient manner required, with the added capabilities offered by a DXC. X.25 and LAN routed traffic can be *packet* switched, while LAN bridged, SNA, voice and video, and other delay-sensitive traffic can be *circuit* switched. The primary advantage is seen when using this switch as a hub concentrator for many types of traffic through dynamic allocation of available bandwidth. It allows an integrated platform for both data transport and network management. Thus, the network designer can design one network, and not multiple networks for both circuit and packet switching, thus consolidating equipment and operating costs of both. But one must also ask — can a Volkswagen beat a drag racer in a race if you need speed, or can a drag racer enter a miles per gallon race? The point is that this solution is not without the drawbacks of both technologies as we have discussed previously.

6.6 REVIEW

The capabilities of and differences between multiplexing and switching are important. There are many methods of multiplexing, such as Space Division (SDM), Frequency Division (FDM), Time Division (TDM), and addressing multiplexing, and each has multiple hardware devices to satisfy the various user needs for traffic aggregation. Looking at the future of multiplexing, switched services and LAN/MAN/WAN routing devices have already eroded a large part of the market once owned by multiplexers. The list of features and functions of various multiplexer hardware helps decide what to use for what need. Circuit-switching services and technologies are quite valuable to constant data-rate traffic, as well as valuable for dedicated circuit backup. Packet switching technologies span from the older X.25 packet switching to newer techniques in fast packet and cell switching such as frame relay, SMDS, and ATM. After understanding the advantages and disadvantages of each type of technology, it is apparent that many network designs require a "hybrid" of both dedicated and switched technologies.

Part

4

Protocols and Interfaces

This section provides the reader with an overview of the major protocols and interfaces of all seven layers of the OSIRM. We start by looking at the physical layer. Then special attention is paid to the data link, network, and transport layers. Since the thrust of this text is on WAN design, further detail on the session, application, and presentation layers are left to the reader to master. Bridge and router protocols reside somewhat outside the traditional OSIRM, as do the IEEE 802.X LAN protocols, and both subjects are covered in detail. LAN switching and virtual LANs (VLANs) are introduced. The section ends by taking the reader from legacy SNA environments through peer-to-peer SNA communications (APPC/APPN) to multiprotocol environments, including standards like Data Link Switching (DLSw) and RFC 1490.

Chapter

7

Common Protocols and Interfaces – Part 1

As introduced in Chapter 4, a *protocol* is similar to a language, conveying meaning and understanding through some form of communications. Protocols are sets of rules governing communications between data machines and between protocol layers. The definition of protocol also implies documentation, negotiation, and the establishment of rules. For one computer to talk to another, each must be able to understand and translate the other's protocol. Protocols are defined in seven major sections: the physical layer, data link layer, logical link control and media access control layers, bridge protocols, router protocols, network and transport layer protocols, and upper- or user-layer protocols. Discussions of both interfaces and protocols will be covered in this chapter. Interfaces play an important part in network design by providing the physical and logical interface between the user and the network equipment. Protocols play a very important part in data transmissions, for without them, islands of users would be unable to communicate.

Lower-layer protocols provide the logical link and physical interface to the transport medium. Details concerning physical interface signaling, timing, and pin level configuration are outside the scope of this text. Data link layer protocols allow communications with the physical medium. Included in the data link layer are both the Logical Link Control (LLC) and the Media Access Control (MAC) sublayers, which define LAN communications. Bridge, router, transport, and Internet mid-layer protocols will be covered in the next chapter.

7.1 BASIC CONCEPTS

Interfaces provide boundaries between different types of hardware, while protocols provide rules, conventions, and the intelligence to pass data over these interfaces. Interfaces and physical media provide the path for data flow, while the protocols "manage" that data flow across the path and interfaces. Both interfaces and protocols must be compatible for accurate and efficient data transport. Often, interfaces are referred to only in the physical layer of the OSIRM. Protocols can also act as interfaces, defined as interface protocols. Such protocols define the interface between the DTE-to-DCE signaling and transfer that information to higher-layer protocols for user presentation. Many network designs now incorporate multiple levels of protocols and interfaces, from the physical layer to the application layer according to the seven-layer OSIRM.

The concepts behind the use of multiple protocol layers are important. The concepts of physical, data link, and network layer protocols can now be defined on a high level. Less time will be spent on the details of session, presentation, and application layer protocols, since our thrust is toward a design that implements protocols such as frame relay, Distributed Queue Dual Bus (DQDB), Fiber Distributed Data Interface (FDDI), and Asynchronous Transfer Mode (ATM), which have their roots in the lower-layer protocols. Some implementations of session, presentation, and application layer protocols will be discussed later in the next chapter.

7.1.1 Physical Layer Concepts

The terms *Data Termination Equipment* (DTE) and *Data Communication Equipment* (DCE) refer to the hardware on each side of the communications channel interface. DTE is typically a computer or terminal which acts as an end point for transmitted and received data. DCE is typically a modem or communication device for data transport. The DTE communicates with the DCE, which then interfaces with and provides the DTE with access to the network. Delving into network design, the farther we go into the network, the more these terms blur. DTE and DCE are also used to identify a standard cable configuration, and it is not uncommon to find a DTE-to-DTE cable connecting two devices. This is called a *null modem* connection and is often used to connect two DTE devices such as a terminal and a computer. Figure 7.1 shows a common end-to-end network configuration where DTE 1 talks to DCE1, which in turn formats the transmission for transfer over the network to the end DCE 2 which then interfaces to the end DTE 2.

Physical layer protocols provide both electrical and mechanical interfaces to the transport medium. Physical layer standards define electrical and mechanical interfaces, as well as procedures and functions for their operation. The physical layer can also activate the transmission media, maintain transmission of data over that link, and deactivate the link upon end of transmission, while doing this through interfaces with the data link layer. The physical layer is concerned only with assuring the transmission and reception of a data stream between two devices.

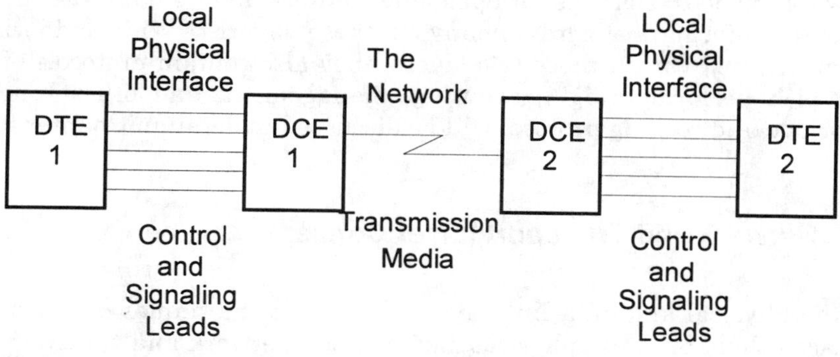

Figure 7.1 DTE-to-DTE Communications over DCE

The intelligence managing the data stream and the protocols residing above the physical layer are transparent to the physical layer. Physical cable-connector characteristics, voltages and currents, and timing and signaling are functions of the physical layer. And the physical layer interfaces with many physical network media devices spanning many standards and architectures. Functional specifications define data, control, timing, and grounding assignments. Procedural specifications define the procedures that govern the activation, use, and interpretation of these interface characteristics.

7.1.2 Data Link Layer Concepts

The data link layer is layer 2 in most computer architecture models, including the seven-layer OSIRM. The data link layer interfaces between the first physical layer and the third network layer protocols, interpreting the data flow across the physical media and feeding the network layer protocols information on the outcome of these services. The primary function of the data link layer is to establish a data link across the physical medium, manage reliable data flow across this medium, and terminate the link after completion of accurate data flow. The data link control functions establish a peer-to-peer relationship across the network. This layer may also provide functions and services such as error control, detection, and correction; flow control; framing and character formatting; synchronization; sequencing for proper delivery; connection control; and management functions.

Data link functions and protocols use many circuit topologies including point-to-point, multipoint, switching, and broadcast. Since computer communications via LANs utilizes special functions of the data link layer, both the MAC and LLC sublayers will be emphasized. The MAC sublayer protocols deserve special attention since they form the basis of local and metropolitan area network standards.

Network devices such as bridges and routers manipulate the protocol transfer of information across many of these layers. While adhering to protocols defined within these two layers, they also contain protocols of their own, which perform bridging, routing, management, and other functions. Each bridge and routing protocol will be discussed in detail in Chapter 8.

7.1.3 Network and Transport Layer Concepts

Once the physical and data link layers have built the frames of information and placed them onto the physical medium, the network and transport layer protocols take over and pass information through the network in packets and ensure end-to-end reliable delivery. A broad range of network and transport protocols from many different architectures will be explored and explained.

7.2 PHYSICAL LAYER PROTOCOLS AND INTERFACES

There are several major types of physical interfaces that primarily involve the physical layer of the OSIRM. The more commonly known interfaces include: RS-232C; EIA-449; EIA-232E; EIA-530; ITU-T Recommendations V.24/V.28, X.21, X.21bis, I.430, I.431, T1/E1, and D4/ESF; High Speed Serial Interface (HSSI); High Performance Parallel Interface (HIPPI); ESCON; and Fibre Channel. Some physical interfaces are integrated with link and network layer protocols such as the IEEE 802.X LAN standard interfaces. Selected standards will be discussed. Physical wiring interfaces and framing standards such as T1/E1 and D4/ESF will also be discussed.

7.2.1 Physical Media

There are three major types of physical media: unshielded copper wire, shielded copper wire, and fiber optics. Air may also form part of the transmission media, such as with cellular wireless or microwave.

Unshielded copper wire is typically present as unshielded twisted pair (UTP). UTP is the typical wiring type found in most buildings and is the least expensive of all cabling types. Unfortunately, UTP has high error rates and is subject to crosstalk, noise, and interference.

Shielded copper wire can be present as shielded twisted pair (STP), coaxial (coax), twin-axial (twin-ax), and broadband (used in CATV). The shielding protects the cable from the interference and high error rates experienced by UTP. All forms of shielded copper wire are more expensive than UTP.

Fiber optics is fast becoming the standard for all new facilities transmission cabling. The price of fiber optics and its connection devices continues to drop. Fiber optics has the added advantage of resistance to electromagnetic signals and is not affected by crosstalk, interference, or the elements.

Each progressive transmission medium has a better error rate and can carry much more high-bandwidth and high-speed protocols and applications. In fact, new technologies like Wave Division Multiplexing (WDM) can push a single strand of fiber-optic cable to transmit over 10,000,000,000 bits of data per second, where UTP is limited to the range of 10,000,000 bits per second over long distances (at short distances even 155 Mbps ATM may be possible based on a trade-off of distance for speed).

In IBM cabling terms, Type 1 cabling is two-wire STP, Type 2 cabling is two-wire STP or four-wire UTP, Type 3 cabling is four-wire UTP, Type 5 cabling is fiber, Types 6, 8, and 9 cabling are braided large gauge two-wire copper.

7.2.2 RS-232-C, EIA-232-E, EIA-449, and ITU-T V.24/ V.28

RS-232-C and EIA-232-E are defined by the Electronic Industries Association (EIA) as synchronous interface standards for use with the physical layer of the OSIRM. Adopted at a time when analog transmission was the prevalent industry standard, RS-232-C is probably the most common interface standard, and provides a D-shaped 25-pin connector DTE interface to voice-grade modems (DCE). The EIA-232-E is a more recently adopted standard which, though offering a significant upgrade to the RS-232-C standard, has had limited acceptance. The EIA-530 standard is also replacing the EIA-449 standard.

The ITU-T V.24/V.28 standard is very similar to RS-232-C and provides the international version of the RS-232-C standard. ITU-T V.24 defines the physical interface and V.28 defines the electrical interface. Many of the EIA standards parallel multiple ITU-T standards. For example, the RS-232-C standard contains the electrical, mechanical, and signal definitions for physical connectivity. The ITU-T V.24 (signal definition), V.28 (electrical), and ISO mechanical standards are required to define a similar interface.

Since the 232 standards are over 35 years old and are based on the technology of that time, limitations show up on implementation, such as a maximum distance of 15 m (50 ft) and a speed of 19.2 kbps on standard RS-232-C. RS-449 was adopted later to alleviate these distance and speed restrictions and improve performance by using a 37-pin connector. This provides balanced signaling and tighter cabling and electrical specifications.

Two other standards were developed to further extend the distance and speed of the RS-232-C interface. The RS-423A offers an improvement of up to 300 kbps speed and operates in "unbalanced" transmission mode, while the RS-422A offers speeds up to 10 Mbps and operates in "balanced" transmission mode. Note that EIA-449 is a mechanical interface and uses a 423/422 electrical interface. EIA-530 is also mechanical and uses a DB-25 interface instead of the EIA-449's DB-37 and DB-9.

7.2.3 ITU-T X.21, X.21bis

The ITU-T developed the X.21 standard in 1972 as a physical interface specification for digital networks using digital transmission facilities (unlike RS-232-C which was designed during the analog network era). X.21 also eliminates the restrictions imposed by RS-232-C by using balanced signaling and two wires for each circuit (as opposed to two wires total for transmit and receive in RS-232). This allows for full duplex transmission of user data and control and circuit status information. X.21 also adds more logic at the DTE and DCE interfaces. X.21 spans the gap between the physical and data link layers of the OSIRM, even touching, at times, upon the network layer for circuit-switched networks. The call-management capabilities of X.21 will be discussed later. X.21 uses a 15-pin connector and operates only in synchronous transmission. It provides an unbalanced or balanced mode of operation. The major capabilities present in RD-232-C but lacking in X.21 are the ability to pass control information during data transfer and the separation of transmit and receive signal-element timing circuits and signal rate selectors. The X.21bis interim standard was developed as a migration from the RS-232-C, EIA-232-D, and V.24 standards to X.21.

7.2.4 ITU-T I.430 and I.431

The ITU-T has defined many standards for the Integrated Services Digital Networks (ISDN). Two standards are defined for the physical interface to ISDN: Basic Rate Interface (BRI), or basic access, defined in the ITU-T I.430 standard, and Primary Rate Interface (PRI), defined in the ITU-T I.431. Both standards define the electrical characteristics, signaling, coding, and frame formats of ISDN communications across the S/T (user access interface) reference point as shown in Chapter 4. The physical layer provides transmission capability, activation and deactivation of terminal equipment (TE) and network termination (NT) devices, D-channel access for TE, maintenance functions, and channel status indications. The basic infrastructure for these physical implementations, as well as the definition for S/T, TE, and NT, are defined in ITU-T recommendation I.412.

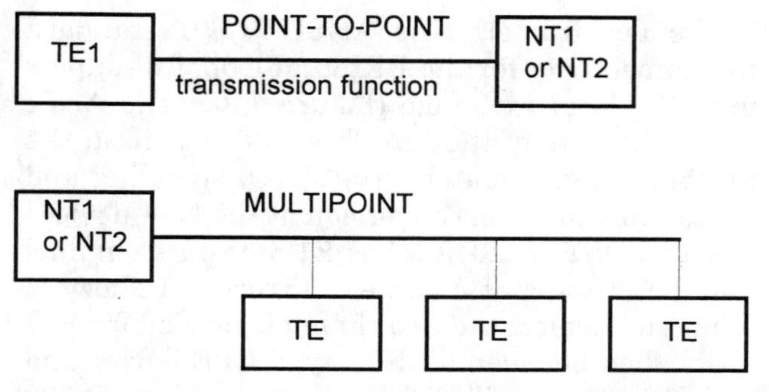

Figure 7.2 ISDN BRI Point-to-Point and Multipoint Configurations

Note that BRI and PRI interfaces are part of the specifications for Narrowband ISDN (N-ISDN). The physical interface in ISDN is one part of the D-channel protocol, and defines a full-duplex synchronous connection between the TE layer 1 terminal side of the basic access interface (TE1, TA, and NT2 functional group aspects) and the NT layer 1 terminal side of the basic access interface (NT1 and NT2 functional group aspects). Figure 7.2 shows both a point-to-point configuration with one transmitter and one receiver per interchange circuit, as well as a multipoint configuration with multiple TEs both for BRI. Both bus distances cannot exceed 1000 m except when using a short passive bus as opposed to an extended passive bus in multipoint mode, when the limitation is 180 m. These bus configurations are explained in Appendix A of the I.430 standard. The bit rate in both directions is 192 kbps for BRI (2B+D).

Basic Rate Interface (BRI). Offers two 64 kbps user data (bearer) channels and one 16 kbps control, messaging, and network management channel (D-channel). This interface is also referred to as 2B+D (the B stands for "bearer" channel, bearing the user's data information). The BRI is primarily used for customer access devices such as the ISDN voice, data, and videophone or simply for access to a protocol converted to a public network service like frame relay.

Primary Rate Interface (PRI). Offers 23 64 kbps user data channels and one 64 kbps signaling channel. This interface is also referred to as 23B+D. PRI is primarily used by customer devices requiring large amounts of bandwidth such as the Private Branch Exchange (PBX) and LAN servers. PRI is becoming the access method of choice for private access to the Internet.

The BRI interface consists of two B-channels and one D-channel (2B+D) using an ISO standard 8877 eight-pin, subminiature modular plug and an RJ-45 jack. This connector represents one of the first open-standard, end-user interfaces. The 192 kbps transmission rate is accomplished by 4000 frames per second with 48 bits per frame. The ANSI T1.601 standard provides the U reference point connectivity for the BRI local-loop, full-duplex connectivity via twisted pair to the local exchange (Figure 7.3). The ANSI standards also define many other aspects of the interface different from the I.430 standard, due to the two-binary, one-quaternary (2B1Q) signaling and framing scheme, and will require some protocol conversion at the NT1 device.

PRI provides a single 1.544 Mbps DS1 or 2.048 Mbps E1 data-rate channel over a full-duplex synchronous point-to-point channel. Figure 7.4 shows a PRI point-to-point configuration, and depicts the two channels needed for PRI data transfer. The link is established between an NT2-type CPE device and the Local Exchange Carrier (LEC) switch. ITU-T Recommendations G.703 and G.704 define the electrical and frame formats of the PRI interface, respectively. The 1.544 Mbps rate is accomplished by 8000 frames per second of 193 bits per frame over a standard T1 line. Twenty-four channels of 64 kbps each compose the T1, containing 23 B-Channels at 64 kbps each and one D-channel (equivalent to a B-channel) at 64 kbps. Twenty-four frames are transmitted in each multiframe, utilizing Bipolar 8 Zero Substitution (B8ZS) code.

Figure 7.5 shows the transmitted framing of the T1 PRI interface. The CEPT E1 PRI interface is somewhat different from this, offering 30 B-channels, one D-channel, and a channel reserved for physical layer signaling, framing, and synchronization.

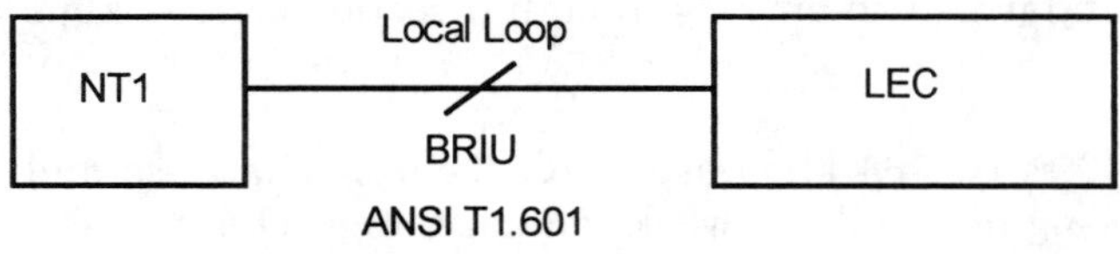

Figure 7.3 Standard ISDN BRIU and Local-Loop Interfaces

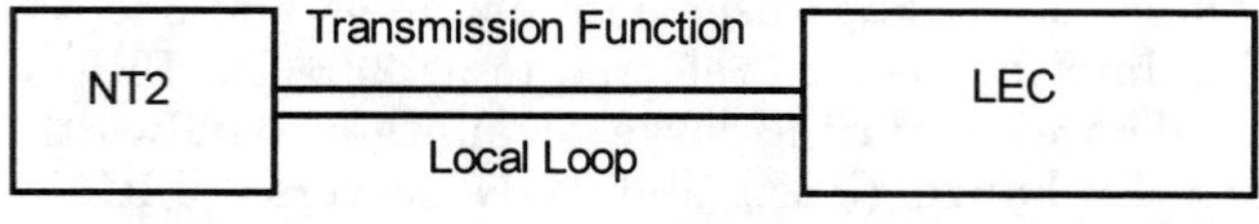

Figure 7.4 ISDN PRI Point-to-Point Connection

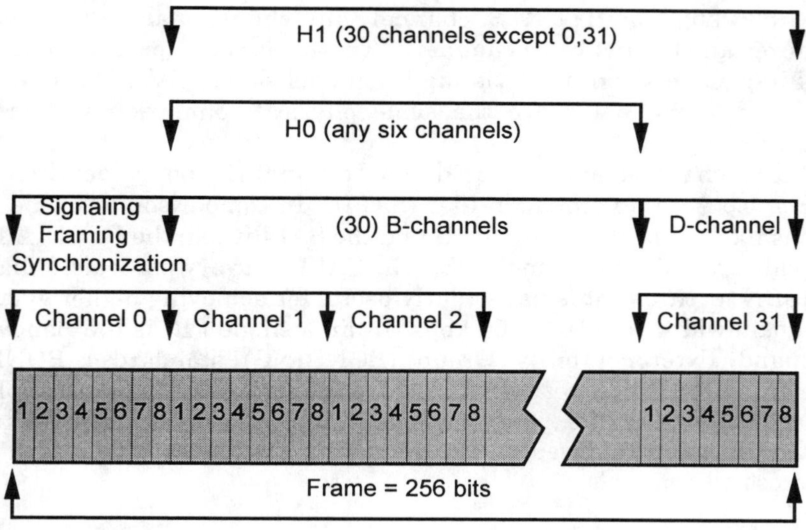

Figure 7.5 ITU-T T1 PRI Frame Structure

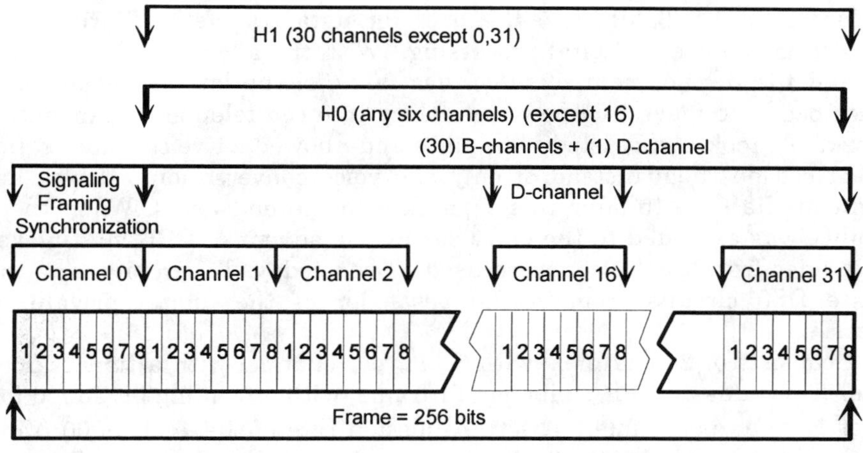

Figure 7.6 CEPT E1 PRI Frame Structure

The frame structure for the CEPT E1 PRI interface is shown in Figure 7.6. These 32 frames are transmitted via high-density bipolar 3 zeroes (HDB3) signaling. The primary attribute distinguishing ISDN service is the concept of common channel signaling, or out-of-band signaling using the D-channel.

H-channels are used in PRIs and defined in I.431. Two types are defined. H_0-channel signals have a bit rate of 385 kbps and H_1-channels have a bit rate of 1,536 kbps for H_{11} (U.S. channel rate) channels and 1,920 kbps for H_{12} (European channel rate) channels. These channels (except for the H_{12} channel implementation) use existing D-channel slots. Also note that the D-channel and B-channel share the same physical connection and medium through TDM.

ISDN local channels are composed of a Terminal Endpoint Identifier (TEI) and a Service Access Point Identifier (SAPI). In comparison to frame relay, the TEI is like the physical circuit ID and the SAPI is like the DLCI. All TEIs are the same number for a single TE. The SAPI will vary per logical channel.

One ISDN feature that is particularly useful for achieving higher aggregate channel bandwidth rates than 64 kbps within a single PRI is the Bandwidth-ON-Demand INteroperability Group (BONDING) standard. BONDING enables an ISDN device to act as an inverse multiplexer function by splitting a single data stream (i.e., 384 kbps) over multiple (6) 64 kbps channels. BONDING has the required delay calculating mechanisms to assure equal delay across all channels.

7.2.5 T1/E1 and D4/ESF Framing and Formatting

T1 circuits operate at a speed of 1.544 Mbps. With overhead they generally offer less than 1.536 Mbps to the user for data transfer. T1 technology derives from the use of digital processing. With the advent of the *transistor effect* and the development of *integrated circuits*, the large-scale telephone utilities began to move this new technology into the telephone transmission network. T1 took two twisted wire pairs and allowed 24 voice conversations to be placed on them instead of only one voice conversation. It was little thought at the time to offer this capability to the end users. When the T1 capability was extended to the end user by the advent of CPE multiplexers, private lines from the Telcos were used. Even today, T1 circuits (and their sub-rate DS0 circuits) remain the bestseller of the digital private line services.

A T1 consists of 24 channels with 8 bits per channel with a time frame of 125 μs. This adds up to 192 bits per T1 frame, with a framing bit added for a total of 193 bits per frame. The transmission rate of the T1 is 8000 frames per second, and includes an 8 kbps overhead channel. E1 is the European standard of the T1, and differs by offering 2.048 Mbps bandwidth. The 8 kbps framing overhead on each T1 channel can be used to great advantage, depending on what framing protocol is used. The D4 12-frame superframe concept allows the 8 kbps overhead on each T1 channel to be used for frame synchronization and signaling. The physical T1 port (often called a T1 framer port) is a DS1 channel as defined under the DSX-1 standard. Framed T1 runs at 1.544 Mbps over a DSX-1 interface. D4 framing formats can provide nonchannelized or channelized (as in DS0) circuits. D4 framing can also be used to access fractional T1 and DXC services.

There exists an alternate method of using the 8 kbps overhead channel. Extended Superframe Format (ESF) is an enhancement to D4 framing. The ANSI standard for ESF is T1.403. With ESF, both the carrier and the user can "nonintrusively" monitor the performance of private lines. The ESF divides the 8 kbps overhead channel into three network-management and reporting functions: 2 kbps performs the frame synchronization and signaling, 2 kbps provides a Cyclic Redundancy Check (CRC-6) code for providing error detection of end-to-end format and logic errors, while the last 4 kbps is the Facility Data Link (FDL) used as an open control channel.

The obvious advantage to ESF is the capability for remote monitoring and problem detection, without having to take the circuit out of service in order to test (as in D4 framing). This is called "nonintrusive" monitoring and testing. If ESF is implemented in conjunction with intelligent network equipment, errors affecting performance can be detected and corrected transparently to the user. ESF has played a valuable role with services such as frame relay and SMDS, where network management information provided by ESF can supplement and, in some instances, make up for existing deficiencies or lack of capabilities.

A word on Fractional T1 (FT1). While FT1 is popular, its sales have not come close to reaching those of T1. Users seem to favor using FT1 for tail circuits on complex, large networks. Fractional T1 is built as an interim step between a few (usually around a half dozen) dedicated circuits versus a full T1 (24 channels). It is a cost tradeoff. T3 is still in its infancy for widespread customer use, but more and more users who have large-bandwidth applications are looking into full and fractional T3 services. Currently, the price breakpoint for T3 seems to be the need for enough bandwidth for eight T1s or more to justify the DS3 facility. This varies based upon carrier tariffs.

DS3 circuits can either use asynchronous or synchronous protocol multiplexing. The asynchronous transmission protocols are defined in ANSI T1.107 and the synchronous transmission protocols (SYNTRAN) are defined in ANSI T1.103. Timing is usually derived by the CPE from the network elements, and is often referred to as loop timing.

7.2.6 AMI and B8ZS Line Coding

Line coding varies depending on the speed of access. DS0 channels can be configured as either 56 kbps or 64 kbps. 56 kbps channels use a technique called Alternate Mark Inversion (AMI). A process called "bit stuffing" is used to set the Least Significant Bit (LSB) in every byte to 1, and thus it is not available for user traffic. Bipolar Eight Zero Substitution (B8ZS) is used in the case of 64 kbps, or "clear channel" service. B8ZS allows the entire bandwidth of 64 kbps to be used. This is a requirement for 64 kbps frame relay network access. Always remember that either a CSU or a DSU is capable of providing either AMI or B8ZS coding, so make sure you have the correct device.

7.2.7 High-Speed Serial Interface (HSSI)

High-Speed Serial Interface (HSSI) is a physical interface operating at speeds up to 52 Mbps. The HSSI interface was primarily developed by Cisco Systems and T3Plus Networking, Inc. This high-speed interface was designed to become the standard interface between the DS3 rate of 45 Mbps and the OC-1 SONET interface of 51.84 Mbps for everything from WAN connectivity to a DTE-to-DCE direct-channel interface. It can be used to extend 45 Mbps DS3 mainframe channels to remote devices, providing a valuable high-speed interface between computer and communications equipment and, in effect, extending the WAN with larger bandwidth pipes. Currently, the HSSI interface is a CPE hardware interface. HSSI is a nonproprietary standard and is slated for ANSI standardization. The ANSI standard would use a 50-pin tab connector, shielded twisted-pair cabling, similar to the Small Computer Systems Interface II (SCSI-II), and could operate at up to SONET speeds. The HSSI interface is also software configured to handle a high-speed frame relay interface. HSSI can be found in ANSI X3.2.

7.2.8 HIgh-Performance Parallel Interface (HIPPI)

The HIgh-Performance Parallel Interface (HIPPI) is a high-speed broadband parallel point-to-point channel (interface) for supercomputer networking. HIPPI was designed by a few scientists at the Los Alamos National Laboratory who required high-speed parallel transfer speeds for graphic-intensive applications. HIPPI is standardized in ANSI X3T9.3/90-043, 1990. The standard defines HIPPI data transfer speeds of 100Mbytes per second or 20Mbytes per second over 50 twisted pair copper cable with a maximum distance of 25 meters. Serial-HIPPI specifications can reach baud rates of up to 1.2 gigabits per second over fiber-optic media. HIPPI circuits can be connected through multiple circuit switches in a crossbar topology.

7.2.9 Enterprise Systems Connection Architecture™ (ESCON)

ESCON provides high-speed, direct-channel connectivity for VM- and VSE-based system processors, Direct-Access Storage Devices (DASD), and peripherals. Primary support is for IBM 3990 storage control and application software. ESCON transfers data through synchronous, variable-length frames as opposed to the older byte-by-byte, Bus-and-Tag parallel interface. ESCON operates over fiber-optic cable, rather than the copper wire used in Bus-and-Tag. ESCON uses both device and link-level framing protocols, and can operate in either a cached or noncached mode. Cached transfer operates at 10 or 17 Mbytes per second channel speeds. Non-cached data transfers will operate at the full device speed.

ESCON also uses a device called a *director*. A director acts as a high-performance switch and router for all attached devices. ESCON topology, when using the director switch/router, resembles a logical star. This configuration is shown in Figure 7.7.

The advantages of ESCON include:

- Data center local or remote connectivity
- DASD extension (9 km versus 400 ft maximum distance between peripherals)
- Improved application and resource availability
- Increased transfer speed of data
- Increased control of data transfer
- Increased network and system performance
- Network management across all DASD and peripherals
- Easy configuration
- Electronic vaulting of critical data — disaster recovery
- User transparency to system reconfiguration
- Fiber-optic cables to replace copper

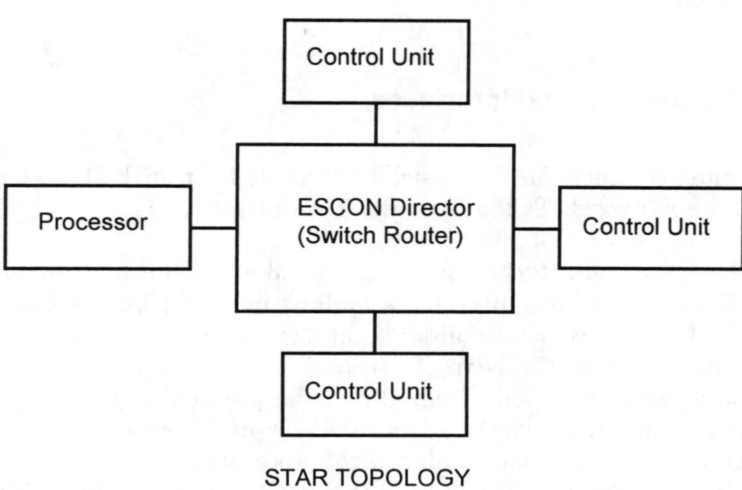

Figure 7.7 ESCON Star Topology with Director

IBM products have slowly moved users toward ESCON as the IBM standard high-end interface. Third-party ESCON controllers, switching devices, and converters are also available. Converter devices are required to convert between parallel bus-and-tag to ESCON channels, and thus make ESCON implementations more cost effective. Two converter models are available: 9034 ESCON Converter Model 1 and 9035 ESCON Converter Model 2. Although ESCON solves many problems, it is still a young interface. Many of the DASD and tape control unit peripherals still need to increase their internal speeds to take advantage of ESCON. The industry standards challenge for ESCON will be to map ESCON speeds to ATM and SONET interfaces. Routers are beginning to appear that can directly connect to IBM host processors through an ESCON interface.

7.2.10 Fibre Channel

The Fibre Channel Standard (FCS) defines a high-speed data-transfer interface for connecting and transferring data between computing devices ranging from workstations to supercomputers. FCS works over both electrical and optical media, and supports full-duplex data rates from 133 Mbps to 1062 Mbps over distances up to 10km. Topologies include point-to-point, loop, and switch matrix. FCS also has a built-in sliding window protocol for end-to-end delivery of data. FCS supports a variety of higher-level protocols such as HIPPI, IP, IEEE 802.2, and SCSI. Details on this technology can be found in ANSI X3.230-1994, Fibre Channel Physical and Signaling Interface (FC-PH).

7.2.11 IEEE 802 Physical Interfaces

The three most common MAC physical interfaces for the IEEE 802 architecture model are Ethernet, Token Bus, and Token Ring.

Ethernet. The physical interface for IEEE 802.3 and Ethernet provides more than just the synchronous interface standard provided by RS-232 or V.35. Recognition of the presence or absence of the control of the Carrier Sense Multiple Access with Collision Detection (CSMA/CD), data transport, collisions, and the translation of signaling from physical to MAC layer (layer 2 sublayer) are provided by the physical layer of Ethernet. These will be discussed in the section on data link control protocols.

There are five physical types of Ethernet access: 1BASE5, 10BASE2, 10BASE5, 10BASET, and 10BROAD36. Each type defines both the wiring and the device terminating the end of the wiring. 10BASE5 was the thick-cable Ethernet with the drop cable needed by each user to access via a tap.

The "10" refers to 10 Mbps Ethernet, while the "5" refers to the 500 m maximum length of a segment. 10BASE2 was introduced in the 1980s as thin-wire Ethernet (or "Cheapernet"), offering a thinner coaxial cable with the same method of access. The "2" refers to 200 m cable length. The physical connectors are called BNC and AUI, respectively.

The most common connectivity is via twisted-pair wiring and the 10BASET standard, where users access the medium through their telephone RJ45 wall jack, no more than 100 m of 0.5-mm gauge telephone twisted-pair into a star topology central hub. The "T" stands for twisted-pair cable. Both baseband coaxial and broadband coaxial were designed to operate at 10 Mbps, while unshielded twisted-pair (UTP) was designed to operate at 1 Mbps. A transceiver module may be needed to adapt to the 10BASE2 thin-wire or 10BASET twisted-pair Ethernet connection. Hubs are used to concentrate the star distributed twisted-pair cable connections. Other Ethernet proprietary implementations may require an external radio frequency modem or fiber-optic inter-repeater link. Another standard in process is the 10BASEF and 10BASEFB. The "F" stands for fiber. These standards specify fiber-optics with Ethernet networks and backbone Ethernet. The distance for Ethernet could be extended to 2 km, the same as for FDDI. Finally, 100 Mbps Ethernet has emerged.

For physical connectivity, cables run from the computer to the LAN and contain multiple-wire pairs with 15-pin interface connectors (there is also a RJ45 connector available). For coaxial cable wiring schemes, a tapping screw and tap block are needed to pierce the outer shielding and contact the center coaxial cable conductor and ground on the outer shield. An Attachment Unit Interface (AUI) provides the physical connection to transfer the MAC PDU from the user attached device to the LAN access device called a Medium Attachment Unit (MAU). This MAU attaches to the physical network medium via a Medium Dependent Interface (MDI). All Ethernet interfaces operate at a 10 Mbps bus speed for IEEE 802.3 and Version 1.0 and 2.0 Ethernet frame format.

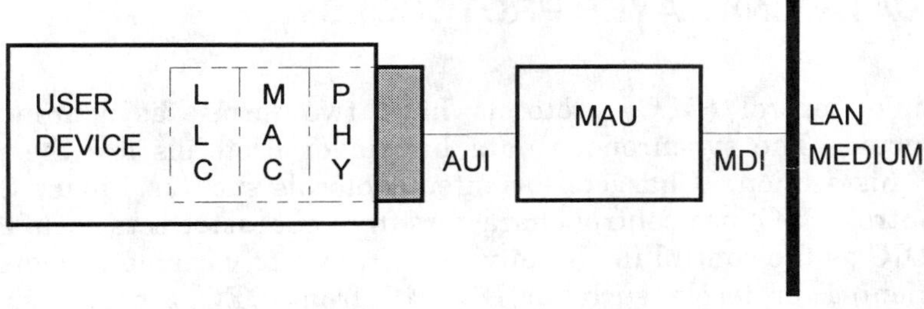

Figure 7.8 Token Ring Physical Connectivity

Token Bus and Token Ring. There are nine types of Token Bus physical interfaces. These interfaces fit into two categories: the broadband coaxial and the carrier-band coaxial, both supporting 1, 5, and 10 Mbps. Physical interface for IEEE 802.4 Token Bus and IEEE 802.5 Token Ring is the dB connector, interfacing the IBM Type 1 shielded twisted-pair cable. Coaxial cable connections are also available. Token Ring wiring is usually run in Type 1 (2-pair STP), Type 2 (4-pair STP), Type 3 (UTP), and Type 5 (fiber-optic cable). Token Ring interfaces at either 4 Mbps or 16 Mbps through an IEEE 802.5 interface, and uses 802.2 Type 1 LLC support. It also can interface via shielded twisted pair at 1, 4, and 16 Mbps. Figure 7.8 shows an example of Token Ring physical connectivity.

Table 7.1 shows a comparison of LAN physical media based on speed, maximum distance, and signaling. Baseband and broadband LANs are compared in Table 7.2.

TABLE 7.1 Physical Media Comparison

PHYSICAL MEDIA	STANDARD NAME	SPEED Mbps	MAX DISTANCE, m	SIGNAL MODE
50-ohm Coaxial	10BASE5	10	500	Baseband
50-ohm Coaxial	1BASE5	1	500	Baseband
Thin Coaxial	10BASE2	10	200	Baseband
UTP	1BASE5	1	500	Baseband
UTP	10BASET	10	100	Baseband
STP	Token Ring	4/16	100 (lobe)	Baseband
Broadband Coaxial	10Broad36	10	3600	Broad-band
Fiber-optic Cable	---	16	4500	Baseband
STP (data grade)	Token Ring	16	700(lobe) + 800 inter-MAU	Baseband

7.3 DATA LINK LAYER PROTOCOLS

Data Link Control (DLC) protocols have two forms: asynchronous and synchronous. The synchronous data link layer protocols are the primary focus of this section. Character-oriented protocols such as Binary Synchronous Control (BSC) use control characters from character sets such as ASCII or EBCDIC as the control fields set within frames of variable formats. Byte-count-oriented protocols such as DDCMP from DEC are similar to the character-oriented protocols but use count fields to indicate the number of bytes being transmitted. Finally, bit-oriented protocols such as SDLC, HDLC, ISDN BRI and PRI, and X.25 use specific bit *patterns* for frames. The individual bits define the protocol specifics and control the transmission. Bit-oriented protocols are of the most interest to us, because they represent the primary DLC protocols. Data link layer functions specific to frame relay, ATM, and SONET are discussed in later chapters.

TABLE 7.2 Comparison of Broadband and Baseband LANs

ATTRIBUTE	BASEBAND LANs	BROADBAND LANs
Media Type	Coaxial, UTP, STP, Fiber	Coaxial Cable
Number of Signals Carried	One (1 user has entire BW)	Multiple (FDM)
Type of signal	Digital (voltage on/off)	Analog (variation of carrier frequency)
Speeds	1 to 16 Mbps	1 to 5 Mbps per channel (20 – 30 channels)
Distance limitation	2000 ft (then digital repeaters required)	6000 ft. (MANs)
Installation & maintenance required	Easy install - minimum maintenance	Careful design, tuned components
Type of data carried	Data only	Data, voice, video
Typical topical distribution	Intrabuilding or intra-campus	Metropolitan area

7.3.1 Binary Synchronous Control (BSC or Bisync)

The Binary Synchronous Control protocol, BSC or Bisync, was introduced by IBM in the mid-1960s as an asynchronous half-duplex, point-to-point or multipoint, character-oriented protocol for bidirectional transmissions of character-oriented data. Each variable-sized frame consisted of control codes such as Start of TeXt (STX) and End of TeXt (ETX) to manage transmission of character-coded user information. All codes are derived from a single character set, EBCDIC, the model for the American Standard Code for Information Interchange (ASCII). Figure 7.9 shows a typical BSC text frame consisting of the following characters: a frame pad (PAD), two SYNchronous idles (SYN), a Start Of Header (SOH), header information, Start of TeXt (STX), nontransparent data (denoting a fixed- or variable-bit pattern), an End of TeXt (ETX), a Block Check Count (BCC), and another PAD. Note that when using BSC, every block sent requires a receipt acknowledgment, drastically limiting throughput.

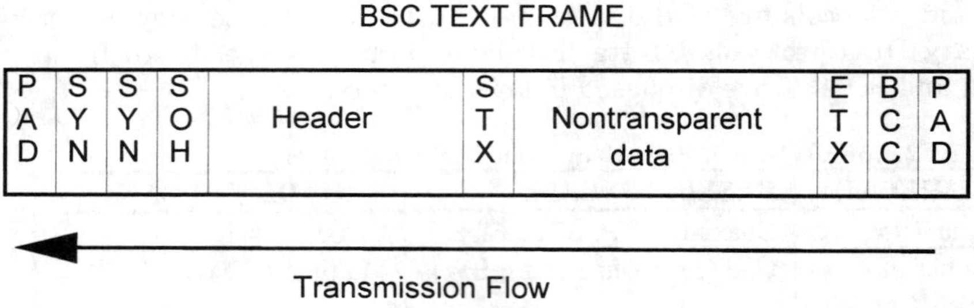

BSC TEXT FRAME

PAD	SYN	SYN	SOH	Header	STX	Nontransparent data	ETX	BCC	PAD

← Transmission Flow

Figure 7.9 BSC Text Frame Format

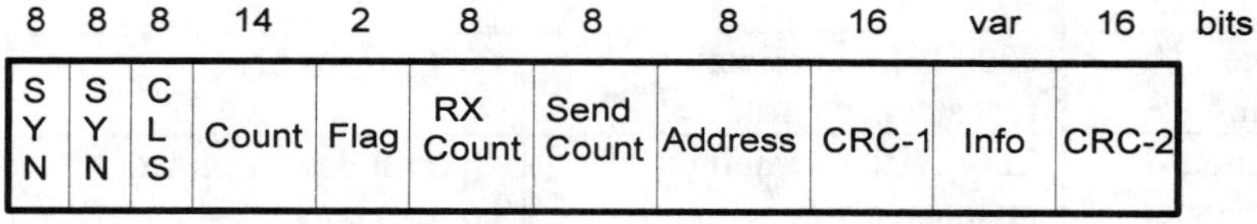

8	8	8	14	2	8	8	8	16	var	16	bits
SYN	SYN	CLS	Count	Flag	RX Count	Send Count	Address	CRC-1	Info	CRC-2	

Figure 7.10 DDCMP Standard Frame Format

7.3.2 Digital Data Communications Message Protocol (DDCMP)

The Digital Data Communications Message Protocol (DDCMP) developed by Digital Equipment Corporation (DEC) provides a byte-count-oriented protocol transmitted either asynchronously or synchronously over half- or full-duplex circuits on point-to-point or multipoint topologies. This protocol is similar to BSC, and uses a count field to indicate the number of bytes in the information field, synchronization characters, a flag, CRCs for error management, address and information fields, and the send and receive count fields. Figure 7.10 shows a standard DDCMP frame showing placement of these fields. DDCMP also provides for supervisory and information frames, where this information would replace the information field. No one coding scheme was standardized because each vendor had a self-interest to "proprietize" the coding for its unique products, lock in users, and protect its customer base.

7.3.3 Synchronous Data Link Control (SDLC)

In 1973 IBM was the first vendor to produce a bit-oriented protocol, called Synchronous Data Link Control (SDLC) . This de facto standard has been modified and adopted by the International Standards Organization (ISO) as the High-Level Data Link Control (HDLC) or ISO4335 protocol and by the American National Standards Institute (ANSI), as the Advanced Data

Communications Control Procedure (ADCCP) or ANSI X3.66. The ITU-T also has developed two standards based upon SDLC.

The ITU-T Link Access Procedure Balanced (LAPB) is the X.25 implementation of SDLC, and the ITU-T Link Access Procedure-D (LAPD) is the ISDN and frame relay (LAPF) HDLC-based implementation of SDLC. Since LAPB and LAPD are subsets of HDLC, the discussion will center on HDLC. HDLC has spawned a variety of HDLC-like protocols, including LAP, LAPB, LAPD, LAPF, LAPM, and LAPX. Figure 7.11 shows the relations and progression of various DLCs derived from SDLC. The framing of the SDLC frame is very similar to the HDLC framing that will be covered in the next section.

The present version of IBM's SDLC primarily uses the unbalanced normal response mode of HDLC together with a few proprietary commands and responses for support of loop or ring topology polling. SDLC operates independently on each communications link, and can operate in either multipoint or point-to-point, switched or dedicated circuit, and full- or half-duplex operation. The primary difference between SDLC and HDLC is that SDLC does not support the extended address field nor the extended control field.

SDLC is steadily replacing the less efficient BSC protocol. Some improvements of SDLC over BSC include: the ability to send acknowledgments, addressing, block checking, and polling within every frame rather than in a separate sequence; the capability of handling long propagation delays; no restrictions to half duplex; not susceptible to missed or duplicated blocks, not topology dependent, and not character code sensitive.

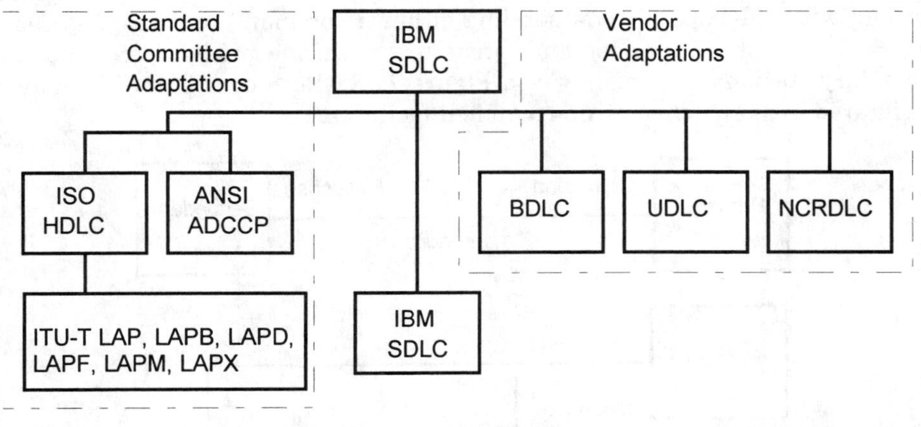

Figure 7.11 SDLC Legacy

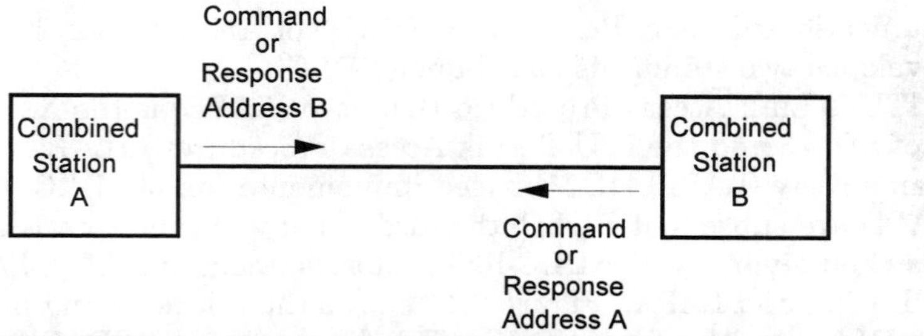

Figure 7.12 HDLC Balanced Mode

7.3.4 High-Level Data Link Control (HDLC)

HDLC protocol is not only the most popular protocol for data link control implementations (level 2), but it also forms the basis for ISDN and frame relay protocols and services. HDLC is an international standard, adopted under ISO TC97. HDLC is a bit-oriented; simplex, half-duplex, or full-duplex; and synchronous protocol passing variable-bit length streams over either a point-to-point or multipoint configuration. HDLC can also operate over either dedicated or switched facilities.

There are two types of point-to-point link structures: a primary station in "balanced mode" transmitting commands to and receiving responses from the secondary station, as in Figure 7.12, and as a combined transmitting and receiving station in "unbalanced" mode acting as a primary and secondary station, with the capability of sending either a command or a response as in Figure 7.13. The multidrop link structure with one primary and multiple secondary stations is also shown in Figure 7.13. Both configurations may be configured over switched or nonswitched facilities.

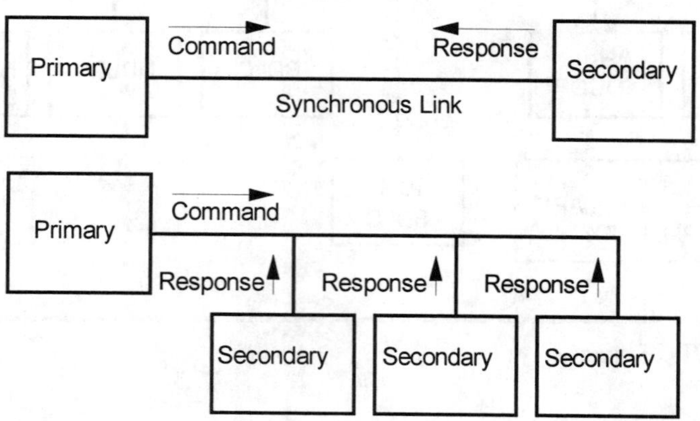

Figure 7.13 HDLC Unbalanced Mode

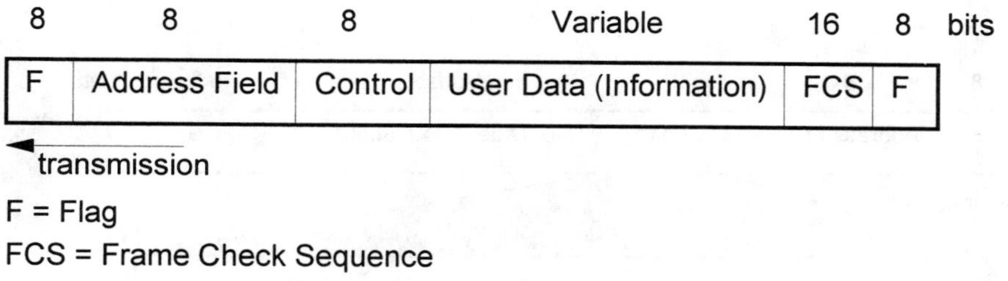

Figure 7.14 HDLC Frame Format

HDLC has three types of data-transfer modes. The two most common types are "unbalanced" Normal Response Mode (NRM) and Asynchronous Balanced Mode (ABM). NRM is used in multidrop and point-to-point links with the secondary station awaiting a poll from the primary one. ABM is used in the "balanced" configuration between combined stations, and allows only one secondary station to be active at any time. A third type or method is via "unbalanced" Asynchronous Response Mode (ARM), which requires the secondary stations in an "unbalanced" mode to have explicit permission from the primary station to initiate transmissions.

A standard HDLC frame format is used for both information exchange and control of transmission. This frame is represented in Figure 7.14. This frame format supports both basic and extended control field formats. Two flag fields of proprietary bit patterns encapsulate the frame, an address field provides the address of the secondary station (but is not needed for point-to-point configurations), the information field, of course, contains the data being transmitted, and the frame check sequence (FCS) verifies the accuracy of the fields within the frame. Also included in this frame is a *control field* to identify one of three types of frames available. The first bit (or 2 bits with supervisory and unnumbered frames) of each control field is used to identify the type of frame: *information*, *supervisory*, or *unnumbered*. These basic control field formats in an 8-bit version is found in Figure 7.15. The 16-bit version of the information, supervisory, and unnumbered frames is found in Figure 7.16.

The *information* frame is used to transport user data between stations. Within this frame, the N(S) and N(R) fields designate a modulo 8 send-and-receive count for the number of frames to be transmitted (S) and received (R), respectively. The P/F field designates a poll requesting transmission from the secondary station or a final bit indicating the end frame in the transmission sequence. The *supervisory* frame manages flow control and error control through positive and negative acknowledgments using four modes of operation: Receive Ready (RR), Receive Not Ready (RNR), REJect (REJ), and Selective REJect (SREJ). " S" bits establish one of these modes, and all other fields operate the same as before. The actual bit transmission order is also shown in the figure.

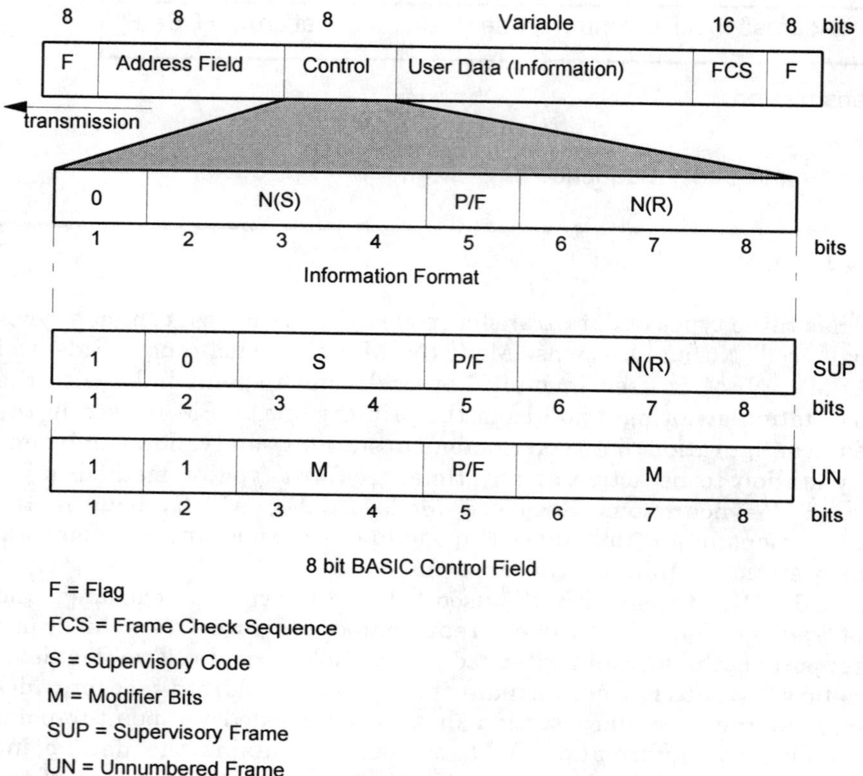

Figure 7.15 HDLC Frame with Control Field Breakouts (8-bit version)

The *unnumbered* frame specifies a variety of control functions through the mode-setting commands just discussed: NRM, ARM, and ABM. The "M" modifier bits specify which type of unnumbered frame to use.

Other implementations of HDLC are also used. It is interesting to note that HDLC is often used in satellite transmissions, because the window can open between 2 and 127 frames in size before an acknowledgment is needed. This is important due to the 500-ms turnaround times for up- and down-link transmissions.

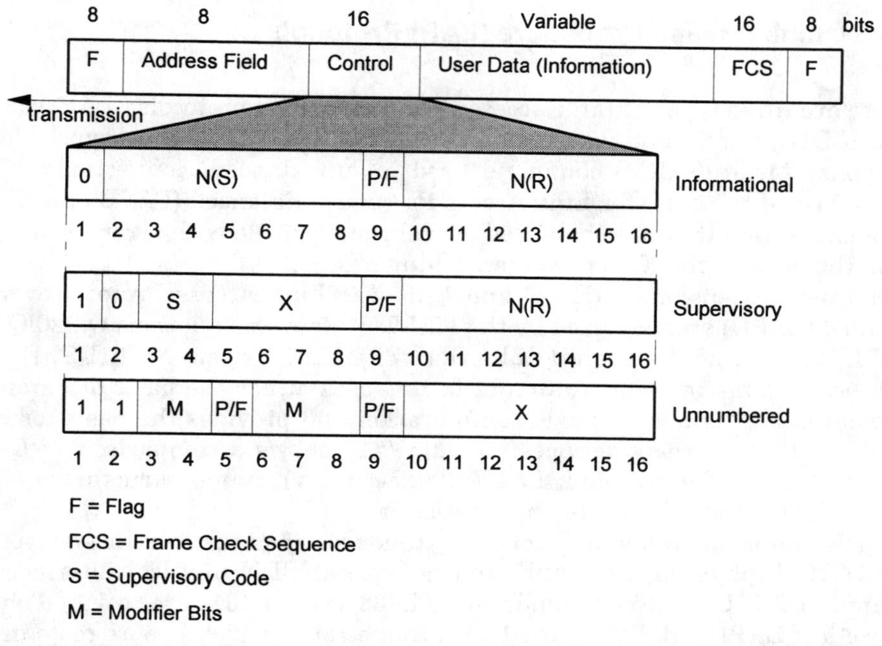

Figure 7.16 HDLC Frame with Control Field Breakouts (16-bit version)

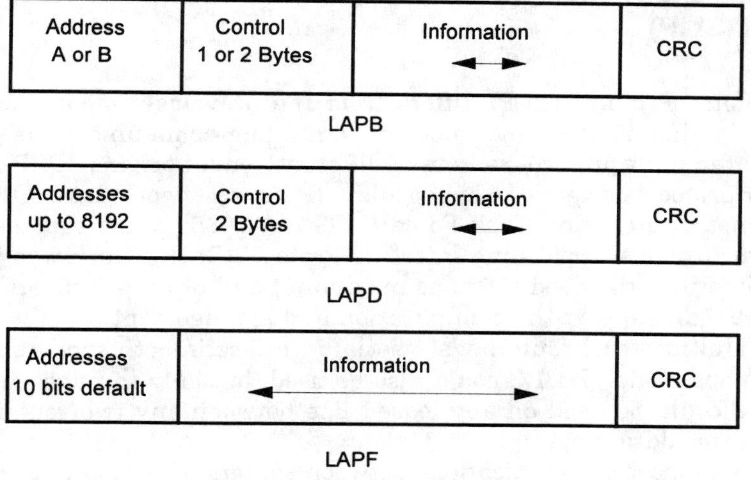

Figure 7.17 LAPB (X.25), LAPD (ISDN), and LAPF (Frame Relay) Comparison

7.3.5 Link Access Procedure (LAP) Protocols

There are three types of Link Access Procedure (LAP) protocols. LAP was the first ISDN protocol and was designed based on the HDLC Set Asynchronous Response Mode (SARM) command used in "unbalanced" connections. This mode formed the basis for Link Access Procedure Balanced (LAPB), an HDLC implementation that uses balanced asynchronous mode with error recovery to form the basis of the X.25 packet switching protocol.

The next extension of HDLC and LAP was Link Access Protocol over D-channel (LAPD) standardized by the ITU-T in Recommendations Q.920/Q.921 and I.440/I.441 as the Digital Subscriber Signaling System No.1 (DSS1) data link layer. This implementation of HDLC uses either the basic or extended asynchronous "balanced" mode configuration and provides the basis for both ISDN and frame relay services. Figure 7.17 shows a comparison of LAPB (X.25), LAPD (ISDN), and LAPF (frame relay) frame structures. The tradeoffs of both will become apparent later.

ISDN and frame relay protocols and standards span the first three layers of the OSIRM: physical, data link, and network. ISDN physical interfaces as defined in ITU-T Recommendations I.430 and I.431 are covered here. Aspects of LAPD will be explored with frame relay, which has its roots in the ISDN and LAP protocol suites.

7.3.6 Point-to-Point Protocol (PPP) and Serial Line Interface Protocol (SLIP)

Point-to-Point Protocol (PPP) differs from the previously mentioned router protocols in that it was developed for serial-line communications between routers, often multiprotocol routers of different vendor origins. PPP is a data link layer protocol designed to encapsulate IP inter-network data. Created by the Internet Engineering Task Force (IETF) in 1988, it has superseded the older asynchronous Serial Line Interface Protocol (SLIP) which was theoretically limited in both speed (56 kbps maximum) and protocol support (TCP/IP only). PPP can support the configuration and management of links between multiple multiprotocol routers via a serial interface in both synchronous and asynchronous mode. HDLC could also be used, but only through encapsulation. PPP could be used on any leased line between any two routers. PPP also supports addressing.

PPP can support communications between routers using many protocols in addition to TCP/IP, such as DECnet, OSI Internet protocols like CLNP, IPX, and AppleTalk. PPP has many advantages, such as providing addressing information exchange between routers having different addressing schemes, employing data compression techniques, providing link quality monitoring via the LQM protocol, and offering levels of encryption. Its security features allow the network to check and confirm the identity of users attempting to establish a connection. PPP operates like many of the services and protocols that rely on clean, reliable transmission media: it discards any packets received in error, letting the higher-level protocols sort out the retransmission. PPP is attractive for router network design when a small number of network routers are used without another Internet protocol, and with a higher-level protocol to account for discarded data. PPP does not have to tie up the entire physical circuit; it can be shared with other serial-line protocols only on a session by session basis – two encapsulations (e.g., SLIP, PPP, FR, etc.) cannot be used simultaneously. PPP defines both a Link Control Protocol (LCP) for link establishment, configuration, and testing and an Internet Protocol Control Protocol (IPCP, specifically, IPXCP for IPX, ATCP for AppleTalk, etc.) for network control. PPP has been adopted by hub and router vendors alike and is often the protocol of choice for remote-switched access.

7.4 LLC AND MAC SUBLAYER PROTOCOLS

The Logical Link Control (LLC) and Media Access Control (MAC) sublayers roughly associate to the upper and lower layers of the data link control layer (layer 2) of the OSIRM. Figure 7.18 shows this relationship. Together with the physical layer, data link standards make up the core IEEE 802.X protocol standards. The MAC layer manages communications across the physical medium, defines frame assembling and disassembling, and performs error detection and addressing functions. The LLC layer interfaces with the network layer through Service Access Points (SAPs), as shown in Figure 7.19. This section will define the MAC and LLC sublayer functions, along with the IEEE 802.3 through 802.5 protocol operations over both sublayers. A detailed discussion of SMDS and IEEE 802.6 will be covered in Chapter 12.

While the IEEE 802.2 standard defines the logical link control layer, further developments with the IEEE 802.3 through 802.6 standards define the MAC layer protocols. Multiple MAC protocols can exist under the same LLC. Figure 7.20 shows the physical relationship between LLC and MAC interface points, where a multiple-host application LLC interfaces to an Ethernet LAN is via a single MAC address. A Network Interface Unit (NUI) also provides a single MAC address to the same Ethernet LAN, and supports a terminal and workstation on separate LLC addresses. The host also connects to a Token Ring LAN, while another NUI, with workstation, attaches to the Token Ring LAN.

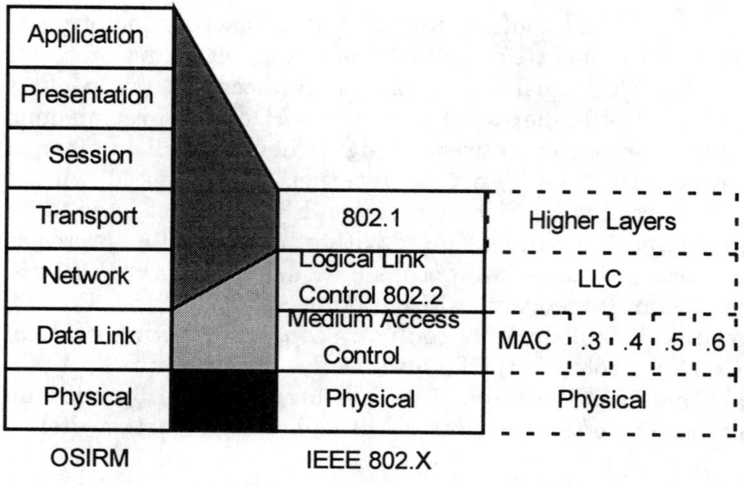

Figure 7.18 LLC and MAC Layer Protocol Stack of IEEE 802.X Compared to the OSIRM

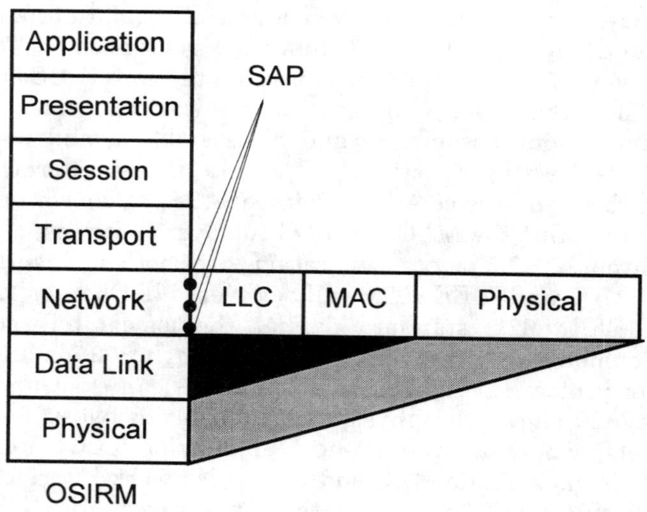

Figure 7.19 LLC and Service Access Points (SAPs)

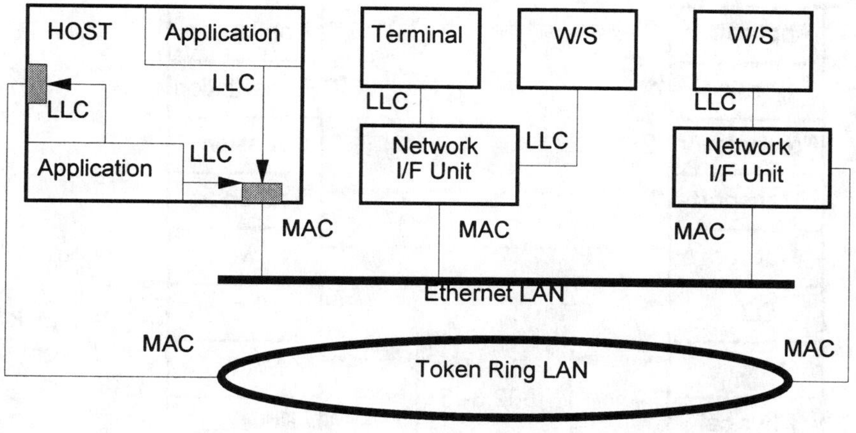

Figure 7.20 Illustration of LLC and MAC Physical Interface Points

7.4.1 Logical Link Control (LLC) Sublayer

The Logical Link Control (LLC) protocols are designed for peer-to-peer communications over multipoint bus and ring topologies. The IEEE 802.2 standard defines the LLC sublayer within the layer 2 data link layer. In LLC, primary and secondary stations do not exist — all stations are *common* to the transmission medium, with no intermediate switching. The LLC sublayer protocol allows a 802.3, .4, or .5 protocol to carry multiple, logical sub-network traffic of each protocol over the same physical medium, such as the LAN.

The two major modes of service interfacing with the network layer are connection-oriented and connectionless. Connection-oriented service uses the previously mentioned SAP peer-to-peer communications and provides acknowledgments, flow control, and error recovery. There are two classes of connectionless services provided in the LLC: class 1, or *unacknowledged* connectionless, which requires both the sending and receiving station address to be contained in each packet, and class 2, or *acknowledged* connectionless, which requires the acknowledgment of each individual frame. Both types of connectionless services provide no acknowledgments, flow control, or error control, but rely on higher-level protocols to perform these functions.

The LLC and MAC sublayers of the layer 2 data link layer, along with the other layers of the OSIRM, are shown in Figure 7.21. From this reference it is clear that the LLC sublayer serves a peer-to-peer protocol function between end users, and that the MAC and physical layers interface to the LAN transport media.

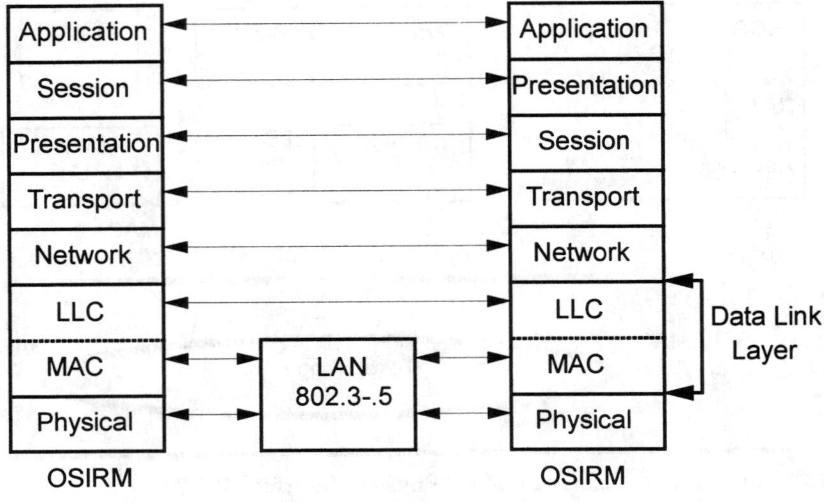

Figure 7.21 LAN Layers of the OSIRM

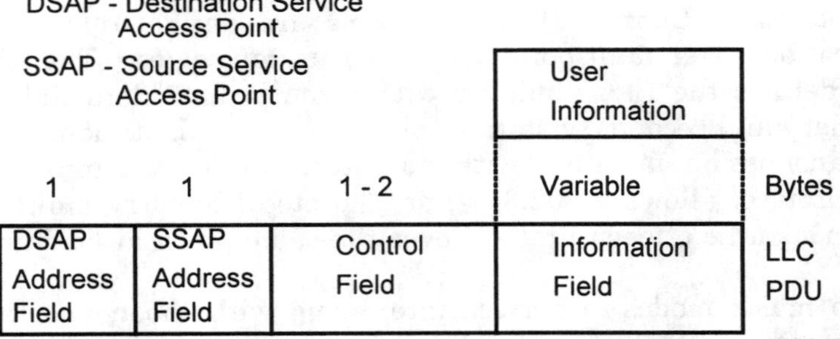

Figure 7.22 LLC Protocol Data Unit (PDU)

When the logical data link layer receives user data in the form of an information field, it adds a header to this field and forms what is called a Protocol Data Unit (PDU). Figure 7.22 shows the formation of the LLC PDU. The information field can be variable in size. The PDU header contains both a destination address and a source address of the origination port for a network hardware device or application for network software. Both are referred to as Service Access Points (SAPs). It is important to note that the size of these address fields determines the number of possible addresses on the network. There are two options, a 2-byte or a 6-byte address field, with each defined as individual or group, with universal or local authority.

The physical and logical link layers of many vendor-proprietary LAN standards follow those of the 802.X standards. As a final note, IEEE 802.1 is defined by the ISO and ITU-T as the Higher Layers and Management Interface (HILI) standards. These standards are focused on bridging protocols, and one example, the Spanning Tree Protocol (STP), will be defined in Chapter 8. The IEEE 802.X standards above 802.6 are left for further study by the reader.

7.4.2 Media Access Control (MAC) Sublayer

The Media Access Control (MAC) sublayer in the OSIRM data link layer (layer 2) manages and controls communications across the physical media, manages the frame assembling and disassembling, and performs error detection and addressing functions. It is the point where distributed processing begins. The four most common MAC layers include:

- 802.3 CSMA/CD Ethernet
- 802.4 Token Bus
- 802.5 Token Ring
- 802.6 Metropolitan Area Networks (MANs)

Other completed standards include:

- 802.9a isoEthernet
- 802.10 LAN Security Working Group
- 802.11 100BASEVG

The following MAC standards are still under development:

- 802.12 Wireless
- 802.14 CATV-based LAN

There are two Technical Advisory Groups (TAGs)

- 802.7 Broadband Technical Advisory Group
- 802.8 Fiber-optic Technical Advisory Group

There is also one MAC layer bridge protocol 802.1d bridge (Spanning Tree) designed to interface any 802 LAN with any other 802 LAN. This protocol will be covered in Chapter 8.

When the MAC layer receives the Logical Link Control PDU, it adds a header and trailer for transmission across the MAC layer (and physical medium). Figure 7.23 shows the LLC PDU as formatted into a MAC PDU. Each of the specific IEEE 802.X MAC frames conforms to this format and is described in the following sections. This new frame is now called a MAC

PDU. MAC addresses are unique and identify physical station points on the network. Each station reads this MAC address to determine if the call should be passed to one of the LLC entities. Each Network User Interface (NUI), discussed in the section on physical interfaces, has its own SAP and address.

Since there are many potential combinations of Ethernet types and protocols, the LLC control header was extended. The IEEE defined an extension to the 1-byte SAP field to allow more than 64 SAP values to be identified. In a normal MAC frame, the LLC DSAP and SSAP would be 1 byte, and the LLC control 1 to 2 bytes. When the DSAP and SSAP values equal AA_H, and the LLC control field equals 03_H, then there are two fields added to the MAC frame header – an Organizationally Unique Identifier (OUI) for defining an organization that will assign a Protocol Identifier (PID) for the type of Ethernet. One example would be an Ethertype frame running DECnet Phase IV protocol, where the OUI and PID values would be 00000_H and 6003_H, respectively. Figure 7.24 illustrates the SubNetwork Access Point (SNAP) structure. The list of available LLC1/SNAP header types is published in RFC 1340. Use of the SNAP is shown in later chapters where many Ethertypes and protocol types are identified as they are transported over services like SMDS.

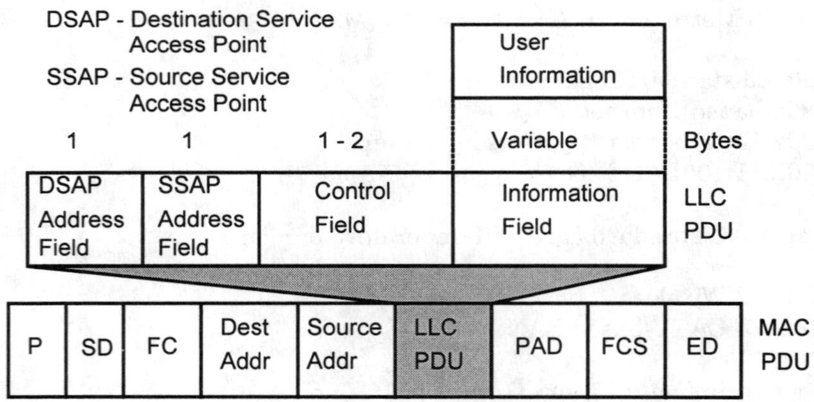

Figure 7.23 LLC PDU Formatted into the MAC PDU

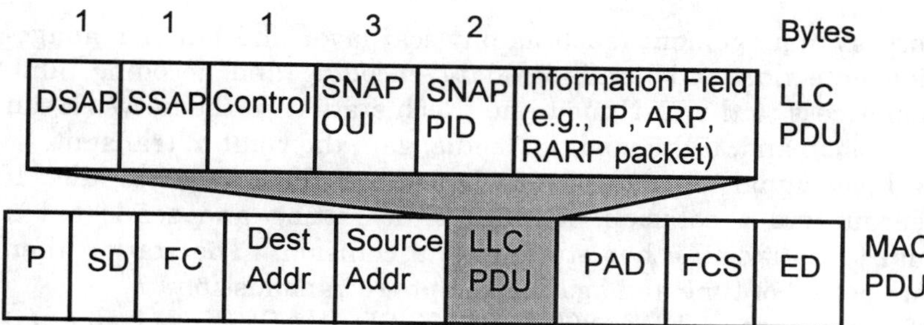

P = Preamble
SD = Starting Delimiter
FC = Frame Control
FCS = Frame Check Sequence
ED = Ending Delimiter
DSAP = Destination Service Access Point
SSAP = Source Service Access Point

Figure 7.24 IEEE LLC1 and SNAP Header

Now let's take a look at the three most common of the MAC protocols: Ethernet, Token Bus, and Token Ring.

7.4.3 802.3 CSMA/CD (Ethernet)

Ethernet was invented by Dr. Robert M. Metcalfe in the late 1970s at the Xerox Palo Alto Research Center. The first Ethernet specifications were published by the multivendor consortium of DEC, Intel, and Xerox (DIX) in 1980, and the first products for Ethernet appeared in 1981. This standard used a Media Access Control (MAC) protocol called Carrier Sense Multiple Access with Collision Detection (CSMA/CD) within a standard Ethernet frame, across a common physical medium bus with channel-attached MAC-addressed stations. The IEEE later adopted Ethernet as the IEEE 802.3 standard. This is a classical case of vendor-driven standards development. The use of CSMA/CD allows the LLC sublayer to send data (given a collision does not occur) at rates theoretically reaching 10 Mbps. In actuality, it can reach about 3.5 Mbps under maximum load conditions.

CSMA/CD allows for stations to both transmit and receive data in a "best-effort" data delivery system – no guarantee of data delivery is made. During a collision the end stations initiate a "back-off" algorithm and follow a mathematical formula to randomize each station's next attempt to retransmit. The medium can be either baseband or broadband. The specific data link functions of Ethernet include encapsulation and de-encapsulation of user data, media access management (such as physical layer and buffer management), collision detection and handling, data encoding and decoding, and, finally, channel access to the LAN medium. Each station on the network can attempt transmission and, if the medium is idle, gain the right to transmit. If they receive a busy signal, they transmit when the medium becomes idle. If the station encounters a collision, it stops transmitting and sends out a jamming signal to notify all other stations of a collision. The station then waits a random period of time and again attempts retransmission.

Figure 7.25 shows the IEEE 802.3 CSMA/CD MAC PDU frame (a) compared to an Ethernet frame (b).

The preamble field provides synchronization. It is the "carrier" that is detected by other stations, which in turn stops them from transmitting. The Starting Frame Delimiter (SFD) is a "start-of-frame" character. The destination and source address provide the MAC-layer destination and source address. Each address is created by combining a 24-bit OUI from the manufacturer of the Ethernet interface card with a 24-bit unique address to form a 48-bit hardware-coded MAC address. The length field identifies the length of the data field in bytes. The information field is the LLC PDU. The pad provides extra characters to achieve a minimum frame length value. Finally, the frame check sequence is the standard CRC-32. The maximum size of the 802.3 frame is 1500 bytes. This is an important number to remember when we start segmenting MAC frames into IP packets.

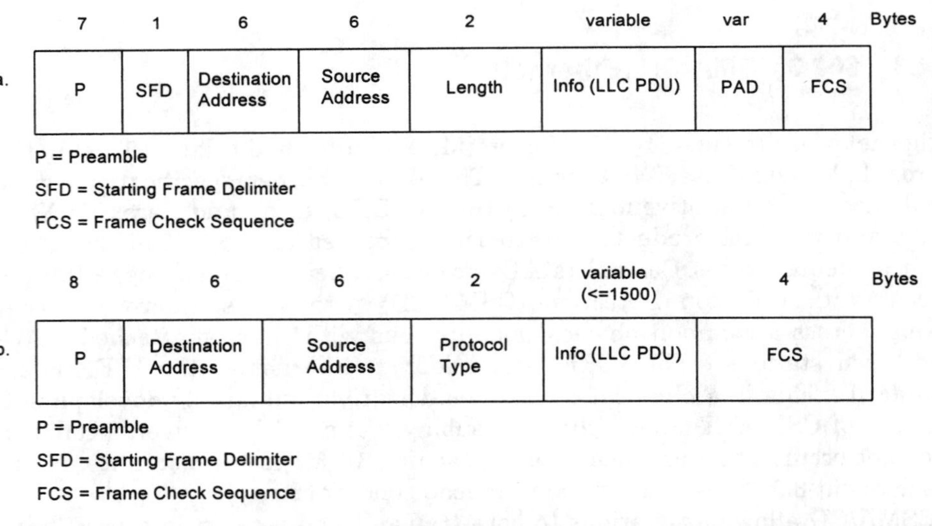

Figure 7.25 (a) IEEE 802.3 CSMA/CD and (b) Ethernet MAC PDU Frame

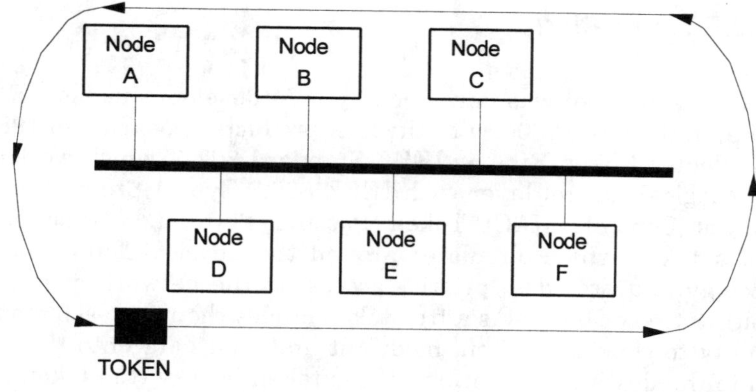

Figure 7.26 Token Bus Token Passing Routine

7.4.4 802.4 Token Bus

The IEEE 802.4 Token Bus standard defines the MAC protocol for a token-passing bus topology. A logical ring is formed on the physical bus, and each station knows only the preceding station on the bus. A token is passed down the bus, from station to station in logical ring sequence and by descending station address. This token contains the destination address of the next station. When the destination station receives the token, it can use the medium to transmit information for a limited time before having to turn the token over to the next station on the bus (in sequence). Figure 7.26 shows the Token Bus token-passing routine. Token Bus is the least used MAC protocol today.

Figure 7.27 shows the IEEE 802.4 Token Bus MAC PDU. This is similar to the Ethernet MAC PDU, with the omission of the PAD functionality and the addition of both a Frame Control (FC) character to identify the frame type and an End Delimiter (ED) which indicates the end of a frame.

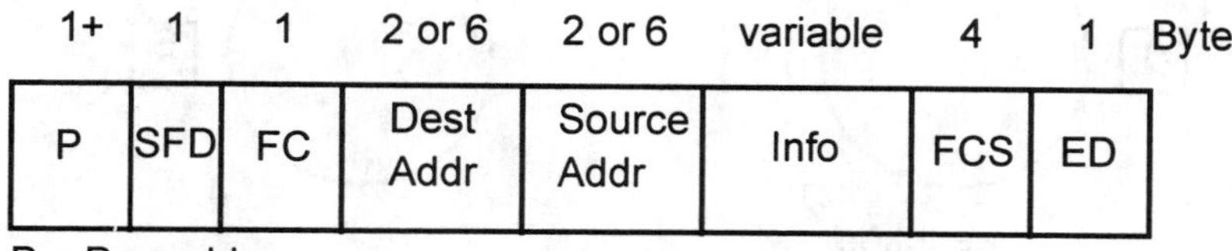

Figure 7.27 IEEE 802.4 Token Bus MAC PDU

7.4.5 802.5 Token Ring

The Token Ring protocol was developed by IBM development labs in Zurich, Switzerland, in the late 1960s, with the first products appearing in 1986. The IEEE has adopted Token Ring as IEEE Standard 802.5, which works on the IEEE 802.2 logical control layer with IEEE 802.2 Type 1 protocol and 802.5 Media Access Control (MAC) Token Passing Protocol. Basic operation consists of a token which circulates around the physical "hub" and logical "ring" topology and provides "priority access" to the network medium. The token is either free or busy. As a free token circles the ring, each station has the capability to seize the token, modify it and load data onto the bus, and send it on to the destination station. If the token is busy (the token contains data destined for a different station), the station regenerates it and passes it on to the next station without modification. Thus, only one station on the ring can transmit data over the common medium at a given time. Priorities can be assigned to the token for specific stations on the ring. At heavy load conditions, the Token Ring protocol is much more bandwidth efficient than other LAN protocols (because there are fewer idle tokens — as opposed to Ethernet, where there are many collisions during heavy load conditions). Figure 7.28 shows the Token Ring token-passing routine.

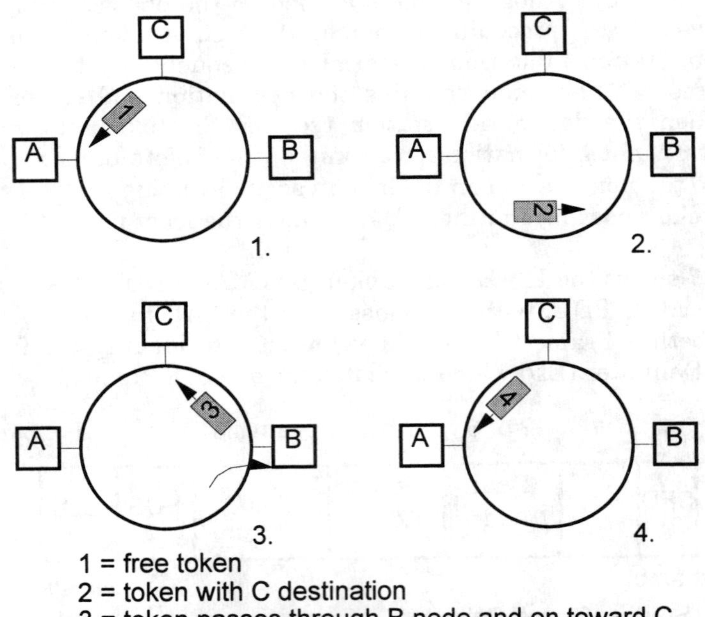

Figure 7.28 Token Ring Passing Routine

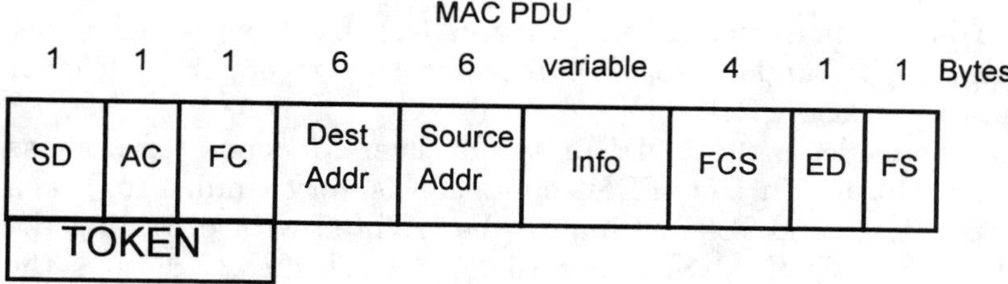

SD = Starting Delimiter
AC = Access Control
FCS = Frame Check Sequence
ED = Ending Delimiter
FS = Frame Status

Figure 7.29 IEEE 802.5 Token Ring MAC PDU

Figure 7.29 shows the IEEE 802.5 Token Ring MAC PDU. This is similar to the Token Bus PDU, with the omission of the preamble and the addition of the Access Control (AC) field, for priority and reservation access control, and the Frame Status (FS) character. Also, note that when an empty token is sent, only three characters are needed: the Start Delimiter (SD), Access Control (AC), and an End Delimiter (ED) field in place of the rest of the Token Ring PDU.

The maximum frame size for a Token Ring frame using the 4 Mbps medium is 4,000 bytes, for the 16 Mbps medium it is 17,800 bytes. Again, this number is important in future discussions of segmentation of MAC frames into network layer protocols like IP.

7.4.6 Fiber Distributed Data Interface (FDDI)

The Fiber Distributed Data Interface (FDDI) was designed to provide either a high-performance LAN or a campus backbone. Shared FDDI MANs can be connected via DS3 or OC-3 SONET pipes to form a wider area network, subject to distance constraints. FDDI is a LAN and MAN standard defined by ANSI (and CBEMA Committee) as X3T12. It is also recognized as an ISO standard. FDDI operates over both physical- and MAC-layer protocols, providing a 100 Mbps transmission over a dual, counter-rotating optical fiber ring between nodes. Although the bandwidth provided on the ring is 100 Mbps, the actual throughput is usually much lower. Still, this makes FDDI a high-speed LAN technology. Up to 500 dual-attachment connection devices can interface to the FDDI ring in series. FDDI rings support a maximum of up to 1000 stations, with a maximum distance between stations of 2 km and a maximum ring total circumference (path) of 100 to 200 km. Many more network stations can be supported by FDDI than lower-speed LAN technologies, leading to better performance curves and less LAN degradation per user. There is also a standard for FDDI protocol over copper — Copper Distributed Data Interface (CDDI).

In an OSIRM comparison, the FDDI protocols cover the same territory as the Token Ring protocol. In fact, FDDI operation is very similar to Token Ring protocol operation, and Token Ring can be credited with providing the basics of FDDI. This FDDI ANSI standard X3T12 specifically defines the Physical Medium Dependent (PMD) (X3.166) layer for single or multimode operation through full-duplex connectors, optical transceivers, and optional bypass switches. The physical layer of FDDI consists of a class A dual attachment physical interface via the PMD sublayer. The PHYsical protocol (PHY) (X3.148) layer implements a Nonreturn to Zero Inverted 4-bit-to-5-bit (NRZI-4B/5B) encoding/decoding algorithm and also performs handshaking between each station's PHY protocol. Physical interfaces to the transmission medium are via multimode or single-mode fiber.

The MAC (X3.139) layer serves as peer-to-peer communications for the LLC layer and the SMT layer over the ring, as well as routing and traffic allocation. The Station ManagemenT (SMT) (X3T12/84-48) layer is still under study, and will provide addressing, bandwidth allocation, fault isolation and ring reconfiguration, and initialization of station control functions. This important layer provides the means of inserting and removing stations from the ring. SONET interface and transport is still under study. Figure 7.30 shows these differences, where the Layer ManagemenT (LMT) layer provides the station interaction management between physical and MAC layer protocols.

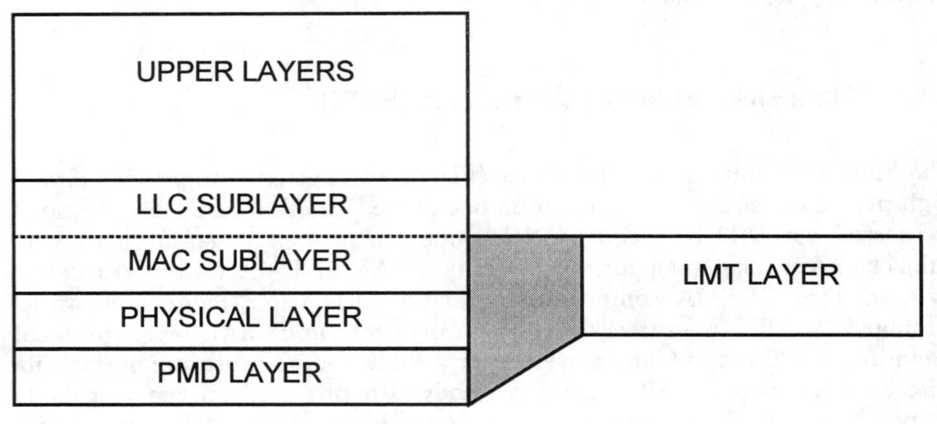

Figure 7.30 FDDI Protocol Stack

16+	2	2	6	6	var	8	1	3+	Symbols
Pre-amble	SD	FC	Dest Addr	Source Addr	Info	FCS	ED	FS	

MAC FDDI

SD = Starting Delimiter
FC = Frame Control
Info = Information Field
FCS = Frame Check Sequence
ED = End Delimiter
FS = Frame Status

Figure 7.31 FDDI MAC Layer Frame Format

Protocol Data Units (PDUs) similar to those used in Token Ring are formed in the same manner as other LAN protocols, and use the FDDI MAC layer frame format found in Figure 7.31. FDDI fields are labeled in symbols which represent four bits each, and all fields shown in this figure have been discussed. The information field (data packet) ranges from 128 to 4500 bytes. The address fields conform to the Token Ring standard. The maximum frame length is 9000 bytes.

Basic FDDI operation is similar to that described in the section on Token Ring, with the exception of free-token seizing and the release of the token after transmission. Each idle station on the FDDI ring has a chance to seize a passing free token. Figure 7.32 shows an example of FDDI token passing. If there is a free token passing by station A, the station can (1) seize the token and (2) transmit a frame to station C. The original token will be taken off the ring, and a new token not released until station A has transmitted its full frame. This is the major difference between FDDI and Token Ring. A new token will be released onto the ring (3) after the completion of frame transmission from station A, even though the destination station C has not received the full frame (4). In this manner, high-speed transmissions can be accomplished without the need for the transmitting station A to clear the original token. The frame that was transmitted by station A will eventually come back around (station C reads the frame as it passes) and station A must purge the frame from the ring (5).

Two classes of stations use the FDDI ring. Figure 7.33 shows both types of stations and their use of the FDDI ring. Class A stations are classified as *primary stations* and utilize both the inner and outer fiber rings. They are called Dual Attachment Stations (DAS) since they attach to both fiber rings. Class A stations can route around network failures by utilizing a combination of both primary and secondary rings. These stations can also utilize a bypass switch, which enables the ring to remain intact even though the station has lost power. Class B stations cannot provide reroute, and use only *the primary (outer) ring*. They are called Single Attachment Stations (SASs). Each SAS attaches to the ring via only two fibers, and can be isolated by the hub during failure conditions. These stations are shown connecting to the FDDI LAN through a wiring hub, also called a Dual Access Station (DAS) concentrator. Under normal operation, stations use the primary ring for data transfer.

During a link failure (shown in Figure 7.34) all class A stations can automatically reconfigure to use the secondary ring. This capability is called *self-healing*. Class B stations will be offline because the primary ring they use is inactive during a failure condition. Any station on the link can be taken down without affecting the FDDI ring.

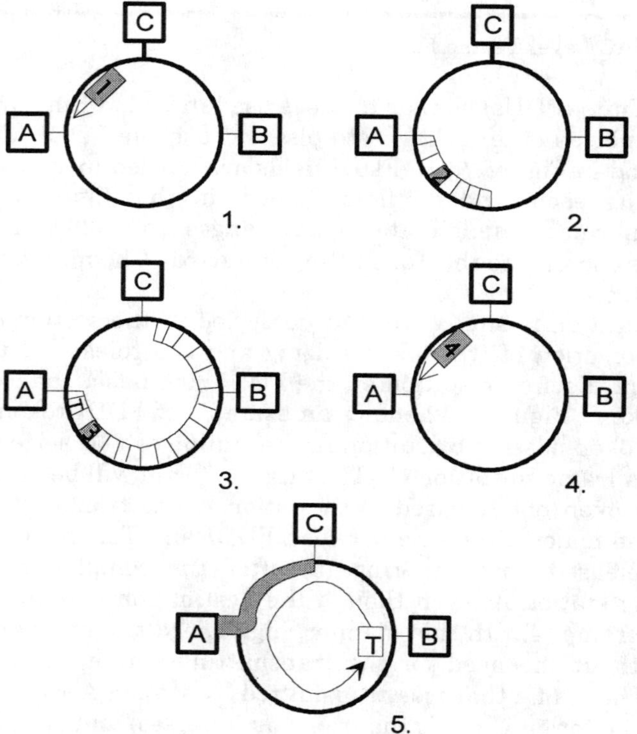

1 - A absorbs the token
2 - A transmits frame to C
3 - A adds new token to end of frame (B ignores token)
4 - C reads in frame, and frame continues to A
(B has chance to transmit)
5 - A takes frame off network (C has chance to transmit)

Figure 7.32 FDDI Token-Passing Routine

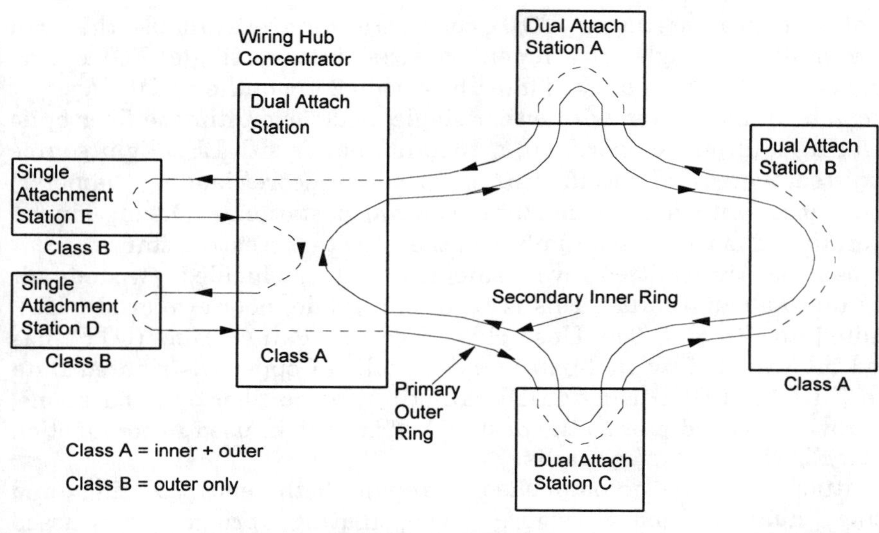

Figure 7.33 FDDI Station Classes and Rings

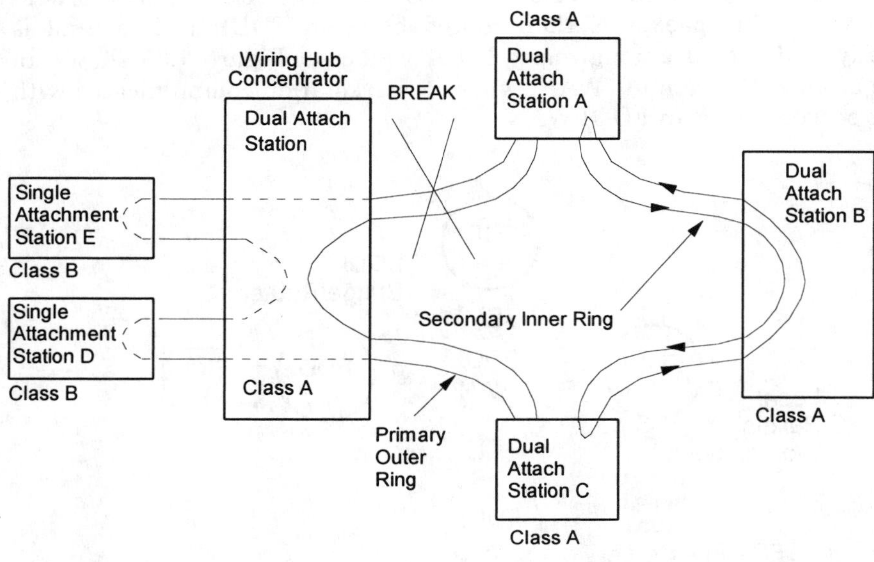

Figure 7.34 FDDI Link Failure Scenario

The secondary (inner) ring acts as an online backup to the primary (outer) ring. This is due to physical connections on the dual FDDI ring to share a single MAC layer and a single MAC address. FDDI networks can also be configured in a star-wiring arrangement, where a patch panel is used for concentration of workstations. FDDI concentrators are available that can aggregate multiple single attachment devices into a single FDDI ring attachment. Each of these devices must be within 2 km of the FDDI ring.

FDDI can be implemented with either single mode or multimode fiber-optic cable. During multimode operation, a 1300-nm bandwidth LED light source is transmitted over ANSI-specified 62.5/125 micron (core/cladding diameter) multimode fiber, with a 2-km maximum between stations. During single-mode operation, a laser is used in place of the LED to increase distance.

FDDI can be transmitted over shielded and unshielded twisted-pair distances up to about 100 m. This is with data grade, not voice grade, UTP wire limited to 50 m. The Unshielded Twisted Pair Forum (UTF) has developed the shielded twisted-pair standard called Copper Distributed Data Interface (CDDI). FDDI using CDDI can still use the fiber-optic backbone, but can provide twisted pair to the desktop. This is then used in conjunction with 32-bit FDDI PC interface cards.

WAN attachment is accomplished through both encapsulating and translating dual-attached bridges. Encapsulating bridges (discussed previously) are designed to perform encapsulation of the MAC LAN packet into an FDDI packet. This new packet is then forwarded through the router network. This is a proprietary approach. Translating bridges bond the MAC LAN packet address to a SubNet Access Protocol-Service Access Point (SNAP-SAP) packet. This packet is then routed between FDDI devices, and is universally understood among many FDDI vendors. Figure 7.35 shows an example of an FDDI campus WAN, where a workstation communicates with a remote server across an FDDI WAN.

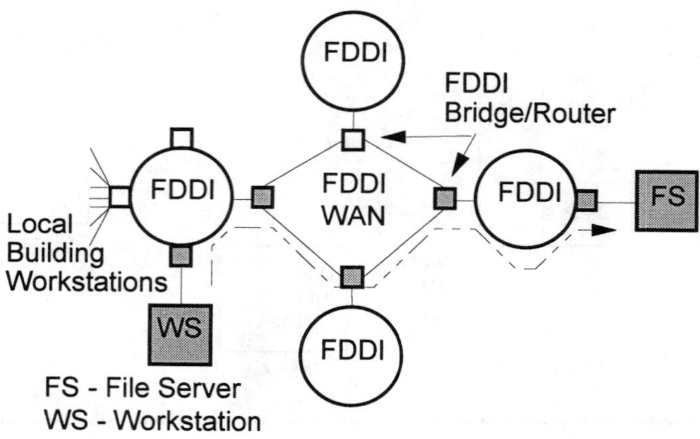

Figure 7.35 FDDI Campus Backbone or WAN

The many advantages of implementing an FDDI LAN include

+ Accommodate large numbers of users on a single LAN segment
+ 100 Mbps shared bandwidth
+ Large geographic area coverage (long-distance LAN)
+ High reliability through self-healing
+ Fiber immune to copper cable interference — high transmission quality
+ Direct efficient attachment for hosts
+ Supports more stations than standard LAN protocols
+ Built-in network management (SMT)
+ Support for multimedia services on LAN
+ Economics of Dual Access Stations (DAS)

There are also a few disadvantages of FDDI LANs:

– Expensive to install (cost of hardware and fiber runs)
– Need to use existing copper wiring at lower data rates and distances (except CDDI)
– Speed conversion problems

7.4.7 FDDI-II

Development is still under way on a mechanism called Hybrid Ring Control (HRC) which will allow FDDI LANs to transport multiplexed asynchronous packet data and isochronous circuit-switched data. Figure 7.36 shows the new FDDI-II protocol structure. The physical layer will probably change to SONET, but, as of now, it still uses the old FDDI-I 100 Mbps interfaces. There is now a hybrid multiplexer layer between the physical and MAC sublayer. The MAC sublayer has been split into a packet-processing MAC sublayer (from the old FDDI-I standard) and a new isochronous MAC sublayer. Frames are now called cycles. The PMD layer passes a cycle onto the FDDI-II ring every 125 μs. The hybrid multiplexer layer strips off the header and passes the cycle to the appropriate MAC layer. The station management remains to be worked out for compatibility between different vendor hardware.

Multiple 6 Mbps portions of data can be dynamically allocated to DS1 channels to support voice, data, and video. This 6 Mbps (actually 6.144 Mbps) chunk of data consists of multiple 64 kbps channels. Each cycle can carry up to 16 channels, and each channel up to 6.144 Mbps. Isochronous traffic can also use the 6.144 Mbps channels. This service is good for interconnection of PBX equipment to the LAN and WAN, and combines telecommunications and data communications mixed media on the same fiber. Other planned enhancements include the WBS subchannels, dedicated packet groups, and cycle formatting. Future protocol support may include XTP, HCR, and HIPPI. To date, the deployment of FDDI-II has been stalled by the lack of a vendor to produce a chipset (due to the high development costs associated with advanced technology chipset development) and the offering of low-speed LAN ATM network interface cards. FDDI does not provide address screening and security features such as those found in SMDS. FDDI also contains some distance limitations.

FDDI-II may eventually correct the lack of FDDI isochronous service capability and allow FDDI to compete more effectively with ATM. But it does seem that FDDI will coexist with ATM for some time. In fact, FDDI and ATM can be viewed somewhat as competing technologies. FDDI can also coexist with ATM on a feeder basis.

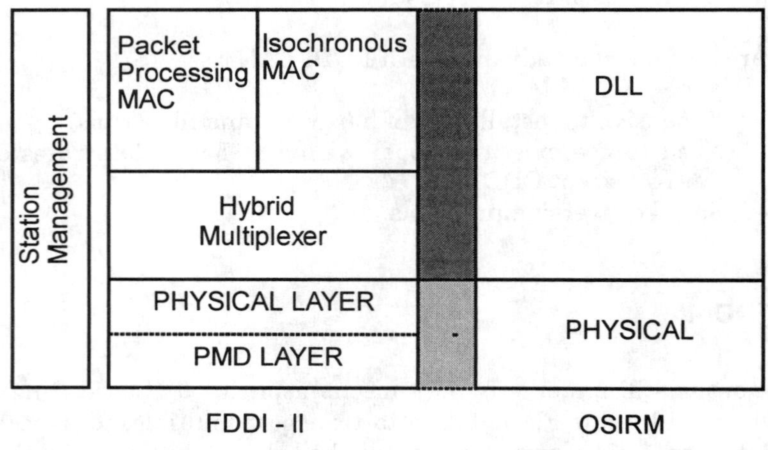

Figure 7.36 FDDI-II Protocol Structure

7.4.8 100-Mbps Ethernet: 100BASET and 100VG-AnyLAN

Ethernet 10 Mbps is clearly the most popular LAN technology in use today. It provides low-cost hardware and an IEEE standard that is very common. Two IEEE approaches at offering 100 Mbps Ethernet have emerged – 100BASET and 100VG-AnyLAN.

100BASE-T Fast Ethernet speeds up the existing CSMA/CD media access control mechanism of common 10 Mbps Ethernet to 100 Mbps. Thus, the time to transmit a bit on the medium is reduced by a factor of 10. 100BASET is an IEEE 802.3 standard. Frame format, data content and size, and media access control mechanism are all the same, and it is fully compatible with 10 Mbps Ethernet. Three major segment types exist: T4, TX, and FX. T4 segment type uses four-pair twisted wiring. TX uses two-pair twisted media. FX uses two-strand fiber-optic cable. Both the TX and FX ANSI physical media standards are referred to as the 100BASE-X standard, which was the standard originally developed for FDDI. All three use a 40-pin MII connector.

100VG-AnyLAN is also called VG, Fast Ethernet, Fast Token Ring, and Demand Priority. 100VG-AnyLAN uses a new media access control mechanism which uses a switching hub device that controls access to the medium by a "demand priority" mechanism. The new IEEE standard for 100VG-AnyLAN is 802.12, while 100BASEVG is an IEEE 802.11 standard. The 10 Mbps Ethernet frame format remains the same, and the standard also supports Token Ring frame types. 100VG-AnyLAN can operate over four-pair UTP (up to 100 m), two-pair STP (up to 200 m), and fiber-optic cable (up to 2000 m). A deterministic demand priority scheme is used to create a predictable order by which nodes share the network. A round robin polling scheme is used, along with a dual priority system that distinguishes between high or normal priority.

100BASET is best used as an upgrade to existing 10 Mbps Ethernet when cabling permits but continued interoperability is required. The IEEE 100VG-AnyLAN standard allows an easy migration from existing Ethernet and Token Ring speeds of 10 Mbps and 4/16 Mbps.

There also exists a proprietary standard called 100Mbps TCNS developed in 1990 as a 100 Mbps extension to ANSI standard 878.1 ARCNET. Here a token bus passing access method is used. UTP, STP, coaxial, and fiber-optic cable are supported, but typically at less than 100 m. The IEEE has been working on a standard that would specify a 16-Mbps isochronous Ethernet (IEEE 802.9a) designed to support multimedia, something which the current Ethernet cannot do well, but this version has never caught on.

The Fast Ethernet standards above may become the new wave for workstation LAN attachment. By most estimates the 100BASET standard equipment will outsell 100VG-AnyLAN. But these 100 Mbps Ethernet standards are being challenged by ATM, which now sports the LAN Emulation (LANE) standards. At the time of printing there was no clear leader.

7.5 SWITCHING IN THE LAN ENVIRONMENT

There is no question that Ethernet is the king of the LAN today. It is extremely cost effective, with adapter cards typically priced at less than $100. The 10 Mbps limit, or realistically 3 to 4 Mbps when the medium is shared, is not a limit for some communities of users. But workstation client-server and multimedia applications continue to push the envelope, requiring greater amounts of bandwidth every day. Even 10 or 16 Mbps shared among a few users (or even as few as one user) is sometimes not enough – thus creating a situation of *media constraint*. Add to this the fact that many LANs carry traffic that does not originate nor terminate on their segment. As more users are added to the LAN, or each user requires more bandwidth, the network load or number of collisions increases and network performance begins to suffer. We note that when the average user's bandwidth requirements begin to exceed 100 kbps on a regular basis, then the number of users per LAN should be less than 50. When this number goes to greater than 500 kbps, the number of users is further decreased to less than 10. Users that require more than 500 kbps on a regular basis are good candidates for a single-segment LAN. Figure 7.37 illustrates the evolution of LAN segmentation and switching providing "legacy-to-luxury" and increased bandwidth to each user.

Traditional passive or repeater hubs provide a common back-plane for LAN aggregation and are less expensive than switching hubs. Unfortunately, they only provide layer 1 repeater functionality. Their shared bandwidth efficiency decreases quickly as the individual user bandwidth requirements and amount of LAN segmentation increases. Now the requirement to switch traffic between LAN segments and dedicate bandwidth to each user segment requires a more dynamic device and methodology. Enter the LAN switch and Virtual LAN (VLAN).

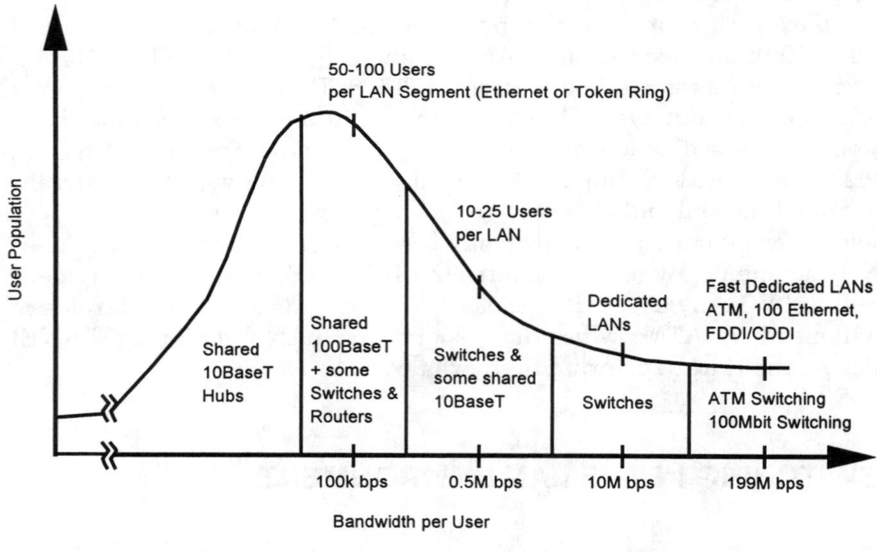

Figure 7.37 Legacy-to-Luxury (© Cisco Systems 1995)

7.5.1 Ethernet and Token Ring LAN Switch

How do you get more bandwidth to each user? Power users, work groups with bandwidth-intensive applications, and servers can be accommodated by *segmenting* the LAN to have fewer users per shared medium. The term used for segmenting a LAN with many users into small or single-user LANs is *microsegmentation*. A LAN switch can take multiple segments with much fewer users and act as an aggregation and switching backbone. LAN switching of traffic only between source and destination LAN segments can save much bandwidth, rather than routing traffic across multiple LAN segments that serve as neither source nor destination segment. This switching function is performed at layer 2 (the MAC sublayer), and is similar to the transparent bridging discussed earlier. LAN switching allows the manager to preserve his or her strategic investment in legacy LAN speed devices while adding the elements of scalability and control. The LAN switch offers its own high-speed back-plane, much higher than 10 Mbps, and can offer multiple LAN segments to smaller work-groups or even to single user segments. In this manner each LAN segment or port is its own collision domain. This is a sharp contrast to the traditional LAN hub, where the entire hub served as a single collision domain.

7.5.2 When Should You Use a LAN Switch?

Network scaling issues accompany any network growth, and routed networks are no exception. Routing protocols must constantly be analyzed for design efficiency. Routing protocols broadcast information across the network to all other routers in an attempt to discover network services and to update their neighbors through distributing routing information. They interact with protocols like ARP and SAP used for address resolution. Routers communicate via routing protocols like OSPF, RIP, BGP, IGRP, IS-IS, NLSP, RTMP, AURP, and PNNI. Their communications multicast and broadcast information that, if mis-configured, can cause a lot of overhead across a large internetwork. Excessive broadcasts, or “broadcast storms”, are typically caused by mis-configured or defective systems (routers, hosts, etc.) and can take entire networks out of commission. The goal of the designer is to limit the propagation of broadcasts without denying the benefits they afford. The next chapter will explore these concepts in more detail.

How can you design the network to reduce the amount of routing required, yet control the amount of contention for MAC layer (LAN) bandwidth? LAN segments can be placed first into LAN switches – devices that will segment and switch local traffic at the MAC (layer 2) layer and reduce WAN routing requirements. LAN switches rarely have WAN interfaces. Instead they rely on routers to provide the broadcast function across the WAN, but the LAN switches now allow the network to scale much larger. LAN switches allow the broadcast domains of a network to scale much larger than with shared hubs, while routers provide the ability to scale the WAN.

When should you consider a LAN switch (versus a router or ATM switch)?

- ⇒ Workstation-to-workstation and workstation-to-server traffic is no longer mostly local.
- ⇒ Large routed networks where the router update protocols are generating high levels of overhead.
- ⇒ Scalability is required – as the number of users and switches increases (much more complex in router-based networks) to avoid LAN bottlenecks.
- ⇒ An increased number of users per router port (assuming delivery of constant user bandwidth) is required.
- ⇒ Mission-critical applications are moving to LANs – increasing throughput and availability requirements.
- ⇒ Client-server technology is stretching boundaries of LANs (inter-LAN).
- ⇒ Work groups are becoming more dynamic – enter the VLAN.
- ⇒ Higher-speed and performance LAN segments with fewer users per segment (more available bandwidth per user) are needed.
- ⇒ Increased manageability of each LAN port through SNMP is needed.
- ⇒ Port, protocol, and address flexibility is required.
- ⇒ Support for mobile roaming users to access shared server resources is required.
- ⇒ Current Ethernet and Token Ring investments need to be preserved.
- ⇒ The bandwidth requirements of the individual user cannot be accommodated in a shared media environment but are not sufficient to justify ATM.

But LAN switches are not roses without thorns. Beware, these devices can be difficult to manage and administer configurations, and hard to troubleshoot when there are problems. Make sure each device is fully manageable and experts are performing the administration and management. Explore the creation of zones where the server is placed on its own segment and operates as a centrally located resource to all other segments. Also beware that as the bandwidth available to users increases, so too does the bandwidth they require.

7.5.3 Types of LAN Switching

Ethernet switching typically employs Application Specific Integrated Circuits (ASICs) to aggregate multiple single segment LAN users onto a single switched (typically bus or cross-bar) back-plane that can run at speeds in excess of 1 Gbps. Thus, each client or server can transmit at the entire wire rate of 10 Mbps or 100 Mbps Ethernet for an entire segment's worth of bandwidth, and the LAN switch filters and forwards the traffic. Local traffic is switched to the destination LAN segment and remote traffic is switched out a port to another device (typically a router) via a protocol like ATM, FDDI, or 100 Mbps Ethernet. Each LAN switch acts as a multiport bridge. When a LAN switch port receives a layer 2 MAC PDU, it

- Examines the source and destination address
- Learns where the source resides (so that when another destination tries to send frames to that source the switch remembers where it is)
- Either
  - ⇒ *Forwards* the data out to the destination address

    Or
  - ⇒ *Filters* it out if it goes back out the same interface it was received on (if the destination address is on the same LAN segment as the source address)
- If the destination address is unknown the LAN switch, like a bridge, will forward the packet out to all interfaces other than the source interface

Servers can be connected via multiple single-user Ethernet segments when more bandwidth is needed. Thus, Ethernet switching allows better throughput and extends the life cycle and investment of the existing LAN and wiring structure.

Ethernet switch designs use either symmetric or asymmetric switching. Symmetric switching provides switching between like bandwidth LANs (e.g., 10 Mbps to 10 Mbps). Asymmetric switching provides rate adaptation switching between unlike bandwidth LANs (i.e., 10 Mbps to 100 Mbps). Here the entire packet is held until bandwidth is available to transmit to the destination (LAN segment) address. There are two general types of Ethernet switches – cut-through and store-and-forward. Cut-through switches act as cell switches, where they start to forward the MAC frame to the destination address before receiving the end of the frame. This technique is good for minimizing delay but bad for propagating errors. Store-and-forward switches read in the entire MAC frame before forwarding it to the destination address. They also perform error checking on packets and discard errored packets. This method is used then moving frames from a lower-speed LAN to a higher-speed LAN as with asymmetric switching, and is the more common and more expensive approach.

Token Ring switches have also arrived that offer similar benefits to Ethernet switches. Token Ring switches mostly use either transparent bridging or Source Route Bridging (SRB). Eventually, ATM switches will probably outsell and outperform these LAN switches, but in the interim LAN switches offer good high-performance desktop integration.

7.5.4 Virtual LANs and LAN Emulation

Virtual LANs are defined by switching devices that group users into a virtual community in which it appears that all users within that community share a local LAN segment. Virtual communities can be software-defined work groups, cross-functional teams, and cross-departmental project teams – all groups that need to communicate in a virtual shared environment independent of physical limitations. VLANs allow logical networks to be formed independent of where each device is physically located. In this manner, administrative changes can be made dynamically without reassigning IP addresses or changing physical wiring structures. One example of a VLAN feature is the capability for automatic address registration across the VLAN.

Figure 7.38 shows a switching hub and VLAN network. Users A, B, and C each represent a 16 Mbps Token Ring network that is switched within the switching hub. The switching hub may be switching them at 16 Mbps speed, or using a protocol like 100VG- AnyLAN to switch them at 100 Mbps. Other switching hubs are switching 10 Mbps or 100 Mbps Ethernet users D and E at 100 Mbps Ethernet speeds, or 100 Mbps FDDI users F, G, and H at a similar speed. The router is providing routing between each of these hubs and LAN technologies, while the switching hubs are conducting layer 2 (MAC sublayer) switching and administering the VLAN logical work-groups. In our example, users A, D, and G belong to a virtual LAN work-group, users B, E, and F another VLAN work-group, and users C and H yet another VLAN work-group. Each VLAN within a switching hub can be assigned a subnet address for all users attached to that VLAN. These subnets can span multiple LAN switches. VLANs can be created *across* subnets, so that users within a specific VLAN can be from different subnets. This is also shown in the illustration where user A from subnet 300.200.100.0 can talk to user D in subnet 300.200.50.0 within a single VLAN. Notice also that the router is the only place in this network where security measures (e.g., packet or circuit firewall) can be applied.

There are three methods of implementing VLANs: ATM LAN Emulation (LANE), IEEE 802.10, and proprietary implementations. VLANs tend to require that all ports in the VLAN use the same media. Mixed media VLANs imply translation functions (translational bridging a la IEEE 802.1) being performed by the LAN switch or router. ATM LANE is performed with four components. A LAN Emulation Client (LEC) provides a translational bridge from the LAN protocol to ATM. A LAN Emulation Server (LES) acts to resolve unknown and broadcast addresses by maintaining and replying to known address resolution requests. The Broadcast and Unknown Server (BUS) maintains all ATM addresses and handles all point-to-point and point-to-multipoint addressing, emulating the LAN broadcast and multicast functions absent from ATM technology. The LAN Emulation Configuration Server (LECS) provides the address of the LES and BUS to every LEC when they initially attach to the ATM network (emulated LAN management and address registration functions).

IEEE 802.10 VLANs can use the standard 802.10 PDU frame header originally designated for Secure Data Exchange (SDE). The VLAN ID is carried within the IEEE 802.10 header, specifically within the Security Association IDentification header (SAID) field as shown in Figure 7.39. This approach offers a low-latency packet-tagging approach as pioneered by Cisco. The only major drawback is that it is a LAN standard and does not currently interwork with ATM.

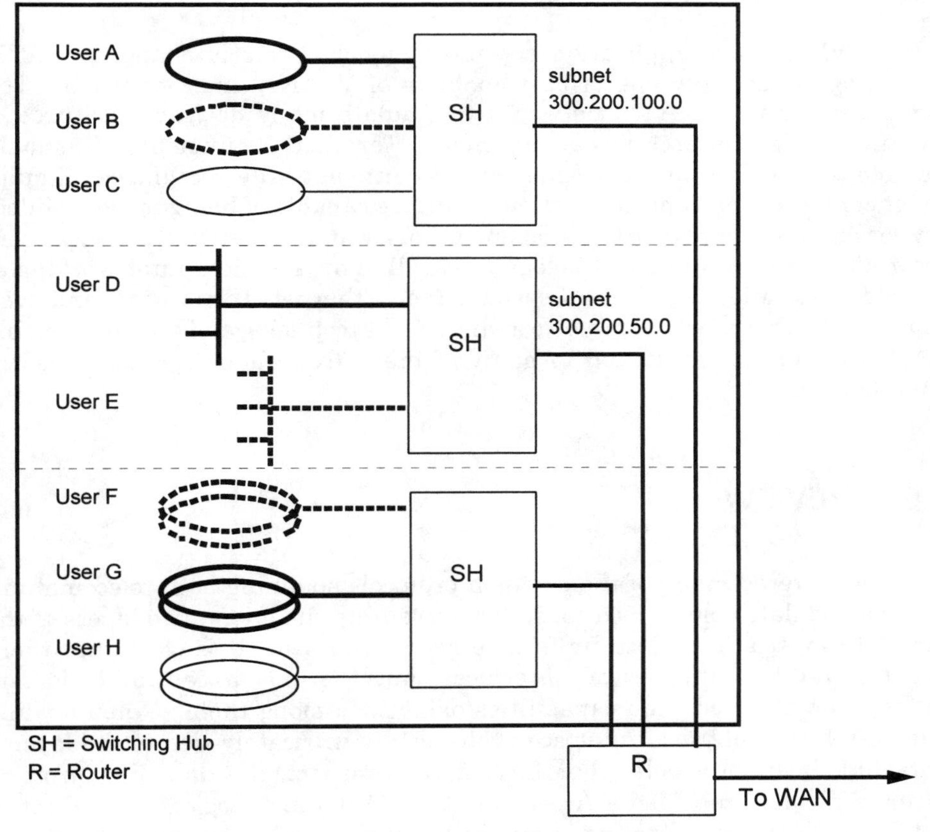

Figure 7.38 VLAN Example

There are also many proprietary methods of implementing a VLAN. One of the more popular is Cisco's Inter-Switch Link (ISL). All frames are tagged with a proprietary VLAN identifier and all trunking between VLAN devices are proprietary.

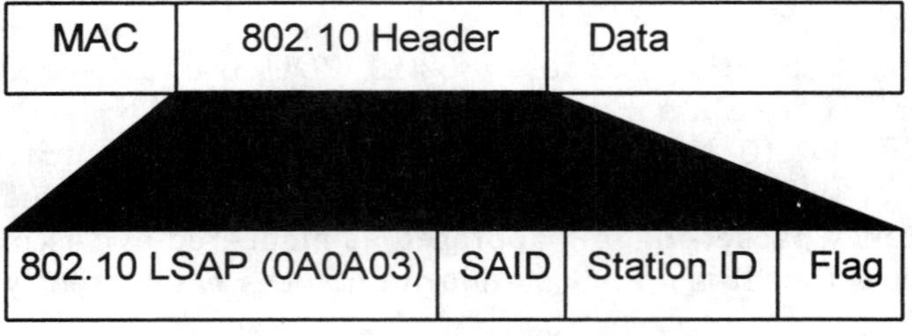

Figure 7.39 VLAN Using IEEE 802.10 Framing

Most VLANs are application specific today, but this is changing. ATM technology is actually one of best enablers of VLANs, and vice versa. The capability for newer ATM networks to emulate many desirable features of existing LANs is often a key requirement. Terminal Equipment (TE) should be able to interface to ATM LANs and be automatically recognized. Equipment configurations and connection should be capable of being moved, added, and/or changed by network management, or even automatically. Many users view ATM as a unifying technology that will allow seamless inter-working of the older, so-called legacy LAN systems (i.e., Ethernet, Token Ring, and even FDDI) with the latest, high-performance ATM technology. Thus, ATM using LANE will offer competition to many of the LAN technologies discussed in this chapter.

7.6 REVIEW

We have covered many of the common protocols spanning both telecommunications and data communications. Protocols from the lowest two layers of the OSIRM (physical and data link) have been discussed. It is clear that there are many different physical interfaces, but there is a central logic and progression of speeds and capabilities exhibited among them. When dealing with LANs, the physical interface protocols are intricately tied to the layer 2 data link layer protocols. For LAN data transport, the data link protocol layer is divided into Media Access Control (MAC) and Logical Link Control (LLC) sublayers, performing local media access and managing end-to-end data transport, respectively. New protocols such as FDDI and 100 Mbps Ethernet have provided a tenfold increase in available bandwidth, and Ethernet switching has emerged to play a key role in rapid expansion of multiple LAN environments and single segment users with an eye toward preserving existing infrastructure. VLANs will also play an important part in future LAN and WAN design. Bridge, router, and higher-layer protocols will be explained in the next chapter.

Chapter

8

Common Protocols and Interfaces – Part 2

Most of today's networks contain bridging and routing devices. These devices communicate through a language of their own – exchanging information about the state of the network through protocols that parallel those found in the OSIRM designed for data communications. These router protocols and their design are just as important as those of the OSIRM network and transport layer protocols that negotiate the transport, networking, and internetworking of data. And no discussion of protocols would be complete without a detailed examination of the legacy SNA networking world. Most of the world's data networks have some portion of equipment running legacy protocols. These legacy environments are merging with the newer TCP/IP-based routed environments. SNA inter-networking protocols are presented in this chapter from their traditional or legacy configurations through new multiprotocol routed and peer-to-peer communications protocols like Data Link Switching (DLSw), Advanced Program-to-Program Communication (APPC), and Advanced Peer-to-Peer Networking (APPN).

8.1 BRIDGE PROTOCOLS

The IEEE 802.1 Spanning Tree Learning Bridge Protocol (STP) and IBM Source Routing Protocol (SRP) are the two major protocols for network bridging. These protocols operate at the physical (layer 1) and Media Access Control (MAC) sublayer (layer 2) to provide a limited form of relaying packets over the local and wide area network media. True bridging protocols operate as relay points only. They provide a LAN extension similar to the repeater function but with limited additional intelligence. Some bridges used fixed (static, or manually configured) tables to make forwarding decisions, while others, such as the IEEE 802.1 Spanning Tree Protocol, employ dynamic, forwarding tables capable of updates. Bridging schemes such as these allow the bridges to dynamically change packet relaying based upon network topology changes. Ethernet relies on the spanning tree approach when scanning for address destinations on the WAN. Token Ring almost always uses SRP to accomplish the same, but not 100 percent of the time.

8.1.1 IEEE 802.1 Spanning Tree Learning Bridge Protocol (STP)

The IEEE Standard 802.1 Spanning Tree Learning Bridge Protocol (STP) is a bridging protocol based upon the IEEE 802.1 Transparent Spanning Tree algorithm. STP defines forwarding table operation for bridges that span multiple networks, provides the function of frame (packet) forwarding, and has the capability for the bridge device to "learn" station addresses and network topology changes. Each bridge has a forwarding table, which is updated dynamically by the STP to correct forwarding problems such as forwarding loops or unavailable circuit paths. A flat common addressing scheme is used to assign a unique data link address to each device attached to a networked bridge, and to eliminate transmission broadcast "loops". Each data frame passing through a bridge is examined and forwarded on through a process called *filtering*. If it is destined for the local LAN, it is filtered off to the local LAN segment and sent on to the user device. The resulting "tree" spans each sub-net and assures that there is only a single route between any two LANs. If the topology is changed, a new spanning tree is created by the protocol. STP performs traffic management by employing packet filters to forward or drop packets based upon their source and destination addresses, protocol type, and multicast or broadcast address. Some vendors implementing this protocol accommodate load sharing across multiple physical links, but beware of these implementations as they are purely proprietary and are difficult to implement in mixed vendor networks.

STP is a true bridging protocol and is inefficient and disadvantageous when used as a large networking protocol. STP is better utilized when the network is made up of many point-to-point circuits. STP does have a few disadvantages. STP elimination of loop paths ties up expensive leased-line resources. Also, spanning tree table building after network failures takes considerable time and introduces long user delays.

8.1.2 IBM Source Routing Protocol (SRP)

The IBM SRP allows LAN workstations to specify their routing for each packet transmitted. Thus, each packet transmitted by a workstation on the LAN to the bridge contains a complete set of routing information for the bridge to route upon. The workstation learns this optimal path routing from the discovery packet it broadcasts throughout the bridged network. Thus it becomes a combination of bridging and routing, but the distinction is that the routing is performed at the data link layer, not the network layer. The connection is built at OSIRM layer 2, and thus the connection must be reestablished if there is a topology change in the source routes. The addressing scheme is hierarchical in nature. Each device makes its ring number part of the data link address, thus creating a hierarchy of addresses for each level of devices. The bridge then routes according the packet instruction, and routing is performed at the data link layer (layer 2) rather than the network layer (layer 3).

The information for source routing to perform its function is contained in the routing information field (an extension of the source address field) within the MAC sublayer frame. Figure 8.1 shows the structure of this field, which starts with a 2-byte control header, and then contains consecutive ring and bridge numbers, each 12 bits and 4 bits long, respectively, to identify the path towards the destination ring. The maximum size of the address field is 230 bits, which would allow up to 14 ring or bridge numbers. Since most implementations require the use of two ring/bridge numbers per "hop", there is a maximum of 7 bridges or "hops". IBM's Token Ring implementation of source routing has a seven-hop count maximum. The more uncommon IEEE 802.5 standard states a maximum of 14 or 15 hops, but this is almost never used. If the routing information field is zero, the bridge does not pass the frame (performs filtering). Any frame with the Routing Information Indicator (RII) bit in the address header set to 1 is routed to the next bridge in sequence.

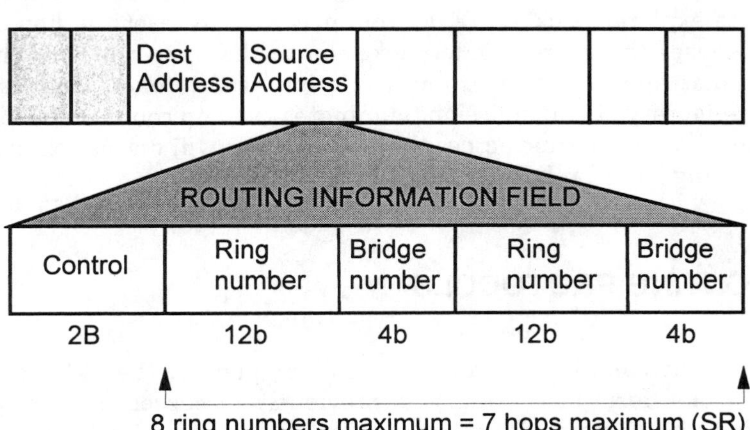

Figure 8.1 MAC 802.X Frame Source Routing Field

8.1.3 Source Route Transparent (SRT) Bridging

There is also a standard called Source Routing Transparent (SRT) bridging defined by the IEEE. IEEE SRT marries the IEEE STP and the IBM SRP into one bit-selective bridging protocol. The selective bit is transmitted to the router within the MAC-frame information field. SRT can then interact with the source route bridging of token ring while performing transparent bridging to other LAN implementations. Many bridges achieve forwarding rates of over 14,500 frames per second sustained over a long period of time using this technique. STP is used primarily for LAN-to-LAN and LAN-to-WAN connectivity, but should be used with caution as performance and response time are much poorer than with routing protocols. Note that SRP has more overhead than SRT, but the processing is reduced for each bridge it traverses. SRT can also allow SNA source routing into Ethernet TCP/IP networks and DECnet networks, as we will see later in this chapter.

8.1.4 Source Routing Extensions

Many vendors such as Bay Networks and Cisco Systems have implemented extensions to the SRB protocol. These routers, while providing bridging capability, can transmit bridged traffic across an entire WAN composed of multiple routers, and still the entire network will only count as a single hop. Network end stations can support both local source route bridging and inter-network routing, while eliminating the seven-hop count restriction on source route bridging. Routing tables are built dynamically through use of the source route explorer packets. Each router is able to reset the hop count to zero as it passes the source route packet on to the next router. While this method is just another form of encapsulation of the token ring packet, it improves reliability of transmission, eliminates the hop count restriction, and can decreases response time across the network. We will discuss extensions to SRB later using Data Link Switching (DLS).

8.2 ROUTING PROTOCOLS

As networks increase in size and protocol complexity, they almost always implement some form of routing. As previously discussed, routers perform both *routing* and *bridging* functions. Both methods require that the router performs address translation. There are multiple routing protocols that build forwarding tables using different metrics. Some perform routing based on the shortest path to the destination node, some use least-cost routing, and others are based upon complex algorithms. Routers use a series of algorithms to perform the task of routing, along with dynamic routing tables to manage this routing. Almost all routers support bridging protocols, as it is preferable to perform translation bridging with a router as opposed to encapsulation bridging with a bridge.

8.2.1 Routing Protocols Defined

Routing, or gateway protocols, provide router-to-router communications between *like* routers using routing tables. Communications can take place between autonomous systems [Exterior Gateway Protocol (EGP)] and within autonomous systems [Interior Gateway Routing Protocol (IGRP)]. We will cover RIP, IGRP, EGP, BGP, OSPF, and IS-IS. Serial line protocols provide communications over serial or dial-up links between unlike routers. HDLC, PPP, and SLIP were covered in Chapter 7. Gateway and serial line protocols work in parallel – the gateway protocol passes the routing table information and "keep alive" packets, and the serial line protocol (or media access protocol) passes the true user data. Protocol stack routing and bridging protocols operate across the network to manage the flow of frames.

Gateway protocols are actually used once the destination address is resolved. Routers then need to determine the best way to reach that address through a network of nodes. This determination is made based on a variety of parameters. One example is to assign a specific *cost* to each link in a network. It is then the job of the routing protocol to find the least-cost route. This cost may or may not be economic, but may reflect some performance information such as the delay or latency of the link.

Routing algorithms generally exchange information about the topology, that is, the links that are connected and their associated costs, in one or two generic methods – distance vector and link state.

Distance vector algorithms use neighbor nodes to periodically exchange vectors of the distance to every destination in the network. This process eventually converges on the optimal solution. Distance vector algorithms employ the Bellman-Ford algorithms; each device builds its table, then sends an update, and eventually everyone will agree.

Link state algorithms have each router learn the entire *link state* topology of the entire network. This is currently done by flooding only changes to the link state topology through the network. Flooding involves copying the message from one node to other nodes in the network in a tree-like fashion such that only one copy of the message is received by every node. Link state algorithms flood all router tables until each device agrees they have the same one. Then each device builds its own forwarding table from its own perspective. The link state approach is more complex, but converges much more rapidly. *Convergence* is the rate at which a network goes from an unstable state to a stable state. When the topology of the network changes due to a link or node failure, or the addition of a new node or link, this information must be updated at other nodes. The amount of time required to update all nodes in the network about the topology change is called the convergence time.

8.2.2 Distance Vector Routing Protocols

The first routing protocols to emerge on the market were based on distance vectors. The distance vector method was used in the initial data communication networks such as the ARPANET and is used by the Internet's Routing Information Protocol (RIP) A key advantage of the distance vector is its simplicity. A key disadvantage is that the topology information message grows larger with the network (depending on the addressing scheme used and the ability to do address summarization), and the time for it to propagate through the network increases as the network grows. Convergence times on the order of minutes are common. Some examples of address summarization are (1) IP RIP automatically summarizes at the edges of a class (A, B, C) network, (2) OSPF can be configured to summarize on more arbitrary area boundaries, and (3) IPX RIP doesn't do any summarization at all. Figure 8.2 shows an example of the use of distance vector routing determination for routing table exchange.

Distance vector protocol allows router A to talk to its nearest neighbors, namely routers B and C, for an intermittent time period (e.g., 30 seconds). Router A will constantly exchange its routing tables with routers B and C, and vice versa. Thus, router A in effect broadcasts its status to router C who, in turn, broadcasts to routers D and E, and so forth throughout the network.

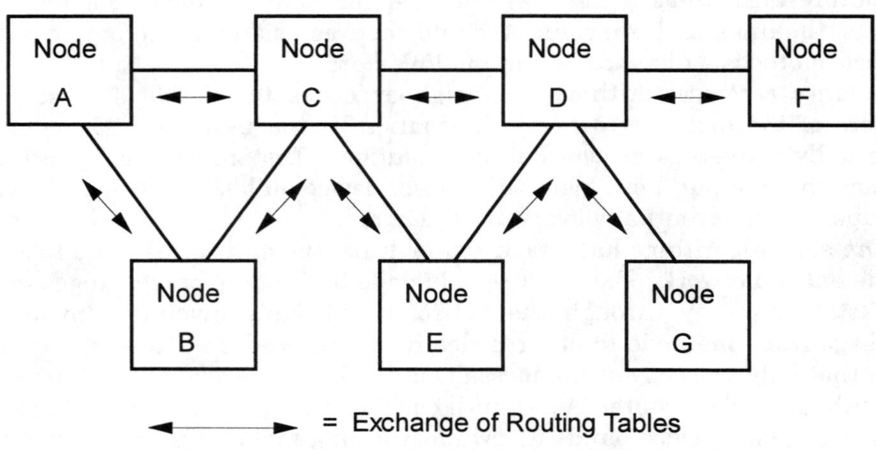

Figure 8.2 Distance Vector Routing Table Exchange

Problems can arise due to convergence, where the transfer of these routing tables between nodes takes 30 seconds or more per hop. In a large network, this can amount to a multiple-minute delay, causing a different network status at multiple locations throughout the network.

There are many implementations of the distance vector routing protocols. One of the first developed was the Routing Information Protocol (RIP), developed for the XNS protocol suite. RIP is the most basic and operates in a connectionless mode at the application layer, interfacing with transport layer protocols through UDP. Its decision for routing is based upon hop count only, where each router is one hop. RIP computes this hop count while ignoring the length of the hop and the capacity available in that and other hops. This can cause problems when a higher-bandwidth path is available and desirable for transport, as in Figure 8.3. Here, router A would like to send a 500K file to router E. Since the path through router D requires only two hops, it will be chosen (regardless of distance) instead of the higher-bandwidth path (and three hops) through routers B and C. RIP also requires an abundant amount of overhead to update neighboring routing tables every 30 seconds. Rather, this is not just an update; for each router in the network transmits its entire routing table to each of its neighbors every 30 seconds. This problem obviously compounds as the network becomes larger. RIP protocol also has a hop-count restriction of 16 hops, and is prone to routing loops (nodes stuck transmitting back and forth to each other because each believes the other has the shortest path to the destination) if misconfigured. The use of split horizons and poison reverse can improve performance and reduce the chance for loops, and hold-downs can be tweaked per the environment.

The Interior Gateway Routing Protocol (IGRP) is another type of routing protocol proprietary to Cisco Systems routers. This protocol operates similar to RIP, but is superior because it understands bandwidth limitations between hops, as well as time delays. IGRP is tunable to make it faster than RIP if desired (i.e., no use of hold-downs). This is the classic distance vector trade-off of network stability versus time. While this protocol improves upon RIP, it also doubles the transmit time of information between nodes, amplifying the opportunity for a convergence problem.

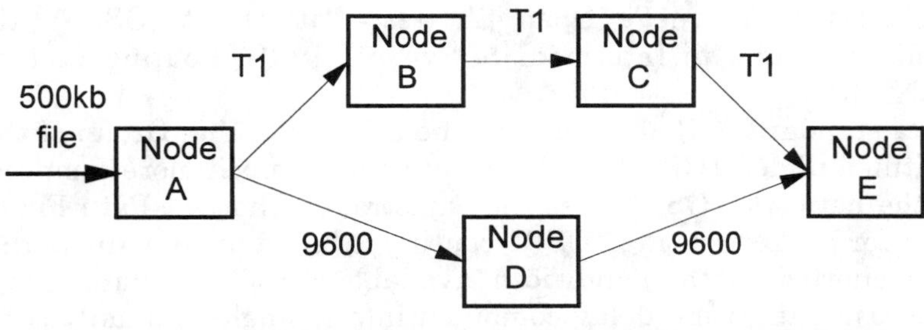

Figure 8.3 RIP Routing Example

EGP and Border Gateway Protocol (BGP) are exterior routing protocols, that is, they are used between separately administered networks. Internet Service Providers (ISPs) use BGP to share routing information between their networks, and in situations where it matters, like sites that are dual homed (most singly homed Internet subscribers are statically routed, and since it is a binary decision, the route is either there or not there and no path selection occurs). EGP (the protocol, not the class of protocols including BGP) is deprecated.

8.2.3 Link State Routing Protocols

More recently developed and even more efficient as a routing protocol is the *link state* algorithm. The link state advertisement method was designed to address the scalability issues of the distance vector method. Routers using link state routing protocols request changes in link states from all nodes on the network. Routing tables are exchanged with neighbors, but every device on the network must be at least one other devices' neighbor. In this manner, each router will eventually be updated with everyone else's routing tables. This makes good use of the routing process and eliminates having various network states running simultaneously throughout the network. When a link is added or deleted from the network, an advertisement of its cost is flooded through the network. Each node has complete knowledge of the network topology in time *t* (usually tens of milliseconds to seconds) after any change and computes the least-cost routes to every destination using an algorithm such as the Dijkstra algorithm. Link state updates are sent using 64-byte packets (depending on the specific protocol) in a multicast mode, and require acknowledgments. The actual neighbor reachability exchanges are this small, with the actual link state updates potentially larger. This protocol will also notify users if their address is unreachable. This method is more memory intensive for the router, and requires large amounts of buffers and memory space. More router CPU cycles are also needed, as more complex algorithms must be used.

There are three major implementations of link state routing protocols on the market: the Internet's Open Shortest Path First (OSPF), the OSI Intermediate System to Intermediate System (IS-IS) Routing Protocol, and Novell's NLSP.

OSPF, a standard IGP developed by the OSPF Working Group of the IETF and identified under TCP/IP (DARPA), provides a much more comprehensive view of the network. OSPF uses the Dijkstra, or Shortest Path First (SPF), algorithm for packet routing. OSPF routing is based upon many parameters, including shortest path, bandwidth available, cost in dollars, congestion, interface costs, and time delay combined into a single manually configured metric. All costs for links are designated on the outbound router port.

Routers are sectioned into "areas", with each area maintaining its own topological database. These areas are then connected to a backbone area.

OSPF routing supports three types of networks: point-to-point, broadcast, and NonBroadcast MultiAccess (NBMA). Point-to-point networks join a single pair of routers. Broadcast networks attach more than two routers, with each router having the ability to broadcast a single message to multiple routers through a single address. Nonbroadcast networks, such as X.25, attach more than two routers but do not have broadcast capability. OSPF also supports sub-netting and filtering, which we will discuss later in address design. OSPF is only useful with TCP/IP networks. OSPF also supports bifurcated routing: the ability to split packets between two equal paths.

The OSI IS-IS protocol is now a standard. IS-IS is the OSI standard equivalent to OSPF, and provides similar benefits. There is also a Cisco version of the IS-IS standard that has been around since 1992 and is very similar to OSPF.

The End-System-to-Intermediate-System (ES-IS) protocol is used to route between end nodes and intermediate nodes, while the Intermediate-System-to-Intermediate-System (IS-IS) protocol is used to route between network nodes. ES-IS protocol is complimentary to IS-IS, and comparable to ARP for IP. Another analogy is to compare OSPF to IS-IS, as ARP is to ES-IS. An extension of IS-IS, Integrated IS-IS (also called Dual IS-IS, as proposed by DEC), can support both OSI and TCP/IP networks simultaneously. This protocol helps TCP/IP users migrate to the OSI platform. DECnet V has standardized support on both versions. OSI IS-IS standards are popular in the international community, where OSI is the predominant standard. IS-IS standards do not have a hop-count limit. In fact, there is no concept of a hop count in OSPF or IS-IS – the interface costs build up cumulatively throughout the network. There is one real distinction between the protocols – OSPF provides a wider range of interface costs than IS-IS.

8.2.4 Routing Protocols Comparison

Table 8.1 shows a comparison matrix between communications protocols and their native routing protocols.

TABLE 8.1 Communications and Routing Protocols

Communications Protocols	Native Routing Protocols
OSI	ES-IS, IS-IS, Integrated IS
TCP/IP	BGP, RIP, OSPF, Integrated IS-IS, IGRP
XNS, Novell IPX	RIP, NLSP for IPX
Banyan VINES	RTP, SRTP
AppleTalk	RTMP
DECnet IV	DECnet
DECnet V	see OSI

8.3 NETWORK AND TRANSPORT LAYER PROTOCOLS – THE INTERNET PROTOCOL SUITE (TCP/IP)

Now that we have the groundwork of the physical and data link layer protocols, we can delve into the world of end-to-end network and transport layer protocols. Since many of the network and transport protocols work closely in unison, each architecture implementation will be examined. We start with the Internet suite of protocols – Internet Protocol (IP) and Transmission Control protocol (TCP). Later in this book, the influence that IP has had on SMDS and ATM will become apparent.

8.3.1 Origins of TCP/IP

The U.S. Advanced Research Projects Agency (ARPA) began development of a packet-switched network in 1969, and demonstrated the first packet switching capability in 1972. It was named the ARPANET. The ARPANET continued to grow, and in 1983 introduced the Transmission Control Protocol/Internet Protocol (TCP/IP), replacing the earlier Network Control Protocol (NCP) and Interface Message Processor (IMP) protocol. Also in 1983 the ARPANET was split into a military network and a nonmilitary research network; the latter was the origin of the Internet. In 1986, the National Science Foundation (NSF) founded the construction of a 56 kbps network connecting its six new supercomputer centers. It was upgraded to DS1 in 1988. In 1990 the National Science Foundation (NSF) embarked upon a program to upgrade the entire Internet backbone to DS3 speeds (45 Mbps) for supercomputer interconnection. In 1994 the NSF began upgrade of the Internet backbone for supercomputer communication to OC-3 speeds (150 Mbps). The backbone speed continues to increase. The OC-3 network is not a general-purpose network for use as "the Internet backbone", however, plans are in place for the major Internet backbone Service Providers (ISPs) to upgrade to OC-3 by the time of publishing. The Internet has its own standards body, called the Internet Engineering Task Force (IETF), which is described in Chapter 3.

8.3.2 Structure of TCP/IP

Figure 8.4 illustrates the Internet protocol suite built atop the Internet Protocol (IP) and the layered Internet protocol architecture. The User Datagram Protocol (UDP), Internet Control Message Protocol (ICMP), routing control protocols, and the Transmission Control Protocol (TCP) interface directly with IP, corresponding to the transport layer in the Internet architecture. This section focuses on TCP and IP.

Both TCP and UDP provide the capability for the host to distinguish among multiple applications through port numbers. TCP provides a reliable, sequenced delivery of data to applications. TCP also provides adaptive flow control, segmentation, and reassembly, and prioritized data flows. UDP only provides an unacknowledged datagram capability.

A number of applications interface to TCP and UDP, as shown in Figure 8.4. The File Transfer Protocol (FTP) application provides for security log-in, directory manipulation, and file transfers. TELNET provides a remote terminal log-in capability. The Simple Network Management Protocol (SNMP) supports configuration setting, data retrieval, and alarms. The Trivial FTP (TFTP) protocol provides a simplified version of FTP, which is intended to reduce implementation complexity. The Remote Procedure Call (RPC) and Network File Server (NFS) capabilities allow applications to interact over IP. Domain Name Services (DNS) provide a centralized name service, and can run over UDP or TCP.

Routers send error and control messages to other routers using ICMP. ICMP also provides a function in which a user can send a *ping* (echo packet) to verify connectivity to an IP-addressed host.

The Address Resolution Protocol (ARP) directly interfaces to the data link layer, for example, Ethernet. The purpose of ARP is to map a physical address (e.g., an Ethernet MAC address) to an IP address. Routing protocols were discussed previously.

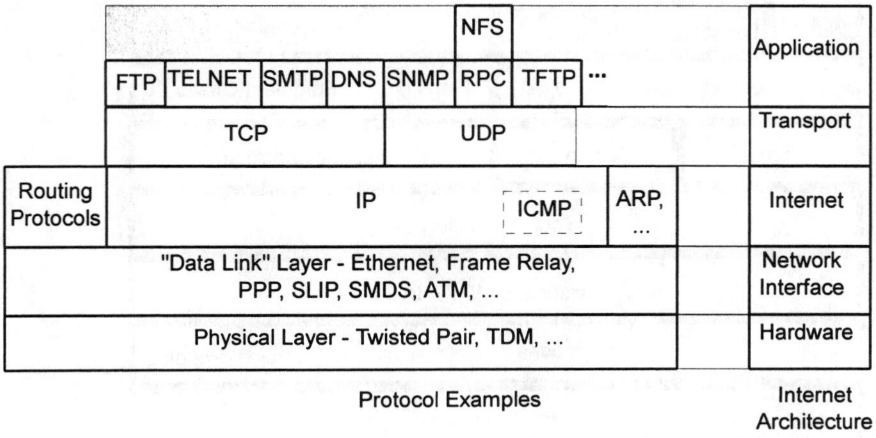

NFS
FTP TELNET SMTP DNS SNMP RPC TFTP ...
TCP UDP
Routing Protocols
IP
ICMP
ARP, ...
"Data Link" Layer - Ethernet, Frame Relay, PPP, SLIP, SMDS, ATM, ...
Physical Layer - Twisted Pair, TDM, ...
Protocol Examples

Application
Transport
Internet
Network Interface
Hardware
Internet Architecture

Figure 8.4 Internet Protocol (IP) Suite

8.3.3 IP Packet Formats

Figure 8.5 illustrates the format of the IP packet. The version field specifies the IP protocol version. The header length field specifies the datagram header length in units of 32-bit words, the most common length being 4 words, or 20 octets. Use of the Type Of Service (TOS) field varies across the industry. Either each bit is treated as an individual flag (a 3-bit precedence of 1 to 7 – 1 bit to indicate delay sensitivity, 1 bit to indicate high throughput, and 1 bit to indicate a request for high reliability), or a 3-bit field is used with values of 0 through 7 (or 1 through 8, even) and 8 levels of precedence or service qualities. The total length field specifies the total IP datagram length for the header and the user data. The identification, flags, and fragment offset fields control fragmentation (or segmentation) and re-assembly of IP datagrams. The Time To Live (TTL) field specifies how many routers the packet can pass through in the Internet before it is declared "dead". Intermediate nodes or routers decrement TTL, and when it reaches zero, the packet is discarded. The protocol field identifies the higher-level protocol type (e.g., TCP or UDP), which identifies the format of the data field.

The header checksum ensures integrity of the header fields through a calculation that is easy to implement in software. Source and destination IP addresses are required, and the user data is placed in the data field. The nonmandatory fields for options and padding can specify routing and time-stamp information.

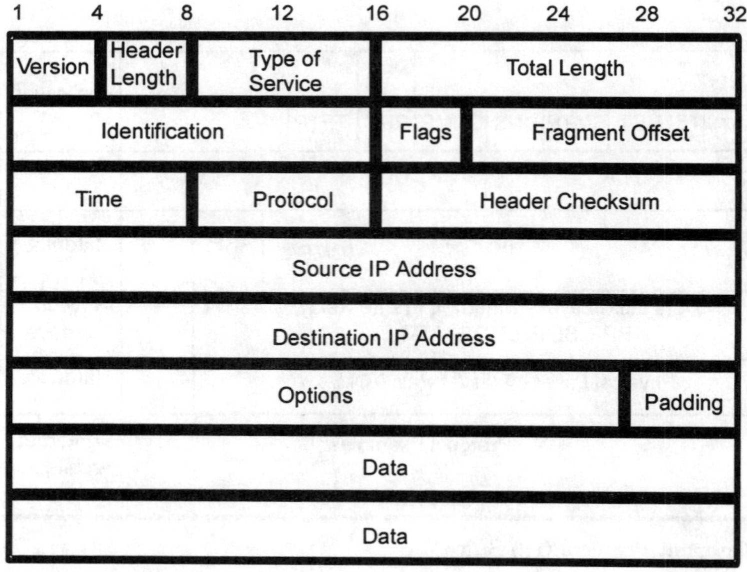

Figure 8.5 IP Datagram Format

8.3.4 Internet Protocol (IP) Addressing

The Internet is a huge worldwide network that uses 32-bit IP addresses as a global network addressing scheme. Each user, or "host" in Internet parlance, is assigned a unique IP address of 32 bits, or 4 octets, represented in the following dotted decimal notation:

XXX.XXX.XXX.XXX

where XXX ranges from 0 to 255 decimal, corresponding to the range of 00000000 to 11111111 binary. There are 2^{32}, or over 4 billion, IP addresses.

IP addresses are grouped into classes A, B, and C as shown in Figure 8.6, where the class determines the maximum network size, measured in number of hosts. A class A address supports a network of up to 16 million host addresses (2^{24}), a class B address supports up to 64,000 (2^{16}) hosts, while a class C address supports up to 256 (2^8) host addresses. Internet addresses are assigned and managed by a central authority, the Internet Assigned Numbers Authority (IANA), to ensure that they are unique. A network may assign the host addresses however it wishes, as long as the assignment is unique. If unique addresses are not maintained, problems with address conflicts can arise when networks are interconnected. More on IP address assignment and design will be covered in Chapter 22.

IP works with TCP for end-to-end reliable transmission of data across the network. TCP will control the amount of unacknowledged data in transit by reducing either the window size or the segment size. The reverse is also true, where window or segment size values can be increased to pass more data if error conditions are minimal. Let's now explore the TCP.

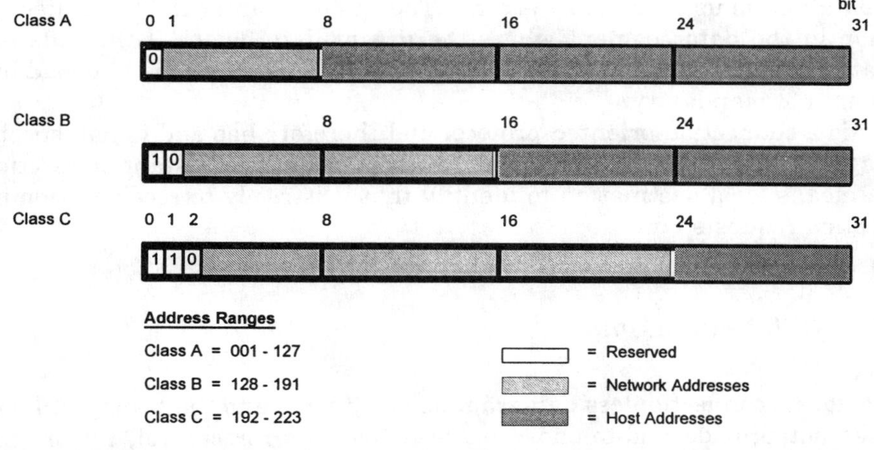

Figure 8.6 Internet Assigned Address Classes

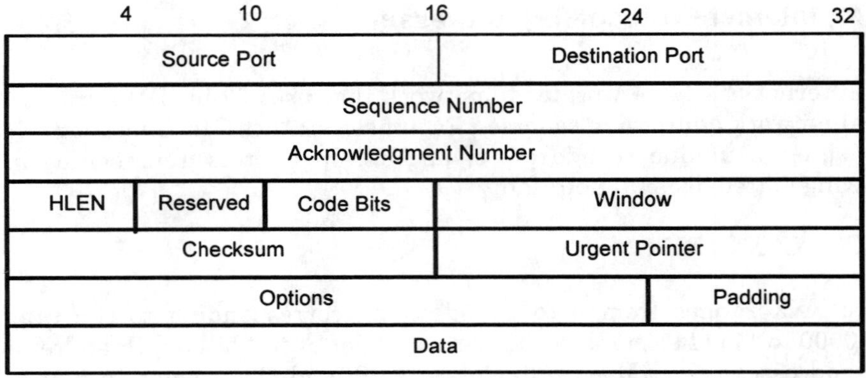

Figure 8.7 TCP Segment Format

8.3.5 TCP Frame Format

Figure 8.7 illustrates the TCP frame format. The source and destination TCP port numbers identify a specific application program in the source and destination hosts. The sequence number field identifies the position of the sender's byte stream in the data field. The acknowledgment number field identifies the number of the next octet to be received. The HLEN provides the length of the header. The code bits field determines the use of the segment contents (e.g., SYN for synchronize sequence numbers and RST for reset connection). The window field tells the amount of data the application is willing to accept. The checksum is applied across the TCP header and the user data and is used to detect errors. The urgent pointer field specifies the position in the data segment where the urgent data begins if the code bits indicate that this segment contains urgent data. The options and padding fields are not mandatory.

TCP is a connection-oriented protocol and therefore has additional, specific messages and a protocol for an application to request a distant connection, and a means for a destination to identify that it is ready to receive incoming connection requests.

8.3.6 TCP/IP Functions

IP provides a connectionless datagram delivery service to the transport layer. IP does not provide end-to-end reliable delivery, error control, retransmission, or flow control; it relies on TCP to provide these functions.

A major function of IP is in the routing protocols, which provide the means for devices to discover the topology of the network, as well as detect changes of state in nodes, links, and hosts. Thus, IP routes packets through available paths around points of failure. IP has no notion of reserving bandwidth; it only finds an available path. Most of the routing algorithms will minimize a routing cost, as discussed previously.

8.3.7 Example of TCP/IP Operation

Figure 8.8 shows an example of a TCP/IP network transferring data from a workstation client to a server. Both TCP and IP are built upon the principle that the underlying network is a connectionless datagram network that can deliver packets out of order, or even deliver duplicate packets. TCP handles this by segmentation and re-assembly using the sequence number in the TCP header, while IP does this using the fragment control fields in the IP header. Either method, or both, may be used. A user's data "ABCD" is segmented into four TCP segments on the left-hand side of the figure. A router is initially routing this traffic via an X.25 network and sends datagram A via that route. The router then becomes aware of a direct connection to the destination router, and routes the remaining datagrams via the direct route. This routing action causes the datagrams to arrive at the destination server out of order, with datagram "A" traversing the X.25 network and arriving significantly later. TCP resequences the datagrams and delivers the block of data to the destination in the original order. IP performs a very similar process using fragmentation and re-assembly. IP does no reordering or retransmission, and re-assembly occurs only at the final destination host.

This operation by TCP/IP of accepting datagrams out of order, and being able to operate over an unreliable underlying network, makes it quite robust. None of the other standard modern data communication protocols has this attribute – IPX/SPX approximates it, as does the CLNP/TP4 protocol stack.

8.3.8 Traffic and Congestion Control Aspects of TCP/IP

TCP works over IP to achieve end-to-end reliable transmission of data across a network. TCP flow control uses a sliding window flow-control protocol, like X.25; however, the window is of a variable size, instead of the fixed window size used by X.25. Figure 8.9 illustrates a simplified example of key concepts in the dynamic TCP window flow-control protocol between workstation and a server. The sender starts with a window size equal to that of one TCP segment. The IP datagrams are delivered to the destination workstation, resulting in a delivered segment which is acknowledged. The sender then increases the window size to two segments. When these two segments are received they are both acknowledged, and the sender increases the window size to three segments. The network has become congested at this point, and the third segment is lost. The sender detects this by starting a timer whenever a segment is sent. If the timer expires, then the segment is resent. Upon such a retransmission time-out, the sender resets its window size to one segment and repeats the above process. Specific implementations will vary, and there is constant fine-tuning of the algorithms and their implementation. Fortunately, the architecture permits the sender and receiver to use different algorithms so improvements can actually be deployed.

The tuning and refinement of the TCP dynamic window flow control protocol has been the subject of a great deal of research. The above operation is often referred to as the Van Jacobson "Slow Start" TCP protocol.

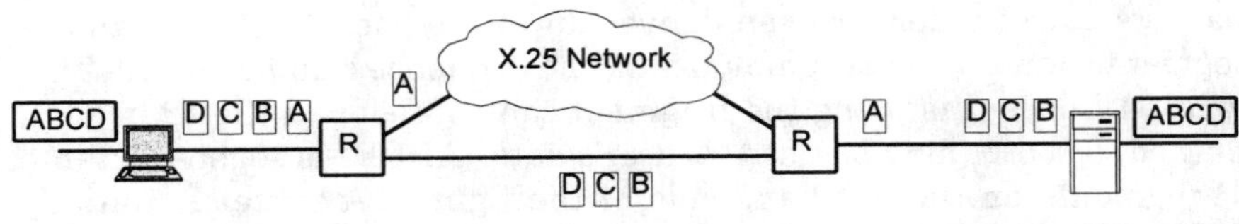

Figure 8.8 Example of Data Transfer Using TCP/IP

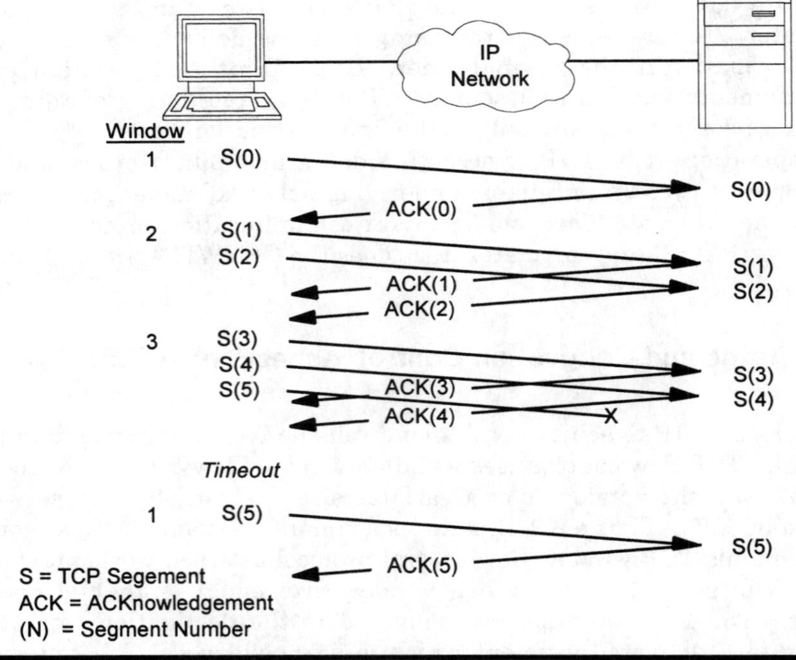

Figure 8.9 Example of TCP Dynamic Windowing Flow Control

8.3.9 Service Aspects of TCP/IP

TCP/IP implementations typically constitute a router, TCP/IP workstation and server software, and network management. TCP/IP protocol implementations span UNIX, DOS, VM, and MVS environments. A majority of UNIX users employ TCP/IP for inter-networking. Many Network Operating System (NOS) vendors are now integrating TCP/IP into their NOS platforms. Examples include Novell NetWare, Banyan Vines, and Windows 95. TCP/IP is also used internationally.

Operation of IP over a number of network, data link, and physical layer services is defined. At the network layer, IP operation over X.25 and SMDS is defined. At the data link layer, IP operation over frame relay, Ethernet, Token Ring, FDDI, and ATM is defined. IP operation over circuit-switched and dedicated physical layer facilities is also defined.

8.3.10 IP Next Generation (IPng) - IPv6

Many users will claim "The Internet is out of addresses!" While it is difficult to obtain a large block of addresses (i.e. Class B or C), it is not impossible. Over 50 percent of the available IP addresses in IPv4 have not been assigned by any of the NIC manufacturers yet. With more rational address assignment policies now in place, and with the implementation of CIDR and the availability of routing protocols that support variable-length sub-net masks, the IPv4 address space should last well past the end of the decade. Even with 100,000 networks (a reasonable estimate) and 2,000 machines per network (a very high estimate), we have used only 200,000,000 addresses (approximately 4 or 5 IP addresses for every person who is purportedly using the Internet), leaving 4 billion addresses of headroom. The frugal use of address space (i.e., RFC 1597) and network address translation, while clearly not agreed upon universally, also help with address conservation.

In July 1994 the IETF issued RFC 1752 – The Recommendation for the IP next generation protocol – IPng. IPng supersedes IPv4, and is formally referred to as IPv6. The "formal" RFCs for IPv6 include RFC 1883 for IPv6 general definition, RFC 1884 for addressing, RFC 1885 for ICMPv6, and RFC 1886 for Domain Name Services (DNS) extensions. IPv6 contains the following additions and enhancements to IPv4:

* Expands the address size from 32 to 128 bits
* Simple dynamic auto-configuration capability
* Easier multicast routing with addition of "scope" field
* Anycast feature – send packet to anycast address and it is delivered to one of the nodes which allows nodal routing control
* Capability to define quality of service to a traffic flow added

* Reduction of overhead – some header fields are optional
* More flexible protocol design for future enhancements
* Authentication, data integrity, and confidentiality options
* Easy transition and interoperability with IPv4
* Support for all IPv4 routing algorithms (e.g., OSPF, RIP, etc.)

IPv6 is designed to accommodate traditional applications such as:

◊ IP datagram service
◊ FTP file transfers
◊ E-mail
◊ X-windows
◊ Gopher

along with new applications such as:

- Nomadic computing
- Wireless
- Network-available entertainment
- 500 channel TV
- Video-on-demand
- Home device control (electrical and mechanical)

The automatic configuration capability of IPv6 is good for mobile users that do not want to use Virtual LANs (VLANs). It is also a handy feature that eliminates the requirements for LAN administrators to constantly reconfigure the network. Some manual configuration is required. IPv6 is already being implemented in the Internet.

There are three types of IP addresses: unicast, anycast, and multicast. All addresses in IPv6 are assigned to an interface. Unicast addresses are assigned to a single interface. Anycast addresses are assigned to a group of interfaces and the packet will be delivered to at least one of these interfaces. Multicast addresses are assigned to a group of interfaces such that when a packet is sent all interfaces receive it. Space is also reserved for NSAP, IPX, and neutral addresses. With 128-bit addressing there is the possibility for 340×10^{36} individual addresses.

The header format for IPng is shown in Figure 8.10. Notice that the version field value equals 6. The priority field allows eight values (0, 1, 2, 3, 4, 5, 6, and 7) for prioritizing traffic that can back-off during congestion, and eight values (8-15) that can be assigned to traffic that does not back-off in response to congestion (e.g., "real-time" constant bit-rate traffic like video). The flow label field works in concert with the priority field to determine quality of service. The payload length field specifies the length of the payload. The next header field identifies the type of header immediately following this header (same values used as with IPv4). The hop limit field is a count that decrements by 1 each time the packet is forwarded. If the count reaches zero, the packet is discarded. The source and destination addresses are the same as for IPv4, except that they are 128 bits. Variable-length extension headers may be added up to a total of 40 bytes. Also note that many details were not yet resolved or agreed upon as of this printing.

8.4 LEGACY SNA

Before we look at how to migrate SNA networks into LAN and WAN multiprotocol networks, we need a solid understanding of legacy SNA systems. Legacy SNA systems are still growing. SNA still maintains the predominant corporate mainframe architecture, accounting for over 50 percent of worldwide data communications networks. Mainframe and VTAM sales and deployment increase every year. VTAM and NCP software form the core communications software for all SNA communications. Traditional SNA architecture is master-slave and thus hierarchical in nature. SNA is now moving toward a more distributed, peer-to-peer architecture called Advanced Peer-to-Peer Networking (APPN), which we will explore in great detail in the next section. Multiprotocol environments with legacy and non-SNA protocols are a fact of life for many large corporations. This migration from the older SNA environments to the newer client-server applications takes time. Complete applications have to be rewritten and, in many cases, new hardware purchased, installed, and managed much differently.

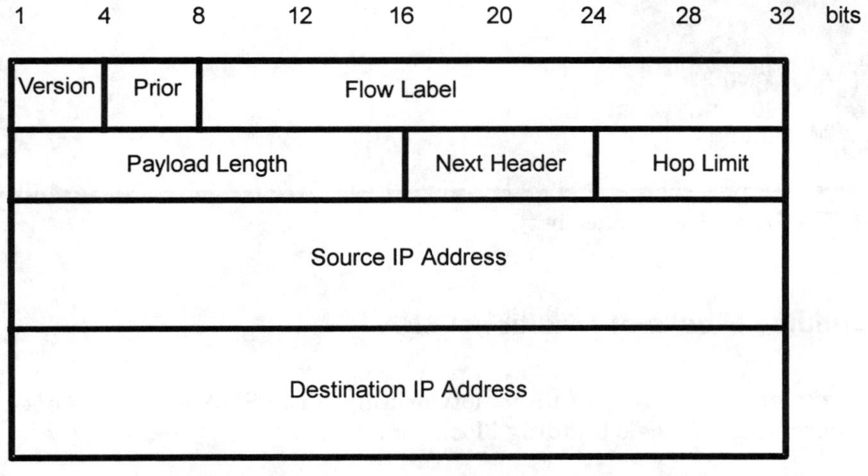

Figure 8.10 IPng Packet Format

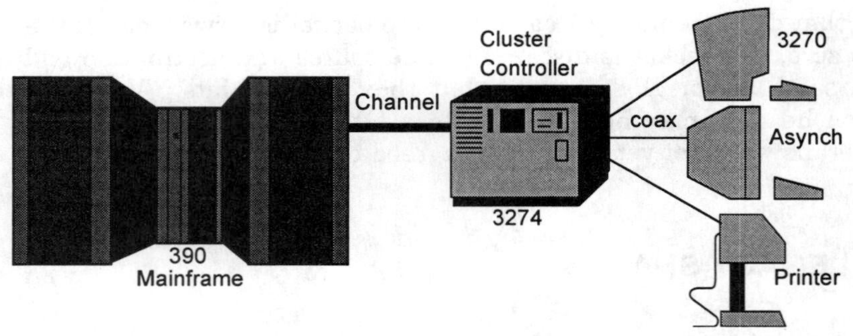

Figure 8.11 Cluster Controller Operation

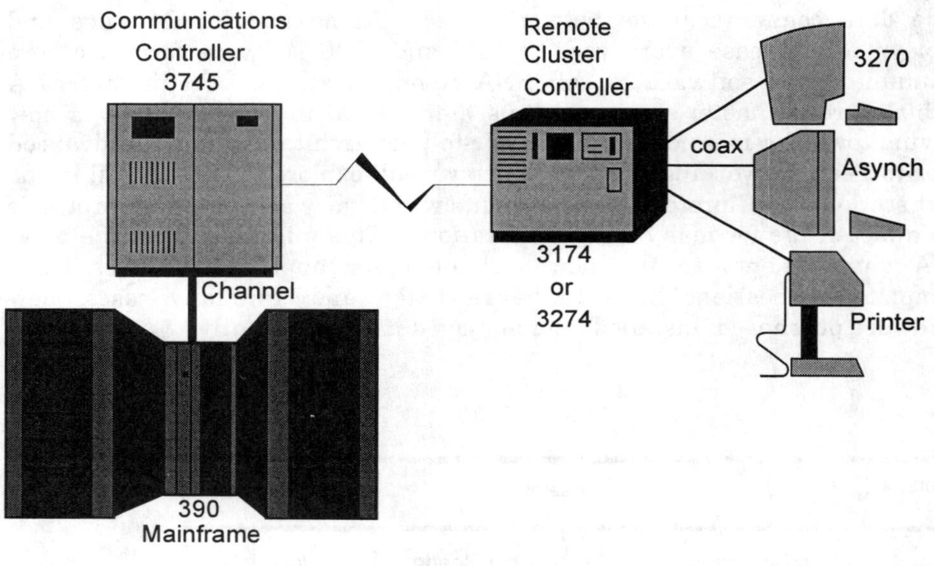

Figure 8.12 FEP Local Host Connectivity

8.4.1 Building Blocks of Traditional SNA

Before we explore the details of inter-networking in the SNA world, we need to first understand the basic building blocks of SNA.

A **Host Processor** is also called a Central Processing Unit (CPU). Devices include the IBM 3090, 4381, and 9370. Mainframes run ACF/VTAM VxRy (current release is V4R2) software.

Cluster Controller or Terminal Controllers control a cluster of 8 to 32 typically coax-attached terminals (IBM 3278, 3290, 3270 PC) and printers (IBM 3268, 3287). Attachment device protocols include BSC and SNA/SDLC. CCs can be either channel-attached to the mainframe (IBM 3274 Model 41D or 41A, as shown in Figure 8.11) or remote-connected to the mainframe through a communications controller (IBM 3274 Model 41C). IBM 3276 and the newer IBM 3174s (with attached workstations instead of terminals) can also be called cluster controllers as shown in Figure 8.12.

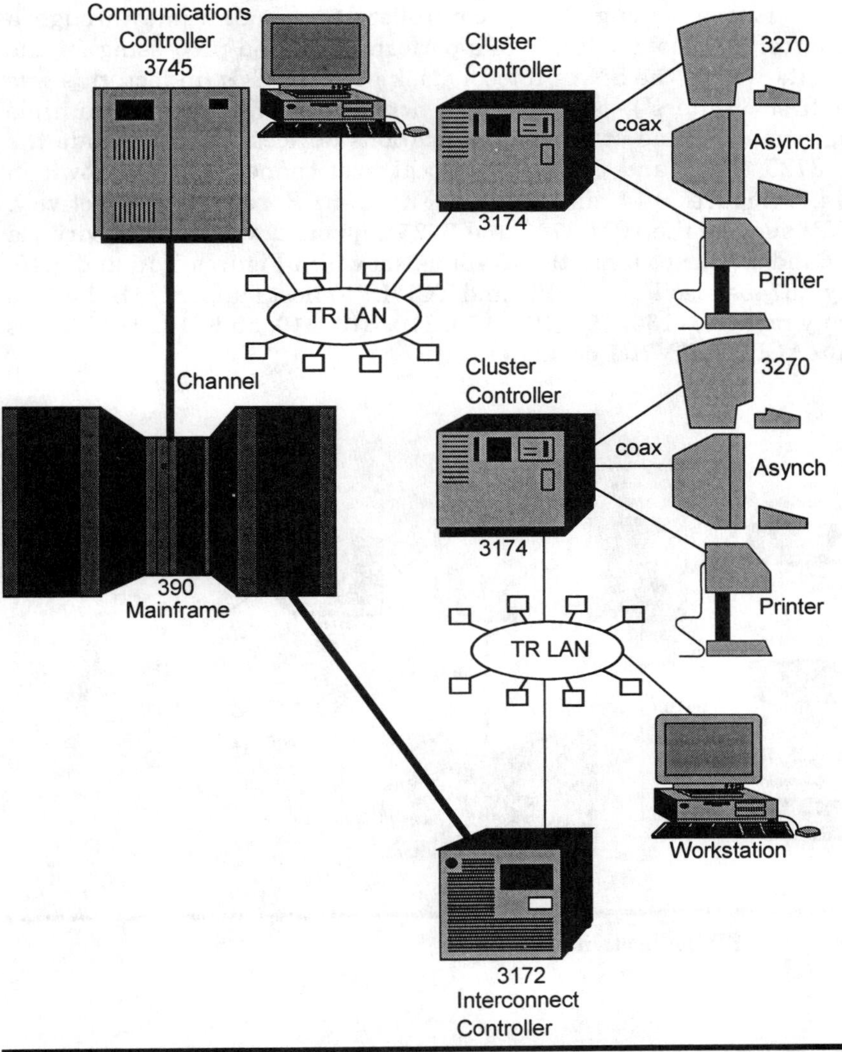

Figure 8.13 3174 Establishment Controllers Token Ring Connectivity

Establishment Controller Units, or ECUs (such as the IBM 3174), are a form of cluster controllers that can act as a gateway for mainframe connectivity to a Token Ring or Ethernet LAN for VTAM access. This configuration is shown in Figure 8.13. IBM 3174s provide TCP/IP-to-host support for both Ethernet and Token Ring, including frame relay and Remote Source Route Bridging (RSRB) capability. 3714s also support APPN, acting as a Network Node (NN) and providing directory services for downstream End Nodes (ENs).

Communications Controllers (CCs) or **Front-End Processors** (FEPs) provide access for connecting cluster controllers to a mainframe through a Network Control Protocol (NCP). FEPs perform front-end processing for the host, route data within the SNA protocol stack between CCs (in fact, this was one of the first "routers"), and can also act as concentrators to multiple controllers, terminals, and other communications devices. FEPs include the IBM 3745, 3720, 3725, and 3705. FEP local host connectivity is shown in Figure 8.14. Figure 8.14 also shows FEP-to-FEP remote connectivity. Certain FEPs such as the IBM 3745 and 3725 support device connectivity via Token Ring and Ethernet (only the 3745) as shown in Figures 8.15 and 8.16, respectively. 3745s also have APPN and TCP/IP-to-host support. IBM 3745s come in many models – 130, 150, 160, 170, 210, 310, 410, and 610. IBM 3745s typically run ACF/NCP V7R1 or higher.

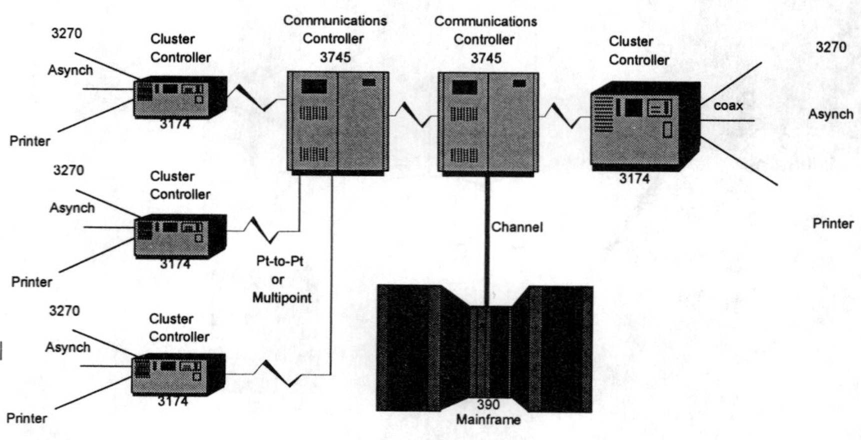

Figure 8.14 FEP-to-FEP Connectivity

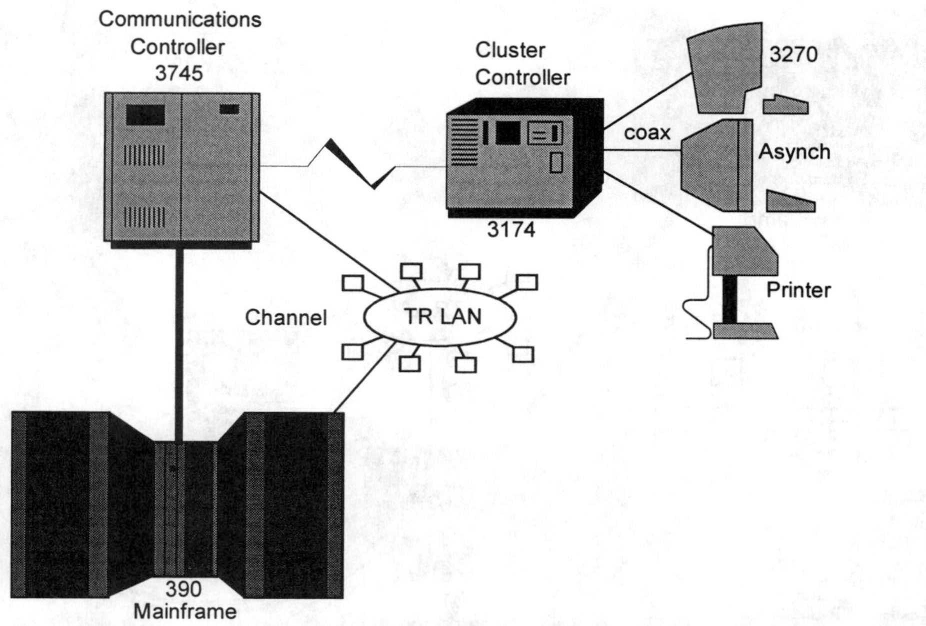

Figure 8.15 FEP Token Ring Connectivity

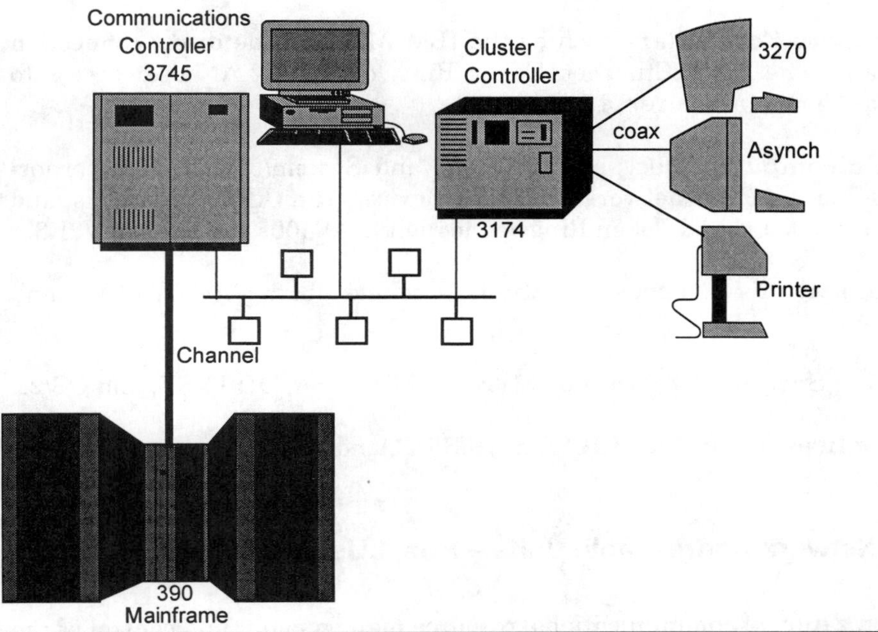

Figure 8.16 FEP Ethernet Connectivity

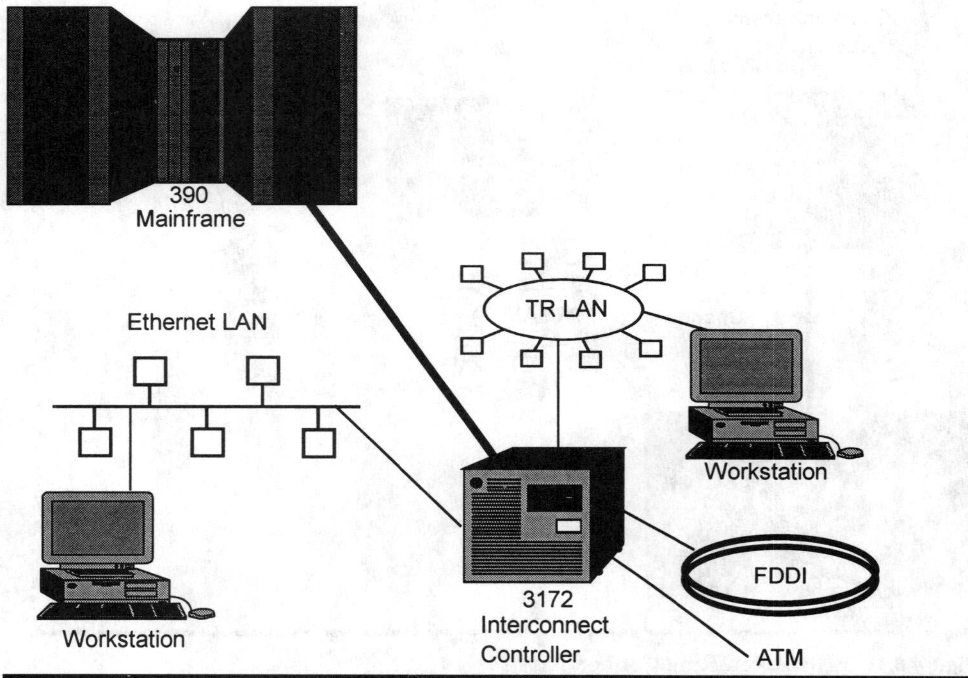

Figure 8.17 3172 Ethernet and Token Ring Connectivity

Interconnect Controllers such as the IBM 3172 provide direct connection for a mainframe to an Ethernet, Token Ring, or FDDI LAN user access to VTAM, as shown in Figure 8.17.

IBM Minicomputers such as the AS400 and System/36 form the cornerstone of most APPN networks. These devices run APPN protocols and support both SDLC and Token Ring connectivity. AS400s run OS/400 V2R3.

Communications Access Methods include both ACF/VTAM and ACF/TCAM.

Operating Systems (OS) include MVS/XA, MVS/ESA, DOS/VSE, and OS/2.

Host Applications include CICS/VS, IMS/DC, and TSO.

8.4.2 Network Addressable Units – PUs, LUs, and Domains

Synchronization of communications, resource management, and control of the network are managed by Network Addressable Units (NAUs). The three types of NAUs are the logical unit (LU), the physical unit (PU), and systems services control point (SSCP). LUs are "sessions" between end-user access ports on the network. LUs provide for the access and transfer of information across the domain and to other domains. PUs manage LUs. There are five types of PUs as shown in Table 8.2. Note that the higher number of the PU, the closer it is to the host. The SSCP defines the single point for domain control. A network device PU, LU, and SSCP is combined to form the network addressable unit (NAU), which forms the network address for a given device. Sessions are then established between NAUs.

TABLE 8.2 PU Types Comparison

PU Type	Device Type
PU1	3271, 6670, 3767
PU2	3174, 3274, 3276, PC, 3770, AS400
PU2.1	3174, S36, S/38, AS/400, PC, TPF, VTAM V4R1
PU4	37X5, 3720 (including NCP)
PU5	4300, 308X, 3090 (including VTAM)

Figure 8.18 shows a typical SNA network depicting the logical layers of devices LUs, PUs, and the other naming conventions of SNA. Each device in the network is labeled a *node*. These nodes can be host subareas, communications controllers, or even peripherals. Subareas are groups of devices that communicate, such as a host and its direct or remote-connected cluster controllers, or a communications controller and its associated remote controllers. The entire area controlled by one host is called the *domain*. The primary communications protocol here is SDLC. We see that SNA PU 2 devices are typically 3174 cluster controllers providing a concentration and bridging function locally for 317X terminals, and SNA PU 4 devices are front-end processors providing routing of native-mode SNA across local or wide areas. A 3172 interconnect controller and the mainframe form the PU 5 functionality.

8.4.3 SNA Legacy Software Communications

Virtual Telecommunications Access Method (VTAM) is the software that resides in the host computer and communicates with the "dumb" terminals attached to the 3174. The FEP runs software called Network Control Program (NCP) that provides the routing function for VTAM.

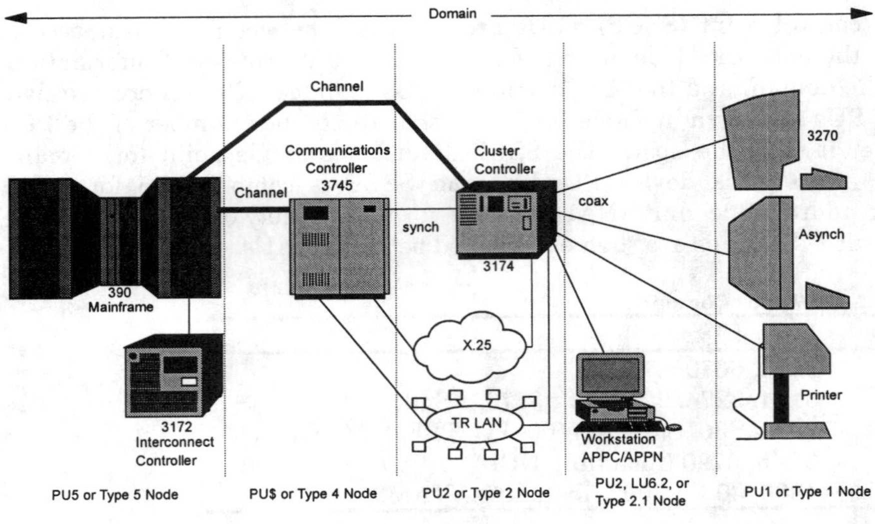

Figure 8.18 SNA Domain

8.5 IBM SNA/SDLC MIGRATION TO LAN/WAN INTERNETWORKING

It has long been a well-known fact that SNA/SDLC protocols and traditional non-SNA, internetworking or routed protocols do not mix well on the same local or wide area network. This is no longer true! SNA routing protocols and standards have changed drastically in the last few years. Technology and protocol advances have provided new opportunities for heterogeneous environments. But don't think it will be easy! Applications are migrating to client-server, workstation-based environments, but these migrations take years to occur. Homogeneous SNA protocols are still alive and well in many networks.

Access still remains a major portion of network cost, and users want to integrate SNA and non-SNA traffic over the same LANs, WANs, and public data services. How then should SNA traffic be moved onto a common LAN protocol and then across the WAN on a common routed backbone protocol? Why combine SNA traffic with non-SNA traffic? One of the advantages of placing SNA traffic over a WAN is that broadcast packets and unnecessary polling overhead can be eliminated, similar to a more dynamic method of filtering. Broadcast packets cause excessive overhead with source routing; the larger the network, the more overhead used. Sometimes, users are forced to use an alternate design. 9600 bps multipoint lines become highly utilized, and services like frame relay with 56 kbps access circuits and 16 kbps

Committed Information Rates (CIRs) are available at a small incremental cost but have the advantage of boosting throughput and thus the response time and number of users dramatically.

There are many methods of tying SNA networks into the non-SNA WAN environment – all the major efforts will be introduced. SNA in multiprotocol environments is a complex subject, difficult to cover in a chapter, let alone an entire book. Many users have already upgraded LAN-capable SNA devices with Token Ring or frame relay interfaces. These devices then interface to the WAN through the Token Ring LAN or directly by frame relay service. Some of the older IBM devices, such as the 3X74s, S/36s, S/38s, 3600s, 4700s, and 5520s, cannot be upgraded with Token Ring or frame relay capability. This isolates them from the LAN internetworking arena, and causes more elaborate schemes to be used for interconnection. SDLC is another option, but acts as a point-to-point protocol, where Token Ring (LLC) and TCP/IP can be combined in a routed environment. When multiple SDLC lines are placed on a Token Ring network, much bandwidth is wasted. Also, the SDLC address space is not large enough to support LAN networking, so other methods have been developed to pass SDLC traffic over the WAN. Therefore SDLC must be encapsulated and passed through the WAN. There are other methods of passing SNA traffic through a common non-SNA access and eventually through the backbone network that we will discuss. Let's now explore the standard methods for passing and integrating traditional SNA traffic with routed traffic across the LAN and WAN.

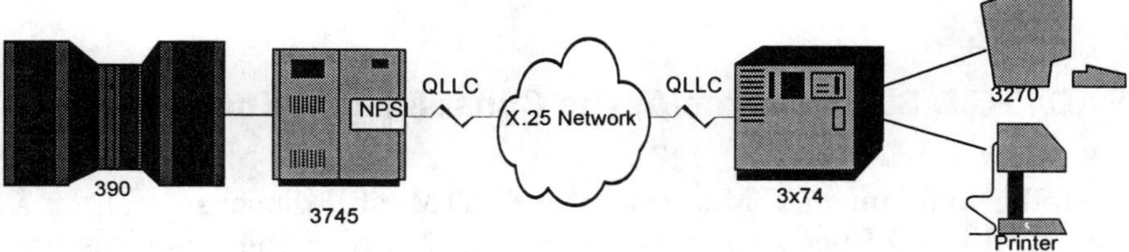

Figure 8.19 SNA X.25 NPSI

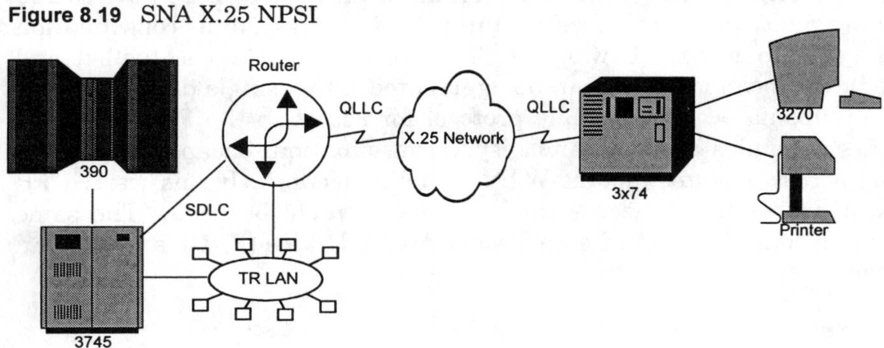

Figure 8.20 QLLC Conversion (SNA over X.25)

8.5.1 SNA over X.25 – NPSI

One method for sending SNA traffic from a FEP (3745) to remote 3x74s is to encapsulate it within X.25. IBM offers software and hardware called the Network Control Protocol (NCP) Packet Switching Interface (NPSI) as one option for encapsulating SDLC traffic for transport across the WAN. NPSI encapsulates SNA traffic into X.25 packets. The X.25 traffic can be sent over a private or public X.25 service, or encapsulated into IP and be transported over a routed TCP/IP environment, as shown in Figure 8.19. This allows access to a packet-switched network or a WAN capable of routing X.25 protocol. The NPSI is a cost-effective method for transporting SNA traffic over an X.25 network, but the protocol encapsulation is very inefficient with a large amount of overhead.

8.5.2 QLLC Conversion – SNA over X.25

The requirement for NPSI can be eliminated by attaching a Token Ring interface to the 3745, and translating from MAC to QLLC protocol within a router to the X.25 network or convert standard SDLC to QLLC. The remote 3X74 and workstation devices send their data to the X.25 network via QLLC. QLLC conversion is shown in Figure 8.20.

8.5.3 PAD/FRAD SDLC/Bisync/Async Consolidation/Encapsulation

Automatic teller machines (ATMs), the "other" ATM, still dispense cash on a daily basis to billions of people across the world. Many of these devices use the bisync protocol to communicate their transactions back to the controller. Now combine these devices with async terminals and other SDLC devices and the requirement for cost-effective integrated access, and consolidation methods come to mind. Low-speed SNA traffic using Async (polled and nonpolled), Bisync, and SDLC can be aggregated into a single device and the protocol encapsulated into a single protocol for access to the WAN. Figure 8.21 shows examples of async and bisync consolidation, encapsulation, and tunneling across a point-to-point WAN or a FR network. If this were a FR network, a Frame Relay Access Device (FRAD) would be used. The same configuration could be used when a Packet Access Device (PAD) is used in an X.25 network.

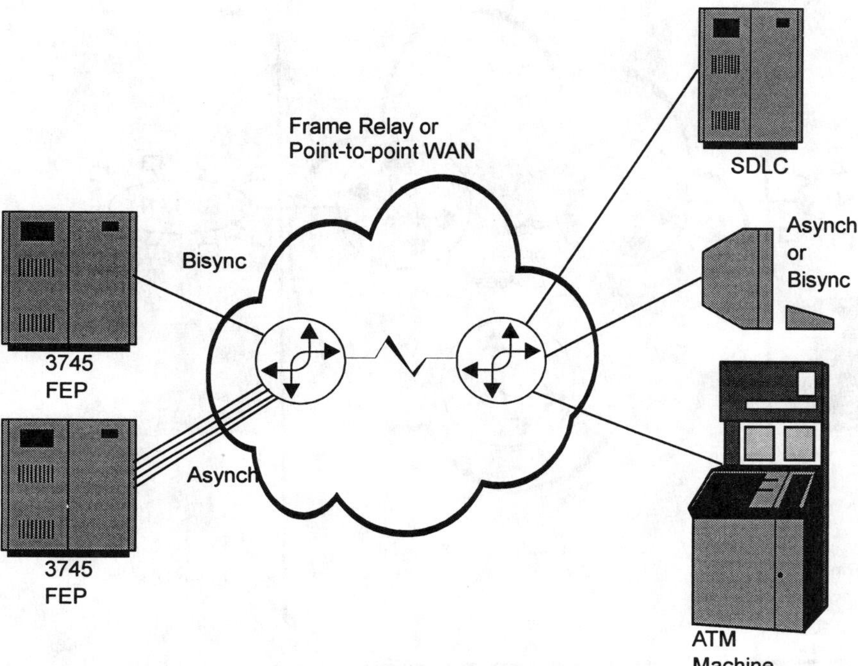

Figure 8.21 Async, Bisync, SDLC Conversion/Encapsulation

8.5.4 Traditional Source Route Bridging (SRB) and Remote SRB (RSRB)

SNA traffic can be bridged between Token Ring LANs and across the WAN. Replacing point-to-point SDLC links with a Token Ring connection eliminates polling across the entire WAN and eliminates the need for interruptive VTAM/NCP "gens" when adds, moves, and changes are required. When SRB is used, the LLC frame is passed intact across the WAN – no translation is performed. SRB is shown in Figure 8.22. Note that the three bridges in the WAN count as three "hops". While SRB offers a simplistic approach, it has many problems associated with it:

⇒ Potential session time-outs
⇒ 7 hop-count limit
⇒ Sessions are statically defined and cannot be rerouted
⇒ No metrics are available for performance routing (e.g., distance, cost)
⇒ does not work well across a frame relay WAN

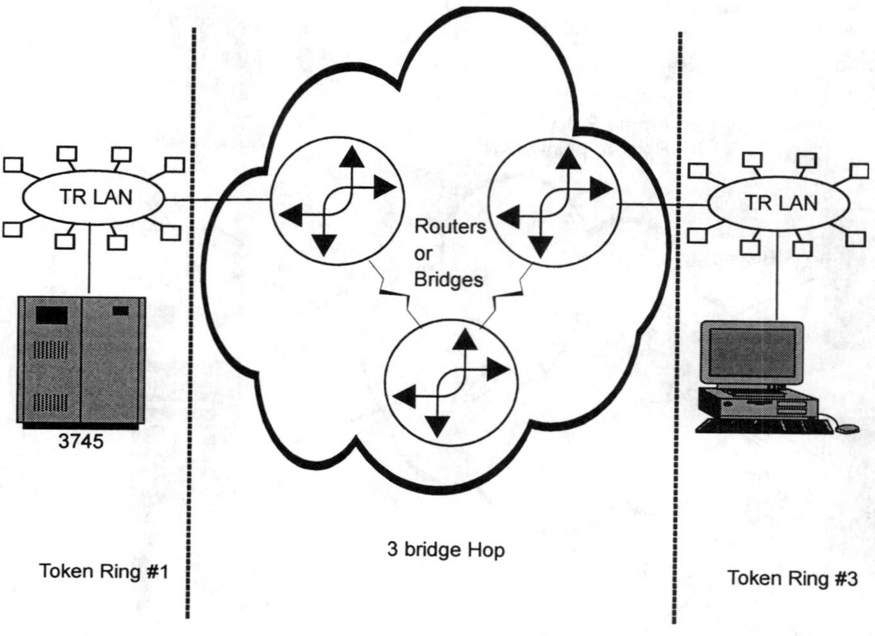

Figure 8.22 Source Route Bridging (SRB)

Recent improvements in routers have solved many of the problems of SRB and RSRB. Router capabilities like virtual rings that solve hop-count limits, the ability to route around failed links, and serial tunneling are just a few features available. Cisco's method of RSRB provides Token Ring-to-Token Ring connectivity. Many of these methods will be explained in subsequent sections in this chapter.

8.5.5 SDLC to LLC2 Protocol Conversion

There are various methods to consolidate IBM 3X74 devices into a single FEP. The two predominant options include SDLC to LLC2 protocol conversion and serial tunneling solution.

In SDLC to LLC2 conversion, remote 3X74 devices can connect via SDLC to a TCP/IP router. The router will then convert the SDLC traffic into Token Ring format LLC2. The LLC2 traffic will be sent to the remote destination router directly or encapsulated within TCP/IP. The destination router will then place it onto the FEP Token Ring segment in the LLC2 format. This process eliminates the requirement for a Token Ring interface card in the 3X74. LLC2 encapsulation is performed at logical link layer 2. SNA SDLC traffic is essentially encapsulated or mapped to an LLC2 frame by the router. SDLC to LLC2 conversion is shown in Figure 8.23.

An external device other than the WAN router is sometimes used to convert the SNA SDLC to LLC2 framing. Some devices are available that can aggregate multiple cluster controller links into a single SDLC point-to-point or multipoint circuit or Token Ring LAN. This improves performance, reduces polling, and saves bandwidth, and the circuit can now be placed over the WAN-routed network (through the router). Most router vendors have the capability to convert SNA/SDLC to the Token Ring LLC format, and many routers also support both the synchronous pass-through of SDLC and HDLC from origin to destination through the IEEE 802.1 spanning tree protocols. The same method is used by many routers to route IBM LU6.2, NetBIOS, IPX, and TCP/IP protocols. IBM uses a proprietary source-routing protocol, or implements true SNA Type 5/Type 4 host/FEP node emulation, as previously discussed. If IP encapsulation is used to transport SNA traffic, up to 50 bytes of overhead per message will be added. The smaller the size of the message, the worse the throughput. Another router option is to simply add to the SDLC address. This, however, will only increase the message overhead by up to 10 bytes or so.

8.5.6 SNA SDLC Serial Tunneling (Synchronous Pass-Through) over IP

As discussed previously, SNA routing is performed through the proprietary configuration of host VTAM and FEP resident Network Control Program (NCP). One method of *routing* point-to-point 3270 traffic from an IBM 3174 cluster controller is through SDLC serial *tunneling*, also called *synchronous pass-through*. Here the router encapsulates the SDLC traffic into an IP packet and routes it through the network. Inter-LAN traffic is handled through either 317X cluster controllers or 37XX front-end processors acting as bridges, converting the LAN packet to an SDLC frame.

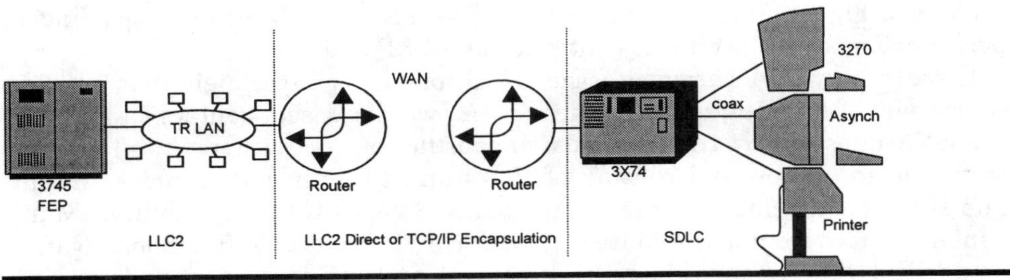

Figure 8.23 Async, Bisync, and SDLC Conversion/Encapsulation

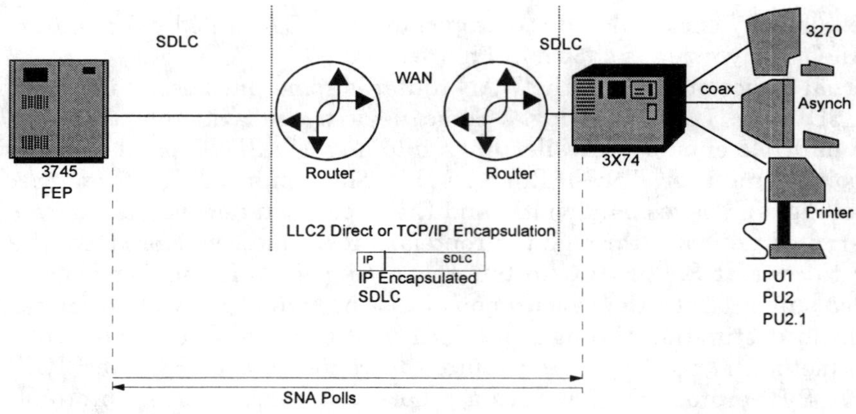

Figure 8.24 Synchronous Pass-Through or Serial Tunneling

Synchronous or transparent pass-through, or tunneling, provides point-to-point port mapping with IP encapsulation of the SNA SDLC traffic. This method adds some additional overhead and may affect time-outs, but this is usually reduced with polling and local acknowledgments. There may also be a problem with constant and occasional polling when information passes over the network from primaries to secondary. Figure 8.24 shows an example of synchronous pass-through. Every router vendor implements its own version of SDLC tunneling, and the DLSw standard was founded on SDLC tunneling. Many router vendors also offer some form of prioritization for SDLC tunneled or DLSw traffic.

Remote SDLC/3270 polling with retransmission. This eliminates polling overhead with a technique called *spoofing* or local acknowledgment. In this case, the access device passes only blocks containing SNA data over the dedicated SNA line. Polling is done locally with both primary or secondary modules performing the polling functions. When polls travel across the WAN, they increase network congestion. Spoofing provides the same benefits as synchronous pass-through, yet eliminates some overhead and time-out problems. Figure 8.25 shows an example of spoofing, where the spoofing is performed at both the cluster controller and FEP ends.

There are two variations to the synchronous pass-through that provide some level of spoofing or SNA routing. As we discussed, routers can handle the SNA question by two methods: encapsulation (or packetization) of SNA traffic or emulation and routing of PU2s and PU4s in native mode. Many non-IBM routers, moreover, are supporting SNA's LU4 compatibility. Many benefits derive from using routers to perform PU2 and PU4 functions. Native mode PU4 routers provide routing control and efficiencies gained by both priority routing through the router network and the avoidance of double packetization of data using native mode. Also, a router network provides the ability to consolidate many support systems under one network. Network management can be provided under SNMP utilizing IBM NetView feeds to the host.

Remote SNA switching with host pass-through. This replaces the primary and secondary polling nodes with primary and secondary SNA nodes in the router, where the secondary device-connected routers emulate SNA type 5 nodes and the primary device-connected routers emulate SNA type 2/2.1 nodes. This provides dynamic path routing rather than the SNA-specified routing, and eliminates the need to establish SNA cross-domain host sessions. Remote SNA switching forms a virtual SNA environment, but does not provide response time advantages over remote polling. Figure 8.26 illustrates remote SNA switching.

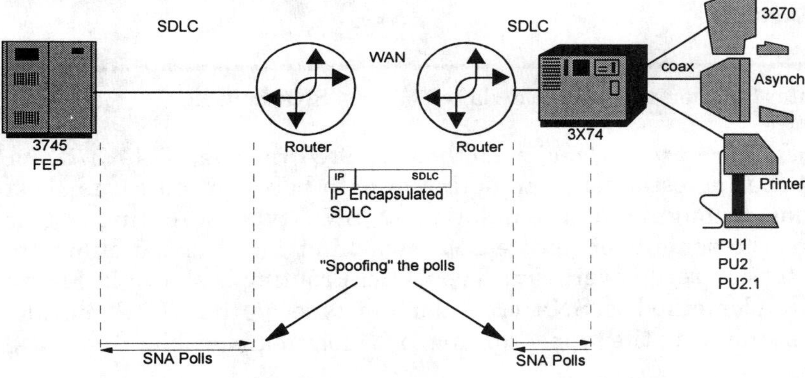

Figure 8.25 Spoofing Example

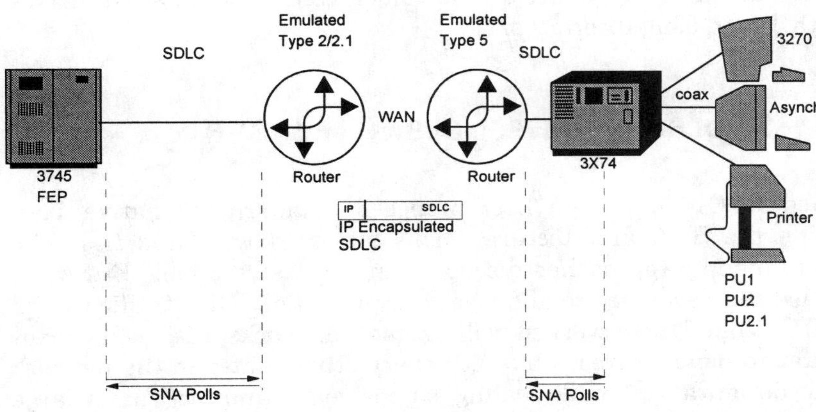

Figure 8.26 Remote SNA Switching

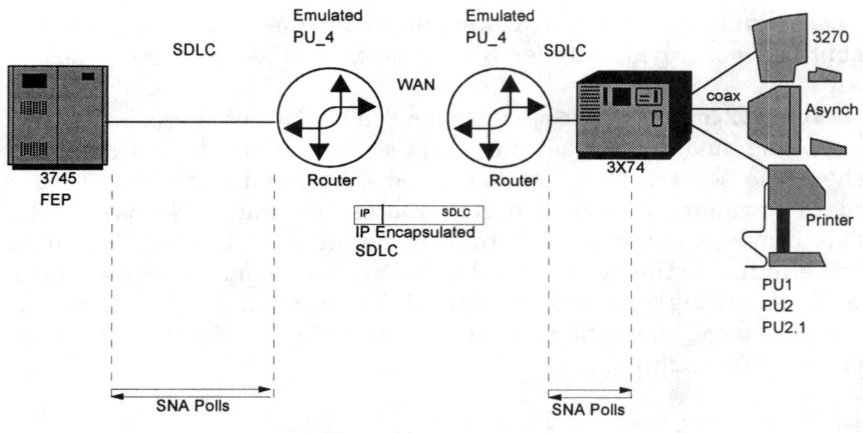

Figure 8.27 Router Solution with PU4 Emulation (Type 4 SNA Routing)

SNA Routing. There are two major methods of SNA routing. SNA 37XX or APPN Type 4 routing establishes an optimum path between routers for host communications through router emulation of SNA type 4 routing. This method retains the benefits of remote SNA switching, but does not eliminate cross-domain session setup overhead. Type 4 SNA routing is shown in Figure 8.27. The second method is SNA cross-domain type 5/4 host/FEP routing. This method is similar to the type 4 routing, but more manageable.

Both methods discussed are extremely vulnerable to changes in any of the SNA domains using SNA routing. The SDLC-to-LLC2 approach is widely preferred to serial tunneling, especially for older IBM 3725s that cannot be upgraded with Token Ring interfaces.

8.5.7 RFC 1434, DLSw (RFC 1795), DLSw+, and RSRB

IBM published RFC1434 as the first proposed standard for native SNA routing outside the SNA architecture. This standard was bred from the synchronous tunneling approaches discussed in the last section. DLSw, or RFC 1795, was then developed to allow basic transport of SDLC traffic routed within TCP/IP. While DLSw worked well in small networks, the requirement for every router to have a direct link with every other router in the network (fully meshed configuration) made scaling expensive and impractical for large networks. DLSw also had excessive explorer traffic overhead. The formal standard for DLSw, RFC 1795, later added some flow control and prioritization features, but the scalability holes present in these two standards were not fixed until Cisco's RSRB and later DLSw+.

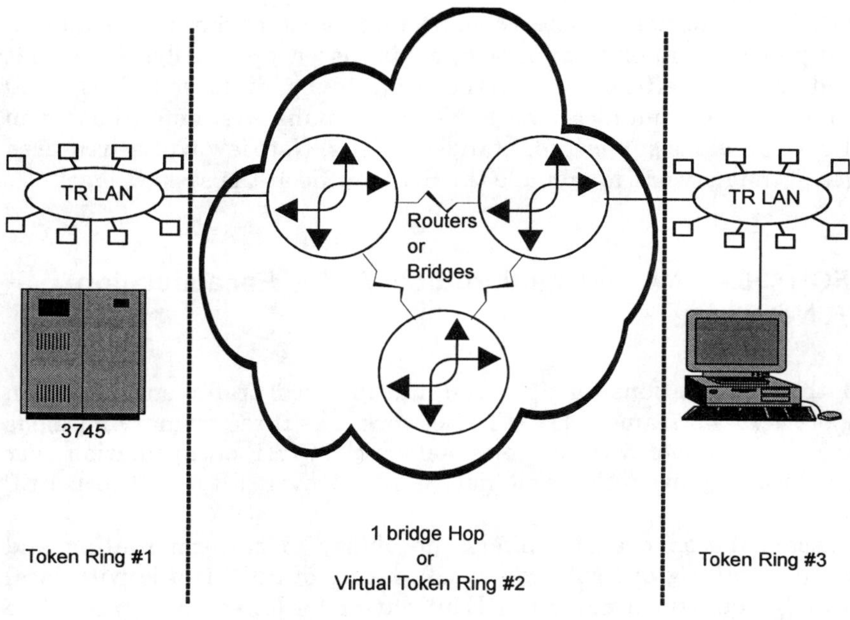

Figure 8.28 DLSW+ SNA Routing

DLSw+ was designed based on DLSw and RSRB. DLSw+ fixes the scalability problems of DLSw by counting the entire TCP/IP network as a single "hop", regardless of how many devices the network uses. Figure 8.28 illustrates the concept of DLSw+. DLSw+ provides the local LLC2 acknowledgments – polls are filtered and terminated locally (spoofing as described before) to assure there are no session time-outs and to decrease the overhead across the WAN. SNA and NETBIOS traffic are encapsulated and routed transparently using TCP/IP across a multiprotocol-routed WAN. Traffic is automatically rerouted around failed links without loss to sessions. Performance is improved through load sharing across multiple routes (within the TCP/IP network), with load balancing, and through the ability to select optimal routes in the router. Routers implementing DLSw+ can also remember specific broadcast routes in cache memory, further improving performance. DLSw+ requires routers at both ends of the WAN to implement the standard. DLSw+ networks are extremely scalable through the use of subnetworks with border peer nodes. These nodes act similar to subnet routers – minimizing the number or WAN connections and explorer packet activity.

Along with TCP/IP encapsulation, DLSw+ offers an IP datagram service called Fast Sequence Transport (FST/IP). FST/IP is used only when the transmission media is extremely reliable, because there is no TCP to assure end-to-end delivery of packets. A data link layer direct encapsulation capability is also included in DLSw, for transport of SNA traffic over a point-to-point HDLC, Frame Relay, or LAN connection. Each of these implementations is really just a tunneling approach, as discussed previously. Note that this method is more efficient than the soon to be discussed RFC 1490 approach for FEP communications. Network managers note that even though DLSw+ provides support for standard MIBs, NetView will be required at the edges of the network to manage the SNA traffic at the session level.

8.5.8 RFC 1490 – SNA and Multiprotocol Traffic Encapsulation across FR Networks

RFC 1490, the specifications for SNA and multiprotocol traffic encapsulation and transport across a frame relay (FR) network, has three primary methods of sending SNA data over a frame relay network: TCP/IP encapsulation over FR, remote bridging over FR, and native LLC2 over FR for direct FEP connection.

TCP/IP encapsulation over FR offers the ability to perform routing and nondisruptive rerouting of SNA traffic, IP routing of SNA traffic with local poll acknowledgment (spoofing), and DE bit setting for low-priority traffic like NetBIOS. An example of TCP/IP encapsulation using RFC 1490 is shown in Figure 8.29. The importance of this method is to provide any-to-any connectivity and to enable the implementation of RFC 1490 without any NCP or 3174 microcode changes.

The second method of routing SNA data over a frame relay network is the use of native LLC2 over FR for direct FEP connection. Figure 8.30 illustrates an FEP 3745 serial port to V.35 FR access port direct mapping with LLC2 encapsulated within FR frames. This capability was first provided on the NCP7.1 release classified as "FR for 3745 FEP native LLC2 over FR (FRF.3)". This capability is supported only on newer FEPs with high-speed port capability, but not supported on older 37XX series (i.e., 3720 and 3725 communications controllers). 3270 LU6.2 traffic is supported as shown in the figure. Many SNA devices now can interface as DTE directly into a FR network. These devices include the 3745, 3746, 3172, 3174, AS/400, 6611 and 2210 bridge/routers, and the IBM RouteXpander PC card. There is also a method of using a LAN-attached router implementing RFC 1490 in front of the 3745 FEP, thus achieving local acknowledgment spoofing and session integrity during WAN reroutes. Designer note: the RFC 1490 method of encapsulation is somewhat inefficient compared to the other methods discussed due to excessive overhead of encapsulations. Avoid the use of low CIR rates that can cause loss of DE data or long delays – all of which can cause SNA session time-outs. Also note that sessions will be lost when rerouted using RFC 1490.

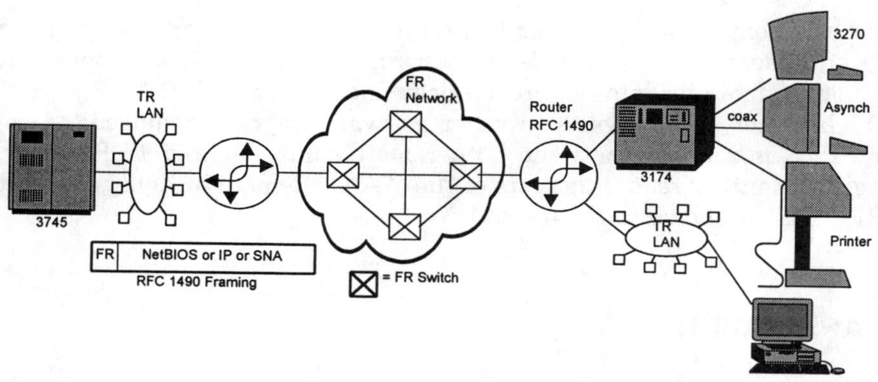

Figure 8.29 RFC 1490 – TCP/IP Encapsulation over FR

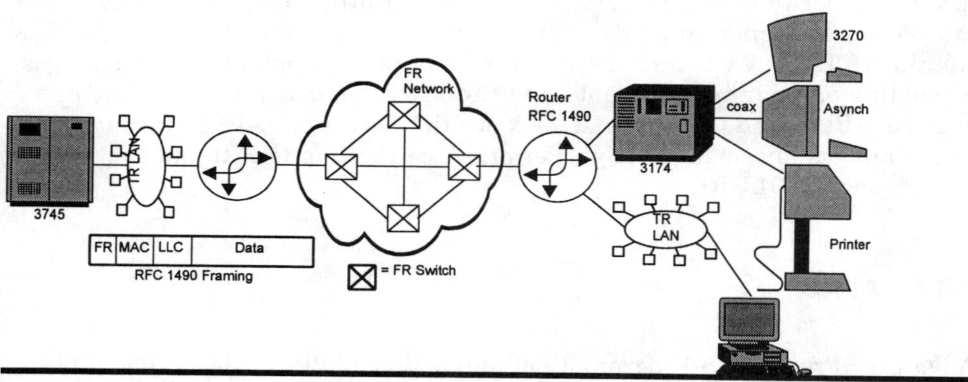

Figure 8.30 RFC 1490 – Native LLC2 over FR

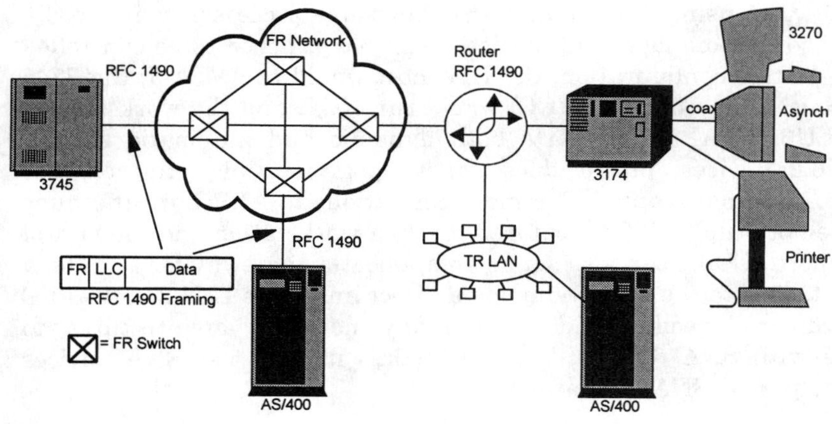

Figure 8.31 RFC 1490 - Remote Bridging over FR

When using remote bridging over FR, routers located at every site perform a triple encapsulation of the SNA data within LLC, MAC, and then FR frames. The remote bridging approach does not require a FEP NCP load of 7.0 or higher, nor is a remote controller software upgrade required. Also, only one PVC is required between both remote controller and FEP router, reducing the monthly recurring costs of the WAN. Remote bridging over FR using RFC 1490 is shown in Figure 8.31.

8.6 APPC/APPN

Advanced Program-to-Program Communication (APPC), also called LU6.2, and Advanced Peer-to-Peer Networking (APPN) are paving the way for the new SNA peer-to-peer communications and migrating SNA into multiprotocol internetworked environments. The minimum cost of entry into APPN is running VTAM V4.1 and NCP V6.2, along with many other changes, depending on your requirements and the age of your equipment. Let's now explore APPC and APPN, and look at the future of APPN through two important enhancements - High Performance Routing (HPR) and Dependent LU Requester (DLUR).

8.6.1 APPC

Advanced Program-to-Program Communication (APPC), also called LU6.2, provides for peer-to-peer intelligent sessions between peripheral PU2.1 nodes. This constitutes an LU6.2 device-to-LU6.2 device session *without involving the host* using VTAM and the front-end processor using NCP. However, usage and management statistics can be gathered to be controlled by the host. In this configuration, the IBM host would run VTAM, the 3745 FEP Communications Controller (CC) would run NCP, and the workstations would run LU6.2. APPC supports both dynamic and automatic routing between LU6.2 devices, but it does not support multiple protocols nor mainframe to terminal traffic. The main limitations to APPC are the huge amount of memory (up to 500K) required to run a workstation and the lack of software support. LU6.2 can also act as an application gateway for a PC on a TCP/IP LAN to talk to the mainframe via a direct link. The LU6.2 and APPC are not hardware specific, and allow many non-IBM architectures to communicate with SNA devices. Also, IBM has its own non-SNA devices which need help to be SNA compatible.

8.6.2 APPN

Advanced Peer-to-Peer Networking (APPN) is an IBM protocol concept or architecture which allows routing LAN traffic independent of a front-end processor or a mainframe between workstations or peer devices called End Nodes (ENs). ENs are typically LU workstations running APPN software.

The routing devices between ENs, such as FRADs and routers, are called Network Nodes (NNs). Figure 8.32 demonstrates this concept, where user EN network devices running Advanced Peer-to-Peer Communications (APPC) are remote-accessing the IBM 3745 communications controllers. These front end processors are running NCP, which in turn is managed through VTAM in the IBM 390 host computer. NNs communicate via sessions called Control-Point-to-Control-Point (CP-CP).

APPN moves users away from FEPs and mainframes and toward routers — the true platform for devices using APPN routing. APPN is the dynamic-routing and control architecture part of both SNA and Systems Application Architecture (SAA). It can provide a migration path from SNA to SAA. The APPN protocol provides a peer-to-peer architecture designed for distributed processing and LANs, adding much-needed independent operational flexibility. APPN allows network devices to share data equally independent of the host, but over fixed communications paths. This is peer-oriented communications and biased toward program-to-program cooperative processing applications. The old method of routing SNA traffic was through IP packet encapsulation. With APPN, users can actually translate SNA traffic and dynamically route it in native SNA mode (without the need for encapsulation).

Unfortunately, the entire network-routed topology is stored at each node, and error check and recovery with retransmission of lost packets is performed at each node in the network. The routing protocol is called Intermediate Session Routing Protocol (ISRP). In large networks ISRP can generate much overhead in status updates, similar to link state routing protocols like OSPF. This requires networks to be separated into domains. APPN does take the first step in SNA routing prioritization, offering a class of service for prioritizing some forms of branch office traffic over others.

APPN support is provided in IBM 3174 cluster controllers, OS/2 Extended Edition, VTAM, and NCP software. APPN can support SDLC, X.25, Token Ring LAN, IBM 3270 and synchronous connections, and frame relay. APPN can run on RS6000 workstations, servers, and IBM LU2 devices (like 3270 terminals).

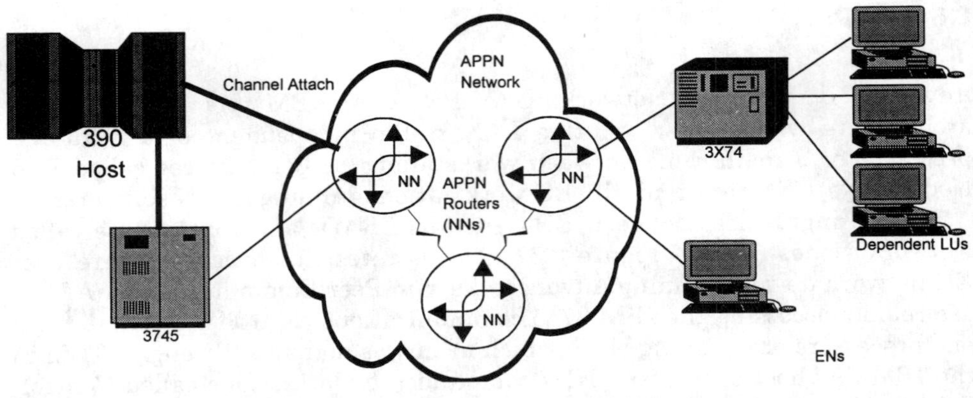

Figure 8.32 IBM APPN ENs and NNs

8.6.3 High Performance Routing (HPR) and Dependent LU Requester (DLUR)

Two important enhancements for APPN are High Performance Routing (HPR) and Dependent LU Requester (DLUR).

IBM's HPR, also called APPN+, picks up where APPN left off, and competes with the TCP/IP routing methods mentioned previously. HPR is defined within RFC 1490. HPR provides a souped-up version of APPN. Error detection and correction is done only in LU6.2 NNs, and connectionless data link layer (layer 2) routing is performed by the Rapid Transport Protocol (RTP) and Automatic Network Routing (ANR). RTP acts as an end-to-end node-routing protocol that offers the improvement of allowing nondisruptive routing around a failure between NNs. Thus, sessions will not be lost when a link fails and reroutes between two NNs. In the case of HPR over FR, HPR can sense an outage and dynamically reroute over a different path while maintaining end-to-end session integrity. APPN+ also offers adaptive rate-based flow control as defined in the ATM standards in Chapter 12 and 13.

Software called Dependent LU Server (DLUS) and Dependent LU Requester (DLUR) can be configured in VTAM V4R2 and the (NN) router, respectively, to allow a migration pathway for older dependent LUs through an APPN network. The DLUS in effect acts as the intelligent device to tell the DLUR how to route through the network.

Some vendors such as Cisco Systems have also come out with a method of direct attachment of VTAM for mainframe host computers to an NN.

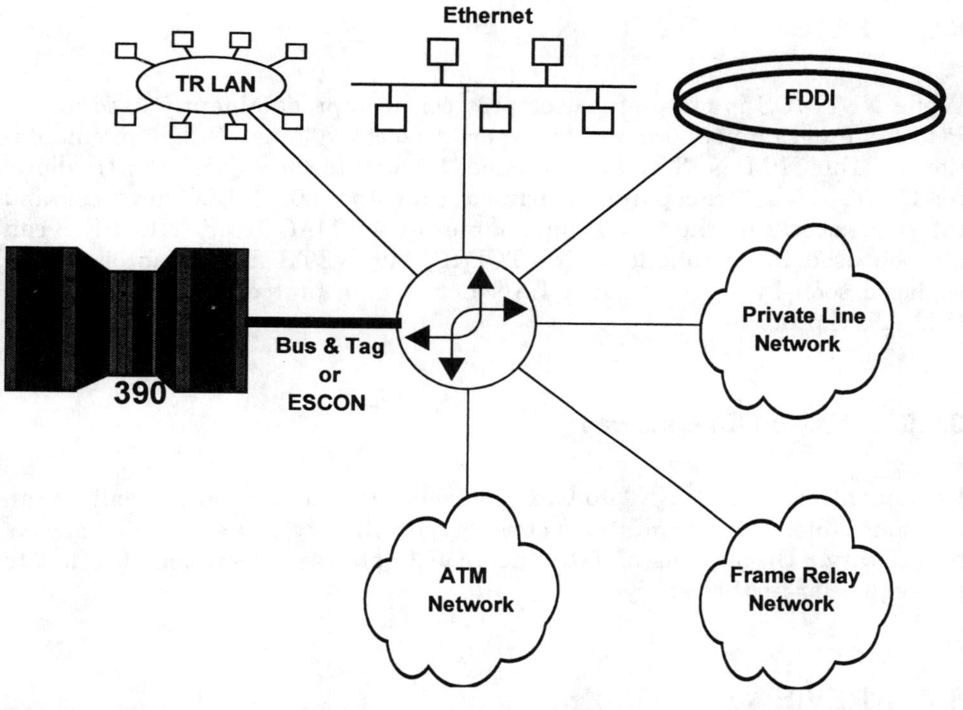

Figure 8.33 Channel Extension – Cisco's CIP

8.6.4 Channel Extension – Cisco's Channel Interface Processor (CIP)

How about direct mainframe connectivity to a router? Cisco has available a method of providing a VTAM-to-TCP/IP gateway that uses the direct interface from the host to the router via the older bus-and-tag interface or the newer 17 Mbps ESCON channel interface. Since TCP/IP and VTAM run in the mainframe, no 3172 and no NCP are required. The router thus connects a host to a private line, LAN (Token Ring, Ethernet, FDDI), frame relay, or ATM network, as shown in Figure 8.33.

Direct mainframe connectivity to a router poses a significant threat to the future of the IBM 3745 FEP and NCP. The FEP was the last firewall between the network and the glass house. This feature has brought peer-to-peer dynamic distributed computing to the doorstep of the mainframe.

8.6.5 NETBIOS/NETBEUI

While NETBIOS is more of a user protocol, it is predominantly used as the PC LAN program network and transport protocol in Token Ring implementations. The IBM NETBIOS Extended User Interface (NETBEUI) allows NETBIOS to be transparently passed over the 802.2 LLC protocol and interface, accessing the token ring adapter at the MAC layer. NETBIOS can also be used in conjunction with TCP/IP, but NETBEUI will probably be replaced soon by more efficient LAN networking protocols, or even by the IBM APPC protocol.

8.6.6 SNA-to-OSI Gateway

Implementing a full SNA-to-OSI gateway is also an option, albeit an expensive one. Implementations of this type will vary, but are almost always proprietary. Discussions of TCP and LU6.2 gateway conversions are left to the reader for further study.

8.7 REVIEW

This chapter completes a discussion on the physical through transport layer protocols spanning both telecommunications and data communications. This chapter focused on bridge, router, and higher-level protocols. Bridge and router protocols are the brains of computer protocol routing and bridging. Each router protocol was covered in detail, showing its own advantages and disadvantages. The predominant network and transport protocols such as TCP/IP and SNA were explained. SNA legacy and peer-to-peer protocol functionality were discussed, along with examples for all major forms of SNA internetworking, including DLSw+, APPC, and APPN.

Chapter

9

X.25 Packet Switching

Now that circuit switching has been covered, we will turn attention to the packet technology forming the basis of many advanced frame and cell technologies. Packet-switched networks have been in existence for over 25 years. X.25 packet switching provides the network environment needed to handle terminal-to-host "bursty" data traffic. X.25 packet switching also serves many other user communities, especially in Europe, where it constitutes the majority of public and private data transport services. The CCITT X.25 packet-switching standard, along with a host of other "X dot" standards, was developed to provide a reliable system of data transport for computer communications over analog-grade transport media. Transport media have drastically improved since X.25 was first developed, and now digital and fiber is replacing much of the older analog communications facilities. Speeds have increased beyond 56/64 kbps, which is the maximum transmit rate of many packet switches. Much of the overhead once associated with ensuring reliable data transfer over these poor transmission media is not needed now. As a result, packet switching has taken a backseat to newer technologies which utilize less overhead and rely on clean transmission facilities, such as frame relay. Yet we must understand the principles of packet switching, since packet-switching concepts form the basis of the newer technologies. Many international networks still use and will continue to use packet switching long after the world becomes fully digital and fiber predominates. And X.25 switching still allows many users to ease the migration of legacy traffic into newer frame and cell-switching technologies.

9.1 A BRIEF HISTORY OF PACKET SWITCHING

To understand the packet switching of today, we must go back to the original premise on which packet-switching technology was built. X.25 packet switching was originally designed as a secure method for the transport of *voice* traffic. X.25 packet switching initially provided the network environment needed to handle bursty, terminal-to-host data traffic over noisy analog telephone network facilities. Over the last 25 years, packet switching technology has evolved into a data-transport platform for statistical multiplexing of low-speed user traffic across large distances and forms the basis of many advanced data communications today. X.25 packet switching built elaborate transmission schemes into its protocol operation to accommodate for poor voice-grade transmission facilities. With the advent of fiber optics, this superfluous overhead is no longer needed and is a hindrance rather than an aid. Today, packet switching has been widely implemented. This is especially true in Europe, where it constitutes the majority of public and private data services.

9.1.1 Packet Switch Beginnings

Packet switching was first invented by Paul Baran and his research team for the RAND Corporation in the early 1960s and published in 1964 as a secure method of transmitting military *voice* communications. This was actually a project to enable the United States military communications system to survive after a nuclear attack. By segmenting an entire message into many pieces of data and wrapping routing and protocol information around these pieces of data, "packets" were created. The routing and control information was to ensure the correct and accurate delivery and reassembly of the original message at the end-user destination. These packets had a fixed maximum size assigned, typically 128 or 256 bytes long. Through the use of multiple independent packets, the entire message could be transmitted over multiple paths and diverse facilities – and reassembled in its original order at the destination. In this manner of transmission, voice wiretapping was virtually impossible because only a portion of the entire transmission could be tapped, and even that portion would be incomplete and garbled.

The next step in packet switch history was taken when the Advanced Research Projects Agency (ARPA) of the United States Department of Defense (ARPA)(DoD) implemented packet switching to handle computer communications requirements, thus forming the basis for the ARPANET. This was also the first time that layered protocols were used, as well as a meshed backbone topology. Packet switching was chosen as the method to implement WAN computer communications, which mainly consisted of connecting large computing centers. Soon after ARPANET, many commercial companies also developed packet-based networks. Today, most of Europe's nonfiber transmission networks are tied together with reliable private and public packet-switched networks.

9.1.2 Early Reasons for Packet Switching

Several factors created the need for packet switching: the need to create standard interfaces between computing devices, the more efficient use of expensive transmission bandwidth, the interconnection of a large number of computing devices, and the ability to extend computer communication over noisy transmission facilities.

The early days of computing saw the development of a new interface and data-communication protocol with each computer. Large computer manufacturers, like IBM and DEC, developed protocols that were standardized across their products (generally speaking). One of the goals of the Open System Interconnection (OSI) standardization effort was to enable standard computer communication interfaces and protocols in a multiple vendor environment.

Packets were designed with Cyclic Redundancy Check (CRC) fields that detected bit errors. If a packet was received in error, then a protocol was defined so that it could be resent until it was successfully received. The advent of low bit-error-rate digital and fiber-optic transmission media means that this function is now cost-effectively done in the end system, since errors rarely occur.

Early packet-switching systems were designed for terminal-to-host communications. The typical transaction involved the users typing a few lines, or even just a few characters, and then sending a transaction to the host. The host would then return a few lines, or possibly an entire screen's worth of data. This terminal-host application was very bursty; that is, the peak transmit rate of each terminal was much greater than its average rate. Packet switching allows many such bursty users to be statistically multiplexed onto expensive transmission facilities.

As the number of computers, applications, and people using computers increased, the need for interconnection increased, creating the accelerating need for bandwidth discussed in Chapter 2. Similar to the growth in telephony, it quickly became absurd to have a dedicated circuit to connect every pair of computers that needed to communicate. Packet switching and routing protocols were developed to connect terminals to hosts, and hosts to hosts.

9.1.3 Principles of Packet Switching

Packet switching is a special case of the general address multiplexing and switching method described in Chapter 5. Packet switching, more specifically X.25 packet switching, provides a service in which blocks of user data are conveyed over a network. These blocks of user data are called the *payload information*. Packet switching adds overhead to the user data blocks, resulting in a block of data called a *packet*. All of the protocols studied in this book have this characteristic including X.25, IP, frame relay, SMDS, Ethernet, FDDI, Token Ring, and ATM.

The functions that use the packet overhead are either link layer, packet layer, or transport layer from the OSIRM summarized in Chapter 4. Older protocols, such as X.25 and IP, perform both the link layer and packet layer function. Newer protocols, such as frame relay, SMDS, and ATM, perform only a subset of link layer functions. Further, SMDS uses addressing functions that have a networkwide meaning.

Link layer functions always have a means to indicate the boundaries of the packet, perform error detection, provide for multiplexing of multiple logical connections, and provide some basic network management capability. Optional link layer functions are: flow control, retransmission, command/response protocol support, and link-level establishment.

Network layer functions always have a means to identify a uniquely addressed network station. Optional network layer functions include: retransmission, flow control, prioritized data flows, automatic routing, and network layer connection establishment.

Packet switching performs the same function as the statistical multiplexer described in Chapter 5, where the packet switch allows multiple logical users to share a single physical network access circuit by providing buffers which are used during times of overflow. Packet switches can control the quality provided to an individual user by allocating bandwidth, allocating buffer space, controlling the traffic offered by users, or by controlling flow.

Packet switching also extends the concept of statistical multiplexing to an entire network. In order to appreciate the power of packet switching, compare the full mesh network of dedicated circuits in network Figure 9.1a versus that of the packet switched network in Figure 9.1b. The dedicated network has three lines connected to every host, while the packet network has only one line connecting the host to the packet switch. A virtual circuit connects every user through the packet-switched network, as shown by dashed lines.

The dedicated circuit network (a) has higher overall throughput, but will not scale well. The packet-switched network (b) requires additional complexity in the packet switches and has lower throughput, but reduces circuit transmission costs by over 40 percent in this simple example with the nodes placed on the corners of a square. Sharing of network resources allows savings over the cost of many dedicated, low-speed communications channels, each of which is often underutilized the majority of the time. The concept of a virtual circuit carries through into both frame relay and ATM technology.

Packet switching employs queueing to control loss and resolve contention at the expense of added, variable delay. The packet may take longer to get there with packet switching, but the chances of loss are much lower, assuming a reasonable buffer size, during periods of network congestion. There are two types of flow and congestion control used to manage packet data protocols: implicit and explicit congestion notification.

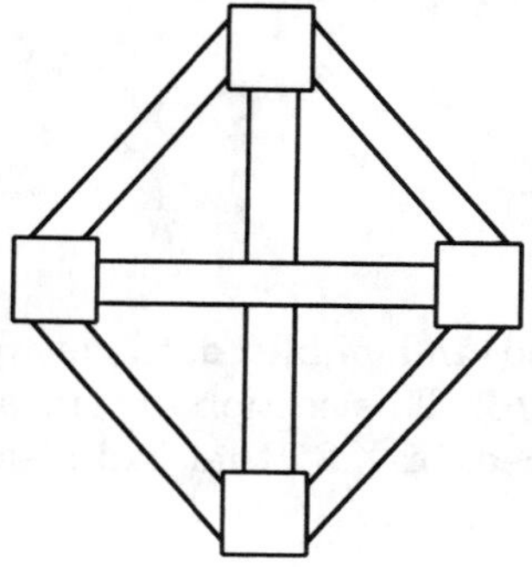

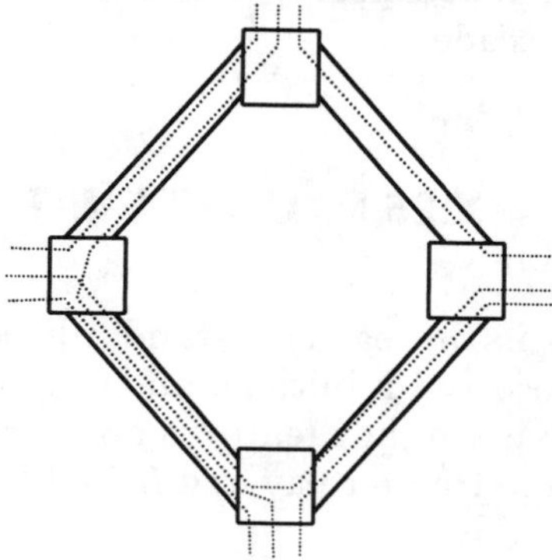

Figure 9.1 The Power of Packet Switching

Implicit congestion notification usually involves a layer 4 transport protocol, such as the Internet Transmission Control Protocol (TCP), in either the network device or the user premises equipment. These protocols can adaptively alter the rate of packets sent into the network by estimating loss and delay.

Explicit congestion notification occurs when the protocol notifies the sender and/or receiver of congestion in the network. If the sender or receiver reacts to the explicit indication of congestion quickly enough, then loss can be avoided entirely.

9.1.4 X.25 Packet Switching Today

X.25 packet switching continues to play an important role in the 1990s environment of distributed processing. X.25 packet switches provide low-speed (56 kbps and lower), efficient networking for bursty data transport applications. Many packet switches today can provide networking speeds up to T1 and E1, with packet sizes up to 4096 bytes. Packet-switched networks use the same architecture as the switched networks defined in this text.

X.25 packet switching serves many user communities, especially in Europe, where it constitutes the majority of public and private data services. Over 10 percent of U.S. public data networking is via packet-switched networks, whereas in Europe it is just the opposite — over 60 percent of public and private data networking is done through packet-switched networks. This is due to the high cost of leased and private lines and the poor quality of transmission facilities in many European countries. The shift is happening, albeit slowly. In many European and Pacific Rim countries, as digital and fiber transmission facilities have become more prevalent, technologies like ISDN and SMDS have begun to proliferate. Packet switching remains a very popular technology, and will likely continue to be popular through the end of the decade.

9.2 X.25 PACKET SWITCHING DEFINED

X.25 is the earliest standardized packet-switched and public data network protocol, with initial standards first defined in 1976. This section provides an overview of key features and terminology developed for X.25 that can also be seen in frame relay and ATM technologies today.

9.2.1 Origins of X.25

In the beginning, there were proprietary protocols; then the CCITT standardized upon the first international physical, link, and packet layer protocol – X.25. The CCITT X.25 packet-switching standard, along with a number of other "X dot" standards, was developed to provide a reliable system of data transport for computer communications over the noisy, unreliable analog-grade transmission medium.

Speeds have increased beyond 56 kbps, the maximum transmit rate of early packet switches. Many packet switches today can provide networking speeds up to and including DS1 and E1, with packet sizes up to 4096 bytes.

9.2.2 Standards Structure of X.25

The CCITT set of "X dot" standards for the physical, link, and packet layer protocols shown in Figure 9.2 are known collectively as X.25. The suite of physical, link, and network layer protocols standardized by X.25 has been adopted as part of the OSIRM. These standards define the protocol, services, facilities, packet-switching options, and user interfaces for public packet-switched networks.

The physical layer is defined by the X.21 and X.21bis standards. X.21 specifies an interface between DTE and DCE. X.21 also specifies a simple circuit-switching protocol that operates at the physical layer, which is widely implemented in the Nordic countries.

The data link layer standard is based upon the High-level Data Link Control (HDLC) ISO standard. X.25 modified this and initially called it a Link Access Procedure (LAP), subsequently revising it again to align with changes in HDLC resulting in the Link Access Procedure-Balanced (LAP-B).

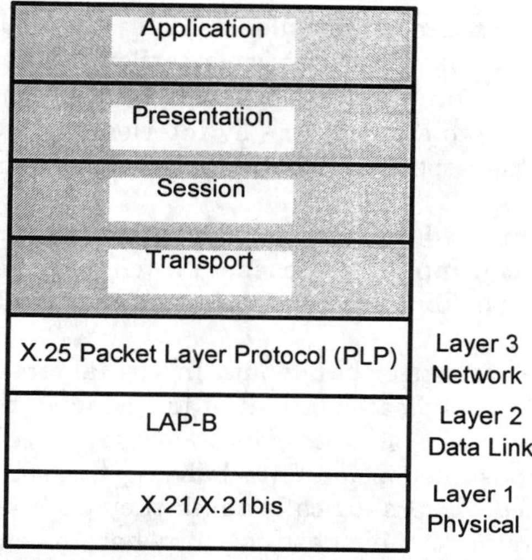

Figure 9.2 X.25 Packet Switching Compared to the OSIRM

The packet layer standard is called the X.25 Packet Layer Protocol (PLP). The packet layer defines Permanent Virtual Circuit (PVC) and virtual call, or Switched Virtual Circuit (SVC) message formats and protocols. The concept of PVCs and SVCs from X.25 is also used in frame relay and ATM.

User connectivity to the packet-switched network takes on many forms. The suite of "X dot" standards is: X.121, X.21, X.25, X.28, X.29, X.3, and X.32. X.121 defines the network layer numbering plan for X.25.

CCITT Recommendations X.3, X.28, and X.29 define the method for asynchronous DTEs to interface with X.25 networks via a Packet Assembler/Dissembler (PAD) function. A PAD takes strings of asynchronous characters from the DTE, delimited by a carriage return, and assembles these into a synchronous X.25 packet. The PAD delivers a stream of asynchronous characters to the DTE from a received X.25 packet. Recommendation X.3 defines PAD parameters, such as terminal type, line length, break key actions, and speed. Recommendation X.28 defines the terminal-to-PAD interface, while X.29 defines the computer-to-PAD interface. Recommendation X.21 defines a dedicated physical interface, and X.32 defines a synchronous dial-up capability. Each of these standard network and user interfaces will be shown later in this Chapter.

9.2.3 What Does X.25 Packet Switching Provide?

X.25 packet switching performs the same function as a statistical multiplexer, where the packet switch allows multiple logical users to share a single physical network access circuit, but also includes the additional intelligence of providing buffers for use during times of overflow, queuing, and addressing of user ports. X.25 packet switching provides logical user access and logical channel multiplexing onto a single line by interleaving low-speed user channels into a single high-speed data channel which then interfaces to the network.

Figure 9.3 is a simplified version of this concept, showing seven 9600 bps X.3/X.28 circuits as user inputs to a packet switch and one direct X.25 access circuit. The single 56 kbps circuit is the output trunk to the transport network.

Packet switches allocate user bandwidth in virtual circuits. This gives the user the perception of a dedicated circuit of full bandwidth when in actuality the network resources are shared over a virtual circuit. Virtual circuit bandwidth is only consumed when data is being transmitted, otherwise the bandwidth is not used. Users logically think they each have a full 9600 bps dedicated virtual circuit to their destination, when in reality they share the same network resources. Together, the total user bandwidth, if each user transmitted simultaneously, would be 67.2 kbps, or almost twice the network transport bandwidth available. Packet-switch networks are designed based upon the statistical chance that not all users will want to transmit at the same time, nor for the same duration. Pauses in the transmission of data among users make this possible. In a circuit-switched network, these pauses represent idle channel time and wasted bandwidth capacity. Thus, even though 56 kbps would be available in a circuit-switched network, the entire bandwidth may rarely be used.

Oversubscribing users, like the overbooking of flights by airlines, by sharing of network resources in this manner, allows saving the cost of many low-speed communications channels, each of which could be vastly underutilized most of the time. When used in packet switching, the switch will queue the waiting packets until bandwidth becomes free. The packet switch includes buffers for those times when the inputs exceed the outputs and this queuing takes place. Buffering can be done and some time delay by buffering can be tolerated, because data packet switching is non-time-sensitive.

9.2.4 Packet-Switch DTE and DCE Concepts

Packet switching's first practical commercial application was designed for host computers to communicate through multiple nodes over a packet-switched network. Figure 9.4 shows this concept of and DCEDTE and DCE devices connected across a packet-switched network. The X.25 protocol defines the protocols and procedures that manage the transfer of data between the DTE, typically a user terminal, and the DCE, typically the network node. The end-user DTE accesses the X.25 network through a communications controller, FEP, or host. A DCE packet assembler/dissembler (PAD) is often used within the network for DTE access. We will discuss each of these in detail.

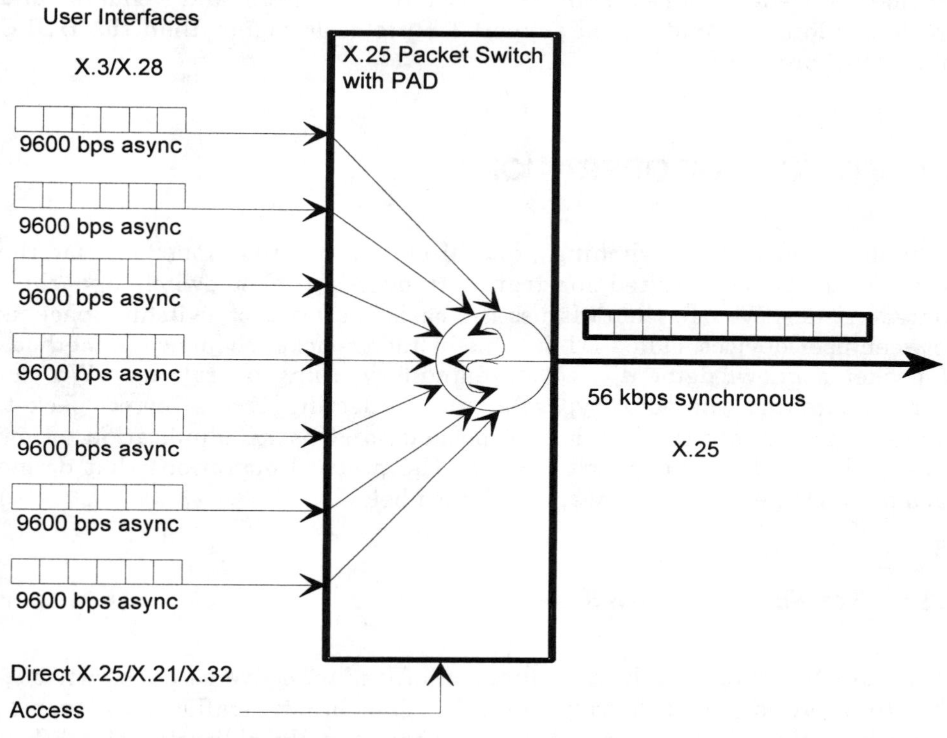

Figure 9.3 X.25 Packet Switch

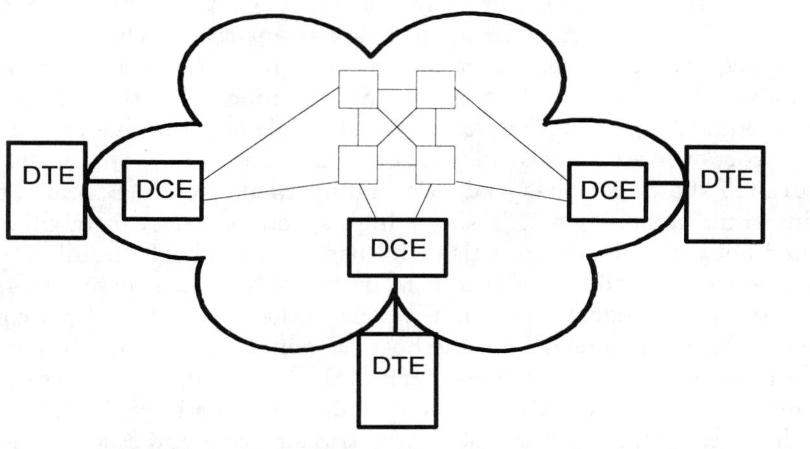

Figure 9.4 DTE and DCE Concepts

The CCITT X.25 standard defines services, facilities, and packet-switching options, as well as user interface standards for packet-switched networks. It provides a well-developed standard interface for users and vendors, and provides additional end-to-end support for protocols higher than the HDLC and LAP-B protocols.

9.3 THEORY OF OPERATION

To understand packet-switching protocol details, we first must look at the types of traffic best suited for transport over a packet switch and their characteristics. We can then discuss the basic operation of switching packets between user devices, called DTE. This includes packet sequencing, methods of packet acknowledgment, and store-and-forwarding operations. We can then understand the four types of traffic-affecting errors: erred packet, improper packet sequencing, loss of packets, and packet duplication. How does packet switching deal with each? The protocol operations that define each method of error recovery are explained below.

9.3.1 Traffic Characteristics

Most data transmissions have a duration of less than five seconds, attributable to what is called "bursty traffic". This bursty traffic often travels predominantly in one direction, rather than equally bidirectional. When packet-switched networks were first built, they provided an ideal transport for the typical terminal user who had many pauses between transmissions, thus causing the data to be bursty in nature. Packet-switched networks also best accommodate traffic that is not delay-sensitive. Therefore, the two primary requirements that best suit packet networks are *burstiness* and *delay-insensitive* traffic. Because of the dynamic allocation of bandwidth techniques used by packet switches, bursty, delay-insensitive traffic is ideal for transport over a packet-switched network.

Figure 9.5 shows 30 low-speed terminal users at sites A, B, and C communicating simultaneously with a single high-speed user host through a packet-switched network. The terminals could use low-speed X.3 circuits to request information downloads from the host, or possibly X.32 synchronous dial-up access through a modem. Terminal traffic *to* the host is very light compared to the data traffic received *from* the host. For instance, a small inquiry to the host can generate a long response back to the terminal. Also, there is a high probability that not all of the terminals will be requesting information at the same time. In fact, they will probably be transmitting and receiving less than 3 percent of the time. The single 56 kbps multiplexed X.25 line from the host into the packet-switched network shows the efficiencies of asymmetrical traffic patterns where the host will transmit to terminals much more traffic than it receives.

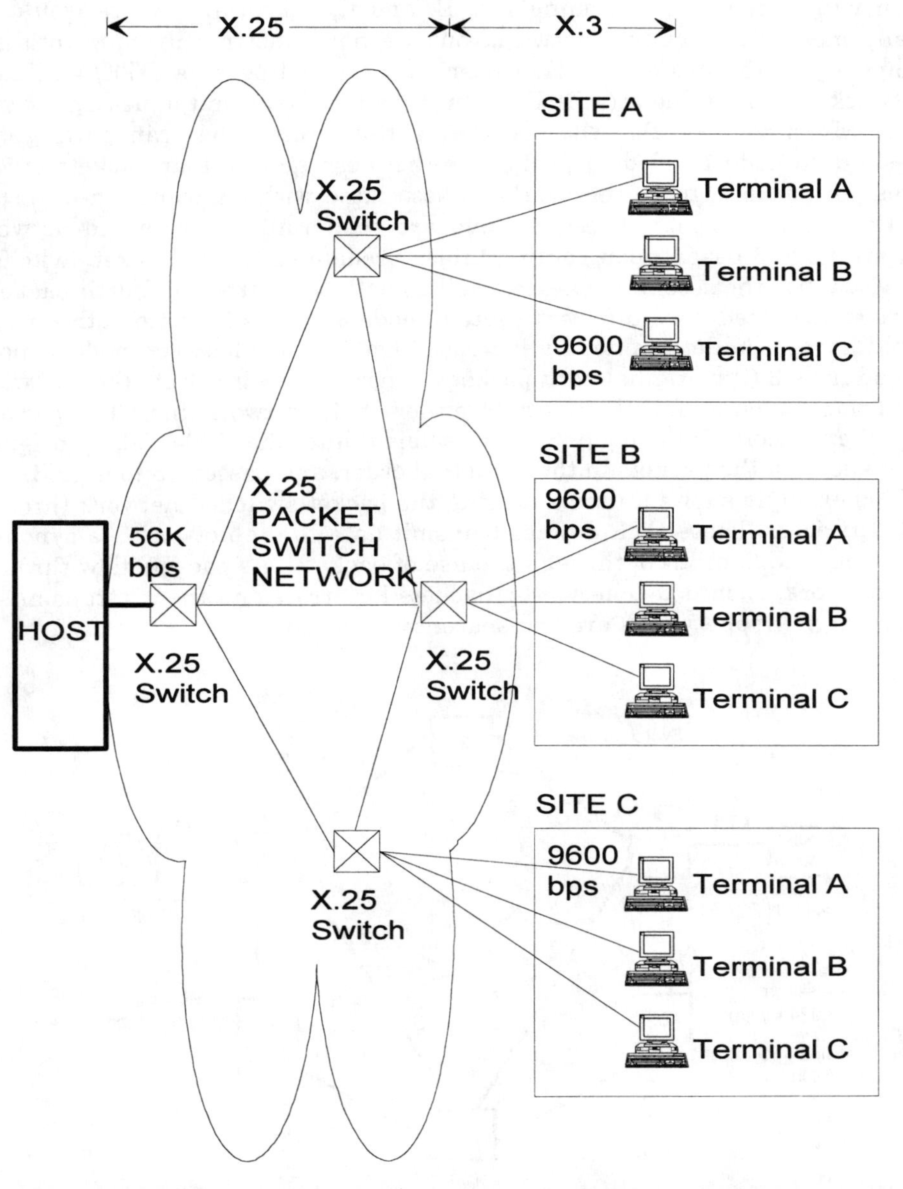

Figure 9.5 Terminal Communications over a Packet-Switched Network

9.3.2 Basic Operation

Figure 9.6 shows a sample packet-switched network with six nodes (1–6), each with three users (terminals A, B, and C). Typically, there would be many more users on this network, but we have shown only nine total for simplicity of the example. Each user device is acting as a DTE, and each network node is acting as a DCE. User A wants to transmit a message of size 1024 Mbits to user B. User A begins this process by transmitting the message to node 1. Node 1 packetizes the message into four packets of 256 kbps per packet (ignore the overhead associated with transmission until the section on protocols). These packets are then routed across the network toward node 3 based upon routing tables predefined in the packet switches. Observe that the second packet, as well as both the third and fourth packets, were transmitted via a different route to node 3. This alternate path routing could have been determined by increased traffic loads between node 1, node 5, and node 3 (the original path packet #1 took), or a variety of other network conditions, such as failed circuits in either of those two paths. The packets are then received by node 3, reassembled into the 1024 Mbits original message with the packets in their original order, and passed on to user B.

This example shows a user accessing the packet-switched network through DTE devices. These DTE devices transmit data to the network via synchronous mode X.25 protocol through the use of packets. As packets flow through the network, each node checks the packets for errors and then retransmits if necessary. All operations are transparent to the user.

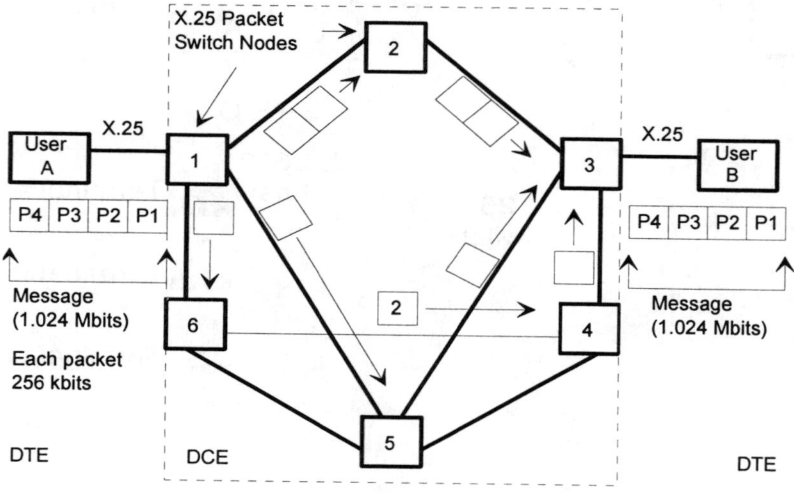

Figure 9.6 Sample Packet-Switched Network

An elaborate acknowledgment and retransmission scheme is provided in packet switching, primarily because of the large amount of errors which could be experienced when using voice grade lines. This scheme provides flow control and error detection and correction, and limits the traffic flow by buffering to prevent congestion. Since packet switching was built on the premise of using voice grade lines for transport, much overhead, error correction, and buffering were built into the X.25 protocol. Since the advent of fiber, many of these capabilities are no longer needed.

9.3.3 Acknowledgments

Under normal conditions, all packets are acknowledged by each receiving node as they pass through the network. The last example in Figure 9.7 demonstrates the acknowledgment function. Figure 9.7 shows the acknowledgments (ACK) which accompany each packet as it propagates through the network. Now let's look at this operation from a logical diagram approach.

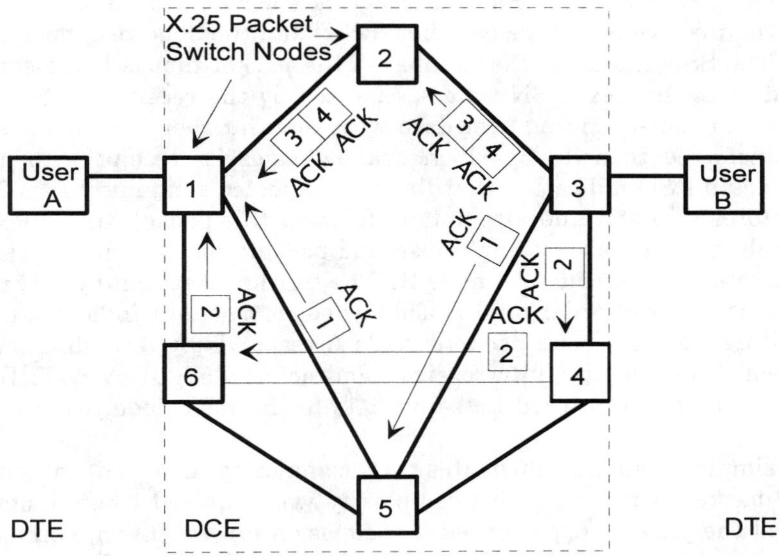

Figure 9.7 Packet Switch Acknowledgment Function

9.3.4 Packet Sequencing

Basically, packet switching utilizes queuing and store-and-forward protocols with packet-sequencing information contained within each packet. Sequencing errors can be caused by delay incurred by message division (different packet delays) over simultaneous long and short hops. Packet sequencing, traffic and congestion control will be detailed later in this section.

9.3.5 Example of X.25 Store-and-Forward Operation

Let us take our last example and expand upon the store and forward capability of X.25 packet switching. Let us also take two of the nodes, node 2 and node 3, and label them nodes A and B.

The LAP-B protocol uses a store-and-forward approach to ensure reliable delivery of packets across noisy, error-prone transmission links. The example of Figure 9.8 illustrates the store-and-forward approach for recovering from errors between two packet-switching nodes, labeled A and B.

Two types of packets are exchanged between the nodes: Link Data (LD) and ACKnowledgment (ACK). Each message has a pair of numbers associated with it: the Receive Sequence Number (RSN) and the Send Sequence Number (SSN). The SSN indicates the number of the packet that is being sent. The RSN indicates the next SSN that is expected by the receiver. The example begins with node A sending user data with send number 1, which is successfully transferred to node B, which acknowledges its receipt with an ACK containing an RSN indicating that the next expected send number is 2. Node B now stores packet 1 and attempts to forward this packet to the next node. Meanwhile node A was sending the second packet; however, it was corrupted due to errors and discarded by node B. The third packet sent by A is received by B, but it is out of order, and B acknowledges this, but indicates that it is still waiting for the second packet. Node A responds by resending packets 2 and 3, which are successfully received and acknowledged by node B, which can now attempt to forward these packets to the next node using the same process.

This simple example illustrates the complexity involved in store-and-forward packet switching. This complexity was required when a significant portion of the packets experienced transmission errors. Even more sophisticated schemes were invented in which only the errored packets were retransmitted.

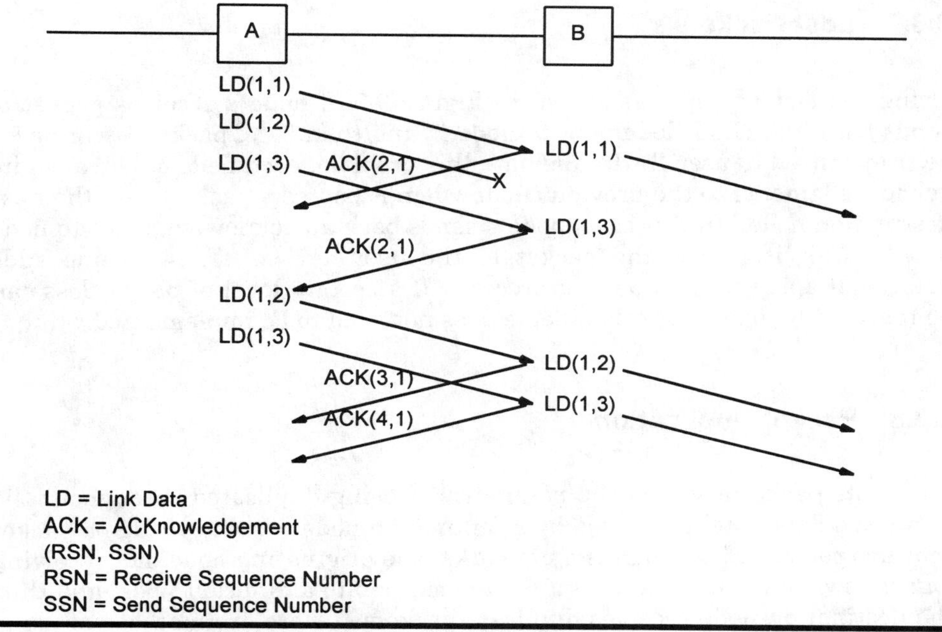

Figure 9.8 Example of X.25 Store-and-Forward Operation

9.3.6 Packet Error

Now let's take the last example and show how the packet error affected the network. In the last example, it was assumed that all four packets arrived at node 3. Figure 9.9 shows the result of an erred packet. If an error (E) occurs in packet 3 before it arrives at node 3 (a), node 3 will detect the error and not send back an acknowledgment to node 2 (b). If after a predetermined time (the time-out period) node 2 does not receive an acknowledgment, it retransmits packet 3 (c) and packet 4. Node 3 then sends back an acknowledgment (ACK) when the correct packets are received (d). This one-way windowing can help or inhibit flow control. If the window size is seven (W = 7), and packet 2 is acknowledged, then packets 3 through 7 have to be transmitted. Large window sizes can boost throughput on high-grade lines, or could cause long delays on noisy (error-prone) lines. A Negative ACKnowledgment (NACK) can also be sent by the receiving node (in this case node 3) telling node 2 that the packet was in error. This NACK will reduce the time node 2 will wait before retransmitting the packet in error.

9.3.7 Lost Packets

Using the last example as shown in Figure 9.9, if node 3 receives packet 3, sends back an acknowledgment to node 2, and then fails, packet 3 will never be transmitted to user B. To alleviate this problem, each node only transmits acknowledgments to the previous node when it passes a packet on to the next destination node. In this case, node 3 sends back an acknowledgment to node 2 only after it passes the packet to the user device. This scheme adds additional delay to the queuing process. If a certain level of packet loss can be reasonably tolerated, this scheme does not need to be implemented.

9.3.8 Packet Duplication

The same packet also has the possibility of being duplicated throughout the network. This could be caused by a failure of a node to acknowledge a packet that has continued through the network. The originating node, not receiving an acknowledgment, generates a retransmission to a different node, and thus the destination node receives duplicate packets. There are methods of using portions of the packet overhead to prevent this from happening.

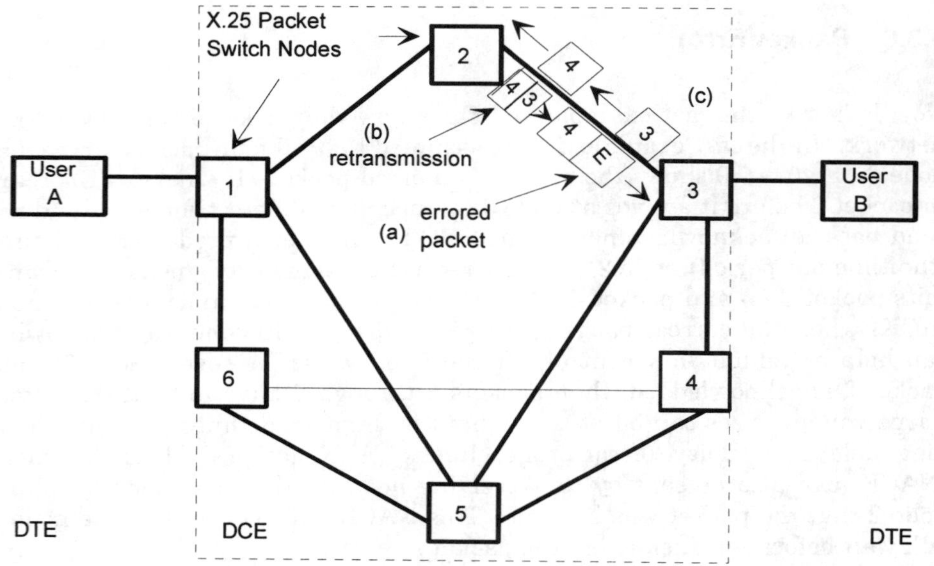

Figure 9.9 Packet Switch Erred Packet Example

9.4 X.25 INTERFACE PROTOCOL STRUCTURES

The X.25 interface protocols define two levels of control procedures. The subscriber link access procedure defines the physical movement of data between two user locations. This is a local device protocol and is used to connect user devices to a network node. The packet layer DTE/DCE interface defines the transfer of information across the physical medium at the network layer. This level contains user information in packets. The data-link layer uses a version of HDLC that assures end-to-end error-free transmission. This level also provides virtual circuits to the user.

9.4.1 CCITT Recommendation X.25

CCITT Recommendation X.25 defines the standard for packet switching. This standard is supported in the ISO OSIRM (under ISO 7776 data link layer and ISO 8208 packet layer standards). It spans the physical, data link, and network layer protocols. The X.25 protocol acts as the interface between DTE and DCE for terminals and computers operating in the packet switching mode and connected to a public data packet-switched network by a dedicated circuit. Thus, the DTE devices communicate through DCE devices using X.25 protocols. The CCITT Recommendation X.25 covers the physical interfaces, link access procedures, packet layer interface, permanent virtual circuit procedures, packet formats, user facilities procedures, and many annexes for specialization of the protocol. Figure 9.10 shows the relation of DTE and DCE functions to the OSIRM. This is an asymmetric relationship between the DTE and DCE.

9.4.2 X.25 and the OSI Reference Model

Figure 9.11 shows the OSIRM and the layers used by packet-switch protocols and specified by CCITT Recommendation X.25. These include the physical layer protocol; X.21 or X.21bis (the data link layer protocols), Link Access Procedures (LAP) and Link Access Procedures Balanced (LAP-B) (both for single circuits for DTE-to-DCE or LAP-B for multiple circuits), and the network layer protocol called the Packet Layer Protocol (PLP), which provides procedures for establishment of virtual calls and multiple simultaneous virtual calls over a single physical channel. Both the X.21 (including X.21bis) and LAP-B protocols are discussed in Chapter 5. X.25 also supports the V-series of modem physical interfaces, as well as recommendations X.31 and X.32 semipermanent ISDN connections. Layers 4 through 7 are either OSI-compatible protocols or user specific. Figure 9.12 shows the packet-switch-related protocols supported at each layer of the OSIRM.

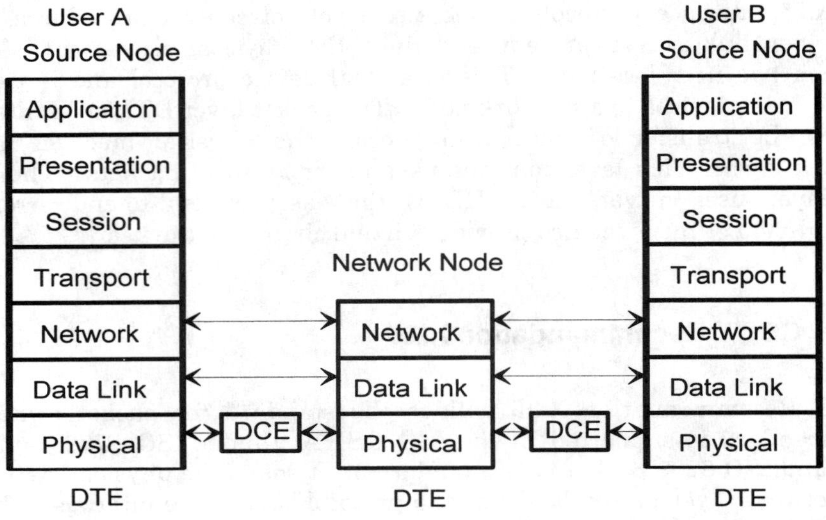

Figure 9.10 X.25 Packet Switching Compared to the OSIRM

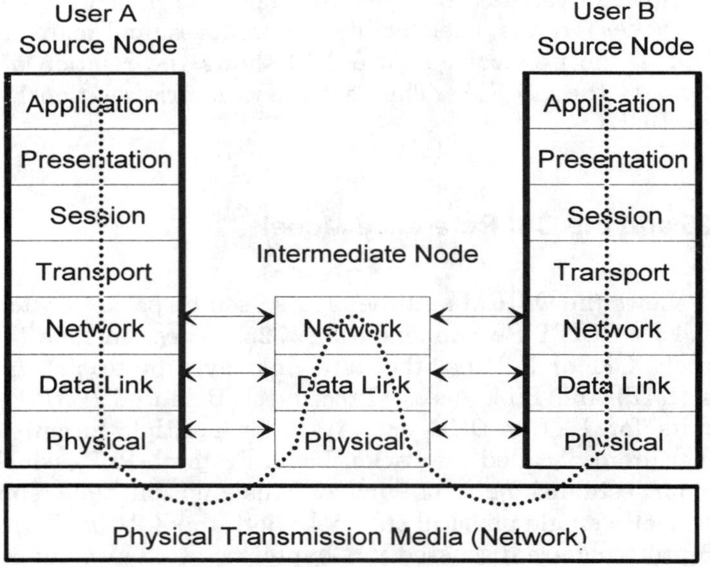

Figure 9.11 OSIRM Layers Used in Packet Switching

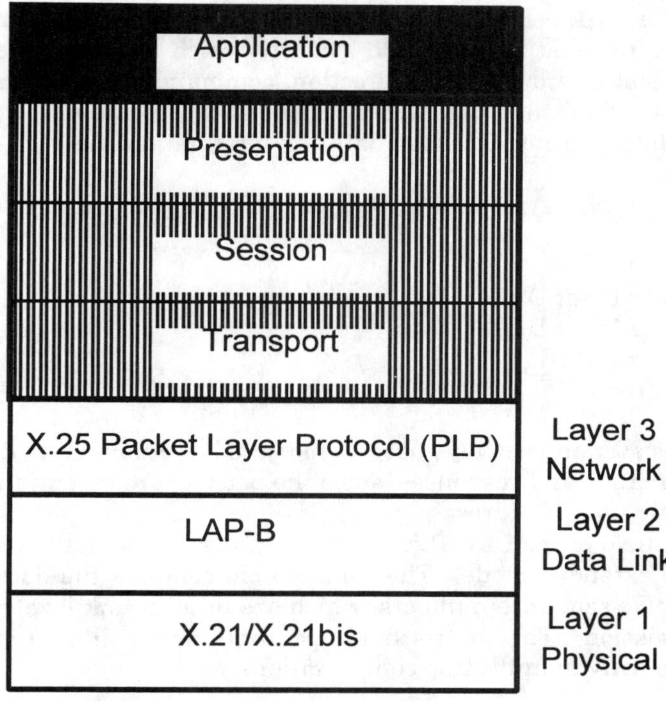

Figure 9.12 OSIRM Specific Implementations

9.4.3 Data Link Frame Structure

X.25 network access can be accomplished over a single circuit or multiple circuits between the DTE and DCE. The single-link procedure (SLP) uses standard ISO HDLC framing and the multilink procedure (MLP) uses LAP-B over multiple channels based on the ISO MLP standard. An example of the SLP frame (HDLC frame structure) is shown in Figure 9.13. A breakout of the multilink (MLP) frame differences is also shown. Note that this is the same frame structure defined in the ANSI ADCCP specifications. All fields are used in the same manner as described for HDLC frames in previous chapters.

9.4.4 The Packet Layer DTE/DCE Interface

Each packet to be transferred across the DTE/DCE interface is carried or packaged within the data link layer HDLC (LAPB) frame information field as shown in Figure 9.14. Here we see the SLP HDLC or LAPB frame from the last example, illustrating the X.25 packet, which takes the form of the information field and details the direction, command, and response types of address fields. Note that the X.25 layer 3 packet, including packet header and packet data, forms the user data, or information, field of the layer 2 LAPB frame.

The LAPB address system is always used and is comprised of one of four types:

- Point-to-Point DTE
- Point-to-Point DCE
- Multidrop DTE
- Multidrop DCE

The address system is always used to indicate direction and to differentiate between commands and responses, since the packets are essentially the same except for their LAP-B address.

The control field of the LAP-B frame may be one, or optionally two, octets in length in the extended mode. The control field contains the data link layer send and receive sequence numbers, which are used in link-level flow control and retransmission. The control field also contains a poll/final bit, which is also used primarily in multidrop configurations.

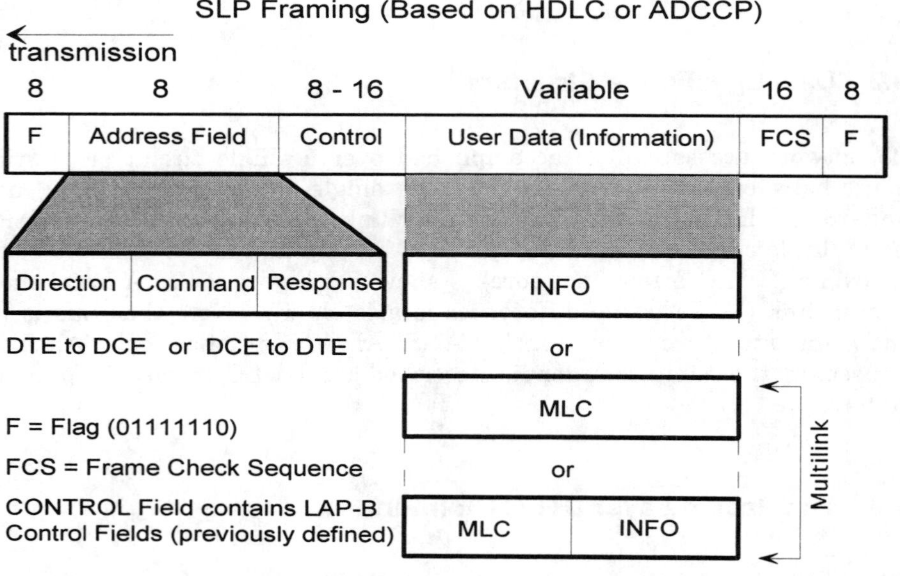

Figure 9.13 SLP Framing

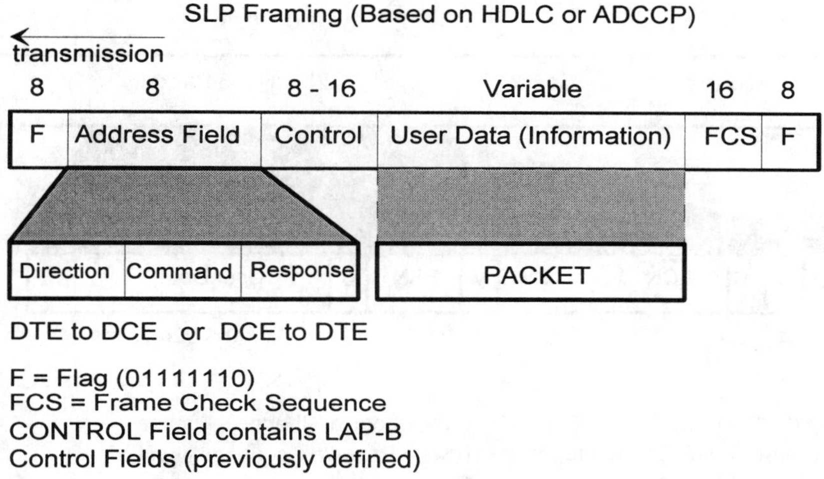

Figure 9.14 SLP HDLC or LAPB Frame Showing Packet Payload

The Frame Check Sequence (FCS) is computed by the sender, and is recomputed by the receiver to detect if there were any bit errors in the received LAP-B frame. The Flag (F) sequence delimits the beginning and end of the LAP-B frame. An operation of the data link layer is to avoid the occurrence of the flag sequence within user data. If a sequence of six 1s is detected in the data, a zero is inserted prior to the sixth 1 upon transmission. Upon receipt, the inserted zeroes are removed by looking for sequences of five 1s followed by a "stuffed" zero bit.

9.4.5 X.25 Layer 3 Packet Format

The X.25 packet layer is composed of a header and a user data, or information, field as shown in Figure 9.15. The Qualifier (Q) bit allows the transport layer to separate control data from user data. The D bit is used in delivery confirmation during call setup. The next two bits indicate the packet type, with 01 indicating a data packet with three-octet header. A four-octet header is also standardized. The X.25 packet layer address has a 4-bit group number and an 8-bit logical channel number, together forming a 12-bit Logical Channel Number (LCN), or virtual circuit number. Virtual circuit zero is reserved, and therefore there can be up to 2^{16} minus 1 = 4095 virtual circuits. The packet layer Receive and Send Sequence Numbers (RSN and SSN) provide packet layer flow control. The More (M) bit supports segmentation and reassembly by identifying packet segments with a value of 1, with the last segment having a value of zero.

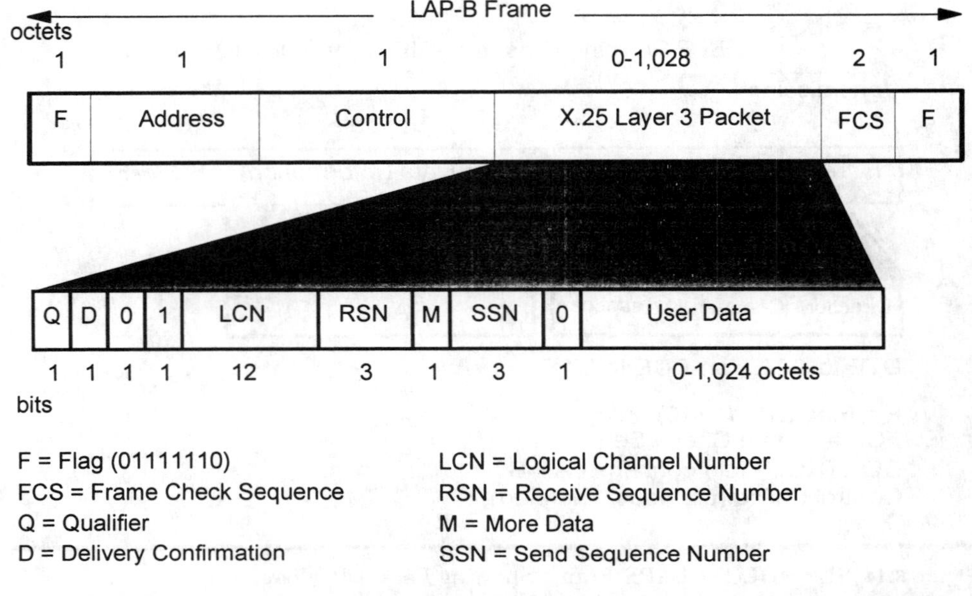

Figure 9.15 LAP-B Frame and X.25 Packet Layer Payload

9.5 NETWORK LAYER FUNCTIONS

Now let's look at the packet-switch protocols from the network perspective. Each physical interface can establish one or multiple virtual circuits to remote physical interfaces. Each of these circuits is then assigned logical channel numbers similar to phone numbers but with local significance only. Virtual circuits assure sequence integrity in the delivery of user data, established either administratively as a PVC, or as an SVC through call control procedures. Over these PVCs flow both normal data and call control packets. An X.25 "call" is set-up using a global X.25 address, and a SVC channel number is negotiated and allocated between each switch. The X.25 global address is only present in call set-up and tear-down, and all data in between is identified by its SVC channel number. Thus, the X.25 address is global significant, and the SVC channel number is locally significant. This section describes the X.25 protocol as it defines the network layer features and functions. Both X.25 services, virtual circuit and datagram, will be explained in detail. Datagrams are messages unto themselves that do not require call control procedures. Datagrams may be sent in a best-effort mode, or have an explicit receipt notification.

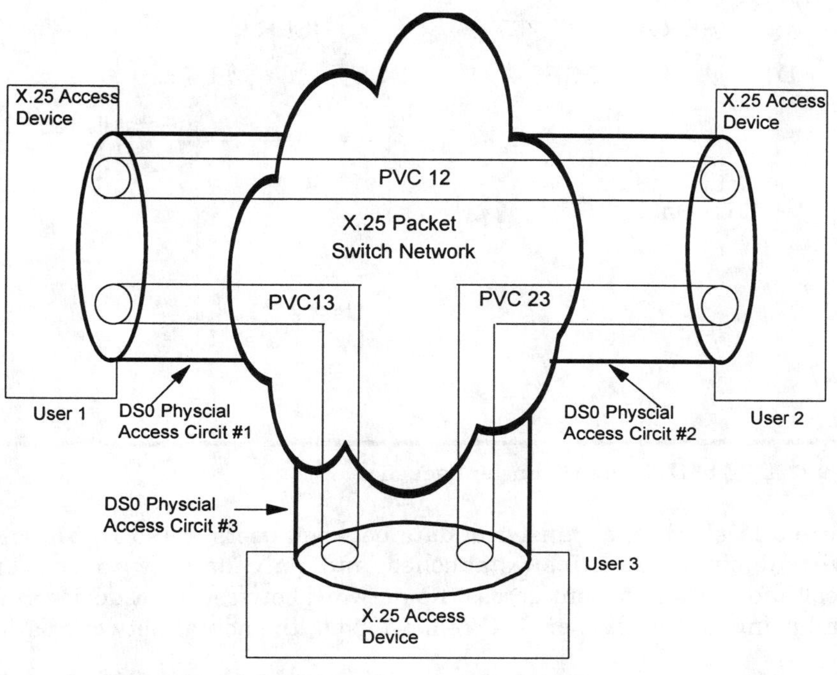

Figure 9.16 Packet Switch Networking Example

9.5.1 Permanent Virtual Circuits and Virtual Calls

The network layer provides the user with up to 4095 logical channels designated either as Permanent Virtual Circuits (PVCs) or Virtual Calls (VCs) over one LAPB physical channel. PVCs are virtual circuits permanently established between a source and destination node. This is similar to having a private or leased line dedicated at all times between two specific users. These PVCs guarantee a connection between two points when demanded by the user. The user always sees the virtual circuit as a dedicated circuit for his or her use only, whereas the network provides the same circuit as a shared resource to multiple users upon demand.

Figure 9.16 illustrates three users of a public X.25 packet-switched network. Each user has a single physical DS0 access circuit to the network, labeled 1, 2, and 3. Within each access circuit there are multiple Permanent Virtual Circuits (PVCs), labeled 12, 23, and 13, that allow each site to communicate with the other two. Each of these PVCs is static, thus their end points are predefined. Each PVC carries traffic in a bidirection. Switched Virtual Circuits (SVCs) operate in the same manner, but are established and disabled on demand.

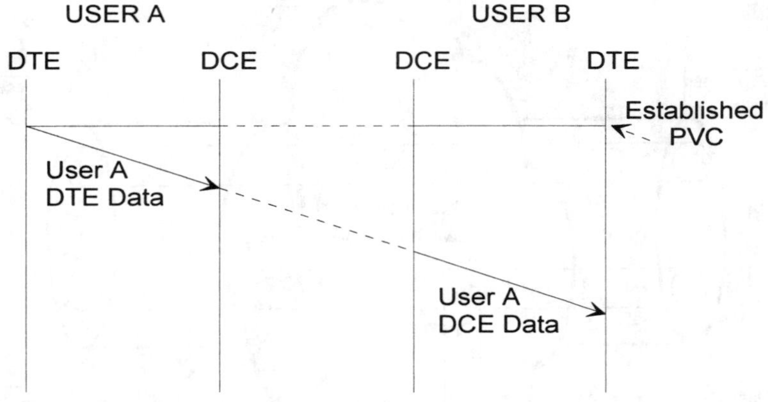

Figure 9.17 DTE to DTE Data Transfer Sequence

Figure 9.17 shows the transfer of data between users A and B. Notice that the virtual circuit remains established and only data (with the proper protocol information) is sent across the network between DTE devices. While the end points of the PVC or SVC remain fixed, the actual network path may vary.

Virtual Calls (VCs) or Switched Virtual Calls (SVCs) act as circuit-switched calls, with the characteristic of being connected and disconnected after the data has been sent between the source and destination node. Therefore, one source can connect to many destinations at different times, as opposed to always being connected to one destination. This is similar to the method of making a telephone call, with the phone off-hook, and talking during the duration of the call. Each time a call is made, regardless of the destination, it is reestablished through the entire network. Figure 9.18 shows a standard packet sequence for the establishment of a SVC virtual call, data transfer, and then call clearing. Note that the data transfer stage can last any amount of time.

SVCs can add even more delay than when using a PVC. SVCs, in addition to encountering connection blocking and connection delay, can encounter queuing and retransmission delays. These delay factors must be taken into account during the design.

9.5.2 Virtual Calls and Logical Channel Numbers

Logical Channel Numbers (LCNs) are assigned to each of the incoming and outgoing virtual calls for each DCE and DTE, respectively, as well as to all PVCs. Out of the 4095 logical channel numbers available per physical circuit, PVCs are assigned the lowest numbers, followed by one-way incoming virtual calls, then two-way incoming and outgoing calls, and the highest numbers are reserved for one-way outgoing virtual calls. Figure 9.19 illustrates an interpretation of logical channel administration as defined in the CCITT X.25, Annex A. These LCNs hold only local significance to that specific physical port, but must be mapped to a remote LCN for each virtual call. The packet network then uses search algorithms to assign these LCNs to each virtual call. These are also shown in Figure 9.19.

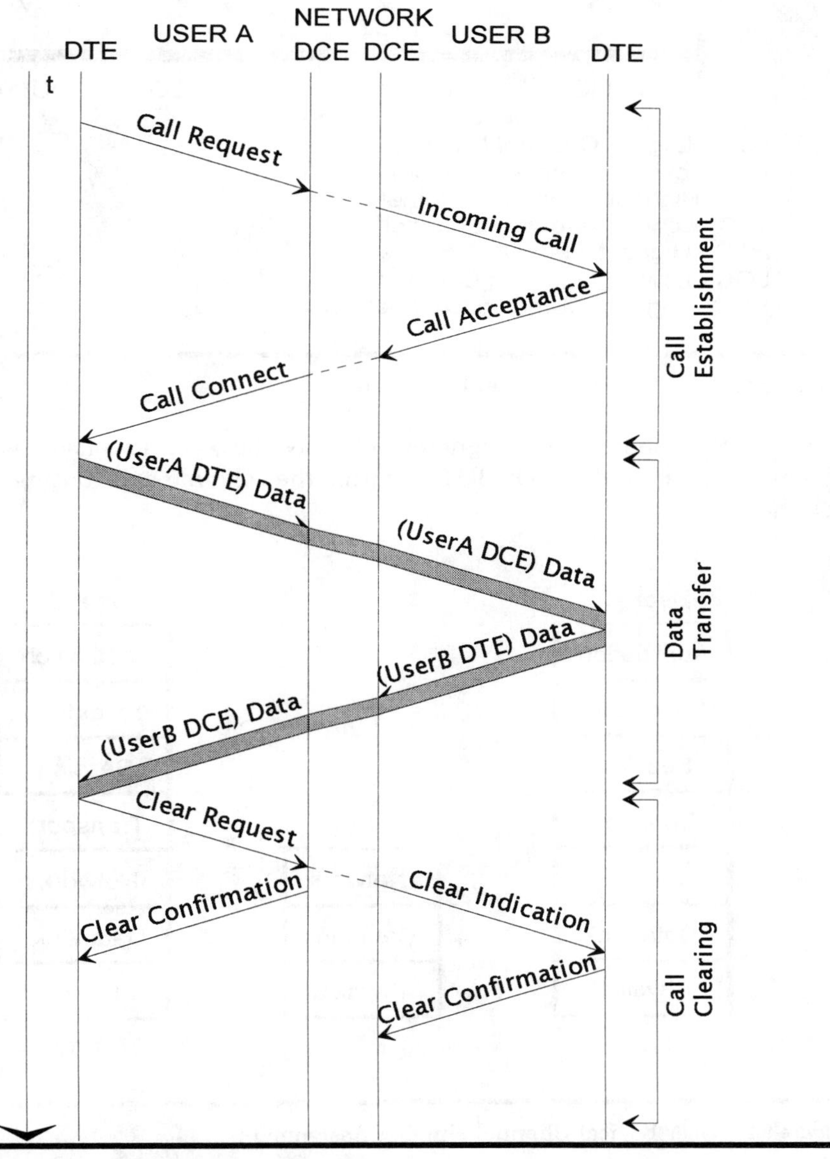

Figure 9.18 Standard X.25 Packet Transfer Sequence

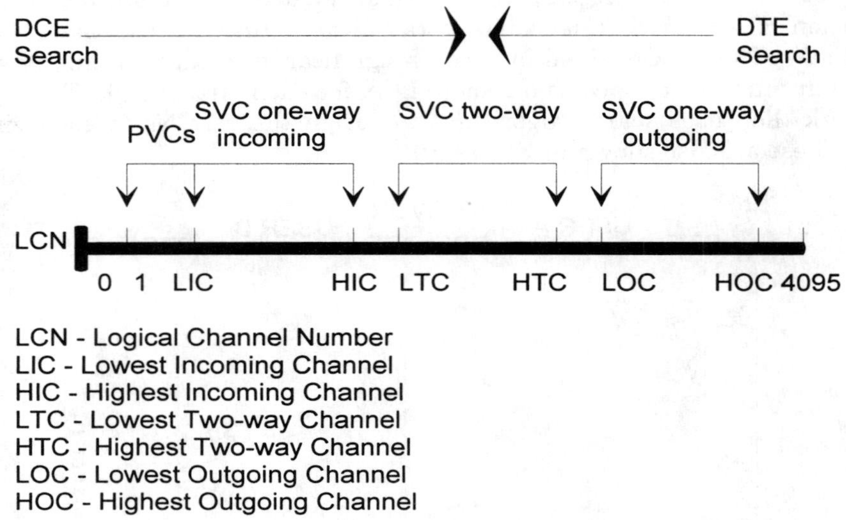

Figure 9.19 X.25 Logical Channel Definition

Figure 9.20 shows the assignment of LCNs between two users. Note that the network layer of the OSIRM performs the relaying and routing of packets via the LCNs.

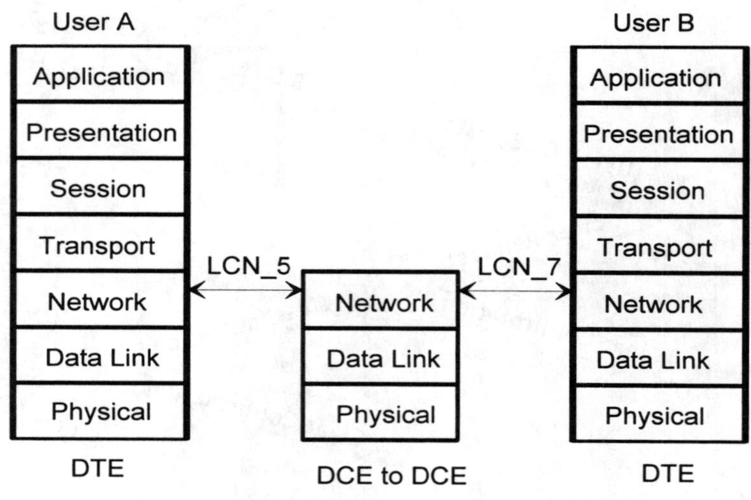

Figure 9.20 User Logical Channel Number Assignment

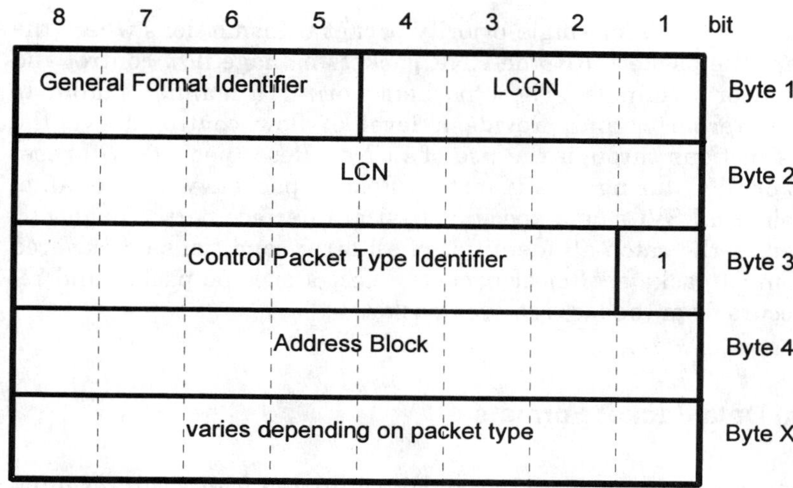

Figure 9.21 Packet Format for Call Request and Incoming Calls

9.5.3 X.25 Control Packet Formats

Control packets are used for virtual call setup and termination. Figure 9.21 shows the format for a control packet. The General Format Identifier indicates the general format of the rest of the header, indicating whether the packet will be a call setup, clearing, flow control, interrupt, reset, restart, registration, diagnostic, or data packet. The Logical Channel Group Number has local significance for each logical channel. We have already discussed LCNs. The Control Packet Type Identifier relates the packet type (indicated in the general format identifier) from DCE to DTE and from DTE to DCE. The fourth and any additional bytes contain information that is packet-type specific. Control packets perform many functions, including: call request and incoming call packets; call accepted and call connected; clear request and clear indication; DTE and DCE clear confirmation, data, interrupt, interrupt confirmation, receive ready (RR), receive not ready (RNR), reset confirmation, and restart confirmation; reset request and reset indication; restart request and restart indication; diagnostic; DTE Reject (REJ), registration request, and registration confirmation. The example in Figure 9.21 shows the packet format for call request and incoming calls.

A quick explanation of these control packets is in order. Clear packets are used to clear the user-to-user session (DTE-to-DTE). Interrupt packets are used when the user wants to bypass the normal flow control protocol.

Interrupt packets are used for single-priority packet transmissions where the DTE must accept the packet. RR and RNR packets manage flow control and are initiated by user terminals. These packets work in a manner similar to their HDLC counterparts, and provide a level of flow control above the normal HDLC functions through the use of LCNs. Reset packets will reset the entire PVC or SVC during data transfer. Restart packets will reset all of the PVCs and clear all SVCs on a specific physical interface port. Diagnostic packets are used as the catch-all identifier of all error conditions not covered by the other control packets. Reject packets reject a specific packet and retransmission occurs from the last received packet.

9.5.4 Normal Data Packet Formats

Normal data packets are transferred *after* call setup and *before* call termination. PVCs only require normal packet formats, as the virtual circuit is permanent and does not need to be set up or terminated. Figure 9.22 shows the format of a normal data packet. The Qualified Data (Q) bit distinguishes between user data and a user device-control data stream. The Data (D) bit is set to 0 if the flow control and acknowledgments have local significance, and set to 1 to designate end-to-end significance. The LCGN and LCN together provide the 12 bits needed to form the Virtual Circuit Number (VCN). The P(R) and P(S) fields designate the receive and send sequence count, respectively. The More Data (M) bit is set to 0 throughout the length of the message, and is set to 1 on the last packet of the message, indicating the end of the message. The M bit is used to chain packets together, which serve as a single message, such as a 737-byte message that gets segmented into many 128-byte packets. The data field is prespecified to a maximum size (e.g., 16, 32, 64, 128, 256, 512, 1024, 2048, and 4096 bytes) and contains the actual user data (or padding).

9.5.5 Flow Control and Windowing

The send and receive sequence numbers in the X.25 packet layer are also used to provide flow control between the packet layer source and sink. Figure 9.23 illustrates a simple example of X.25 packet layer flow control. The send sequence number is a sequential number for the current packet. Numbers are incremented modulo the maximum window size. This example uses a modulo of 4, which means that sequence numbers are incremented in the order 0, 1, 2, 3, 0, 1, 2, 3, 0, and so on.

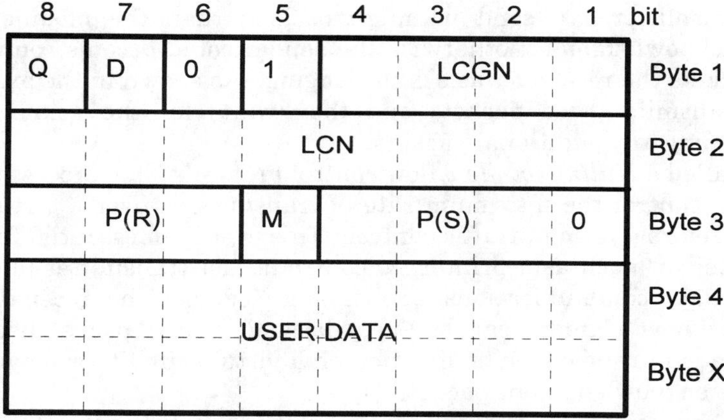

Figure 9.22 Normal Data Packet Format

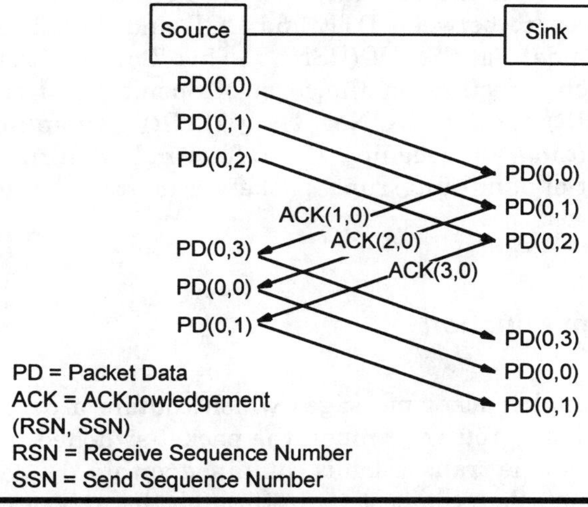

Figure 9.23 Example of X.25 Flow Control

The receive sequence number in the ACKnowledgment indicates the next send sequence number expected in the next packet from the other end for that virtual circuit. Therefore, the receive sequence number acts as an acknowledgment for all packets up to one less than the receive sequence number.

The transmitter can send no more packets than the modulo minus 1 without acknowledgment; otherwise the sender could become confused as to which packets the receiver was acknowledging. As shown in the example, the sender transmits three packets and then waits for the acknowledgment before sending any additional packets.

This is called a *sliding window* flow control protocol. This process allows the receiver to control the maximum rate of transmission over a virtual circuit, and is therefore a form of traffic control. This is still an essential function for a slow receiver (such as a printer) to control a fast transmitter (a computer) in many data communications applications today. The receive sequence number acknowledgment can be "piggybacked" in the packet header for a packet headed in the opposite direction on a virtual circuit, or may be sent in a separate acknowledgment packet.

Window size is directly proportional to traffic load on the logical channel, so resources should be used wisely, balancing the cost of providing more logical channels and bandwidth against maintaining performance. The default window setting is 2.

While this method operates at both the data link and network levels, it allows the network to throttle individual logical channels rather than an entire physical circuit. Some protocols, such as TCP/IP, have the intelligence to reduce the window size during network congestion and increase the window size after the congestion has been relieved.

The control packet forms the basis of the flow control element of X.25. These packets operate between DTE and DCE and limit the rate of packet acceptance by updating the PD(RSN). This flow control is negotiated separately in each direction, in the form of opening and closing windows. Receive Ready (RR) and Receive Not Ready (RNR) play an important role in postponing or closing and opening the DTE window during problem DCE conditions. Out-of-band interrupt packets can also be used to control transmissions.

9.5.6 Datagram Function

Datagrams are single-packet messages which contain a destination address and are independently routed through the packet-switched network. All the information for a single transaction is contained within the datagram packet. These packets each select the best route through the network, do not require acknowledgments, are unsequenced, and thus are a form of connectionless service. Datagrams are ideal for when the user interface data transfer is for a very short period of time and where response time must be fast, or is not even needed, and where user control over the transmission is not required. Datagrams are also used when sending broadcast messages to many destinations. Some applications are more suited to datagrams, such as point of sale, credit card validation, or inquiry-response registration systems.

Datagrams were dropped from the X.25 standard, but are compatible with the X.28 and X.29 standards. In fact, some internal network protocols, which are not controlled by the standard, still use datagrams. Datagrams are also used in the 802.X LAN standards.

9.6 USER CONNECTIVITY

User connectivity to the packet-switched network takes on many forms. The network user interface is accomplished through seven important standards: X.121, X.21, X.25, X.28, X.29, X.3, and X.32. We also need to understand the optional user facilities available, as well as the fast connect option.

9.6.1 User Network Interface

CCITT Recommendations X.3, X.28, and X.29 have been defined as link-level protocols which provide asynchronous terminal DTE interface to X.25 networks. These standards are for interactive terminal DTE that does not have X.25 synchronous capability and can only communicate via low-speed asynchronous mode. CCITT Recommendation X.25 also provides synchronous user connectivity, and X.32 provides synchronous dial-up capability. Figure 9.24 shows three examples of asynchronous and BSC DTE terminal connectivity options to an X.25 packet-switched network. Each of the interface protocols is defined as follows:

CCITT Recommendation X.121. Defines the international numbering plan for packet-switched networks.

CCITT Recommendation X.28. Defines the operational control of these functions between the (nonpacket mode) character mode terminal DTE device and the DCE PAD. Through the use of X.28 protocol, the DTE (through the PAD) establishes a virtual circuit, initializes the service, and exchanges the control and data packets. The X.28 protocol manages these controls and exchanges of data flows between the DTE and PAD through a terminal-user command language.

CCITT Recommendation X.29. Defines the same controls but for the host computer destination (or origination). Information exchange can happen at any time over the virtual call. X.29 uses machine commands that identify packets between the host and the PAD.

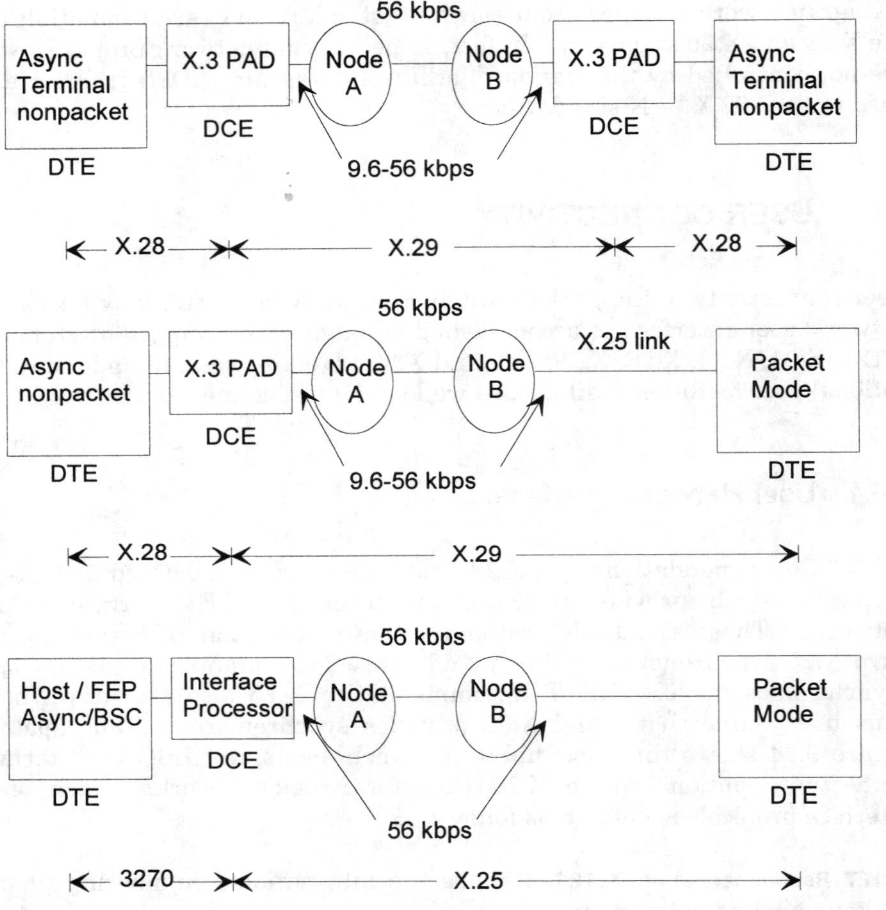

Figure 9.24 Asynchronous and BSC DTE Terminal Connectivity Options

CCITT Recommendation X.3. Defines a Packet Assembler/Disassembler (PAD) concentrator function for start-mode or character-mode DTE devices. These terminal management functions include the bps rate, terminal specifics, flow control, and escape sequences.

CCITT Recommendation X.32. Defines X.25 synchronous dial-up mode for DTE services.

There are two types of "user-to-network" interfaces using these protocols: packetized virtual circuits and packetized datagram. Each spans all three OSIRM levels as discussed. Virtual circuits assure sequencing of user data and an ordered flow of messages which require multiple packets. Packetized datagrams are messages unto themselves and do not follow the ordered packet flow of virtual circuits.

The other type of user access device is the packet assembler/dissembler (PAD), which takes asynchronous inputs from various terminals and assembles their individual transmissions into a single, synchronous X.25 circuit to the packet network. The PAD acts as a point-to-point statistical multiplexer, and PAD buffers are used to accumulate and accommodate the information streams not passed due to network congestion. The same device can also be used to disassemble the X.25 synchronous channel into individual asynchronous user interfaces. Many packet switches have the PAD functionality built into them, and provide for asynchronous user ports directly into the packet switch. Thus, the switch performs a function similar to the front-end processor and host. More common are the standalone PAD devices, including single-port cards for personal computers.

9.6.2 User Applications

The primary application used with packet switching is the terminal-to-host application access and vice versa. Packet switching was designed for terminals and PC interactions, and compressed voice can also be passed through HDLC over the packet-switched network. We have discussed the PAD as one of the methods of connecting remote IBM 327X and IBM 5251 terminal clusters to mainframes. There are three additional methods of connectivity:

- Software package and hardware protocol converter
- BSC 3270, which uses both software and hardware protocol conversion
- Asynchronous dial-up to packet network

SNA hosts use the IBM X.25 frame format, called Qualified Logical Link Control (QLLC), to format the SNA data within the X.25 protocol. Hosts can communicate with both packet-capable and non-packet-capable equipment. Terminal handlers implement the packet protocol for device interfaces not conforming to the X.25 standard. Some routers allow bridging and routing over the same X.25 network interface. SVCs encapsulating TCP/IP hosts through X.121 addressing can access other TCP/IP hosts on the router. They can also address DDN IP hosts and the DDN addressing algorithm.

9.6.3 User-to-User Protocols

Users communicate with other users through byte streams, but these byte streams go through many changes as they are passed through a host or computer and then through the packet-switched network. The protocols to control these user applications are transparent to X.25 and related protocols, as discussed.

9.6.4 Optional User Facilities (Section 6.0 of the Standards)

The CCITT X.25 standard defines procedures for optional user facilities that provide functions to end users at the packet layer. These facilities are specified in the control packet format. Some examples include

On-line facility registration permits the DTE to request registration of facilities from the DCE through use of the registration request packet. The DCE will in turn report back to the DTE what facilities are available.

Incoming and outgoing calls barred prevents outgoing calls to the DCE or incoming calls to the DTE.

Additional options include extended packet sequence numbering, D-bit modification, packet retransmission, one-way logical channel outgoing and incoming, nonstandard default packet and window sizes, default throughput classes assignment, flow control parameter negotiation, and fast select, to name a few. More can be found in the X.25 standard under Section 6.0.

9.6.5 Fast Connect Option

There also exists a fast connect option for fast packet transactions. In fast connect mode, each packet has the call request format together with the data so the establishment of a virtual circuit is not required. This is similar to a datagram. There are two types of fast connect: fast select call and fast select with immediate clear.

Fast Select Call. The fast select packet from user A has both call request and user data (up to 128 bytes of data), and user B can respond with a call-accept packet which also contains user data from user B. The rest of the call connection and disconnect works the same as a switched virtual call. This operation can be seen in Figure 9.25.

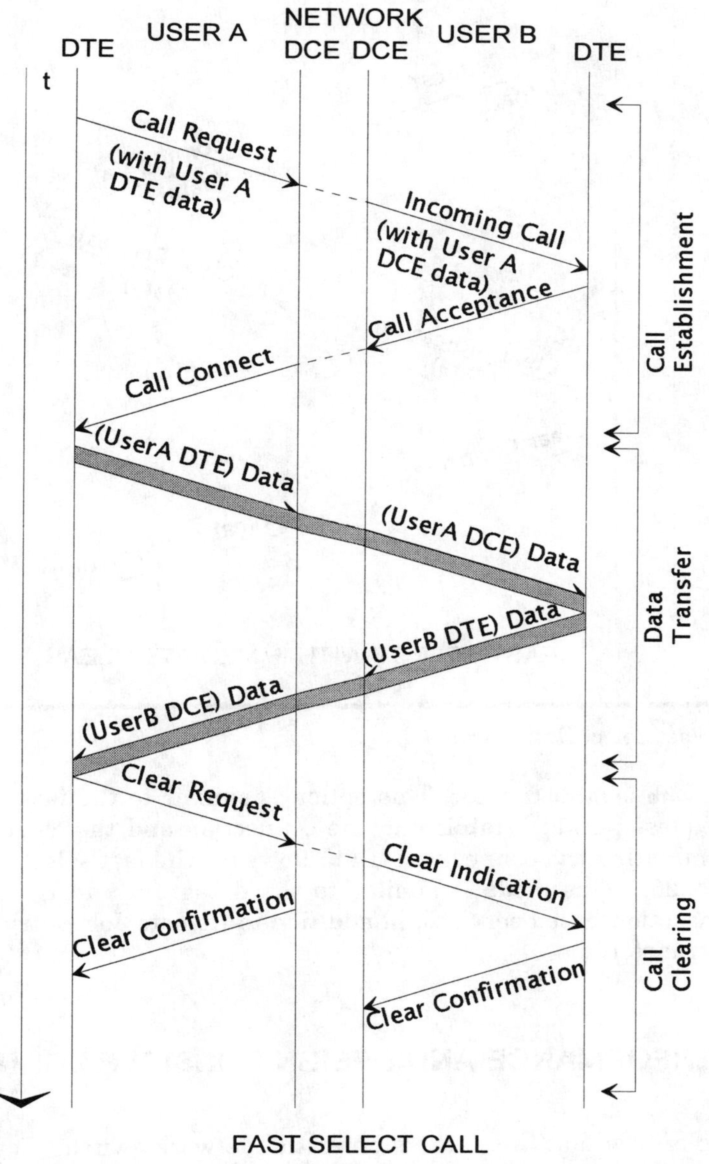

Figure 9.25 Fast Select Operation

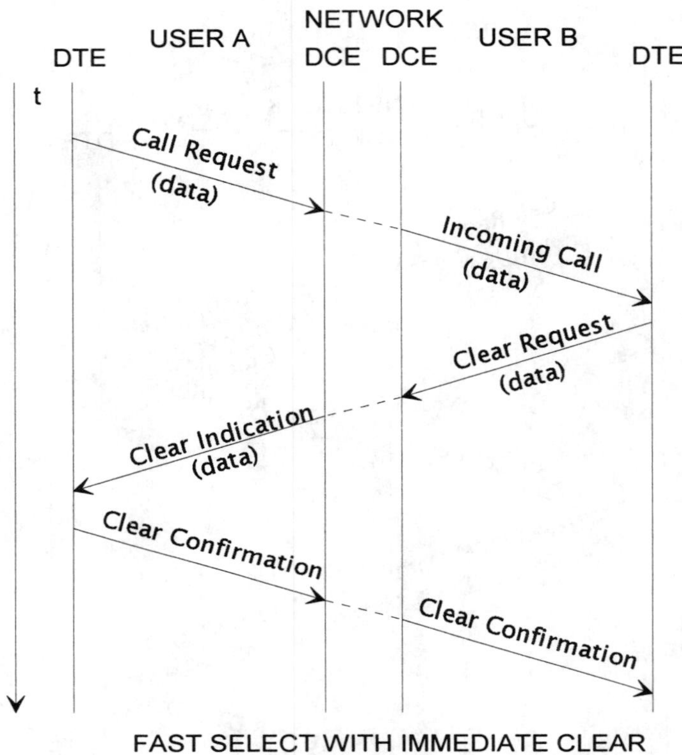

Figure 9.26 Fast Select Data Flows

Fast Select with Immediate Clear. This option is similar to the fast select, with the call request packet establishing the connection and the clear indication packet terminating the connection. Data flows for the fast select can be seen in Figure 9.26. This mode is similar to the datagram and is designed for single transaction-based services, in addition to Remote Job Entry (RJE) and bulk data transfer.

9.7 PERFORMANCE AND DESIGN CONSIDERATIONS

Regardless of how fast the packets enter the network switch, they go into a queue before being switched through each node. If the queue is full, the node will buffer the packet until it can pass through the queue and bandwidth is available. The amount and length of queuing is directly related to the blocking delay through the network. Some packet switches degrade in throughput as their queues fill up and thus throughput decreases. The greater the packets per second passed the greater the delay or congestion.

Errors in the network transport can also cause more queuing and delay. Overhead is also a major consideration. The overhead incurred per packet is anywhere from 64 to 256 bits per packet. Since typical messages are 256 to 1028 bits, overhead would account for 25 percent of the total transmission bandwidth. This directly reduces efficiency.

Performance in a packet-switched network is measured in packets per second throughput in relation to the delay incurred from switch ingress to egress. These figures calculate to throughput and delay characteristic curves, which should be supplied by any prospective vendor. Packet delay through a typical packet switch node is 50 to 200 ms due to packet processing. Typical packet processing per node is anywhere from 300 packets per second at the low end and up to 10,000 packets per second. Switches should be favored that have constant packet per second processing at all levels of traffic throughput. Also, the switch performance should be constant, irrespective of packet size. Some packet switches drastically degrade performance and packet processing as the packet size increases above 128 or 256 kbits. These larger packets are characteristic of batch processing, which uses packet-switched networks because it cannot justify dedicated or leased-line circuits. This type of traffic absolutely requires good performance and constant throughput, regardless of packet size.

Another consideration is protocol conversion. The greater the amount of protocol conversion that the switch or PAD has to perform, the lower the throughput and performance. Also, as the amount of PAD padding increases, the actual data throughput of the service degrades because of the increased processing power required.

9.8 X.75 INTERNETWORKING PROTOCOL

CCITT Recommendation X.75 defines the protocol structure and procedures for internetworking multiple X.25 Packet-Switched Private Data Networks (PSPDNs). Thus, the access of any user to an individual X.25 network is extended across multiple X.25 networks, providing the capability to share network resources and data across the international arena. X.75 can also be used to connect the larger backbone packet switches to one another. X.75 provides address translation in conjunction with the X.121 addressing protocol standard. X.75 functions reside in the network layer above X.25 functions. All functions of the X.75 protocol are similar to the X.25 protocol (e.g., LCGNs, LCNs, PVCs, SVCs). X.75 also supports the multilink procedures to support multiple links between STE. STE is Signaling Terminal Exchange, and acts as the internetwork interface point and performs both packet-transfer procedures and packet signaling.

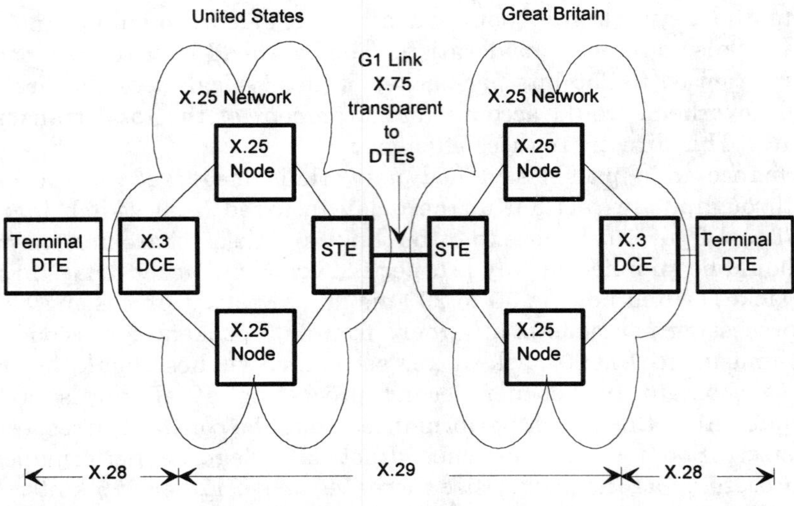

Figure 9.27 X.75 Packet Switch International Gateway

Figure 9.27 shows nonpacket DTEs from two separate X.25 networks in the United States and Great Britain communicating via the X.75 protocol. The actual communications still take place over the X.28 and X.29 protocols, and the X.75 network protocol is transparent to the users. The DCE in this case is part of network node functionality, and communicates directly X.25 into the X.25 network. This is an example of X.75 being used as an international packet-switched service. The links between these STEs can either be an A1 link, which is used between two adjacent nodes, or a G1 link, which is used between a source STE (United States) and a destination STE (Great Britain). Many countries now have some form of private and public packet-switched networks and use X.75 to link these networks. Most vendors and X.25 networks implement different versions of the X.75 standard, changing or supporting one or more of the options available. One cannot assume that just because the network supports X.75 that it will be able to communicate with another X.25 network supporting X.75.

9.9 ADVANTAGES AND DRAWBACKS

Advantages of X.25 packet switching include

- Format, code, and speed conversions between unlike terminal devices
- Inherent secure transmission scheme

- Fault tolerant technology (all packets don't need to follow the same path)
- Packetized long messages and short messages, which do not interfere with each other
- Dial or leased-line connections for access
- Rapid exchange of short messages, and consistent delay of long messages under steady load
- Network functions transparent to users
- Good for transport of small batch files
- Asynchronous and synchronous interfaces
- Transmission speeds 150 bps to 56 kbps
- New networking speeds up to 256 kbps, T1, and E1
- Reduce vulnerability to network failure (routes around failures and risk distributed over multiple switches)
- Better circuit utilization than circuit switching
- Reduce access costs for multiple users (versus dedicated access)
- International connectivity with lower-cost circuits

Primary drawbacks of X.25 packet switching include

- ⌧ Low-speed access limitations
- ⌧ High delay potential
- ⌧ High overhead

9.10 REVIEW

As packet switching emerged as a technology from the voice encryption requirements of the military, it laid the groundwork for many of the newer frame and cell-switching technologies. These will be discussed in the next few chapters. Packet-switched networks provide the best technology for geographically dispersed locations which require any-to-any connectivity, and a mix of protocol and traffic types, and where end-to-end data integrity is of paramount importance. While X.25 packet switching has been the leading switched-data technology for over 30 years, fiber optics and virtually error-free digital transmission facilities are quickly making it obsolete in the United States as the transport technology of choice. In fact, for many applications X.25 packet switching has yielded to frame relay. As the digital and fiber-optic infrastructure is laid, so the robustness of the public network is allowing the interrelation of technology such as frame relay and cell switching with the error detection and correction required only at the ends of the transmission. In the global market, however, packet switching continues to dominate, and probably will until the end of the century. Packet switching requires physical and user interfaces, features, and functions, data link protocol, and network protocol operations, making X.25 packet switching both a private and public network protocol. User-to-user interface and transport protocols operate in conjunction with X.25, and with the X.75 internetworking protocol. Finally, performance and design considerations for packet networks show that performance relates to packets per second throughput compared to the delay in the packet switch. These principles for performance will apply to the upcoming packet and transmission technologies as well — Frame Relay, ATM, and SONET.

Chapter

10

Frame Relay, Part 1 – Theory

Since the first edition of this book, public frame relay services have taken the United States by storm, similar to the X.25 public packet-switching services explosion in the 1970s and the private statistical multiplexing networks advance in the 1980s. This popularity is due in part to the user community-driven forums and equipment manufacturer communities. Cooperation between the American National Standards Institute (ANSI) and the International Telegraph and Telephone Consultative Committee (CCITT) (now the ITU-T) with these user community forums has made frame relay an overnight success. To understand frame relay as a service, we must first look at the origins and theory of operation. Frame relay is defined through three classifications: frame relay as an *interface*, as a *signaling protocol*, and as a *network service*.

The user can interpret the multiple standards that define the interface, one common signaling protocol, and network service through an understanding of each standards committee's definition and each provider's implementation of frame. There are two types of frame relay offerings, private and public networking, defined by these standards bodies. Frame relay protocol structure and transmission theory is covered here in detail. A discussion on frame relay addressing and the user interface specifications rounds out this chapter and leads to a discussion of the operations and services in the next chapter.

Changes in frame relay in the premises and public service network environments have caused an entire rewrite of these two chapters from the first edition. Much of the detail on the ISDN version of FR access found in the first edition was omitted, as almost all frame relay implementations are now non-ISDN. Even the first implementations of ISDN to frame relay are mapping ANI or E.164 addresses directly to Permanent Virtual Circuits (PVCs).

10.1 ORIGINS AND STANDARDS OF FRAME RELAY

X.25 packet switching, private networks using Time Division Multiplexing (TDM) or statistical multiplexing (STM), and legacy networks running HDLC and SDLC dominated the data communications marketplace from 1980 through the earlier part of the 1990s. In order to keep pace with the increased bandwidth and connectivity requirements of today's applications, a new data communications technology that provide higher throughput at lower cost was required. Frame relay has emerged to provide higher throughput, higher bandwidth, more cost-effective packet-style data transport, and take advantage of new digital and fiber-optic transmission facilities.

Frame relay combines the advantages of both time division and statistical multiplexing on a single-access circuit, while maintaining low end-to-end network latency. It allows many of the security features of private lines but greater granularity of bandwidth assignment and dynamic allocation of bandwidth. Frame relay is sometimes described as X.25 packet switching on steroids. This is somewhat accurate, as frame relay provides a next-generation packet-type service at higher speeds than X.25. While frame relay has its origins in HDLC and ISDN, it also provides a scaled down and streamlined protocol from X.25 packet switching, eliminating error-correction and flow-control overhead, and relying on low-error-rate transmission facilities and higher layer protocols (i.e., TCP) to recover from lost or corrupted data.

Frame relay has become the leading technology in the continual evolution of fast packet network transport. Frame relay provides an upgrade to existing packet-switch technology by allowing user transport speeds up to T1 (1.544 Mbps — with theoretical speeds up to 45 Mbps) while switching frames of fixed or variable size over PVCs and SVCs. Frame relay fills the technology gap between X.25 packet service and SMDS and ATM broadband transport service, and in many cases it complements these emerging broadband standards. In fact, frame relay over ATM and frame relay interworking with ATM are two options now available.

Frame relay standards are derived from the ISDN Link Access Procedure for the D-channel (LAP-D, or as later modifications were called LAP-F) in ITU-T/CCITT Recommendation Q.921, which led to I.233, Q.922, and Q.933. Later, the ANSI T1.617 and T1.618 specifications standardized the service description, protocol, and status signaling for frame relay used today.

Frame relay also created the need for a separate industry group, the Frame Relay Forum, chartered with developing implementation agreements in order to facilitate interoperability. Today, almost every WAN manufacturer and data communications service provider have announced support for the frame relay protocol.

10.2 FRAME RELAY DEFINED

The building blocks of a frame relay service include:

⇒ FR user access port
⇒ FR network access port
⇒ FR user access circuit or User-to-Network Interface (UNI)
⇒ Permanent Virtual Circuit (PVC)
⇒ Committed Information Rate (CIR)
⇒ Data Link Connection Identifier (DLCI)
⇒ Switched Virtual Circuit (SVC)

A FR user-access port connects to the FR network-access port through the use of a FR user access circuit, also called a User-to-Network Interface (UNI). One or multiple Permanent Virtual Circuits (PVCs) reside within a single UNI. Each PVC is bidirectional, and each direction has an assigned Committed Information Rate (CIR). Each endpoint of the PVC has an identifier called a Data Link Connection Identifier (DLCI). One concept used consistently throughout the next few chapters is that of the data services "cloud". The cloud figure represents a variety of network environments, including the service provider's transport network from access port to egress port (UNIs), the local exchange environment, and even separate networks that the user sends data to and receives data from. The cloud symbol is typically used when the transport environment is transparent to the user (i.e., its interworkings are not controlled or influenced by the end users). Figure 10.1 illustrates the FR network environment, with three users accessing the FR network through a UNI, each with a PVC to the other site, and each PVC end point identified by a DLCI. Let's now explore each of these aspects of frame relay through detailed definitions.

10.2.1 FR User-Access Ports and Circuits (FR UNIs)

The FR user access port is a physical port on the Customer Premises Equipment (CPE) such as a router. This FR user-access port is connected to a single FR access circuit, typically a digital DS0 (56 kbps), fractional T1 (128, 256, 384, 512, 768, 1024 kbps being the most commonly used rates), or a DS1 (1.544 Mbps) physical transmission circuit. This FR access circuit is then connected to a FR network-access port, which is the physical port on a FR switch at the service provider's premises. This FR access circuit is named by the standards as a User-to-Network Interface (UNI). Large sites with multiple devices or large bandwidth requirements in excess of DS1 require multiple FR access circuits. Figure 10.2 illustrates these principles. A CSU/DSU provides channel access. The entire FR access circuit – the interface between the network and the user – is referred to in the standards as the User-to-Network Interface (UNI). FR access port speeds can be DS0, Fractional-T1, or DS1 speeds. Some providers offer higher-speed connections, and DS3 FR access is entirely possible. Note that each user only requires a single FR user-access port to communicate with *many* other FR user-access ports that connect to the FR network. This point will be amplified later.

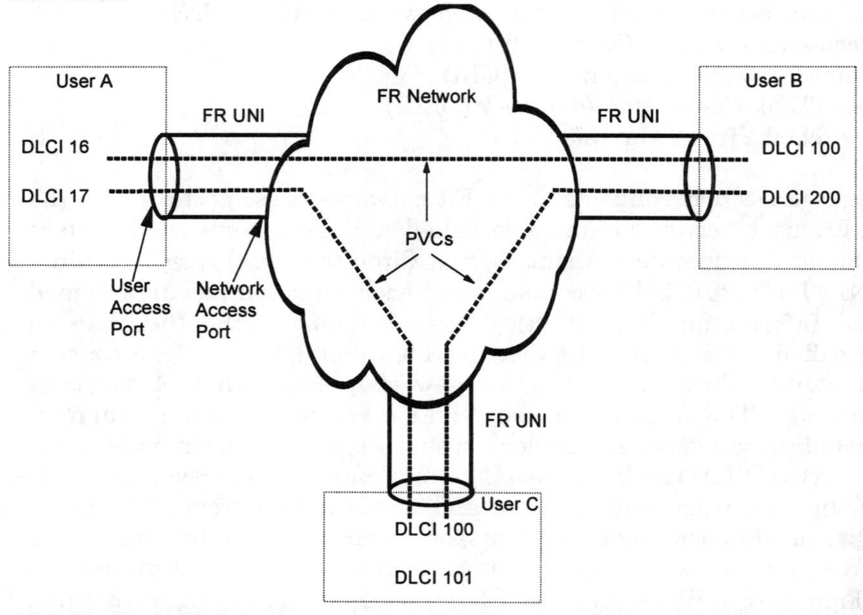

Figure 10.1 Frame Relay UNI and PVCs

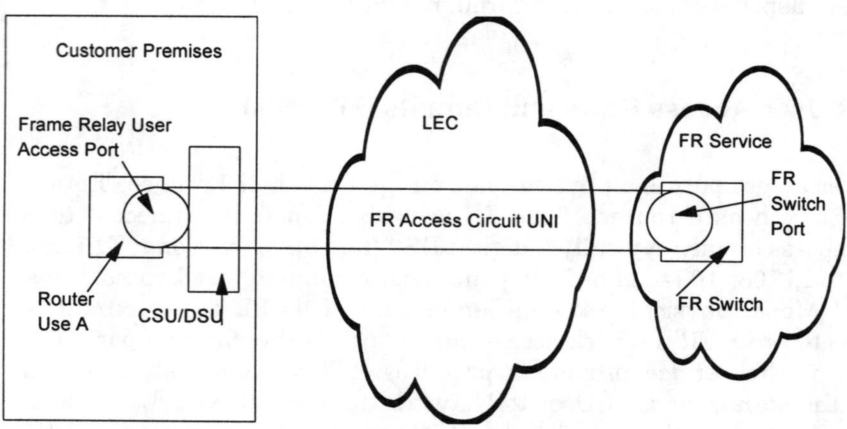

Figure 10.2 Frame Relay Principles

10.2.2 Permanent Virtual Circuit (PVC)

Each FR UNI supports one or more Permanent Virtual Circuits (PVCs). PVCs are virtual circuits, or virtual private lines, provisioned point-to-point from one FR user-access port to another FR user-access port. While each end of the PVC will terminate on a FR switch port, the user sees one end-to-end PVC from user port to user port (as seen in Figure 10.3a). The user devices view a PVC from FR user-access port to user-access port, when in reality they are defined between two FR access ports. Think of a PVC as a static logical path from one user-access port to another [switched virtual circuits (SVCs) add an element of dynamic allocation, as discussed later]. From the user's view, these PVCs travel in a point-to-point virtual line between FR user-access ports 1 and 2. This virtual private line is similar in connection characteristics to a dedicated private line (although its bandwidth allocation, throughput, and traffic transport characteristics may be very different). Any data transmitted over this virtual circuit arrives in the exact sequence as it was sent, and end-to-end security of the circuit is the same. In actuality, these PVCs are switched by FR switches within the FR network, as shown in Figure 10.3b, transparent to the user. PVCs are provisioned and then remain static until changed by the user or provider via administrative changes (as opposed to signaling, which will be discussed with SVCs).

Imagine a single physical FR access circuit (UNI) as the highway, with three PVCs (1, 2, and 3) as the lanes that cars can travel down, as shown in Figure 10.4. Now let's say that the FR UNI is a DS0 (56 kbps) physical circuit. Three PVCs are provisioned within that 56 kbps physical access circuit (UNI), and each is assigned a "rate" of 16 kbps. This "rate" will later be defined as a Committed Information Rate (CIR). The combined *simultaneous* transmission speeds of all three PVCs cannot exceed the physical limitation of 56 kbps, but each PVC will be "guaranteed" at least a 16 kbps minimum throughput. PVCs can be oversubscribed so that the total CIR rate exceeds the physical port speed, and this capability will be discussed later.

Obviously, one of the benefits of frame relay is statistical multiplexing, and we will see later how a user can assign CIR rates to attain high levels of statistical multiplexing. Remember that the total bandwidth available to all PVCs within an access circuit at a specific instant in time is still no greater than the port connection speed of the physical circuit. Your total transmission speed of all PVCs combined cannot exceed the physical transmission speed at any one instant in time! Also note that a PVC does not consume bandwidth when it is not transmitting data. Each FR access circuit can contain up to 1024 PVCs in theory, but service providers and CPE typically support a maximum of one hundred.

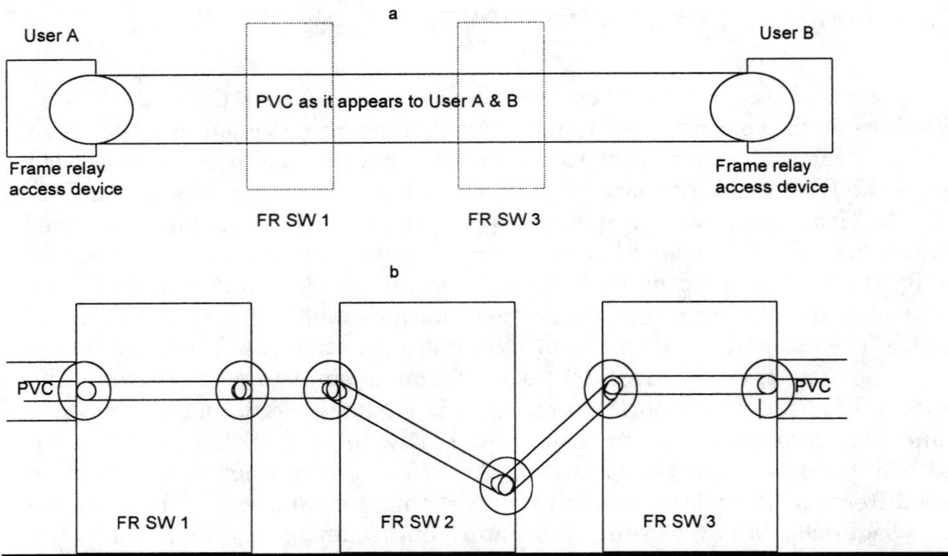

Figure 10.3 Frame Relay Permanent Virtual Circuits (PVCs)

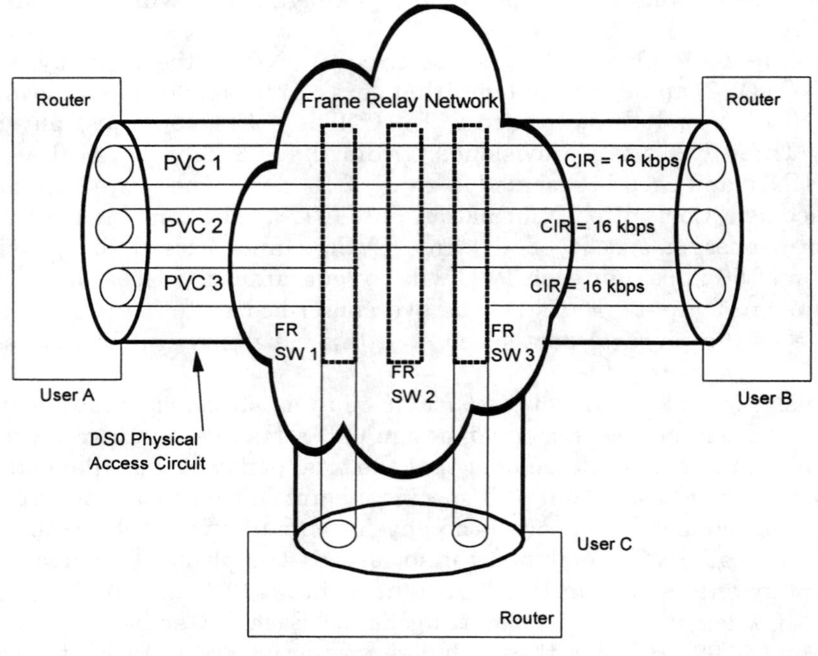

Figure 10.4 Frame Relay PVC Operation Example

10.2.3 Committed Information Rate (CIR)

Many frame relay services define the transmission parameters of each PVC in terms of a Committed Information Rate (CIR). The CIR, in strict terms, is a quality-of-service measurement that provides a "statistically guaranteed" minimum rate of throughput to its PVC at any one period in time. It provides a method for sizing your bandwidth offered to each PVC and comes close to assuring a minimum throughput (and thus end-to-end latency) for protocols and applications. CIR rates are unidirectional, in that each PVC has a CIR rate for *each direction.* This concept is shown in Figure 10.5. Users A and B each has a single FR-access-circuit-to-FR-network switch 1 and 3, respectively. Over these access circuits are provisioned two PVCs between user A router and user B router. PVC 1 is provisioned with the same 16 kbps CIR in both directions. PVC 2 is provisioned with a 4 kbps CIR from user A to user B, and a 16 kbps CIR from user B to user A. Thus, each user is "guaranteed" 16 kbps throughput in both directions on PVC 1, but only 4 kbps minimum throughput from A to B on PVC 2. If the applications on both CPEs burst traffic over these two PVCs simultaneously, the maximum *combined* throughput cannot exceed the 56 kbps physical circuit speed in either direction. More likely, one user (PVC) will statistically be bursting at different instances than the other, and will therefore often receive more than the assigned CIR bandwidth, in fact, possibly close to the entire access circuit bandwidth. From this example you can see that if PVC 1 is the only PVC actively transmitting traffic, it could potentially be transmitting at the full 56 kbps (based on an CIR of 56 kbps), rather than the minimum 16 kbps.

CIRs that are able to assign different rates to each direction of the PVC are called unidirectional or *simplex* CIRs, and will be discussed later. CIRs vary in speed, typically in 56 kbps or 64 kbps increments, but as small as 4 kbps. Also, 0 kbps CIR rates are also available and will be discussed in detail later. CIR rates will eventually be user configurable "on-the-fly", providing the user instant dynamic allocation capability of access bandwidth.

10.2.4 Data Link Connection Identifier (DLCI)

The Data Link Connection Identifier (DLCI) provides each PVC with a unique identifier at both the CPE device and the FR switch. Each end point of a PVC is assigned a DLCI number, similar to assigning an IP address to a physical port, except that IP addresses are recognized globally and the DLCI only has local significance on that specific PVC between the FR port and the CPE port. More will be said on DLCIs later in this chapter.

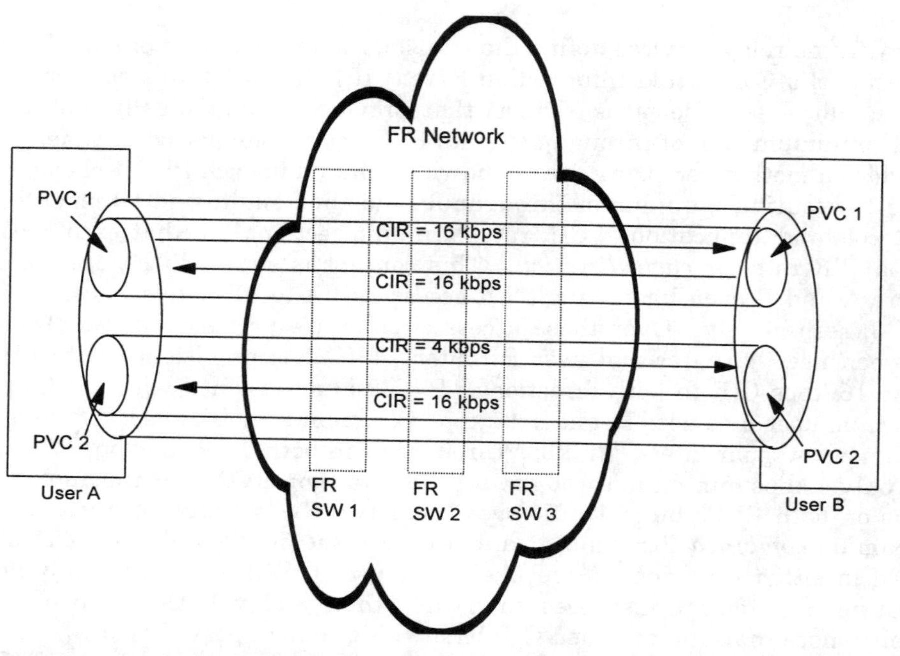

Figure 10.5 Frame Relay PVC CIR Rates

10.2.5 Frame Relay Functions – Putting It All Together

Frame relay provides an upgrade to existing packet switching technology, by supporting speeds up to DS3 (45 Mbps). Frame relay supports PVCs for static user configurations and SVCs for the infrequent user who requires virtual circuits on-demand. Frame relay is a service that delivers frames in order with high probability. Frames with detected errors are simply dropped and, therefore, frame relay can operate effectively only on low-error-rate media such as that used in digital and fiber-optic transmissions.

In its simplest form, frame relay acts as a data link protocol to higher layer protocols, such as TCP/IP. Frame relay does not perform the overhead-intensive functions of error management and flow control that X.25 does, and consequently operates at higher speeds. End systems must implement and be responsible for these error-management and flow-control functions, usually at the transport layer, for example, TCP. With TCP/IP, user files are broken down into IP packets which are sent using a transport-layer (layer 4) window flow-control protocol, i.e., TCP. These IP packets are further broken down into pieces that form the data portion of the FR frame.

These frames are then sent in serial fashion from one end of the PVC to the other, from one DLCI to the other. Frames are received at the destination address where the IP packets are reconstructed into their original form and TCP acknowledges their receipt. Frame relay and its relation to the OSIRM will be covered later.

Frame relay virtual circuits (PVCs and SVCs) may be point-to-point or point-to-multipoint (called multicast) as defined in the network topologies in Chapter 6. Frame relay virtual circuits may be arranged into closed user groups for security purposes.

Now let's look at the many facets of frame relay in more detail.

10.3 THE MANY FACETS OF FRAME RELAY – INTERFACE, SIGNALING PROTOCOL, AND SERVICE

We now look at frame relay as an *interface* or *public frame relay access method,* a *network-signaling protocol*, and a *network-provided service*. These concepts are shown together in Figure 10.6. Here we see the differences of viewing frame relay as an *interface* to a public FR network, as a method of *protocol addressing and signaling* using DLCIs and signaling protocols via the data link layer (frame relay *signaling protocol*), and as a FR *network service*. This figure shows a public frame relay network providing a service to the customer premises equipment through frame relay interfaces.

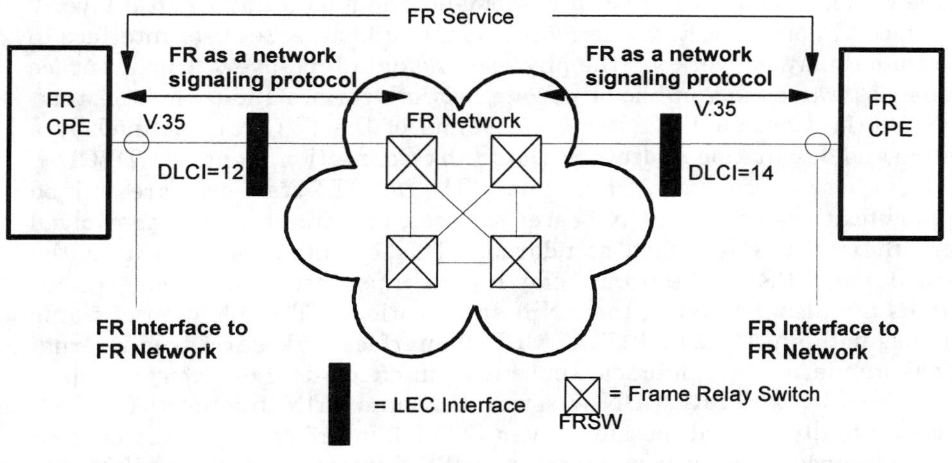

Figure 10.6 Frame Relay Interface/Access, Protocol, and Network Service

As we progress through this chapter frame relay should be approached through these three viewpoints. We will explore the business and technical benefits of each approach. The primary use of frame relay is as an interface to a public data service. The service architecture could be frame relay, IP, or ATM-based. Frame relay standards define three implementations of the technology: that of the *interface* or *public frame relay access method,* as a *network-signaling protocol*, and as a *network-provided service*. It is important to note that while frame relay does provide statistical multiplexing, it is *not* a switching technique. After discussing these viewpoints and the advantages of each, a discussion of the transmission and signaling protocol theory and operation will follow.

10.3.1 Frame Relay Access to a FR Network

Users want one-to-one, one-to-many, many-to-one, or many-to-many connectivity via various types of circuit interfaces. In previous chapters, these circuit interfaces were shown to communicate over either fixed or switched circuits. Frame relay offers the best of both types, with the capability to define fixed-virtual circuits (PVCs) over a switched network service efficiently and quickly via frame transmission techniques. Frame relay service can give the impression that each device on the network is logically connected to every other device. The greater the mesh in the backbone network, the greater this impression.

The first classification of frame relay is as an *interface* or *access method.* For the network designer, frame relay defines both a packet-access technique which provides bandwidth-on-demand and a data link OSIRM layer 2 interface. In one aspect, frame relay refers to a fast-packet user interface to the frame relay network via the physical and data link layer. This interface transmits frames to a public or private network service and on to a destination interface over a PVC. The end points of the PVCs are defined by a source and destination address or Data Link Connection Identifier (DLCI).

As discussed previously, frame relay ITU-T/CCITT standards are defined as modifications of the ISDN bearer services, and frame relay has evolved from these ISDN interface standards. This evolution is evident in the comparison of PRI to the frame relay layer 1 interface. Frame relay specifications are also defined in the ANSI specifications. The adoption of frame relay as both an ANSI and ITU-T/CCITT interface makes it a true international standard. In a practical sense it is, in effect, *only an interface*, operating over BRI and PRI ISDN, V-series, DDS and DDN, fractional T1, X.21, and eventually T3 and, possibly, even SONET interfaces, with the current preponderance of services using the non-ISDN interfaces (such as V.35 into digital transmission facilities).

The standard frame relay access configuration to a public service is shown in Figure 10.7. Using a typical LAN-attached workstation, the LAN in turn interfaces to the WAN-attached router. This router talks to the CSU/DSU via a V.35 interface. The router in turn interfaces via a local loop through the Local Exchange Carrier (LEC) serving as Point-of-Presence (PoP) to the frame relay switch in the FR provider's PoP. The frame relay switch can either be at the LEC PoP, IXC PoP, or service provider location. The local loop is typically DS0, fractional T1, or T1.

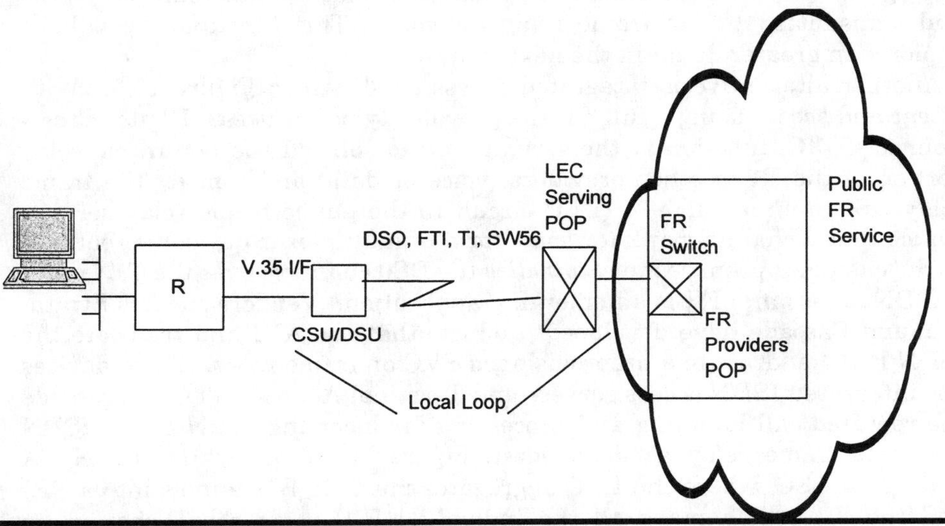

Figure 10.7 FR Public Service Access Connectivity

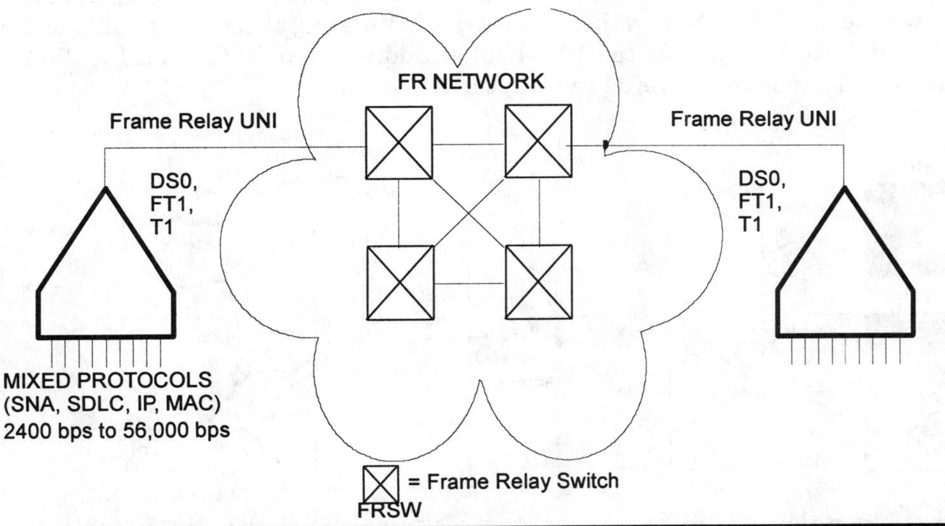

Figure 10.8 Frame Relay Access Device (FRAD) Example

Many users want to connect older, legacy protocols and applications to frame relay. These protocols must somehow be encapsulated into the frame relay protocol to be transported. Figure 10.8 shows one type of equipment used to accomplish this task – the Frame Relay Access Device or Assembler/Disassembler (FRAD). Each FRAD is used to combine mixed subrate protocols ranging in this example from 2400 bps to 56,000 bps, which are aggregated into a single frame relay access circuit (within multiple PVCs) and transmitted to the frame relay network. This functionality will be explored in greater detail in the next chapter.

Another alternative is integrated access as shown in Figure 10.9. With integrated access using a full T1, the provider typically uses a Digital Cross-Connect (DXC) function at the serving PoP to split off the non-frame relay portion of the T1 to other providers (voice or data) and connect the frame relay DS0 or Fractional-T1 (FT1) circuit to the public frame relay service. Notice that a channel bank (or some form of multiplexer device) is required at the customer premises to *channelize* the DS0 channels over the T1.

ISDN access into FR is an emerging application. Vendors such as Stratacom and Cascade have developed products that use ANI and translate the ISDN E.164 address to a preprovisioned PVC on frame relay. These devices use integrated ISDN access servers and Terminal Adapters (TAs) to provide the required call handling and processing for incoming ISDN calls. ISDN access to frame relay as depicted in Figure 10.10a shows an ISDN TA dialing an LEC, where the LEC aggregates multiple B channels into a PRI and the FR switch maps all the individual E.164s on the D-channel to DLCIs on individual PVCs. All address signaling information is carried on the D channels, and all "data" is carried on the B-channels. Figure 10.10b shows the same ISDN Terminal Adapter (TA) dialing through an LEC to a FR switch that translates the E.164 caller address to a DLCI on a FR PVC. An ISDN primer was covered in Chapter 7.

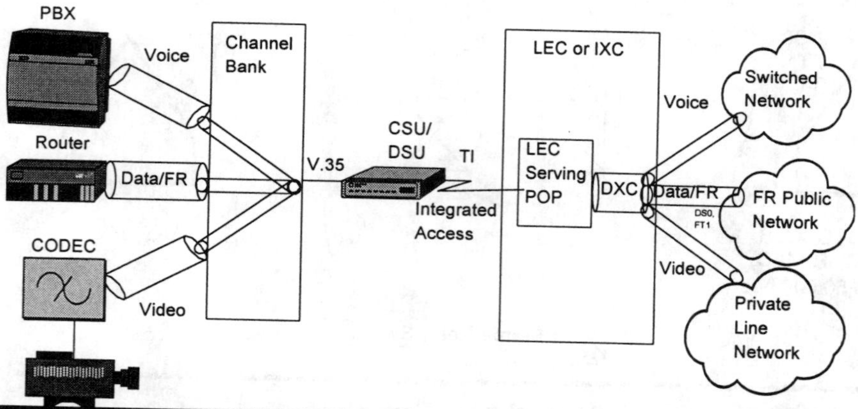

Figure 10.9 FR Integrated Access

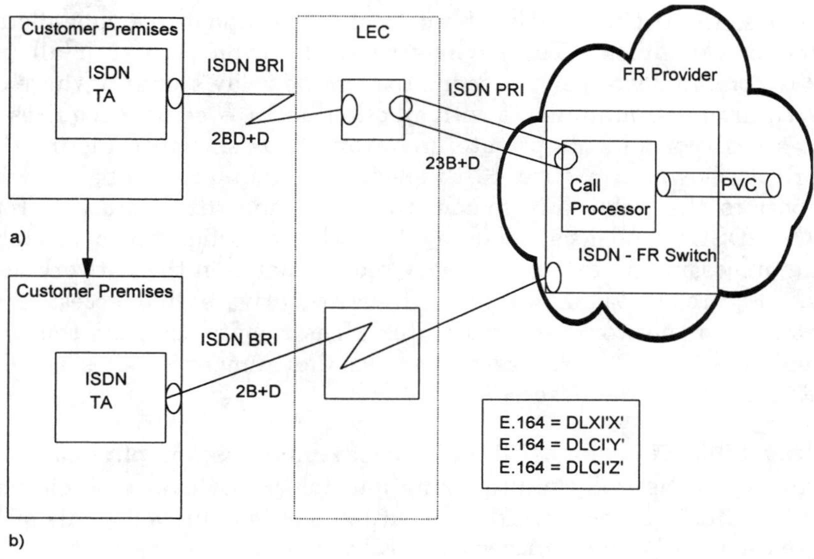

Figure 10.10 ISDN Access to FR Switch

Frame relay access provides a cost-effective solution for the transport of bursty data, such as LAN traffic. FR's statistical multiplexing capability makes it an ideal choice for aggregation of multiple private lines up to T1 speeds. Multiple logical circuits are combined within a single physical circuit, thus better utilizing network bandwidth while lowering both CPE hardware and network service access costs.

Frame relay as a network access offers the following benefits:

⇒ Equipment and local loop savings
⇒ Maximizes link efficiency
⇒ True international standard

Equipment and Local Loop Savings. By allowing multiple users access to a single shared physical access circuit, tremendous savings in network interface equipment, local loops, and (potentially) long distance IXC bandwidth costs can be achieved. Take, for example, the network shown in Figure 10.11. In Figure 10.11a, the Headquarters (HQ) site currently communicates with each of sites A, B, C, and D over dedicated private lines. Each private line has an average utilization of 25 percent. With this private line solution, the HQ site requires four 56 kbps network access ports, four local loops, and four long-distance IXC circuits. Using the frame relay network scenario shown in Figure 10.11b, the HQ site would provision only a single 56 kbps FR physical access port and provision a logical 16 kbps PVC to users A, B, C, and D. Thus, the HQ site would save the cost of three router ports, three CSU/DSUs, three local loops, and three long-distance dedicated private lines. The savings would be even greater if all users wanted to communicate peer-to-peer. In a frame relay scenario where each user is required to communicate with all other users, *each* user requires four 56 kbps access ports in the private line example as shown in Figure 10.12. With FR as shown in Figure 10.13, each user requires a single 56 kbps access port to the public FR switch, thus reducing the number of router ports, CSU/DSUs, and local loops by 15! This also has the byproduct of reducing processing power and memory requirements in the network access devices. Figure 10.14 shows the FR versus private line access circuit requirements for networks up to 10 sites. It is easy to see from this graph the advantages of FR port aggregation as the number of sites requiring meshed connectivity increases.

Maximizes Link Efficiency. FR makes maximum use of physical circuit bandwidth by statistically multiplexing multiple PVCs over a single physical circuit. Thus, link bandwidth total utilization is improved. This quality can drive the price/performance ratio of FR very low.

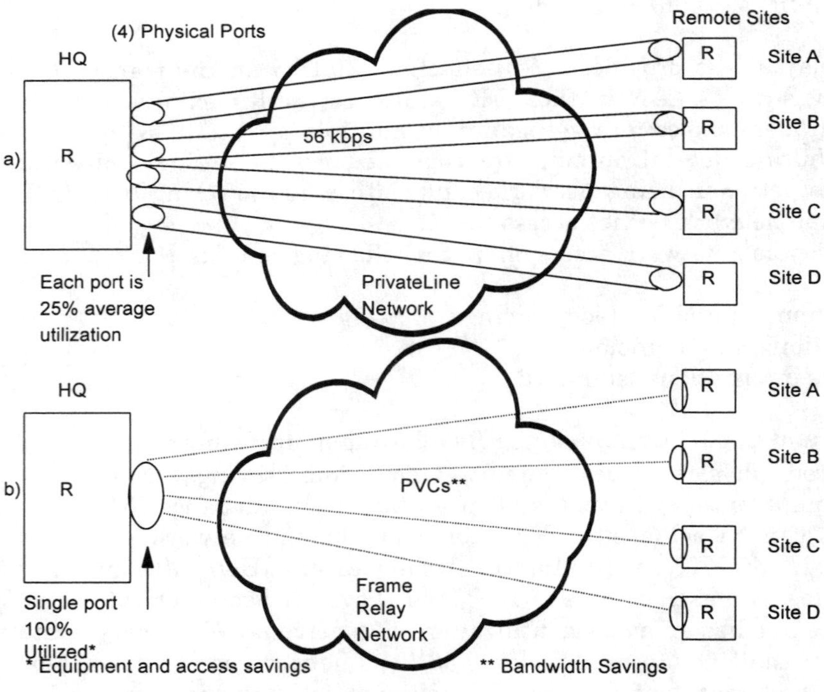

Figure 10.11 Frame Relay Equipment and Bandwidth Savings

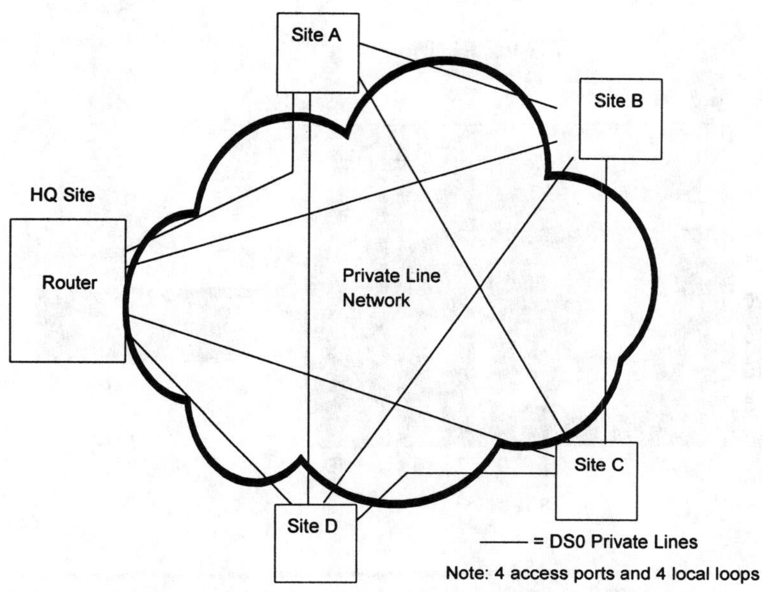

Figure 10.12 Frame Relay Equipment and Bandwidth Savings with Peer-to-Peer Communications – Private Line Example

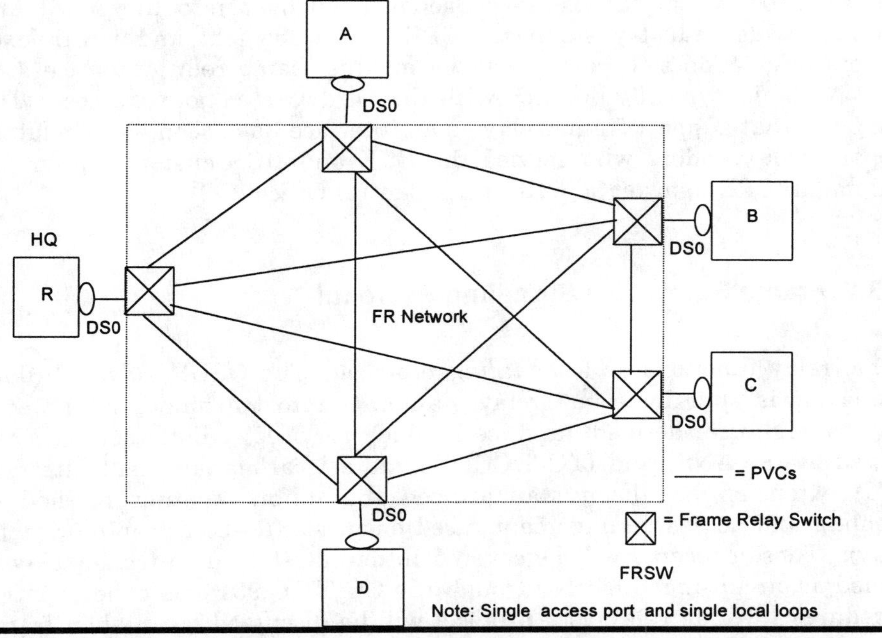

Figure 10.13 Frame Relay Equipment and Bandwidth Savings with Peer-to-Peer Communications – FR Example

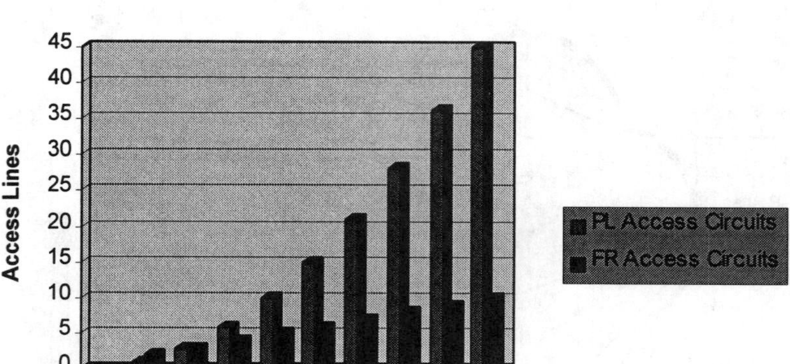

Figure 10.14 Frame Relay vs. Private Line Meshing Efficiencies

True International Standard. FR standards were originally developed by the ITU-T (CCITT) and defined as an international network interface standard. These standards have been carried over into the ANSI and maintain wide industry support. CPE router, switch, and multiplexer vendors have endorsed frame relay by making frame relay interface software available, typically bundled with the hardware at no extra cost. The standards that support frame relay as an interface have seen wide industry support from vendors who service the DTE and DCE customer premises equipment (CPE) market as well as the Central Office (CO).

10.3.2 Frame Relay as a Signaling Protocol

Frame relay functions as a *signaling protocol.* The OSIRM layer 2 (data link layer) is split by frame relay standards into two major areas: core services and user-defined (and selectable) services. Both services are defined by the ANSI and ITU-T/CCITT, and a local management interface (LMI) extension has been standardized that offers another method of signaling and access management (used on most FR access configurations today). These concepts will be covered in detail later when frame relay is defined as circuit-mode ISDN through the CCITT Q.931 connection control procedures. Frame relay as a protocol will be discussed later when frame relay protocols are compared to the OSIRM.

An important point to note is that transport of the frame relay protocol is transparent to higher layer protocols, only in the aspect that the higher level protocols are not viewed or modified from ingress to egress. This is not to say that frame relay transport does not *affect* higher-level protocols, as we will see in the next chapter on performance issues.

The many benefits of using frame relay as a signaling protocol are

- ⇒ In-band CPE management
- ⇒ In-band link management
- ⇒ Transparent to higher layer protocols
- ⇒ Improved performance over packet switching
- ⇒ Protocol flexibility
- ⇒ Flexibility of bandwidth allocation

In-Band CPE Management. A single PVC can be provisioned as a virtual management channel within the physical user-access circuit. In this manner frame relay providers can manage each user site "in-band" through IP or SNMP (or a proprietary solution using the FR PVC), without requiring a separate out-of-band management circuit. This could significantly reduce cost for frame relay access from remote locations or where the number of network nodes is less than 10.

In-band Link Management. The PVC provisioned as a virtual management channel within the physical user-access circuit can also be used to monitor circuit health "in-band". In-band management types include LMI, Annex D, and Annex A.

Transparent to Higher Layer Protocols. Many applications can be transported over FR due to its transparency to higher layer protocols. Again, this does *not* mean that variations in frame relay transport cannot affect higher layer protocols.

Improved Performance. FR offers increased performance over older packet technologies (e.g., X.25 packet switching) by eliminating error detection and correction and packet retransmission overhead not needed with fiber-optic transmission facilities and by relying on higher layer protocols to retransmit lost data. This protocol reduction in overhead is gained at the expense of discarding incorrect or excess data. Actual overhead of FR frames can range from 8 percent on small frames to less than 1 percent on large frames!

Protocol Flexibility. FR supports a wide variety of applications transport and meets the throughput requirements of both advanced and legacy computing applications and platforms. Transport frame sizes can vary, with standards-specified minimums and maximums dependent upon FR service provider switching equipment and CPE.

Flexibility of Bandwidth Allocation. PVCs can be changed and provisioned much quicker than physical private lines. PVC CIR rates can be allocated for maximum use of the existing bandwidth and optimal performance.

A few of these advantages can also become disadvantages. Incorrect design of a frame relay network PVC and CIR structure can cause many problems. Discarded frames during congestion and lack of error correction can cause many user data retransmissions; and this can be compounded by data fragmentation due to encapsulation. Bottom line, a dedicated private line or dial access may still be the best solution. Design issues such as these will be covered in the next chapter. Now we will look at frame relay as a service.

10.3.3 Frame Relay as a Network Service

Frame relay has become, in a very short time, one of the primary LEC and IXC data service offerings. FR continues to provide a good interim solution and feeder technology to broadband data technologies such as ATM. Users are demanding higher-speed and higher-performance switched data services to interconnect LANs and WANs. Client-server computing and distributed processing continue to proliferate, and applications are becoming more bandwidth intensive. Network-attached devices are becoming more intelligent, offering to offload much of the network intelligence as well as handle the higher-level protocol functions with their increased processor and memory capabilities.

Frame relay service offers significant improvements to throughput and delay over the use of traditional X.25 service. It also provides dynamic bandwidth allocation (bandwidth-on-demand), which cannot be achieved through private-line or circuit-switched networks. Frame relay service does not provide the error correction or flow control attainable in X.25. The standards do offer some congestion notification (FECN and BECN), but a frame relay service relies on the user applications to interpret congestion and to provide congestion control and recovery. It also relies on higher-level user protocols, such as TCP/IP, to provide the retransmission and guarantee delivery rather than duplicating flow control at the network layer. Frame relay service does provide the concentration and statistical multiplexing of X.25 packet switching, while providing the short delay and high-speed switching of TDM multiplexers. Permanent Virtual Circuits (PVCs) and Switched Virtual Circuits (SVCs) are established from one-to-one or many-to-one (multicast) end points, with a dynamic route through the "cloud". Frame relay service becomes a major player in WAN-switched networks where it provides a cost-effective virtual private network to a plethora of LAN users.

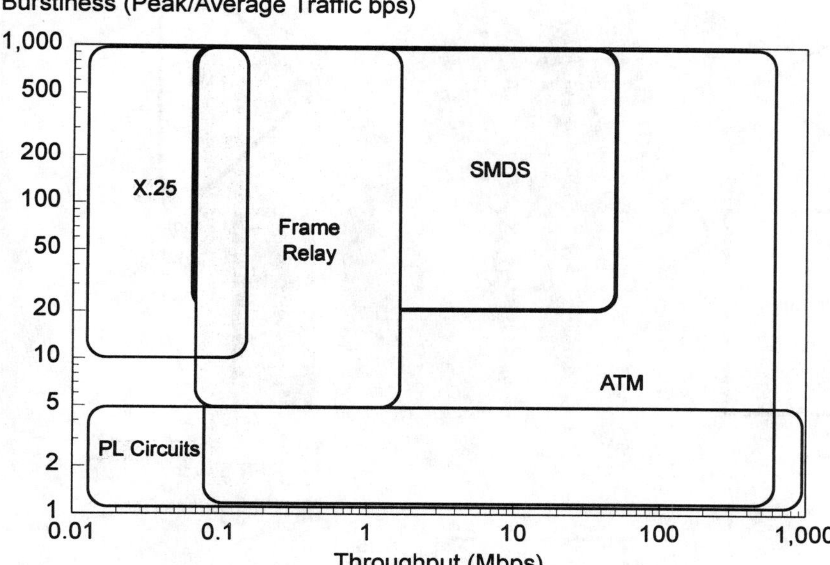

Figure 10.15 Frame Relay Compared to Competing Services

While frame relay service provides many of these improvements, it relies on a virtually error-free digital transmission facility. This reliance on digital (and better yet fiber-optic) transmission media is a major consideration in frame relay network design, and a major contributing factor to the popularity of frame relay services, as many of the providers today have large SONET-based fiber-optic infrastructures underlying the FR network.

The FR service market has become a multibillion-dollar market, and shows no sign of yielding soon to other broadband services such as SMDS or ATM. Figure 10.15 shows competing services, but with frame relay providing cost-effective DS0 to T1 access for very bursty (high ratio of peak to average traffic patterns) types of traffic. Also, notice that frame relay can potentially increase to DS3 speeds, and SMDS (DXI) and ATM (FUNI) to lower access speeds. The proliferation of frame relay in comparison to SMDS and ATM cell-switching service has been nothing short of phenomenal. Frame relay growth rates continue to double yearly. Frame relay is best suited for LAN interconnection service because of its high speeds and low delay over physical lines sharing multiple virtual circuits. Frame relay bridges the gap between connection-oriented and connectionless protocols. In sum, frame relay is a high-bandwidth, cost-effective, bandwidth-on-demand transport solution available now.

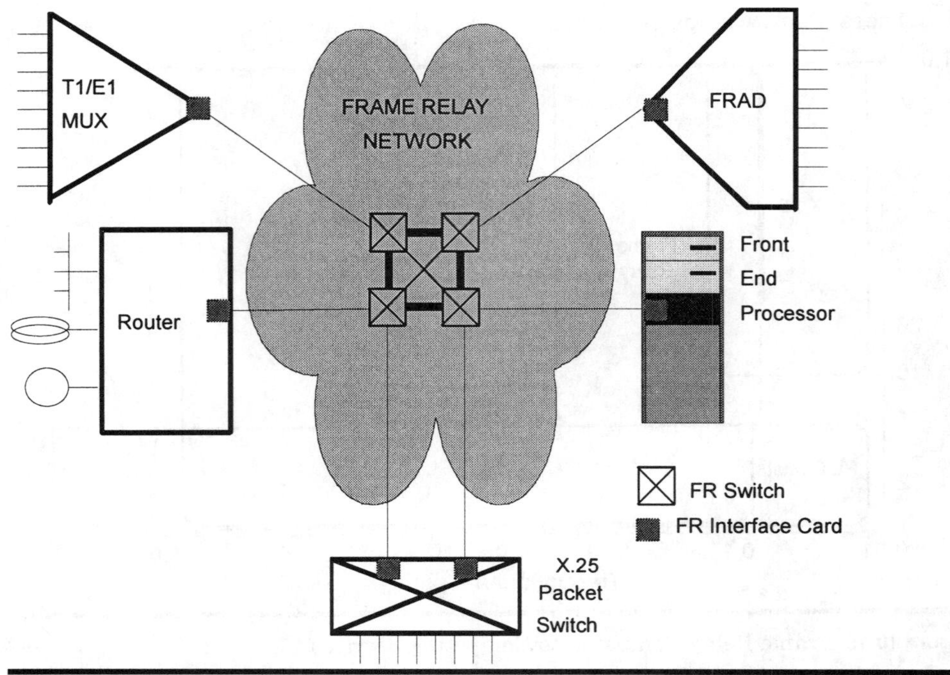

Figure 10.16 Frame Relay Network Access Elements

A typical frame relay public data transport network will support a variety of user access devices, including T1/E1 multiplexer, bridge, router, gateway, front-end processor, an X.25 packet switch, and a Frame Relay Access Device or Assembler/Disassembler (FRAD) as illustrated in Figure 10.16. Each of these devices must have the capability to convert or encapsulate their native protocols into frame relay, as shown by the FR interface card. These devices have traditionally operated independently and have rarely interfaced through a common transport media, other than perhaps a digital data network made up of dedicated point-to-point circuits. A frame relay service network provides a common integrated transport platform and network access protocol.

A frame relay private or public data service is composed of signaling and access protocols. In its purest form, frame relay service is a layer 2 data transmission system with rudimentary congestion control and quality-of-service features. Frame relay is a connection-oriented service in that it has predefined static PVCs.

Frame relay as a network service offers the following benefits:

⇒ Circuit savings
⇒ Higher circuit availability
⇒ Higher network availability
⇒ Prevention from technology discontinuity

⇒ Latency Increases or Reductions
⇒ Dynamic circuit and network architecture
⇒ Lower WAN costs through meshing capability
⇒ Fills the need for high-speed LAN-to-LAN connectivity
⇒ One network - multiple protocols
⇒ Managed service and guarantee of availability

Circuit Savings. Using our last example, FR can save money when existing dedicated (private line) network connectivity spans LATAs, states, and countries. Most frame relay public pricing rates and tariffs are non-mileage-sensitive. Private line IXC rates are mileage sensitive. Taking the last example and extending the private line across LATA, state, and national boundaries, one can quickly see how a non-mileage-sensitive frame relay network rate structure could be advantageous, especially over long distances. Cost savings using FR in a meshed environment can be significant.

Higher Circuit Availability. Frame relay utilizes all available bandwidth with multiple virtual sessions over a single physical access. Frame relay service is provisioned over, and takes advantage of, digital or fiber-optic, virtually error-free transmission facilities. FR also provides a self-healing network architecture, where PVC paths are automatically switched around failures within the FR network "cloud".

Higher Network Availability. Private line networks are subject to failures. Outages which can extend to hours and even days are a fact of life. The longer the circuit distance between two locations, the greater the probability of an outage, fiber cut, or some type of disruption affecting that circuit. Frame relay minimizes or eliminates the WAN point-to-point bottleneck. Most vendors provide the feature of automatic rerouting of PVCs around circuit failures. Figure 10.17 demonstrates this concept. In the private line network shown in Figure 10.17a, if the circuit is cut between the HQ site and user B, the two locations cannot communicate and user B is isolated. In the frame relay network shown in Figure 10.17b, since each user has a single physical access to a frame relay switch and the frame relay switches have PVCs back to the HQ site, when the physical (or logical) circuit is cut between the HQ site and user B, the frame relay switches automatically reroute around the failure either over path 1, 3, or 4. These switches will gracefully reroute back to the original path when it becomes available. This capability gives frame relay a much higher inherent availability than private lines using digital transmission, although many private-line vendors are offering SONET-based service that automatically routes around failures (but still cause an interruption of service).

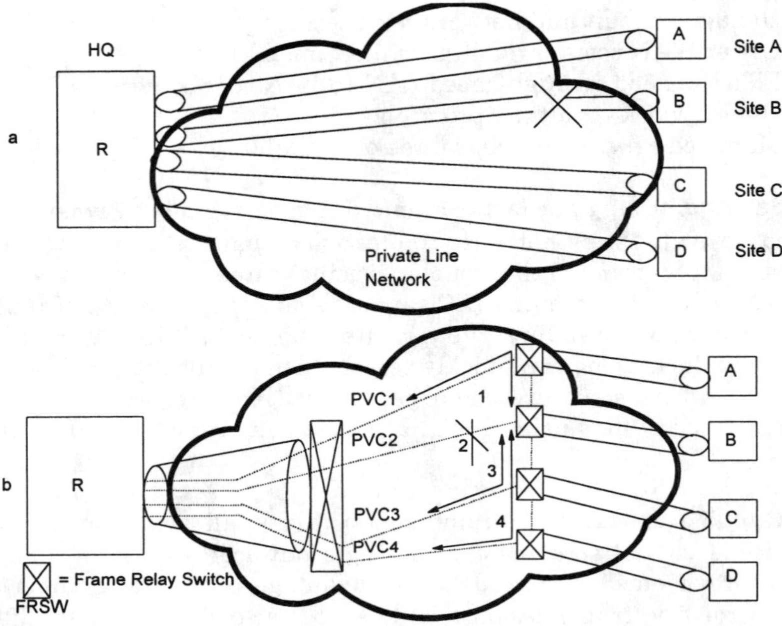

Figure 10.17 Automatic Reroute of PVCs around Failures

Prevention from Technology Discontinuity. When purchasing frame relay service from a provider, you take out an insurance policy against technological discontinuity. Frame relay is backwards compatible with older technologies, and can be a service and protocol offering over an ATM-technology-based architecture. In fact, FR can either be transported over ATM or interwork (FR to ATM and vice versa) with ATM. Frame relay fills the gap between X.25 and broadband services, and has become the next logical step in the broadband services revolution and evolution. Why purchase switches and build a FR network, when you can let the frame relay provider take on the burden of updating its public network with the most current technology? International frame relay service is also available.

Latency Increases or Reductions. Frame relay service offers high speed with low delay compared to X.25. Make no mistake, frame relay does have an inherently higher end-to-end latency (delay) than private line in most cases. This is due to the increased buffering delay of the frame relay switches and the requirement of some FR switches to read in the entire frame before transmitting it on to the next switch (called serialization delay). Thus, on an equidistant point-to-point private line compared to a point-to-point frame relay PVC of equal bandwidth, the frame relay circuit will almost always have longer delay. This increase in delay can range from milliseconds to seconds. The good news is that meshing PVCs may actually decrease latency between two sites, if the previous connectivity was through a longer private line. This concept will be discussed in more detail in the design section of Chapter 11.

Dynamic Circuit and Network Architecture. Once a user has established a port to the frame relay network, it is easy to provision additional PVCs to new remote sites without requiring a new dedicated circuit from every existing site requiring connectivity to every new site on the network. Frame relay, in this context, provides a sort-of bandwidth-on-demand. This concept is illustrated in Figure 10.18, where the addition of a new PVC 5 between users C and D does not require any additional ports or circuits, and can be provisioned typically in a few days.

Lower WAN Costs and Meshing Capability. Frame relay in its truest sense is a private network transport technology that has been adapted to public network service. It offers a statistically multiplexed function through its use of virtual circuits. It is this virtual circuit-meshing capability that allows the many-to-many communications paths required for true meshed service. Frame relay combines private line characteristics with the benefits of a public network service, with transport speeds up to DS1 (DS3 soon available). The number of circuits required to support a fully meshed multiplexer network in comparison to the number of circuits needed for a frame relay network is:

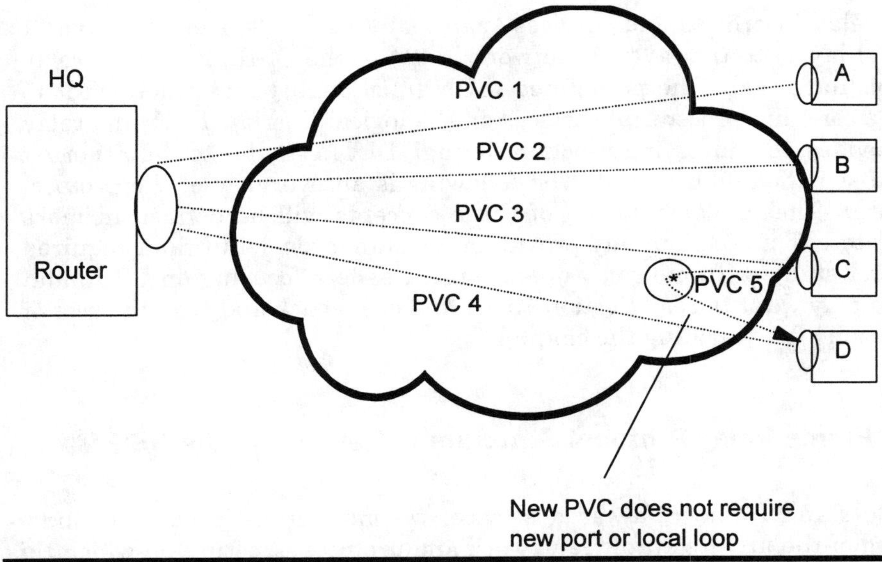

Figure 10.18 Ease of FR Provisioning

$$\text{Fully meshed network} = \frac{(n)(n-1)}{2}$$

Fills the Need for High-Speed LAN-to-LAN Connectivity. Frame relay networks transport traffic ranging from bursty LAN-to-LAN transmitting large file transfers to low volume terminal traffic. Frame relay service offers improved productivity and response to changes in the business traffic patterns and applications.

One Network – Multiple Protocols. FR offers the capability to place multiple protocols, such as TCP/IP, SNA, NETBIOS, and IPX, over a single network-transport protocol.

Managed Service and Guarantee of Availability. Many providers of FR service offer complete managed offerings. This includes everything from reactive management to proactive management down to the router level on the premises. Some companies, such as NetSolve, offer management inclusive of the router and LAN ports with an availability guarantee.

10.4 TRANSMISSION AND SIGNALING PROTOCOL STRUCTURE

Frame relay interfaces and services span many protocols, from the layer 1 (physical layer) to the layer 3 (network layer) of the OSIRM. Frame relay protocols have taken the predefined ISDN functionality and redefined it to split the core and procedural services on the logical link layer. Frame relay also provides an addressing function through DLCIs similar to the Ethernet and cell-switched addressing. The following is an overview of the protocol structure. The implementation of these concepts will be defined in more detail later. This section may provide more standards detail than required for a first study of frame relay operations. Readers focusing on FR fundamentals may want to read Section 10.4.1 and come back and read the rest of this section after finishing the chapter.

10.4.1 Frame Relay Protocol Structure in Relation to the OSIRM

To understand frame relay as a service, we must first develop an understanding of the architectural framework and protocol structure on which this service is offered. An explanation of frame relay standards developed under the OSIRM gets us started. Figure 10.19 shows the OSIRM layers and protocol structure of frame relay transport. Frame relay transport comprises only the first two layers of the OSI model, the physical and data link layers. Frame relay operates on the principle of logical end-to-end links. Thus, its primary protocol functions operate at the logical link sublayer of the OSIRM Link Layer 2. The end-to-end protocol operations of all layers above the physical and data link are "transparent" to the frame relay network. The physical layer interface can range from a DS0, through fractional T1 (FT1) and, finally, up to and including a full T1 (with future specifications for DS3 speeds being defined). Signaling is similar to standard synchronous channel connections. Layer 2 utilizes the ITU-T/CCITT link access procedure (LAP-D) data link layer protocol. Layers 3 and 4 are typically controlled within the network-access device. This forces higher layer protocols (such as TCP) to perform the error correction, addressing, and sequencing. Most frame transmissions are sent in unacknowledged mode, but acknowledged mode is available. These will be discussed later.

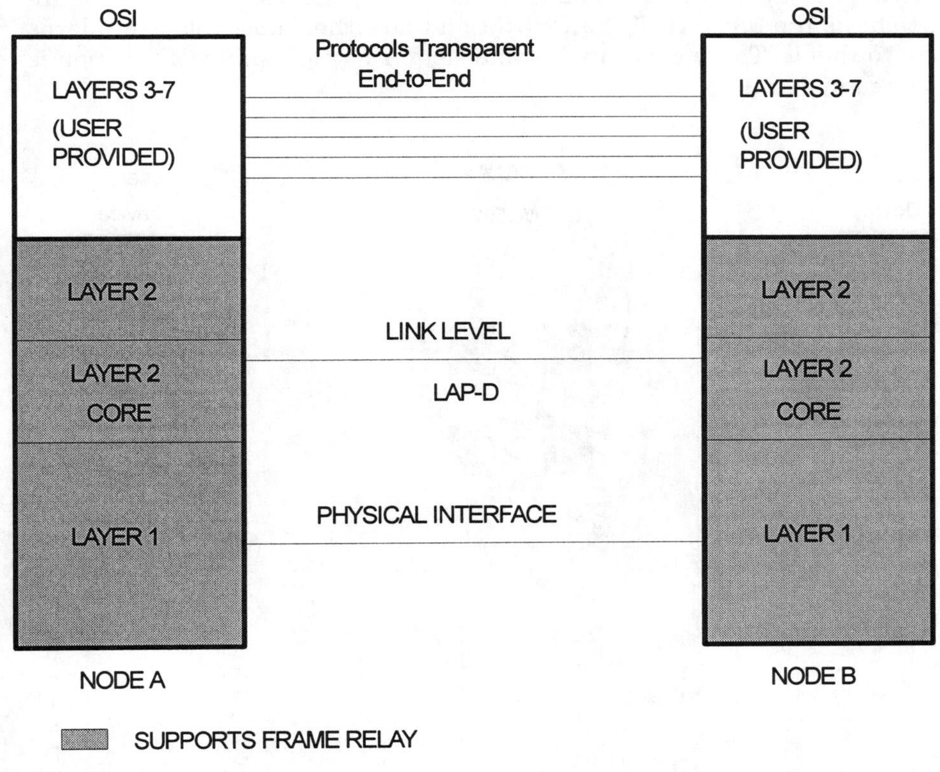

Figure 10.19 Frame Relay and the OSIRM

Frames are transmitted between nodes at the OSI layer 2 data link layer. These frames contain addressing, error detection, and control for the frames themselves, but not the data contained within. As discussed previously, frame relay does check for frame validity with the Frame Check Sequence (FCS), and frames are discarded if in error. FR nodes establish permanent virtual circuits (PVCs) and route the data through this point-to-point serial connection. Frames are routed by destination addresses (DLCI). No retransmissions are requested at this layer. Figure 10.20 shows an example of an end-to-end frame relay network, illustrating the OSIRM layers used at each point of transport across the WAN. Notice that the FR switches operate at layer 2, while the transport of data across the UNI operates at layer 1.

Core functions of OSIRM layer 2 include frame error checking through the FCS. User physical connectivity and frame relay transport services are provided through the physical and data link levels, while the network services touch upon the data link layer to provide the user services. Figure 10.21 shows the 3 layers of the OSIRM and how the frame relay standards relate to them. These concepts become clearer as each protocol function is explained in detail.

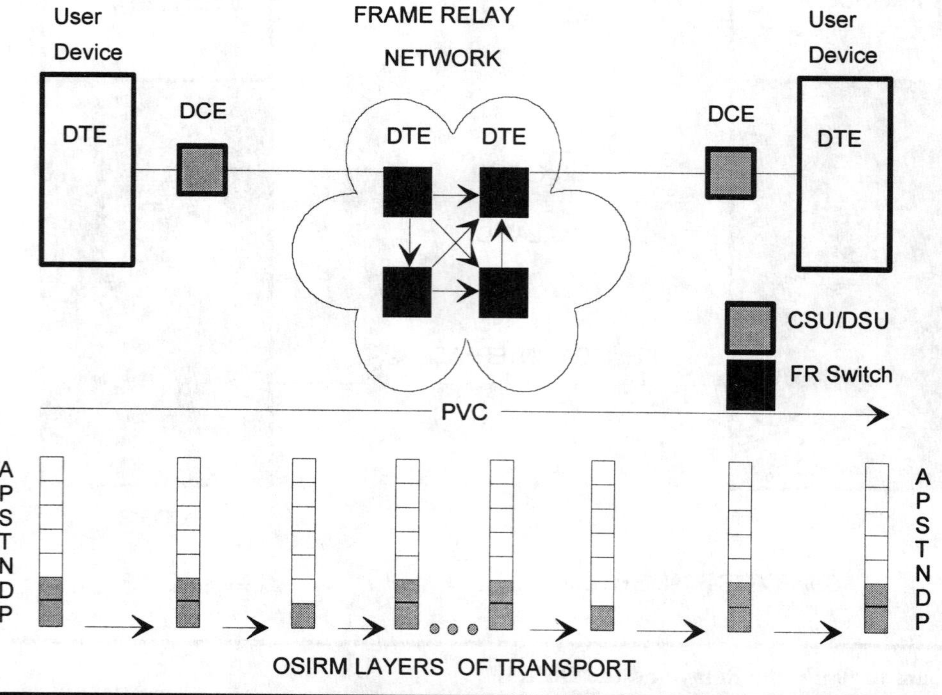

Figure 10.20 End-to-End Frame Relay Network

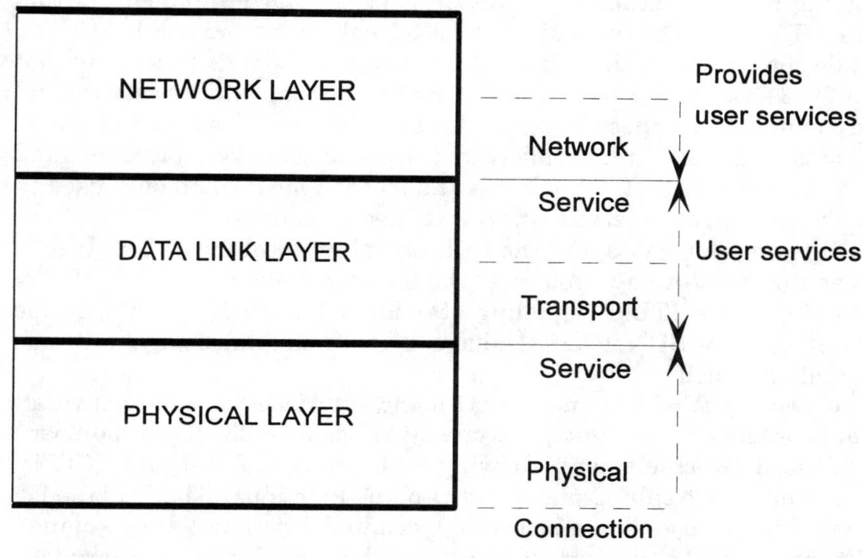

Figure 10.21 OSIRM Interfaces to Frame Relay

10.4.2 Layer 2 Protocol Structure Details

Frame relay service, as it relates to ISDN packet-mode bearer service, is concerned with two logically separate levels of the data link layer, defined as the control plane (C-plane) and the user plane (U-plane). Each provides different services, and each will be discussed in the context of how they relate to the protocol structure. The concept of control and user planes has been defined as a fundamental practice for ISDN protocols. The frame relay version of the ISDN standards has attempted to establish one set of protocols for all C-plane frame relay services, and separates the U-plane from the C-plane to allow user customization of frame relay services. These concepts have been carried through to non-ISDN implementations. Further in-depth study of the original intent of the ISDN control plane standards than that presented here is left to the reader.

Figure 10.22 illustrates the structure of the protocols that support frame relay in relation to the protocol planes and standards. The user plane of frame relay implements a subset of the OSIRM data link layer functions as specified in ITU-T Recommendation Q.922. The U-plane provides the data transport of the user data via the physical access line and through logical links.

Frame relay also has a control plane which is involved with reporting on the status of PVCs, or the establishment of SVCs. The C-plane can perform frame relaying by two methods: Virtual Calls (VCs) and Permanent Virtual Connections (PVCs). The virtual connection calls are defined by CCITT Recommendation Q.922 at the data link control layer (layer 2) and Recommendation Q.931 at the network layer (layer 3). Virtual calls are set up and released dynamically by these two standards. The second method of frame relaying is through PVCs administrated by the network provider and established at subscription time. This is the method most commonly used in today's public frame relay service offerings. Recommendation Q.933 defines the status signaling for PVCs and the call control protocol for SVCs. It may operate over the frame relay protocols (Q.922), or be signaled via the ISDN protocol (Q.921). The ITU-T signaling standards for ISDN (Q.931), frame relay (Q.933), and B-ISDN (Q.2931) have a common philosophy, message structure, and approach.

There are two types of C-plane and U-plane interfaces: user-to-network and network-to-network element connectivity. Figure 10.23 shows the user interface to the network element, showing each relevant ANSI and CCITT standard, as well as the split C-plane and U-plane functions. The U-plane is split into core functions and user-selectable terminal functions. The C-plane is also split into layer 2 and layer 3 services, or the procedures necessary for signaling. In addition, Figure 10.24 shows the network-to-network element interfaces.

Core services and procedural services have been separated in the next two sections. This separation roughly corresponds to the U-plane and C-plane distinction, respectively. These services will be defined as they appear in the CCITT and ANSI standards.

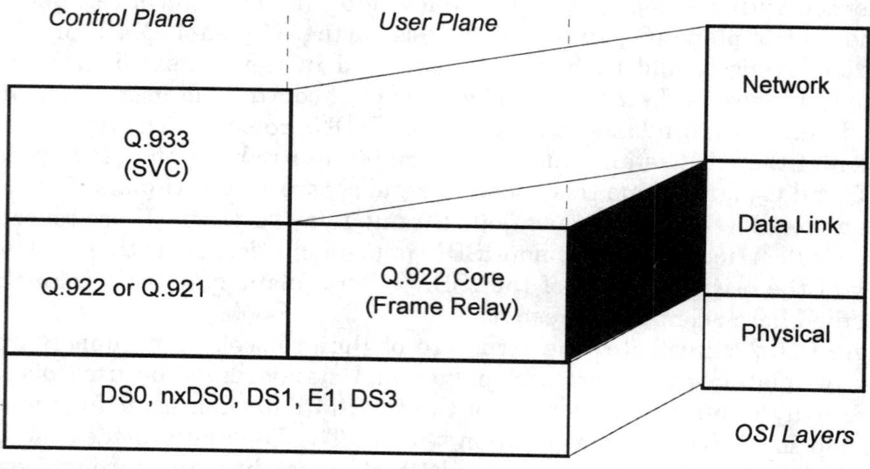

Figure 10.22 Frame Relay Protocol Structure

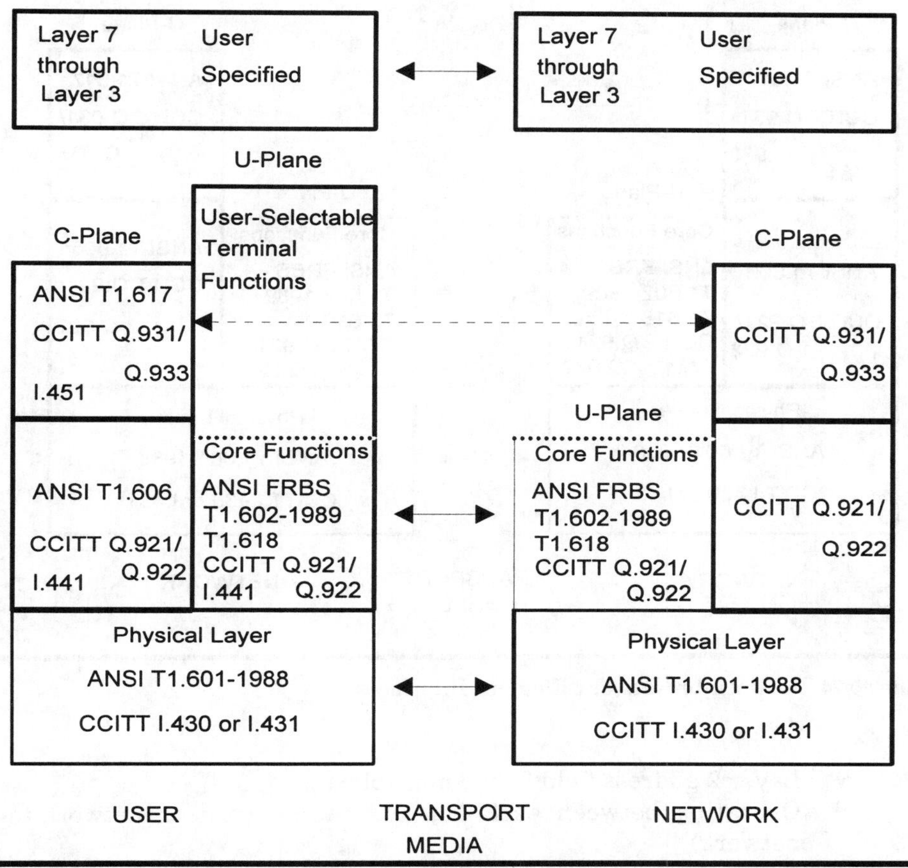

Figure 10.23 User-to-Network Element Interfaces

10.4.3 Core Services

The core functions, defined by ANSI T1.602-1989 and ITU-T/CCITT Recommendation Q.921 with the user-selectable terminal functions, make up the core services. The core services roughly correspond to the U-plane functionality, which defines user-selectable frame-relaying services. Together they span the data link layer of the OSIRM, and define the user's interface to the frame relay network. Some of the services provided by the U-plane are as follows:

- Error detection
- Congestion management
- Bit-level transparency
- Frame delimiting

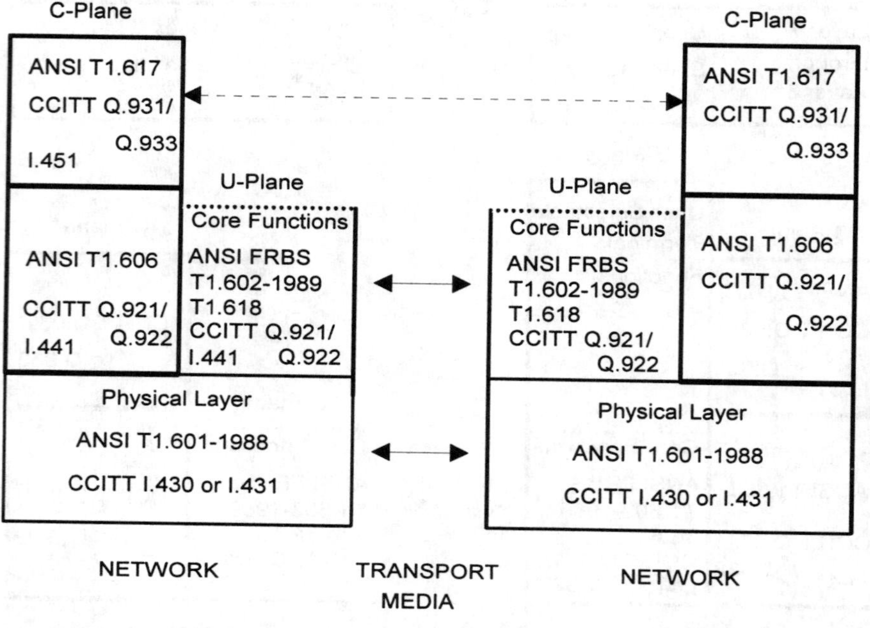

Figure 10.24 Network-to-Network Element Interfaces

- Layer 2 address field frame multiplexing
- Operating between each hop (user-to-network or network-to-network)

Figure 10.25 depicts the end-to-end transport via the U-plane. Notice that, again, all protocols above level 2 are transparent to the frame transport. These core services are discussed later in the next section on transmission theory.

10.4.4 Procedural Sublayer Services

The procedural sublayer defines procedures for data transport from the user device to the network and between network devices. It is different from core services in that it operates with the entire network in mind, providing end-to-end connectivity across the network, and bridging the OSIRM layers 2 and 3. This is where true signaling information is managed. In the standards, this relates roughly to the control plane (C-plane) and manages call control and the negotiation of network parameters. Some services provided by the C-plane are:

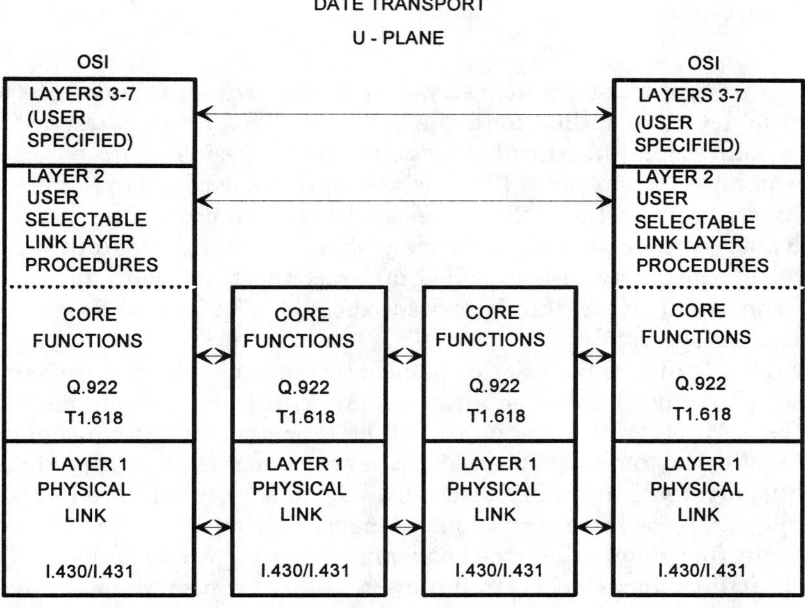

Figure 10.25 End-to-End Transport via the U-Plane

- Error recovery
- Flow control
- Timer recovery
- Mmode setting
- Acknowledgments
- XID exchange
- User-to-user, end-to-end service (the entire PVC)

These control services will be discussed in the next section on transmission theory.

10.5 TRANSMISSION PROTOCOL THEORY

With an understanding of the protocol structure of frame relay protocols, discussion can now center on how frames are assembled and disassembled, the many types of frames and the data contained in each, addressing structures and schemes, and detailed frame structure and operation.

10.5.1 Overview

The high throughput of frame relay is achieved with the side effects of losing error detection (other than the simplistic CRC) and correction and foregoing addressing overhead functions found resident in traditional packet-switching technologies. This is the equivalent of removing the OSI layer 3 functions from the X.25 packet-switching protocol. One of the primary advantages gained is the relatively short delay incurred during data transport. Frame relay also provides fast reconnect and statistical multiplexing, consistent with the benefits expected of TDM and statistical multiplexers, respectively.

Highly reliable digital facilities or fiber-optic transmission are preferred in the frame relay environment because virtual error-free transmission media is essential. All error correction, as well as flow and congestion control, is handled at the customer premises CPE level rather than within the network. Thus, errored frames are discarded by the service and are left to the user's application for retransmission. Congestion control is also left to the user. While this eliminates overhead and delay (typically found in X.25 networks), it introduces an entirely new role for the user premises equipment. In some parts of the world where the transmission facilities are not yet digital or fiber, such as Eastern Europe and much of the Pacific Rim, traditional X.25 packet services will probably prevail for quite some time until the transmission infrastructure is upgraded to error-free fiber-optic media.

High throughput and statistical multiplexing seem to offer an advantage to the user, but the price paid for these benefits may be high. With the advent of frame relay and virtual LAN services, the well-defined line between data transport services and LAN/WAN extension services becomes somewhat fuzzy. As we have discussed, these transport services leave the responsibility of end-to-end data delivery guarantees to the user's CPE. Many users are not ready nor able to sign up to this responsibility, thus public network providers offering frame relay services have provided tried and tested network systems and solutions to capture public FR service users.

Frame relay differs from TDM and FDM multiplexer networks in that the statistical properties of frame relay allocate bandwidth only as needed. In a multiplexer, channels are permanently allocated to specific users, and, in effect, bandwidth is wasted during idle times on some channels while another channel could be using that extra unused bandwidth. This allocation works best for LAN connectivity, where sporadic and bursty traffic could literally demand the entire channel during a given time, with little or no bandwidth requirements the rest of the time. When coupled with a frame relay public network service using frame relay switching, the ultimate result is achieved: a switched public network bandwidth-on-demand service that operates on a shared bandwidth program. Statistical multiplexing can achieve this, either on premises or via the network employing frame relay switching.

Figure 10.26 shows a comparison of (a) conventional TDM multiplexing to (b) frame relay. When multiple users are time-division-multiplexed onto a single physical channel, they each receive specific time slots. Each user must use their full "slice" of bandwidth available or the bandwidth is wasted. If only one user out of four wants to transmit data in a single time period, as during time interval 3, only one-fourth of the bandwidth is used. During time intervals 2 and 4, only one other user is sending data, so one-half of the total available bandwidth is wasted. With frame relay access, each user (protocol) is assigned a virtual channel. If there are four virtual channels assigned to four users, and only one user needs to transmit at a single time period, that one user gets *all* the bandwidth, as shown in (b) during time interval 3. If two users want to transmit during the same time period, they can each receive half the bandwidth (the exact division of bandwidth resources is determined by the CIR assignments) as shown during times 2 and 4. In this case, these users could transmit their data from end-to-end in half the time it would have taken with option (a).

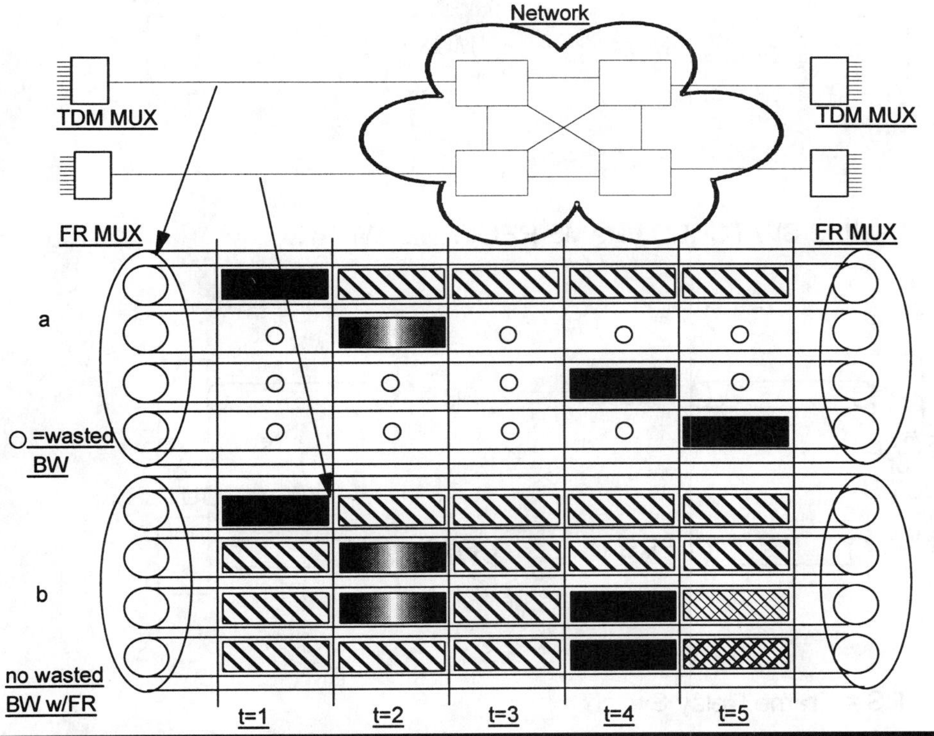

Figure 10.26 Frame Relay Compared to TDM Multiplexing

This example becomes even more compelling with the option of usage-based pricing, where the user pays for the entire channel and any empty preassigned slots not needed are wasted. When frame relay users access the network, they do not pay for bandwidth not needed, but only for what is used.

As mentioned previously, frame relay networks can be much more efficient compared to private line networks based on the number of access circuits. Figure 10.27 shows a standard private multiplexer network compared to a public switched frame relay network.

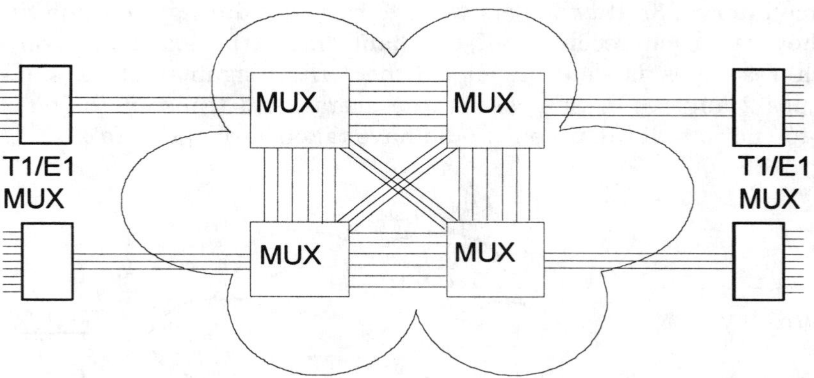

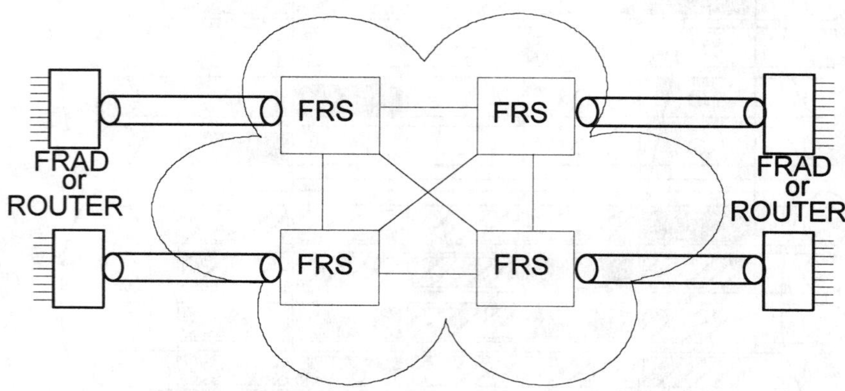

Figure 10.27 Multiplexer Network Compared to Frame Relay Network

Both approaches provide the same amount of user access, but fewer access and long-distance circuits are needed with frame relay (use PVCs instead of physical circuits) because the backbone network bandwidth is statistically shared.

Another major aspect of frame relay in comparison to older packet technologies (X.25) is that frame relay switches merely pass frames along to the destination identifier (DLCI). Thus, depending on the specific vendor implementation, intermediate nodes often do not perform any packet (or frame) disassembly or error correction. DLCIs change at each node in the network, but transparent to the users. PVCs are established within and throughout the frame relay network from switch to switch, but the users see one single end-to-end PVC. PVCs are never changed other than through the service provider or eventually user intervention. Switched virtual frame relay circuits (SVCs) will allow users to modify their own network configurations and even enable dynamic allocation of virtual circuits to fixed and dial-up connections. To date, SVCs have been defined but have not seen widespread implementation in public frame relay services network.

Advances in 50 Mbps HDLC framer chips are pushing frame relay transport rates up to T3 speeds. This will amplify the benefit of multiple users on a single access line, which in turn leads to reduced network access costs.

10.5.2 Example of Frame Relay Operation

Frame relay has been called "X.25 on a diet" because it is a much simpler protocol. Figure 10.28 illustrates a key aspect of the simplification that frame relay provides. Node A on the left-hand side of the figure is transmitting frames to a destination through an intermediate node B. There are no sequence numbers in the frame, with the numbers in the example being shown for illustrative purposes only. Node B simply relays the frames to the outgoing link toward the destination. Node B may begin relaying the frame (in much smaller size cells) even before the entire frame is received, in a technique called *fast packet switching* that was popularized by Stratacom. If a frame is received in error, as shown for the fifth frame in the example, the intermediate node simply does not relay it. This simplified relay-only protocol allows very simple, fast intermediate nodes to be built; however, it requires more intelligence in the higher-layer protocols such as X.25 or TCP, and in the end systems to recover from lost frames. Frames can be lost due to transmission errors or congestion. When frame relay operates over modern transmission media, such as fiber optic systems, loss of frames due to errors becomes a rare occurrence. Loss then occurs primarily due to congestion in frame relay networks. Since loss occurs infrequently, the end systems seldom need to invoke error-recovery procedures, which are usually in place anyway regardless of the performance of the underlying network.

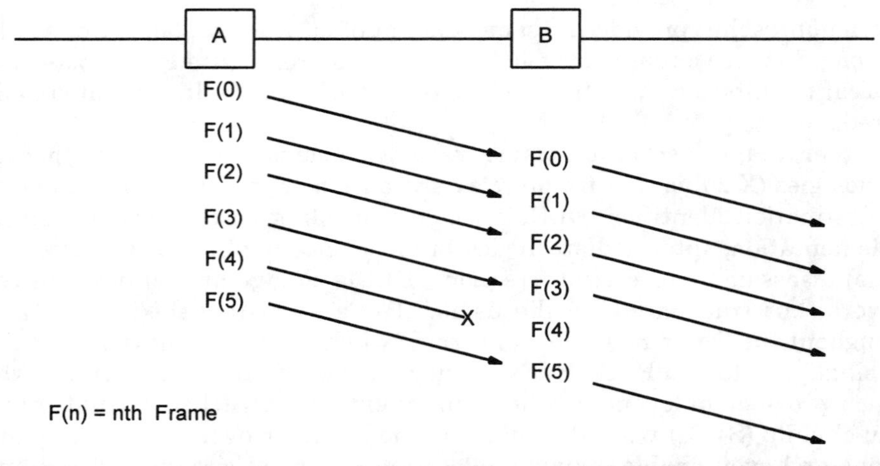

Figure 10.28 Frame Relay Operation

10.5.3 Basics of SAP and DLCI

Before discussing the recent frame relay standards implementations, we need to understand the basic foundations of the LAP-D and framing structures. We first will review ITU-T/CCITT Recommendations Q.920 and Q.921 and then move to the newer Recommendation Q.922 and ANSI T1.618 standards. Note that the original implementations of frame relay were designed in the standards to be ISDN, but later used only DLCI and were non-ISDN based. This section presents the concepts of DLCI, along with the ISDN version using SAP and TEI. Almost all North American versions of frame relay use the non-ISDN implementation.

ITU-T/CCITT Q.920 defines the terms and basic concepts of DLCI data link addressing. The Service Access Point (SAP) is the logical-level data link interface from the user to the network. The SAP provides services to layer 3 protocols. There are multiple data link connection endpoints associated with each SAP and, at the link layer, these are referred to as Data Link Connection Identifiers or DLCIs. Figure 10.29 depicts the relationship between the SAP and the DLCI, showing how multiple DLCIs communicate at the data link layer from one SAP to another.

When using the ISDN version of frame relay, two data link addressing values are assigned within the DLCI called the SAPI and the TEI. The SAPI, or Service Access Point Identifier, defines the service-access point on the user or network side and how the data link layers relate to the layer 3 management entity through call control procedures, or packet mode communications of either Q.931 or X.25, or the layer 2 management features. The TEI, or Terminal Endpoint Identifier, defines the specific endpoint for the given SAPI, thus completing the virtual circuit. The selection of the SAPI and TEI values are detailed in ITU-T/CCITT Recommendation Q.921. A good analogy is to compare the SAPI to the DLCI and the TEI to the physical circuit ID.

Figure 10.30 defines the address field structure of the ITU-T/CCITT Q.921 Recommendation. Notice the 6-bit SAPI address and the 7-bit TEI address. One bit is reserved for a command response indicator and 2 bits for extended addressing (both covered later). While these basics are important, the true blend of ITU-T/CCITT and ANSI standards for the framing and address formats is in the ITU-T/CCITT Draft Recommendation Q.922 and ANSI T1.618, as well as with the LAP-F functionality.

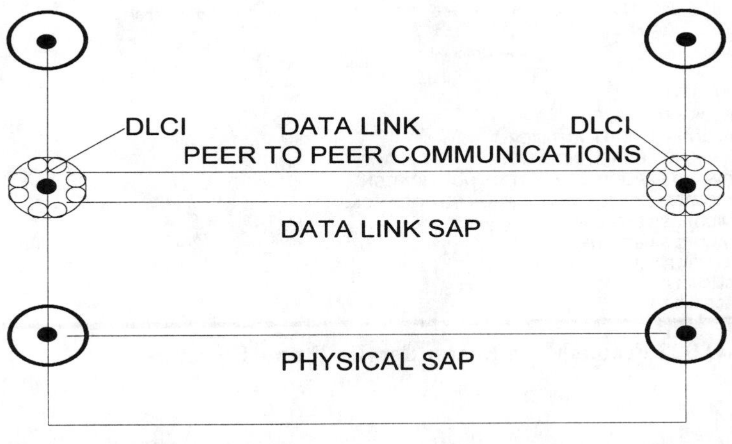

Figure 10.29 SAP-to-DLCI Relationship

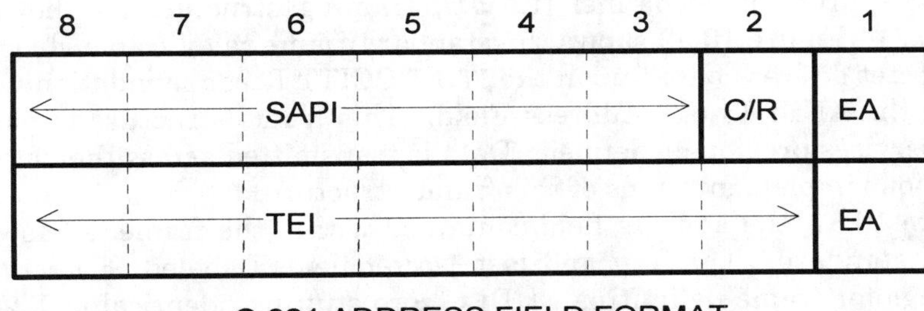

Figure 10.30 ITU-T/CCITT Q.921 FR ISDN Address Field Structure

Figure 10.31 LAP-D Frame Structure

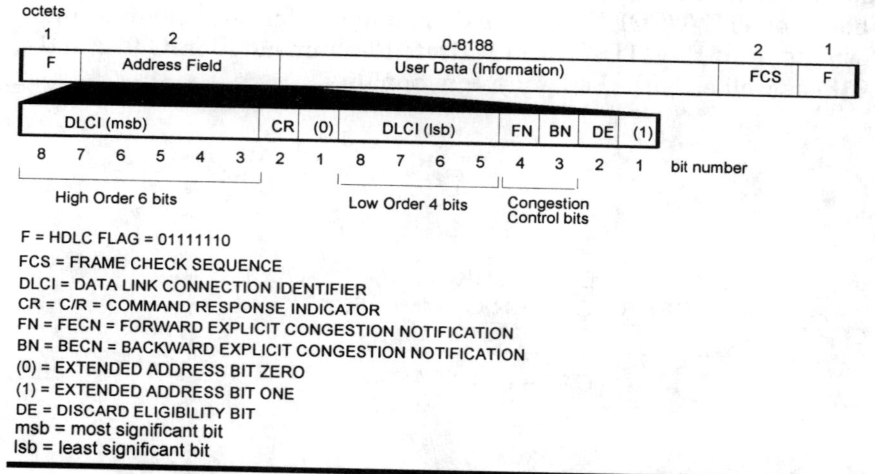

Figure 10.32 Q.922 Frame-Mode Bearer Service Frame Structure

10.5.4 Frame Format

The frame format used by frame relay services is a derivative of the ISDN Link Access Protocol D-channel (LAP-D) framing structure as shown in Figure 10.31. Figure 10.32 shows the standard frame relay frame structure with a 2-octet address based upon the ITU-T/CCITT Recommendation Q.922 including the ANSI T1.618 Address Field. This frame structure is part of the core services previously defined. Data is transmitted across the network using various implementations of this frame structure.

In figure 10.31, the address field contained within the frame is based on the ANSI standard. The first and last 1-octet fields (labeled "F") serve as HDLC flags for frame delimiting. HDLC zero stuffing, identical to X.25, is performed to avoid mistaking user data for a flag. The second field is the address field, taking up 2 octets. Although Figure 10.33 depicts a 2-octet address field, there are also 3- and 4-octet address formats that will be shown in the next section. The third field is for user data. The user data field can be up to 8188 octets (8192 minus 2 bytes each for the address and FCS field). The standard states that all implementations must support a maximum frame size of at least 1024 octets. The Frame Check Sequence (FCS) field is 2 octets long, and is the same used in HDLC, X.25, and a number of other protocols.

Now for a detailed review of the address field.

10.5.5 Address Field Structure

The address field resides within the frame as shown in Figure 10.32. The original address field defined for frame relay was modeled after the LAP-D DLCI address frame, where the DLCI was composed of the SAPI and TEI. The structure has changed to accommodate congestion control signaling in the FECN, BECN, and DE bits.

The Data Link Connection Identifier (DLCI) is split into two fields, together forming a 10-bit DLCI that identifies up to 1024 virtual circuits per interface. This DLCI identifies the logical channel connection within the physical channel or port for a predetermined destination. The DLCI may have local significance on an access circuit or global significance to the FR network (local is much more common). A point-to-point frame relay virtual circuit may have different or similar DLCIs for the access circuit on each end. *Global DLCI* assignment is when each user CPE device must have a separate DLCI for each destination. This limits the size of a frame relay network to approximately 1000 nodes. Instead, FR service providers use *local significant* DLCI assignment where the DLCI is significant to the FR access port only. In this manner, DLCI numbers may be reused on each FR access circuit across the network. Almost all North American frame relay implementations use *local significant* DLCI assignment method.

The Command/Response (C/R) bit is not used at this time, being reserved for future functions (thus, it may be set to either value). Some devices, like the IBM 3745, use the C/R bit and therefore it must be passed through the network intact. Ask your users if they require this.

The Forward Explicit Congestion Notification (FECN) bit is a toggle that tells the remote *user* that network congestion was encountered by the frame transmitted across the physical media, and that the user should take action to prevent data loss. FECN is set in frames traversing the network from sender to receiver that encounter congestion. FECN can be used in receiver-based flow control protocols, such as DECnet.

The Backward Explicit Congestion Notification (BECN))bit works the same, but notifies the *sender* of congestion in the data on the returning path. An increase in the frequency of FECN and BECN bits received is a good indication of the congestion throughout the network. FECN and BECN operation will be covered later.

The Discard Eligibility (DE) bit, when set at 1, indicates that the frame should be discarded during congestion conditions, as opposed to discarding other frames with a higher priority (those set at 0). This bit is used by carriers to determine what data they will discard first when the total traffic exceeds the Committed Information Rate (CIR) and exceeds network bandwidth and buffering resources.

Unfortunately, the FECN, BECN, and DE bits are not often used (depending on the FR device used in the network), not because they do not send out an alert of a congestion problem, but because many CPE applications accessing the network cannot understand or make use of this information yet, and consequently usually ignore it. Even if the equipment could act on the FECN and BECN messages, there has been little or no development in associating these link layer messages with network and transport layer protocols. In the case of DE discards, data is lost; either lost within the network or at the network ingress or egress access point. And the user must rely on higher layer protocols, such as TCP, to provide flow control and recovery from lost data. More on this topic will be covered in the next chapter.

The Extended Address (EA) bits act as address field delimiters, set at 0 and 1, respectively. These bits are used to extend the DLCI addressing range to 3- and 4-octet formats.

Each user CPE device with multiple logical and physical ports must have a separate DLCI for each destination on the egress port it wants to transmit to. These DLCIs are built into the switching/routing tables of each CPE and switching device on the network. The DLCI only has local significance because it establishes a virtual circuit to one of 1023 other virtual ports in the network switch. Therefore, each network may have up to 1024 active DLCIs, or 1024 active virtual circuits per physical access port. This is not exactly true, as there are a few other DLCI numbers reserved (see Table 10.1), and often FR service providers limit the number of DLCIs to less than 1000. The realistic CPE router limitation is less than 100 PVCs per physical port due to processor and memory limitations. Some options are available for circumventing these limitations, such as combining the DLCI with a physical port and node number, NPA/NNX addressing scheme, or some other IP addressing scheme to allow a larger base of common addresses. Either way, the DLCI changes on multiple hops through the network, and only identifies a point-to-point virtual connection between two ports, whether they are defined as user or network ports.

Some vendors, such as Stratacom, use additional addressing schemes such as edge and node identifiers, while other router vendors translate DLCI addresses into Internet Protocol (IP) addressing schemes. When frame relay network design is discussed, the addressing options available for implementation should be reviewed. The ANSI specification provides the Extended Address (EA) bits with the capability to extend the DLCI address by 2 bits, thus breaking the barrier of the 1024 DLCI address limitation.

10.5.6 Proposed Address Structures of ANSI T1.618

ANSI Standard T1.618 defines two additional methods of extending the address field. The current version discussed, the default, is the use of 2 octets for the address field. There are options for identifying 3- and 4-octet address fields. A representation of the 3-octet extended addressing is seen in Figure 10.33. A representation of the 4-octet extended addressing is seen in Figure 10.34. The Data Link Control Indicator (D/C) indicates that the octet serves as an extended address DLCI.

ANSI T1.618 also defines the methods of assigning DLCI values based on the bearer channels (B-channel and N-channel) and on the D-channel when using the ISDN implementation of frame relay. Both methods can use the 2-octet address scheme, but 3- and 4-octet extended addressing is defined only for the bearer channels. When using the D-channel, only DLCIs from 512 to 1007 can be assigned using frame relay connection procedures.

When using the B-channel or N-channel bearer channels, the DLCI values have a much stricter rule base. Table 10.1 shows the differences in using the 2-, 3-, and 4-octet DLCI addressing structures and how these DLCIs are assigned.

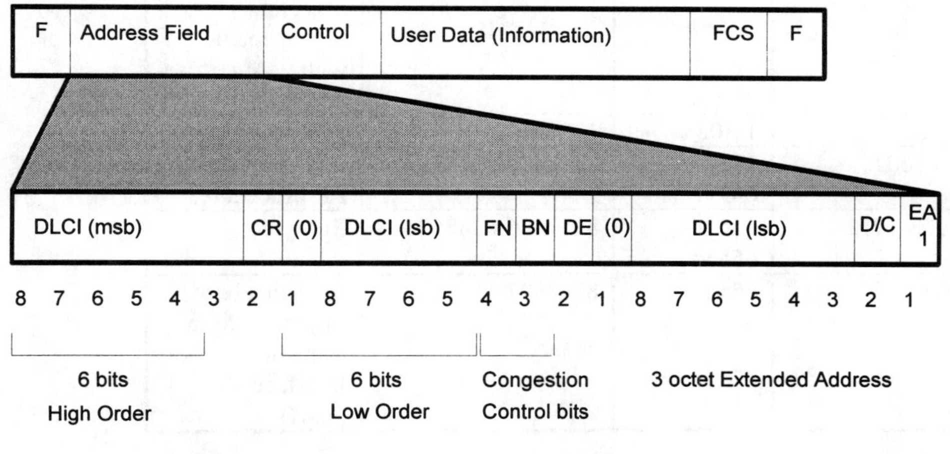

Figure 10.33 Three-Octet Extended Addressing

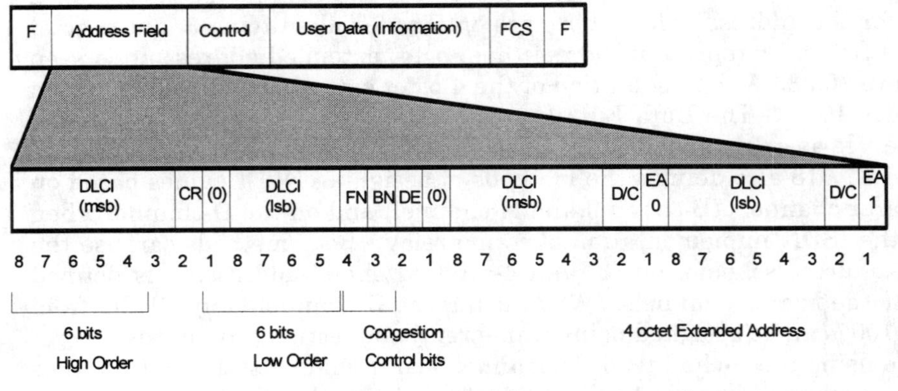

Figure 10.34 Four-Octet Extended Addressing

TABLE 10.1 DLCI Addressing Structures and Assignments

2-Octet DLCI value	3-Octet DLCI value	4-Octet DLCI value	Function
0	0	0	In-channel Signaling or Management with Annexes A, D, and NNI
1-15	1-1023	1-131071	Reserved
16-1007	1024-64511	131072-8257535	Assigned using FR procedures
1008-1022	64512-65534	8257536-8388606	Reserved
1023	65535	8388607	In-channel Layer Management Interface (LMI)

10.5.7 Data Field or Payload Structure

The data field or "payload" structure can vary in size up to 4096 or 8188 octets long. This number varies by service provider, but the limit of 4096 is the most common, driven by the integrity of the Frame Check Sequence (FCS) only up to 4096 octets. The data can be either pure data — when using a direct connection to a device that provides a frame relay interface — or it can be encapsulated packets of a different protocol. In the second case, an X.25 or SDLC packet, complete with the appropriate X.25 or SDLC (SNA) packet header, subnetwork addressing, and user data, can be encapsulated within the frame relay data field. A similar payload may contain an entire or part of an IP packet. This subnetwork packet is then unencapsulated at the distant end. Figure 10.35 shows the frame relay frame structure breakout with an encapsulated X.25 packet or an encapsulated SDLC packet.

FRAME RELAY FRAME STRUCTURE
(from User to Network)
Using CCITT I.441/Q.921 Frame Structure
Including Data Encapsulation Types

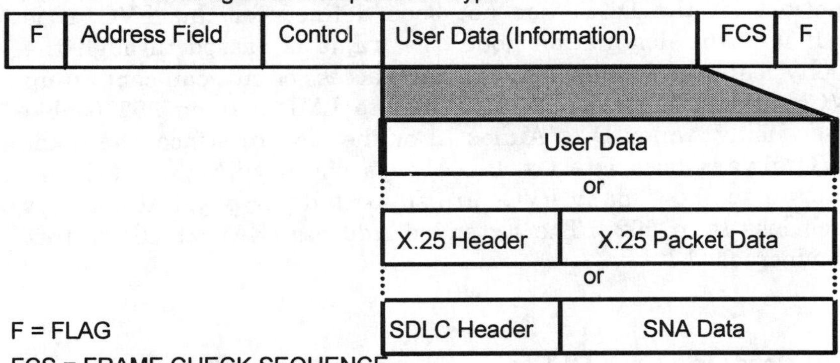

F = FLAG
FCS = FRAME CHECK SEQUENCE
DLCI = DATA LINK CONTROL IDENTIFIER
CR = C/R = COMMAND RESPONSE INDICATOR
FN = FECN = FORWARD EXPLICIT CONGESTION NOTIFICATION
BN = BECN = BACKWARD EXPLICIT CONGESTION NOTIFICATION
(0) = EAB (0) = EXTENDED ADDRESS BIT ZERO
(1) = EAB (1) = EXTENDED ADDRESS BIT ONE
DE = DISCARD ELIGIBILITY BIT

Figure 10.35 Frame Relay Frame Structure with X.25 or SDLC Encapsulated Packet

10.5.8 Frame Check Sequence (FCS)

The FCS field assures the data integrity of the frame. If there is an error, the frame is discarded. The protocol does not correct the frame, so the packet will have to retransmitted. Error detection and correction are handled at higher layers. The FCS is defined in ANSI Standard T1.618 as a 16-bit Cyclic Redundancy Check (CRC-16).

10.6 FRAME RELAY ADDRESSING

A Data Link Connection Identifier (DLCI) provides each PVC with an addressing scheme. Each end point of a PVC is assigned a DLCI. Each frame within a PVC is sent from an originating DLCI to a destination DLCI, where the frame check sequence (FCS) is verified. If the frame does not pass the FCS, it is simply discarded, with no indication to the network or user. If the frame does pass the FCS, the DLCI is located in a routing table; routing tables then match addresses, either DLCI to DLCI, or DLCI to IP. If the DLCI has been predefined for this PVC, the frame will be routed to its final destination. If the DLCI has not been defined for this PVC, it is discarded. If it is the destination node, the frame is passed through the logical and physical port to the user. Each FR access circuit can contain up to 1024 PVCs. Some of these are dedicated to LMI, leaving 992 usable DLCIs. When using Annex D or Annex A, or the NNI interface, the management PVC always uses DLCI = 0. Always check with the CPE and switch vendor to see how many PVCs are supported per physical port. It may be much less than 992. The Extended Address (EA) bit allows this number to be increased.

10.6.1 FR Addressing with DLCIs

Figure 10.36 depicts a user CPE device residing in Dallas, which needs to exchange data with two other locations – Washington and Boca Raton. The Dallas CPE connects one T1 frame relay access line into the public FR network cloud. The DLCI address for Washington is 85, and the DLCI for Boca Raton is 120. Washington and Boca Raton also want to send data to Dallas, and they use DLCI address 22 and 35, respectively. All DLCI addresses are assigned using an extension of the ITU-T/CCITT Recommendation Q.931 call control procedures.

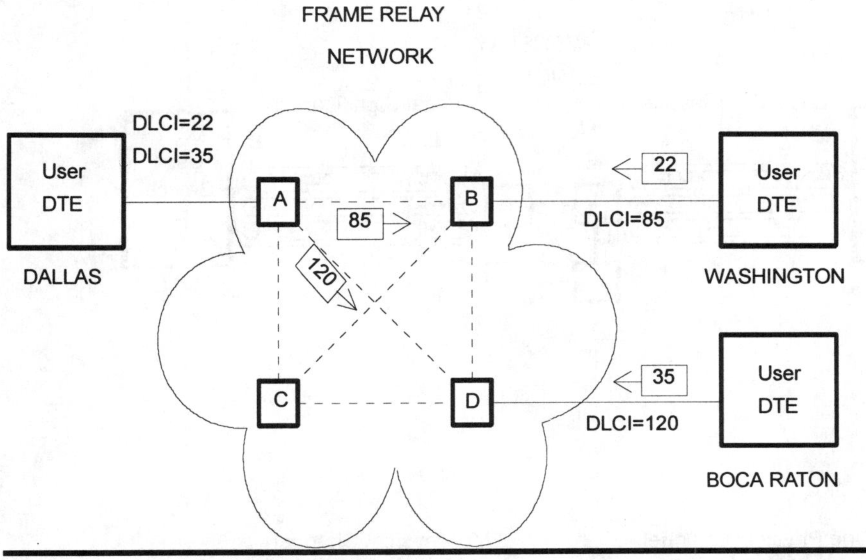

Figure 10.36 DLCI Addressing

Figure 10.37 shows a virtual frame relay network using DLCI addressing. It can be seen that user device A communicates with a frame relay switch (1) through a single physical connection using multiple DLCIs for each virtual circuit (in this example there are three PVCs from user A to user B). Each of these DLCIs have local significance, meaning that each set of DLCIs is established between each device on the network, and that the same DLCI number may be reused in all ports across the network. Different addressing schemes are used inside the FR network.

10.6.2 Frame Handling and Switching with ISDN FR Access

When using an ISDN implementation of frame relay, the Frame Handlers (FHs) and Remote Frame Handlers (RFHs) perform much of the frame-relaying service between the physical ports and the mapping of the logical DLCIs between all ports in a group. It is the responsibility of the frame handler to identify the local physical channels that terminate on either the local exchange (case B) or in the frame relay network (case A). The DLCIs assigned to a frame handler for a group will be unique. The frame handler will also

- Map in-bound to out-bound DLCI
- Perform FCS and correct for retransmission
- Discard corrupted frames
- Write out-bound DLCI value into the frame-address field
- Coordinate transport of frame out of the physical channel

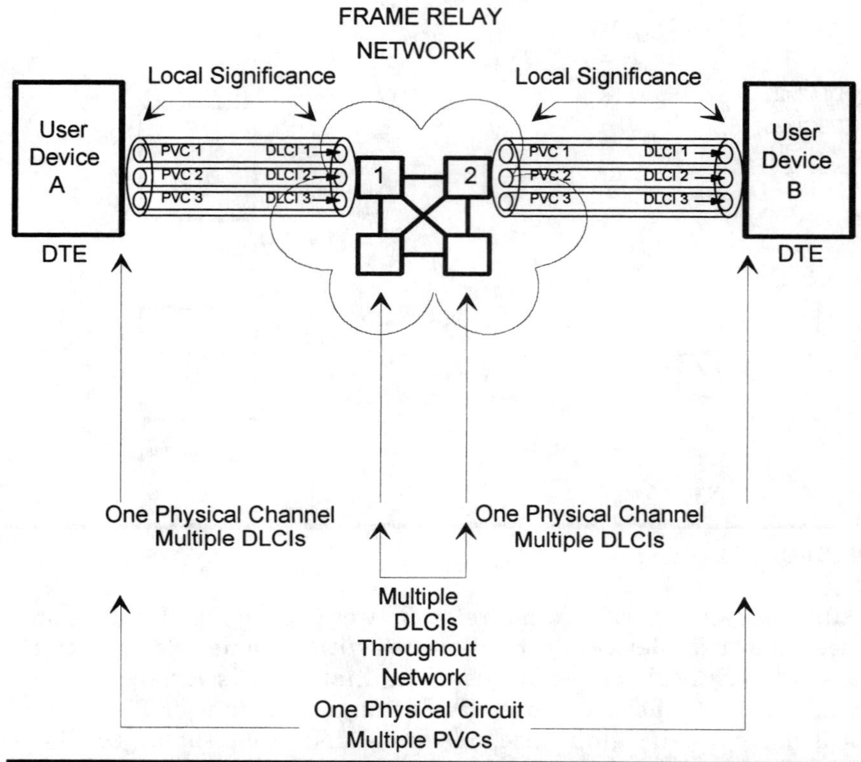

Figure 10.37 Frame Relay Network DLCI Addressing Example

Figure 10.38 shows a frame relay frame handler (or remote frame handler) during ISDN access to FR operation. A frame relay network device is acting both as a frame handler for case B integrated access and as a remote frame handler for case A access. The case B integrated access TE3 is using the D-channel for both signaling *and* data flow. TE3 is sending frames on DLCI = 11 to TE4 on DLCI = 13. Call establishment is done via SAPI0. The case A access is via the B-channel for data transfer and call setup, using DLC = 0 for call establishment. TE1 is sending frames on DLCI = 10 to TE2 on DLCI = 12.

10.6.3 Logical Channel Multiplexing via Frames

Through the use of the DLCI addressing, multiple user logical data streams can be multiplexed and demultiplexed within the same physical data channel. Each physical channel can contain up to 1023 logical channels, each identified by a DLCI value (or more with extended addressing). Logical channel

1024 is reserved for CLLM (note that CLLM is rarely ever used). These multiplexed users are assembled into frames and transmitted across the network. These frames retain their order of transmission and reception. Each protocol is negotiated during the call establishment procedure.

Figure 10.39 shows a standard frame representing the physical media connectivity, the data link layer core aspects connectivity, as well as the LAP-D and Q.922 signaling and communications procedures. The figure also shows how the data link control procedures are multiplexing the various user DLCIs into each frame. In this example, there are various logical channels attempting to transmit. The figure shows DLCI 23, 32, 41, and 210, and assumes there are others between 41 and 211. These users are employing their own level 3 and higher user-defined protocols. Frame establishment is also shown using the Q.931 procedures with DLCI 1023 being used for the link management (LMI) procedures and DLCI 0 used for Annex A, Annex D, and NNI.

Each logical channel can operate with a different data link control procedure and a different network layer service. The many different types of data link control procedures that can be carried on a logical channel are:

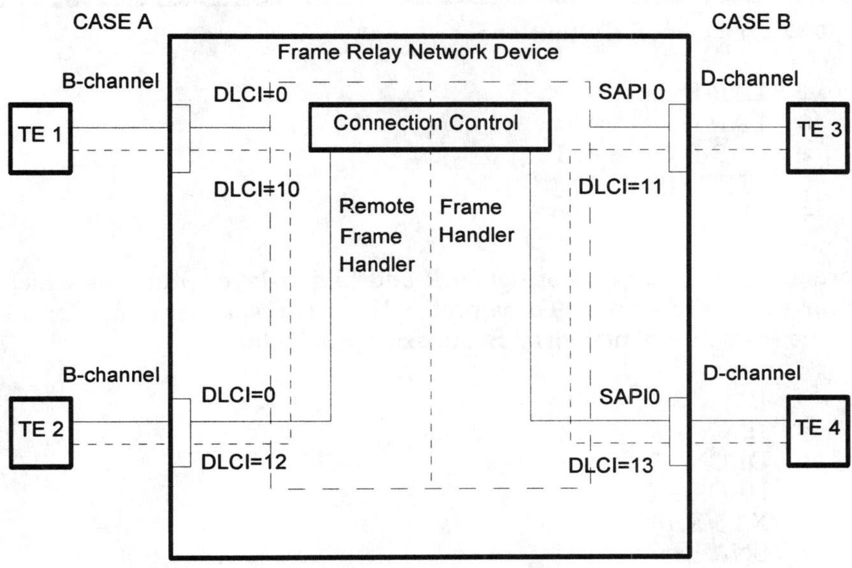

Figure 10.38 Remote Frame Handler Operation

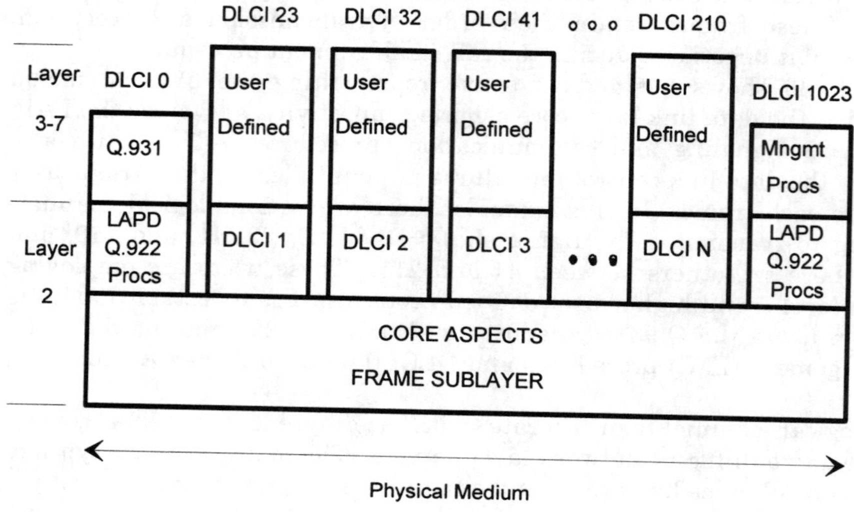

Figure 10.39 Frame Level Multiplexing

- LAP-B
- LAP-D
- LAP-D Extended
- IEEE 802.2
- SDLC

There are different types of network and higher-layer protocols which can ride over a logical channel. These protocols are transparent to data transport across the frame relay network. Some examples include:

- IP
- IPX
- DECNET
- DEC LAT
- X.25/X.75
- SNA
- ASCII

These protocols can be offered over various types of traffic and circuits including:

- Priority traffic
- Revenue-bearing traffic

- ✦ Time-sensitive traffic
- ✦ Single-destination traffic
- ✦ Multiple-destination traffic
- ✦ Permanent Virtual Circuits (PVCs)
- ✦ Switched Virtual Circuits (SVCs)

10.7 USER-DEFINABLE SERVICES

Core service functions were defined in the last section. They showed the OSIRM layer 2 (data link layer) split by frame relay standards into two major areas: core services and user-defined (and selected) services. Now we will look at user-definable services in more detail.

10.7.1 User Interface

By eliminating the need for multiple access lines by using a *single access* into a switched infrastructure, whether a private or public frame relay network, users can reduce a significant portion of networking costs. Since access charges constitute the majority of data networking costs, reductions due to frame relay access can be significant enough to justify the purchase of additional hardware, services, and even support systems. The user can realize huge cost savings, but must also plan for supporting the control mechanisms not inherent in frame relay, such as congestion control and error correction at the higher layers. The actual physical user interface is typically an RS-449 or V.35 connection to a router or switch, although with the drop in local BRI access charges ISDN interfaces are fast being deployed. With frame relay, the user can minimize the number of interfaces to the network by using multiple V.35, or four-wire, if a CSU/DSU is needed.

10.7.2 User Applications

There are many user applications that will work well over frame relay. These applications cannot be overly delay sensitive, nor sensitive to "jitter", defined as variations in delay. Typical synchronous traffic might include long network connection times, excessive call setup and takedown times, long transmission sessions, nonbursty traffic patterns, and PVC connections. This is different from typical packet-network characteristics, which may include short network connection times, short call setup and takedown times, short transmission sessions, and bursty traffic patterns. Make sure the applications are well matched to frame relay. User applications which traverse frame relay networks and utilize frame relay services must accompany network and transport layer protocols that have the intelligence at the higher levels to perform both congestion control and error detection, correction, and retransmission of data due to these conditions. More on application design specifics in the next chapter.

10.7.3 Interface Signaling

Most of the methods of user-to-network interface signaling have already been covered, but additional elements or functions in the channel may require additional signaling. Transmission equipment such as CSUs, DSUs, and other channel-conditioning devices may require in-band or out-of-band signaling. This should be transparent to the frame relay transmission, however, while providing maximum throughput, line efficiency, and minimum response time degradation and delay.

ANSI has also defined some Annex recommendations. Though not necessary for standards compliance, they can make user management much more efficient and thorough. These issues include PVC status, congestion recognition and signaling, fairness and guaranteed user throughput, as well as other future expansions and enhancements. Now we will look at a few of these enhancements.

10.7.4 PVC Management

When a Permanent Virtual Circuit (PVC) is established between two physical ports and one or multiple DLCI addresses are established over this link, there is a need for both the network access device (user) and the network switching device (provider) to manage the status of the link. PVC management is defined by ANSI, ITU-T, and the LMI extensions. These specifications define three main areas of PVC management: PVC status signaling, DLCI verification, and physical interface keep-alive heartbeat.

A PVC is managed by status signaling defined in ITU-T Recommendation Q.933, LMI, Annex A, and ANSI Standard T1.617, Annexes D and A. Status signaling provides for status inquiry and reporting of the physical link, or PVCs, as identified by the DLCI value. The status response may be for selected PVCs, or a full status (FS) for all PVCs. PVC status is defined by 3 bits: new, delete, and active. The new bit is set to 1 for a new PVC, otherwise it is set to 0. The delete bit indicates whether the DLCI is configured 1 or 0. The active bit indicates whether the PVC is operational or not. Status signaling occurs on DLCI 1023 for LMI (or DLCI 0 for Annex A or D and NNI).

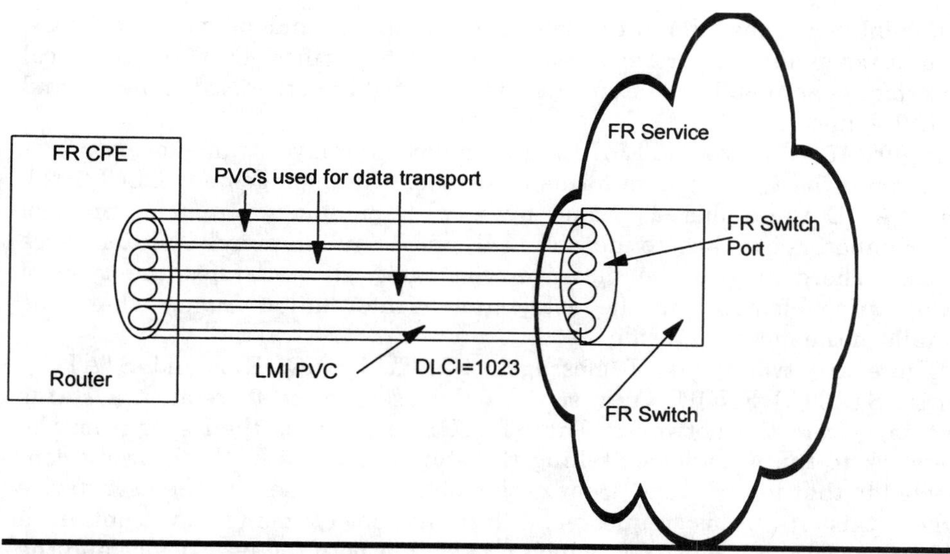

Figure 10.40 LMI Network Configuration

The maximum number of usable DLCI codes to identify PVCs is limited by the maximum frame relay frame size for the Full Status (FS) message.

Annex B of ANSI Standard T1.617 defines additional procedures for permanent virtual connections that apply to implementing both PVCs and SVCs on the same interface, case B with D-channel signaling implementations, and case A with in-channel signaling and PVC-only implementations. The primary benefit of this Annex is the notification of and recovery from PVC outages. Annex D provides additional procedures for PVCs using unnumbered frames. It is used for operational purposes with case A in-channel signaling only.

The other forms of PVC management commonly used are the Local Management Interface (LMI) extensions and proprietary methods.

10.7.5 The Local Management Interface (LMI) Extension

The Local Management Interface (LMI) extension defines a protocol for managing the frame relay access circuit from FR CPE to the FR public network switch. The LMI provides a keep-alive signal between the FR CPE and the FR network access port, makes the initial frame relay circuit and equipment configuration simpler by allowing automatic notification of connectivity, and provides a status report for active or deactivated DLCIs. Figure 10.40 shows this concept. The LMI extensions define DLCI address number 1023 as the LMI address. The PVC status and configuration information features provided by the LMI include notification of PVC availability or unavailability, deletions, additions, and presence of PVCs, and a keep-alive heartbeat sequence which verifies that the physical interface is active. LMI extensions are specified in both ANSI Annex A and ITU-T Annex D.

Figure 10.41 shows the LMI Extension data link layer frame format. It is similar to the Q.931 frame format, but uses the management DLCI 1023, the LAP-D unnumbered "frame byte" with poll-bit set to 0, a protocol discriminator "byte set" to identify LMI, and a "null dummy" Call Reference (CR). There is also the message-type byte, which defines the type of information elements in the user data or information frame, where the details of the message reside.

There are two types of messages: STATUS_ENQUIRY and STATUS. First, STATUS_ENQUIRY is sent by the user device to request a status message from the network. The STATUS message is then sent from the network to the user device telling the status of PVCs in the network connected to that user device. Information elements are sent to the user device when this status is requested. Information elements can contain a KEEP_ALIVE_SEQUENCE, which proves that both the user device and the network element are active; a PVC_STATUS, which gives the configuration and status of an existing PVC; or a REPORT_TYPE to indicate either the type of inquiry requested by the user device or the status message content. Figure 10.42 shows the same LMI extension frame but includes a sample STATUS message format.

FRAME RELAY FRAME STRUCTURE

(from User to Network)

Using the Local Management Interface (LMI) Extension Framing

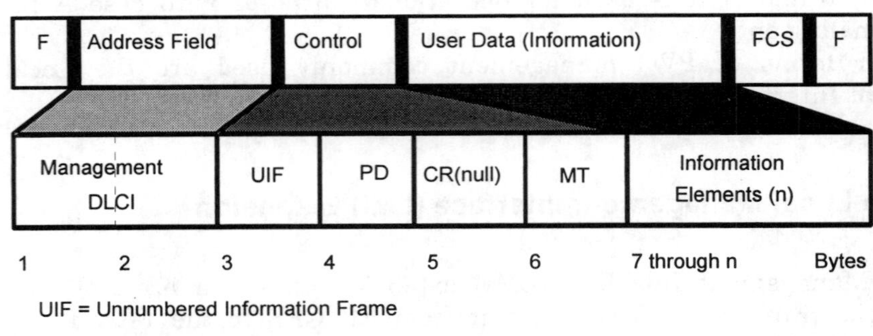

UIF = Unnumbered Information Frame

PD = Protocol Discriminator LMI

CR (null) = Call Reference (null)

MT = Message Type

Figure 10.41 LMI Extensions Frame Format – Frame Check Sequence

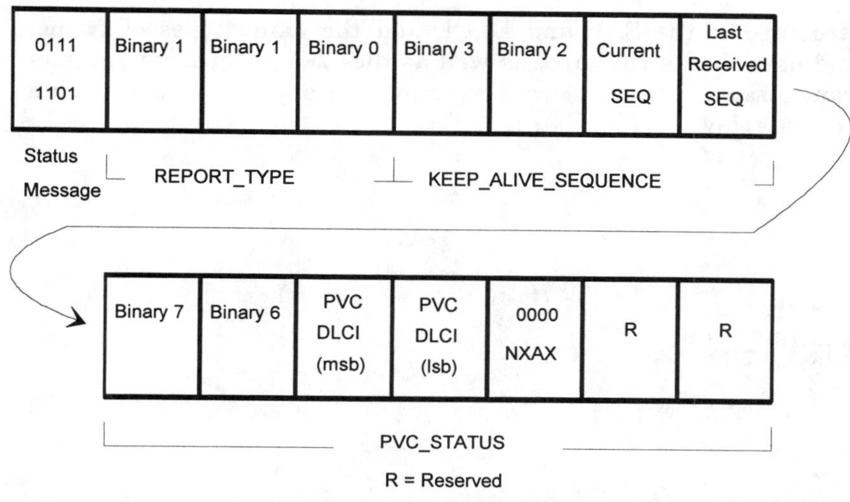

Figure 10.42 LMI Extension Frame Including Sample STATUS Message Format

Notice that the message, REPORT_TYPE, KEEP_ALIVE_SEQUENCE, and PVC_STATUS have filled the information portion of the frame.

The message and information elements discussed previously are used to perform the "heartbeat process" consisting of heartbeat polling, keep-alive sequencing, and adding or changing new PVCs. These procedures ensure synchronization between the user and network devices, report new virtual circuits, report the deletion of old virtual circuits, and ensure link integrity between the user and network device. The LMI procedures also provide this information so that additional monitoring and maintenance can be accomplished by the user devices. Annex D implementations also use the heartbeat polling, where every third (this is configurable) message sent contains a full status, and a PVC status message is sent if something happens between polling intervals.

10.8 REVIEW

The chapter began by reviewing the basic building blocks of frame relay: the UNI, PVC, CIR, and DLCI. From there we defined frame relay as an interface, a signaling protocol, and a network service. The standards that govern frame relay include ITU-T, CCITT, ANSI, and the LMI extensions written by the "Gang of Four" frame relay vendors, and each was covered. As frame relay is defined as an OSIRM layer 2 protocol, it contains two separate functional elements: core services that provide the user-selectable services and the procedural sublayer for frame relay transport and signaling. We covered frame relay transmission theory including the basic protocol structure of the SAP and DLCI, and the many types of frame, address, and data field structures, as well as the LMI Extensions parameters for transmission. Next, we will examine the application and design aspects of frame relay.

Chapter

11

Frame Relay, Part 2 – Application, Services, and Design

Frame relay user interface standards have developed from the ISDN frame mode bearer services. From this standard the American National Standards Institute (ANSI) and the International Telegraph and Telephone Consultative Committee (CCITT), now called the International Telecommunications Union (ITU-T), defined two different implementations of user connection modes, which are the user interface options to the frame relay network. Both the non-ISDN and ISDN-like connection modes are important, as ISDN access to FR has finally become available. Clearly, the most common implementation is the non-ISDN standards using LMI, Annex D, and Annex A. Next, frame relay parameters such as CIR, EIR, and DE are discussed as they relate to PVC and port sizing, followed by the traffic congestion and control parameters of FECN, BECN, DE, and CLLM. A predominant number of FR ports installed today are on public frame relay services. Public service offerings have many options, and their frame and cell backbone architectures have varied impacts on user applications. Thus, the two major types of architecture design algorithms, closed-loop and open-loop, will be covered. Additional design issues include window sizing, moving from private lines to FR, FR primary and alternate access methods, and network management will be covered. There are also performance and delay issues which require study. Performance is a major design criterion and consideration in a frame relay network, and thus we study the parameters affecting it. The chapter concludes with a look at FR pricing structures.

11.1 MULTIPLE STANDARDS DEVELOP

The standards for frame relay have developed through the help of multiple standards committees, user groups, vendor consortia, and a variety of other interest groups on an international scale. This broad-based cooperation has caused frame relay to quickly become an established standard. Frame relay standards about to be examined have been established worldwide in a very short time, driven by a common user-to-network interface (UNI) and service. Since vendor implementations of frame relay interfaces, protocols, and services span numerous standards, it becomes extremely important for the network design engineer or manager to understand what the standards define and where to find specific details on their implementation! In the next few sections we will examine how the ITU-T and the ANSI Telecommunications Committee standards define frame relay, as well as how each standard has developed.

Frame relay is a protocol defined by both ANSI and ITU-T. Frame relay originated in the ITU-T in 1988 as a derivative of its Recommendation I.122. This derivative was actually from the Link Access Protocol-D (LAP-D) signaling portion of the new Integrated Services Digital Network (ISDN) signaling standard. Frame relay is also a transport technique offered by many network providers through a service referred to as frame relay. In the context of providing a network service, frame relay is a connection-oriented frame mode bearer service as defined in the ISDN standards by both ANSI and ITU-T. The ANSI T1S1.1 Committee, an architecture and services team under the Services, Architecture, and Signaling T1 Subcommittee, first standardized on a frame relay interface in T1S1/88-2242, which is a frame relay Bearer Service – Architectural Framework and Service Description. This standard does not include voice or video, and is compliant with the HDLC (High-Level Data Link Control) protocol. This provided a common, cost-effective interface to existing equipment on the market. The ITU-T then standardized frame relay under the I-series recommendation I.122 Framework for Additional Packet Mode Bearer Services.

Both ANSI and ITU-T ISDN standards use the LAP-D data link layer – Layer 2 of the OSIRM, and the ANSI standard has provisions to supplement frame relay using the LMI extensions. The frame relay service is defined in ITU-T I.122 and ANSI T1S1. The relation to ISDN is part of ITU-T Recommendations Q.921 and Q.931. Service descriptions are defined by both ANSI T1.606 and ITU-T, while congestion management is defined in the ANSI T1.606 Addendum. The core aspects are defined in ANSI T1.618 as well as ITU-T Q.922. And finally, the access signaling and framing is defined in both the ANSI T1S1/89-186 recommendation and ITU-T Q.931.

Frame relay is sometimes confused with the term “fast packet”. Fast packet is a generic term used for many high-speed packet technologies, such as frame relay and cell relay, and has been used to represent multiplexer upgrades to faster X.25 packet switching. Fast Packet is also the trademarked name of StrataCom's Fast Packet Technology, which defines the transmission of voice and data using a packetized format. Frame relay and frame switching are synonymous only with the ITU-T switching implementation of frame relay called type II.

Due to the disparity between the ANSI and ITU-T standards for frame relay interfaces, protocols, and services, we will look at each implementation separately: the ANSI standards, the ITU-T standards, as well as some proprietary solutions. The LMI specifications, which span both standards organizations, will also be covered. It becomes apparent quickly that frame relay is more than just passing frames between a user and their network provider. In fact, it takes more than one standards body to produce a workable interface, network, and service for the complete end-to-end implementation of frame relay. Many of the ANSI and ITU-T standards actually rely on one another to provide the complete interface, architecture, and services to embody the full complement of frame relay implementations.

11.1.1 ITU-T/CCITT Standards

ITU-T standards are first defined as part of a working group's recommendations. These recommendations are then formalized into draft recommendations and given numbers with letter prefixes. These draft recommendations, pending acceptance, are then published as ITU-T recommendations. The "I" recommendations tend to provide the *framework* for services, protocols, and operations while the "Q" recommendations tend to define the *detailed* operations of subjects such as signaling, transport, and implementations. As noted, frame relay shares much of its architecture and protocol structures with the ITU-T ISDN standards. This ISDN consequence will be discussed first, followed by a description of each recommendation that plays a role in frame relay.

Frame relay is referred to as an end-user service under the ISDN bearer services standards. This defines frame relay as an "interface" between the user and the network service. The relaying of HDLC frames was first defined in ITU-T Recommendation I.122, which was a broad standard and could apply to many services, including ISDN. ITU-T Recommendation I.441/Q.921 defines the frame relay implementation of the LAP-D core protocol functions, and further defines the HDLC framing process. Here the addressing of frame relay is defined through Data Link Connection Identifiers (DLCIs), enabling multiple logical channels (PVCs) per a single physical user interface. ITU-T Recommendation I.441 also calls for three additional functions to be implemented in the upper half of the layer two in the OSIRM, namely, link utilization, flow control, and error recovery. These are the main functions implemented by the older X.25 packet-switching protocol, and are overhead-intensive. Thus, they are rarely implemented when using these recommendations, and these functions are often performed by the user DTE equipment or other higher-level protocol implementations such as TCP/IP.

ISDN standards are at the root of frame relay protocol operation. All ISDN frame relay standards rely on ISDN standards which use the OSIRM layer 2 LAP-D data link layer standard, using the D-channel for signaling and the B- or D-channel for the transmission of information, depending on whether it is Type I or Type II. Both types of the standard will be considered. As discussed in the section on ANSI, the ITU-T Recommendation I.122 defines the frame relay bearer services under the ISDN recommendations. There are two main types of frame relay defined by this recommendation. Type I private or virtual private frame relay and type II public frame relay. These types define the service descriptions and network architecture by which the services are offered. The Q.931 standard was developed by the ITU-T to handle the access-signaling portion of frame relay. This standard relates directly to the ANSI T1.617. The Q.922 standard was developed to handle the core aspects of frame relay. It is an enhancement of the Q.921 standard and relates to ANSI standard T1.619. The Q.921 standard defines the frame format and corresponds directly with ANSI T1.602.

11.1.2 ANSI Standards

ANSI standards are first defined as part of a technical subcommittee recommendation. These recommendations are then formalized into drafts and given numbers with the prefix denoting the type of standard (for our study, we will focus upon the T1 standards). These drafts, pending acceptance, are then published as ANSI standards.

Upon close examination, the reader will find that many of the ANSI standards defined below bear a close resemblance to the ITU-T Recommendations defined in the last section. In fact, many of the ANSI standards are designed to complement the ITU-T ISDN Recommendations. The Exchange Carrier Standards Association (ECSA) has coordinated the efforts of the ANSI T1S1 Committee in the development of frame relay specifications. While many frame relay implementations comply with ANSI standards, it is the LMI specifications with extensions that made early implementations of frame relay possible. These interface specifications are enhanced by the LMI extensions as defined by the "Gang of Four" (StrataCom, Digital Equipment Corporation (DEC), Cisco Systems, and Northern Telecom) whose switching equipment continues to be an integral part of most public frame relay offerings today. ANSI T1.617, T1.618, and T1.606 provide customer interface standards for access speeds of DS0, Nx56 kbps, Nx64 kbps, and DS1, primarily defining the user-to-network interface (UNI) and the network-to-network interface (NNI). T1.607 concentrates on the frame relay circuit switching procedures. T1.617 defines frame relay call control procedures, and T1.618 defines the framing and transmission of frame relay (also includes new congestion-control techniques). Annex D and NNI, along with LMI, are by far the most common implementations. Both permanent virtual circuits (PVCs) and Switched Virtual Circuits (SVCs) provide call connection service via the ANSI standards.

11.1.3 LMI Extension and Proprietary Solutions

When the ITU-T and ANSI standards were under development, four vendors selling in the commercial/government marketplace did not wait for standards to evolve but decided to write their own specifications defining frame relay standards between the user and the network elements. The four vendors, known as the "Gang of Four", were StrataCom, Digital Equipment Corporation (DEC), Cisco Systems, and Northern Telecom (NorTel). As is often the case, these vendors saw the need to get a product to market, along with the projected revenue stream which could be achieved with an early release of a frame relay product. These factors drove them to adopt an interim set of specifications, called the LMI extensions. These extensions have features which, even though they are of a proprietary implementation, complement and supplement both the ANSI and ITU-T standards, as well as represent the views of private and public network suppliers. This common platform of the Gang of Four for interoperability has become the de facto standard in the industry for the interconnection of CPE equipment, via a frame relay access interface, to frame relay switches. Other vendors eventually joined the original Gang of Four and formed the Frame Relay Forum (FRF), which remains the driving force for FR implementation agreements which become de facto standards or are submitted to ANSI and ITU for processing into standards. Bellcore also participates in the creation of FR standards.

These proprietary LMI features handle the information exchange between the network and user-attached devices, providing standards for such things as support of automatic reconfiguring of devices and fault detection. LMI features also enhance service by providing the user with status and configuration information on the PVCs active at that time. OSIRM level 1 connectivity is also addressed, along with customer network-management functions. Figure 11.1 depicts the user-to-network interface (UNI) as defined by the LMI specifications. Specifically, it shows where the LMI standards exert their influence. The standard defines only permanent virtual circuits (PVCs) between data termination equipment (DTE) and frame relay networking equipment. It does not define data communication equipment services, but enhancements are provided in the various extensions for frame relay service.

There are two major types of LMI extensions, the standard set and optional extensions. The standard extension set is used by almost every major CPE vendor offering a frame relay interface for its equipment. Many of the optional extensions are not used, and some remain under development. All LMI extensions should be used in conjunction with the ANSI standards.

Many of the LMI extensions have already been implemented in recent ANSI standards. As the ANSI and ITU-T standards evolve, they will also incorporate the same functionality as found in the LMI extensions (primarily because of vendor influence in these standards committees). Some standards even have written "annexes" which contain sample implementations of extensions and options to the base standard.

11.1.4 Standard LMI Extensions

The LMI common extensions are based upon the message formats of the ITU-T Recommendation Q.931, and define enhanced versions of these messages for configuration and maintenance. These standard LMI extensions perform the following functions:

- Notify user of PVC status (active and present DLCI)
- Notify user of add/delete/change PVC (removal or failure of DLCI)
- Notify user of physical link "keep-alive" signal and logical link status

The LMI standard extensions identify:

- Maximum frame size of 8196 octets (4098 if doing CRC)
- Support for 1024 DLCI addresses
- Common extensions
- Setting of FECN/BECN bits, DE congestion bit
- Support for multicasting
- Global addressing
- Maximum of 1024 logical connections (PVCs only)

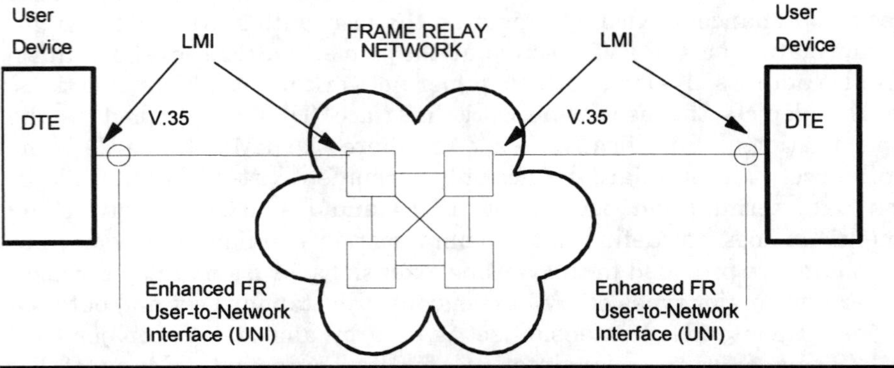

Figure 11.1 Frame Relay User-to-Network Interface with LMI

All of these extensions are transmitted through the network on DLCI 1023. This is the logical channel that has been designated for LMI extensions.

11.1.5 Optional LMI Extensions

The optional LMI extensions define four key areas of enhanced user functionality additions. These four optional extensions include:

- Multicast capabilities
- Flow control
- Global addressing conventions
- Asynchronous status updates

Multicast capabilities. The multicast capabilities allow multiple LAN interconnected user devices to function with simpler address resolution. Multicast replaces the need to poll a LAN/WAN for a destination address for sending packets. Multicast simultaneously broadcasts to all routers in a predefined multicast group. Multiple DLCIs are received for each multicast group. The network device then replicates the transmitted frame into multiple frames of a predefined multicast group of DLCIs.

Flow control. Enhancements to congestion indication and user notification of such conditions are provided in this extension. This style of flow control is similar to XON-XOFF, but can be used only for unidirectional data flow. This mode of flow control should be used in conjunction with the ANSI standard for a homogeneous implementation of frame relay standards. The primary users of this extension will be bridges and routers that cannot implement the ANSI standard congestion and control mechanisms.

Global addressing convention. This capability allows the network to provision DLCIs on a port-by-port basis; in effect, using one DLCI for each port or end device so that any user on the network can communicate and use the same DLCI for a given destination every time. This extension allows only a total of 1024 DLCIs for the entire network. Each DLCI is assigned to one specific network port, providing the same termination point for each given DLCI number. The termination point always remains the same, regardless of origination port. This is much different from the 1024 DLCIs per port as defined in the ANSI standard, and is used only in small private network implementations due to its total network port limitation.

Asynchronous status updates. This enhancement allows the network to notify the user device of a change in logical channel DLCI status. This acts as an option to the ANSI standards for flow control and congestion control.

The optional functional extensions listed above will notify users of any changes to the multicast group, multicast virtual circuit availability or lack thereof, and the configured source DLCI for the broadcast endpoint. Other optional extensions provide an asynchronous update to DLCI changes, explicit notification of a deletion of any PVC, including multicast, network buffer status, and minimum transmission bandwidth. There is also the capability of notifying the user device of the minimum bandwidth provisioned by the network for each Permanent Virtual Circuit (PVC). Most vendors conform to either type of frame relay implementation.

The LMI extension document mentioned above was published in late 1990. Since then, no revisions have been issued. Each vendor has published specific implementation specifications for the standards at the back of the document in the Appendices. Since that time, additional support has been added by all four vendors of the Gang of Four, and they should be contacted for details. The document is called *Frame Relay Specifications with Extensions*, Document Number 001-208966, Rev. 1.0, September 18, 1990 (StrataCom, Digital Equipment Corporation (DEC), Cisco Systems, and Northern Telecom).

11.2 FR PARAMETERS AND SIZING

Committed Information Rate (CIR) and Excess Information Rate (EIR) are at the core of sizing FR access. CIR and EIR are tied together and calculated by the frame relay switch. CIR rates in public frame relay networks are chosen for each PVC based on perceived traffic minimum and maximum patterns, and the settings of these variables depend on the network architectures, as does the setting and discard of Discard Eligible (DE) bits. CIR, EIR, and DE form the building blocks of traffic and congestion control (or avoidance) in FR networks.

11.2.1 Calculating the Committed Information Rate (CIR) and Excess Information Rate (EIR)

The CIR is a quality-of-service measurement that provides a "statistically guaranteed" rate of throughput on the transmit or receive path of a PVC during any one period of time. Many frame relay services define the transmission parameters of each PVC in terms of a CIR, and define CIR as the minimum throughput achievable under all network conditions. However, the term *committed* is somewhat ambiguous in that it does not specifically state the frame loss or delay objective, but CIR can be used to estimate a minimum latency that applications can expect across the frame relay network. Transmission errors can cause frames to be lost, and finite buffer space in networks that are overbooked can result in lost frames due to momentary, statistical overloads.

The CIR is computed as the number of bits in a committed Burst size, *Bc*, that can arrive during an averaging interval *T* such that CIR = *Bc*/*T*. If the number of bits that arrive during the interval *T* exceeds *Bc*, but is less than an excess threshold, *Bc* + *Be*, then the subsequent frames are marked as Discard Eligible (DE). The Excess Information Rate (EIR) is defined as (*Bc* + *Be*)/*T*. The bits that arrive during the interval *T* in excess of *Bc* + *Be* are discarded by the access FR node. However, this discarding situation can be avoided for a given access rate, R_A, if Be is set to $R_A \times T$ minus *Bc*.

At present, there is no uniform method for setting the interval *T*. If *T* is set too small, such that *Bc* is less than the length of a single frame, then every frame will be marked DE. If *T* is set too large, the buffer capacity in the FR access node required to police CIR may not be practical. Setting *T* to a value on the order of the round trip delay is a good guideline to achieve good TCP/IP throughput over frame relay. In public FR service it is the responsibility of the provider to set the value of *T*, and the value of 1 is often used to match the private line measure of bps.

11.2.2 CIR Sizing

CIR rates in public frame relay networks are chosen for each PVC based on perceived traffic minimums and peak maximum. This measurement is made for both traffic transmitted and received by the FR access port, with heavier emphasis on the traffic received (total traffic on egress from the network to a single premises). For example, a user provisions a single PVC over a 56 kbps FR interface circuit. The CIR rate assigned in each direction is 32 kbps. Thus, at any one time the user can transmit up to 32 kbps with a very small chance (typically .001 percent) of network blockage or lost data, assuming no congestion (thanks to solid engineering). Actual blocking is dependent on how the FR network is loaded and engineered. With an open-loop architecture, frames that exceed the CIR are typically marked DE. With a closed-loop architecture, the switch will not allow the CIR to be exceeded unless there is end-to-end bandwidth available across the network to transmit the frame. Data already sent to the frame relay switch in excess of the CIR will be buffered until more bandwidth becomes available. Some carriers allow the user to exceed this bandwidth but do not guarantee delivery of data above the CIR rate (i.e., marking of DE frames). These providers, such as MCI, offer the subscriber the capability to use additional bandwidth over and above the CIR, marking all traffic above the CIR as DE. In effect, this is a statistical approach assuming that not all the customers will need bandwidth at all times. To account for peak periods, these carriers typically overengineer capacity in their backbone networks. Some carriers such as Sprint offer CIR and non-CIR services, thus allowing users to subscribe to CIR and use the DE bit to discard traffic in excess of the CIR during network congestion. Few providers offer usage and fixed (CIR) pricing.

CIR rates are typically chosen based on the type of traffic and protocol being transmitted and the time required to get information from origin to destination. Figure 11.2 illustrates the example where two 32 kbps CIR rate PVCs are provisioned through a single router and over a single 56 kbps physical access circuit. A PVC is assigned between user A and user C, and one between user B and user D. Users A and B need to send a 200,000-byte file using TCP/IP to users C and D, respectively. If user A is the only one transmitting a 200,000-byte file in a given time period, say 1 minute, it will take approximately 25 seconds if user A can burst above its 32 kbps CIR to the full 64 kbps port speed. Now say both users A and B are bursting 200,000 byte files simultaneously. Since their PVCs share the same FR access circuits, each has available only their CIR rate of 32 kbps, and both files take a minimum of 50 seconds to reach their destinations. These transmission times don't take into account the delay due to the transmission media, propagation delay, switching and routing delay, higher protocol windowing delay, and DE bit setting. Loss of frames marked DE due to congestion could increase the total transmission time even further.

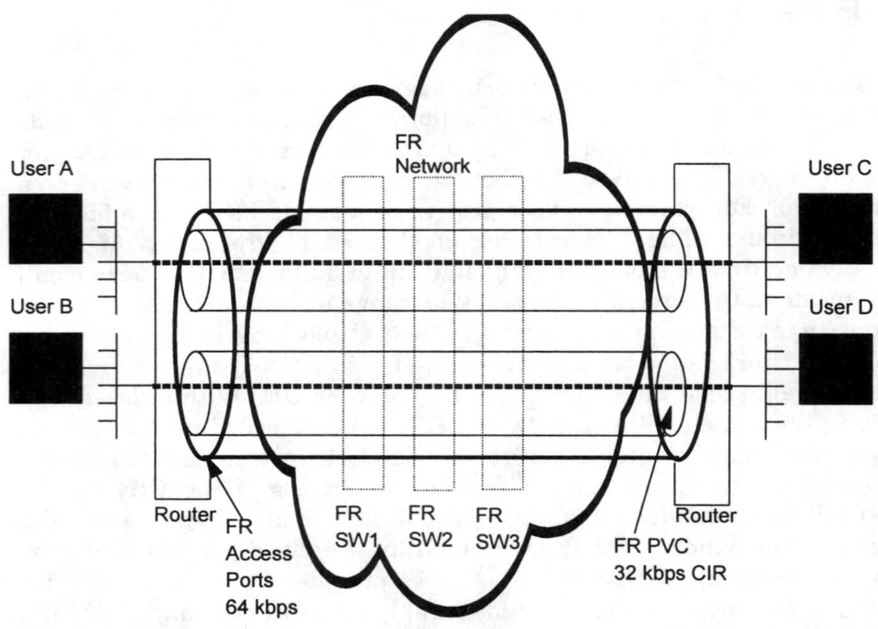

Figure 11.2 Frame Relay CIR Sizing Example

$$\frac{200 \text{ kbyte}}{} * \frac{8 \text{ bits}}{1 \text{ byte}} * \frac{1 \text{ second}}{64 \text{ kbits}} = 25 \text{ seconds}$$

$$\frac{200 \text{ kbyte}}{} * \frac{8 \text{ bits}}{1 \text{ byte}} * \frac{1 \text{ second}}{32 \text{ kbits}} = 50 \text{ seconds}$$

As you can see, it is best to size your CIR to attain the minimum throughput you can stand under congestion conditions for your mission-critical traffic. This is like a "threshold of pain" you will experience in end-to-end throughput and thus transmission time for traffic to travel from users A and B to users C and D. If you are not getting the average throughput required for user satisfaction, try either tuning your transport protocol and application or increasing the size of your CIR. Also note that end-to-end latency will also affect this number.

Some public frame relay network providers offer the option of utilization reports. These reports tell the user by PVC, for each direction, what the peak, average, and maximum average traffic load is at any time period throughout the day. Reports of this type are valuable for sizing of FR access ports and in the setting of PVC CIR rates.

11.2.3 FR Access Port Sizing

FR access ports come in many speeds, from 56 kbps, through 56/64 kbps increments, up to and including DS1(1.544 Mbps) and DS3 (45 Mbps). All PVC CIR rates both into and out of the FR access port should be added separately. This combined CIR speed in either direction should not exceed the port speed in either direction, unless you plan to oversubscribe the port (discussed later in this chapter). Remember that FR is a full duplex service, with mutually exclusive CIR rates in both the transmit and receive directions. Take the example shown in Figure 11.3. Four remote sites have PVCs to the HQ site, and each PVC rate is 32K CIR. Each of the remote sites has a 64 kbps FR access port. If you plan to have 100 percent subscription at the headquarters site, you would need four times the CIR rate on that FR access port, or 128 kbps. If you were to provision less, say a 64 kbps FR access port at the HQ location, you would have a statistical chance that if *all* four sites were to burst (send a large file) to the HQ site simultaneously, data could be discarded at the egress FR switch even though it was not marked DE. Thus, if you felt there was a high probability of simultaneous, long data transfers from the remote sites to the HQ sites, you may want to stay with the 128K FR access port speed. Either way, the total configuration must meet all design objectives as outlined in the next few sections.

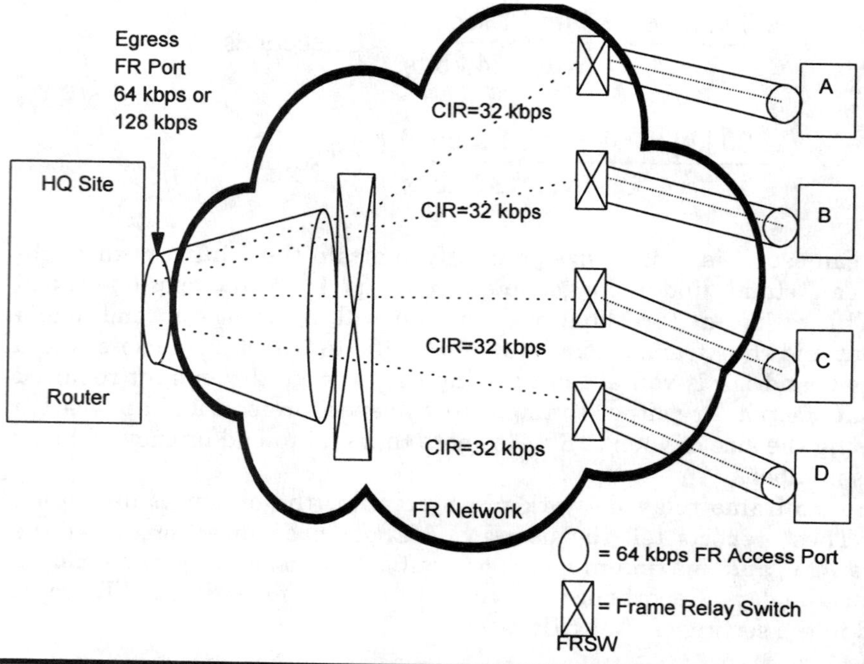

Figure 11.3 FR Port Speed Sizing Example

Most networks do not have exactly overlapping traffic patterns, and some level of oversubscription of the headquarters' FR egress port can be achieved. In fact, the average utilization of most private lines is 10 to 20 percent. If five such private lines were placed on a single FR access the total CIR rate could be 500 percent oversubscribed for matching aggregate CIR to aggregate private line port speeds. In networks without a definable headquarters or master site where most data would be sent to and received from, a study of this type must be done for each site. Refer to the traffic matrix approach defined in Chapter 16.

11.2.4 Unidirectional, Asymmetrical, or Simplex PVCs

Even though a PVC offers a full-duplex connection, CIR rates are assigned unidirectionally. Each PVC is assigned two CIRs – one for each direction – transmit and receive. Most FR users provision the same CIR rate in both directions, and most pricing schemes do not allow users to take advantage of unidirectional assignment of different CIR rates. There is the capability in some frame relay networks to assign different CIRs to each direction of the PVC. These are called *unidirectional*, *asymmetrical*, or *simplex* CIRs. These unidirectional CIR assignments fit well when traffic patterns dictate a small size request in one direction that triggers a large file transfer in the opposite direction as in an inquiry/response application. Figure 11.4 shows an example of an asymmetrical PVC where site A communicates with site B. Site A interfaces to the frame relay network with a 56 kbps FR access circuit (UNI), and site B with a T1 access circuit. Since most of the requests or inquiries for files come from site A to site B, and the files are sent from site B to site A, the PVC between users A and B is assigned a 4 kbps CIR in the direction from user A to user B, and a 32 kbps CIR in the direction from user B to user A.

11.2.5 Bursting over CIR

One of the primary benefits of FR is the statistical multiplexing gain from handling bursty traffic over multiple PVCs. This bursty traffic, such as LAN-to-LAN file transfers, can occur at any time on any of the PVCs. The files will typically be larger in size than can be transferred over the physical access circuit speed within one second, so they must take multiple seconds. In most cases, the transmitted traffic throughput will exceed the assigned CIR. This is referred to as "bursting".

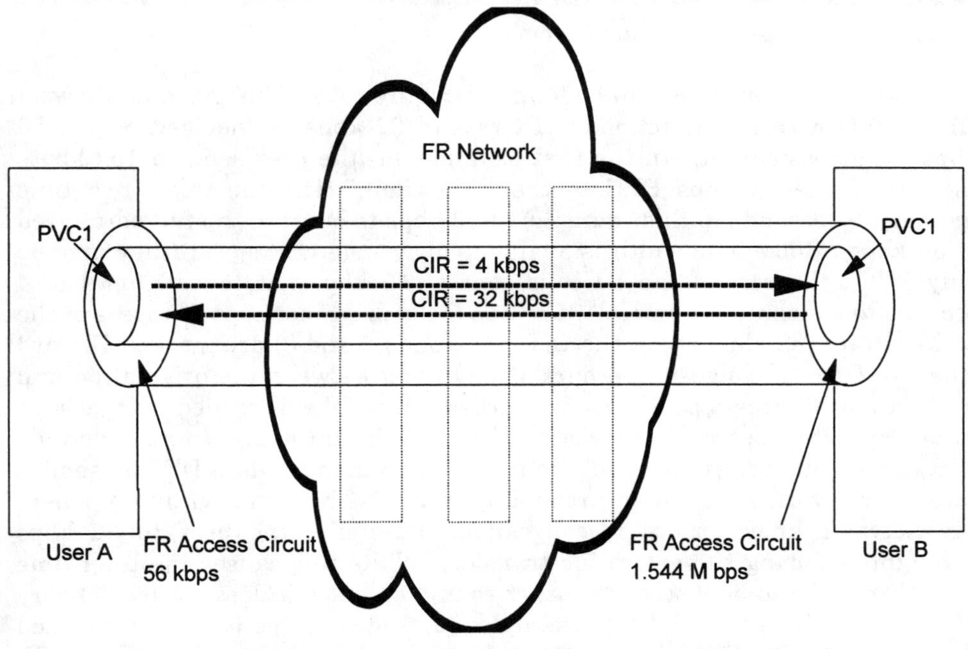

Figure 11.4 Frame Relay Asymmetrical PVC Example

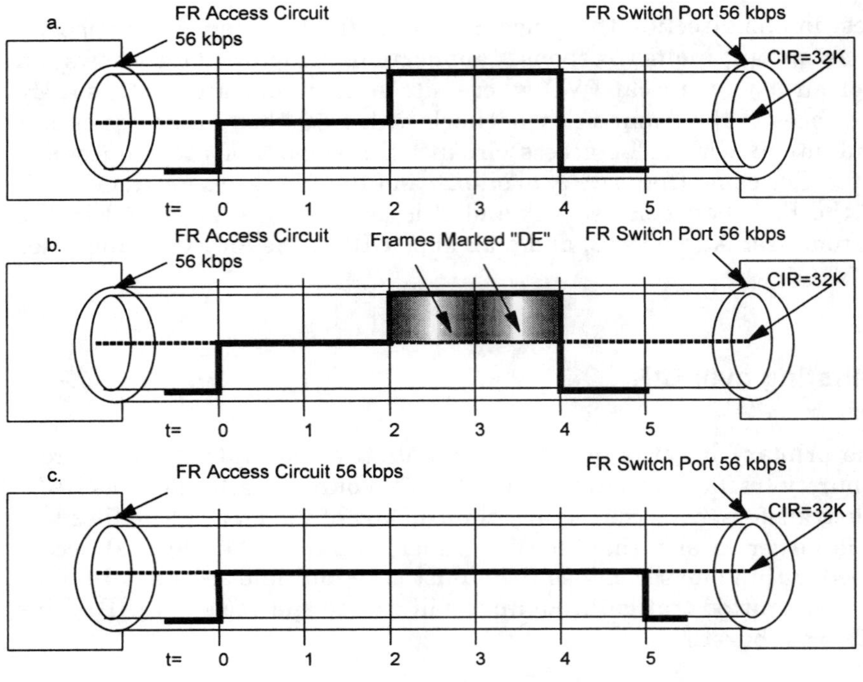

Figure 11.5 Frame Relay Bursting Example

An example of bursting can be found in Figure 11.5. This example shows a single PVC with a bidirectional CIR rate of 32 kbps provisioned over a 56 kbps FR access circuit. In the first example, (a) the user sends a 192 kbyte file across the 32 kbps PVC to the FR switch. The file takes two time increments (seconds in this example) at 32 kbps to burst to the full port speed of 56 kbps. Since bandwidth is available above the CIR speed (they are the only PVC), the rest of the burst is sent at 56 kbps. It takes a total of 4 seconds to transmit the entire 192k Byte file. All frames sent in excess of the 32 kbps rate (32 kbps above the CIR at seconds 2 and 3) are marked Discard Eligible (DE). If congestion occurs at any point between the origination and destination FR access ports, traffic marked DE will be discarded first as seen in example (b). Some FR networks will limit the throughput to the defined CIR rate during congestion conditions, rather than mark data DE and send it into the network with a high probability of loss. This is shown in (c), where the network knows there is congestion and limits the user to 32 kbps throughput during the entire file transfer. While this causes the total time for file transfer to be 8 seconds rather than 4 seconds, it does assure delivery of the data. If in the first two examples (a) and (b) some of the DE-marked data was actually discarded, the time for higher-layer protocols such as TCP to retransmit the 56 kbyte file may have taken much longer than 8 seconds.

Bursting over CIR may not have a good effect on applications during congestion conditions, but most of the time multiple PVCs sharing the same UNI access circuit will not transmit data at the exact same moment. This leads to good statistical multiplexing on access ports, and in these instances FR can provide significant response time savings. This is especially true when a user has been conditioned to the response time of a 56 kbps private line, and now has a 56 kbps PVC provisioned over a T1 FR access circuit. Statistically, most of the time, they may get more than their CIR rate, and often the entire T1 worth of bandwidth will be available. For the last example, this would cut down the transmission time of the 56 kbyte file to 0.3 seconds! (Assuming the higher layer protocols like TCP can acknowledge data that quickly.) Quite a throughput improvement.

11.2.6 Discard Eligible (DE)

There are many ways to limit the amount of bandwidth provided to a user at any time. This may be a critical factor during congestion conditions, when many users with both high-bandwidth and low-bandwidth requirements are contending for limited resources. One method of delimiting the bandwidth to select users on a priority basis is through the intelligent and selective use of the Discard Eligibility (DE) bit. This bit provides a two-tier priority scheme. Other methods employ proprietary implementations. User frames with DE set to 1 are discarded first. Higher-priority users would have DE set to 0. But a DE of 0 does not guarantee that the frame will not be discarded – only that it may be potentially discarded after all frames marked with a 1 are discarded.

The Discard Eligible (DE) bit may be set by either the customer or by the network. If a network node becomes congested, it will first discard the frames with the DE bit set to 1 in an attempt to control further congestion. Beware, however, of the danger of discarding frames marked with the DE bit set to 0 during long periods of congestion. The applications will react by retransmitting lost frames and congestion can intensify.

11.2.7 Oversubscription

There are two different philosophies in the setting of the CIR. The first is called *regular* booking, where the sum of the CIRs is no more than the access rate, and the second is called *overbooking*, or *oversubscription*, where the sum of CIRs exceeds the access line rate.

In regular booking the CIRs can be added up across trunk routes, resulting in predictable, deterministic performance at the expense of a PVC being limited to its CIR during congested intervals. In overbooking, the trunking performance becomes statistical; however, each individual PVC can be provided with a higher CIR rate than in the regular booking case, since the sum of the PVC CIRs can exceed the access line rate.

Thus, oversubscription is the capability to oversubscribe or overbook the CIRs coming into a single physical access port. In effect, it raises the percentage of statistical multiplexing on a FR access circuit even higher. For example, 200 percent oversubscription would allow eight 32K CIRs (256 kbps worth of CIR) to be provisioned over a single 128 kbps physical access port. Oversubscription of 500 percent would allow 20 32K CIRs to be provisioned over a single 128K physical access port. The amount of oversubscription allowed by a frame relay service provider can be an important factor if there are many low-speed user CIRs contending for a single physical network access port, such as at a headquarters or hub site in a hub-and-spoke network. High oversubscription rates can yield greater throughput and savings in equipment and local loop costs. Oversubscription is typically chosen when users intimately understand their PVC traffic patterns and utilization. For example, a 56 kbps FR access port has four PVCs, each with a 32 kbps CIR. This is an example of 200 percent oversubscription. But if two of the PVCs were dedicated to IP file transfer traffic between the hours of 0800 and 1800, and the other two PVCs were dedicated only to IP file backups during 0100 and 0400, then their traffic patterns would be mutually exclusive. Thus, during both day and night each set of PVCs could burst and still receive 100 percent of their CIR in throughput. Oversubscription can be very dangerous if used when traffic utilization patterns are unknown, as it could drastically degrade performance to all users and does not guarantee that each PVC will receive even its full CIR rate at any given point in time.

11.2.8 PVC Reroute Capability

In most frame relay networks, if a physical path on which a PVC rides is broken (e.g., a fiber cut), the FR switches at both ends of the physical path can route the PVC via an alternate switch to the end switch destination. The overall interruption is typically contained to milliseconds. This capability does not exist for the UNI, only within the FR-switched fabric.

11.2.9 Moving from PL to FR

One final note on the migration from a private line (PL) network to a FR network. You must always fully understand the number of sites, CIR sizing, level of meshing, application characteristics, future site growth plans, application and site connectivity requirements, and applications. Ask many questions. Is the client moving to client-server and/or distributed computing architecture? What are the average, peak, and sustained peak throughput requirements? What is their threshold of pain (maximum tolerable delay) for getting the traffic to the destination? What is their minimum and maximum interaction time (e.g., 50 ms for interactive traffic)? What is their total transfer time (the time in ms it takes to transmit a file over a dedicated circuit versus over a PVC with a stated CIR rate)? What is their typical screen refresh time (e.g., 100ms for a typical client-server screen update)? How mission-critical is the nature of the traffic? What is their availability requirement of each application, site, and the entire network (e.g., network = 99.5%, site availability = 99.4% for remote sites, HQ site = 99.6%, and applications = 99.3%)? These are but a few of the questions that will help you produce the best design that meets the user's requirements.

11.3 TRAFFIC AND CONGESTION CONTROL ASPECTS OF FRAME RELAY (CIR, EIR, FECN, BECN, CLLM): DESIGN ISSUES

Now that we have covered other user-definable aspects of frame relay, we turn our attention to the more detailed traffic and congestion-control aspects of frame relay. Flow control is handled at two levels; implicitly at the application and transmission protocol layers, and explicitly within the frame relay protocol, with the use of Forward Explicit Congestion Notification (FECN), Backward Explicit Congestion Notification (BECN), and Consolidated Link Layer Management (CLLM).

11.3.1 Congestion in Frame Relay Networks Defined

Congestion increases with an increase in traffic load across the network. Network congestion occurs when the traffic attempting to be passed across a specific portion of the network fabric is greater than the available bandwidth (after overhead). Typically, network transport hardware will have some buffering capability, but when this capability is exceeded, a congestion condition occurs. In basic frame relay transport, as discussed in the previous chapter, when the network reaches a congestion point it will begin to discard frames using DE bit priorities until there is no longer a congestion condition (or until it has discarded all DE traffic, remains congested, and next begins to discard non-DE marked frames). When network congestion causes the network to discard frames, the user or network access devices must have the intelligence of higher-level protocols to provide end-to-end error detection and correction and retransmission of missing data (frames).

There are two types of congestion-control methods used to manage frame relay data transport: implicit and explicit congestion notification.

Implicit congestion notification implies the use of a layer 4 transport protocol, such as the DoD Transmission Control Protocol (TCP) or IBM's System Network Architecture (SNA), in either the network device or the user premises equipment. These protocols work similarly to the transmit and receive windowing in X.25 packet switching, but manage the end-to-end transmission of packets instead of FR frames. TCP automatically reduces the window size, or the number of packets transmitted, according to network delay or frame loss. This allows the end users (or the network access device) to accommodate network congestion and avoid discarding frames and causing retransmissions, but it also implies that the user takes the responsibility for managing congestion control. Many of the approaches discussed in the following sections can be used in conjunction with TCP implemented at the user device level. Thus, flow control could be adjusted by the TCP upon receipt of congestion information from the frame relay network. With SNA, Receiver Not Ready (RNR) notifications are sent from the FRAD to the SNA device (e.g., an IBM 3174 controller) during periods of congestion.

The burden on these protocols can be reduced somewhat through the use of PVC bandwidth prioritization within the CPE. Some CPE can actually prioritize individual PVCs within a network-access circuit, allowing some PVCs to be less affected by congestion conditions while other are more severely affected.

Explicit congestion notification comes in three flavors: Forward Explicit Congestion Notification (FECN), Backward Explicit Congestion Notification (BECN), and Consolidated Link Layer Management (CLLM) addressing. ANSI standard T1.618 clearly defines congestion control with the FECN/BECN bits and manages message notification through the CLLM mechanism. Each method will be discussed in detail.

There may also be an absence of flow control, in which case the higher-layer protocols will transmit data across the WAN at a fixed rate, regardless of whether data is lost or discarded.

11.3.2 FECN and BECN

Congestion notification is provided in the frame relay address field by the FECN and BECN bits. The FECN bit is set by the FR network nodes when they become congested, and this informs the receiver flow-control protocols of the congestion situation, while the BECN bit is set in FR frames headed in the downstream direction to inform transmitter flow-control protocols of the congestion situation. An increase in the frequency of FECN and BECN bits received is a good indication of growing network congestion. At present, very little use is being made of this technique of congestion control in end and intermediate systems. One concern is that by the time the FECN/BECN arrives at the controlling end, the congested state may no longer exist in the FR node that sent the FECN/BECN notice. The main concern is when the FECN/BECN notice is delivered to the CPE router, which is not the primary source of flow control. Currently, no technique exists for the CPE router to convey the FECN/BECN message to TCP or the application that could provide flow control.

Figure 11.6 depicts a frame relay network connecting a host in Dallas with many remote user devices in Charleston via a FR network. In the process of downloading massive files from the mainframe in Dallas to the users in Charleston via a PVC (shown as the dashed line), congestion occurs on the Atlanta-to-Raleigh trunk. The FECN and BECN bit setting is performed on all DLCIs traversing the Atlanta-to-Raleigh trunk to notify them of the congestion condition. The Atlanta node sets the FECN bit to 1 and notifies the Charleston PVC user receiving traffic from Dallas of impending congestion. The Atlanta node also sets the BECN bit to 1 on frames destined from Charleston to Dallas, informing the Dallas PVC user of the same congestion condition. Either the Dallas user could throttle back, or the Charleston user could flow control and the Dallas sender use a higher-layer protocol. Either action reduces the frame rate and will eventually cause the congestion condition to abate and the FECN and BECN to clear.

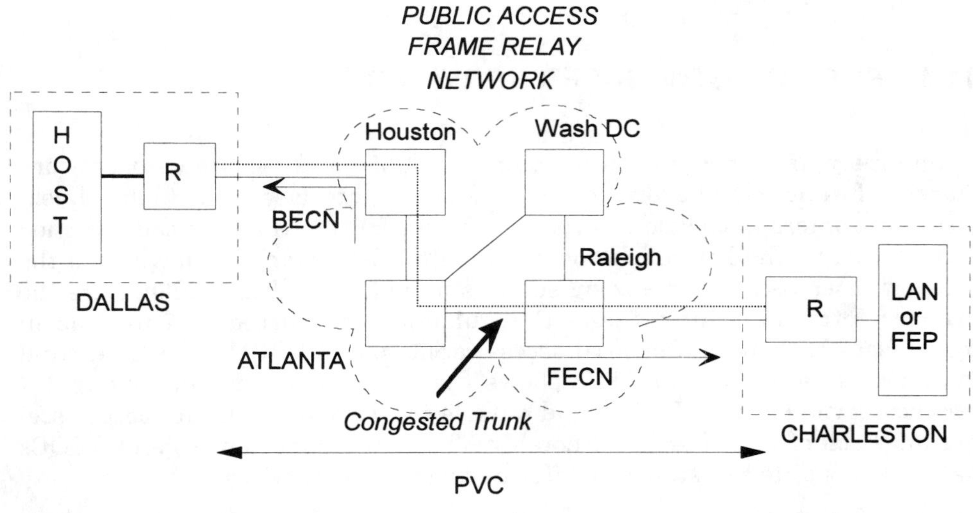

Figure 11.6 Congestion Control Example

11.3.3 Consolidated Link Layer Management (CLLM)

The second form of congestion management defined by ANSI T1.618 is the Consolidated Link Layer Management (CLLM) function. CLLM reserves one of the DLCI addresses on a frame relay interface for transmitting control messages to user devices when there are no frames to transmit, yet a congestion notification still needs to be sent. The CLLM message is a contingency for notifying users of congestion activity outside the conventional framing structure, since there is no provision in the standards for empty frames that contain only congestion-control information. The CLLM can contain a list of DLCIs that correspond to the congested frame relay bearer connections — all users affected are then notified of congestion. Multiple CLLM messages can be transmitted in a network with many DLCIs that require congestion notification.

An example of CLLM in use is depicted in Figure 11.7. ANSI T1.618 defines the message based on the ISO 8885 definition of the use of message identification (XID) frames for the transport of congestion management information. This figure shows the same network configuration as in the last example, but now Atlanta is notifying Dallas of network congestion through DLCI number 1023.

One further note on the use of CLLM: since both the ANSI-defined CLLM and the frame relay Specifications with Extensions, which defines the Local Management Interface (LMI), both use DLCI 1023, they are mutually exclusive and cannot be used simultaneously.

11.4 PUBLIC NETWORK FR SERVICES

Frame relay has emerged full force on the public and private data network market. Frame relay hardware ranges from PC interface cards to multiplexers, from routers to backbone switches offering FR interfaces to cell-switched architectures. The IntereXchange Carriers (IXCs) historically have been the primary inter-LATA frame relay services providers, and the RBOCs are the primary intra-LATA providers. Deregulation has blurred this line, as in many cases IXCs now offer local access services, and RBOCs interLATA and interstate services. Figure 11.8 shows the connectivity provided by an FR service provider across LATAs and outside the LATAs (alternate access scenario). Each of the IXCs (most notably AT&T, MCI, and Sprint) and RBOCs have taken a different stance on offering frame relay services.

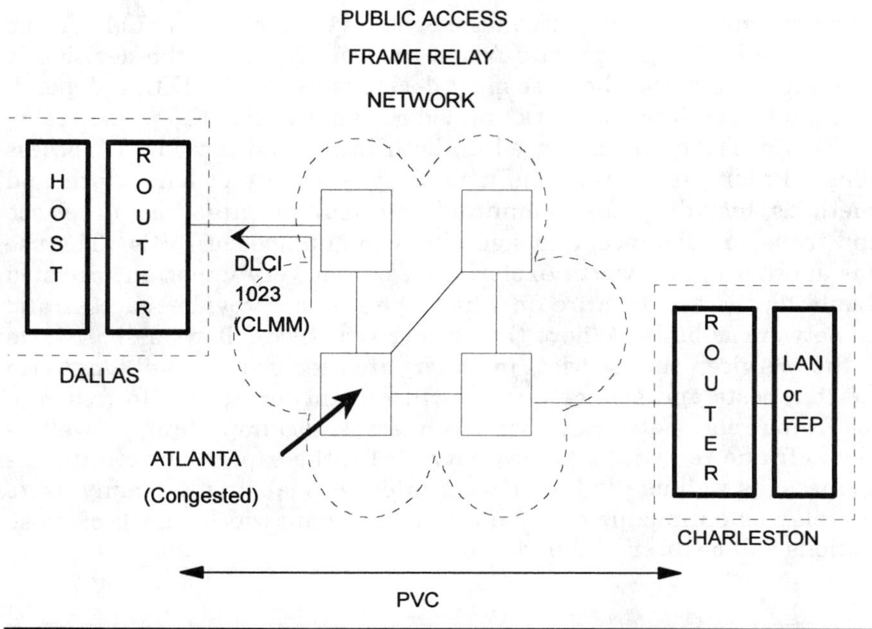

Figure 11.7 Consolidated Link Layer Management (CLLM) Function

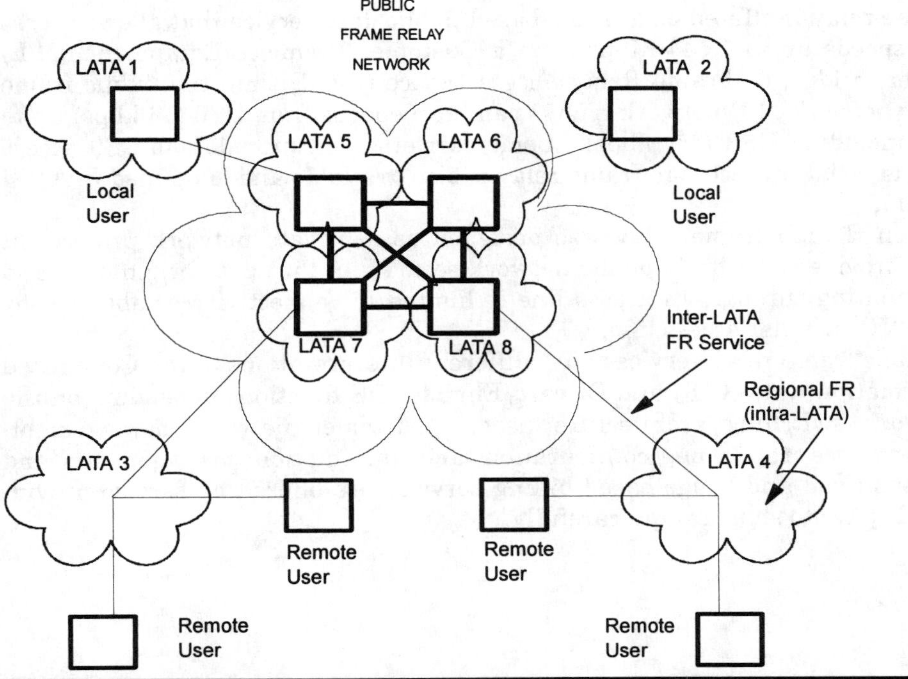

Figure 11.8 Public Services Frame Relay Network Topology

First, the user must choose between the benefits of accessing a public frame relay network or building a private frame relay network. If the decision is made for a public network, the user must decide between the IXC, independent information services network provider, and/or RBOC frame relay services. This decision will be based on both intra- and inter-LATA access and pricing. Pricing is, in turn, influenced by a variety of bandwidth and access methods including the committed information rate (fixed), service access and transport distance, and sometimes the number of PVCs. The use of SVCs is another option worth exploring. Another very important decision factor should be the architecture on which the service provider's access and backbone network is built. Where the pricing structure follows a short-term view of the service, the service provider architecture is the long-term insurance that costs and service quality will remain constant. How each of the public frame relay network services connect is also important, as well as international frame relay interconnectivity. With the expansions of international business, as well as the high cost of international circuits, many users see frame relay as optimizing costly international bandwidth. Each of these service options will be discussed in detail.

11.4.1 Service Aspects of Frame Relay

Frame relay is offered as a frame-based public data service that allows access line speeds up to 1.544 Mbps from a Customer Premises Equipment (CPE) router, bridge, or Frame Relay Access Device (FRAD) into the public frame relay network. FR network trunks can be of speeds from DS0 (56 kbps) up to and including DS3 (45 Mbps). Some carriers even provide sub-DS0 access speeds. Dial-up access to frame relay is also available and is defined in ANSI T1.617.

Even though frame relay was designed as a private network protocol, it does provide some basic public network security in that data originating and terminating through an access line is limited to connectivity established by the PVCs for that access line.

Public frame relay services offer different interpretations of the Committed Information Rate (CIR) and Discard Eligible (DE functions depending on the network switching architecture used. Customer network management, performance reporting, configuration and information management, and various fixed and usage-based billing services are offered by service providers. It pays to shop around carefully.

11.4.2 Public versus Private

Now that the user is interested in frame relay as the transport technology of choice, does he or she build a private frame relay network, or subscribe to a public frame relay service? This decision is determined by cost efficiencies, operations and network management, alternate service and product offerings (standalone or bundled), and the corporate position on outsourcing. Some companies are retaining private networks to carry voice traffic and converting their data transport to public frame- and cell-relay services. Others are taking a more conventional approach and keeping part of the network private and slowly migrating to public frame- and cell-based network services.

Public frame relay service provides a consolidation of private line meshing, instead performing the meshing through PVCs within the FR network and requiring each user to have a single access circuit to the public network. Figure 11.9 shows the difference between a frame relay network service and a private network solution. Frame relay networks provide virtual-circuit access to any other node on the network, a virtual fully meshed network without paying for many private lines, a reduction in facility costs in the number of network access ports, and dynamic bandwidth allocation between PVCs. Obviously, service-level availability increases with the number of nodes in the service provider's network.

Private frame relay network designs are based on three types of technologies:

1. DS1/DS3 multiplexers employing fast-packet frame relay technology and interface cards
2. Bridges or routers employing dedicated links for frame relay interfaces into a network
3. Fast-packet switches employing dedicated DS1/DS3s (expensive for large networks)

These types vary widely, and existing customer premises equipment will often influence the decision. The network design manager and engineer should consider all of the alternatives presented here before deciding on what type of technology to use when deploying a frame relay network. When frame relay was first supported over a multiplexed backbone, inefficiencies were inherent in the bandwidth allocation schemes. Over the past few years, multiplexer vendors have worked out these problems to where bandwidth allocated to frame relay traffic is truly statistically multiplexed.

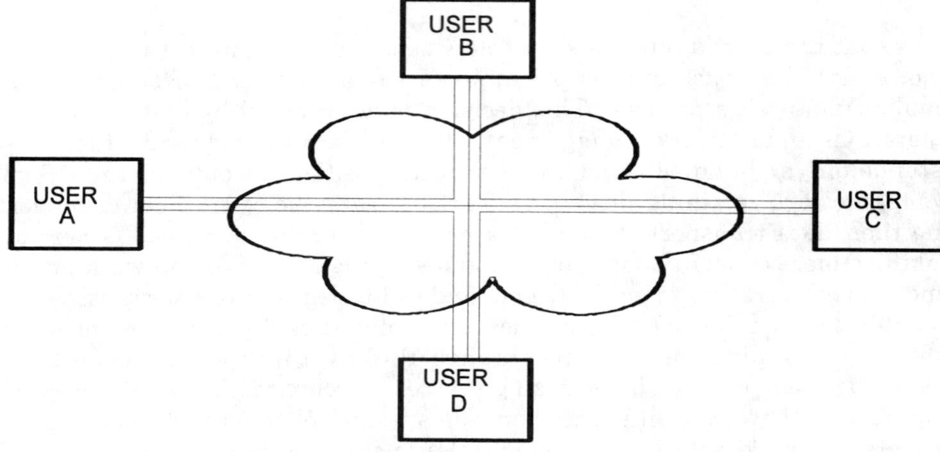

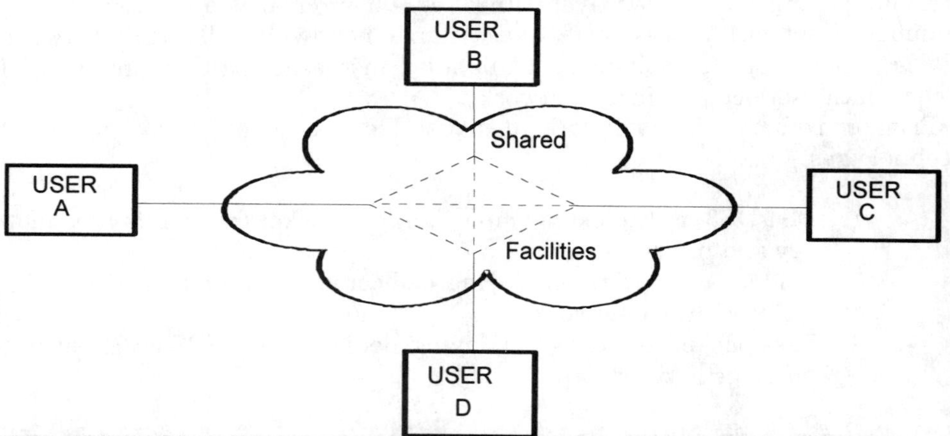

Figure 11.9 Public Service Frame Relay versus Private Network Solution

11.4.3 Public Frame Relay Service Offerings

There are three main groups providing public frame relay services: what were traditionally the IXCs, the RBOCs and LECs, and Internet access providers. Since the 1996 Telecommunications bill was passed, many FR service providers span two or all three of these categories. These days almost all FR service providers offer some form of value-added services in addition to frame relay transport, such as voice service bundles, flexible pricing schemes (e.g., fixed CIR and usage based), and higher and more flexible access speeds. The major frame relay service providers in the United States include Ameritech, AT&T, Bell Atlantic, BellSouth, Cable & Wireless, CompuServe, GTE, MCI Communications, MFS, NYNEX, Pacific Bell, Sprint, and US West. This list is not complete; it includes only those with the largest market share or geographic coverage at time of publication.

IXC frame relay public service offerings have the following additional advantages for users:

- Ubiquitous public network access
- Little network capital investment required (CPE only)
- Distributed switching backbone and architecture
- Extensive IXC bandwidth capacity
- Extensive IXC PoP coverage
- Universal access
- Flexibility of access locations and interface speeds
- Frame relay offered in combination with other switched services
- Migration path to other technologies often offered
- Usage-based and flat-rate billing options (users take advantage of best one) with tariff structures
- Carrier-provided CPE in many instances
- Outsourcing packages available
- Skilled service and equipment support structures
- Inherent reliability, redundancy, and survivability
- Intercompany switched and permanent virtual sessions

Additional benefits of public networks over private networks discussed in earlier chapters should be reiterated here, such as: value-added services, network redundancy, and network management. Most, if not all, frame relay services conform to ANSI T1.617, ANSI T1.618, ANSI T1.606, and LMI Extensions and support the following capabilities:

- PVCs and SVCs
- Access rates of DS0, Nx56/64 kbps, DS1, E1,
- PVC CIR rates as low as 4 kbps increments (and 0CIR PVCs)
- Some analog access rates
- Up to 1023 DLCI addresses
- 2, 3, or 4 octet DLCI addresses
- 4096 octets frame size
- FECN, BECN, DE bit support for network and CPE devices
- Multicasting
- Global or local addressing
- Closed user groups of DLCI addresses
- PVC in-band local status
- Interenterprise, intercarrier frame relay internetworking (i.e., NNI)
- End-to-end delay of service less than 250 ms

- Extended addressing options
- High availability and low error rate
- Interworking with other services (i.e., ATM)
- Proactive, 7 × 24 network management with performance engineering

Most of today's IXC frame relay public service offerings are based upon either the StrataCom Integrated Packet Exchange IPX-32 with BPX, the Bay Network's BCN and BNX frame relay switches, the Alcatel TPX1100, the Cascade STX-9000s, or the AT&T BNS-2000. It is the author's opinion that architectures based on a standard cell-switched backbone typically offer the best performance and can offer quick upgrade to, or internetworking with, ATM. The correct selection of a frame relay vendor often depends on the customer and application requirements. Almost all of the frame relay providers are offering both frame relay and ATM-based services.

11.4.4 Switched Virtual Circuits (SVCs)

Both ANSI and ITU-T have published standards for Switched Virtual Circuit (SVC) frame relay operation. The standards (based on ISDN Digital Subscriber SSNo.1) define a signaling interface to build a switched virtual circuit. SVC service offers an excellent opportunity to users requiring:

- Short connect, low volume, and transfer times with infrequent connectivity and traffic patterns (like video conferencing)
- Connectivity provisioned on-the-fly
- Backup for PVC failure over dial access (POTS line or ISDN) to FR switch

Switched Virtual Circuits (SVCs) allow a sending DTE to transmit the address of the receiving DTE along with the data at call setup time. When the first switch receives this address and data, it establishes the connection-oriented, virtual path to the receiver. This method eliminates the need for preconfigured PVCs. Some of the functions available on SVCs include DLCI control and addressing scheme assignments, user channel negotiation, and service parameters negotiation (maximum frame size, throughput, transit delay) all on a switched service offering. Wide implementation of SVC services has been slow, primarily due to the complexity of SVC management, late standardization, and the requirement for strict security and administration. SVCs are outlined along with PVCs in ITU-T Recommendation I.122. SVCs, to date, are not interoperable across NNI interfaces.

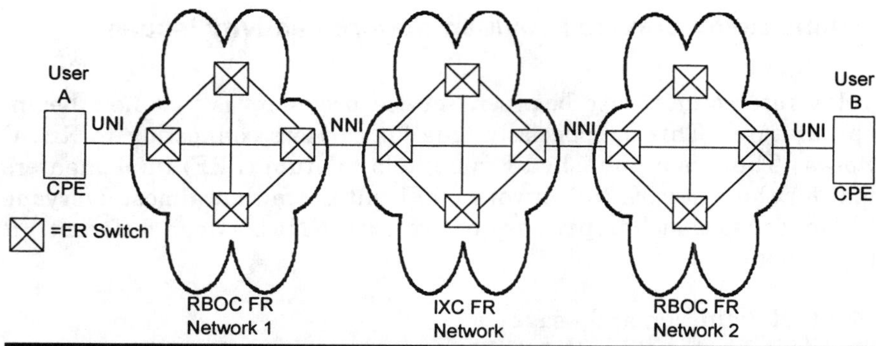

Figure 11.10 Frame Relay NNI Network Example

11.4.5 Network-to-Network Interface (NNI)

The FR Network-to-Network Interface (NNI) is defined by the standards as a method for two frame relay networks to interconnect, pass frame relay traffic, and manage the logical connections (PVCs) which originate on one frame relay network and terminate on another. Figure 11.10 illustrates an NNI network example. User A interfaces to RBOC 1 FR network via a FR UNI. RBOC 1 interfaces to the IXC FR network with a FR NNI. The IXC also interfaces to RBOC 2 FR network with a FR NNI. Finally, RBOC 2 FR network interfaces to the destination user B with a FR UNI. Users A and B view their connection as a single PVC between their CPE. Each FR provider has visibility, query capability, and bidirectional polling of the end device or switch in the adjacent FR network through the NNI interface. NNI circuits are also used to connect dissimilar switch types, as is usually the case between different FR services, providing multivendor interoperability.

FR NNI standards include

- ⇒ ITU Recommendations I.372 Frame Mode Bearer Services NNI Requirements, 1992
- ⇒ ITU Recommendation I.370 Congestion Management in Frame Relaying Networks, 1991
- ⇒ ITU Recommendation Q.933 DSS1 Signaling Specification for Frame Relay Basic Call Control, 1992
- ⇒ Bellcore TR-TSV-001370 Generic Requirements for Exchange Access FR PVC Service
- ⇒ FR Forum NNI Agreement, 1992

11.4.6 Frame Relay Service Provider Interconnectivity Issues

Frame relay interconnectivity between service providers is just now beginning to proliferate. This is especially true for carriers connecting to RBOC FR networks. There is a published Frame Relay Forum (FRF) Implementers Agreement for the Network-to-Network (NNI) interface that almost everyone follows. The issues that hamper ease of use with NNI between different FR switch types include:

- CIR definition and usage
- Switching architecture differences (open- vs. closed-loop congestion algorithms)
- Congestion-control implementation (different uses of DE)
- Transfer of network management and billing information problems
- Ability to pass LMI information
- Number of DLCIs per port / IP addressing

Many of these problems have either been resolved or accommodated in most of today's FR NNI implementations, or have limited the functionality of the NNI interface to just passing traffic and SNMP alarm indications. Most of the IXCs and LECs offer some form of NNI, and those that do not offer some form of lower-speed dedicated or dial access for remote access sites that cannot access the frame relay cloud directly.

11.4.7 Regional, National, or International?

Before deregulation, the RBOCs were not able to provide data services inter-LATA, or between two LATAs. Thus, RBOCs have traditionally offered intra-LATA FR and have been forced to partner with CAPs and IXCs to offer Inter-LATA and interstate FR service. This has changed with deregulation. Figure 11.11 shows three examples of regional FR networks. Example (a) demonstrates a five-site intra-LATA network where one site serves as the HQ site to four remote sites. All switching is performed by a single FR switch. It is easy to see that there are three major single points of failure in this scenario – the FR switch, the access from the HQ site to the FR switch, and the HQ site device (router) itself. Example (b) shows the same network, but now there are two FR switches and much greater diversity is added to the network. Dial backup could also be added to either scenario to increase diversity. Also notice on example (b) that a trunk is provisioned to an IXC FR switch allowing inter-LATA FR service extension.

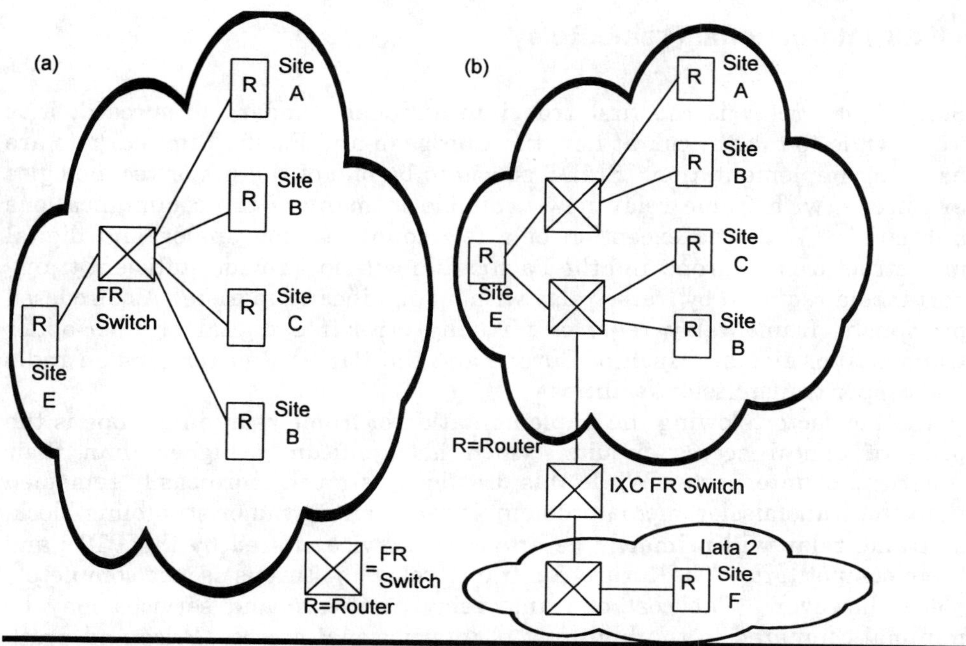

Figure 11.11 Regional Frame Relay Network

When does regional FR make sense?

* All sites are within a small geographic area and they require high degree of meshing – such as between one or multiple close proximity LATAs.
* Many sites are in one geographic area (LATA or state) – typically worth looking at with >5 sites intra-LATA traffic.
* Density of RBOC FR switches – the regional frame provider has more than one switch per LATA you want to terminate traffic in, otherwise you are still vulnerable on the back-haul from the local serving PoP to the FR switch
* Pricing is cheaper than with an equivalent private line and throughput is just as good.
* Most sites are intra-LATA with at least a few inter-LATA or interstate.
* Increased delay does not adversely affect applications.

Regional FR pricing has been very competitive; in fact, in a few areas such as PacBell's California territory, it is even cheaper than traditional local loops. Pricing for regional FR service has been based on the port connection, access circuit speed, and number of PVCs (with decreasing price, the greater the number of PVCs). This is interesting, as the FR provider actually plans to provide the entire port speed, allowing the users to segment their port speeds into bandwidth increments (CIRs) to fit their user profiles, as long as they do not exceed their FR port speed (100 percent maximum subscription).

11.4.8 International Frame Relay

Since frame relay is the first true international standard to succeed, it is worthwhile to take a look at how the European and Pacific Rim markets are handling implementation. SMDS seems to be one of the major technologies in Europe, with frame relay now available in many of the communications hub cities. With the exception of a few countries, the analog and digital infrastructure in Europe and the Pacific Rim will not provide sufficient transport media required by frame relay without significant upgrade. As discussed previously, frame relay requires virtually error-free digital or fiber-optics transmission media. Much of Europe and the Pacific Rim remains on radio and copper transmission facilities.

Another factor slowing the implementation of frame relay in Europe is the price of digital access circuits, which is significantly higher than their American counterparts. While this drawback is much more easily remedied than the transmission media problem, it represents a major stumbling block, as frame relay will primarily be an access service offered by the PTTs and their competitors. The future for frame relay in Europe is not completely bleak, however. The cost of frame relay hardware and services may be minimal compared to the high cost of international access. Price and availability prove to be the driving forces in the success of international frame relay. Trans-Atlantic and Pacific Rim fiber-optic cables provide the transmission media needed, and the secondary expense of turning up frame relay access is in the hardware. This upgrade of transmission facilities, along with completed ITU-T frame relay standards, will move many European countries toward frame relay.

The introduction and migration toward ISDN in some countries may speed the resolution of these roadblocks, but if the implementation and widespread use of X.25 packet switching provides any indication, international frame relay may not be as valuable an interim solution for bandwidth-flexible services such as SMDS or ATM as in the United States. However, the international community is far from implementing ATM technology, so frame relay may provide the needed interim solution. Many FR service providers in the United States and international PTTs have joined to offer international frame relay access. The leaders include British Telecom North America, AT&T, MCI, Sprint, Infonet, and Cable & Wireless.

11.5 PUBLIC FRAME RELAY NETWORK ARCHITECTURES

The switching architecture used in the public frame relay network backbone will determine the characteristics of end-to-end delay (latency), handling of CIR and DE traffic, and will definitely have an effect on the higher-layer protocols (such as TCP/IP and IPX). Some FR network service providers use cell-switching architectures to slice and dice the frames into fixed-length cells as soon as there is enough data to fill a cell (good because cell sizes can be as small as 24 bytes). This technique can decrease the end-to-end network latency for large frame sizes. Others perform pure frame relay switching, reading the entire frame into the switch before relaying it to the egress port or another FR switch (this can add a lot of store-and-forward delay if large frames are being used), with the last switch in network reassembling the frames before sending them to the end user. The major difference between leading FR network service providers today is whether they use an open-loop or closed-loop congestion control or avoidance algorithm between FR switches. The difference between these two approaches can really affect your applications, especially during periods of severe network congestion.

11.5.1 Open-Loop Architecture

Open-loop algorithm systems operate on the concept of congestion control after congestion begins to occur. In an open-loop architecture, each user (PVC) is allocated a committed burst size or CIR. Users can transmit all their traffic and not mark any frames discard eligible (DE) if the committed burst (CIR) is not exceeded. If the CIR is exceeded by a given value for a period of time *t*, the first frames to be discarded during congestion are those marked for DE. Any transmission of frames that exceeds both the CIR *and* the excess burst rate will begin discard automatically until the level of congestion is brought down to the point where DE-set frames are discarded and non-DE frames are passed. It is then up to the applications to use some method to back-off-and-retransmit while the network recovers from congestion. The user will need to use large buffers to store the data that applications have already transmitted from the CPE to the network, but has not gone through the network to the destination CPE because of the congestion within the network or at the egress port. Traffic enforcement will be practiced on all users until minimum or no congestion conditions return.

Take the example shown in Figure 11.12, where FR CPE 1 is communicating over a public FR network with FR CPE 2. CPE 1 has a 64 kbps UNI port over which is provisioned a single PVC with a 32 kbps CIR. The same CIR rate is provisioned in both directions. Now say that CPE 1 bursts enough data toward CPE 2 so that it could fill the 56 kbps circuit for 7 seconds. In the open-loop algorithm, the ingress FR switch A immediately allows the user to burst over the assigned CIR to the full port speed. FR switch A will mark every other frame discard eligible (DE). Since each of the switches do not keep track of the congestion conditions anywhere else in the network, it is conceivable that congestion could be occurring on link B-C (effectively allowing only a 32 kbps throughput for this PVC) at the same time as FR switch A is accepting all the user data at a 56 kbps rate. Thus, if the congestion condition still existed at the time switch B transmitted the data on to switch C, then half the user data (those frames marked DE) could be dropped. Notice that this has the effect of an open-loop where each switch does not know the congestion status of any other switch.

Pure noncell frame switches typically use open-loop congestion algorithms. Frame relay switches that do not use cell switching will typically read the entire frame into buffers before transmitting it to the user or next switch. The engineering of open-loop architectures is also unique, where switch egress, or network, trunks must have sufficient bandwidth reserved for both normal CIR traffic and some percentage of traffic marked DE. This typically leads to overengineering the switched backbone.

Be aware, however, of the danger of discarding frames marked with the DE bit during long periods of congestion. All traffic that has been discarded has to be retransmitted, along with new traffic requiring transmission. Applications that react by retransmitting lost frames will cause congestion to intensify even further. Window-sizing flow-control protocols such as Transmission Control Protocol (TCP) can be used to scale down the volume of retransmissions and spread the load over a greater time period. This slows the effective offered load and decreases the throughput gracefully until congestion clears.

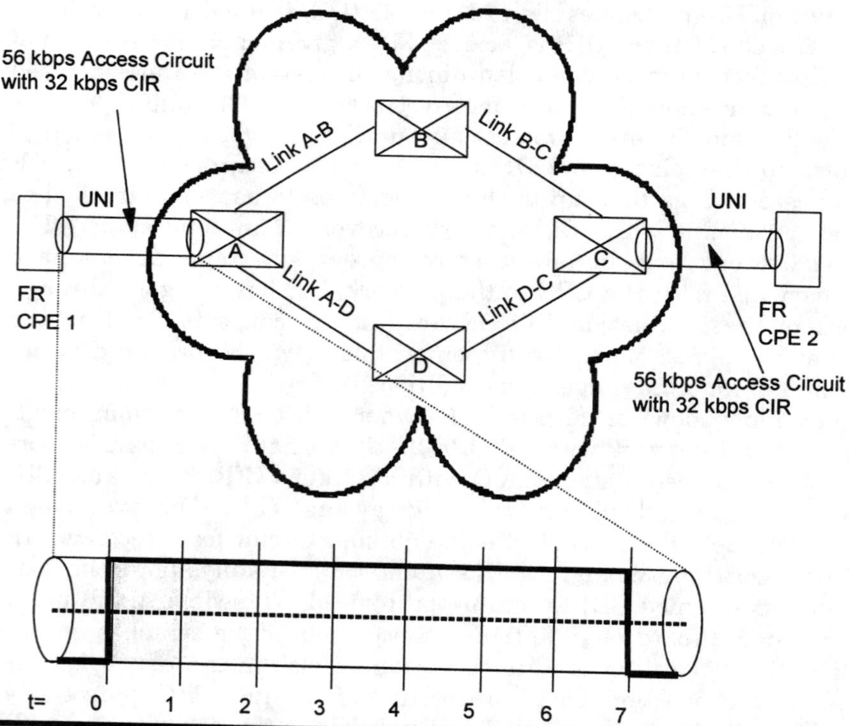

Figure 11.12 Open-Loop Algorithm Example

11.5.2 Closed-Loop Architecture

A closed-loop architecture is typically found in switches that convert frames to fixed-size cells on the backbone. These switches immediately slice frames into cells and transmit the data, thus incurring less serialization delay. The closed-loop architecture creates a closed environment, where every switch within the FR network fabric knows the congestion condition from origin to destination. The FR network prevents the user from experiencing lost data due to congestion by slowly throttling back the available transport bandwidth at the user entry point to the FR network (UNI) to the predefined CIE rate. This congestion prevention is used in place of allowing the user to continue to burst and marking DE frames, knowing that discard and retransmission of some frames is inevitable. It is always better to avoid congestion than to have to control it. Closed-loop algorithms do just that – avoid congestion. One example is StrataCom's Foresight algorithm. The Foresight algorithm uses a gradual step function, gracefully increasing or decreasing the traffic allowed into the network. This allows less marking of DE frames and guarantees a more constant end-to-end delay with less jitter.

Take the example shown in Figure 11.13, where FR CPE 1 is communicating over a public FR network with FR CPE 2. CPE 1 has a 64 kbps port over which is provisioned a single PVC with a 32 kbps CIR. The same CIR rate is provisioned in both directions. Now say that CPE 1 bursts enough data toward CPE 2 that it could fill the 56 kbps circuit for 10 seconds. In the closed-loop algorithm, the ingress FR switch (A) slowly increases the available bandwidth to the user in small increments (say 4 kbps for this example). The user can actually use the entire 64 kbps port bandwidth, but the FR switch only increases the available bandwidth in short increments to assure that all frames accepted can reach the end destination (switch C). When congestion begins to occur on Link B-C at time interval 4, FR switch B sends a congestion warning to FR switch A, which in turn (one time interval later) begins to throttle back CPE 1 as shown in the figure. If the congestion condition continues to intensify CPE 1 traffic flow will continue to be gracefully throttled back until it reaches no less than its guaranteed CIR rate of 32 kbps. Note that part of the fixed cell overhead is used to send these link and port congestion state notifications back and forth between FR switches. Notice that this has the effect of a closed-loop environment where each switch knows the congestion status of every other switch.

This method also allows the FR provider to attain a much greater usage of network resources than by the open-loop method. Another side benefit is easier capacity and growth planning. The real advantage to the user is that it achieves a close, somewhat predictable Quality-of-Service (QoS) delay level to every user. This implementation is better for Constant Bit Rate (CBR) traffic that is jitter sensitive and Variable Bit Rate (VBR) traffic bursts from multiple users.

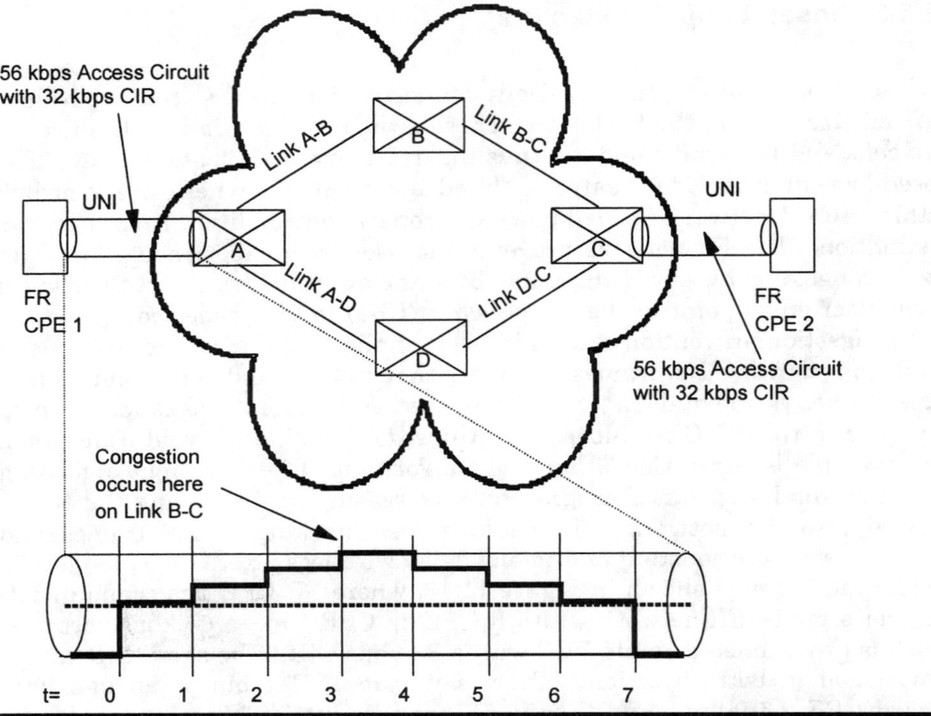

Figure 11.13 Closed-Loop Algorithm Example

11.5.3 FR over a Cell-Relay Backbone

When frames are segmented into cells and transmitted as soon as there is enough data to fill up a cell, the end-to-end delay can be decreased. Thus, the frame relay switches do not have to wait until entire frame is read into buffers before segmenting into cells and transmitting. Serialization delay is decreased and end-to-end jitter is also reduced. Don't worry about the increase in cell overhead when compared to frames – most FR providers will either overengineer their backbone or provision DS3 trunks at a minimum.

11.5.4 Input/Output Buffers

Some FR switches will store data (frames) that exceeds CIR in large input buffers. These buffers transmit the data either when the congestion has cleared, or when bandwidth within the defined CIR is available. This can cause a marginal amount of delay if the CIR is consistently exceeded and traffic is blocked from entering the network, but in many cases the delay will be more tolerable to the end-transport protocols, as they do not have to accommodate and discover packets lost to DE discard.

11.6 ACCESS DESIGN ISSUES

There are many methods of accessing a frame relay network. We first look at the more common direct or dedicated access via a DS0, FT1, or DS1 circuit using a bridge, router, multiplexer, gateway, and switch. The Frame Relay Access Device (FRAD) plays a unique role in enabling legacy and newer internetworking protocols to share access to a FR network. Some remote sites do not require nor can afford dedicated access to a frame network, yielding to the more cost-effective dial access. Dial access also doubles as a backup method for dedicated access circuits. Finally, network management plays a key role in managing the access portion of the network, where most of the outages in a FR network occur.

11.6.1 Network Access Devices

A variety of hardware devices exist on the market that make frame relay network access possible. These devices range in complexity and include bridges, routers, gateways, FRADs, multiplexers, and even voice switches. This is not a complete list, just the more popular devices. While many frame relay service providers offer a frame relay cloud, which promises ubiquitous access, it befalls the user to employ intelligent premises devices to concentrate, aggregate, multiplex, and translate existing traffic and protocols into the FR protocol and provide the access interface to the FR network. Some users will even deploy a "hybrid" solution, using one or more of the devices described.

In all of these devices, much of the protocol conversion, processing, and switching is done through *software*. Most devices just require a software upgrade, and the CSU/DSU can remain the same (as it is transparent to the frame relay protocol). This advantage minimizes the hardware investment required to upgrade to FR. The size of the hardware is influenced primarily by the number of access and egress ports on the device, and is often not representative of the functionality provided. Be wary of the number of software releases published by vendors in the frame relay market. Each vendor can release from 3 to 4 major releases and 15 to 20 "dot" or bug fix/feature enhancement releases per year!

When purchasing frame relay access or switching hardware, ensure that the equipment is compatible with the standards discussed here. Support should be available for the DLCI and all frame relay header bits, FCS review, the use of FECN, BECN, and DE bits, congestion control conforming to the standards, and multiple protocol support.

Many bridge and router vendors provide frame relay support in their products. Since the architecture of these devices lends itself to offering multiple, multipurpose ports (as opposed to access and trunk side distinctions using traditional multiplexers and switches) they view frame relay as a software implementation on synchronous cards. FR protocol support is typically bundled with the devices' operating system software.

Many multiplexer vendors offer some form of frame relay network access. As noted in the last chapter when discussing fast-packet switching, many multiplexer vendors are providing fast-packet capabilities in their products by packetizing all originating traffic into a fixed-length packet for transmission across the network. While this is an efficiency upgrade to common TDM multiplexing, it still provides a proprietary implementation that must be replicated at the destination end. There are other disadvantages with this implementation. Multiple dedicated circuits are still required for access to the network. Also, packets are not built with multimedia from all users accessing the multiplexer, but instead are built for one user at a time. This implementation is not true statistical multiplexing, but mainly an implementation of multiplexing using packets for transport. The actual multiplexing is accomplished by the interleaving of packets from different access circuits and bandwidth is allocated by the number of frames, not bits.

This multiplexing technique, while not providing true frame relay, still allows efficiencies. The primary difference between this style of fast-packet and frame relay switching is that fast-packet multiplexers still have dedicated paths for the data, while frame relay routes are based upon the DLCI in the address field. Also, multiplexers employing frame relay must allocate a portion of their trunks to frame relay, and many times this bandwidth is dedicated whether it is used or not. A true frame relay device has the flexibility of "dynamically allocating" all available bandwidth to whatever application needs it at a given time. There are also cost efficiencies gained through the addition of only an interface card, rather than the purchase of a new router.

11.6.2 Frame Relay Access Device (FRAD)

There is one device as unique to frame relay as the Packet Assembler Disassembler (PAD) is to X.25 packet switching – the Frame Relay Access Device or Assembler Disassembler (FRAD). Figure 11.14 shows a FRAD aggregating multiple network access devices [SNA/SDLC, Bisynchronous (BSC), Asynchronous, X.25, and 2780/3780 RJE terminals], hosts, and other various network elements into a single frame relay access circuit. The FRAD performs the framing function, placing the user protocol into a FR frame. The FRAD then provides the connectivity to a private or public switched FR network. Access speeds are via DS0, fractional T1 (FT1), or full T1. A FRAD can also provide an interface for LAN protocols such as Token Ring or Ethernet.

FRADs contain the powerful capability to carry SNA and LAN traffic over a single interface or network access circuit, and some even provide "spoofing" or some level of PU4/PU5 emulation. FRADs can interface directly to a FR-capable FEP or through a Token Ring LAN.

FRADs can perform a level of congestion control outside the frame relay network through SDLC congestion-control techniques as discussed in previous chapters. By generating and acknowledging the polls of each individual session, the FRAD can reduce or eliminate polling from being transmitted across the frame relay interface and thus drastically reduce the congestion caused by polling on each session. Conversion from legacy networking equipment to a FRAD configuration can allow you to keep much of your existing infrastructure in place. This conserves much of your current investment and minimizes change to the users. FRADs can make the replacement of multipoint and private lines almost transparent.

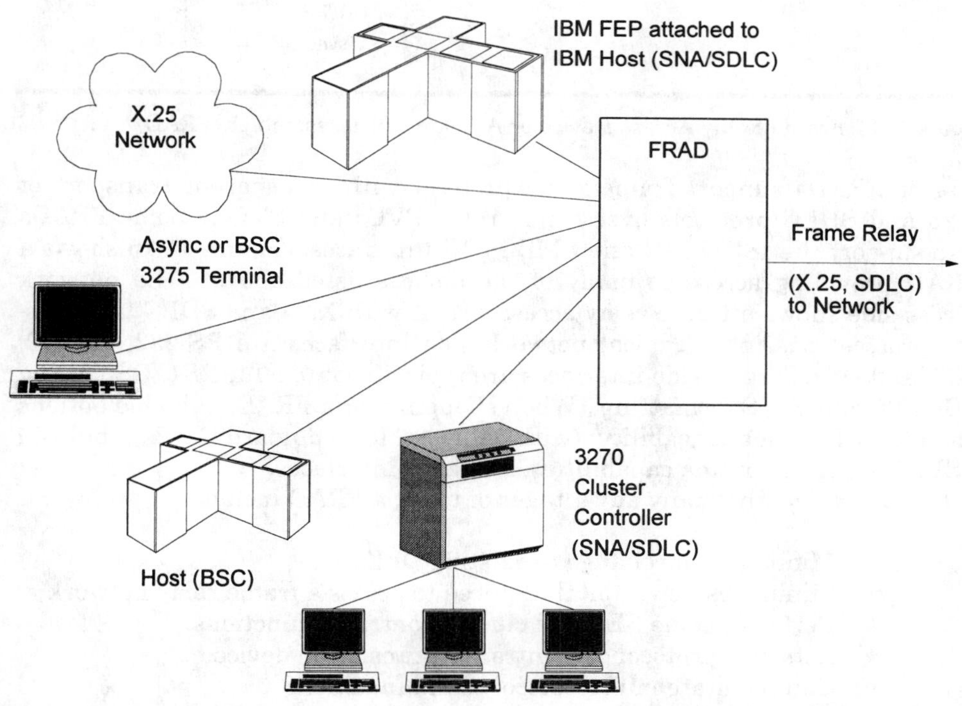

Figure 11.14 FRAD Connectivity Example

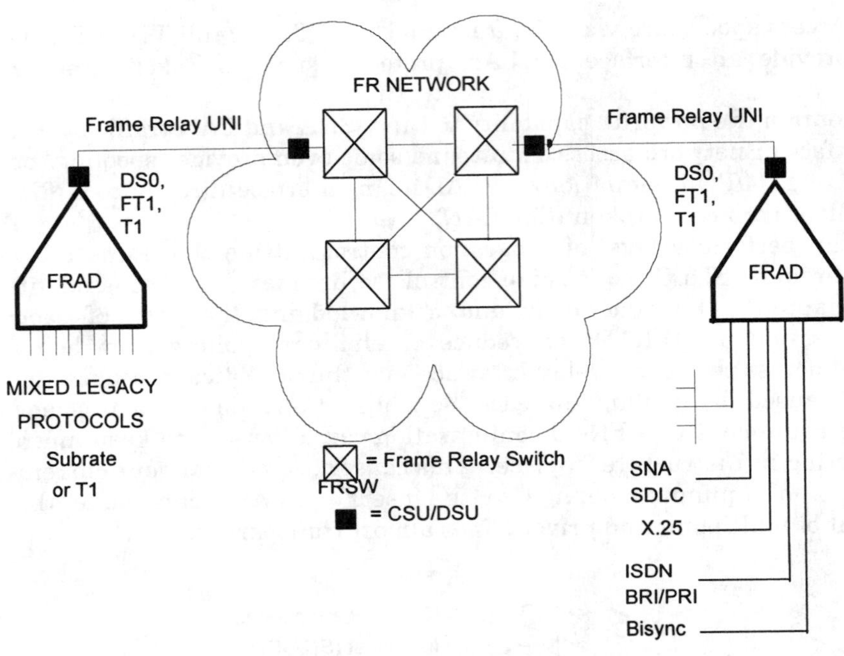

Figure 11.15 Frame Relay Access Device or Assembler/Disassembler (FRAD)

Most FRADs support frame relay protocol with transparent transport of X.25 and SDLC protocols over frame relay PVCs and SVCs. Some FRADs also support the ISDN PRI and SMDS SNI interfaces. Figure 11.15 shows a FRAD providing access to many of the devices listed above. The network access side shows a frame relay access circuit with X.25 and SDLC transparent protocol passing. Typical network side interfaces are RS-232, RS-449, V.35 and DS1. Trunk side interfaces are typically DS0, FT1, DS1, DS3, using ESF, SF, and B8ZS formatting. When shopping for a FRAD, valuable options include SNMP manageability (with support for standard MIBs), built-in CSU/DSU, basic routing capabilities, and LAN interfaces.

To summarize, the many advantages of using a FRAD include

- ★ Minimal to no change to existing CPE
- ★ Minimizes new capital required to access a frame relay network
- ★ Performs some FEP and cluster-controller functions
- ★ Acts as a protocol concentration/translation device
- ★ Can facilitate multiprotocol communications

Many users have requested voice and video capability over FR. A device that can be used to assist transmission of video over frame relay is the video coder/decoder (codec). A codec can transmit pixel updates for only that portion of the video that changes. Thus, data is only transmitted in bursts when movement occurs and pixels require update. Since the term "FRAD" has multiple meanings (i.e., frame relay access device, frame relay assembler/disassembler), many special-function FRADs have emerged to aggregate user-application protocols for access to frame relay networks. Some vendors offer the capability of placing low-quality voice over FR, such as Motorola, Hypercom, and Micom. This feature is especially attractive (as is voice over the Internet) with international communications. But beware of placing voice traffic over frame relay until the effects of jitter, latency, and congestion control are fully understood.

11.6.3 Dial Access and Dial Backup

Many networks have users that require either infrequent or mobile access to corporate resources. These users are typically located at remote sites that do not need continuous connectivity and cannot justify the expense of a dedicated private line. In this case, dial access can provide a cost-effective alternative to dedicated access. Dial access can also be used as a backup to dedicated access. Let's now look at both dial access and backup.

Dial access provides the capability to dial into a dedicated network device, such as the FR switch and terminal server as shown in Figure 11.16. When access is required, the user FRAD dials a phone number (over POTS) of the dedicated FR switch port within the FR network service. Once the link is established, data is transmitted. When no data communications are required, the link is terminated.

Dial access can also provide dial backup should a primary, dedicated link fail or something else goes wrong (such as the connection between the FR CPE and FR network switch). Dial backup is the capability for the remote site to dial up an alternate circuit for disaster recovery should the primary access circuit fail (via the router or a dial backup modem or CSU/DSU). Dial backup outside the FR network is shown in Figure 11.17. All FR CPE, especially at remote sites, should have some form of dial access with an external modem. This is your insurance policy should a user or administrator inadvertently change the FR access device configuration. And it can prevent an expensive dispatch in both dollars and time.

Dial backup can be initiated outside the FR network, as shown in Figure 11.17, or dial backup can be provided to another FR switch within the public FR network. This is shown in Figure 11.18, where the remote site dials a local phone number to access a port on FR switch 2. FR switch 2 has static-defined PVCs, which in turn are assigned to each user as they dial into the switch for the duration of the call. When the call is terminated, the PVC or SVC is dropped and another user can dial in and access the same VC. In this manner, one FR port can be accessed by many users but only one simultaneous user. Some providers offer a rollover routing feature in case one line is busy (similar to most modem pool arrangements), then the network will reroute the call to the next available port or PVC.

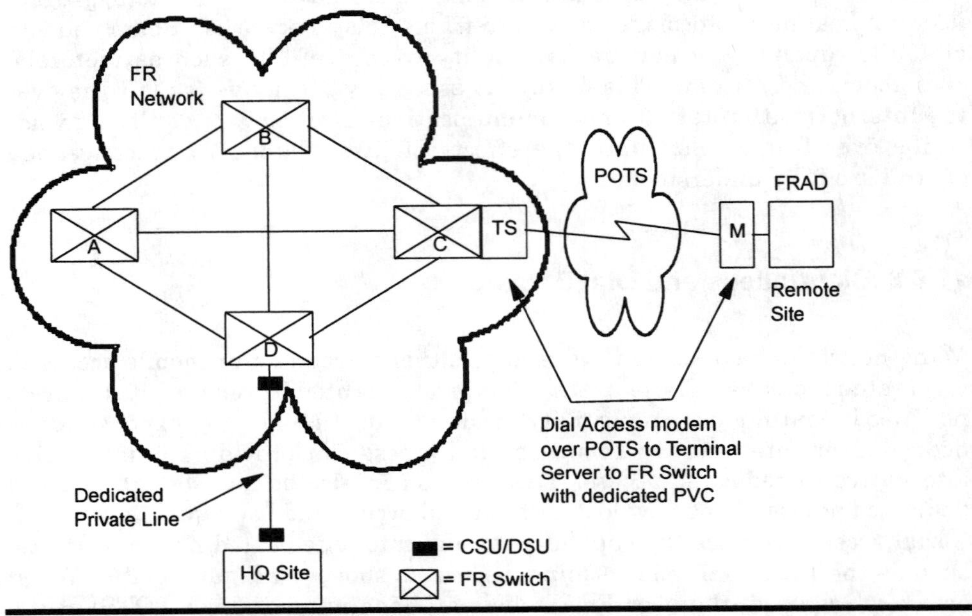

Figure 11.16 Dial Access to FR

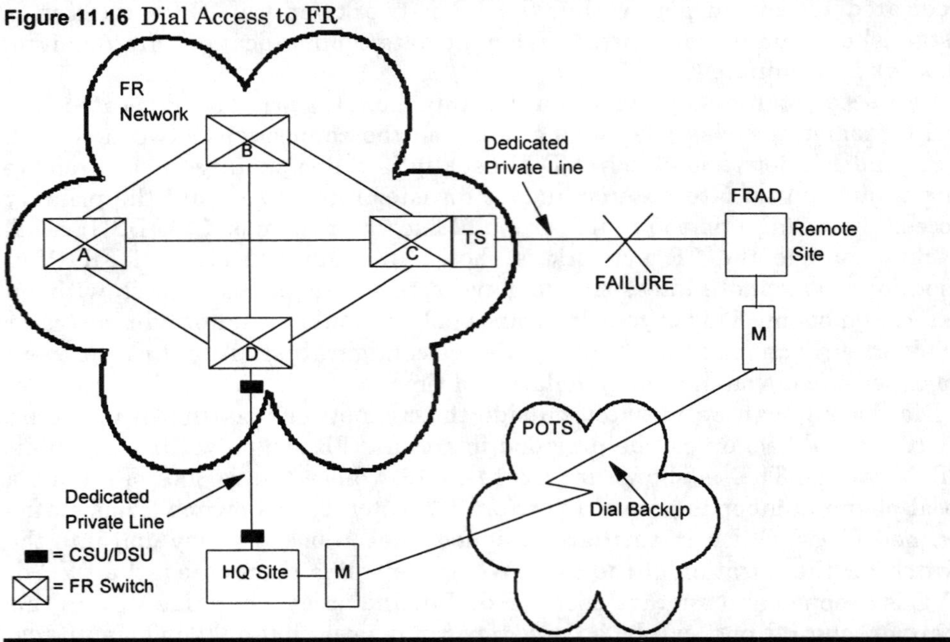

Figure 11.17 Dial Backup with FR

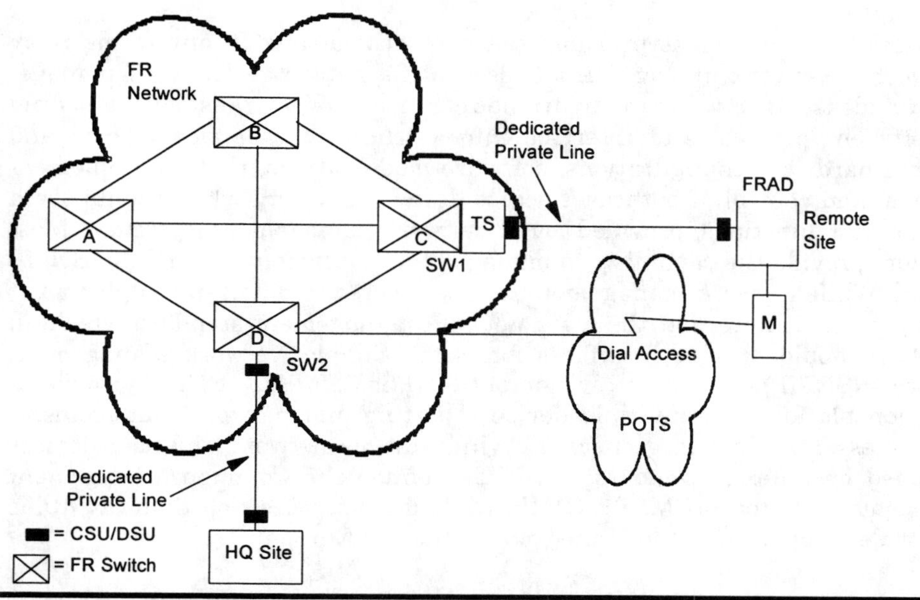

Figure 11.18 Dial Backup into FR Network

There are three forms of dial access in use today:

- Standard Analog Dial (14.4 kbps or 28.8 kbps most common)
- Digital Switched 56 and T1
- Digital ISDN (BRI and PRI)

Dial access protocols typically used include:

- PPP
- SLIP
- TCP/IP
- X.25
- Asynchronous (Telnet)

Dial access will eventually be combined with SVC capability for true end-to-end dynamic access, even across multiple providers' networks (such as across an NNI). SVCs allow paths to be established and terminated without preprogrammed paths.

11.6.4 Network Management

Network management is probably the most critical link in any frame relay network. Network management tools run the network. Network management adds the true value to any frame relay network — transforming it from an efficient protocol and interface into a true public service. Local and remote hardware configurations, software modifications, protocol implementations, and control of both user-access devices and network elements are a few of the functions provided by a network-management system. Most vendors provide the capability to manage their equipment through an SNMP agent. While network management will be covered in detail in Chapter 23, it is important to note that the main network-management standard which all vendors should provide interfaces for is the Simple Network Management Protocol (SNMP). The next revision of SNMP is SNMPv2. SNMP provides a common platform for multiple device reporting and network management. This is essential in a large network with multiple network and user devices supplied by different vendors. OSI has defined the Common Management Information Protocol (CMIP). CMIP, while more feature rich than SNMP, is less widely deployed in the United States than in Europe.

11.7 PERFORMANCE DESIGN ISSUES

The first measure of performance should be built into the digital and fiber-optic transmission network that carries frame relay services. Since frame relay does not provide the OSI layer 3 services found in X.25, the transmission network should have performance characteristics that produce minimal or no errors.

The link layer core parameters define the controls that most affect performance within the network. Maximum frame size can affect performance and degrade throughput if it is set too low. Throughput is another parameter that can be set to allow for no more traffic than what can be handled by the network, thus putting the onus on the users to manage throughput class rather than poor network performance controlling it for them. Burst-size settings that are too large and CIRs that are set too low and consistently exceeded will affect performance if the network is congested and drops DE traffic. Delay plays a major role in a FR network, particularly propagation, transmission, queuing, serialization, and packetization delays. Buffering will have an impact on network delay, as will choice of window size in the higher-layer protocols. Finally, the benefits of maintaining a consistent delay (reducing jitter) will be discussed.

11.7.1 Transmission Error Rates and Lost Frames

Bit errors have the same detrimental effect as congestion. They cause the frames in error to be discarded and thus require retransmission, which can cause increased delay and congestion. The network again relies on the higher-level transmission protocols to perform network recovery. This demonstrates the disastrous effects that poor transmission facilities have upon a frame relay network, causing much retransmission of data. Transmission facilities, such as fiber-optic cables with error rates of 10^{-13}, are desirable for the best performance.

There are two performance measurements defined in ANSI T1.606-1990. Residual Error Rate (RER) is defined as the percentage of total transmitted FPDUs to the total correct FPDUs delivered between two boundaries. This is calculated by the formula:

$$1 - \frac{\text{total correct FPDUs delivered between boundaries}}{\text{total offered FPDUs between boundaries}} = \text{RER}$$

The second measurement is the lost frames incurred in a given period of time between two boundaries. This is usually measured in frame losses per second.

11.7.2 Propagation Delay

Propagation delay is incurred by the sending of data over the transmission facility. It is approximately 8 ms per 1000 miles. This is a constant factor added into all transmission delay calculations.

11.7.3 Transmission Transit Delay

Since the frame size is variable, the total transmission delay is also variable. Both voice and compressed video do not tolerate delay, and therefore frame relay is not a good transport mechanism for these types of data. All applications using frame relay must be able to tolerate variable transmission delay, as well as the retransmission of data. Variations in end-to-end delay are referred to as *jitter*.

The primary performance measurement for frame relay is *transit delay* as defined in ANSI T1.606-1990. This is also referred to as end-to-end *latency*. Latency defines the transit delay of a Frame relay Protocol Data Unit (FPDU) from the first bit crossing the first of two boundaries (transmit) to the last bit crossing the last of two boundaries (receive). This is shown in Figure 11.19.

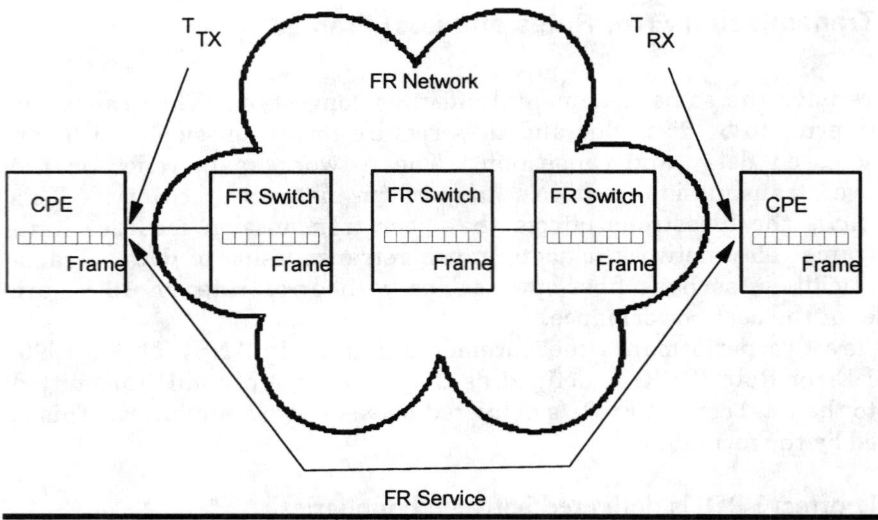

Figure 11.19 Frame Relay Service Transit Delay

Transit delay is measured by:

$$t_{\text{transmit}} - t_{\text{receive}} = t_{\text{transit delay}}$$

This relatively short transit delay is typically 5 to 10 ms per node with routers, compared to 30 to 50 ms higher delay in similar transport devices. Typical one-way, cross-country transit delay across a public FR network for 128-byte frames should be less than 150 ms. Additional delay is inserted during protocol and addressing conversions, as well as during the data exchange. Protocol conversions and encapsulations usually take place in the user access device and are not part of the end-to-end transit delay through the network, although users can perceive this additional delay caused by overhead, they may believe it to be the fault of the network.

11.7.4 Queuing, Serialization, and Packetization Delay

Queuing in a frame relay network becomes a function of the network device buffers which process the frames. There is very little queuing as compared to X.25 packet switching. Remember, the frame relay protocol is designed to discard frames (first DE, then all others) when congestion conditions occur and warn the sending and receiving devices that a congestion condition has occurred. In this aspect, there is no queuing. Some vendors have implemented buffers which serve as queuing devices for a short period of time, but this is often limited to milliseconds. Delay is also incurred when a FR switch must read into input buffers an entire FR frame and check the CRC before it can be transmitted on to the next switch. This is called *serialization delay*. Delay can also be incurred in buffers during the queuing process (the entire frame is read into the input buffer, but must be held until bandwidth is available to transmit the frame across the network). If used incorrectly, large amounts of both serialization and queuing delay can be extremely detrimental to session-oriented traffic (e.g., SNA). Any additional queuing required should be performed by user devices such as a Packet Assembler/Disassembler (PAD) and Frame Relay Assembler/Dissembler or Access Device (FRAD). *Packetization* delay can be found in these edge devices, where delay is incurred waiting to fill a FR frame with data. When the queuing capacity is exceeded, the frame relay device will generally begin to discard data, usually even before the data enters the network. The order in which data is discarded can be managed in different ways, such as: by the DE bit, hardware configurations and flags, or proprietary implementations – but only if the data passes from the access device, past any buffers, and into the network.

11.7.5 Overhead and Throughput

As mentioned before, there is very little overhead when using frame relay, and the percentage of overhead decreases as the frame size increases. This is due to the absence of the end-to-end services now provided by higher-layer protocols in the end devices. Eliminating this unneeded overhead increases performance, since more information can be transmitted over the physical channel. The larger the frame size accepted by the network, the greater the throughput. Throughput can be calculated based upon the number of data bits successfully transferred from one boundary to another within a set period of time.

11.7.6 Window Sizing and Effects on Higher-Layer Protocols

Performance of higher-layer protocols will almost always be affected when a user migrates from using private lines or dedicated circuits to frame relay. Frame relay networks, in an apples-to-apples distance comparison, will almost always exhibit greater end-to-end delay and jitter and lower throughput during simultaneous periods of PVC bursting. Not only will frame relay increase delay, it can also adversely affect the higher-layer protocols and the way they communicate. Since delays can be exaggerated and variable, applications that are session-oriented may time-out. Excessive frame discard of DE traffic can cause the same effect. Protocols that require an acknowledgment for every packet transfer (e.g., window size of 1), such as Novell IPX, may have terrible performance over frame relay service that has a high DE traffic discard rate. In this case special Network Loadable Modules (NLMs) have been designed to allow users to "tune" their networks for better frame relay performance. Examples of tuning include increasing the window size, increasing the packet size, or increasing the time-out delay. Before switching to frame relay, ask your WAN protocol vendors what you can expect and what tuning you need for optimal performance.

Remember that frame relay is not just cheap bandwidth. The price of using frame relay will show through when everyone with a PVC wants to use the single FR access port that was equal to your old dedicated private line. This is why your PVC's CIR rate should be equated to your private line equivalent minimum threshold of pain.

11.7.7 Buffering and Throughput during Congestion

Two bottlenecks can exist — network congestion can occur when either a network node receives more frames than it can process or it transmits more frames than the network can accept — with all buffers being filled. When the information overflows the buffers, packets begin to be discarded. Congestion is left to be handled by the network layer. This is another reason for intelligent application transmission protocols. The network will rely on these higher-level protocols, such as TCP and OSI Transport Class 4, to provide for retransmission of discarded data. Unfortunately, much of the traffic best suited for frame relay transport is bursty in nature, and prone to large bursts which will easily flood the network and overflow buffers. As congestion increases, there is a direct negative effect upon throughput. Thus, implementations that allow large sustained bursts above CIR and data discard based upon DE settings, coupled with large maximum frame sizes, are the most detrimental to throughput during periods of frame loss or congestion.

11.7.8 Bursting and Jitter Effects on Applications

Applications such as LAN-to-LAN file transfer traffic that consistently burst above CIR will mark a large number of frames DE. If many of these frames are discarded either within the network or at the egress port, delay performance will vary. As discussed previously, variations in delay are called jitter, and the amount of jitter will increase in direct relation to an increase in the amount of frames discarded. The overall effect is variable and nonpredictable application delay and network performance. While this can cause file transfer times to vary, its greatest effect is on terminal-type traffic. Long delays and variations in delay can have a disastrous effect on SNA traffic that has time-outs and on terminal traffic where the user can perceive delay. The two worst things you can do to a user of this type of traffic is to offer wide variations in delay (and thus to response times) or have long delay times. Users can tell when delays exceed 250 ms and variations in delay on the order of seconds are extremely noticeable.

11.7.9 Traffic Prioritization

Some devices, particularly routers, allow multiple prioritization among the PVCs within a FR access port. Thus, routers can prioritize individual protocols, such as SNA over TCP/IP traffic. This will be explained in greater detail in Chapter 20. Traffic prioritization must be used with care. Low-priority traffic can be drowned out by higher-priority traffic if appropriate bandwidth resources are not allocated.

11.8 PRICING, RATES AND TARIFFS

Rates and tariffs have played an important role in the success or failure of most public network services. FR has been no exception. One of the most important purchase criterion for FR service is price. FR services must not only be price competitive to other FR provider competition, but also to competing technologies. The cost elements and service options are listed below. Cost increases with the port-access speed and CIR rate. Overall cost per user decreases as the number of PVCs increases. The greater the number of PVCs and meshing, the greater the overall savings. It can be seen that FR is much more cost effective the greater the distance, meshing, and number of PVCs.

11.8.1 Elements of FR Pricing

Fixed rate FR pricing has many possible elements, but typically contains the following:

⇒ Two channel termination charges, called "chan terms" (similar to those encountered when provisioning private line services) based on FR access circuit speed and sometimes based on mileage

⇒ Flat rate cost per PVC – distance sensitive or insensitive from origin to destination ***or*** cost per PVC based on CIR ***or*** mileage-based rate per PVC (sometimes based on the chosen CIR rate)

⇒ Recurring monthly port cost based on physical access circuit rate

Variable rate (or usage based) FR pricing has the following elements:

- Usage charge based on the number of kbytes or kiloframes received
- SVC variable rate based upon distance and usage per call

Additional pricing options include:

- Unidirectional pricing
- Charges for changing PVC rates and adding PVCs/SVCs

Some providers ignore the CIR rate and allow the user to ascribe CIR rates for all PVCs, as long as their combined rate does not exceed the port speed (100 percent subscription).

Regional (RBOC offered) FR pricing seems to follow the same rule as national (IXC) pricing, with a few exceptions. The PVC pricing for most regional frame relay networks is typically non-mileage-sensitive. In fact, it may even be cheaper than a local loop of the same access speed. Usually there is a monthly recurring cost per PVC. For example, monthly recurring costs of $5 for each PVC up to five, $3 per PVC from six to ten, and $1 per PVC greater than 11.

11.8.2 Tariff or Nontariff?

All non-LEC frame relay services were historically not specified under tariff and therefore are classified as public pricing. Some of these pricing schemes have been disclosed to the public, some have been kept secret and provided only per each bid. As of time of publishing, there was work under way to tariff all FR pricing.

11.8.3 Usage-Based Pricing an Option?

When are you a candidate for usage-based pricing? When you:

- Understand your traffic patterns and flows
- Fully understand your protocol operation
- Have a fairly static network design

Usage-based pricing should **not** be considered when:

- The average and/or peak traffic load is unknown
- You do not understand your WAN or LAN protocols and window sizes

For many users, the initial frame relay deployment should be limited and focused on fixed pricing, allowing the user to learn his or her own traffic patterns. When these patterns are known, the user can decide upon mass deployment of frame relay and consider usage-based pricing.

Some guidelines for comparing fixed to usage pricing include:

① Simplicity versus complexity in pricing should match your knowledge of network traffic and protocol patterns.
② The more you know about your traffic, the more flexible you can be on selection of pricing scheme.
③ Flat pricing with non-mileage-sensitivity is most common.
④ Flat pricing can provide predictable recurring monthly costs for planning purposes; usage pricing is much more detailed and can vary month to month.
⑤ Usage pricing could cost less than fixed cost – find the break-even point and decide which is least expensive.

If usage-based pricing is used, carefully study the price caps. Some users of usage-based services end up paying much more money per month than they would have paid with a flat-rate fee or even a leased dedicated private line. Prices should not penalize users who are trying the service and are not familiar with their historical traffic patterns.

11.8.4 Comparison Pricing Guidelines

The previous edition of this text compared pricing by provider, but since FR pricing changes almost on a daily basis and the pricing structures vary widely between providers, it is best to investigate what pricing you can obtain on a network-by-network basis. Make the network provider quote two sizes of network, your current configuration (or 1 year snapshot) and your (2 to 3 year) planned network size. Be specific on the exact port, PVC, CIR, and locations you want.

The leading FR public network providers as of publish time included AT&T, MCI, Sprint, and Worldcom. Some things to ask FR network providers include:

✓ Flat-rate pricing, usage-based pricing, or both.
✓ Will they provide an installation plan with a dedicated project manager?
✓ How will the PVCs be provisioned and managed?
✓ How will you be notified of maintenance?
✓ What are the price elasticity points?

Figure 11.20 shows the basics of price elasticity. There is a break-even point where FR fixed-CIR-rate service equals usage-based pricing for a given number of kbytes received per month. At lower utilization, fixed pricing is more expensive, and at higher utilization, less expensive. The same lines can be drawn against private lines, switched 56/DS1, etc.

11.8.5 Zero CIR

Zero CIR is like betting on the come in Craps. You are guaranteed nothing, but have the opportunity to win the entire port speed (everything). But not only do you compete with other 0 CIR PVCs on your FR access port, but also with *all* other DE-marked traffic within the FR network. This service seems to work best for non-time sensitive traffic and non-mission-critical traffic. Pricing is usually cheap, but as someone once said – "you get what you pay for".

The typical sizing design for highly utilized or heavy traffic volume sites is a higher CIR. Smaller or remote locations with lower average utilization often require lower CIR rates. 0 CIR is usually used only for low utilization or non-mission-critical or non-delay-sensitive traffic.

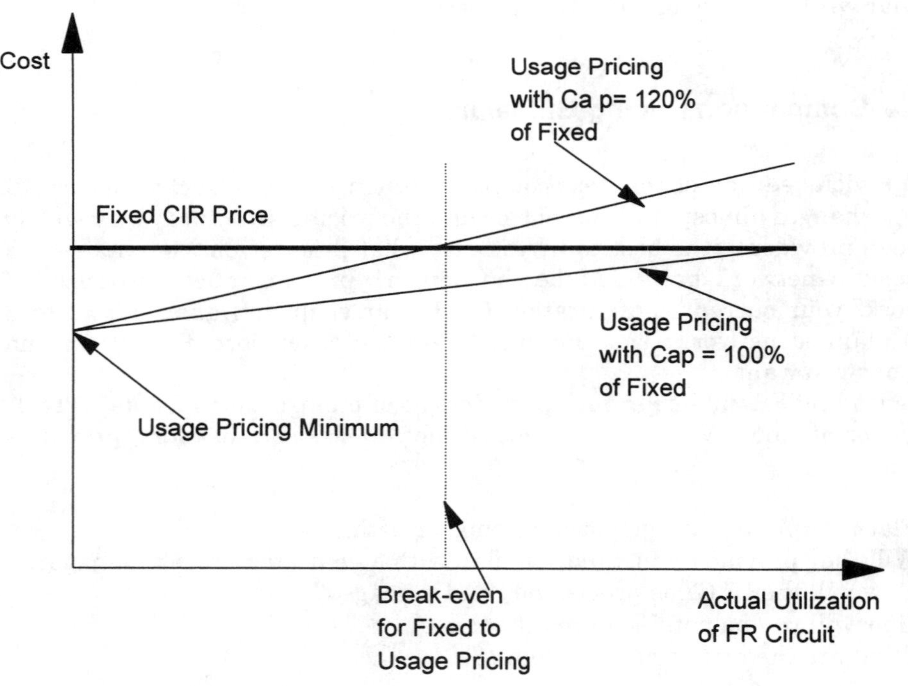

Figure 11.20 Frame Relay Price Elasticity

11.8.6 Build versus Buy

Sometime in the process of pricing a FR network you will consider the prospects of build versus buy. Do you purchase your FR service from a network provider or build the FR network yourself? Chapters can be written on this analysis, but the overriding question to ask is – is building, installing, and managing a FR network my core competency? If the answer is not a strong "yes", it seems to strongly recommend the purchase of a public FR service.

11.9 REVIEW

Frame relay is based on many standards developed by both ANSI and ITU-T, along with the proprietary (and now standard) LMI extensions. There are many FR parameters that require understanding to correctly size access to a FR service. These include EIR, CIR, and FR access-port speed; rate and direction of PVC sizing; bursting capability; DE; and oversubscription opportunities. Many of these parameters are classified as user-definable services. There are also core services and signaling protocols. Implicit and explicit congestion notification and control within a FR network using FECN, BECN, and CLLM were explained. We next took a detailed walk through a public frame relay network service. Private and public networking aspects, public service offering features and functions, SVCs, and FR network interconnectivity using NNI were explained. We reviewed the benefits and drawbacks of using regional, national, and international FR networks and hybrids of all three. The architecture and routing protocols of a public FR network can affect the user all the way down to the application layer, so we explored the two leading methods of congestion control and avoidance – open- and closed-loop algorithms – along with the benefits of a cell versus FR switched backbone. Proper access design can have a profound impact on the performance of a FR network, so a quick trip was taken through the various access devices used to interface to a frame relay network. Dial access and backup methods were explored. We then turned our attention to some detailed examples of how to improve performance within a FR network, such as analyzing and minimizing delay, reducing the effects of buffers, turning window sizing, and use of traffic prioritization. The chapter closed with a discussion of FR pricing.

Chapter

12

SMDS

This chapter is designed to provide the reader a solid overview of SMDS technology, protocols, architectures, and service features. The service aspects of SMDS and specifics of the Distributed Queue Dual Bus (DQDB) protocol as defined in the IEEE 802.6 standard are covered. Focus is applied to the service definitions of SMDS, access methods and the addressing and traffic-control methods for that access, protocol and architecture structures of SMDS and the DQDB, bridging and routing TCP/IP over SMDS, and performance and design considerations for SMDS public networks.

12.1 SWITCHED MULTIMEGABIT DATA SERVICE (SMDS) DEFINED

Traditional switched, multiplexed data transport and the extension of Local Area Networks (LANs) across a Wide Area Network (WAN) merge with the implementation of SMDS. SMDS offers the ability to eliminate the geographic restrictions of distributed high-speed data communications at native LAN speeds. As LANs continue to proliferate in offices worldwide, the need for networking high-speed services in the multimegabit range continues to grow. LAN/WAN administrators and managers are looking for alternatives to costly inter-premises dedicated private lines. SMDS offers an attractive alternative.

Switched Multimegabit Data Service (SMDS), in its most common form as a public, connectionless, cell-switched data service, allows data to be switched between multiple public-addressed subscribers at multimegabit per second speeds. SMDS offers a method of high-speed LAN and MAN interconnection across the WAN that, through the aggregate of a single network interface per subscriber, is more economical and efficient than a dedicated (private line) network. SMDS offers the capability to virtually extend the LAN, at direct connect LAN speeds, across the MAN and WAN.

Two major developments have occurred to SMDS since the last edition of this book that have caused a change of focus on SMDS. First, the official IEEE protocol standard, IEEE 802.6-1990, has been published. This document is an excellent reference to DQDB architecture and protocol structure of SMDS. Thus, less attention will be paid in this edition to DQDB architecture and its self-healing operation. Instead, more attention will be paid to the access methods (SIP, DXI, FR, ISDN), bridging and routing with other protocols, performance of public SMDS networks, and design considerations, as these topics are much more important to the typical user of SMDS service than the architecture within the "cloud".

The second major change is that SMDS service, while defined prior to frame relay, has become neither a leading nor a ubiquitous data service in the United States as was the forecast. In fact, revenues for frame relay service are far exceeding those of SMDS service (this is just the opposite in Western Europe, where SMDS service, second to ISDN, has exceeded frame relay). What caused frame relay to bypass SMDS so quickly? This occurrence is partly due to a lack of cost-effective rates and partly to slow deployment of the technology by leading switch vendors. SMDS did, in fact, begin to become popular around the same time as frame relay, but the lack of an intercarrier interface (ICI) during the time that switch vendors were integrating SMDS interfaces into their products allowed frame relay to gain momentum and steal the wind out of the SMDS sails. Frame relay has since reinforced businesses' confidence in carrier-provided public data services. But as intercompany communications bandwidth requirements increase beyond simple e-mail and Internet file transfers, SMDS may play a key role in offering a more dynamic, address- and security-rich, scalable solution. These facts also reinforce that emphasis must be placed on SMDS internetworking with other protocols and SMDS as connectionless access to what is fast becoming the next generation transport technology – ATM.

Also, it is important to note that DS1 speed access service is becoming much more prevalent and cost effective, making SMDS service even more economically attractive. This is especially true of SMDS DS1 Data eXchange Interface (DXI) access, which offers an (HDLC-like) frame-based user interface and relies on the network switch to provide frame-to-cell conversion.

Let's first take an historical look at the origins of SMDS.

12.1.1 Origins of SMDS

The MAN and DQDB saga began when the IEEE began work in 1982 on standards for transmission of voice, compressed video, LAN interconnectivity, and bulk-data transfer. These ideas were first presented to the cable television (CATV) community, which didn't tune into the idea. These same cable companies now have a wealth of bandwidth in cable TV and only nominally use it. Burroughs, National, and Plessey initiated a second effort in 1985 with the slotted ring concept. This effort died when the leveraged buyout of Sperry Univac cut required funding, and again MAN technology waited. The most recent effort began with a Bell Labs MAN standard proposal and was developed in parallel with the ex-Burroughs FDDI venture called MST (Multiplexed Slot and Token). This new Bellcore MAN standard became the IEEE Project 802.

The IEEE 802.6 standard is based upon the distributed queue dual bus (DQDB) technology. The DQDB architecture (which resembles the Bell Technology Lab's dual coax with reservation MAN architecture, called Fastnet) was invented at the University of Western Australia and hardware was first produced by QPSX LTD (a University of Western Australia and Telecom Australia spin-off).

As SMDS was created as a Metropolitan Area Network (MAN) service by Bellcore, it is in the purest sense a service definition and not a protocol. The first realization of SMDS was defined using the DQDB technology, as specified in the IEEE 802.6 standard. The IEEE 802.6 DQDB standard defines connectionless data-transport service using 53-byte slots to provide integrated data, video, and voice services over a MAN, which is typically a geographic area of diameter less than 150 km (90 miles). This cell-switching architecture combines the best of two worlds, (1) connectionless datagram public data-transfer services similar to packet switching and (2) speeds in excess of 155 Mbps. The SMDS implementations based upon the IEEE 802.6 standard were the first public services to use ATM-like technology. Although the IEEE 802.6 standard also defines connection-oriented isochronous services, SMDS today supports only a connectionless datagram service primarily targeted for LAN interconnection. Some vendors provide their own proprietary version of isochronous transport.

SMDS is a form of cell switching. Cell switching is defined in terms of standards, underlying architectures, initial services implementation (such as SMDS), and protocols. Cell switching has taken two development paths: connectionless data transport in the form of IEEE 802.6 (DQDB), and connection-oriented and connectionless in the form of Asynchronous Transfer Mode (ATM). SMDS services use the IEEE 802.6 DQDB CL (ConnectionLess) service. While SMDS provides LAN/WAN interconnection, a network design offering SMDS service over a DQDB architecture is not limited to a geographical area. While ATM may well become the long-term WAN transport technology of choice, either technology will serve the purpose of eliminating, in the near future, data networks composed of private lines.

Central-office switch vendors such as Siemens Stromberg-Carlson were are the primary players for the first versions of cell switching to hit the telecommunications market: Switched Multimegabit Data Service (SMDS) using the DQDB architecture as access. These switches first made use of DQDB's ConnectionLess (CL) service. Versions of SMDS service have been offered by IXCs, LECs, and PTTs worldwide, including MCI Communications, British Telecom, Telecom Ireland, and the Deutsch Telekom.

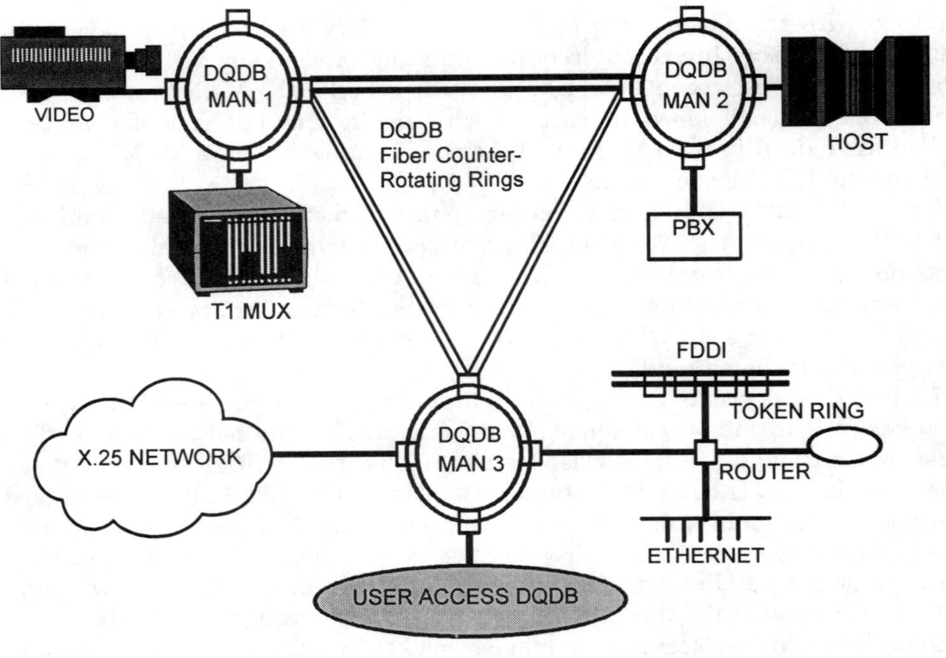

Figure 12.1 DQDB Metropolitan Area Network (MAN) – IEEE 802.6

12.1.2 What Is a MAN?

The interconnection of multiple SMDS or DQDB subnetworks forms a Metropolitan Area Network (MAN). The MAN can provide shared media for voice, data, and video transmissions over a local geographic area (typically less than 150 km in diameter), as well as high-speed extension of each LAN and WAN attached. These buses provide a high-speed, fiber-optic-based, shared medium access protocol across point-to-point, bus, and looped bus topologies. Cells are routed through the MAN wideband channels similar to packets in a packet-switched network, except that the bandwidth available is much higher (broadband transport speeds of 155 Mbps are available as opposed to 56 kbps and 1.544 Mbps). All transmission is assumed to be via optical fiber. Figure 12.1 portrays an example of a metropolitan area network providing connectivity to a large variety of multimedia users.

Major technology trends are pushing multimegabit, multimedia data communications to the desktop. As the costs of multi-MIP machines continue to drop, desktop personal computers and workstations are providing processing power equivalent to the mainframes of old. They continue to gain in processing power and drop in cost. In fact, a 286 PC, more than 10 times slower than some Pentium-processor-based PCs, provides more processing power than the IBM 7090 used in the Apollo space project! Users are demanding higher-speed data transport with bandwidth-on-demand to support bandwidth-intensive applications such as imaging, three-dimensional motion graphics, and interactive computer simulations. True distributed processing has arrived in the form of the client-server LAN. LANs provide large amounts of local capacity with good performance at a low cost. But with the advent of high-speed local networking among many users, the need emerges to connect these local environments over metropolitan and wide distances in real time using large bandwidths. Thus enters the MAN to fit this need. Demand pull is forcing the WAN to "catch up" to the high-speed LAN and MAN environments by use of technologies and services like SMDS over SONET and ATM.

Users want their application performance to be transparent to the data transport technology and MAN and WAN service. The MAN is viewed by the user as a utility for point-to-point and point-to-multipoint transport. The network resources accessed over the SMDS network must appear local.

MANs are the next step in the evolutionary process from LANs to WANs. MANs offer high-speed public-switched services including data, voice, and video. MANs are also expected to pass several LAN/WAN protocols without protocol conversion (using, in effect, encapsulation techniques). While MAN technology was originally defined for LAN/WAN interconnection, it has become a major interim solution between packet technologies and ATM switching. A MAN's primary function is as a public network offering, but there are also provisions that port the capabilities to Customer Premises Equipment (CPE). Local Exchange Carriers (LECs) and IntereXchange Carriers (IXCs) are providing SMDS MAN connectivity in the United States, while the European and Asian PTTs are also finding a vested interest in SMDS, in fact, more so than in the United States.

MANs interconnect LANs and WANs, while providing switching, concentration, and high-speed data transport. The MAN operates on a shared DQDB bus. This bus operates as a LAN, where each station on the bus has equal access to all available bandwidth. MANs implementing DQDB architecture to support SMDS will cut switched-network costs. By eliminating numerous dedicated point-to-point circuits, similar to the functions provided by frame relay, SMDS networks perform statistical multiplexing and efficiently use bandwidth-on-demand.

Perhaps the predominant business case for these services is the enticement for users to eliminate numerous private lines in favor of fewer high-speed trunks utilizing the bandwidth-on-demand capability of SMDS. This drastically reduces the fixed cost of private lines, while achieving the benefit of paying for only the bandwidth used, when it is used. This trend may drive many corporations even further toward outsourcing.

12.1.3 SMDS Service – Public versus Private

SMDS is primarily a public data network offering, but could also be used in a private network. SMDS will connect multiple nodes, referred to as Customer Access Nodes (CANs). SMDS can provide transport for a variety of customer network access methods, including packet-switched networks, synchronous data transport, ISDN, and LANs such as Ethernet and Token Ring.

SMDS is publicly offered by several RBOCs (Ameritech, Bell Atlantic, BellSouth, GTE, Pacific Bell, and SNET) and only one IntereXchange Carrier (IXC), MCI Communications. As SMDS service proliferates, many providers plan to eventually migrate SMDS service transport to an Asynchronous Transfer Mode (ATM) network over a SONET fiber backbone. SMDS public data networks provide access to the central office environment. In contrast to the typical voice central office, SMDS networks transport a variety of data, voice, and video in a high-speed switched environment through a public data offering. The RBOCs currently offer service between LATAs using the IXCs.

National and international SMDS carrier networks will be able to interface via the eXchange Access SMDS (XA-SMDS) specification defined by Bellcore. This standard provides a seamless interface for multiple SMDS networks and is the cornerstone of SMDS standards. The specification is defined in TR-TSV-001060 SMDS Generic Requirements for Exchange Access and Inter-company Serving Arrangements.

12.2 SUBSCRIBER INTERFACE AND ACCESS PROTOCOLS

There are six major methods for users to access an SMDS network. Each of these methods is presented in Figure 12.2: SMDS Subscriber Network Interface (SNI), SMDS Interface Protocol (SIP) or Access DQDB, Data eXchange Interface (DXI), SIP Relay Access, and ATM UNI Access. Each of these access methods is explained in this section, along with evolution of the CPE environment. First, we need to review the heart of the SMDS protocol – the Level 3 Protocol Data Unit (L3_PDU).

12.2.1 SMDS L3_PDU

The first level of user data encapsulation when using SMDS is within the L3_PDU. The L3_PDU carries the real protocol value of SMDS. The most common version of the L3_PDU shown in Figure 12.3 is detailed in RFC 1209, The Transmission of IP Datagrams over the SMDS Service. Here we see the SNAP fields encapsulated within the LLC frame, which in turn is encapsulated within the SIP L3_PDU. The SMDS Interface Protocol (SIP) function will be explained soon. The High-Layer Protocol Identifier (HLPI) field value is 1. All other fields compose the standard IEEE 802.2 LLC frame and have a fixed value depending on whether you are sending IP or ARP packets. The Org Code, Ethertype, and IP/ARP fields compose the SNAP. The three most common types of transport for the L3_PDU are the DXI frame, 802.6 cell, and ATM cell. There is a noticeable alignment between the 802.6 and ATM cells that we will see later.

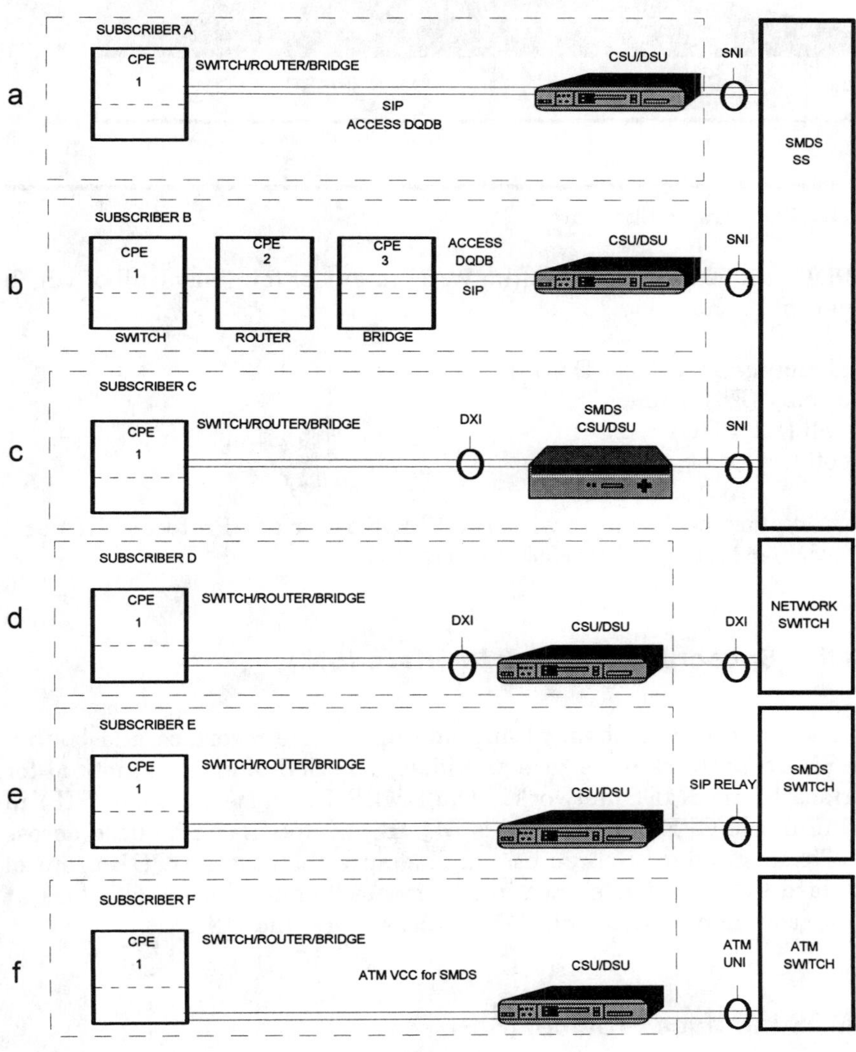

Figure 12.2 SMDS Interface Access Protocols

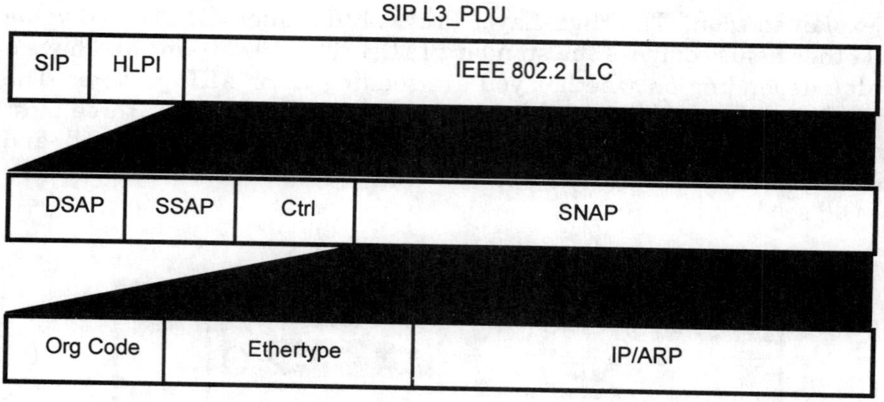

SIP L3_PDU

SIP	HLPI	IEEE 802.2 LLC

DSAP	SSAP	Ctrl	SNAP

Org Code	Ethertype	IP/ARP

Figure 12.3 L3_PDU Frame Structure

An L3_PDU can be moved across the WAN in any of four ways, all of which are transparent to the user:

⇒ Data eXchange Interface (DXI) frame
⇒ Frame relay (FR) frame
⇒ 802.6 cell (L2_PDU)
⇒ ATM cell

Let's now explore each, along with the SMDS Interface Protocol (SIP) and SMDS Subscriber Network Interface (SNI).

12.2.2 SMDS Subscriber Network Interface (SNI)

The SNI is the subscriber physical and administrative interface and boundary to the SMDS network or service provider. The SNI offers one method for CPE interface to an SMDS network. The SMDS Interface Protocol (SIP) in single and multiple CPE access ("access DQDB") protocols can be used across this SNI. These standard SNI access methods use the access DQDB protocol and a standard CSU/DSU as shown in Figures 12.2a and b. Now let's look at the two more common methods of SMDS access – SIP and DXI.

12.2.3 SMDS Interface Protocol (SIP)

The SIP was the original, and is now the predominant, access protocol that operates across the SNI, although the DXI protocol, which we will discuss next, is gaining popularity. SIP provides for many CPE devices to communicate over the SNI using the DQDB protocol. SIP operation is primarily the exchange of L3_PDUs between CPE and SMDS network switching nodes. This operation is called an "access DQDB", which is distinguished as CPE-to-MAN Switching System access, as opposed to SS-to-SS access. The SMDS access DQDB is based on the open bus topology. One (single-CPE access) or multiple CPE (multi-CPE access) devices may be attached to one access DQDB via DS1, DS3, E1 or E3 circuits. These CPE devices may be a variety of devices, such as bridges, routers, gateways, or switches. If all CPE devices attached to a given access DQDB require autonomy, no other alien CPE may be attached to the same access DQDB. Thus, if there are multiple customers at a site, each customer must be provided a separate access DQDB into the SMDS network. Figure 12.2a shows an example of SIP access across an SMDS SNI for a single CPE (single-CPE access). Figure 12.2b shows multi-CPE access. Figure 12.4 illustrates an end-to-end network using DXI over a SNI.

12.2.4 Data eXchange Interface (DXI)

The Data eXchange Interface (DXI), a variation of SIP, was first developed by the SMDS Interest Group as a cost-effective access method that required only the upgrade of the CSU/DSU equipment and software on the CPE device (typically a router) rather than a hardware upgrade to the CPE device. This allowed for easy integration and upgrade capability to SMDS for the existing router base. Thus, the router equipment is not required to do the "slicing and dicing" of the SMDS L3_PDU into L2_PDUs, and the task is relegated to select SMDS CSU/DSU vendors, as shown in Figure 12.2c. Here the router placed the user data into an L3_PDU, and uses a logical level protocol – Data eXchange Interface (DXI) – to move the L3_PDU to the SMDS CSU/DSU. When the SMDS CSU/DSU receives the L3_PDU, it strips off the DXI header, takes the original user data and then chops it into L2_PDU segments and encapsulates it into the SMDS L2_PDU frame for transmission to the SMDS network.

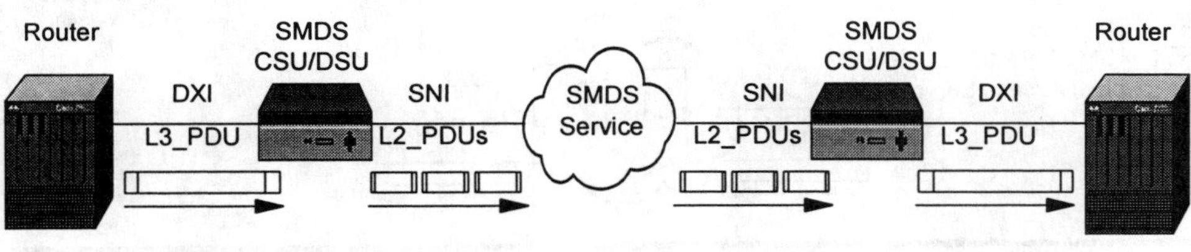

Figure 12.4 Data eXchange Interface (DXI) Access over an SNI

F	Address	Control	DXI Header	L3_PDU	CRC	F	
1	1	1	2	0 to 9232	2 or 4	1	Bytes

Figure 12.5 Data eXchange Interface (DXI) Protocol Structure

The DXI Local Management Interface (LMI) protocol is used for signaling across the DXI. A High Speed Serial Interface (HiSSI) can also provide transport for DS3 DXI access, and is used by providers such as MCI Communications. DXI standards are defined in the Generic Requirements for Low Speed Access, TA-TSV-1239 and Frame Relay Access to SMDS, TA-TSV-1240.

The DXI is an enhanced version of the standard HDLC protocol and frame, as shown in Figure 12.5. As shown, the SMDS CSU/DSU performs the L3_PDU-to-L2_PDU segmentation and reassembly. MCI Communications improved the specification by eliminating the need for a special CSU/DSU for speeds of 56 kbps to 1.544 Mbps, and this specification was later ratified in 1993 with the Bellcore Technical Advisory 1239 – Generic Requirements for Low Speed SMDS Access. This standard has spawned a new SMDS DXI service that allows for DXI access straight from the CPE, through the CSU/DSU, and into the SMDS network switch as shown in Figure 12.2d. The SMDS network switch performs the functionality of the SMDS CSU/DSU in example c. This service provides lower SMDS speeds for greater ubiquity and cost-effective service. Some providers, such as MCI Communications, have provided this direct L3_PDU DXI interface to their SMDS service, and a special DXI CSU/DSU is not required. DXI SMDS service is offered by some LECs, such as Bell Atlantic and Pacific Bell. Both vendors provide an access server technology to convert the customer DXI into an SMDS Interface Protocol (SIP) as shown in Figure 12.6.

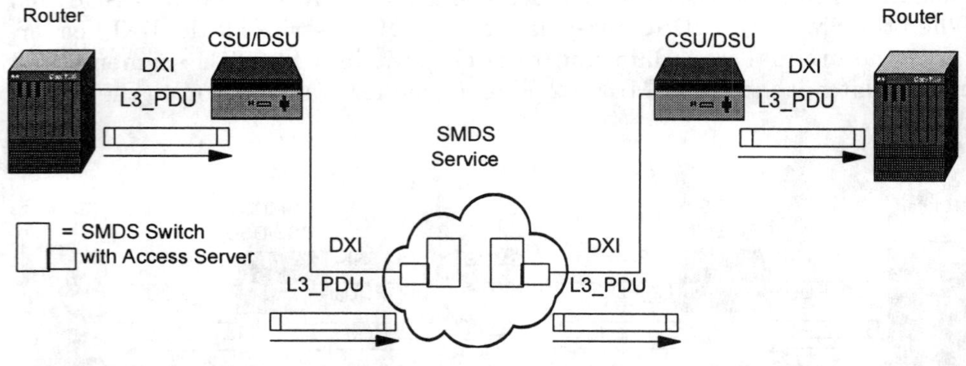

Figure 12.6 Data eXchange Interface (DXI) Access Server Configuration

F	DLCI = SRI PVC ID	L3_PDU	CRC	F	
1	2	0 to 9232	2	1	Bytes

Figure 12.7 Frame Relay SRI PVC Protocol Structure

F	HEADER	L3_PDU	CRC	F	
1	2	< 4096	2 or 4	1	Bytes

Figure 12.8 LAP-F Frame Relay SRI PVC Protocol Structure

12.2.5 Frame Relay Access

What alternatives are available when your frame relay users want to talk to your SMDS users? SIP Relay is the method of using a frame relay protocol as an access to an SMDS service. Again, an HDLC deviation is used similar to the DXI access protocol, but with the frame relay information as the L3_PDU and the frame header address (Data Link Connection Identifier or DLCI) as the SIP Relay Interface PVC (SRI PVC). Figure 12.2e shows the frame relay SIP PVC access, where the CSU/DSU simply relays the L3_PDU to the SMDS switch. Note that this method passes L3_PDUs into the FR frame and extracts them out of a FR frame at the destination end. The protocol format for SRI PVCs is shown in Figure 12.7, and the network access connectivity is shown in Figure 12.2e. This implementation is defined by the Frame Relay Forum (FRF) implementers agreement as Link Access Procedures Frame-mode (LAP-F), the format of which is shown in Figure 12.8. This allows the use of a single interface port for both frame relay and SMDS access to a public network.

Figure 12.9 illustrates a frame relay user in Georgia who has established PVCs over a frame relay network to frame relay users in Texas and New York. Now the Georgia user wants to communicate with a user in California. But the user in California is already using SMDS service with the same service provider that is providing frame relay to the other three users. The provider will offer the user in Georgia a SRI PVC through the frame relay network. The job of the internetworking unit within the carrier's network is to receive the L3_PDU frame, and if it is connected to a DXI switch, convert the L3_PDU back into a DXI frame. If it is connected to a SIP SNI, it slices the L3_PDU into 802.6 L2_PDU cells. In our example, the InterWorking Unit (IWU) translates the SRI PVC into a SIP and forwards through an SS onto an SMDS SNI to the SMDS user in California. Access classes (defined later in this chapter) and CIRs are not defined on the SRI PVC, so for engineering purposes, assure that the SRI PVC and SIP have similar bandwidth requirements. The Annex D specification is used for signaling. SIP relay and signaling operations are further defined in Bellcore Technical Advisory 1240.

12.2.6 SMDS to ATM Access

Figure 12.2f illustrates ATM VCC connectivity for access to SMDS service through an ATM UNI access protocol. The standards for SIP access can be found in Bellcore Technical Reference 772. It is interesting to note that there is also a SIP variant for ATM access that allows use of one or move Virtual Channel Connections (VCCs) to be allocated as SMDS SIPs. ATM terms will be covered in detail in the next two chapters.

12.2.7 The Customer Premises Environment (CPE)

Users have many methods of interfacing applications to the SMDS network. Routers, bridges, brouters, and gateways typically provide four levels of protocol interfaces between the user and the SMDS network.

The user environment, called Customer Premises (or Provided) Environment (or Equipment) – CPE – typically contains multiple applications using diverse protocols, and riding multiple subnetworks. These subnetworks could be either colocated or geographically diverse. They may be composed of local area networks, wide area networks, leased or private lines, public multiplexer networks, or packet networks. The data speeds could range from low-speed asynchronous bursty traffic to high-speed bulk data transfers. Traffic patterns and quantities will vary along with intranetwork and internetwork protocols.

The customer's requirements can either be satisfied by interfaces directly into the SMDS network or by concentration via a variety of devices. Typical CPE devices include modems, DSUs, CSUs, bridges, brouters, routers, gateways, and a variety of proprietary interconnection devices supporting one or more connectionless network-level protocols. There are also a few SMDS interface cards for existing equipment. Even the CRAY supercomputer has an SMDS terminal adapter available built by Fujitsu.

Many vendors now support the SIP, DXI, and frame relay SIP interfaces. Vendors of the DXI interface typically assure vendor interoperability over both RS-449 and V.35 physical interfaces, as well as support for DS3 and HiSSI interfaces.

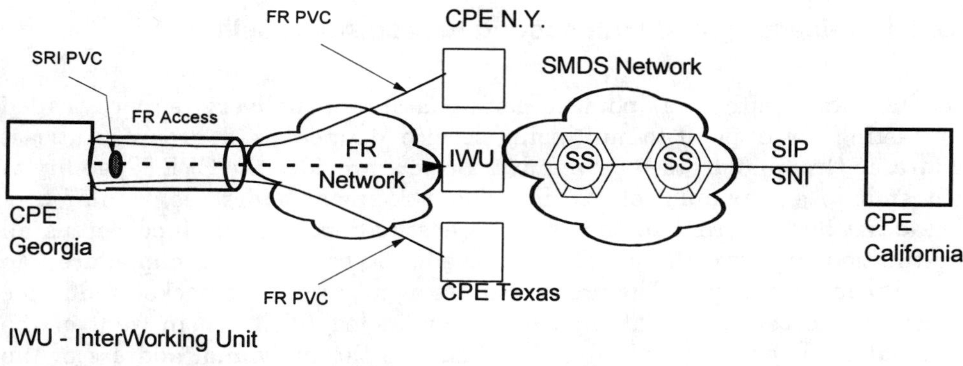

Figure 12.9 Frame Relay SRI PVC Access Example

12.3 ADDRESSING AND TRAFFIC CONTROL

The addressing scheme used by the SMDS network is formatted using the same structure as the North American Numbering Plan (NANP), which uses the ITU Recommendation E.164 numbering plan which contains up to 15-digit addresses. This scheme was chosen to speed the integration of SMDS into the telephone network addressing infrastructure for integration of voice and data operations. As a result, the source and destination addresses have 15 digits reserved to accommodate *any* E.164 address. The NANP (world zone) has 10-digit numbering schemes plus it adds a 1 (for world zone 1) for a total of 11 digits. Within these 11 digits, SMDS uses the first 7 digits (including the world zone 1) to define one switching system from which individual and group addresses can be defined. The last 4 digits of this number are used to find a specific access line on the switching system.

CPE interface methods to an SMDS network device via multiple access protocols across the SNI include SIP, DXI, SIP relay, ISDN, and ATM, all of which will be discussed in this chapter. The SMDS service provider will assign each SNI one or more unique addresses. The subscriber will have full control over the use of each individual address, and may assign multiple SMDS addresses per CPE. SMDS can assign a group address to multiple devices so that they can multicast their data to other members of their group address. The standard specifies that up to 16 subscribers are possible per SNI. However, no user in the network will have the same address.

There are many addressing functions available, such as unicasting and multicasting. Source address validation and address screening are performed on all SNIs, and access classes are offered as a means of controlling traffic patterns and congestion.

12.3.1 Unicasting and Multicasting (Group Addressing)

SMDS offers either a point-to-point datagram delivery service called unicasting, or a point-to-multipoint service defined as a group multicast address. Group-addressed data unit transport provides the CPE capability to transmit to a maximum of 128 individual recipient addresses, similar to a broadcast but different in that specific destinations are specified versus all destinations in a broadcast. The source address can send a group address to a group-address agent. The group-address agent copies the packet and sends a copy on to each destination, with an appended BOM cell in front of the original L3_PDU. The new BOM cell carries the individual address of the member of the group the copy is intended for. Each Switching System (SS) can support up to 1024 of these group addresses, and each address on the network could be assigned up to 32 group addresses. One addressing example is to assign all the SMDS nodes (members of the same group address) the same IP network and subnet address. Then each of these nodes would ARP each other as if they were on the same physical LAN with common higher-layer protocols.

12.3.2 Source Address Validation and Address Screening

SMDS service operates on the E.164 source and destination addresses. The specific structure of the E.164 address can be found in Chapter 22. The SMDS source address is screened by the network to ensure that it is valid for the source SMDS access line. SMDS customers can screen incoming data and only accept data from specific source SMDS addresses or block data from specific SMDS addresses. SMDS users can also limit the destination SMDS addresses that can be reached from their SMDS access lines. SMDS customers can have ubiquitous connectivity, or they can use these screening tools to achieve tightly controlled, closed user groups. Source address validation is an incredibly valuable feature not contained in protocols like IP. One example of this usefulness is the mandatory validation of source addresses, a feature that if implemented in IP over the Internet would have provided a great security feature.

When a data unit is transmitted via the SNI to the SS, the source address is verified to assure that it was assigned to the SNI from which it originated. This will be performed for each data unit sent. If the source address is not assigned to the SNI that originated the call, the L3_PDU is not delivered. The SMDS network also has the capability of authorization and address screening for both source and destination if closed user group network service is required. It is the network designer's job to assure that virtual private networks are built within the public data network, in effect provisioning a private virtual network, and that the subscriber receives every feature required by the private SMDS network. Care must be taken when establishing address screening and group addressing to eliminate conflicts in both.

The standard ranges and limitations of each subscription parameter are shown in Table 12.1. Carriers often deviate from these Bellcore standards in their SMDS services.

Table 12.1 SMDS Access Classes for DS3 Access

Subscription Parameters	Ranges and Limitations
SNI Addresses	16 maximum per SNI
Group Addresses	128 maximum addresses per group, 32 group memberships per address
Address Screens	4 maximum per SNI

12.3.3 SIR Access Classes as Traffic and Congestion Control

SMDS controls congestion and traffic through the use of an open loop flow control mechanism called Sustained Information Rate (SIR) regulated through the assignment of access classes. Thus, the SIRs are designed to control congestion conditions. SMDS SIR is based on the aggregate of all data originating on the SMDS access line regardless of it's destination. SIRs are defined by access class.

12.3.4 Access Classes

Access classes are assigned to SNIs based upon many factors, but primarily to control congestion conditions and ensure an efficient access traffic engineering design by placing limits on the bursts of data. Access classes are a method of providing bandwidth priorities for times when there is network congestion at the SNI. Network congestion occurs when there is an attempt by the network to transfer one or more SMDS data units without an interval of time between the units. This means that more data is attempting transfer than can be supported by the SIP across the access path. The access class places a limit per user on the rate of sustained information transfer available. When the user creates a burst of traffic across the shared SMDS access link, the access class determines the duration of time that the user controls the link. In actual practice on an SNI, the SMDS CSU/DSU chooses the access class and then clocks and meters the traffic from the router to average the traffic to meet the SIR rate. When using an entire DS3 access, the user will be able to burst to the entire DS3, then back-off to the average SIR, then burst, then back-off, and so forth. Thus the user achieves the average access speed and throughput of the SIR. But beware of the effect this may have on throughput.

The only time the access class is not equal to the access bandwidth is with DS3 access classes. For DS3 access lines, five access classes are defined in Table 12.2. This table shows the class number assigned to the user, the maximum rate of transfer that the user can use over extended intervals (SIR), and the LAN traffic each was designed to support. Data arriving at a rate higher that the SIR is discarded at the originating SMDS switch. Access classes are regulated by a credit manager scheme. The table also shows the maximum burst size in kbytes per access class. These values can help designers determine the average delay they can expect to see over the SMDS access.

Table 12.2 SMDS Access Classes for DS3 Access

Access Classes	SIR (Mbps)	LAN Mapping	Burst Size in kbytes
1	4	4 Mbps Token Ring	10.4
2	10	10 Mbps Ethernet	13.0
3	16	16 Mbps Token Ring	17.6
4	25	16 to 34 Mbps Subrate	33.7
5	34	No enforcement	Unlimited

Note that access classes 1 through 3 line up with standard LAN speeds, so that traffic from a single LAN cannot experience loss due to the SIR credit manager operation. It is apparent that T1 access does not warrant an access class, as the maximum amount of bandwidth achievable using SIP over a T1 SNI trunk is about 1.17 Mbps (due to overhead). Note that 34 Mbps is the maximum amount of bandwidth that can be achieved using SIP over a DS3 SNI trunk (due to overhead).

For example, suppose user A decides to aggregate one 16 Mbps Token Ring LAN, three 10 Mbps Ethernet LANs, and five T1 synchronous data channels through a router. The router aggregates these CPE units into one DS3 SNI trunk into an SMDS SS. Since the combined aggregate of these inputs (ignoring the inefficiencies of Ethernet and that it never achieves a 10 Mbps data transfer rate) would be approximately 53.5 Mbps, the network provider assigns access classes to each CPE LAN. The five T1 circuits are not assigned an access class, and are given an aggregate 7.5 Mbps. This leaves 26.5 Mbps for the LANs. Since in this case the 16 Mbps Token Ring is a mission critical LAN for the Stock Market, it is assigned an access class 3, which is a 16 Mbps class. This leaves 10.5 Mbps for the remaining three Ethernet LANs. Since we know that the maximum data an Ethernet LAN can transmit is 3.5 Mbps (due to collisions at low utilization), we assign an access class of 1 to each Ethernet LAN.

Thus, the total access class assignments will not exceed the available bandwidth of the DS3 trunk: 34 Mbps. Realistically, the router will perform some statistical multiplexing, and the characteristics of the user traffic on each LAN would dictate the bandwidth actually used by each CPE, but this analysis is good for defining the access class use. The problem from the opposite direction is where low access classes could be assigned to each of the noncritical applications, still leaving a full 16 Mbps of bandwidth for the Token Ring LAN without assigning it an access class. Either method will work. Egress access classes are identical to ingress access classes, as shown in Table 12.2.

The 34 Mbps for access class 5 is the maximum throughput achievable on a 45-Mbps access line after Physical Layer Convergence Protocol (PLCP), and L2_PDU or ATM cell overhead are taken into account. SIR uses a credit manager, or "leaky bucket", type of rate enforcement method. Basically, no more than M out of N cells may contain nonidle slots or cells. For class 5 $M = N$, while for the lower numbered classes, the relationship is SIR = $M \times 34/N$ Mbps. The value of M controls the number of consecutive slots or cells that can be sent at the DS3 rate.

SMDS has a L3_PDU loss objective of 10^{-4}, which is several orders of magnitude greater than that caused by transmission errors. This is consistent with the character of the SMDS service, emulating that of a LAN but providing MAN or WAN coverage.

12.3.5 SMDS Addressing

The public phone network uses an addressing, or numbering, scheme called E.164 that basically has a country code part and then a nationally assigned part for each country, as detailed in Chapter 9. This is the familiar international dialing plan. Internationally, and usually nationally, this is a geographic numbering plan, since the digits taken from left to right hierarchically identify the geographic location of the user. For example, in North America the first two digits identify world zone 01, the next three digits identify the area code, the next three digits identify the exchange switch, and the last four digits identify the user-access line on the switch. This convention greatly simplifies the routing decisions in telephone networks and has allowed the goal of universal connectivity to be achieved in the telephone network.

Today, SMDS 10-digit numbers do not coincide with the national phone number 10-digit system. Some moves by carriers such as MCI Communications are trying to change the system to be more in line with public phone network numbers. Figure 12.10 shows one example of a potential SMDS numbering plan.

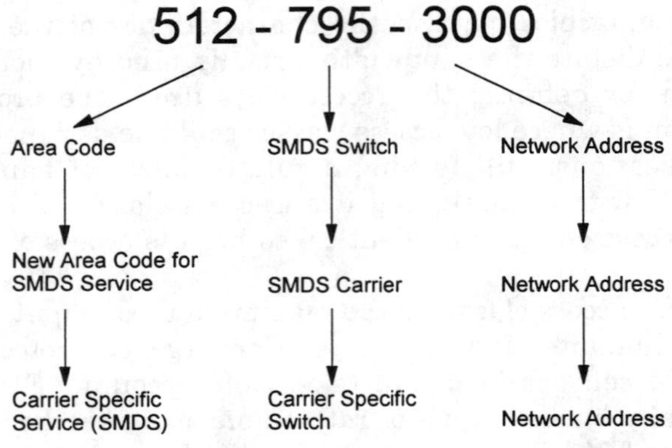

Figure 12.10 SMDS Addressing Example

12.4 SMDS AND DQDB PROTOCOL STRUCTURES

The IEEE 802.6 standard is one of the 802.X series of LAN and MAN standards, which has been further modified for operation over the WAN. We first look at the IEEE 802.6 protocol model in comparison to the OSI Reference Model (OSIRM). A detailed explanation of the SMDS and DQDB protocol and message structure follows.

12.4.1 IEEE 802.6 Compared to the OSIRM

IEEE 802.6 is part of the IEEE defined 802.X suite of LAN and MAN protocols. The IEEE 802.6 MAN protocol spans both the physical layer (layer 1) and media access control (MAC) sublayer (layer 2) of the OSIRM. It also interfaces to the logical link control (LLC) sublayer. Figure 12.11 depicts how the IEEE 802.X standard (Layer 2) and other 802.X IEEE protocols relate to the OSIRM layers.

12.4.2 Structure of SMDS and IEEE 802.6

SMDS and the IEEE 802.6 DQDB protocol have a one-to-one mapping to each other as illustrated in Figure 12.12. The SMDS Interface Protocol (SIP) has Protocol Data Units (PDUs) at levels 2 and 3. These PDUs are labeled L2_PDU and L3_PDU for level 2 and level 3, respectively. The level 2 SIP PDU is a 53-byte cell that corresponds to the DQDB MAC PDU of the IEEE

802.6 standard. The level 3 SIP PDU can contain one customer data packet of up to 9188 bytes and is treated the same as the upper layers in IEEE 802.6. SMDS protocols work independently of network and higher-layer protocols. There is also a strong correspondence between these layers and the OSIRM as shown in Figure 12.12.

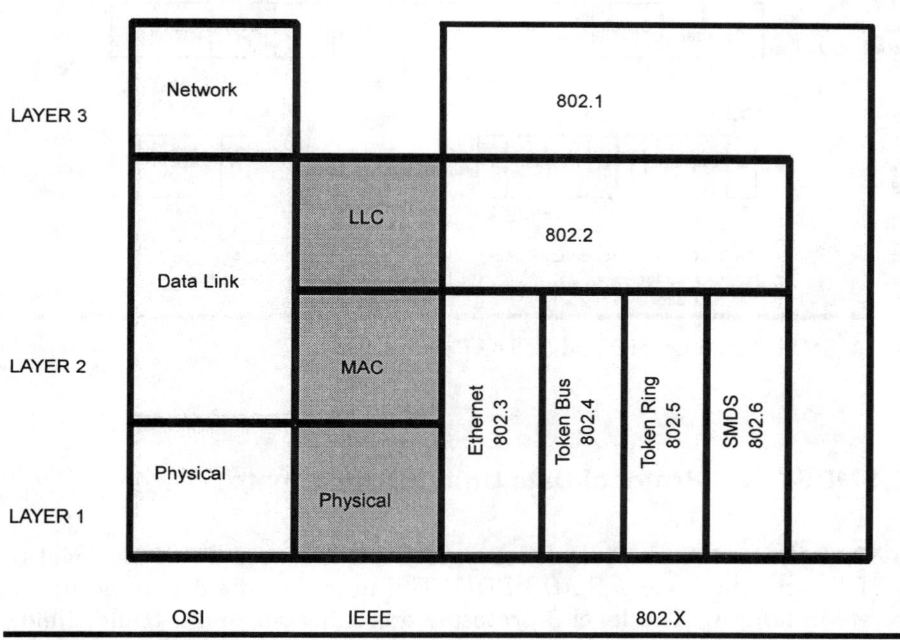

Figure 12.11 802.X to OSI Comparison

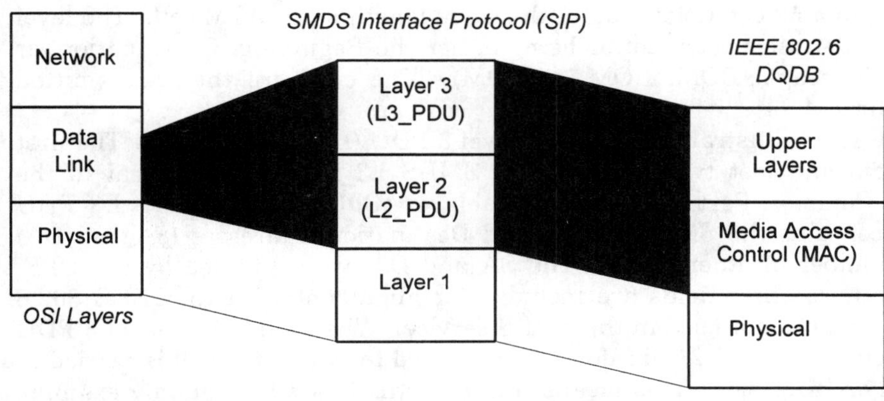

Figure 12.12 Protocol Structure of IEEE 802.6 DQDB and SMDS

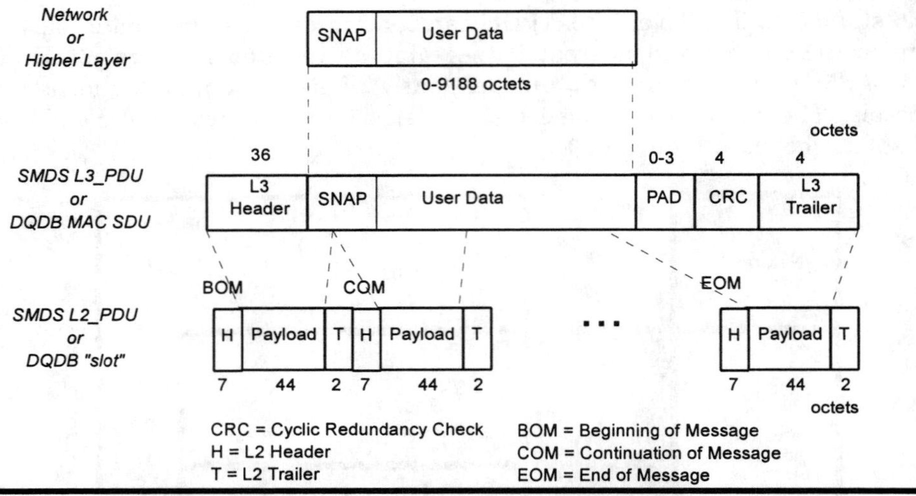

Figure 12.13 SMDS/802.6 Level 2 and 3 PDU Relationships

12.4.3 SMDS/802.6 Protocol Data Unit (PDU) Formats

Figure 12.13 illustrates the relationship between the user data, the level 3 SMDS PDU, and the level 2 SMDS PDU. The user data field may be up to 9188 octets in length. The level 3 protocol adds a header and a trailer field, padding the overall length to be on a 4-octet boundary. Level 2 performs a segmentation and reassembly function, transporting the level 3 payload in 44-octet segments. The level 2 PDU has a 7-octet header and 2-octet trailer resulting in a 53-octet slot length, the same length as an ATM cell. The level 2 header identifies each slot as being either the Beginning, Continuation, or End Of Message (BOM, COM, or EOM). The cells are then transmitted header first.

Figure 12.14 illustrates the SMDS level 3 PDU (L3_PDU) format. The first two octets and last two octets of the SMDS L3_PDU are identical to the AAL3/4 Common Part Convergence Sublayer (CPCS). The SMDS L3_PDU header contains the SMDS Source and Destination Addresses (SA and DA) and a number of other fields. The SA and DA are populated by the CPE. Most of these other fields are included for alignment with the IEEE 802.6 protocol and are not used in the SMDS service. When the SMDS level 3 PDU is segmented by level 2, all information needed to switch the cell is carried in an SSM or BOM slot. This means that an SMDS switch need only examine the first slot to make a switching decision.

The addressing plan for SMDS and CBDS is based upon the ITU-T Recommendation E.164; in the United States the proposed format is similar to the North American Numbering Plan (NANP) used for telephone service.

As the SMDS E.164 address is globally unique, SMDS provides the capability for ubiquitous connectivity. The E.164 address scheme will be covered in detail in Chapter 22. The IEEE 802.6 standard also allows the option for 48-bit IEEE Media Access Control (MAC) addresses to be employed in the DA and SA fields.

Figure 12.15 illustrates the 48-octet SMDS level 2 PDU format encapsulated in a 53-octet DQDB slot. The other four octets of SMDS level 2 overhead in the DQDB payload are used for the SMDS Segment Type (ST), Message IDentifier (MID), payload length, and a Cyclical Redundancy Check (CRC) on the 44-octet payload. The SMDS level 2 overhead and function are identical to the ATM AAL3/4 SAR. The ST field identifies either a Single Segment Message (SSM), Beginning Of Message (BOM), Continuation Of Message (COM), or End Of Message (EOM) slot. The MID field associates the BOM with any subsequent COM and EOM segments that made up an SMDS L3_PDU. The MID value will be the same for each cell that makes up a packet, and all cell sequence integrity is done through the MID. When an SMDS switch receives an SSM or BOM segment, the destination address determines the outgoing link on which the slots are transmitted. This is especially important in 802.6 implementations, because the protocol interleaves cells during transport and the MID offers the method of re-sequencing these cells at the egress port.

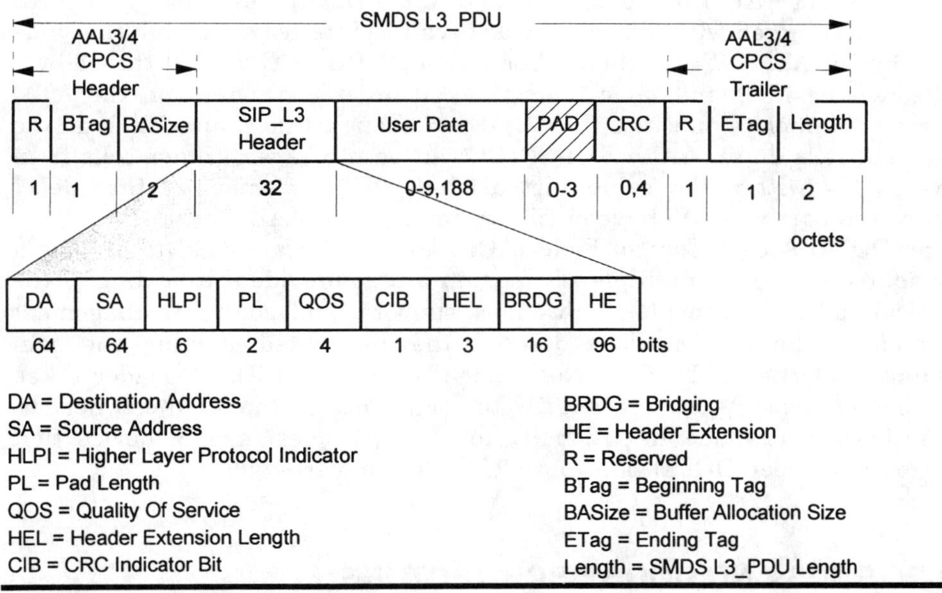

Figure 12.14 SMDS Level 3 PDU Format

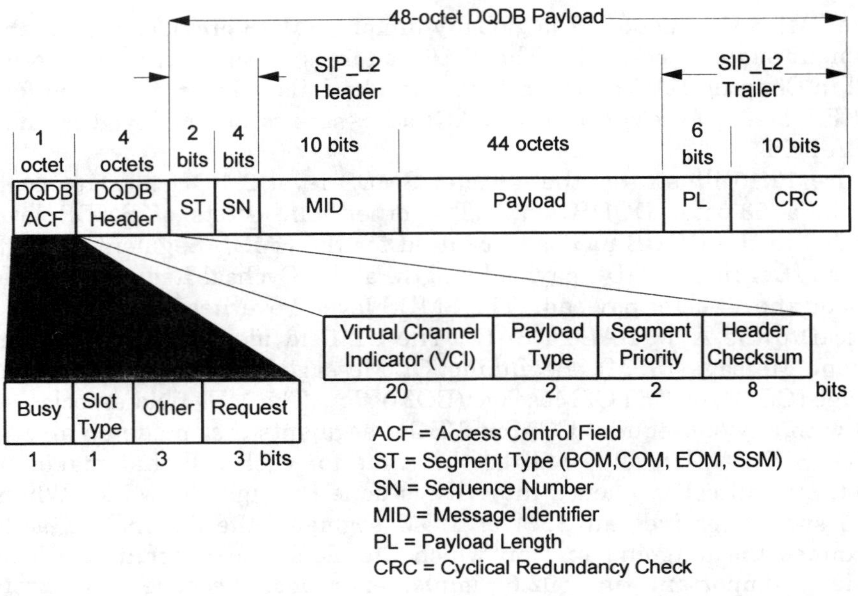

Figure 12.15 DQDB Slot Structure

AAL 3/4 and AAL 5 implementations of the MID are different. With AAL 3/4, cells associated with different packets can be interleaved within the same 802.6 bus or ATM VCC. When AAL5 on an SMDS VCC is used the 48-byte cell loses the MID and must keep the cell order concurrent on the ATM Virtual Channel Connection (VCC). Even though this limitation must be observed, cells on an AAL5 SMDS VCC can be mixed with other cells from other VCCs within the same Virtual Path (VP). Remember that delay between cell arrivals will have much less impact with AAL5 service.

The DQDB Access Control Field (ACF) and header are used to provide a distributed queue for multiple stations on a bus, provide self-healing of the physical network, provide isochronous support, and control management functions. The next sections describe the distributed queuing and self-healing properties of DQDB. Note that the DQDB ACF and header taken together are exactly 5 bytes, exactly the same size as the ATM cell header. This choice was made intentionally to make the design of a device that converted between DQDB slots and ATM cells simpler.

12.5 SMDS AND DQDB ARCHITECTURE

SMDS is defined as a service, and therefore can be offered with multiple access protocols and over multiple backbone transport technologies. When public SMDS services were first appearing around 1993, their backbones were built on the DQDB architecture. As these networks proliferated, ATM networks began to form. Today, SMDS service is offered over both DQDB and ATM network transport architectures.

In this section we will look at SMDS network architectures that consist of building blocks such as SMDS CPE, Switching Systems (SSs), the Inter-Carrier Interface (ICI), and the DQDB architecture. Customer Access Nodes (CANs) are used in European implementations only and are left to further study. Details on SMDS transport over ATM can be found in Chapter 14.

12.5.1 SMDS Backbone Architecture

SMDS public network backbone designs can be composed of multiple MAN Switching Systems (SSs) connected by InterCarrier Interface (ICI) transport. The old InterSwitching System Interface (ISSI) standard considered by Bellcore was never finished and the newer ICI is now the standard. Users interface to the network via SMDS CPE over the SMDS access protocols. Figure 12.16 represents an SMDS public data network supporting multiple customer premises environments on multiple access protocols. Access lines represent SIP using DXI, ATM, and frame relay. In Europe, the CAN resides on the customer premises.

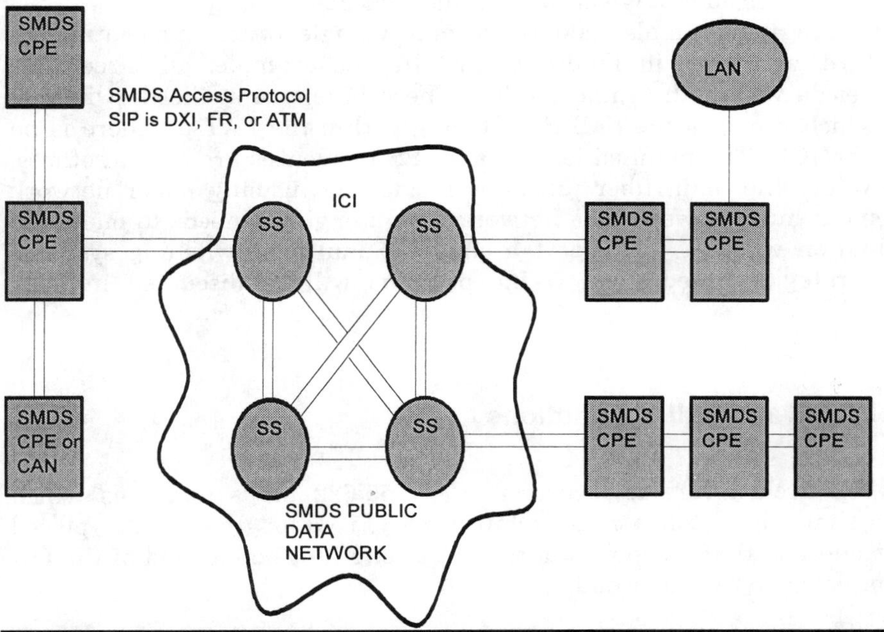

Figure 12.16 SMDS MAN Public Data Network

Access DQDB refers to the use of the DQDB protocol as the basis for the SMDS interface protocol providing access to the SMDS service. Bellcore standards define the SMDS Switching System (SS) as a collection of equipment that provides high-speed packet switching function in a network supporting SMDS. Multiple SSs are interconnected by the ICI to form a complete network. CPE could include any of those mentioned in the last section.

Switching Systems (SSs) can be configured in a distributed architecture where multiple SSs would form the SMDS network, such as shown in Figure 12.17. Each LATA has CPE which communicates with its local SS via the System Network Interface (SNI). These switching systems are linked by the ICI and form the SMDS backbone network. SSs operate in either a store-and-forward mode where the SS reads in the entire L3_PDU on the SNI before transmitting it on to the next SS or end CPE device. This technique of *reassembly* adds store-and-forward delay. One method of eliminating this delay is through *pipe-lining*, where the switch immediately starts forwarding part of the L3_PDU before the entire L3_PDU is received into the switch. This operation is similar to many frame relay switches that read the entire L2 frame into the switch before transmitting it to the next switch. Pipe-lining can be used in traditional IEEE 802.6 and AAL 3/4 implementations. MID sequencing must be assured at each SMDS switch. The MID can be used to avoid rebuilding the entire L2_PDU at each switching point. It is interesting to note that, as in frame relay, the smaller the data unit (frame or L3_PD) is, the less advantageous pipe-lining becomes.

Switching systems can also take the form of a single switch in a centralized architecture, as shown in Figure 12.18. In this example, all three CPE devices reside within the same LATA. There is one centralized switching system which provides the SMDS switching within the LATA. There is no need for an ICI. The planned locations for SS residences are central offices. This is where the main fiber junctions reside, and usually major network management hubs as well. The network design engineer needs to make the determination whether to support a single or multiple switching systems. Design strategies based upon traffic patterns will be discussed in later chapters.

12.5.2 DQDB and SMDS Functions

The DQDB architecture is based on a 45/155/622 Mbps dual bus which operates similarly to token ring architecture. Fixed-length cells are placed within time slots that move from a time slot generator on one end of the bus to a terminator on the other end.

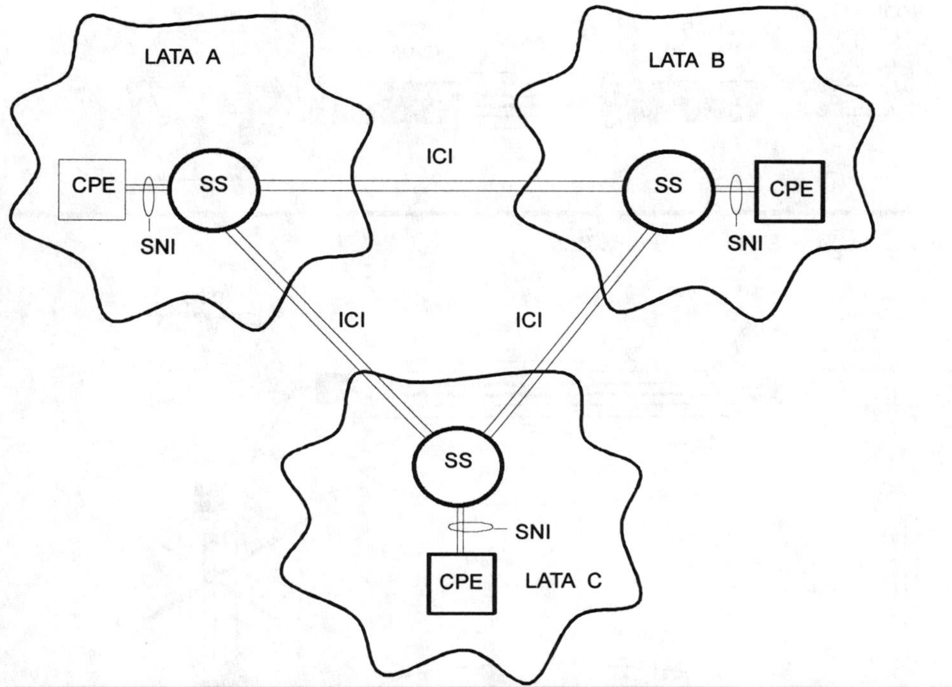

Figure 12.17 SMDS Distributed Architecture

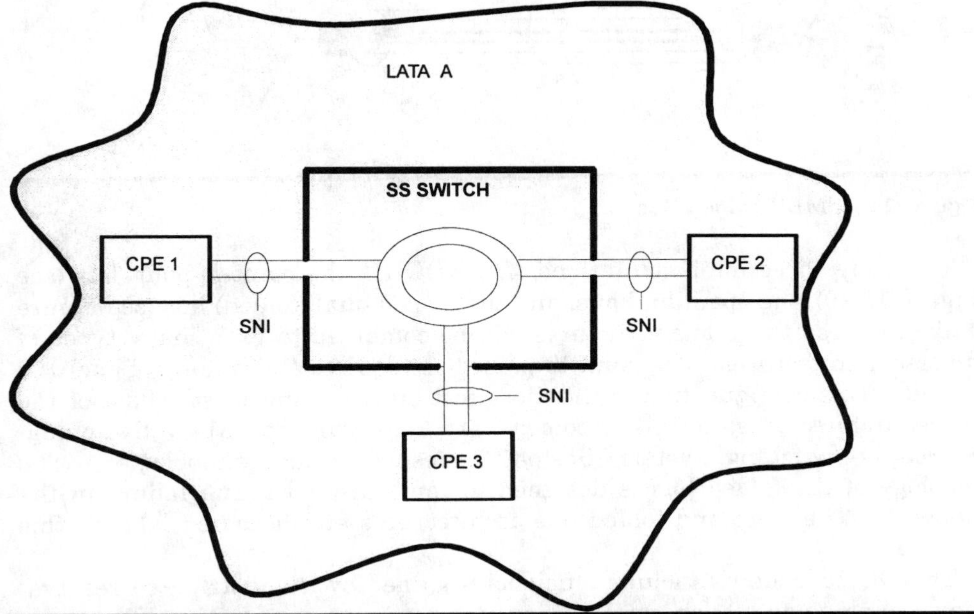

Figure 12.18 SMDS Centralized Architecture

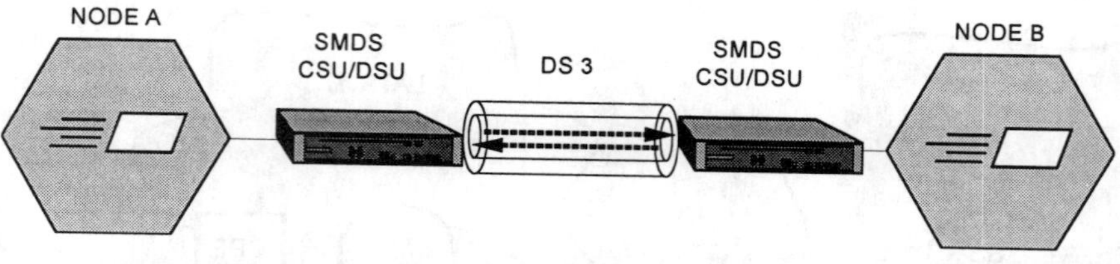

Figure 12.19 SMDS Point-to-Point Bus

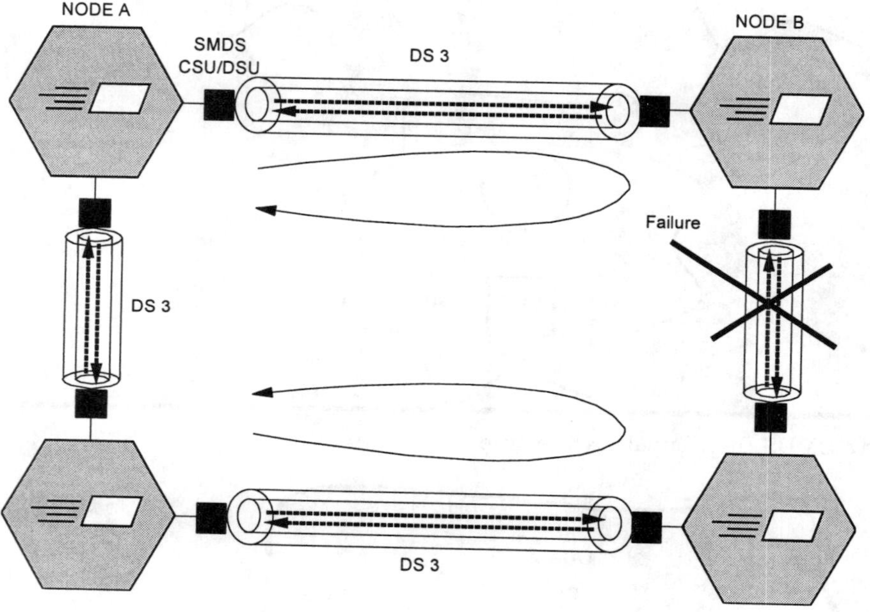

Figure 12.20 SMDS Folded Bus

There are three implementations of the DQDB: the point-to-point bus (see Figure 12.19), the open-dual bus, and the looped dual (folded) bus (see Figure 12.20). These three bus structures can be combined to form many types of diverse architectures. The point-to-point bus requires a minimum of one DS3 circuit. This configuration is the most cost effective and least robust of the three architectures, but it becomes very important for MAN Switching-System-to-Switching System (SS-to-SS) meshed trunking topologies. The topology of the folded bus is designed to route around a link failure in the network. The open and folded bus architectures are discussed later in this section.

The DQDB benefits include efficiencies gained by the distributed reservation technique and its channel efficiency during normal operation. Transmission can occur over single and multimode fiber optics. Since SMDS networks are designed to accommodate a broad range of traffic, some overdesign is built into the network. As with frame relay traffic design, there are statistical methods for planning traffic patterns (explained in later chapters), but some large peak periods of traffic could encounter some delay.

12.5.3 DQDB Architecture – Bus Defined

This section describes the distributed queuing and self-healing ring properties of the IEEE 802.6 DQDB protocol with reference to Figure 12.21. Refer to the IEEE 802.6 standard for further details on the different implementations of the DQDB architecture. There are two unidirectional buses, A and B, that interconnect a number of nodes, often configured in a physical ring. Even though the physical configuration may be a ring, logical operation is bus-oriented. Nodes read from both buses, usually passing along any data onto the next node in the bus. Each node may become the Head Of Bus (HOB) or End Of Bus (EOB) as indicated in the figure. The HOB generates 53-octet slots in a framing structure to which the other nodes synchronize. The EOB node simply terminates the bus.

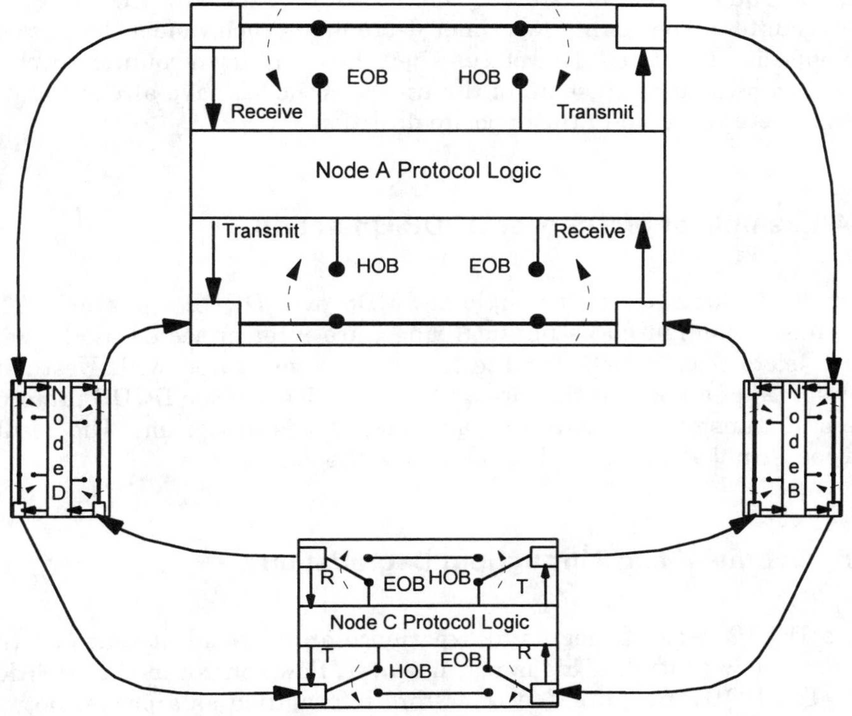

Figure 12.21 Dual DQDB Architecture

Another distinction that warrants discussion is that although the bus appears to pass *through* each node on the bus, in fact it only passes *by* each node. This provides for a highly reliable network, as a node failure will not affect the operation of the rest of the network. Neither bus operation would be interrupted. If a node fails or is powered down, it is designed so that it passively passes data. Therefore, each node effectively has four ports, two for each bus. Normally one node would be the HOB for both buses, as shown for node C. However, in the event of a failure of one of the buses connecting a pair of nodes, the DQDB protocol ensures that the nodes on either side of the break become the new HOB within a short period of time.

The looped architecture provides a common point for timing into the network to ensure network synchronization, as well as a self-healing, fault isolation mechanism inherent to the architecture.

The busy and request bits in the DQDB Access Control Field (ACF) implement a distributed queue. Each node has two counters: one for requests and the other as a countdown for transmission. If a slot passes through the node with the request bit set, then the request counter is incremented; otherwise the request counter decrements. Thus, the request counter reflects how many upstream nodes have slots to send. When a node has data to send, it writes a logical 1 to the request bit in the first slot received that has the request bit equal to 0 and loads the countdown register with the value of the request counter. The countdown timer decrements each time a slot passes by in the opposite direction. Therefore, when the countdown counter reaches 0, the slot can be sent because all of the upstream nodes have already sent the slots that were reserved in the opposite direction.

12.5.4 Example of SMDS over DQDB Operation

Figure 12.22 illustrates an example of SMDS over DQDB operation. Three DQDB buses, configured as physical rings, are interconnected as shown. A series of slots from a node on the far left are generated with Destination Address (DA) of a node on the far right. The nodes use the DQDB protocol to queue and transmit the slots corresponding to this datagram. The result is that a reassembled datagram is delivered to the destination.

12.5.5 Overhead and Throughput Degradation

When a DQDB network begins to experience an overload, it relies on three methods of flow control. This is not, however, flow control in the traditional sense. The DQDB network does not store information as a packet network, rather it decides what type of data receives the priority of transmission.

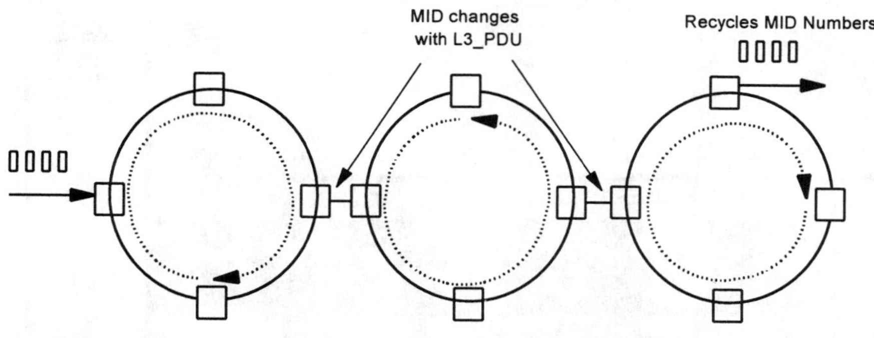

Figure 12.22 Example of SMDS/DQDB Operation

Prearbitrated access enables the service provider to allocate bandwidth to isochronous connections with constrained jitter. This allows priority bandwidth to be provided to the services that are most affected by delay priority bandwidth – namely video and voice. This is the equivalent to a level 1 priority, and should be assigned with careful consideration. Video and voice are prime examples of data requiring primary access to bandwidth because of their intolerance for delay.

Queued arbitrated access would be level 2 in the bandwidth priority scheme. Queued arbitrated access has distance limitations. These are displayed in Table 12.3. These distances are derived from the size of one 53-octet slot. The longer the distance between the stations, the less effective the priority queuing. This is usually allocated to lower-priority services, or services that can tolerate delay and retransmissions more easily than video or voice. This service also assumes that bandwidth balancing is disabled. Bandwidth balancing will be discussed later.

For example, in Figure 12.23 there are three users on a DS3 DQDB. User A is located 150 meters from the MAN Switching System (SS), and should have no problem with employing queued arbitrated access with priority. User B is farther away but still within the 2000-meter distance limitation. User C may use arbitrated queuing, but is not guaranteed priority and may become the last in the priority queue behind users A and B. Note that queuing fairness only becomes an issue at utilization rates higher than 80 percent, such as during periods of high network activity.

TABLE 12.3 Queued Arbitrated Access Distance Limitations

DISTANCE (meters)	SPEED (Mbps)
2000	44.736
546	155.520
137	622.080

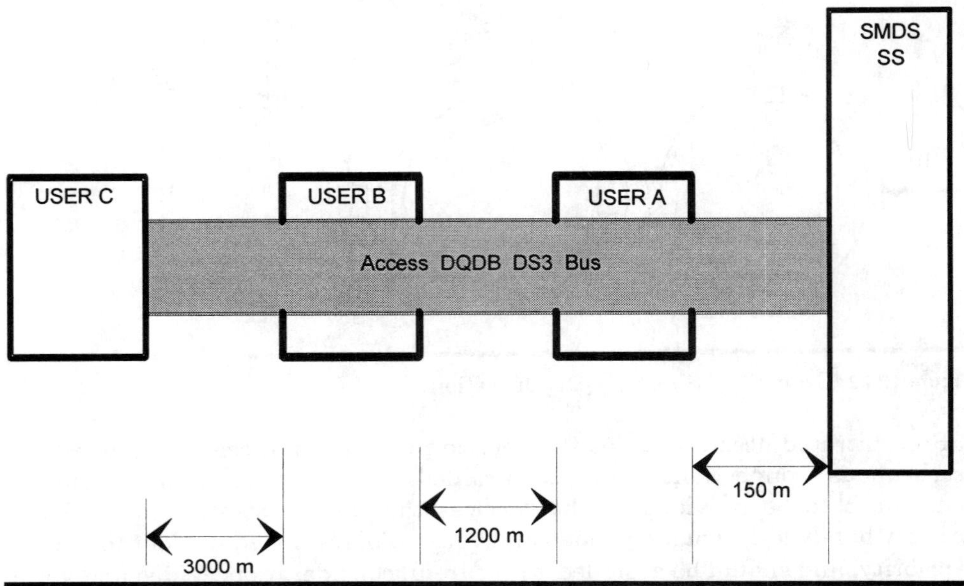

Figure 12.23 Queued Arbitrated Access with Priority Example

If user C does exceed the maximum distance limitation as in the previous example, and the service provider wants to provide equal access to all three users, bandwidth balancing could be applied. Bandwidth balancing would allow users A, B, and C to receive an "equal share" of the available bandwidth by equally dividing bus bandwidth among all users on the bus.

The network designer should strive to design the subnetworks and CPE that interface with the DQDB bus in a manner to ensure that peak traffic conditions do not cause excessive delay and loss of traffic. This can be accomplished by the effective use of these techniques.

12.6 SMDS INTERNETWORKING – BRIDGING AND ROUTING

Internetworking for TCP/IP over SMDS is accomplished primarily with either bridging or routing. Bridging can be accomplished either with MAC bridging or simple encapsulation. Routing can be accomplished with simple encapsulation of IP. Both will be explained below with reference to the network shown in Figure 12.24.

In our examples, we use Transmission Control Protocol with Internet Protocol (TCP/IP). TCP/IP remains the predominant internetworking and transport protocol in the educational, scientific, and military environments. TCP/IP spans multivendor networks, providing a common platform for end-to-end data management and error correction, as well as internetwork addressing. Many users find that TCP/IP will sufficiently meet LAN-to-LAN internetworking needs for the next five years. TCP/IP is the predominant internetworking protocol today.

12.6.1 SMDS Bridging with TCP/IP

SMDS bridging is one method of extending the LAN environment through SMDS using a bridge. Some protocols require bridging such as DEC LAT and NetBIOS. The local end-user device will send the IP packets within the IEEE 802.3 Ethernet frames to the local bridge. The bridge will use encapsulation bridging into SMDS SIP frames as shown in Figure 12.25. This figure depicts a user employing TCP/IP to establish communication and data transport from the application through first the LAN, and then a router and, finally, to the SMDS network. The egress side of the network would usually resemble the ingress side displayed here.

The bridge does not perform internetwork protocol functions, but instead only encapsulates data on one end and unencapsulates it at the distant end. The MAC interface is not translated into a SIP, but is instead encapsulated and transported between SIPs. All TCP and higher-level interfaces in this process remain the same (i.e., transparent to the bridge and SMDS network). Thus, the IP and MAC layer protocols (IEEE 802.3 Ethernet in this example) will be encapsulated within the SMDS SIP by the local bridge and forwarded to a remote bridge, where they will be deencapsulated and sent to the remote end-user device. The OSI layer 4 is for all intents and purposes transparent to the router or switch, and ensures end-to-end transport of data between users. Layers 5, 6, and 7 are also transparent and are handled between users by the application. RFC 791 and 793 define the specifics of bridging IP over SMDS, and are left to the reader for further study. Although SMDS supports this bridging function, routing is preferred over bridging.

12.6.2 SMDS Routing with TCP/IP

Figure 12.26 depicts the same LAN connectivity as in the previous example but now using a router in place of the bridge. The difference in this example is that the router provides the conversion from the MAC protocol to the SMDS SIP. Using the SIP, the router now uses a DQDB providing SMDS to allow high-speed connectivity over large geographic areas. Notice that the router does pay attention to the LLC and IP addresses when making its routing decision, rather than just forwarding the frames received as in the bridging example. Thus, the router makes the SMDS transport look like just another LAN segment.

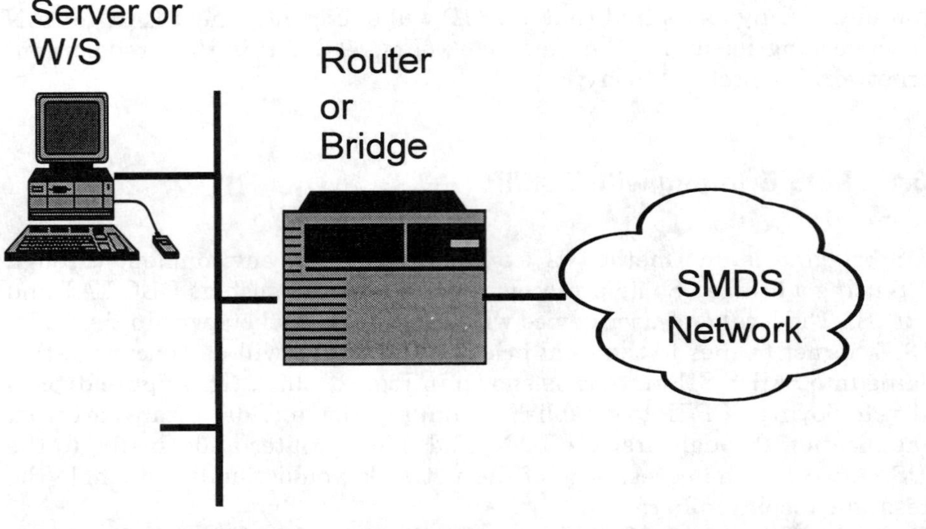

Figure 12.24 SMDS Reference Network for Comparison

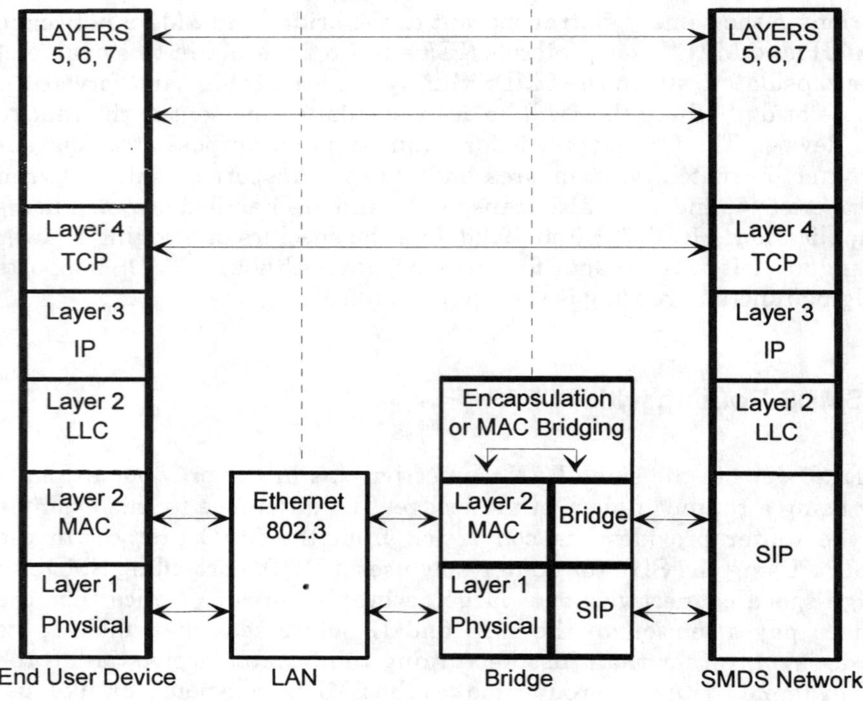

Figure 12.25 SMDS Bridging with TCP/IP

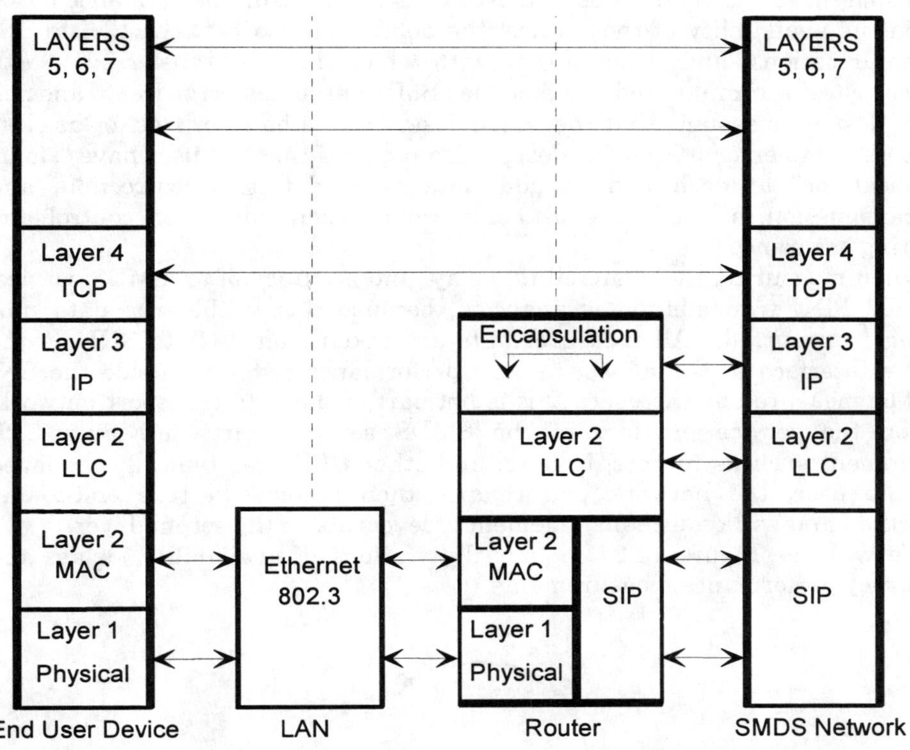

Figure 12.26 SMDS Routing with TCP/IP

Layers 4, 5, 6, and 7 are the same as the last example, are transparent, and are handled between users by the application. RFC 791 and 793 define the specifics of routing IP over SMDS, and are left to the reader for further study. SMDS can also provide multicast support for IPX and AppleTalk protocols.

12.7 PERFORMANCE

Performance objectives in SMDS service are very important to both the service provider and the end user. Since these performance objectives are not publicly announced, it is up to the user to ensure that the provider is indeed providing quality service. This is especially true for SMDS networks that span the country and even the globe.

The main focus on performance for SMDS networks is SNI-to-SNI connection at the L3_PDU level. The CPE or the service provider will measure the performance of the service. As discussed, the SMDS network should be transparent to the user. Thus, the user CPE will measure performance based upon the availability of the service, the delay incurred between SNI-to-SNI communications, and the accuracy with which data is transferred. With these criteria in mind, and the fact that SMDS assumes error-free transmission, designers assume that the transmission media be error free (or as close as possible to error free). The design also requires that the user have "smart applications" at each end to add data error detection, correction, and retransmission, as well as end-to-end transmission congestion control and routing assurance.

When measuring the availability, delay, and accuracy of an SMDS service, the L3_PDU transmission is analyzed, because this is the true data unit being transmitted. All measurements are taken from SNI to SNI, as the user's interface to the network. Any performance criteria outside the SNI will be measured by the user; this is not part of the data transport network. When the service provider of the SMDS service starts providing CPE equipment such as routers, bridges, and other CPE gear typically managed by the user, the network performance then becomes a true end-to-end function, and will require management of levels above the second layer.

We will use Figure 12.27 for our illustrations of availability, delay, and accuracy performance measurements.

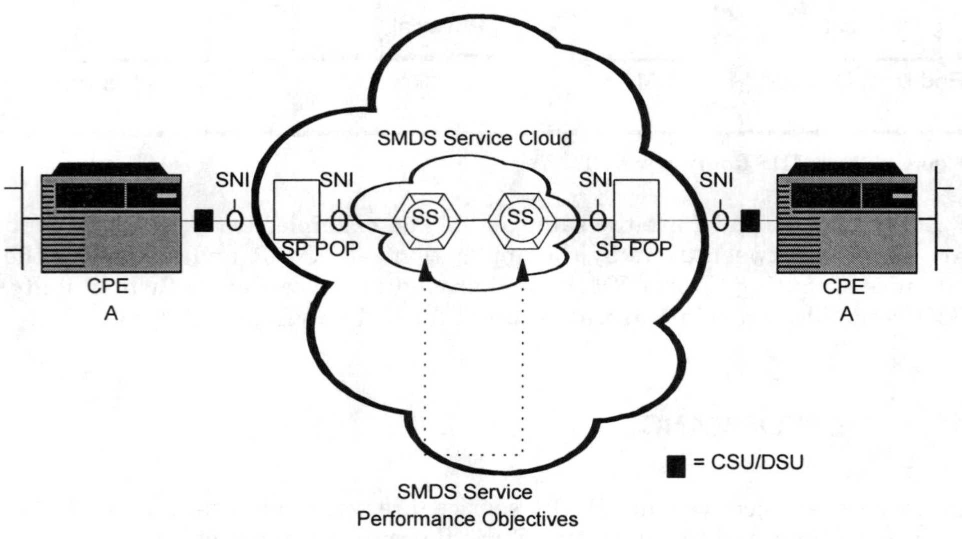

Figure 12.27 SMDS Network Availability, Delay, Accuracy Performance Measurements

12.7.1 Availability

Availability is measured by the ratio of actual service time to scheduled service time on a user-to-user basis (SNI to SNI). There are four methods of measuring the availability of the service: (1) network availability should be at least 99.9 percent, (2) scheduled service time should be 7×24, (3) Mean Time To Repair (MTTR) should be less than 2 hours, and (4) Mean Time Between Service Outages (MTBSO) should be greater than 1092 hours or no more than 2.5 service outages per year. Each of these availability measurements will change based upon user requirements, network configuration, equipment locations, and vendor specifications. Each user should establish a threshold of pain for these availability measurements and require the service provider to pay penalties if they are not met.

Figure 12.26 shows that the availability measurements listed previously are for the SMDS network only, again SNI to SNI. This definition is very subjective. Does it include access to a provider's Point of Presence (PoP) that does not contain an SMDS switch, or measured only once it is into the first SMDS switch? Does it include elements of the local access, such as the local loop? The answers to these questions are important, as many more problems typically occur in the local loop than in the SMDS service "cloud", and a 99.9 percent availability could be actually much less to the end user.

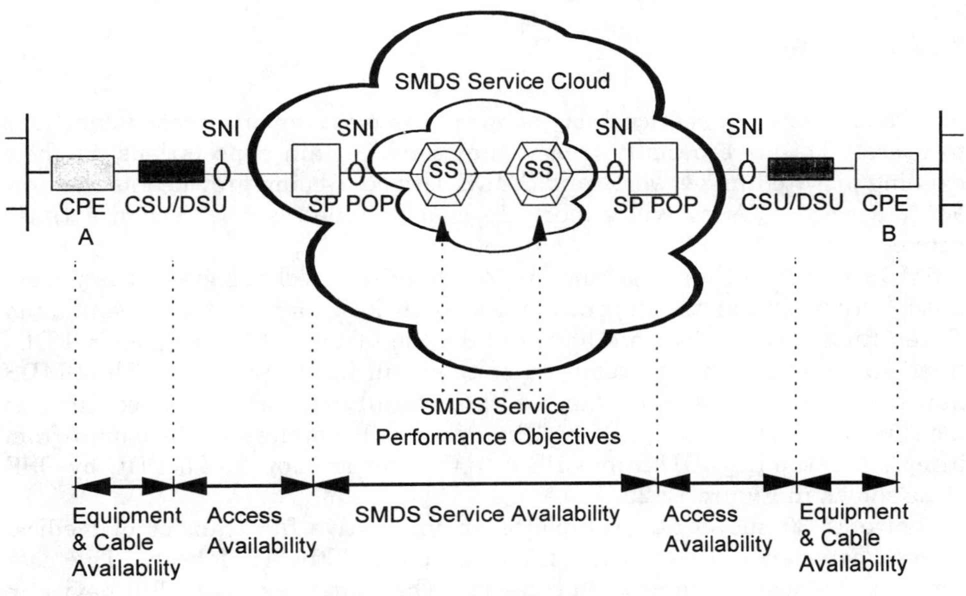

Figure 12.28 SMDS Network Availability Measurements

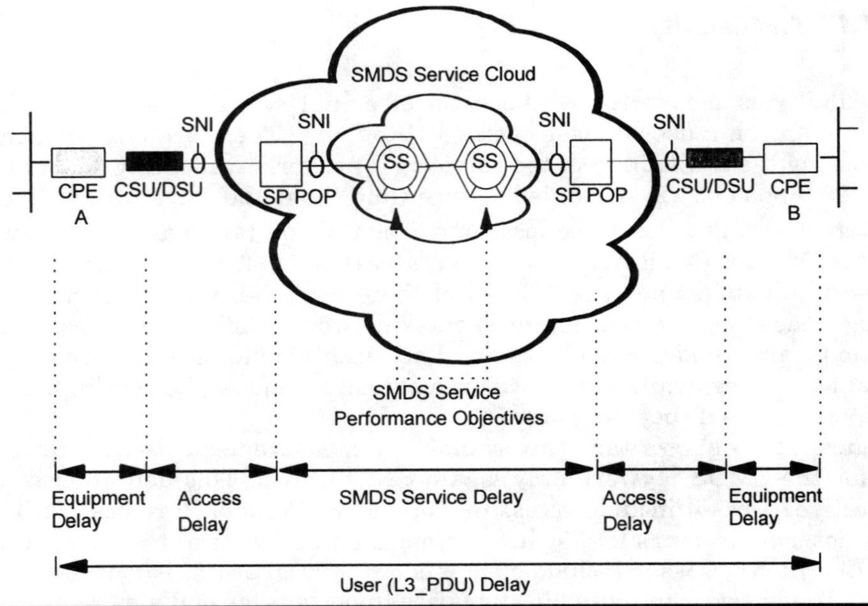

Figure 12.29 SMDS Network Delay Measurements

12.7.2 Delay

End-to-end network service delay is one of the most important considerations to users. This is especially true if they have certain expectations on their existing private line network, and SMDS service is being provided as the new WAN service. Users will expect the same, if not faster, response times between SNIs.

SMDS response times are similar to a hybrid of technologies: at low load, quick access similar to Ethernet and at high load, orderly access similar to Token Ring. SMDS does not have to take the tokens off the ring as in FDDI (in FDDI, tokens must be removed or they will fill up the bus). The SMDS network response time portion of the overall network response time is measured in terms of L3_PDUs. The delay will therefore be measured from inception of the L3_PDU from CPE A to the reception of the L3_PDU by CPE B, as shown in Figure 12.29.

Figure 12.30 shows an example of an interactive file transfer of medical images between a Token Ring LAN station and the IBM host. The user contacts the host to request file transfer. The router acts as a CPE device in the building where the LAN resides. It takes the Token Ring PDU and translates (or encapsulates) it to the access DQDB bus protocol for transport over the SMDS network. The SMDS network provides the transport through SMDS switching systems, and delivers the transaction directly to the front-end processor, in this case an IBM 3745, which employs a direct access DQDB to the SMDS network. The FEP then interfaces to the host computer. The host application processes the request and transmits the file back to the requesting station. Obviously, there are many additional higher-level protocol functions that take place, but this illustration shows the "end-to-end" delay components.

In this example, there are many areas where delay is added to the total transmission time. The Token Ring LAN access and transmission time, router protocol conversion or encapsulation and routing function, the SMDS network transmission delay, and the FEP and mainframe processing delay. Also, the transmission media in each of these steps add delay. This is referred to as the total user delay, not the SMDS network delay. The SMDS network delay begins at the router SNI and ends at the FEP/mainframe SNI, and is measured by the passage of L3_PDUs between those interfaces. There is also delay inherent in the transmission medium used within the SMDS network.

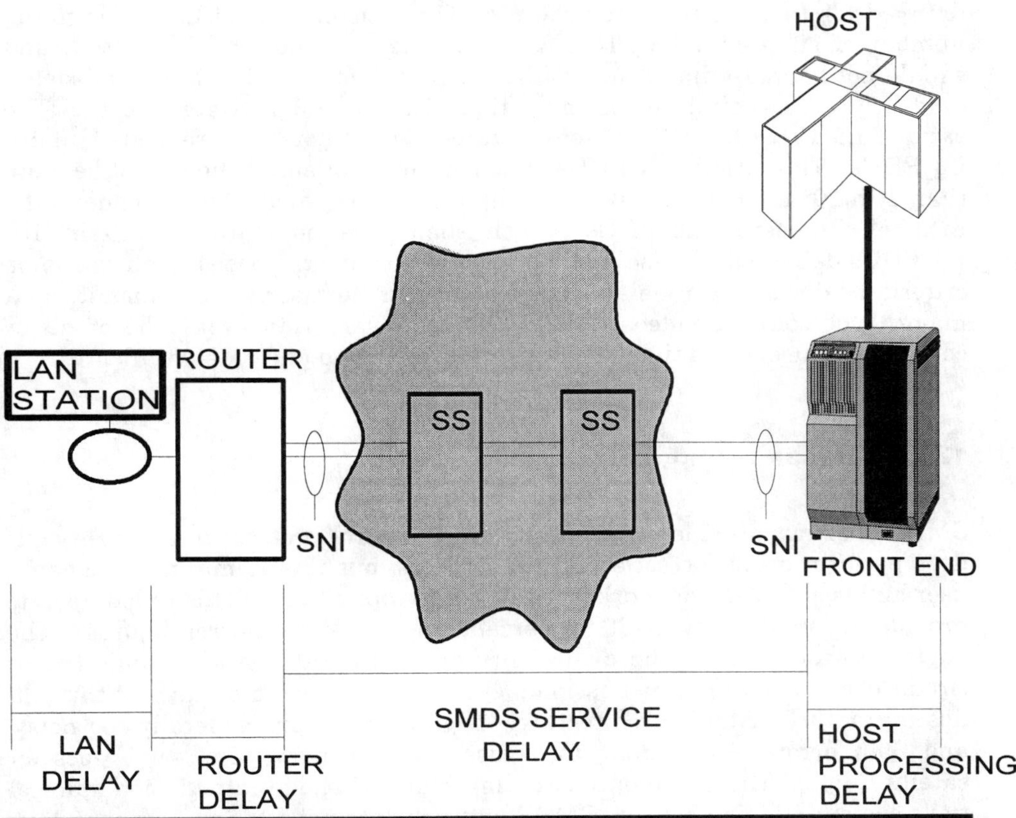

Figure 12.30 SMDS Interactive File Transfer Example

The delay for the L3_PDUs is defined for individually addressed and group-addressed L3_PDUs. With individually addressed L3_PDUs, the delay based on two CPE units using DS3 SNI access lines should be less than 20 ms within the same LATA. The delay based on two CPE devices using a DS3 SNI access line should be less than 80 ms within the same LATA. The delay based on two CPE units that both use T1 access trunks should be less than 140mS (for cross country application, add transient delay). With group-addressed L3_PDUs, the delay times should be less than 100, 160, and 220 ms, respectively. The maximum lifetime allowed for an L3_PDU is 500 ms. These delay figures are very important when analyzing the feasibility of an SMDS network over other technologies, such as ATM.

12.7.3 Accuracy

The accuracy of the network is achieved by the number of delivered or dropped L3_PDUs across the network. The ratio of errored L3_PDUs to the number of successful L3_PDUs is called the "errored L3_PDU ratio", and should not be more than 5 in 10^{13} L3_PDUs delivered. The ratio of misdelivered L3_PDUs should not be more than 5 in 10^{8} L3_PDUs delivered. The ratio of L3_PDUs which are *not* delivered should not be more than 1 in 10^{4} L3_PDUs. The ratio of L3_PDUs which are missequenced should not be more than 1 in 10^{9} L3_PDUs delivered. The last accuracy calculation made is the ratio of duplicated L3_PDUs, which should be no more than 5 in 10^{8} L3_PDUs delivered. These numbers would be adjusted based upon the same criteria as discussed in delay. For example, if the user were transmitting a majority of voice or video traffic, the misdelivery ratio would be of major concern because of the time-sensitive nature of voice and video traffic.

12.7.4 Reliance on Fiber

SMDS does not provide error correction or control protocol functionality. It does perform error correction on the address, but this is minimal. When a user builds an SMDS network, digital or fiber-optic transport is relied upon to provide an availability of 99.99 percent and low circuit-error figures. The engineer should verify the availability and error ratio of each digital fiber circuit used. SONET transmission facilities are preferred because of the self-healing nature of their architecture. Digital radios are generally too noisy, and their errors too random, to be used as transport. The same goes for satellite shots. These standards are important to design into the communications system. Remember, the SMDS network does not perform flow control or data error checking. It *assumes* the transmission paths are virtually error free and that error checking and correction is performed by the higher-layer protocols! If the cell takes an error in the SDU (data portion), it will be passed on to the user. The concept is that a tradeoff exists between error correction for performance and high throughput for cost efficiencies.

12.7.5 "Smart Applications" Concept

SMDS networks provide only layer 1 and 2 protocol functionality. Users of existing data services, such as X.25 packet-switched networks, rely on the network to perform the error detection, correction, and end-to-end data transport control. This extra functionality is traded off for a major decrease in throughput. The SMDS network does very little of these functions, and when it does, it does so for the addressing of PDUs, not the actual data *within* the PDU. What this means to the user is that smart protocols must be used at the CPE, such as TCP/IP and DECnet, to ensure end-to-end transmission.

Transmission systems may need the enhancement of Physical Layer Convergence Procedures (PLCPs) to enhance the physical level interfaces. Protocols that are transported over SMDS need to be reviewed for window size settings and timer settings that may be impacted by variations or lengthy network delay.

12.8 DESIGN CONSIDERATIONS

SMDS design considerations include the transport to be used, limiting the distance between nodes and taking into account the nodes' position on the bus, network timing, network bandwidth capacity and overbuilding, and network management. Ease of migration from SMDS services to ATM services is also a consideration.

12.8.1 Transport

When discussing addressing, it was noted that access classes were assigned to CPE to avoid network congestion of multiple transfers of data units. There the user also has a choice on the number of data units which may be in transit between the CPE and SS at any given time. If the user chooses only one, the SS will attempt to buffer the information when the maximum value of data units is exceeded. The user can also choose from two to sixteen at a given time, for which the SS would also perform buffering, with a greater chance of data loss. The user can also choose to not specify a limit, but this precludes the SS from buffering, and is not a wise choice for most users.

DQDB connectivity is established over 34 and 140, 45, and 155 Mbps links using CCITT G.703, ANSI DS3, and CCITT G.707-9 SDH standards, respectively. Fiber-optic transmission media should be used to assure the best performance. SONET infrastructure in the form of ring architectures is now used in almost all of the leading LEC and IXC digital data networks.

SMDS service offerings can be found at subrate (DXI), DS1, and DS3 speeds. Thus, all SMDS access classes (4, 10, 16, 25, and 34 Mbps) can now be offered across the WAN. Future offerings may include STS-N speeds.

12.8.2 Distance between Nodes

The overall distance between SMDS nodes and their position on the DQDB has a major influence on the amount of potential delay they may incur. Figure 12.31 shows that nodes on the center of the bus (from head and tail of buses) will incur greater delay than nodes at the head or tail of the bus. The "end" nodes will do so by having to wait for more cells to pass before they find an empty one (the head and tail nodes will be able to get the empty cells first). This has a drastic effect as the number of users and traffic on the ring increases.

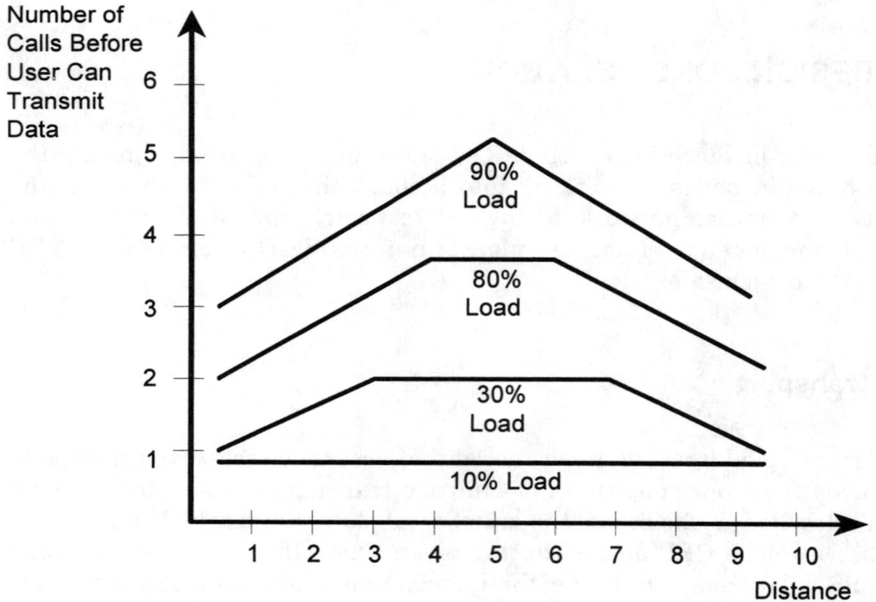

Figure 12.31 SMDS Delay

Also note that there are several problems that complicate the IEEE 802.6 standard. First, the nodes that are closer to the head end of the bus have first access to the request bits, and can dominate the traffic on the bus. Secondly, provisions must be made for stations to join and leave the bus and handle bit errors. The IEEE 802.6 standard defines procedures to handle all of these cases.

12.8.3 Timing

Network timing can either be provided by an external source to the DQDB network (the network user) or provided by one and only one node per DQDB bus. If there is more than one DQDB ring, a master node will be chosen from which to draw network timing. External timing will always have priority over nodal timing. A stratum level 1 clock source is desirable, but any source up to and including stratum level 3 will suffice. Due to operating speeds, an accurate clock source is vital to operations.

12.8.4 Capacity Planning

The most desirable way to build an SMDS network is to overbuild. The traffic base for this service is often LAN interconnect and extension. As seen in previous chapters, the traffic output from a LAN can vary up to 100 times the original projections. This is due to the very bursty nature of LAN-to-LAN information transfers. The design engineer must build enough capacity into the network for it to withstand times of extremely high traffic volumes, despite the statistical multiplexing characteristic of multiple-LAN traffic on the same transmission. This becomes a tradeoff of cost avoidance and profit. Cost avoidance is planning enough capacity on the network to eliminate many private individual circuits, and profit is what will be gained or lost by doing so.

For example, it would not be good to eliminate 46 DS1 private lines for a router and one DS3, with the hope that their average utilization peak is only 50 percent. If their peak were to exceed the 50%, the DS3 would be out of capacity, and either the application would have to buffer the traffic, or the data would be lost. Now imagine – it is 1:30 p.m. and all the LANs attached to the network decided to perform massive file transfers. The utilization just went up 300 percent: ergo, there were not enough buffers and transport to handle even a third of the traffic and the LAN's file transfers were delayed considerably. In a large network, this situation could bring the network to its knees. The designer needs to ensure a balance between the cost avoidance of extra circuits and equipment to plan for peak periods (and reduce delay during those times) and the profit or loss incurred if the user's traffic is effectively transported or not. This is why proper capacity planning is important, and we will discuss this in later chapters in greater detail.

If bandwidth hogging (bus fairness) is a problem, use a bandwidth balancing parameter of eliminating the use of 1 slot in N. At the same time, the connectionless priority could be restricted to 0 to add a higher priority to connection-oriented traffic.

12.8.5 Network Management

SMDS networks, by author bias, should be managed under a standard network management protocol. The Customer Network Management (CNM) used should allow the user to measure performance and subscription standards, as well as address administration, as stated earlier in this chapter. In the United States this is Simple Network Management Protocol (SNMP). In other parts of the world such as in Europe Common Management Information Protocol (CMIP) and CMIP Over Logical link control (CMOL) are the standards. For SNMP Version 1 and 2, the MIB I or MIB II modules for SNMP management should be used. There are also MIBs for DS1, DS3, SIP, and SMDS subscription. Network management will be covered in detail in Chapter 23.

12.8.6 Future PARs

Table 12.4 shows the 802.6x extensions. The current status of each can be found by contacting the IEEE.

TABLE 12.4 802.6x Extensions

802.6x	Feature or Enhancement
a	Multiport bridge interface
b	DS3 premises extension
c	DS1 physical layer
d	SONET physical layer
e	Eraser node
f	PICS pro forma
g	Layer management
h	Isochronous
i	Remote bridging
j	Connection oriented
k	Additions to 802.1

Future directions of SMDS also include speeds up to 622 Mbps, isochronous enhancements for end-to-end transparent cell transport (let the carriers sort it out), additional premises physical layer support, and efficient methods of guaranteeing bandwidth.

12.8.7 Migration Path from SMDS to ATM

When Bellcore specified recommended standards for SMDS, they kept in mind the need to migrate to Broadband-ISDN (B-ISDN) standards and integrate with ATM transport in the near future. The features and functions of SMDS and the conformance to 53-octet DQDB and ATM cell size were designed to provide a service which could migrate with a minimum loss of feature and function, quality of service, and performance, as well as minimize the need to replace existing equipment. As services emerge that are based on ATM transport, vendors supporting these new services will need to provide an incentive for users to migrate.

Major efforts to aid in the migration and integration of SMDS to ATM include:

- SMDS is fiber-oriented – based on cell-relay data format
- 802.6 and B-ISDN committees worked together – share membership
- 802.6 method of dividing up bandwidth on ATM places 802.6 segments into ATM cells

It was originally thought that many of the vendors providing SMDS hardware, primarily central office vendors, would be the same players providing ATM hardware. This has happened in the central office switch vendor communities and at the premises. Companies like Cascade that now lead the charge with ATM switching products offer SMDS interfaces to their ATM switches. Even the premises vendors of router products like Cisco and Bay Networks have offered both SMDS and ATM interfaces. One example of a bilateral push for both technologies is Siemens Stromberg-Carlson. It was the first central office vendor with an SMDS switch, and it has also announced an ATM switch product.

12.9 REVIEW

In this chapter the first implementation of cell switching via the IEEE 802.6 standard was explained. Starting with a history of cell switching that began with the development of the DQDB architecture, it was shown how SMDS was the first major service offering derived from the IEEE 802.6 MAN standard, and now provides for connectionless public data service. The discussion then moved to a study of access methods to SMDS service. These methods include the SMDS Subscriber Network Interface (SNI), SMDS Interface Protocol (SIP) or access DQDB, and frame relay access. Next, methods of addressing and traffic control were explained, including unicasting, multicasting, address screening and access classes. SMDS and DQDB protocol structures were discussed with focus on all three levels of Protocol Data Units (PDUs). We learned how to translate the 802.6 MAC protocol interface to the SMDS subscriber network interface, delving into the L2_PDU and L3_PDU frame structures, which are the heart of the data-transport service within SMDS. With the preponderance of TCP/IP users, we discussed bridging and routing with TCP/IP over SMDS. Performance consideration and parameters that were discussed for SMDS include availability, delay, and accuracy. Most importantly, considerations for designing an SMDS network were outlined, highlighting capacity planning as the critical key to success. The chapter ends with a discussion of network management considerations and migration capabilities to ATM.

Chapter

13

ATM, Part 1

Cell relay historically defined two major technology platforms: 802.6 Distributed Queue Dual Bus (DQDB) and Asynchronous Transfer Mode (ATM), over which a variety of services such as Switched Multimegabit Data Service (SMDS) and Broadband ISDN (B-ISDN) were to be offered. In the last chapter we discussed SMDS, primarily known today as a public data service. In the next two chapters we discuss ATM as a transport technology over which many services can be offered.

ATM means many things to many people, such as an interface and protocol, a networking technology, a method of integrated access, a public virtual data service, or a network infrastructure. The B-ISDN standards model defines the ATM protocol structure. This chapter defines the terms and standards which create the framework for ATM. ATM operational theory from cell structure through asynchronous multiplexing techniques will now be discussed. This coverage begins with the building blocks of ATM — transmission paths, virtual paths, and virtual channels. Next the ATM cell and its transmission and switching will be examined through a series of simple examples.

This chapter next explores in detail the theory behind ATM and the foundation of the entire ATM-based B-ISDN protocol stack. The primary layers of the B-ISDN protocol reference model are: the PHYsical layer, the ATM layer, where the cell structure occurs, and the ATM Adaptation Layer (AAL), that provides support for higher-layer services such as circuit emulation, LAN Emulation (LANE), frame relay, and SMDS. The PHY layer corresponds to OSI Reference Model (OSIRM) layer 1, the ATM user-plane layer and the AAL correspond to OSIRM layer 2, while other layers correspond to OSI layer 3 and above, for example, the control-plane layer used in ATM signaling. It is logical to start at the bottom with the physical (PHY) layer, and then move to the ATM layer, which defines virtual paths and virtual channels. Traffic contracts and Quality Of Service (QoS) parameters are covered, including how they relate to specific applications. The ATM Adaptation Layer (AAL) and all higher-layer functions of the protocol model will be explained in detail in the next chapter. Throughout both chapters all layers of the ATM/B-ISDN protocol stack will be defined, along with the many methods of user and network connectivity. This includes the performance, benefits, and design considerations of ATM.

13.1 ATM DEFINED

Asynchronous Transfer Mode (ATM) is a cell-based switching and multiplexing technology designed to be a general-purpose, connection-oriented transfer mode for a wide range of services. ATM has also been applied to LAN and private network technologies as specified by the ATM Forum for Token Ring, Ethernet, and FDDI LAN Emulation (LANE).

ATM handles both connection-oriented traffic directly (cell-based) or through adaptation layers, or connectionless traffic through the use of adaptation layers. ATM virtual connections may operate at either a Constant Bit Rate (CBR) or a Variable Bit Rate (VBR). Each ATM cell sent into the network contains addressing information that achieves a virtual connection from origination to destination. All cells are then transferred, in sequence, over this virtual connection. ATM provides two modes for the establishment of virtual connections: Permanent or Switched Virtual Connections (or Circuits) (PVC or SVC). ATM is asynchronous because the transmitted cells need not be periodic as time slots for data are required to be in Synchronous Transfer Mode (STM).

ATM offers the potential to standardize on one network architecture defining the multiplexing and switching method, with SONET/STM providing the basis for the physical transmission standard at very high speeds. SONET/STM will be defined in Chapter 15. ATM also supports multiple Quality of Service (QoS) classes for differing application requirements on delay and loss performance. Thus, the vision of ATM is that an entire network can be constructed using ATM and ATM Adaptation Layer (AAL) switching and multiplexing principles to support a wide range of all services, such as:

- ★ Voice
- ★ Packet data (SMDS, IP, FR)
- ★ Video
- ★ Imaging
- ★ Circuit emulation
- ★ LAN Emulation

ATM provides bandwidth-on-demand through the use of SVCs or ABR (Available Bit Rate) services, and also supports LAN-like access to available bandwidth across the WAN.

13.2 THE MANY FACES OF ATM — ARCHITECTURE, TECHNOLOGY, AND SERVICE

ATM technology takes on many forms and means many different things to different people, from providing software and hardware multiplexing, switching, and cross-connect functions and platforms, to serving as an economical, integrated network access method, to becoming the core of a network infrastructure, to the much-touted ATM or Cell Relay Service (CRS). Let's now explore each.

13.2.1 As an Interface and Protocol

Asynchronous Transfer Mode (ATM) is defined as an interface and protocol designed to switch variable bit-rate and constant bit-rate traffic over a common transmission medium. The entire B-ISDN protocol stack is often referred to as ATM, and we will soon see how ATM protocols are based on the B-ISDN protocol stack. ATM offers the technology and protocol structure to enable you - the user - to utilize existing and extend capabilities such as LAN, conferencing, FTP, and many others in a more cost-effective and efficient manner than with separate networks and access facilities.

13.2.2 As a Technology

ATM is often referred to as a technology, comprising hardware and software conforming to ATM protocol standards, which provides a multiplexing, cross-connect, and switching function in a network. ATM technology takes the form of a network interface card, multiplexer, cross-connect, or even a full switch. Today, ATM is most prevalent in the switch market and as a WAN interface on traditional data communications products like routers and hubs; ATM end systems and applications are beginning to appear in mass quantity.

13.2.3 As Economical, Integrated Access

Public ATM service providers offering ATM-based services are now appearing on the scene, enabling users to capitalize on a basic advantage of ATM — integrated physical and service access to reduce cost. The development of circuit emulation technology based upon ATM will make this benefit available to users who already have a large number of TDM access lines today. The TDM access lines can be multiplexed onto an E3, DS3, or even

SONET access line, leaving large amounts of bandwidth available for ATM applications at small incremental cost.

13.2.4 As an Infrastructure

ATM technology can also have an advantage as the core of a network infrastructure. ATM hardware and associated software together can provide the backbone technology for an advanced communications network. In fact, many experts view an ATM-based architecture as the future platform for data and eventually voice. ATM also provides a very scalable infrastructure, from the campus environment to the central office. Scalability is available in the dimensions of interface speed, available bandwidth, number of ports (i.e., port density), switch size, network size, and addressing.

13.2.5 As a Service

ATM is not a service, but services can be offered over an ATM architecture. The Cell Relay Service (CRS) involves the direct delivery of ATM cells. Other services involve ATM Adaptation Layers (AALs), and include circuit emulation services as defined using AAL 1, variable-rate video as defined using AAL 2, Switched Multimegabit Data Service (SMDS) as defined using AAL 3/4, and frame relay as one of the service-specific connection-oriented services defined for AAL 5. These ATM adaptation layers and their implementation will be defined in the next chapter.

13.3 THE ATM CELL AND TRANSMISSION

The primary unit in ATM is the *cell*. This section defines the basics of the ATM cell and presents a detailed explanation. Several examples are used to illustrate the basic concepts of ATM.

13.3.1 ATM Cell

ATM standards define a fixed-size cell with a length of 53 octets (or bytes) comprising a 5-octet header and a 48-octet payload, as shown in Figure 13.1. The figure also shows a caption of the standard block cell format as defined in the standards. The bits in the cells are transmitted over the transmission path from left to right in a continuous stream. Cells are mapped into a physical transmission path, such as the North American DS1, DS3, or SONET (i.e., STS-3c/OC-3, OC-12); European, E1, E3 and E4; or ITU-T STM standards; and various local fiber and electrical transmission payloads.

All information is switched and multiplexed in an ATM network in these fixed-length cells. The cell header identifies the destination, cell type, and priority. The Virtual Path Identifier (VPI) and Virtual Channel Identifier (VCI) hold local significance only, and identify the destination. The Generic Flow Control (GFC) field allows a multiplexer to control the rate of an ATM terminal. While the GFC has been defined since the B-ISDN standards, there have been no ATM Forum implementation standards or agreements produced on how to actually use or implement it. The Payload Type (PT) indicates whether the cell contains user data, signaling data, or maintenance information. The Cell Loss Priority (CLP) bit indicates the relative priority of the cell similar to Discard Eligible (DE) bits in frame relay service. Lower-priority cells may be discarded before higher-priority cells by the Usage Parameter Control (UPC) at the ingress if cells violate the predetermined user contract, or by the network if congestion is experienced.

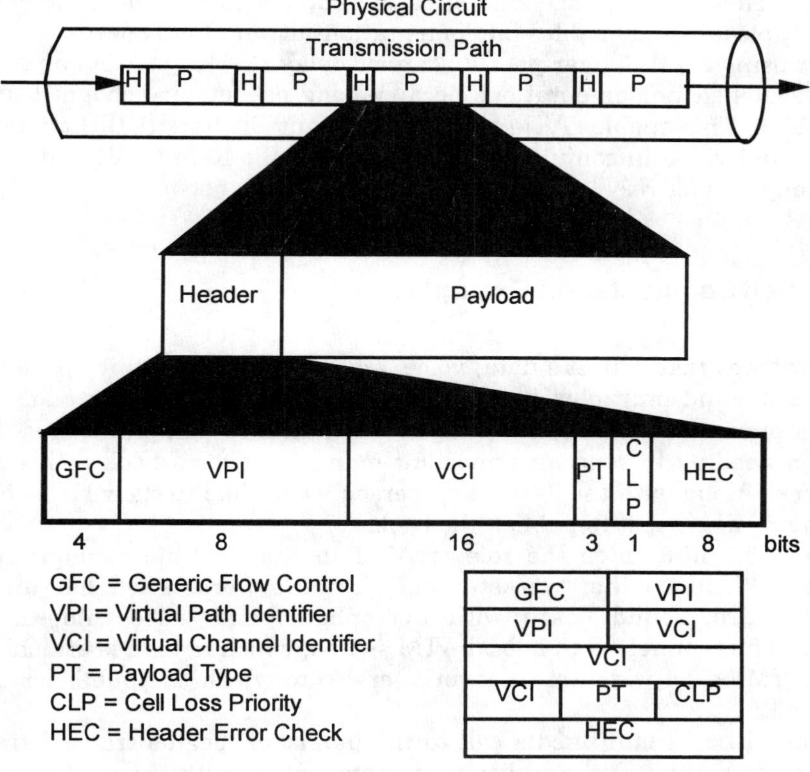

Figure 13.1 ATM Cell Transmission and Format

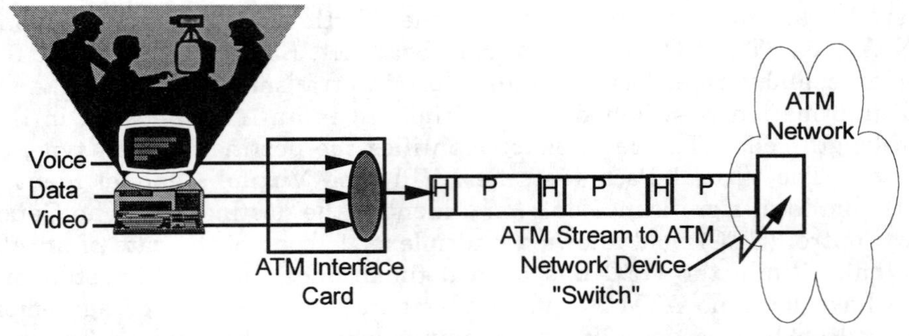

Figure 13.2 Multimedia Communications Example Using ATM

Because of the critical nature of the header, the cell Header Error Check (HEC) detects and corrects errors in the header. The payload field is passed through the network intact, with no error checking or correction. ATM relies on higher-layer protocols to perform error checking and correction on the payload. The fixed cell size simplifies the implementation of ATM switches and multiplexers and enables implementations at very high speeds.

When using ATM, longer packets cannot delay shorter packets as in other packet-switched implementations because long packets are chopped up into many cells. This enables ATM to carry Constant Bit Rate (CBR) traffic such as voice and video in conjunction with Variable Bit Rate (VBR) data traffic, potentially having very long packets within the same network.

13.3.2 Cell Segmentation Example

ATM switches take a user's data, voice, and video, then chop it up into fixed length cells, and multiplex it into a single bit stream which is transmitted across a physical medium. An example of a multimedia application is that of a person needing to send an important manuscript for a book to his or her publisher. Along with the letter, this person would like to show his or her joy at receiving a contract to publish the book.

Figure 13.2 illustrates the role of ATM in this real-life example, where Jeanne is sitting at her workstation. Jeanne's workstation has an ATM interface card, sound board with microphone, and video camera. The workstation is connected to a local ATM switch, which in turn is attached to a public ATM-based wide area network service to which the publisher is also connected.

Jeanne places a multimedia call to the publisher, begins transmitting the data for her manuscript, and begins a conversation with the publisher, with Jeanne and the publisher able to see each other — providing text, voice, and video traffic, respectively, in real time. The publisher is looking through the manuscript at her workstation, all the while having an interactive dialogue with Jeanne. Let's break this scenario down into its working ATM components.

Video and voice are very time-sensitive; the information cannot be delayed for more than a blink of the eye, and the delay cannot have significant variations. Disruption in the video image of Jeanne's face or distortion of the voice destroy the interactive, near real-life quality of this multimedia application. Data, such as a file transfer using IP, can be sent in either connection-oriented or connectionless mode. In either case, the data is not nearly as delay-sensitive as voice or video traffic. Data traffic, however, is very sensitive to loss. Therefore, ATM must discriminate between voice, video, and data traffic, giving voice and video traffic priority and guaranteed, bounded delay, simultaneously assuring that data traffic has very low loss.

Examining this example in further detail, a virtual path is established between Jeanne and the publisher, and over that virtual path three virtual circuits are defined for text data, voice, and video. Figure 13.3 shows how all three types of traffic are combined over a single ATM Virtual Path (VP), with Virtual Circuits (VCs) being assigned to the text data (VCI = 51), voice (VCI = 52), and video (VCI = 53). In this example, then the virtual path has the QoS required for the most stringent VC. Note that VCIs 0–31 are typically reserved as specified by the ATM Forum standards, and that all three of these virtual circuits could have been on separate virtual paths.

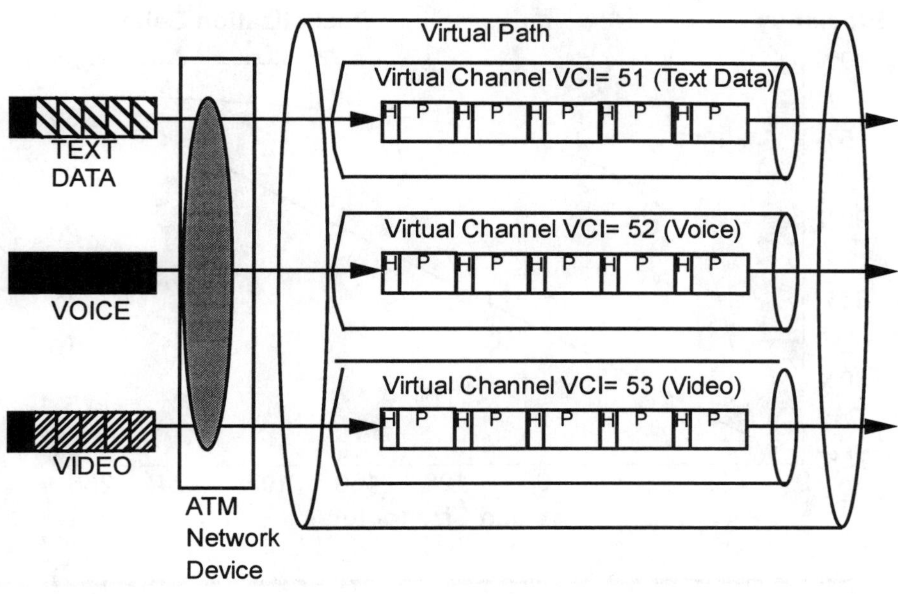

Figure 13.3 Virtual Channels Supporting Multiple Applications

13.3.3 Why 53 Bytes? Choice of Payload Size

When a standard cell size was under discussion by the ITU, there was a raging debate between a 32-octet versus a 64-octet payload size. The decision on the 48-byte payload size was the compromise between these positions. The choice of the 5-octet header size was a separate tradeoff between a 3-octet header and an 8-octet header.

There is a basic tradeoff between efficiency and packetization delay versus cell size, illustrated in Figure 13.4. Efficiency is computed for a 5-octet cell header. Packetization delay is the amount of time required to fill the cell at a rate of 64 kbps, that is, the rate to fill the cell with digitized voice samples. Ideally, high efficiency and low delay are both desirable, but cannot be achieved simultaneously. As seen from the figure, better efficiency occurs at large cell sizes at the expense of increased packetization delay. In order to carry voice over ATM and interwork with two-wire analog telephone sets, the total delay should be less than about 12 ms, otherwise echo cancellation must be used. Two Time Division Multiplexing (TDM)-to-ATM conversions are required in the round-trip echo path. Allowing 4 ms for propagation delay and two ATM conversions, a cell size of 32 octets avoids the need for echo cancellation. Thus, the ITU-T adopted the fixed-length 48-octet cell payload as a compromise between a long cell sizes for time-insensitive traffic (64 octets) and smaller cell sizes for time-sensitive traffic (32 octets).

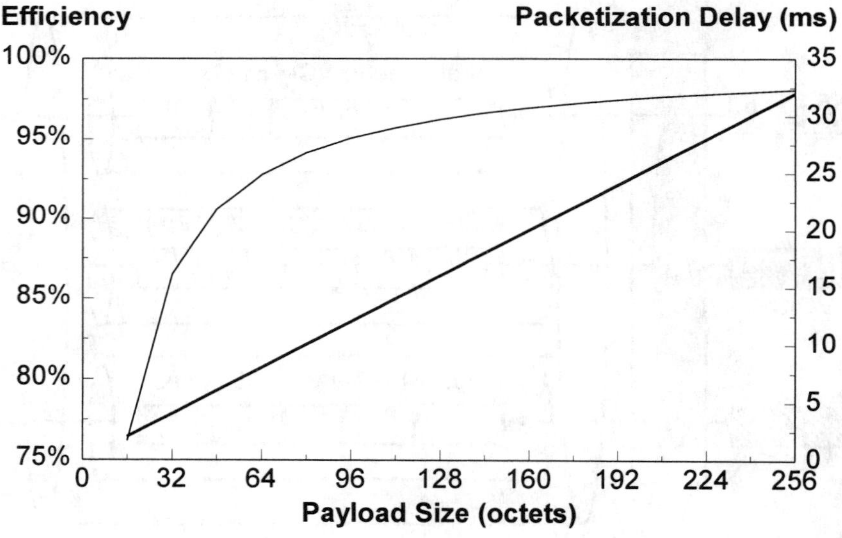

Figure 13.4 Delay versus Cell Size Tradeoff

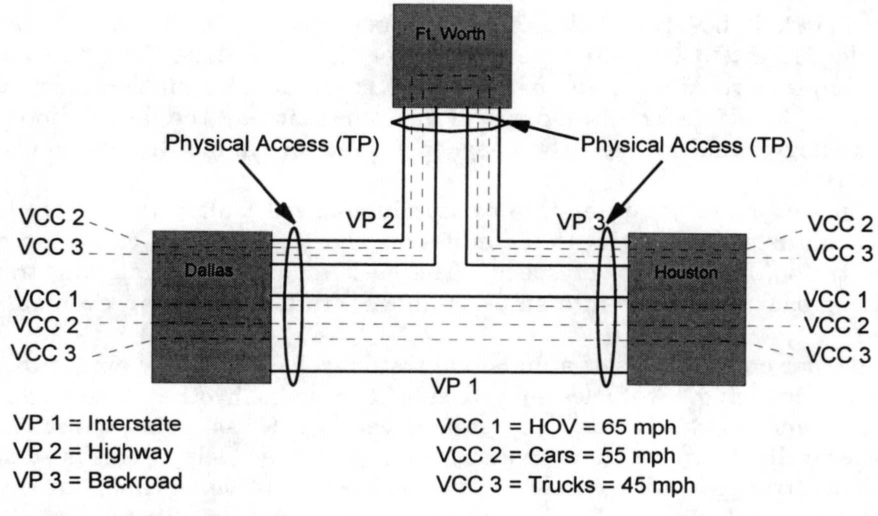

Figure 13.5 Transportation Example of ATM Principles

13.4 ATM NETWORKING BASICS

Three major concepts in ATM are: the transmission path, the Virtual Path (VP), and, optionally, the Virtual Channel (VC). These form the basic building blocks of ATM.

13.4.1 Transmission Path, Virtual Path, and Virtual Channel Analogy

Let us look at a simple example of these concepts in relation to vehicle traffic patterns. These analogies are not intended to be exact, but to introduce some concepts that are elaborated on in later chapters. Think of cells as vehicles, transmission paths as roads, virtual paths as a set of directions, and virtual channels as a lane discipline on the route defined by the virtual path. Figure 13.5 illustrates the example described in this section.

Three transmission paths form the set of roads between three cities: Dallas, Fort Worth, and Houston. There are many interstates, highways, and back roads between any two cities, which creates many possibilities for different routes; but the primary routes, or virtual paths, are the interstate (VP1) from Dallas to Houston, the highway from Dallas to Fort Worth (VP2), and a back road (VP3) from Fort Worth to Houston. Thus, a car (cell) can travel from Dallas to Houston either over the highway to Fort Worth and then the back road to Houston, or take the direct interstate. If the car chooses the interstate (VP1), it has the choice of three lanes: car pool or High Occupancy Vehicle (HOV) (VCC1), car lane (VCC2), or the truck lane (VCC3). These three lanes have speed limits of 65 mph, 55 mph, and 45 mph, respectively, which will cause different amounts of delay in reaching the destination. In our analogy, vehicles strictly obey this lane discipline (unlike on real highways).

In our example, the interstate carries high-speed traffic: tractor trailers, buses, tourists, and business commuters. The highway can carry car and truck traffic, but at a lower speed. The back roads carry locals and traffic avoiding backups on the interstate (spill-over traffic), but at an even slower speed.

Note that our example of automotive traffic (cells) has many opportunities for missequencing. Vehicles may decide to pass each other, there can be detours, and road hazards (like stalled cars in Texas!) may cause some vehicles (cells) to arrive out of sequence or vary in their delay. This is evident in normal transportation when you always seem to leave on time, but traffic causes you to be delayed. Automotive traffic must employ an Orwellian discipline where everyone follows the traffic routes exactly (unlike any real traffic) in order for the analogy to apply.

The routes also have different quality. When you get a route map from the American Automobile Association (AAA), you have a route selected based on many criteria: least driving (routing) time, most scenic route, least cost (avoids most toll roads), and avoid known busy hours. The same principles apply to ATM.

Now, let's give each of the road types (VPs) and lanes (VCCs) a route choice. A commuter from Dallas to Houston in a hurry would first choose the VP1, the interstate. A sightseer would choose the highway to Fort Worth (VP2) to see the old cow town, and then the back road to Houston (VP3) to take in Waxahachie and Waco on the way. When commuters enter the interstate toward Houston, they immediately enter the HOV lane (VCC1) and speed toward their destination.

Figure 13.6 adds a railroad (VCC4) running from Dallas to Houston along the same interstate route (VP1) in the previous example. Assuming no stops between Dallas and Houston, the railroad maintains the same speed from start to finish, with one railroad train running after another according to a fixed schedule. This is like the Synchronous Transfer Mode (STM) or Time Division Multiplexing (TDM) discussed in Chapter 6. Imagine there are passengers and cargo going between Dallas and Houston, each having to catch scheduled trains. The arriving passengers and cargo shipments originating at Dallas must wait for the next train. Trains travel regardless of whether there are any passengers or cargo present. If there are too many passengers or cargo for the train's capacity, the excess must wait for the next train. If you were a commuter, would you want to rely on the train always having capacity, or would you prefer to have a car and statistically have a better chance of making it to Houston in an even shorter time period using ATM?

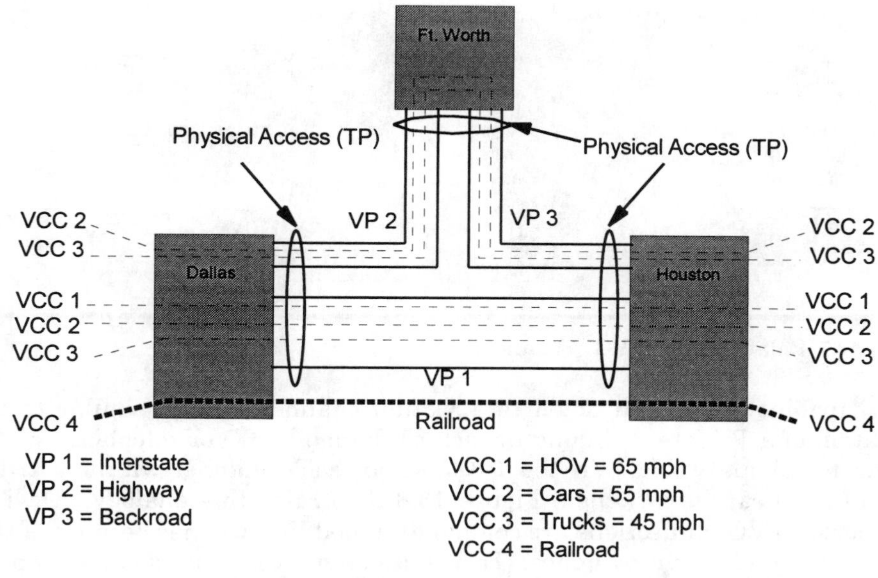

Figure 13.6 Transportation Example — STM versus ATM

Studying this analogy, observe that the private vehicles (and their passengers) traveling over VCC1, VCC2, or VCC3 have much more flexibility (ATM) than trains (STM) in handling the spontaneous needs of travel. The trains are efficient only when the demand is accurately scheduled and very directed, such as during the rush hour between suburbs and the inner city.

Note that the priorities, or choice, of each VCC can vary throughout the day, as can priorities between VPs in ATM. An additional VCC can be configured on a moment's notice (VCC) and assigned a higher priority, as in the case of an ambulance attempting to travel down the median during a traffic jam to get to the scene of an accident. No analogy is perfect, and therefore extensions or comparison of other aspects of transportation may not be valid.

13.4.2 Transmission Path, Virtual Path, and Virtual Channels

Bringing our analogy forward into ATM transmission terms, Figure 13.7 depicts graphically the relationship between the physical Transmission Path (TP), Virtual Path (VP), and Virtual Channel (VC). A transmission path contains one or more virtual paths, while each virtual path contains one or more virtual channels. Thus, multiple virtual channels can be trunked within a single virtual path. Switching can be performed on either a transmission-path, virtual-path, or virtual-circuit level.

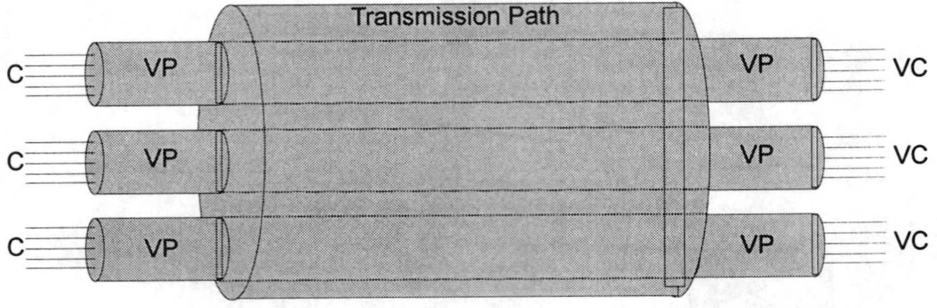

Figure 13.7 Relationship of VC, VP, and TP

This capability to switch down to a virtual channel level is similar to the operation of a Private or Public Branch eXchange (PBX) or telephone switch in the telephone world. In the PBX/switch, each channel within a trunk group (path) can be switched. Figure 13.8 illustrates this analogy. Devices that perform VC connections are commonly called VC switches because of this analogy with telephone switches. Transmission networks use a cross-connect, which is basically a space-division switch, or effectively an electronic patch panel. ATM devices that connect VPs are commonly often called VP cross-connects in the literature by analogy with the transmission network.

These analogies are useful for those familiar with TDM/STM and telephony to understand ATM, but should not be taken literally. There is little technical reason for an ATM cell-switching machine to restrict switching to only VCs and cross-connection to only VPs, and today's ATM switches are able to do both simultaneously.

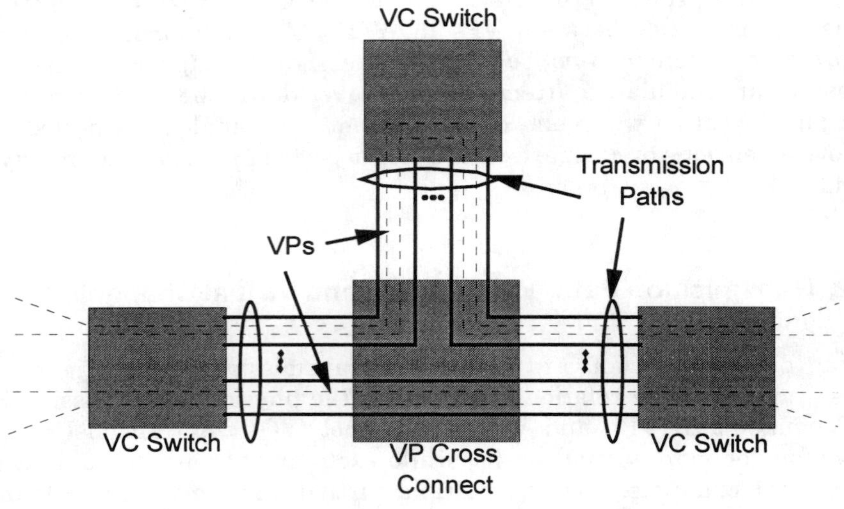

Figure 13.8 Switch and Cross-Connect Analogy

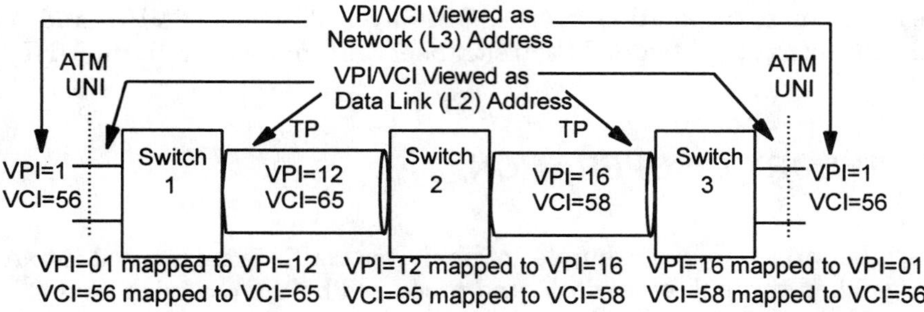

Figure 13.9 Illustration of VPI/VCI Usage on Link and End-to-End Basis

13.4.3 Virtual Path Connections (VPCs) and Virtual Channel Connections (VCCs)

At the ATM layer, users are provided a choice of either a VPC or a VCC, defined as follows:

Virtual Path Connections (VPCs) are switched based upon the Virtual Path Identifier (VPI) value only. The users of the VPC may assign the VCCs within that VPI transparently since they follow the same route.

Virtual Channel Connections (VCCs) are switched upon the combined VPI and Virtual Channel Identifier (VCI) value.

Both VPIs and VCIs are used to route cells through the network. Note that VPI and VCI values must be unique on a specific Transmission Path (TP). Thus, each TP between two network devices (such as ATM switches) uses VPIs and VCIs independently. This is demonstrated in Figure 13.9. Each switch maps an incoming VPI and VCI to an outgoing VPI and VCI. In this example, switch 1 and switch 2 have a single TP between them. Over this TP there are multiple VPs. At the ATM UNI, the input device to switch 1 provides a video channel over VPI 1 and VCI 56. Switch 1 then assigns the VCI 56 to an outgoing VCI 65, and the incoming VPI 1 to outgoing VPI 12. Thus, on VPI 12 switch 2 specifically operates on virtual channel (VC) number 65 (VCI 65). This channel is then routed from switch 2 to switch 3 over a different path and channel (VPI 16 and VCI 58). Thus, VPIs and VCIs are tied onto each individual link across the network. This is similar to frame relay, where Data Link Connection Identifiers (DLCIs) address a Virtual Circuit (VC) at each end of a link. Finally, switch 3 translates VPI 16 into VPI 1, and VCI 58 on VP 16 to VCI 56 on VP 1 at the destination UNI. The destination VPI and VCI need not be the same as at the origin. The sequence of VPI/VCI translation across the switches can be viewed as a network address in an extrapolation of the OSI layer 3 model. VPIs and VCIs switched internal to network TPs are transparent to the user on the UNI.

13.5 THEORY OF OPERATION

This section presents two examples of how user traffic is segmented into ATM cells, switched through a network, and processed by the receiving user.

13.5.1 A Simple ATM Example

Let's look in more detail at the last example (Section 13.3.2), where Jeanne is simultaneously transmitting text, voice, and video data traffic from her workstation. The workstation contains an ATM interface card, where the "chopper" slices and dices the data streams into 48-octet data segments, as shown in Figure 13.10. In the next step, the "postman" addresses the payload by prefixing it with the VPI, VCI, and the remaining fields of the 5-octet header. The result is a stream of 53-octet ATM cells from each source: voice, video, and text data. These cells are generated independently by each source, such that there may be contention for cell slot times on the interface connected to the workstation. The text, voice, and video are each assigned a VCC: VCI = 1 for text data, VCI = 2 for voice, and VCI = 3 for video, all on VPI = 0. This example is greatly simplified, as there may be many more than just three active VCI values on a single VPI.

Figure 13.10 shows an example of how Jeanne's terminal sends the combined voice, video, and text data. A gatekeeper in her terminal shapes the transmitted data, sending a cell at intervals of eight cells (about 80 μs at the DS3 rate), normally allowing one voice cell, then five video cells, and finally what is left — two text data cells — to be transmitted. This corresponds to about 4 Mbps for high-fidelity audio, 24 Mbps for video, and 9 Mbps for text data. All data sources (text, voice, and video) contend for the bandwidth, each shaping interval of eight cell times, with the voice, video, and then text data being sent in the above proportion. Cells are retained in the buffer by the gatekeeper in case all of the cell slot times were full in the shaping interval. A much larger shaping interval is used in practice to provide greater granularity in bandwidth allocation.

13.5.2 An ATM Switch Example

An illustration of an ATM switch is shown in Figure 13.11. A continuous video source is shown as input to a *packetizing* function, with logical destination VPI/VCI address D. The continuous bit stream is broken up into fixed-length cells composed of a header and a payload field (indicated by the shading). The rate of the video source is greater than the continuous DS3 bit stream with logical destination address A, and the high-speed computer directly packetized input addressed to B. These sources are shown *time division multiplexed* over a transmission path, such as SONET or DS3.

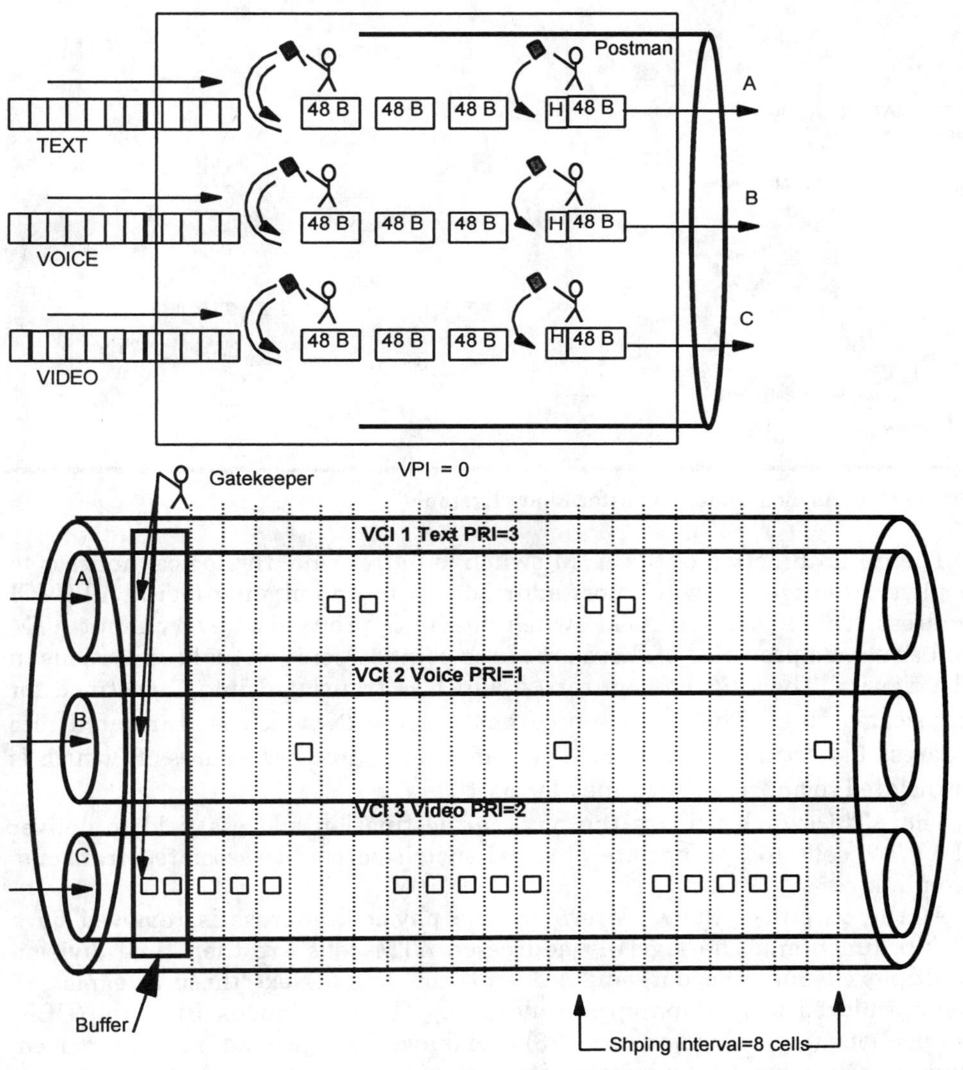

Figure 13.10 Asynchronous Transfer Mode Example

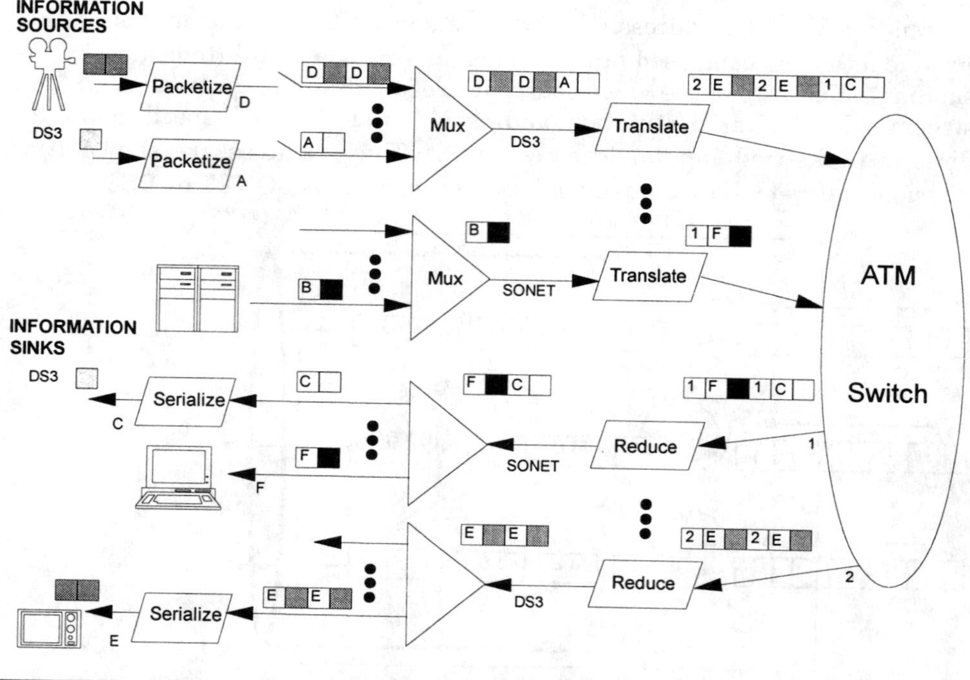

Figure 13.11 Asynchronous Transfer Mode Example

The initial function of the ATM switch is to *translate* the logical address to a physical outgoing switch port address and to an outgoing logical VPI/VCI address. This additional ATM switch header is prefixed to every input ATM cell as shown previously. There are three point-to-point virtual connections in the figure. The DS3 has address *A* which is translated into C destined for physical port 1. The video source has address D, which is translated into address E, destined for port 2. The computer source has address B, which is translated to address F, destined for port 1.

The ATM switch utilizes the physical destination address field to deliver the ATM cells to appropriate physical switch port and associated transmission link.

At the output of the ATM switch, the physical address is removed by a *reduce* function. The logically addressed ATM cells are then time division multiplexed onto the outgoing transmission links. Next these streams are demultiplexed to the appropriate devices. The Continuous Bit Rate (CBR) connections (i.e., video and the DS3) then have the logical addresses removed, and are re-clocked to the information sink via the *serialize* function. Devices, such as workstations, can receive ATM cells directly.

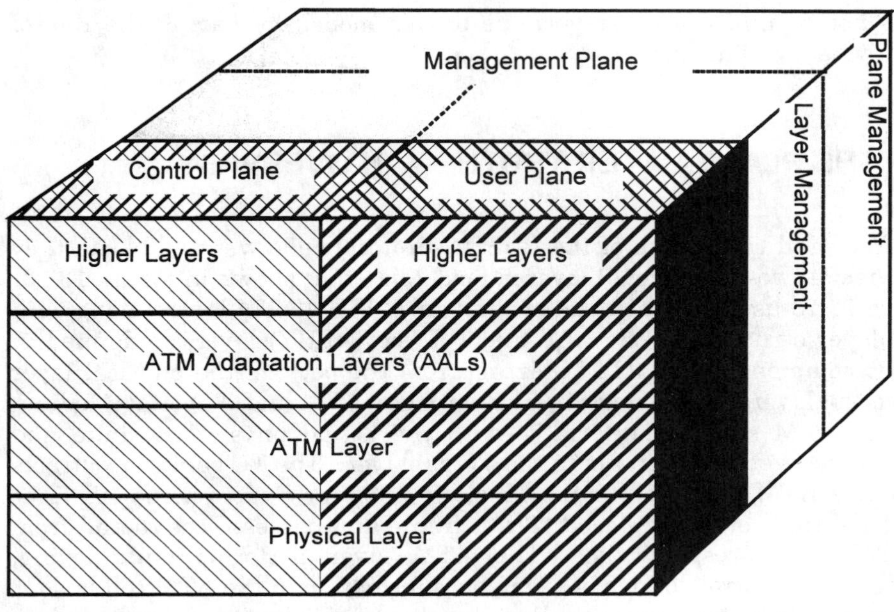

Figure 13.12 B-ISDN Protocol Model

13.6 B-ISDN PROTOCOL REFERENCE MODEL

This section describes the protocol model for B-ISDN that is built on ATM. Figure 13.12 depicts the B-ISDN protocol reference model from ITU-T Recommendation I.321, which is used to structure the remaining recommendations. A significant portion of the architecture exists in this protocol dimension. This subsection introduces the B-ISDN protocol reference model. Each section will be introduced by a shaded version of the model in Figure 13.12, illustrating what the section will cover.

The top of the cube illustrates the planes, which are defined on the front and side of the cube. The user plane and control plane span through the higher layer, down through the AALs (which can be null), to the ATM layer and physical layer. Therefore the physical layer, ATM layer, and AALs are the foundation for B-ISDN. The user and control planes may make use of common ATM and physical layer protocols; however, the end purpose differs in the AALs and higher layers.

The management plane is further broken down into layer management and plane management. As shown in the figure, layer management interfaces with each layer in the control and user planes. Plane management has no layered structure and is currently only an abstract concept with little standardization at this point. It can be viewed as a catchall for the things that do not fit into the other portions of this model, by having the role of overall system management.

13.7 THE PLANE-LAYER TRUTH — AN OVERVIEW

If the front and right sides of the B-ISDN protocol cube were unfolded, they would yield a two-dimensional layered model like that shown in Figure 13.13.

Figure 13.13 lists the functions of the four B-ISDN/ATM layers along with the sublayer structure of the AAL and PHYsical (PHY) layer, as defined in ITU-T Recommendation I.321. Starting from the bottom, the physical layer has two sublayers: Transmission Convergence (TC) and Physical Medium (PM). The PM sublayer interfaces with the actual physical medium and passes the recovered bit stream to the TC sublayer. The TC sublayer extracts and inserts ATM cells within the Plesiochronous or Synchronous (PDH or SDH) Time Division Multiplexed (TDM) frame and passes these to and from the ATM layer, respectively. The ATM layer performs multiplexing, switching, and control actions based upon information in the ATM cell header and passes cells to, and accepts cells from, the ATM Adaptation Layer (AAL). The AAL has two sublayers: Segmentation And Reassembly (SAR) and Convergence Sublayer (CS). The CS is further broken down into Common Part (CP) and Service-Specific (SS) components. The AAL passes Protocol Data Units (PDUs) to and accepts PDUs from higher layers. PDUs may be of variable length, or may be of fixed length different from the ATM cell length.

The physical layer corresponds to layer 1 in the OSI model. The ATM layer and AAL correspond to parts of OSI layer 2, but the address field of the ATM cell header has a network-wide connotation that is similar to OSI layer 3. A precise alignment with the OSI layers is not necessary, however. The B-ISDN and ATM protocols and interfaces make extensive use of the OSI concepts of layering and sublayering as we shall see. Figure 13.14 illustrates the mapping of the B-ISDN layers to the OSI layers and the sublayers of the PHY, ATM, and AALs that we describe in detail later.

It is interesting to look at the number of instances of defined standardized protocols or interfaces that exist for each layer, and whether their target implementation is in hardware or software. Figure 13.15 depicts the number of instances at each layer by boxes with the arrows on the right-hand side showing how the layers are either more hardware- or software-intensive. The arrows illustrate the fact that ATM implementations move from being hardware-intensive at the lower layers (PHY and ATM layer) to software-intensive at the higher layers (AALs and higher layers). This shows how ATM is the pivotal protocol, for which there is only one instance, for a potentially large number of physical media, several AALs, and an ever-expanding set of higher-layer functions. The inverted pyramid on the left-hand side of Figure 13.15 illustrates this concept. In other words, ATM allows machines with different physical interfaces to transport data independently of the higher-layer protocols using a common, well-defined protocol amenable to high performance and cost-effective hardware implementation.

Layer Name		Functions Performed	
Higher Layers		Higher Layer Functions	Layer Management
AAL	Convergence Sublayer (CS)	Common Part (CP)	
		Service Specific (SS)	
	SAR Sublayer	Segmentation And Reassembly'	
ATM		Generic Flow Control Cell Header Generation/Extraction Cell VCI/VPI Translation Cell Multiplexing/Demultiplexing	
Physical	Transmission Convergence (TC) Sublayer	Cell Rate Decoupling Cell Delineation Transmission Frame Adaptation Transmission Frame Generation/ Recovery	
	Physical Medium (PM)	Bit Timing Physical Medium	

Figure 13.13 B-ISDN/ATM Layer and Sublayer Model

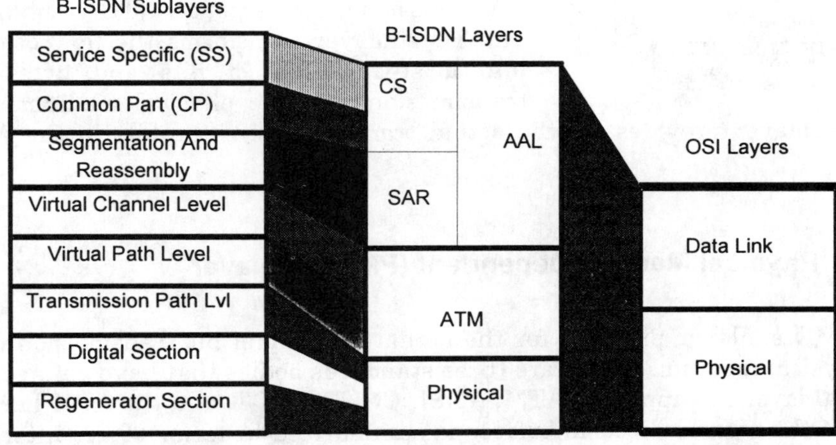

Figure 13.14 B-ISDN Layers and Sublayers and OSI Layers

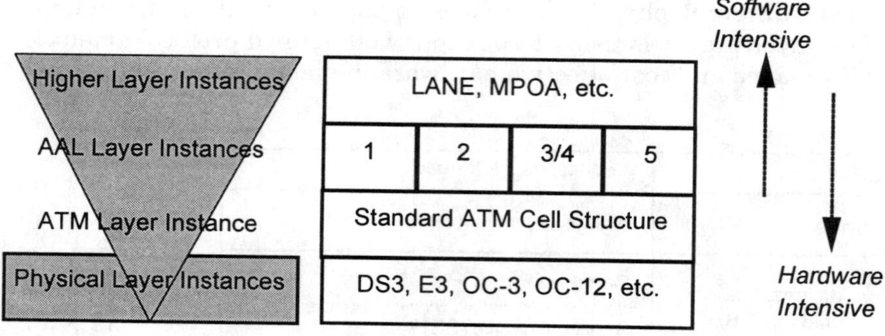

Figure 13.15 ATM Protocol Model Hardware to Software Progression

Now the journey begins up through the layers of the B-ISDN/ATM protocol model, starting with the physical and ATM layer in this chapter, and concluding in Chapter 14.

13.8 PHYSICAL (PHY) LAYER

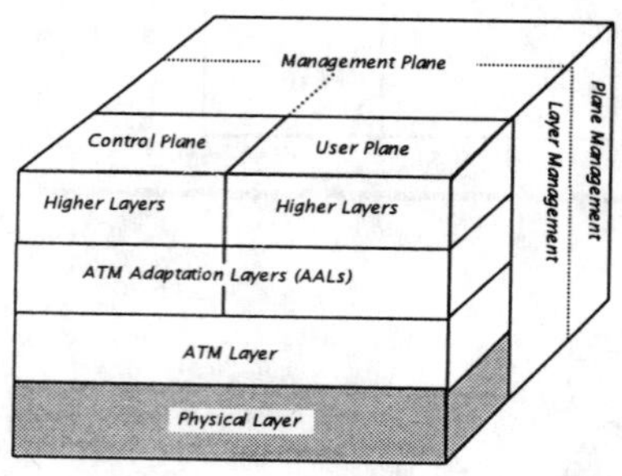

This section covers the key aspects of the PHY layer. The PHY layer provides for transmission of ATM cells over a physical medium that connects two ATM devices. The PHY layer is divided into two sublayers: the Physical Medium Dependent (PMD) sublayer and the Transmission Convergence (TC) sublayer. The TC sublayer transforms the flow of cells into a steady flow of bits and bytes for transmission over the physical medium. The PMD sublayer provides for the actual transmission of the bits in the ATM cells.

13.8.1 Physical Medium Dependent (PMD) Sublayer

The PMD sublayer provides for the actual clocking of bit transmission over the physical medium. There are three standards bodies that have defined the physical layer in support of ATM: ANSI, CCITT/ITU-T, and the ATM Forum. Each of the standardized interfaces is summarized in terms of the interface clocking speed and physical medium following.

13.8.1.1 ANSI Standards

ANSI standard T1.624 currently defines three single-mode optical ATM SONET-based interfaces for the ATM UNI:

- STS-1 at 51.84 Mbps
- STS-3c at 155.52 Mbps
- STS-12c at 622.08 Mbps

ANSI T1.624 also defines operation at the DS3 rate of 44.736 Mbps using the Physical Layer Convergence Protocol (PLCP) from the 802.6 Distributed Queue Dual Bus (DQDB) standard.

13.8.1.2 CCITT/ITU-T SDH Recommendations

CCITT/ITU-T recommendation I.432 defines two optical Synchronous Digital Hierarchy (SDH)–based physical interfaces for ATM which correspond to the ANSI rates mentioned in the last section. These are:

- STM-1 at 155.520 Mbps
- STM-4 at 622.08 Mbps

Since the transport rates (and the payload rates) of the SDH STM-1 and STM-4 correspond exactly to the SONET STS-3c and STS-12c rates, interworking should be simplified. ITU-T standardizes additional electrical, physical interface rates of the following type and speeds:

- DS1 at 1.544 Mbps
- E1 at 2.048 Mbps
- DS2 at 6.312 Mbps
- E3 at 34.368 Mbps
- DS3 at 44.736 Mbps using PLCP
- E4 at 139.264 Mbps

13.8.1.3 ATM Forum Interfaces

The ATM Forum has defined four physical layer interface rates:

- DS3/44.7 Mbps
- 100 Mbps
- 155 Mbps

Two of these are interface rates intended for public networks and are the DS3 and STS-3c standardized by ANSI and the ITU-T. The SONET STS-3c interface may be supported on an OC-3, either single-mode or multimode fiber. 25 Mbps and 51 Mbps rates will also soon be available, and ATM

Frame UNI (FUNI) is now available. The following three interface rates and media are for private network application:

- ⌘ FDDI-based at 100 Mbps – TAXI™
- ⌘ Fiber-channel-based at 155.52 Mbps
- ⌘ Shielded twisted pair (STP) at 155.52 Mbps

The FDDI-based PMD and fiber channel interfaces both use multimode fiber, while the STP interface uses type 1 and 2 cable as specified by EIA/TIA 568. The ATM Forum is specifying ATM cell transmission over common building wiring, called unshielded twisted pair (UTP) types 3 and 5.

13.8.2 Transmission Convergence (TC) Sublayer

The TC sublayer converts between the bit stream clocked to the physical medium and ATM cells. On transmit, TC basically maps the cells into the TDM frame format. On reception, it must perform "cell delineation" on the individual cells in the received bit stream, either from the TDM frame directly, or via the Header Error Check (HEC) in the ATM cell header. Generating the HEC on transmit and using it to correct and detect errors on receive are also important TC functions. Another important function that TC performs is cell rate decoupling by sending idle cells when the ATM layer has not provided a cell. This is a critical function that allows the ATM layer to operate with a wide range of different speed physical interfaces.

Two examples of TC mapping of ATM cells will be covered: direct mapping to a SONET payload and the PLCP mapping to a DS3. The use of the Header Error Check (HEC) and why it is so important will be shown. The description of the TC sublayer will be completed with an illustration of cell-rate decoupling using unassigned cells.

13.8.3 Examples of TC Mapping

In this section we give an example of direct and Physical Layer Convergence Protocol (PLCP) mapping by the Transmission Convergence (TC) sublayer of the physical layer.

13.8.3.1 SONET STS-3c Direct Mapping

The SONET mapping is performed directly into the SONET STS-3c (155.52 Mbps) Synchronous Payload Envelope (SPE) as defined in Chapter 3 and as shown in Figure 13.16. ATM cells fill in the STS-3c payload continuously since an integer number of 53-octet cells do not fit in a single STS-3c frame.

This results in better efficiency than carriage of M13-mapped DS3s, or even VT1.5 multiplexing over SONET. Not all the SONET overhead is supported by the standards or implementers. The ATM layer uses the HEC field to delineate cells from within the SONET payload. The cell transfer rate is 149.760 Mbps. The mapping over STS-12c is very similar in nature. The difference between SONET and SDH is in the TDM overhead bytes.

13.8.3.2 DS3 PLCP Mapping

Figure 13.17 illustrates the DS3 mapping using the Physical Layer Convergence Protocol (PLCP) defined in IEEE 802.6. The ATM cells are enclosed in a 125-μs frame defined by the PLCP, which is defined inside the standard DS3 M-frame. The PLCP mapping transfers 8 kHz timing across the DS3 interface, which is somewhat inefficient in that the cell transfer rate is only 40.704 Mbps, which utilizes only about 90 percent of the DS3's approximately 44.21-Mbps payload rate. Note that the PLCP does not use ATM's cell delineation because the PLCP frame indicates the exact location of each cell. Some ATM switch vendors allow the user to disable PLCP in favor of using cell delineation to achieve better efficiency and usage of the DS3 frame.

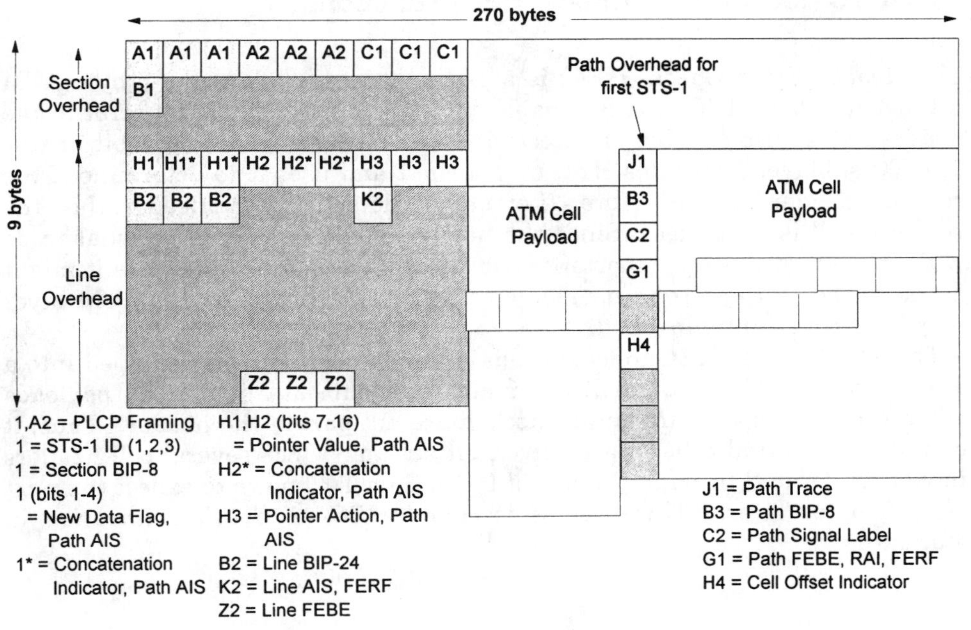

Figure 13.16 B-ISDN UNI Physical Layer — STS-3c

PLCP Framing		POI	POH	PLCP Payload	
A1	A2	P11	Z6	ATM Cell 1	
A1	A2	P10	Z5	ATM Cell 2	
A1	A2	P9	Z4	ATM Cell 3	
A1	A2	P8	Z3	ATM Cell 4	
A1	A2	P7	Z2	ATM Cell 5	
A1	A2	P6	Z1	ATM Cell 6	
A1	A2	P5	X	ATM Cell 7	
A1	A2	P4	B1	ATM Cell 8	
A1	A2	P3	G1	ATM Cell 9	
A1	A2	P2	X	ATM Cell 10	
A1	A2	P1	X	ATM Cell 11	
A1	A2	P0	C1	ATM Cell 12	Trailer
1 Octet	1 Octet	1 Octet	1 Octet	53 Octets	13 or 14 Nibbles
			Object of BIP-8 Calculation		

Definitions

PLCP = Physical Layer Convergence Protocol
A1 = 11110110
A2 = 00101000
P0-P11 = Path Overhead Identifier (POI)
POH = Path Overhead
Z1-Z6 = Growth Octets = 00000000
X = Unassigned
B1 = PCLP Bit Interleaved Parity -8 (BIP-8)
G1 = PLCP Path Status
= AAAAXXXX = FEBE B1 Count
= XXXXAXXX = RAI
C1 = Cycle Stuff Counter
Trailer Nibbles = 1100

Figure 13.17 B-ISDN UNI Physical Layer — DS3

13.8.4 TC Header Error Check (HEC) Functions

The Header Error Check (HEC) is a 1-byte code applied to the 5-byte ATM cell header. The HEC code is capable of correcting any single-bit error in the header. It is also capable of detecting many patterns of multiple-bit errors. The TC sublayer generates HEC on transmit and uses it to determine if the received header has any errors. If errors are detected in the header, then the received cell is discarded. Since the header tells the ATM layer what to do with the cell, it is very important that it not have errors; otherwise it might be delivered to the wrong user or an undesired function in the ATM layer may be inadvertently invoked.

The TC also uses HEC to locate cells when they are directly mapped into a TDM payload. The HEC will not match random data in the cell payloads when the 5 bytes that are being checked are not part of the header. Thus, it can be used to find cells in a received bit stream. Once several cell headers have been located through the use of HEC, then TC knows to expect the next cell 53 bytes later. This process is called *HEC-based cell delineation* in standards.

13.8.5 TC Cell Rate Decoupling

The TC sublayer performs a cell-rate decoupling, or speed-matching function, as well. Physical media that have synchronous cell time slots (e.g., DS3,

SONET, SDH, STP, and the fiber-channel-based method) require this function, while asynchronous media such as the FDDI PMD do not. As we shall see in the next section, there are special codings of the ATM cell header that indicate that a cell is either *unassigned* or *idle*. All other cells are *assigned* and correspond to the cells generated by the ATM layer. Figure 13.18 illustrates this operation between a transmitting device and a receiving ATM device. The transmitter multiplexes multiple VPI/VCI cell streams, queuing them if an ATM slot is not immediately available. If the queue is empty when the time arrives to fill the next synchronous cell time slot, then the TC sublayer inserts an unassigned or idle cell. The receiver extracts unassigned or idle cells and distributes the other, assigned cells to the destinations.

ITU-T Recommendation I.321 places this function in the TC sublayer of the PHY layer and uses idle cells, while the ATM Forum places it in the ATM layer and uses unassigned cells. This may present a potential low-level incompatibility if different systems use different cell types for cell-rate decoupling. Look for ATM systems that support both methods to ensure maximum interoperability. The ITU-T model views the ATM layer as independent of whether or not the physical medium has synchronous time slots.

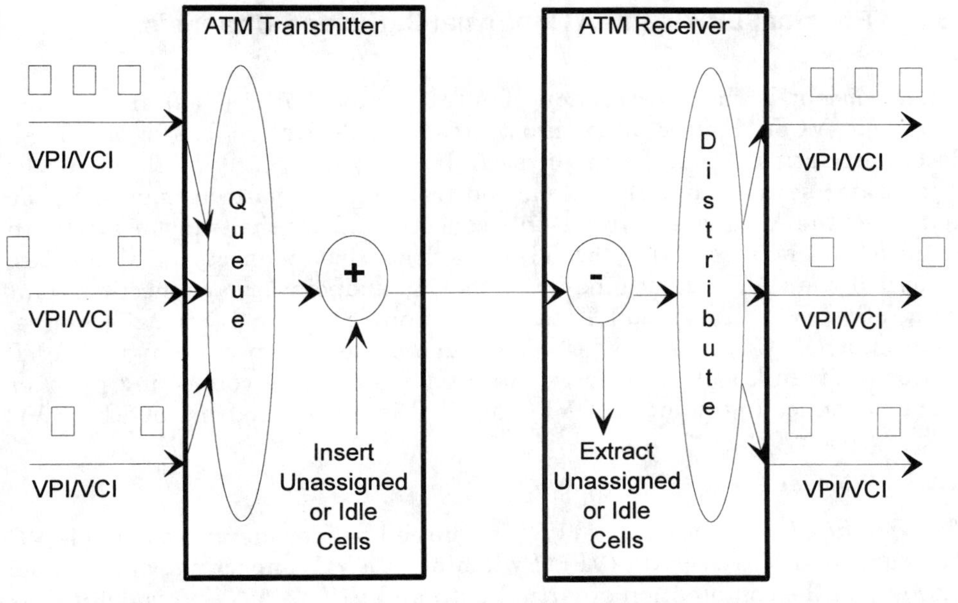

Figure 13.18 Cell Rate Decoupling Using Unassigned Cells

13.9 ATM LAYER — PROTOCOL MODEL

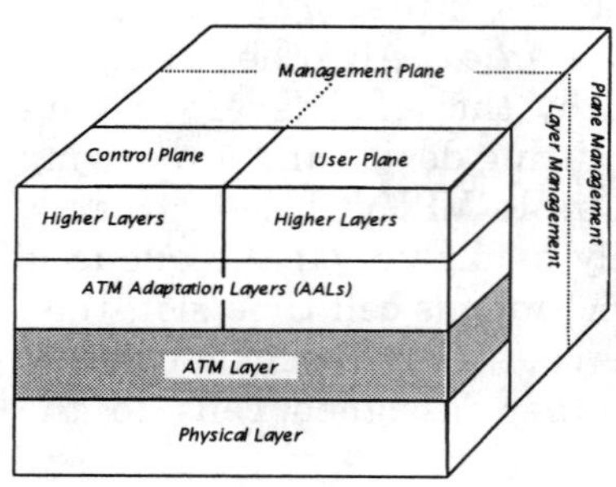

This section moves to the focal point of B-ISDN, the ATM Layer. First, the relationship of the ATM layer to the physical layer and its division into a Virtual Path (VP) and Virtual Channel (VC) level are covered in detail. This is a key concept, which is the reason that several analogies were presented earlier in the chapter. Several examples are provided in this section portraying the role of end and intermediate systems in a real-world setting rather than just a formal model. This is accomplished by explaining how the ATM layer VP and VC functions are used in intermediate and end systems in terms of the layered protocol model. An example is then provided showing how intermediate systems perform ATM VP or VC switching or cross-connection, and how end systems pass cells to the ATM Adaptation Layer (AAL).

13.9.1 Physical Links and ATM Virtual Paths and Channels

A key concept is the construction of ATM Virtual Paths (VPs) and Virtual Channels (VCs). Figure 13.19 illustrates this derivation based on ITU-T Recommendation I.311. The physical layer is composed of three levels: regenerator section, digital section, and transmission path, as shown in the figure. At the ATM layer, we are only concerned about the transmission path because this is essentially the TDM payload that connects ATM devices. Generically, an ATM device may be either an endpoint or a connecting point for a VP or VC. A Virtual Path Connection (VPC) or a Virtual Channel Connection (VCC) exists only between endpoints as shown in the figure. A VP link or a VC link can exist between an endpoint and a connecting point or between connecting points. A VPC or VCC is an ordered list of VP or VC links, respectively.

13.9.1.1 VC level

The *Virtual Channel Identifier (VCI)* in the cell header identifies a single VC on a particular Virtual Path (VP). Switching at a VC connecting point is done based upon the combination of virtual path and VCI. A *VC link* is defined as a unidirectional flow of ATM cells with the same VCI between a VC connecting point and either a VC endpoint or another VC connecting point. *A Virtual Channel Connection (VCC)* is defined as a concatenated list of VC links. A VCC defines a unidirectional flow of ATM cells from one user to one or more other users.

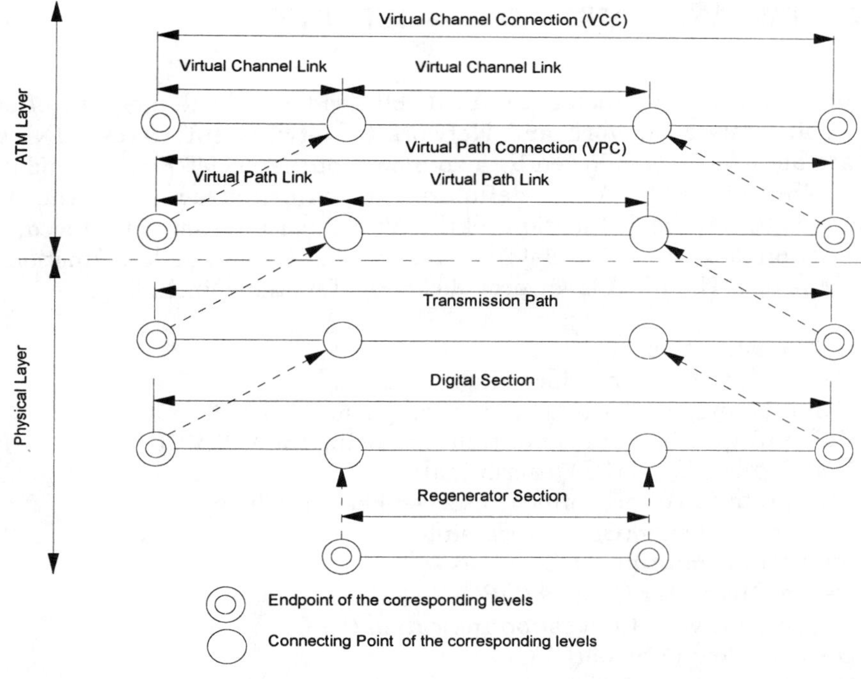

Figure 13.19 Physical Layer, Virtual Paths, and Virtual Channels

A network must preserve cell sequence integrity for a VCC; that is, the cells must be delivered in the same order in which they were sent. A Quality of Service (QoS) is associated with a VPC or VCC. (See McDysan and Spohn's *ATM: Theory and Application* for more detail on QoS assignments.)

13.9.1.2 VP Level

Virtual Paths (VPs) define an aggregate bundle of VCs between VP endpoints. A *Virtual Path Identifier (VPI)* in the cell header identifies a bundle of one or more VCs. A VP link provides unidirectional transfer of cells with the same VPI between VP endpoints or connecting points. Switching at a VP connecting point is done based upon the VPI — the VCI is ignored. A VP link is defined as a VP between a VP connecting point and either a VP endpoint or another VP connecting point. A Virtual Path Connection (VPC) is defined as a concatenated list of VP links. A VPC defines a unidirectional flow of ATM cells from one user to one or more other users.

Standards do not require a network to preserve cell sequence integrity for a VPC; however, the cell sequence integrity requirement of a VCC still applies. A Quality of Service (QoS) is associated with a VPC. If a VPC contains VCCs in different QoS classes, then the VPC assumes the QoS of the VCC with the highest quality. Thus, in our example with the author-to-publisher communication, a VCC rather than a VPC would be used for QoS.

13.10 ATM LAYER AND CELL — DEFINITION

Now for a detailed look inside the ATM cell header and the meaning of each field. The User-to-Network and Network-to-Network Interfaces (UNI and NNI) are defined first, followed by a summary of the ITU-T Recommendation I.361, ANSI, and ATM Forum definitions of the cell structure at the ATM UNI and NNI. The basic functions of the ATM layer are then introduced, and each function is described in detail. This section details the key functions of the ATM layer. The ATM layer provides many functions, including:

- Cell construction
- Cell reception and header validation
- Cell relaying, forwarding, and copying using the VPI/VCI
- Cell multiplexing and demultiplexing using the VPI/VCI
- Cell Payload Type (PT) discrimination
- Interpretation of predefined reserved header values
- Cell Loss Priority (CLP) processing
- Support for multiple QoS classes
- Usage Parameter Control (UPC)
- Explicit Forward Congestion Indication (EFCI)
- Generic Flow Control (GFC)
- Connection assignment and removal

The most important of these functions will be covered in this chapter.

13.10.1 ATM UNI and NNI Defined

Figure 13.20 defines the ATM reference configurations at the User-to-Network Interface (UNI) and the Network-to-Network Interface (NNI). The ATM UNI occurs between the user equipment or End System (ES), or Broadband Terminal Equipment (B-TE), and either the Terminal Adapter (TA) or Network Termination (NT), or Intermediate System (IS).

The ATM Forum terminology of private and public UNIs is mapped to the ITU-T reference point terminology in this figure. The ATM UNI may be a private ATM UNI, which would occur at the R or S reference points in ITU-T Recommendation I.413 and ANSI T1.624, or a public ATM UNI, which would occur at reference points T or U as shown in the figure. The Network-to-Network, or Network-Node, Interface (NNI) defined in ITU-T Recommendation I.113 is normally thought of as the standard interface between networks, which will most likely also be the interface used between nodes within a network. The ATM Forum distinguishes between an NNI used for private networks and public networks as shown in the figure.

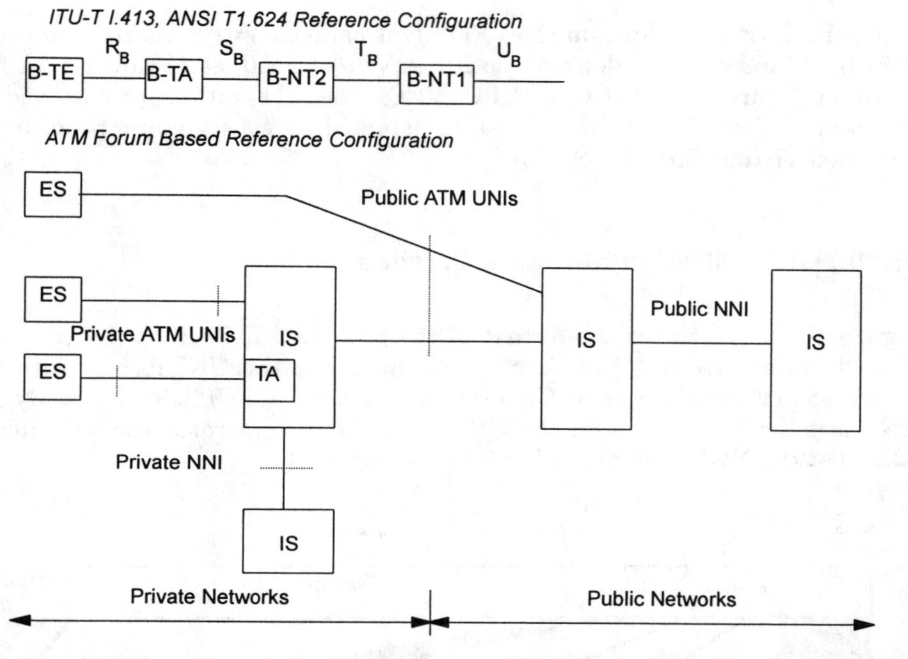

Figure 13.20 ATM UNI and NNI Reference Configuration

Two standardized coding schemes exist for cell structure: the User-to-Network Interface (UNI) and the Network-Node, or Network-to-Network Interface (NNI). The UNI is the interface between the user [or customer premises equipment (CPE)] and the network switch. The NNI is the interface between switches or between networks. UNI and NNI coding schemes are introduced and each field is defined in this section. ITU-T Recommendation I.361 is the basis of these definitions, with further clarifications given in ANSI T1.627 and the ATM Forum UNI and Broadband InterCarrier Interface (B-ICI) specifications.

13.10.2 ATM UNI Cell Structure Detailed

Figure 13.21 illustrates the format of the 53-byte ATM cell at the User-Network Interface (UNI). The cell header contains a logical address in two parts: an 8-bit Virtual Path Identifier (VPI) and a 16-bit Virtual Channel Identifier (VCI). The cell header also contains a 4-bit Generic Flow Control (GFC), 3-bit Payload Type (PT), and a 1-bit Cell Loss Priority (CLP) indicator. The entire header is error-protected by a 1-byte Header Error Check (HEC) field. This section details the meaning of each header field. A fundamental concept of ATM is that switching occurs based upon the VPI/VCI fields of *each* cell. Switching done on the VPI only is called a Virtual Path Connection (VPC), while switching done on both the VPI/VCI values is called a Virtual Channel Connection (VCC). VPCs/VCCs may be either provisioned as Permanent Virtual Circuits (PVCs), or established via signaling protocols as Switched Virtual Circuits (SVCs).

13.10.3 ATM NNI Cell Structure Detailed

Figure 13.22 illustrates the format of the 53-byte ATM cell at the Network-Node Interface (NNI). The format is identical to the UNI format with two exceptions. First, there is no Generic Flow Control (GFC) field. Secondly, the NNI uses the 4 bits used for the GFC at the UNI to increase the VPI field to 12 bits at the NNI as compared to 8 bits at the UNI.

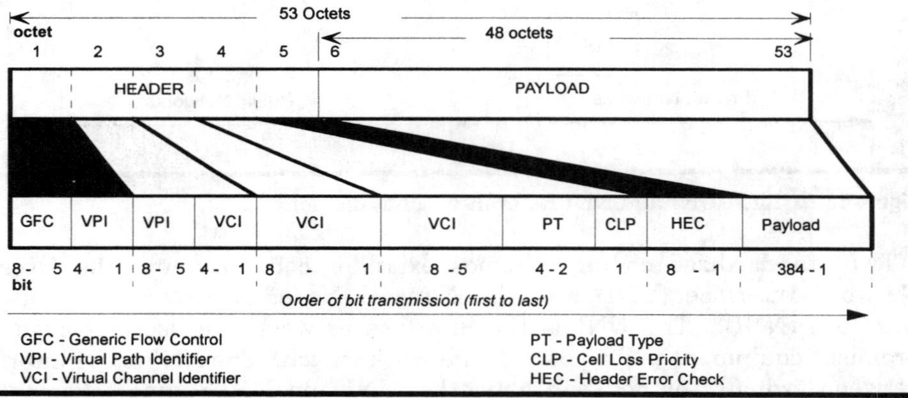

Figure 13.21 ATM User-to-Network Interface (UNI) Cell Structure

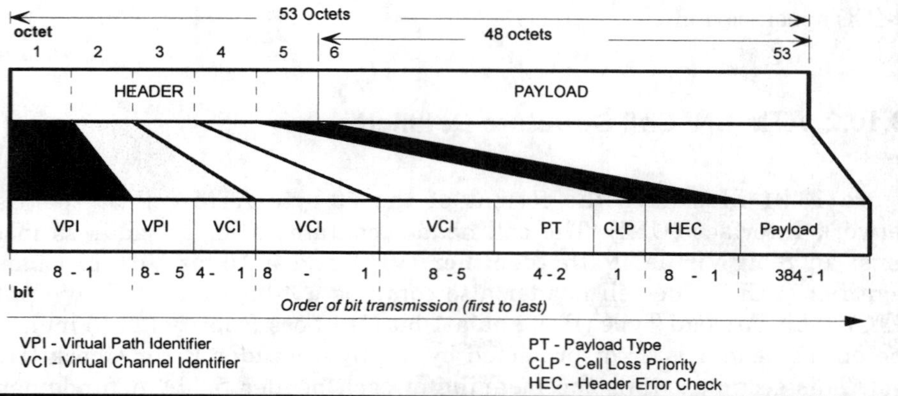

Figure 13.22 ATM Network-Node Interface (NNI) Cell Structure

13.10.4 Definition of ATM Cell Header Fields

This section provides a description of each header field.

Generic Flow Control (GFC) is a 4-bit field intended to support simple implementations of multiplexing. In the early 1990s, GFC was being specified to implement a DQDB-like, multiple-access-type protocol. However, it appears unlikely that this type of GFC will be standardized. The current standards define the *uncontrolled* mode, where the 4-bit GFC field is always coded as zeroes. If too many nonzero GFC values are received, layer management should be notified.

Payload Type (PT) is a 3-bit field that discriminates between a cell payload carrying user information or one carrying management information.

Cell Loss Priority (CLP) is a 1-bit field that indicates the loss priority of an individual cell.

The Header Error Check (HEC) field provides error checking of the header for use by the Transmission Convergence (TC) sublayer of the PHYsical layer as defined earlier.

13.10.5 Relaying and Multiplexing Using the VPI/VCI

As shown through several earlier examples, the heart of ATM is in the use of the VPI and VCI for relaying or switching. ATM also effectively performs multiplexing and demultiplexing of multiple logical connections with different quality requirements using the fixed-length ATM cell.

The number of bits allocated in the ATM cell header limit each physical UNI to support of no more than $2^8 = 256$ virtual paths and each physical NNI to support of no more than $2^{12} = 4096$ virtual paths. Each virtual path can support no more than $2^{16} = 65{,}536$ virtual channels on the UNI or the NNI.

Although the UNI and NNI cell formats specify 8 and 12 bits for the VPI, respectively, and 16 bits for the VCI on both interfaces, based on current ES's and applications not needing that many VCs, an implementation need only support a smaller number of the lower-order bits in the VPI and VCI. Thus, a real ATM application may differ markedly from the above maximums. This means that the number of virtual paths and virtual channels actually supported in a live ATM network may be far less than the maximum numbers defined above. This has important implications in interoperability if one ATM device expects the next ATM device to operate on VPI/VCI bits, but that device ignores these bits. One way to handle this is to allow each system to query the other about the number of bits that is supported. This function is supported in the ATM Forum Interim Local Management Interface (ILMI).

13.10.6 Meaning of Preassigned Reserved Header Values

A key function of the ATM layer is the identification of preassigned, reserved header values. Figure 13.23 shows the preassigned (also called predefined) header field values for the UNI. The 4-bit GFC field can be used with all of these values. The ITU-T has reserved the first 16 VCIs for future assignment as preassigned, reserved header value functions.

The physical layer usage of ATM cells is still in the process of standardization. Metasignaling, general broadcast, and point-to-point signaling are now defined and can be found in McDysan and Spohn's *ATM: Theory and Application*, as well as the current proposals for resource management.

The NNI has an additional 4 bits in the VPI field. The NNI preassigned, reserved header fields have not been completely standardized. The current version of the ATM Forum B-ICI specification only requires that the F4 OAM flows, point-to-point signaling, invalid patterns, and unassigned cells be supported.

13.10.7 Meaning of the Payload Type (PT) Field

Figure 13.24 depicts Payload Type (PT) encoding. We see the first bit is an AAL indication bit (currently used by AAL 5 to identify the last cell), the second bit indicates upstream congestion, and the third bit discriminates between data and operations cells. Payload types carrying user information may also indicate whether congestion was experienced by Explicit Forward Congestion Indication (EFCI) or whether the cell contains an indication to the AAL protocol. The management information payload type indicates whether the cell is either a segment or end-to-end Operations Administration and Maintenance (OAM) cell for a VCC or Resource Management (RM) cell.

13.10.8 Meaning of the Cell Loss Priority (CLP) Field

A value of 0 in the Cell Loss Priority (CLP) field means that the cell is of the highest priority — or in other words, it is the least likely to be discarded. A value of 1 in the CLP field means that this cell has low priority — or in other words, it may be selectively discarded during congested intervals in order to maintain a low loss rate for the high-priority CLP = 0 cells. The value of CLP may be set by the user or by the network as a result of a policing action.

Usage	VPI*	VCI	PT	CLP
Unassigned Cell	00000000	0	XXX	0
Idle Cell *	00000000	0	000	1
Reserved for Physical layer *	00000000	0	PPP	1
Metasignaling (I.311)	XXXXXXXX	1	0A0	C
General broadcast signaling	XXXXXXXX	2	0AA	C
Point-point signaling	XXXXXXXX	5	0AA	C
Segment OAM F4 Flow Cell	YYYYYYYY	3	0A0	A
End-to-end OAM F4 Flow Cell	YYYYYYYY	4	0A0	A
Segment OAM F5 Flow Cell	YYYYYYYY	>0	100	A
End-to-End OAM F5 Flow Cell	YYYYYYYY	>0	101	A
Resource Management Cell	YYYYYYYY	>0	110	A

* Defined as invalid pattern by ATM Forum
X = "Don't Care"
Y = Any VPI value
A = Use by appropriate functio
C = Originator set CLP
P = Reserved for PHY Layer

Figure 13.23 Preassigned, Reserved Header Values

PT Coding	PT Coding
000	User Data Cell, EFCI = 0, AAL_indicate = 0
001	User Data Cell, EFCI = 0, AAL_indicate = 1
010	User Data Cell, EFCI = 1, AAL_indicate = 0
011	User Data Cell, EFCI = 1, AAL_indicate = 1
100	OAM F5 segment associated cell
101	OAM F5 end-to-end associated cell
110	Resource management cell
111	Reserved for future functions

EFCI = Explicit Forward Congestion Indication
AAL_indicate = ATM-layer-user-to-ATM-layer-user indication

Figure 13.24 Payload Type (PT) Encoding

13.11 THE TRAFFIC CONTRACT AND QUALITY OF SERVICE (QOS)

A traffic contract is an agreement between a user and a network regarding the Quality of Service (QoS) that a cell flow is guaranteed – if the cell flow conforms to a set of traffic parameters defined by the leaky bucket rule. The principal QoS parameters are: average delay, variation in delay, and loss ratio. The traffic parameters define at least the Peak Cell Rate (PCR), and may optionally define a Sustainable Cell Rate (SCR) and Maximum Burst Size (MBS). A Cell Delay Variation Tolerance (CDVT) parameter is also associated with the peak rate, but is not usually specified by the user. A leaky bucket algorithm in the network checks conformance of a cell flow from the user by pouring a cup of fluid for each cell into a set of buckets leaking at rates corresponding to the PCR, and optionally the SCR. If the addition of any cup of cell fluid would cause a bucket to overflow, then the cell arrival is considered *nonconforming*, and its fluid is not added to the bucket. Additional considerations in setting the depth of the leaky buckets to account for tolerances in the traffic parameters are also described.

ITU-T Recommendation I.371 and the ATM Forum UNI Specification version 3.1 define the formal concept of a traffic contract. The traffic contract is a sort of "contract with the user". In essence, a separate traffic contract exists for every VPC or VCC. The traffic contract is an agreement between a user and a network across a UNI regarding the following interrelated aspects of any VPC or VCC ATM cell flow:

- The QoS that a network is expected to provide
- The traffic parameters that specify characteristics of the cell flow
- The conformance checking rule used to interpret the traffic parameters
- The network's definition of a compliant connection

The definition of a compliant connection allows some latitude in the realization of checking conformance of the user's cell flow. A compliant connection can identify some portion of cells to be nonconforming, but no more than the portion that the ideal conformance checking rule would identify as nonconforming.

13.11.1 Reference Model

The basis of the traffic contract is a reference configuration, which in the standards is called an *equivalent terminal* reference model, as illustrated in Figure 13.25.

ATM cell traffic is generated by a number of cell sources, for example, a number of workstations, which each have either a VPC or VCC connection endpoint. These are all connected to a cell multiplexer – which in a distributed implementation could be a local ATM switch, router, or hub. Associated with the multiplexing function is a traffic shaper, which assures that the cell stream conforms to a set of traffic parameters defined by a particular conformance-checking algorithm. The output of the shaper is the physical (PHY) layer Service Access Point (SAP) in the OSI layered model of ATM.

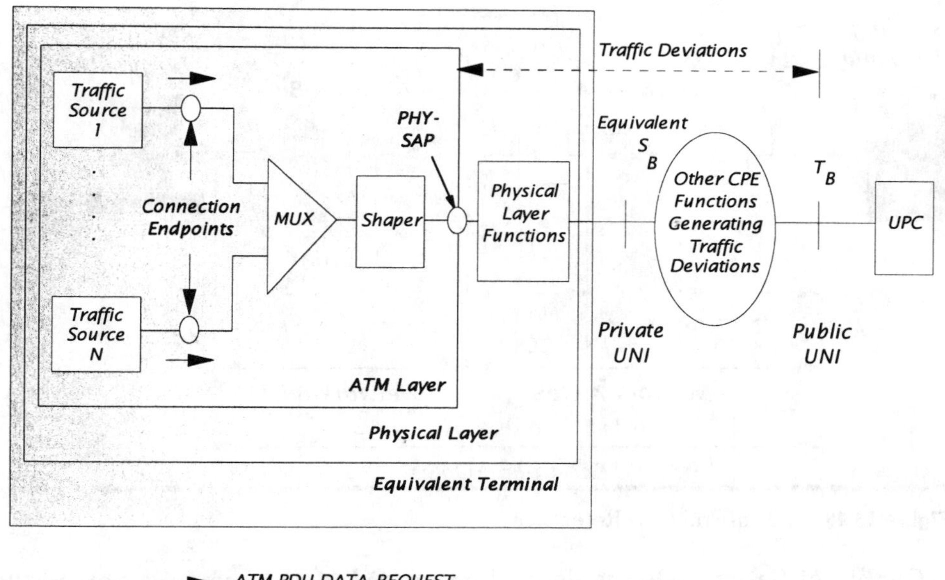

Figure 13.25 Equivalent Terminal Reference Model

After the shaper function, some physical layer (and other) functions may change the actual cell flow emitted over a private ATM UNI (or S_B reference point) so that it no longer conforms to the traffic parameters. This ATM cell stream may then be switched through other CPE, such as a collapsed ATM backbone, before it is delivered to the public ATM UNI (or T_B reference point).

The end-to-end QoS reference model may contain one or more intervening networks, each with multiple nodes as depicted in Figure 13.26. Each of these intervening networks may introduce additional fluctuations in the cell flow due to multiplexing and switching, thereby impacting QoS. In principle, the user should not have to be concerned about how many intervening networks there are and/or what characteristics they have, but should always be provided the guaranteed end-to-end QoS for all configurations. However, this principle and reality have not yet been aligned in standards or inter-working of multiple networks.

13.11.2 Quality of Service Parameters

Quality of Service (QoS) is defined by specific parameters for cells that are conforming to the traffic contract. In order to simplify a user's request for a certain QoS, certain classes are defined.

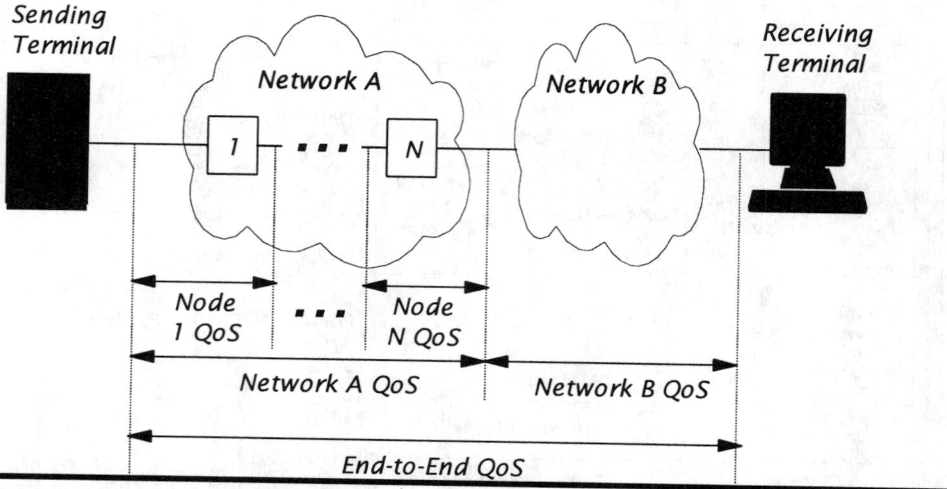

Figure 13.26 End-to-End QoS Reference Model

Quality of Service (QoS is defined on an end-to-end basis – a perspective that is actually meaningful to an end user. The definition of *end user* can be the end workstation, a customer premises network, a private ATM UNI, or a public ATM UNI.

QoS is defined in terms of the one of the following measurement outcomes. The measurement is done with respect to cells sent from an originating user to a destination user.

- A **Transmitted Cell** from the originating user.
- A **Successfully Transferred Cell** to the destination user.
- A **Lost Cell** which does not reach the destination user.
- An **Errored Cell** which arrives at the destination but has errors in the payload.
- A **Misinserted Cell** which arrives at the destination but was not sent by the originator. This can occur due to an undetected cell header error or a configuration error.

Cell transfer delay can be affected by coding and decoding, segmentation and reassembly, and end-to-end nodal and transmission delay, the components of which are illustrated in Figure 13.27.

Delay can occur on the sending and receiving sides of the end terminal, in intermediate ATM nodes, and on the transmission links connecting ATM nodes.

Cell Delay Variation (CDV) is currently defined as a measure of cell clumping, which is heuristically how much more closely the cells are spaced than the nominal interval.

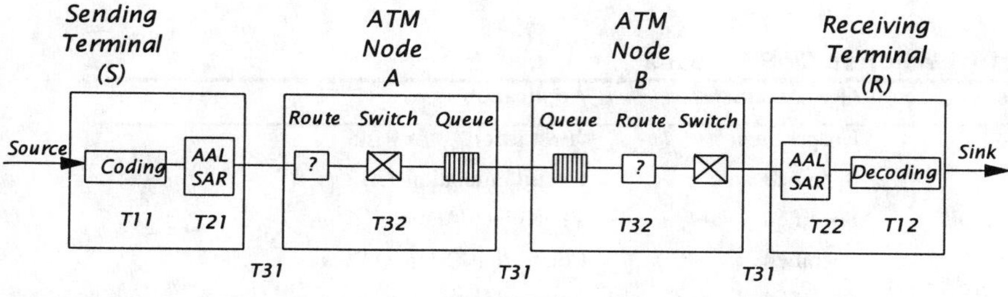

Figure 13.27 Illustration of Sources of Delay

Quality of Service (QoS) classes are defined primarily in terms of the following parameters defined by ITU-T Recommendation I.350 for each ATM VPC or VCC:

- Average delay
- Cell delay variation
- Loss on CLP = 0 cells for ATM
- Loss on CLP = 1 cells for ATM
- Error rate

For those connections that do not (or cannot) specify traffic parameters and a QoS class, there is a capability defined by the ATM Forum as *best effort* where no QoS guarantees are made and no specific traffic parameters need be stated. This traffic can also be viewed as "at risk" since there are no performance guarantees. In this case, the network admits this traffic and allows it to utilize capacity unused by connections that have specified traffic parameters and have requested a QoS class. It is assumed that connections utilizing the best-effort capability can determine the available capacity on the route allocated by the network.

13.11.3 QoS Classes

In order to make things simpler on users, a small number of predefined QoS classes are defined, with particular values of parameters (defined above) prespecified by a network in each of a few QoS Classes. The ATM Forum UNI Specification version 3.1 defines the five numbered QoS classes and example applications summarized in Table 13.1.

Table 13.1 ATM Forum QoS Classes

QoS Class	QoS Parameters	Application
0	Unspecified	"Best Effort", "At Risk"
1	Specified	Circuit Emulation, CBR
2	Specified	VBR Video/Audio
3	Specified	Connection-Oriented Data
4	Specified	Connectionless Data

A QoS class is defined by at least the following parameters:

- Cell loss ratio for the CLP = 0 flow
- Cell loss ratio for the CLP = 1 flow
- Cell delay variation for the aggregate CLP = 0 + 1 flow
- Average delay for the aggregate CLP = 0 + 1 flow

The CLP = 0 flow refers to only cells which have the CLP header field set to 0, while the CLP = 1 flow refers to only cells that have the CLP header field set to 1. The aggregate CLP = 0 + 1 flow refers to all cells in the virtual connection.

13.11.4 Specified QoS Classes

A specified QoS class provides performance to a ATM virtual connection (VCC or VPC) as specified by a subset of the ATM performance parameters. For each specified QoS class, there is one specified objective value for each performance parameter, where a particular parameter may be essentially unspecified – for example, a loss probability of 1. Initially, each network provider should define the ATM performance parameters for at least the following service classes from ITU-T Recommendation I.362 in a reference configuration that may depend on mileage and other factors:

- Service class A: circuit emulation, constant bit-rate video
- Service class B: variable bit-rate audio and video
- Service class C: connection-oriented data transfer
- Service class D: connectionless data transfer

In the future, more QoS classes may be defined for a given service class. The following specified QoS Classes are currently defined by the ATM Forum:

Specified QoS Class 1 supports a QoS that meets service class A performance requirements. This class should yield performance comparable to current digital private line performance.

Specified QoS Class 2 supports a QoS that meets service class B performance requirements. This class is intended for packetized video and audio in teleconferencing and multimedia applications.

Specified QoS Class 3 supports a QoS that meets service class C performance requirements. This class is intended for interoperation of connection-oriented protocols, such as frame relay.

Specified QoS Class 4 supports a QoS that meets service class D performance requirements. This class is intended for interoperation of connectionless protocols, such as IP or SMDS.

Figure 13.28 gives a concrete example of how the QoS parameters for cell loss ratio for the CLP = 0 flow and cell delay variation might be assigned for the four specified QoS classes. A network operator may provide the same performance for all or a subset of specified QoS classes, subject to the constraint that the requirements of the most stringent service class are met. Note that class 1 requirements meet the requirements of all of the other classes, a requirement stated in Appendix A of the ATM Forum UNI version 3.1 Specification.

13.11.5 Unspecified QoS and "Best-Effort" Service

In the unspecified QoS class, no objective is specified by the network operator for the performance parameters (however, an internal objective may be set). Services using the unspecified QoS class may have explicitly specified traffic parameters.

An example application of the unspecified QoS class is the support of *best-effort* service, where effectively no traffic parameters are specified. For this type of best-effort service, the user does not effectively specify any traffic parameters and does not expect a performance commitment from the network. One component of the best-effort service is that the user application is expected to adapt to the time-variable, available network resources. The interpretation and clearer definition of the best-effort service is an ongoing activity in the ATM Forum. The current name for this type of service is the Unspecified Bit Rate (UBR). An adaptive, flow-controlled service is currently being defined by the ITU and the ATM Forum as the Available Bit Rate (ABR). Note that ANSI dropped the CLASS Y name, and has adopted an explicit rate-based (versus the credit-based rate) flow control for congestion avoidance.

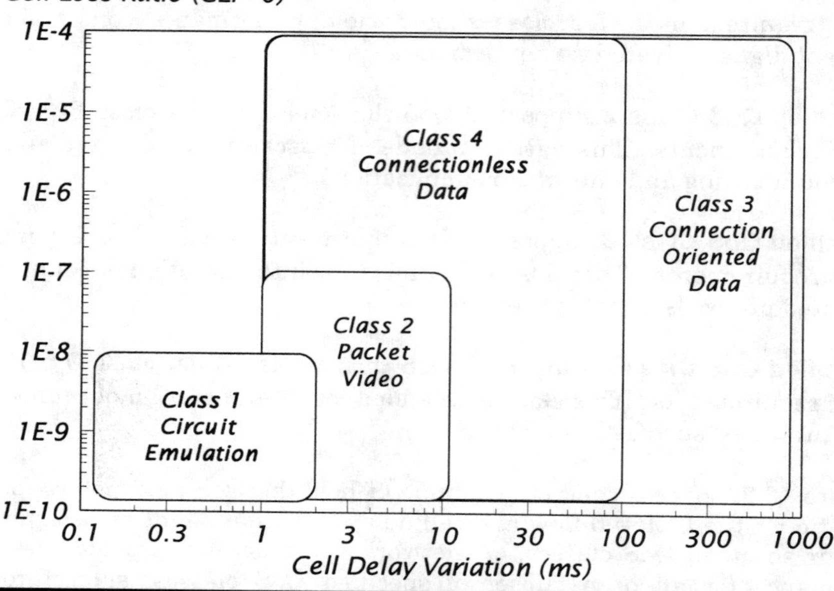

Figure 13.28 Example of QoS Class Value Assignments

ATM uses a leaky bucket algorithm as the key to defining the meaning of conformance checking for an arriving cell stream against the traffic parameters in the traffic contract.

13.12 TRAFFIC DESCRIPTOR

The traffic descriptor is a list of parameters which captures intrinsic source traffic characteristics. It must be understandable and enforceable. ATM traffic descriptors include (as defined by the ATM Forum UNI Specification version 3.1):

- A mandatory Peak Cell Rate (PCR) in cells/second in conjunction with a CDV tolerance in seconds.
- An optional Sustainable Cell Rate (SCR) in cells/second (always less than or equal to PCR) in conjunction with a Maximum Burst Size (MBS) in cells

The following statements summarize the current state of the ATM Forum agreements. Figure 13.29 illustrates the following key traffic contract parameters:

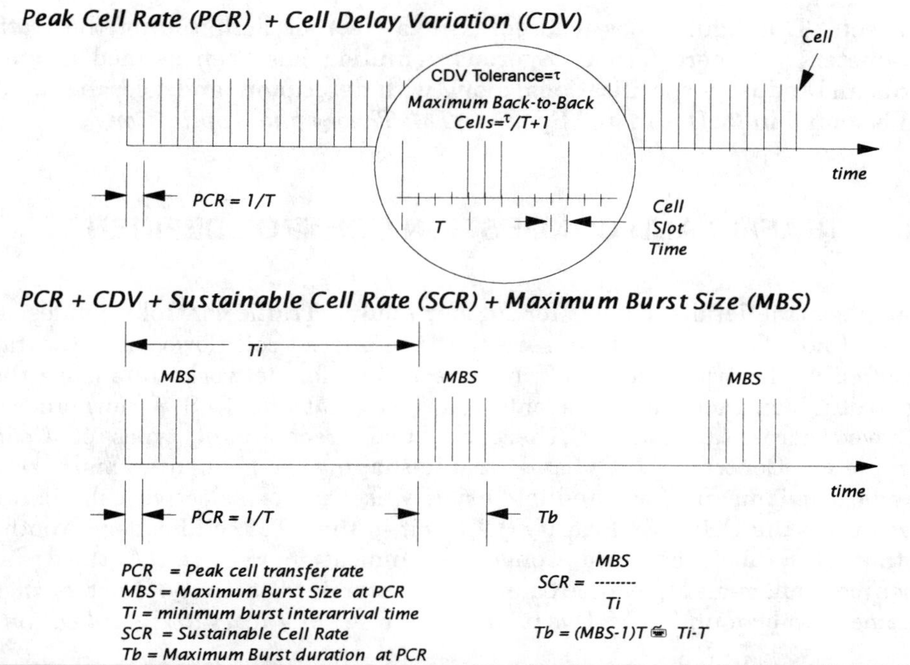

Figure 13.29 Illustration of Principal ATM Traffic Parameters

- Peak Cell Rate (PCR) = $1/T$ in units of cells/second, where T is the minimum intercell spacing in seconds (i.e., the time interval from the first bit of one cell to the first bit of the next cell).

- Cell Delay Variation (CDV) tolerance = τ in seconds. This traffic parameter normally cannot be specified by the user, but is set instead by the network. The number of cells that can be sent back-to-back at the access line rate is $\tau/T+1$, as shown in the figure.

- Sustainable Cell Rate (SCR) is the maximum average rate that a bursty, on-off traffic source that can be sent at the peak rate, such as that depicted in Figure 13.29.

- Maximum Burst Size (MBS) is the maximum number of cells that can be sent at the peak rate.

Figure 13.29 also depicts the minimum burst interarrival time as *Ti*, which is related to the SCR and MBS as defined by the equations at the bottom of the figure. The maximum burst duration in seconds is given by *Tb*, which is also defined at the bottom of the figure. These definitions may be helpful in understanding the traffic parameters but are not part of the formal traffic contract. This figure does not represent a rigorous definition of the traffic parameters. A more formal, rigorous definition has been defined in standards and industry specifications, along with descriptors and tolerances, and can be found in McDysan and Spohn, *ATM: Theory and Application*.

13.13 TRAFFIC AND CONGESTION CONTROL DEFINED

Traffic control details are left for further study. Traffic control provides the means that allow a user to ensure that the offered cell flows meet the rate specified in the traffic contract, and the means for networks to ensure that the traffic contract rates are enforced such that the QoS performance is achieved across all users. There are two predominant types of Usage Parameter Control (UPC) and traffic-shaping implementations. One standardized means for handling priority is that of selective cell discard based upon the Cell Loss Priority (CLP) bit in the ATM cell header. Another is that of Explicit Forward Congestion Indication (EFCI). A third, fast resource management, is an area of current standards activity. Each of these schemes can be found in McDysan and Spohn, *ATM:Theory and Application*.

13.14 METHODS OF CONGESTION CONTROL

The standard method for ATM congestion control is selective cell discard. There are longer time scale methods of congestion control, namely resource allocation, network engineering, and network management controls. Alternate methods exist to adaptively control the flow of user traffic into the network using either flow control or backward congestion notification. Specific congestion control for ATM can be categorized according to response: management, avoidance, and recovery. Each of these may operate at the cell level, the burst level, or the call level as illustrated in Table 13.2.

Table 13.2 Congestion Control Categories and Levels

Category	Cell Level	Burst Level	Call Level
Management	UPC Discard	Resource Allocation	Network Engineering
Avoidance	EFCI, UPC Tagging	Rate, or Credit Flow Control	Overbooked CAC, Call Blocking
Recovery	Selective Cell Discard, Dynamic UPC	Loss Feedback	Call Disconnection, Operations Procedures

Congestion management works to ensure a condition of congestion is never reached. ATM uses the following congestion management methods:

- Resource allocation
- Usage Parameter Control (UPC) discard
- Fully booked Connection Admission Control (CAC)
- Network engineering

Congestion avoidance methods include:

- Explicit Forward Congestion Indication (EFCI)
- Usage Parameter Control (UPC) tagging
- Connection Admission Control (CAC) overbooking
- Call blocking
- ATM layer rate or credit-based flow control

Congestion recovery procedures are initiated to prevent congestion from severely degrading the end-user-perceived Quality of Service (QoS) delivered by the network. These procedures are typically initiated when the network has begun to experience loss or markedly increased delay due to congestion.

Congestion Recovery includes:

- Selective cell discard
- Dynamic UPC
- Loss feedback
- Disconnection
- Operations procedures
- Resource management cell feedback (e.g., ABR)

13.15 REVIEW

The chapter began with definitions of ATM terminology and concepts. Examples were presented throughout the chapter in an attempt to compare ATM concepts to everyday life examples. The presentation then moved on to define the basic building block of ATM — the cell — and the method of constructing cells by assigning VPI and VCI addresses to a header field which prefixed the user payload. With these basics in hand, the chapter progressed through two examples of ATM protocol operation. ATM has many facets, and is referred to as an interface, a technology, integrated access, a network infrastructure, and even a service. Each of these aspects was summarized to set the stage for the rest of the book. The building blocks of ATM networking, the Transmission Path (TP), the Virtual Path (VP), and the Virtual Channel

(VC), were covered. The concepts of both Virtual Path Connections (VPCs) and Virtual Channel Connections (VCCs) were then introduced.

The foundations of B-ISDN are in the PHYsical (PHY) layer, the ATM layer, and the Common Part (CP) ATM Adaptation Layers (AALs). The chapter started with an overview of how these layers fit into the overall B-ISDN protocol model, and went on to investigate the sublayer structure of the PHY and ATM Adaptation layers. The PHY layer broke down into Physical Medium Dependent (PMD) and Transmission Convergence (TC) sublayers. Examples of how the PMD supports different physical media and interface rates and how the TC sublayer effectively makes the PHY layer appear as a pipe that can transfer cells at a maximum rate to the ATM layer were covered.

The ATM layer protocol model was covered, including an explanation of Virtual Path (VP) and Virtual Channel (VC) links, connections, and concepts complete with network examples from several points of view. The ATM cell was dissected, clearly defining every field in the header, reviewing some of the basic functions, and identifying where to reference detailed treatment of particular aspects of ATM in other areas of this book. The chapter next introduced the concepts of traffic and congestion control and indicated where these would occur in user equipment or networks.

The notion of congestion as demand in excess of resource capacity was defined. The degree of congestion impacts contention for resources, which can reduce throughput and increase delay, as occurs in vehicular traffic jams. Congestion can occur at multiple levels in time and space. In time, congestion can occur at the cell level, the burst level, or the call level. In space, congestion can occur at a single node or multiple nodes. Congestion-management attempts to ensure that congestion never occurs, which may be done at the expense of reduced efficiency. Congestion-avoidance schemes attempt to operate in a region of mild congestion in order to obtain higher efficiency at nearly optimal performance, while congestion recovery is tasked with moving the network out of a severely congested state in the event that the previous two philosophies fail, sometimes using rather drastic measures.

Chapter

14

ATM, Part 2

This chapter continues with the discussion of ATM-based, higher-layer protocols. First, we look at the ATM Adaptation Layer (AAL), which plays host to service class definitions that define protocol transport over ATM. An in-depth study of ATM Adaptation Layers (AALs) 1 through 5 relating them to the ITU-T service class definitions is also provided. The chapter provides an overview of the higher layers and the Service Specific Convergence Sublayer (SSCS) portion of the ATM Adaptation Layer (AAL). It includes the user and control planes, along with the management plane. The principal purpose of the control and management planes is to support the services provided by the user plane. Next, the chapter moves on to the very important control plane, which is central in performing the functions needed in a Switched Virtual Connection (SVC) service. The B-ISDN signaling protocol, Service Specific Coordination Function (SSCF), and Service Specific Connection-Oriented Protocol (SSCOP) SSCS protocols are then covered. Finally, the management plane, composed of overall plane management and management of each of the user and control plane layer components, is covered. The Data eXchange Interface (DXI) provide low-speed ATM access protocol rates of *n*xDS0, DS1, and E1. Finally, we look at public ATM services and providers, and the author's view of the challenges and future facing ATM.

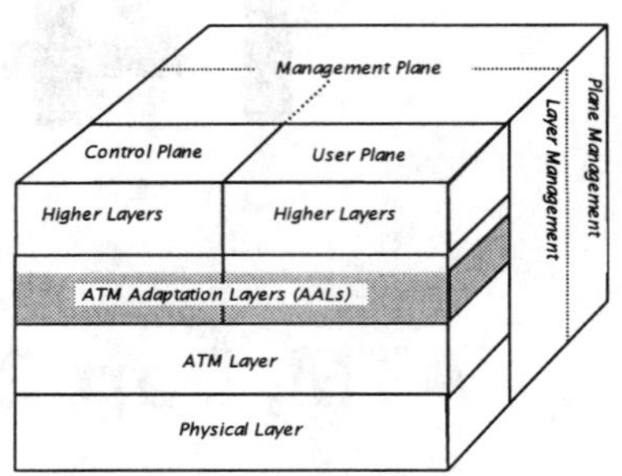

14.1 ATM ADAPTATION LAYER (AAL) — PROTOCOL MODEL

ITU-T Recommendations I.362 and I.363 define the next layer of the ATM/B-ISDN protocol stack, the ATM Adaptation Layer (AAL). AAL service class attributes and example applications will be covered first, followed by the generic AAL protocol model. The Common Part (CP) AALs format and protocol are described in detail with examples of each.

14.1.1 The AAL Protocol Structure Defined

The B-ISDN protocol model adapts the services provided by the ATM Layer to those required by the higher layers through the ATM Adaptation Layer (AAL). Figure 14.1 depicts the structure and logical interfaces of the AAL. Services provided to higher layers by an AAL Service Access Point (SAP) are shown at the top of the figure, across which primitives regarding the AAL Protocol Data Units (AAL-PDUs) are passed. The AAL is divided into the Convergence Sublayer (CS) and the Segmentation And Reassembly (SAR) sublayer. The CS is further subdivided into Service Specific (SS) and Common Part (CP) components. The SSCS may be null, which means that it need not be implemented. The CPCS must always be implemented along with the SAR sublayer. These layers pass primitives regarding their respective PDUs among themselves as labeled in the figure, resulting in the passing of SAR-PDU primitives (which is the ATM cell payload) to and from the ATM layer via the ATM-SAP.

This protocol model may seem somewhat abstract now; however, specific examples clarifying these concepts will soon be provided. This section provides an explanation of the Common Part CS (CPCS) and SAR models. It is nearly impossible to generalize the CS and SAR functions since, as we shall see, there are significant differences between every AAL.

The protocol primitives will not be covered in detail here. Instead, their actions resulting in the transfer of PDUs either between sublayers or across a SAP will be viewed. Standards use the primitives: request, indicate, response, and confirm. Refer to the definition in Chapter 4 of the OSI layering principles for a further explanation and references on this subject.

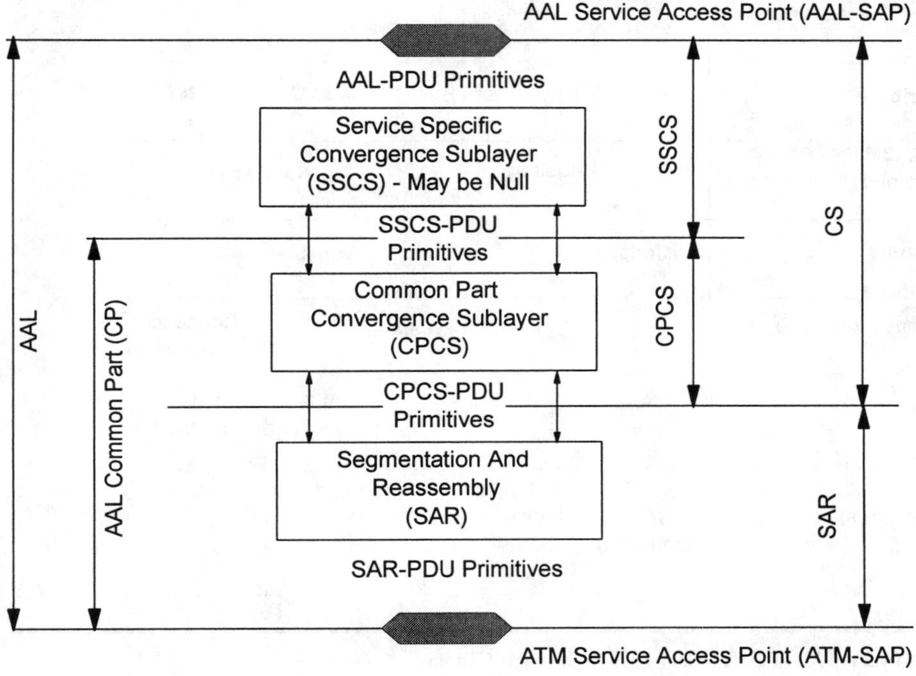

Figure 14.1 Generic AAL Protocol Sublayer Model

14.1.2 AAL Service Attributes Classified

ITU-T Recommendation I.362 defines the basic principles and classification of AAL functions. The attributes of the service class are the timing relationship required between the source and destination, whether the bit rate is constant or variable, and the connection mode is connection-oriented or connectionless. Figure 14.2 depicts the four currently defined AAL service classes, labeled A through D, summarized as follows:

- Class A — constant bit-rate (CBR) service with end-to-end timing, connection-oriented
- Class B — variable bit-rate (VBR) service with end-to-end timing, connection-oriented
- Class C — variable bit-rate (VBR) service with no timing required, connection-oriented
- Class D — variable bit-rate (VBR) service with no timing required, connectionless

	Service Class			
Attribute	Class A	Class B	Class C	Class D
Timing relation between source and destination	Required		Not Required	
Bit Rate	Constant	Variable		
Connection Mode	Connection-Oriented			Connection -less
AAL(s)	AAL1	AAL2	AAL3/4 or AAL5	AAL3/4 or AAL5
Example(s)	DS1, E1, nx64 Kbps emulation	Packet Video, Audio	Frame Relay, X.25	IP, SMDS

Figure 14.2 ATM ITU ATM/B-ISDN Service Classes

The mapping of service classes to AALs is only partially complete in the standards. The next section indicates the AAL(s) that can support the attributes of the defined AAL service class and also gives several application examples for each service class and AAL.

14.1.3 ATM Adaptation Layer (AAL) — Definition

AAL1 through AAL4 were initially defined by the CCITT to directly map to the AAL service classes A through D. ITU-T Recommendation I.363 states the standards for the AALs. AAL1 has been defined by the ITU-T and further clarified in the ANSI T1.630 standard for Continuous Bit Rate (CBR) applications. The history of AAL development for Variable Bit Rate (VBR) services is interesting. Initially, AAL3 was being developed for connection-oriented services and AAL4 for connectionless services. As the details were being defined, it was realized that AAL3 and AAL4 were common enough in structure and function that they were combined into a single class called AAL3/4. More recently, AAL5 was conceived by the computer industry in response to perceived complexity and implementation difficulties in AAL3/4, which had become aligned with the IEEE 802.6 layer 2 PDU (L2_PDU). Initially, AAL5 was named the Simple Efficient Adaptation Layer (SEAL) for this reason. AAL5 was adopted by the ATM Forum, ANSI, and the CCITT in a relatively short time compared to the usual standards process and has become the predominant AAL of choice in a great deal of data communications equipment. AAL5 is currently standardized for the transport of signaling messages and frame relay. AAL3/4 will likely be chosen for the support of SMDS since it is essentially identical to the IEEE 802.6 L2_PDU.

We describe the Common Part Convergence Sublayer (CPCS) and Segmentation And Reassembly (SAR) sublayer for each of the currently standardized Common Part (CP) AALs:

- AAL1 — constant bit-rate (CBR) traffic
- AAL3/4 — variable bit-rate (VBR) traffic
- AAL5 — lightweight variable bit-rate (VBR) traffic

14.1.3.1 AAL1

AAL1 specifies how TDM-type circuits can be emulated over an ATM network. Circuit emulation is specified in detail for DS1, DS3, and *n*xDS0 support in ANSI T1.630. AAL1 supports circuit emulation in one of two modes: the Synchronous Residual Time Stamp (SRTS) or Structured Data Transfer (SDT) method. The SRTS method supports transfer of a DS1 or DS3 digital stream, including timing. SDT supports an octet-structured *n*xDS0 service.

Figure 14.3 depicts the CPCS for AAL1 in support of SRTS and SDT.

A key concept in SRTS is that both the origin and destination have a very accurate frequency clock of frequency fn. The signal (e.g., DS1) has a service clock frequency fs with the objective being to pass sufficient information via the AAL so that the destination can reproduce this clock frequency with a high degree of accuracy. The method standardized for doing this is illustrated in the top part of Figure 14.3. The network reference clock fn is divided by x such that $1 \leq fnx/fs \leq 2$. The source clock is divided by N as shown in the figure to sample the 4-bit counter Ct driven by the network clock fnx once every $N = 3008 = 47 \times 8 \times 8$ bits generated by the source. This sampled counter output is transmitted as the Residual Time Stamp (RTS) in the SAR PDU. ITU-T Recommendation I.363 and ANSI T1.630 show how this method can accept a frequency tolerance for the source frequency of 200 parts per million (ppm).

The Structured Data Transfer (SDT) method is more straightforward, as shown in the bottom part of Figure 14.3. SDT has two modes depending upon whether the sequence number is odd or even. The SDT CPCS uses a 1-octet pointer field in even sequence numbers of the 47-octet SAR-PDU payload to indicate the offset into the current payload of the first octet of an nxDS0 payload. The value of n may be as large as 92 in the P-format since the pointer is repeated every other cell when supporting AAL1.

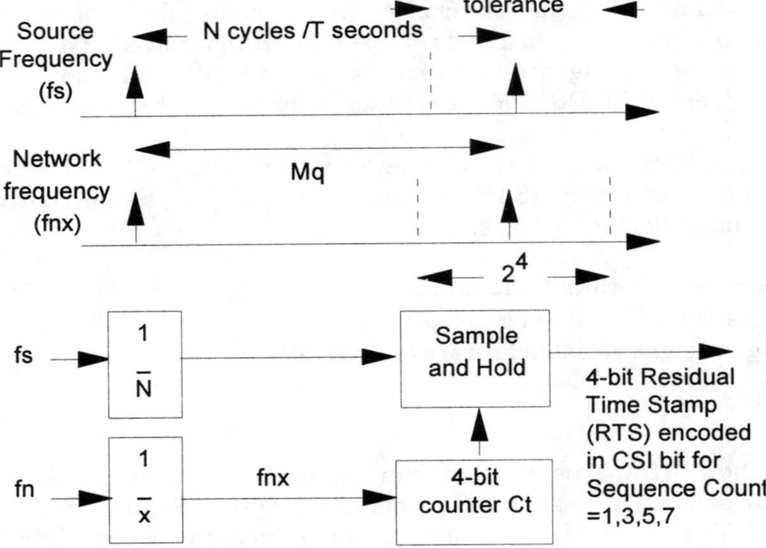

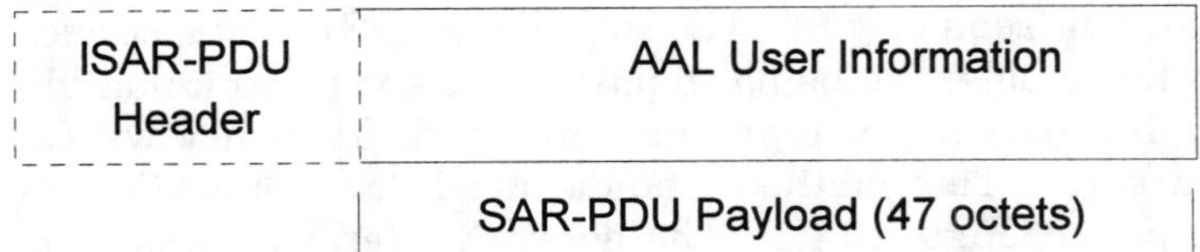

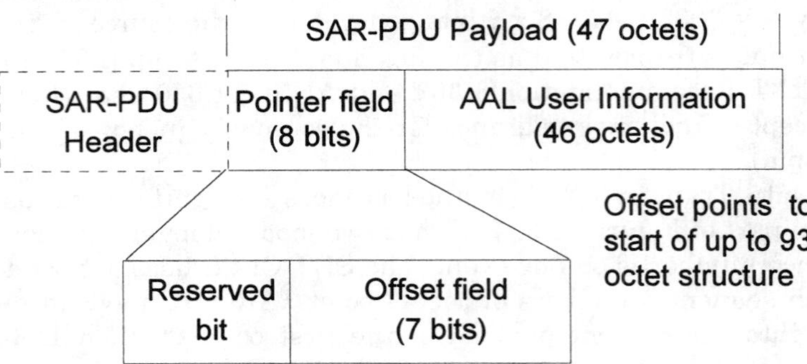

Figure 14.3 AAL1 Common Part Convergence Sublayer (CPCS)

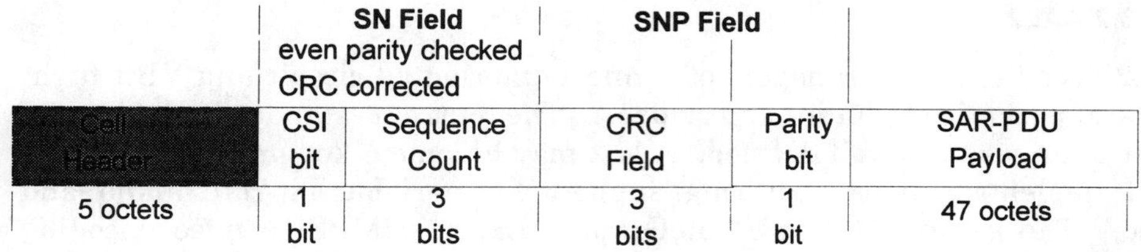

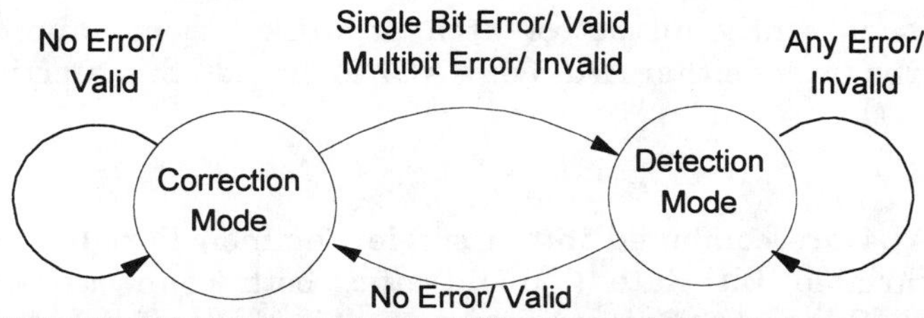

Figure 14.4 AAL1 Segmentation And Reassembly (SAR) Sublayer

Figure 14.4 depicts the SAR for AAL1. The 1 octet of overhead is broken down into four fields as shown in the figure. Since 1 octet is used by the AAL1 SAR, this leaves 47 octets for user data. There are two major fields: the Sequence Number (SN) and the Sequence Number Protection (SNP) field. The 3-bit sequence count is incremented sequentially by the origin. The receiver checks for missing or out-of-sequence SAR-PDUs and generates a signal alarm when this occurs. The Convergence Sublayer Indication (CSI) bit in the SN field is used differently in the SRTS and SDT modes. In SRTS mode, the 4-bit RTS is sent in odd-sequence-numbered PDUs. In SDT mode, the CSI bit is used to indicate if the pointer field is present in even-sequence-numbered SAR-PDUs. The 3-bit CRC field computes a checksum across the SN field. The parity bit represents even parity across the first 7 bits in the 1-octet SAR-PDU overhead.

The sequence number is critical to proper operation of AAL1 since an out-of-sequence or missing SAR-PDU will disrupt at least 47 octets of the emulated circuit bit stream. A well-defined procedure is standardized to correct many problems due to bit errors in the sequence number field, or to accurately detect errors that are not corrected. The operation at the receiver is illustrated in the state machine at the bottom of Figure 14.4. While in the correction mode, the receiver can correct single-bit errors using the CRC, but, if after CRC correction the parity check fails, then either a single or multiple bit error has been detected and the receiver switches to detection mode. The receiver stays in detection mode until no error is detected and the sequence number is sequential (i.e., valid).

14.1.3.2 AAL2

AAL2 specifies ATM transport of connection-oriented circuit and VBR high-bit-rate packetized audio and video. The current standard at time of publication was not well defined. AAL2 may become a key protocol in future ATM implementations requiring support for variable bit-rate audio and video. The second Motion PhotoGraphic Experts (MPEG) video encoding standard, called MPEG2, can be operated at a variable bit rate. The standardization and specification of interoperable video and audio encoding using ATM is currently an active area of work. Some approaches are investigating the use of either AAL5 or AAL1 to provide this function.

14.1.3.3 AAL3/4

AAL3 and AAL4 are combined into a single Common Part (CP) AAL3/4 in support of Variable Bit Rate (VBR) traffic, both connection-oriented or connectionless. Support for connectionless service is provided at the Service Specific Convergence Sublayer (SSCS) level. For example, the IEEE 802.6 L3_PDU could be carried over AAL3/4 in a manner that would interwork with 802.6 L2_PDUs.

Figure 14.5 depicts the CPCS-PDU for AAL3/4. The header has three components as indicated in the figure. The 1-octet Common Part Indicator (CPI) indicates the number of counting units (bits or octets) for the Buffer Allocation Size (BASize) field. The sender inserts the same value for the 2-octet Beginning Tag (BTag) and the Ending Tag (ETag) so that the receiver can match them as an additional error check. The 2-octet BASize indicates to the receiver how much buffer space should be reserved to reassemble the CPCS-PDU. A variable-length PAD field of between 0 and 3 octets is inserted in order to make the CPCS-PDU an integral multiple of 32 bits to make end-system processing simpler. The trailer also has three fields, as shown in the figure. The 1-octet ALignment field (AL) makes the trailer a full 32 bits to simplify the receiver design. The 1-octet ETag must have the same value as the BTag at the receiver for the CPCS-PDU to be considered valid. The length field encodes the length of the CPCS-PDU field so that the pad portion may be taken out before delivering the payload to the CPCS user.

Figure 14.6 depicts the SAR for AAL3/4. The SAR-PDU encoding and protocol function and format are nearly identical to the L2_PDU from IEEE 802.6. The SAR-PDU has a 2-octet header and trailer. The header contains three fields as shown in the figure. The 2-bit Segment Type (ST) field indicates whether the SAR-PDU is a Beginning Of Message (BOM), a Continuation Of Message (COM), an End Of Message (EOM), or a Single Segment Message (SSM). The 2-bit Sequence Number (SN) is incremented by the sender and checked by the receiver. The numbering and checking begins when an ST of BOM is received. The 10-bit Multiplex IDentification (MID) field allows up to 1024 different CPCS-PDUs to be multiplexed over a single ATM VCC. This is a key function of AAL3/4 since it allows multiple logical connections to be multiplexed over a single VCC. This function is essentially the same one used in the 802.6 L2 protocol where there was effectively no addressing in the cell header. The MID is assigned for a BOM or SSM segment type. The trailer has two fields. The 6-bit Length Indicator (LI) specifies how many of the octets in the SAR-PDU contain CPCS-PDU data. LI has a value of 44 in BOM and COM segments, and may take on a value less than this in EOM and SSM segments.

14.1.3.4 AAL5

The Common Part (CP) AAL5 supports variable bit rate (VBR) traffic, both connection-oriented or connectionless. Support for connectionless or connection-oriented service is provided at the Service Specific Convergence Sublayer (SSCS) level. For example, signaling SSCS protocols and frame relay and multiple protocols (including IP) can be operated over AAL5.

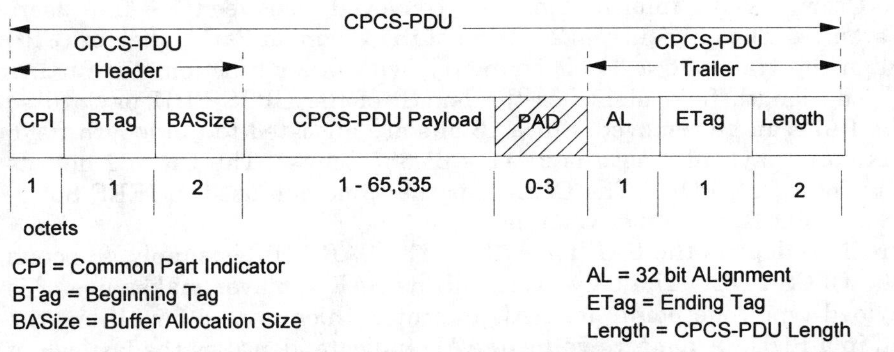

Figure 14.5 AAL3/4 CPCS Sublayer

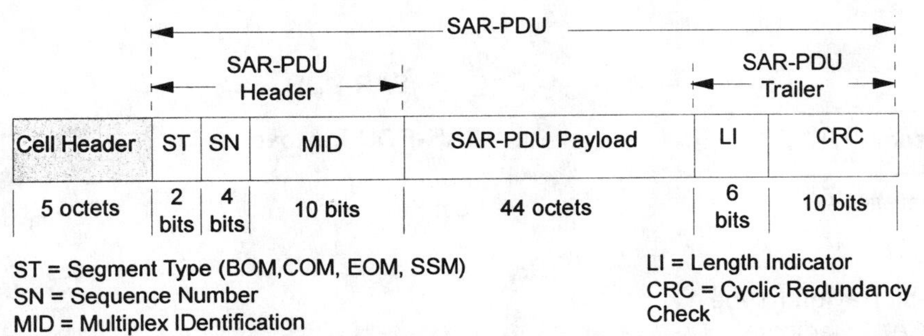

Figure 14.6 AAL3/4 Segmentation And Reassembly (SAR) Sublayer

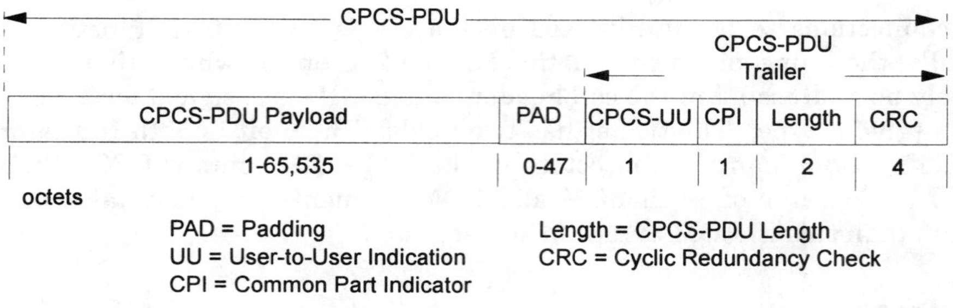

Figure 14.7 AAL5 Common Part Convergence Sublayer (CPCS)

Figure 14.7 depicts the CPCS for AAL5. The payload may be any integer number of octets in the range of 1 to $2^{16}-1$ (65,535). The padding field (PAD) is of a variable length chosen such that the entire CPCS-PDU is an exact multiple of 48, so that it can be directly segmented into cell payloads. The User-to-User (UU) information is conveyed between AAL users transparently. The only current function of the Common Part Indicator (CPI) is to align the trailer to a 64-bit boundary, with other functions for further study. The length field identifies the length of the CPCS-PDU payload so that the PAD can be removed. Since 16 bits are allocated to the length field, the maximum payload length is $2^{16}-1$ = 65,535 octets. The CRC-32 detects errors in the CPCS-PDU. The CRC-32 is the same one used in IEEE 802.3, IEEE 802.5, FDDI, and Fiber Channel.

Figure 14.8 depicts the SAR for AAL5. The SAR-PDU is simply 48 octets from the CPCS-PDU. The only overhead the SAR sublayer makes use of is the payload type code points for AAL_indicate, which is zero for all but the last cell in a PDU. A nonzero value of AAL_indicate identifies the last cell of the sequence of cells indicating that reassembly should begin. This was intended to make the reassembly design simpler and make more efficient use of ATM bandwidth, which was the root of the name for the original AAL5 proposal, called the Simple Efficient Adaptation Layer (SEAL).

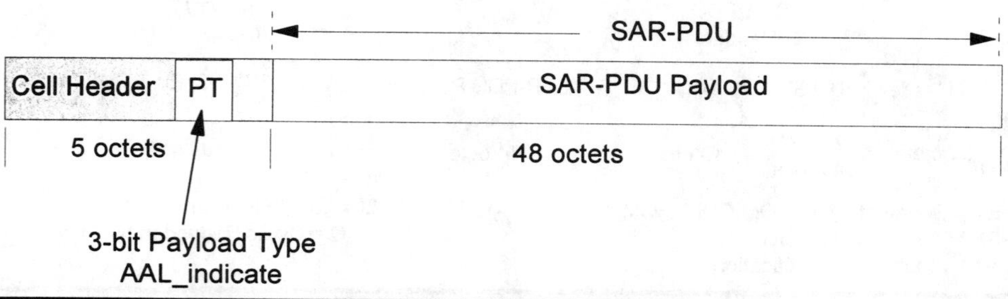

Figure 14.8 AAL5 Segmentation and Reassembly (SAR) Sublayer

14.2 USER PLANE OVERVIEW

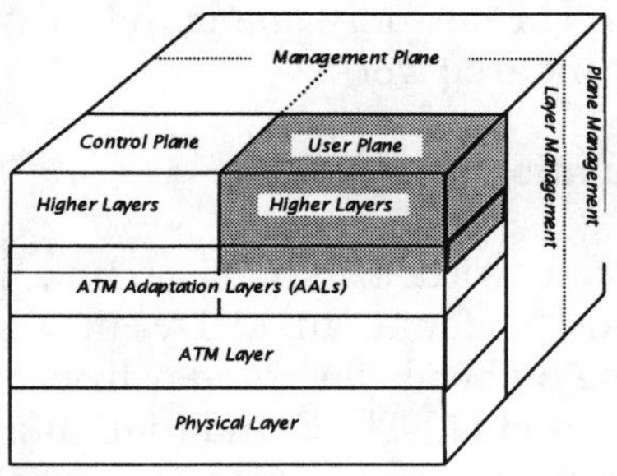

As shown in the shaded portion of the figure to the left, this section covers the general purpose and function of the user plane. The control and management planes exist to support the user plane. The state of standardization in the Service Specific Convergence Sublayer (SSCS) and higher layers of the user plane is also summarized. A great deal of standardization work still remains to be done in the area of higher-layer user plane functions.

14.2.1 User Plane — SSCS Protocols

To date, two Service Specific Convergence Sublayer (SSCS) protocols have been developed specifically for the user plane:

- Frame relay SSCS
- SMDS SSCS

There is no SSCS required for support of IP or circuit emulation over ATM since the common part AAL directly supports them. There is some discussion and the likely possibility that the Service Specific Connection-Oriented Protocol (SSCOP) defined for signaling could be used to provide an assured data transfer service in the user plane. It is anticipated that SSCS protocols will be developed for the following user-driven applications:

- Desktop-quality video
- Entertainment-quality video
- Multicast LAN support
- LAN emulation
- Reliable data delivery (like the X.25 capability)
- Interactive, cooperative computing support
- Database Concurrency, Commitment, and Recovery (CCR) function support

A large amount of additional standardization work is still being developed to support the applications listed above. It is likely that many more SSCS protocols will be required to support these applications before the B-ISDN protocol suite is mature.

14.2.2 User Plane — Higher Layers

The area of higher-layer protocol support for ATM has only one standard to date, which underscores the need for further standards work:

☺ IETF RFC 1483 — Multiprotocol encapsulation over ATM

IETF RFC 1483 explained in detail, complete with examples of how it enables current applications to use ATM, can be found in McDysan and Spohn's *ATM: Theory and Application*. That the higher-layer standardization is not as far along as the lower layers is to be expected. The foundation must first be built before adding the walls and finally the roof. Of course, work continues on the foundation layers by defining new physical layers, new ATM capabilities, and possibly even new AALs in the ever expanding B-ISDN/ATM mansion. ATM Forum LAN Emulation working group LANE 1.0 has been approved. There are, however, some key activities in progress including:

😐 ATM Forum System Aspects and Applications (SAA) working group. A detailed specification for packing MPEG into AAL5 has been passed.
😐 ATM Forum Private Network-to-Network Interface (P-NNI) working group
😐 IETF work group supporting IP over ATM
😐 IETF work group for routing over ATM networks

It is suggested that users follow the progress of these activities and provide inputs to these groups on requirements. Users need these functions, but they are not defined yet; that is why they don't have smiles on their faces in the above list. You have a voice in the standards process — use it!

14.2.3 Frame Relay Over ATM

Frame relay and ATM interworking are specified in ITU-T Recommendation I.555, the ATM Forum B-ICI specification, and two Frame Relay Forum Implementation Agreements (IAs):

Network Interworking (FRF.5)
Service Interworking

Each of these scenarios have their associated access configuration, protocol, Service Specific Convergence Sublayer (SSCS), status signaling, traffic and congestion control, mapping, and service interworking considerations.

Frame relay (FR) and ATM interworking can operate in one of two scenarios using three access configurations as shown in Figure 14.9. In ITU I.55, these are defined as two scenarios. In scenario 1, FR is interworked *over* ATM. In scenario 2, FR interworks *with* an ATM end system. The first two access configurations of FR CPE interfacing via a FR UNI to the Interworking Function (IWF) or through a frame relay network apply to both scenarios. The third access configuration of a direct connection of an ATM end system via an ATM UNI to a network that terminates the VCC on the IWF applies to scenario 2 only.

The FR to ATM Interworking Function (IWF) converts between the Q.922 core functions and the FR Service-Specific Convergence Sublayer (FR-SSCS) defined in I.365.1, and the AAL5 Common Convergence Sublayer (CPCS) and Segmentation And Reassembly (SAR) sublayer from I.363, as shown in Figure 14.10a. The IWF must also convert between the Q.933 Annex A PVC status signaling for a single, physical FR UNI port and the VCCs that correspond to the DLCIs. The FR-SSCS Protocol Data Unit (PDU) is the CPCS SDU of the AAL5 Common Part, as described previously. Figure 14.10b illustrates the FR/ATM interworking protocol of an ATM end system. This function is identical to the right-hand side of the FR/ATM IWF. The ATM end system must support Q.933 Annex A frame relay status signaling.

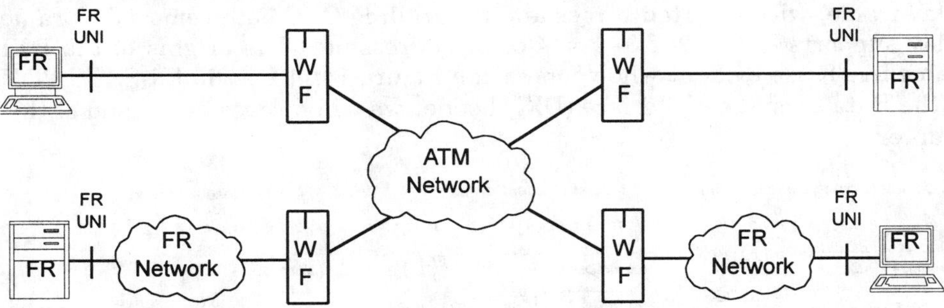

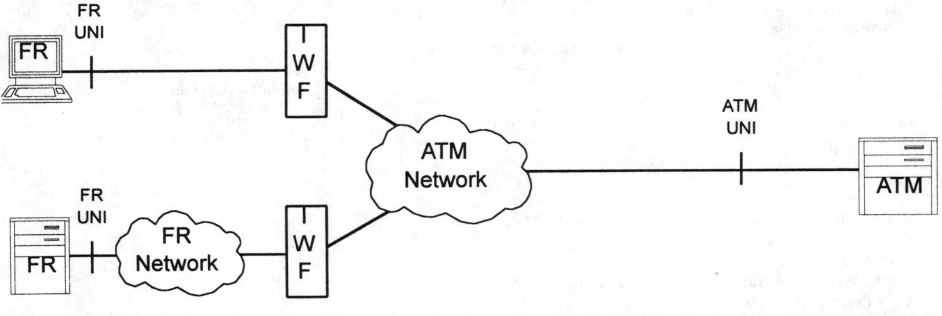

Figure 14.9 FR/ATM Interworking Scenarios and Access Configurations

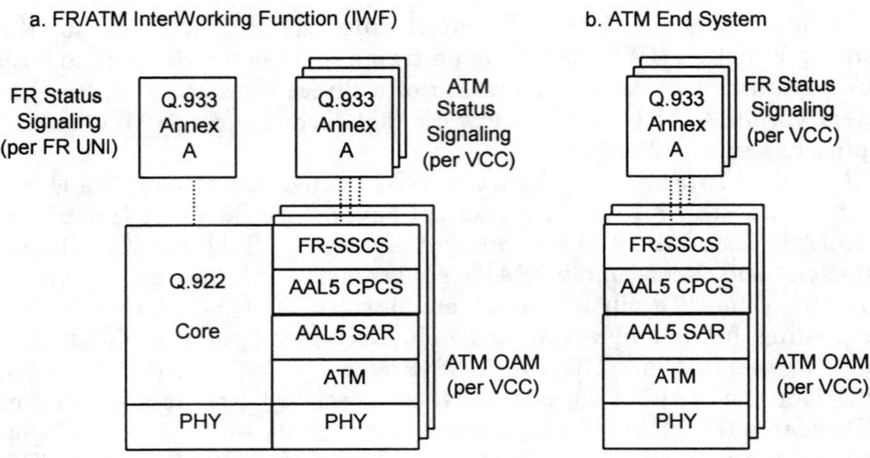

Figure 14.10 FR to ATM Network Interworking Control Planes

Figure 14.11 illustrates the FR-SSCS PDU format (essentially a frame relay frame) with inserted zeroes and the trailing CRC both removed. Frame relay supports either 2- , 3- , or 4-octet addressing. The origins of the DXI frame in FR are evident when comparing Figure 14.11 for the FR-SSCS PDU to the Data eXchange Interface (DXI) header we will discuss at the end of this chapter.

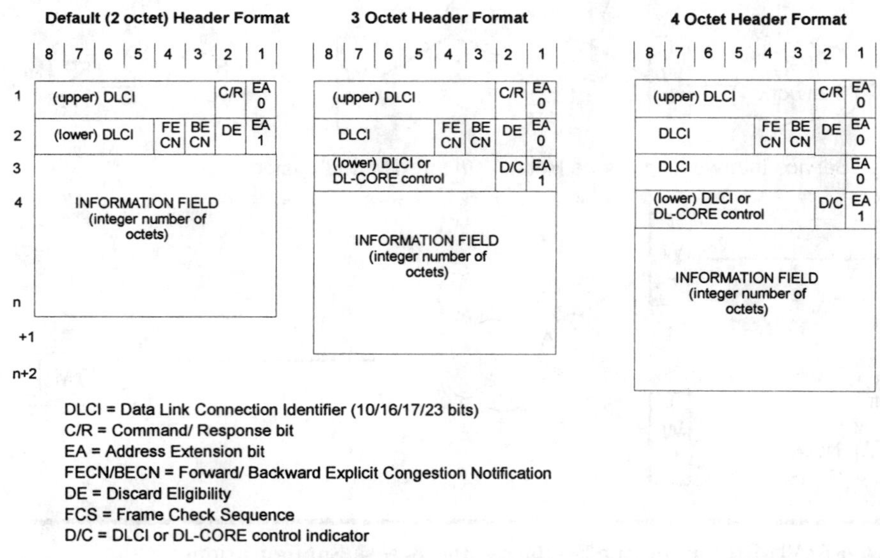

Figure 14.11 FR-SSCS PDU Formats

The FR-SSCS supports multiplexing through the use of the DLCI field, with the ATM layer supporting connection multiplexing using the VPI/VCI. There are two methods of multiplexing FR connections over ATM: many-to-one and one-to-one. Many-to-one multiplexing maps many FR logical connections identified by the Data Link Connection Identifiers (DLCIs) over a single ATM Virtual Channel Connection (VCC). One-to-one multiplexing maps each FR logical connection identified by DLCI to a single ATM VCC via VPI/VCIs at the ATM layer.

Control and addressing functions and data are either mapped or encapsulated by the interworking function. For example, in the FR-to-ATM direction, the DLCI, DE, FECN, and BECN fields are encapsulated in the FR-SSCS PDU. The FR DE bit is also mapped to the ATM CLP bit, and the FR FECN bit is mapped to the ATM EFCI bit. FR BECN is encapsulated in the FR-SSCS. BECN may also be mapped if the EFCI was set in the last cell of a frame reassembled from the ATM-to-frame relay direction. The frame relay FCS is mapped to (that is, replaced by) the AAL5 CRC function.

In the ATM-to-frame relay direction the CLP bit may be logically ORed with the DE bit as a configuration option on a per-DLCI basis. The AAL5 CRC is checked, and the FR FCS is recomputed for delivery to a frame relay UNI. The FR-SSCS PDU carries the encapsulated FECN, BECN, and DE bits intact.

The FR traffic parameters include access line rate (Ra), committed burst size (Bc), excess burst size (Be), and measurement interval, which define a Committed Information Rate (CIR) and an Excess Information Rate (EIR) in T1.617. Appendix A of the ATM Forum B-ICI specification maps these FR traffic parameters to the ATM traffic parameter in terms of Peak Cell Rate (PCR), Sustainable Cell Rate (SCR), and Maximum Burst Size (MBS).

The ATM Quality of Service (QoS) class for the VCC must also be selected. Usually QoS class 3 as defined by the ATM Forum for connection-oriented data would be used.

Note that the multiprotocol encapsulation for frame relay of RFC 1490 differs from the multiprotocol encapsulation being defined for ATM. RFC 1483 specifies that for direct interworking with frame relay end-system support for RFC 1490 NLPID encapsulation should be provided. This means that an ATM end or intermediate system must also support NLPID if interworking with FR is required.

The issue of status signaling interworking with ATM is resolved in FRF.8. The ATM ILMI and ATM layer Operations Administration and Maintenance (OAM) functions do not support all of the frame relay status signaling functions. The ATM Forum plans to address this issue.

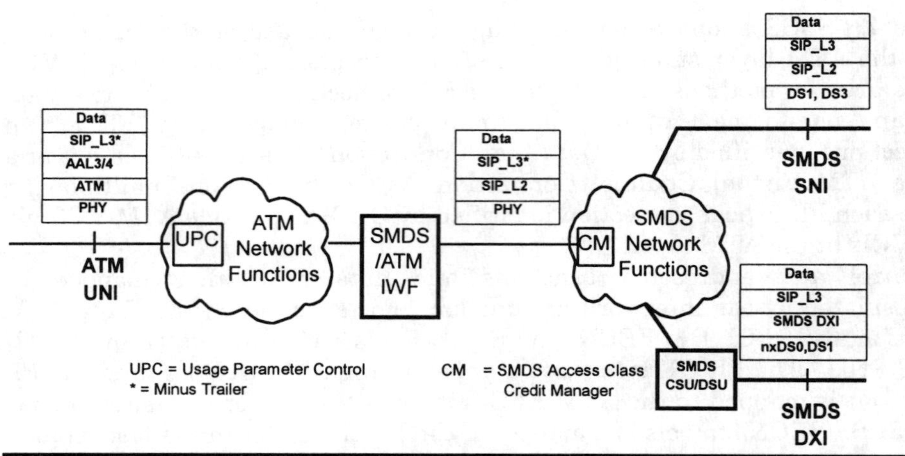

Figure 14.12 Logical Configuration for SMDS Access over ATM

14.2.4 SMDS Access Interworking Over ATM

The ATM Forum B-ICI document defines how SMDS can be transported between carriers. The ATM Forum, SMDS Interest Group (SIG), and European SIG (E-SIG) are jointly defining how SMDS can be accessed across an ATM UNI. Access configuration, functions performed, and expected protocol specification based upon the B-ICI specification are described in this section.

Figure 14.12 depicts the access configuration and logical placement of function for accessing SMDS features over an ATM User-to-Network Interface (UNI). An ATM end system accessing SMDS over ATM must format an AAL3/4 CPCS PDU containing the SMDS Interface Protocol layer 3 (SIP_L3) PDU, as shown on the left-hand side of the figure. The ATM network performs Usage Parameter Control (UPC) to emulate the SMDS access class as will be described later. The ATM network relays the cells to an SMDS Interworking Function (IWF), which may be implemented in a centralized, regionalized, or distributed manner. The SMDS/ATM IWF converts the AAL stream into the SMDS protocol stack and passes this to an SMDS network, which implements the SMDS service features, including access class enforcement. The SMDS network can interface to a subscriber using the SMDS Subscriber Network Interface (SNI) or the SMDS Data eXchange Interface (DXI), as shown in the figure.

Several of the functions which the IWF performs include:

- Conversion between SIP_L3 and the AAL3/4 CPCS
- Conversion between 802.6 layer 2 PDUs (slots) and ATM AAL3/4 SAR
- Multiplexing of 802.6 Multiplex IDs (MIDs) into a single ATM VCC

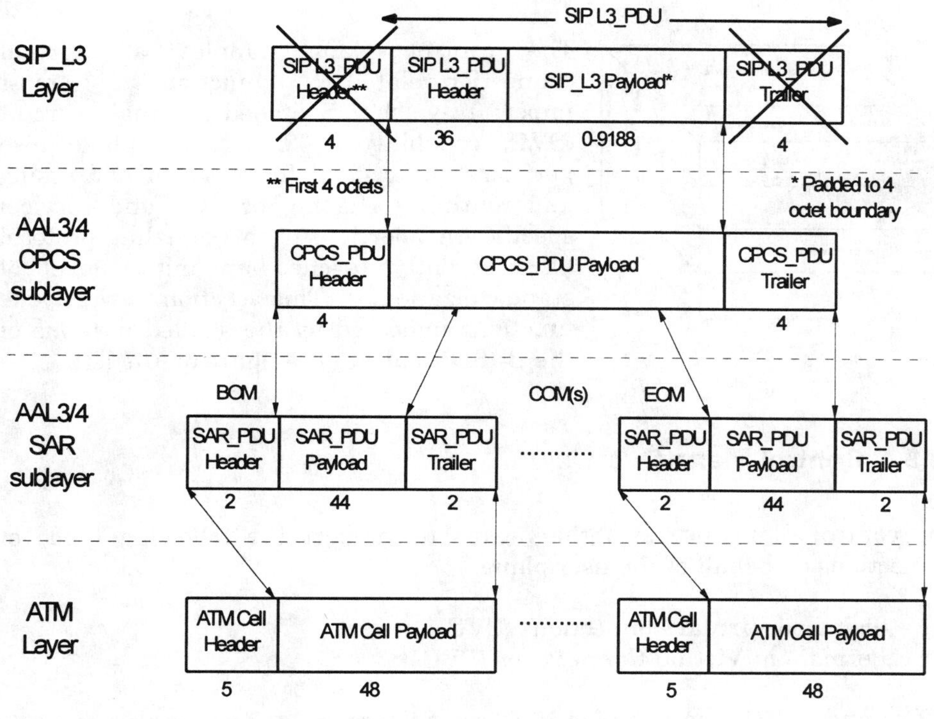

Figure 14.13 SMDS over ATM Protocol Interworking Detail

Figure 14.13 illustrates how the SMDS Interface Protocol (SIP) is carried over ATM using the IWF. The 4-octet header and 4-octet trailer of the SMDS SIP_L3 PDU are removed prior to being inserted in the AAL3/4 CPCS PDU. Padding of the truncated SIP_L3 PDU must be performed to ensure that 4-octet alignment is achieved in the AAL3/4 CPCS PDU. The operation of AAL3/4 Segmentation And Reassembly (SAR) using Beginning, Continuation, and End Of Message (BOM, COM, and EOM) mapping to ATM cells is also illustrated in the figure.

The mapping between the SMDS access class credit manager parameters and the ATM traffic parameters is a key function. This may be performed as described in Section B.2 of Appendix B in the ATM Forum version 3.1 UNI Specification using the peak and sustainable cell rates, or using the peak rate only as described in Appendix A of the SIG/E-SIG/ATM Forum specification.

14.3 CONTROL PLANE AAL

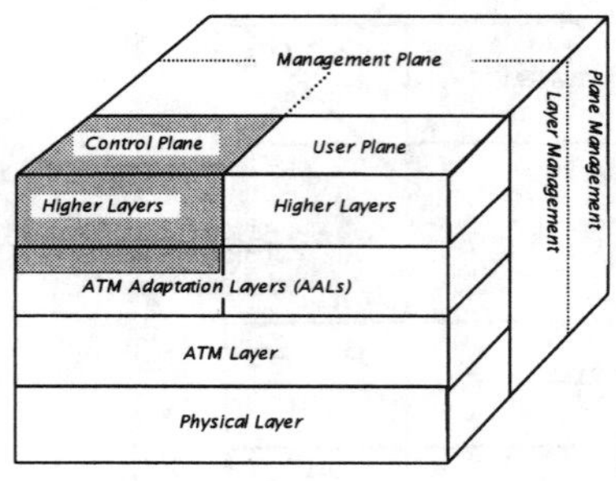

The control plane handles all virtual connection-related functions, most importantly the Switched Virtual Circuit (SVC) capability. The control plane also performs the critical functions of addressing and routing. The higher-layer and service-specific AAL portions of the signaling protocol have recently reached an initial level of standardization. This section covers the functions indicated by the shaded portions of the B-ISDN cube in the figure on the left.

14.3.1 Control Plane Overview

The control plane provides the means to support the following types of connections on behalf of the user plane:

* Switched Virtual Connections (SVCs)
* Permanent Virtual Connections (PVCs)

SVCs and PVCs can be either point-to-point, point-to-multipoint, or multipoint-to-point Virtual Path Connections (VPCs) or Virtual Circuit Connections (VCCs), as defined in Chapter 4. A VPC or VCC provides a specified Quality of Service (QoS) with a certain bandwidth defined by traffic parameters in an ATM-layer traffic contract. The entire B-ISDN architecture must support the user's application needs to be successful.

14.3.2 Control Plane Architecture and Signaling

The signaling protocol architecture of the control plane is very similar to that of Narrowband Integrated Services Digital Network (N-ISDN) as depicted in Figure 14.14.

The specifications for the Signaling AAL (SAAL) are being developed in the ITU-T and are being adopted by ANSI and the ATM Forum. ITU-T Recommendation Q.2931 (previously called Q.93B) specifies the B-ISDN signaling on the ATM UNI. Q.2931 was derived from both the Q.931 UNI signaling protocol specified for N-ISDN and the Q.933 UNI signaling protocol for frame relay. The formal name for the ATM UNI signaling protocol is the Digital subscriber Signaling System 2 (DSS2), while the name for ISDN UNI signaling was DSS1. ITU-T Recommendation Q.2130 (previously called Q.SAAL.2) specifies the Service Specific Coordination Function (SSCF) for the UNI. ITU-T Recommendation Q.2110 (previously called Q.SAAL.1) specifies Service Specific Connection-Oriented Protocol (SSCOP). The ISDN User Part (ISUP) is being adapted in a similar way to broadband as the UNI protocol was in defining the broadband NNI signaling, which is called B-ISUP. The B-ISUP protocol operates over the Message Transfer Protocol 3 (MTP3), identical to that used in Signaling System 7 (SS7) for out-of-band N-ISDN and voice signaling. This will allow B-ISDN network signaling the flexibility to operate over existing signaling networks or directly over new ATM networks. The series of ITU-T Recommendations Q.2761 through Q.2764 specify the B-ISUP protocol. ITU-T Recommendation Q.2140 specifies the SSCF at the NNI. The NNI signaling uses the same SSCOP protocol as the UNI.

14.3.3 Control Plane Addressing and Routing Defined

There are two capabilities that are critical to a switched network: addressing and routing. *Addressing* occurs at the ATM VPI/VCI level and at the logical network level. Since the VPI/VCI is unique only to a physical transmission path, there is a need to have a higher-level address that is unique across at least each network. Ideally, the address should be unique across all networks in order to provide universal connectivity. Once each entity involved in switching virtual connections has a unique address, there is another even more onerous problem of finding a route from the calling party to the called party. This problem is solved by using *routing*.

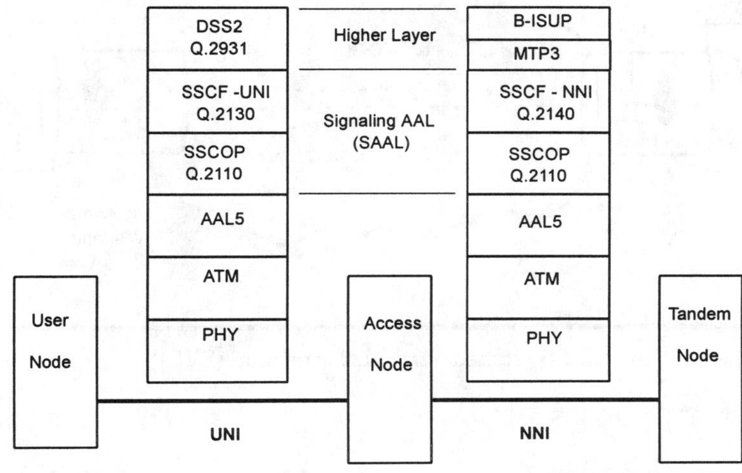

Figure 14.14 Overview of Control Plane Architecture

14.3.4 ATM Layer VPI/VCI Level Addressing

The signaling protocol automatically assigns the VPI/VCI values to ATM addresses and physical ATM UNI ports based upon the type of SVC requested according to the following set of rules: either point-to-point or point-to-multipoint. A physical ATM UNI port must have at least one unique ATM address. An ATM UNI port may also have more than one ATM address.

Recall that a VCC or VPC is defined in only one direction; that is, it is simplex. A point-to-point SVC (or a PVC) is a pair of simplex VCCs or VPCs: a forward connection from the calling party to the called party, and a backward connection from the called party as illustrated in Figure 14.15. The forward and backward VCC or VPC can have different traffic parameters. A point-to-point SVC is defined by the forward and backward VPI (and VCI for a VCC) as well as the ATM address associated with the physical ATM UNI ports on each end of the connection. The VPI and VCI assignment can be different for the forward and backward directions of a VPC or VCC at the same end of the connection as well as being different from the other end of the connection. A convention where the VPI (and VCI for a VCC) is identical at the same end of a connection may be used, and is the most common implementation method.

A point-to-multipoint SVC (or PVC) is defined by the VPI and the ATM address associated with the physical ATM UNI port of the root node, and the ATM address and VPI and VCI for each leaf node of the connection, as shown in Figure 14.16.

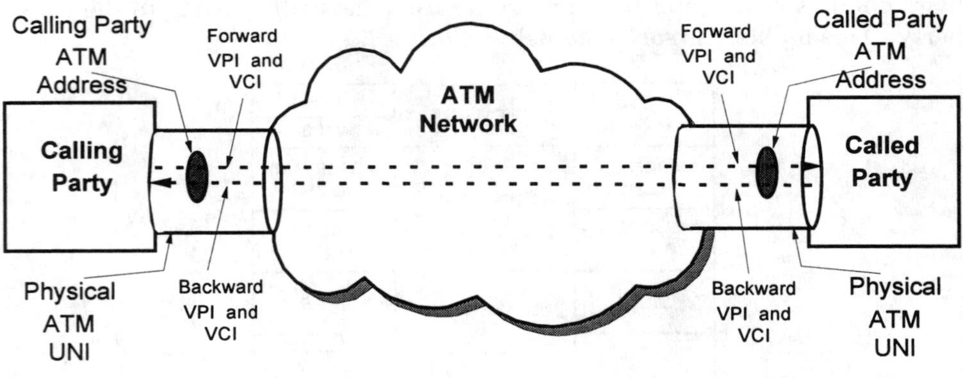

Figure 14.15 Point-to-Point Switched Virtual Connection (SVC)

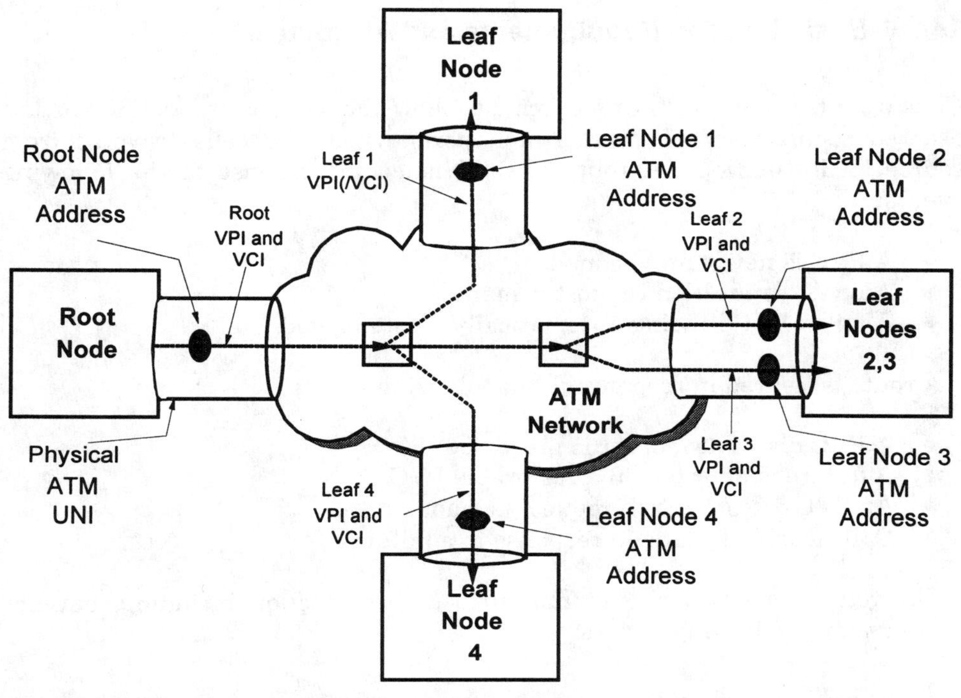

Figure 14.16 Point-to-Multipoint Switched Virtual Connection (SVC)

There is essentially only a forward direction because the backward direction is allocated zero bandwidth. Note that more than one VPI/VCI value and ATM address can be assigned to a physical interface as part of the point-to-multipoint connection. This means that the number of physical ATM UNI ports is always less than or equal to the number of logical leaf endpoints of the point-to-multipoint connection. The implementation of a point-to-multipoint connection should efficiently replicate cells within the network. A minimum spanning tree is an efficient method of constructing a point-to-multipoint connection, as illustrated in Figure 14.16.

14.3.5 ATM Control Plane (SVC) Addressing

Currently two types of ATM Control Plane (SVC) addressing plans are being considered in the standards bodies to identify an ATM UNI address: the Network Service Access Point (NSAP) format defined in ISO 8348, CCITT X.213, and CCITT E.164 standards. Details on both can be found in McDysan and Spohn's *ATM: Theory and Application.*

14.3.6 Basic Routing Requirements and Attributes

Cells from the same VPC or VCC must follow the same route, defined as the ordered sequence of physical switch ports which the cells traverse from source to destination. A route is established in response to the following events:

- A PVC is newly provisioned.
- An SVC connection request is made.
- A failed PVC is being automatically reestablished.

A route is cleared in response to the following events:

- A PVC disconnect order is processed.
- A failure is detected on a restorable PVC.
- An SVC disconnection request is made.
- Call clearing is done in response to a failure.

The route traversed should minimize a cost function including, but not limited to, the following factors:

- Delay
- Economic expense
- Balance utilization (when multiple links are present between a node-pair)

There are desirable attributes to follow when designing an ATM layer routing scheme. Attributes of the routing scheme include at least the following:

- Simplicity
- Automatic determination of least-cost route(s)
- Ease of managing changes in the network in terms of new links and nodes
- Scaling of the routing scheme to a large network

14.3.7 A Simple ATM Layer VCC Routing Design

A simple routing design for VCCs utilizes routing based upon the VPI value only. Each physical node is assigned a VPI value, which means that it is a VPC endpoint, as illustrated in Figure 14.17.

Every node can route traffic to a destination node using a VPC connecting point with the VPI corresponding to the destination node number. This routing is accomplished by each node — knowing that the tandem nodes will connect this VPC through to the destination node.

The principal advantage of this method is that it is very simple — no VPI or VCI translation is required. This method has two main disadvantages: it is inefficient since VPIs are allocated on routes that are not used and it limits the number of VPCs that can be assigned to user applications.

14.3.8 Control Plane Protocol Model

Figure 14.18 illustrates the protocol model for the Signaling AAL (SAAL). The Common Part AAL (CP-AAL) is AAL5 was previously defined. The SSCS portion of the SAAL is composed of the following two protocols:

- Service Specific Coordination Function (SSCF)
- Service Specific Connection-Oriented Protocol (SSCOP)

The SSCF provides the following services to the SAAL user:

- Independence from the underlying layers
- Unacknowledged data transfer mode
- Assured data transfer mode

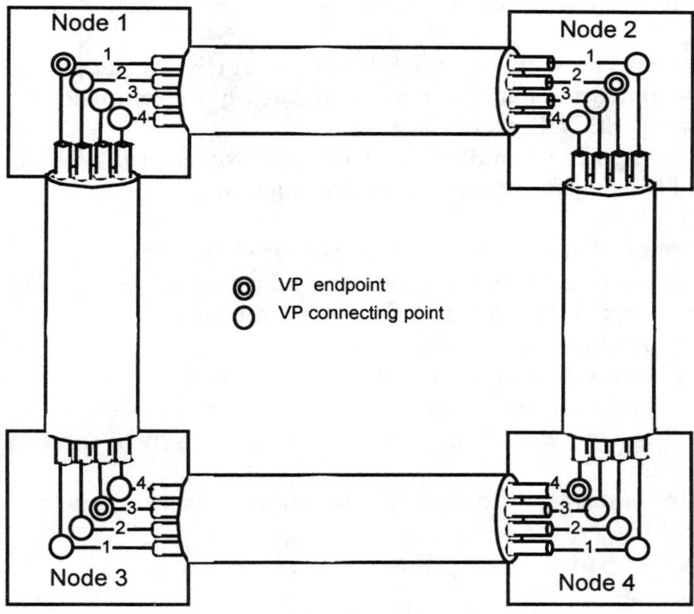

Figure 14.17 Illustration of Simple VPC-Based Routing

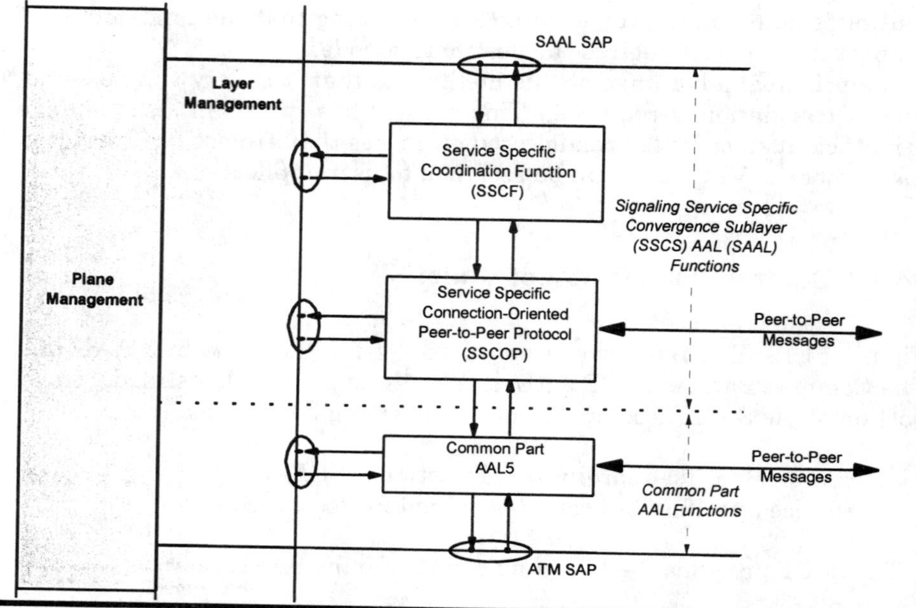

Figure 14.18 Signaling AAL (SAAL) Layered Protocol Model

- Transparent relay of information
- Establishment of connections for assured data transfer mode

The SSCF provides these capabilities primarily by mapping between a simple state machine for the user and the more complex state machine employed by the SSCOP protocol.

The Service Specific Connection-Oriented Protocol (SSCOP) is a peer-to-peer protocol that performs the following functions:

- Guaranteed sequence integrity, or ordered delivery
- Error correction via error detection and retransmission
- Receiver-based flow control of the transmitter
- Error reporting to layer management
- Keep-alive messaging when other data is not being transferred
- Local retrieval of unacknowledged or enqueued messages
- Capability to establish, disconnect, and synchronize an SSCOP connection
- Transfer of user data in either unassured or assured mode
- Protocol level error detection
- Status reporting between peer entities

SSCOP is a fairly complicated protocol, but is specified in the same level of detail as a successful protocol like HDLC. The unassured mode is a simple unacknowledged datagram protocol, similar to the User Datagram Protocol (UDP).

SSCOP PDUs also employ a 24-bit sequence number that allows very high sustained rates to be achieved in a window-flow-controlled protocol such as the Transmission Control Protocol (TCP).

The SAAL primitives are provided at the SAAL Service Access Point (SAP). The CP AAL5 interfaces with the ATM layer at the ATM SAP. There is a one-to-one correspondence between an SAAL SAP and an ATM SAP. The signaling SSCF and SSCOP protocols and the CP-AAL are all managed as separate layers, by corresponding layer management functions as indicated on the left-hand side of Figure 14.18. Layer management is responsible for setting parameters in the individual layer protocols and monitoring their state and performance. Plane management coordinates across the layer management functions so that the overall end-to-end signaling capability is provided.

14.3.9 Control Plane — Signaling Functions

Many of the control plane signaling functions are currently defined by the ATM Forum and the ITU-T. The current version of the ATM Forum UNI Signaling Specification version 3.1 and the ITU-T Q.2931 standard are closely aligned.

The major functions defined in ITU-T Recommendation Q.2931 are:

- Point-to-point connection setup and release
- VPI/VCI selection and assignment
- Quality of Service (QoS) class request
- Identification of calling party
- Basic error handling
- Communication of specific information in setup request
- Subaddress support
- Specification of Peak Cell Rate (PCR) traffic parameters
- Transit network selection

The ATM Forum UNI Specification version 3.1 does not require the following capabilities from Q.2931:

- No alerting message sent to called party
- No VPI/VCI selection or negotiation
- No overlap sending
- No interworking with N-ISDN
- No subaddress support
- Only a single transit network may be selected

The ATM Forum UNI Specification version 3.1 defines the following capabilities in addition to Q.2931:

- Support for a call originator setup of a point-to-multipoint call
- Extensions to support symmetric operation
- Addition of sustainable cell rate and maximum burst size traffic parameters
- Additional information elements for point-to-multipoint endpoints
- Additional NSAP address structures

There is a general intention stated by both the ITU-T and the ATM Forum to align the specifications of future releases.

The ITU-T has specified a capability set 2 that defines a set of capabilities that will be standardized next. These capabilities must first be described in more detail before protocol standardization can begin. The following general functions are part of capability set 2:

- Specification of a call model where each call may have multiple connections, for example, in multimedia
- Support for a distributed point-to-multipoint call setup protocol
- Renegotiation of traffic parameters during the course of a connection
- Support for multipoint and multipoint-to-point calls
- Specification of metasignaling, which establishes additional connections for signaling

Information on the signaling messages and their key parameters, the basics of the signaling protocol can be found in McDysan and Spohn's ATM:Theory and Application.

14.4 MANAGEMENT PLANE

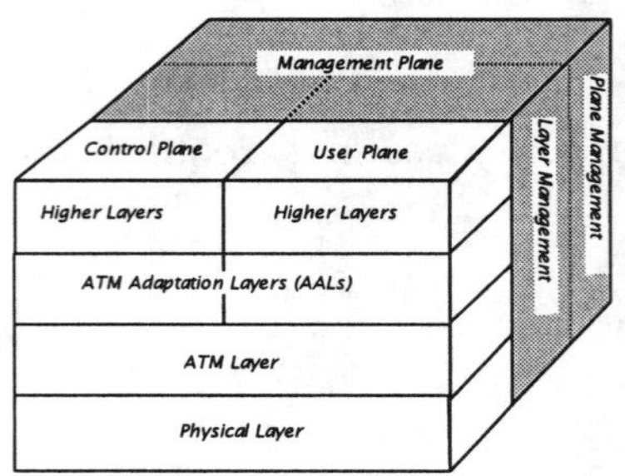

The management plane covers the layer management and plane management functions as shown in the B-ISDN cube on the left. Layer management interfaces with the PHYsical, ATM, ATM Adaptation Layer (AAL), and higher layers. Plane management is responsible for coordination across layers and planes in support of the user and control planes through layer management facilities. This ensures that everything works properly. Layer management will be discussed first, followed by plane management.

14.4.1 Layer Management

Layer management has a management interface to the PHYsical, ATM, AAL, and higher-layer protocol entities in both the control and user planes as depicted in Figure 14.19. This two-dimensional view is constructed by cutting the B-ISDN cube open from the back and then folding it out flat. This view illustrates the oversight role of plane management as well. Plane management only interfaces with layer management, which provides interfaces to the user and control plane layers. Standards for these management interfaces are being defined by the ITU-T and ANSI for telecommunications equipment using the Common Management Information Protocol (CMIP), and by the IETF for data communications equipment using the Simple Network Management Protocol (SNMP).

Layer management has the responsibility for monitoring the user and control plane for faults, generating alarms, and taking corrective actions, as well as monitoring for compliance to the performance stated in the traffic contract. The operation and maintenance information functions found within specific layers are handled by layer management. These functions include fault management, performance management, and configuration management. The standards for PHY layer management are very mature. The standards for ATM layer fault and performance management are nearing the first stage of usability. Standardization for management for the AAL and higher layers is just beginning.

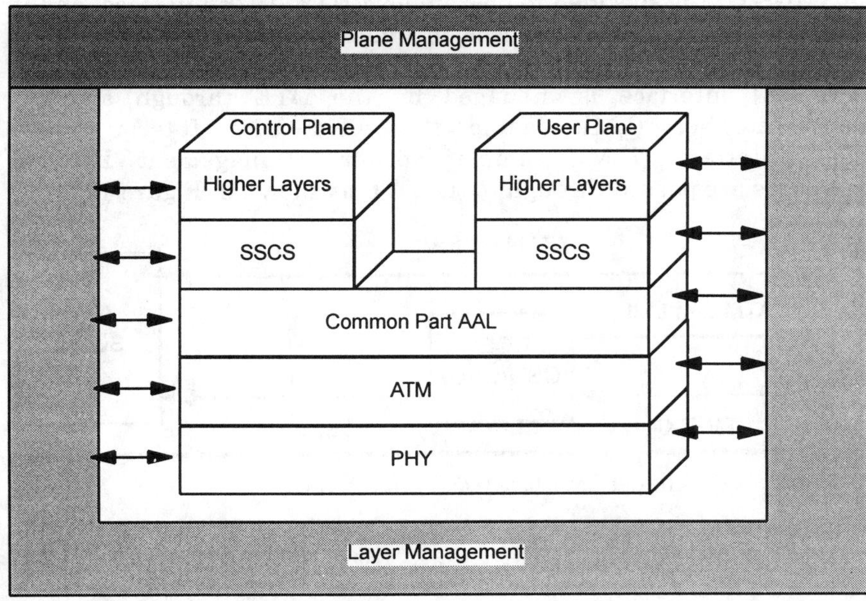

Figure 14.19 Layer Management in Relation to the User and Control Planes

14.4.2 Plane Management

Plane management has no defined structure, but instead performs management functions and coordination across all layers and planes in the entire system. The Telecommunication Management Network (TMN) architecture developed by the ITU-T for managing all types of telecommunications networks is being extended to perform the B-ISDN plane management role.

14.5 DATA EXCHANGE INTERFACE (DXI)

Many users have asked the following question: What if I want the capabilities of ATM over the WAN, but I can't afford the cost of a DS3 or OC-3 access line? The answer could be the ATM Forum specified ATM Data eXchange Interface (DXI), which supports either the V.35, RS449, or the HSSI DTE-DCE interface at speeds from several kbps up to and including 50 Mbps. ATM DXI specifies the interface between a DTE, such as a router, and a DCE, usually called an ATM CSU/DSU, which provides the conversion to an ATM UNI, as illustrated in Figure 14.20. The ATM DXI is normally thought of as a DTE-DCE interface specification. The Frame Relay UNI (FUNI) protocol was defined for longer distance access over *n*xDS0, DS1, and *n*xDS1 access lines. The SMDS DXI is specified to operate as a DTE -DCE interface, and it is likely that the ATM DXI will be used in this manner as well. The ATM DXI is an example of relatively simple network interworking with ATM.

The ATM DXI interface is managed by the DTE through a Local Management Interface (LMI), while the ATM UNI Interim Local Management Interface (ILMI) Simple Network Management Protocol (SNMP) messages are passed through to the DTE as shown in Figure 14.20.

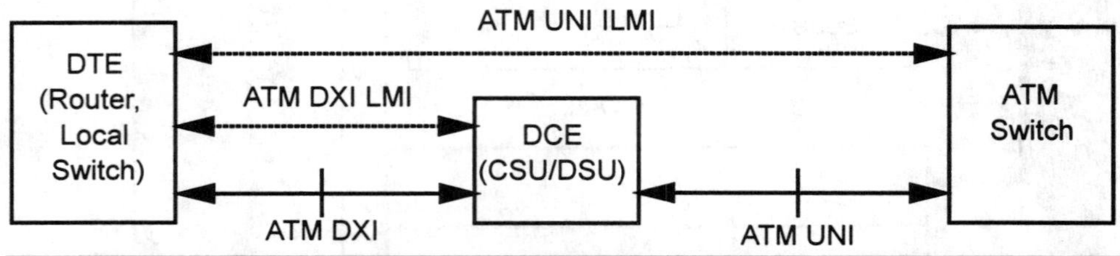

Figure 14.20 ATM Data eXchange Interface (DXI) Configuration

Table 14.1 Summary of ATM DXI Mode Characteristics

Characteristic	Mode 1a	Mode 1b	Mode 2
Maximum number of VCCs	1023	1023	16,777,215
AAL5 Support	Yes	Yes	Yes
AAL3/4 Support	No	Yes	Yes
Maximum DTE SDU Length			
AAL5	9232	9232	65,535
AAL3/4	N/A	9224	65,535
Bits in FCS	16	16	32

Let's now take a look at the three major modes of DXI: mode 1a, mode 1b, and mode 2, whose characteristics are summarized in Table 14.1. The maximum number of VCCs supported is determined by the number of addressing bits: 10 for mode 1 and 24 for mode 2. AAL5 is supported in all modes, while AAL3/4 is a configuration option in modes 1b and 2 with maximum DTE Service Data Unit (SDU) length for each AAL, as indicated in Table 14.1. The number of Frame Check Sequence (FCS) bits required usually determines whether ATM DXI support will be a software upgrade for 16 bits in mode 1 or a hardware change for 32 bits in mode 2. The mode 1 option will likely be the choice for existing hardware, while mode 2 will likely be supported by much of the newer hardware.

The protocols and operation of modes 1a, 1b, and 2 will now be covered.

14.5.1 ATM DXI — Mode 1a and Mode 1b

ATM DXI Mode 1 supports two implementations. Both mode 1a and 1b define DCE support for AAL5 as shown in Figure 14.21. The DTE Service Data Unit (SDU) is encapsulated in the AAL5 CPCS and then segmented into ATM cells using the AAL5 Common Part Convergence Sublayer (CPCS) and Segmentation And Reassembly (SAR) sublayer functions as defined in Chapter 12. The 2-octet DXI header defined later in this section prefixes the DTE SDU. The 2-octet Frame Check Sequence (FCS) is the same as that used in frame relay and HDLC, and hence much existing DTE hardware can be modified to support mode 1.

Mode 1b adds support for the AAL3/4 CPCS and SAR on a per-VCC basis, as shown in Figure 14.22. The DTE must know that the DCE is operating in mode 1b AAL3/4 since it must add the 4 octets for both the CPCS PDU header and trailer, as indicated in the figure. This decreases the maximum-length DTE SDU by 8 octets. The same 2-octet DXI header used for the AAL5 VCC operation is employed.

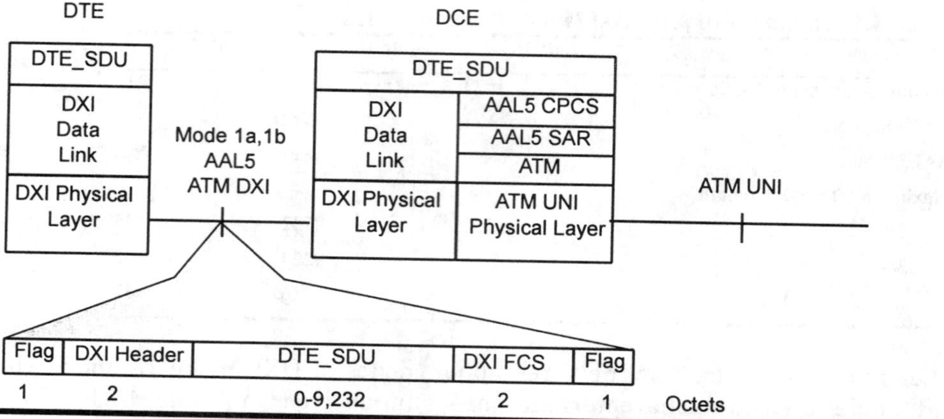

Figure 14.21 Modes 1a and 1b DXI Using AAL5

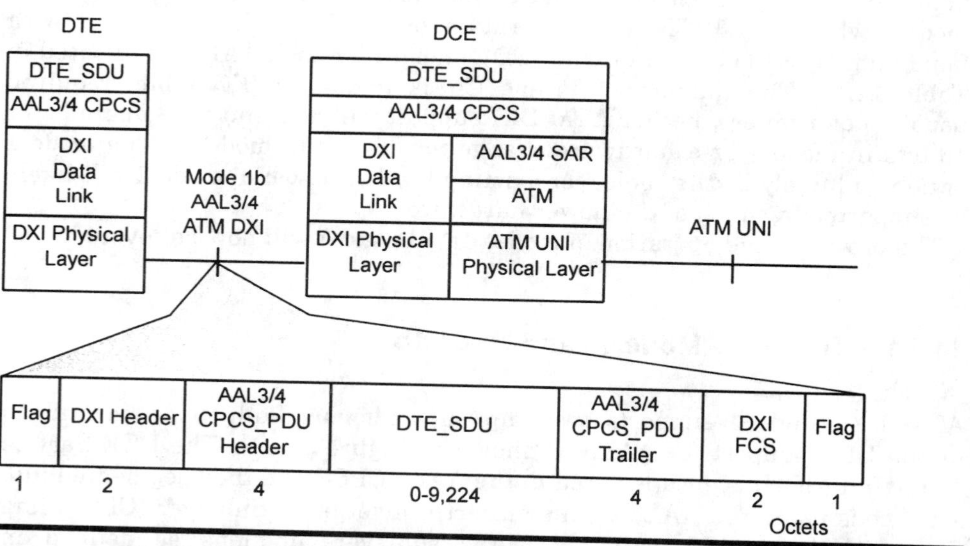

Figure 14.22 Mode 1b ATM DXI Using AAL3/4

14.5.2 ATM DXI — Mode 2

Mode 2 uses the same interface between DTE and DCE regardless of whether the VCC is configured for AAL5 or AAL3/4, as shown in Figure 14.23.

The DTE must place the DTE SDU inside the AAL3/4 CPCS header and trailer, and then the DCE performs the appropriate function depending upon whether the VCC is configured for AAL3/4 or AAL5. The DCE operates the same as in mode 1b for a VCC configured for AAL3/4, performing the AAL3/4 SAR on the AAL3/4 CPCS_PDU as shown in the top part of Figure 14.23.

The DCE must first extract the DTE_SDU from the AAL3/4 CPCS_PDU for a VCC configured to operate in AAL5, as shown in the bottom half of the figure. The net effect of these two transformations is that a mode 2 DCE can interoperate with a mode 1 DCE. The mode 2 DXI frame has a 4-octet header and a 4-octet FCS, which will usually require new hardware. Because the FCS is longer, the maximum DTE_SDU length can be larger. The 32-bit FCS used in the DXI is the same as that used for FDDI and AAL5.

14.5.3 ATM DXI Header Formats

Figure 14.24 illustrates the details of the 2- and 4-octet DXI header structure. The DXI Frame Address (DFA) is mapped into the low order bits of the VPI/VCI by the DCE. The Congestion Notification (CN) is mapped from the last ATM cell of the PDU's Payload Type (PT) congestion indication. The DTE can set the CLP bit so that the DCE will in turn set the CLP bit in the ATM cell header with the same value, thus allowing the user to mark some PDUs as low loss priority. A great deal of similarity can be found when comparing these formats to the frame relay Service Specific Convergence Sublayer (SSCS) formats later in this chapter.

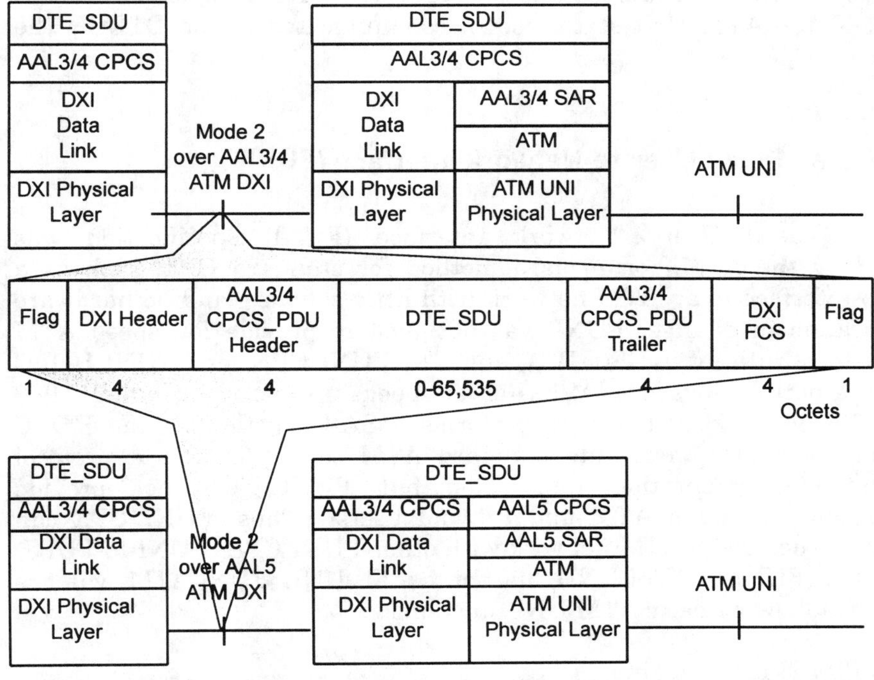

Figure 14.23 Mode 2 ATM DXI Using AAL3/4 or AAL5

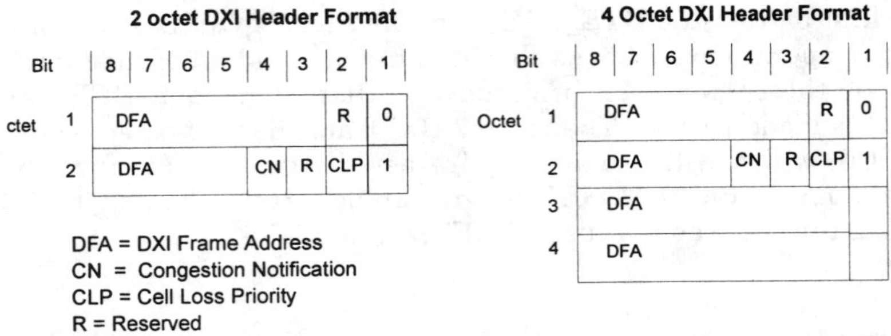

Figure 14.24 ATM 2- and 4-Octet DXI Header Formats

14.5.4 Local Management Interface (LMI) Summarized

The DXI Local Management Interface (LMI) defines a protocol for the exchange of SNMP GetRequest, GetNextRequest, SetRequest, Response, and Trap messages between the DTE and the DCE. The LMI allows the DTE to set or query (Get) the mode of the DXI interface as either 1a, 1b, or 2. The LMI also allows the DTE to set or query the AAL assigned on a per-VCC basis as indexed by the DXI Frame Address (DFA). A shortcoming of the current LMI is that the ATM UNI status is not communicated to the DTE by the DCE.

14.5.5 Frame Relay User-to-Network Interface (FUNI)

The Frame-based User-to-Network Interface (FUNI) specification was developed by the ATM Forum as a method for standard CPE, such as a router, to interface to an ATM network with little software and no hardware reconfiguration or change. FUNI was designed to provide low-speed ATM access protocol rates of *n*xDS0, DS1, and E1. FUNI CPE send FUNI HDLC frames to a network-based ATM switch at speeds up to and including 2.048 Mbps. The network switch then performs a SAR function on the HDLC frames and converts them into standard ATM cells. This is a protocol encapsulation segmentation into cells, but FUNI does not provide interoperability between ATM and FR end users. Thus, FUNI CPE can communicate across an ATM network with other FUNI CPE (FUNI-to-FUNI) or ATM UNI (FUNI-to-ATM UNI), but not to a FR UNI. FUNI ATM switches support the following basic ATM UNI functions:

- VPI/VCI multiplexing
- Signaling
- Network management

- Traffic policing
- Operations, Administration, and Maintenance (OAM) functions
- VBR and Unspecified Bit Rate (UBR) traffic

Future enhancements to the FUNI will include MIB definitions and switched-on-demand FUNI connections.

14.6 ATM PUBLIC SERVICES

There are many factors to consider when choosing a public network ATM-based service: the type and speed of access, the CPE support, the Quality of Service (QoS) classes offered, interworking support, network management support, and billing options. The decision factors for choosing an ATM-based service will now be covered. First, public ATM network architectures are examined, and then public network ATM services are reviewed.

14.6.1 Public ATM Network Architectures

As ATM technology proliferates, it provides an evolutionary path from the traditional networks based on a TDM architecture to an ATM-based architecture. An architecture based upon ATM technology utilizes ATM switches in both the Central Office (CO) and on the Customer Premises Equipment (CPE). ATM can also be employed in cross-connects, routers, gateways, workstations, and IWFs, as shown in Figure 14.25. Also, most public ATM-based networks employ a SONET or SDH backbone. Figure 14.25 shows a network example where users either interface to the ATM network directly via an ATM UNI, an ATM DXI interface, or a frame relay interface, achieve access to an SMDS connectionless server, or interface through multiple other protocols through an MultiProtocol (MP) interworking function.

14.6.2 ATM Service Suite

The suite of possible ATM services includes the following:

- ATM Cell Relay Service (CRS)
- Virtual Path or Virtual Channel Connections (VPC or VCC)
- Point-to-point or point-to-multipoint connections
- Permanent Virtual Connection (PVC)
- Switched Virtual Connection (SVC)

- Bandwidth reservation
- Frame relay network and service interworking with ATM
- SMDS access over ATM
- Multiprotocol (e.g., IP) interworking over ATM
- X.25 interworking over ATM
- Voice over ATM

14.6.3 Public ATM Services and Providers

Commercial and private ATM service offerings have been announced and are offered by the traditional Local Exchange Carriers (LECs), Competitive Access Providers (CAPs), Independent Service Providers (ISPs), IntereXchange Carriers (IXCs), value-added service providers, and international Postal Telephone and Telegraph (PTT) operators. These include Ameritech, Bell Atlantic, Bell South, GTE, MFS Datanet, NYNEX, Pacific Bell, SBC, US West, AT&T, BT, LDDS Worldcom, MCI, MFS Datanet, Sprint, Telecom Finland, and Time Warner.

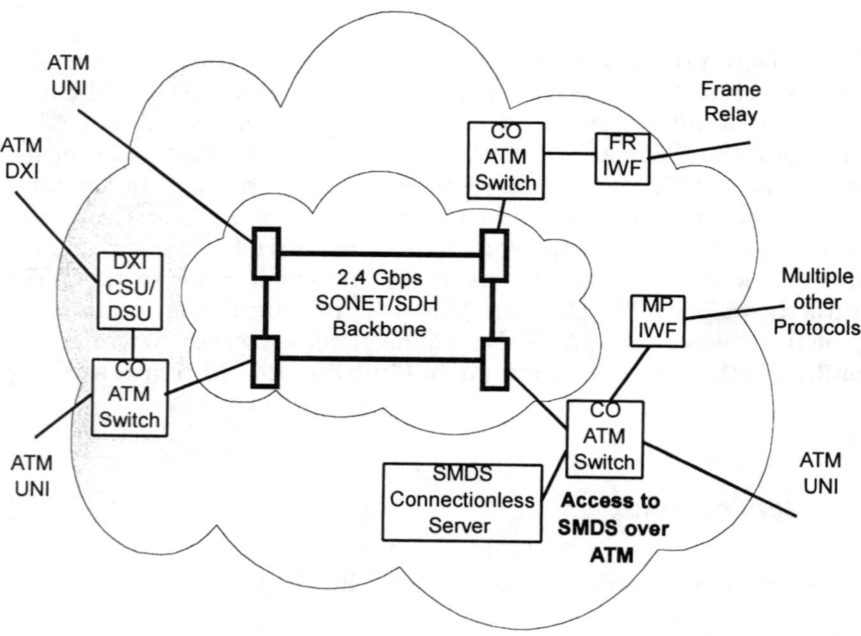

Figure 14.25 ATM-Based Network Services Using a SONET Backbone

Most backbones are composed of DS3s, with plans to later upgrade to OC-3 with T1/E1 and DS3/E3 access speeds. Current service offerings include CBR service, VBR service, PVC Circuit Emulation, and DS1/DS3 channel extension. Methods of choice for public data providers can be found in Chapter 18.

14.7 CHALLENGES

What are the possible directions for ATM? What is the best case? What is the worst case? What is the likely scenario? What standards work is still in progress and nearing completion? This section provides some answers to these questions.

Several major challenges face ATM:

◊ Voice over ATM
◊ ATM support of standard/legacy LAN products
◊ Interconnection of classic IP sub-nets
◊ Further standards for video over ATM
◊ True end-to-end service guarantees over a public network
◊ Wide area ATM backbone public infrastructure issues
◊ Interworking between ATM QoS and IP RSVP
◊ SVC interworking with frame relay and N-ISDN
◊ Costs in line with TDM, FR, and SMDS applications

The ATM Forum has established a number of technical work groups to focus on subjects such as:

⇒ Private Network-to-Network Interface (P-NNI)
⇒ Available Bit Rate (ABR) service introduction
⇒ LAN Emulation Service (LES System Aspects)
⇒ Application Program Interface (API)
⇒ SAA Video Coding

The Private Network-to-Network Interface (P-NNI) will define a routing topology update and signaling protocol that will move users closer towards plug-and-play operation in a multivendor network. The definition of an Available Bit Rate (ABR) service defined by the ATM Forum and the ITU will create a more LAN-like bandwidth on demand environment.

Some of the greatest challenges that lie ahead for ATM are in the area of networking and applications. These are probably the least understood and least standardized — yet most critical — areas to the success of ATM. Applications must be written that interface directly to AAL and QoS classes are a key to ATM success, such as multimedia and IP support for multiple

QoS classes. In this vein, the ATM Forum SAA group is defining the semantics of an Application Programming Interface (API) for ATM. Several proprietary APIs have already been developed. Today, the foremost applications of ATM networking operate in the local environment. Anything that brings ATM closer to the user will drive its success.

The ATM Forum is adopting a structure to get early input from users in the protocol and interface specification process using the Enterprise Network Roundtable (ENR). This is a great experiment that will hopefully deliver needed capabilities to users sooner, and provide a high degree of interoperability.

The IETF has assigned working groups to two major efforts of ATM development:

⇒ Routing Over Large Clouds (ROLC) or large data networks such as ATM, SMDS, and Frame Relay public network services
⇒ IP Maximum Transfer Unit (MTU) over ATM

In summary, ATM networks will offer many capabilities that may yield to success:

⇒ Collapsed Backbone - the ability to collapse multiple LANs on the back-plane of an ATM switch
⇒ Integrated Access - the circuit emulation capabilities that allow circuit-based voice, video and data to share expensive access lines
⇒ Virtual Private Networking and Public Connectivity - carrier-provided virtual networks built on ATM architectures that are more cost-effective than private networks.
⇒ High-Performance Internetworking - an alternative to or hybrid with routers for high-speed and channel extension connectivity
⇒ Protocol Internetworking – with ATM, frame relay, IP, and SMDS interfaces via a portfolio of interworking services.
⇒ High-Performance Server Connections - Moving ATM to the desktop and providing true competition for FDDI, Switched Ethernet, and Fast Ethernet.
⇒ ATM Work groups - ATM adapter cards in high-end workstations and servers.
⇒ Video over ATM

It is forecast that ATM networks will coexist with existing STM based networks for a long time. ATM seems to be the next step in the evolution of universal public networking technologies. ATM should be the star in the ever-evolving multiprotocol network, probably for at least the next five years.

Look for each of these capabilities to play a key role in the future success of ATM.

14.8 REVIEW

This chapter took up where the last one left off, on introducing higher layer ATM protocol functions. An in-depth study of ATM Adaptation Layers (AALs) 1 through 5 was provided along with an overview of the higher layers of the ATM Adaptation Layer (AAL). Overviews were provided for the user plane, along with the control and management planes which support the services provided by the user plane. Frame relay to ATM interworking and access to SMDS via ATM were described.

The AAL protocol model was then introduced in terms of the Convergence Sublayer (CS) and the Segmentation And Reassembly (SAR) sublayer, and the CS was further divided into a Service Specific (SS) and Common Part (CP). The CPCS and SAR were explained in detail focusing on the three AALs that are currently standardized: AAL1, AAL3/4, and AAL5. Definitions of the format and operation, as well as an example, were provided. An example of emulating the DS1 bit stream from a video codec using AAL1 was provided, and the multiplexing that can be performed by AAL3/4 and AAL5 was compared. Finally, two examples illustrated how AAL3/4 can make more efficient use of a VCC in some cases than AAL5 through increased overhead and complexity.

The Data eXchange Interface (DXI) provides a low-speed ATM access protocol. The chapter summarized public ATM services and providers and concluded with a discussion of the challenges ahead and possible future directions.

Chapter

15

SONET

Without debate, fiber optics has thrown a whole new light on the future of communications. The costs of fiber-optic transmission facilities are decreasing as fast as new methods of using fiber-optic cables are growing. Superhighways of fiber-optic cable now ring most major cities and provide terabits worth of bandwidth across the United States. Fiber optics also spans the globe. By the year 2000, fiber will become the predominant transmission medium in many leading industrialized countries. With the advent of these fiber highways come concomitant technologies to effectively utilize this seemingly limitless bandwidth. The market demands of technologies and services such as FDDI, SMDS, and ATM are driving this need for ultra-high-speed transport.

Synchronous Optical NETwork, or SONET, is the harbinger of this new technology wave. SONET represents the North American standard, while the Synchronous Digital Hierarchy (SDH) represents the standard for the rest of the world. SONET and SDH provide a fiber-transmission protocol that offers channel speeds up into gigabits per second. This chapter explores the many facets of SONET and SDH. We start with protocol structure and standards, covering the details of the operation, administration, maintenance, and provisioning (OAM&P) through the interfaces and hardware that allow SONET and SDH to be used as the terabit transport for such services as SMDS, ATM, and other services not yet dreamed of.

15.1 TERMS DEFINED

Synchronous Optical NETwork (SONET) is a Bellcore term for the North American version of the Synchronous Digital Hierarchy (SDH), standardized by the ITU-T worldwide. Its standards are now represented by ANSI and ECSA. SONET was conceived as a method of providing a high-speed, low-error-rate, international, fiber-optic multiplexed transmission standard for interface between the PTTs, IXCs, and LECs. For all standard purposes, SONET is a transport interface and method of transmission only. Thus, it is not a network in itself, but rather network infrastructures are built using SONET technology. As an international standard for network transport, protocol, and architecture, SONET is eliminating the different transmission schemes and rates of North America, Europe, and the Pacific Rim through a common international rate structure. It also provides a technology that allows the major IXCs and PTTs to internationally standardize and control broadband network transport media through a common fiber interface called a *midspan meet*.

Probably the greatest benefits of SONET lies in its in-band operations, administration, maintenance, and provisioning (OAM&P), which will be discussed in this chapter.

The SONET standards continue to evolve through the guidance of Bellcore and the RBHCs, LECs, IXCs, and PTTs. These groups have a vested interest in making SONET work with standards and services like SDH/PDH, SMDS, and ATM. Vendors and service providers consider SONET a common interconnectivity medium for direct fiber services such as SMDS and ATM. With these capabilities, SONET lowers transmission costs and increases transmission efficiency. As these enhanced services grow, so concurrently does the deployment of SONET transmission facilities. And we see some of the IXCs partnering with bypass carriers who are deploying SONET-based gear to offer direct-connect capabilities and services like LAN extension. SONET is proving to be a true international standard for fiber transport interconnectivity. The benefits and drawbacks of SONET will be summarized at the end of this chapter.

SONET uses a transfer mode that defines switching and multiplexing aspects of a digital transmission protocol. The switching technology comprises two types of transfer modes: synchronous and asynchronous. Synchronous Transfer Mode (STM) defines circuit switching technology, while Asynchronous Transfer Mode (ATM) defines cell relay technology. SONET uses both synchronous and asynchronous transfer modes through the use of a fixed data-transfer frame format including user data, management, maintenance, and overhead.

Major terms associated with SONET equipment are Path-Terminating Equipment (PTE), Line-Terminating Equipment (LTE), and Section-Terminating Equipment (STE). The primary user interface at the CPE is the PTE. The next level of access device is the LTE. Both can be terminal, switching, multiplex, or cross-connect devices. STE is primarily regeneration equipment. This points to one of the primary benefits of SONET – the capability to easily consolidate and segregate, or multiplex, traffic through "grooming", similar to a Digital Cross-Connect (DXC).

Let's first take a look at how the ITU-T (previously the CCITT) defines the implementation phases of SONET standards.

15.2 STANDARDS

In 1984, MCI Communications requested that the Exchange Carriers Standards Association (ECSA) develop a standard for a "midspan fiber meet" for IXC interfaces to LECs. Bellcore also requested a method of connecting add/drop multiplexers with DXCs. Both of these requirements, including that of a hierarchical network bandwidth scheme, were formalized in ANSI T1.101, T1.102, T1.105 and T1.106 (Phase I), as well as ITU-T/CCITT G.707, G.708, and G.709. These standards define the topics covered in this chapter.

SONET standards have been introduced in three phases. Each phase presents additional levels of control and operations, administration, maintenance, and provisioning (OAM&P).

15.2.1 Phase I

Phase I as approved by the CCITT in 1988, defines basic transmission rates and characteristics, frame formats and testing, and an optical interface multiplexing scheme. This phase primarily defines the hardware specifications for point-to-point data transport. Phase I supports the initial requirement of an Optical Carrier-*N* (OC-*N*) “midspan fiber meet” at payload level only. It also defines the standard Data Communications Channel (DCC) with basic functions, as well as the basics of the framing and interfaces defined in this chapter.

15.2.2 Phase II

Phase II builds upon the midspan fiber meet for multiple-vendor connectivity and management. Phase II defines:

- OAM&P procedures
- Synchronization
- SONET to B-ISDN interconnectivity
- Pointer adjustments for wander and jitter
- Central Office (CO) electrical interfaces and network advantages
- Imbedded operation channels
- Common Management Information Service Elements (CMISE)
- Point-to-point, add/drop multiplexer capabilities
- Mapping operations into OC-3 from FDDI and ATM tributaries

It also further defines DCC protocols.

Phase II also defines the intraoffice optical interface (called an IAO), which allows equipment to be interconnected at the central office. This interface ranges from 20m to 20km and commonly operates at OC-1, OC-3, and OC-12 rates.

15.2.3 Phase III

Phase III builds upon Phase II by providing all of the OAM&P required for a midspan fiber meet. Additional network management, performance monitoring, and control functions are added, as are DCC standard message sets and addressing schemes for identifying and interconnecting SONET network elements. This allows the passing of DCC information among various vendor implementations of SONET. Phase III also provides for ring and nested protection switching.

15.3 SONET STRUCTURE

The SONET Optical Carrier (OC-*N*) structure follows a strict structure and hierarchy, which maps to the electrical hierarchies of many nations. These OC-*N* levels are then multiplexed to form higher-speed transport circuits that range into the gigabits range and provide an alternative to aggregating multiple DS1 and DS3 transmission facilities. SONET solves many of the network management problems associated with DS3 transmissions. The SONET architecture also maps somewhat to the OSI Reference Model (OSIRM), as do the messaging and file transfer protocols, and offers the only international standard for digital-to-fiber optic communications.

15.3.1 Basic Structure

The basic or primary structure of SONET is built around Synchronous Transport Signal level 1 (STS-1) transport through an Optical Carrier (OC-*N*) signal over fiber optics. An aggregate 51.84 Mbps STS-1 bit stream, when converted from "electrical" to "fiber optic" is called Optical Carrier-1 (OC-1), and is composed of a transmission of 810-byte frames sent at a rate of 8000 times per second. Here the electrical DS3 signal is converted to an OC-1 optical signal, and vice versa. Current SONET speeds range from 51.84 Mbps (OC-1) to 9.95328 Gbps (OC-192); true fractional speeds are achievable, providing virtually any division of bandwidth required. Any subrate signals below OC-1 are multiplexed to form a single OC-1 channel.

TABLE 15.1 SONET STS-N Speed Hierarchy

STS level	Bit Rate (Mbps)	DS0s	DS1s	DS3s
1	51.84	672	28	1
3	155.52	2,016	84	3
6	311.04	4,032	168	6
9	466.56	6,048	252	9
12	622.08	8,064	336	12
18	933.12	12,096	504	18
24	1,244.16	16,128	672	24
36	1,866.24	24,192	1008	36
48	2,488.32	32,256	1344	48
96	4,976.64	64,512	2688	96
192	9,953.28	129,024	5376	192
255*	13,219.20	171,360	7140	255

(* theoretical maximum speed)

TABLE 15.2 SONET Equivalent to Digital Hierarchy

SONET	T-Carrier	USA	Europe	Japan
VT1.5	DS1	1.544	2.048	1.544
VT6	DS2	6.312	8.448	6.312
OC-1	DS3	44.736	34.368	32.064
OC-3	–	–	139.264	97.728

15.3.2 SONET Hierarchy

Table 15.1 shows the SONET speed hierarchy by STS-level, illustrating the number of DS0s, DS1s, and DS3s equivalents. Table 15.2 shows the closest SONET equivalent speed compared with the digital hierarchy existing today between countries. All values are in Mbps.

15.3.3 Multiplexing

SONET provides direct multiplexing of both SONET speeds and current asynchronous and synchronous services into the STS-*N* payload. Payload types range from DS1 and DS3 to OC-3c and OC-12c ATM and SDH/PDH payloads. For example, STS-1 supports direct multiplexing of DS1, DS2, and DS3 clear channel into single or multiple STS-1 envelopes, which are called tributaries. Multiple STS-1 envelopes are multiplexed into an STS-*N* signal.

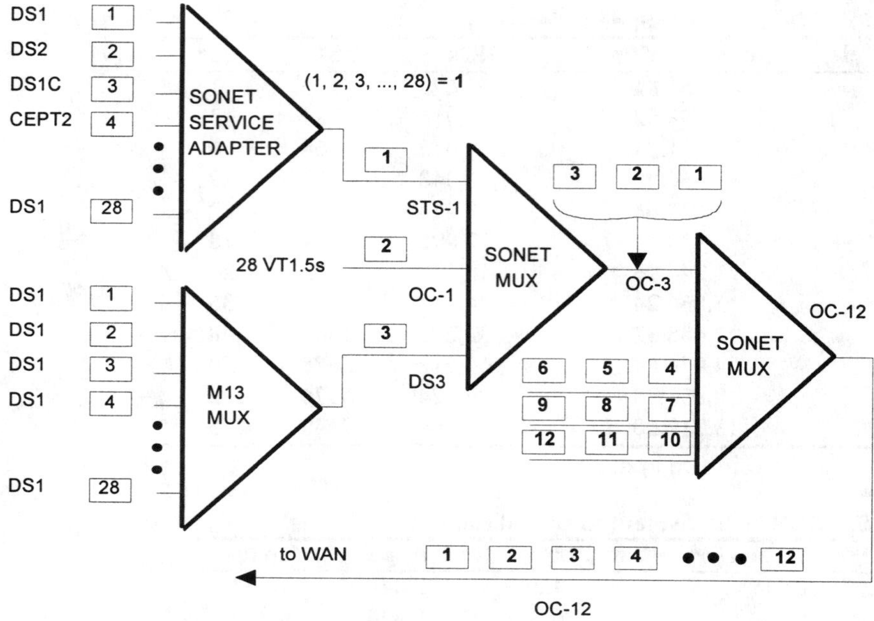

Figure 15.1 SONET Multiplexing

Figure 15.1 shows the method of multiplexing, where users 1 through 28 represent individual DS1, DS2, DS1C and CEPT2 Virtual Tributary (VT) user access circuits, which are first adapted to an STS-1 stream. These streams are then combined with OC-1 and DS3 streams into a SONET mutliplexer, where they are converted to an OC-3 stream. Finally, they are converted to an OC-12 trunk and transmitted across the WAN. This figure also shows an M13 multiplexing 28 DS1s into a single DS3, which the SONET multiplexer converts to an OC-*N* format. Five Mbps worth of overhead is bit-stuffed into the signal to boost the contents and meet the STS-1 rate of 51.84 Mbps. Notice also that the synchronous order in which the subrate channels are transmitted remains constant.

The other major advantage of SONET is that each individual signal down to the DS1 level can be accessed without the need to demultiplex and remultiplex the entire OC-*N* level signal. This is commonly accomplished through a SONET Digital Cross-Connect (DXC) or multiplexer similar to those discussed in Chapter 6.

It is important to note that SONET multiplexing requires an extremely stable clocking source with a stable reference point. Thus, the frequency of every clock within the network must be the same or synchronous with one another. This central clocking source must be at least a Stratum level 3 source, with a Stratum 1 preferred for greatest accuracy.

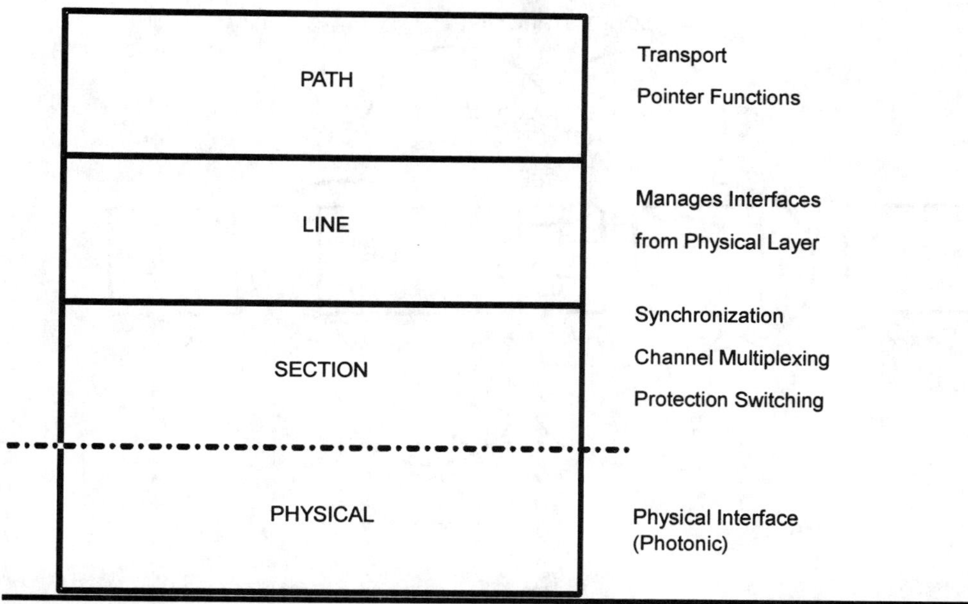

Figure 15.2 Four-Layered SONET Architecture

15.3.4 SONET Architecture Layers

There are four layers to the SONET architecture: physical (or photonic), section, line, and path. These layers can be seen in Figure 15.2. Three of these layers – section, line, and path – roughly correspond to the layers of overhead present in the SONET frame. First, the physical layer defines the physical fiber type, path, and characteristics. The more common examples of the physical interface include 1550-nm dispersion-shifted fiber and 1310-nm conventional glass fiber. The physical layer also includes the many electrical interfaces which become virtual channels within the STS-1 frame.

Secondly, the section layer builds the SONET frames from either lower SONET interfaces or electrical interfaces. Thirdly, the line layer provides synchronization, channel multiplexing, and protection switching. This layer provides the communications channel between line-terminating equipment at the point of STS-1 multiplexing to higher rates, as well as providing management between LTE and STE. The path layer manages the actual data transport across the SONET network, as well as the pointer function. Each layer will be discussed in detail in a subsequent section. Figure 15.3 shows an entire SONET network with each of these interface points shown.

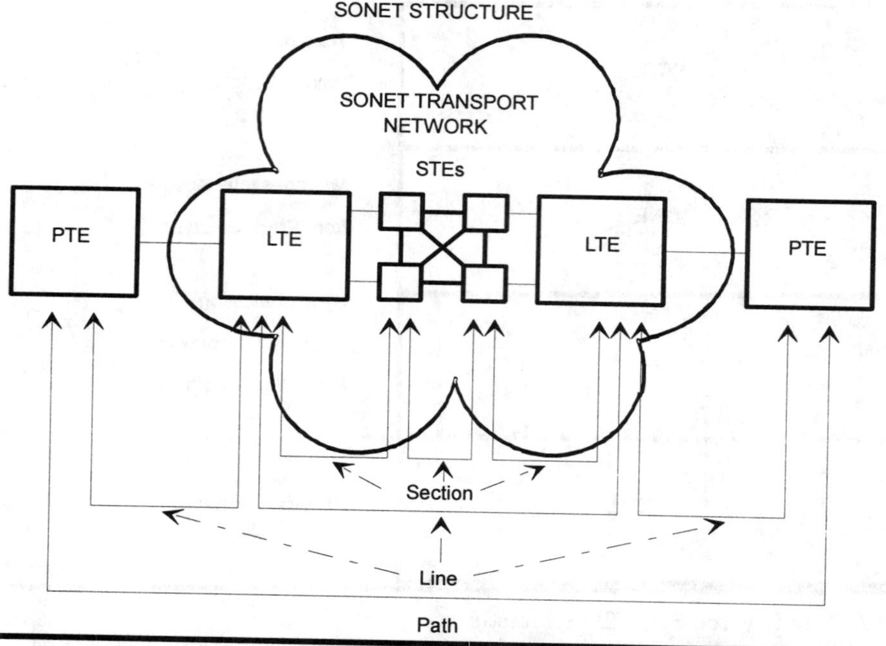

Figure 15.3 SONET Network Structure

15.3.5 SONET Protocol Stack

Figure 15.4 shows the protocol stack used by SONET as defined by Bellcore TR-TSY-00253. This stack parallels the seven-layer OSI reference model. These protocols constitute the Operating Systems (OS) interface to SONET. Phase 1 provides a subset of this stack for file transfer, but uses the RS-232-C, LAPD, and X.25 for file transfer and messaging. Phase II changes the lower levels to 802.3, 802.2, and TCP/IP or ISO 8473. Phase III establishes the standard shown in this figure.

15.3.6 OC-*N* Midspan Fiber Meet

The OC-*N* midspan fiber meet allows CPE, LEC, and IXC hardware from different vendors to interface with each other via SONET. This interface covers basic payload-only connections to payload transport, operations and maintenance information exchange, and automatic protection switching. It provides a single platform base for access from the central office to the CPE. Figure 15.5 illustrates the concept of a midspan fiber meet for both the typical asynchronous interface as well as the new SONET interface.

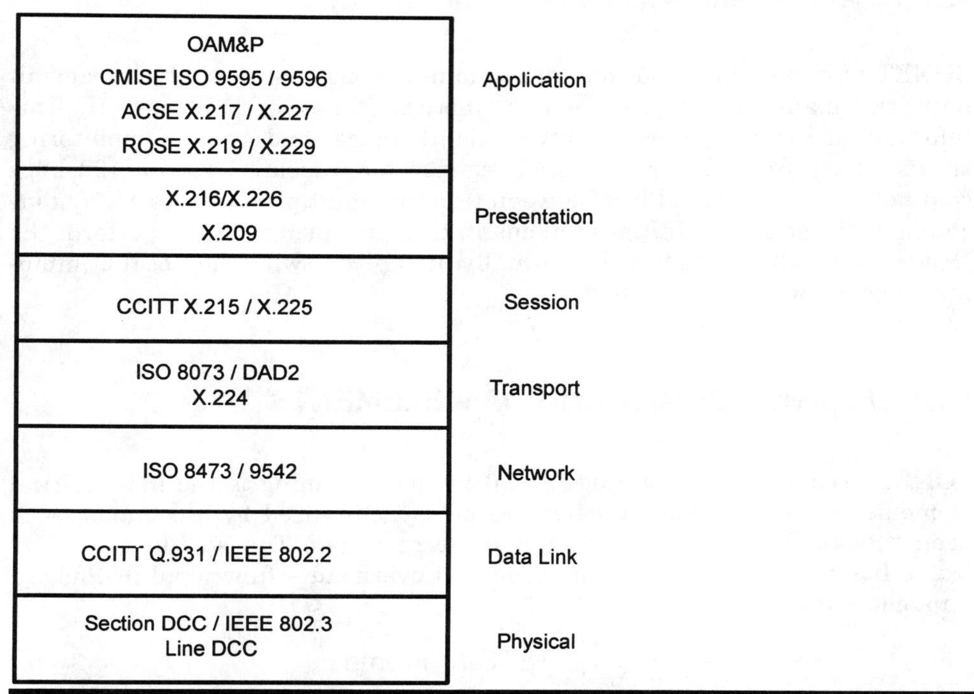

Figure 15.4 SONET Protocol Stack

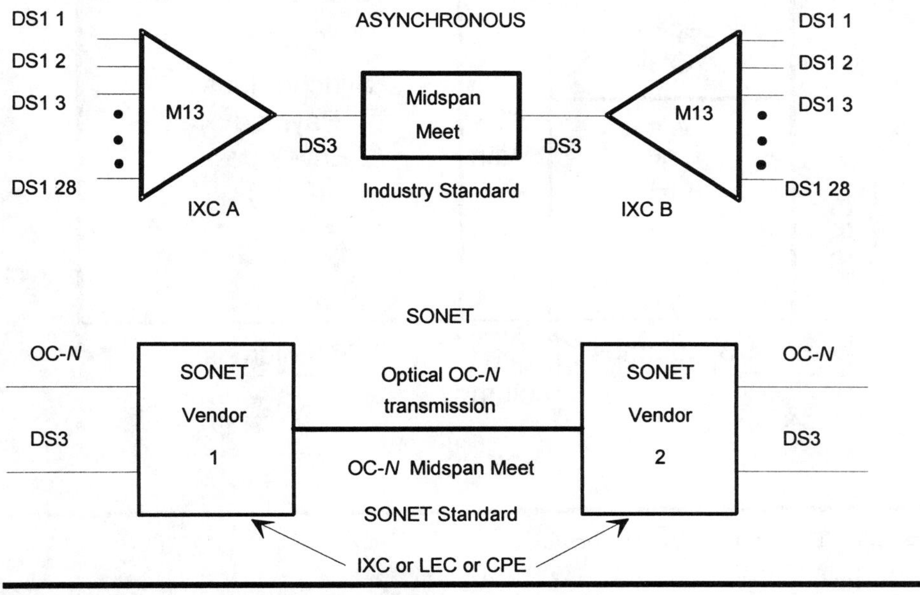

Figure 15.5 SONET Midspan Meet

15.3.7 Data Communications Channels (DCC)

SONET transmissions also contain communications channels which transmit network management information between network elements. This information includes alarm, control, maintenance, and general monitoring status. Each SONET terminal and regenerator (repeater) uses a 192 kbps channel, and each optical line between terminal multiplexers uses a 576 kbps channel for the DCC. Initial implementations are using X.25 to perform the DCC functionality, which will eventually be replaced with the Local Communications Network (LCN) interface.

15.4 FRAME FORMAT AND OAM ELEMENTS

SONET uses a unique framing format for which timing is the most critical element. SONET frame payloads are not synchronized by a common clock even though SONET is a synchronous technology. The standard SONET frame has two major pieces – payload and overhead – functional in Phase I implementations.

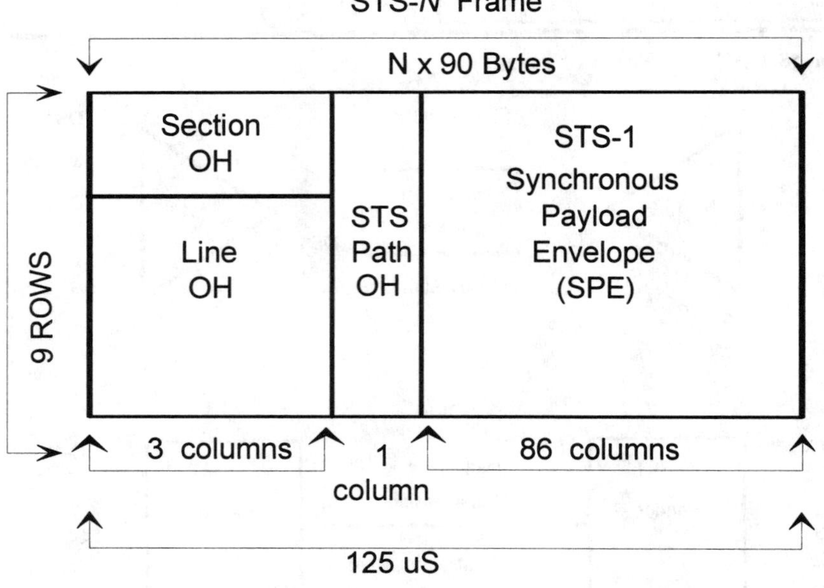

Figure 15.6 STS-*N* Basic Frame Format

15.4.1 Basic Frame Format

The SONET STS-*N* frame format is shown in Figure 15.6. Notice that the frame comprises multiple overhead elements (section, line, and path) and a Synchronous Payload Envelope (SPE). The frame size for an STS-1 SPE is 9 rows × 90 columns (1 byte per column) for a total of 783 bytes per frame (excluding the 27 bytes section and line overhead) or 6480 total bits. The total STS-1 frame of 810 bytes is transmitted each 125 μs, resulting in the basic SONET/STM rate of 51.84 Mbps.

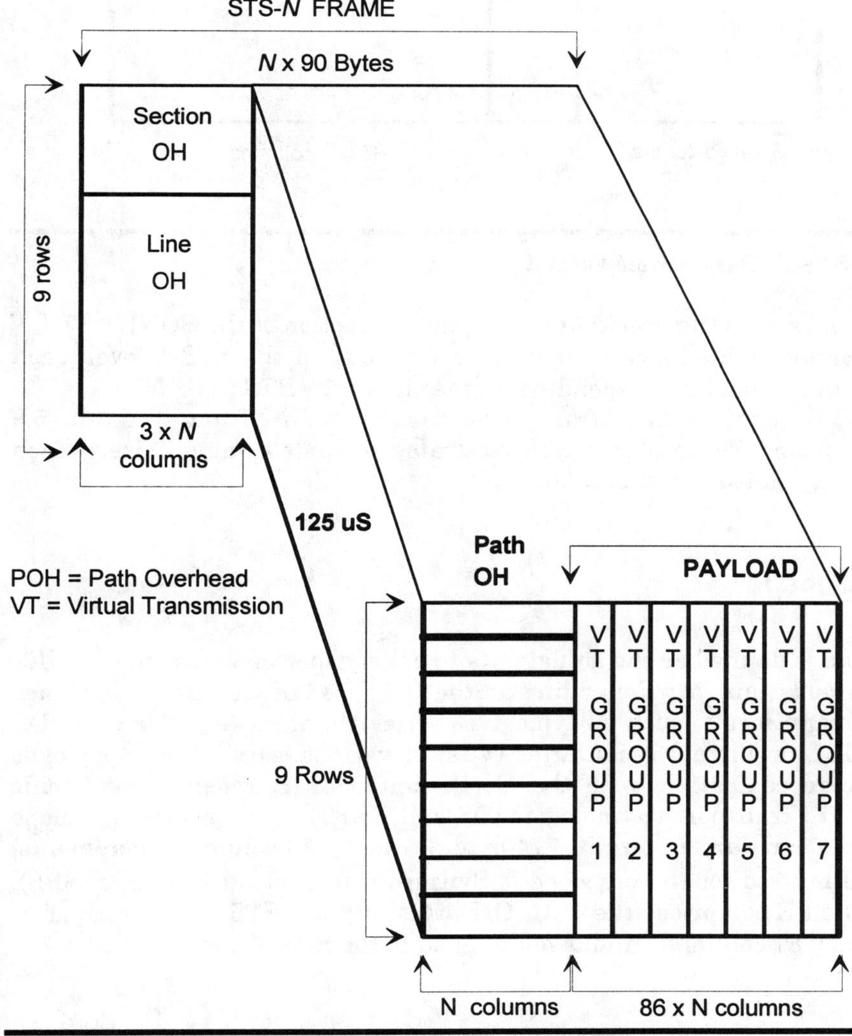

Figure 15.7 STS-*N* Frame Format Breakout

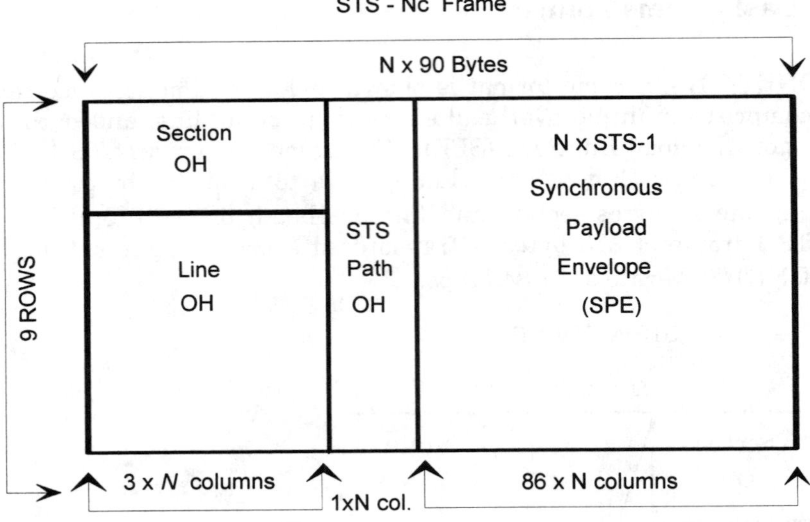

Figure 15.8 STS-Nc Basic Frame Format

Figure 15.7 shows the breakout of the payload section of the SONET STS-*N* frame of undetermined size. For frames larger than the STS-1 level, each column is multiplied by *N* depending on the size of the STS (STS-*N*).

Figure 15.8 shows the basic frame format of the STS-*Nc* frame. Figure 15.9 shows the frame format for a STS-*Nc* frame of undetermined size. Each shows the payload size in a breakout.

15.4.2 Payload

The payload is defined as the actual data to be transported across the SONET path. Payloads can vary depending on the OC speed of transport. Payloads can take many forms, such as typical T-carrier channels (e.g., DS3), FDDI, SMDS, ATM, or Virtual Tributaries (VTs) of various sizes. Thus, payloads are backward compatible with the North American, European, and Pacific Rim standard transport technologies (DS and CEPT). The payload envelope of the frame can vary in size in 774-byte (9 rows × 86 columns) increments, and the term used for the envelope is Synchronous Payload Envelope (SPE). The STS-1 SPE comprises the Path OH bytes and the STS payload capacity (*N* × 9 rows × 87 columns), and is not aligned to the STS frame.

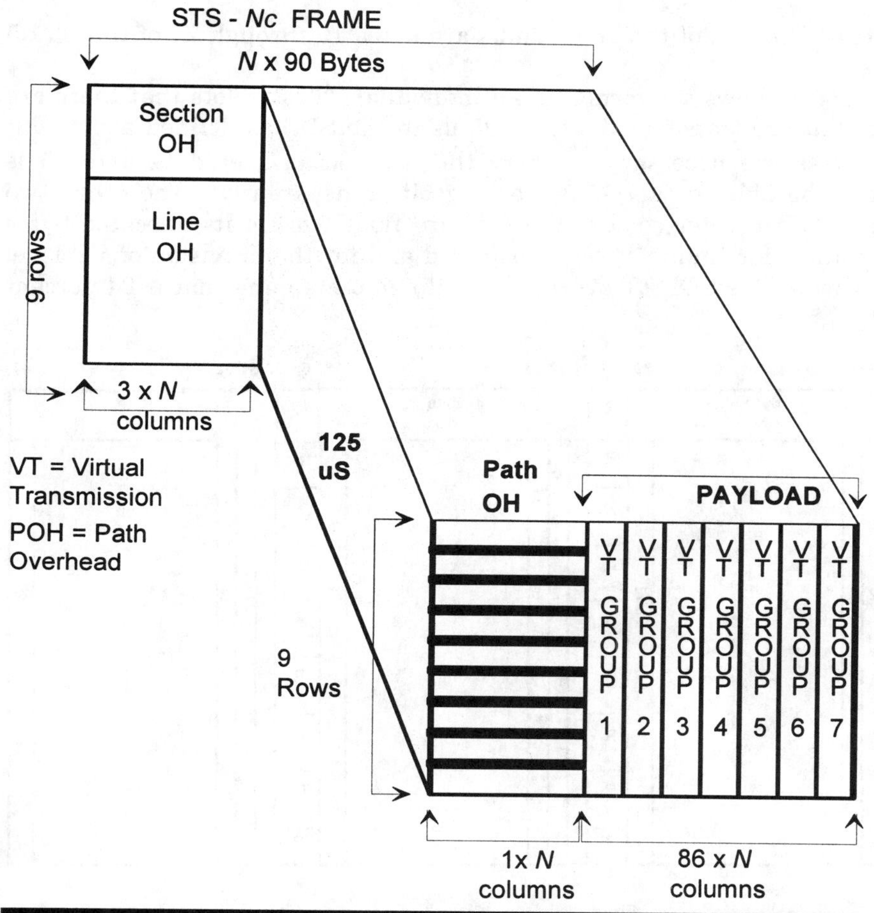

Figure 15.9 STS-*Nc* Frame Format Breakout

When a SONET frame is first created, it is easy to identify the beginning of the SPE data frame. When a frame is transmitted across the network, the line and overhead of each frame can be changed based upon timing changes throughout the network. Frame starts and stops begin to slip, and even the best synchronization schemes cannot keep the frame transmissions in perfect synchronization. Buffers should not be used to correct this problem of frame slip because this would introduce unwanted delay (125 μs at each transit node), which would also accumulate over time. So SONET uses "pointers" to provide synchronization.

Figure 15.10 illustrates how VT1.5s are mapped into an STS-1 SONET Synchronous Payload Envelope (SPE). The first column of 9 bytes is the STS-1 path overhead. The next 28 columns are bytes 1 through 9 of the (28) VT1.5 payloads, followed by a column of stuff bytes. Similarly, columns 31 through 58 are bytes 10 through 18 of the (28) VT1.5 payloads, followed by a column of stuff bytes. The last of the 28 columns are bytes 19 through 27 of the VT1.5 payloads.

Figure 15.11 shows the format of an individual VT1.5. Note that there are 27 bytes that are transferred every 125 μs in the SPE as defined above, but only 24 bytes are necessary to carry the user data. User data byte 25 is included to be able to carry the framing bit transparently. The other two bytes provide a pointer so that the VT can "float" within its allocated bytes and thus allow for timing to be transferred and for the provision of VT level path overhead. The SONET overhead results in a mapping that is 84 percent efficient.

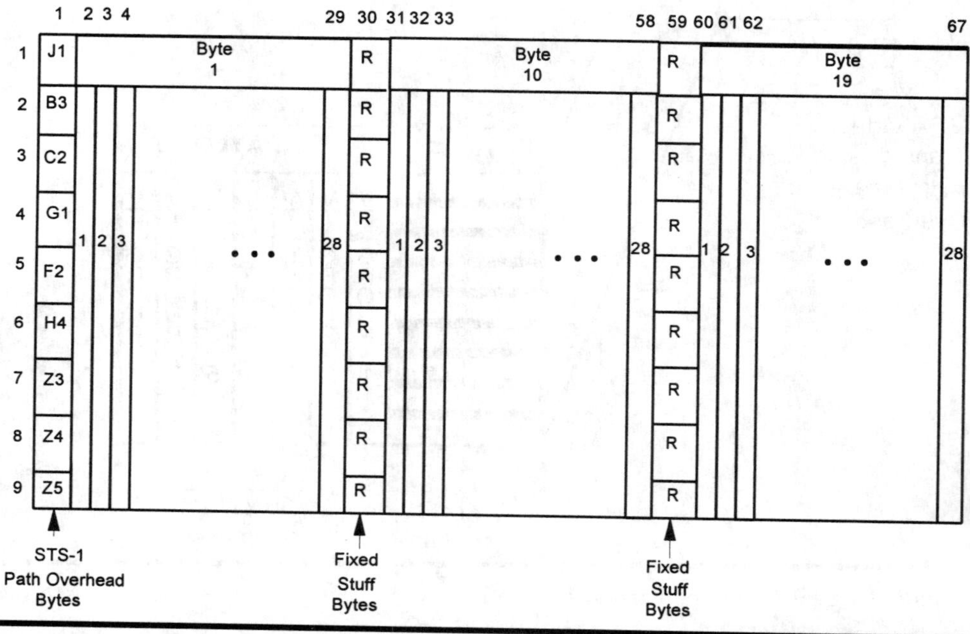

Figure 15.10 VT1.5 Mapping within STS-1 Frame

15.4.3 Virtual Tributary

Virtual tributaries are the building blocks of the SPE. The label VTxx designates virtual tributaries of xx Mbps. These virtual tributaries are labeled as VT1.5 for DS1, VT3 for DS1C (3 Mbps), VT2 for CEPT E1, and VT6 for DS2 (6 Mbps). Table 15.3 shows these VTs and their respective equivalents.

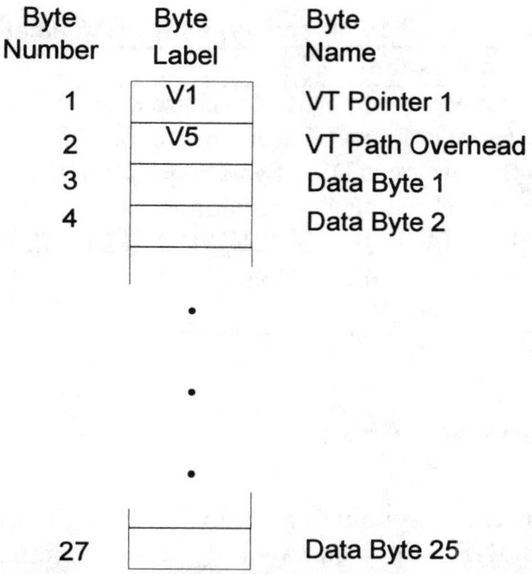

Byte Number	Byte Label	Byte Name
1	V1	VT Pointer 1
2	V5	VT Path Overhead
3		Data Byte 1
4		Data Byte 2
•		
•		
•		
27		Data Byte 25

Figure 15.11 Format of a VT1.5

TABLE 15.3 Virtual Tributary Classes with Equivalents

VTxx	Data Rate (Mbps)	Electrical Channel Equivalent
VT1.5	1.544	DS1
VT2	2.048	E1 (CEPT1)
VT3	3.152	DS1C
VT4	Open	Open
VT5	Open	Open
VT6	6.312	DS2

VTs are combined to form VT groups. These VT groups consist exclusively of three VT1.5s, four VT2s, two VT3s, or one VT6 within a 9-row by 12-column portion of the SPE. A complete SPE is then composed of seven VT groups, 2 bit-stuffed unused columns, and the path overhead column. There are seven VT groups of 6 Mbps groups per STS-1. These VT groups can be mixed to make up an STS-1, which can either contain multiple VCs or a single asynchronous DS3. VTs can either operate in "locked mode", which fixes the VT structure within an STS-1 and is designed for channelized operation, or "floating mode", which allows these values to be changed by cross-connects and switches and is designed for unchannelized operation. STS-3s can handle even larger payloads, such as ATM, FDDI, and SMDS payloads. STS-12 payloads will often be extremely large bandwidth-intensive applications, such as medical imaging or HDTV.

The common tributary is VT1.5, which supports a virtual tributary of 1.5 Mbps through a DS1 transport envelope. VTs run from the VT1.5 through a VT6 (DS2). Table 15.4 shows the many types of traffic payloads possible.

TABLE 15.4 Virtual Tributary Traffic Payload Types with Applications

Payload Type	Applications
VT1.5 through VT6	Asynchronous DS1, Asynchronous DS1C, Asynchronous DS2, Asynchronous 2.048, Synchronous DS1, Synchronous 2.048
STS-1	Asynchronous DS3, Syntran
STS-3	DS4NA, DQDB/SMDS, FDDI, FDDI-II, NTSC Video, ATM/B-ISDN
STS-12	Imaging, HDTV

15.4.4 Synchronization and Pointers

The SONET answer to frame synchronization is through the use of pointers. Pointers are used by SONET devices to easily identify subchannels down to the DS0 level within a SONET transmission. These pointers are located within the line overhead portion of each frame. The Synchronous Payload Envelope (SPE) is allowed to "float" anywhere within the SPE-allocated portion frame, and will often overlap multiple frames. The pointer number (pointers H1, H2, and H3) indicates the start of the SPE frame. If the frame experiences jitter or wander, the pointer will shift within the frame parallel to the SPE shift, thus maintaining its pointer integrity. The H1 and H2 pointers are then updated at each terminal across the network.

Figure 15.12 illustrates an example of an SPE that spans two STS-1 frames. In this figure, the H1, H2, and H3 pointers in the line overhead identify the start of the SPE-3 frame. The next STS-1 frame H1 and H2 identify the beginning of another STE, but the H3 octet holds the value of the last byte in STS-3. This continues on through the transmission. Also note that it is common for STEs to span two frames. Pointers are also used to identify virtual tributaries (VTs) within an SPE.

15.4.5 Overhead and the Control Field

The SONET overhead structure parallels the existing telephone network, with three layers to match section, line, and path segments. As we have seen, the first three columns of the frame contain this transport overhead. Each layer assures the correct transmission of the layer below it. Figure 15.13 shows the three types of SONET equipment, Path-Terminating Equipment (PTE), Line-Terminating Equipment (LTE), and Section-Terminating Equipment (STE); and the overhead structure by which they are managed.

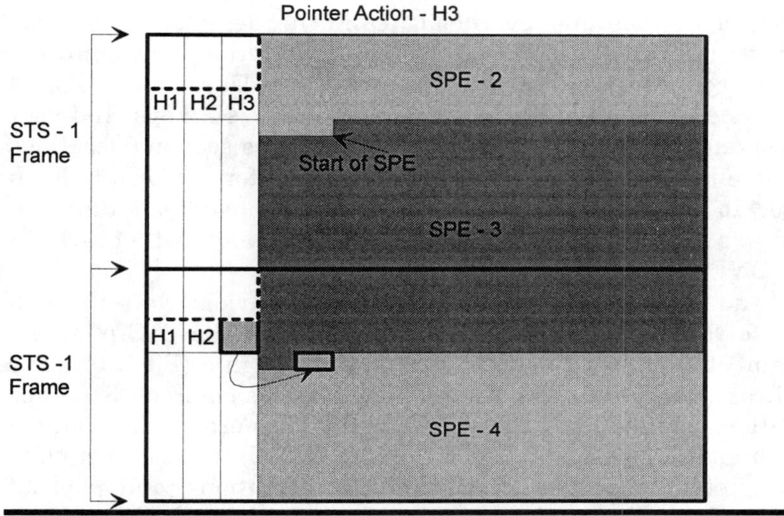

Figure 15.12 Synchronous Payload Envelope (SPE) Operation

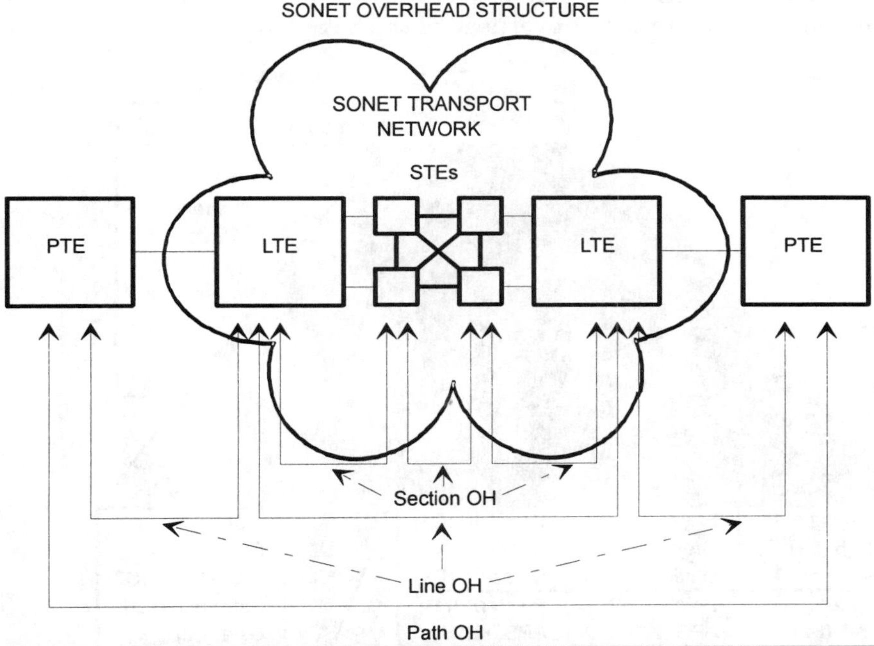

Figure 15.13 SONET Overhead Structure

The section layer provides management of network segments between regenerators, which includes both switching and nonswitching elements. This function is similar to that of the electrical repeater discussed in Chapter

5. The section layer contains overhead (OAM headers) for multiplex equipment framing information (A1 and A2), span performance monitoring BIP-8 parity check counts (B1), STS identification (STS-ID) number (C1), 64 kbps local maintenance communications channel (E1), 64 kbps end-user channel (F1), and data communications channel (192 kbps section operations channel) for remote monitoring and control (D1, D2, D3) for the DCCs. Each STE regenerator in the network performs the section overhead function. Figure 15.14 shows the breakout of the section, line, and path overhead sections of the SONET frame.

The line overhead provides for reliable transport of payload data through parity checking (error monitoring) between elements at the STS-*N* signal level. These elements perform switching functions through a (Bit Interleave Parity) BIP-8 check (B2), interoffice data communications channel (576 kbps embedded operations channel) (D4 through D12), 64 kbps order-wire channel (E2), 128 kbps automatic line protection switching (ALPS) to backup circuits (K1 and K2) for network recovery during outage conditions, and payload pointers to show where the payload section begins (H1 and H3) and to identify the pointer action byte (H3) for control of synchronization. Growth or B-ISDN functionality (Z1 and Z2) is also included. The line and section overhead make up the transport overhead of the STS-*N* frame.

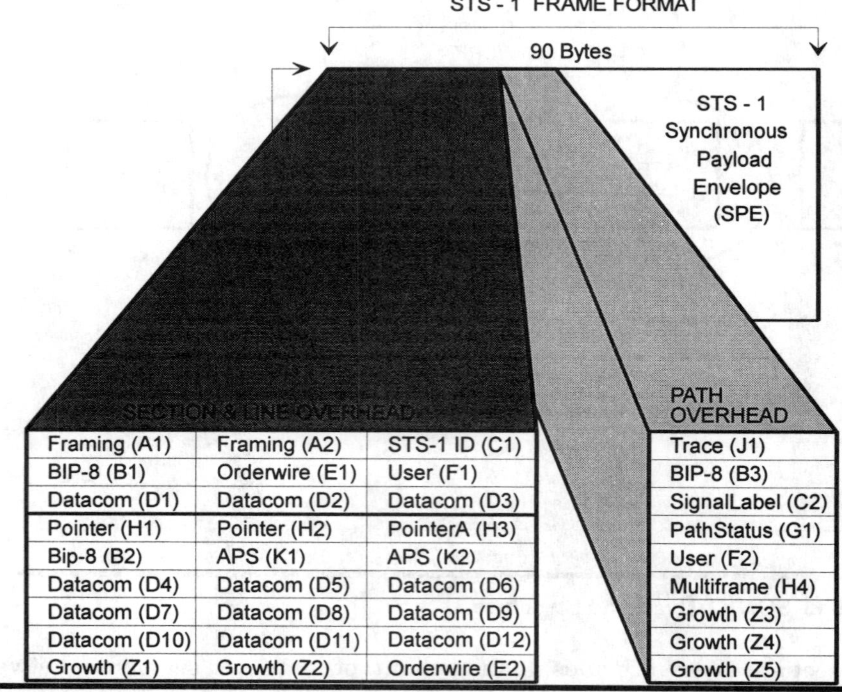

Figure 15.14 SONET Overhead Breakout

The path overhead provides the end-to-end performance monitoring similar to a network layer protocol at the VT and STS-1 signal level. The path overhead operates between PTE devices, providing a BIP-8 (B3), STS payload envelope mapping (C2) similar to a protocol identifier for layer 3 and higher protocols, 64 kbps user channel (F2) or network provider (class C), path error statistic conveyor (G1), multiframe payload identifier (H4), trace from receiver back to transmitter (J1) to verify connection, and growth bytes (Z3, Z4, Z5). The path also maps the DS3 format to the OC-3 format and is associated with the STS payload capacity. It is an essential part of the SONET add/drop multiplexer (SADM). Path overhead is assembled at each PTE and rides through the network until it is disassembled at the receiving PTE. Path overhead defines four service classes:

- Class A – Payload independent functions (required)
- Class B – Mapping dependent functions (not required for all PTs)
- Class C – User specified overhead functions
- Class D – Future use

15.4.6 Bit Interleave Parity Check (BIP-8)

Parity is provided through a 1-byte Bit Interleave Parity (BIP-8) code at each section, line, and path segment of the frame. The *section* BIP assures error-free transport between regenerators, the *line* BIP assures error-free transport between terminating devices, and the *path* BIP assures error-free transport between line termination equipment.

15.4.7 Bit Stuffing

When the incoming tributary data rates cannot fully meet the STS-N rate, the SONET device performs bit stuffing to achieve the desired bandwidth. This is as simple as inserting extra bits into the data stream, which are then stripped off at the destination SONET device.

Bit stuffing is also used for frame synchronization. This technique is used when the access hardware and network hardware are using different timing sources having clock frequency differences. This method locks the user into a point-to-point transmission in that any bits stuffed at the transmitting multiplexer must be demultiplexed and unstuffed in reverse order at the other end.

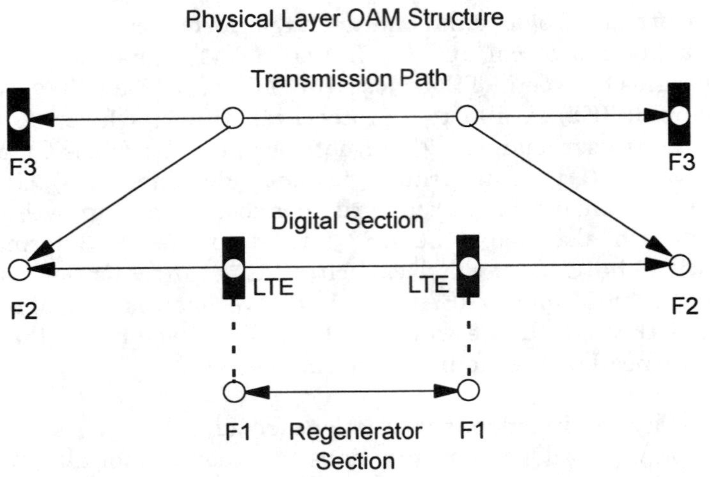

Figure 15.15 SONET OAM Structure

15.4.8 OAM Structure

The Operations, Administration, and Maintenance (OAM) functions of SONET are divided into three levels. These levels are labeled F1, F2, and F3 for the regenerator, digital section, and transmission path, respectively. Figure 15.15 shows this concept. These tags depict where information flows between these layers. The F1 layer defines OAM flows between regenerator sections, and between regenerators and LTE. Reporting is available for loss of frame and degraded error performance. The F2 layer defines OAM flows between LTEs at the termination of section end points. Reporting is available for loss of frame synchronization and degraded error performance. The F3 layer defines OAM flows between PTE elements that perform payload assembly and disassembly, error check operations, and cell delineation over the transmission path.

15.5 SONET HARDWARE

SONET hardware distinctions are possibly the most difficult aspect of SONET to understand. Many devices produce the same functionality, and even the vendors are split on the choice of hardware markets and the future of SONET equipment types. Some hardware both extends the distance of the CPE into the SONET network and allows the user and provider to monitor and control the network in the same manner, rather than through proprietary T1 and T3 systems. The most common equipment term used is the SONET terminal. The word *terminal*, or terminal *adapter*, is used at times to represent a SONET multiplexer, DXC, and even a switch. More often, there is a DXC interface or terminal adapter to lower-speed interfaces and protocols, and these devices are combined through a SONET terminal or switch. OC-*N*–to–OC-*N* SONET devices, those that provide the interface of OC-12 and OC-48 speeds to higher-speed tributaries like OC-192, are most often called terminals as well.

The primary benefit of SONET Central Office (CO) terminal equipment – terminals, multiplexers, terminal multiplexers, DXCs, and switches – is the reduction of equipment required for DS1, DS3, and OC-*N* connectivity and interswitch trunking. SONET terminal equipment is pushing the envelope to increase the bandwidth-to-fiber ratio even higher, using Wave Division Multiplexing (WDM) to achieve what are now common emerging terminal speeds of OC-192 (9.6 Gbps). We will now study the many types of terminals constituting the core SONET network.

15.5.1 SONET Terminating Multiplexers

Terminating multiplexers provide user access to the SONET network. Terminating multiplexers – also called terminal adapters, edge multiplexers, or just terminals – operate similarly to the M13 multiplexer, and provide the user variable speed public network SONET access. Terminating multiplexers, also called PTE, turn *electrical* interfaces into *optical* signals by multiplexing multiple DS1, DS1C, DS2, DS3, or E1 VTs into the STS-*N* signals required for OC-*N* transport. These devices are configured in point-to-point configurations. The most common is the point-to-point, four-fiber configuration over the "line", where two fibers are connected between two terminals, as shown in Figure 15.16. There are two pairs of fiber, each with physical geographic diversity. One pair acts as the full-time working transmission facility. The other pair acts as the full-time protection pair, remaining idle and empty while the working channel passes data, and automatically (in milliseconds) rerouting traffic from the working pair if an interruption is sensed. Both pairs operate in full duplex. Two-fiber configurations are possible, but this does not offer the redundancy that is achieved with four-fiber trunking. 1 for *N* (1:*N*) configurations are also possible.

SONET terminals are typically connected in fiber rings, with each device connected to another through the two-pair fiber configuration previously defined. Figure 15.17 shows an example of SONET four-fiber, bidirectional line-switched fiber ring connectivity, with (a) demonstrating normal operation, (b) showing automatic reconfiguration during outage on the working pair, and (c) illustrating automatic reconfiguration during fiber cut of *both* working and protected fiber pairs. To extrapolate further, the failure of either a single node or span, or both, would not take down the entire ring. Nonintrusive maintenance can also be performed on the spans.

Figure 15.18 shows end-user LTE terminal adapters (multiplexer) which each interface up to 84 DS1s into a single OC-3 interface for SONET transmission.

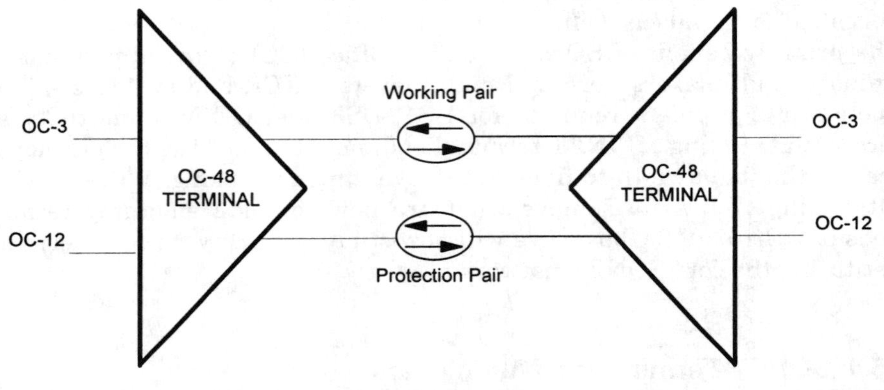

Figure 15.16 SONET Terminal Trunking

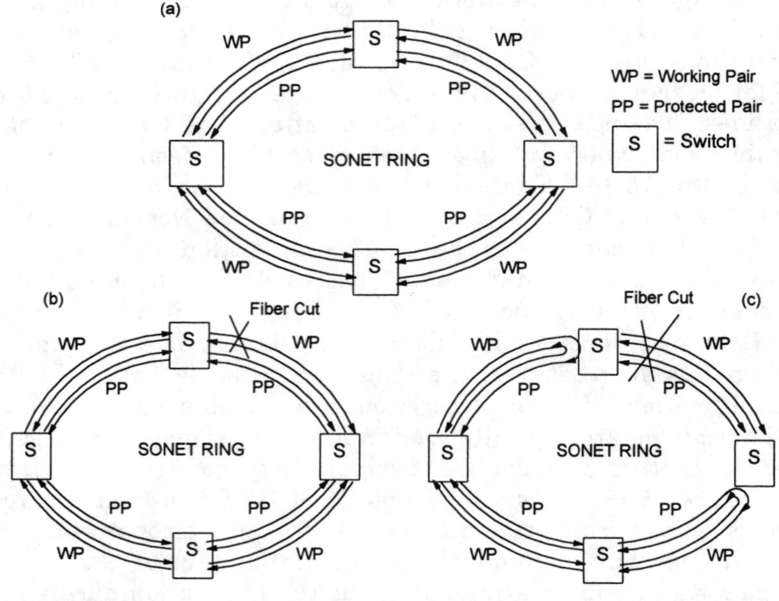

Figure 15.17 SONET Four-fiber Protected Ring Connectivity

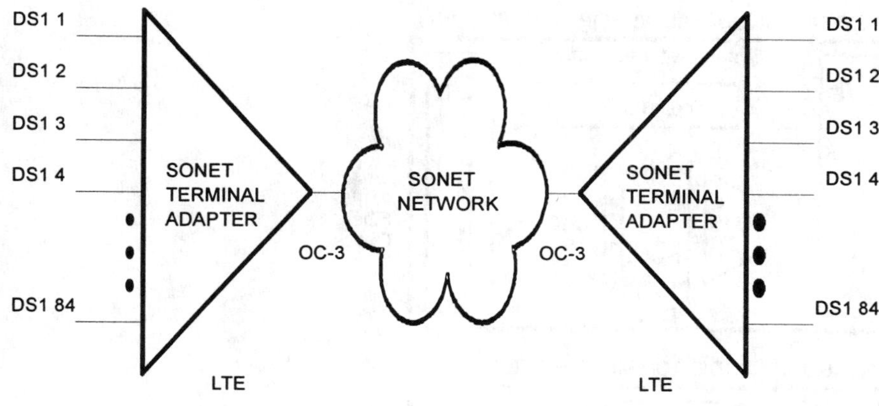

Figure 15.18 SONET Line Terminating Equipment (LTE)

15.5.2 SONET Concentrators

SONET concentrators operate the same way as electrical concentrators and hubs, concentrating OC-3, OC-12, and OC-48 interfaces into higher-transmission rates like OC-192. It also allows the full SONET OAM&P features to all access circuits.

15.5.3 SONET Add/Drop Multiplexer (SADM)

The current system of electrical transport and multiplexing is asynchronous at DS3 and lower speeds. This requires a huge investment in asynchronous equipment (multiplexers, DXCs). This method not only involves extensive overhead, but also the need for large numbers of multiplexers and DXCs. Multiple back-to-back M13 multiplexers and patch panels are used to break out low-speed channels from the aggregate DS3 signal. SONET eliminates these multiple equipment implementations and requirements through the use of a SONET Add/Drop Multiplexer (SADM).

SONET add/drop multiplexers or terminals work in a similar manner to their electrical equivalents, but allow the provider to drop and add not only the lower SONET rates, but also electrical interface rates down to the DS1 level. Drop-and-insert, drop-and-continue, and broadcast mode are standard features. The optical signal is converted to electrical, and these functions are performed electrically. This provides a much more dynamic network with better transport efficiency than the older point-to-point terminal multiplexers.

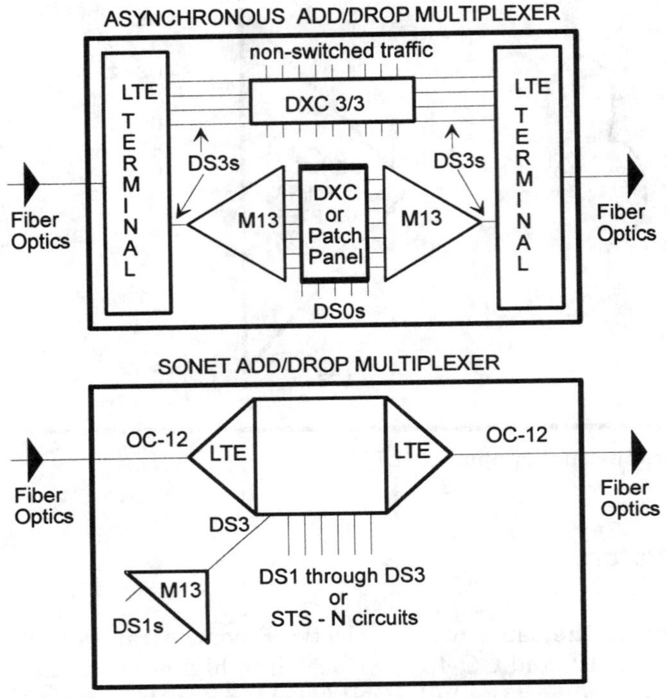

Figure 15.19 Comparison of Asynchronous Add/Drop Multiplexing and SONET

Figure 15.19 shows a comparison of the asynchronous and SONET methods of add/drop multiplexing. Notice that the asynchronous digital method requires the M13 multiplexer to break down a DS3 into 28 DS1s, which are then placed into a cross-connect or patch panel for drop-and-insert capability. The SDXC allows direct drop-and-insert of any DS3 through DS1 VT within the OC-*N* signal (in this case an OC-12). Note that SADMs require point-to-point connectivity to both LTE terminal devices. Also notice the reduction of equipment while still providing additional functionality.

SADMs are generally used for distributed point-to-point network connectivity. They are central office devices forming the building blocks of the SONET network. SADMs allow ease of expansion and are often used in SONET ring architectures. They generally operate at the higher transmission speeds of OC-3 through OC-192.

Some additional capabilities of SADMs include:

- Operation and protection channels
- Optical hubbing
- Ring and time slot capabilities
- Dynamic bandwidth allocation

15.5.4 SONET Digital Loop Carrier Systems (DLCs)

Digital Loop Carrier systems (DLCs) are used to concentrate multiple DS0 traffic from remote terminals into a single OC-3 signal. These devices are typically situated at the LEC and handle both voice and data traffic, providing an interface for non-SONET CPE, LEC, and CO switches to the SONET public network. DLCs also have many of the capabilities typically found in the LEC voice systems, such as operational and maintenance capabilities, and can handle access for many of the data services such as N-ISDN and B-ISDN. These devices are also used when a remote terminal cannot transmit an OC-*N* signal to the IXC CO switch and must go through the LEC.

15.5.5 SONET Digital Cross-Connects (SDXCs)

SONET Digital Cross-Connects (SDXCs) operate similarly to standard digital DXCs, in that they allow switching and circuit grooming across all levels of the transmission down to the DS1 level, including those that interface to the SDXC without being on the incoming or outgoing transmission. In fact, SDXCs originated as a simple SONET STS-1 interface on a non-SONET DXC. SDXCs provide SONET OC-*N* level cross-connect provisioning capabilities and can also act as a SONET hub to provide both asynchronous and synchronous user or network access. Thus, they can reside on either the user line interface side or the trunk side of a SONET terminal. SDXCs have helped migrate existing legacy LEC and IXC asynchronous networks to SONET. Most grooming and routing of SONET circuits is done through SDXCs. Figure 15.20 shows an example of a SONET DXC (SDXC). SONET DXCs also provide an interface to other switched architecture feeds such as ATM, wireless, and voice switches. Figure 15.21 shows a combined SONET terminal and DXC.

SONET DXCs use pointers rather than traditional DXC slip buffers to mark the beginning of a DS1 frame and allow insertion/extraction with minimal delay. The additional SDXC features include:

- Network monitoring and testing
- Network provisioning
- Maintenance
- Network restoration

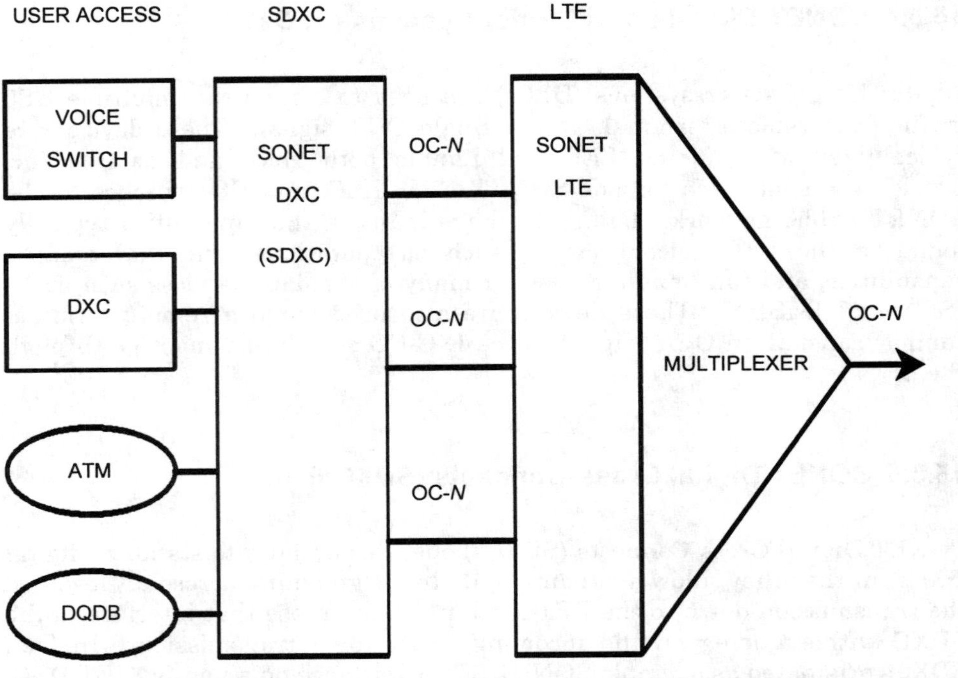

Figure 15.20 SONET DXC (SDXC)

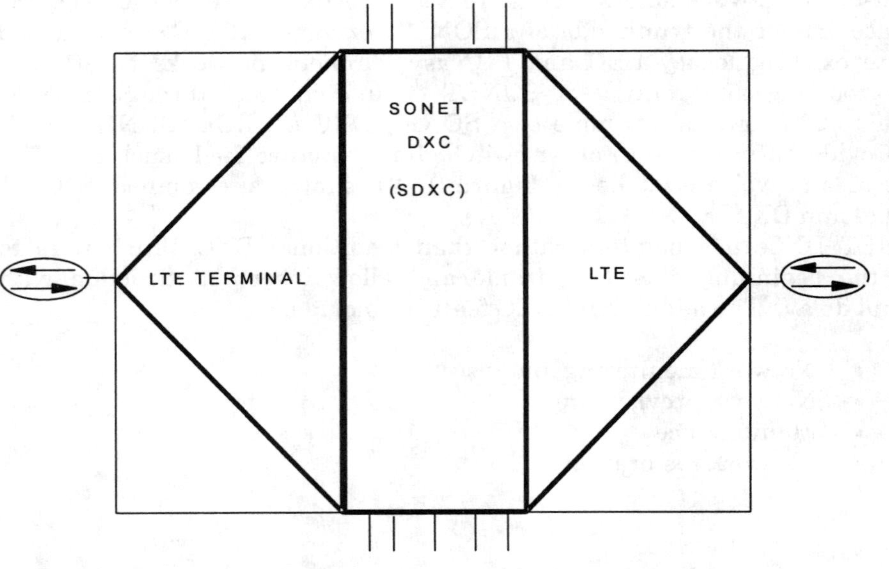

Figure 15.21 SONET Broadband Switch Interfaces

SDXCs come in two flavors: broadband (BDXC) and wideband (WDXC). The lower-speed device is the WDXC, which provides cross-connect capability for floating VTs within an STS-*N*. WDXCs can also provide a transparent connection between multiple DS1 interfaces and DS3 or OC-*N* termination. The higher-speed device is the BDXC. The BDXC can both cross-connect at DS3 (asynchronous or synchronous) and STS-1 signals and provide concatenation of multiple STS-1 signals to STS-*N* levels. SONET DXCs and ATM DXCs are similar and can coexist in the same network, but SONET DXCs can provide restoration for ATM switches that do not have restoration features. In this case, the ATM switch would provide the network access and conversion to ATM over optical OC-*N* channels, and the SDXC would serve as an optical DXC. SDXCs can also act as international SONET gateways.

One recent trend is the elimination of the SDXC as a discrete element by the use of a technique called basic time-slot assignment (TSA). TSA, premiered in Hitachi Telecom's Advanced Multiservice Terminal SONET product family, allows add/drop capability of STS-1 level traffic at each SONET element, along with pass-through and broadcast drops. This ADM function can operate for both line-to-tributary and tributary-to-tributary, and eliminates the need for a separate cross-connect. Broadcast capability across multiple network elements is also available. Figure 15.22 shows an example of TSA operation.

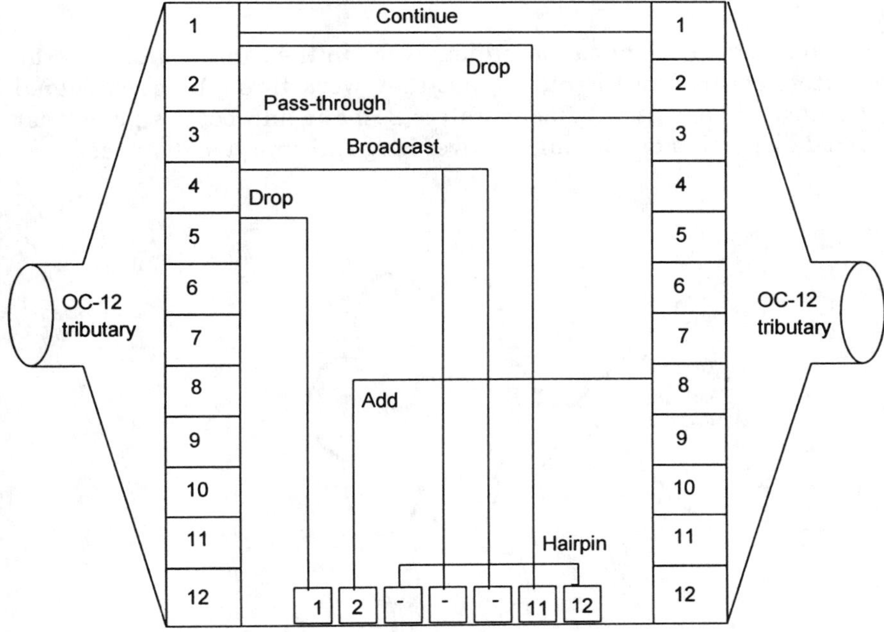

Figure 15.22 SONET Time-Slot Assignment (TSA) Example

15.5.6 SONET Broadband Switches

SONET broadband switches have taken a backseat to the broadband and wideband SDXCs. SONET broadband switches provide the switching capability found in major voice switches, but operate at the higher OC-*N* levels. Switching options typically include revertive and nonrevertive, and unidirectional or bidirectional. Many SONET terminal and switch vendors are now including SDXC capabilities within their switches. A need also exists for this functionality in the CPE environment interfacing many LAN and MAN technologies. This device will also require the capability to allocate bandwidth-on-demand, and provide both digital data network interfaces as well as SONET interfaces. Figure 15.23 shows an example of a SONET broadband switch (LTE) which interfaces through a terminal adapter to many CPE broadband services.

Switches are typically connected via four-fiber, line-switched rings, as previously shown. Eventually, SONET switches will be replaced by photonic switches, which will provide both terabit transmissions and the capability to switch at any subrate down to DS0. This is the inevitable evolution of many of the devices covered in this chapter.

15.5.7 SONET Regenerators and Optical Amplifiers

SONET regenerators and optical amplifiers work in the same manner as the signal repeaters covered in Chapter 5, but they work through optical signal regeneration over fiber optics. Regenerators reshape and boost signals that have incurred dispersion or attenuation over long transmission distances.

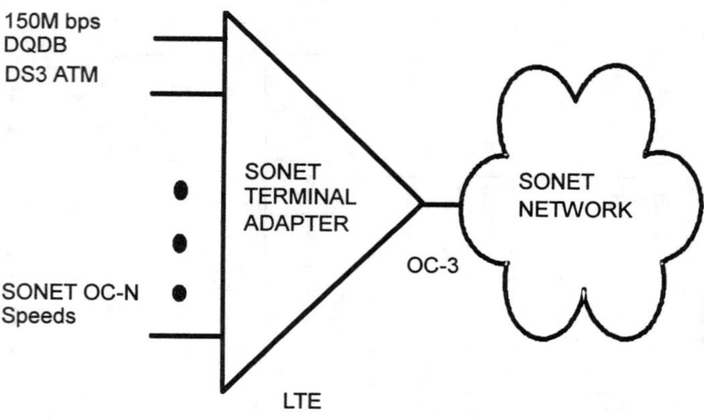

Figure 15.23 SONET Broadband Switch Interfaces

15.5.8 SONET Equipment Vendors

SONET hardware terminal vendors can be separated into three camps. In the first are the vendors pushing the SONET DXC. In the second are those who offer drop-and-insert multiplexer products. In the third camp, vendors advocate integrated SONET message switches. Their view is that the new SONET switches now emerging will have all the capabilities of the SONET DXCs. Some of the major vendors of SONET equipment include AT&T Network Systems, Alcatel Network Systems, Ascom Timeplex, DSC Communications, Fujitsu, Hitachi Telecom, NEC America, Northern Telecom (NorTel), Rockwell, Telco Systems, and Tellabs.

A shift has taken place among the central office vendors toward all SONET-compliant equipment. These vendors are offering hardware that complies with Phase I and II of the SONET standard, with software modifications following for Phase III compliance. Most LECs and IXCs have moved to new transport builds composed of all SONET hardware.

The other major consideration for these providers is the size of their existing DXC base and the upgrade capability to SONET. Some vendors were well positioned to upgrade, having a majority of DXC 3/3s infrastructure with SONET upgrade capability. Most systems today are being installed at OC-48 speeds, with some deployment of OC-192 systems, and are all new hardware devices.

In the international arena, many PTTs plan to use SONET primarily for transport and cross-connects and use technologies such as DQDB and ATM as the switching architecture.

15.6 INTERFACES

The Network-Node Interface (NNI) specifies the link between existing in-place digital transmission facilities and the SONET network node, as well as the process for converting the electrical signal into optical pulses for network transmission. This is the primary interface from the electronic world into the optical world.

15.6.1 Interface Options

There are three major SONET interface options:

① Direct CPE or CO hardware interface
② Gateway device to convert to OC levels
③ Conversion within the SONET switch itself

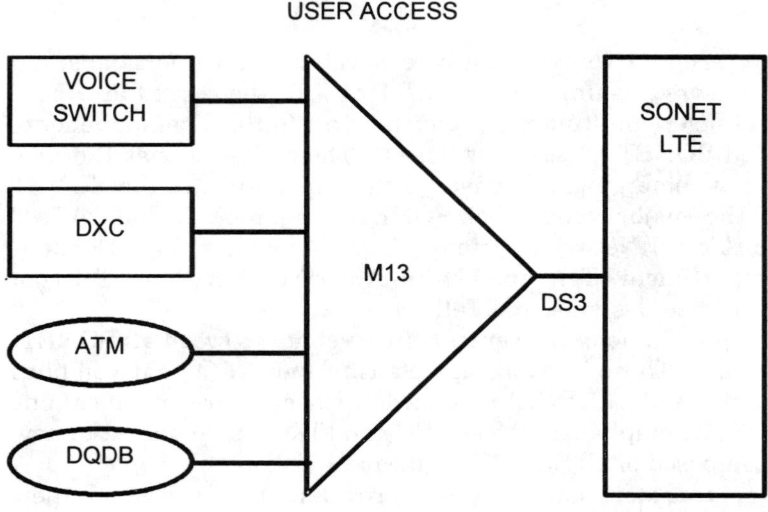

Figure 15.24 M13 Multiplexer Access to SONET LTE

All three interface options are supported by the major IXC and LEC deployments of SONET in major metropolitan centers across the country. Most access to the SONET network is through the LTE, commonly a SONET add/drop terminal or multiplexer (SADM).

An M13 multiplexer can also be used for access to the SONET network. M13s can aggregate multiple DS-level inputs into a single DS3 for access. They can also be used for synchronization across the SONET network through a single DS1 within the DS3, but this can cause data slips, which in turn could cause lengthy delays and degradation of data rate. Figure 15.24 shows an example of the M13 multiplexer concentration via DS3 access.

15.6.2 User Access

Many vendors providing SONET access hardware are following the TR-08 SONET access standard. This seems to be the predominant standard. Typical SONET access interfaces include:

- SONET STS-*N*
- SONET OC-*N*
- SONET OVTG (fiber)
- European or Asian SDH
- Channel bank
- LEC telephone service device

- DXC 3/1, 3/3
- M13 multiplexer
- ISDN
- DS0 through DS3 (including fractional T1/T3, E1)
- LAN/MAN

Thus, large-scale access circuit integration can be accomplished. The applications using this high-speed access include distance learning video-on-demand, disaster recovery capacity-on-demand, and the financial and health services industries. In fact, most users are beginning to request OC-48 tributary access to SONET services!

15.6.3 Services Support

Typical services to ride over SONET networks include:

- Digital Data Service (DDS)
- N-ISDN
- ATM
- X.25/X.75
- Frame relay
- FDDI/FDDI-II
- 802.6/SMDS

With SONET, users will be able to dial up whatever bandwidth increments are needed. This achieves true bandwidth-on-demand, up to gigabit speeds! The standards bodies that work high-speed data services are now considering SONET to provide the much needed backbone infrastructure on which to base these services. An example of this prospect is the work currently underway by the FDDI committee to provide an FDDI-to-SONET interface, with an SMDS-to-SONET interface not far behind. There are parallel efforts between the ANSI SONET T1X1.5 standards committee and the B-ISDN standards body (T1S1.1) for compatibility of ATM services over SONET, or mapping of AAL1 service to SONET VTs.

15.7 ADVANTAGES AND DISADVANTAGES

The advantages to deploying a SONET-based network far outweigh the disadvantages. Some of the many advantages provided by SONET include:

- Abundant support provided for broadband services
- True fractional DS3 service can be offered

- Lower transmission costs
- Easy, long-range planning for network providers
- Efficient management of bandwidth at the physical layer
- Aggregation of low-speed data transport channels into common high-speed backbone trunk transport
- Standardization of global transmission networks
- Long life-span technology
- Internetworking simplicity
- Standard optical interface and format specification
- Reduction in the quantity and cost of the service provider's equipment
- Increased reliability and restoration
- Increased bandwidth management through "grooming"
- Smart OAM&P features with uniformity
- Vendor and service provider interoperability
- Economic method of access to subrate multiplexed signals
- Resources for managing the transmission network carried at different levels
- Add/drop channels without the need to demultiplex or remultiplex
- Reduced overall network transport delay
- ATM, FDDI, FDDI-II technologies supported
- B-ISDN, SMDS, and other new high-bandwidth services supported
- Cabling and equipment reductions
- Ability to build private SONET networks

Some of the challenges and drawbacks of SONET deployment include:

- Strict synchronization schemes
- Early deployment of *asynchronous* fiber will eventually have to be replaced by *synchronous* fiber to mesh today's synchronous networks with SONET
- Lack of control systems
- Lack of bandwidth management
- Need new hardware for add/drop multiplexers
- Nearly complete software dependence
- Hardware maintenance staff must be retrained for software access only
- Development on the OAM&P standards requires significant and continual software changes

Overall network synchronization is one of the greatest challenges to running a SONET network. Network management runs a close second.

15.8 PERFORMANCE AND DESIGN CONSIDERATIONS

SONET provides the means for end-to-end in-service traffic performance monitoring through the three types of overhead discussed. SONET also uses pointers to eliminate the slip buffer delay of asynchronous transport. This significantly reduces transport delay from 193 bits down to 24 bits, almost an 8:1 reduction! It is interesting to note that with standard 56 kbps or T1 transport, most of the delay was incurred just getting data into the pipe. With SONET transport, the delay limit is primarily dictated by propagation delay — at this time an unsolved limitation. Within the SONET standard, there are many performance parameters defined that can be reported by SONET-compliant equipment. These include:

- Severely Errored Framing (SEF) sections
- Errored Seconds (ES)
- Severely Errored Seconds (SES)
- Coding Violations (CV)
- Line Depredated Minutes (DM)

While SONET provides the many advantages listed previously, there remain many performance issues, some of which have been solved while others require refinement or still need to be addressed. These issues include:

- Error and jitter performance
- Protection switching
- Alarm/status indication and surveillance
- Provisioning
- Performance monitoring
- Pointer monitoring

In addition, SONET can take a Stratum 3 clock, but requires a minimum of a Stratum 1 clock source to minimize slips and maintain transmission integrity. Beware of timing problems and loops that may appear on circuits upstream of the clocking source. Testing in these areas can be broken down into four major components: Bit Error Rate Testing (BERT), SONET equipment alarms, pointer adjustments and alignment, and section/line/path parity checks.

A note on SONET design: the SONET standards have been designed so that SONET can exist in both metropolitan rings and wide area network meshed networks. The metropolitan rings will provide higher transport and access speeds, while the WAN-meshed connectivity will provide large areas of coverage and remote access to the SONET network. Service providers are still debating the method of deploying SONET rings and meshed configurations. Some are building small, high-density ring networks which turn out to be more survivable than meshed networks. Others are building SONET rings with add/drop multiplexers and DXCs providing the wide area network connectivity over point-to-point circuits. Much of the network restoration in these configurations will be through the broadband DXCs which employ both online and spare dedicated circuits.

15.9 REVIEW

In this chapter the SONET standards were reviewed, with Phase I defining the basic operation and frame structure; Phase II defining additional functions, OAM&P, and the IAO interface; and Phase III defining SONET vendor interfaces and additional OAM&P for the midspan fiber meets. Next, the frame structure and multiplexing hierarchy of SONET were discussed, first to understand the highly structured STS-*N* and OC-*N* hierarchy, and how the messaging and file transfer protocols fit into SONET, and then the actual composition of the SONET frame and OAM&P elements. The full line of SONET terminal hardware available was analyzed to provide the reader with the capability of objectively choosing the concentrator, SADM, SDXC, switch, or regeneration device and desired trunking for any given design. SONET vendors providing this hardware were highlighted. User interface options, user access to a SONET network through various interfaces, and the services that can use SONET were explored. Finally, an analysis of the advantages and drawbacks of SONET networks was undertaken, covering some performance and design considerations inherent in SONET network designs.

Part

5

Requirements, Planning, and Choosing Technology

Part 5 now covers the aspects of defining user requirements, conducting an analysis of the traffic requiring transport, establishing a capacity plan for the next two to three years, and drawing comparisons of circuit *versus* packet *versus* frame *versus* cell *technologies. One of the most difficult aspects of a network design is fully understanding user requirements. The user's view of the network is often that of someone who simply picks up the phone and dials, and, if there is a problem, calls the phone company. Thus, the user views the network as a utility, and requires the network manager to make that utility and its operation as transparent as possible. In the voice world, there are very few variations to the telephone. In the data world, there are multitudes of variables that apply to the average user data connection. Data network design in its purest form is interpreting the user requirements and building the utility to provide the level of service required. Chapter 16 helps us outline the right questions that when asked of the users will determine their exact communication service needs. Chapter 17 provides methods to analyze user traffic to provide a preliminary capacity and configuration plan. This plan will later serve as the blueprint to the access and then backbone network design. Chapter 18 presents a comparison of technologies discussed thus far. The next few chapters leave many of the detailed calculations to more in-depth traffic analysis books, but provide the important calculations required to complete the network design.*

Chapter

16

Requirements Definition

Requirements analysis is the first and most important step in the network design. The network design is the product, and the user is the customer. The network is built for the customers, and it must conform to their needs, wants, and desires. No single aspect of the design is more important than fully understanding the users' needs, for they ultimately dictate the technology, protocols, hardware, software, and resources devoted to both access and backbone design. The two major views of requirements are those of the *user* and those of the *designer*. The user looks at the network from the outside (premises) in, and the designer looks at it from the inside (backbone network) out, thus creating two myopic views which must merge to provide a comprehensive complementary analysis beyond simple network ingress and egress design. Many questions must be asked before beginning the design. Both parties must "get to know each other" to begin the "marriage" of user and designer. This working relationship is essential to the success of the network's design and use. Changes and inaccuracies in user requirements can have devastating effects on both the access and backbone network design. While user requirements change, the designer needs to set a time limit when the addition of any new requirements is frozen and the current ones analyzed. This chapter will examine how to look at the requirements from both the user's and the network design engineer or manager's perspective. But, first, we explore the many aspects of user requirements that set the stage for the traffic-analysis and capacity-planning phases.

16.1 USER REQUIREMENTS — THE USER'S VIEWPOINT

How often do users proclaim "I want it all now"? Users want as much network functionality as they can get. Bandwidth requirements are exploding as high-speed LANs and MANs proliferate and applications move toward distributed computing platforms. Users who once carried on low-speed terminal emulation sessions across the WAN are now more than ever accessing and sharing multimegabit data files across the WAN. Users who were once content to read e-mail messages are now scanning the Internet and retrieving huge text files with graphic images that cause the amount of data transmitted across their LAN to their workstation to increase by orders of magnitude. WAN link speeds of 9600 bps have yielded to speeds of 56 kbps, 1.544 Mbps, and 45 Mbps. Multiuser 4 Mbps and 10 Mbps LANs are yielding to single-user 100 Mbps LANs. But as these communications speeds increase, so does the increasing tangle of protocols, architectures, support and management systems, and a multitude of other factors influencing and controlling the data flow between users. The line between network access devices and those once dedicated only to LAN communications has blurred and the two functions have merged. This is an exciting age, when users are taking more control of their data networks. Media and application enablers such as the Internet have only served to increase user interest in the WAN. Corporate and public communication data networks are playing catchup to the users demands. Networks where once the WAN bandwidths were the limiting factor are now facing protocol throughput problems that cannot be solved by simply adding more bandwidth in the WAN. As discussed in the beginning of the book, the user has become smarter and more sophisticated. Users no longer stand for the smoke-and-mirrors approach experienced with hierarchical MIS organizations in the past. Historically, the MIS application backlog averaged from 1 to 2 years. Multimillion-dollar budgets for mainframes were tightly controlled and MIS was a mystery. These days, however, if corporate MIS does not solve the connectivity problem in a timely manner, users buy their own routers, switching hubs, and workstations out of departmental budgets for a few thousands of dollars, and heterogeneous communications environments proliferate. Bottom line – if the user's true requirements are not satisfied, the user will go elsewhere. This begins the education process for both user and designer. First, however, we must clarify the level of user expectations and satisfaction.

16.1.1 User Expectations and Satisfaction

User expectations must be properly managed to ensure satisfaction not only at install but through continued service of the network. The best way to ensure this is by jointly establishing with the user and then meeting the initial levels of customer satisfaction. Clearly understand what is expected on both sides and then set expectation levels accordingly. If this is a new network, make sure users know that initial service is in its test stages. Establish graduated levels of new technology introduction: technology trial, then alpha test, then beta test, and finally full production. These levels of user access are defined as:

Technology Trial: A test environment where both the user and network designer are learning from each other. Network downtime and reconfiguration are expected often. This phase is primarily for both parties to learn about the new technologies. The network services are limited in scope and functionality. The target group should be limited to experienced users or people not heavily impacted by downtime. This phase is certainly not to be tested on mission-critical users or applications.

Alpha Test: A prerelease version of the network service where the customer is still learning from the network provider, but the provider now has the network design completed and the hardware is fully operational. Downtime is minimal, and very few users are on the network. This is a small-scale version of the "real thing", often an internal trial run, and expected to be "buggy". Again, users should not be severely impacted by downtime.

Beta Test: Final test phase before offering commercial or public service availability. Most, if not all, of the bugs should be out of the system by the beta test and users should experience little or no downtime. The beta test phase is close to the actual network offering, but since it is new, everyone expects some minor instabilities.

Production. The network officially goes live! All of the bugs (hopefully) have been eliminated and the network is running with full functionality. There is no downtime (unless scheduled in advance).

The final version of the production network should be transparent to the average user. Each user should feel that he or she has full connectivity when required and with the required amount of bandwidth, to every destination he or she communicates with. Let's look at the user "dream sheet" of expectations:

- No delays
- No cost to user
- No protocol or functional interworking restrictions
- No physical or logical constraints
- No network errors (or very low error rate)
- Ubiquitous access with portability
- No network/circuit/site/application downtime
- Network performing all protocol conversion
- All internetwork interconnectivity is as requested (i.e., Internet access)
- Broadcast and multicast capability
- Confirmation of receipt (fax, interactive SVCs)
- Security and privacy
- Easy to use
- Full training and documentation

These are among a few of the typical expectations and network perceptions of users. After a short time, the network is viewed as a utility, something that always works — not a luxury, but a necessity. Back to the telephone example: the user picks up the phone and expects to get dial tone. Above all, remember that the user is the customer and the network designer is the provider. The primary responsibility of the network manager or designer is to provide network capabilities and performance as close as possible to the user's expectations. Keep a professional, friendly attitude toward users, treat them as partners, and they will treat you in the same way. From the network provider perspective, user perception is reality.

The problem with many of the new technologies is that they require the user to understand the mid- to high-layer protocols more than ever before. The protocol used across the WAN can be just as much a limiting factor as the WAN bandwidth. It is the job of network engineers and managers to make this environment as transparent as possible to the user, while still providing the feature functionality in a user-friendly manner to the desktop applications. The network should look like the transparent cloud in Figure 16.1, where users A, B, C, and D can communicate with whomever and whatever they require. Sit now in the designer's seat and understand user requirements from the network side or viewpoint.

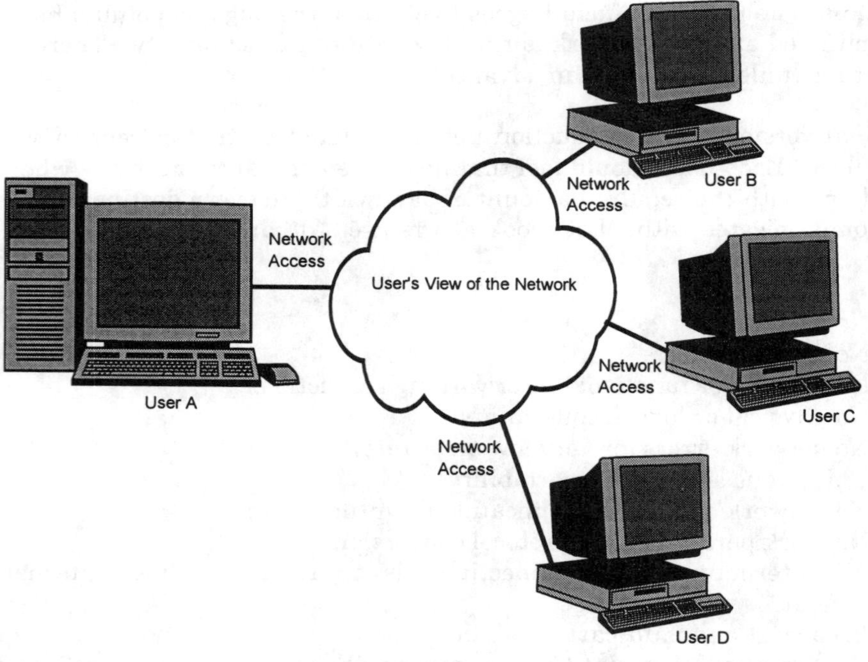

Figure 16.1 User's View of the Network

16.1.2 User Involvement in Technology

Never before have users known as much about networking technologies as they do now. Users have become the driving forces behind consortia, forums, user's groups, and other organizations that have actually driven many of the standards defined in this text. The user becomes more informed each day. In some cases, the user is more experienced than the network designer or manager. Do not overlook this important source of input for network planning and design. Instead, draw upon this expertise. Users have a wealth of knowledge concerning their applications – avail yourself of it! Make sure the requirement-gathering process is an educational process for user and designer. The network process is a partnership where the sharing of information is bidirectional. Now that the pep talk is over and the user and designer are identified as partners, the next step is to get down to business and define requirements for the data network.

16.2 USER REQUIREMENTS — THE DESIGNER'S VIEWPOINT

The rest of this chapter discusses user requirements from the designer's viewpoint. Obviously, the network designer has to understand much more than the input and information provided by the user, as user information is often incomplete and sometimes inaccurate. While scanning the following sections, the reader should compile a working list of each user's requirements. Refer back to earlier chapters for clarification on technologies, hardware, and services to meet these requirements. The reader should also understand both user and network designer constraints. Once the user requirements are identified, a comprehensive traffic analysis for purposes of capacity planning will be explained in the next chapter. The designer will never receive all of the user requirements, and even if he or she does, the requirements will change throughout the development of the design and life of the network.

16.3 TRAFFIC SIZING

Traffic comes in many shapes and sizes, conforms to many protocols and formats, travels in many types of patterns, and requires special methods of processing and handling. The next few sections cover these aspects and more. The format of this and later sections, and the approach of this chapter, is provided in a questioning tone. The network designer should ask the questions identified here for each application planned for the network. These values should also be compared to existing transport means, such as speed of the transmission facility now being used.

16.3.1 Message or Data Size Basics

The two common formats for data traffic are the units of measure and the packaging of these units. Units of measure progressively explained include: bit, byte, octet, message, and block. These units can be packaged into files, packets, frames, or cells or left as plain units for transfer across a physical medium using transmission packaging (e.g., DS1). Another name for a data package is a protocol data unit (PDU), which is how the SMDS and ATM standards define the term.

Data is measured by the number of units or packages transmitted per unit of time. Some examples include packets/frames/cells per second, bytes per second, messages per hour, or even by the number of transactions per second (using a fixed or variable unit of measure for each transaction). These values translate into channel transmission rates, and the transmission rate determines the amount of time it takes to transmit a unit of data. Table 16.1 shows examples of data size and transmission times based on network bandwidth available (these times assume no overhead — and could be considerably less). In network design, *average* packet or message size is often used as the measurement.

TABLE 16.1 Data Transmissions Comparison

Data Sent	Data Size	Transmission Speed	Time To Send Data (seconds)
Basic text file	30 kbps	56 kbps	0.5 seconds
(10 pages)		DS1	.02 seconds
Basic	250 kbps	56 kbps	4.5 seconds
spreadsheet		DS1	.16 seconds
Single page	1 Mbps	56 kbps	18 seconds
graphics		DS1	.65 seconds
Average	3 Mbps	56 kbps	54 seconds
FAX		DS1	2 seconds
CAD/CAM	10 Mbps	56 kbps	3 minutes
graphics file		DS1	6.5 seconds
Compressed	100 Mbps	56 kbps	30 minutes
video		DS1	1 minute

16.3.2 Tuning Data Size across the Network

The actual data size of each package is the size of the data for each user compared with overhead and framing in the packaging. Many technologies set limits of minimum and maximum packaging size, such as a maximum X.25 packet size of 4096 bytes or a maximum frame relay frame size of 8096 bytes. Also, determine if the packet/frame/cell size needs to be identical at each end of transmission.

Many protocols, such as Transmission Control Protocol (TCP) and X.25 packet switching, provide windowing for acknowledgments of data sent and received. Users of these protocols need to provide the window size required: minimum, average, or maximum. But frequently, users require expert recommendations because they often do not have the foggiest idea. Many of the technologies discussed tend to segment data as it transits the network. Confirm if the segmentation of user data can be tolerated by the user applications, or if the user applications require segmentation.

16.4 TRAFFIC CHARACTERISTICS DEFINED

This section defines the major traffic characteristics. There are four predominant traffic characteristics: burstiness, delay tolerance, response time, and total capacity or throughput. The performance requirements of an application are derived from a combination of these four, along with other important considerations depending on the transmission medium and protocol used, such as session and usage patterns, call setup and response time, routing, data accuracy, prioritization, and quality of service requirements.

16.4.1 Traffic Burstiness

Burstiness is a commonly used measure of how infrequently a source sends traffic. A source that infrequently sends traffic is said to be very bursty, while a source that always sends at the same rate is said to be nonbursty. Burstiness is defined as the ratio of peak to average rate of traffic based on a specific sampling period for the data.

$$\text{Burstiness} = \frac{\text{Peak Rate}}{\text{Average Rate}}$$

For example, if the peak traffic rate for the busy hour was 10 Mbps and the average traffic rate was 500 kbps, the traffic would have a burst factor of 20, or be very bursty. LANs can achieve very high burst rates per user of 100 to 1000. Evidence the occasional user of e-mail that sends a 20 kbits file every hour. The file transfer should take less than 1 second on a 10 Mbps LAN, so the burtiness over a 1-hour period would be extremely high. Now take, for example, a 50 minute video-conference call. Now the bit stream may be a continuous 256 kbps video stream over a 256 kbps point-to-point circuit. Thus, in this case the burstiness would be extremely low (approaching 1) because most of the time the peak rate was almost equal to the average rate (unless the samples were very long).

16.4.2 Traffic Delay Tolerance

How tolerant is traffic to delay? Can you wait an extra second or minute for your e-mail to be sent to the destination (high delay tolerance)? Can you wait 10 seconds (which may seem like an eternity) for your video-conference picture to catch up with the voice (low-delay tolerance)? Delay can be attributed to many factors, as described in Chapter 17, but the bottom line is to determine the maximum delay the application and user can tolerate.

16.4.3 Response Time

Variations in delay lead to variations in response time. Applications and users require different response times, from real time for applications like business video conferencing to batch for file transfers or electronic mail. Will your users get upset if their terminal emulation log-on has a 1-second response time on Monday and a 4-second response time on Tuesday? Can the user or application experience variable delay and response time, also called application "jitter"?

16.4.4 Capacity and Throughput

Capacity and throughput are similar, but not the same. *Capacity* is the actual amount of resources available across a given path. *Throughput* is a measure of how much *data* can be passed across a medium in a stated period of time, and typically this refers to user data. For example, the capacity of a T1 synchronous line is 1.544 Mbps in both the transmit and receive direction. If a TDM multiplexer using D4/ESF framing used this line, the actual throughput would be 1.536 Mbps (1.544 Mbps minus the 8-kbps framing overhead). Some multiplexers use additional available capacity for in-band signaling, network management, and other proprietary functions, thus reducing the maximum throughput even more. In the *circuit* world, throughput is commonly measured in bits and bytes (or even in peak periods). In the *packet* world, throughput is measured in packets/frames/cells per second. For example, on a 56 kbps capacity line a typical packet switch using 128-byte packets could pass up to 55 Packets Per Second (PPS):

$$(56\text{ kbps}) * \frac{1\text{ byte}}{8\text{ bits}} * \frac{1\text{ packet}}{128\text{ Bytes}} = 55\text{ PPS}$$

Thus, the theoretical maximum for 128-byte packet sizes over a 56 kbps circuit is 55 PPS, but in actuality due to overhead packets, this number is usually lower than 50 PPS. The same formula for packet switching can be used for frames- and cells-per-second throughput.

Some technologies utilize the available bandwidth more efficiently than others, providing for higher throughput. One example is Token Ring, which more efficiently utilizes the available bandwidth during the transmission of larger file transfers than Ethernet due to its token reservation technique. Another example is FDDI, which eliminates the need for token reservation. Either way, a data network should be designed with good throughput and extra capacity for the future. These steps are part of the capacity-planning process, discussed in detail in the next chapter.

16.4.5 Application Traffic Attributes Summarized

What are examples of applications that require different values of these four performance measures? Table 17.2 summarizes the approximate attributes for a number of applications.

16.4.6 Sessions and Usage Patterns

What is the relationship between network devices? What are the characteristics of the user's sessions with the network? Some characteristics include:

- ✓ Number of sessions or virtual circuits
- ✓ Number of call setups
- ✓ Number of times it turns on
- ✓ Number of calls
- ✓ Polling intervals
- ✓ Reporting intervals

- ✓ Maximum output rate
- ✓ Maximum rate receivable

What are the time patterns of user sessions? Time patterns occur in:

- ✦ Peak work/traffic hours (Figure 16.2a)
- ✦ Specific hours of bulk data transfer (Figure 16.2b)
- ✦ Random times, but predictable averages (Figure 16.2c)

These time intervals can typically be anywhere from milliseconds to hours. What are the traffic patterns during the peak usage times?

- ? Peak burst of traffic (not same as peak traffic condition)
- ? Average peak condition
- ? Maximum peak condition
- ? Sustained peak condition
- ? Constant data flows
- ? Change of protocols

TABLE 17.2 Application Traffic Attributes

Application	Burstiness	Delay Tolerance	Response Time (ms)	Throughput (Mbps)
E-mail	High	High	Batch	.004 to .020
Voice	Medium	Low	Real-Time	.004 to .064
File Transfer	Often High	High	Batch	.01 to 600
CAD/CAM	High	Medium	Near Real-Time	1 to 100
Transaction Processing	High	Low	Near Real-Time	.064 to 1.544
Channel-to-Channel	Low	Low	Real-Time	10 to 600
Imaging	High	Medium	Real-Time	.256 to 25
Business Video	Low	Low	Real-Time	.256 to 16
Entertainment Video	Low	Low	Near Real-Time	1.5 to 50
Broadcast Ubiquitous Video	Low	Low	Real-Time	.128 to 45
Various	Low	Low	Real-Time	.064 to 2.048
Isochronous Traffic				
LAN-LAN	High	High	Real-Time	4 to 100
Server Access	Avg.	High	Real-Time	4 to 100
Hi-Fi Audio	Low	Low	Real-Time	.128 to 1

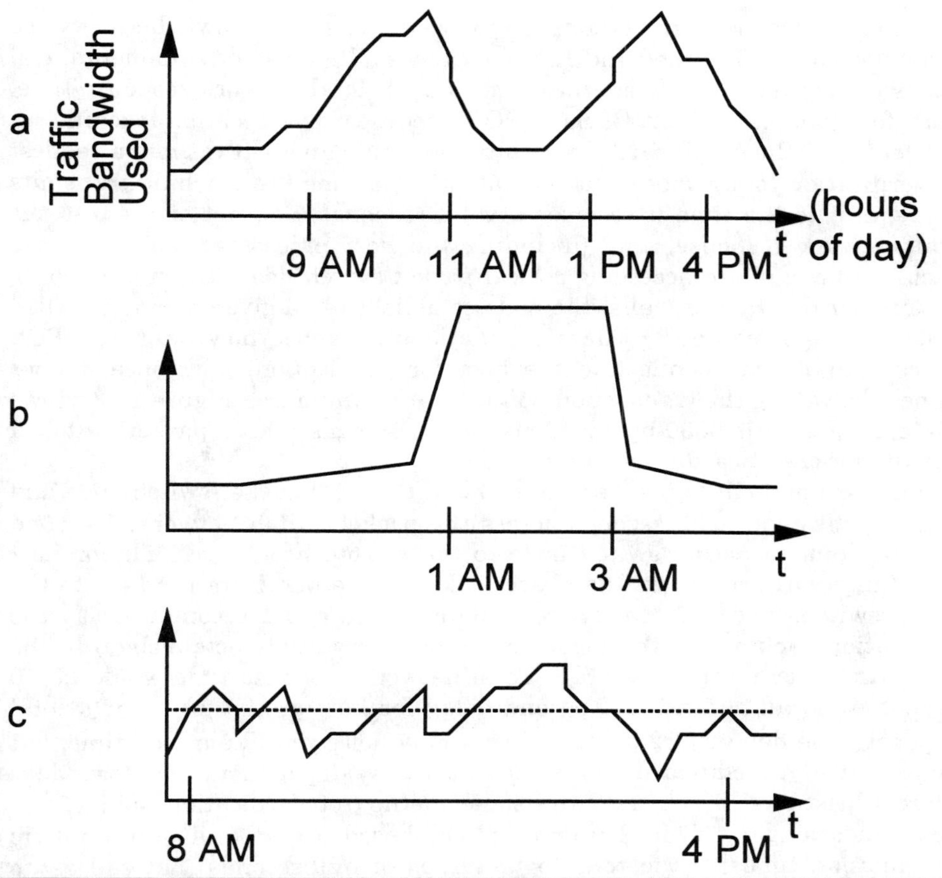

Figure 16.2 User Traffic Patterns

One way to get a handle on existing traffic flows is to evaluate the average, average peak, and maximum peak of traffic on the network at time slots throughout the day, say at 10-minute intervals. This sampling technique, when graphed on an *x-y* axis, will resemble those figures seen above. This can easily be accomplished through an inexpensive network modeling tool with reporting capability.

16.4.7 Call Setups per Second and Response Time

Any time users are contending for the same resources, there is the potential for blockage. Many of the newer frame and cell networks are designed to prioritize traffic and notify higher-level protocols when network response time is not quite what is required. But tracking the number of call setups and total response time is important when analyzing switched-network elements like X.25 packet and ISDN switches. In these environments, call setups per second can be generated based upon total network response time. Take, for example, a Point-Of-Sale (POS) credit-card verification machine. A retailer "zips" the credit card through the machine and it transmits a request for verification to a remote host computer. The time the machine transmits the request to the time it receives a valid response (i.e., not errored) is the total network response time (including the host processing time). If the machine is one of ten accessing a local packet-switch node (through a PAD), the number of requests (calls) the node establishes in a given second is called "call setups per second". These calculations influence how often the POS device actually can connect to the host for verification, and, once it does connect, how long the transaction will take at a minimum. Figure 16.3 shows this example with 9600-bps POS users accessing an X.25 packet-switched network for credit-card verification.

In this example, it takes 3 seconds to dial the local packet-switch node and transmit the request, 2 seconds across the packet-switch network, 1 second from the remote packet-switch node to the remote host, 2 seconds for host processing (verification and database lookup), 1 second from the host to the packet switch, 2 seconds back across the network, and 1 second to relay the information back across the modems (connection already established) to the automatic teller machine (ATM). Total network response time would be 10 seconds, with an additional 2-second delay for host processing – for a total response time delay of 12 seconds. This may not seem like a long time, but compare it to a credit-card transaction at a busy department store two days before Christmas, which uses the same method of verification, and it will seem much longer. Typical frame and cell-based networks have round-trip transmission times in the tens to hundreds of milliseconds (but call setup through the network might still take a second or so).

Networks of this type are designed based upon standard Poisson distribution arrival rates, where the network is designed to accommodate overload periods of traffic for a short period of time at a certain grade of service with the understanding that there will be underutilized periods when queued or lower-priority data can be processed at even better grades of service. Traffic arrival rates and handling will be covered in more detail in Chapter 17.

Notice that there is little to no room for delay in this type of application. In fact, delays have a way of escalating in packet- and frame-switched systems, because calls and frames store up in the buffer queue and new calls or frames cannot even get into the queue until the old ones are out. In frame relay and cell switching, excess calls that exceed the buffers are simply "dropped", with the presumption that higher-layer protocols will retransmit the data later as necessary.

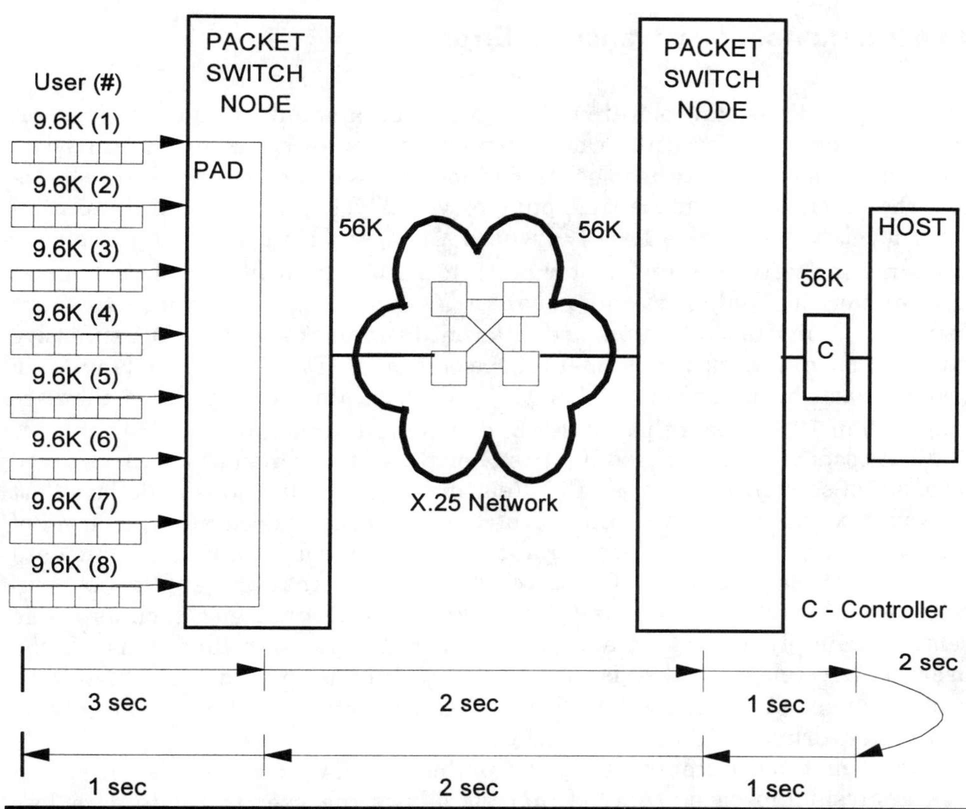

Figure 16.3 Total Network Response Time

16.4.8 Routing

Another important factor is data unit routing. What route does cell, frame, packet, or entire call or message take from origin to destination, and what are all of the possible routes it may take? For circuit-based technologies, the origin and destination are often fixed. Even circuit-switched services can provide planned origin and destinations. But with switched services such as frame relay and SMDS, there are logical addressing schemes where any user may be able to "talk" to any other user. How do you plan for the call routing in this scenario? The best method is to calculate "best-guess" traffic utilization averages and peaks based on common user groups, known traffic patterns, and projections provided by the users. Thus, a deterministic approach to network design will prevent frustration in your capacity planning staff.

16.4.9 Data Accuracy (Minimum Errors)

Some applications can tolerate only a minimum amount or no data error, or, in other words, a stated data accuracy, to certify an accurate transmission. Excessive delay could cause the user to lose the session and need to reestablish the session, experience time-outs, or worse yet, lose data. Minimum bit error levels are stated as 1×10^{-X}, where X ranges from a value of 3 in poorer transmission networks to a factor of 12 to 15 better in fiber-optic networks. The higher the value of the negative X exponent, the fewer errors are incurred. Note that bit errors are different from packet errors, but excessive bit errors may cause detrimental packet-error rates. For example, a transmission bit-error rate of 1×10^{-3} will drop almost all packets that are longer than 128 bytes if the errors are distributed randomly.

What costs will be incurred if parts of or the entire transmission is received late, out of sequence, or not at all? Relating these implications to dollars (lost revenue and productivity) is one of the best methods of deciding what level of data accuracy to provide. Is error and flow control required, or can data simply be discarded (as in frame relay) assuming that the application will take care of error detection and recovery? Some technologies such as frame relay can simply discard data during error and congestion conditions. If the user cannot tolerate this, is he or she willing to provide the high-level protocols needed for end-to-end flow and error control, or is he or she relying on the network or CPE devices to do this?

A good method of approaching the problem of data accuracy is through a risk analysis approach. A risk analysis allows the user to relate data loss risks to financial loss. For example, the loss of a T1 transmitting data from a banking institution for 10 seconds could cause the bank to lose up to $200,000 in lost transactions. An even worse case would be the stock market for international trading, where millions could be lost in seconds, or brokerage houses, where large penalties are paid for network-induced late trades. Other risks that could relate directly to costs include: downtime of users or computers, routing of data to the wrong destination (possibly a competitor), and loss of customers due to downtime. Productivity losses are less tangible, but sometimes even more detrimental than financial losses. These figures all add up to a bottom-line value for the assurance that data will be delivered error-free and to the correct destination.

16.4.10 Prioritization

Users with multiple applications, traffic flows, and hardware devices that use shared resources may want to prioritize their traffic. Find out what the users view as their priority scheme for each application, between applications, and even among multiple users. Find out which network elements carry the mission-critical traffic, as well as those that have redundant systems for periods of failure. *Mission-critical* traffic is defined as data containing the day-to-day critical business information, which would cause severe financial or operational loss if corrupted or not delivered. Examples include: billing, command and control, monetary transactions, and account information. Prioritization is important for services such as SMDS and ATM, which offer quality of service (QoS) features. Priority schemes can be as simple as giving the higher priority traffic all the throughput during periods of network problems, or prioritizing traffic between PVCs, VCs, or VPs.

16.4.11 Application Quality of Service (QoS) Requirements

Various applications have different QoS requirements. For example, some well-known requirements exist for voice after 30 years of experience in telephony. If voice has greater than about 15 ms of delay, then echo cancellation is usually required. Packetized voice can accept almost a 1 percent cell-loss rate without being objectionable to most listeners. Newer applications do not have such a basis, or well-defined requirements; however, there are some general requirements that the following paragraphs summarize.

Video application requirements depend upon several factors, including the video-coding algorithm, the degree of motion required in the image sequence, and the resolution required in the image. Loss generally causes some image degradation, ranging from distorted portions of an image to loss of an entire frame, depending upon the extent of the loss and the sensitivity of the video-coding algorithm. Also, variations in delay of greater than 20 to 40 ms can cause perceivable jerkiness in the video playback.

Combined video and audio is very sensitive to differential delays. Human perception is highly attuned to the correct correlation of audio and video, which is apparent in the discrepancies of some foreign language dubbed films. File transfer applications are also sensitive to loss and variations in delay, which result in retransmissions and consequent reduction in usable throughput. The sensitivity is related to the time-out and loss-identification algorithm and the retransmission strategy of the application.

As we have discussed previously, users of interactive applications are sensitive to loss and variations in delay due to retransmissions, and inconsistent response time (also called "jitter"), which can decrease productivity. Consistent response time (or the lack thereof) can affect how users perceive data service quality.

Distributed computing and database applications can be very sensitive to absolute delay, loss, and variations in delay. The ideal for these types of applications is infinite bandwidth with latency close to that of the speed of light in fiber. A practical model is that of performance comparable to a locally attached disk drive or CD-ROM, which ranges from 10 to 100 ms. Each of these sensitivities to delay must be taken into account when determining a target QoS for each user and application.

16.5 PROTOCOLS

The full suite of user protocols must be defined for both existing and planned applications. This includes all protocols for each architecture supported, serving all seven layers of the OSI reference model, which may include everything from the lower level physical media requirements to the upper level presentation software and operating systems. Multiple protocols per layer are often present. Previous chapters have identified and explained approximately 90 percent of the user protocols that are normally encountered.

Next, define what protocols are to be used on both the application side and the network side. What functions are specific to applications that warrant special consideration? Also, define how users will internetwork these protocols. The bridging, routing, or switching required will depend heavily upon the protocols. For example, some protocols such as NetBEUI and DEC LAT are not network-layer addressable protocols and must be bridged, while others such as FTP can be routed through the use of TCP/IP at the network level. Will the user require protocol encapsulation, conversion, translation, or just bridging? Are higher-level directory services required (e.g., X.400, X.500)? Also, know if there are any special or proprietary implementations of these protocols and how they operate.

16.5.1 Connection/Session Oriented

Is connection-oriented or connectionless service required? Connection-oriented services could include channel-to-channel (host-to-host) or synchronous dedicated circuit (multiplexer), and connectionless services could be LAN/MAN (bridged or routed) traffic — standard LAN protocols are all connectionless.

Is polling/selection or nonpolling used? Examples of polling or selection services include selective or group polling (E-mail), stop-and-wait polling, sliding windows for packets or frames (e.g., BSC, HDLC, SDLC), and transaction processing (e.g., order entry). These are typically based on hierarchical or client/server architectures. Nonpolling services and applications include Request to Send (RTS)/Clear to Send (CTS), Xon/Xoff, multiplexed, token-based reservation and nonreservation (priority and nonpriority), and CSMA and CSMA/CD random access with sensing (priority and nonpriority). Ethernet is the only common CSMA/CD protocol and it is always nonpriority.

16.5.2 Protocol Routing

Routing accomplished by a protocol can either be fixed or dynamic. This depends on many factors often outside the user's control and is a function of the network technologies and protocols. An example of fixed-protocol routing is PVCs in frame relay, where a user-assigned PVC will always route from one fixed point to another. An example of dynamic protocol routing is X.25 packet switching (including datagram services), where the packets will route dynamically the "best way", including around a failure. Dynamic protocol routing can occur either in a true dynamic nature through the network and transparent to the user, or it can be initiated by user commands (as in high-speed circuit switching). The capability to dynamically reroute around network failures is often a requirement, so determine if the dynamic rerouting is serviced on a *packet* level or a *(virtual) circuit* level.

16.5.3 Application Architecture

Applications will generally follow a specific application architecture which establishes the standard user and programmer interface. When the developers use an application architecture, they set the standard method of protocols for programming, file transfer, and data-access methods for consistency across the network. Some examples of application architectures include:

- TCP/IP Internet Architecture
- IBM Systems Application Architecture (SAA)
- DEC Network Applications Support (NAS)
- Novell's NetWare

These application architectures tend to be found in more distributed application designs. While many network designs are transparent to this level of protocol, many of the architectures listed also define protocol levels affected by the network. The network designer and manager must understand protocols down to the application program interfaces (APIs) as problems with an application architecture that could have repercussions down to the physical media. Also, determine whether traffic is centrally processed, or if the processing is distributed over multiple locations.

16.5.4 Addressing and Naming Schemes

What are the user addressing and naming schemes currently being used? Are they flat addressing conventions or are they hierarchical in nature? Are they permanent? If not, can changes, modifications, and new adaptations be made easily? Can they fit in with a global addressing scheme? Comprehensive addressing questions can be asked after the reader has completed Chapter 22 on address and routing design, but these are good starting questions.

16.6 TIME AND DELAY CONSIDERATIONS

Probably one of the most important aspects of data communications networking is timing or delay considerations. Decreasing network delay and improving the total transmission time is a major responsibility for the design engineer, and this can relate to significant cost savings. Response times are measured in application-to-application, network request and response, and the total network end-to-end response time.

Delays in transmission times affect throughput. Sometimes, short delays are tolerable. Some technologies such as packet switching use buffering to queue excess data until it can be transmitted, thus incurring some delay in the storage. Other technologies such as frame relay use minimal buffering and simply block or discard excess data. Interrupts and resets are additional forms of delay.

While timing plays an important part in the accuracy of data transport across the network, especially with new synchronous technologies like SONET, it becomes increasingly important to have accurate timing sources.

16.6.1 Access Time

Figure 16.4 shows a comparison of LAN/MAN access times for the IEEE 802.X and FDDI technologies. These curves assume that there are 100 stations on the LAN generating the same amounts of traffic with an average packet size of 256 bytes.

For circuit-switched and multiplexed services not having to contend for a token or access to the common bus, the access time should be almost instantaneous (except during blocking). *Access time* differs from *response time* in that it only provides a measure for when the user can place data on the medium. *Response time* takes into account the round-trip delay from source to destination, or the time it takes a user to send a request until he or she receives a response/reply.

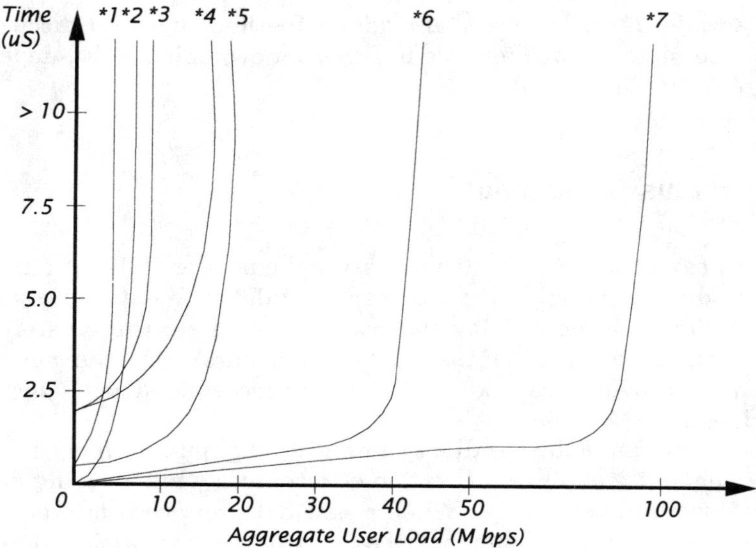

Figure 16.4 LAN/MAN Access Times Comparison

16.6.2 Response Time

Is delay in response time a major factor? What is the element of delay that most impacts response time? What is the response time requirement versus costs of delay and blocking? Response time is a double-edged sword. Normally, users will be quite aware of their response time (probably to the nearest second or hundreds of milliseconds). If a new network service is provided that decreases the time required to receive a response (response time), they will, of course, be happy. Let us take the example of a new LAN service such as 100 Mbps Ethernet, where they are the only test users during the first three months of service. Their response time decreases from 10 seconds to 1 second with the new LAN access speed. They are ecstatic, until the Ethernet LAN adds more users, and their response time starts to creep back up toward 3–4 seconds. They still have better than half the response time they originally enjoyed before the higher-speed LAN was installed, but they still complain that their response time has been degraded (and will continue to degrade as more users are added to the bus). As discussed previously, one possible answer for this is Ethernet switching hubs, depending on the traffic patterns.

16.6.3 Delay versus Throughput

How much delay can be tolerated when accessing the network? What amount can be tolerated during the end-to-end transport of data? What is the round trip delay? Usually, the more delay that can be tolerated, the greater the throughput. What is the cost of time delay in dollars? Do the network devices chosen to provide transport add any appreciable delay (such as routers or bridges)?

Users want minimum delay and maximum throughput. Thus, a good network design should maximize utilization of resources while keeping delay in line with the user's expectations. When a new data service is offered, and few users are on the network, it may be necessary to introduce artificial delay to control user expectations. This is only temporary until more users start using the service. This provides that the first users will experience a *constant* delay over time, rather than a decrease in performance as users are added. The lesson here is to manage the users' expectations concerning response time.

One example of an application that is costly in bandwidth is a card-swipe reader. This device uses an entire call for call setup, data transfer of two packets, and call tear-down. One alternative for this is to use the packet switch option of fast select. This will allow the entire process to occur in a single transaction.

16.6.4 Performance – Packet-per-Second Processing, Forwarding, and Filtering

Network hardware can measure performance through packet-per-second (PPS) processing, forwarding, and filtering rates. Packet-per-second processing is how fast the switch interprets the packet header and does what it needs to do with the packet (either interprets, terminates, or switches it). Typical access switches operate at the 2000 to 5000 PPS rates with backbone switches exceeding 500,000 PPS. Packet-forwarding rates are provided by bridges and routers to represent how fast they interpret packets and forward them to their MAC destination. Typical rates are 3000 to 4000 PPS forwarded, with many vendors now exceeding these rates. Packet-filtering rates show how fast a bridge can determine if a packet is addressed to a point inside the LAN (filtered) or whether it should be passed on to the next bridge. Typical filtering rates are from 9000 to 14,000 PPS.

These rates are commonly displayed as bridging throughput, such as 500,000 PPS bridging throughput. There are also routing throughput rates in excess of 100,000 PPS. Many of these high rates are based upon small packets (e.g., 64 bytes), many of the rates go down as the size of the packet increases, and some are based on packets with no data in them. The source route bridging protocol, for example, usually offers the highest PPS bridging rate, and the source transparent bridging protocol for Ethernet throughput is much better than that for Token Ring. FDDI packet-forwarding rates are usually 75,000 PPS (for 22-byte packets). Obviously, as more protocol conversion and routing takes place, the PPS rate is driven down proportionally.

The most important aspect when designing for packet performance is the total PPS processing of each line and that of the entire device. For example, if a user requirement is 500 PPS over a DS1 line, and there are 20 DS1 lines, then the requirement is 10,000 PPS. Therefore, a device that handles 500,000 PPS can easily handle the load (assuming vendor claims are accurate and the lab results are meaningful in a real-world environment). There are many ways a device can be limited by performance, including interface-specific, protocol-specific, and traffic-specific.

16.6.5 Blocking versus Storage versus Queuing

Invariably, every network will eventually encounter some network congestion. It is important to understand how the user applications and protocols will handle these congestion conditions. Congestion can have three major effects on user traffic. When a technology uses blocking, the user traffic flow is blocked until sufficient bandwidth is available to continue the transmission. This is the most drastic method of dealing with congestion, yet it is the method employed by many of the new technologies discussed in this text. Other technologies just "drop the information out onto the floor" during congestion conditions, assuming that the user has employed some form of higher-level protocol at the CPE transport through application level to stop the flow of information until congestion clears. Others notify the user and simply block the transmission flow until the congestion clears or the user slows down transmission of data. The determination to use or not use blocking is very important, as many delay-sensitive applications cannot handle blocking.

Storage and queuing are similar and often used together. Queuing is the method of allowing data to be stored in buffers in the order it was received (FIFO) until there is sufficient bandwidth to transmit it to its destination; it is sent out in the same order it was received. The primary example of queuing discussed already is the packet switch, which queues packets until transmission bandwidth is available. Storage is used in store-and-forward networks, and typically signifies the use of memory buffers in a FIFO arrangement. Both queuing and storage increase delay through the network.

Blocking, storage, and queuing vary by technology and by implementation within each technology. Please refer to hardware vendor's implementation specifics.

16.6.6 Interrupts and Resets

The use of interrupts is rare but still should be taken into account. Interrupts occur when the user's traffic carries software-defined interrupts such as break keys. Ask if the user plans on using such interrupts, and, if so, what interrupts will be used. Also, ask if the interrupts need to be sent ahead of data. A second form of interrupt is the reset, which some applications will perform. Both interrupts and resets should be transparent to the transport network.

16.6.7 Congestion

Congestion in public data networks is a normal situation and should be planned for. Congestion will warrant different levels of response depending upon its severity or duration. Congestion is defined as the condition where the offered load (demand) from the user to the network is approaching, or exceeds, the network design limits for guaranteeing the Quality of Service (QoS) specified in the traffic contract. This demand may exceed the resource design limit because the resources were overbooked, or because of failures within the network. Resources that can become congested include CPE and switch ports, buffers, transmission links, and processors. Congestion can occur simultaneously on multiple resources for a cumulative affect. The resource where demand exceeds capacity is called a bottleneck, congestion point, or constraint. Once congestion occurs, there are certain responses, or controls, that exist to deal with it. The detection of congestion is termed an indication, feedback, or notification. The reaction to congestion can occur in either *time* (packet-by-packet, frame-by-frame, or cell-by-cell standalone or burst basis) or *space* (a single node, the source, the receiver, or multiple nodes).

There are longer time-scale methods of congestion control, namely, resource allocation, network engineering, and network management controls. Alternate methods exist to adaptively control the flow of user traffic into the network using either flow control or backward/forward congestion notification (as with frame relay and ATM).

16.7 CONNECTIVITY

With a handle on the types and characteristics of traffic the user requires for transport, we now take the next step to define user connectivity requirements. In many cases, user connectivity will be defined by existing connectivity methods. First, we look at the differences between user-to-network and network-to-network connectivity. Geographic connectivity requirements play an important factor in traffic patterns, as the current infrastructure and design of cabling and local connectivity. Finally, remote access requirements are introduced and given greater study in later chapters.

16.7.1 User-to-Network and Network-to-Network Connectivity

The user typically requires a single interface to the entire computing and communications environment or network. This user-to-network interface allows local or remote access to other users with high-level protocols, transparent to the lower-level protocols and the transport in between the local and remote applications. A graphical and textual user interface is typically required when communicating with the network. Symbols and icons of the graphical interface are often preferred to text-mode command prompts, forming a requirement for a true *human* rather than *machine* interface to the bit/byte/packet/cell world.

Other questions must be asked about the user-to-network interface. Some have been covered before. What is the speed (data-access and data-transfer rate) of connectivity? What types of devices will be connected? What is the distance involved between user equipment and data-communications equipment? What vendors and models are now used? What are the vendor's software and hardware vendor specifics? What mode of addressing is required for the access and backbone portions? What are the physical, data link, etc., protocols required for basic connectivity?

Once the user-to-network interface has been defined, any network-to-network interface requirements for internetworking new and existing networks to the data-transport network must also be defined. To what extent is ubiquitous connectivity required? Any-to-any connectivity can take on many forms and layers of protocols. Will the connectivity community be homogeneous or heterogeneous? Will private, public, or a hybrid network access and transport be required? Also, there is the question of what form of technology will be used for network interfaces and internetworking arises. Examples include:

- Multipoint or point-to-point
- Multiplexing or concentration
- Switched (circuit, packet, frame, or cell)

- Bridged or routed
- Hybrid

16.7.2 Geographical Requirements

Where do the applications reside? Are there specific geographical location restrictions based on topology, transport media availability or quality, user communities, existing facilities, or any other limitations? Are the users fixed or mobile?

16.7.3 Structure – Central versus Distributed

What type of structure is required? The technologies described in this book apply to both distributed and centralized processing. Is the design hierarchical in nature? Hierarchical LAN/MAN designs are the first step in building WANs because of the importance of the segmentation of data user groups. Now the proliferation of LAN switching is making hierarchical LAN design virtual in nature.

Figure 16.5 shows an example of a hierarchical LAN/MAN configuration. Here, Ethernet LANs are built in a three-tier hierarchy. Tier 1 is the local floor LAN segment, tier 2 is the departmental LAN segment (department 1 comprises floors 1, 2, and 3 of building A, department 2 comprises floors 4 and 5 of building A, and so on), and tier 3 is the building LAN segment. The fourth tier is the FDDI MAN connecting users in both buildings. This allows segmentation of user traffic and prevents "flooding" the FDDI MAN with information transfers it never needs to process. Combine these junction points between LAN segments with switching hubs and you have the next generation of "virtual" LAN design, where any user on any LAN can be switched to any other user without the requirement for routing. Virtual LAN design is a complex subject that is just now beginning to achieve recognition. Figure 16.6 shows an example of how to design a LAN/MAN *without* this hierarchical design. The FDDI ring could be a collapsed backbone within a single device, such as an intelligent hub, router, or switch. Further study on VLAN design is left to the reader.

16.7.4 Current Infrastructure

What is the current infrastructure being used? Are user communities heterogeneous or homogeneous? What impact will implementing a new platform or architecture have on existing facilities? The designer must understand the existing voice, data, and other media structures to effectively utilize all existing resources in the new network. Migration from an existing architecture to new platforms is often an arduous and difficult process. The designer must consider the use of temporary gateways as the first step at internetworking the current infrastructure with a new architecture.

16.7.5 Remote Access

Do remote users operate in a fixed or mobile environment? If users are in a fixed environment, what type of access facilities are available – dedicated or switched? If users are mobile, what geographic or virtual connectivity areas do they typically travel through? What access facilities are available in these areas, and how do they communicate today?

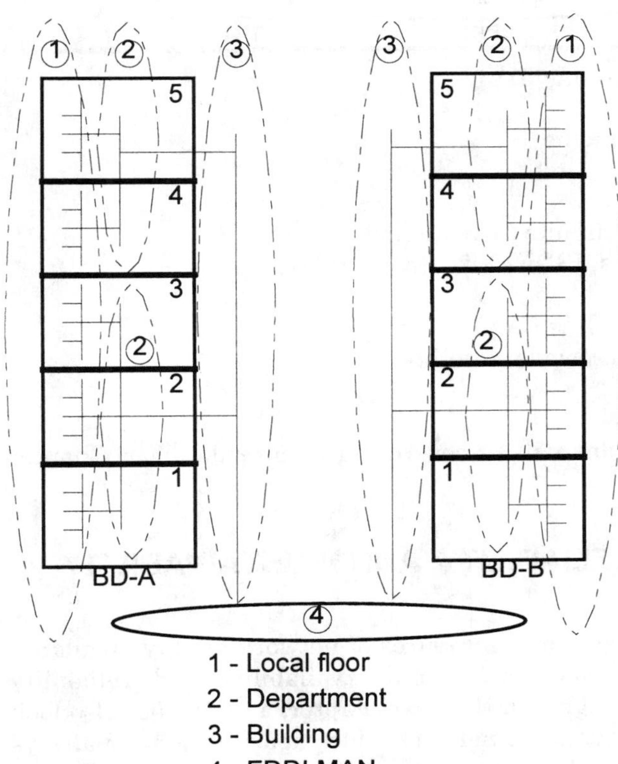

Figure 16.5 Hierarchical LAN/MAN Designs

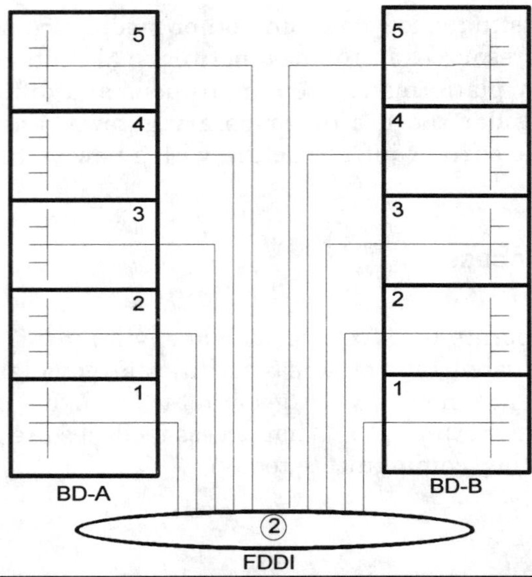

Figure 16.6 Nonhierarchical LAN/MAN Design

Remote access facilities could be

* Multipoint circuits
* Point-to-point dedicated circuits (private line)
* Dial access (asynchronous, ISDN, X.25, frame relay)
* Wireless acces
* s (cellular, PCS/PCN, wireless LAN)
* Radio-based systems (microwave, satellite)
* VSAT

Remote-access design options will be covered in greater detail in Chapter 20.

16.8 AVAILABILITY, RELIABILITY, AND MAINTAINABILITY

A user is concerned with three major measures of network quality: availability, reliability, and maintainability. While availability and reliability calculations are defined thoroughly in the next chapter, a user must also look at availability as related to available network-wide capacity. A user always wants to have enough capacity to transmit his or her message (regardless of the message size) in a reasonable amount of time. The network allocates capacity across the network, rather than to a specific user. Some services have methods of allocating specific capacity to users, such as with SMDS, ATM, and RSVP for IP.

Maintainability is defined as the measure of effort a user or network provider must put into the network to maintain its operating efficiency. Maintainability can include

⇒ Defining how the designer will expand the network as requirements increase
⇒ Expandability and flexibility of the hardware platform
⇒ Ease of software upgrades
⇒ Built-in tools for network monitoring, troubleshooting, trending, and reporting

Does the protocol require fault tolerance, and what is the level of error tolerability? How much sharing of resources and capacity is tolerable? Does the user protocol require guaranteed delivery? These are some of the questions that are asked of the user regarding the reliability of existing systems.

16.9 AMOUNT OF USER CONTROL

To what degree does the user need control of network resources? Many public network service providers are struggling with this question. Today, many users want more and more control over their traffic than in the past. In practice, many users want the comfort level of "seeing" the network while allowing the vendor to actually administrate the network under the "control" of the customer. Customers require the capability of intelligent network management and tools that they can use to monitor the health of and reconfigure network resources. The designer must draw the line as to which resources users can access and which they cannot. One option is to allow users to "see" the network status of resources but in a manner which will not permit the resources to be directly modified. An interesting aspect of services such as frame relay is that they provide users with network status for conditions such as network congestion (which they may or may not be able to control). Remember, also, that too much information can be dangerous, so carefully evaluate what the user really will need to see of the network. The best solution is to provide a true level of transparency while providing optimal user "control" of network resources even if the vendor administrates it.

Control can take on either a centralized or distributed nature. In private networks, control rests within the corporation. Public networks are typically managed and controlled by the service provider. Centralized control is often the case for networks managed by local or regional network-management centers. Distributed control is often the case where many LANs are communicating over a WAN. The newer technologies require a little of both in a hybrid mode.

16.10 EXPANDABILITY, SCALABILITY, AND EVOLUTION

The network must be able to react to change. Therefore, it must be designed with the capability to expand, evolve, and be scaled either up or down. The network plan should define an evolutionary cycle, not a revolutionary change. It should also provide the capability to change configuration rapidly to meet changes in a dynamic user environment. This change could involve hardware and software configurations, addition or deletion of services, constant technology updates and upgrades, and protocol flexibility. Strict change procedures should accompany any change, so that the scope of the change, no matter how trivial it may seem, is understood by the network manager. Expansions and migrations should be planned in advance, based on user projections for expanding current applications or adding new ones. Dates should be achievable yet provided in the broadest form available (e.g., 2H99).

One method of ensuring that the network can handle future growth is to overbuild the network with capacity and processing power. But this can become expensive, and can prove to be misguided if the excess allocations are in the wrong location, the technology changes, or the network requirements were overestimated in the first place. Effective network capacity planning is the answer to this problem, along with education of the users on how to plan for and use the evolving technologies covered in this book. Another option is to use a public data service as the network of choice, thus placing the burden of escaping network technological obsolescence in the backbone network onto the public service provider.

16.11 SERVICE ASPECTS

Service aspects such as network management, billing, security, user support, and disaster recovery are important topics with a broad range of standard and proprietary solutions. Network designers must understand the capabilities offered by each technology and protocol and make their decisions based on the criteria defined in this book.

16.11.1 Network Management

Most users require fast end-to-end fault identification and isolation during network failure conditions. This can be accomplished through a proactive network monitoring and management system that provides configuration capabilities and dynamic capacity allocation through a user-friendly network management interface. Much more will be said on network management in Chapter 23.

16.11.2 Billing

For public data networks, billing is based on either public pricing or tariffs. Does the user require special billing arrangements? Are costs allocated by individual, by department, or companywide? Does the customer agree with these methods? Is itemized billing required, and to what extent does each user analyze network costs?

For strictly internal company networks, how are the network and traffic transport costs charged back to the user departments? If it is strictly an internal enterprise network, can a charge-back scheme be implemented? What method of expense allocation accounting is preferred? Can bills for different services be consolidated.

16.11.3 Redundancy and Disaster Recovery

What level of redundancy and disaster recovery is required? The highest level of redundancy and disaster recovery is one fully redundant system element for every live system (1:1). A more conservative approach is one redundant system for *N* systems (1:*N*) or (*N*+1) systems. Is the user prepared to incur the higher cost of such redundancy, or will fewer systems suffice? Is outsourcing of disaster recovery to a public data service provider an option? Remember, disaster recovery plans should be periodically tested at least twice per year to ensure they indeed work and provide true backup.

16.11.4 Security

What level of security is required? What levels of passwords and access are required? What resources require what levels of access, and how are they accessed? Does the user require end-to-end security? How sensitive is the information being passed? With the advent of corporate Internet connectivity, can someone actually compromise your operations though any part of the network access? Do you have the appropriate firewalls, packet and circuit filters, and application filters? What is your security policy? Can you track down and catch an intruder once you have identified an intrusion? As more corporate LAN users access the Internet, corporatewide security will become more of a major concern. A single WAN connection to the Internet can open up your entire corporate network to a security breach.

16.11.5 User Support

User support should be tailored to the user's needs. Users with highly complex routing protocols, proprietary protocol implementations, and executive level users will require many more resources than a standard, single protocol user, mostly because of the complexity of the problems that can occur. The more complex the protocols and the more mixed the protocol environment, the greater will be the complexity and level of support required. User expectations should be managed from the day the network is first announced through the day the user gains actual access to the network. The levels of user support should be agreed upon before the design is complete.

It is sometimes difficult to understand what the user defines as "excellent service" or "quality service". These values vary based on the user's past experience with similar networks. One gauge of user support requirements is to monitor existing systems support and the level of dedication and time required. Ask what services the users currently operate, or what access will be required with the new network. It is important to establish lines of communications with users so that they can alert the network designer of future requirements as they occur. Start the long-term planning process in the initial design.

16.12 BUDGET CONSTRAINTS

Though users try to spend as little money as possible on the network, they still want as many network resources as possible. Either way, the designer must design the network within a given budget, accommodating the largest number of users and applications within the available budget. This becomes a balance between cost, capabilities, and connectivity. How far can you push the economics and still provide functionality and connectivity? The growth in budgets for data-related services in many large corporations is larger than for voice. But how do we justify these large data-network expenditures?

A network becomes cost-justified if it improves operating efficiency, helps users meet corporate objectives, provides a potential revenue increase, and avoids larger expenditures. Additional criteria include improving customer service and creating new services for the user. Ultimately, the question must be asked — can the network expenses be related back to the user and will the network meet the desired criteria?

There is also the concern of who controls the network budget, the network manager or the users. Most often, it is the network manager. This is heavily influenced by how much control the user has over network expenditures. The rule is, the more critical the application, and the closer it gets to the revenue stream, and the more control the user will have over what is purchased. When users have budgetary control, more care is exercised about what is placed on the network. When the network manager has control and the user is a customer, the user tries to place everything possible over the network. This is the point where departmental charge-back schemes may be implemented. The manager can also allocate a communications budget to each department based on the requirements discussed in this chapter. Either way, network costs must be controlled. Customers and users may have an existing hardware base, so the cost of additional equipment, or savings thereof, may not be the major consideration. What happens when the budget cannot meet the requirements? Outsourcing may then become a viable option.

16.13 POLITICS

Politics can cause a perfectly good network plan to go awry. Politics is part of the everyday business world, and it is also part of the requirements process. The user requirements should be scanned for hidden political agendas and decision criteria based upon political rather than technical or economical factors. This is not to say that we should have the equivalent of the McCarthy purges of the 1950s, looking for "communist" bits in every data stream. The network designer should be aware, however, and be prepared to dig a little deeper into the requirement should it appear that executive politics, vendor or application favoritism, turf wars, or any other politically based bias is negatively influencing the network-design decision process.

16.14 REVIEW

There are two viewpoints to requirements: that of the user and that of the designer. Obviously, the designer viewpoint is much more extensive, and has warranted a more detailed discussion. Many characteristics of traffic affect the network design. The characteristics of protocols and their routing, architecture, and the importance of their addressing schemes play a major role. Understanding the transmission time and delay requirements for all traffic types is critical. Methods of connectivity were also discussed, and the calculations to help the designer meet availability, reliability, and maintainability of users was outlined. A brief look was taken at the amount of user control provided by the service aspects of each network design. Two issues which plague every network designer were discussed: budget constraints and politics. The network designer, therefore, must compile all of the user requirements in the manner presented above and feed them into the traffic analysis phase.

Chapter

17

Traffic Engineering and Capacity Planning

Capacity planning used to be fairly straightforward for voice networks and private line data networks. Traffic growth and volume figures were calculated, and the appropriate number of dedicated circuits were added or subtracted with each iteration. If capacity exceeded projections, more bandwidth was ordered. With the advent of distributed computing and communications environments, the number of capacity contingencies has grown at an exponential rate. Advanced protocols, dynamic traffic patterns and characteristics, and peer-to-peer internetworking has changed capacity planning into more of a heuristic guesswork approach than one based on concrete calculations. The traffic matrix is no longer a two-dimensional spreadsheet, but a multidimensional matrix including variables such as protocol types, multiple protocols, multiple traffic-flow patterns, multiple technologies, circuit options, and more. These new technologies and traffic types have caused capacity planners to throw away the old traffic design books and simply overengineer the network. But new tools continue to emerge on the market that take into account multiple protocol environments and can provide a fairly accurate picture for building large advanced public data networks, supporting services such as frame relay, SMDS, and ATM. In this chapter, some new views on traffic analysis are mixed with some older traditional methodology in an attempt to carry the network designer into the next generation of traffic engineering, analysis, and capacity planning — presenting a new method for creating a traffic matrix, including enhanced calculations applied to traffic patterns for both old and new technologies, other methods of modeling traffic sources and switch performance, using some useful approximations for estimating performance that may hopefully get the designer closer to accurately predicting the required network capacity.

17.1 THROUGHPUT CALCULATIONS

Every user-access circuit is regulated by throughput. Throughput is the actual amount of user protocol data that is transmitted over the access circuit and received by the network node. Throughput can also be measured end to end across the entire network. Access-circuit speeds are represented as a total capacity number, for example, a DS1 private line circuit has the capability to transmit up to 1.544 Mbps. The actual throughput that the user receives can be much less than that, depending on the protocols (i.e., TCP/IP compared to FR) and equipment used. Each protocol contributes, in the most basic sense, a particular amount of overhead. Basically, the throughput is the total transmission speed minus the protocol overhead. Overhead takes many forms, from pure header and trailer data wrapped around the user data (packet encapsulation and reformation) to time spent waiting for acknowledgments when data is not even being transmitted. When engineering a network, users should be concerned with the total throughput they will receive, not the total circuit capacity.

The common units of measurement for throughput are bits, bytes, packets, frames, or cells per second. These rates can be applied not only to transmission, but also to processing, filtering, and forwarding capability of network equipment. The amount of overhead affects the total throughput provided to the user over an access line. The technology used and the number of encapsulations incurred before actual transmission of the user data takes place also contribute to overhead.

17.1.1 Packets, Frames, and Cells per Second

If one were to ignore the intricacies of each higher-layer protocol, the maximum achievable throughput could be calculated. The following terms will be used throughout these calculations. The terms *packets*, *frames*, and *cells per second* will be used throughout the calculation. Let's first take an example using X.25 packet switching. The maximum achievable Packet Per Second (PPS) rate on a physical circuit can be calculated as follows:

$$\text{PPS} = (P_K \text{ bits per second})\left(\frac{1 \text{ byte}}{8 \text{ bits}}\right)\left(\frac{1 \text{ packet}}{\text{x bytes}}\right)$$

For example, a DS0 circuit ($P_K = 56{,}000$) has a maximum PPS transmission when using a 128-bByte (x = 128) packet size of:

$$(56{,}000)\left(\frac{1}{8}\right)\left(\frac{1}{128}\right) = 55 \text{ PPS}$$

Again, using 128-byte frames, this number would be 55 frames per second. The same calculations are carried forward for frames and cells per second, adjusting for the speed of the medium and the overhead involved.

17.1.2 Effects of Overhead

The PPS calculated in the last example is actually somewhat misleading. It does not account for the overhead incurred in the switching and protocol handshaking operations. For example, take a 512 kbps frame relay fractional T1 access line. The frame size of 1024 bytes with overhead of 13 bytes (using extended addressing) per frame is used. The total frame size would be 1024 + 13 = 1037 bytes. The actual frames per second throughput would be:

(512 kbps)(1/8)(1/1037) = 61.72 frames per second

Consider the same example using a frame size of 56 bytes. The same amount of overhead is 13 bytes, for a total frame size of 56 + 13 = 69 bytes. The actual frames per second throughput would be:

(512 kbps)(1/8)(1/69) = 928 frames per second.

At first blush, it appears that throughput has been improved, but, actually, it has degraded drastically. The overhead in the first example was only 1.25 percent, whereas in the second example it jumped to 18.84 percent! These calculations are shown below. This illustrates that the larger frame sizes are more efficient and provide higher line throughput than the smaller ones, but only up to a certain point. A low CIR PVC used with large frame sizes together with many DE frame discards could prove to be disastrous.

Overhead (example 1) = 13/1037 = 1.25 percent
Overhead (example 2) = 13/69 = 18.84 percent

In packet switching, the larger the packet size, the higher the probability of error, causing data to require retransmission. For any given Bit Error Rate (BER), the probability of error increases with packet (or frame) size. If BER is high enough, and packet/frame size is large enough, you will almost be guaranteed to make an error for every packet/frame. This is why 128 bytes was chosen as the best compromise for packet switching. For noisy lines, throughput can be increased by decreasing packet size to 64 bytes. The added overhead is offset by reduced retransmissions. The same problem applies to frame relay, where choice of frame size is a function of both the protocol being transported and the probability of frame discard.

Figure 17.1 illustrates the theoretical range for packet/frame size versus delay incurred. Cell-relay technologies such as SMDS and ATM have a fixed overhead per cell, effectively reducing throughput by approximately 17 percent (by Distributed Queue Dual Bus (DQDB) standards, 9 bytes overhead out of the 53 total). This throughput reduction is made up for with large access-circuit speeds (typically DS3 and higher). It also shows the inefficiency of lower-speed cell services and the reason an HDLC-like protocol was chosen for Data eXchange Interface (DXI) services.

17.2 TRAFFIC ENGINEERING BASICS – TRAFFIC CHARACTERISTICS AND SOURCE MODELS

Now that we have viewed performance from a throughput and overhead perspective, we turn our attention to methods of approximating and estimating performance based on the traffic sources. These analytical methods focus on the modeling of real traffic patterns through source models.

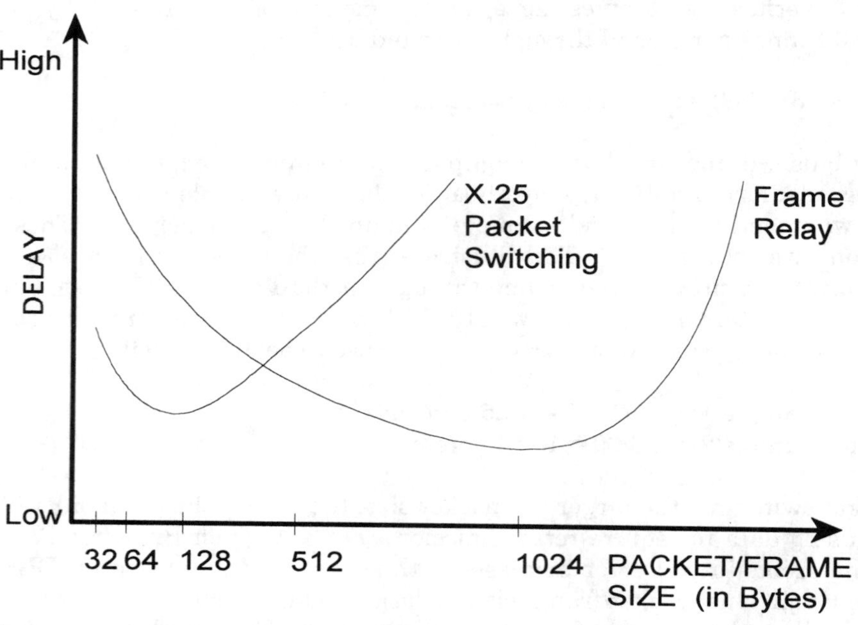

Figure 17.1 Theoretical Delay Curves for Packet/Frame Transmissions

17.2.1 Source Model Traffic Parameter Characteristics

There are two basic philosophies for characterizing source traffic parameters: deterministic and random. Deterministic parameters are based upon a specific traffic contract, with conformance verifiable on a unit-by-unit basis, for example, frames for frame relay and cell-by-cell for ATM. The agreement as to the traffic throughput that achieves a given performance is unambiguously stated.

The probabilistic (also called stochastic) model is typically measurable only over a very long-term average. Since the method and interval for computing the average can differ, conformance testing defines the details of the measurement method. Specification of the statistical model is also required.

Both statistical methods are useful approximations to the deterministic traffic contract behavior. These methods are very useful in analysis if a simple statistical model is chosen. Most of the following examples are based on an ATM cell as the base unit of measure.

17.2.2 General Source Model Parameters

This section defines some general source model parameters used throughout the remainder of this chapter. There are some general terms used here out that need to be defined.

Burstiness is a commonly used measure of how infrequently a source sends traffic. A source that infrequently sends traffic is said to be very bursty, while a source that always sends at the same rate is said to be nonbursty. The formula that defines burstiness in terms of the peak traffic unit (i.e., packet, frame, cell) rate and the average unit rate is defined as:

$$\text{Burstiness} = \frac{\text{Peak Rate}}{\text{Average Rate}}$$

The *source activity probability* is a measure of how frequently the source sends, defined by the probability that a source is bursting:

$$\text{Source Activity Probability} = \frac{1}{\text{Burstiness}}$$

Utilization is a commonly used measure of the fraction of a transmission link's capacity that is used by a source, theoretically measured over an infinite period of time; however, in practice, it is measured over a long time interval. The definition of utilization is given in terms of the peak (packet, frame, or cell) rate and transmission link (access-circuit) rate as follows:

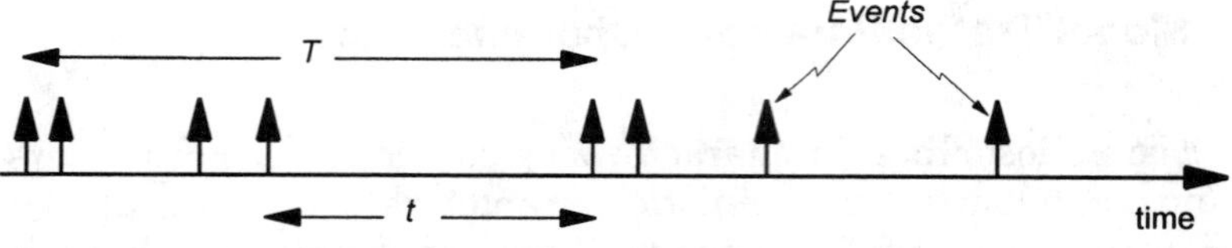

Figure 17.2 Illustration of an Arrival Process

$$\text{Utilization} = \frac{\text{Peak Rate}}{\text{Link Rate}}$$

and is calculated after all (protocol and switching) overhead is accounted for.

17.2.3 Poisson Arrivals and Markov Processes

Random arrival processes are described in general, and the Poisson (or Markov) process in particular, with reference to Figure 17.2. Poisson arrivals occur such that for each increment of time (T), no matter how large or small, the probability of arrivals is independent of any previous history. These events may be either individual cells, a burst of cells, cell or packet service completion, or other, arbitrary events in models.

The probability that the interarrival time between events t, as shown in Figure 17.2, has a certain value called the *interarrival time probability density*. The following formula gives the resulting probability that the interarrival time t is equal to some value x when the average arrival rate is λ events per second:

$$\Pr(t = x) = \lambda\, e^{-\lambda x}$$

This is called a *memoryless process*, because the probability that the interarrival time will be x seconds is independent of the *memory* of how much time has already expired. This fact greatly simplifies the analysis of random processes since no past history, or memory, must be kept. These types of processes are commonly known as *Markov processes*, named after the Russian mathematician of the 19th century.

The probability that n independent arrivals occur in T seconds is given by the famous *Poisson distribution*:

$$\Pr(n, T) = \frac{(\lambda T)^n}{n!} e^{-\lambda T}$$

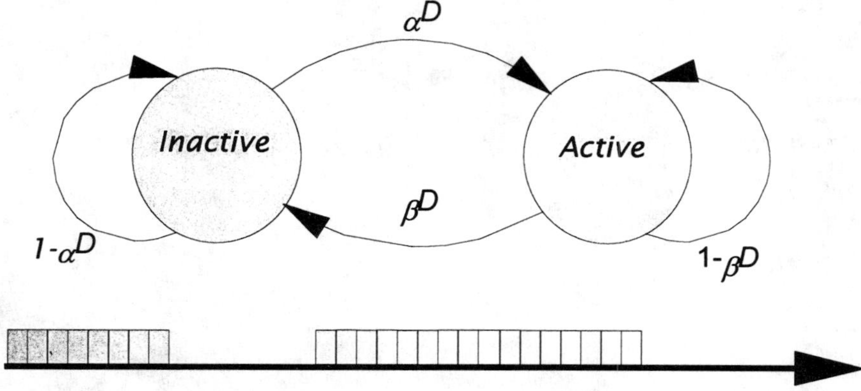

Figure 17.3 Discrete Time Markov Process Model

These two thoughts are combined in a commonly used model called the Markov Modulated Poisson Process (MMPP). There are two basic types: the *discrete* (which corresponds to frame or cells) and the *continuous* (which corresponds better to higher-layer PDUs, which generate bursts of frames or cells). The next two figures give an equivalent example for the discrete and continuous models.

The labels on the arrows of Figure 17.3 show the probability that the source transitions between active and inactive bursting states, or else remains in the same state for each cell time. In other words, during each cell time the source makes a state transition, either to the other state, or back to itself, with the probability for either action indicated by the arrows in the diagram.

The burstiness, or peak-to-average ratio, of the *discrete* source model is given by the following formula:

$$b = \frac{\alpha + \beta}{\beta}$$

where α is the average number of bursts arriving per second, and β is the average rate of burst completion. Often we think in terms of β^{-1}, which has units of the average number of seconds per burst. We define D as the cell quantization time having units of seconds per cell. Therefore, αD defines the probability that a burst begins in a particular cell time, and βD defines the probability that a burst ends in a particular cell time. The average burst duration d (in units of packets, frames, or cells) is then computed from the standard geometric series as follows:

$$d = \frac{1}{(\beta)(D)}$$

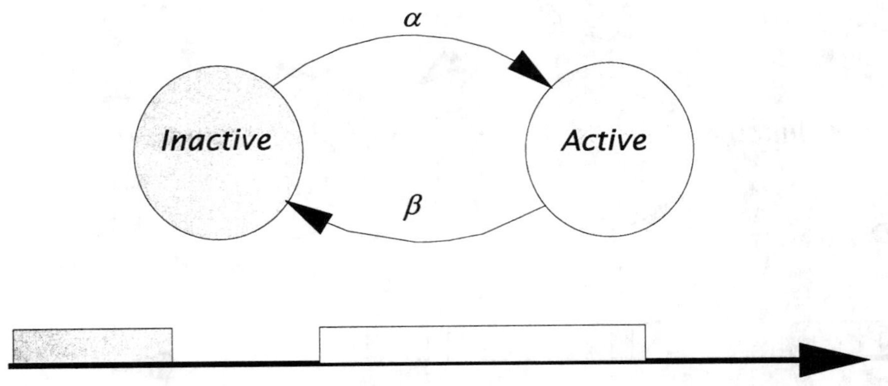

Figure 17.4 Continuous Time Markov Process Model

The second, *continuous* time case is illustrated in Figure 17.4. The time elapsed from the beginning of the burst to the end of the burst is modeled instead of modeling the individual cells. Some accuracy is lost in that the quantization inherent in segmentation and reassembly is not considered; however, we utilize in this book the simplicity in modeling it provides. The diagram is called a *state transition rate diagram* since the variables associated with the arrows refer to the rate exponent in the negative exponential distribution introduced earlier in this chapter. Both the discrete and continuous Markov models yield equivalent results except for the (unit) quantization factor D.

The corresponding burstiness b for the continuous process is:

$$b = \frac{\alpha + \beta}{\beta}$$

and the average burst duration in seconds is given by the following formula:

$$d = \frac{1}{\beta}$$

Note how these formulae are identical to the discrete case except for the absence of the discrete cell time D in the denominator of the equation for the average burst duration of the continuous model.

Another distribution that is sometimes used to model extremely bursty traffic is that of the hyperexponential, which is effectively the weighted sum of a number of negative exponential arrivals. This turns out to be a more pessimistic model than Poisson traffic because bursts and burst arrivals are more closely clumped together.

Recent work based upon actual LAN traffic measurements indicate that these traditional traffic models may be overly optimistic and represent ideal conditions. These results show that the LAN traffic measured at Bellcore is *self-similar,* which means that the traffic has similar properties regardless of the time scale on which it is observed. This is in sharp contrast to the Poisson and Markovian models, where the traffic tends to become smoother and more predictable as longer and longer time averages are considered.

17.3 TRADITIONAL TRAFFIC ENGINEERING

In this section we will look at traditional traffic modeling, starting with the basis of voice traffic modeling, the traditional Erlang analysis. These fundamentals will help us lay the foundation for exploring basic cell traffic modeling.

17.3.1 Statistical Behavior of User Traffic

Traffic patterns can be calculated in many ways. User information arrives at the network node based on statistical arrival rates. Not all users need to communicate with all other users at the exact same time. Therefore, statistical approximations can be used to model these traffic patterns. These calculations can either be based on mathematical calculations that generalize the messages or packets and their arrival rates and then calculate the required bandwidth to support the total traffic. Or, they can be performed through packet-level modeling where each type of packet transmission is calculated, and bandwidth is sized from the aggregate. This chapter presents aspects of both methods.

The primary parameters to be concerned about are the call arrival rate λ, usually in calls per hour, and the average hold time or duration of message τ per call. With these numbers, demand on the access node can be predicted in units called *erlangs*. Erlangs can be used in voice network modeling as well as circuit-switched data network designs, and have been used successfully for many years.

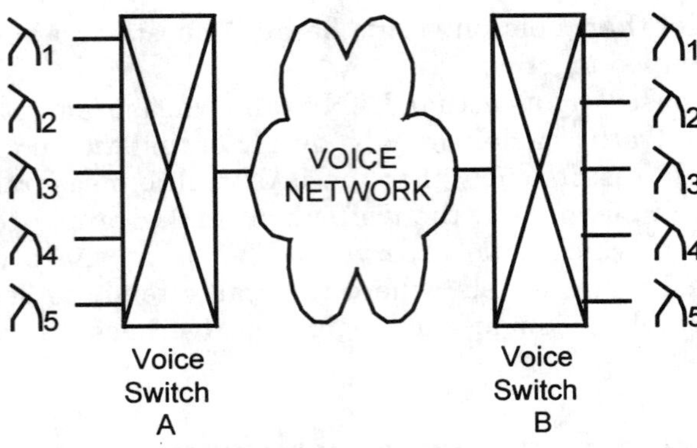

Figure 17.5 Voice Network

17.3.2 Voice Traffic Modeling (Erlang Analysis)

The standard for statistically calculating an estimate of user demand based on random call arrival and holding was modeled by A. K. Erlang in the 1920s. This unit of measure, called the erlang, is calculated as:

$$E = \lambda\tau = \text{one erlang}$$

where λ = the call arrival rate in calls/hour, and τ = average holding time in hours.

This measurement was developed for analog voice communications, where calls would arrive at a voice switch or circuit switch (see Figure 17.5) at λ and whose total transmission time would be τ hours. In this example, there are five users at switch A. If each user calls every 12 seconds and talks for 6 seconds before hanging up, the total utilization of the transmission line is 0.5 erlang [(1/12)(6) = 0.5]. It is obviously possible to offer 1 erlang for every user, but the laws of statistics show that much lower numbers of circuits can be maintained, since every user will not try to place a call at the same time. The actual utilization on an access line is normally much less than 1 erlang. One erlangs is also equal to 36 Call Century Seconds (CCSs). CCSs were first standardized by Bell Labs. A camera took a picture of the call peg counters on the electromechanical switches every 100 seconds — thus the term call century seconds.

The number and duration of calls vary, and therefore so must the erlang calculation. The formula for calculating erlangs with multiple call duration is:

$$\sum_{n=1}^{k} \tau_n = \text{average erlangs},$$

where k is the total number of calls completed in an hour and τ_n is the length of the call in hours.

Thus, if 100 calls of 150-second duration, 200 calls of 100-second duration, and 300 calls of 50-second duration took place over a one-hour period, the number of erlangs would be 13.89.

Since all blocked calls are "cleared", blocking should be calculated from the erlang calculations shown previously. The formula to calculate the probability of blocking is:

$$B = \frac{E^N / N!}{\sum_{k=0}^{k=N} E^k / k!}$$

where $B = B(N, E)$ = percent of blocking as a function of the number of lines available and the number of affected Erlangs and

$$N! = N(N\text{-}1)(N\text{-}2)...(3)(2)(1)$$

For example, 20 calls per hour at 3 minutes per call would equal 1 erlang (or 36 CCS). The number of trunks required for 2 percent blocking would be four. There are erlang B (lost calls cleared) tables in most voice and packet-switch design books that graphically demonstrate blocking versus erlangs for various volumes of traffic. As the call arrival rate increases, the probability that a new call will be blocked or dropped increases.

17.4 QUEUED DATA AND PACKET-SWITCHED TRAFFIC MODELING

While erlangs work well predicting voice network and circuit-switched traffic rates, they do not work well with packet-switched networks. In packet-switched networks, some level of queuing is employed so that packets are queued in buffers and transmitted when congestion ceases, rather than being immediately blocked. Also, packet-switched networks provide a mix of protocol and traffic types, whereas voice and circuit-switched networks provide point-to-point, transparent homogeneous transport of information. Therefore, packet switching demands a different analysis of traffic handling. Knowledge of the way packet/cell modes of traffic are measured combined with a knowledge of the user traffic will allow the network designer to calculate the patterns provided to the access network so that a model of the access node can be simulated. We will now see how the statistical characteristics of the traffic directly affect the access design. We start with the notation used in queuing systems, and move through the common models for traffic modeling. Next, we discuss some of the complex calculations for approximating traffic, overflow and performance issues and analysis, and modeling of statistical multiplexer gain and LAN/MAN systems.

17.4.1 Queueing System Models Notation

There are three major queuing formulas for dealing with voice, TDM, and packet (queuing) models. Each of these formulas follow the same format. This usual categorization of queuing systems is given by the notation shown in Figure 17.6. This is industry standard technical notation that will be used throughout the book.

17.4.2 Queued Data and Packet-Switched Traffic Modeling

The three major modeling formulas include:

Erlang-B : $M / G / s / s$,
which is used for voice-blocked calls cleared and TDM modeling.

Erlang-C : $M / G / s / k$,

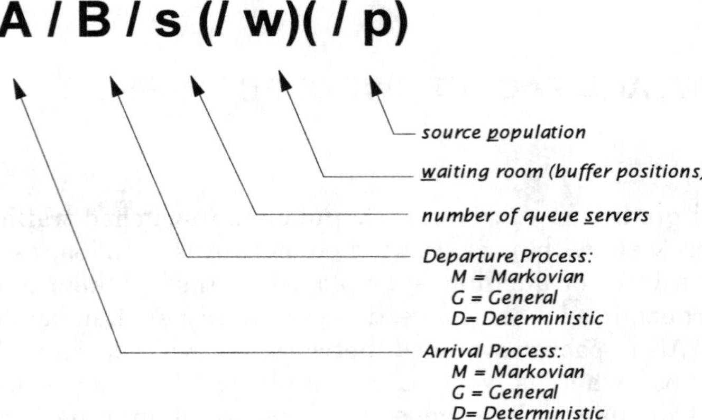

Figure 17.6 Queuing System Notation

which is used when k > s (the waiting room is greater than the number of servers) for voice with blocked calls held, or for operator services.

Packet : $M / G / 1$,
which is used for one server and infinite waiting and population, commonly used to model packet, frame, and cell networks.

The third formula is of primary concern: packet modeling with *M*/*M*/1, where *M* designates a Markovian process (or Poisson arrival distribution — previously *G* designated the Gaussian arrival distribution). Thus, formulae are based on a single server with Poisson arrivals or equivalently negative exponential service times, and first-in-first-out (FIFO) service. Figure 17.7 shows this relationship between arrival rates λ service times, and a single server μ. Buffers and buffer overflow will be discussed later.

17.4.3 Markovian Queueing Systems Models

Two particular examples of queuing systems are presented, namely, the *M*/*D*/1 and *M*/*M*/1 systems. From this notation, each of these queuing systems has Markovian arrivals (negative exponential or memoryless burst arrivals) at a rate of λ bursts per second. The *M*/*M*/1 system has random-length bursts with a negative exponential distribution (Markov), while the *M*/*D*/1 system has constant-length bursts. The parameter μ^{-1} defines how many seconds (on average) are required for the transmission link to send each burst. For the *M*/*M*/1 system, this is an exponentially distributed random number of this average length, while in the *M*/*D*/1 system, this is the constant or fixed length of every burst. Both systems also have a single server (i.e., physical transmission link) and an infinite population (number of potential bursts) and infinite waiting room (buffer space). The units of the buffer in the *M*/*D*/1 model are units (packets, frames, cells), while in the *M*/*M*/1 case the units of the buffer are bursts of units. Figure 17.8 illustrates these physical queuing systems and their specific relationship to a cell-based technology (such as ATM).

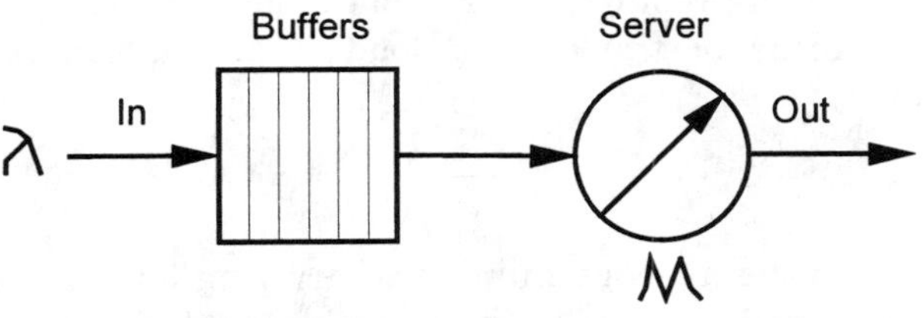

Figure 17.7 *M*/*M*/1 Single Server Model

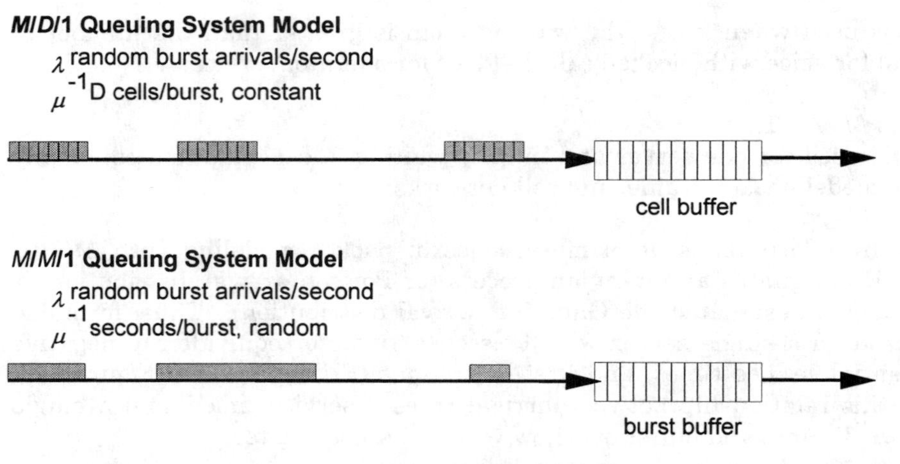

Figure 17.8 Application of *M/D/*1 and *M/M/*1 Queueing System with Cells

This is a good example of the tradeoffs encountered in modeling. The *M/D/*1 system accurately represents the fact that the buffers in the switch are in units of cells; however, the bursts are all of fixed length. The *M/M/*1 system does not model the switch buffers accurately since it is in units of bursts and not cells; however, the modeling of random burst lengths is more appropriate to many traffic sources, such as with frame relay. The *M/M/*1 model is also very simple to analyze, and therefore it will be used extensively to illustrate specific tendencies in frame relay and ATM systems. In general, if the traffic is more deterministic than the *M/M/*1 model (for example, more like the *M/D/*1 model), then the *M/M/*1 model will be pessimistic (there will actually be less queuing and less delay in the modeled network). If the traffic is more bursty than the *M/M/*1 model, then the *M/M/*1 results will be optimistic (there will actually be more queuing and more delay in the modeled network).

17.4.4 Utilization and Capacity Calculations

In many of the following results, the system delay and loss performance will be presented in terms of the offered load or utilization ρ, given by the following formula:

$$\rho = \frac{\lambda}{\mu}$$

Recalling that λ is the average number of arriving bursts (packets, frames, or cells) per second, and that μ^{-1} is the average number of seconds per burst, it is seen that the offered load ρ is unitless. Thus the offered load has the interpretation of the average fraction utilization of the resource capacity that is in use.

The service rate μ is computed as follows for a burst of B bytes at a line rate of R bits per second:

$$\mu = \frac{8B}{R}\left(\frac{\text{bursts}}{\text{second}}\right)$$

The utilization calculated determines the average amount of time to serve each message (τ):

$$\tau = \frac{B}{R}$$

The probability that there are n bursts waiting in the *M/M/*1 queue is given by the following formula:

$$\text{Prob}\,[n \text{ burst in } M\,/\,M\,/\,1 \text{ queuing delay}] = \rho^n (1-\rho)$$

When dealing with *M/M/*1 queues, as in packet switching, there is an average of N users in the queue:

$$N = \left(\frac{\rho}{(1-\rho)}\right),$$

where ρ is the probability that the queue is not empty and $(1 - \rho)$ is the probability that the queue is empty. Figure 17.9 shows how the increase in utilization (p) causes an increase in the average queue size (N).

The average queuing delay (i.e., waiting time), or w, in the *M/M/*1 system is given by the following formula:

$$\text{w} = \text{Avg}\,[M\,/\,M\,/\,1 \text{ queuing delay}] = \frac{\rho\,/\,\mu}{1-\rho}$$

then the average delay (d_{avg}) equates to the sum of the waiting time and the service time during stable queue conditions:

$$d_{avg} = w + \tau = \tau\,/\,(1 - \rho)$$

*M/D/*1 queuing predicts better performance than *M/M/*1. Indeed, the average delay of *M/D/*1 queuing is exactly one-half of the *M/M/*1delay. The probability for the number of cells in the *M/D/*1 queue is much more complicated, which is one reason the *M/M/*1 model will be used in many of the following examples.

17.4.5 Markovian Queuing Packet-Switching System Example

Take the following example for a packet-switched network. If a packet switch has 5 users, each transmitting 10 messages per second at 1024 bits per message, with the packet switch operating over a 56 kbps trunk, the following applies:

λB = (5)(10)(1024) = 51,200 bps
p = 51,200 bps / 56,000 bps = 91.4 percent utilization
τ = 1024 / 56,000 = .0183 Seconds
N = (0.914) / (1 – 0.914) = 10.63 users in queue
w = (10.63)(.0183) = .195 seconds average wait time
d_{avg} = .0183 + .195 = .213 seconds average delay

Note that the queuing delay is an order of magnitude much greater than the transmission delay. Now, one portion of overall network delay is known, that which is within the packet-switch queue. Based on the queuing theory shown, the utilization of a trunk is directly influenced by the delay in queuing.

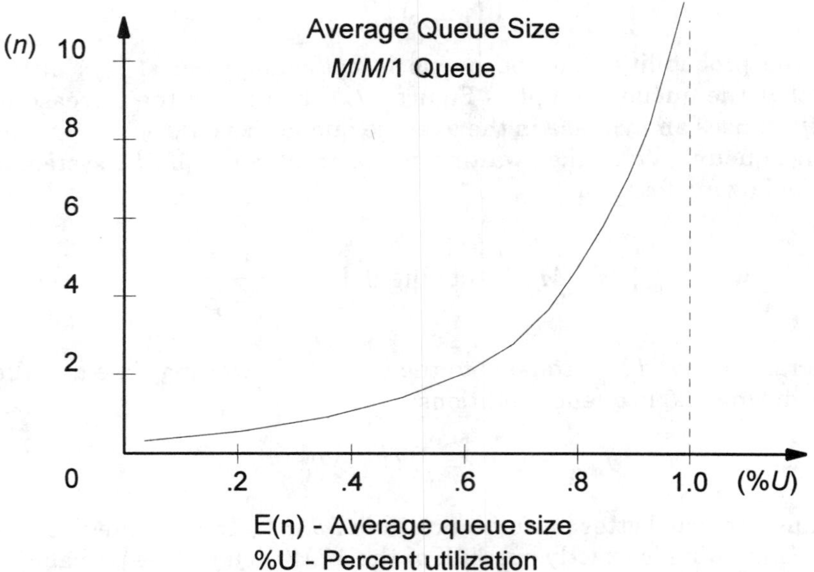

Figure 17.9 Relationship Between Utilization and Queue Size

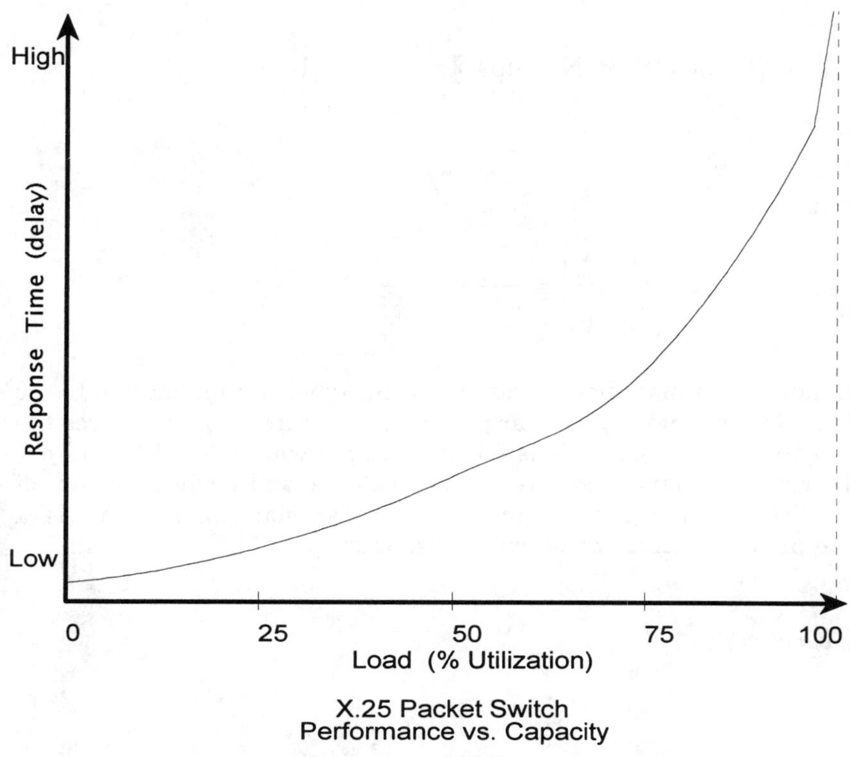

Figure 17.10 Relationship Between Utilization and Response Time

Figure 17.10 shows that as system utilization (p) increases, so does the delay through the system (d_{avg}). This shows that the greater the utilization, the longer the delay. The cause and effects are simple; if delay in queuing becomes a problem, either move some users to additional trunks or increase the size of the trunk.

17.4.6 Bernoulli Processes and Gaussian Approximation

A Bernoulli process is essentially the result of N independent coin flips (or Bernoulli trials) of an "unfair coin." An unfair coin is one where the probabilities of heads and tails are unequal, with p being the probability of that "heads" occurs as the result of a coin flip and $(1 - p)$ being the probability that "tails" occurs. The probability that k heads occur [and hence $(N - k)$ tails] as a result of N repeated Bernoulli trials ("coin flips") is called the *binomial distribution,* as given by:

$$\Pr[\text{k "heads" in N "flips"}] = \binom{N}{k} \rho^k (1-\rho)^{N-k}$$

where

$$\binom{N}{k} \equiv \frac{N!}{(N-k)!k!}.$$

The Gaussian, or Normal, distribution is a continuous approximation to the binomial distribution when *Np* is a large number. Figure 17.11 compares the binomial and Gaussian distributions for an example where $N = 100$ and $p = 0.1$. The distributions have basically the same shape, and for large values of *Np*, in the $Np(1 - p)$ region about *Np*, the Gaussian distribution is a reasonable approximation to the binomial distribution.

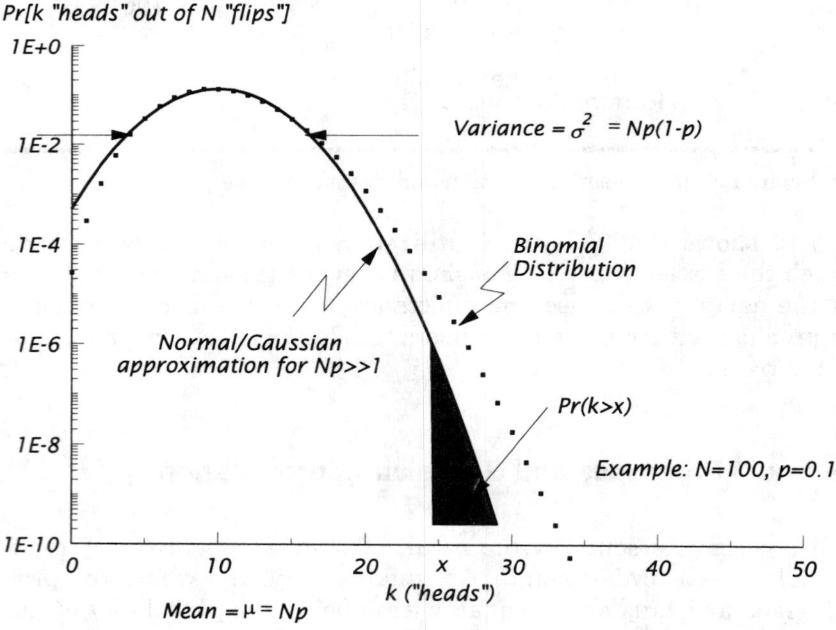

Figure 17.11 Normal Approximation to Binomial Distribution

This is helpful in analyzing relative performance in that the probability area under the tail of the Gaussian, or normal, distribution is widely tabulated and implemented in many spreadsheets and mathematical programming systems. We approximate the tail of the binomial distribution by the cumulative distribution of the normal density, $Q(\alpha)$. We will use the following approximation several times to estimate loss probability or statistical multiplex gain:

$$\Pr[k > x] \approx Q\left(\frac{x-\mu}{\sigma}\right) = Q(\alpha) \approx \frac{1}{2}e^{-\alpha^2/2}$$

where $Q(\alpha) \equiv \frac{1}{\sqrt{2\pi}} \int e^{-x^2/2} dx$

17.4.7 Traffic Engineering Complexities

Realistic source and switch traffic models are not currently amenable to direct analysis, with the results presented in this book providing only approximations under certain circumstances. Such approximate methods may have large inaccuracies, which can only be ascertained by performing detailed simulations or actual tests. Simulations are time consuming and, in the case of modeling complex high-speed technologies like ATM, cannot effectively model low cell-loss rates since an inordinate number of cells must be simulated. For example, in order to simulate a cell-loss rate of one in a billion, at least 100 billion to 1 trillion cells must be simulated. Even with today's computers this is a lot of computations to obtain a single point on a loss curve. Where possible, methods for extrapolating loss rates and estimating the occurrence of unlikely events should be used instead. Also, constantly changing source, switch, and network characteristics create a moving target for such traffic engineering models. For greater detail on traffic engineering with ATM see McDysan and Spohn's *ATM: Theory and Application.*

17.4.8 Buffer Overflow and Performance

While it is important to understand the limits of the queue and delay imposed, it is also important to calculate when a buffer will overload and data will be lost. The probability that there are k packets in the $M/M/1$ queue is approximated by:

$$P_k = \rho^k(1-\rho)$$

With this value, we can calculate the probability of overflowing a buffer capable of holding B packets of variable length ($\Pr[u \geq B]$). This value can be approximated as:

$$\Pr[u \geq B] = \sum_{k=B}^{\infty} P_k = r^B$$

17.4.9 Cell Buffer Overflow Analysis

This section analyzes several simple models of switch delay and loss performance as impacted by various aspects of a switch buffer architecture. For simplicity, Poisson arrivals and negative exponential service times are assumed. Output queuing delay performance then behaves like a classical $M/M/1$ system. Input queuing incurs a problem known as Head Of Line (HOL) blocking. HOL blocking occurs when the cell at the head of the input queue cannot enter the switch matrix because the cell at the head of another queue is traversing the matrix.

For uniformly distributed traffic with random message lengths, the maximum supportable offered load for input queuing is limited to 50 percent, while fixed message lengths increase the supportable offered load to only about 58 percent. On the other hand, output queuing is not limited by utilization as in input queuing. Figure 17.12 illustrates this result by plotting average delay versus throughput for input and output queuing. For a more detailed analysis of input versus output queuing, which shows that these simple types of models are valid for switches with a large number of ports, see McDysan and Spohn's *ATM: Theory and Application*.

The consequence of this result is that almost all TDMs and cell switches have some form of output buffering. If input buffering is used on a cell switch that you are considering, check to make sure that some means to address Head Of Line (HOL) blocking is implemented. Examples of methods to address HOL blocking are: a switch fabric that operates much faster than the cumulative input port rates, schemes where an HOL-blocked cell can be bypassed by other cells, or the use of priority queuing on the input.

The next example gives a simple, useful approximation for the output buffer overflow probability. For simplicity, an $M/M/1$ queuing system, which has an infinite buffer, is assumed, instead of a $M/M/1/B$ system, which would have a finite buffer. The overflow probability for a buffer of size B cells is approximately the probability that there are B/P bursts in the infinite queue system. Comparison with simulation results and exact analysis has shown that this is a reasonable approximation. When the average higher-layer Protocol Data Unit (PDU) burst size is P cells, the approximate buffer overflow probability is given by the formula:

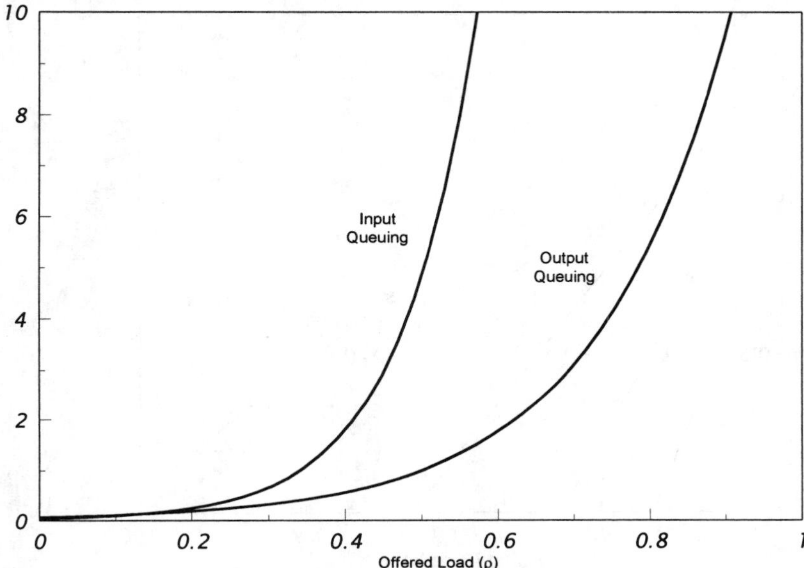

Figure 17.12 Delay versus Load Performance for Input and Output Queueing

$$\Pr ob\left[Overflow\right] \approx p^{B/P+1}$$

Figure 17.13 plots the approximate buffer overflow probability versus buffer size for various levels of throughput ρ assuming a PDU size of $P = 1$ cells. The performance for other burst sizes can be read from this chart by multiplying the x axis by the PDU burst size P.

Note that for a specific overflow probability objective and a fixed buffer size the load must be limited to a maximum value. We illustrate this concept by solving the above equation for the overflow probability in terms of the required buffer size B to achieve an objective Cell Loss Ratio (CLR). The result is the following:

$$B \approx P\frac{\log(CLR)}{\log(\rho)}$$

Buffer overflow probability in frame and cell networks increases as the higher layer PDU sizes increase. When the PDU size approaches the buffer size, the loss rate is almost 100 percent. Figure 17.14 illustrates the impact of higher-layer PDU size (P) on buffer overflow performance for various output buffer sizes (B frames or cells).

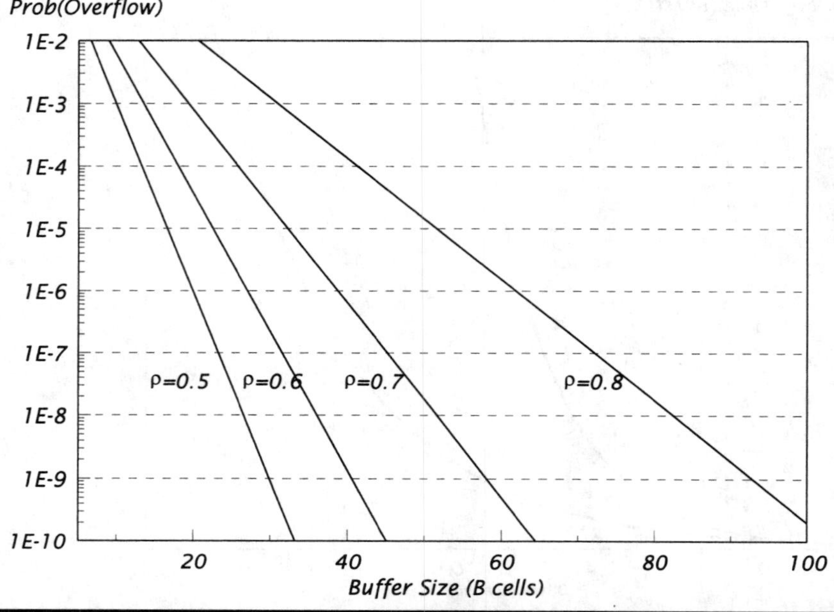

Figure 17.13 Switch Buffering Performance

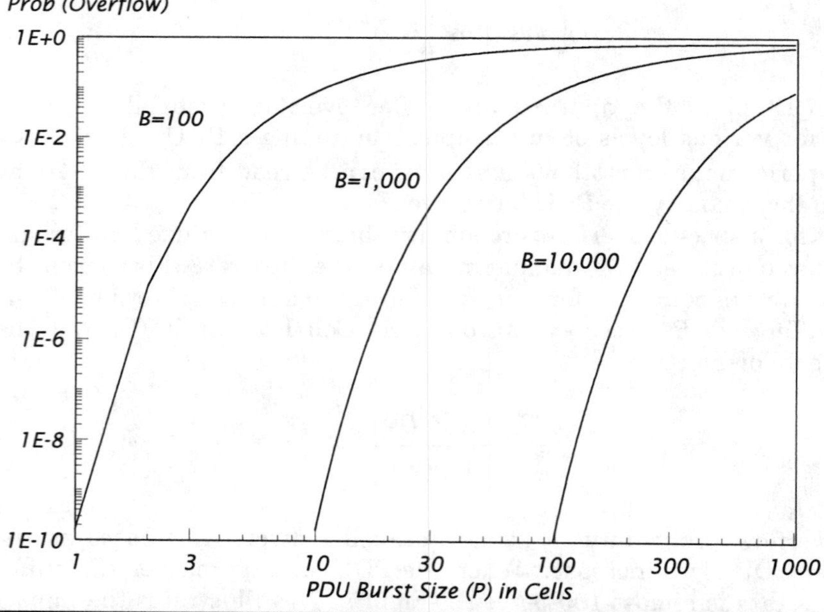

Figure 17.14 Overflow Probability versus PDU Burst Size

The shared output buffer scheme has a marked improvement on buffer overflow performance because of sharing a single, larger buffer among many ports. Since it is unlikely that all ports are congested at the same time, the loss will be substantially less than an equivalent number of individual output buffer positions dedicated to each port.

Since the exact analysis of shared buffer performance is somewhat complicated, a simple approximation is presented based on the normal distribution. In the shared-buffer architecture, N switch ports share the common buffer, each with approximately the $M/M/1$ probability distribution requirement on buffer space. The sum of the individual port demands determines the shared-buffer probability distribution. The normal distribution approximates a sum of such random variables for larger values of N. The mean and variance of the normal approximation are then given by the following:

$$Mean = \frac{N\rho}{(1-\rho)^2} \qquad Variance = \frac{2N\rho^2}{(1-\rho)^2}$$

Figure 17.15 shows a plot of the overflow probability versus the equivalent buffer size per port for shared buffers on switches of increasing port size (N), along with the dedicated output buffer performance for large N from Figure 17.14 for comparison purposes. The offered load is $\rho = 0.8$ or 80% load. The total buffer capacity on a shared buffer switch is N times the buffer capacity on the x axis. Note that as N increases, the capacity required per port approaches a constant value. This illustrates the theoretical efficiency of shared buffering. Of course, a practical implementation has limits in terms of the shared buffer access speed.

17.4.10 Statistical Multiplexing Gain

One key capability that cell-based services like ATM enables is that of statistical multiplexing, which attempts to exploit the on/off, bursty nature of many source types as illustrated in Figure 17.16. On the left-hand side there are several sources and sinks of ATM cell bursts: a video display, a server, a camera, and a monitor. The lower trace in the figure shows a plot of the sum of these cell bursts. In this particular simple example, only two channels are required at any point in time. As more and more sources are multiplexed together, the statistics of this composite sum become increasingly more predictable.

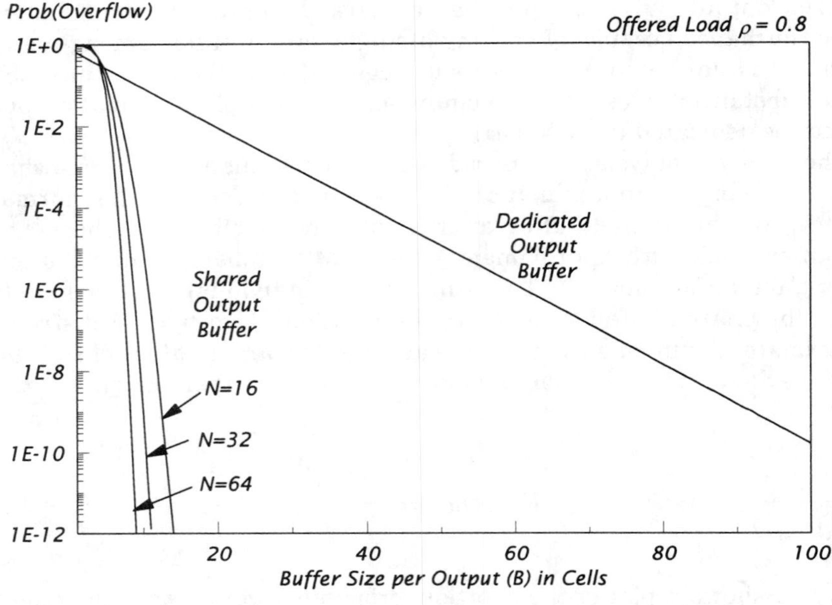

Figure 17.15 Shared versus Dedicated Buffer Performance

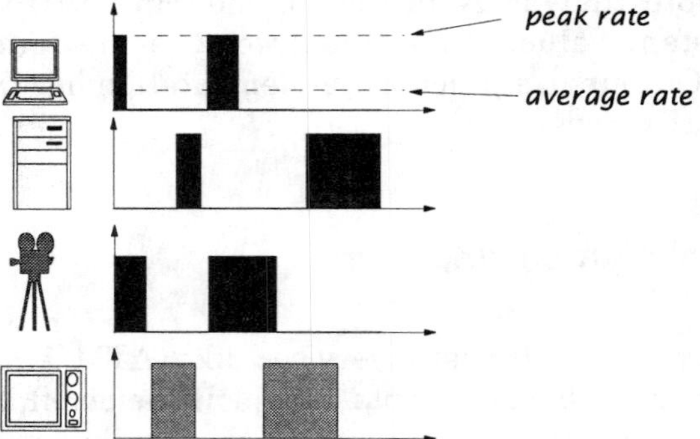

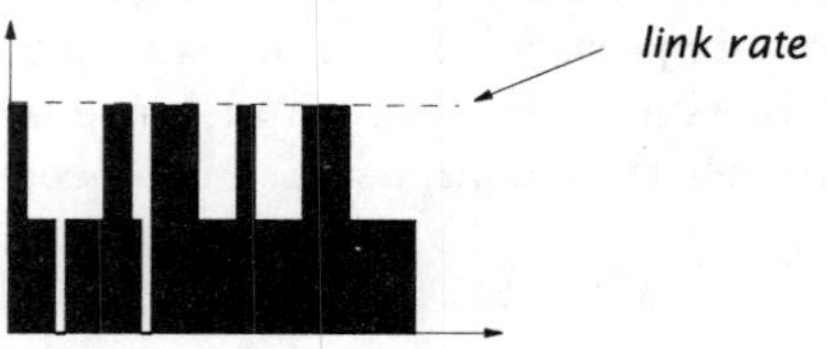

Figure 17.16 Illustration of Statistical Multiplex Gain

The statistical multiplexing gain G is defined as the following ratio:

$$G = \frac{\text{Number of Sources Supported}}{\text{Required Number of Channels}}$$

The statistical multiplex gain G can be computed from the binomial distribution, or estimated from the Normal distribution with the following parameters:

$$Mean = \frac{N}{b} \qquad\qquad Variance = \frac{N}{b}\left(1 - \frac{1}{b}\right)$$

where N is the number of sources
b is the burstiness (peak/average rate)

The required number of channels, C (in units of the number of peak rate sources), to achieve an objective Cell Loss Ratio (CLR) of $Q(\alpha)$ is given by:

$$C \approx N / b + a\sqrt{N(b-1)} / b$$

The parameter η defines the peak source-rate-to-link-rate ratio, which means that the link capacity is $1/\eta$. Therefore the statistical multiplex gain reduces to $G = N/C = N\eta$. Setting C in the previous equation equal to this link capacity $1/\eta$ and solving for N using the quadratic formula yields the result:

$$G \approx \frac{N(\sqrt{\alpha^2(b-1) + 4b/\eta} - \alpha\sqrt{b-1})^2}{4}$$

Figure 17.17 plots the achievable statistical multiplex gain G versus the peak-to-link rate ratio η with burstiness b as a parameter for a cell loss ratio of 10^{-6}. This figure illustrates the classical wisdom of statistical multiplexing: the rate of any individual source should be low with respect to the link rate η, and the burstiness of the sources b must be high in order to achieve a high statistical multiplex gain G.

Figure 17.18 illustrates how many sources must be multiplexed together in order to achieve the statistical multiplex gain predicted in the previous example. This confirms the applicability of the key statistical multiplex gain assumption that a large number N of sources, of low average rate $1/b$ and modest peak rate, with respect to the link rate η, must be multiplexed together in order to achieve a high statistical multiplex gain G.

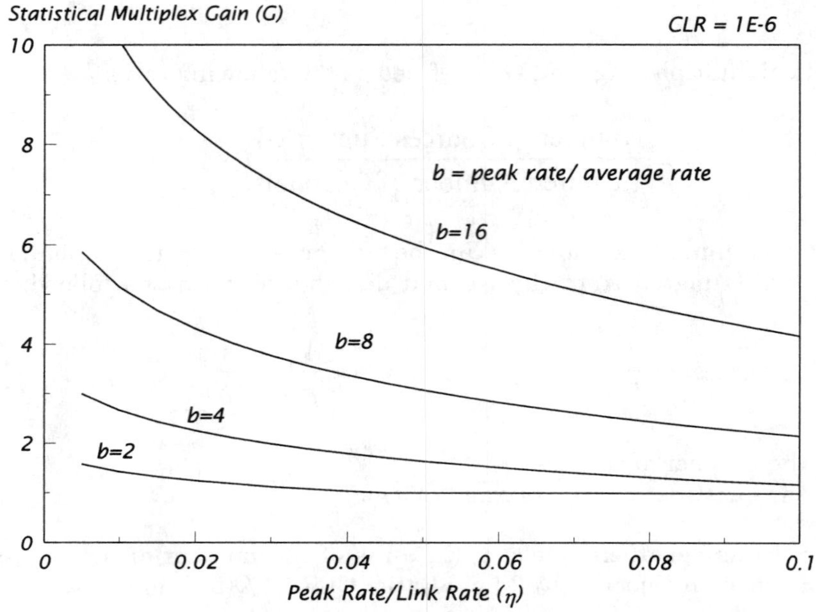

Figure 17.17 Achievable Statistical Multiplex Gain

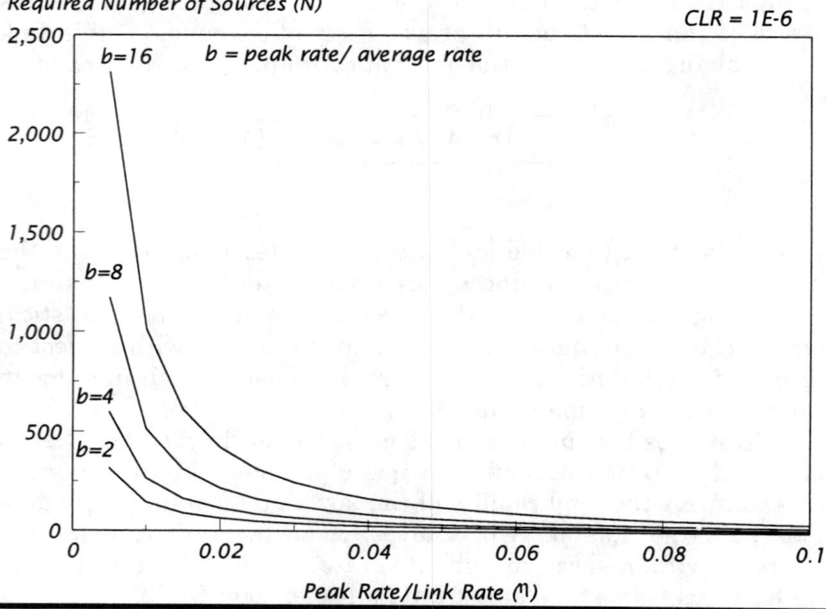

Figure 17.18 Statistical Multiplex Gain Example

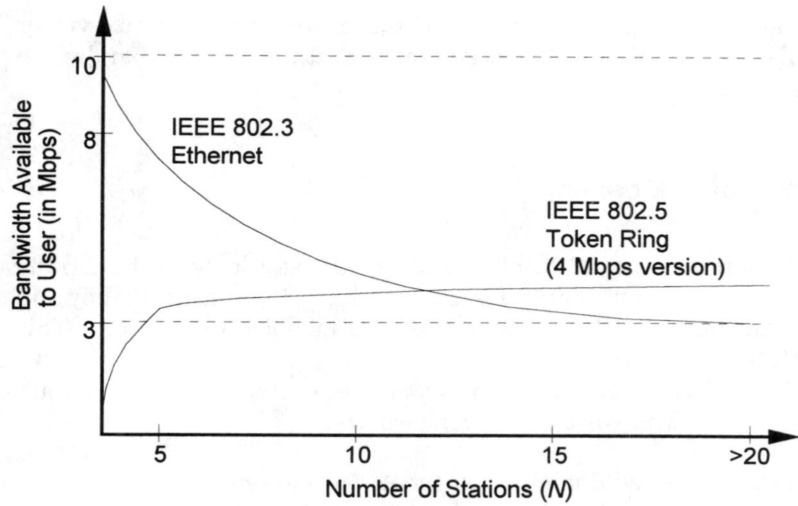

Token Ring -- throughput increases when *N* increases because less time spent token passing
Ethernet -- throughput decreases when *N* increases because of increased chance of collision

Figure 17.19 LAN Throughput Comparison

17.4.11 LAN Traffic Modeling

LAN traffic modeling is a difficult process and is subject to further study, although some of the techniques discussed in the section on DQDB MAN traffic modeling are applicable. Many LAN traffic characteristics, such as performance and throughput based on number of users, have been thoroughly studied and are provided by LAN equipment vendors. Figure 17.19 shows a comparison of Token Ring 4 Mbps LANs to Ethernet 10 Mbps LANs. Notice that the Token Ring throughput increases when the number of users increases because less time is spent token passing, whereas on the Ethernet (CSMA/CD) LAN the throughput decreases as the number of users increases due to the increased likelihood (and number) of collisions. FDDI and IEEE 802.6 SMDS response curves resemble that of the Token Ring, yet are more efficient. More detailed calculations can be obtained by the LAN traffic analyzers on the market, which are increasingly becoming more sophisticated.

LAN bridge designs are concerned primarily with frames forwarded per second and frames filtered per second. Any design should also take into account packet and frame forwarding and filtering buffers, as well as the depth of LAN address table memory. Proprietary bridge and router overhead, as well as routing algorithm traffic (especially the distance-vector routing protocol), can generate substantial traffic that reduces the bandwidth available to user traffic.

17.4.12 DQDB Traffic Modeling

The DQDB bus operates as a LAN, but handles calls similarly to the Erlang method, where messages contending for the bus have to wait until they can reserve a space on the bus. Call arrival rates are modeled differently. This new method will be explored.

The traffic characteristics of a LAN (bursty traffic) attached to a MAN are shown in Figure 17.20. The variables of concern are:

B = Bandwidth consumed during burst (peak rate) in bps
t_s = Average time slot used for transmission in seconds
n = Number of time slots between starts of bursts
t_b = Time of each burst (average) in seconds (μ^{-1}) = $8(D_b)/B$
D_b = Burst duration (bytes)

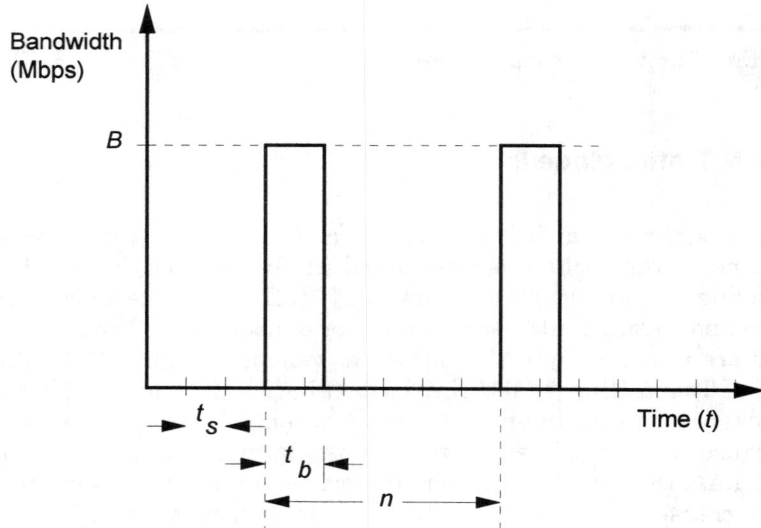

Figure 17.20 Characteristics of LANs Attached to MANs

Note that a burst may contain one or more packets. For more than one packet per burst, use $(t_b)(x) \Rightarrow t_b$, where x equals the number of packets per burst.

Previous calculations can be taken one step further to model an IEEE 802.6 DQDB MAN where the traffic characteristics of the individual LANs attached are known. The required capacity of a DQDB MAN to handle all user traffic is calculated with the sum of the λ's (packets per second) of the local, remote traffic from and to the MAN, and the pass-through traffic. The formula is:

$$\sum l_l + \sum l_{rf} + \sum l_{rt} = \lambda'$$

where $\sum l_l$ = local traffic

$\sum l_{rf}$ = traffic *from* remote MAN

$\sum l_{rt}$ = traffic *to* remote MAN

such that $\lambda' = 1 / (n)(t_s)$,

where all λ's are the sum of the users in that category and λ' represents the minimum required capacity of the local MAN. The capacity of the MAN would obviously be higher than the capacity required.

Since MANs often provide high-bandwidth connectivity to a small number of users, the traffic approximations just discussed become valid (where aggregations tend to have Poisson distributions). Huge bursts on the MAN can dwarf the normal large packet transmissions normally seen on the LAN.

Now let's look at a LAN/MAN traffic model that allows for the approximation of the number of LANs, based on traffic characteristics, that can be attached to a MAN.

The probability that a LAN time slot will be busy (ρ_b) is calculated as:

ρ_b = Avg number of slots consumed by burst / n = $(t_b/t_s)/n$ = $8(D_b)/[(B)(n)(t_s)] = \lambda' / \mu$

Suppose a DS3 DQDB network has the following characteristics:

B = Class of Service (4, 10, 16, 25, and 34 Mbps) = 16 Mbps

t_s = 53 octet time slot of 125 μs

$n = 5$

$D_b = 1024$

The probability that a slot will be busy = [(8)(1024)] / [(16 Mbps)(5)(125 μs)/13] = .8192 = 81.92 percent.

And the probability that a LAN will transmit onto a particular MAN slot, in theory, is

$$\rho_m = (\rho_b)(\rho_{\text{inter-LAN}})$$

where $\rho_{\text{inter-LAN}}$ represents the fraction of inter-LAN bursts.

If there are N LANs connected to the MAN, the probability that k out of N LANs will be transmitting bursts onto the MAN at any given time is represented by the binomial distribution:

$$\binom{N}{k} \rho_m{}^k (1 - \rho_m)^{N-k} = \rho_N(k)$$

Assume that the MAN is y times faster than each LAN (e.g., $y = 4$ for a DS3 SMDS MAN connecting to multiple 10 Mbps Ethernet LANs). If the number of LANs currently sending bursts exceeds y, then some or all of the LAN bursts will have to be queued or discarded. Approximating the DQDB MAN as an $M/M/1$ queue with average utilization (or throughput) of:

$$\rho_{\text{MAN}} = (N)(\rho_m) / y,$$

then the average $M/M/1$ delay is proportional to $1 / (1 - \rho_{\text{MAN}})$.

We can optimize the ratio of throughput to delay, usually called the queuing power (P), as follows:

$$P = \text{throughput/delay} = \mu(1 - \mu)$$

$$P = [(N)(\rho_m) / y] - [(N)(\rho_m) / y]^2$$

The queuing power versus network utilization is plotted in Figure 17.21.

If $\partial P / \partial N$ is set to 0 ($\partial P / \partial N = 0$), the optimum number of LANs that can be connected to the MAN (N_{opt}) can be solved for:

$$N_{opt} = \frac{y}{2\rho_m}$$

17.5 DESIGNING FOR PEAKS

When calculating the arrival rate of calls (λ), a figure was used called "busy hour". Any network must be designed to handle the busiest traffic periods, or data will be blocked or lost. Take, for example, the IXC long-distance carriers, which need to design networks based on the nation's busy hour.

How long would you keep your long-distance carrier if there was a good chance that your calls would be blocked from 9 to 10 AM each day during the average five-day work week (one of the nation's busiest hours for phone calls)? The IXCs specifically design their networks to handle periods of peak usage (such as Mother's Day — the busiest calling day of the year) or understand the potential for blocking and loss during that time period. Data networks must be designed with a similar thought process.

17.5.1 Standard Busy Hour Calculations

When λ is calculated and applied to the formulas for traffic load, it is assumed that the designer will use a call arrival rate measured or estimated during the peak busy period. This period is called the busy hour, and an hourly measurement is fine for most voice networks.

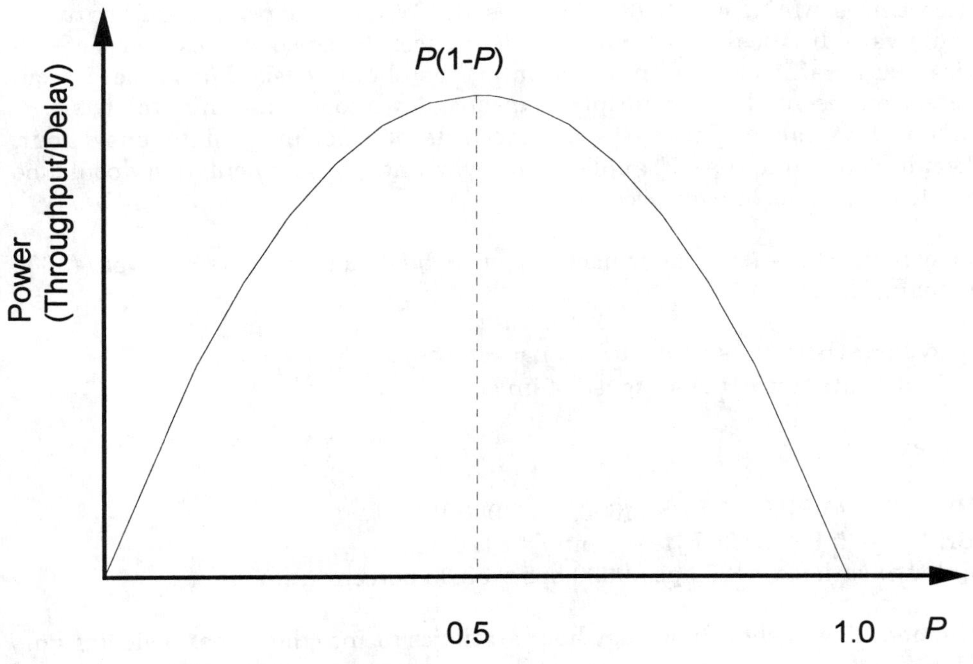

Figure 17.21 Queuing Power versus Network Utilization

17.5.2 Data Equivalent of Busy Hour

Data networks have their own equivalent of busy hour. Take, for example, the New York Stock Exchange (NYSE), which each day after 4 pm Central Time transmits huge amounts of information about the day's transactions across the world. Or the data center that performs its switch/billing/file updates at 2 am each morning. These are the times when the highest throughput is required for these networks. Thus, a network is designed to accommodate the peaks of its particular "busy hour". Often a cost tradeoff is used to balance the need of a larger network that may accommodate all traffic during busy hour with little to no delay compared to a less robust network that buffers or delays transmissions during busy hour.

The other major component of data is its burstiness. The bandwidth allocated to a phone call is usually the same: 56 or 64 kbps for a standard voice channel, and down to 8 kbps for compressed voice. But in data, an average user may transmit anything from a 2-kbit text file to a 2-Mbit graphics file. To complicate matters, multiple users may be simultaneously accessing a MAN, which in turn uses the WAN, and peak traffic patterns could vary drastically with virtually no notice. Because of these characteristics, data traffic can be analyzed on a "busy hour" basis, but is more accurately represented with multiple snapshots down to a "busy minute" basis.

Now let's take a look at some methods of calculating data busy hour, keeping in mind that if applications warrant, these calculations could be made in minutes or even seconds.

busy hour PPS = (busy hour packets sent + busy hour packets received) (3600 seconds / hour)

busy hour (BH) (busy hour PPS × packet size) × 8 bits
link utilization = BH bps / speed of link

For example,

BH PPS = (5 PPS + 5 PPS)(3600) = 36,000 PPS
BH bps = (5 PPS)(128 bytes)(8 bits) = 5120 bps
link utilization = 5120 bps / 9600 bps = 53.33 percent utilization

Chapter 20 will show how busy hour statistics fit into the access node design.

17.6 DELAY

When a network begins to slow down because of buffering, retransmissions, and/or any other time-affecting factor, its users will begin to experience *delay* and may experience *loss* of traffic. Delay and loss will cause response time and throughput to degrade, application time-outs and retransmissions to occur, and may even cause users to lose data. The potential impacts of delay and loss can affect an application's design when performance is a major consideration, which is true in most networks. Loss will impact the usable throughput for most network and transport layer protocols. This is true for almost all applications that are either bandwidth- or latency-limited. The accumulation of delay variation in multiple hop networks is important to delay-variation-sensitive applications, such as video, audio, and real-time interactive traffic. Variations in delay are also called jitter. Appreciable variations in delay, on the order of 50 ms or more will be observed by most users, particularly for terminal users who are in command-response mode.

17.6.1 Causes of Delay

While actual transmission-path delay does contribute an element of delay to the network, the primary contributors to delay include

- Propagation path length
- Line speed
- Number of access hops
- Hardware and software interface buffers
- Load on every component across the path
- Hardware/processor elements traversed (each adds delay)
- Window sizes
- Bit-setting selections (e.g., D-bit)
- Memory and buffers
- Pad functions
- Address database look-up
- Address verification
- Changes in traffic load
- Filtering, forwarding, and processing packets, frames, and cells

Most network design tools routinely model delay, but they also need to account for the components of delay listed above. There are many ways to decrease delay by decreasing network load, capacity, or routing, as well as adjusting device-specific tuning parameters.

17.6.2 Circuit-, Message-, Packet-, and Cell-Switching Delay Basics

In circuit switching, the delay incurred by a user is based upon the message size and the time it takes to transmit it over the available bandwidth. For example, if a graphics file of 2 Mbits is being transmitted over a 128 kbps frame relay trunk, the total delay in transmission (assuming zero network and protocol delay elements) would be

2 Mbits / 128 kbps = 15.625 s

Message switching delay closely resembles that found in frame relay networks. This is where the total delay is calculated the same as in circuit switching, but multiplied by the number of nodes the frame must traverse, minus 1. For example, assume that a user is transmitting the same 2 Mbit file through the 128 kbps port on the user device. The frames are being passed through a four-node frame relay network (not counting the origination and destination nodes), with the middle two nodes passing the information at T1 speeds. The total delay would be [(2)(2 Mbits/128 kbps)] + [(2)(2 Mbits/1.544 Mbps)] = 33.84 seconds. This calculation assumes that the user has the entire bandwidth of each link (and may vary for different implementations of frame relay).

Packet-switching delay is based on many of the packet-switching calculations examined above. The total message delay is calculated as:

$$[\left(\frac{p}{c}\right)(n+1)] + \left(\frac{r}{c}\right),$$

where p = packet size of first packet
n = number of nodes
c = capacity available in the transmission medium
r = remaining number of bits to be delivered in message

For example, if the 2 Mbit graphics file is transmitted over the four-node network connected by 56 kbps trunks, using packet sizes of 1024 bits, total delay in transmitting the entire graphics file would be [(1024/56,000)(4 + 1)] + (1,998,976/56,000) = 35.79 seconds.

Cell-switching delay best resembles packet-switching delay. There is some queuing (as in packet switching) but with a *fixed* number of cells. Data exceeding the available throughput is discarded, with no retransmissions. The *entire* frame/cell needs to be completely read and processed before it can be transmitted out.

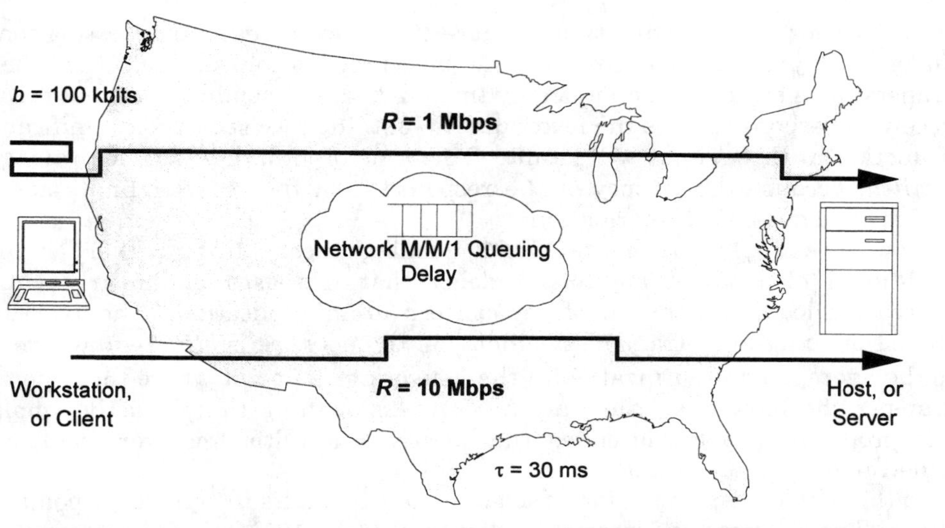

Figure 17. 22 Propagation Delay, Burst Length, and Peak Rate

17.6.3 Impact of Delay on Applications

Two situations occur when a source sends a burst of data at a certain transmission rate across a network with a certain delay, or latency: these situations are called bandwidth limited and latency limited. A *bandwidth-limited application* occurs when the receiver begins receiving data before the transmitter has completed transmission of the burst. A *latency-limited application* occurs when the transmitter finishes sending the burst of data before the receiver begins receiving any data.

Figure 17.22 illustrates the consequence of sending a burst of length b equal to 100,000 bits (100 kbits) at a peak rate of R Mbps across the domestic United States with a propagation delay τ of 30 ms. It takes 30 ms for the bit stream to propagate from the originating station to the receiving station across approximately 4000 miles of fiber since the speed of light in fiber is less than that in free space, and fiber is usually not routed along the most direct path. When the peak rate between originator and destination is 1 Mbps, and after 30 ms, only about one-third of the burst is in the transmission media, and the remainder is still buffered in the transmitting terminal. This is called a bandwidth-limited application because the lack of bandwidth to hold the transmission is limiting the transmitter from releasing the entire message immediately.

Now let's look at the case where the transmitter has sent the *entire* transmission before the receiver has received any data. When the peak rate is increased to 10 Mbps, the situation changes significantly — the entire burst is sent by the workstation before it can even reach the destination. Indeed, only about one-third of the bits propagating through the fiber transmission system are occupied by the burst! If the sending terminal must receive a response before the next burst is sent, then we see that a significant reduction in throughput will result. This type of situation is called *latency limited*, because the latency of the response from the receiver limits additional transmission of information.

Now let's apply the basic *M*/*M*/1 queuing theory from earlier as an additional element of end-to-end delay that increases nonlinearly with increasing load, and thus is of key concern to an application. The average *M*/*M*/1 queuing-plus- transmission delay in the network is $b/R/(1-\rho)$, where ρ is the average trunk utilization in the network. The point where the time to transfer the burst (i.e., the transmission-plus-queuing time) exactly equals the propagation delay is called the latency/bandwidth crossover point, as illustrated in Figure 17.23.

In the previous example, for a file size of b = 100 kbits the crossover point is 3.33 Mbps for zero utilization, and increases to 10 Mbps for 66 percent utilization.

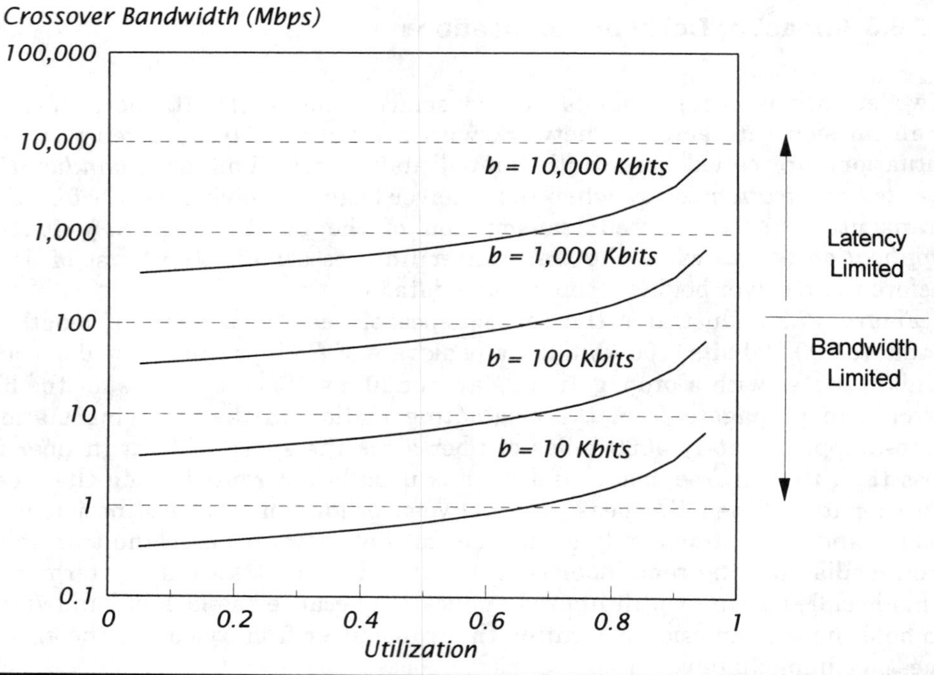

Figure 17.23 Latency/Bandwidth Crossover Point

17.6.4 Impact of Loss on Applications

Loss can be another enemy of applications. For many applications, the loss of a single frame or cell results in the loss of an entire packet (or an entire PDU). This is because the higher-layer network protocol (such as an IP packet) or ATM SAR sublayer in the AAL will fail in attempts at reassembly. Loss (or even excessive delay) can result in a time-out or negative acknowledgment in a higher-layer protocol, such as at the transport layer (TCP). If the round-trip time is long with respect to the application window size, then the achievable throughput can be markedly reduced. This is a basic aspect of all flow- and congestion-control methods. The amount of buffering required in the network is proportional to the product of the delay and bandwidth. In our example of Figure 17.22, the delay-bandwidth product is 300 bits for a 1-Mbps link (30 ms × 1 Mbps) and 3000 bits for a 10-Mbps link.

This situation is analogous to what occurred in early data communications over satellites, where the data rates were low, but the propagation delay was very high. The delay-bandwidth product is high in satellite communications because the propagation delay is high, while in terrestrial B-ISDN and ATM communications the delay-bandwidth product becomes large because the transmission speeds are high.

Higher-layer protocols recover from detected errors, or time-outs, by one of two basic methods: either all information that was sent after the detected error or time-out is retransmitted, or only the information that was actually in error or timed out is selectively retransmitted. Resending all of the information means that if N packets were sent after the detected error or time-out, then N packets are retransmitted, reducing the usable throughput. This scheme is often called a *Go-Back-N* retransmission strategy. The second method is where the packet that has a detected error, or causes a time-out, is explicitly identified by the higher- layer protocol; then only that packet need be retransmitted. This scheme is often called a *selective-reject* retransmission strategy. The usable throughput is increased because only the erred or timed-out information is retransmitted. However, this type of protocol is more complex to implement.

A simple model of the performance of these two retransmission strategies is presented to illustrate the impact of cell loss on higher-layer protocols.

The number of cells in the retransmission window W is determined by the transmission rate R, the packet size p (in bytes), and the propagation delay τ as follows:

$$W = \left\lceil \frac{2\tau R}{8p} \right\rceil$$

The probability that an individual packet is lost due to a random cell loss, probability π derived from the Cell Loss Ratio (CLR), is approximately the following:

$$\pi \approx \left\lceil \frac{p}{48} \right\rceil \text{CLR}$$

In the Go-Back-N strategy, if a single packet is in error of a window of W packets, then the entire window of W packets must be retransmitted. For the Go-Back-N retransmission strategy, the usable throughput η(Go-Back-N) is approximately the inverse of the average number of times the entire window must be sent, which is approximately:

$$\eta(\text{Go - Back - }N) \approx \frac{1-\pi}{1+\pi W}$$

In the selective reject strategy, if a single packet is in error, then only that packet is retransmitted. For the selective reject retransmission strategy, the usable throughput η(Selective-Reject) is approximately the inverse of the average number of times any individual packet must be sent, which is:

$$\eta(\text{Selective - Reject}) \approx (1-\pi)$$

This formula is valid for the case in which only one packet needs to be transmitted within the round-trip delay window. It also applies to a more sophisticated protocol that can retransmit multiple packets, such as ATM's Service Specific Connection-Oriented Protocol (SSCOP).

Figure 17.24 plots the usable throughput (or "goodput") for Go-Back-N and selective-reject retransmission strategies for a DS3 cell rate R of 40 Mbps, a packet size p of 200 bytes, and a propagation delay of 30 ms. The resultant window size W is 1500 packets. The retransmission protocols have nearly 100 percent usable throughput up to a Cell Loss Ratio (CLR) of 10^{-6}. As the CLR increases, the usable throughput of the Go-Back-N protocol decreases markedly because the probability that an individual window (of 7500 cells) will be received error free decreases markedly. As the CLR increases toward 10^{-2}, the probability of an individual packet having a lost cell starts to become significant, and even the selective-reject protocol's usable throughput begins to degrade.

These examples illustrate the importance of selecting a QoS class with loss performance that meets the application requirements. For example, Transmission Control Protocol (TCP) uses a Go-Back-N type of protocol and hence works best with low loss rates.

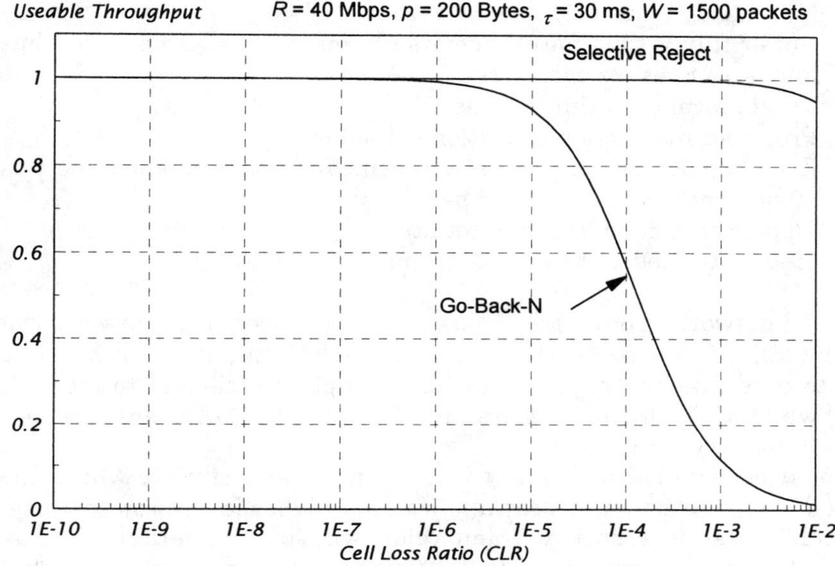

Figure 17.24 Usable Throughput versus Cell Loss Ratio

17.6.5 Data Services Delay

Sometimes delay components are not readily visible. For example, a PAD or a FRAD receiving asynchronous transmissions may packetize or frame this traffic at 128 bytes at a time, or it may wait until it receives 4 kbytes and then split the message into packets and transfer (store-and-forward). Thus, greater delay is incurred when an entire message must be read into a node before being transferred. This example is very important when designing frame relay networks. In most frame relay networks, when a frame relay device receives a frame, it must read the entire frame into memory, calculate the CRC to verify the frame, and then transmit the entire frame on to the next node or to the user. The larger the frame size, the greater the delay incurred, and the more buffer space required. Some combination frame/cell switches eliminate this delay by segmenting the frames into cells and immediately transmitting them across the WAN.

Let us take a remote user accessing a packet switched network via dial access and calculate total network delay. The total network delay is composed of many elements, such as:

- Call setup delay (20 ms – Call RQ, Call CN, ENQ, Auth, Resp, Ack, Clear RQ, and Clear CF)

- Node delay (variable)
- Buffer filling time for characters (32 ms per 4 async on 1200 bps line — so 8 ms for each access line)
- Packet formation time (50 ms)
- Processor instruction execution (11–33 ms)
- Each hop across network (e.g., if utilization on a 56 kbps line was 10 percent, the delay would be 28 ms)
- Modem-to-modem (80 ms) initiate
- Modem-to-modem terminate (10 ms)

for a total network round-trip delay on a three-hop network of (2)[(20)+(8)+(28)] + (3)[(50)+(11)] + 80 + 10 = 385 ms, best case. It is important to note that the modems in this example contributed to much of the delay, while CSU/DSUs in a frame relay or LAN/MAN environment would contribute very little delay.

Delay would be handled differently in a frame relay network, where the result depends on the how the user applications higher-level protocols deal with delay. Most services, such as frame relay, will state a guaranteed delay objective, such as the percentage of PDUs/frames which are delivered within a specified time (ms), for example, 90 percent of PDUs delivered within 1 ms, the rest delivered within 5 ms. This figure is driven by both what the user application requires and what the network devices can provide. Another example is buffering, which tells the user how many packets or frames/PDUs can be buffered and at what size (including CRC check), as in the last example on frame relay frame size and its effect on delay.

With larger frame sizes, the service that is providing the transport may segment or lose the frame. Also, delay may be incurred in storing portions of frames in buffers until they can be received and retransmitted in their entirety. In most frame relay switches, the entire frame is received and verified (via a CRC) before being retransmitted. There is also the danger of large frames being segmented by other protocols, such as IP, SMDS, and even ATM. This causes additional overhead in proportion to the frame size. The effects of protocol conversions, encapsulations, and translations on delay must all be accounted for by the network designer.

17.7 AVAILABILITY AND RELIABILITY

Two quality measures of hardware and software must be known by the network designer: availability and reliability. These values are found through vendor-provided calculations such as Mean Time Between Failures (*MTBF*) and Mean Time To Repair (*MTTR*). Note that Mean Time To *Respond* is sometimes calculated by service providers, and should not be confused with *repair*. Read the service contract. *MTBF* is calculated based on stress tests, the results of which are projected into the future, as well as through theoretical model projections, possibly using compilations based on the individual parts that make up the system. Other methods of measuring availability and reliability performance will also be explored.

17.7.1 Availability

Availability is the amount of time the system is working when compared to the measured lifetime of the system. Availability is calculated by:

$$A_i = \text{Availability} = \frac{MTBF_i}{MTBF_i + MTTR_i}$$

$$= \frac{\text{time system is working}}{\text{time system exists between failures}}$$

For highly reliable systems, this number should be at least .999, or 99.9 percent. This is commonly referred to as "three nines". Networks that provide public service offerings often have availability figures of 99.95 percent or higher. Each additional nine increases the order of magnitude by 10, thus an increase from 99.99 percent to 99.999 percent is a drastic increase in availability. But what does it cost for an extra 9? It may be more than one is willing to pay, as the cost increase in hardware, software, and services to provide 99.99 percent may also be tenfold. Availability is related to available capacity, whereas users always want to have enough capacity to transmit their units of data (regardless of the message size).

Another way to look at availability is through its complement or reciprocal: *unavailability*.

$$U = \text{Unavailability} = 1 - \frac{MTBF}{MTBF + MTTR} = \frac{MTTR}{MTBF + MTTR}$$

Unavailability is a calculation of the time the system will be unavailable or, in other words, its probability of failure. The system is unavailable *MTTR* hours out of every *MTBF* + *MTTR* hours.

Another way to look at the number of failures during a given period is by the formula:

Average number of failures in $t = t \,/\, (MTBF + MTTR) \cong t \,/\, MTBF$,

where t is the number of hours of operation. *MTTR* is included in the formula because each failure must be repaired. When *MTBF* is much greater than *MTTR* (*MTBF* >> *MTTR*), *MTTR* can be omitted from the equation. Thus, if the *MTBF* was 1000 hours (a very poor *MTBF*) and the number of failures must be determined within a year (8760 hours), there would be the likelihood of 8.76 failures that year, or .024 failures per day (almost one failure each month). If there are 100 nodes in your network, .024 failures per day means that there are 2.4 failures per day throughout the entire network. Now it can be seen why an MTBF of 1000 hours is quite poor! Consider a good MTBF of 40,000 hours, which would calculate to one failure every 4.57 years! Now this 100-node network has less than 2 failures per month.

For multiple network elements with different *MTBF*s, as in a hybrid network, availability (A_i) and unavailability (U_i) would be calculated for each element and then one of the following formulas would be used, depending on whether the elements were in serial or parallel.

For a serial network as seen in Figure 17.25, the availability with two devices would be calculated as:

$$A_s = (A_1)(A_2) = \left(\frac{MTBF_1}{MTBF_1 + MTTR_1}\right)\left(\frac{MTBF_2}{MTBF_2 + MTTR_2}\right)$$

Thus, the greater the number of nodes, the greater the chance of network failure.

The unavailability would then be calculated as:

$$U_S = (U_1)(A_1) + (A_1)(U_2) + (U_1)(U_2)$$

For a parallel network as seen in Figure 17.25, the unavailability with two devices would be calculated as:

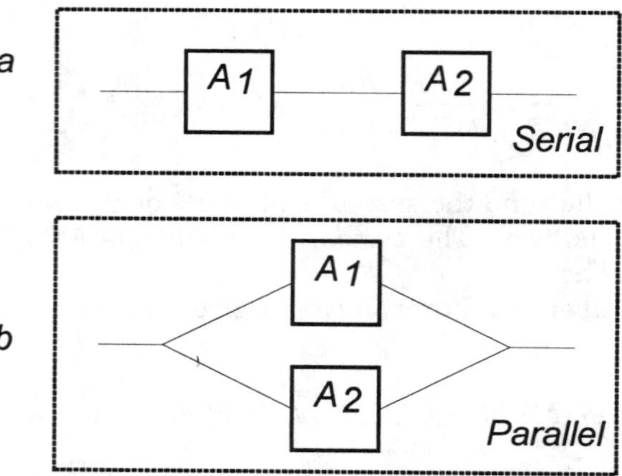

Figure 17.25 Availability

$$U_p = (U_1)(U_2) = (1 - A_1)(1 - A_2) = 1 - A_1 - A_2 + A_1A_2$$

The availability would then be calculated as:

$$A_p = (1 - U_p) = A_1 + A_2 - A_1A_2$$

Thus, the greater the number of nodes, the less chance of network failure. Meshing also has the potential to increase *network* or *system* reliability.

17.7.2 Reliability

Reliability is the distribution of time between failures. Reliability is often specified by the Mean Time Between Failure (*MTBF*) for Markovian failures. A high-reliability *MTBF* figure means that the system contains many reliable components which together constitute a reliable system. Reliability is specified as the probability that the system does not fail prior to *t* hours.

$$\text{Reliability} = e^{-t/MTBF}$$

Take a sample *MTBF* of 10,000 hours and a time interval *t* of 1 year (8760 hours). The reliability would be 41.64 percent. If we were to increase the *MTBF* to 20,000 hours, the reliability jumps to 64.53 percent. For multiple network elements with different *MTBF*s, as in a serial hybrid network (such as a bus environment), the total failures calculation would be:

$$R(total) = e^{-t[(\frac{1}{MTBF_1})+(\frac{1}{MTBF_2})+(\frac{1}{MTBF_3})}$$

As an example, if we had *MTBF* figures of 20,000, 25,000, and 30,000 hours, respectively, measured over one year, the network would yield a 34 percent reliability! Thus, reliability can also be cumulative, but is always as weak as the weakest network element and always decreases as network devices are added. It can be seen that reliability is a tradeoff with redundancy when adding additional network resources.

Two additional performance measurements to MTTR are

Mean Time To Isolate (MTTI). The time it takes to identify the cause of the problem or outage.

Mean Time To Repair (MTTR). After finding a problem, how long does it take to repair the problem or outage? This figure is usually stated in minutes.

Mean Time Between Service Outages (MTBSO). How long (historically) it has been since the system has been down for a service outage? This figure is usually stated as greater than 2000 hours. Over 2000 hours translates to 2.5 hours down time per year (250 days × 8 hours per day).

Also, with 1:*N* live spares, the overall *MTBF* can be much higher, by a factor of 10 to greater than 100! Always select 1:*N* sparing if possible.

17.7.3 Additional Performance Measurements

In service or maintenance contracts, negotiated penalties apply if performance objectives provided by the vendor are not met. Also, each network performance parameter must be tested before placing users or applications on it. Not only must the level of error tolerability be determined, but also how much sharing of resources and capacity is tolerable. Some common methods of measuring performance on packet-, frame-, and cell-switched services include:

- Less than *x* packets, frames, PDUs among *y* are
  - Delivered without error
  - Delivered to wrong customer
  - Lost
  - Duplicated
- Total lost frames/packets/cells per time period
- Total network delay
- Guaranteed aggregate throughput per channel based on characteristics of data (e.g. 1.22 Mbps per T1 using 16-byte frames)
- Guaranteed overhead limits (based upon packet/frame/cell size)
- Measure of DDS service in error-free seconds (99.99 percent desirable)
- Load-balancing/load-sharing limitations
- Masking, filtering, and forwarding rates for access and backbone
- Error detection/correction effects upon overhead and throughput
- Level of redundancy built into network

17.7.4 Plan for Failures

Is there extra capacity to allow for failures in the network backbone nodes, access nodes, links, network hardware, and network software? Make sure that the system is designed to survive failures. Select hardware and software with high availability and reliability figures. Implement designs that minimize weak failure points by adding additional redundant subsystems and implementing network meshing. It may also be prudent to force a failure early in the life of the network (or before it goes "live") to determine if fault-tolerant system backups are working properly. Always periodically test your backup hardware and systems.

17.8 REACTION TO EXTREME SITUATIONS

Another important consideration in network design is the desired behavior of the network under extreme situations. We will consider the extreme situations of significant failure, traffic overload, and unexpected peak traffic patterns.

It is very important to consider what will happen during a significant failure, such as one or more critical trunk failures, or failure of an entire switch. The general guideline is that any element of the network should not become isolated by a single trunk or switch failure. If you can survive with some loss of connectivity, costs can be significantly reduced in a private network; however, public networks are usually designed to survive single circuit and equipment failures. The exception and most vulnerable point is usually the user's access to the public network, in both single-point-of-failure CPE or access circuits (such as the local loop, which typically has the greatest failure rate often attributed to "back-hoe fade"). This can be solved with equipment diversity, circuit diversity, or dial or dedicated backup facilities. You may have different performance objectives under failure situations than under normal circumstances. Also, you may desire that some traffic be preempted during a failure scenario so that support for mission-critical traffic is maintained. A failure without redundant facilities can effectively reduce either a bandwidth or switching resource, and hence can be a cause of congestion.

Traffic overloads and unexpected traffic parameters can also cause congestion. For example, offered traffic in excess of the service contract (like CIR in frame relay) may create congestion. Some network services like ATM mark this excessive traffic (under normal circumstances) for selective cell discard, and those cells in excess of the contract will be discarded first. But if the network is overbooked with contracted traffic parameters, the selective cell discard may not be enough. As pointed out earlier, congestion can drive a switch or multiple points in a network into overload, reducing overall throughput significantly if congestion collapse occurs. If you expect this situation to occur, then a mechanism to detect congestion, correlate it with its cause, and provide some feedback in order to isolate various traffic sources and achieve the required measure of fairness is desirable. If you are uncertain as to how long such overloads will persist, then some slow-reacting feedback controls may actually reduce throughput because the reaction may occur after congestion has already abated (such as we saw with higher-layer protocols like TCP).

In order to support time-varying traffic patterns, there are two fundamentally different approaches: one based upon the telecommunications concept of reserving bandwidth and the other based on the communications concept of fairly shared resources. A Switched Virtual Channel (SVC) capability allows an application to request the network to reserve bandwidth for its exclusive use, very similar to circuit switching. In order to use the current SVC protocols, you will need to estimate your bandwidth accurately since it can only be changed by tearing down the call and setting it up again. Future SVC protocols will allow the bandwidth to be dynamically negotiated without the call being taken down. Both of these scenarios will require the user to estimate the bandwidth requirement and communicate this to the network.

Another possibility would be that of dynamic flow control where feedback from the network regarding congestion is used to throttle back sources in a fair manner, which also isolates applications that are "good citizens" from those that aren't following the flow-control rules. The choice of approach will depend upon the characteristics of your applications, and which approach is adopted by the vendor and service providers.

17.9 NETWORK PERFORMANCE MODELING

Most users are concerned with modeling the performance of a network. There are two basic modeling approaches: simulation and analysis. A simulation is usually much more accurate, but can become a formidable computational task when trying to simulate the performance of a large network. Analysis can be less computationally intensive, but is often inaccurate. What is the best approach? The answer is similar to nodal modeling — it depends on how much information you have and how accurate an answer you require.

Simulation models are very useful in investigating the detailed operation of a system, which can lead to key insights into equipment, network, or application design. Detailed simulations generally take too long to execute to be used as an effective network design tool.

A good way to bootstrap the analytical method is to simulate the network technology or switch performance under the expected mix of traffic inputs. Often an analytical approximation to the empirical simulation results can be developed as input to an analytical tool. An assumption often made in network modeling is that the nodes operate independently, and that the traffic mixes and splits independently and randomly. If better information is not available, then this is a reasonable assumption, and simulation may be the only recourse. Analytical models become very complex without the assumption that nodes are independent of each other.

The inputs and outputs of a network model are similar for any packet-switched network design problem. The inputs are the topology, traffic, and routing. The network topology must be defined, usually as a graph with nodes and links. The characteristics of each node and link relevant to the simulation or analytical model must be described. Next the pattern of traffic offered between the nodes must be defined. For point-to-point traffic this is commonly done via a traffic matrix. The routing, or set of links that traffic follows from source to destination, must be defined.

The principal outputs are measures of performance and cost. The principal performance measures of a model are loss and delay statistics. A model will often produce an economic cost to allow the network designer to select an effective price-performance tradeoff.

Now let's take a look at the first step in traffic modeling – the traffic matrix.

17.10 CREATING THE TRAFFIC MATRIX

Now that the user requirements have been defined and we have categorized the traffic modeling and engineering, we can compile and sort these requirements into meaningful data to develop a network design. In the most simple terms, we can create a traffic matrix of who needs to talk with whom, and what traffic patterns need to go where. We can then analyze the traffic matrix and start the capacity-planning cycle.

17.10.1 Asymmetric versus Symmetric Distribution

Is the distribution of traffic by direction asymmetric or symmetric? *Asymmetrical* traffic lacks directional symmetry through an imbalance of flows, speeds, or a variety of other characteristics. It originates from large sites to small, or vice versa, and does not follow a normal distribution. Access devices vary in quantity, design, engineering, and loading. On the other hand, symmetric traffic often originates from communities of similar interest, such as specific geographic regions, and is uniformly spread across these sites within each region, and the bidirectional quantity is similar. In *symmetrical* networks, many of the access devices are similar in quantity, design, engineering, and loading. Hierarchical networks, such as those using the SNA protocols, are often symmetrical in nature. Distributed networks often resemble asymmetrical rather than symmetrical traffic distributions. LAN traffic and WAN traffic made up of LAN traffic feeds tends to be asymmetrical and very hard to diagnose. In this instance, average and peak traffic patterns should be used in the traffic matrix. Figure 17.26 illustrates symmetrical and asymmetrical traffic distributions.

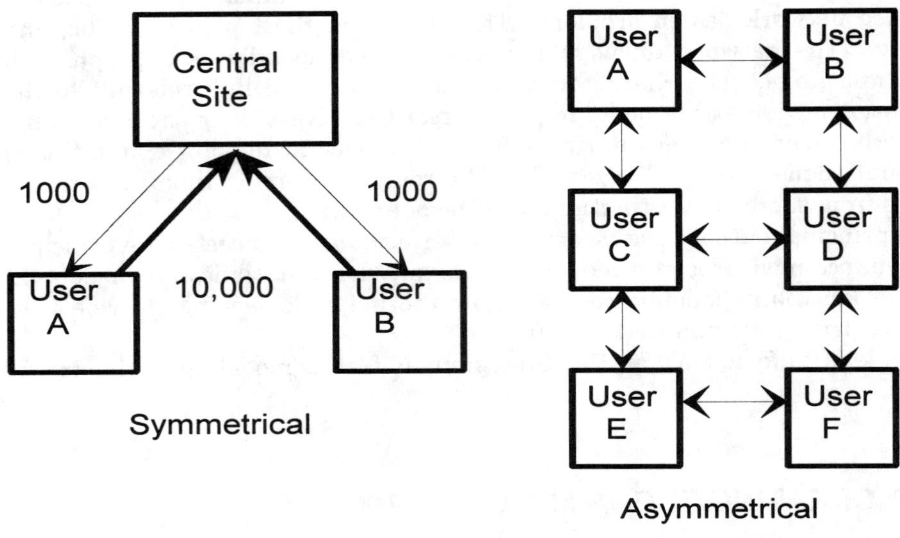

Figure 17.26 Symmetrical and Asymmetrical Traffic Distributions

17.10.2 Creating the Traffic Matrix

The traffic matrix is an essential part of the access node design, and illustrates traffic flows not otherwise readily apparent. Traffic interfaces to the network through an access node or access point. Access nodes could take the form of a concentrator (e.g., PAD or FRAD), DXC, access multiplexer, hub, bridge, router, access switch, or any other device concentrating user inputs but not operating as a switching backbone. The traffic matrix helps define details about the access node requirements, such as location, size, operation, protocol support, performance characteristics, and device type.

The traffic matrix is, in effect, a spreadsheet or table mapping traffic flows from origin to destination. The FROM nodes are listed vertically down the left side of the matrix, and the TO nodes are listed horizontally across the top. Figure 17.27 shows a sample traffic matrix with simple data units (e.g., bytes, calls, packets) per second for each site. Each box represents a traffic flow from the FROM node i to the TO node j (this is sometimes referred to as the ij matrix). All traffic that remains local to a node will be found in the A-A box, B-B box, and so forth. Notice that node A has 20 intranodal traffic units per second, while node B has only three. Notice also that node B sends two traffic units per second to node A.

TO LOCATION (j) / FROM LOCATION (i)

i \ j	A	B	C	D	E	F
A	20	0	2	1	20	12
B	2	3	3	*	6	5
C	2	0	12	2	8	3
D	8	*	1	10	22!	5
E	12	4	0	31!	6	3
F	22	8	2	1	2	2

Traffic Flow Units (e.g., packets, frames, bytes, calls per second)

Figure 17.27 Traffic Matrix

It is good practice to start with a local geographic area as node A and work out from there, so that letters that are lexically close represent nodes in a geographic region. Keeping to this scheme as much as possible simplifies the process. Traffic flows, or profiles, will be represented by any of the previously discussed formats, including packets, frames, bytes, calls, or even protocols, priorities, or other dependencies. Traffic measurements used should have a similar message (packet) length and should be measured in "mean busy hour" throughput (in bps) or in the peak-to-mean ratio. Traffic patterns are often provided in units per second (i.e., packets, frames, cells) during average, peak, and maximum traffic patterns throughout a 24-hour period and designed for busy hour traffic as previously discussed. Traffic measurements should be measured from either the network or the application point of view. Thus, a matrix can be built that shows specific application traffic flows (such as FTP or Telnet file transfer protocol traffic) or generic packet flows, such as Ethernet packets from a LAN interface. Also mark invalid and preferred routes. Figure 17.28 shows the same matrix, with the additional detail of invalid routes indicated with an *, while preferred routes are indicated with an !

TO LOCATION (j) / FROM LOCATION (i)

i \ j	A	B	C	D	E	F
A	20	0	2	1	20	12
B	2	3	3	*	6	5
C	2	0	12	2	8	3
D	8	*	1	10	22!	5
E	12	4	0	31!	6	3
F	22	8	2	1	2	2

Traffic Flow Units (e.g., packets, frames, bytes, calls per second

Figure 17.28 Traffic Matrix

17.10.3 Interpreting the Matrix

In its simplest use, the matrix shows the connectivity required between each site. Let M be the binary matrix, with a 1 indicating connectivity and a 0 indicating no connectivity. The following are then true:

M = connectivity for one node (i.e., direct connectivity)
$M \times M$ = connectivity for a 2-hop path
$M \times M \times M$ = connectivity for a 3-hop path
$M + M^2 + M^3$ = all paths up to path length of 3 hops

Note that this method can include "cycles" or loops (paths which traverse the same node more than once), which should be eliminated. For example, each level of connectivity between nodes may require a private line, PVC if frame relay, VC or VP if ATM, or tandem node.

All traffic identified as remaining local to a given node would be placed into the same access node. Circles are then drawn around boxes that represent a small geographic area which could be served by a single concentrator. This is done by grouping nodal traffic distributions in a local geographical area together to form larger access nodes. This reduces the number of access devices required.

Figure 17.28 shows the same matrix from the last example. Node A has 20 units of traffic (this could be 20 PPS, 20 frames per second, or 20 kbps average traffic during busy hour), which remains local and node B only has three units of traffic. Also note that node A sends no traffic to node B, and node B sends only two units of traffic to node A. Since in this example node A and node B are in the same geographic region, the traffic from both nodes is combined at node A where a single access node is placed. The small amount of traffic originating at node B is "backhauled" to node A. Some amount of backhaul access is required in many public data services where there are limited access points into the switched network. This also assumes that no other large amounts of traffic are generated or sent to node B from other nodes.

This process continues until the number of access nodes required to begin the design is established. Ideally, one would like to place a separate concentrator node at each site, but often economics do not justify this, so the network design usually settles for smaller nodes at less concentrated regions and larger ones in more dense regions, or backhaul from less to more concentrated regions.

Network designs for multimedia and multiprotocol networks are much more complicated. These complex designs often require many traffic matrices combined into a multidimensional matrix (e.g., a *z*-axis forming a three-dimensional matrix to accommodate interdependencies such as priority of information, budget tradeoffs, or protocols), or in large networks, design tools to perform these calculations. Ideally, this analysis would be performed by a design tool. Design tools will be covered in Chapter 24.

17.11 CAPACITY PLANNING AND NETWORK VISION

Capacity planning was once done on a 5- to 10-year cycle. It is now a 1- to 3-year cycle, and many times even shorter. There are two elements to the plan, a *short-term* objective and task-oriented plan usually revised each year, and the *long-term* 3- to 5-year plan, which should also take into account the strategic vision of corporate communications for the next 5 to 10 years. As the cost of computing hardware decreases, the entropy of capacity requirements increases. This makes capacity planning for communications networks a challenging task. Short- and long-range capacity planning can provide the corporation with a competitive advantage, assuming that the plans fit in with the long-range strategic business plan. Each design must provide the flexibility to change technology as business needs change without major network restructuring. Both plans must take into account the business needs, customer needs, and the technologies.

One method is to migrate multiple network platforms to a consolidated network platform that conforms to industry standards. Decide early on whether to maintain the existing architecture and build upon it, or plan to build a new integrated network architecture in the future. One of the best architectures is that which is built in a hierarchical nature that caters to flexible peer-to-peer communications and can be replaced in layers over time. Plan for port expansion, CPU capacity, hardware storage requirements, memory storage requirements, growth in user application traffic, and many other critical growth areas discussed in this chapter. Many design tools have the capability to model future network changes and assist in both the short-term and long-range capacity planning process.

17.12 REVIEW

Going beyond the voice world and standard circuit-switched traffic modeling, the queued data and packet-switched traffic modeling of data services and technologies such as packet switching, frame relay, DQDB (SMDS), and even ATM were introduced. We started the chapter with some basic throughput calculations. We next moved to the key aspect of traffic engineering philosophy: *source modeling*. Various source models affect the accuracy and complexity of the traffic-engineering calculations. In general, the more accurate the model, the more complicated the calculation. There are models that average, but deterministic models that use actual data structures and equipment propagation delays are far more complex, but have a vastly better level of accuracy. This book opts for simplicity in modeling and introduces only a few of the popular, simple source models. After traditional erlang traffic engineering was introduced, we next turned to the key aspects of modeling switch performance, including a comparison of buffering methods and statistical multiplexing. The network has been sized to accommodate standard and peak traffic conditions, and to determine what theoretical level of delay and loss will be tolerable. Guidelines were provided to aid in the choice of link speed, burst duration, and loss ratio. Methods for calculation of delay loss and error rate in a multiple switched-node network were described, along with some suggestions and alternatives for managing delay variation. The tradeoffs and critical factors include cost, risk, and performance. Part of the network design should consider what will happen under extremes, such as failures, overload, and unexpected peak traffic patterns, and each subject was explored in detail. The availability, reliability, and other performance measurements required of vendor products with which to build the network have been identified. Calculating the traffic matrix, or possibly even multiple traffic matrices, allow the designer to determine network access resource requirements and size access nodes. This has identified capacity needs, including how much capacity, what the utilization will be, how performance will be affected by these decisions, and how to improve performance. Finally, a network vision and organized plan was set forth to accommodate future growth in capacity. Next, the best technology must be chosen to suit network access requirements, and a choice of the vendor(s) to supply this technology established, and only then can the access network design be completed.

Chapter

18

Technology and Service Comparisons

The next step in the design process is to choose the access and backbone technology or hybrid of technologies or the public network service that will offer this choice of technologies. Previous chapters have covered a working knowledge of circuit-, packet-, and cell-switching technologies, the standards which define them, and the services which can be offered. This knowledge will be coupled with the user's requirements and the level of capacity required from the network. The most popular technologies vying for command of the WAN include private lines, circuit switching, IP, X.25 packet switching, frame relay, SMDS, and ATM.

This chapter draws comparisons between these technologies and services, their protocols and interfaces, and the details of each switching technique. Comparisons are based upon objective measures, suitability to application needs, network attributes, and services provided to end users. Some comparison to traditional LAN technologies such as FDDI and 100 Mbps Ethernet are also provided. A good understanding of these high-speed data transport technologies is essential for the network design engineer to make a wise design decision. Thus, the access and backbone portion of the network design can be accomplished using the best mix of technologies to meet the user's requirements and to ensure designing the correct capacity requirements.

18.1 CIRCUIT-, MESSAGE-, PACKET-, AND CELL-SWITCHING METHODS

This section summarizes all of the circuit-, message-, packet-, and cell-switched data communications methods that have been developed throughout history. Motivations for the choice between circuit switching versus packet switching in terms of some simple application examples are also provided.

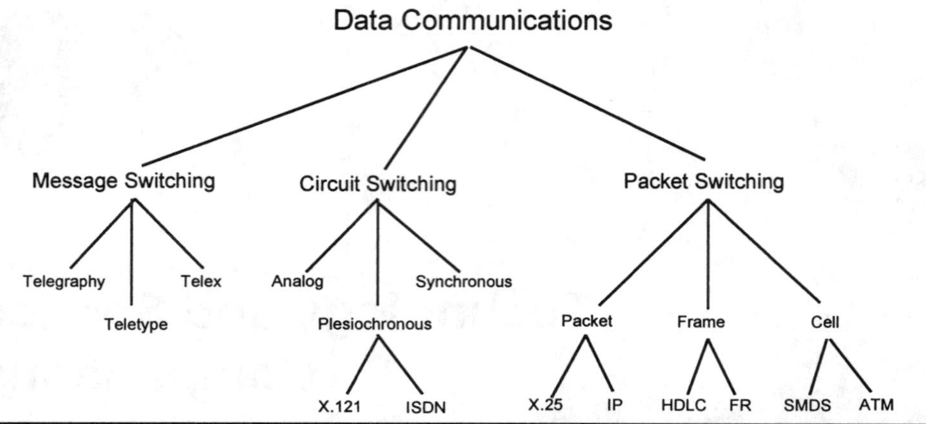

Figure 18.1 A Taxonomy of Historical Data Communication Methods

18.1.1 A Taxonomy of Data Communication Methods

There are basically three switching methods that can be used to communicate data: circuit switching, message switching, and packet switching. All other categories of data communications can be placed into this taxonomy as illustrated in Figure 18.1. The packet-switching branch is further broken down into packet, frame, and cell switching. The large number of techniques under the packet-switching branch is indicative of the industry focus on this method.

Message switching started the era of modern data communications in 1847 with the invention of the telegraph by Morse and the system of message relays. Message switching evolved into paper tape teletype relay systems and the modern telex messaging system used for financial transfers and access to remote locations. But although digital data communications began with the telegraph, which initially employed human operators to perform the message-switching function, it is not a prevalent data communications technology today. The telegraph was eventually replaced by the teletype, which yielded to the Telex system of today, without which you could not wire money or reach remote locations. True message switching today has evolved to become a higher-layer protocol, and in many cases, an application that operates over packet switching in modern data communication networks. One example is the ISO X.400 messaging system. The Simple Mail Transfer Protocol (SMTP) of the Internet also provides a higher-layer protocol for messaging.

Circuit switching in data communications started over 50 years ago through modems designed for use on analog transmission systems. This evolved into plesiochronous digital transmission systems over the past 30 to 40 years. The main technologies in use today are digital private lines, X.21 fast circuit switching, and ISDN BRI and PRI circuit switching.

Packet switching was developed in the past 30 years to overcome the expense and poor performance of transmission systems. Three major classes of packet switching have evolved over time. The first packet switching systems of X.25 and IP were designed to operate over very poor transmission networks. A simpler protocol like HDLC could be used for local connections when the quality of the links was better. HDLC in turn has evolved into the wide area with frame relay. The desire to achieve even higher performance and flexibility lead to the development of SMDS, which is further enhanced by the development of ATM. Improvements in transmission technology, electronics, and protocol design are key enablers in this latest generation of data communications technology.

18.1.2 Dedicated or Switched Networks?

Should you choose a dedicated network connection or a switched service? Figure 18.2a illustrates the tradeoffs between a dedicated facility between two points and a switched facility. This figure shows that there is a point when a dedicated facility between two points will be more economical than a switched facility for a certain amount of daily usage. For example, if the usage duration is high, such as 2 minutes per transfer, but the total daily usage is only about 2000 seconds or about 30 minutes, then a switched service is probably more economical. This crossover can be different if the individual usage duration is so small that the required switching capability is too expensive. Some services like ISDN are offered with both per call and usage charges. If the point-to-point usage indicates switching is economically desirable, then there are two types of switching to choose from: either connectionless like the Internet Protocol (IP) or Switched Multimegabit Data Service (SMDS), or connection-oriented, like Integrated Services Digital Network (ISDN) and frame relay. Bottom line – it is important to understand the tariff structure and cost of each service. As a general rule of thumb, the average transaction duration should be an order of magnitude or greater than the circuit (either physical or logical) setup time when choosing a CONS, otherwise consider a CLNS, as shown in the setup time regions of Figure 18.2b.

Figure 18.3 illustrates this example of usage duration by showing the time required to transfer an object of a certain size for a range of representative PDH circuit transfer rates. There obviously exists a linear relationship. The range of transfer times is divided into three regions based upon applicability of technology: connectionless, connection-oriented, and bulk data transfer (e.g., overnight mail). Note that there is a gap in the transfer time between 1.5 Mbps and 45 Mbps in the PDH and SDH transmission granularity. This is an example of where the flexibility of packet or cell transfer over fixed-rate circuits is evident.

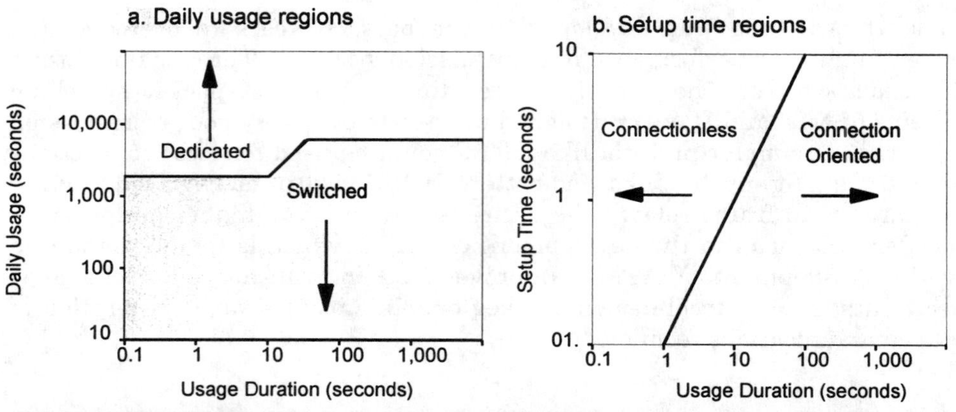

Figure 18.2 Ranges of Data Service Application

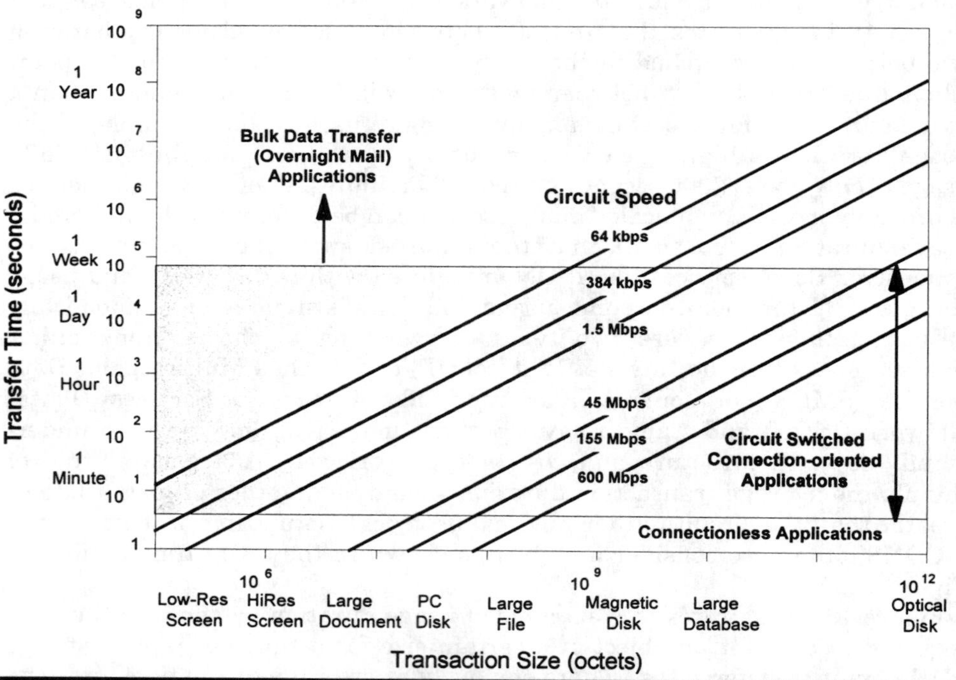

Figure 18.3 Transfer Time versus Transaction Size for Circuit Rates

18.2 PACKET-SWITCHING SERVICE ASPECTS

This section compares the service aspects of packet-switching technologies. These include the philosophy of data delivery, congestion control, flow control, protocol functions, and how the service relates to the OSI Reference Model (OSIRM).

18.2.1 Data Delivery Philosophy

A fundamental aspect of a packet-switching service is whether the packets are guaranteed to be delivered or not. An assured data service guarantees delivery of the packets, while an unassured data service does not. The assured mode is tolerant of errors. The unassured mode is also called a datagram service, a term that originated in the older X.25 standards.

X.25 assures that packets are delivered reliably on a link-by-link basis. Frame relay and SMDS operate in unassured mode. ATM can offer assured mode service through the Service-Specific Connection-Oriented Protocol (SSCOP).

The packet-switching service may guarantee that data arrives in the same sequence as it was transmitted, or may reorder the packets upon delivery. If a packet service has sequence integrity, the order of transmitted packets is preserved end-to-end.

18.2.2 Switching Approach

The packet-switched network may operate as either a Connection-Oriented Network Service (CONS) or a ConnectionLess Network Service (CLNS) as defined in Chapter 4. Connection-oriented packet services may be operated as either Permanent Virtual Connections (PVCs) or Switched Virtual Connections (SVCs).

18.2.3 Traffic, Congestion, and Flow Control

A packet service may reserve bandwidth for a connection-oriented service or it may enforce other limits on access to the service. This bandwidth reservation may take the form of a Committed Information Rate (CIR) as with frame relay, access classes as with SMDS, or Peak Cell Rate (PCR) and Sustainable Cell Rate (SCR) traffic-control functions per virtual connection (VCC) as with ATM.

Table 18.1 Comparison of Protocol Function

Function	X.25	IP	FR	SMDS	ATM
Switching Type	Packet	Packet	Frame	Cell	Cell
Mode	CONS	CLNS	CONS	CLNS	CONS w/CLNS
CONS Types	PVC, SVC	N/A	PVC, SVC	N/A	PVC, SVC
Assured Mode	Yes	No	No	No	via SSCOP
Sequence Integrity	Yes	No	Yes	Yes	Yes
Retransmission	Yes	No	No	No	via SSCOP
Traffic Control	None	None	CIR, EIR	Access Class	PCR, SCR
Flow Control	Yes	No	No	No	No
Congestion Control	Transmit	No (but possible)	Transmit, Receiver	No	Receiver

A packet service may implement flow-control. The flow-control method may be window-based as with X.25, congestion-based as with frame relay (FECN/BECN) and ATM (forward congestion notification), or rate-based and credit-based as with ATM. Alternatively, a packet service may have no flow control whatsoever, such as with IP. A packet service may detect and react to congestion on either a link-by-link basis, or on an end-to-end basis. The reaction to congestion may be receiver-controlled, transmitter-controlled, both, or neither.

18.2.4 Comparison of Protocol Functions

Table 18.1 shows a comparison of public data service protocol functions. The terms used in the table were summarized in the preceding sections.

18.2.5 OSI Functional Mapping

Figure 18.4 depicts an approximate mapping of data communications protocols, services, and their common interfaces to the OSIRM. These protocols were covered in previous chapters.

OSIRM	Protocol	Service	Interface
Application	Operating System File Management X.400 / X.500	Distributed File Sharing, Multimedia, Messaging	User, Software
Presentation	NCP, NetBIOS, NETBeui, FTP, NFS, FTAM	Multimedia	Software
Session	SPX, NetBIOS, NETBeui, FTP, SMTP	LU6.2	Software
Transport	TCP, XNS, SPX	TCP/IP	Software
Network	IP, IPX, XNS, IEEE 802.1, X.25 (packet), ISDN, ARP	ISDN, X.25, IP, SMDS, ATM AAL	Software
LLC	IEEE 802.2 LLC, HDLC, SDLC, X.25(link), PPP, FR, SIP_L2	X.25, PPP, ATM, FR	Software
MAC	IEEE 802.X, SMDS SIP, FDDI	ATM, FDDI, High SpeedCkt Switching	Ethernet, Token Ring, FDDI X3.139
Physical	DS0, FT1, DS1, DS3	DS0, FT1, DS1, DS3, HSCS	Copper/Coax/Fiber Media systems and interfaces

Figure 18.4 Mapping of Services and Protocols to the OSIRM

18.3 GENERIC PACKET-SWITCHING NETWORK CHARACTERISTICS

This section covers aspects of addressing, switching, routing, and network design. A tabular presentation summarizes the comparison of the networking aspects of data communication services.

18.3.1 Network-Addressing Philosophies

Addressing may be geographically oriented like the telephone numbering plan, network-oriented like the Internet, or hardware-oriented. Addressing schemes employed include IP, X.121, E.164, NSAP, and IEEE MAC, as covered in earlier chapters and in more detail in Chapter 22.

The IP address is 32 bits and is assigned on a network basis. The E.164 addressing plan used in SMDS is 15 Binary Coded Decimal (BCD) digits and is currently assigned on a geographic basis. The 48-bit IEEE MAC addresses are assigned on a vendor chip basis. X.25 utilizes a Logical Channel Number (LCN). Switched X.25 connections utilize a 14-digit X.121 address, which is allocated to networks based upon the first four digits, with the network provider specifying use of the remaining digits.

Frame relay frames are assigned a Data Link Connection Identifier (DLCI). Frame relay SVCs utilize the E.164 numbering plan. ATM cells are assigned a Virtual Path Identifier (VPI) and Virtual Channel Identifier (VCI) that can have meaning on an end-to-end basis through translation at intermediate nodes. Switched virtual ATM connections may utilize either E.164 or NSAP addresses. The ISO NSAP addressing plan is assigned on a network administrator basis.

18.3.2 Routing Approaches

The routing of packets in data communications services may range from static to dynamic. The routing may be unspecified for the service, or may be standardized. Examples of standard routing protocols are the Open Shortest Path First (OSPF) and the Routing Information Protocol (RIP) of the Internet. Both routing protocols were covered in Chapter 8.

18.3.3 Network Access and Topology

A packet service may provide user access via a shared medium or a dedicated medium. The access medium may be dedicated to a single type of service, or may be shared between multiple service types. The service may provide either point-to-point, multicast (that is multipoint-to-multipoint or broadcast), or point-to-multipoint connectivity as defined in Chapter 5.

18.3.4 Protocol-Specific Functions

A key characteristic of packet services is the existence of standard methods to carry other protocols, defined as protocol interworking. For example, an Internet Engineering Task Force (IETF) Request for Comment (RFC) standard is defined for how IP can be carried over each data communication service protocol.

Table 18.2 Comparison of Networking Aspects

Aspect	X.25	IP	FR	SMDS	ATM
Addressing Plan Layer 3	X.121	IP	-	E.164	E.164, NSAP
Addressing Plan Layer 2	LCN	-	DLCI	MID	VPI/VCI
Maximum Packet Length	< 1024 octets	< 65,535 octets	< 8192 octets	< 9188 octets	< 65,535 octets*1
IP Encapsulation	RFC 877	Native	RFC 1490	RFC 1209	RFC 1483
Routing Standard	None	RIP, OSPF, BGP	None	ISSI	P-NNI
Access Medium	Dedicated	Dedicated	Dedicated	Shared or Dedicated*2	Dedicated
Access Sharing	No	No	Yes	Yes	Yes
Point-to-Point	Yes	Yes	Yes	Yes	Yes
Multicast	No	Yes	Yes*4	Yes	No
Point-to-Multipoint	No	No*3	No	No	Yes

*1 depends on AAL
*2 multiple users share same access bus
*3 multicast can be achieved by point-to-multipoint operations
*4 limited in number

18.3.5 Summary of Networking Aspects

Table 18.2 compares the networking aspects of public data communication services. The preceding sections defined the terms, concepts, and acronyms listed in this table.

18.4 PRIVATE VERSUS PUBLIC NETWORKING

Is a dedicated private network or a shared public network better for your suite of protocols and applications? Or would a combination of private and public networks be better? Some objective criteria for assistance in making this sometimes difficult decision are provided in this section.

One key element to be considered is the overall cost. Overall costs should include planning, design, implementation, support, service, maintenance, and ongoing enhancements. These can require the dedication of significant resources for a private network, but are often included in public network service offerings.

The current network will likely consist of mainframes and controllers, minicomputers, and/or LANs interconnected by bridges, routers, and hubs supporting workstations and servers. Almost every existing network contains some form of legacy SNA protocols. Their interconnections may use private lines, or an existing private or public data service. Identify if there are some applications, or concentrations of traffic, at certain locations that require connectivity with other locations. Try to construct a traffic matrix of what throughput is required between major locations. You can then build a trial network design for a private network to achieve the delay and loss performance that your application requires. In a private network, it is important to estimate the capital and ongoing expenses accurately. It is a common mistake to overlook or underestimate the planning, ongoing support, and upgrade costs of a private network.

If you have the site locations and estimated traffic between sites, a carrier will often be able to respond with fixed-cost and recurring-cost proposals. These proposals often offer both fixed- and usage-pricing options. The performance of the public service will be guaranteed by the service provider, while in a private network this can be controlled to some extent by the network designer. In a public network, switches and trunks can be shared across several customers, reducing cost and achieving economies of scale which are difficult to achieve in private networks. Carriers will often implement a shared trunk speed higher than any access-line speed, and consequently can achieve lower delay and loss than in a private network due to the economy of scale inherent in the large numbers required for statistical multiplexing gain. This decreases costs for the individual user with performance that is suitable for most applications. If your application has unique performance requirements that are not met by any of the carrier's Quality of Service (QoS) offerings, then you may be forced to build a private network, regardless of cost. Be very sure that your current and future application requirements will justify this decision.

For comparable performance, the decision then becomes a matter of choosing which costs less yet meets your current and future requirements, and assessing risk. Of course, the least costly (and least risky) design might be a hybrid private and public network. In the very general sense, large volumes of high-utilization point-to-point traffic may be better handled via a private network or circuit switching, while diverse, time-varying connectivity may be supported better in public packet-based networks. If you are uncertain about your traffic patterns, then a fixed-price charge scheme is often the most economical choice.

If a public network service is chosen, then a key question is whether fixed or usage-based billing should be selected. Not all carriers offer these billing options, so if your application can be more economically supported by a choice of billing options, then this should be an important factor in your selection process. A fixed-rate option would charge a fixed monthly price for a certain traffic contract, which specifies a target throughput and QoS. Examples would be frame relay where the minimum CIR predictable frame delivery rate is guaranteed, or ATM where the Quality of Service (QoS) is expressed in terms of cell loss and delay. A usage-based option would specify the guaranteed throughput and QoS, but the actual bill should be based upon the units of data that were successfully received by the destination station, with a discount penalty for poor network performance. Usage billing is usually subject to a minimum and maximum charging amount, usually 100 percent or more of the equivalent fixed rate.

Most users who are unfamiliar with their traffic patterns will chose a fixed-rate option with a guaranteed QoS level. Only after users become intimately familiar with their traffic patterns and volumes will they migrate to usage rates with maximum price caps to protect them from times of unpredictable excess traffic or growth. Accurate traffic forecasts are rare, and due to the accelerating bandwidth principle forecasting future traffic is difficult. Check to see what the minimum charge is for usage-based billing, and if there is a cap on the usage-based option in relation to the fixed-rate option. If the minimum is low and the cap is reasonable, then usage-based billing may be your best choice. Knowledge of your network traffic volumes and patterns is valuable here.

If the public service provides traffic-measurement capabilities, you can use them to obtain more accurate traffic data and make a better informed decision in the future. One example is the network-management product from NetSolve called ProWatch IV℠. One feature of this product provides the user with detailed monthly traffic reports on a per-virtual-circuit basis — ideal for sizing the FR network.

18.5 PUBLIC NETWORK SERVICE SELECTION

How does one choose a public-network service? Design methodologies and selection criteria have been defined throughout each technology chapter. Some additional rules of thumb are provided in this section, but are by no means exclusive. Each technology transports data differently. The primary transport technologies reviewed in this section include X.25 packet switching, frame relay, SMDS, ATM, and SONET. IP traffic may be transported over any of these technologies. Private line transport mode is provided as a baseline.

When do you require a specific technology? Here are a few guidelines.

18.5.1 When Do You Need a Private Line?

A private line, or dedicated circuit between two points, *may* be required when

- ⇒ Connectivity is required between only two locations
- ⇒ Average link utilization between two points is very high (> 30 percent average utilization during the busy hour of the busy day) such as with LAN extension
- ⇒ Building a star network configuration to a single hub site

⇒ Integrated access of voice, video, and data is required over a single circuit from an existing CPE device like a PBX, Channel Bank, or multiplexer
⇒ Traffic characteristic is constant-bit rate (CBR), like video conferencing

The quality of private-line circuits has drastically improved in recent years with the advent of all fiber-optic and SONET-based transmission facilities and high-quality PL services like AT&T's FASTAR.

18.5.2 When Do You Need X.25 Service?

X.25 public service *may* be required when

⇒ Traffic is bursty and delay-insensitive in nature
⇒ Reliable data transport is required at speeds from 150 to 56,000 bps
⇒ Poor quality communications facilities are used
⇒ Error checking and flow control are required to be built into the protocol
⇒ International connectivity to nonfiber countries and cities is required

18.5.3 When Do You Need FR Service?

Frame relay *may* be required when

⇒ Consolidation of multiple protocols (i.e., IP, IPX, and SNA) over a single network access circuit and technology
⇒ Traffic is variable-bit rate (VBR) and very bursty, non-delay-sensitive
⇒ Multiple locations (usually greater than three) require interconnectivity (meshing)
⇒ Multiple traffic prioritization down to the protocol or session level through DE-bit setting or PVC prioritization
⇒ In-band management capability like SNMP is required
⇒ Flexibility for rapid network reconfiguration (at PVC level)
⇒ International connectivity over fiber-optic facilities

18.5.4 When Do You Need SMDS?

SMDS *may* be required when

⇒ Many-to-many connectivity is required for distributed applications and user groups
⇒ Public-network addressing scheme is desired
⇒ Intercustomer and interpartner communication is required
⇒ For dynamic user environments (closed and shared user groups)
⇒ Native LAN interconnect speeds that reach up to 16 Mbps

18.5.5 When Do You Need ATM?

ATM *may* be required when

⇒ Very high-speed connectivity (DS3 minimum, with DS1 DXI as an option)
⇒ Native LAN interconnect speeds of 100 Mbps (and higher)
⇒ NxDS1 usage patterns that justify a DS3 dedicated private line
⇒ Multiple QoS levels are required within virtual channel and circuit traffic streams
⇒ Multiple service interconnection (i.e., FR to SMDS)
⇒ Private line, frame relay, and SMDS service transport and interworking

At T1 speeds, FR is more efficient than ATM DXI. Frame relay would only require 5 bytes of overhead for a 128-byte frame (2 percent overhead) where ATM would require 84 bytes (66 percent overhead). CPE equipment for ATM DXI is also more expensive than similar FR equipment. A new standard called Frame UNI (FUNI) for low-speed ATM subrate access is now available. FUNI ATM services will offer ATM QoS capabilities with the ease of service and protocol interworking along with much lower overhead than DXI (approximately that of frame relay) on low-speed lines. But the success of FUNI is in the hands of the CPE vendors and users.

18.5.6 When Do You Need a Public Data Service?

What do you look for in a public date service?

⇒ Redundant/diverse facilities (no common facilities)
⇒ SONET redundant, self-healing architecture

⇒ Guarantees of availability or refund of predefined damages if not met
⇒ Pricing: volume discounts, x-year commitment, city pair discounts
⇒ Multiprotocol interoperability support

18.5.7 Transport Transmission Characteristics

Figure 18.5 illustrates a comparison of circuit-switched, X.25 packet-switched, frame relay, cell-switched (ATM), SONET, and private line transmissions. Notice in circuit switching that variable bandwidth is not available to the user, whereas in frame and cell switching, bursty data can be allocated the appropriate bandwidth-on-demand by the CIR. Packet, frame, and cell technologies also allow for the capability to dynamically route around failures at the packet level, rather than at the circuit level, and circuit reconnect time is in milliseconds rather than seconds. Usually, in circuit switching, the entire call has to be reestablished in the event of a failure or disconnect.

Which technology is better suited to smaller or larger networks? As the number of meshed or semimeshed circuits increase, which technology is better suited? Figure 18.6 illustrates one method of viewing technology selection based on network size. There are obviously many similar charts that can be drawn to compare technologies based on network characteristics.

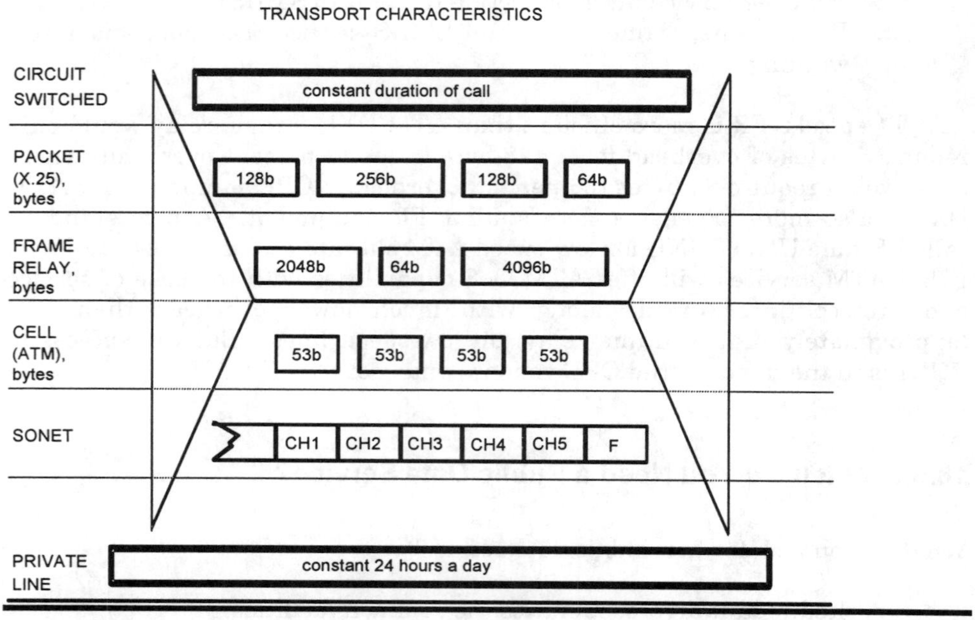

Figure 18.5 Circuit, Packet, Frame, Cell, and Private Line Transmissions

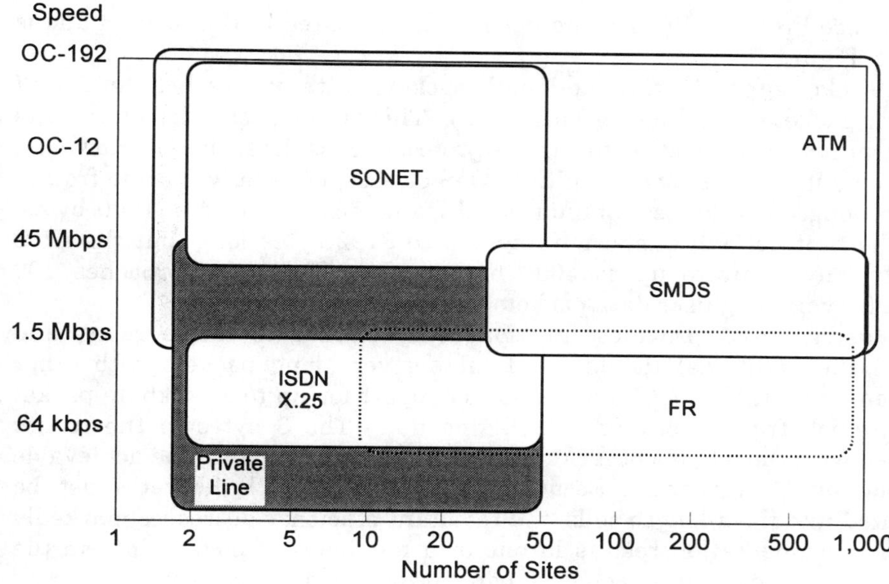

Figure 18.6 Private Line, Circuit, Packet, Frame and Cell Transmissions Comparison

18.6 BUSINESS ASPECTS OF PACKET-, FRAME-, AND CELL-SWITCHING SERVICES

This section compares several business aspects of data communication services. These include the tradeoff between efficiency and features, impacts on user hardware and software, a quantification of the savings due to integration, an assessment of the market demand, and pricing comparisons of various data communications services.

18.6.1 Efficiency versus Features

One thing that you may want to consider is the tradeoff of efficiency versus features. Both may have an impact on your higher-layer protocols and thus on your applications. Increasing the number or quality of features often comes at the expense of decreased efficiency. In this section, the efficiency and features of three major data protocols used in private or public networking are compared: frame relay, ATM (using AAL5), and 802.6/SMDS (using AAL3/4). Protocol efficiency (but not the impact of the Physical Layer

Convergence Protocol (PLCP) on efficiency) is compared in this section and is shown in Figure 18.7.

Frame relay supports variable-length packets, with an overhead of 5 to 7 bytes per packet (excluding zero insertion). This is the most efficient protocol with respect to overhead of the three protocols considered here. However, frame relay may not support multiple QoS classes, especially if some frames are very long. The longest standardized frame size required is 1600 bytes, while the protocol will support frames up to 8192 bytes long (but the CRC check is only accurate up to 4000 bytes). Its efficiency approaches 100 percent for very long user data packets (for example, IP packets).

ATM using AAL5 provides functions very similar to frame relay, and provides the additional flexibility of mixing very long packets with other delay-sensitive traffic. AAL5 also allows support for up to a 64-kbyte packet length, which frame relay and SMDS do not. The 8 bytes in the trailer combined with the 5 bytes of ATM cell header overhead reduce the achievable efficiency by 17 percent. Because the variable-length packet must be segmented into fixed-length cells, the resultant efficiency decreases markedly when this segmentation results in one or a few bytes of packet data in the last cell. Its efficiency approaches 90 percent for very large packets.

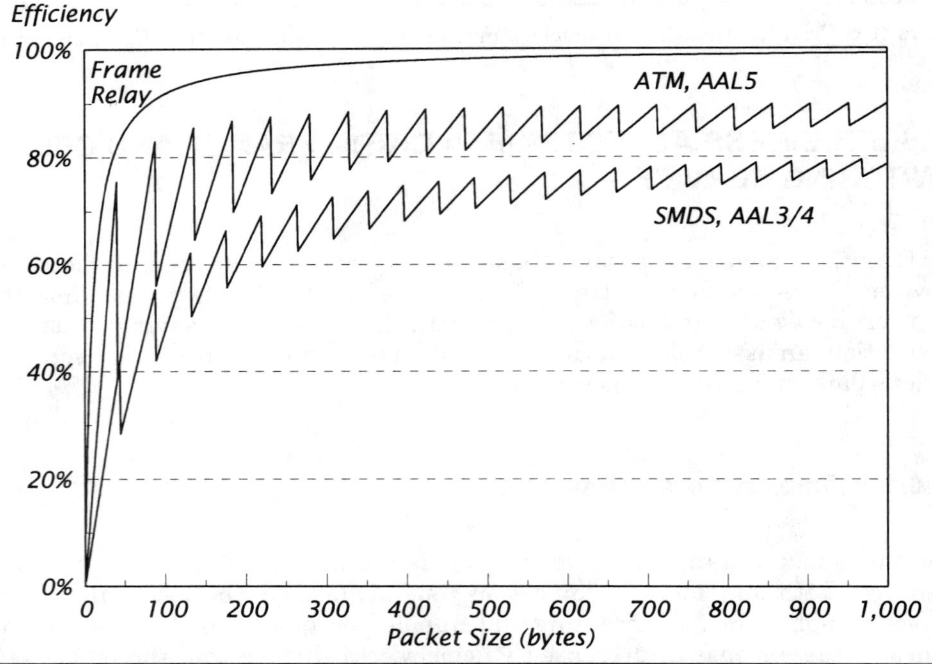

Figure 18.7 Protocol Efficiency versus Packet Size

SMDS currently utilizes the IEEE 802.6 Distributed Queue Dual Bus (DQDB) and AAL3/4 cell formatting. DXI is also available on access. The ATM AAL3/4 provides an additional level of multiplexing in the MID field and a per-cell CRC, consuming an additional 4 bytes per cell. The first cell in an SMDS packet contains 44 bytes of information, including the source/destination addresses and other fields. Much of the flexibility and many of the features of SMDS derive from this header. Packets may be up to 9188 octets long, slightly longer than the maximum in frame relay. This flexibility reduces efficiency, with the best limited to about 80 percent maximum efficiency for very large packets. Figure 18.7 plots the resulting efficiency of each protocol versus user packet size. Note how very short packets are handled very inefficiently by ATM Adaptation Layers (AALs) 3/4 and 5. In one further example, a study performed on current Internet traffic produced calculations showing that the efficiency of offering this traffic over ATM would be approximately 60 percent because of the large proportion of very short packets!

Which protocol is best for your application? It depends. If you need a feature that only the less efficient protocols support, then the choice is clear; you can't use a more efficient protocol if it doesn't support a critical feature. If your network will require support for multiple QoS classes for different concurrent applications, then ATM is probably a good choice. If you need to connect to other networks via a public service, or require an additional level of multiplexing, then 802.6/SMDS or frame relay are probably good choices, either as a standalone service or carried over an ATM-based service. If raw efficiency is key, and support for multimedia applications is not required, then frame relay is a good solid choice.

18.6.2 CPE Hardware and Software Impacts

What are the hardware and software cost and change impacts of adding a new protocol to your WAN or LAN? X.25 and IP already work on most existing hardware platforms. Software support for both of these protocols is also widely available. Few hardware changes are generally required for frame relay at lower speeds (DS0). Upgrading a data communications network to SMDS generally requires new hardware and software (as well as administration of the numbering plan). Hardware includes new interface cards, switches, hubs, routers, and potentially new CSU/DSUs. Software includes operating systems, device drivers, and applications. The SMDS Data eXchange Interface (DXI) is usually packaged as a separate CSU/DSU that interfaces to existing hardware at lower speeds, but it is now finding its way into many standard internetworking products.

ATM also requires new hardware and software support. The ATM Data eXchange Interface (DXI) interface offers ATM at DS1 speeds. This interface promises to be a lower-cost, smaller-hardware change entry point for ATM, similar to the SMDS DXI interface, that enables an earlier start for the deployment of ATM. ATM FUNI is yet another low-speed option that promises minimal CPE change.

18.6.3 Integration Savings

X.25, IP, and SMDS primarily pass data traffic only. There are several commercial and public domain software packages that can pass voice over IP in a MAC, Windows, and UNIX operating system environment. There are also public domain video-over-IP packages such as Mbone and CU-Seeme that are now commercially available. The IP RSVP feature, which offers QoS capability for transmitting voice, data, and video traffic integration over IP, will be supported by such industry leaders as Cisco, SUN, and Microsoft and may possibly give ATM a run for the money. Frame relay is also designed to pass only data, but capability has been demonstrated to pass low-quality video. ATM supports transport of voice, data, and video. The need for multimedia and mixed services over a single integrated access line or shared switch port is a key advantage of ATM. Technologies that integrated multiple forms of traffic (voice, data, and video) and can prioritize between them can achieve and sustain higher bandwidth utilization patterns than single traffic pattern technologies. This integration capability has cost savings which must be measured against the additional cost of new hardware, duplicate facilities, and, in most cases, new wiring.

18.6.4 Ubiquity and Market Demand

X.25 has been around for many years. It is much more widely available in Europe, Latin America, and Asia than in North America. Part of the reason for this is the relatively expensive cost of a private line and the lack of fiber-optic transmission facilities in most areas of the world. Furthermore, X.25 is slow and has high processing overhead and long delays but it has accuracy and guaranteed delivery – both critical for low quality transmission environments.

IP networks continue to experience phenomenal growth, which indicates the pent-up demand for ubiquitous data communications access. IP currently cannot support multiple classes of service or reserve bandwidth, but capabilities for RSVP and other integrated services standards are emerging. Most IP service is over the Internet, or over a transport-protocol service such as frame relay, where access is paid through an Internet Service Provider (ISP) in either a flat rate or usage-pricing configuration.

Frame relay has seen phenomenal growth over the last few years. It has seen substantial interest from large corporations constructing virtual private networks as well as small companies wishing to mesh many small remote offices without the cost of many private lines.

SMDS has seen limited growth so far in the United States, but much wider acceptance in Europe. SMDS as a standalone service platform does not seem destined for the same huge success in the United States as frame relay, but maybe SMDS will be successful as an access class to ATM (see Chapter 14). SMDS does not support isochronous traffic, has no congestion-control mechanisms, and is limited to transporting data traffic.

ATM PVC service will likely be used by corporate customers in a manner similar to frame relay to construct virtual private networks. ATM is just now beginning to be deployed nationwide by many of the IXCs. Due to its high cost of entry, ATM can be difficult to economically justify in many cases. There is a reasonable amount of activity at the LAN and server level to feed to ATM private or public switched networks. The true promise of ATM may be realized through SVCs, which will require assignment of addresses and carrier interconnection. IP service is most often offered over another service such as private line, frame relay, or ATM. An IP over ATM capability will be a major boon for ATM, and the initial usage of IP over ATM is predicated to operate over an ATM SVC network capability. In fact, IP over ATM has already found its way into some high-speed test beds, and has become part of public data services. ATM also is backward compatible with the frame relay and SMDS technologies and can interconnect these different protocols over virtual private networks.

18.6.5 General Pricing Structures

Services such as frame relay, SMDS, and ATM can either be classified as enhanced services, and thus would not be offered under a structured tariff, or else would be offered under a tariff. The pricing and billing policies of these enhanced data services are based on many factors, including:

- Port access speed
- Total virtual connection bandwidth per port
- Traffic contract parameters
  - Committed Information Rate (CIR) for frame relay
  - Access class for SMDS
  - Peak and sustainable cell rates for ATM
- Quality of Service (QoS) class
- Local access line charges based on speed and distance
- Fixed-rate or usage-based billing option
- Different rates based upon priority
  Discard Eligible (DE) for frame relay
  Cell Loss Priority (CLP) for ATM
- Bulk discounts

- ➢ Time-of-day discounts
- ➢ Points-of-Presence (PoPs) available for customer access
- ➢ Access circuit charges based upon distance to serving PoP

Usage-based billing rates may be measured in packets, frames, cells, or just bytes delivered over a time period rounded off to some accuracy. For example, the charge may be based on millions of cells delivered per month.

Fixed charges include a port charge, access charges (for the circuit from the customer premises to the service provider switch), installation charges, and other fees. A fixed-rate billing option may also include a charge based upon the virtual connection bandwidth, priority, and QoS class.

In some cases, the service provider offers an option for fixed or usage pricing. Usually, an intimate understanding of the traffic patterns allows a user to take advantage of usage-based pricing. This is due to the fact that many service providers offer usage-based rates which favor the intelligent user.

Private line costs often limit users to low-speed dedicated circuits for LAN-to-LAN traffic, creating a WAN bottleneck. If these circuits are analyzed, it is often seen that they are flooded during the busy hour but are not utilized much during off-peak, nonbusiness hours. These applications are ideal candidates for virtual networking. For many users, the initial deployment of any virtual data service should be limited, allowing the users to learn their traffic patterns. Once the traffic is understood, the choice of usage-based pricing, flat-rate pricing, or a hybrid of both can be made intelligently.

Users should look for price caps on a usage-based service so that it can be no greater than a certain percentage above the comparable flat-rate fee or leased line service. Pricing should not penalize users who are just trying out the service and who are not familiar with their traffic patterns. There will still be access charges, but a virtual data network using fewer dedicated access circuits in the local loop will decrease bottom-line access costs.

Intra-LATA, inter-LATA, and interstate data services (frame relay, SMDS, ATM) are offered as either public pricing or under a tariff. Public pricing varies, so make sure you get a true "apples-to-apples" pricing comparison for your network. Some "public" pricing is published openly, some are bundled, and some are still double secret. Tariffs are public and available to anyone. Regulatory structures constantly change (like FR service public pricing and tariff), so shop around.

Network management reports, often SNMP standards-based, are also an important part of any public data service. In fact, these monthly reports should closely track the usage-based billing invoices to provide effective cost-control.

18.6.6 Private Line Pricing Example

Private line pricing characteristics usually include

⇒ Fixed charge
⇒ Mileage sensitivity
⇒ Linear rate structure
⇒ Significant increases over longer distances

Private line rates include DS0, FT1, T1, FT3, DS3, OC-3, and OC-12. The number of circuits to achieve a break-even point for purchasing a single DS1 instead of multiple DS0s is now around 5–10 (and as low as 3–4 in some metropolitan areas). The number of circuits to achieve a break-even point for purchasing a single DS3 instead of multiple DS1s is now around 7–13 (again, less in metropolitan areas). Inverse multiplexers covered in Chapter 6 have extended the life of DS1s with channel extension rates of 6 Mbps and higher.

18.6.7 Frame Relay Pricing Example

Frame relay pricing is broken down into LEC and IXC.

IXC Carrier Pricing characteristics usually include

* Flat rate charge per port
* Flat rate charge for each PVC
* No mileage component (usually)

Typically, the more meshed the network configuration, the more cost effective the overall design compared to a private line network. Some carriers also offer usage-based pricing at a few cents per megabyte of data received, but beware that the data received includes overhead plus the file being sent (the amount depends on the protocols being used).

With mileage-based private line and non-mileage-based frame relay rates, private lines and frame relay have a crossover point, as shown in Figure 18.8, where the frame relay service becomes more cost effective at greater distances. Here we see that in an apples-to-apples comparison, frame relay-loaded costs of a CIR equal to the private line speed is cheaper between two cities at distances greater than 500 miles. The greater the meshing, the greater the cost savings because the port and access charges are already established for FR, but required for each new point-to-point connection with private lines.

Local (LEC) Provider Pricing characteristics usually include

⇒ Price based on number of PVCs
⇒ Price reduced every n PVCs
⇒ Cost per port connection

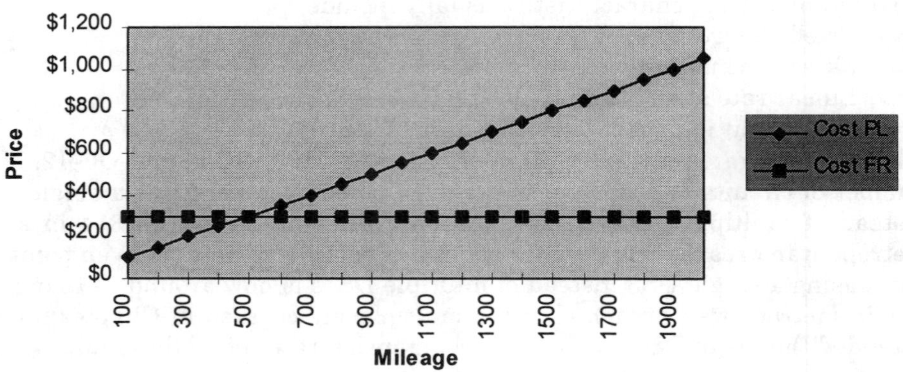

Figure 18.8 Price of Frame Relay Service Compared to Private Lines

LECs typically do not charge per CIR rate. Many of these rates can be close to their equivalent private-line local-loop rates, making a regional FR meshed network an attractive alternative.

"ZERO CIR" service is one option where the provider transports all frame relay frames with the DE bit marked for discard. Thus, there is no CIR guaranteed. All data could potentially be discarded. This service is sometimes more cost effective for remote locations that have low-speed requirements, intermittent access, and delay-tolerant applications. But beware, the actual throughput may be 0 kbps. Remember that CIR does not always "guarantee" delivery of a CIR (non-DE) frame; it just means that CIR frames may be dropped only after all DE frames are discarded.

NNI service may be another option for users of an LEC FR service that require inter-LATA transport. Some LECs charge a flat rate for NNI access; others bundle this into a single per-site rate. Beware of performance issues when using a shared NNI.

Volume, term, and some city pair discounts can often be obtained, but watch yourself. Do not lock yourself into a long-term contract in an era of falling data rates and even faster falling private-line and local-loop costs. Also, lease CPE when it makes sense, which may make upgrades easier. Technical obsolescence moves at a fast rate, and it may be worth the lease money to make your service provider shoulder much of the upgrade burden.

18.6.8 SMDS Pricing Example

SMDS pricing characteristics usually include

⇒ Flat monthly port connection fee
⇒ A usage fee (for your protection, make sure it has a maximum monthly cap)

A specific SIR rate is chosen per port. Administrative fees for features such as group addressing may be required.

18.6.9 ATM Pricing Example

ATM pricing characteristics are broken down into the type of service required. VBR service is offered with a defined SCR (minimum peak BW) and PCR (maximum peak BW), but with only the SCR guaranteed. With ABR (Available Bit Rate) service you pay for a minimum throughput level. With UBR (Unspecified Bit Rate) service there is no such specification. VBR can come in both connection-oriented (CO) and connectionless (CL) modes. A maximum burst duration and CDV rate is assigned for each VC. CBR service may be charged as a specific defined bandwidth similar to a traditional dedicated private line. The primary elements of ATM service fees include a flat monthly fee per access port and circuit (depending on speed) and a fee per virtual circuit (VC) based on speed. There could also be usage- and mileage-sensitive cost components. All services aforementioned above may include additional nonrecurring and bundling charges.

18.6.10 Summary of Business Aspects

Table 18.3 provides a comparison of business aspects of the currently available public data services.

18.7 HIGH-SPEED LAN PROTOCOLS COMPARISON

Moving closer to the user, we inevitably come to the discussion of high-speed LAN technologies. The key contenders in 100 Mbps and higher-speed LAN technologies includes FDDI, 100 Mbps Ethernet 100VG-AnyLAN and 100BASE-T, and ATM. Table 18.4 shows a comparison of these technologies.

Table 18.3 Comparison of Business Aspects

Aspect	X.25	IP	FR	SMDS	ATM
Efficiency (1-4, best to worst)	2nd	3rd	1st	4th	1st, 2nd, 3rd, and 4th
Multiple Service Support	None	None	Possible	Some	Best
CPE Hardware Use	Existing	Existing	Existing	Existing	New
CPE Software Use	Existing	Existing	New	New	New
Ubiquitous Access	Yes	Yes	No	TBD	TBD
Market Demand and Geographic Coverage	Low	High	High	Low	Moderate
Evolution Potential	Low	Some	Some	Some	High
Price	Inexpensive	Inexpensive	Inexpensive	Varies	Expensive
Technological Obsolescence Factor	High	Low	Low	Medium	Low

Table 18.4 Comparison of FDDI, 100VG-AnyLAN, 100BASE-T, and ATM

Attribute	FDDI	100VG-AnyLAN	100BASE-T	ATM
Standard	ANSI X3T12	IEEE 802.11	IEEE 802.3u	ATM Forum, ITU, IETF
Throughput	100-Mbps Simplex	100-Mbps Simplex	100-Mbps Simplex	1-Mbps to 1.2-Gbps Duplex
Packet or Frame Type	FDDI frame	Ethernet or Token Ring	Ethernet	Cell
Evolution Potential	Little	Some	Some	Best
Reserved Bandwidth	No	No	No	Yes
Isochronous Support	No	No	No	Yes
Multiple Traffic Classes	No	Yes	No	Yes
Projected Cost	High	Low	Low	Medium
Use of Existing Wiring	Yes (CDDI)	Yes*	Yes*	Yes*
Scalable in Speed	No	No	No	Yes
Scalable to Wide Area	No (MAN)	No	No	Yes

* with the caveat of distance, category of wiring, and number of wire pairs required

18.8 APPLICATION PERFORMANCE NEEDS

This section compares the various services introduced in this book to meet the performance needs of applications with their several distinctive characteristics. First, the relative throughput of each service type and its underlying technology is summarized. Then the tradeoffs between burstiness, throughput, and delay are examined.

The data communications network industry is offering an increasingly wider range of services —some very attractive features are being provided such as enhanced user control and management, increased maximum bandwidth, improved price-performance ratios, and the support for multiple applications by the same service. This section analyzes the attributes of user application needs for throughput, burstiness, and delay tolerance over a wide range of public data services.

18.8.1 Throughput

Figure 18.9 shows the history of maximum available throughput for commercially available data services. The time frame is the historical or projected year in which the maximum data rate was widely offered and became cost effective. From this perspective, there is some differentiation in maximum throughput with ever-increasing maximum bandwidths on the horizon. However, throughput is not the only dimension of performance that must be considered.

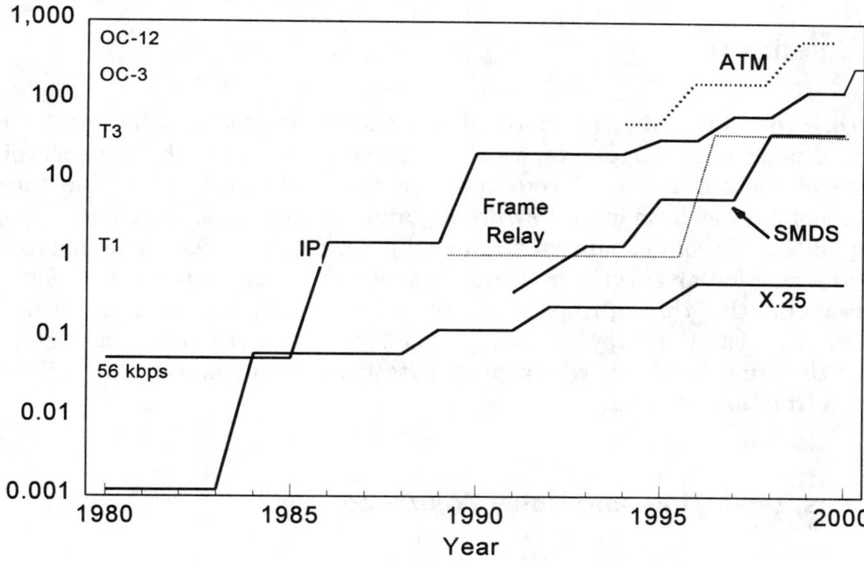

Figure 18.9 Comparison of Maximum Data Rate by Service

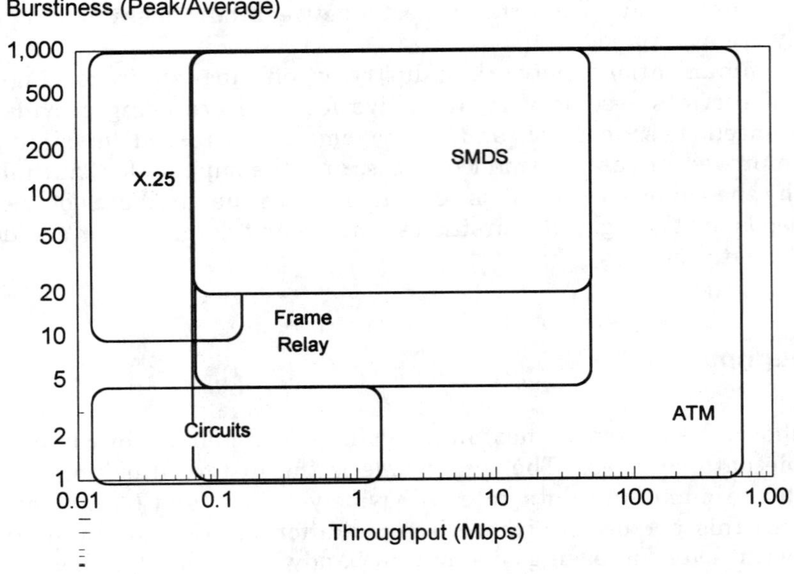

Figure 18.10 Service Applicability to Burstiness and Peak Throughput

18.8.2 Burstiness

Figure 18.10 plots the characteristic of burstiness, defined in Chapter 16 as the ratio of peak to average rate, on the vertical axis versus the supportable peak rate of the service, or throughput, on the horizontal axis. The term *circuits* encompasses both circuit switching and private lines, the choice being based upon the economics summarized earlier in this chapter. The enclosed region for a particular service indicates that it is applicable to that region of burstiness and the throughput characteristic. A number of the services overlap in their range of applicability. As described in the previous section, note that the time frame in which peak rate throughput has been available progresses from left to right.

18.8.3 Response Time and Delay Tolerance

Figure 18.11 depicts the applicability of services in another dimension, namely the range of nodal delay on the vertical axis versus peak throughput on the horizontal axis. The chart shows that circuit switches have essentially constant nodal delay. Any form of packet switching will introduce some variations in delay, and, typically, the lower the speed of the packet-switching trunks, the more the variation in delay, as shown by the general trend of the services to support better (i.e., lower) nodal delays as the peak throughput increases. SMDS was designed to support data-only services and thus is not well suited to supporting specific values of delay (voice). Frame relay can support more specific values of delay through the use of prioritization. ATM can support delay close to that of dedicated circuits up to ranges exceeding those of the other services through the implementation of priority queuing in support of multiple Quality of Service (QoS) classes.

Figure 18.12 depicts the applicability of services in the dimension of range of nodal delay on the vertical axis and burstiness on the horizontal axis. As can be observed from the previous charts, dedicated circuits are best suited to applications that are not bursty and have a strict delay tolerance, such as video, audio, and telemetry data. The X.25 service depicts the classic wisdom of packet switching targeted to bursty applications that can accept significant variations in delay. Frame relay and SMDS support a broader range of application burstiness, while frame relay has the potential to support better delay tolerance through prioritization. ATM supports the broadest range of burstiness and delay tolerance through the implementation of multiple QoS classes.

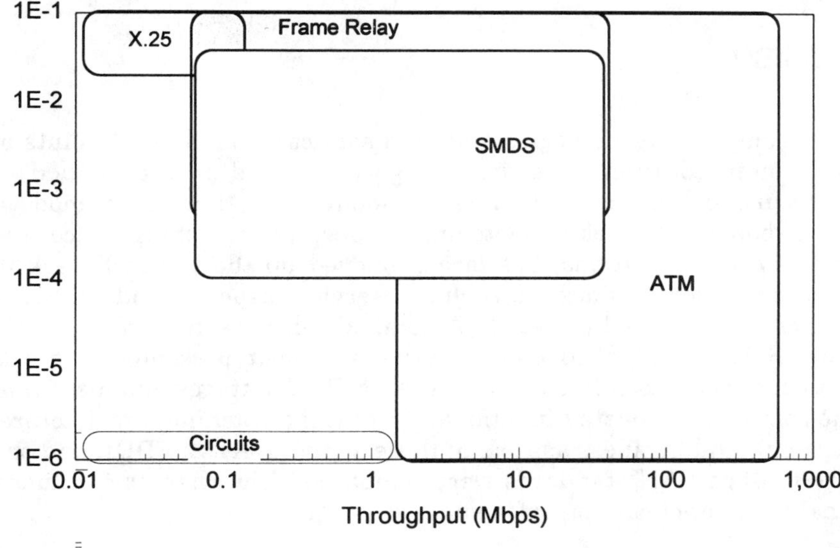

Figure 18.11 Service Applicability to Delay Tolerance and Peak Throughput

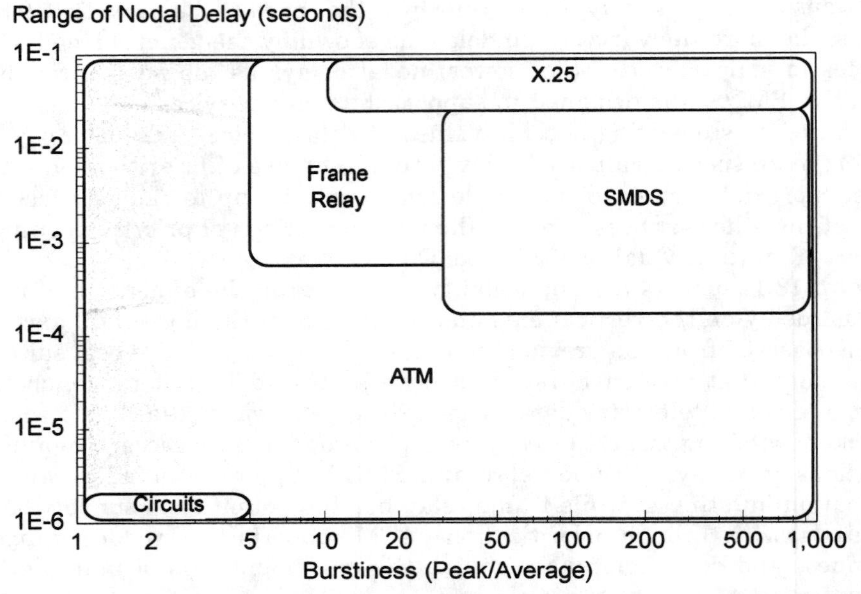

Figure 18.12 Service Applicability to Delay Tolerance and Burstiness

18.9 REVIEW

This chapter compared technologies and data services from several points of view. Data communications was first categorized based on the method — message, circuit, or packet switching — identifying that most modern methods are based on packet switching. Message switching, once the cornerstone of communications, has largely moved up the protocol stack to the application layer. Packet-switching service aspects and network characteristics were covered in detail. A detailed comparison of the X.25, IP, frame relay, SMDS, and ATM data services was next presented. It was shown that each technology has its specific area of advantages and disadvantages. The comparison covered functional, technical (switching, architecture, and addressing), and business aspects of these services. ATM, FDDI, and the emerging 100-Mbps LAN standards were compared. The chapter concluded with an analysis of application performance requirements.

Part 6

Choosing the Service Provider

Choosing a service provider is like getting married (and I can now say this from experience). Proposals for a relationship are extended through solicitations (RFIs and RFPs) providing a list of requirements by which to build a long-lasting relationship. The provider (the user's future partner) responds to the RFI/RFP with a list of what it can provide, when it can provide it, and at what cost. The capabilities of each provider are examined carefully, and ultimately one is chosen (or, as in some cases, multiple patrons are engaged) to build the network. The contract is written and the future (network) is committed to the vendor as the vendor commits its services to the user. Both find out how they must live with each other. Partnerships are often for the life of the network, although the capability of "divorcing" the network from the vendor may become necessary if service becomes poor or the vendor's priorities change.

Chapter

19

The Service Provider Selection Process

Sometime after the requirements have been defined, the technology (or technologies) has been selected, and the high-level design process has begun, the vendor(s) or service provider(s) must be chosen. Vendor selection should be done with care. The success of the network and network manager's job may directly relate to vendor performance. In this chapter, the Request for Proposal (RFP) process is summarized. Requests for Information (RFIs) may have been issued as well, but it is now time to select vendors to propose specific solutions to specific network requirements. Conformance to standards, the business parameters of the company, and the industry as a whole is critical. The RFP is the one chance to "get it all in writing". If a requirement or conformance is not included in the RFP, and subsequently is not in the contract, the vendor does not have to provide it. The watchword is: be thorough in the selection and contract process.

This chapter presents a method of choosing vendors based on weighted technical and business needs. Critical issues include what tradeoffs to expect, how to derive various levels of support from the vendor, how to ensure industry standardization in the equipment purchased, and how to ensure vendors will deliver on their promises. The vendor-user relationship must benefit the strategic and technical direction of both parties to be a lasting relationship. In this chapter, both end users and network designer are "users" when considering vendor relationships. We see that vendor responsiveness to user needs is critical. Vendor selection can affect the future business success of the company.

The network is designed, the purchase orders are written, and the network sites are awaiting the equipment's arrival. Vendor XYZ promised that the hardware would arrive in six weeks. It has now been over three months and still no equipment. The recent trade magazine shows that vendor XYZ is having financial problems. A call is placed to the sales representative at vendor XYZ. He or she tells you, "no problem, the stuff is on its way; you are only hearing rumors". A week later the hardware arrives and the bill is paid. The next month, XYZ goes out of business. When finally the equipment you bought is up and running, it does not work properly. When it is interfaced to another vendor's equipment, it does not work because the interfaces are proprietary. The network is eventually scrapped, the network designer loses his or her job. This story, of course, is exaggerated to emphasize the point that a thorough vendor analysis must be completed prior to choosing a vendor. This chapter helps separate promises from reality. Don't be an XYZ fatality!

19.1 THE REQUEST FOR INFORMATION (RFI)

A Request for Information (RFI) is designed to obtain enough information from potential suppliers to enable the user to eliminate suppliers who cannot provide the needed requirements. Thus, the user arrives at a short list from which a final candidate is chosen. The RFI simply offers prospective suppliers a version of the desired end result and allows them the opportunity to provide their style of solution. This is the "feeling out" stage, and many vendors can be provided an opportunity to respond. There are usually parameters placed on the selection of vendor and technology, and guidelines are offered. The user will typically provide:

- Traffic volumes and characteristics (as explained in this chapter)
- Traffic matrix
- Existing applications and technologies to replace or integrate
- Business and network performance objectives
- Future plans and requirements
- Evaluation criteria
- All information in electronic and hard-copy format

The user will typically request from the supplier respondents:

- A specific response for each request or line item
- Vendor capabilities
- Service and product delivery dates
- Complete supporting documentation
- General pricing

19.2 THE REQUEST FOR PROPOSAL (RFP) PROCESS

The evaluation of the RFI responses hopefully narrowed down the potential vendors. It is now time to begin the Request for Proposal (RFP) process. Generally the rule is that RFIs go out to only 10 to 15 vendors, and RFPs to 3 to 5 vendors. RFIs are used

- To clarify buyer needs
- As a legal agreement of vendor provisions and capabilities
- To weed out competition
- To finalize the network design and direction
- To solve pricing discrepancies

RFPs are a means of requesting multiple vendors to formally commit detailed solutions, propose the appropriate technology, and quote services to satisfy designated requirements. Before issuing the RFP, the buyer must:

- Understand the technology alternatives
- Properly define what is required from the vendor
- Clearly define the technology, business, and financial issues with priorities
- Clearly define support requirements

Make sure that user requirements are clearly articulated and define what you will and will not accept. All correspondence should be thoroughly documented. This may seem harsh for two businesses who are trying to establish a lasting relationship, but it is necessary to build a professional relationship and to avoid finger-pointing later. Also understand that vendors rarely meet their delivery dates.

During the RFP process, try to have vendors with sales, marketing, and technical contacts respond to the RFP. The intelligent user will work with vendors to complete RFPs. At this stage, it is very important to avoid confusion and misrepresentation among vendors in order to arrive at the best choice. Make sure the comparisons between vendor responses are "apples to apples".

19.2.1 The RFP Structure

RFPs vary based upon the systems being bid, from simple requests for a specific piece of hardware or software to an entire communications system complete with vendor support and possibly even an outsourcing agreement. A general RFP format includes

- Synopsis or business objectives
- General contractual terms and conditions (explanations/interpretations/rules of engagement)
- Scope of work
- Timeline schedule with milestones and deliverables
- Qualifications of bidder
- Current systems, technologies, architectures, protocols, services, and applications
- Hardware and software technical specifications or proposed configurations
- Equipment specifics and environmental requirements
- Equipment substitutions
- Vendor-required engineering and installation
- Implementation plan
- Performance objectives
- Service support
- Warranty or availability requirements
- Summary of financial bid
- Payment options
- Work and responsibilities
- Proposal assumptions
- Training requirements
- Vendor credibility and reference requirements
- Legal considerations

19.2.2 The Sample Network(s)

In the case of publishing an RFP for a complete network design, even though you have included the network application and transport requirements in the RFP, each vendor may come back with a difference size network. The number of nodes and trunks may vary widely. One of the best ways to ensure all vendors provide similar responses is to provide a sample network design, or at least a minimum and maximum configuration. For example, if you are building a statewide frame relay network and want to connect 10 cities, four of which are large cities and six, smaller (remote) cities, you may want to specify a design that provides for four switches and a design for 10 switches. In this manner, the responses can be compared closer to apples-to-apples in cost and configuration. Otherwise, you may get back five designs from five vendors, each with a different number of switches, which would be difficult to compare.

19.2.3 Solicitation

Solicit the RFP to the vendors chosen in the RFI process. Number all questions for response. Offer equal and fair guidance to all vendors. Set a maximum return date for all responses and stick to it. If vendors want your business, they will respond in time. Make sure you have given ample time for a comprehensive response. Keep in mind holidays. A time to respond that is too short will yield shoddy responses that can be vague or noncompliant. Set up a question-and-answer session with each respondent to clarify and amplify any areas that are not quite clear. A good rule of thumb is to allow two times the length of time it took to create the RFP for vendor questions, and at least two more weeks for a good response. Requiring a very short due date will only hurt the quality of all responses. Don't hurry the process, it takes long enough for the vendor to gather all the information requested.

19.2.4 Analyzing and Evaluating the RFP Response

Each respondent to the RFP should respond paragraph by paragraph. Responses will be varied, but this seems to be the best format. Beware of terms like "substantial compliance", "intend to comply", and "will be contained in future releases". Look for terms like "full compliance" with an explanation of how they comply and to what extent. Vendors should clearly specify what they do *not* support. Replies should contain

- Price of product
- Maintenance
- Training and learning curve
- Ongoing expenses
- Tax financing
- Contract termination fees
- Warranties
- Documentation
- Purchase or lease decisions
- All non-recurring and recurring costs

These factors should be included in the vendor response. In the next section, each factor will be examined for a determination of which vendor to choose.

19.3 CHOOSING THE VENDOR(S)

There are many reasons for choosing one vendor over another. The vendor is not chosen only for compliance with industry standards or the ability to meet the users' needs. Factors such as politics; business, financial, and operational needs; future position or potential partnership with the vendor; goals of both businesses; and a variety of others may outweigh the technical abilities of the vendor. This is particularly true of a larger corporation or user dealing with a large national or international vendor.

The relationship established with the choice of a vendor must be both practical for the business needs and affordable to the user and vendor. The most successful contracts represent a win-win solution for both parties. Contract relationships are sometimes termed as "sleeping with the vendor". You have to know who you are sleeping with, just as you would know whom you were marrying. Look into the vendor's past for not only the product you are purchasing, but financial history, payment history, billing accuracy, shipping and receiving procedures and policies, past customer base, and industry experience. Ask for references and, more importantly, *check* references.

Some evaluation criteria for hardware vendors include

- Vendor history
- Product versatility
- Processor and packet/frame/cell-processing speeds and capabilities
- Interface and protocol support
- Local or remote support ability
- Standard versus proprietary protocol support and operation
- Performance characteristics
- Features and functions
- Network management
- Security
- Price to performance

Remember, price is often not the most important evaluation factor, because the labor and resources committed to making the network operate often exceed hardware costs. Do not allow the focus to become myopic to cost – technical decisions based strictly on cost constraints may place the design in jeopardy. Do not condone foolhardy or frivolous spending, but bargaining away technology and performance for low cost is foolhardy. There is often a point on all technology in which cost outweighs benefit. It is your job to find the balance point.

TABLE 19.1 Requirements Matrix Weighting

REQUIREMENT	WEIGHT	SCORE	TOTAL PTS
Total costs	10	7	70
Pricing and billing options	5	8	40
Features and functions (protocols and interfaces)	10	10	100
Vendor and product reputation and philosophy	5	4	20
Architecture flexibility and technology migration path	5	6	30
System capacity and performance	15	8	120
Availability, reliability and disaster recovery	15	4	60
Network management	25	8	200
CPE hardware support	5	8	40
Customer and field service and support aspects	5	4	20
TOTAL	100	-	700

19.3.1 The Requirements Matrix and Weighting Methods

Once a requirements matrix has been established, a weight is assigned to each requirement based on its importance. More important criteria are given a greater weight, less important, a lower weight. Some requirements such as total cost are often weighted more heavily than others, such as security. With the advent of Internet access and transport and the inherent security risks, security has lately taken a much higher priority.

Table 19.1 shows a sample weighting of 10 typical requirements for an RFP, specifying a three-node router network. Each was provided a weight from 1 (1%) to 99 (99%), with a total weight of all requirements of 100 (100%). Each requirement was then assigned a rating from 1 to 10, with 10 being the highest score and 1 the lowest. In the table below, the vendor scored a total of 700 points out of a possible 1000 points.

The weighting could be adjusted to provide an equal weighting for all requirements, or more requirements could be added. Either way, the vendor with the highest number of total points is probably the best choice for you. Another method of requirements analysis is the cost-benefit analysis, where the costs of each requirement are weighed against the benefits realized by the requirement. This is similar to the weighting method shown previously.

Some companies perform an exposure analysis, which measures the expenses if the contract is a total failure. This includes both the capital expenditures and the operational and personnel costs involved in the project from conception. Maximum exposure is usually measured from 1 to 2 years with the vendor stretching out delivery and then finally not delivering or, worse yet, going bankrupt after spending the user's prepaid money.

19.3.2 What Tradeoffs Are Critical?

The weighting method is an excellent way to determine which vendor to choose. But how can it be determined which tradeoffs are critical and warrant higher weighting factors? This section presents a broad range of criteria to consider when choosing a data communications public service. This list is by no means comprehensive, but does represent the most commonly proposed options. These options can be converted to vendor questions for the RFI and RFP process. You should make your own detailed list, prioritize it, and use it to select the service or product that best meets your needs. There may be a large equipment base already existing in the corporation that will need integration and interoperability. If this is the case, integration must be factored into the requirements analysis.

Pricing and Billing Options

- Order intervals
- Fixed or usage billing
- Minimums and maximum caps on usage billing
- Delivery options for bills (hard-copy, fax, e-mail, disk/tape)
- Frequency of billing
- Capability to bundle all services (equipment, management, transport/circuit costs) in one bill

Features and Functions (Protocols and Interfaces)

- Processor capability (PPS/FPS/CPS)
- Packet/frame/cell filtering/forwarding capability per protocol and in total
- Bus and data transfer speeds
- Bridging/routing protocols supported
- Physical interfaces required/supported
- Access classes and speeds (DS0 through STS-*Nc*)
- Multiple-service access through single interface
- Memory requirement and expansion capability
- Local- and remote-load software for operation
- Classes of Service (CoS) and Quality of Service (QoS) offered and fully supported to standards
- Prioritization handling
- Traffic parameters supported (i.e., CIR, SIR, PCR, SCR, MBS)
- Multiple fully redundant, load-sharing power supplies

- Security features
- In-band or out-of-band network management

Vendor and Product Reputation and Philosophy

- Industry leader or follower
- References and recommendations (be sure to check)
- Large range of internetworking products or single solution source
- Commonality of common logic across entire product line
- Service-level guarantee with promise of refund

Product Architecture Flexibility and Technology Migration Path

- Ability to migrate to future technologies (with minimal impact to CPE) like ATM
- Future product line migration path (no disjointed software or hardware upgrades/revisions/fixes and proven architecture)
- Standards-based for future investment protection
- Plug-and-play CPE to Network compatibility
- Type of network architecture/equipment used

Architecture/System Capacity and Performance

- Fault tolerant robust network (1:*N* or 1:1 switch and component redundancy and availability)
- PPS/FPS/CPS transmission over lightly loaded and heavily loaded ports, cards, and nodes
- Minimal back-haul to closest switch (many switches)
- Ease of expansion
- Amount of end-to-end network delay (latency) at normal and peak traffic conditions (understand buffering and prioritization methods' effects on traffic like SNA)
- High performance interfaces
- Minimal data loss rate
- High throughput
- Type of equipment used by network
- Network architecture with high MTBF and low MTTR
- Minimal switching delay and buffer delay per switch

Availability, Reliability and Disaster Recovery

- Fault tolerance (no single physical or electronic point of failure)
- Multiple processors per interface card (look at processor MIPS, bus speed, PPS/FPS/CPS processing, memory, etc.) or live backup processors

- Symmetric multiprocessing (gives scalable performance that can be both sustained over long periods of time and routing tables and protocol conversion that are done at port level with no bus transfer needed)
- Easy device configuration and customization (local and remote)
- Minimum/maximum network availability
- Redundancy in all components and systems
- Parallel back-plane/bus for reliability
- Daughter-board expansion built in for future processor and memory upgrades
- Independent load sharing over data paths
- Redundant power supplies, common logic boards, local media
- Hot swap functionality (replace cards while online without service interruption)
- Dynamic reconfiguration while on line
- No single point of failure (1:*N* system redundancy)
- Automatic isolation of failed components, cards, and buses
- For FDDI, support of optical bypass and redundant rings
- Disaster recovery options
- Number of switches, location, and back-haul required
- Network-loadable firmware upgrades

Network Management

- SNMP-compliant, CMIP-compliant, or proprietary
- Network management system compatibility and portability with current systems
- Customer Network Management (CNM) features
- Reporting capabilities
- NMS costs and reporting costs
- Monitoring and real-time configuration capabilities
- Change management procedures
- Performance management and engineering

Premises Hardware Support

- CPE supports industry standards
- Flexible CPE leasing/rental/purchase plans
- Software and firmware revision testing and implementation
- All relevant standards met, or if standards do not exist, the percentage of completed draft standards
- Upgrade-capable equipment (software, hardware, new technologies)
- Free initial training provided
- Ongoing support

Total Cost Involved

- Total cost of the network for the configuration provided
- Price performance ratio – processing power and cost per unit (i.e., packets/frames/cells per second and cost per packet/frame/cell per second)
- Modularity expansion or upgrade costs
- Price per port or trunk (DS1, DS3, OC-*N*)

Service Aspects - Operations and Support

- Defined and measurable quality of service levels
- 7×24 customer support and troubleshooting expertise
- Same level of service regardless of customer size
- Large support staff size with demonstrable talent
- Ease of software and hardware installation
- Documentation provided
- Customer intimacy

19.3.3 Public Service Network Offerings versus Private Networks

Users must at some point decide whether to access a public network or to build their own private network. If the decision is made to use a public network service, the user must decide between IXC, independent service providers, and LEC services. This decision will be based primarily on intra-LATA, inter-LATA, interstate, or international access and connectivity requirements, availability, and cost of services.

Public network service offerings have the following advantages over private networks:

- Less capital investment may be required
- Large shared backbone capacity – efficiencies of scale
- Extensive Points of Presence (PoPs) and switches
- Broad choice of interface speeds
- Integrated access capabilities – support for multiple services over a single access circuit
- Sophisticated network management support and performance management capabilities
- Portfolio of services (X.25, FR, SMDS, IP, ATM) to minimize technological obsolescence
- Smooth migration between services – minimal CPE changes required
- Usage-based and flat-rate billing structures
- Carrier-provided CPE offerings
- Outsourcing possibilities

- Skilled service and equipment support structures
- Inherent reliability, redundancy, and survivability of a virtual private shared backbone
- Access to public resources, i.e., Internet
- Internetwork, intercompany, and intranet connectivity and communications

Another very important decision factor should be the architecture that the service provider employs for the access and backbone network. Whereas the tariff or public pricing structure is key in the initial selection, the service provider's architecture is the long-term insurance that costs will remain stable, that service quality will be delivered, and that new features and technologies will be offered in a timely manner. With the expansions of international business, as well as the high cost of international private-line circuits, many users see virtual data services such as IP, FR, and ATM reducing the cost of international data communications. Earlier chapters described additional benefits of public networks as compared to private networks, such as value-added services, economy of scale, network redundancy, and network management.

19.3.4 Adherence to Industry Standards

In today's age of data communications standardization and open systems, it becomes increasingly important to choose vendors who adhere to de facto standards and justify this commitment to standards by continuing to develop products around them. Beware of vendors who are banking on a single-standard product (especially a proprietary-standard product), even though they may promise eventual standards compliance. These rules also apply to regulatory, protocol, and manufacturing compliance on both a national and international scale. Compliance to the standards previously listed leads to interoperability from the client-server level through the network access and into the network. A complete guide to standards support is found in Chapter 3.

19.3.5 Vendor Promises and Support

Vendors will make many promises when courting a contract. Just make sure that all verbal commitments are fully explained in writing and included in the contract. If it is not in writing it does not have to be (and often is not) honored. To verify information, research the vendor. Ask around. Talk to other customers of the vendor, and even to its competitors (and weigh their responses accordingly). Ask the vendor for a few good references and then ask for one or two that had problems with their service. From them you may get a clearer picture of the vendor. Documentation of all vendor correspondence should be compiled and stored for future reference.

One of the most hotly contested issues among vendors and buyers is support. When the vendor is first courting the user, look for vendors who both educate and consult your staff on the technologies and issues involved, and sell a solution rather than just trying to sell a product. Look for the following support from the vendor:

- On-site maintenance services
- 7 days by 24 hours (7×24) support by trained staff (test this support before you buy!) that understands your network
- How much assistance will be provided with the installation and turn-up?
- Percentage of staff assigned to support – does the vendor have a specific project manager assigned to its success?
- Built-in training support for your entire staff
- Size of vendor support staff
- Ongoing training by the vendor for your staff (includes fixes to unknown problems, features and functions, and options)

19.3.6 Vendor Expertise

What expertise does the vendor hold in sales, marketing, product, design, and systems-level support? Have their account references been checked? Also check the manufacturer's position in the industry. A vendor may have to delay a product delivery because it has been short of power supplies from its overseas power-supply vendor (who has gone out of business)! Make sure the vendor's supply sources are easily accessible and that it has alternate sources for its parts.

19.3.7 Vendor Delivery Dates and Reality

Again, check the vendor's references for its delivery track record. Does it often miss deliveries, postpone deliveries? Does it build products at order levels or does it build at 80 percent of orders? If the latter, the vendor may look good to the financial industry but shipments could be delayed. What have been some of its other customers' experiences with late deliveries? How does the vendor ship and track these shipments? In the United States, it is common to have two-week to two-month average delivery cycles from the date the order is placed to the date the equipment ships from the vendor. In Europe and Asia, the average delivery time is much longer, typically two to four months. This average is getting shorter, as many international vendors are now competing in national markets where project timelines and delivery dates are more competitive and much shorter.

19.3.8 Product Announcements and Product Futures

Be aware of all product announcements and the future product direction of each vendor. Product announcements should be received free of charge through data sheets, advertisements, and electronic mail bulletins. If information is sensitive in nature and not yet public, a user-vendor mutual nondisclosure form can be used, which states that neither party will divulge information about the other without express written consent or until after a specific date. This contract is legally binding and strictly enforced. Nondisclosure agreements can be either selective or blanket agreements.

Also ask for the future product direction of the company. Discern its dedication to R&D activities, and what percentage of its profit goes toward research and new product development. Make sure that the vendor's spending direction for new products is the same as your product requirements direction.

19.3.9 The Proprietary Vendor and Futures

While the same vendor can provide backward compatibility, it can also lock the user into an obsolete product. The vendor could get lost with technological change, and take the user with it. Avoid proprietary vendor implementations, with the exception being cutting-edge, prestandards products. While proprietary implementations provide specialized solutions for the short term, they cause atrophy in the long term. Lastly, look at the overall future potential of the vendor. This includes market position, product futures, financial condition, strategic partnerships, existing and potential competition, and a myriad of other company "health" factors, which will paint the true picture of whether the vendor is in for the short haul or the long haul.

19.4 THE VENDOR-DESIGNER RELATIONSHIP

A user-vendor relationship can be a rewarding experience. As mentioned before, this is similar to a marriage, where both parties benefit under good conditions. Both must clearly understand each other's business needs, and maintain good communications channels to head off any misunderstandings. If you do not like or trust your salesman, then a "divorce" is eminent.

There are some rules to follow to achieve these goals. Don't let the vendor experiment with your network. This is especially true when you are trying to stabilize your network, and the vendor is experimenting with untried solutions such as new software revisions. All upgrades should be planned to eliminate these surprises, and strict change management procedures should be followed.

Maintain good interpersonal relationships. Make sure it is clearly understood what is expected of the vendor and of the user. Speak honestly and cooperatively with the vendor, and work together to achieve your goals. Understand the levels of peer-to-peer relationships and the roles and responsibilities of the account team. Frequent presales and postsales support calls, as well as user visits to vendor facilities and labs are desirable. The vendor should make available an engineering staff contact, such as a knowledgeable network engineer, and provide some level of continued on-site support personnel for large accounts; 7 day by 24 hour (7×24) maintenance support is left to maintenance contracts.

Make sure you are purchasing the products you want, not what the vendor wants you to purchase. When signing vendor development contracts, make sure you do not get locked in for long periods of time. These days, 3 years may be too long a time to be locked in. Balance a good price for a long-term commitment with what you may pay in early cancellation penalties. Have the vendor produce good documentation before project/product hand-off to the user.

Look for vendors who are choosy about their business partners, and how the vendor relates the chosen customers to its long-term strategy. Does the vendor deal only with interexchange carriers, or does it also deal with local access providers? The primary customer base of a vendor can tell much about how the vendor is positioning itself for the future.

The relationship between vendor and user will usually last a long time; therefore, the vendor will have a profound impact on the user's business. The two are tied together. If the primary vendor for a communications network suddenly goes out of business, it could mean substantial budgetary impacts on the user's business to either replace the existing product base or migrate to a new one.

19.5 STRATEGIC USER-VENDOR AGREEMENTS

Strategic agreements between users and vendors take many forms, depending on the level of commitment of each party. Flexibility is the most important aspect of the agreements listed below. Both user and vendor will learn through the process, and both will be required to adapt to each other's needs. Large users typically have enough buying clout to impact the R&D direction of the vendor. These agreements can offer many advantages, such as guaranteeing a revenue stream for both parties, providing the lowest prices, skipping the repetitive and resource-intensive and expensive RFP process, and building upon the strengths of both user and vendor. Often, the vendors achieve greater control, for without them there is no product. The following are some common terms of agreement defined:

Affiliate. No legal contract, but work together for business purposes

Alliances. Nonexclusive contractual agreement, separate funding but may lead to a joint product or service venture

Joint Venture. Central or pooled funds and exclusive contract language

Strategic Vendor-User Partnership. Work together to solve complex problems, may involve any level of those relationships listed above

19.6 SERVICE LEVELS

It is important to define the service expectations of the vendor. This includes the vendor's service perspective – how service is defined, how that service is provided, and measurements for both. What are the categories of service provided, and what are their priorities? What priority is the user to the vendor — what size account — and how does the user compare to other users? It is a fact of life that the customers that represent the largest amount of revenue typically are provided the greatest amount of vendor resources. What is the vendor's response and repair times, parts and sparing plan, software and hardware support hours? Are spares centrally located or dispersed to areas of dense customer service areas? These elements are critical to maintaining a highly available network.

Vendors provide many service levels to users. Four general levels of service can be provided, and the user must decide which best suits the business strategy and is most cost effective. The four levels of service are: nonparticipant, value-added, full service, and joint development.

Nonparticipant vendors deliver their products to their customers and do not provide continued service after receipt of delivery. These are typically off-the-shelf products not requiring vendor installation or maintenance. They are also often low-cost items with sales based on price, availability, and speed of delivery. An example of nonparticipant vendors is Black Box, a company that specializes in delivery of well-known low-end and midrange data communications products.

Value-added vendors include some level of service and support with their products. These vendors are judged by factors other than price and availability, such as quality, feature function, and support staffs, and make it a part of their business to interface with each customer. These vendors offer some long-term commitment to their products and services, as well as to the customers who purchase them. While value-added vendors provide customer support, they typically draw the line when it becomes a financial burden to do so; customer service is an added value for their product, not part of their revenue-generating business.

Full-service vendors are differentiated by their dedication to, and relationship with, each customer. These vendors typically have large corporate accounts and support users who require a dedicated account team and are willing to pay for it. Often this service is only provided to the vendor's largest customers. Full-service vendors interface much more with the end user, and may be involved with the actual implementation of the hardware purchased. Full-service vendors provide customer service and account teams and relate this service directly to revenue. These vendors often prefer long-term relationships with the user based on joint service offerings and future business potential. Service in this case is often measured and conforms to strict guidelines. Outsourcing and out-tasking fit into this category.

The ***joint development vendor*** not only works with the users, but also develops products in and around the users. The 1990s have been a time for mergers and strategic partnerships among many businesses in the data and voice communications industry. Vendors that can partner with large businesses can gain a strategic advantage in the marketplace. Small vendors can claim interoperability with major users and cut a niche into the market at the expense of time spent on development work with the user.

Sometimes a vendor will not be able to provide all the service or product that is required. A good design will incorporate alternate sources and strategies for network support that will not leave you out in the cold. It is the network manager's job to find and implement these alternatives.

19.7 NETWORK AND SYSTEMS MANAGEMENT CAPABILITIES

Network and systems management should be one of the most important decisions in the vendor-analysis process. Networks are now moving toward a single network management platform with distributed analysis and data and alarm collection from all equipment and elements present in the network. More important, they need one network management *system* to monitor all elements of both the LAN and WAN. This incorporates the need for integrated network management into the RFP process. Some users may already have an existing hardware base which will be integrated with the new — mixing protocols, operating systems, billing, alarms, and operating platforms, making integrated network management all the more important. This creates a need for a network management platform that can do many things – provide proactive and reactive global fault detection, analysis, and correction; measure network performance; help with proactive performance engineering, security control and accounting measures, alarm and event correlation, local and remote configuration capability. Each of these features should be provided to a variety of bridges, routers, gateways, multiplexers, switches, concentrators, LAN servers, and other wide and local area network elements. This may appear to be the "holy grail" for some companies.

There are two network-management protocols that provide the integrated capability needed in today's computing networks: TCP/IP's Simple Network Management Protocol (SNMP) and OSI's Common Management Information Protocol/Common Management Information System (CMIP/CMIS). Both management protocol schemes enable integrated network management for network elements on a communications network. These protocols can be managed through platforms such as HP OpenView, SUNNet Manager, and Cabletron Spectrum.

The vendor must also provide its plans for the support of SNMP or CMIP/CMIS. SNMP is available in both versions 1 and 2. SNMPv1 and SNMPv2 implementations must support Management Information Base (MIB) I and II plus extensions, along with any proprietary hardware MIBs.

Much of the burden still lies with the user, who must both interpret the information provided by the network manager and develop interfaces for the translation of this data into a workable form. Just monitoring SNMP feeds on an HP OpenView platform will not suffice. Some important network-management requirements that should be incorporated include:

- Flexible alarm presentation and log structure
- Intelligent interpretation of alarm and management data
- Real-time geographical network status
- Integration of all OSIRM layer of alarms
- Real-time performance graphics
- Point-and-click graphics
- Statistical collection
- Remote and local downloads
- Remote and local nodal configuration
- Remote and local board diagnostics
- Remote and local inventory management capabilities
- Local hard drive/floppy storage
- Multiple security levels other than system log-on
- Data scope functions
- Accounting and billing collection (ASCII or binary)
- Integration of nonproprietary implementations

19.8 FUTURE BUSINESS OF YOUR COMPANY

It cannot be stressed enough that the future success or failure of a business can ride on the success or failure of the vendor(s) chosen for the data and computer communications networks (not to mention the designer's job). For this reason, a user will rarely give the entire business to a single vendor. A multivendor environment is a healthy and safe one. It creates a competitive environment so that vendors work harder for the business and a secondary supplier is available in case the primary supplier falters. Occasionally a business relationship, partnership, or joint strategic direction will dictate a single vendor solution. If all vendors meet the criteria presented in this chapter, especially standards compliance, there should be minimal difficulty in network integration and interoperability.

19.9 REVIEW

This chapter is designed to assist the reader in choosing a vendor or service provider capable of providing the features, functions, and services required per the network design. This decision is based upon the criteria defined in previous chapters. After the RFI is analyzed and the choice of vendors is narrowed down to a "short list", the RFP is issued. RFP responses are then analyzed based on a host of weighted criteria including cost, performance, features and functions, manageability, and perception of the vendor's ability to provide the required services. A look at real-world user-vendor issues revealed the importance of items such as delivery dates, product announcements and features, and the vendor-designer and vendor-user relationships that are required for successful vendor implementations and ongoing relationships. Finally, existing vendor network-management capabilities were reviewed along with how the vendor becomes an integral part of the future network. The next phase of the design comprises the access and backbone network designs. The choice of vendors can and often does follow the access and backbone designs.

Part

7

Network Design and Management

Now that the requirements have been analyzed, the capacity plan produced, and the vendors chosen, the time has come to perform the access and backbone network design. Thus far, each technology and protocol chapter has provided detailed design criteria which must be followed during the design process. These specifics will be used to accomplish the design. This section will step the reader through both the access and backbone portion of the network design. While it is impossible to focus on every aspect of network design for every protocol, technology, and service discussed, the next two chapters provide insights into the key issues which may be encountered. Documentation should be completed at each step of the design process. After designing both the access and backbone portion of the network, the next step will be to implement the design. Although the access network design is often completed before the backbone and drives the backbone design, early versions and phases of network designs may be configured as an access network only, with a backbone built at a later date, and either step can be completed first as long as the rules presented in these two chapters are maintained. Most often the applications drive the access design, and the access design drives the backbone technology or service. These steps are not always followed in this order, and sometimes the entire design must be completed before a vendor can be chosen. Other times these steps will happen simultaneously.

Chapter

20

Access Network Design

This chapter will help you design the access portion of the network. *Access* is defined as the environment and elements providing the interface between local and wide area network environments. Access in a strictly local environment may define the devices that interface multiple LANs or workstations to one another. Network access includes the point where the premises access devices interface to the data transport network. Access may also include some portion or all of the actual data transport to the backbone network.

The first step in access network design is to define access requirements as identified in Chapters 16 and 17. Next, the capacity required across the total network and in each access device should be defined, always planning for future capacity. The style by which local access is mapped follows next. Ubiquitous access and hierarchical schemes are explored, along with collapsed backbones and ATM LAN switching. An overall access network topology can then be planned to accommodate the applications, access devices, and access and network circuit design, and to allow interfacing either to access devices or the backbone network, which could take the form of a public network service. The requirements for mobile, remote, and ATM access are increasing, and a discussion of each is included. Finally, diversity alternatives and integrated access options are provided along with examples.

20.1 ACCESS AND BACKBONE LEVEL DESIGN DEFINED

There are three general layers in a network design: (1) the user or application, (2) concentration or access, and (3) backbone. These layers are shown in Figure 20.1 and are explained below. Generally, the user- or application-layer design concentrates on all layers of the OSI reference model (and corresponding levels of other architectures), but focuses on LAN protocols, interfaces, and technologies. The access- and backbone-layer designs typically concentrate on linking and internetworking the first three OSIRM layers (physical, data link, and network) and sometimes providing the OSIRM fourth layer (transport) with end-to-end connectivity. Higher-layer support (fifth, sixth, and seventh layers) are usually controlled by the application software, but also may reside as services within the access and backbone layer.

20.1.1 User or Application Layer Design

This layer defines the user or application access to the local network resources. For physical interface this level typically includes the PC LAN (workstation and server) network-interface card (NIC), FEP interface to the Token Ring LAN, or any other device where data originates or terminates. Usually few "network" services exist at this layer, but this depends on the level of protocol structure operated by the user or application. This area provides the greatest diversity of interfaces, protocols, architectures, technologies, and standards of any network layer. The user layer of design is based not only on protocols that access and transport data across the network, but also on file transfer and session-oriented protocols. Much of the user and application layer design was covered in Chapters 7 and 8.

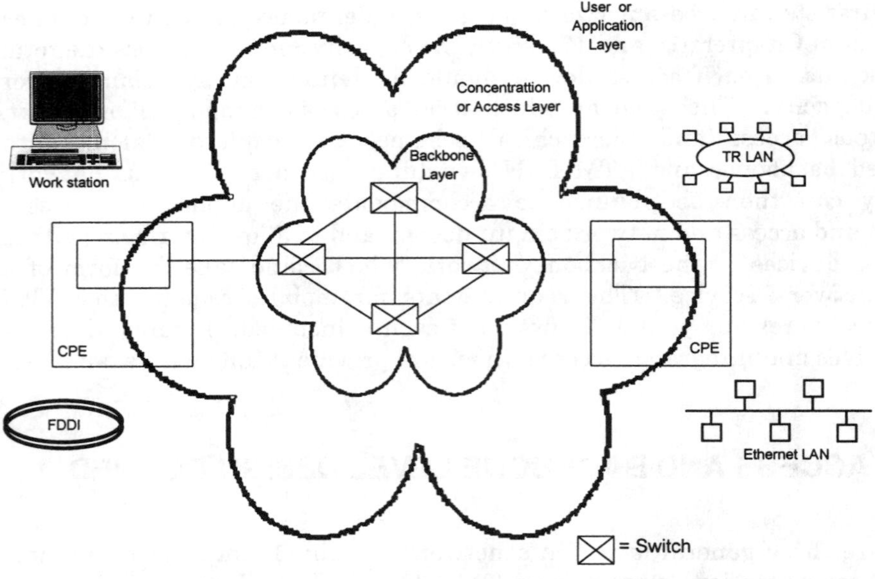

Figure 20.1 Three Network Design Layers

20.1.2 Access Layer Design

This layer defines the user access into the backbone layer or WAN. Typical access devices include routers, bridges, PBXs, switches, or any device that provides a focal point for standardization of interfaces, protocols, architectures, technologies, features, functions, and services required. Protocols are typically transport, network, data link, and physical, and are similar, if not identical, among all network access devices. This is also the point where the user interfaces and interacts with switched-data services and the WAN. Access devices are sometimes called terminal or network devices, terminal adapters, or Data Communications Equipment (DCE). As a general rule, terminal devices or Data Terminal Equipment (DTE) terminate data, while terminal adapters (DCE) pass or modify data.

20.1.3 Backbone Layer Design

This layer defines the backbone transport between access layer elements. It is generally transparent to the access portion of the network, unless the user skips or omits the access network portion and interfaces directly with the backbone (as is sometimes true with high-speed data services like ATM or SONET). The backbone provides a standard platform interface, protocol, architecture, technology, and quality of service. It also provides user features, functions, and services. To the user, the backbone can be the carrier-provided switched service, becoming the "network cloud" to which the access devices send and receive traffic. One example of a backbone layer service is frame relay, where the user-access device (a router or maybe a front-end processor) interfaces with a backbone frame switch. This method of interface is the most common of today's backbone public data services such as X.25 packet switching, frame relay, SMDS, and ATM.

20.2 NETWORK ACCESS REQUIREMENTS

What are the requirements for network access? The access design is primarily based on the traffic analysis and capacity plan. These steps were provided in the last few chapters for requirement analysis and capacity planning and will not be reiterated here. However, it should be emphasized that there is a need to coalesce user requirements onto a common platform defining the interfaces, protocols, architecture, technology, features, functions, and services required.

20.2.1 Interfaces and Physical Connectivity

Perhaps the widest variance of any connectivity requirements will be at the physical media level. The access device design needs to accommodate both the user-side interfaces (determined in Chapter 16 and 17) and the network- or backbone-side interfaces. If you are building a private network composed of access nodes only, the network interfaces will be the point-to-point links between access nodes. These are often synchronous links utilizing the most efficient protocols available to the devices chosen. When interfacing to a public network, the network side will often be determined by the public network access (gateway) and backbone interface.

The existing wiring configurations at each access site will dictate many connectivity options. Many of the physical interface protocols used were covered in Chapter 7. The primary options include unshielded twisted pair (UTP), shielded twisted pair (STP), thin and thick coax, and glass (single mode or multimode) or plastic (multimode) fiber-optic.

Twisted-pair wire (shielded and unshielded) can be used for both analog and digital transmission. Many existing locations will probably have twisted-pair telephone wiring as the main building wiring. Recent advances have increased the data rates that can be transmitted over twisted pair wires, such as Ethernet, Token Ring, and even FDDI.

Coaxial cable was the second generation of wiring to proliferate, but in some cases (i.e., Wang, Unisys, and legacy SNA networks) was the predecessor of twisted pair. Coax cable is used extensively for Ethernet. Many buildings have existing coax cable wiring to each floor. Previous to fiber deployment, coax cable was used for interbuilding wiring. Coax can handle much higher bandwidths than twisted pair wiring, up to 500 MHz.

Fiber-optic cable provides the highest bandwidth available, into the terabits-per-second data-transfer rates. Data is transmitted through light-wave pulses converted from electrical signals. Advantages to fiber are the obvious high-bandwidth capability, security, the lack of copper-media-affecting disturbances, and the logistical advantages of smaller, lighter cable.

Physical and electrical interfaces range from the telephony/telecommunications world to the computer LAN arena. The physical telecommunications transmission media (facilities) comprise the electrical- and physical-access path. Common physical and corresponding electrical and mechanical interfaces include DB-25 (RS-232, RS-449, and RS-530), DB-37 (EIA-449), M-34 (V.35).

For computer and LAN communications, each LAN architecture provides multiple interfaces. (These were also discussed in detail in Chapter 7.) Most personal computers contain Network Interface Cards (NICs) that have RJ-45 outputs. A twisted-pair cable will run from the interface card to an RJ-45 wall jack. This wall jack is wired through the building to the telephone closet, where it is terminated on a 66 punch-down block (a row of wire prongs extended from the main distribution frame for "punching down" the wires, while stripping back the insulation of the wire to provide contact with the prong). This punch-down block interfaces the user to the destination device, which can be an IBM connector for a multistation access unit (if IBM Token Ring), an RJ connector on an Ethernet concentrator (hub), or some other type of terminal concentrator, controller, or hub. Most wiring closet designs will also include some form of patch panel before the concentrator for testing and ease of reconfiguration. Figure 20.2 shows one example of user connectivity to the network-access device. The PC interfaces to the wall jack in the office via a LAN interface card with an RJ-45 interface plug. This wall jack is wired to the patch panel in the local wiring closet (the point at which everyone else on the LAN is also wired). The patch panel is wired to a 66 block, where patching capability is provided. The four wires are run down to a LAN concentrator or hub, where all four wire circuits terminate onto the LAN media. The hub is then passed to a port on the access device.

Other legacy connection devices that may be required are an RS-232 line driver or a limited-distance modem (LDM), a balun for impedance matching, and external radio-frequency modems or fiber-optic inter-repeater links for distance connectivity. There are also many LAN, modem (analog, ISDN, cable), and wireless solutions available. These connections eventually require interfacing to the network-access devices, such as repeaters, CSU/DSUs, modems, bridges, switches, and routers.

20.2.2 Protocols

What protocol support is required? Protocol support can range from providing transparent transport for a homogeneous protocol environment like IP, to translating and converting multiple protocols from multiple architectures, to actual protocol interworking as in ATM. First, each protocol that operates over each interface must be defined by identifying its syntax, semantics, timing, and proprietary implementations and idiosyncrasies. Next, determine what portion of each protocol is used. Identify and use protocols that are not dependent on physical media or hardware when possible.

Identify the characteristics of the file-transfer protocols for impacts, specifically, their packet sizes in each direction (such as NFS, which from the file server's perspective transmits large packet sizes and receives small ones back, or IPX, where the window and packet size can vary drastically). Determine each protocol's mean data unit size and ratio of transmit-to-receive data units. Then determine which protocols can be bridged, routed, or switched, and which cannot. Isolate the media-access protocols, and determine if they will be passed transparently to the network, encapsulated (tunneled), translated, or converted by the network. Also, many protocols have interdependencies on other protocols which limit their handling and operation. Analyze which protocols will be affected by error detection, correction, notification, flow control, or buffering. Analyze the effects of the end-to-end latency on each protocol.

There will most likely be many dissimilar protocols in the user layer, and most will not communicate directly with any other, or, if they do, they do so via some form of protocol conversion or gateway. These protocols should be mapped with their interdependencies and conflicts clearly understood. Look at the protocol requirements from the perspective of the access node. What protocol requirements are expected from the access portion of the network? For example, packet-switching protocol specifics would be the speed in bits or bytes per second, the number of packets, calls, resets, and interrupts allowed, the VC call memory allocations, packet size and window size per VC. All of these parameters are expected to be set by the access device (PAD) and the network switch and must be defined. Frame relay specifics would be the minimum and maximum frame size, end-to-end delay, setting of DE, oversubscription and its potential effects on throughput, routing protocol used (i.e., RIP, OSPF, IGRP), and number and speed of PVCs. Other technologies have similar protocol-specific parameters that must be identified.

This brings up the question of the amount of control that the access network needs to exert over the user or application, or more importantly the amount of access-network-device-to-user interaction required. These interactions will be different depending on the protocol(s) being used. The network designer is required to clarify all of these interdependencies before progressing with the access design. It is obvious how important these details become for an accurate network design.

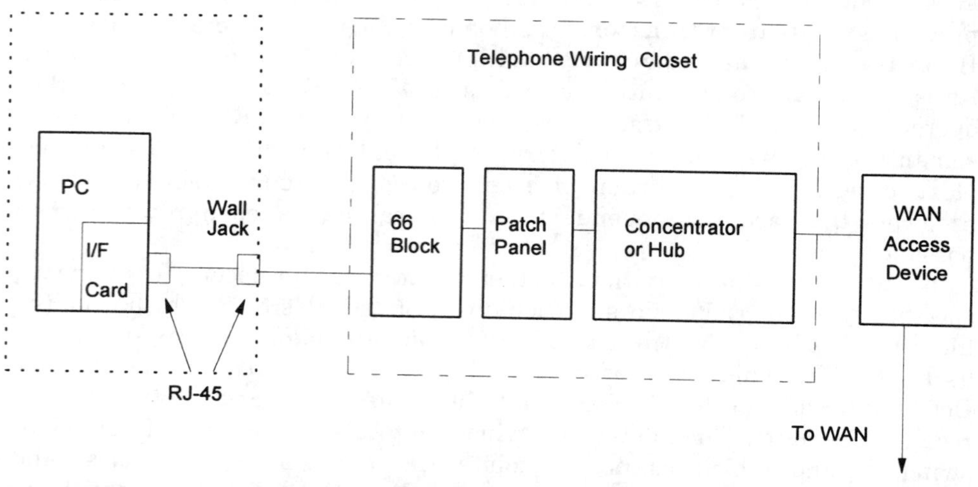

Figure 20.2 User Access Device Connectivity

20.2.3 Architecture and Technology

Next determine what architecture the protocols interact with, and how these architectures themselves interact. Most of this design will be protocol-to-protocol specific. Again, determine what level of encapsulation, translation, bridging, routing, or switching is required, and the threshold levels for each. Ask where these functions will be accomplished: at the physical input or output of the access device (transport media), within the access device, or within the network backbone.

Another question: Is the technology base a single technology or the intermix of multiple technologies? Obviously, the more complex the mix of technologies, the more complex the access design and the more limited the number of device options available. When doing the access design, refer back to the Chapter 19 technology comparison and make sure that the choice of technology has not changed. Unless the future plans or economics dictate, do not use a more complex device than what is required. For example, do not use a bridge when a repeater is required or a router if only a bridge is required. These days, the distinction is no longer whether to buy a bridge or a router, but rather what type of router or switch to buy. Review equipment types from Chapter 5 and pick the best type, or mix of types, to meet your application and economic requirements. Remember, the more meshed and dynamic the topology, the more intelligent the access devices must be and more dynamic their configuration.

20.2.4 Features, Functions, and Services Required

When the user interfaces to the WAN through an access network device, certain features, functions, and services are required over and above the normal interface and protocol support. These features and functions are specific to the combination of interface and protocol selected, such as FECN, BECN, and DE bit usage with frame relay. Another example is the access class of SMDS. The protocol may support these functions, but how do the user and access device use them to implement flow control? And how do they affect the user's applications (such as discarding traffic in an open loop FR transport environment)? Many of these questions can be answered when it is determined where the user traffic hits the service. The service interface point is often the place where features and functions operate. Does the access node provide the first advantages of the data service, or does it begin in transport to the backbone, or even at the backbone? Where do the value-added services begin; at the access or in the backbone? Once these questions are answered, the initial loading phase of access design can begin.

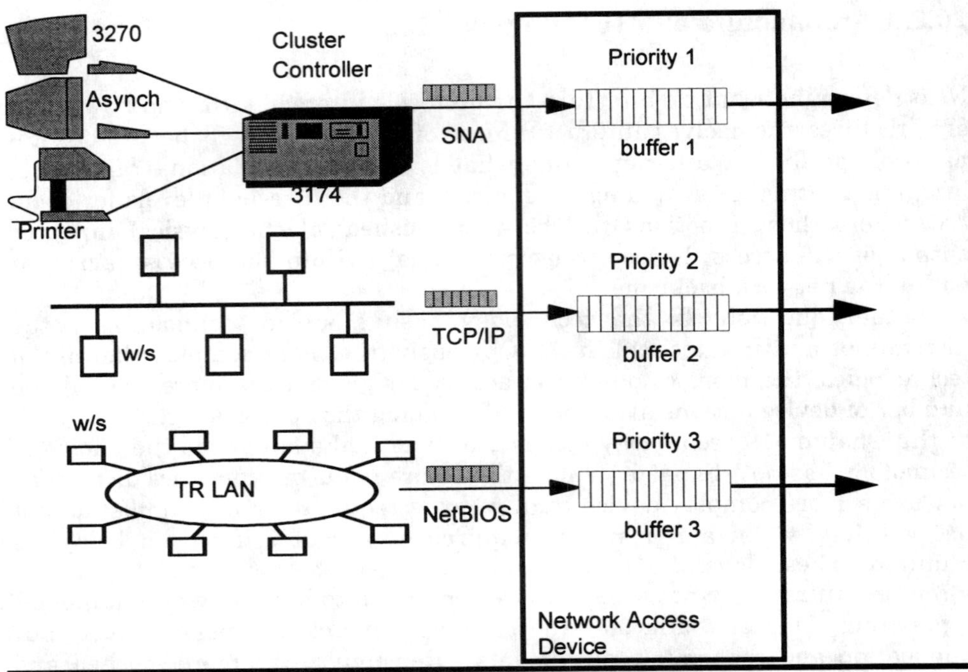

Figure 20.3 Traffic Prioritization

20.2.5 Traffic Prioritization at the Access Device

Some access devices, such as routers, switches, and intelligent multiplexers, allow prioritization of user traffic. This prioritization is often performed in conjunction with large variable-size buffers, so that traffic with a lower priority can be queued. The most common term used is "priority queuing". Priority can be assigned by protocol, packet/frame/cell message size, physical or virtual port, or (LU) device. When used correctly and in conjunction with passing SNA and non-SNA traffic together over the same access circuit (as in Figure 20.3), priority queuing can prevent SNA time-outs by larger file transfer traffic such as with TCP/IP. This is close to assuring a quality of service (QoS) over a service like frame relay. In this example we see three types of traffic, with SNA-based accounting traffic taking the highest priority (1), TCP/IP file transfers second (2), and NetBIOS traffic the lowest (3). The SNA traffic will receive the bandwidth required to transmit its traffic before the other two protocol streams (or be allowed to use a majority of available bandwidth), and the TCP/IP file transfers will have priority over NetBIOS traffic. Priority queuing implementations vary, but beware that if the SNA traffic requires most of the bandwidth most of the time, the lower-priority traffic (especially the NetBIOS traffic) may achieve marginal to no throughout for long periods of time while sitting in the queue waiting to be transmitted.

Thus, care must be observed when using this approach, as incorrect allocation of high-priority buffers or high-utilization patterns of higher-priority traffic can cause lower-priority traffic to be drowned out. This could further cause a cascade or avalanche effect if the lower-priority protocols are sensitive and have short retransmission sequences, causing effective throughput, or "goodput", to be drastically degraded.

Prioritization can also be carried through on the WAN side of the access device. Specific PVCs within a single frame relay access circuit can be provided different priorities, along with the traffic being transmitted over that PVC.

20.3 ACCESS NETWORK CAPACITY REQUIREMENTS

Chapter 17 assisted the designer in calculating the loading on each access device based on known inputs. If the user applications and inputs are well known, the access-node configurations are either already known or easily determined. If so, proceed to connect the access devices via one of the backbone designs as defined in the next chapter.

However, when interfacing an access design to a large private or public data network, the user-access application and transport specifics such as utilization and efficiency are usually not clear or well defined. In fact, most network designers are faced with very few facts on the user specifics of access requirements. This is especially true when designing a network from scratch, and the user inputs are estimations or, worse yet, speculations. In this case, some broad approximations of user traffic can be placed into a model to make a mathematical guess or educated assumption at the number of access and backbone ports required, their speed, and utilization. This assumes that the user protocol characteristics are either the same or similar, and that a single technology and set of protocols is used for internetworking these users (as implemented from Chapter 18). These requirements must take into account service-specific aspects, such as the ACK/NACK overhead in SNA, TCP window sizes, IPX burst capability, and CIR in frame relay, which provide logical constraints that may be and probably will be exceeded by the user at any time.

20.3.1 Access Device Loading and Link Utilization Principles

Now we look at how to calculate the access-network design required when only raw access bandwidth numbers are provided. These calculations are protocol and technology independent, and require modification for statistical multiplexing, queuing, or any other buffering or efficiency increases from the input to output of the access device. These calculations are most applicable to calculating multiplexer devices, as well as frame relay and ATM network-access devices. It is also obvious that much network tuning per access port is required.

A certain user community, such as one or more LANs within a building, will transmit a given number of bytes of information per day over the network M through a given number of access-node ports n. A model for the access network can be built with n user input ports and T backbone access trunks. A limit must be set on the size (in ports) of the access devices, as well as the access and trunk speeds available. Once this access model is done, modifications can be made to these variables by adding factors that model queuing delays, statistical multiplexing, and internodal traffic.

Figure 20.4 shows an example where M = number of Mbytes/day/network = 950,000 and the number of access ports in the network n= 2000. For simplicity, we designated that all access ports speeds s = 1.544 Mbps (DS1). If we divided all transmitted traffic equally among all access ports, the average, one-way utilization for each port (or link) would be calculated below as 5.7 percent. The formula for average utilization per port is shown below. Naturally, some ports (such as the headquarters site in a star network) would have higher utilization than others, such as higher port-access speeds for headquarters and processing sites and lower speeds for remote-access sites.

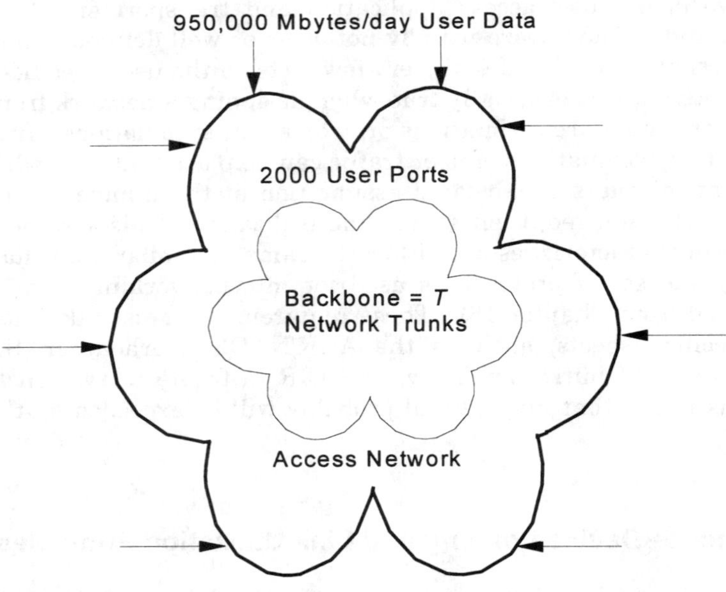

Figure 20.4 Access Port Sizing

This utilization would also have to be adjusted for overhead (actual available throughput on a DS1 is 1.536 Mbps). These calculations are acceptable for an estimate, but cannot take the place of true protocol- and device-specific design modeling.

$$\frac{M}{n} \times \frac{1 \text{ day}}{24 \text{ hours}} \times \frac{1 \text{ hour}}{3600 \text{ seconds}} \times \frac{8 \text{ bits}}{1 \text{ byte}} \times \frac{1}{\text{port speed}} = \text{avg \% Utilization per port}$$

$$\frac{950{,}000}{1000} \times \frac{1 \text{ day}}{24 \text{ hours}} \times \frac{1 \text{ hour}}{3600 \text{ seconds}} \times \frac{8 \text{ bits}}{1 \text{ byte}} \times \frac{1}{1.544 \text{ Mbps}} = 5.7\% \text{ Utilization}$$

Now add a busy-hour calculation where 20 percent of the total traffic occurs during the busy hour. The new calculation would include a factor of 5 hours per day to attain the 20 percent busy-hour peak.

$$\frac{M}{n} \times \frac{1 \text{ day}}{5 \text{ hours}} \times \frac{1 \text{ hour}}{3600 \text{ seconds}} \times \frac{8 \text{ bits}}{1 \text{ byte}} \times \frac{1}{\text{port speed}} = \text{avg \% Utilization per port}$$

$$\frac{950{,}000}{1000} \times \frac{1}{5} \times \frac{1}{3600} \times \frac{8}{1} \times \frac{1}{1.544} = 27.35\% \text{ Utilization}$$

Notice that port utilization has increased from 5.7 to 27.35 percent during the busy-hour period (again assuming a flat traffic distribution – this utilization would be even greater in a star network with a headquarters site). Take this one step further and look at the utilization during the busy minute and second. The busy minute or busy second could be calculated by converting the number of hours to seconds in the hour denominator. When this is done, "bursty" traffic can have a drastic effect on the bandwidth utilization of a dedicated circuit, running at the 100 percent link utilization mark for periods in excess of 1 second (if the protocol and its buffering scheme will operate that fast – some protocols could not fill up an entire DS1 circuit even if one were the only user on it).

20.3.2 Access Node Design

Now look at the average access node design. Since only a general idea what the traffic will be at each node is known, further assumptions can be made based on the fact that each access node will be configured in a similar manner. Access design can start out this way, and the access design can be further refined and modified as more detailed site-specific information becomes available. After all nodes are operational, look at the traffic requirements of each and tune the network as necessary, for example, by decreasing or increasing CIR or ports speed in frame relay.

Figure 20.5 shows a sample access node. To find the access node input-to-output utilization, a comparison is made concerning the number of ports, the speed of each port, and the port utilization to the output trunk utilization. The formula would read

$(T)(S)(\%UT) = (p_i)(s)(\%Up)$
where the
# of trunks required = T
# of ports of type $i = p_i$
speed of trunks = S
speed of port = s
% utilization of trunks = $\%UT$
% utilization of port = $\%Up$

For example, inputs and outputs to an access node are designed with the average (this could be peak or busy-hour average) input utilization is 27 percent on eight DS1 input ports, you want an average output utilization per trunk of no more than 50 percent, and the output trunks are also DS1s. Thus, you would require almost 5 DS1 trunks to accommodate all eight access ports at an average of 27 percent utilization each, and maintain less than 50 percent trunk loading. If all trunks were to simultaneously exceed 27 percent, the utilization on the trunks would increase, to the limit of 100 percent, and could support simultaneous transmission of all access ports at 54 percent utilization each (or some sum thereof).

$(T)(1.544)(.5) = (8)(1.544)(.27)$, then $T = 4.32$, or 5 trunks are required.

This calculation can be taken one step further, where there are now multiple access speeds and port utilizations, but the trunk speeds remain constant. The formula would now read

$$(T)(S)(\%UT) = \sum (p_i)(s)(\%Up_i)$$

Here is another example where the inputs are five DS1, 10 FT1 (256 kbps), and twelve DS0 (56 kbps) circuits. Assume that the access utilization remains the same at 27 percent utilization, the total number of trunks needed would be

$(T)(1.544)(50\%) = (5)(1.544)(.27)+(10)(.256)(.27)+(12)(.056)(.27)$
T = 3.83, or 4 DS1 trunks are required.

As the input port utilization increases, so does the number of trunks required to support the traffic.

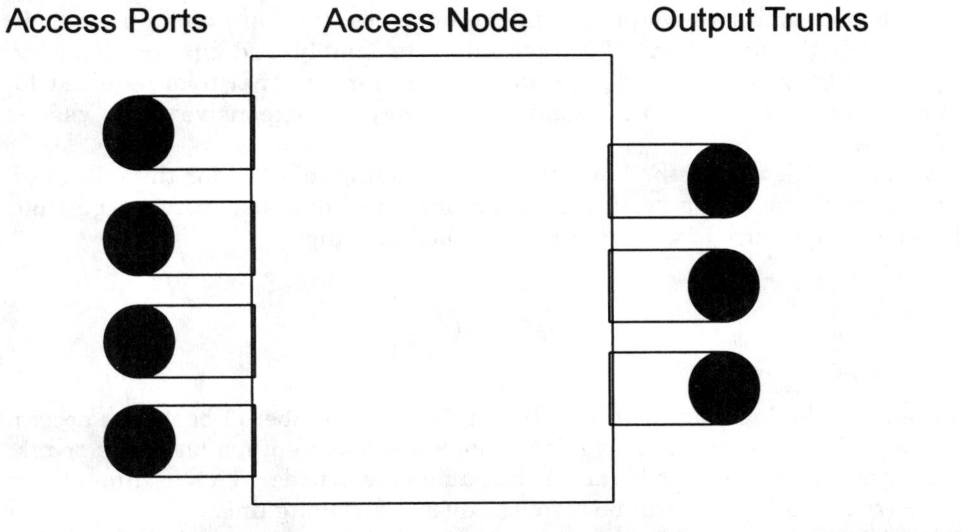

Figure 20.5 Simple Access Node

Obviously, these numbers will vary based on statistical multiplexing efficiencies, time variances in utilization and busy-time periods, protocols, and usage patterns, to name a few. LAN inputs and loading factors were explained in Chapter 17. It is important to note that the designer should not only design to the bandwidth required during normal transmission, but also design to the peak bandwidth during the busy hour/minute/second.

20.3.3 Utilization, Loading Factors, and Anticipating Failures

The link utilization and link efficiency relies heavily on the protocols operating over the link and the technology being used. These can vary from frame relay and HDLC, which are very efficient, to BSC and asynchronous protocols, which are relatively inefficient. The utilization of a link is affected by the number of end-user devices using the same link, the propagation delay, packet sizes and overhead due to flow control, error control, window and buffer sizes, and many other protocol- and technology-proprietary factors.

The utilization of a link will range from the average utilization to the busy hour/minute/second and even millisecond peak period utilization. *Bursting* is the term used for extended peak utilization conditions – such as a large file transfer that transmits data up to the maximum port speed (100 percent utilization) for a few seconds in duration. The network designer can plan for high utilization periods through three major methods of link loading. The first is to overbuild the capacity. This is the simple yet expensive method of throwing more capacity at the link (a link can constitute multiple circuits between the same two endpoints) in the hopes that it can handle periods of excessive high utilization. The second is to simply add up the capacity required during peak periods and double the number of trunks required to support the bursty traffic. Again, this may be expensive and wastes bandwidth.

The most efficient method of link (trunk) loading to allow for the failure of one link without losing traffic is by loading the links at a percentage that allows for the failure of a single trunk by the following:

$$L_f = \left[\mu - \left(\frac{\mu}{N} \right) \right]$$

where L_f is the load factor of each trunk, N is the number of backbone access trunks of the same speed, and μ is the maximum percentage load on a trunk given a failure of another trunk in the same access node. This assumes that traffic from a failed link can be rerouted over a surviving link.

For example, a network where the trunk overhead accounts for 50 percent of the bandwidth (μ) is a drastic case! For two links of T1 speed, the loading factor would be 25 percent or 386 kbps maximum traffic load (thus, one link could fail and the other link could carry the traffic at a 50 percent utilization). Now, take the same example for four links with the same overhead. This is shown in Figure 20.6. Each trunk is loaded with no more than 37.5 percent traffic, or 579 kbps, because if one link fails, the remaining links have to carry an additional 12.5 percent of the total traffic, resulting in a 50 percent utilization of the remaining three links. This formula could be modified based on the level of reliability of failure analysis and appropriate link loading. Typical 9600 bps loading for packet switching is at 60-65 percent, and for 56 kbps is at 75–80 percent. The network-access devices in packet networks are typically utilized at much lower levels than the network trunk side. In frame relay, loading is often high because of the statistical nature and low overhead inherent in the protocol.

The last example using an overhead of 50 percent was a bit high, but some technologies actually provide that much overhead. For example, an ATM channel over a DS3 can be considered. The maximum throughput of a DS3 (44.736 Mbps) is 43.008 Mbps (at 4 percent overhead due to framing). The overhead of the ATM packet structure of a 53-byte packet is 5 bytes. Thus, the aggregate overhead is approximately 14.6 percent. This does not take into consideration the higher-layer protocol overhead within the cell. It may not be uncommon to have over 40 percent overhead on the actual user data which originates as a file.

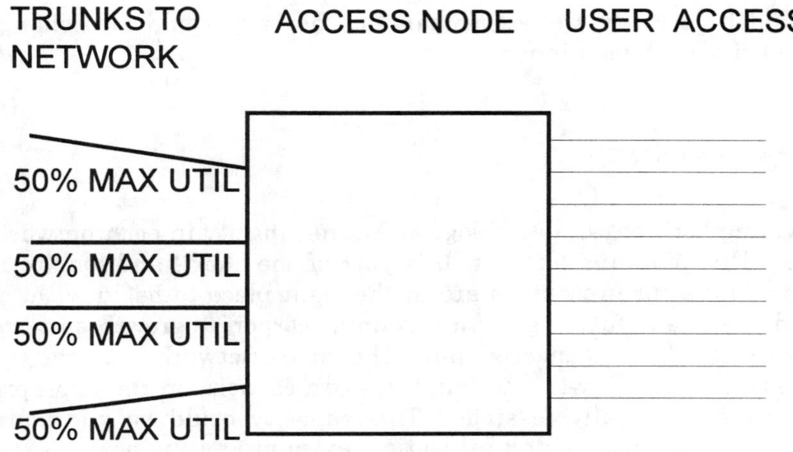

Figure 20.6 Network Trunk Sizing

The utilization of WAN links is usually measured in packets or frames. For example, an Ethernet LAN that is sending over a T1 WAN link takes 3000 PPS (of the smallest packets) to fully utilize a T1, and for 64-byte packets, or larger, the throughput would be less. If the throughput begins to degrade, and the packet size remains the same, it may be necessary to reallocate LAN resources to additional WAN links, segment the LAN, move to a faster-speed trunk, or add more WAN circuits. Either way, define allowable margins and enforce them.

20.3.4 Efficiencies of Statistical Multiplexing

As discussed before, statistical multiplexing can also increase the efficient use of available bandwidth. Statistical multiplexing is found in packet switches, routers, cell switches, and of course electrical and light-wave statistical multiplexers. LAN and MAN operation can also be considered as a form of statistical multiplexing, because users who need the bandwidth get it when it is available on a time-sharing basis. If one station on the LAN/MAN requires all of the bandwidth, that station gets most or all of it for a period of time (again depending on the architecture). The ratios of statistical multiplexing are expressed as $X{:}Y$, where X is the user input and Y is the access device output. For example, if eight T1 user input circuits are transmitting an average of 12.5 percent utilization each, and a single output T1 trunk could be driven at 100 percent utilization, the ratio would be 8:1. On the other hand, if there were four inputs at an average utilization of 25 percent each, the ratio would be 4:1. In the same manner, the ratio could also change based on the load of each user input.

20.3.5 Future Capacity

Plan for providing both physical and logical future capacity in each network-access device. This planning for growth is part of the short- and long-term capacity plan. Make sure resources are in the right place to begin with, as well as placed in areas of future growth. Examine corporate growth patterns and engineer them into the capacity plan. The smart network designer will anticipate these areas of growth and build in extra capacity in the appropriate areas when economically feasible. This capacity could be additional hardware or ports, low initial trunk utilization, extra processing power, extra floor or rack space, or just adding the capability to expand a specific area of the network.

20.4 STYLE

Style has been discussed previously in terms of network topological styles. This section discusses how the design of the geographically local environment and access devices may have a major impact on the WAN, both in loading and topology. A first look will be taken at the geography of user requirements as defined in the traffic matrix, and then consideration will evaluate the distribution of those resources within each geographic region in either a hierarchical or matrix (ubiquitous access) style. We will investigate a hierarchical ATM switch design and the migration from collapsed backbones to ATM switch backbones. Finally, we will look at new forms of LAN switching and architecture design.

20.4.1 Based on Geography

The geographic placement of local access nodes will be based primarily on geographical user and application distribution. Use the traffic matrix built in Chapter 17 to determine the actual physical placement of access nodes. Access groupings can be organized by CPE, LATA, state, nation, and continent. Many options are available for geographically remote areas where a full-access node may not be required, such as dial-access and remote-node capability.

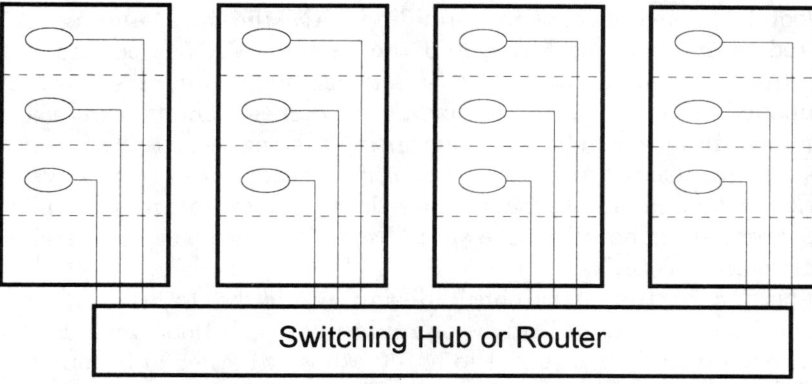

Figure 20.7 Ubiquitous Access Example

20.4.2 Ubiquitous Access (Matrix)

There are two major styles of providing connectivity to local area resources (subnets): *ubiquitous* and *hierarchical* access. The ubiquitous, sometimes called "flat", access approach allows all users to transmit and receive data from all areas of the network. This is also called the "matrix approach". One example of ubiquitous access is shown in Figure 20.7, where a single intelligent switching hub or router provides access for the entire building's LAN connectivity. Any user on any LAN can pass data through the hub or routing device, as well as access any other device in the network. This style of access is good for organizations that are spread out and nonstructured (nonhierarchical) in nature. The ubiquitous access style provides a one-dimensional, flat network and is often used with smaller networks. This type of network becomes difficult to manage as it grows in size, especially when multiple interfaces, technologies, architecture, protocols, and vendors are involved. Problems with performance degradation are not easily diagnosed and the network can become more difficult to manage. It also offers a very large single point of failure that can take *every* user down at one time.

20.4.3 Hierarchical

Hierarchical designs provide a user access hierarchy where traffic destined for its own local, metropolitan, and wide area remains in that geographical area, rather than accessing the common switching or routing point to the backbone as in the ubiquitous access approach. Figure 20.8 illustrates a building with a four-tier hierarchy: each user is connected to a floor LAN, each floor LAN is connected to a building LAN, the four building LANs are connected to one campus MAN, and the campus MAN is connected to the WAN. In this example, connectivity between segments, or subnetworks, is accomplished via bridges, routers, or LAN switches. The hierarchical design is often used in larger networks warranting the segmentation of user traffic. In this design, users typically do not require access to every server in the network, instead going through their local server for most applications. Thus, servers are generally more specialized. This is also a good architecture for implementing VLANs.

A deviation of the hierarchical design would be to use intelligent or switching hubs instead of bridges or routers on each floor, and the building LAN or MAN would be internal to a 100 Mbps Ethernet hub, router, or 155 Mbps ATM switch. This is shown in Figure 20.9. Here the hubs act as concentration and possibly LAN switching points within each floor and between floors. LAN and WAN routing and switching are performed in the hub, router, or switch. Remember that hub ports are usually less expensive than router ports due to their limited functionality requirements.

The segmentation of hierarchical networks starts at the work-group subnet. This unit provides interconnection of resources (workstations) between LANs — (e.g., a flat distance-vector protocol like RIP in conjunction with IP routing and multiple operating systems) typically through a LAN hub, switch, or router. The next higher level is the departmental subnet where routers and switches connect a larger local area. This unit provides LAN-to-LAN inter-networking and connection to WAN routing and switching. The next higher level is MAN and WAN networking. Departmental subnets should be arranged to provide flows of connectivity which form the enterprise backbone. The enterprise backbone could be the network as portrayed in the last figure, or many such networks connected over the WAN. Typically, the enterprise network is the latter, with many local designs connected via access nodes (the routers or the hubs in these examples) to a carrier providing a public network service (e.g., IP, FR, SMDS, or ATM backbones).

The hierarchical access style allows the capability of connecting low-speed LANs to high-speed LANs, MANs and WANs. It allows the designer to understand performance bottlenecks and thus manage or architect the network to alleviate these bottlenecks. The rule that the transport is only as fast as its "slowest link" still applies, and with a hierarchical style the bottlenecks can be eliminated by assuring that each level of the hierarchy is at least as fast as the previous one. Hierarchical-style networks help to protect users from broadcast storms and make it easier for administrators to regulate and firewall traffic flows between segments. Some other tips to follow when deploying this style are that servers on local LAN segments should never route packets, but instead routers should be used. And regardless of which style is chosen, support and management of all elements of the WAN is required.

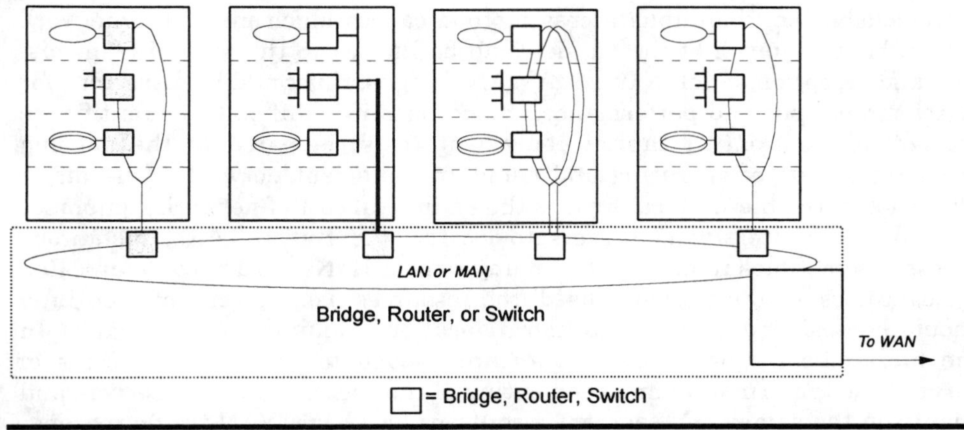

Figure 20.8 Hierarchical Access

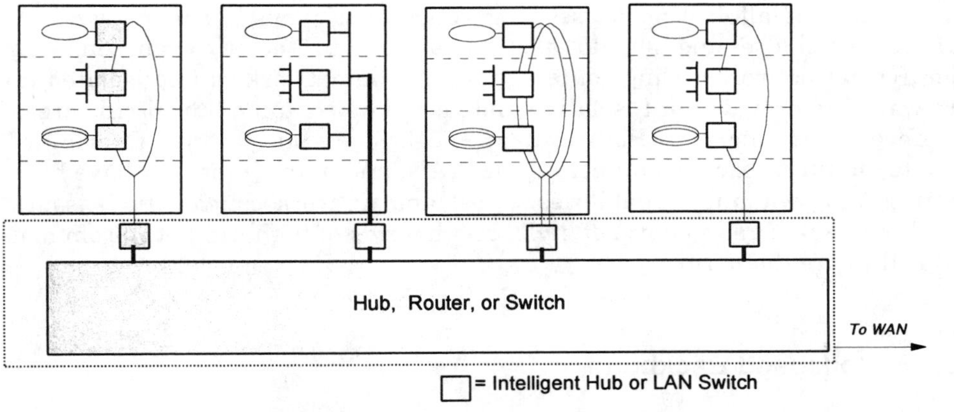

Figure 20.9 Hierarchical Access with Switching Hub, Router, or Switch

20.4.4 Hierarchical versus Ubiquitous Access

The hierarchical approach to local access design provides many advantages over the ubiquitous access style, including:

- Cost-efficient use of network media
- Performance does not from degrading
- Protection from broadcast storms
- Hierarchical address schemes can be used (see Chapter 21)
- Access control filters in routers to police segments
- Ease of security administration
- Isolation and diagnosis of problems are easier

Obviously, the ubiquitous access method causes much more internetwork traffic, because much of the traffic could be limited to the area of transmission and reception of data. In large WAN designs, this could be disastrous for WAN throughput and performance. Sometimes it is difficult to quantify the tradeoff of up front of capital equipment costs compared to the ongoing (recurring) costs of operating and using an inefficient network. The major drawback of the hierarchical style is the additional cost of network equipment (switches or routers) and servers to localize the traffic. Also, ubiquitous access is sometimes required when many remote LANs need to communicate.

Regardless of which style is used, the resources (i.e., servers) of each LAN should be designed in line with hierarchical or ubiquitous access layers. In the hierarchical style, more servers are needed to ensure local access of server-based information and segmenting of that access. Putting servers and clients on the same LAN segment also keeps backbone WAN traffic reasonably low. In ubiquitous access, all servers can talk to all other servers so all resources can be shared across the entire local access network. VLANs offer one method of alleviating these geographic restrictions. The network or subnetwork addressing should also correspond to the style chosen. In hierarchical networks using routers, parts of the network can be isolated or fire-walled to provide fault isolation and keep data contained to specific areas to prevent data storms. Both routers and bridges can perform filtering of data to eliminate excess data across the WAN, and many hubs now have both routing and switching capabilities. Cost and network control (turf) issues also become factors in choice of style, and hybrids of both are not uncommon but rather are the norm.

20.4.5 Collapsed Backbone

A single, shared-medium LAN segment runs out of bandwidth quickly as more users require interconnections to shared resources such as servers or as communication traffic volume increases due to the re-engineering of the corporation. The bridging of LAN segments does not scale well beyond a certain point, driven by the number of bridges and hops (7 maximum) and geographic diversity limitations. An architecture employed by many users confronted with this problem was to effectively implement a hierarchy or star network collapsed on a router as shown in Figure 20.10a. As the demand for speed and connectivity increases, there is a requirement for a single technology device that can increase the bandwidth available in a hierarchical collapsed-backbone architecture. One example is a collapsed backbone, as shown in Figure 20.10b. This example demonstrates using ATM as the collapsed backbone. An IP architecture could also be used. The ATM architecture also has the potential to move away from this hierarchy to a more distributed backbone architecture. ATM offers the key functions of automatic configuration, fault recovery, address resolution, address assignment and network management for a collapsed backbone. It also serves as a single technology to consolidate and unify network management in this environment.

20.4.6 LAN Switching Migrations to ATM

Let's now look at the migration from LAN segmentation and hubbing, through router LAN hubbing, and into ATM-switched LANs. This is just one view of how the future of local architectures may look with ATM switching.

Phase 1 – LAN segmentation with hubbing. Hub devices on each floor aggregating LAN segments and sending them to the ground floor to a router for WAN connectivity as illustrated in Figure 20.11. Routing is thus performed between floors by the router in the basement. This was the first step in creating a collapsed backbone, and the beginning of server "farms" in a central location near the router.

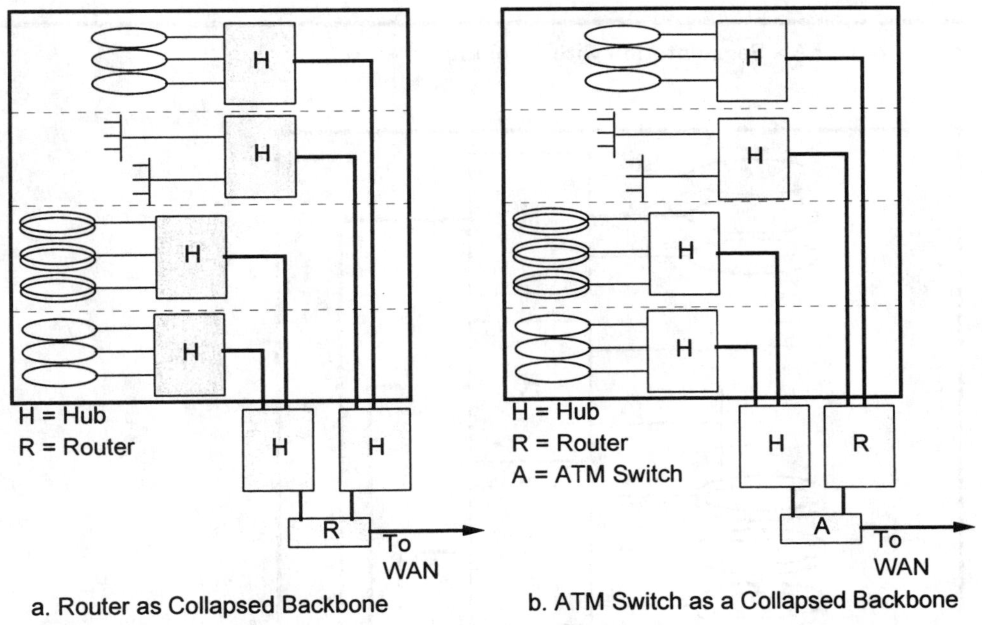

Figure 20.10 Use of ATM in the Enterprise Collapsed Backbone

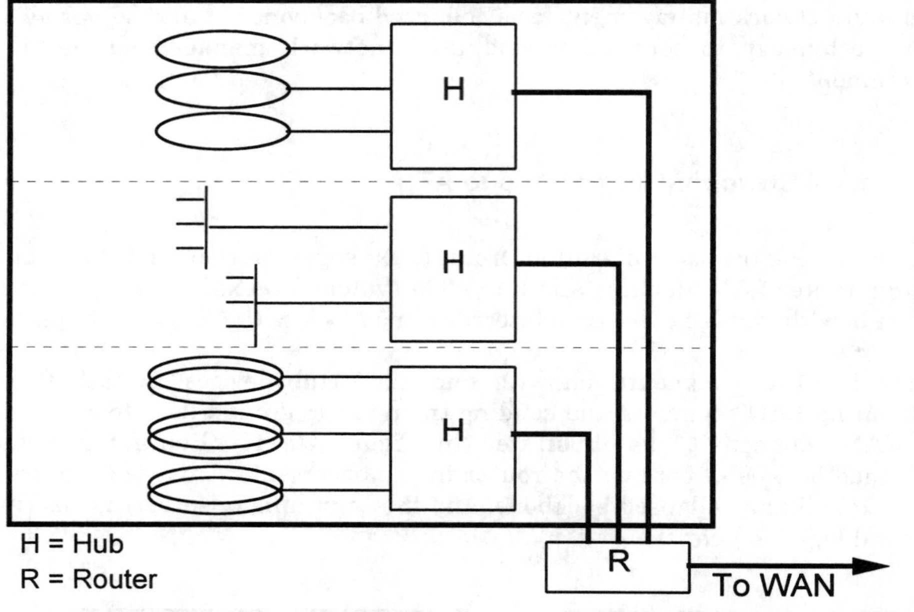

Figure 20.11 LAN Segmentation with Hubbing

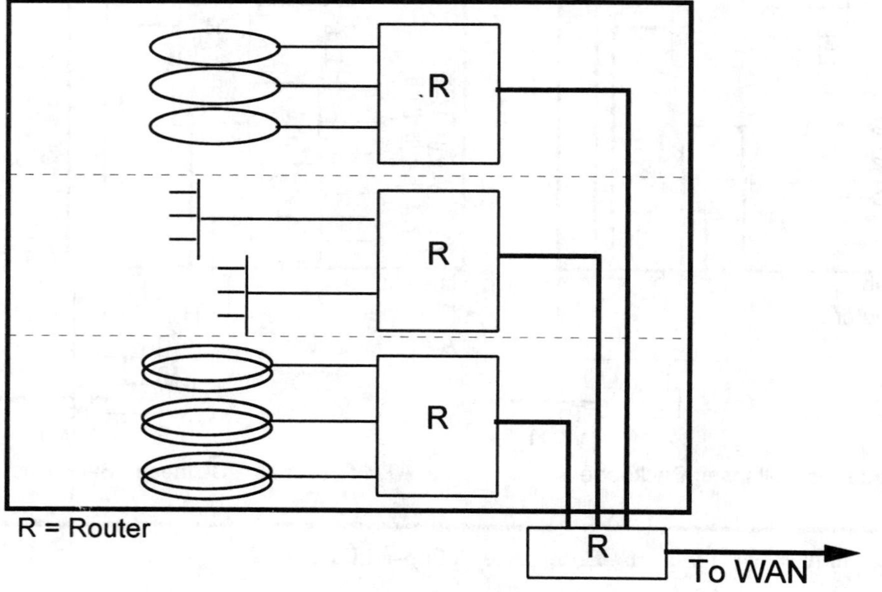

Figure 20.12 LAN Segmentation with Routing

Phase 2 – LAN segmentation with routing. Routers move to each floor and provide multiple or now single LAN segment routing. A master router that advertises addresses to the WAN resides on the ground floor as illustrated in Figure 20.12.

Phase 3 – LAN switching with hubs or routers. All switching devices (hubs or routers) on each floor are aggregated by a LAN switch in the basement. Segmentation and microsegmentation of LAN segments cause there to be fewer machines per segment or even work groups without servers, or server farms on a single LAN segment as shown in Figure 20.13.

Phase 4 – LAN switching per work group or floor. Now the LAN switches move closer to the work group, are optimized for the work group, and provide LAN switching on each floor, at close to native LAN speeds. This enables higher-speed LAN-to-LAN communications and less complex routing to slow down processes, and the router still provides the WAN connectivity as illustrated in Figure 20.14.

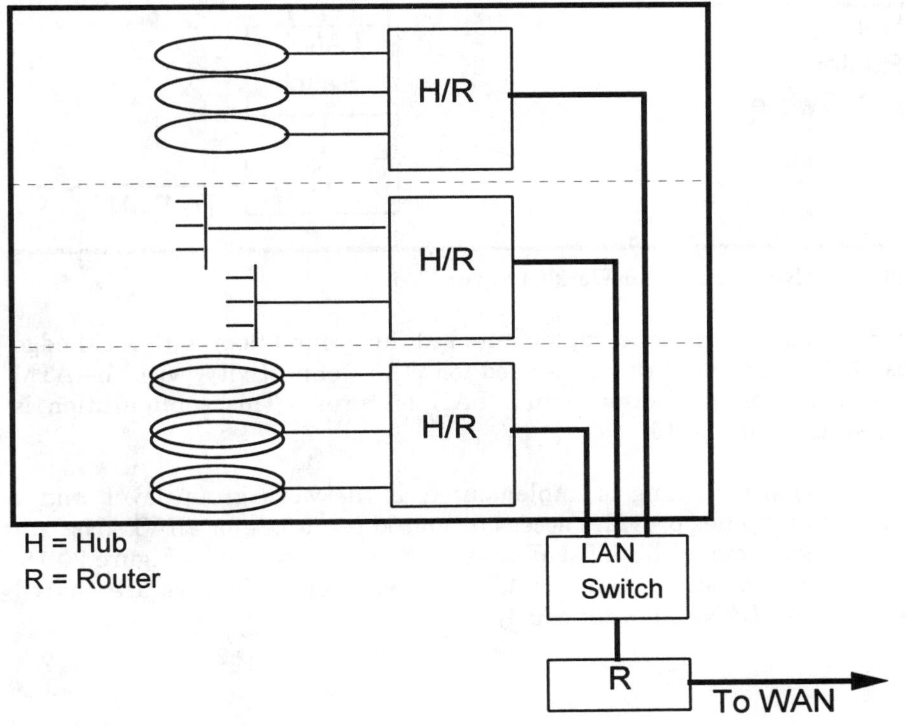

Figure 20.13 LAN Switching with Hubs or Routers

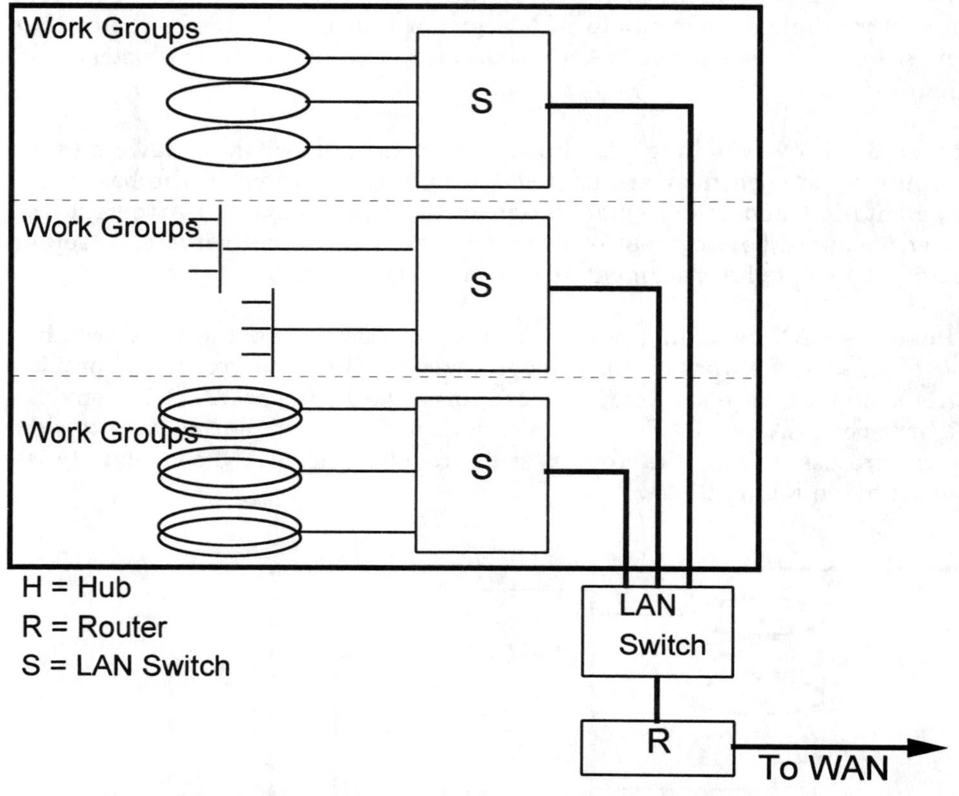

Figure 20.14 LAN Switching per Work Group or Floor

Phase 5 – ATM switching is implemented in the ground floor with ATM edge devices. A high-powered router is used for WAN connectivity, with the ATM switch focusing on providing virtual LAN features. This configuration is illustrated in Figure 20.15.

Phase 6 – ATM switching is implemented at the work group level, and a group of ATM switches provides access to shared resources for all VLANs. An ATM switch connects to the ATM WAN service as illustrated in Figure 20.16. VLANs are shared across many or all ATM locations. Servers are shared across multiple VLANs simultaneously.

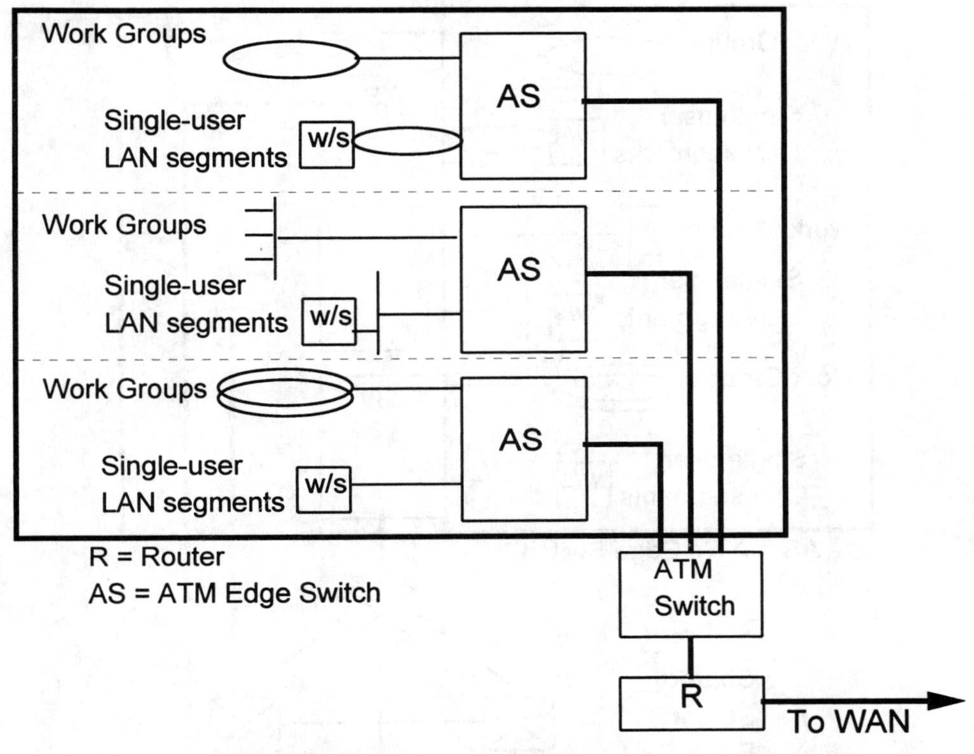

Figure 20.15 ATM Switching with Edge Devices

20.5 COMPLETING THE ACCESS NETWORK DESIGN

The steps for completing the access-network design include verifying the user-application intelligence, confirming the design and choice of the access device(s), choosing the number and type of access devices, completing the circuit design to and from the access node, and verifying the total access topology. Most of these steps may have already been fixed from design practices explained in previous chapters, but are presented here in a wrap-up fashion to ensure that every step is summarized in completing the access design portion of the network.

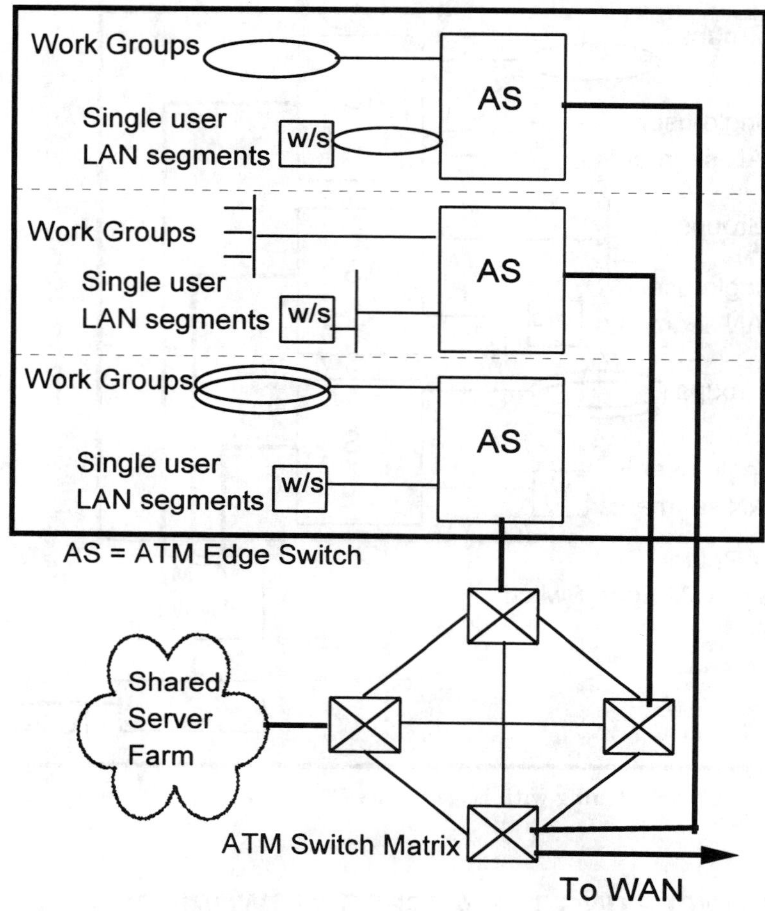

Figure 20.16 ATM Work Group Switching

20.5.1 User/Application Intelligence Verification

When the access network design was performed, it was assumed that there was some level of intelligence in the user devices and applications. The greater this level of intelligence, the less is required from the network, and the more the network can concentrate on passing data. If not done in the initial requirements phase, some time should be spent reanalyzing the user application intelligence to confirm the expectations of both the user and the network from the application and protocols standpoint. Remember, frame relay is a transmission protocol only, and a higher-layer protocol like TCP is required for retransmission of lost frames. Most user applications, unless specifically designed to do so, do not automatically route around an access-circuit failure, and therefore the CPE must initiate a dial backup routine to reestablish service. Issues like these are critical, as services like FR and SMDS do not retransmit lost data.

Confirm that the required intelligence is in the access device selected, and that this device will be able to communicate that intelligence to the backbone network. One example of misconceptions that may arise is operating system support from LAN to LAN. Most routers can convert between LAN protocols, such as Ethernet to Token Ring, but cannot allow LANs with different operating systems to interoperate. This process is complex because of the different framing and addressing formats. Some users may overlook (rightfully so, if the network is viewed as a utility) this level of detail and just expect different types of LANs to interoperate.

20.5.2 Access-Device Level

The next level of verification is of the access device itself. The access device should be the feeder portion of the network design, where user applications, devices, and protocols of a defined geographic area are fed into a single or multiple device(s). This access device(s) will then communicate with other access devices or directly with the backbone. The typical access node will aggregate and transmit voice, data, and video traffic from many different interfaces, protocols, architectures, and technologies to the backbone via a single protocol and technology. Access devices, therefore, should reduce the number of access ports, protocols, conversions, and data formats fed to the backbone. With technologies such as frame relay, access to the WAN is in terms of multiple logical channels rather than single physical channels per port. ATM is one technology that can offer true integrated access of all forms of communication – specifically voice, data, and video.

20.5.3 Number and Type of Access Nodes

The number of access nodes is determined by the traffic matrix, the optimized grouping of traffic, and the placement of access nodes. In flat architectures, fewer nodes tend to cause longer access circuits, but decrease total network delay. More nodes increase the chance of a failure somewhere in the network (see availability calculations in Chapter 16), but networks can be designed with hardware and circuit redundancy to minimize or eliminate the impact of node loss to the user. The network design should always allow for a multiple node-failure scenario, as well as alternate trunks for a minimum of a single access trunk failure. Loading factors that accommodate for trunk failures have been discussed already, and the same formulas can be used to calculate the number of nodes required to survive a single node failure.

By now, the reader should be able to choose the type of access node required. Here are a few extra tips on the selection of access hardware. Using a single device with multiprotocol support may preclude buying two devices that each support a single protocol. This would reduce the number of network-access points and equipment costs while providing maximum functionality. Most router and switch vendors make almost all common protocols available for their devices either at no cost or at a very low cost. Consider using a switching hub over a router if you have a flat LAN architecture, many single user LANs, or a homogenous LAN environment. For remote sites, consider less expensive remote-access products that offer reduced memory and processing power and a subset of routing (or bridging) capabilities. Since client-server traffic (TCP/IP, NetBIOS, and other protocols) usually constitutes the majority of user traffic, this is a major consideration in LAN/WAN access design.

IP and FR access devices can be any normal access device discussed so far: multiplexers, switches, bridges, or routers. Access devices for SMDS are more limited, and include routers, Macintosh PCs, and even some multiplexers, but these devices often require hardware/software upgrades to support this new service. Most SMDS access types require special DSUs specifically designed to perform L3_PDU-to-L2_PDU segmentation. But SMDS interfaces are beginning to proliferate to all types of LAN/MAN/WAN access devices, even the CRAY supercomputer. ATM interfaces and functionality are available on most user/customer premises equipment, and some high-end CPE access devices provide SONET interfaces.

Host-to-host connectivity has been offered through the channel-to-channel bus-and-tag adapter at 3 Mbytes per second. Channel extension can be accomplished through either high-speed dedicated DS1 and DS3 circuits, or through high-speed LAN/MAN/WAN access. The latter is beginning to predominate with FDDI or IEEE 802.6. More vendors, including IBM and Cisco, now have FR and SMDS interfaces for their processors and host computers, including some direct interconnect options as discussed in Chapter 7.

20.5.4 Access Circuit Topology and Design

The best way of designing the access and backbone circuit sizing is with a network design tool. Barring access to such a tool, circuits can be chosen and prioritized based on a variety of factors including:

- ★ Shortest path
- ★ Minimum congestion
- ★ Minimum delay

- ★ Minimum loss
- ★ Minimum/maximum throughput
- ★ Utilization
- ★ Spanning tree minimum hop count
- ★ Minimum cost

Once the circuit topology is decided, the placement of nodes should be reviewed. Based on the total ingress/egress traffic into/out of a node, the decision to add/delete nodes or change nodal configurations can be made. This is an iterative process, and takes multiple iterations to achieve an optimum design. This is especially true with multiple protocol layers, each affected by changes in the filtering, forwarding, routing, and switching. The best advice is to understand the limits of the protocols being used (e.g., hop counts, overhead, etc.) and make sure they are not violated by changes in topology.

The procedure goes something like this: assign the capacity in circuits between access nodes, taking care to account for every constraint. Use a design tool to fail parts of the network and determine where additional capacity may be required. Add the capacity and fail another part of the network. Continue until the design meets the correct criteria for availability and reliability. Now optimize the network wherever possible. Analyze backhaul (the amount of distance extension required to reach the nearest access node) and determine if it is cost-justifiable to eliminate any nodes or links (keep original user requirements in mind) or if additional ones are required. After optimization is complete, return to failure analysis and repeat the process. A good design tool will perform these steps and many more (design tools will be discussed in Chapter 24).

20.5.5 Access Network Topologies

Access network topologies can vary:

- ☆ Direct connect to backbone nodes *without* direct trunks between access nodes
- ☆ Direct connect to backbone nodes *with* direct trunks between access nodes
- ☆ Ring (loop) connected to backbone
- ☆ Trees with "root" connected to backbone
- ☆ Multipoint with bus connected to backbone
- ☆ Star with hub connected to backbone
- ☆ Hybrid meshed configuration

Many of these topology styles have been defined in Chapter 5, and will be covered in more detail in the next chapter.

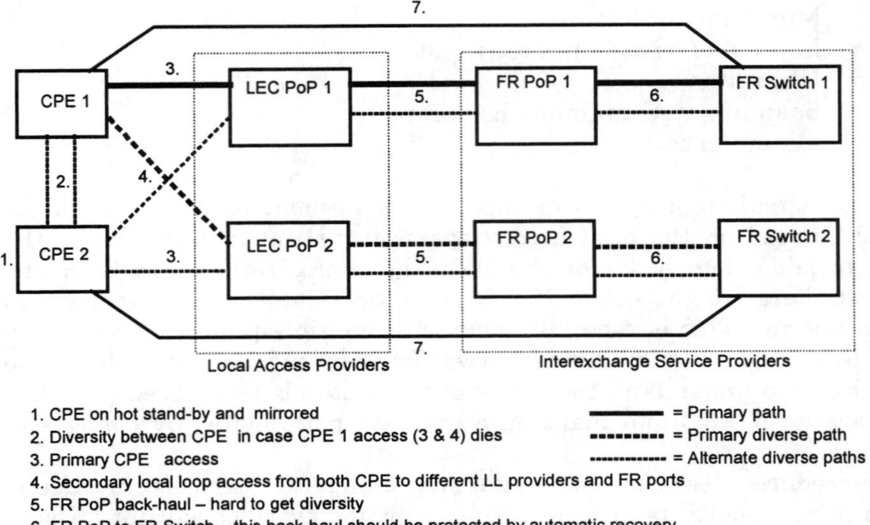

Figure 20.17 Access Diversity Options

Also, when building bridged networks (or nonrouted networks) beware of creating loops. As point-to-point connections grow across the WAN, the likelihood of loops increases. Loops can cause duplication of packets. Protocols such as Spanning Tree Protocol (STP) works for local bridges, but remote bridges can cause loops and multiple nonunique paths. STP will place some links (if loops found) on standby mode and the subsequent routing may cause increases in delay and hops. As stated before, be aware of the effects of all protocols used in the access-network architecture, as well as the architecture impact on the protocols.

20.6 DIVERSE, REMOTE, AND TELECOMMUTING OPTIONS

Let's now review a few access options – access diversity, remote access, and telecommuting.

20.6.1 Access Diversity Alternatives

Access diversity can take the form of equipment, local loop, back-haul, and switch-access port diversity. Figure 20.17 shows the areas of focus for diversity that we will discuss in this section. In this example of frame relay service access, we notice that diversity is required in the CPE, LEC PoP, FR PoP, and into the FR switch.

All access to backbone circuits should have diverse homing based on the availability and redundancy required. If at least two diverse circuits are used, they should have the capability to load share and load balance. Test failure and survivability on all circuits before placing live traffic on them. Make sure that the network contains the desired level of redundancy. Circuits between access and backbone nodes look like access circuits to the backbone, and the shorter the access circuit distance, the better. Long-access circuits incur slightly more delay (due to propagation and transmission delay), are more expensive, and allow more opportunity for failure or interruptions. Run all access circuits through a back-haul analysis to determine if an additional access node should be used.

Look for automatic restoration on all circuits whenever the design and economics permit. This is especially important when accessing a frame switched service like FR. Here, back-haul is defined as the distance from when you enter a serving Point-of-Presence (PoP) to where you actually enter the first frame relay switch. Examples of back-haul protection include the AT&T FASTAR II dynamic recovery service and MCI's VISN. Based on a SONET infrastructure, these services dynamically reconfigure around any circuit failure within minutes or even seconds. Always test automatic restoration plans periodically (otherwise how do you know they will work during a failure?!). Guaranteed and automatic circuit diversity and recovery for mission-critical application circuits and sites are often well worth the cost. Also, look at local loop diversity.

Remember, if all sites home to a single headquarters location, no amount of diversity and disaster recovery is too much, because if that site goes south the entire network is effectively down! Take a serious look at backup for your headquarters or critical server facilities or investigate out-tasking this to someone who provides this option at a fraction of the price it would cost to build it.

20.6.2 Remote Access Alternatives

Remote access takes two forms – remote dedicated access and remote on-demand switched access. Dedicated access methods have already been discussed in this chapter, so we turn our attention to on-demand switched access methods.

A variety of on-demand services exist, and the key to choosing the correct one for your needs depends on a few factors:

- User application
- Transport protocol(s)

- CPE selection
- Access speed and throughput
- Service (presence) availability
- Service reliability
- Economics
- Level of security

Remote access is commonly accomplished through the following protocols:

- X.25/X.3
- PPP or SLIP
- TCP/IP Telnet,

and more popular transport mediums (services):

- Modem through POTS to modem pool or terminal server
- ISDN (BRI and PRI)
- Dial into dedicated FR port
- Internet (beware of security issues)

The two most common forms of dial access are PPP and SLIP. SLIP is used only over asynchronous access, while PPP can run over asynchronous or synchronous, switched or dedicated access. ISDN is a second most common form of dial access. Both are shown in Figure 20.18. Here a PPP session is initiated from one end device to another. Notice the conversion from the ISDN Automatic Number Identification (ANI) to the FR Data Link Connection Identifier (DLCI) for mapping ISDN B-channel to FR PVC. Mapping of DNIS to PVC DLCI is also performed.

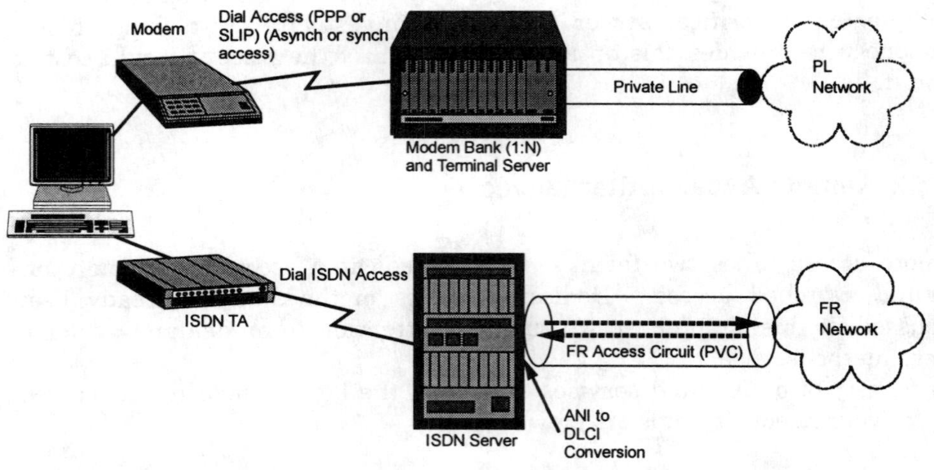

Figure 20.18 Access Diversity Options

Most ISDN implementations are now using a form of "spoofing". Spoofing can be used to disconnect the user from the network when proxy SAP and RIP updates, watchdog, and keep-alive information is the only traffic being sent back and forth across the network – spoofing each of these back to the user. In this way, the host is fooled into believing the session is still connected even though it may be temporarily disconnected. This saves on both connection time and usage, and is advantageous to ISDN implementations that are charged by the minute or total connection time. Another feature, called multilink PPP, allows several PPP logical channels to be bundled and treated as a single PPP connection.

20.6.3 Telecommuting Options

Many corporations and government entities are exploring the option of telecommuting. Telecommuting can take the form of fixed or on-demand access, and is typically for home access or small remote sites that do not justify dedicated access facilities. Connections are characterized by low traffic volumes and intermittent transmission times and volumes. The tried and true method has been primarily modem access to a corporate bank of modems called a modem pool. The explosion in remote access has created many new opportunities that are higher speed, more cost effective, and more reliable. ISDN BRI service, where the remote user dials ISDN access to an intelligent node, which in turn connects to a regional or national network, is beginning to proliferate as a preferred mode of remote dial access.

20.7 CHOICE OF CARRIER TECHNOLOGY AND SERVICE

Carrier technology and service decisions should be based on the decisions made in the access portion of the network design. The primary focus should be on the future of the network. In the next chapter, the backbone network design will be covered and a look taken at the carriers that provide the required backbone technology or service. Each of the technologies discussed is offered by the carriers as a public network service. It is up to the reader to analyze each option based on the information provided in this text. Then choose the best fit for their network requirements.

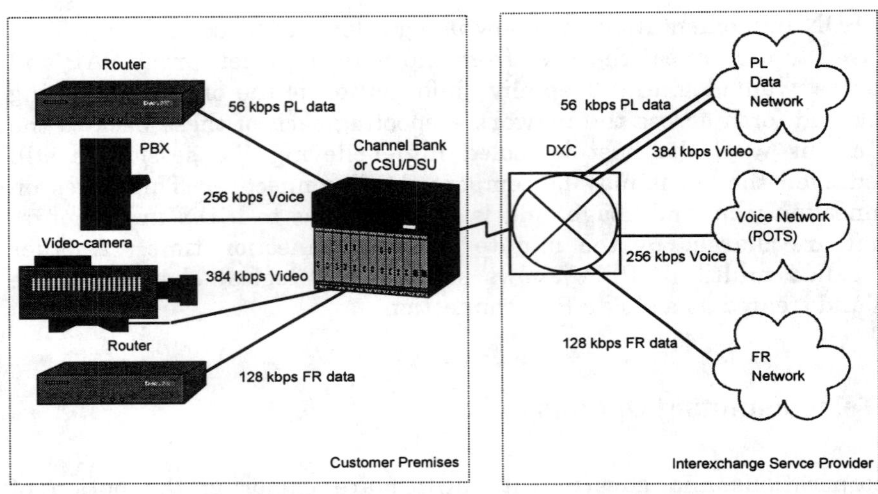

Figure 20.19 Integrated Access Solution

20.8 INTEGRATED ACCESS

Sometimes a site will require multiple service types over a single access facility. Channelized local access can be used to combine a single local loop among multiple applications, such as voice, data, video, and packet/frame/cell services. In this method, multiple DS0 64 kbps channels or *n*xDS0 (FT1) composite channels are combined into a single DS1 access circuit. These channels are combined on the user premises through either a channel bank or CSU/DSU and are then broken out at the carrier digital cross-connect (DXC) into their respective dedicated or switched services.

Figure 20.19 illustrates an example of integrated access, where a router transmitting 56 kbps private line data, a PBX with 256 kbps voice traffic, a video system generating 384 kbps video channel, and a router sending 128 kbps FR traffic are all integrated over a single T1 to the service provider. Here they are broken out again and sent to either the private line data network, the voice (POTS) network, or a FR network service.

20.9 REVIEW

In this chapter, requirements explained in Chapters 15 and 16 were built into the access portion of the network design. First, the requirements in the categories of interfaces, protocols, features, functions, services, and technologies were modeled. The importance of building the access portion of the network to accommodate these requirements was emphasized while assuring that the requirements were indeed supported by the design. It was found that there are many methods of modeling network capacity on a site-specific and global level. The importance of building future capacity into the network was discussed. It was seen that the hierarchical style of topology is best for large, complex access networks and that ubiquitous access is best for small, heterogeneous designs. Networks are moving toward collapsed backbone structures, and local ATM backbones offer one option for serving as a collapsed backbone for LAN switching. The access design was verified by taking into account the user device and application intelligence, the device type and quantity to adequately support the users, and the circuit design to support optimal performance with room for future growth. Finally, integrated access provides one method of combining various voice, data, and video traffic into a single access circuit, and allowing the backbone network or service to strip each type back out and transmit it over the appropriate medium.

Chapter

21

Backbone Network Design

Now that the access network design is completed, the decision must be made whether to interconnect the access design, build a backbone network, or interface to an existing backbone such as a public data network service like IP and frame relay. Another review of the interfaces, protocols, architectures, features, functions, and services is required in the same manner as done for the access network design. The capacity required to support the access network was determined primarily from the outputs of the design stage. Next, a topology and style consistent with the services and technology must be chosen. The resultant topology will in turn determine the number and placement of backbone nodes, the circuit design, and the overall integrated access and backbone network design. During the process of establishing the topology and technology choice, there is a necessity to go into great detail on network addressing, which will be covered in the next chapter. Both network management and network timing are discussed, and this chapter closes with a discussion of methods of fine-tuning the entire network design. Many of the same principles discussed in access design also apply to backbone design and will not be explained in detail but the results will be given and applied.

21.1 BACKBONE REQUIREMENTS

Why is a backbone needed? If an existing meshed point-to-point network is composed of network concentrators or access devices, what economies and benefits may be derived that would drive the design of a backbone? Backbones provide many efficiencies not achievable from a meshed-access network, including:

- ☞ Traffic consolidation – elimination of multiple paths with different types of traffic
- ☞ High-bandwidth switched-services platform
- ☞ Rerouting and redundancy
- ☞ Economies of scale
- ☞ Self-healing architecture
- ☞ Sharing of equipment and facilities by multiple locations
- ☞ Intelligent routing
- ☞ Dynamic bandwidth resource allocation
- ☞ Flexible topologies and styles of design
- ☞ Distributed or centralized network management
- ☞ Flexibility

Public switched-data networks can also act as backbone networks in a hybrid fashion to an access network. Thus, the backbone design aspects of this chapter will refer primarily to public or large private switched-data network designs. The two prominent examples are hierarchical IP and flat FR networks. When viewed from the backbone network, the perspective must be global. As LAN interconnectivity grows in size, possibly company-wide, it is called an *enterprise network*. Either the enterprise network keeps a matrix structure (as in SNA networks), or subnetworks begin to form a hierarchical structure (as in many non-SNA TCP/IP or OSI multiprotocol networks). As the number of point-to-point trunks grows between access nodes, it becomes necessary to design a backbone network layer.

Figure 21.1 shows a private line WAN with six access/concentrator nodes. This is compared to the same network, this time with a three-node backbone providing a switched service to the same six access nodes. The access nodes could be IP, FR, SMDS, or ATM switches, bridges, routers, gateways, or any other network access or switching device discussed so far. The backbone network achieves many of the efficiencies listed above. Now to look at the characteristics of backbone networks and the requirements that drive their design.

21.1.1 Interfaces

The primary interfaces for the backbone design will be either access circuits from the access design portion (see Chapter 19) or direct-user access into the public service backbone. The primary speeds for backbone interfaces are 56 kbps, FT1, DS1, DS3, 100 Mbps, 155 Mbps, and OC-*N*. Many of the specifics on these interfaces have been discussed in previous chapters.

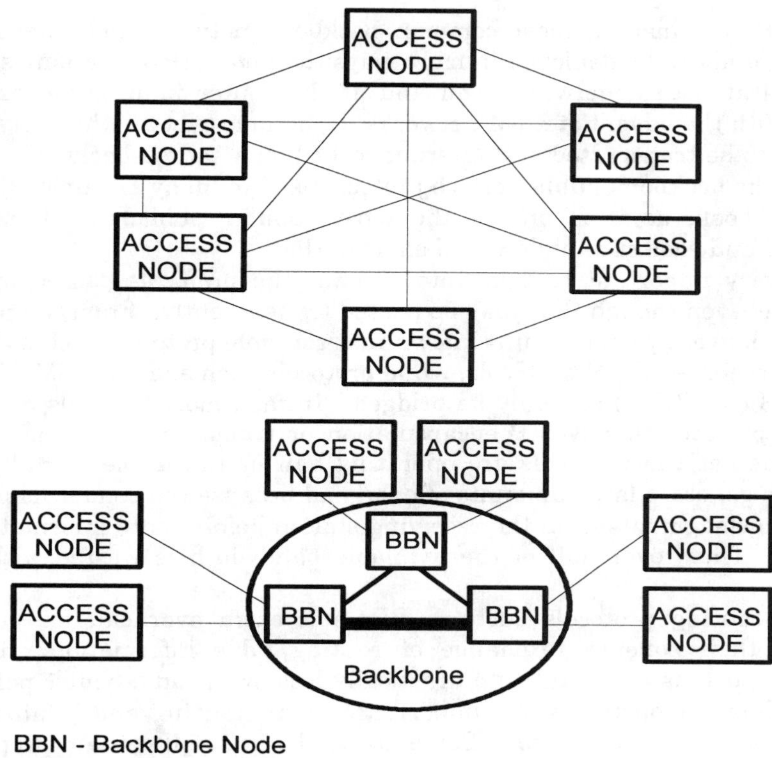

Figure 21.1 Private Line WAN Backbone Compared to Switched Services WAN Backbone

21.1.2 Protocols

Many of the user protocols will be transparent to the backbone, but the design of the backbone may still have an effect on them. Performance degradation, delay, and other protocol factors may ripple back from the backbone to the user protocols. The backbone design must be flexible enough to accommodate multiple protocols and operating systems, whether switching them transparently or actually becoming involved in the intelligent operations of the protocol.

The backbones of the next century are moving toward more intelligence in the control of the network and less intelligence in the actual handling of the traffic, with the exception of ATM interworking and QoS. Backbones must have the capability to interconnect diverse sites, switch or route all the protocols of the access network, and accommodate both in-band and out-of-band protocol transmissions.

TCP/IP remains the most common backbone network and internetwork protocol, and can be deployed in more ways than one. IP addressing schemes are used at both a network level and at the router information exchange level. With the advent of ATM networks, IP becomes yet another networking protocol to be transported and internetworked on a shared backbone. Frame relay is the backbone public service protocol used in many examples throughout this book, as it is one of the most popular publicly-used backbone protocols and easiest to understand short of IP.

It is very important to take into account the protocols passed over the backbone, even though they may be passed transparently. From the previous study of network protocols, it is known that routable protocols such as TCP/IP are the preferred WAN protocols, while protocols such as LAT, IBM SRT, and NetBIOS (NetBEUI) can only be bridged. In fact, most methods of passing bridged protocols involve IP encapsulation or translation bridging. Determine whether the protocols are operating half or full duplex. Half-duplex protocols generate large amounts of overhead because the sender has to wait for acknowledgments from the receiving station before more information can be sent. Thus, over half of the available bandwidth is wasted with turnarounds.

Many routing protocols such as RIP add extra overhead to the WAN through their constant exchange of routing table information. Routing protocols such as OSPF take up drastically less overhead (about 1 percent of RIP). This demonstrates the importance of minimizing and localizing the routing tables in each router. Some access designs will contain proprietary protocols within a local area. These instances show that the backbone designs should always attempt to use standard protocols for wide area networking.

21.1.3 Architecture and Technology

Usually the network backbone is either the same or one technology further advanced than the access network technology. IP, by far the most common backbone technology, is usually ubiquitous across the LAN and WAN. Technologies such as ATM are offering a common platform and architecture for the transport and interworking of almost all existing protocols and traffic types (i.e., private line, IP, FR, and SMDS services over an ATM backbone). Backbone designs should also be *faster* than the access devices, at least on a maximum burst, throughput, or utilization basis. Historically, the WAN has been *slower* than the LAN because multiple LANs were connected via point-to-point bridges. Circuits with speeds of 56 kbps and 1.544 Mbps could not keep up with multiple 10 Mbps and 16 Mbps LANs, even though the maximum throughput of these LANs was closer to 1–3 Mbps and 1–6 Mbps, respectively. Performance would degrade, file transfer would take longer over the WAN, and bottlenecks would occur. While the user could always provision higher-speed IP-based circuits, new WAN technologies such as SMDS and ATM have broken that bottleneck to provide the high-capacity backbone bandwidth users require. Their new challenge is to keep up with LAN technologies like 100 Mbps Ethernet and FDDI.

Long-term planning is easier with the backbone than with access, because capacity additions and technology changes can be more easily migrated into the network in layers. Access, configuration, protocol, service, and technology changes will require replacement of the core switching equipment. This is one of the primary reasons many businesses are building access networks and using public switched-data services as the backbone. Why pay for the technology and be concerned with keeping it current when the network provider will incur most of the costs of remaining technologically current? Technological change is accelerating, moving far too quickly to make heavy investments in any one technology. Figure 21.2 illustrates this concept of a layered migratory backbone, where "user land" is where the users reside and the successive rings represent the backbone layer and then future successive access layers where backbone technology slowly migrates closer to the user. ATM breaks this trend by offering both a LAN and MAN solution.

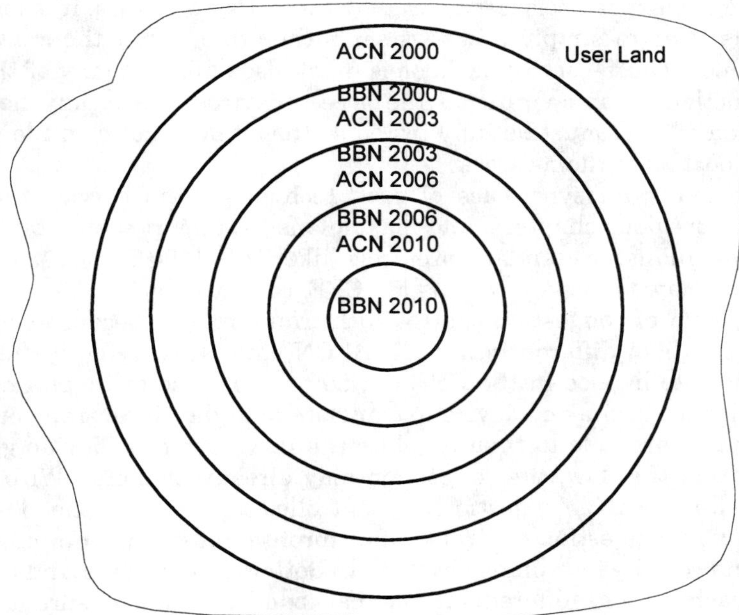

Figure 21.2 Access and Backbone Network Layer Migration Concept

Another prime consideration when designing backbones is whether to build a connection-oriented or a connectionless service and then to determine their impact on each other if layered. Connectionless and connection-oriented services each offer their own advantages in efficiency and throughput, depending on data unit (i.e., frame) sizes, traffic type (voice, data, and video), node-to-node overhead involved, and the delays inherent in setting up a connection. The primary concern is optimizing the packet, frame, or cell size to ensure that the amount of overhead generated is at a minimum in order to guarantee the required quality of service.

21.1.4 Features, Functions, and Services

The features and functions of the backbone will primarily depend upon the technology chosen. The real benefits derived from using a network backbone are the public-network value-added, switched-services available. These services include circuit switching, packet switching, TCP/IP, FR, SMDS, and ATM. Many of these services reside on the backbone and are fed by a user premises access node such as a bridge, router, switch, PAD, or FRAD. With these newer ultra-high-speed services offered by the IXCs and LECs, it is less expensive for the user to simply access them rather than build their own corporate backbone. These service backbones must also support many of the features and functions that operate on the access devices. Also, any new feature or function offered must be fully tested so that it does not degrade or affect the access portion of the network.

Remember the many idiosyncrasies of each technology and service that were presented in previous chapters, and make plans to support them. Make sure devices follow industry standard protocols, like RFC 1490 for multiprotocol over frame relay transport, to assure CPE compatibility. Take, for example, the problem of congestion control with frame relay. Because each vendor implements them differently, FECN, BECN, and DE may be ineffective if there is no intelligence in the CPE device to make use of them, or if there is no intelligence in the end device to translate to higher-level transmission protocols, which are able to then regulate the flow. Even if they do get around to regulating the flow, the congestion may already be gone. With a TCP/IP private line WAN, congestion is controlled strictly by the TCP protocol. Issues like congestion control in multiprotocol environments must be planned for and contingency plans developed. Bottom line: understand the deficiencies of each service offered on the backbone and make sure the customer and user also understand them.

21.2 BACKBONE NETWORK CAPACITY REQUIRED

Backbone capacity is typically measured by ingress and egress bandwidth, backbone bandwidth between switches, processing power, and port density of each switch. Node type is selected based on the amount of local, remote, and pass-through traffic processing, along with the service type required. Capacity is measured by the required amount of ports for all access devices, trunks to other backbone nodes, and the bandwidth on the trunks between those ports. Backbone nodes are designed within utilization and loading parameters similar to access node design. Once the access loading is determined, the total backbone capacity can be found. It is then up to the designer to apply good judgment (and a good design tool) for each backbone node design — this ensures that the loading can handle both normal operating conditions and a single (or multiple) node or link failure analysis. Remember that these design rules are approximations and the design of a complex backbone, like those built with ATM technology, will require a much more detailed study of traffic types and patterns.

21.2.1 Backbone Node Selection

First, determine what percentage of the traffic will remain in the access design and what needs to be passed over to the backbone. This is found by interpreting the traffic matrix one step further: perform a "backbone traffic matrix" in the same manner as the access matrix, but this time instead of user-application traffic, consider the access-node traffic passed to the backbone. Select a starting location for each backbone node you think may be required. Then determine what percentage of traffic passed to each backbone node goes in and back out of the same backbone node. Finally, determine how much traffic enters the backbone node and leaves to go to another backbone node.

Figure 21.3 shows an example of typical traffic patterns for a 12-node network with single trunk access nodes. Notice that each access node is trunked to a single backbone node. Forty percent of the user traffic remains local (to and back out of the same *access* node), 30 percent of the traffic remains within the same state or province (to and back out of the same *backbone* node), and 30 percent of the traffic must transit the backbone. Now, take this one step further. Assume that each access node is dual-trunked: one trunk to two separate backbone nodes. This is shown in Figure 21.4. The same amount of traffic accesses each access and backbone node; however, only half the previous amount actually transits the backbone links. This takes the utilization of the backbone links down to 15 percent and allows either fewer links to be used (reducing the design by two backbone-to-backbone trunks) or it keeps the links for even greater diversity and redundancy. These considerations will be used together with topology styles defined later in this chapter to choose the number and location of the backbone nodes and trunks.

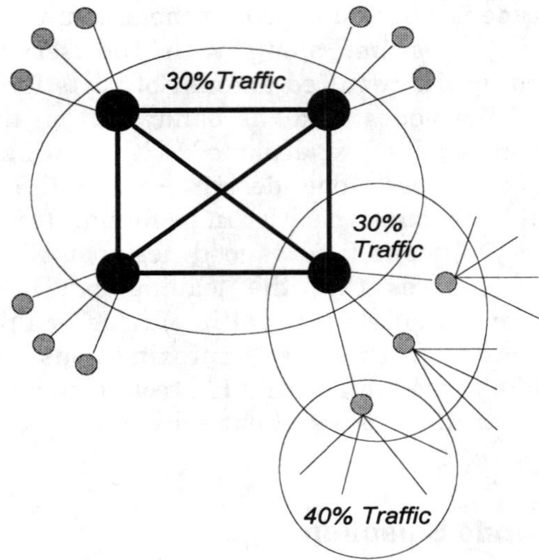

Figure 21.3 Typical Traffic Patterns — Single-Trunk Access Nodes

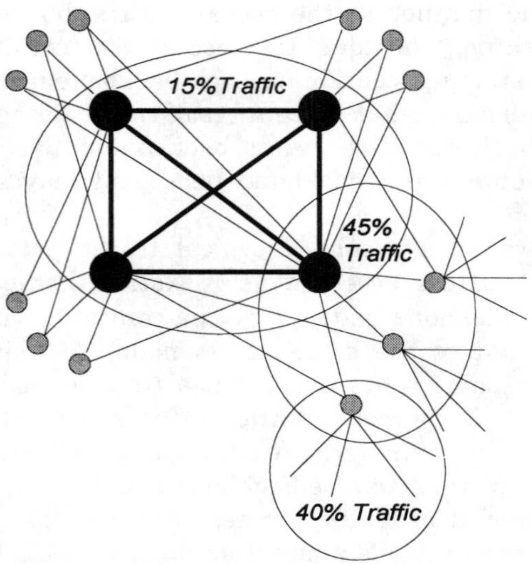

Figure 21.4 Typical Traffic Patterns — Dual-Trunked Access Nodes

21.2.2 Utilization, Loading Factors, and Anticipating Failures

The same calculations from Chapter 20 for the access network can now be used for the backbone network to calculate node and link utilization and loading. These calculations are made for trunks into the backbone nodes (labeled as "user ports" in Chapter 20) and the trunks between the backbone nodes (labeled as "trunks" in Chapter 20). Yet these calculations will be more precise because the traffic patterns between the access nodes are already known or approximated, and thus the backbone nodal design will be more accurate (or even less if the access design was calculated incorrectly!). The theory here is that if the initial calculations were off, the errors will be multiplied in the backbone design. Also, at this stage, loading factors should be in the same units of measurement, for example: packets, frames, or cells per second.

It is easier to change the utilization and loading of the backbone if required. It is much harder to change utilization and loading on access nodes (as it directly affects the user). A good design will accommodate for change in both. Performance problems can also be isolated and fixed more easily on a backbone network than on the access side, where user traffic can be temporarily rerouted around the "construction area". It is also easier to throw more capacity (bandwidth or circuits) at the backbone. These changes require the point at which additional capacity is needed in the nodes and trunks. Response times at the beginning of service must be good and not degrade over time.

Some styles of backbone designs provide for high reliability during failure conditions by overbuilding the network and providing excess capacity at each network node. The practical limit for designs of this type should be 125 percent to 140 percent of average load conditions. Anything more is overkill and would be very expensive. In these scenarios, the calculations for node failure are the same as those for link failure defined in Chapter 20. Again, a good design tool can help determine loading and utilization requirements, along with failure analysis.

21.2.3 Total Backbone Capacity

Given the backbone-access traffic patterns, backbone capacity can be calculated in two ways. It can be calculated as the total capacity of the backbone network with a chosen number of nodes as a given, or it can be calculated by the total number of backbone nodes required, given the capacity required. The next set of calculations performs the first method, and the second is left to the reader (a simple manipulation of formulae).

Take the case where users are single-trunked to a network backbone, once a topology configuration is decided upon, and if the number of nodes in the backbone N and capacity of each node c is known, the total capacity of the backbone T based on the type of traffic it will carry can be determined. There are four major types of traffic patterns:

1. Most or all traffic that enters a node leaves the same node and does not transit any other backbone node. There are times when a majority of, or *all,* traffic that enters a node will leave the same node, as shown in Figure 21.5. In the case where most of the traffic that enters leaves the same backbone node, the backbone trunking from this node to other backbone nodes is minimal; many good network designs operate by this concept, where the backbone nodal trunks are primarily used for backup and redundancy. The formula for calculating the total backbone capacity in this arrangement is: $T = (N)(c)$. Figure 21.6 shows a four-node backbone network with 12 access nodes. Each backbone node can process up to 50 units (packets/frames/cells) per second (UPS). For this network, $T = (4)(50) = 200$ UPS.

2. Traffic originating on a backbone node is transmitted symmetrically to every other backbone node. This is the case for broadcast or public networks. The backbone nodes' trunks are primarily used for switching and the links between them are heavily used. The formula for calculating the total backbone capacity in this arrangement is: $T = (N+1)(c)/2$. Figure 21.7 shows a four-node backbone network with 12 access nodes. Each backbone node processes 50 UPS. For this network, $T = (4+1)(50)/2 = 125$ UPS.

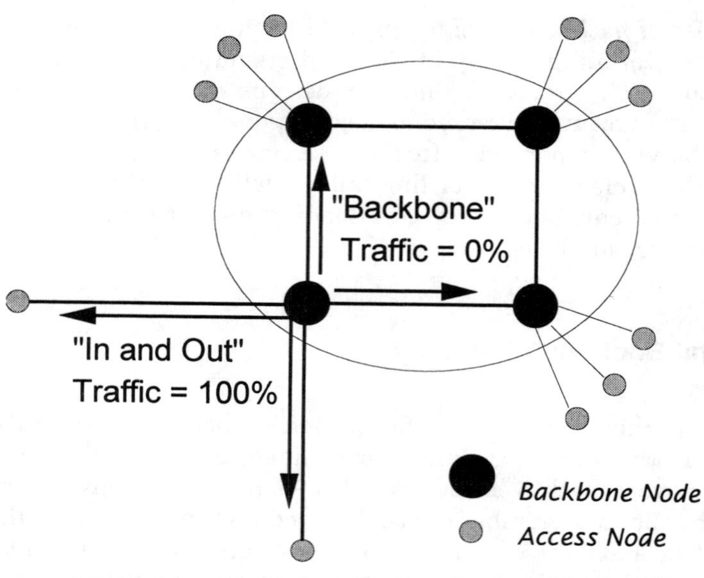

Figure 21.5 Backbone with 100 percent Traffic Remaining with Access BB Node

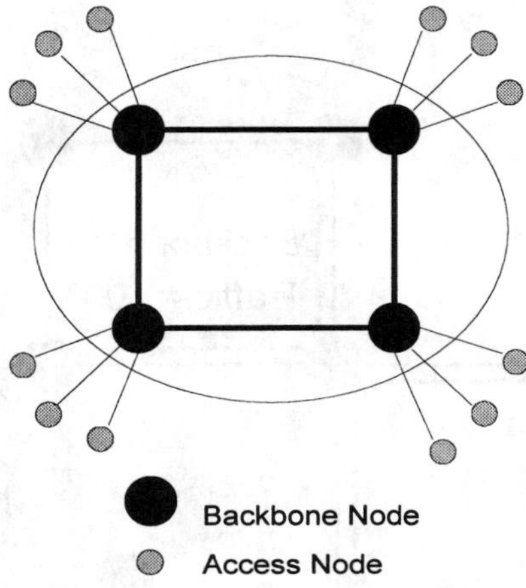

Figure 21.6 Backbone with Single-Trunk Access Nodes

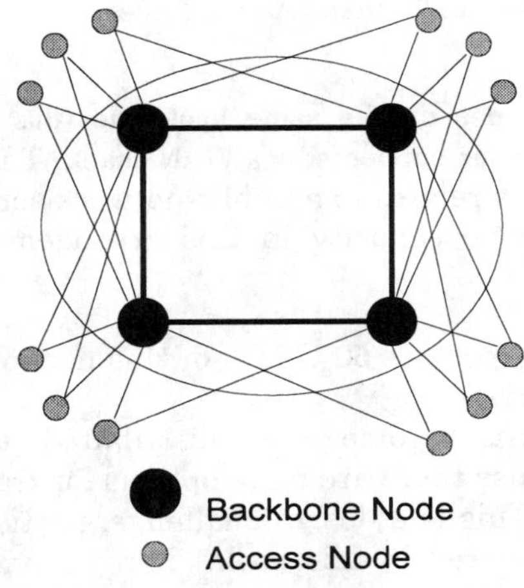

Figure 21.7 Backbone with Dual-Trunked Access Nodes

3. All traffic patterns are asymmetrical and are divided into user classes such as terminal-to-host and LAN-to-LAN (IP) communications. The backbone nodes' trunks are again primarily used for switching or routing and the link usage varies. The formula for calculating the total backbone capacity in this arrangement is $T = (N^2)(c)/(2N{-}1)$. Again, refer to Figure 21.7. Each backbone node processes 50 UPS. For this network, $T = (4^2)(50)/((2)(4)\text{-}1) =$ 114 UPS.

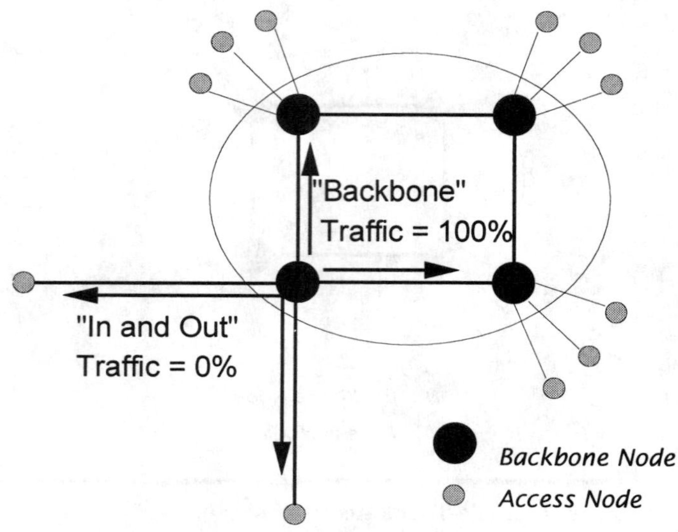

Figure 21.8 Backbone with Dual-Trunked Access Nodes

4. Users never talk to nodes on the same backbone (this is a multiple backbone scenario with backbone nodes connected via WAN links). The applications for this are varied, but again this relates to a public-network service. The formula for calculating total backbone capacity in this arrangement is: $T = (N)(c)/2$. Refer to Figure 21.8.

Each backbone node processes 50 UPS. For this network, $T = (4)(50)/2 = 100$ UPS.

As the traffic patterns become more distributed, the network capacity decreases. This is because there are more options for traffic to use the limited bandwidth resources. This is a design challenge, particularly with the next-generation networks covered in this book. Many novice network designers are finding that the only way to add extra capacity to this type of network is to overengineer from the beginning. Remember that these calculations are approximations only, and should be confirmed through a good design tool.

21.2.4 Route Determination

WAN elements such as circuit, packet, frame, and cell switches; bridges; routers; and other associated devices can all route or switch data based on preexisting physical routes over access and backbone links. In IP the exact route is dynamic and not predefined. In FR, these routes are either static or dynamic and either preprogrammed (as with permanent virtual circuits) or assigned dynamically (as SVCs). Some are routed "best way" as long as they get to the required destination. This choice of routing is accomplished node-to-node, hop-by-hop, and is based on a variety of variables (hop count, cost, bandwidth, priority, quality of line). Once these variables have been defined, the designer should document and keep consistent route definitions. For example, the priority of traffic flow may be (from low to high) copper, coax, short-range microwave radio, VSAT, wireless communications, or fiber optics. After these priorities are met, traffic will be routed via the minimum hop count. Most devices offer some form of prioritization by transmission facilities or physical path (e.g., by WAN port).

Do not let the users control the routing on the backbone network. A prime example is the throughput class in X.25 packet switching. Users could misuse this parameter and cause loss of network control. Another example is the SMDS throughput class, which should be defined by the backbone.

Some technologies like TCP/IP allow the traffic to route around network problems or congestion. The user is then notified of the condition, requiring the transport protocol to throttle back the traffic flow or use a different route. Some technologies like FR use FECN and BECN bits to notify users of congestion. The user can then reroute, limit the traffic flow, or ignore the notification. Other technologies such as ATM and X.25 can lose a trunk between backbone switches and the backbone network will automatically route individual packets or cells around the node failure transparent to the user (except for the loss of the packet or cell, which may be noticed by an ATM user but not an X.25 or TCP/IP user).

21.2.5 Future Capacity

User requirements for bandwidth can increase from 25 to 250 percent on the average annually (number of users, number of segments, and bandwidth required), and therefore extra capacity should be built into the backbone. Loading factors should be low early in the life of the network, and the network should have the capability to quickly add capacity when and where required. Again, this means both increased processing power and extra trunking bandwidth capacity at each backbone site. When turning up a new service, make sure that this extra capacity is available. For example, in frame relay, measure all the CIRs of each user input to the switch, calculate the total burst that may reach the backbone, and determine if the backbone can handle that burst or drop traffic. Then plan on providing more than what is required based on the growth rate as defined above. If you follow the design practice of building a backbone with a higher level of technology and larger bandwidth pipes than the access actually requires, the design will prove effective.

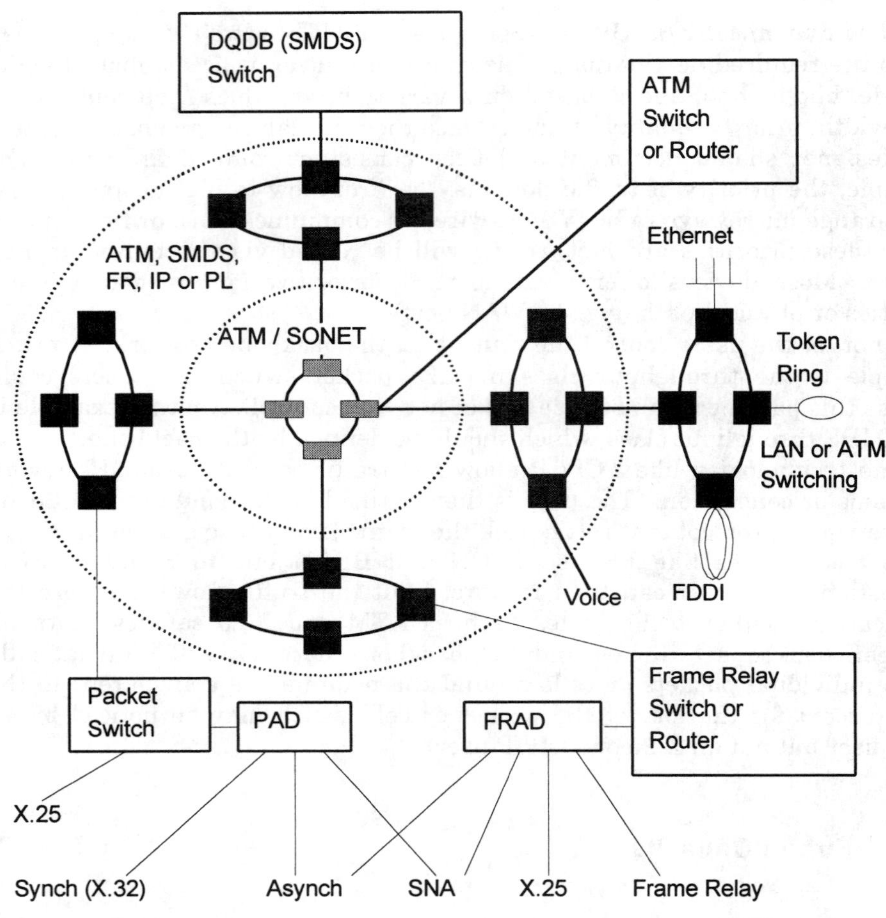

Figure 21.9 Future Data and Computer Communications Network

What will the future data communications network look like? Figure 21.9 shows a possible scenario. Notice that all voice and data ride over this network, and the traditional voice network hierarchy of the LECs and IXCs disappears and is replaced by an all-digital data-access network built upon a SONET transport medium and, possibly, an ATM-based infrastructure. Also, notice the layering of the network, which allows for expanding (adding) and contracting (reducing) layers of technology. Access can directly connect to any layer of the network, even to the ATM/SONET core.

21.3 STYLES OF TOPOLOGIES

Backbone topologies come in two styles — those planned and those that just grow. All private and public data networks seem to fit these stereotypes. Private networks, especially LANs that grow into MANs and then into WANs, tend to take on very asymmetrical shapes, with definable communities of interest. On the other hand, public networks respond to user needs and are often designed largely on the procedures outlined in this book. It is easier to plan a backbone design and then build the network than to try and modify an existing mesh of WAN connectivity. Either way, the backbone network topology should be a function of the user applications, the access-network topology, traffic volume, and range and profile of connectivity (local to global). Do not cement yourself to a single technology or a single protocol suite. Now we examine some of the more popular backbone topologies and the designs that go with them.

21.3.1 Star

The *star* design, also called *hub-and-spoke*, is similar to the star topology, where there is a central node serving as the hub node and all other nodes are connected via point-to-point circuits to the central node. All communications pass through the central node. A minimum of N-1 links are required to support N node(s) including the hub. This star style is often used in an environment such as a LAN hub or ATM switch/hub. The central node is often a multiport, scalable device that can handle large amounts of concentration, bridging, switching, or routing. While this configuration provides a maximum of two hops, it is unreliable and susceptible to an entire network failure when the hub node fails. However, despite star-network inefficiencies, this type of management has certain advantages. Figure 21.10 illustrates a star-style backbone configuration.

A special version of the star topology is the distributed star. This is typically used in LAN environments that use hubs as concentrators and tie the hubs together. Figure 21.11 shows an example of the distributed star topology linking three hubs each with three Ethernet LANs. This topology is also called a star-wired ring.

21.3.2 Loop

The loop backbone design is similar to the loop or ring topology. Each network node is connected to two other network nodes. A minimum of N links are required for N nodes. This style is often used for distributed networks where nodes primarily talk to local nodes or point-to-point communications are required over short distances (or cannot operate over extended distances such as MAN links). There is no maximum to the number of hops across this network, but it is reliable up to the point of two link failures, which would then separate the network into two pieces. Capacity planning is difficult with loop topologies, and upgrades are difficult if the traffic patterns are not symmetric and consistent across different access nodes. The DQDB loop configuration is one example of this backbone topology. Figure 21.12 illustrates the loop style topology.

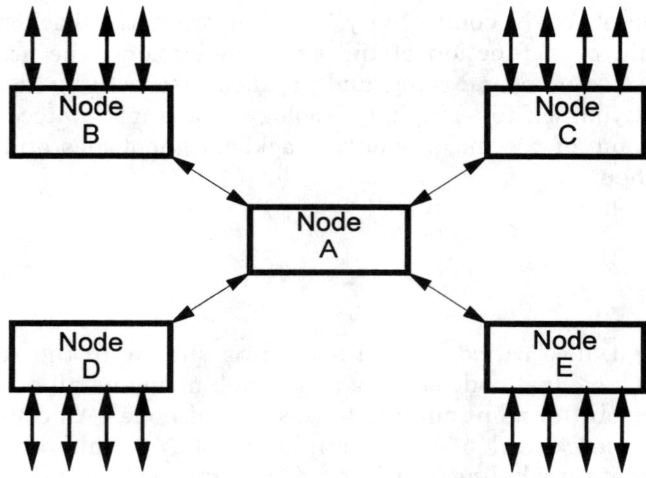

Figure 21.10 Star Backbone Topology

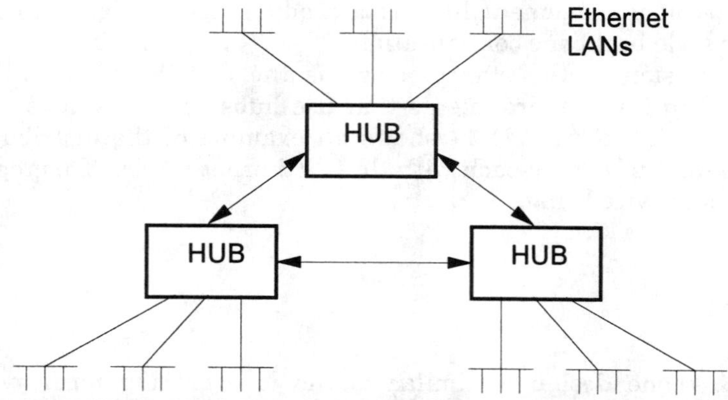

Figure 21.11 Distributed Star Backbone Topology

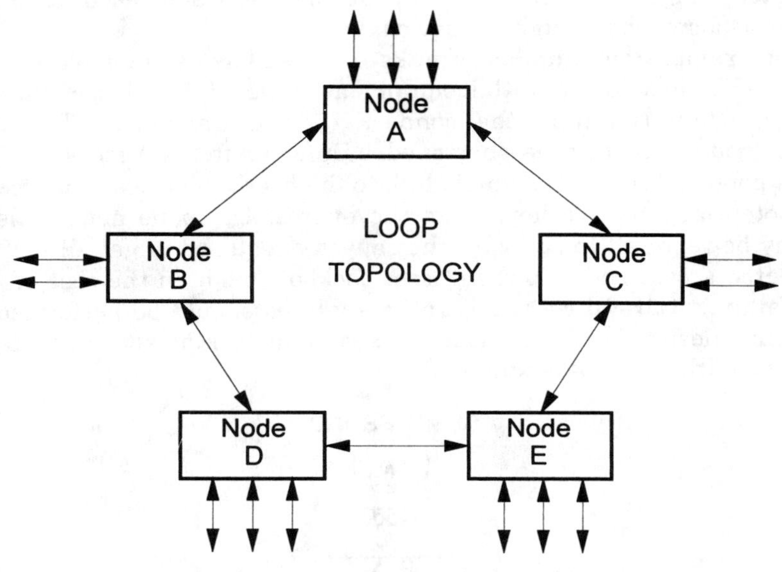

Figure 21.12 Loop Backbone Topology

21.3.3 Meshed and Fully Meshed

While the meshed network was discussed in Chapter 5, the degree to which a mesh is built depends upon the hardware and software expense of the ports, incremental cost of the links, network resource availability, and the amount of reliability and redundancy required. The number of links required for a fully meshed design is $N(N-1)/2$. The number of links required drastically increases with the number of network nodes (thus pointing to the advantages of virtual private network services like frame relay). Obviously, a fully meshed network is highly desirable, but often cost prohibitive and rarely required. Again, design tools have the capability of modeling various scenarios of meshing. Figure 21.13 shows both a partially meshed and fully meshed backbone.

21.3.4 Daisy-Chained Access Nodes

Consider, as an example of daisy-chained nodes, the packet network depicted in Figure 21.14a. All network-access devices are dual-homed to two high-capacity backbone switches. While this provides for high availability, it wastes bandwidth if the applications are regional or their processing is distributed. Figure 21.14b shows an alternative, where each access device also acts as a switch through a daisy chain.

In this example, the number of links required has been decreased from 54 to 32. This has lowered the equipment costs of the larger centralized switches, while retaining the connectivity requirements. The distance between nodes will also be shortened. Unfortunately, these gains are not without potential costs. If a single link to the backbone is lost, an access node could potentially be five hops from the nearest backbone node. Also, each link may be required to carry all the capacity required to get all traffic from the isolated access nodes to the closest backbone node in the case of a single trunk failure. Careful cost and traffic analyses should be performed before using this design, as it almost always adds complexity and decreases reliability, with little cost reduction.

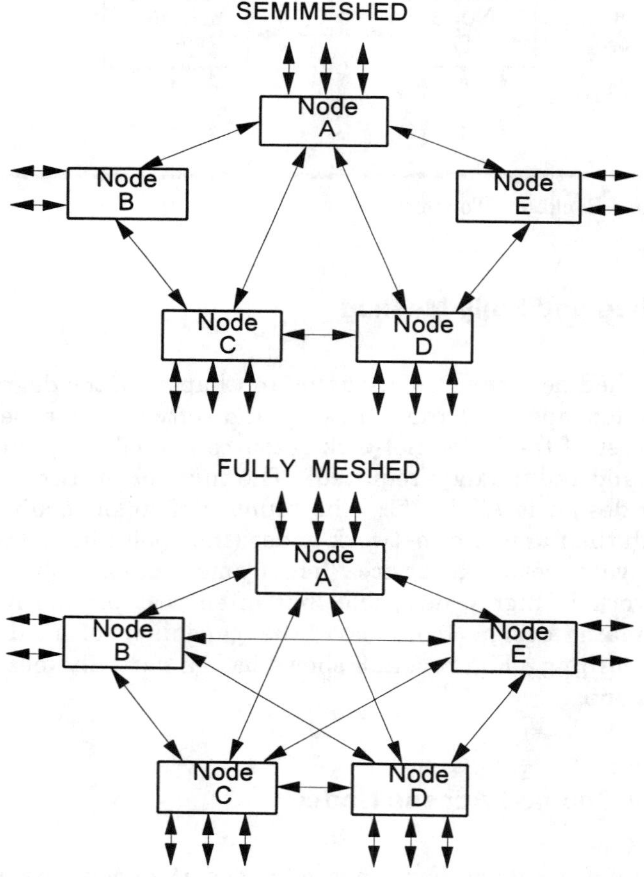

Figure 21.13 Semimeshed and Fully Meshed Backbone Topologies

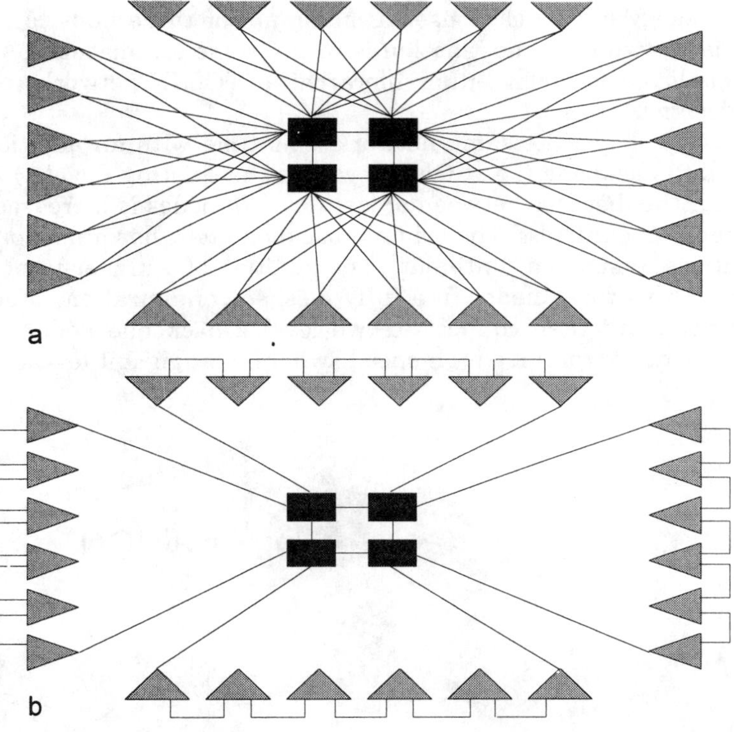

Figure 21.14 Daisy Chain Access to Backbone Network

21.3.5 Backbones within Backbones

In the last section it was assumed that the location of network backbone nodes was dictated by the requirements of the access nodes. In many cases, however, the backbone nodes and their topology are separate from the access-node topology. In fact, many network providers often build multiple backbones within backbones in a hierarchical nature. This approach has both advantages and disadvantages, as we will soon see.

Figure 21.15 shows an example of a network where 10 access nodes receive user CPE traffic, and the design is based on DS1 and DS3 circuits. Each LATA is served by two access nodes. These network access nodes are configured in a loop-access topology, where each access node is connected to two other access nodes. These access nodes are then, in turn, connected to two different backbone nodes. Up to this point, all circuits are of DS1 speed. The backbone nodes are also configured in a loop backbone topology and provide a majority of the inter-LATA high-bandwidth transport. The backbone provides high-capacity DS3 circuits between backbone nodes. This network topology allows each user a maximum of three hops to get to any destination, or two if the destination is in the same or adjacent LATA. This topology could be used for either hierarchical TCP/IP networks or flat FR network designs.

Figure 21.16 shows the same network, this time with an additional high-speed (level 2) backbone (i.e., SONET) within the existing (level 1) backbone. Assume that the distance between access (level 0) nodes is increased, and the LATAs are now countries. The original backbone now has a network node at each country and spans a continent. The addition of a higher-level backbone will be built with three nodes in a fully meshed configuration. Each level 1 backbone node will then connect to two level 2 backbone nodes. The new level 2 backbone can provide high-speed switching at gigabit levels.

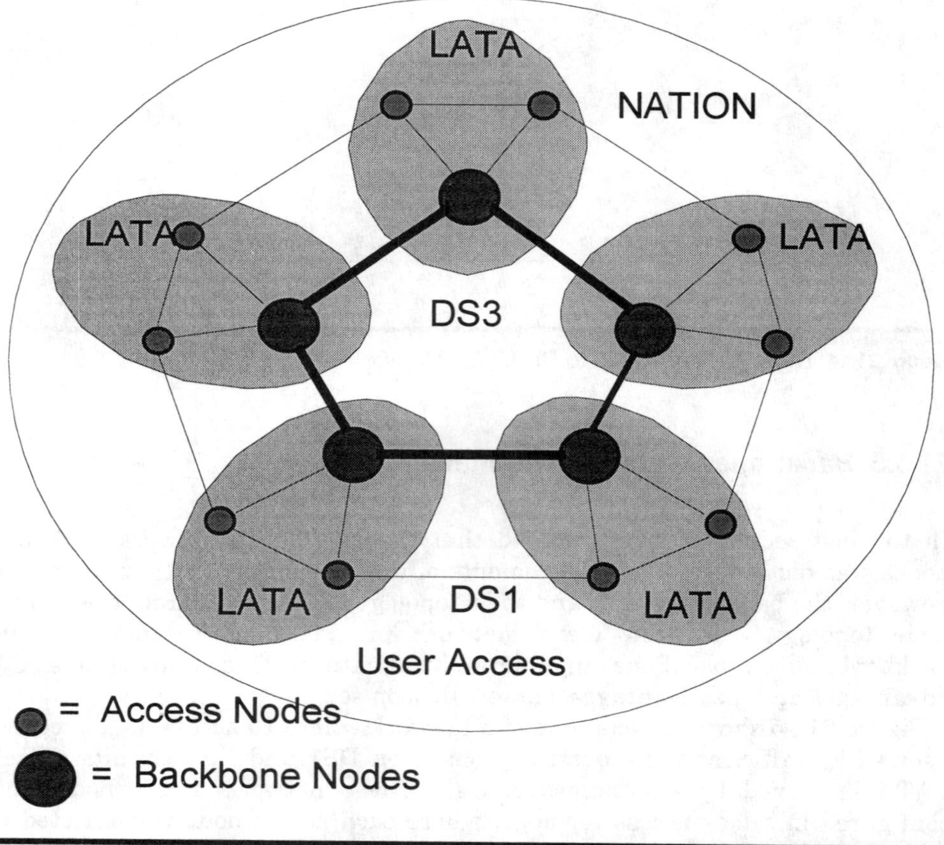

Figure 21.15 Single-Access and Single-Backbone Network Configuration

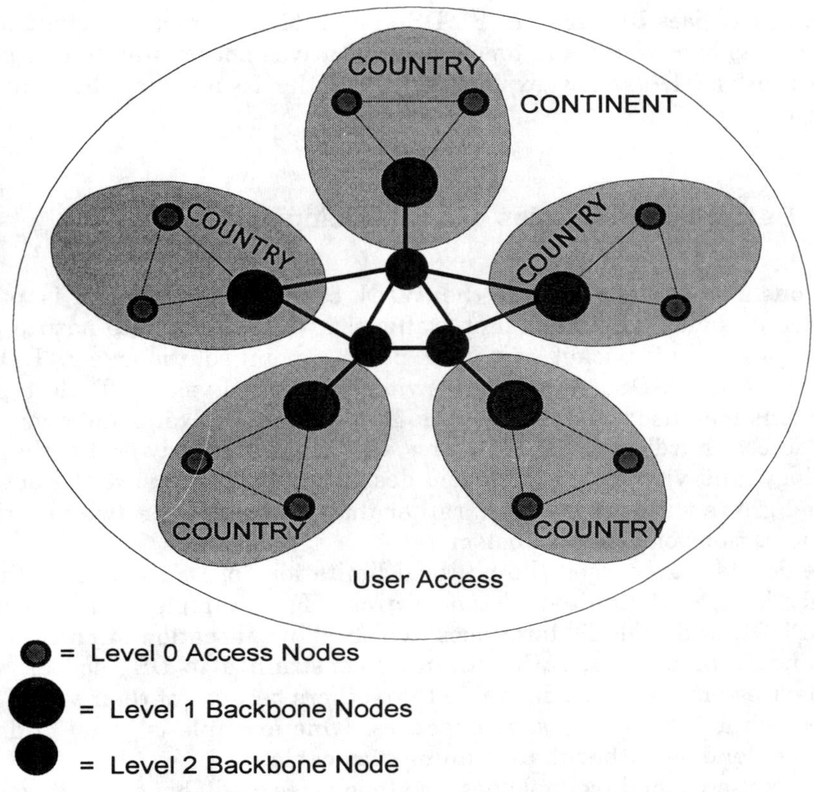

Figure 21.16 Single-Access and Multiple-Backbone Network Configuration

From this analysis, it is plain that networks are built using hierarchical structures offering not only redundancy and availability, but also a reduced hop count (and the processing delay that goes along with it) and an increased speed of traffic that transits long distances across the network.

21.4 BACKBONE TOPOLOGY STRATEGIES

As discussed in the last chapter, there are two styles of connecting local LANs: hierarchical and ubiquitous (or flat) access. Now we will look at the entire WAN, specifically enterprise backbone topology strategies. The enterprise backbone provides not only interconnection of the departmental subnets, but also LAN/MAN/WAN interconnectivity through routers or switched networks (e.g., IP, SMDS, and ATM).

As users require more and more bandwidth, dedicated-access facilities' bandwidth begins to fill up. WAN bottlenecks typically occur in the access facilities. Services like IP, FR, SMDS and ATM offer more efficient utilization of access bandwidth and topology alternatives not found in many private line networks. Let's now explore a few of the issues that drive network topologies.

21.4.1 Desirable Topologies per Technology

With constant bit-rate traffic, the WAN connection of choice is often a dedicated or switched circuit. For traffic of a variable bit-rate nature, WAN technologies include packet switching, point-to-point solutions (e.g., HDLC or PPP), IP, FR, SMDS, ATM, and switched-data services. Both types of connections may use switches, bridges, routers, multiplexers, and a variety of other access hardware. Combining the right topology with the right technology, and vice versa, will avoid design flaws. Make sure the device so designed grows with the network, rather than limiting it through proprietary implementations of older technologies.

Some devices can exceed the physical limitations of DS1 and DS3 circuits, but only in a local (limited distance) area. For example, routers can use HSSI, FDDI, and SONET interfaces, which allow allocation of bandwidth in Mbps and Gbps chunks, rather than be constrained to DS1 speeds. Also, some devices may be more desirable than others because of their value-added services, while others may save expenses. One example is using bridges as distance extenders rather than running coax cable.

For packet-switched technologies, the topologies available are quite flexible. IP is the most flexible, allowing almost any potential configuration. In FR, all links are point-to-point unless they ride another switched-service platform. Also consider using integrated circuit- and packet-switched equipment, which provides good integration of packet- and circuit-switching capabilities.

The next generation of backbones will most likely be composed of ATM DXCs and switches, with the capability to transport and interwork IP, FR, and SMDS services. These devices together with SONET switches will be used to cross connect and switch electrical speeds to optical speeds in the gigabit range. In fact, many MAN architectures consist of SONET fiber-based ringed transmission facilities.

21.4.2 Requirements Drive the Topology

One method for designing the topology of a network is to add the links that are absolutely required first, and proceed to add more links until all possible links are added where capacity is required for data flow. The designer then eliminates links and combines traffic over other existing links based on many factors such as shortest path, link cost, and quality of facilities. This method can also be performed by a design tool. Always review all technologies and routing algorithms available, and do not confine yourself to a single transport technology or protocol during the design process.

This method is called *shortest path*. Figure 21.17a shows six links that have been added in order of the *largest* flow required to the *smallest* flow required (links 1 through 6, respectively). Figure 21.17b shows the selection of links 1, 2, 3, 4, and 5 to remain, and 6 to be deleted because it was too expensive not to route the traffic through node B (over links 1 and 3) rather than directly from node A to node D and vice versa. Figure 21.17c shows the final iteration where link 2 was eliminated due to only analog transmission facilities being available (traffic from B to C was rerouted from B to D to C and vice versa) and link 5 was eliminated due to its excessive distance (and traffic rerouted from A to B to D to C and vice versa). While this is a simplistic view of a network-topology design, it does provide some insight into the method of selection for topologies and aggregation of backbone links.

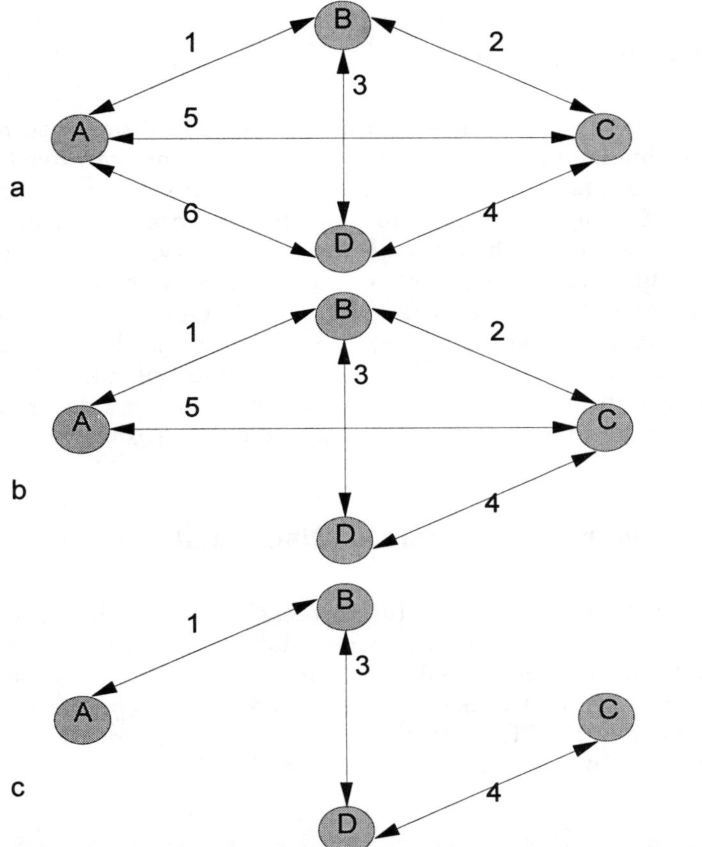

Figure 21.17 Shortest Path Design Methodology

Never lose sight of the original user requirements during the backbone design. Understanding the effects that your backbone design will have on user applications is critical in optimizing the backbone design. This is a two-way process. Note that high-bandwidth access and backbone transport may not be required if the application can stand a bit of delay during times of congestion. But, if the opposite is true, and a backbone is designed with too few links, the extra network transport delay incurred across the backbone may have an adverse effect on the application. When signing up for a carrier-offered service, the user needs to fully understand the carrier's access and backbone design and its potential effects upon user applications. For example, if a carrier is quoting a 500-millisecond total delay across its public data network, how does this affect your file-transfer sessions? Is the delay variable? Will this delay, when added to your access and egress delay to the carrier's service, affect your applications? These questions and many more from previous chapters must be asked of the carriers.

21.4.3 Hybrid Topologies

Many users today mix both leased or dedicated facilities with packet, frame, and cell technologies. Hybrid networks that employ both fixed and switched topologies are common. Switched services are often used as backup to leased facilities. If designing a private network, make sure it can be integrated (hybridized) with a public network-switched services. Public and private network hybrids allow control of critical resources to be retained while taking advantage of public services functionality and pricing. When designing a hybrid backbone network, attempt to keep all speeds fairly constant, and beware of bottleneck bandwidth points. Beware of multiple encapsulation schemes in hybrid networks, and understand that similar network devices must often be used at both network ingress and egress points.

21.4.4 Topology of the Future — Distributed Design

The primary feature of distributed processing networks is the placement of the intelligence to process and switch data into the access devices, rather than the backbone devices. As seen previously, most backbone designs are either point-to-point trunks or are used as access to a public network service. Services such as IP, FR, SMDS and ATM offer efficiencies to networks with distributed designs, so investigate the use of each.

21.5 NETWORK MANAGEMENT

Network management is much easier to administer at the network level than at the access concentrator or even user-device level. A single WAN management platform could manage the addressing, bandwidth-management (e.g., congestion control, throughput classes, synchronization), administration, and performance-management activities. Network management for the entire network is covered in detail later in Chapter 23.

21.6 TOTAL NETWORK TIMING

Timing is always an important aspect of each design with any technology whose success relies on error-free synchronization. Timing is also important between the CPE and network-access devices. External timing (such as from a dedicated clock source) should be used when possible, because internal equipment timing sources, while accurate to the originating device, may not be accurate to all network elements. The higher the transmission speed, the more critical timing becomes. Timing problems can cause line interference, data unit slips which lead to loss of data, interruption of service, and a general decrease in the reliability of transmission.

Clock sources are rated in Stratum levels from 1 to 5, where Stratum 1 is the *most* accurate and 5 the *least* accurate. Always use a clock source as accurate as possible for all equipment. Use internal timing sources only when an external Stratum source is not available. Analyze timing sources on a regular basis and always look for potential timing loops (a device that provides a clock source and receives back its same clock as its own source). Some Stratum 1 examples include the Basic Synchronous Reference Frequency (BSRF) and the DoD Loran-C (Global positioning system). Clock sources rated Stratum 1 assure no more than one slip per day. Note that clocking sources can be regenerated.

21.7 TUNING THE NETWORK

Network tuning should be performed at the same time you are designing the backbone-network design, as well as at specific intervals in the lifetime of the network. Four specific areas, when tuned, will increase the efficiency and throughout of both the access and backbone design. These include optimizing packet, frame, and cell size, limiting the segmentation of user data by lower-level protocols, decreasing the overall port-to-port transfer delay, and using window size changes to flag potential network degradation. There are also tuning parameters specific to each protocol, such as TCP window sizes when using IP, and CIR size when using frame relay, that are explored. These tuning parameters do not include the many hardware, software, and protocol tuning parameters covered in previous chapters.

21.7.1 Optimizing Packet/Frame/Cell Size

In packet-, frame-, and cell-switched networks there is a tradeoff between large and small packet/frame/cell sizes (we shall refer to "packets" from this point on). When small packets are used (and each packet has a small amount of data), the amount of overhead increases. This causes a disproportionate amount of overhead generated versus data passed, and the data throughput of the line degrades. Remember the definition of throughput — how much *data* a user can pass across a given circuit or device. Small packets have the advantage of better response time and less data corruption due to errors, and therefore a reduced chance of retransmission.

Consider the case of larger packet sizes. A higher throughput can be achieved by placing larger blocks of data within each packet and thus creating a larger packet. While this improves throughput, there is a point where excessive retransmissions due to lost packets, errors, or buffer and transmission delays will cause an actual degradation in throughput.

Figure 21.18 shows a bell-shaped curve depicting the phenomenon of small versus large packet sizes based on achievable throughput to assist the designer in selection of the ideal packet size.

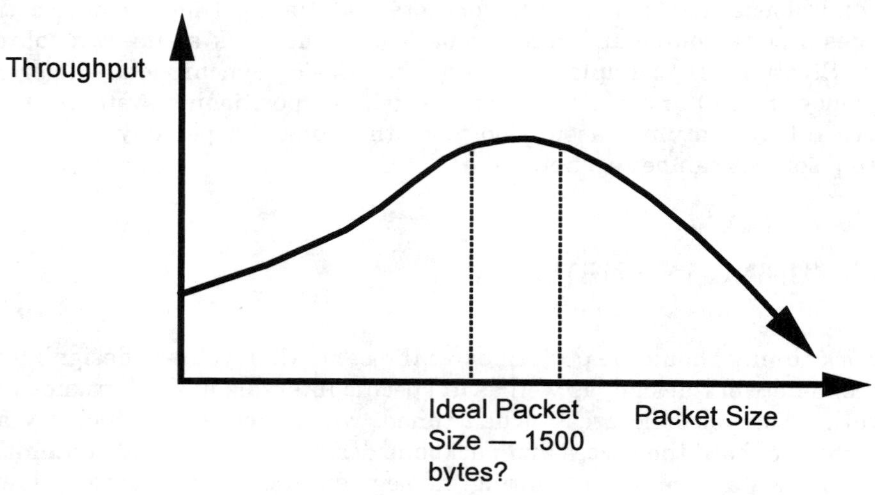

Figure 21.18 Ideal Packet Size Curve

This example uses an IP packet network, where the throughput decreases with very small packets (too much overhead) and with very large packets. As an example, IP over FR begins to segment packetized user files of less than 1500 bytes in length, and the closer the packet size is to the 64 kbyte maximum, the worse the fragmentation. This example does not show the effect of increased use of buffers and the delay imposed on the transmission for large packet sizes. In the example, the optimal packet size across a frame relay network would be around 1500 bytes.

Packet size tuning is a balancing act, where additional factors influencing the size include:

* How long it takes to read in a packet
* Buffer space taken by held packets
* Packets per second (pps) dropped
* Time to forward packet to next device or destination
* Mix of protocols to bridge/route

In addition, each technology and service has its own operational factors such as frame relay, where, in some implementations, each node must read in the entire frame before transmitting. In this case, midsize and smaller frames process faster through the network. The best method for achieving optimal packet size is to tune the network based on the performance observed and refer to a trending analysis or design tool for accuracy.

21.7.2 Limiting Protocol Segmentation

Try to reduce the amount of segmentation at both the user file-transfer level and at the access and backbone-technology transport level. Let's review the IP example. When IP traffic is sent across an IP backbone, segmentation is not performed and high throughput can be achieved. When IP addressing is used on higher-level protocols with large file or message sizes and sent across a FR network, segmentation occurs. Take the example of an NFS file of 6000 bytes that is encapsulated within 1500-byte IP packets. Each frame is cut up into four data units of 1500 bytes each and encapsulated with the IP header and then sent across a FR network. This fragmentation causes even more overhead in the transmission. X.25, with an average packet size of 128 bytes, could add an exorbitant amount of overhead to this file transfer. Ethernet has a maximum packet size of 1500 bytes. Thus, when many layers of encapsulation are encountered across the network, packets may have to be broken down at each new protocol level and decrease throughput.

21.7.3 Port-to-Port Data Transfer Delay

If data is routed at a portion of the maximum data rate, such as 12,600 PPS of a maximum 14,880 PPS (of an Ethernet LAN), the throughput is down to 85 percent, or 15 percent overhead is introduced by the device. This delay becomes more appreciable the larger the file size. Much of this delay and overhead depends on internal architecture and software protocol handling of the device. Actually, large file transfers should not use the minimal-size packets for which the 14,840 PPS figure applies, but much larger packets for higher data throughput. Many devices implement multiple ports per interface card, thus reducing this effect. Also, the higher the bus speed, the faster the data rate between interface boards and the central (or distributed) processor(s). Most types of equipment now have very low port-to-port transfer delays, typically on the order of a few milliseconds.

21.7.4 Window Sizes

Window sizes can be tuned at each level of the X.25 packet-switched network, or at the network layer (i.e., TCP) portion of the protocol stack (usually in the user or access device). These windows provide transmission-flow control. The window size determines how many packets can be outstanding in the network before an acknowledgment is received from the last unacknowledged packet sent. This procedure is fully explained in Chapter 8. In packet switching, high-error lines should use a window size of 2 and low-error full-duplex lines should use a window size of 7. TCP, on the other hand, will adjust its window size automatically based on the current network throughput. If there are more errors in the network, it will *decrease* window size, if fewer errors, it will *increase* window size. Increased window size provides increased throughput, but requires more memory and buffers in the network hardware and software, and can cause more problems than it solves. Network performance problems can be determined by trending the window size changes and determining where additional throughput may be required in the network.

21.7.5 Bursting

Most protocols are designed to allow the application the capability to burst above a predefined traffic parameter setting. Many applications naturally send bursts of data over dedicated facilities when they have the entire bandwidth. Statistical multiplexers allow a form of bursting.

Frame relay was designed to allow network access for multiple variable-bit rate users. These are the same users who once paid for low-speed private lines to connect local computing and the communications environment. When these users have a dedicated 56 kbps private line, their bursts of data would take three seconds to transmit. The rest of the time the line would remain at low utilization. This is shown in Figure 21.19a. Now, they can attach their LAN to a router and share a frame relay access to a public-switched network service with four other LANs. Each of their bursts now only takes 200 ms to transmit the entire file, because during these bursts there is a good chance that they can get all the bandwidth available on the T1 up to their CIR (shown in Figure 21.19b). In fact, they may even be able to burst *above* the CIR during times of low network utilization (such as peak 3). In this case, their file transfer takes even less time (150 ms).

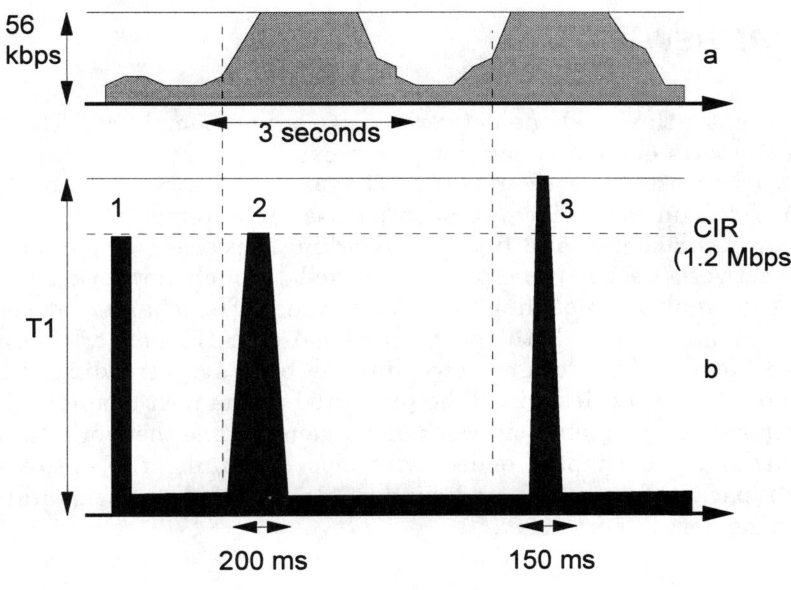

Figure 21.19 Effect of Frame Relay Service CIR on User Traffic

The concept just described works well as long as the user does not try to use the frame relay interface for cheap bandwidth. If the user overloads the service and places many users on the same frame relay interface, the user will have to contend for the same resources at the same time, against many more users. Let's say that the owner of the frame relay interface and router decides to place 16 LANs on the interface. If the increased traffic load of each LAN is proportional, our user will still be able to burst, but chances are he or she will only receive 128 kbits worth of shared bandwidth during his file transmission. Now the user is back to the original problem of the old 3-second delay during bursts. These calculations all assume a constant total network load. A different scenario needs to be analyzed for usage-based service. This FR example shows that while users can intelligently use the

CIR and maximize throughput, their savings are passed off to other users in the form of delay. CIR rates are allocated to allow the maximum burst on the line and still guarantee transmission. They were not designed to use the average transmission speed and definitely not the baseline speed of the circuit. Two measures of bursts are the committed burst size for forward and backward traffic and the excess burst size for forward and backward. Each user should be mapped according to these criteria to get an accurate picture of what the circuit can expect during peak periods.

21.8 REVIEW

In this chapter the backbone network design is now completed. This network design supports enough capacity to meet existing user access requirements, as well as future network growth. The backbone style and topology was chosen based on many factors, such as user requirements, the access and backbone technologies, and future networking concerns. The importance of strong network design principles, confirmed through network performance and trend analysis modeling, was reviewed. The chapter attempted to present examples from both the hierarchical (ex., IP) network design view and the flat (ex. FR) design viewpoints, as both are very different. More detail on IP network design will be presented in the next chapter. The need and importance of global network management and network timing was stressed, and the chapter ended with tips on tuning the entire network through: packet, frame, cell, and window sizing, avoiding segmentation, and minimizing port-to-port delay.

Chapter

22

Addressing and Routing Design

After the topology is established, it is necessary to go into great detail on network addressing. Multiple techniques will be explored. The examples used take this exercise into a brief discussion of IP and IPX address design. The most widely used WAN protocol remains IP. Since IP networks are so predominant, this chapter first focuses on the IP address structure and design, and next on IPX address structure design. There are many books available on addressing, and specifically IP address design. This chapter is meant to be an introduction to some basic principles of IP and IPX address design.

22.1 OVERVIEW OF ADDRESSING

Ubiquitous access to an intelligent data-communications network that spans the globe has become a rallying cry of many users. Users want to access the data network as a large "cloud" and thus be able to talk to any other user connected to that cloud without requiring any knowledge of the internals of the network cloud. A prerequisite to this capability is the assignment of a globally unique or network-recognized unique address to each user. The public voice network has these characteristics, with several lessons from that domain applicable to data networks, such as with the Internet. If a user cannot reach any other user on the public data network, as is taken for granted in telephony and has become a *fait accompli* on the Internet, then the resulting data service will have little utility.

Addresses are used to direct traffic from an origination point to a single or multiple destination point(s). Addresses differ from names in that addresses form a data structure in a communications system that defines the specific physical or logical location of an entity, device, or single access point, whereas *names* provide a humanly readable symbol of a network entity or device. Addresses can be assigned to entities or devices, and a route defines the other devices with which a given address can be reached (thus specifying from and to). Routes can be created to define the other devices or entities from which a given address can be reached. Addressing schemes should be nonproprietary when possible and should be used consistently across the network. In this section, we will discuss various types of common addressing schemes and how they influence the network design.

22.1.1 Levels of Addressing

Addresses can be assigned in either a flat or a hierarchical scheme corresponding to the access and backbone style of design. For example, IP addresses are arbitrary in nature within the scheme of the Internet address classes, while E.164 SMDS addresses are hierarchical with geographic significance (individual IP address assignments can also be hierarchical with geographic significance). It is obviously much easier to control and filter hierarchical addresses, but there is also the disadvantage of requiring change of addresses every time a user changes his or her location.

22.1.2 Types of Addresses

Throughout the technology chapters, many types of addressing have been discussed. A summary is found in Table 22.1.

TABLE 22.1 Addressing by Technology

Technology	Type	Size
Circuit Switching	None	None
X.25 Packet Switching	LCI	12 bits
X.121	LCI	14 BCD digits
Frame Relay (ANSI)	DLCI	2 octets (4 for ITU)
802.6	E.164/D15	16 bits
802.6	E.164/D15	48 bits
802.6/SMDS	E.164/D15	Individual 60 bits
802.6/SMDS	E.164/D15	Group bit
802.6/SMDS	E.164/D15	NPA/NXX
802.X LAN	MAC	16 to 48 bits
ATM	VPI/VCI	8/16 bits

Each network architecture has its own type of addressing. One example of a predominant architecture is DECnet. DECnet Phase IV addressing has both an area level 2 address and a node-specific level 1 address, and can support up to 63 areas with each area supporting up to 1023 systems. System names can be up to 6 alphanumeric characters each. These architecture-specific addressing schemes must be mapped to any network-addressing scheme (such as network IP address design, which will be discussed next) to eliminate any addressing discrepancies. The other architectures have similar address designs.

22.1.3 Address Assignment and Resolution

A key requirement in any communications network is that unique addresses be assigned to each of the entities that want to communicate. This is the case in the telephone network where every phone in the world has a unique number, and in the 48-bit IEEE 802.3 Media Access Control (MAC) assignments that are built into every Ethernet interface. Every user or "host" in the Internet is assigned a unique IP address.

Ensuring that the address assignments are unique and that they efficiently administer an address space presents some challenges. Not only must addresses be handed out, but a means for users to return addresses and request blocks of addresses is also required. Furthermore, if there is more than one administrative authority, then the scope of assignments allocated to each administration must be clearly defined. It is sometimes difficult to predict the demand for addresses. For example, area codes have been realigned because the demand differs from what was forecast years ago. If an administrative authority hands out blocks of addresses too freely, then the network can run out of unique addresses well before the limit determined by the number of bits in the addresses, as has occurred with many of the IP address blocks.

Once you have your own address and the address of someone that you wish to communicate with, how do you resolve the address of the desired destination into information about how to get it there? First, consider the following simple analogy. Let's say that you have spoken to an individual on the telephone for the first time and have agreed to meet him or her at a party to which you both have been invited by the same host. Once you arrive at the party, you can find the individual (resolve the address) in one of two ways: you can jump up on stage, grab the microphone, and broadcast your presence, or you can locate the host and ask to be introduced to the individual. Broadcast is commonly used in shared-medium LANs to resolve addresses. A problem arises when the volume of broadcast traffic begins to approach the level of user traffic. The concept of having someone who has the information (the host) resolve the address (match an address with a user) is called a *Domain Name Server (DNS).*

22.2 IP ADDRESS DESIGN

IP is by far the most common WAN addressing scheme. The design of an IP network based upon the addressing format is a critical issue. A network may have a large number of hosts. If every router in a network needed to know the location of every host, then the routing tables could become quite large. A key concept used in routing IP is that of "subnetting". Subnetting allows the host address space to be broken down into multiple subnetworks by masking the bits in the host address field to create a separate subnetwork for each physical network.

The Internet assigns 32-bit numbers to each user employing an organizational hierarchy. Entire blocks of numbers which need not have any geographic meaning whatsoever are assigned to an organization. A user may move geographically, and it becomes the job of the intelligent network to find him or her using a routing discovery protocol. The organization may structure its block of addresses however it chooses, either geographically, organizationally, or in some other manner. The Internet has also achieved worldwide nearly ubiquitous access and addressing as well.

22.3 IP ADDRESS DESIGN PRIMER

An IP address is a 32-bit integer. This integer is divided into four integers, each 8 bits long. Each of these 8-bit integers is separated by a dot. For example, 198.62.193.32 is a single address. Each of these 8-bit integers can be represented by a decimal (0 through 255), hexidecimal (0 through FF), or binary (00000000 through 11111111) number. Thus, an IP address "A.B.C.D" has one of the following three formats:

- Binary: 00000000.00000000.00000000.00000000 through 11111111.11111111.11111111.11111111 or
- Decimal: 0.0.0.0 through 255.255.255.255 or
- Hex: 0.0.0.0 through FF.FF.FF.FF

The ranges can also be expressed as:

- Binary: 00000000-11111111.00000000-11111111.00000000-11111111.00000000-11111111 or
- Decimal: 0-255.0-255.0-255.0-255 or
- Hex: 0-FF.0-FF.0-FF.0-FF

22.3.1 Network Mask

There are four classes of IP addresses, each defined by a mask. These are labeled A, B, C, and D. The most common are classes A, B, and C. Network masks separate the number of network nodes from host numbers. These masks are expressed as:

Class A = FF.0.0.0
Class B = FF.FF.0.0
Class C = FF.FF.FF.0

The class A mask has an address structure that allows a possibility of 256 networks (or nets), each with greater than 4 billion nodes (or hosts).

The class B mask has an address structure that allows a possibility of 65,536 networks (or nets), each with 65,536 nodes (or hosts).

The class C mask has an address structure that allows a possibility of 4 billion networks (or nets), each with 256 nodes (or hosts).

Class A addresses are usually assigned by the NIC for very large corporate networks or to service providers like AT&T. Class B addresses are assigned to midsize networks or providers, and class C addresses are for smaller networks.

As an example, a class C address of 198.62.193.0-255 would have a network mask of FF.FF.FF.0.

Let's take an example network where our design calls for four routers (1 headquarters and three remote sites), and each site requires up to 10 hosts per router. Figure 22.1 illustrates this network. Our network mask of choice might be a .240 mask. How many networks and hosts does a 240 mask provide?

16 networks less all 0s and all 1s = 14 networks
16 hosts less all 0s and all 1s = 14 hosts per network
Total hosts throughout = 14 × 14 = 196 maximum hosts

Types of hosts include:

* PCs
* Workstations
* Router ports (LAN and WAN)
* Print servers
* Terminal servers

Note that all 0s and all 1s conditions are defined as experimental and are not accepted by most router manufacturers, and some devices will not even route these addresses.

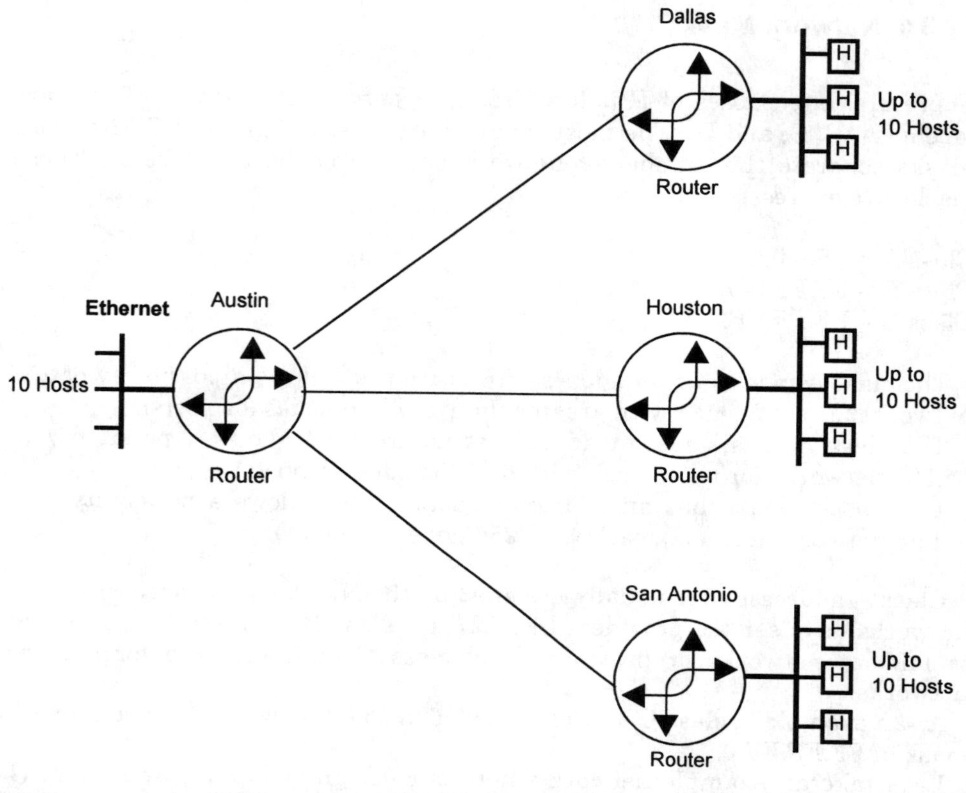

Figure 22.1 Sample Four-Site Network

Therefore, since we only need a maximum of 10 hosts per site we can use the mask of 240, since it will allow us to assign up to 14 hosts per site. A mask of 248 would have allowed us only up to 8 hosts per site. So, if we have a class C address of 198.63.193.0 we can add a mask of 255.255.255.0 and a subnet mask of 198.62.193.240.

There are two main rules to using masks: the mask always moves from left to right in bit order, and every mask needs to contain contiguous 1s (no 0s between 1s). Thus, a mask of 111111111.11111111.11111111.11000000 would be correct, but a mask of 11111111.11110000.11111111.11000000 would be incorrect.

22.3.2 IP Address Topologies

There are many methods of implementing an IP address scheme. The first determination is whether the network will follow a hierarchical or matrix topology. With a matrix topology, each user (workstation, host, server) will be assigned a single IP address. Communications will be peer-to-peer. As discussed previously, this style of addressing scheme would be fine for a small network with few users, but becomes unmanageable with large networks.

For larger networks, a more manageable design is the hierarchical topology. IP addresses are assigned in blocks based upon geographic region and where (by level) the user resides in the hierarchy. Boundaries are drawn by what are called masks and subnet masks. These masks provide a method of segmenting and reducing the number of network addresses that network devices (access and backbone) need to know.

For example, the matrix IP addressing would resemble the old style of sending mail, where the sender would simply place a person's name, address, city, and state on the letter. Each post office or stop would pass the mail along to the city, where the person would then be located by name and address. This was fine for a small number of cities with few people where everyone knew each other, but would not work today. The hierarchical mail scheme adds a zip code. Today, each city has a minimum of one zip code, and larger cities have several zip codes. In fact, some companies have their own zip codes (XXXXX-YYYY). Now each city can sort mail based on zip code (XXXXX), and filter out any mail not destined for that city. Then each post office in any area of a city can sort based on the last four digits of the code (YYYY) and is able to filter all addresses for that given zip code extension. The (XXXXX) portion of the zip code acts as the subnet mask, and the (YYYY) acts as the specific user zip code extension. This is an example of what masking does for IP addressing. Let's look at some specific examples.

22.3.3 Addresses Based on Topology

Now that the style of topology for the network has been determined and we understand the fundamentals of IP addressing, it must be determined how many addresses will be allocated at each site for each level of the hierarchy. For example:

1. Each workstation receives 1 host address
2. Each LAN segment receives 64 host addresses
3. Each floor receives 256 host addresses
4. Each building receives 1024 host addresses

These numbers indicate a sample number of host addresses per unit of measure. This allocation would be accomplished, along with segmentation and hierarchical design practices, through the use of subnet masks. Open Shortest Path First (OSPF) routing, one of the more common Interior Gateway Protocols (IGP), can be used in an autonomous system where subnet masks are required. Routers forward and filter traffic based on subnet addresses. They can forward or filter traffic by mapping the IP destination host address to the router's subnet address. Now we will discuss subnet masks.

22.3.4 Subnet Masks

Once you have identified what network mask you will use (class A, B, or C), and decided on the number of networks and hosts required, it is time to assign addressing within the network. Subnet masks further divide single NIC registered class A, B, and C network masks into multiple hosts and "subnetworks". Subnet masks are used in conjunction with network masks as follows:

Take the class B address 108.10.0.0. The network portion of this number is actually 108.10. The network mask of 255.255.0.0 defines two positions, .0.0 to .255.255, to work with. This allows your 108.10 network to define up to 255 networks and 255 hosts, or a total of 255×255 = 65,534 addresses (address 0 and 65,535 are reserved).

Let's go back to our first example. We are building a network with four sites and up to 10 hosts per site. The class C address we are assigned is 198.62.193.0. Using the cross-reference table in Appendix C, we use a 240 subnet mask to further divide this class C mask into usable chunks of addresses that accurately reflect our mix of subnets and hosts. This allows us to have up to 14 nets with 14 hosts each (2 nets and 2 host addresses are reserved). The 14 network addresses we have available are:

198.62.193.16
198.62.193.32
198.62.193.48
198.62.193.64
198.62.193.80
198.62.193.96
198.62.193.112
198.62.193.128
198.62.193.144
198.62.193.160
198.62.193.176
198.62.193.192
198.62.193.208
198.62.193.224

We start by assigning the 14 network addresses available to each network or site. We see in the upper right of the Figure 22.2 the assignment of the 198.62.193.32 network to Dallas. We continue on with the assignment of .48 to Houston and .64 to San Antonio. We then assign .16 to the headquarters in Austin. We next assign subnet masks to the network circuits. Dallas to Austin is assigned the .80 subnet mask, Houston to Austin the .96 subnet mask, and San Antonio to Austin the .112 subnet mask. Note that each network's point-to-point circuit is now a subnet unto itself. Since each end of the subnet requires only one address, with our subnet masking scheme of 14 addresses per subnet, 12 addresses are wasted. We will see later how variable-length subnet masking can help us reclaim some of these addresses. Also note that we used up seven of the total 14 subnet masks.

We next assign specific addresses within each subnet to the hosts within that subnet as shown in Figure 22.3. Remember that a host can be both a workstation and a LAN or WAN router port. We reference our same network example illustrated now in Figure 22.3. We first take the WAN circuit between Dallas and Austin. Within this 198.62.193.80 subnet mask, we have 14 addresses we could assign – 198.62.193.81 to 198.62.193.94 (.80 and .95 are reserved). The port on the Austin end is assigned the address 198.62.193.81. The port on the Dallas end is assigned address 198.62.193.82.

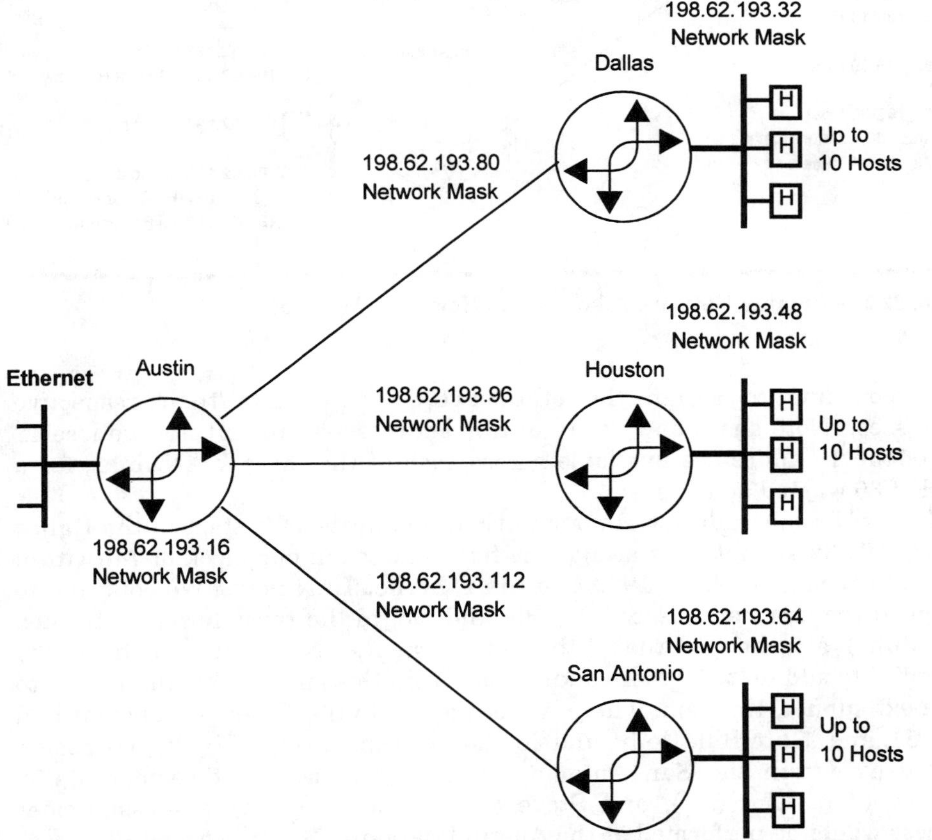

Figure 22.2 Assigning Network Addresses

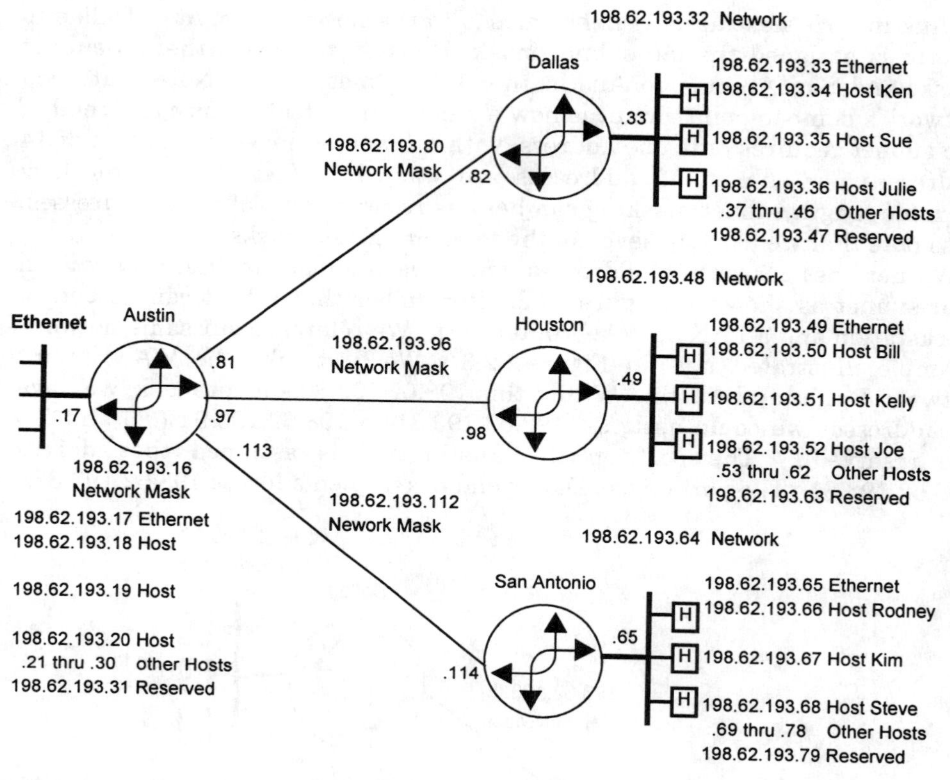

Figure 22.3 Assigning Network Addresses to Hosts and WAN ports

We continue to assign the other two WAN circuits their respective addresses. Note again how wasteful this address assignment is – we lose 12 out of the 14 addresses available across each of the three WAN links, for a total of 36 wasted addresses.

We next assign addresses to our workstation hosts. We start in the Dallas 198.62.193.32 subnet. We assign the first address in our block of 14 (within *this* subnet mask) 198.62.193.33 to the Ethernet LAN port. We continue to assign three more addresses, .34, .35, and .36, to the three hosts (Ken, Sue, and Julie) attached to that Ethernet segment. Note that we have the potential to add up to 10 more addresses within this subnet. We then move to the next subnet, Houston, where we assign .49 to the Ethernet segment and .50, .51, and .52 to Bill, Kelly, and Joe hosts, respectively. Finally, we assign addresses within the San Antonio subnet to the Ethernet segment (.65), Rodney (.66), Kim (.67), and Steve (.68). The same address assignment process would be performed at the Austin location.

This design works well over private line networks or when the size of the network remains under 14 routers. But what happens when the network grows larger? Or is placed over a WAN service like frame relay? Larger network masks can be used, or you can resort to other subnet options.

Optimal mask and subnet mask design depends on the type and size of your network. One method of assigning masks is based on location of devices. For example, assign one network mask for the entire network, one subnet for each device and WAN link, and an individual address to each WAN port, LAN port, and workstation. A subnet could be an entire network, or an individual site with *X* workstations. Let's look at some examples using a class C network mask:

Do you require 64 subnets with four assignable host addresses per subnet? Use a 255.255.255.252 subnet mask.
Do you require 32 subnets with eight assignable host addresses per subnet? Use a 255.255.255.248 subnet mask.
Do you require 16 subnets with 16 assignable host addresses per subnet? Use a 255.255.255.240 subnet mask.
Do you require two subnets with 128 assignable host addresses per subnet? Use a 255.255.255.128 subnet mask.

What if you are running a much larger network with many more users per subnet? Try using a class B network mask with the following subnets:

Do you require 64 subnets with 1024 assignable host addresses per subnet? Use a 255.255.252.000 subnet mask.
Do you require 32 subnets with 2048 assignable host addresses per subnet? Use a 255.255.248.000 subnet mask.
Do you require 16 subnets with 4096 assignable host addresses per subnet? Use a 255.255.240.000 subnet mask.
Do you require 2 subnets with 32,000 assignable host addresses per subnet? Use a 255.255.128.000 subnet mask.

Are you running out of subnet or host addresses, now or in the near future? Then look at variable-length subnet addressing.

Appendix D shows all available subnet masks and their corresponding number of assignable addresses per subnet for class A, B, and C network masks. This table should come in handy when you are designing IP networks and subnetworks.

22.3.5 Variable Length Subnet Masks

Variable-length subnet masks (VLSMs) are used for dividing subnets into variable-size subnets for more efficient use of available addresses. For example, VLSMs break up a class C address into uneven pieces to get more hosts per node. In this manner, greater granularity can be imposed *between nets* on a restricted number of addresses within the entire class C mask.

Using the last example, we now want to reclaim some of the addresses we lost to the WAN links (remember we lost 12 addresses within each LAN link subnet mask). To review, we started with a 198.62.193.0 network mask. From there, we used a subnet mask of 255.255.255.224. This subnet mask gave us 14 subnets with 14 hosts per subnet. We then proceeded to assign the .80 subnet mask to the Dallas-to-Austin link and determined we would lose 12 addresses in the process. If we now take that 198.62.193.80 subnet, we can assign it a "stubnet" mask of 255.255.255.252. In doing so, we change a .224 subnet mask supporting one network and 14 hosts to a .252 subnet (also called "stubnet") supporting four networks with four hosts each. The addressing structure to accomplish this is shown in Figure 22.5. We now can use the .84, .88, and .92 stubnets for *three* WAN links instead of just *one*, using the .89, .90, .93, and .94 host addresses for two other WAN links. In this manner, we just saved six addresses. This is compared to using just the .224 subnet mask in Figure 22.4. Variable subnet masking is valuable for designs using FR because each PVC's DLCI requires its own subnet mask number, and this is one way of extending a limited number of addresses.

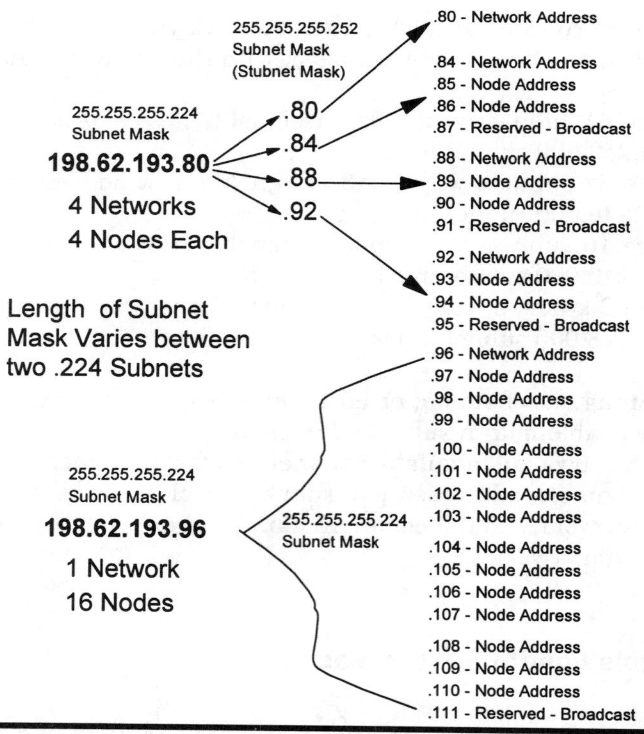

Figure 22.4 IP Variable Subnet Addressing

22.3.6 Design Rules – Subnets and Frame Relay

All routing protocols such as RIP, OSPF, and IGRP only allow one network address per link. Therefore, there is a problem when trying to use a single network mask across a WAN that allows multiple virtual circuits within a single physical circuit. For example, in frame relay, a router has multiple virtual ports aggregated within a single physical port. To IP, each of the virtual circuit (PVC) ports looks like a single physical port (no difference between a physical and logical circuit to IP). The other problem is the overhead incurred when RIP broadcasts across a FR network. If using a FR network in this above design scenario, both split horizons and poison reverse (as covered in previous chapters) must be used.

Subnet masking is not allowed when using RIP. RIP only views and understands addresses from its nearest neighbor. It does not understand subnet mask addresses, because the subnet mask is not part of its limited protocol header. If subnet masks are used in conjunction with RIP, there is a high probability that hosts will not be able to reach certain other hosts. The subnet mask is assumed from the mask assigned to the interface receiving the RIP packet. It is best to avoid using RIP in a network with subnet masks. The alternative is to use a routing protocol like OSPF or IGRP that uses a packet structure which comprehends both destination host address and network (or subnetwork) address.

Subnetwork masks that have many subnets, such as .252 and .240, are typically used when designing large, point-to-point networks with hub or star topologies. Larger masks like 255.255.255.0 (class C subnet masks) are typically used in fully meshed networks.

22.3.7 OSPF versus RIP and Default Gateways

Every IP addressing scheme should be designed in conjunction with the routing protocol. Note that it is more efficient to use RIP routing protocol in the local area subnets and OSPF in the WAN. The fact that summaries have been used in OSPF reduces the amount of address updates which transit the network. RIP is an acceptable routing protocol to use in the local area network because LANs have a lot of bandwidth and can tolerate the periodic RIP updates. Also, most LAN-attached devices support RIP (OSPF is not implemented on most hosts). If a single router is the only interface to the LANs within an area, and if there is only one interface per LAN, RIP routing is not required. A default workstation gateway entry will allow the workstations to find problems with the network through a default gateway address (in our example, the router port to which the LAN connects).

If the packet has a remote destination, the device will send it to a specified IP address on the router (default gateway IP address). Note that the network mask must be the same across the entire network. If all networks and hosts are directly attached to the same router a routing protocol is not required. The default gateway function can be used in cases where each LAN attached to the router has only one interface. Remember that with RIP, each LAN device can both send and receive RIP updates.

IP routes effectively between subnets, but not *within* a subnet. Thus, a network may have different routing protocols within the subnet than those used outside the subnet. Try not to use RIP over the IP backbone, because it generates too much overhead (and the larger the network, the more the overhead) due to transmission of entire routing tables as updates every 30 seconds. Also, RIP does not have password authentication and does not work well if you are using a variable subnet mask within the network. OSPF and EGP use filtering or subnet masking to filter out what addresses are broadcast to the entire network. Filtering can be used on RIP as well. Effective filtering and masking can create efficiencies in the network design.

Global addressing varies based on the service, technology, and protocol being used. In a mixed environment, IP addresses are individually mapped to each technology's specific addressing scheme (such as to DLCIs for frame relay).

22.3.8 Mask Effect on Higher-Layer Protocols

Network and subnet masks are transparent to higher-layer protocols. If TCP is running on two hosts connected by one or more local and/or wide area subnets using IP, IP does not really care about the masks employed. The subnet is, in effect, transparent to it. It is up to the routing protocols like OSPF to understand where each IP address is located within its network and subnet.

22.4 NOVELL IPX ADDRESSING

The second most popular WAN addressing protocol is IPX. Novell IPX is a media-dependent (Ethernet) protocol derived from the original Xerox over Ethernet protocol – XNS. It is a single MAC protocol for support of Ethernet LANs. Special driver software is required for any supported media type. For example, the applications NetWare and Windows NT must know how to handle addresses from Ethernet, Token Ring, Arcnet, etc. IPX was originally designed as a LAN protocol, and was modified for WAN use. Due to its addressing dependency on the MAC address (as we will soon see), IPX operates as both an OSIRM layer 2 (node address) and layer 3 (network address) protocol. In comparison, IP is a layer 3 protocol and is media independent. The other big difference between IP and IPX is that IPX addressing is dynamic, where IP addressing is mostly static. IPX addresses are not preassigned to workstations, but instead are negotiated with the server as required. All IPX workstations are configured with a network address of 0 when they start up. When a workstation wants to send data, it will receive its connection ID from the nearest server. Each workstation derives its node address from its internal MAC address.

22.4.1 IPX Address Structure

The IPX address is composed of three parts as shown in Figure 22.5: the network address, the node address, and the connection ID. The network address is 32 bits long (AAAAAAAA), the node address 48 bits long and conforms to the standard MAC address length (BB-BB-BB-BB-BB-BB), and the connection ID is 16 bits long.

22.4.2 Designing IPX WANs

The typical by-the-book installation calls for each file server to be assigned address 1 and all external addresses A, B, C, D, and so forth, as shown in Figure 22.6. It is much better to plan out your address space well in advance. For example, start with assigning your first file server address FEAD0001, the second file server FEAD0002, and so forth. These numbers must be unique throughout the network. This will provide for a very scalable addressing design.

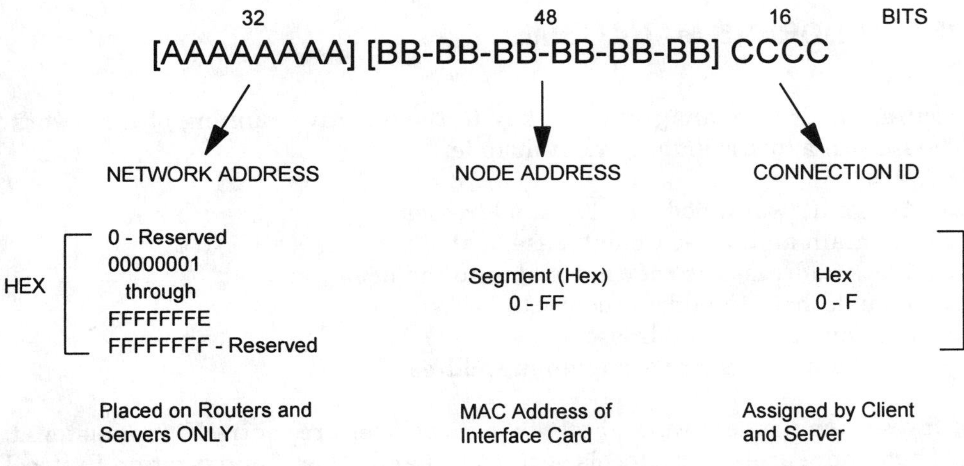

Figure 22.5 IPX Addressing Scheme

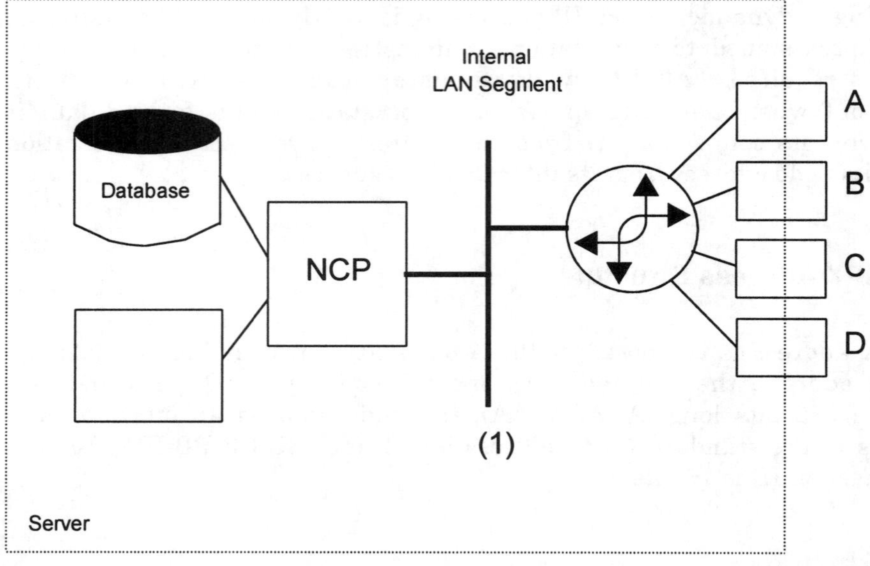

Figure 22.6 IPX Addressing Example

Most initial implementations of IPX had a window size of 1 and a fixed packet size of 512 bytes. The packet burst (p-burst) capability allows the window size to be increased to 65,535 (which would probably never be used) and the maximum packet size to 1024 bytes. Also beware that slow links may cause problems due to RIP and SAP broadcasts.

22.5 ADDRESS MANAGEMENT

Accurate address management is key to the effective running of a network. The roles of address management include:

⇒ Assign network, node, and host addresses
⇒ Maintain an up-to-date database of all addresses
⇒ Track addresses as they move around the network
⇒ Troubleshoot IP address conflicts
⇒ Reassign inactive addresses
⇒ Maintain each user with a unique address

Address management works best when its policies are centrally administered.

Thus, there are also protocols such as Dynamic Host Configuration Protocol (DHCP) and BootP that automate the process of assigning addresses on-demand. Every user device typically does not use an IP address at the same time. These tools are good for mobile workers and telecommuting and for the conservation of addresses.

22.6 CLASSLESS INTERDOMAIN ROUTING (CIDR)

Classless InterDomain Routing (CIDR), pronounced "cider", provides the network designer a method to slow down large-scale address allocation and limit routing table overflow in large networks. RFCs 1517, 1518, 1519, and 1520 define the various aspects and implementations of CIDR. CIDR is referred to as a *classless* protocol, as opposed to a *classful* protocol like RIP and IGRP, because there are no class boundaries imposed on the address scheme. CIDR replaces the address class requirement with an *IP prefix*. This prefix is used to perform route aggregation, where one route in effect summarizes many original IP network numbers. This allows allocation of addresses in bite-size chunks rather than large classes to reduce wasting addresses. CIDR uses an autonomous system number (ASN) to merge multiple networks into a single logical domain.

The benefits of CIDR include:

- ◊ Continuous, uninterrupted growth of the Internet
- ◊ Lesser requirement to update external routing tables
- ◊ Saves routing table space
- ◊ Reduces rapid changes in routing
- ◊ Reduces CPU load of transit nodes
- ◊ Helps the Internet reduce routing overload
- ◊ Increases likelihood that your routes will be carried by all ISPs

CIDR is already implemented in most of the Internet, but users must check with their Internet Service Provider (ISP) to determine if CIDR is supported. Also, make sure your brand of router and software version support CIDR. Designers should refer to the RFCs listed above and CIDR frequently asked questions (FAQ) on the Internet for more detail on design.

22.7 REVIEW

In this chapter, several techniques for network addressing were covered, including a detailed example of IP address design using a network mask and subnet masks. Novell IPX addressing was also covered. Details on frame relay, SMDS, and ATM addressing were previously covered in their respective technology chapters.

Chapter

23

Operations and Network Management

Documentation of the access and backbone network design is important, and it is now time to review and complete it. Proper documentation requires both an engineering plan, which steps a user or manager through the entire network, and an operations and maintenance manual, which provides the support structure for both implementing and maintaining the network. The responsibilities of each department must be identified, and documenting each area will help make implementing the design a success. A detailed analysis of network management is presented, covering the Simple Network Management Protocol (SNMP), OSI's Common Management Information Protocol (CMIP) and its derivations, and other OSI network management plans. ITU's Telecommunications Management Network (TMN) architecture is also covered. Standards for remote monitoring and management of network elements are emerging, and we will study the leading RMON standards. Current trends in network management wrap up the section. Billing and security are briefly discussed, as is training. Finally, some soul searching must be done to decide when to exercise some constraint. At this point we must stop designing and start implementing the network.

23.1 NETWORK DOCUMENTATION

Documentation is one of the most important steps in the network design process. Documentation helps people understand the design and allows them to remember the assumptions made during the design. Documentation should never be an afterthought. Both designer and user will suffer from poor documentation. It must be developed as a joint consensus during the project.

The four primary documents required to support a network design are: the business case document, the user specifications and acceptance document, the engineering plan, and the operations and maintenance (O&M) manual. The first two documents must be completed before the design begins. The engineering plan is developed throughout the design and distributed when the design is completed. The O&M document will be distributed after network design completion, but it requires specific inputs from the engineering plan.

23.1.1 The Engineering Plan

The engineering plan explains the history behind your present connectivity, the reasons for the network design, what the network will support and why it needs support, and the entire design from application to backbone connectivity. Of course, it should include everything discussed in this book about design. Capacity planning could also be included in the plan, or it could be a separate document.

Specific information in the engineering plan includes:

- Requirements matrix
- Node configuration
- Circuit diagrams
- Physical and logical configurations
- Site-specific information
- Bridge/router/hub/switch/gateway/ID addressing
- Segment/port name/ID address plan and design
- Serial and model numbers
- LAN/MAN/WAN addressing (e.g., Ethernet, E.164, TCP/IP)
- Current software and firmware version level

23.1.2 The O&M Document

The Operations & Maintenance (O&M) document presents all information required to install and maintain the network. Many sections of O&M are taken directly from the engineering plan, and many sections represent standard operating procedures for installing and maintaining network equipment. Some of the topics represented in the O&M document include:

- System/network description
- Physical/topological description
- Logical/functional description
- Design of network (reference design document)

* Budgetary impacts
* System/network administration
* Order entry(OE)/order processing (OP) procedures
* Network management (NM) procedures
* Installation and testing
* Billing procedures
* Support structure and escalation procedures
* Hardware/software maintenance and sparing
* Test equipment requirements
* Training
* Vendor specific documentation
* Glossary, acronyms, and references

At the site-specific level, the details provided include:

* Installation power and grounds
* Implementation and cut-over
* Naming and addressing conventions
* Device-specific wiring
* Device-specific testing
* Floor plan construction
* Layout of LAN/MAN
* Topology
* Device locations
* Shared resources locations
* Network management/administration locations
* Maintenance schedules

23.2 ORGANIZATIONAL RESPONSIBILITIES

Many groups within the company participate in the network design and implementation. Active participation from all groups ensures a smooth implementation and continued operation of the network. These group responsibilities are only guidelines, as many of these groups fall under a single engineering and support organization. The list below shows the major groups involved in a network:

Planning. Provides future architecture direction, plans on how future services will integrate and on what technology platforms they will ride, and design concepts for engineering.

Network Engineering. Performs engineering of network from the user requirements through the access and backbone design. This includes the initial design and continued engineering support after the network is operational. Capacity is forecasted.

Systems Engineering. Provides the same service as engineering, but for the software, control systems, and network management of the network, with more of a software and services orientation to ensure interoperability.

Order Entry/Order Provisioning (OE/OP). Orders the required access and backbone circuits and services, tracks circuit orders to completion, notifies the user of potential jeopardy, and provisions the required circuits and services.

Network Administration. Provides all node, circuit, address, and other administrative responsibilities for the network, including configuration management, database management, security administration, and performance reporting.

Billing. Handles the generation of billing to the customer or paying the bills as a customer for the network transport, access, hardware, software, and any other cost aspect of the network.

Operations. Reviews the network design; installs the network devices (hardware and software); performs the operations, maintenance, performance monitoring, preventive engineering, and network management of the network once it is installed, including support structure for trouble reporting and trouble management to vendors and customers.

Testing. Tests and troubleshoots all applications on the network-access devices as well as over the backbone, provides component to system end-to-end network testing, and certifies vendor hardware and software releases. Includes prototyping.

Training. Ensures all personnel are trained on all network systems, and trains users on the network applications and services.

Program and Project Management. Manages the project resources from design conception through implementation (entire life cycle) and maintains overall responsibility for the project and the budget. Most importantly, program management gets the buy-in and cooperation early on from all support groups listed previously in the project and manages their interdependencies. Figure 23.1 shows average project cycles, from technology that rapidly becomes obsolete (curves A and B) to newer technologies (curve C).

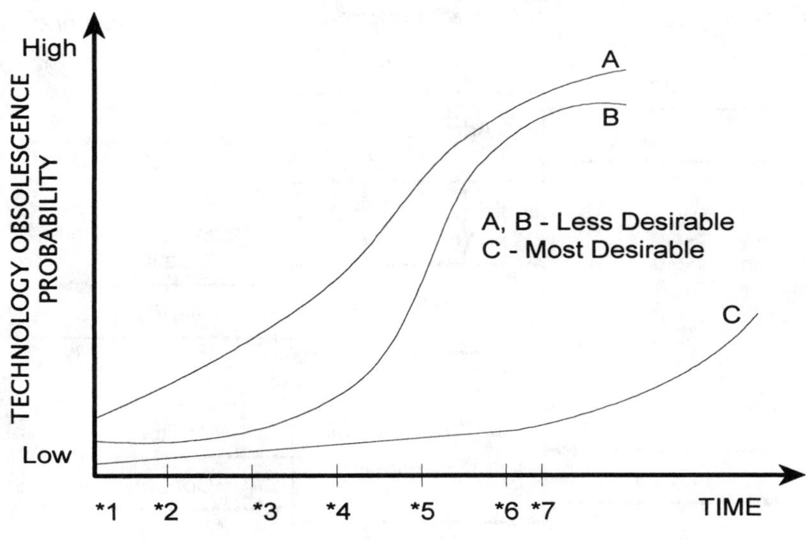

Figure 23.1 Program Management – Project Life Cycles

23.3 OPERATIONS, ADMINISTRATION, MAINTENANCE, AND PROVISIONING (OAM&P) DEFINED

Operations, administration, maintenance, and provisioning functions form the cornerstones of managing a network. First, we will look at the OAM&P functional model for insight into the key areas of operations. Next, each area is defined, followed by a study of centralized versus distributed management.

23.3.1 The OAM&P Functional Model

One of the best examples of a network management functional model is the Operations, Administration, Maintenance, and Provisioning (OAM&P) model as shown diagrammed in Figure 23.2.

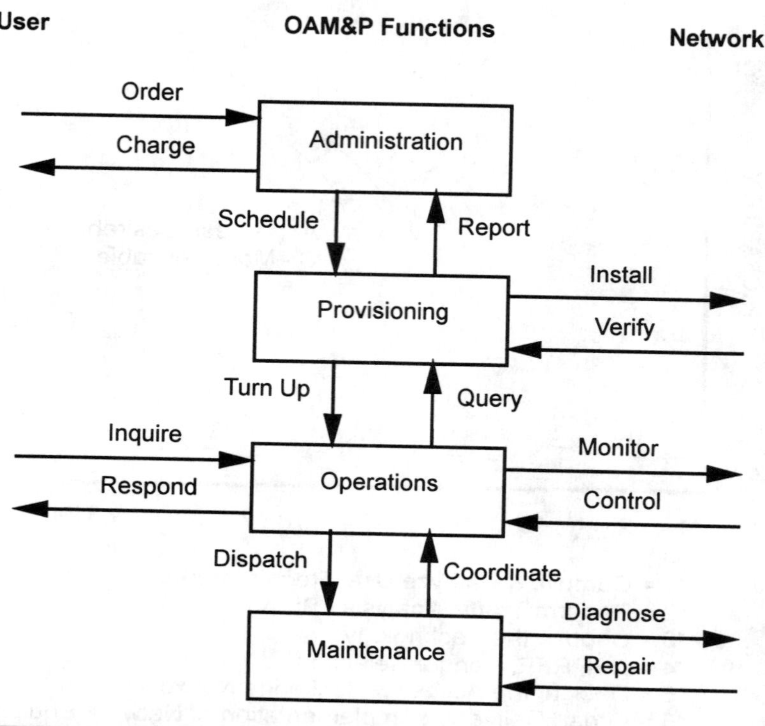

Figure 23.2 OAM&P Process Flow

- **Operations** involves the day-to-day, and often minute-to-minute, care and feeding of the data network in order to ensure that it is fulfilling its designed purpose.

- **Administration** involves the set of activities involved with designing the network, processing orders, assigning addresses, tracking usage, change management, and accounting.

- **Maintenance** involves the inevitable circumstances that arise when everything does not work as planned or when it is necessary to diagnose what went wrong and repair it. It also includes preventive measures.

- **Provisioning** involves installing equipment and facilities, setting parameters, and verifying that the service is operational. It also includes deinstallation.

23.3.2 Operations Defined

Operations is the art of coordinating actions between administration, maintenance, and provisioning of a data-communications service. Reactive monitoring of the network involves watching for faults and invoking corrective commands and/or maintenance actions to repair them. It also involves comparing measured performance against objectives and taking corrective action and/or invoking maintenance. Invoking corrective actions involves operators issuing commands to correct a fault or performance problem, or resolving a customer complaint. A key operational function involves proactively assisting users with performance engineering to resolve troubles and effectively utilize network capabilities to optimize network resources and prevent outages.

23.3.3 Administration

An often overlooked pre- and postdesign task is that of network administration. Prior to completing the initial design, an administrative plan for staging the operations, maintenance, and provisioning activities must be developed. This often involves automated system support for order entry, order processing, work-order management, address administration, and trouble ticketing. Orders must be accepted from users and the provisioning process initiated. Address assignments are made when needed. Once the service is installed, usage data must be collected for traffic analysis and possible accounting use. Based upon forecasts, business requirements, and traffic analysis, changes to the network must be periodically updated. Network planning may make use of automated tools.

23.3.4 Maintenance

Preventive maintenance is always the best method of reducing downtime. If a weakness cannot be caught and resolved before it causes a network outage, it must be quickly isolated and diagnosed to determine the cause(s). Fixes to identified problems must be applied in a manner coordinated by operations. This often involves dispatching, parts delivery, and coordination with service suppliers. An important activity is to perform routine maintenance so that faults and performance degradation are less likely to occur.

23.3.5 Provisioning

New or upgraded equipment and software must be installed. Hardware requires on-site support, while most software upgrades may be done remotely. Circuits or access-line software and hardware installations are also part of provisioning. A key part of processing orders is the setup of protocol-specific service parameters. This may be done manually, but the trend should be toward automation. Once the hardware and software parameters are in place, the final step of the provisioning process is to ensure that the service performs according to the objectives prior to releasing service to the end user.

23.3.6 Centralized versus Distributed Network Management

When designing your network, it is important to consider how the network management systems impact operational philosophy. A key decision is whether to adopt a centralized or distributed Network Management System (NMS) architecture for managing Network Elements (NEs), as depicted in Figure 23.3.

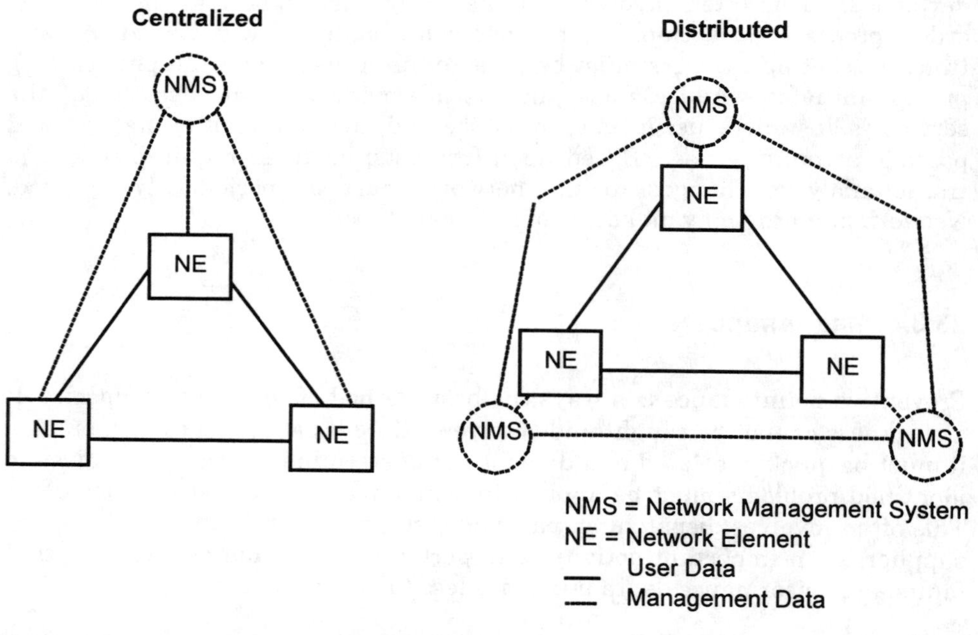

Figure 23.3 Centralized and Distributed OAM&P Architectures

Some will opt for a centralized approach with the expertise concentrated at one or, at most, a few locations with remote site support for only the basic physical actions, such as installing the equipment, making physical connections to interfaces, and replacing cards. In this approach, the software updates, configurations, and troubleshooting can be done by experts at the central site. The centralized approach requires that the requisite network management functions defined in the previous section be well developed, highly available, and effective.

Others may only have a few sites, and hence they may want to have expertise at every site. This approach may be required if the network management system is not sophisticated or the equipment has a number of actions that can only be done at the site. Some lower-level, well-defined automated functions are best performed in a distributed manner. Most RMON and LAN management is performed in a distributed manner.

23.4 NETWORK MANAGEMENT DEFINED

Ambrose Bierce, an American author in the 19th century, published a book called *The Devil's Dictionary*, in which he gave satirical definitions to various words. Network Management (NM) has been defined in Biercian terms as:

> ...the art of making a network appear to be running smoothly
> when in actuality it is teetering on the brink of disaster.

Hopefully, the proactive management of your network will come nowhere near disaster. As we will see in this chapter, there are many ways of managing a network to get the optimal performance and minimal downtime. In this section, we will define the user's view of network management and its evolution into network element management.

23.4.1 Users Demand Better Network Management

Customers are demanding more control of networks with assurances of enhanced reliability and disaster recovery. Vendors of equipment and services have traditionally furnished some type of control and management. As technology has improved and become more complex, users are now demanding better ways to proactively control and manage their systems. The network must appear to be more than just running smoothly with the "brink of disaster" lurking somewhere beneath.

The distribution of computer systems and the "flattening" of the corporate organizational structure has caused more networking to take place. Users are concerned that network management become better, faster, more accurate, less expensive, more integrated, more human-factored, easier to use, and available when they want it and at a price they are willing to pay. Studies show that a majority of LAN and WAN costs (approximately 75 percent) are spent on management and support, with a much smaller proportion on actual hardware and software. Support is defined as the OAM&P, engineering, and management of the network. The results of studies like this cause users to consider out-tasking options that allow them to focus on their core business while out-tasking network management functions.

23.4.2 Evolution of Network Element Management

In the last few decades the cost of embedded processing has been high, so network operations have usually been controlled from one main center. The centralized network was vulnerable to a single point of failure or catastrophe. This center monitored, sent commands, and received messages to and from the network elements that were "out there". This approach was somewhat similar to the centralized mainframe-oriented computing environment. Modern-day PCs and workstations show the opposite trend. More computer power is passing to the end user of which the "client-server" concept is one example. NM is following this trend too. As processing costs have fallen and as distributed processing has become more economical and practical, Distributed Element Management (DEM) is becoming feasible. Each piece of equipment possesses its own processing power to manage operation and status. The centralized management station then collects only the pertinent data required for global systems management.

With frame relay, ATM, and SONET services, the emphasis is on a blend of intelligent CPE and advanced transmission elements that monitor themselves using distributed element management (DEM) systems. Standards committees such as ANSI T1 and X3, IEEE 802.X, and various ITU/ISO committees have created standards for interelement communications management. While the world waits for standards, the real world of vendors and users is usually implementing de facto approaches. This solves today's problems to stay in business long enough to maybe use official standards later. The Simple Network Management Protocol (SNMP) is one good example of an interim de facto standard. SNMP has met the short-term need of users by its simplicity and availability. SNMP was developed by a handful of academics in the research and development community and has captivated many commercial corporate users searching for a way to harness their mushrooming, multivendor TCP/IP and multiprotocol data networks.

In the area of NM, the ITU-T NM standards body went beyond the Common Management Interface Protocol (CMIP) approach with a subset of CMIP called CMIP Over Logical Link Control, or CMOL. Although CMIP is standardized to run over all seven layers of the OSI reference model, CMOL does not follow the seven-layer OSI standard but runs only on the first two layers (physical and data-link layers). In effect, the success of SNMP has caused the original CMIP standards proposal to be scaled back to a subset of CMOL. While CMIP uses elegant object-oriented programming approaches, SNMP, in contrast, uses a remote-debugging paradigm. Remote debugging defines its objects, such as a routing table in a gateway device, in terms of simple management variables, called scalars, and also defines the simple tables constructed from scalars.

Regardless of whether CMIP (or CMOL) or SNMP is used, NM has to be implemented in two places: the management or "manager" station, and the managed device. Since object-oriented programming is "more elegant" and high-powered, it incurs more implementation and run-time costs for both the "management" and the "managed" station. Let's now take a look at the more common network management architectures.

23.4.3 Network Management Architectures

Despite the fact that the CMIP and TMN network management architectures are superior in monitoring, command, and control features over SNMP, most equipment in the United States is developed with the capability for SNMP monitoring. In fact, SNMP-based management has become the de facto standard for the network and higher layers since these exist primarily in end systems and CPE. The TMN network management standard is quickly becoming the worldwide evolving standard for network management. The next few section will summarize the OSI, ITU, and IETF network-management architectures.

23.5 OSI NETWORK MANAGEMENT FUNCTIONAL MODEL

OSI has defined the following five generic functional areas for network management, as defined in the ISO/D15 7498-4 standard, and commonly abbreviated as FCAPS:

- Fault management
- Configuration management
- Accounting management
- Performance management
- Security management

Fault management involves detecting, isolating, and correcting faults in a reactive manner. Performance management involves closely monitoring network elements for changes or patterns that signal that design changes are required or that a fault situation is imminent, and taking action to modify the network. Configuration management involves designing and monitoring the physical and logical state of the network and its resources (addresses, parameters, inventories, etc.) and making changes as required. Accounting management monitors the costs of the network and its resources. Security management involves the monitoring and enforcement of a network security policy detailing access control, user and data authorization and validation, and encryption.

These systems must be tied together with an overall network management brain. It has always been the author's contention that the network designed for the customer must attempt to use industry standard SNMP or CMIP/CMOL standards and stay away from proprietary schemes. Figure 23.4 shows a representation of network-management connectivity. The ties to each element of network management are shown, with the overall element manager represented by SNMP feeds.

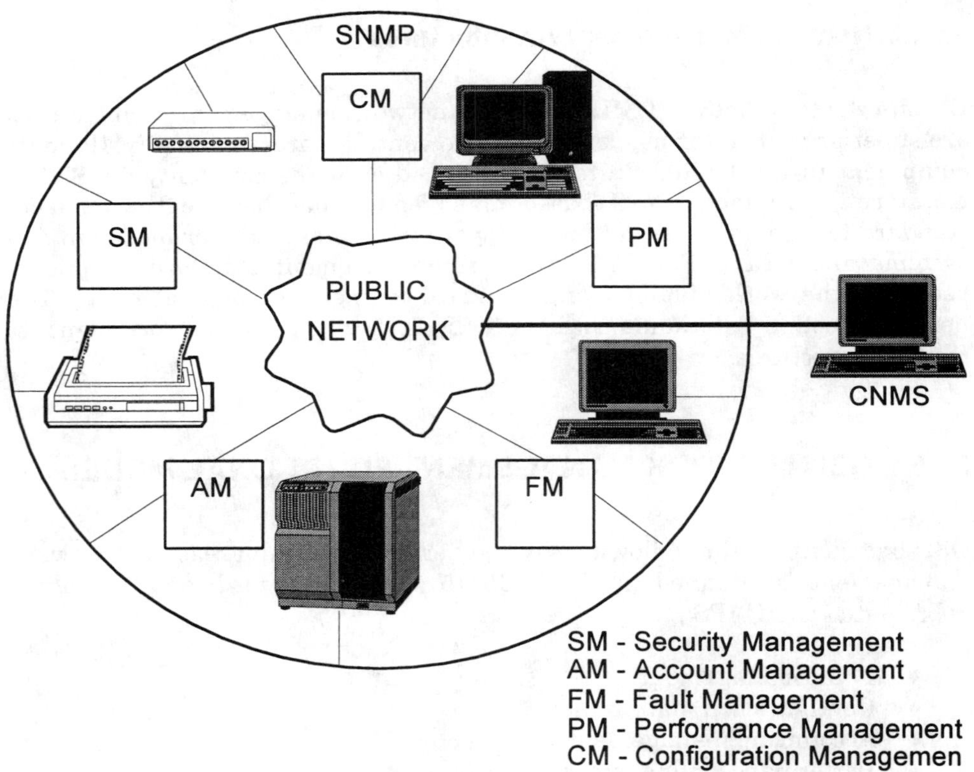

Figure 23.4 OSI FCAPS

There are many other necessities of a good network-management system. Some examples include the capability for remote monitoring and software downloads, geographic diversity with real-time database updates, good statistical and performance reporting, many levels of user access security, a good vendor 7×24 support staff, and a user-friendly, graphical operator interface.

The OSI standard for network management is the Common Management Information Protocol (CMIP). CMIP forms the basis for the entire SONET OAM&P structure.

23.5.1 Vendor Network Management versus OSI and CMIP (CMOL/CMIS)

In addition to the OSI FCAPS model, users need applications-specific network management, including disaster recovery, load balancing, and corrective maintenance. Fault management represents a classic area of confusion. Evolving customer requirements have added several branches to this category, such as restoration, trouble ticket, and inventory management.

The following 10 areas expand the common five-fold OSI definition of network management functions to what various vendors are actually implementing:

Configuration Management. Provides the ability to monitor and reroute on a dynamic basis to meet changing user and network needs. It allows on-demand allocation of bandwidth, preprogrammed configuration scenarios based on changing traffic patterns, and connectivity requirements.

Restoration Management. Relates to, but is different from, configuration management. The restoration management function tracks disaster recovery plans and other contingencies that have been preprogrammed to be executed – manually or automatically - when a line outage or some other disaster occurs.

Information Management. Provides the user with a means to update and maintain the basic physical and logical information contained in the user's databases that define the network. This may include addresses, contacts, circuit layout information, escalation lists, and pager numbers.

Operations Management. Provides information concerning the present operation of the system, including network alarms for all protocol layers and escalation procedures. It also ties into restoration management in disaster situations.

Trouble Management. Provides trouble-ticket management functions in the case of line problems, and historical analysis of past problems tracked by trouble tickets (chronic problems) and their resolution.

Administrative Management. Allows for general administrative chores, notification procedures, file indexing and transfer, system configuration, security access, and administrative messaging via e-mail.

Billing Management. Provides information concerning present bills due, billing formats, alternative billing methods, hierarchy definitions and bill delivery specifications.

Inventory/Provisioning Management. Provides information concerning services inventory, order entry, order status, provisioning details, and delivery dates.

Traffic Management. Provides information on present and past traffic patterns, allowing trunk and circuit analysis, trending, and optimization; cost-performance data analysis; and so forth.

Performance Management. Provides information and reporting on present performance, via real-time transmissions, and correlating it to historical trends in network performance. Then take action! This is the proactive portion of network management – fixing problems *before* they can cause a network outage.

23.5.2 OSI CMIS/CMIP Upstaged by Simple Network Management Protocol (SNMP)

The CMIS and CMIP components of the ISO network-management scheme have been under development for almost 20 years. SNMP is by far the most common management protocol used in North America, while CMIS and CMIP lead in Europe and Asia. SNMP was developed by a group of users in the Internet community (academia, government, military, etc.) for managing their mushrooming Transmission Control Protocol/Internet Protocol (TCP/IP) multivendor data networks. Once considered only as an ad hoc protocol to be eventually replaced by the OSI CMIP protocol, SNMP has taken on a life of its own since the ISO CMIS/CMIP protocols have been slow to gain market acceptance.

SNMP-based monitoring platforms are less expensive than their CMIP counterparts. Most users have deployed two main SNMP management presentation platforms: Hewlett-Packard's OpenView and Sun Microsystems' SunNet Manager. The international market for SNMP is also growing.

Many users are finding that the international network-management standards process is too time consuming, lacks agreement as to what should be developed, tries to be too comprehensive, is too costly, and is too late. The real world demands user-ready solutions that work in less time, at less expense, with less overhead. We will discuss more on SNMP in the next few sections.

23.5.3 New Technology Outpaces Official Standards

The ISO-OSI NM protocol concepts were developed in an era of multikilobit-per-second networking around 1979. However, we are even now passing from the era of multimegabit-per-second networking into a new era of gigabit-per-second networking. While much of the premises equipment today operates with multimegabit communications protocols (as discussed in Chapter 7 and 8), WANs based on ATM and SONET architectures are transporting these multimegabit services and require network management infrastructures even more critically than those in the LANs. Thus, ISO-OSI, which originally planned for kilobit speeds, has moved through megabit speeds and must now deal with gigabit speeds.

The ISO-OSI NM forum tacitly admitted the weakness of CMIP by its actions. As noted, it has scaled back from CMIP to the simpler subset of CMIP called CMOL (CMIP over Logical Link Control): it runs over fewer layers than OSI's seven layers; manages only devices on the same LAN network; and requires the use of proxy agents for dissimilar LAN connection — with the resultant increased overhead, reduced performance, decreased interoperability, and decreased transparency. Most major hardware and software vendors will announce support for standards, especially if their customers see a possible solution to business problems.

23.6 ITU TELECOMMUNICATIONS MANAGEMENT NETWORK (TMN)

The ITU-T and ANSI have been utilizing OSI's standardized Common Management Information Service Elements (CMISE) and the associated Common Management Information Protocol (CMIP) for the Q3 interface in the Telecommunications Management Network (TMN) architecture depicted in Figure 23.5. The other interfaces are also being specified based upon OSI protocols and management principles. This is the standardized vision of interoperable network management of the future.

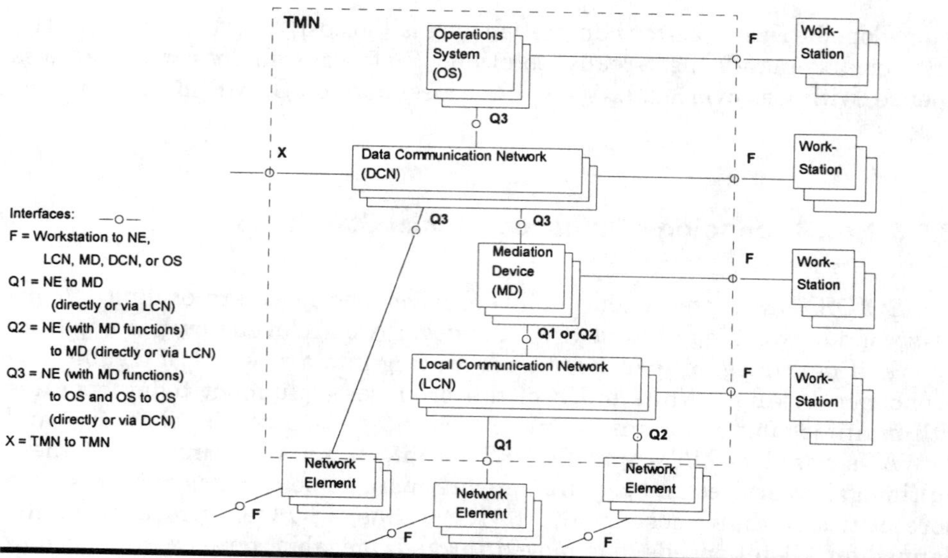

Figure 23.5 Telecommunications Management Network (TMN) Architecture

The software architecture of TMN includes functionally grouped capabilities, called *operations systems functions*, as follows:

- Business-management support of the implementation of policies, strategies, and specific services.
- Service-management functions that are necessary to support particular services, such as subscriber administration and accounting management.
- Network-management support of configuration management, performance management, and maintenance.
- Element-management support for management of one or more Network Elements (NEs), certainly concerned with maintenance, but also involved in performance management, configuration, and possibly accounting.
- Network-element functions at the individual network element or device level that is the source and sink of all network management observations and actions. This includes traffic control, congestion control, layer management, statistics collection, and other protocol-specific functions.

Features that aid in customer billing, network traffic engineering, and setting Quality of Service (QoS) parameters are also supported. The mapping of these software functions onto the hardware architecture is an implementation decision.

23.7 SNMP DEFINED

The IETF SNMP architectural model contains a collection of network-management stations and network elements. SNMP is part of the Internet protocol suite, was first defined in 1990, and is defined in RFC 1157. RFC 1089, 1155 and 1156, and 1212 define SNMP over Ethernet, TCP/IP networks, and MIB definitions, respectively. SNMP today is by far the most widely accepted protocol for managing routers, bridges, switches, and computers (hosts), to name a few. SNMP network-management stations execute a management application which monitors and controls local and remote network elements in a client-server arrangement. Network elements are devices such as hosts, gateways, terminal servers, and the like, which have management agents responsible for performing the network-management functions requested by the network-management stations. SNMP is an application protocol used to communicate management information between the network-management stations and the “agents” in the network elements through virtual connections. The SNMP architecture manages the representation of management information, operations on management information, the form and meaning of exchanges among management entities, the definition of administrative relationships among management entities, and the form and meaning of references to management information.

23.7.1 SNMP Structure and MIBs

SNMP manages network resources through a database called a Management Information Base (MIB). MIBs are composed of managed objects which define the statistical values and parameters of an element’s operation. Each managed object has an Object IDentifier (OID) to distinguish it from other objects.

SNMP as defined in IETF standards has five messages types: GET REQUEST (or simply GET), GET NEXT REQUEST (or simply GET NEXT), SET REQUEST (or simply SET), RESPONSE, and TRAP (which is like an alarm). The SET, GET, and GET NEXT messages are all replied to by the RESPONSE message. A GET is issued from an SNMP management station to an SNMP agent within an SNMP-managed device. The TRAP message is very important since it is the notification of an unexpected event, such as a failure or a system restart. SNMP normally operates over the User Datagram Protocol (UDP), which then usually operates over IP in the Internet Protocol (IP) stack, but may operate over some other protocol.

SNMP utilizes a subset of Abstract Syntax Notation 1 (ASN.1) to define a Management Information Base (MIB) as a data structure that can be referenced in SNMP messages. The syntax of these messages is specified in the Structure of Management Information (SMI) RFC 1155. SNMP network managers access each MIB through a function called a *proxy agent*. The MIB defines objects in terms of primitives such as strings, integers, and bit maps, and allows a simple form of indexing. Each object has a name, a syntax, and an encoding. The MIB variables have a textual Object IDentifier (OID) which is commonly used to refer to the objects. The MIB objects are defined in a tree structure that allows organizational ownership of subtrees to be defined. The branches of the tree are identified by a dotted decimal notation. For example, the prefix of the subtree registered to the ATM Forum is 1.3.6.1.4.1.353. Each of the other branches is identified by the decimal number assigned to the OID as defined in the ATM Forum UNI specification version 3.0. Community name strings can be used as a basic form of secure message authentication. Some examples of Cisco MIB data include interface traffic statistics, QLLC and SDLC events, DSPU, DLSW+, channel, APPN, RSRB, SDLLC, and STUN statistics.

Network-management platforms also offer application programming interfaces (APIs). An API allows third-party developers to offer extensions and additional features on existing platforms. Network managers who are planning to implement SNMP need to understand that it can be difficult to configure devices, administer the agents and manager elements, and that SNMP platforms must be integrated with other tools to perform detailed analysis and management. We will see later how SNMP management systems require a lot of tools augmentation and talent to be valuable.

23.7.2 SNMPv2

A set of upgrades to the Simple Network Management Protocol (SNMP) specifications now define a second, improved version – SNMP version 2 as defined by RFC 1213. The original SNMP standard defined only one variable to be retrieved at a time. The new SNMPv2 can perform bulk retrieval of variables. It also adds better security features and improved performance when manipulating large numbers of objects. Both SNMPv1 and SNMPv2 use the new umbrella MIB module called MIB II.

There is general agreement that SNMP and SNMPv2 are best for CPE and private networks, while CMIP/CMISE is more appropriate for carrier interconnection. Many switches have implemented SNMP since it is simpler; interoperability can be achieved more easily with than the CMIP protocols.

More detail on SNMP can be found in RFC 1098, 1155, 1157, 1212, 1213, and 1215.

23.7.3 Customer Network Management and Proprietary Operating Systems

Customer Network Management (CNM) capability is important for carrier-based services. Capabilities should include at least physical port status, virtual circuit status, order parameters, and selected performance metrics. Delivery of detailed performance counts involves additional complexity and cost. Usage counts from the originating and terminating switch by virtual circuit may also be used to track performance delivered to customers. Status commands, like DLCIs, SRB, current configuration options, DLSW+ peers, performance variables, and diagnostics like trace events, trace routes, interface and state changes, and peer connections are part of many element managers and vendor proprietary operating systems. Proprietary operating systems can also contain diagnostics, monitoring, security, configuration management (software and firmware), and traffic control (i.e., for ATM).

23.7.4 IBM Network Management – NetView

In 1986, IBM took its four or five standalone data-network-management products and combined them into a new offering under the banner of NetView. IBM set up NetView running on the IBM mainframe using MVS or VM operating systems. It was positioned as an enterprise-wide focal point for managing large networks and data centers. All management data has to be translated into IBM SNA protocols before being sent to the focal point at the mainframe for processing. NetView is currently used in conjunction with SNMP and CMIP in networks where there is a large portion of SNA traffic to manage. NetView manages traditional SNA, APPN, and HPR traffic types. NetView for AIX (NetView 6000) is designed for LAN and SNMP-manageable devices like routers and switches. NetView AIX competes with two other leading industry network-management presentation managers – SUN's SunNet manager and Hewlett Packard's OpenView.

23.7.5 Reporting Formats

Network-management reports can be provided through any of the following common means and formats:

- ⇒ Diskette
- ⇒ Paper
- ⇒ Fax
- ⇒ FTP/TFTP

⇒ SNMP agent
⇒ SNMP client
⇒ Terminal
⇒ E-mail
⇒ DOS station
⇒ Internet web interface

23.8 REMOTE MONITORING (RMON)

Remote MONitoring (RMON) is a method of collecting and analyzing information from remote network elements. RMON provides the information required to determine where to place the boundaries between collision and broadcast domains, functions provided by LAN switches and routers, respectively. An RMON agent attached to a local network element captures information and statistics on protocols and traffic activity and communicates the information back, sometimes formatted, to a central RMON management console for processing. RMON probes (dedicated RMON agents) and other RMON agents provide this data when polled. They only send TRAPs to alert the console of a condition but do not send significant data via these TRAPs.

RMON is especially critical when managing a switched LAN environment, because LAN segments, which previously served many users, are now microsegmented. This microsegmentation creates more segments to manage, closer to the user. RMON extends the visibility into these microsegmented LANs, providing traffic analysis at the packet level along with trending capability for performance engineering. When extended to the VLAN environment, physical and logical topology design can be optimized. Remote LAN troubleshooting can be performed proactively, with the engineer looking for things that are abnormal.

RMON probes can provide a great deal of information on the performance of your LAN and WAN traffic patterns and protocol performance trends. This information is especially critical when migrating from a bridged or routed environment to a switched one. The engineer can then optimize the switched or LAN topology. Most importantly, RMON allows the network manager to provide bounding between the collision (MAC) and broadcast (IP/ARP) domains.

RMON can be justified if the application performance on a specific portion of the network is mission critical. RMON can catch utilization patterns that are exceeding thresholds and alert the engineer to take action. All of this monitoring is done remotely, and thus eliminates the need for on-site LAN managers to watch LAN performance, while providing proactive management alerts of potential network outages. Figure 23.6 illustrates a network where remote SNMP devices are monitored through an SNMP management platform. An RMON probe is also placed on the Ethernet LAN.

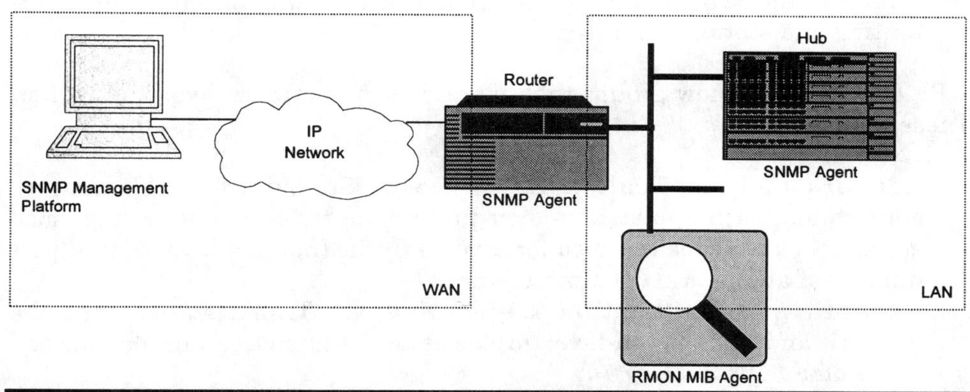

Figure 23.6 RMON Monitoring

RMON standards began with RFC 1098, which defined the Simple Network Management Protocol (SNMP) in 1989, and was later standardized in 1994 as RFC 2222. The first RMON specification – RFC 1271 – was developed in 1994. RFC 1757 was next specified defining the RMON 10 groups, and is the standard used today. RMON2 specifies enhancements to the original RMON RFC. RMON groups operate at the MAC layer, while the newer RMON2 groups operate at the network layer and above.

RFC 1757 defines 10 RMON groups, where each group collects information on variables and sends it back to the central management station for analysis. These groups include:

1. **Statistics Group.** Maintains error and utilization statistics for the specific LAN segment or subnetwork being monitored by the RMON agent. Some examples include CRC/alignment, fragments, multicast, broadcast, and bandwidth utilization.
2. **History Group.** Obtains statistical samples, such as packet count, error count, and utilization and stores them for later retrieval. This also includes a history of conspicuous statistics.
3. **Alarm Group.** Administration control of sampling interval and threshold for any variable monitored by the RMON agent. Some examples include absolute or relative values and rising or falling thresholds.
4. **Host Group**. Host traffic measurements like packets or bytes sent and received, errors, multicast, and broadcasts.
5. **Host TopN Group.** Reporting on top *N* hosts statistics.
6. **Traffic Matrix Group.** Stores the errors and statistics (packets, bytes, and errors) between source and destination nodes on a network.
7. **Filter Group.** Provides a filter engine for packet recognition.
8. **Packet Capture Group.** Buffering criteria for packets that match filter criteria.
9. **Event Group**. Time- and date-stamped logging and printing of events.

10. **Token Ring Group.** Configuration and statistical information on source routing and stations on a ring.

RMON2 provides new groups that operate at the network layer and higher. These groups include:

1. **Network and Application Layer Host.** Statistics for each network address and each application-layer protocol on the segment or ring, such as packets and bytes received for layer 3 traffic (not just layer 2) and port number of an application, respectively.
2. **Network and Application Layer Matrix.** Traffic statistics at the network and application-layer protocols between source and destination nodes on a network.
3. **Protocol Directory.** User-selectable protocols that are monitored and counted.
4. **Protocol Distribution.** Table of statistics for each protocol in directory.
5. **User Definable History.** Sampling of any MIB object monitored by the RMON agent.
6. **Address Mapping.** Listing of MAC to network-layer address bindings such as with ARP.
7. **Configuration Group.** Listing of RMON agent configurations and capabilities.

23.9 TRENDS IN NETWORK MANAGEMENT

What are some of the trends now occurring in network management? Let's now explore the lead that SNMP is taking over the OSI network-management standards, the growth of new technologies in network management, the importance of around-the-clock management, multivendor and multitransport media-management growth, improvements in display management, artificial intelligence (AI) and neural networks, and the role of voice processing in network management.

23.9.1 Will the ISO OSI NM Standards Follow SNMP's Example?

Presently the SNMP protocol as defined by the IETF has many more vendors building to its specs than the OSI CMIP camp. Many vendors develop proprietary MIBs to work in conjunction with standard MIB definitions. SNMP is nonstandard without OSI blessing, but it works, it is cheap, and it is available. Marshall Rose, chair of the Internet's Network Management Protocol working group, gave his opinion:

> SNMP uses a remote-debugging paradigm. Remote debugging defines the objects, such as a routing table in a gateway device, in terms of simple management variables (scalars), and simple tables, which are constructed from these scalars. Although this technique lacks the flair of an object-oriented approach (CMIP) it has a no-nonsense attitude that has proven quite effective in promoting the definition of all kinds of managed objects. ...the products that are out there are doing yeoman's work in the field and providing a robust, competitive market. Talk to your colleagues, see what they are using, and find out what their gripes are ...start managing real networks with real products and draw your own conclusions.

23.9.2 Network Management Elements and New Technologies

To understand the complexity of network management, one must have a bird's-eye view of the private and public network elements that must be managed. Integrated network management must be provided for this hybrid mix of elements:

- CPE/premises elements
- Central-office switching and cross-connect (DXC) elements
- Tandem-level switching and cross-connect (DXC) elements
- International switching/DXC/gateway elements

Networks are growing larger and more complex. Around 1970, the average data network consisted of 20 to 25 terminals connected across a network to the Front-End Processor (FEP) of a mainframe. Today, data networks are much larger on average — sometimes consisting of thousands of terminals applying to multiple FEPs and hosts for access to multiple applications, or thousands of workstations and servers operating in client-server and distributed computing environments using multiple applications and protocols. Technologies that must be managed include Local Area Networks (LANs) using various transmission media: twisted pair (unshielded and shielded), coaxial cable, and fiber, all using multiple LAN protocols (Ethernet, Token Ring, etc.) and internetworking protocols (IP, IPX, etc.). And the entire family of internetworking communications devices between LANs and WANs — bridges, routers, switches, and gateways — must be managed. Value-added services such as frame relay and ATM must be managed, also.

Increasing volumes of alarms and status messages are being received from complex networks composed of larger systems, more complex systems, higher-paced applications (such as just-in-time delivery systems), real-time inventory management, CPU-to-CPU communications, CAD/CAM, large file transfers, increased graphic dumps between workstations, exploding LAN-to-LAN connectivity among similar and dissimilar LANs and, finally, LAN-to-WAN connectivity across the street, the city, the state, the country, and the world.

LAN-to-WAN connectivity is forcing change and has spawned the introduction of new technologies into data networking: frame relay, cell relay (ATM), and Synchronous Optical NETworks (SONET). To help the network manager cope with this veritable explosion of network alarms and status indicators, important new technologies are being employed to assist in the management of modern networks.

CRTs with color graphics are being used instead of printers and CRTs that report status by "text" trouble alarms. Text, unfortunately, is highly mnemonic and often requires documentation to explain the meaning of what went wrong. Network management presentation managers like HP's OpenView use graphical displays with well-designed icons and symbols to display configuration and status for key network elements under Distributed Element Management (DEM) systems. These visual displays and programming paradigms, along with data and alarm correlation tools, are being used to compress and summarize the volumes of data constantly flowing across the network.

Sifting information by new programming methods and using color visual displays of the overall network with icons and network layouts are allowing NM operators to better address strategic networking needs, trend analyses, and planning issues. Rapid mouse-clicking on icons to indicate and/or change their status is also proving helpful and meets human-factors engineering requirements.

23.9.3 Around-the-Clock Operations Increasing

Off-hours or "graveyard shift" traffic is becoming more important with the globalization of networks. Just as the local supermarket is now open 7 days a week and 24 hours a day in many cases, so networks too require the same level of management and availability. Extended hours and around-the-clock operation of world stock exchanges and economic markets from Tokyo to New York to London show this trend. Data critical for global decision making is being passed over networks at all hours of the day and night. Not only are multinational (or now so-called transnational) businesses run monthly from afar but users are now making *daily decisions* from afar. Older human-based systems of NM must be increasingly automated to meet these challenges.

Recent trends in new NM technology applications include:

- High-performance single-user management and engineering workstations
- Improved Graphical User Interfaces (GUIs)
- Windows, menus, icons, color graphics, etc.
- Rapid mouse-clicking on icons to display or change status
- Enhanced human-factors engineering (ergonomics)
- "Exception" report to prioritized alerts, alarms, status

- Alarm and event correlation
- Newly emerging technologies
- Display management
- Neural networks
- Object-oriented coding
- Object-oriented databases
- Self-healing nets/disaster recovery via fiber rings

The sheer volume of network status, alerts, and alarms flowing over a network demands that network managers and operators have all the help they can get to keep control. The information provided to the operator must be summarized, condensed, and made quickly digestible. It should be graphically oriented so the network operator can make operations decisions by observing symbols, color changes, and various condition states on color-CRT screens rather than being forced to decipher, with constant reference to paper documentation, the cryptic messages of network status, alarms, and alerts rapidly scrolling past in a text format on a CRT. Prioritization of alarms is a critical factor. Alarm and event logs should be similarly organized.

Information, too, should be displayed in hierarchical fashion, with the ability to "telescope" from the macro view down to the micro view — for example, looking at the overall network of 100 nodes represented by icons, and then further isolating a problem by rapid mouse-clicking down to the individual icon trunk card level of, let us say, a router in Denver, with the icon showing the router port or IP address as a status light in color on the workstation's windows. Action can then be taken based on status. Icon clicking with the mouse can take the network operator from the macro view to the micro view in 3 to 6 seconds — from the overall network down to the card or individual virtual circuit level of a specific location, device, circuit, and address.

23.9.4 Multivendor, Multitransport Media Networking Growing

Multiple vendor network product and service implementations usually cause interoperability problems. Proprietary designs evolve even within the implementation of standards. Often there is dissimilar hardware, programming, command structures, and displays. As multiple NM platforms have developed, multiple display terminals have also developed. Interoperability is a key issue for users with multivendor networks. Over 90 percent of major commercial users have equipment from at least two different vendors and 50 percent from five different vendors. These are data networks, composed of modems, multiplexers, packet/frame/cell switches, and other communications devices with mixed protocols and architectures. What happens with the addition of voice and legacy protocols (i.e., SNA) into the area of network management? There is no one easy answer to this question. The answer lies in knowing that the hybrid networking environment consists of voice/data, public/private network elements, CPE/POP-based switching systems, and varying degrees of user/vendor control.

To address this multivendor environment, the leading vendors have developed "umbrella" platforms or architectures to deal with the multivendor problem. This approach is called "managing the managers". An Integrated Network Management System (INMS) is developed which monitors existing disparate NM systems through some common interface. However, the problem is not just multivendors but also multiproducts *within* the same vendor.

Most existing NM systems use reactive management techniques instead of proactive ones. Existing NM systems tend to flood the network operator with alarms and status information. And the operator tries to react as quickly as possible. As networks grow more complex, however, the operator is flooded with still more information. Rapid decisions must be made on *more* information, in *less* time, and with *escalating penalties* for mistakes.

Automation of human factors must step in to help. NM systems must be built to adapt to the human mind's ability to process information. People are not good at parallel processing or handling multiple streams of information simultaneously. People are mono, serial processors — one thing at a time, although they can be interrupt-driven. NM systems must take information coming in from the network in parallel fashion, correlate and sort it according to predefined priorities, and adapt it to the human mind's ability to serially process events and actions.

NM systems are beginning to interface to the parallel incoming information sources streaming in from the network. By neural networks and rule-based expert systems, NM systems can reconfigure incoming parallel information streams for serial presentation to the human network operator — thus automating the analysis of information in a warm-and-fuzzy manner.

Some basic requirements for adapting new technologies to NM include:

- Improve display management
- Implement rule-based and neural AI systems
- Employ object-oriented coding and databases
- Handle growing networks with more network elements
- Correlate and summarize network data for decision making
- Move rapidly from macro to micro views of network elements
- Automate the control process
- Improve data presentation and alarm annunciation
- Accommodate emerging technologies and standards
- Replace reactive NM with proactive NM

23.9.5 Improvements in Display Management

Improved graphic-display management software allows the network operator to now scan detailed network diagrams and determine the general health and status of a several-hundred-node network in seconds. This is a major improvement over the chore of reading text-related messages for each network element. Improvements have come largely because of developments in X-Windows, a low-level window manager developed by M.I.T. that runs on UNIX, and with higher-level graphic toolkits such as Open Look, Motif, and Graphic Modeling Systems (GMS). The latest version of the popular X-Windows display manager runs on virtually all UNIX workstations and on many other platforms, from mainframes to PCs. It provides a programming interface to a variety of library functions, called Xlib, that can be used to create and manage windows and their basic functions, such as scroll bars and window resize buttons.

Open Look and Motif are two toolkits for creating X-Windows-based graphical user interfaces (GUIs). They implement calls to Xlib and present mechanisms that allow the end user operate the application. Open Look was developed by Sun Microsystems with the support of AT&T. Motif was originally developed by Digital Equipment Corporation (DEC) and Hewlett-Packard and, since both companies are sponsors of the Open Software Foundation (OSF), Motif receives strong support from the OSF.

User interfaces have become more mouse-, menu-, and windows-oriented, allowing the operator to interact with the actual equipment represented by the icons to program or take in and out of service through vendor-proprietary element managers. Using toolkits and window managers, users can draw complex network diagrams to allow an operator to view the status of hundreds of network nodes and elements simultaneously. Yet with the click of a mouse-button, the operator can, within a few seconds, focus on a particular icon and observe its alarm lights for the state of the actual element or object represented by the icon.

The network operator's attention can be enhanced by the animation of icons to represent "living" systems: turning red, green, blue, or yellow, as well as blinking, showing happy or sad faces, or using speech processing to literally cry out for “Help!” in a strident manner like some video games. Work space on the CRT screen can be maximized by the ability to resize and open or close windows on the network-management workstation. Closed windows, however, continue in real time to monitor the status of the network elements for later recall and display if required. When a window is reopened later, the current, cumulative network status is displayed in nearly real time. This timeliness and availability of information makes network decision making easier and faster. This allows quick resolution of problems with less downtime. This equates to reduced costs and increased revenues.

23.9.6 Artificial Intelligence (AI)/Neural Networks

Since voluminous amounts of network management information must be processed, and network information arrives at the control point in parallel streams as status/alarms originating from perhaps thousands of network elements — such as a modem, multiplexer, router, switch, or CSU/DSU — the parallel streams must be analyzed and patterns and statuses recognized. The "real" alarms, or the "trigger" alarms must be isolated by exception methods from "sympathy" alarms set off by the original "trigger" alarm. Otherwise, thousands of alarms would have to be dealt with.

To move from reactive to proactive NM, rule-based expert systems and neural networks will allow for the detection of deteriorating conditions on the network before a full-fledged outage or breakdown. This allows for proactive effecting of changes before the faults actually occur. Artificial intelligence monitors hundreds of points for traffic flow rates, user transaction response times, and equipment health and status. These data streams are correlated to recognize trends that can predict problems by extrapolation.

The knowledge of experienced network operators can be captured by AI methods by storing various corrective procedures. It also stores "memory" for things *not* to be done. These procedures can be stored and referenced later as holiday or after-hours outages occur so that, in a sense, network operations experience is available in almost real time. Rule bases are produced over time (the experiences of expert human network operators) and these rule bases predict ranges of decisions of things "to do" or "not to do" in certain situations in the network.

To release this overload, a neural network is used. A neural network computer processor gathers and correlates high volumes of measurement data for input to the rule-based expert systems. Unlike traditional computers, which must be programmed to produce certain outputs based on specific input data, neural networks are "trained" to recognize patterns by running sample data. Neural networks can also process many inputs simultaneously, that is, perform "parallel processing" while conventional computers are limited to serial-like processing, performing one operation at a time. Neural nets can correlate multiple measurement data streams against preprogrammed measurement trend-data ranges that could cause network faults and either alarm or take action to fix them. This is proactive network management! Neural network output could also be used by the rule-based expert systems to select corrective courses of action. Thus, "self-healing" networks are possible not only by physical design but by software design as well.

23.9.7 Voice Processing and Network Management

The Speak & Spell computer from Texas Instruments introduced the era of voice processing. Automobiles now use voice processing to supplement visual signals and indicators. The "gas empty" indicator, whether an analog needle that travels to the "empty" position or a digital red light going from "off" to "on", has now been augmented by a human voice speaking to the driver. Network operators, even though they may have existing visual indicators, can now also be reminded at critical points by voice-processing messages so their networks will not run out of gas on some lonely road.

23.10 BILLING

How does the customer receive a bill for service? In what granularity is the bill provided? Does the bill vary based on technology and service? The billing scheme can be based on many factors, such as:

- Technology used
- Specific implementations of protocols
- Time the circuit is used
- Number of data units successfully sent or received (packets, frames, PDUs, cells) during a certain time period
- Tariff or public pricing

Billing schemes fall into three categories: fixed cost, usage based, or a hybrid of both. Charges are either nonrecurring (one-time charges) or recurring (typically monthly). The switched services discussed in this text (with the exception of circuit-switched) are can all be billed based on usage or fixed pricing.

23.11 SECURITY

Network security should be clearly defined in the network-engineering plan, and should be strictly administered. Breaches of security can be classified as query or information gathering, modification, permanent change, or theft. The easiest way to lose control of the network is through insufficient security. There are two primary modes of network security: access and transmission.

Transmission security is performed primarily at the physical layer, and can be implemented through password-protected modems, encoded transmission devices, and at a variety of other network access points. This is to prevent line monitoring, passive wiretapping, and stolen data from an active tap.

Technologies such as ATM and SONET contain their own form of transmission security because even if the circuits are tapped and "read", the data flow is almost meaningless. The way in which ATM and SONET frames are formed distorts the original shape of the data so much that it could not be interpreted.

Security can also be implemented at many protocol layers within the network, within hardware, software, and computer services. Access-control filtering is done primarily at the data-link, network, and application layers. These layers contain the protocol feeds that make security control possible. Perhaps the best security control is at the user or application level. Here, protection from illegal use of the network is gained through:

- User names
- Passwords
- Password life of days, not months or years
- Software access levels
- User lockouts
- User ID card/key
- No user echo of password
- Imbedded nonalphanumeric character
- Tight administration and control
- One-time user passwords
- Fingerprint or eye retina scanner
- Human tissue sample or DNA match
- First born inserted into scanner

Combinations can also be used. Some of these techniques go overboard on security, but use whatever is required based upon the sensitivity and mission-critical nature of the traffic. Also, educating users on how to use the security system will help. Security can be implemented through the access control mentioned above, by hazard protection, and as personnel practices clearly defined in policy and procedures. Remember, network security is only as strong as the weakest link.

Once the network is up and running, a professional security expert should attempt illegal entry. If he or she can get in, someone else can, too. Beware of security holes created during system updates and software upgrades.

Understand the security inherent in each network device. For example, filters can be set in a router to admit or block specific protocol actions, such as FTP file transfers to a specific address. This same capability for network (layer 3) security does not exist in switching hubs or hubs that operate at the MAC layer.

With the proliferation of Internet access, doors are opened into the corporate mainstream network that flash a "come and get me" neon sign to hackers. Evidence the financial services or distribution firm that stands to lose millions of dollars if its data is compromised. Bottom line: it is always worthwhile consulting with a professional security services company. In fact, some of the outsourcing companies now offer some level of security services for Internet and corporate WAN communications.

23.12 TRAINING

The training process should begin as soon as the network design is complete, and can actually begin when the vendor is chosen. Allow the vendor to provide materials for and actually do training as much as possible. If you request vendor training before placing the equipment order, then you have some leverage. The key point to stress is to begin training as soon as possible. Training should cover, at a minimum:

- User training as early on as possible
- Concepts and architecture
- Basic protocol and addressing configuration and operations
- Hardware and software (including database and addressing)
- Installation
- Network management
- Advanced techniques
- Documentation

Training is most critical for those who will actually install and configure the hardware and software. This should be the focus of training before network implementation.

23.13 WHEN TO STOP DESIGNING AND START IMPLEMENTING

The design process is an iterative one, but the designer must know when to stop designing and start implementing. There is new technology emerging on the market every day. Don't give in to the temptation to stop the design process based on a new product some vendor says will be out "next quarter". The design will never be perfect, and modifications can always be made after the network is up and running. If the network is designed based on the guidelines provided in this book, it will be easier to integrate new technology into the network when required.

23.14 REVIEW

Standardization of network management is usually considered later in the technology life cycle because only after you have built the network, determined what can go wrong, and discovered what is needed to make it work can you finalize how to operate, administer, maintain, and provision it. This chapter introduced a model of Operations, Administration, Maintenance, and Provisioning (OAM&P) functions and how they interact to meet the overall needs of network users. Good planning can provide these OAM&P functions in a much more productive manner soon after the introduction of technology; however, there is no substitute for experience.

In this chapter, the importance of documenting both the network design (engineering plan) and the method by which it will be implemented (O&M document) was covered. It takes teamwork among many departments to design and implement a network. The importance and the capabilities of network management were noted: the responsibility to provide thorough network management to the user, and to make the best use of standards-based protocols when implementing network management. Network-management architectures were covered. The OSI architecture defines the functions of Fault, Configuration, Accounting, Performance, and Security (FCAPS). The ITU defines a physical and logical Telecommunications Management Network (TMN) architecture. The IETF has defined the Simple Network Management Protocol (SNMP) and Management Information Base (MIB) and has achieved a high degree of interoperability in the industry. The issues of security, training, and billing are also important. Finally, the design is reviewed one last time before beginning the implementation phase.

Chapter

24

Design and Management Tools

This chapter provides the reader with insight into the selection of network design tools. Design tools provide an accurate method of modeling and designing networks. In this chapter, the criteria by which to choose a design tool will be explained. The chapter will serve to describe types of network tools and state which features belong to each tool, describe typical network design tasks, state standard requirements for a design tool, and analyze and describe the features available on current commercial design tools. The user can then use this chapter to select a design tool that meets their specific requirements.

24.1 DESIGN TOOLS

Over the past decade, many companies have written software design tools. The capabilities of these tools include analyzing existing networks, providing meshed and hierarchical network designs, modeling design change and failure scenarios, and performing clocking analysis. While these tools exist, few are actually used by most network designers and managers. This is in part due to the lack of tool flexibility and the inherent constraints of limited options, and also in part by the sheer difficulty of modeling distributed hybrid networks. Some available tools are also well suited for modeling specific types of networks, such as intelligent multiplexer networks. But, conversely, when an intelligent multiplexer network is meshed with a multiprotocol router-based backbone that has Ethernet and Token Ring LANs attached, the tools hit their limits.

Design tools analyze two types of data networks: circuit-switched and packet/frame/cell-switched networks. When choosing a design tool, certain criteria should be present in the tool. At a minimum, it should support the basic user requirements defined in the last chapter. Before a tool can be successful, the data fed into it must be accurate. Hence the importance of the detailed requirements analysis of Chapters 15 and 16, so that good input will produce good outputs.

Design tools use either mathematical modeling or packet-level simulation. Mathematical modeling uses statistics to predict user traffic flows and model their characteristics. Packet-level simulation is the most common method, however, where the tool inputs are a snapshot of the network at a *single point in time*. Since the traffic on packet networks is often bursty in nature, *multiple* snapshots are required. This type of modeling works well for small networks where the user traffic characteristics are well known, but processing times and the sheer computing power required to perform a large, dynamic network design often makes this process very time-consuming, resource insensitive, and difficult. Some design tools use neither of the above approaches. Instead, they model each user input as a single demand, based on their file-transfer protocol characteristics. The author has found that the best network-design tools focus on heuristic routing algorithms based on user-definable parameters and queuing theory, rather than any one form of mathematical simulation of theory.

24.2 TERMINOLOGY

There are two primary terms used throughout this chapter: transport and demand.

Transport is a term used to define the bandwidth that is used to create user channels. Transport carries user data from point A to point B. Transport comprises the bandwidth (private lines, frame relay, ATM, etc.) between switching devices (digital cross connects, switches, multiplexers, etc.). Transport is also referred to as *backbone*.

Demand is the portion of the transport bandwidth that contains the user data. In private line networks, the demand traffic is the unit of circuit used such as 56 kbps, 64 kbps, fractional-T1, and T1. No distinction is made between the amount of bandwidth required for a particular user, and the amount of bandwidth that is added due to overhead or routing inefficiencies. A session, file transfer, client-server application, or switched circuit are all types of demand. Demand is also referred to as the *circuits* that are carried by the backbone.

24.3 CATEGORIES OF TOOLS

There is a general differentiation among design, configuration-management, and event-management tools. The term *design tool* is used to describe a wide range of applications that are concerned with topics such as optimization of network topology and failure analysis. The term *configuration-management tool* is used to describe a wide range of applications that address topics such as storing records of rack layout, cabling design, and equipment location. The term *event-management tool* is used to describe a wide range of applications that are used for real time network event notification.

24.3.1 Design Tools

The attributes of and the services provided by a design tool include

- Cost model – calculates the cost of the transport portion of the network
- What if analysis – performs changes to the design, gets answers to questions such as cost and failure probability
- Failure analysis – describes completely the effects on demand traffic of a failure of some portion of the transport network
- Visualize – shows network elements and connections on screen and on paper
- Simulate – models the operation of the network devices with respect to physical, data link, network, and so forth, parameters
- Characterize – calculates Key Performance Indicators (KPIs) that describe design, efficiency, utilization, etc.
- Optimize – changes the network design to increase KPIs, use directives, strategies
- Design – produces transport from demand and demand from profiles
- Report – produces utilization, link, equipment, site reports

24.3.2 Configuration-Management Tools

The attributes of and the services provided by a configuration-management tool include

- Keeps detailed records of the setting of network elements, including ports, cards, and devices. Settings include all software-defined attributes of equipment as well as hardware options defined through "straps". Other details such as serial numbers, revision levels, software options, and setup parameters will be stored by a configuration-management tool.
- Keeps detailed records of the layout of racks of equipment. This information will most likely be graphical in nature. The connections made by cables and the routing of cables will be stored.

24.3.3 Event-Management Tools

The attributes of and the services provided by an alarm-management tool include

- Storage of events, some of which will represent faults in the network
- Correlation of events, which reduces multiple events related to a particular failure to a single event relaying the proximate cause of the multiple events
- Presentation of events

24.4 CLASSES OF DESIGN TOOLS

Design tools can be broken down into three categories. Physical-design tools are those tools that take into consideration only attributes of equipment to the physical level. Circuit switching is essentially the only type of network covered by physical-design tools. By contrast, logical-design tools are those tools that take into consideration attributes of equipment beyond the physical level. Networks of this type frequently employ the concept of virtual circuits or datagram delivery. Frame, cell, and datagram networks are the types of networks covered by logical-design tools. Statistical-design tools are those tools that take into consideration applications and the statistical nature of the traffic that they generate. These tools consider delay and throughput requirements of the applications. Their models are inherently statistical in nature.

24.4.1 Physical-Design Tool

A physical-design tool has the capability to design networks that incorporate only physical entities. Transport facilities are always considered as physical when they are primary. Primary refers to a configuration where there is not a lower level of network providing the transport. Figure 24.1 shows a model for a physical design.

Demand circuits are considered physical entities when they consist only of portions of transport circuits that are created at a physical level. For example, a physical time-division multiplexer divides a transport circuit into multiple demand circuits.

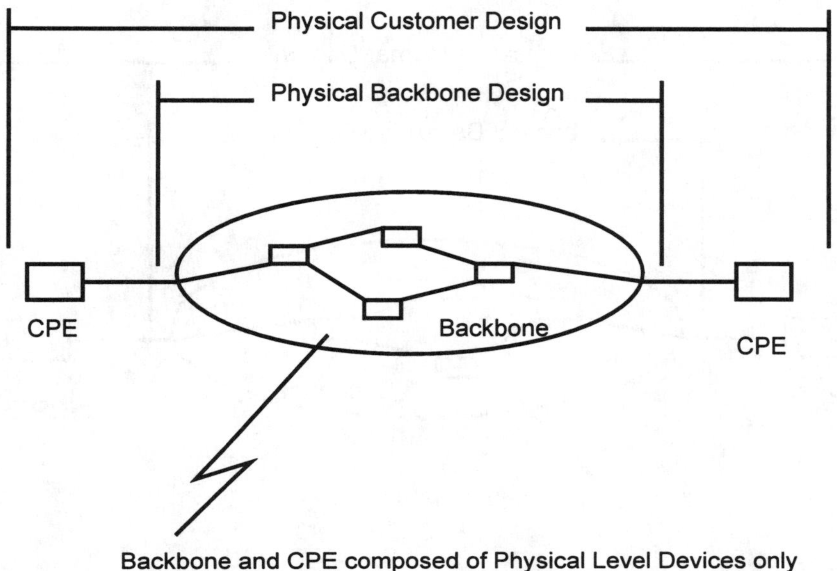

Figure 24.1 Model for Physical Design

24.4.2 Logical-Design Tool

A logical-design tool has the capability to design networks that incorporate logical entities such as permanent virtual circuits and switched virtual circuits. Also included are networks that provide connectionless services such as IP services. This type of tool converts a virtual circuit demand into a optimized physical-transport network. Figure 24.2 shows a model for a logical design.

24.4.3 Statistical-Design Tools

For work with multiprotocol environments, the ultimate demands placed on the data network will be specified in terms of end-user quantifiable entities. Such entities are SNA sessions, client-server sessions, and connections to network servers. For each of these requirements there is a native protocol associated with the application that provides the service. For each native protocol, there are special requirements for data throughput, priority, and latency. A model is needed to convert the user requirements in terms of sessions into logical circuit demand. Figure 24.3 shows a model for a statistical design.

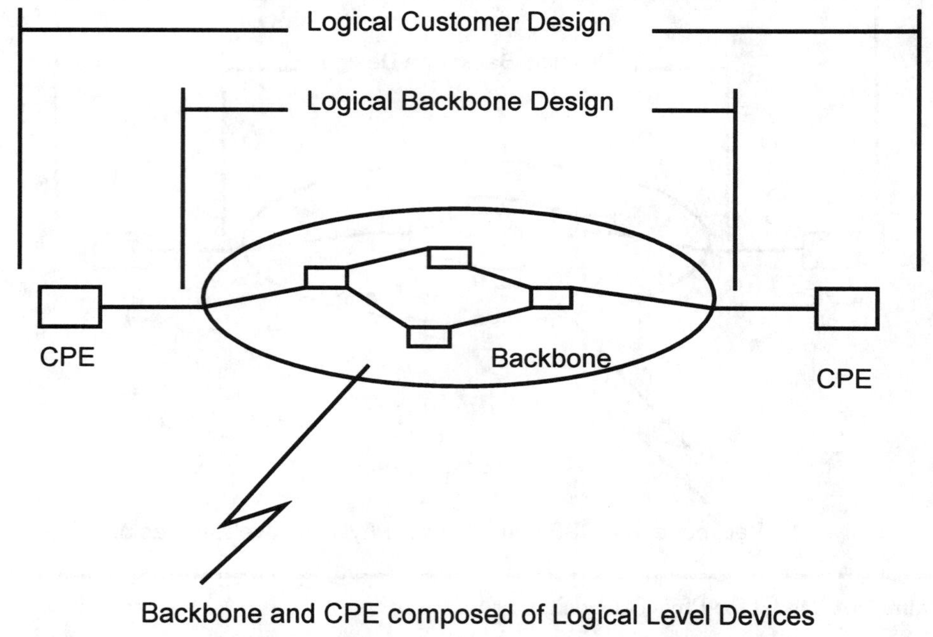

Figure 24.2 Model for Logical Design

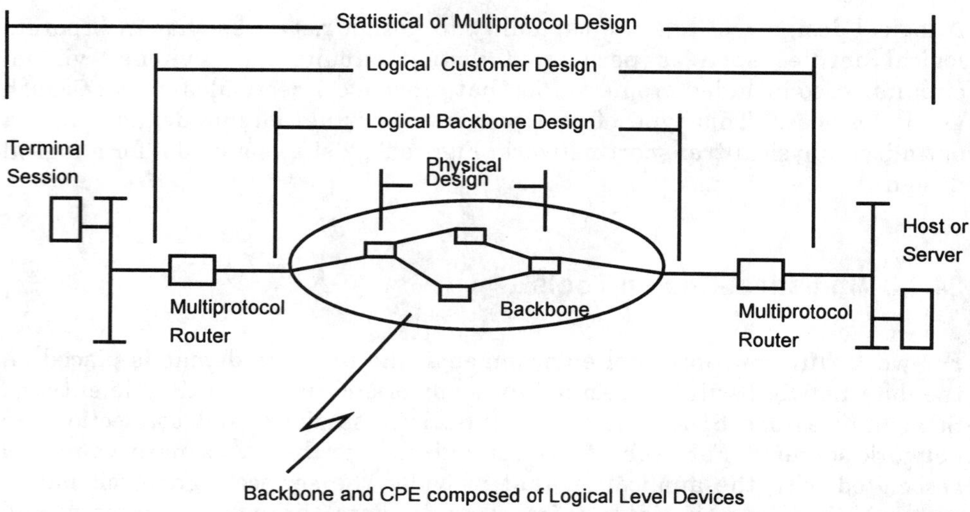

Figure 24.3 Model for Statistical Design

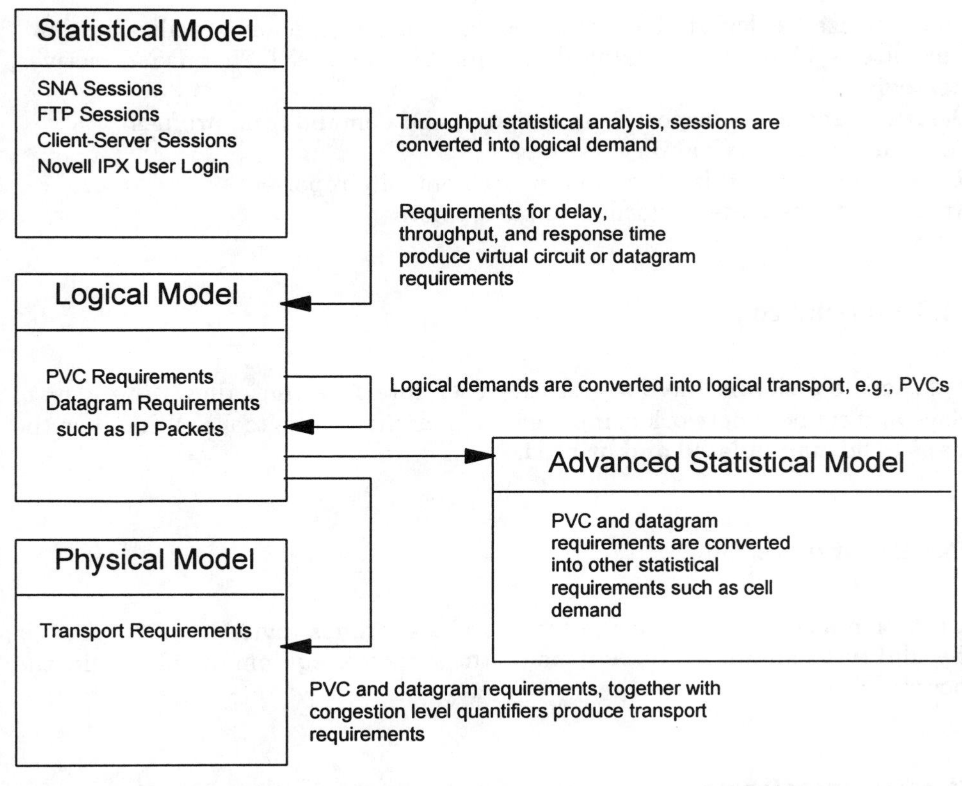

Figure 24.4 Integration of the Three Types of Tools

24.4.4 Integration of the Physical, Logical, and Statistical

In order to perform network design from the level of user demand to the level of physical transport, the three levels of design tool must be integrated, as shown in Figure 24.4. Ultimately, the three levels should exist in one tool.

24.5 COMPONENTS OF DESIGN PROJECTS

Design projects typically require a design tool to perform one or more of the following activities:

Visualize – show network elements and connections, on screen, and on paper
Simulate – model the operation of the network devices with respect to physical, data link, and network parameters

Characterize – calculate KPIs that describe design, efficiency, utilization, etc.
Optimize – change the network design to increase KPIs, use directives, strategies
Design – produce transport from demand, and demand from profiles
Test – evaluate survivability, loading
Report – produce utilization, link, equipment, site reports
Analyze – investigate performance parameters

24.5.1 Visualize

A design tool should have a versatile user interface that allows the user to place and connect network components. In addition, the tool should allow the maps to be manipulated and printed.

24.5.2 Simulate

A function at the core of design tools, and sometimes invisible to the user, is the ability to simulate the actions of the network equipment placed in the model.

24.5.3 Characterize

In order to quantify changes made during the design process, a number of Key Performance Indicators (KPIs) should be calculated by the design tool. Indicators such as utilization, efficiency, cost, survivability, throughput, and delay should be calculated.

24.5.4 Optimize

Services should be provided by the design tool to modify the design in an automated way such that certain parameters of the design are maximized or minimized. For example, the tool should be able to make changes to the design so that cost is minimized, or such that survivability is maximized.

24.5.5 Design

Design is the most important collection of services provided by a design tool. The tool should be able to take as input a set of parameters and produce as output a description of a network design that can be manipulated by the operator, or by automated services of the design tool. Listed below are examples of the input and output for various types of network technologies.

Time Division Multiplexing (TDM)
demand(loc, loc, bw) → [switch locations, transport(loc, loc, bw)]
based on minimum cost or maximum survivability, etc.

LAN to Physical
demand (loc, loc, application profile) → [switch or router locations, transport (type, loc, loc, bw)]
based on delay, priority, etc.

LAN to Virtual
demand (loc, loc, application profile) → demand(loc, pvc bw)
based on delay, priority, etc.

FR Access
demand (loc, pvc bw) → [switch location, transport (loc, loc, bw)]

FR Backbone
demand (loc, loc, pvc bw) → [switch or router locations, transport(loc, loc, bw)]

24.5.6 Test

Services should be available to test the design once created. Tests should include failure and stress analyses. During failure analysis, the output should describe any user traffic that is not carried by the network during the tested outage. Stress analysis should describe the degradation of service in terms of reduced throughput and increased delay due to increased offered load on the network.

24.5.7 Report

A versatile set of reports should be available to describe the components of the network that has been designed. In addition, Key Performance Indicators

(KPIs) should be reported along with details of utilization, throughput, and efficiency of each component or circuit of the network.

24.5.8 Performance Analysis

This area is particularly applicable to tools that address statistical networks. Ideally, a design tool should perform the design in stages. In the early stages, the placement of nodes and links, along with the determination of the size of links, will be calculated based on aggregate parameters such as maximum packet-processing speed. At a later stage of the design, the simulation should switch to a more detailed level. In the later stages of the design, advanced statistical models should be employed to analyze packet throughput and delay and queue depth.

24.6 TYPES OF DESIGN PROJECTS

Design projects include

◊ Digital cross-connect backbone
◊ Private line or dedicated circuit backbone
◊ Data services switched backbone like frame relay
◊ Single-protocol bridged design
◊ Multiprotocol routed or switched design

Each of these is typically approached from both an access and backbone perspective.

24.7 REQUIREMENTS

Next, list all the requirements specific to your network. These may include:

⇒ Interface to the existing database of record (e.g., Oracle database)
⇒ Data flows between the design tool and your configuration and event management systems
⇒ All cost elements (transport, demand, equipment, management, installation)
⇒ Rules or limitations for optimization
⇒ Future expansion
⇒ All nonoptimal transport and demand

⇒ Protocol specifics (e.g., CIR for FR)
⇒ Circuit and session prioritization

24.7.1 User Inputs

Network-design tool user-input parameters vary widely, based on the type of network to be modeled. Some of the more important parameters include:

- ✸ Packet/frame/cell size (average or peak)
- ✸ Number of packets/frames/cells per second (mean and in each direction)
- ✸ Minimum/maximum bandwidth per user access
- ✸ Time between packets (burstiness)
- ✸ File size per transmission
- ✸ Links/trunks required (length, speed, priority, etc.)
- ✸ Cost and priority factors
- ✸ Overhead statistics per protocol
- ✸ Network device (node) specifics
- ✸ Protocol specifics

This information is typically input to the tool through an application profile input file. This file also includes application specifics such as name, description, traffic type, coordinates origin(s) and destination(s), etc.

24.7.2 Tool Support

While the features and functions of design tools vary widely, below are listed some of the more important items to be supported:

- ◎ Multiple protocols (HDLC, X.25, frame relay)
- ◎ Multiple architectures (OSI, TCP/IP, SNA)
- ◎ Layered view of each protocol and architecture
- ◎ Multimedia traffic (voice, data, video — time-sensitive/insensitive)
- ◎ End-to-end view upon selection
- ◎ Support for both hierarchical (LAN/MAN) and meshed (multiplexer) network designs
- ◎ User-friendly interface — Graphical User Interface (GUI) and Applications Program Interface (API), CAD/CAM capabilities, multi-level graphics, international application
- ◎ Location inputs in Vertical and Horizontal (V&H) of serving CO, latitude and longitude, NPA/NXX, LATA, and CRT screen coordinates
- ◎ Conversions for the location finders above

- Display utilization
- Powerful high-level user language accessible by user (user able to make coding changes to tool)
- Online editing of links, nodes, and other properties
- Flexible data structures (circuits/packets/frames/cells)
- Flexible input parameters (distance, cost, quality, bandwidth)
- Flexible parameters for defining link and node placement
- Capability to upgrade/add new technologies, protocols, and parameters
- Modular design (run each step of design separately)
- General-purpose design criteria
- Capability to input national and international tariff and network specifics
- Dial-up capability
- Varied node and link types
- Survivability analysis
- Unlimited number of nodes
- Configuration and clocking design
- Industry-standard platform
- Current software revision
- Multiple homing of links to multiple or same node
- Variable equipment costs
- Fast, efficient algorithms
- Data export including laser printing and plotting
- Multiple save file formats: text and graphics
- Sensitivity analysis
- Tariff manager
- Multivendor, multicarrier device libraries
- Short run and processing times
- Add in for growth
- Thorough debugger, editor, journalizing
- Performance analysis simulator
- Query capability for all of the above
- Traffic generator
- Least-cost topology design
- Assess network delay and throughput
- Applications profiler
- Variable decision matrix
- Price-performance model

24.7.3 Reporting Capability

Design tools need to report their findings to the user so the user can understand what the tool has modeled, what can now be modeled, and how the modeling can be translated to management. Some of the more important reporting characteristics include:

- ➲ End-to-end response time
- ➲ Topology options
- ➲ Throughout, delay, cost (per link and node)
- ➲ Effect of link or node failure
- ➲ Individual link and node views
- ➲ Bandwidth usage per user/port/protocol
- ➲ What changed? analyses (for topology, node/link demand, link load, node throughput, routing differences, and packet throughput)
- ➲ Topology changes
- ➲ Link and node upgrades
- ➲ Protocol type changes (routing, switching)
- ➲ Maximum hop count
- ➲ Delay and throughput analysis
- ➲ Traffic type changes
- ➲ Traffic pattern changes
- ➲ Link and node characteristics changes (PPS processing)
- ➲ Busy hour/minute/second changes
- ➲ Black box support for unrecognized devices
- ➲ Constraints in link and node demand
- ➲ Hybrid topologies
- ➲ Redundancy

24.7.4 User Functionality

User functionality defines the level of control the user can exert over both the design and the design tool. The functions the tool provides to the user should include:

- ☑ Complete design
- ☑ Incremental design
- ☑ Multinetwork design
- ☑ Subnetwork design
- ☑ Built-in redundancy
- ☑ Specific rules of routing
- ☑ Layered (protocol or architecture) design
- ☑ User-specified specific parameter design
- ☑ Manual additions
- ☑ Time interval design
- ☑ Specialized routing
- ☑ Forced homing
- ☑ Connectivity constraints

☑ Import traffic statistics recorded by data analyzers
☑ Macro functions
☑ Zoom-in and zoom-out capability
☑ Printing capability

The tool should also have the capability to import current configuration files in native or ASCII format, ranging from database downloads of existing equipment to entire network maps of available routes and the tariff information for each. All parameters should be displayed and be configurable in both domestic and international measurements, distances, tariffs, maps, etc.

24.7.5 Private Line Customer Network Design Requirements

The input to the tool would be a list of demands, and the output would be the optimal placement of nodes and access lines.

Features of the tool include:

- Ability to gather data on current demand, import into the tool
- Utilization report
- Price components of the design
- Minimum cost design
- Performance analysis
- Maps of proposed design
- Proposal, including details of input to the design
- Easy modification of design
- Graphical user interface

24.7.6 Frame Relay Customer Network Design Requirements

For frame relay networks, the input to this tool would be a list of demands, possibly the same as the input to the multiprotocol customer network design. The output of the tool would be a list of node locations, access line speeds, and PVC speeds. The node locations would be chosen to reduce access costs, and would be a subset of the available public and private frame relay switch locations.

24.7.7 Multiprotocol Customer Network Design Requirements

The network design tool should have the ability to design networks carrying at least the following user protocols:

- SNA
- Vines
- IPX
- IP
- DECNET
- ISO

It is presumed that the design tool will contain a model for each protocol, and that the tool will be able to simulate demand based on user requirements for each protocol.

Input to the tool would include user demand in terms of traffic profiles. A traffic profile specifies the amount of traffic generated by a user, and characterizes the burstiness of the traffic. Parameters such as throughput and delay requirements are also specified. Profiles would be predefined for common applications such as a file server, print server, or client workstation.

The traffic profiles would be converted by the tool into either physical or virtual demands. The physical demands could then be directed as input to the physical -design module. The virtual demands could likewise be directed to the virtual design module described previously as the frame relay access-design module.

24.7.8 Customization Requirements

The tool should be flexible and allow the network designer to create links to other systems.

The tool should include:

1. API for extensibility and customization (with hooks for object messaging)

2. Full support for customized network objects

3. Rule customization and extension (to support new types of connectivity not yet dreamed of by the developers)

4. Extension of existing objects to add attributes needed for integration into existing systems

5. Ability to call other applications (with context) in response to user or object/rule events.

6. Ability to be called and provided with a context (such as a database zoom into a specific object initiating the circuit diagram with specific object selected)

24.7.9 Other Requirements

If possible, the chosen design tool should automate as many of the following as possible.

- Integration of network equipment cost with network bandwidth cost
- Pending order activity (new, disconnect, and change)
- "Auto price" bandwidth
- All nonrecurring charges on installs and rearrangements
- Circuits not on least-cost-routing paths
- Trends on bandwidth activity to support projected bandwidth requirements
- Network utilization reports
- Graphical representations of network bandwidth
- Maintain an inventory of all network equipment
- Costs of routed DS0s, DS1s, and DS3s

24.8 COMMERCIAL TOOLS

Finally, choose a tool. The following six commercial tools are the industry leaders as of the time of publishing.

24.8.1 NetMaker XA from Make Systems

NetMaker XA is the most recent release of a design tool that was originally targeted specifically to design and optimize Network Equipment Technologies (NET) IDNX networks. Figure 24.5 shows the Make Systems design tool. Early releases added libraries to support other TDM equipment and also included some packet equipment. Further revision of the product changed the architecture of the tool, and positioned the tool to take on other equipment types such as adding libraries for router equipment.

24.8.1.1 Hardware Requirements

Sparc 10 with 1.0-Gbyte drive and 128 Mbytes of RAM

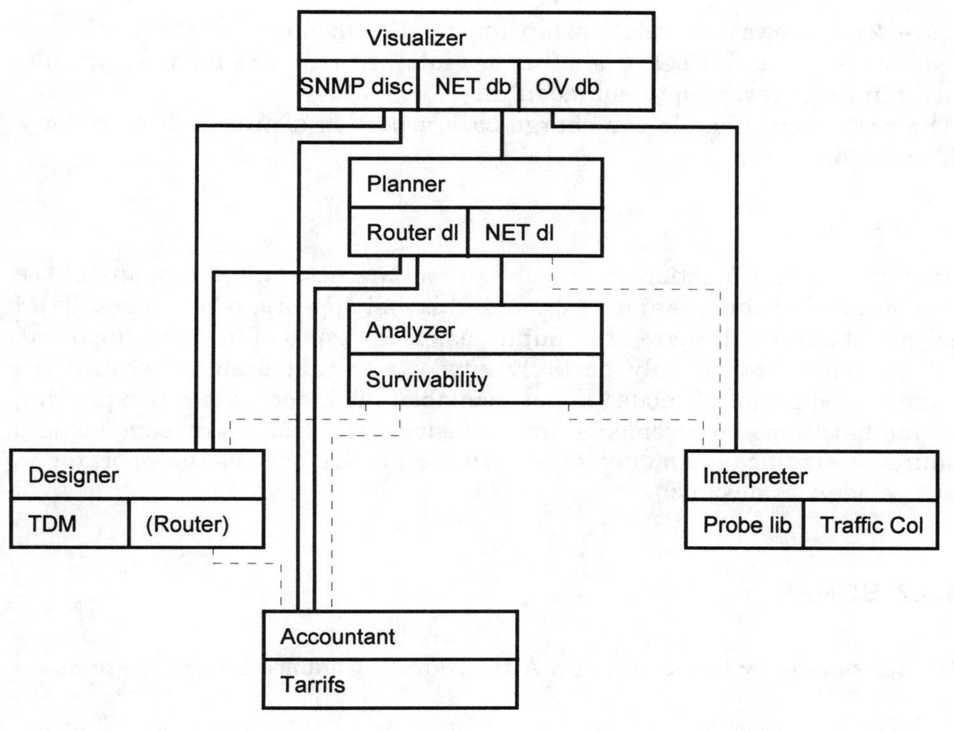

Figure 24.5 Make Systems Design Tool

24.8.1.2 Operating System Requirements

Solaris 1.1.1

24.8.1.3 Features

The Make Systems tool is sold in modules. There are six main modules, and each module has a list of available plug-in additions. The plug-ins enable the module to operate on a specific type of equipment or technology. For example, a designer plug-in addresses routers.

The six major components of NetMaker are:

- Visualizer
- Interpreter
- Accountant
- Planner
- Analyzer
- Designer

Figure 24.5 shows the relationship among the modules in the NetMaker product. All modules below another module are required for that module. Dotted lines represent optional modules.

The accountant module can charge back a portion of transport costs for a particular demand.

24.8.1.4 Summary

The structure and function of this design tool are best suited to many of the tasks outlined in this chapter. Although this tool appears to be the best TDM design tool surveyed, there are limitations on the types of devices supported. At this time, the tool only partially supports virtual designs because the designer module for IP nodes is not available. This tool is not inexpensive, and the hardware requirements are extensive. The tool is also complex and requires a significant amount of experience on the part of the operator to produce network designs.

24.8.2 BONES

BONES is made by Comdisco, now Alta group of Cadence Design Systems

24.8.2.1 Hardware Requirements

SPARC, DEC, or HP workstation
32 Mbytes of RAM
80 Mbytes of free disk space

24.8.2.2 Operating System Requirements

Sun OS 4.1.1 with OpenWindows 3.0 or
Ultirx 4.2 with DECwindows or
HP-UX 8.05 with HP VUE

24.8.2.3 Features

◊ PlanNet
◊ Designer
◊ Interactive Simulation Manager
◊ Application Traffic Generator
◊ Analyzer-Based Traffic Generator
◊ Statistical/Bursty Traffic Generator

Module libraries include:

⇒ FDDI
⇒ Token Ring
⇒ 10Base-T
⇒ Ethernet
⇒ Frame Relay
⇒ 2-Port Bridge
⇒ Multiport Router
⇒ WAN Mesh

24.8.2.4 Summary

Bones is a low-level design tool targeted at detailed performance analysis of individual network components. An overall network design could be performed by connecting several network components, analyzing the performance, and then manually optimizing the design. No automation exists to assist the designer. The focus of this tool is protocol and network component design.

24.8.3 Wandl

Wandl, like the Make Systems product, it targeted primarily at designing NET IDNX networks. This tool adds some interesting frame relay tools though.

24.8.3.1 Hardware Requirements

SUN Sparc

24.8.3.2 Operating System Requirements

Solaris 1.1.1

24.8.3.3 Features

WAN Pricer
T1/T2/FT1 backbone network design and failure simulation
IDNX node card and port assignment
IDNX synchronization timing design
Access network design
Multidrop line design
Voice-network design
Frame relay access network design
Frame relay backbone network design

Let's look at two of the design modules in detail.

The frame relay access network design module selects frame relay switch nodes and performs an optimal design to bring the traffic to the frame relay switch nodes. Channel banks and an LEC frame relay service are used to minimize the access cost. Customers are connected to the frame relay switch nodes using private lines, routers at the customer site, or via an LEC frame relay service. This module produces the optimal access configuration.

The frame relay backbone design module designs and analyzes the frame relay backbone network. Based on the traffic volume, traffic-arrival patterns, packet-size distribution, and protocol distribution between the backbone nodes, this module follows the algorithms used by the hardware to route the traffic over the backbone network. It performs traffic-delay analysis and network-failure analysis. This module builds an optimal backbone network design either from scratch or from an existing network. It minimizes the backbone link cost while satisfying all the delay and reliability constraints.

24.8.3.4 Summary

This tool provides an excellent choice for a frame relay design tool. The tool is not inexpensive; it does provide automation services for design iteration, but they are limited to the areas of frame relay access and backbone design.

24.8.4 COMNET III from CACI Products Company

24.8.4.1 Hardware Requirements

PC or Sparc workstation

24.8.4.2 Operating System Requirements

MS Windows
OS/2
Solaris 1.1

24.8.4.3 Features

This tool is focused on providing detailed performance analysis on a network design.

24.8.4.4 Overall Rating

Comnet III is a low-level design tool, but hides some of the details from the user. The tool provides defaults for many of the low-level parameters. An overall network design could be performed by connecting several network components, analyzing the performance, and then manually optimizing the design. No automation exists to assist the designer.

This tool focuses on a single component of network design, performance analysis. Performance analysis is probably the most complex portion of the design process, but without automation to assist in the iteration process, the analysis is not very useful in the design process. Once a design has reached the implementation phase, the performance analysis would be very helpful.

24.8.5 OPNET Modeler from MIL 3

24.8.5.1 Hardware Requirements

Sun Sparc
DEC workstation or DEC alpha
HP 700
IBM RS6000
Silicon Graphics

24.8.5.2 Operating System Requirements

Solaris 2.2
Ultirx 4.3
DEC OSF/1
HP-UX 8.0 or 9.0
AIX 3.2
IRIX 4.0

24.8.5.3 Features

Hierarchical specification
300 communications and simulation primitives
Library of detailed protocol models including TCP/IP, ATM, X.25, 802.X
Standards-based LAN and WAN performance modeling
Research and development in communications protocols and architectures

24.8.5.4 Overall Rating

Opnet Modeler is intended for low-level design. Programming and definition of finite state machines are required to take full advantage of the services of this tool.

24.8.6 PLANYST from IRI

This tool is positioned mostly as a performance-analysis tool.

24.8.6.1 Hardware Requirements

80486
8 Mbytes of RAM
40 Mbytes of disk

24.8.6.2 Operating System Requirements

DOS and MS Windows

24.8.6.3 Features

- Graphical user interface
- Avoids the need to define underlying queues, protocols, and configurations
- Default models provided for many traffic classes
- Performance results exhibited in tabular and graphical form
- Message delay performance is presented on an end-to-end basis
- Extensive tools are provided for the calibration of FDDI networks
- Detailed performance statistics are exhibited characterizing message delay, buffer occupancy, and retransmission distributions across the network and on an end-to-end-basis

24.8.6.4 Overall Rating

This tool is in the same category as the other low-level tools, but provides a slightly higher-level approach. Instead of simulating detailed attributes of network operation, this tool analyzes the detailed operation of the network. Mathematically, this is a much less intensive approach.

The tool provides defaults for many parameters, making the analysis easier for the operator. This tool, like the others, could be used to design a network by connecting the appropriate network elements, analyzing the performance of the design, and iteratively optimizing the design. As with the other tools, no automation services are provided to assist in the iteration process. Of significant interest are planned enhancements to the tool that will address the need for automation. In addition to automation, the future release will also contain algorithms to produce an optimized network design as a starting point for operator optimization.

24.9 SUMMARY OF DESIGN TOOLS

All of the six tools fit into one of two general categories. Either the tool is targeted at detailed performance analysis, at the packet and device level, or the tool is targeted at price analysis and access design. Most environments require a mixture of the two, with an emphasis on the latter. None of the tools currently provide services to automate the design process.

24.10 HOW OFTEN TO OPTIMIZE?

Remember that the design-tool process does not stop with the initial design. It is a cyclical process to be completed every few months by the network-engineering organization. Design tools can drastically improve the efficiency of an existing network, provide significant cost savings through reducing access and thus reducing costs, and recover underutilized hardware from the network. Network-design tools can optimize efficiency from the local LAN to the entire WAN. These tools can help perform the fine tuning discussed in Chapters 20 and 21. While tools may be valuable for modeling current network topologies and technologies, they may quickly become obsolete when new technology becomes available in the network. And, not only should the tool itself be considered, but ongoing support and updates are also important.

24.11 REVIEW

This chapter has provided us with the capability to choose a network design tool that meets the requirements of user-input parameters, user functionality, feature and function support, and reporting capability. The leading design tools on the market were summarized and the main features and functions required were outlined.

Chapter

25

International Networks

International telecommunications structure has slowly been changing in a manner similar to U.S. telecommunications reform over the past 20 years. Policy changes and regulatory liberalization are sweeping the globe. Global telecommunications corporations find opportunities in countries where new competitive markets are being created by the privatization and liberalization of the traditional PTT monopoly. These countries are moving through a life cycle of monopoly to privatization and liberalization to partial or open competition and deregulation. This evolution into privatization changes the legal status of a PTT or PTO from public or government to private ownership. Sometimes these changes take place in niche markets, such as cellular or digital radio, and sometimes they encompass the entire communications infrastructure of the country. When operating in these new markets, the service provider must understand the politics, laws, economic and labor restrictions, social policies, and limitations to each technology.

This chapter highlights both the business and technology aspects of international network design. The focus will be on the changing role of many national communications systems and regulations. The advantages and drawbacks of providing international network services using both public and virtual private network services will be covered.

25.1 INTERNATIONAL DATA NETWORK TYPES

This chapter discusses many network configurations and services provided by international carriers and dominant public providers. We will now define these terms and their relationship to providers.

PDN. Public data networks provide a common-access network to allow many users to share a common network facility as well as the services it offers (PDN also could refer to a private data network, where a set of common users shares private facilities and services). PDNs support voice, data, or both, and provide access for users who cannot cost-justify building a private data network of their own. Many countries are moving from a single PDN provider (historically the PTT) to a competitive environment with multiple providers.

PSN. Packet-switched networks are shared-data networks where customers are charged based on how much data (measured in packets, frames, or cells) they send across the network. Frame relay, SMDS, and ATM services fall into this category.

IVAN. International value-added networks are privately owned service providers who offer public services not available through the local service (or local PDN). Typical services include basic file or voice transfer, and enhanced services include electronic data interchange (EDI), electronic mail (e-mail), and protocol interpretation and conversion. A user interfaces to an IVAN through direct connect or dial access. Dial access can be plain old telephone service (POTS) or ISDN. IVANs provide a good alternative to private lines. If the country's communications are PTT owned, IVANs will interface to monopoly providers through the local PDN gateway.

IVPDN. International virtual private data network, an international public data network (IPDN) service where facilities and services are offered to customers in a manner where it appears they are operating their own private data network.

IRC. International record carriers were prior to 1980 the only international telex and packet-switch providers that worked with the PTTs through gateways to each country's PDN.

Figure 25.1 shows the evolution of these various service providers.

25.2 THE CHANGING ROLE OF PTTs

The dominant provider for most countries worldwide remains the Post, Telegraph, and Telephone (PTT) entity. Most PTTs are government owned or franchised. They are regulated as public utilities and considered a natural or privatized monopoly. The new term many countries have adopted is Public Telecommunication Organizations (PTOs). While PTTs enjoy a monopoly, they remain under many restrictions, like the need to cross-subsidize service. Cross-subsidization still occurs in many countries where the population is disperse and the classes of service and types of users vary.

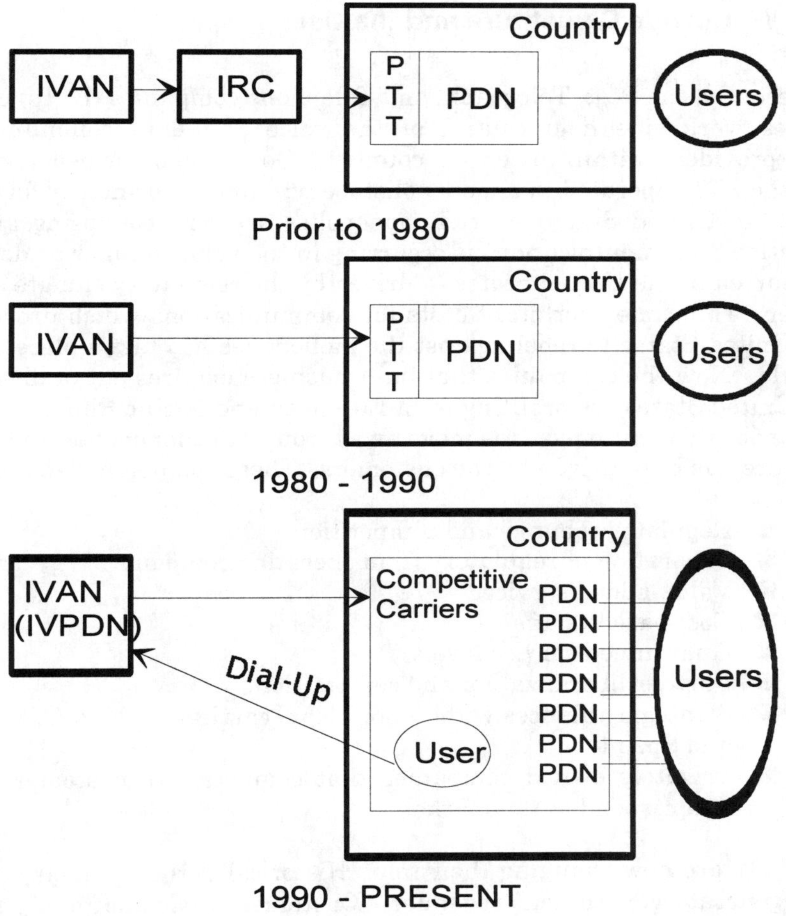

Figure 25.1 Service Providers

Some PTTs are slowly being released to competitive environments like cellular and paging, while their core telecommunications transport services remain monopolistic. In some countries, the PTT or PTO operates in a closed market where the government favors the PTT over potential competition. In this case, they are referred to as the national favorite or hero. Their labor force is often unionized.

The role of the PTT continues to evolve. Voice and data networks are being modernized at an exponential growth rate, and public and private network service providers are scrambling to take advantage of new international markets created by these tides of change. PTTs that remain monopolistic need to prepare for the eventuality of a competitive environment. Let's now look at these changes in detail.

25.2.1 Worldwide Divestiture and the User

Until recently, the Post, Telegraph, and Telephone companies (PTTs) of many countries worldwide held control of the voice and data communications service providers within an entire country. Government owned and influenced, the PTTs operated in a monopolistic environment, primarily for profit.

As in the United States, carrier monopolies are now collapsing and free competition on communications is occurring in the same manner as deregulation occurred in the United States — driven by the regulatory climate and the end user. The same exorbitant costs for communications which drove users in the United States to rebel against the monopolies has taken place all over the world. Now the companies that built business empires out of divestiture in the United States are profiting from European and Pacific Rim divestiture.

As previously mentioned, this move away from PTT monopolies and toward divestiture has been driven by the customers. These customers demanded

- ☎ Regulatory change and competition
- ☎ Separation of regulatory from operating company
- ☎ Value-added services
- ☎ Cost-based tariffs
- ☎ Guaranteed service levels
- ☎ Further liberalization and competition
- ☎ Strategic alliances with major global carriers such as AT&T, MCI, and Sprint
- ☎ Privately owned companies that compete, are customer driven, and respond to the market

The PTTs are now changing their role. Historically, their primary interest was to generate government revenues. Customer service suffered, and the cost of that service was high. Now with privatization, PTTs are reversing their historical priorities and focusing on customer satisfaction and the introduction of new services. This means offering better quality services at lower prices. To date, international providers have had to deal with each PTT, or local competition, one-on-one to form partnerships. This remains true as the PTTs still represent the driving factor in the overseas markets, and basic services remain regulated. As privatization spreads through PTT-owned countries, PTTs are selling government assets to the private industry sector in an effort to obtain the substantial investments required to fully restructure. The PTTs have also tried to gather funds by selling portions or the entire PTT holdings, by offering public stock, and through employee buyout options. These trends continue with privatization.

25.2.2 Dominant Public Providers and PTTs

Table 25.1 shows the dominant public providers, or PTTs if prior to privatization, of the major international voice and data service providers worldwide. Many have been privatized in the last 10 years and are marked so.

This is not a complete list. Most African, Eastern European, Central American, and Caribbean countries are still running on the old PTT model.

25.2.3 The PTTs and Global Players after 1992

The service providers and PTTs mentioned in the previous tables will be the key players in the globalization of data and computer communications. Take a look specifically at Europe. This area has undergone the most radical changes and will continue to revolutionize rather than evolutionize most of its data communications.

There are three primary communities of interest in Europe:

The European Community (EC) consists of Belgium, Denmark, England, France, Germany, Greece, Ireland, Italy, Luxembourg, Netherlands, Portugal, and Spain. This group of nations represents the most diversified group of communications evolving in the world. While this represents the greatest challenge, it also represents the greatest potential.

The European Free Trade Association (EFTA) consists of Austria, Finland, Iceland, Liechtenstein, Norway, Sweden, and Switzerland. This group of nations has some of the most advanced communications infrastructures in Europe, yet they are also highly diversified on standards and interconnectivity. While the possibility of an EFTA-wide common network would greatly enhance the power of the EFTA, a combined EC-EFTA-wide network could signal the beginning of the world's largest economic power — all with the keystone of integrated computer and data communications.

The Eastern Countries (now defunct Eastern Bloc) consist of Albania, Czechoslovakia, Bulgaria, Estonia, Hungary, Latvia, Lithuania, Poland, Romania, and Yugoslavia. While these countries lack the infrastructure that exists in Western Europe, they have the capability to build a modernized network from the ground up. To do this they will require funding assistance from Western Europe or private business moving in to fuel their stagnant economies. And they are receiving it. These countries are making the quantum leap from old technologies to cellular and digital networks in one fell swoop.

TABLE 25.1 Dominant World Public Data Providers

COUNTRY	DOMINANT CARRIER(S) or PTT
Australia	Telstra, Optus Communications Pty. Ltd.
Austria	Radio-Austria A.G. (RADAUS) – PTT
Argentina	Privatized with Consortiums (ENTEL)
Belgium	Regie des Telegraphes et Telephones (RTT) – PTT
Brazil	Empressa Brasileira de Telecomunicacoes, S.A. – PTT
Canada	Teleglobe Canada
Chile	CTC and ENTEL
China	AsiaSat Franchise
Chile	Empresa Nacional de Telecomunicaciones, S.A. (ENTEL) – PTT
Columbia	Ministry of Communications – PTT
Denmark	Kopenhagen Telecom AS (KTAS) – Privatized PTT
Finland	Telecom Finland – PTT
France	France Telecom
Germany	Deutsche Bundepost
Greece	Hellenic Telecommunications Organization – PTT
Hong Kong	Hong Kong Telecom International Ltd. (HKTI)
Hungary	Privatized PTT
India	Videsh Sanchar Nigam, Ltd.
Indonesia	PT Indonesian Satellite Corp.
Ireland	Telecom Eireann – PTT
Italy	SIP, Italcable, Telespazio
Japan	Nippon Telegraph and Telephone, International Telecom Japan, International Digital Communications (IDC)
Korea	Korean Telecommunications Authority (KTA) – PTT
Mexico	Telmex (France Telecom and SBC)
Netherlands	Administration des Postes et Netherlands – Restructured PTT
New Zealand	Telecom New Zealand
Norway	Teledirecktoratet – PTT
Peru	Ministerio de Transportes y Comunicacion – PTT
Philippines	Privatized PTT
Portugal	Companhia Portuguesa de Radio Marconi – PTT
Puerto Rico	Privatization of PTT
Saudi Arabia	Cable & Wireless Riyadh, Ltd.
Singapore	Singapore Telecom (ST) – PTT
South Africa	Department of Posts & Telecommunications – PTT
Spain	Telefonica of Spain
Sweden	Televerket Sverige – PTT
Switzerland	Swiss Telecom – PTT
United Kingdom	British Telecom
Venezuela	CANTV and Consortium

25.3 TRANSMISSION NETWORKS

Many factors are hindering the modernization of worldwide networks. The primary cause is the quality of existing transmission networks and the expense of upgrading to quality digital or fiber facilities. Location also influences the cost and availability of quality transmission facilities. With today's technology, digital transmission facilities are required to move data around the globe, and many satellite facilities no longer provide sufficient quality. Government stagnation and bureaucracy are also factors. In some fast-growing economies, technology acceleration has caused a country to consider upgrading very old facilities to very new facilities, in effect skipping a few generations of technology cycles in the upgrade.

25.3.1 Expensive, Poor Facilities in Developing Areas

The problem plaguing many developing countries is the lack of quality digital transmission facilities. Eastern Europe, Mexico and Central America, and some Far East and third-world countries still have a poor digital infrastructure with little or no existing digital or fiber-optics communications facilities (all old analog). In fact, the wait time for residential phone connectivity in some countries is still 10 years. Fiber is now the predominant intercontinental and intracontinental digital service media, replacing satellite and microwave facilities. International fiber optics were introduced in 1988 with TAT-8 and new builds have far overtaken satellite. But it is still virtually impossible for fiber to reach many underdeveloped areas. It is these areas that are still served by satellite and microwave systems. The other major hurdle with ubiquitous deployment of fiber and fiber-based services is getting the new data communications services and facilities past local regulations.

25.3.2 Importance of Location

The pervasive nature of data communications in all countries is based on location of facilities in areas of large population and in high-growth markets. These are the locations where global network connectivity supports global business. Many European and Asian cities have been labeled as hubs or focal points for inter- and intracountry traffic. These locations serve as the primary origination and termination points for international fiber and satellite. Some examples include: London, Paris, Frankfurt, Zurich, Munich, Dusseldorf, Brussels, Amsterdam, Tokyo, Hong Kong, and Moscow. They are also prime locations for international network-management centers. The quantity and quality of service degrades drastically as the distance from these hubs increases.

25.3.3 Costs

International bandwidth is considerably more expensive than in the United States. Private line costs within Europe and Asia can average a few thousand dollars per month for a DS0 leased line. IVANs can help reduce this private line cost while providing better connectivity. Compare the private line solution to accessing a carrier-provided service. The IVAN would charge per access port, not per circuit. While the connection between the United States and Europe would cost about the same, the intraEurope ports would cost less than half the price of dedicated circuits, and provide the same bandwidth, but would now have ubiquitous access to each other. This is why the IVANs are quite popular in the international market. Ultimately, it is the users who are driving the communications industry, choosing their providers, and insuring their success.

25.4 THE IVAN/IVPDN MARKET

The IVAN market exists for both voice and data, although the two are merging — if ISDN and ATM standards follow through as planned. The IVAN data market can be segmented into five major technologies and services, including:

❶ Routers and bridges using private lines (including IP networks)
❷ X.25 packet switching
❸ Frame relay
❹ SMDS
❺ ATM

These technologies and services will be offered by either the locally predominant carrier, local competition, or foreign service providers. The first two have been discussed; foreign service providers are next.

25.4.1 Foreign Service Providers

An alternative to the locally dominant carrier is a foreign service provider. These companies provide IVAN service when the local PDN cannot adequately service the user's needs. Most common carriers like AT&T, MCI, and

Sprint offer complete end-to-end communications between the United States, European, and Asian locations. The two types of services offered are basic transport and enhanced or value-added services. The IVANs provide international virtual private data network services (IVPDNs) to the foreign country. This connects local data networks to an international data network, as well as offering the services customers require. Often, these services will predominate over the local or domestic virtual network services.

These providers also offer IVANs and IVPDNs. These IVANs and IVPDNs let the international network and service provider handle all the foreign PTT or dominant carrier dealings, provide the appropriate levels of technical support and network management, upgrades as required, and the people required to operate it. This is often the most cost-effective solution, as opposed to building an international private network, especially when switched services are offered. Just make sure that the connectivity and service uses worldwide industry standards. One of the largest international networks is obviously the Internet.

25.4.2 International Outsourcing and Joint Partnerships

Many of the leading service providers and predominant carriers are forming joint partnerships. The focus of these new units is to provide a complete end-to-end international outsourcing package to multinational corporations. The caveat to understand, however, is that there must be a financial incentive to *both* parties of a partnership for the relationship to successful.

25.5 INTERNATIONAL DESIGN

International traffic patterns will vary and are difficult to predict. This is primarily due to the matrix design which has grown from the conglomerate of private line connectivity and packet-switched services. The topologies tend to be flatter, more matrix-oriented than hierarchical, yet still conform to those presented in Chapters 20 and 21. A WAN usually employs gateways between VPNs in each country.

When designing an international network, all of the steps discussed in this book apply and should be followed in the same sequence and order. Designing an international network is similar to designing a national network, with the priority weighted more toward reducing the cost of facilities and transport and less toward creating a "balanced" design. Such conveniences such as diversity and redundancy are often sacrificed in international designs. All architectures discussed may be present, although the OSIRM, TCP/IP, and SNA architectures predominate throughout the world. OSI as a common worldwide standard has still not been realized. The major international standards institute is the International Telecommunications Union (ITU). Worldwide topologies follow those presented in Chapter 20.

Look for business overlaps when planning traffic patterns. One example is the early morning overlap of business hours between the United States and Europe. This yields high voice-traffic volumes. Similar patterns can be found with bank transactions, stock market information transfers, and other industrial and financial traffic.

25.6 REVIEW

This chapter has allowed us to step into the shoes of both the PTTs and the service providers competing for market share in the move toward privatization. The changes in PTT posture have been observed from that of a government-owned monopoly to that of a private enterprise in a deregulated environment. With this change have come opportunities for international network and service providers to compete in areas previously monopolized by the PTTs. These global service providers are helping to shape a new world for communications based on worldwide standards and devoted to customer service satisfaction. Many opportunities have been identified for these providers, as well as new ground rules that they must follow to compete in the international arena. International network designs resemble national designs with a shift in priorities toward cost and quality of facilities. These factors also influence the base technologies that can be used.

Appendix

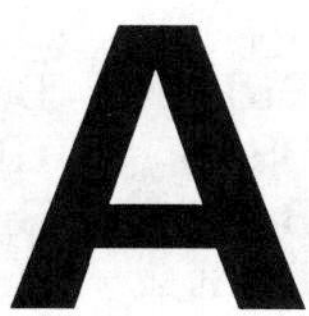

Acronyms and Abbreviations

Comments in parentheses are a clarification or refer to the standard or protocol from which the term is derived. Many acronyms are used by multiple standards; only the most prevalent are mentioned.

AAL	ATM Adaptation Layer
AARP	AppleTalk Address Resolution Protocol
ABM	Asynchronous Balance Mode (HDLC)
AC	Access Control (IEEE)
ACF	Access Control Field (DQDB)
ACK	Acknowledgment
ADM	Add/Drop Multiplexer
AIS	Alarm Indication Signal (SONET)
ANS	American National Standards
ANSI	American National Standards Institute
API	Application Programming Interface
APS	Automatic Protection Switching
ARM	Asynchronous Response Mode (HDLC)
ARP	Address Resolution Protocol
Async	Asynchronous
ATM	Asynchronous Transfer Mode
AU	Access Unit (DQDB)
AUI	Attachment Unit Interface (Ethernet 802.3)
B8ZS	Bipolar with 8 Zero Substitution
BCC	Block Check Characters
BCD	Binary Coded Decimal
BECN	Backward Explicit Congestion Notification (FR)
Bellcore	Bell Communications Research
BER	Bit Error Ratio or Rate
BGP	Border Gateway Protocol
BIP	Bit Interleaved Parity (8)
B-ISDN	Broadband Integrated Services Digital Network
B-NT	Broadband Network Terminator
BO	Bit Oriented (SONET)
BOC	Bell Operating Company
BOM	Beginning of Message (DQDB)

bps	Bits per second or bytes per second
BRI	Basic Rate Interface (ISDN)
BSC	IBM's Binary Synchronous Communications protocol
B-TA	Broadband Terminal Adapter (ATM)
B-TE	Broadband Terminal Equipment (ATM)
CAD/CAM	Computer Aided Design/Computer Aided Manufacturing
CAN	Customer Access Node (SMDS)
CBDS	Connectionless Broadband Data Service
CBEMA	Computer and Business Equipment Manufacturers Association
CBR	Constant Bit Rate
CCI	Carrier-to-Carrier Interface
CCITT	Consultative Committee International Telegraph & Telephone
CD	CountDown counter (DQDB)
CE	Connection Endpoint
CEPT	Conference on European Post & Telegraph
CIR	Committed Information Rate (FR)
CL	Connectionless (SONET)
CLLM	Consolidated Link Layer Management (FR)
CLNP	Connectionless Layer Network Protocol
CLNS	ConnectionLess Network Service (OSI)
CLSF	ConnectionLess Server Function (ITU-T)
CMIP	Common Management Interface Protocol (ISO)
CMIS	Common Management Information Service (ISO)
CMISE	CMIS Element (ISO)
CMT	Connection Management (FDDI)
CNMS	Customer Network Management System
CO	Central Office
COAM	Customer Owned and Maintained
COCF	Connection-Oriented Convergence Function (DQDB)
COM	Continuation of Message (DQDB)
CONS	Connection-Oriented Network Service (ITU-T)
CPE	Customer Premises Equipment
C/R	Command/Response Indicator or bit
CRC	Cyclic Redundancy Check or Test
CS	Convergence Sublayer (DQDB)
CSMA/CD	Carrier-Sense Multiple Access with Collision Detection
CSU	Channel Service Unit
DA	Destination Address field
DAL	Dedicated Access Line
DARPA	Defense Advanced Research Program Agency
DAS	Dual-Attach Station connection (FDDI)
DCE	Data Communications Equipment
DCS	Digital Cross-connect System
DDD	Direct Distance Dialing

DDS	Digital Data Service
DE	Discard Eligibility (FR)
DEC	Digital Equipment Corporation
DH	DMPDU Header (DQDB)
DLCI	Data Link Connection Identifier (FR)
DMPDU	Derived MAC PDU (DQDB)
DPG	Dedicated Packet Group (FDDI)
DoD	Department of Defense
DQDB	Distributed Queue Dual Bus (IEEE)
DS0	Digital Signal Level 0
DS1	Digital Signal Level 1
DS3	Digital Signal Level 3
DSAP	Destination Service Access Point (LLC)
DSG	Default Slot Generator (DQDB)
DSU	Data Service Unit
DT	DMPDU trailer (DQDB)
DTE	Data Terminal Equipment
DTMF	Dual Tone MultiFrequency
DXC	Digital Cross-Connect
DXI	Data Exchange Interface (SMDS, ATM)
E1	European Transmission Level 1
E3	European Transmission Level 3
EA	Extended Address
ECN	Explicit Congestion Notification (FR)
ECSA	Exchange Carriers Standards Association
ED	End Delimiter (IEEE 802)
EGP	Exterior Gateway Protocol
EGRP	Exterior Gateway Routing Protocol
EIA	Electronics Industries Association
EIR	Excess Information Rate
EMA	Enterprise Management Architecture (DEC)
EOM	End Of Message
EOT	End Of Transmission
ES	End System (OSI)
ESF	Extended SuperFrame
ES-IS	End System-to-Intermediate System protocol (OSI)
ETB	End of Transmission Block
ETSI	European Telecommunications Standards Institute
ETX	End of Text
F	Flag
FC	Frame Control field (FDDI)
FCS	Frame Check Sequence (FR)
FDDI	Fiber Distributed Data Interface (ANSI)
FDDI-II	Fiber Distributed Data Interface Version II

FDM	Frequency Division Multiplexing
FEBE	Far End Block Error
FEC	Forward Error Correction
FECN	Forward Explicit Congestion Notification (FR)
FERF	Far End Reporting Failure
FM	Frequency Modulation
FOIRL	Fiber-Optic InterRepeater Link (Ethernet 802.3)
fps	Frames per second
FR	Frame Relay
FRAD	Frame Relay Assembler/Disassembler, or Access Device
FS	Frame Status field (FDDI)
FT1	Fractional T1
FTP	File Transfer Protocol
Gbit	Gigabits (billions of bits)
Gbps	Gigabits per second (10^9 bps)
GFC	Generic Flow Control
GFID	General Format Identifier
GFI	General Format Identifier (X.25)
GGP	Gateway-Gateway Protocol (DoD)
GOS	Grade of Service
GOSIP	Government Open System Interconnection Profile
GUI	Graphical User Interface
HCS	Header Check Sequence (DQDB)
HDTV	High Definition TeleVision
HDLC	High-Level Data Link Control (ISO)
HEC	Header Error Control
HOB	Head of Bus (DQDB) A or B
HSSI	High-Speed Serial Interface
Hz	Hertz or cycles per second
ICF	Isochronous Convergence Function (DQDB)
ICIP	Inter-Carrier Interface Protocol (SMDS)
ICMP	Internet Control Message Protocol
IDRP	InterDomain Routing Protocol
IEC	InterExchange Carrier
IEEE	Institute of Electrical and Electronics Engineers
IETF	Internet Engineering Task Force
IGP	Interior Gateway Protocol
IGRP	Interior Gateway Routing Protocol (Cisco™)
ILMI	Interim Local Management Interface
IMPDU	Initial MAC Protocol Data Unit (DQDB)
IMSSI	Inter-MAN Switching System Interface (DQDB)
I-MAC	Isochronous Media Access Control (FDDI)

intraLATA	intraLocal Access Transport Area
ISN	Initial Sequence Number (DoD)
IP	Internet Protocol (DoD)
IPCP	Internet Protocol Control Protocol (DoD)
IPX	Internetwork Packet Exchange protocol (Novell)
IS	Intermediate System (OSI)
ISDN	Integrated Services Digital Network
ISDU	Isochronous Service Data Unit (DQDB)
IS-IS	Intermediate System-to-Intermediate System (OSI)
ISO	International Standards Organization
ISSI	Inter-Switching System Interface (SMDS)
ISU	Isochronous Service User (SMDS)
ITU	International Telecommunications Union
ITU-T	ITU - Telecommunications standardization sector
IXC	IntereXchange Carrier
kbit	kilobit (thousands of bits)
kbps	kilobits per second (10^3 bps)
km	kilometers (10^3 meters)
LAN	Local Area Network
LAP-B	Link Access Procedure - Balanced (X.25)
LAP-D	Link Access Procedure - D (ISDN/Frame Relay)
LAP-F	Link Access Procedure - Frame Mode
LAT	Local Area Transport protocol (DEC)
LATA	Local Access Transport Area
LB	Letter Ballot
LCGN	Logical Channel Group Number
LCP	Link Control Protocol
LEC	Local Exchange Carrier
LLC	Logical Link Control (IEEE 802.X)
LME	Layer Management Entity (DQDB)
LMI	Local Management Interface (FR)
LSB	Least Significant Bit
LT	Line Termination
LTE	Line Terminating Equipment (SONET)
LU	Logical Unit (SNA)
m	meter
MAC	Media Access Control (IEEE 802.X)
MAN	Metropolitan Area Network (DQDB, FDDI)
Mbit	Megabits (millions of bits)
Mbps	Megabits per second (10^6 bps)
MCF	MAC Convergence Function (DQDB)
MCP	MAC Convergence Protocol (DQDB)

MHz	Megahertz
MIB	Management Information Base (SNMP)
MIC	Media Interface Connector (FDDI)
MID	Message IDentifier (DQDB), Multiplexing IDentifier (ATM)
MIPS	Millions of Instructions Per Second
MMF	Multimode Fiber
MOP	Maintenance and Operation Protocol (DEC)
MPEG	Motion Picture Encoding Group
ms	millisecond (one-thousandth of a second, 10^{-3} seconds)
MSAP	MAC Service Access Point (SMDS)
MSB	Most Significant Bit
MSDU	MAC Service Data Unit (SMDS)
MSS	MAN Switching System (SMDS)
MTU	Maximum Transmission Unit
MUX	Multiplexer
NANP	North American Numbering Plan
NBP	Name Binding Protocol
NCP	Network Control Protocol or Point (SNA)
NE	Network Element
NetBIOS	Network Basic Input/Output System protocol
NFS	Network File Server
nm	nanometer (10^{-9} meter)
NMP	Network Management Process (SMDS)
NMS	Network Management System or Station
NNI	Network-Node Interface (SONET)
NNI	Network-to-Network Interface (FR)
NOS	Network Operating System
NP	Network Performance
NPA	Numbering Plan Area
NRM	Normalized Response Mode (ISO)
NRZ	Non-return to zero
NRZI	Non-return to zero invert ones
ns	nanosecond (10^{-9} second)
NSAP	Network Service Access Point
NTx	Network Termination x (where $X = 1, 2, \ldots$)
OAM	Operations and Maintenance
OC-N	Optical Carrier Level N (SONET)
OH	Overhead
OID	Object Identifier (SNMP)
OOF	Out of Frame
ONA	Open Network Architecture
OS	Operating System
OSI	Open Systems Interconnection

OSI CLNS Connectionless Network System (OSI)
OSIRM OSI Reference Model
OSPF Open Shortest Path First
OTC Operating Telephone Company

PA Prearbitrated segment or slot (DQDB)
PABX Private Automatic Branch Exchange
PAD Packet Assembler/Disassembler (X.25)
PAF Prearbitrated Function (DQDB)
PBX Private Branch Exchange
PDC Packet Data Channel (FDDI)
PDH Plesiochronous Digital Hierarchy
PDN Public Data Network
PDS Packet Driver Specification for public domain
PDU Protocol Data Unit (IEEE)
Ph-SAP Physical layer SAP (DQDB)
PHY PHYsical layer standard (FDDI)
PID Protocol IDentification
Ping Packet Internet Groper
PIR Protocol Independent Routing
PL PAD Length (DQDB)
PLCP Physical Layer Convergence Protocol (DQDB)
PM Performance Monitoring
PMD Physical Layer Medium Dependent standard (FDDI)
POH Path Overhead (SONET)
POI Path Overhead Identifier (DQDB)
PON Passive Optical Network
PoP Point of Presence
POTS Plain Old Telephone Service
PPP Point-to-Point Protocol (Internet)
Pps Packets per second
PRI Primary Rate Interface (ISDN)
PSPDN Packet-Switched Public Data Network
PT Payload Type
PTE Path-Terminating Equipment (PTE)
PTT Postal, Telegraph & Telephone Ministry/Administration
PU Physical Unit (SNA)
PVC Permanent Virtual Circuit or Channel (FR, X.25)

QA Queued Arbitrated (DQDB) segment, slot, access function
QAF Queued Arbitrated Function (DQDB)
QoS Quality of Service
QPSX Queued Packet and Synchronous Exchange

RBOC Regional Bell Operating Company
RCP Remote Console Protocol (DEC)

RDI	Remote Defect Indication (ATM)
REJ	Reject frame
RFC	Request for Comments
RIP	Routing Information Protocol
RISC	Reduced Instruction Set Computer
RJE	Remote Job Entry
RMT	Ring Management (FDDI)
RNR	Receive Not Ready
RQ	Request Counter (DQDB)
RR	Receive Ready frame
RTMP	Routing and Management Protocol (Apple)
RTP	Routing Update Protocol
s	second
SA	Source Address field
SAP	Service Access Point (ISO)
SAPI	Service Access Point Identifier (ISO)
SAR	Segmentation and Re-assembly (ATM)
SAS	Single-Attach Station connection (FDDI)
SD	Start Delimiter
SDH	Synchronous Digital Hierarchy (ITU-T)
SDLC	Synchronous Data Link Control protocol (IBM)
SDU	Service Data Unit (DQDB)
SES	Severely Errored Seconds
SF	SuperFrame
SIG	SMDS Interest Group
SIP	SMDS Interface Protocol (SMDS)
SIR	Sustained Information Rate (SMDS)
SMDS	Switched Multimegabit Data Service
SMF	Single-Mode Fiber
SMT	System Management protocol (FDDI)
SN	Sequence Number
SNA	System Network Architecture (IBM)
SNAP	SubNetwork Access Protocol (SMDS)
SNI	Subscriber Network Interface (SMDS)
SNMP	Simple Network Management Protocol (DoD)
SOH	Section Overhead
SONET	Synchronous Optical Network (ANSI)
SPE	Synchronous Payload Envelope (SONET)
SPF	Shortest Path First protocol
SPM	FDDI-to-SONET Physical Layer Mapping standard
SREJ	Select Reject frame
SRT	Source Route Transparent protocol
SS	Switching System (SMDS)
SSAP	Source Service Access Point (LLC)
SSCOP	Service-Specific Connection Oriented Protocol (ATM)

SSCS	Service-Specific Convergence Sublayer (ATM)
STE	Section Terminating Equipment (SONET)
STM	Synchronous Transfer Mode or Station Management (SDH)
STM-*n*	Synchronous Transport Module level *n* (SDH)
STP	Shielded Twisted Pair
STP	Spanning Tree Protocol (IEEE 802.1d)
STS-*n*	Synchronous Transport Signal Level *n* (SONET)
STS-*Nc*	Concatenated Synchronous Transport Signal Level *N*
SVC	Switched Virtual Circuit or Signaling Virtual Channel
SYN	Synchronous Idle
t	time
TA	Terminal Adapter
TC	Transmission Convergence sub-layer of PHY layer (ATM)
TCP	Transmission Control Protocol (DoD)
TCP/IP	Transmission Control Protocol/Internet Protocol (DoD)
TDM	Time Division Multiplexing
TDMA	Time Division Multiple Access
TE	Terminal Equipment
TP	Transport Protocol (CCITT)
TP4	Transport Protocol Class 4 (ISO)
TR	Technical Report
UDP	User Datagram Protocol (DoD)
UNI	User-to-Network Interface
UNMA	Unified Network Management Architecture (AT&T)
UTP	Unshielded Twisted Pair
VBR	Variable Bit Rate
VC	Virtual Channel or Virtual Call
VCC	Virtual Channel Connection
VCI	Virtual Channel or Circuit Identifier (DQDB)
VC-*n*	Virtual Container-*n* (SDH)
VLSI	Very Large Scale Integration
VP	Virtual Path (ATM)
VPI	Virtual Path Identifier (ATM)
VPN	Virtual Private Network
VT	Virtual Tributary (SONET)
VT*x*	VT of size *x* (currently $x = 1.5, 2, 3, 6$)
VT*x*-*Nc*	Concatenated Virtual Tributary (SONET)
WAN	Wide Area Network
XNS	Xerox Network Systems protocol (XEROX)
ZIP	Routing and Management protocol (Apple)

μs microsecond (10^{-6} second)

Appendix

B

Standards Sources

Alpha Graphics
10215 N. 35th Avenue, Suite A&B, Phoenix, AZ 85051
Ph:602-863-0999 (IEEE P802 draft standards)

American National Standards Institute — ANSI — Sales Department
11 W. 42nd Street, New York, NY 10036
Ph:212-642-4900/FAX:212-302-1286 (ANSI and ISO standards)

Association Francaise de Normalisation, Tour Europe — Cedex 7
92080 Paris La Defense, FR
Ph: 33-1-4-778-13-26; Telex:611-974-AFNOR-F; FAX:33-1-774-84-90

ATM Forum
303 Vintage Park Drive
Foster City, CA 94404
Ph: 415-578-6860; FAX: 415-525-0182; Internet: info@atmforum.com

Bell Communications Research –Bellcore Customer Service
8 Corporate Place, Piscataway, NJ 08854-4156
Ph:908-699-5800 / 1-800-521-CORE (1-800-521-2673)
(Bellcore TAs and TRs)

British Standards Institution
2 Park St., London, WIA 2BS England
Ph:44-1-629-9000; Telex:266933 BSI G; FAX:+44-1-629-0506

Canadian Standards Association
178 Rexdale Boulevard, Rexdale, ON M9W 1R9 Canada
Ph:416-747-4363; Telex:06-989344; FAX:1-416-747-4149

Comite Europeen de Normalisation
Rue Brederode 2 Bte 5, 1000 Brussels, Belgium
Ph:32-2-513-79-30; Telex:26257 B

Computer and Business Equipment Manufacturers Association (CBEMA)
311 First Street N.W., Suite 500, Washington, DC 20001-2178
Ph:202-626-5740; FAX: 202-638-4299, 202-628-2829 (ANSI X3 secretariat)

Dansk Standardiseringsrad
Aurehojvej 12, Postboks 77, DK-2900 Hellerup, Denmark
Ph:45-1-62-32-00; Telex:15-615 DANSTA DK

DDN Network Information Center - SRI International
333 Ravenswood Avenue, Menlo Park, CA 94025
Ph:415-859-3695 / 1-800-235-3155 / e-mail: NIC@NIC.DDN.MIL
(Requests for Comments [RFC] documents)

Deutsches Institut für Normung
Burggrafenstrasse 4-10, Postfach 1107, D-1000 Berlin 30, Germany
Ph:49-30-26-01-1; Telex:184-273-DIN D; FAX:49-30-260-12-31

Electronics Industries Association (EIA)
Standards Sales, 2001 Eye Street NW, Washington, DC 20036
Ph:202-457-4966; Telex:710-822-0148 EIA WSH; FAX:202-457-4985

European Computer Manufacturers Association (ECMA)
Rue du Rhone 114, CH-1204 Geneva, Switzerland
Ph:41-22-735-36-34; Telex:413237 ECMA CH; FAX:41-22-786-52-31

European Conference of Postal and Telecommunications Administrations — CEPT
CEPT Liaison Office, Seilerstrasse 22, CH-3008 Bern, Switzerland
Ph:41-31-62-20-78; Telex:911089 CEPT CH; FAX:41-31-62-20-78

European SMDS Interest Group (SIG)
Merlin House, Station Road, Chepstow
Gwent, UK NP6 5PB
Ph:44-291-620425; FAX:44-291-627119

Exchange Carriers Standards Association (ECSA)
5430 Grosvenor Lane, Bethesda, MD 20814-2122
Ph:301-564-4505 (ANSI T1 secretariat)

Global Engineering
2805 McGaw Ave., Irvine, CA 92714
Ph:1-800-854-7179 (ANSI, IEEE, US. Federal and Military standards and drafts)

Information Handling Services
15 Inverness Way East, Englewood, CO 80112
Ph: 1-800-854-7179; FAX: (303)397-2599

Institute of Electrical and Electronics Engineers (IEEE) — Computer Society
10662 Los Vaqueros Circle
Los Alamitos, CA 90720
Ph: 800-272-6657; FAX: 714-821-4641; Interop: cs.books@compmail.com

Institute of Electrical and Electronics Engineers (IEEE) — Standards Office/Service Center
445 Hoes Lane, Piscataway, NJ 08855-1331
Ph:800-678-4323; FAX: 908-981-9667 (IEEE standards)

International Organization for Standardization
1 Rue de Varembe, Case Postale 56, CH-1211 Geneva 20, Switzerland
Ph:41-22-734-1240; Telex:23-88-1 ISO CH; FAX:41-22-733-3430

International Telecommunications Union — General Secretariat — Sales Service
Place de Nation, CH 1211, Geneva 20, SWITZERLAND
Ph:41-22-730-5860; Telex:421000 UIT CH; FAX:41-22-730-5853
Ph: 41-22-730-5554; FAX: 41-22-730-5337;Internet: helpdesk@itu.ch (Information Services Department) (CCITT and other ITU recommendations)

Internet Access to Request for Comments (RFCs)
Internet: logon "anonymous", password "guest"

Japanese Industrial Standards Committee
Standards Department, Agency of Industrial Science & Technology
Ministry of International Trade and Industry
1-3-1, Kasumigaseki, Chiyoda-ku, Tokyo 100 Japan
Ph:81-3-501-9295/6; FAX:81-3-680-1418

National Institute of Standards and Technology
Technology Building 225, Gaithersburg, MD 20899
Ph:301-975-2000; FAX:301-948-1784

National Standards Authority of Ireland
Ballymun Road, Dublin 9, Ireland
Ph:353-1-370101; Telex:32501 IIRS EI; FAX:353-1-379620

Nederlands Normalisatie-Instituut
Kalfjeslaan 2, P.O. Box 5059, 2600 GB Delft, Netherlands
Ph:31-15-61-10-61

Omnicom, Inc.
115 Park St. SE, Vienna, VA 22180-4607
Ph:703-281-1135; Telex:279678 OMNI UR; FAX:703-281-1505

Omnicom International, Ltd.
1st Floor, Forum Chambers, The Forum, Sevenage, Herts, United Kingdom SG1 1EL
Ph:44-438-742424; Telex:826903 OMNICM G; FAX:44-438-740154

Pacific Rim Frame Relay/ATM/SMDS Interest Group (PR FASIG)
AT&T Taiwan Inc.
12th Floor Overseas Trust Building
249, Sec.1, Tun Hwa South Road
Taipei, 106, Taiwan, R.O.C.
Ph: 886-2-775-6398; FAX: 886-2-775-6356; Internet: attitw.attmail.com

Rapidoc, Technical Indices, Ltd.
Willoughby, Rd., Bracknell, Berkshire, RG12 4DW, UK
Ph: (0344) 861666; FAX: (0344) 714440

Saudi Arabia Standards Organization
P.O. Box 3437, Riyadh 11471, Saudi Arabia
Ph:9-661-4793332; Telex:201610 SASO

SMDS Interest Group (SIG)
303 Vintage Park Drive
Foster City, CA 94404-1138
Ph:415-578-6979; Fax:415-525-0182; e-mail: sig@interop.com

SRI International
333 Ravenswood Avenue, Room EJ291, Menlo Park, CA 94025
Ph:800-235-3155 (Internet Protocol RFCs)

Standardiseringskommissionen i Sverige
Tegnergatan 11, Box 3 295, S-103 66 Stockholm, Sweden
Ph:468-230400; Telex:17453 SIS S

Standards Association of Australia — Standards House
80-86 Arthur Street, North Sydney N.S.W. 2060 Australia
Ph:61-2-963-41-11; Telex:2-65-14 ASTAN AA

Suomen Standardisoimisliitto
P.O. Box 205, SF-00121 Helsinki 12, Finland
Ph:358-0-645-601; Telex:122303 STAND SF

U.S. Department of Commerce — National Technical Information Service
5285 Port Royal Road, Springfield, VA 22161
Ph:703-487-4650 (ITU recommendations, U.S. Government and Military standards)

United Nations Bookstore
United Nations General Assembly Building, Room GA 32B, New York, NY 10017
Ph:212-963-7680; Internet: itudoc@itu.ch (ITU recommendations)

U.S. Department of Commerce - National Technical Information Service
5285 Port Royal Road, Springfield, VA 22161
Ph: 703-487-4650; FAX: 703-321-8547 (ITU/CCITT Recommendations, U.S. Government and Military standards)

Appendix

IP Mask Reference Table

This reference contains a guideline for choosing IP subnetwork mask. The table below is arranged so that the user can select the number of networks and hosts available per mask. Note that the number of actual networks per mask is two less than what is possible because all 1s and all 0s are reserved. The actual network numbers available per mask are provided in the rightmost column.

Mask	B7	B6	B5	B4	B3	B2	B1	B0	Possible Networks (Available Networks)	Hosts	Net numbers
128	1	0	0	0	0	0	0	0	2 (0)	128	0,128
192	1	1	0	0	0	0	0	0	4 (2)	64	0,64,128,192
224	1	1	1	0	0	0	0	0	8 (6)	32	0,32,64,96,etc., to 224
240	1	1	1	1	0	0	0	0	16 (14)	16	0,16,32,etc., to 240
248	1	1	1	1	1	0	0	0	32 (30)	8	0,8,16,24, etc., to 248
252	1	1	1	1	1	1	0	0	64 (62)	4	0,4,8,12, etc., to 252
254	1	1	1	1	1	1	1	0	128 (126)	2	0,2,4,6,8,etc., to 254
	128	64	32	16	8	4	2	1			

Note: All 1s and 0s are technically reserved for network (0) or broadcast (1) (typical configuration) so masks like 128, 64, etc. are invalid.
B = bit position, Nets = number of networks, Hosts = number of Hosts

Appendix

IP Network Addressing Reference

This table can be used to find the network subnet mask that provides a specific number of hosts and networks for classes A, B, and C IP addresses.

128 Subnet Mask Example

Network	Net#	Binary	Address Class A	Address Class B	Address Class C
.000	res	0XXX.XXXX	XXX.000.XXX.XXX	XXX.XXX.000.XXX	XXX.XXX.XXX.000
.128	res	1XXX.XXXX	XXX.128.XXX.XXX	XXX.XXX.128.XXX	XXX.XXX.XXX.128

192 Subnet Mask Example

Network	Net#	Binary	Address Class A	Address Class B	Address Class C
.000	res	00XX.XXXX	XXX.000.XXX.XXX	XXX.XXX.000.XXX	XXX.XXX.XXX.000
.064	1	01XX.XXXX	XXX.064.XXX.XXX	XXX.XXX.064.XXX	XXX.XXX.XXX.064
.128	2	10XX.XXXX	XXX.128.XXX.XXX	XXX.XXX.128.XXX	XXX.XXX.XXX.128
.192	res	11XX.XXXX	XXX.192.XXX.XXX	XXX.XXX.192.XXX	XXX.XXX.XXX.192

224 Subnet Mask Example

Network	Net#	Binary	Address Class A	Address Class B	Address Class C
.000	res	000X.XXXX	XXX.000.XXX.XXX	XXX.XXX.000.XXX	XXX.XXX.XXX.000
.032	1	001X.XXXX	XXX.032.XXX.XXX	XXX.XXX.032.XXX	XXX.XXX.XXX.032
.064	2	010X.XXXX	XXX.064.XXX.XXX	XXX.XXX.064.XXX	XXX.XXX.XXX.064
.096	3	011X.XXXX	XXX.096.XXX.XXX	XXX.XXX.096.XXX	XXX.XXX.XXX.096
.128	4	100X.XXXX	XXX.128.XXX.XXX	XXX.XXX.128.XXX	XXX.XXX.XXX.128
.160	5	101X.XXXX	XXX.160.XXX.XXX	XXX.XXX.160.XXX	XXX.XXX.XXX.160
.192	6	110X.XXXX	XXX.192.XXX.XXX	XXX.XXX.192.XXX	XXX.XXX.XXX.192
.224	res	111X.XXXX	XXX.224.XXX.XXX	XXX.XXX.224.XXX	XXX.XXX.XXX.224

240 Subnet Mask Example

Network	Net#	Binary	Address Class A	Address Class B	Address Class C
.000	res	0000.XXXX	XXX.000.XXX.XXX	XXX.XXX.000.XXX	XXX.XXX.XXX.000
.016	1	0001.XXXX	XXX.016.XXX.XXX	XXX.XXX.016.XXX	XXX.XXX.XXX.016
.032	2	0010.XXXX	XXX.032.XXX.XXX	XXX.XXX.032.XXX	XXX.XXX.XXX.032
.048	3	0011.XXXX	XXX.048.XXX.XXX	XXX.XXX.048.XXX	XXX.XXX.XXX.048
.064	4	0100.XXXX	XXX.064.XXX.XXX	XXX.XXX.064.XXX	XXX.XXX.XXX.064
.080	5	0101.XXXX	XXX.080.XXX.XXX	XXX.XXX.080.XXX	XXX.XXX.XXX.080
.096	6	0110.XXXX	XXX.096.XXX.XXX	XXX.XXX.096.XXX	XXX.XXX.XXX.096
.112	7	0111.XXXX	XXX.112.XXX.XXX	XXX.XXX.112.XXX	XXX.XXX.XXX.112
.128	8	1000.XXXX	XXX.128.XXX.XXX	XXX.XXX.128.XXX	XXX.XXX.XXX.128
.144	9	1001.XXXX	XXX.144.XXX.XXX	XXX.XXX.144.XXX	XXX.XXX.XXX.144
.160	10	1010.XXXX	XXX.160.XXX.XXX	XXX.XXX.160.XXX	XXX.XXX.XXX.160
.176	11	1011.XXXX	XXX.176.XXX.XXX	XXX.XXX.176.XXX	XXX.XXX.XXX.176
.192	12	1100.XXXX	XXX.192.XXX.XXX	XXX.XXX.192.XXX	XXX.XXX.XXX.192
.208	13	1101.XXXX	XXX.208.XXX.XXX	XXX.XXX.208.XXX	XXX.XXX.XXX.208
.224	14	1110.XXXX	XXX.224.XXX.XXX	XXX.XXX.224.XXX	XXX.XXX.XXX.224
.240	res	1111.XXXX	XXX.240.XXX.XXX	XXX.XXX.240.XXX	XXX.XXX.XXX.240

248 Subnet Mask Example

Network	Net#	Binary			
0	res	0000.0XXX	XXX.000.XXX.XXX	XXX.XXX.000.XXX	XXX.XXX.XXX.000
8	1	0000.1XXX	XXX.008.XXX.XXX	XXX.XXX.008.XXX	XXX.XXX.XXX.008
16	2	0001.0XXX	XXX.016.XXX.XXX	XXX.XXX.016.XXX	XXX.XXX.XXX.016
24	3	0010.0XXX	XXX.024.XXX.XXX	XXX.XXX.024.XXX	XXX.XXX.XXX.024
32	4	0010.1XXX	XXX.032.XXX.XXX	XXX.XXX.032.XXX	XXX.XXX.XXX.032
40	5	0011.0XXX	XXX.040.XXX.XXX	XXX.XXX.040.XXX	XXX.XXX.XXX.040
48	6	0011.1XXX	XXX.048.XXX.XXX	XXX.XXX.048.XXX	XXX.XXX.XXX.048
and so forth in increments of 8 until					
.232	29	1110.1XXX	XXX.232.XXX.XXX	XXX.XXX.232.XXX	XXX.XXX.XXX.232
.240	30	1111.0XXX	XXX.240.XXX.XXX	XXX.XXX.240.XXX	XXX.XXX.XXX.240
.248	res	1111.1XXX	XXX.248.XXX.XXX	XXX.XXX.248.XXX	XXX.XXX.XXX.248

252 Subnet Mask Example

Network	Net#	Binary	Address Class A	Address Class B	Address Class C
.000	res	0000.00XX	XXX.000.XXX.XXX	XXX.XXX.000.XXX	XXX.XXX.XXX.000
.004	1	0000.01XX	XXX.004.XXX.XXX	XXX.XXX.004.XXX	XXX.XXX.XXX.004
.008	2	0000.10XX	XXX.008.XXX.XXX	XXX.XXX.008.XXX	XXX.XXX.XXX.008
and so forth in increments of 4 until					
.248	62	1111.10XX	XXX.248.XXX.XXX	XXX.XXX.248.XXX	XXX.XXX.XXX.248
.252	res	1111.11XX	XXX.252.XXX.XXX	XXX.XXX.252.XXX	XXX.XXX.XXX.252

254 Subnet Mask Example

Network	Net#	Binary	Address Class A	Address Class B	Address Class C
.000	res	0000.000X	XXX.000.XXX.XXX	XXX.XXX.000.XXX	XXX.XXX.XXX.000
.002	1	0000.001X	XXX.002.XXX.XXX	XXX.XXX.002.XXX	XXX.XXX.XXX.002
.004	2	0000.010X	XXX.004.XXX.XXX	XXX.XXX.004.XXX	XXX.XXX.XXX.004
.006	3	0000.011X	XXX.006.XXX.XXX	XXX.XXX.006.XXX	XXX.XXX.XXX.006
and so forth in increments of 2 until					
.252	126	1111.110X	XXX.252.XXX.XXX	XXX.XXX.252.XXX	XXX.XXX.XXX.252
.254	res	1111.111X	XXX.254.XXX.XXX	XXX.XXX.254.XXX	XXX.XXX.XXX.254

Glossary

10BASE2 - IEEE 802.3 standard specifying Ethernet over thin coax cable.

10BASE5 - IEEE 802.3 standard specifying Ethernet over thick coax cable.

10BASET - IEEE 802.3 standard specifying Ethernet over UTP.

10BASEF - IEEE 802.3 standard specifying Ethernet over fiber.

100BASEFX - 100 Mbps standard specifying Ethernet over fiber.

100BASET4 - 100 Mbps standard specifying Ethernet over category 3, 4, or 5 cabling. Compatible with 802.3 MAC sublayer format.

100BASETX - 100 Mbps standard specifying Ethernet over category 5 and Type 1 cabling. Compatible with 802.3 MAC sublayer format.

100VG-AnyLAN - IEEE standard specifying 100 Mbps Ethernet and Token Ring over 4-pair UTP.

access unit - In DQDB, the functional unit within a node that performs the DQDB layer functions and controls access to both buses.

address - An identifier of a source or destination in a network. Examples of addresses are IP, E.164, and X.121.

address resolution protocol (ARP) - Protocol used to resolve a destination host MAC address from its known IP address.

address translation - A method of converting a user-protocol address into the standard address format of the network protocol, and vice versa.

agent - Software residing in a managed network device that reports MIB variables through SNMP.

American National Standards Institute (ANSI) - A private, nongovernmental, nonprofit national organization which serves as the primary coordinator of standards within the United States.

analog - Voice or data signals that are continuously variable and possess an infinite number of values (compared to digital, which has discrete variables).

Application Layer (OSI) - Layer 7 of the OSIRM. Provides the management of communications between user applications. Examples include e-mail and file transfer.

Asynchronous Transfer Mode (ATM) - A high-speed, connection-oriented multiplexing and switching method specified in international standards utilizing fixed-length cells to support multiple types of traffic. It is asynchronous in the sense that cells carrying user data need not be periodic.

asynchronous transmission - The transmission of data through start and stop sequences without the use of a common clock.

ATM Adaptation Layer (AAL) - A set of internationally standardized protocols and formats that define support for circuit emulation, packet video and audio, and connection-oriented and connectionless data services.

available bit rate (ABR) - A traffic class of ATM.

B-channel - An ISDN bearer service channel which can carry either voice or data at a speed of 64 kbps.

Backward Explicit Congestion Notification (BECN) - Convention in frame relay for a network device to notify the user (source) device that network congestion has occurred.

bandwidth - The amount of transport resource available to pass information (passband), measured in hertz for analog and bits per second for digital carriers.

bandwidth balancing - A DQDB scheme where a node that is queued for access will occasionally *not* seize an empty QA slot. This helps to ensure effective sharing of QA slots.

Basic Mode - An FDDI mode of ring operation that supports packet-switching services only where MAC PDUs are transmitted directly by the PHY protocol.

basic rate interface (BRI) - An ISDN access interface type composed of two B-channels each at 64 kbps and one D-channel at 16 kbps (2B+D).

B-channel - An ISDN bearer service channel that can carry either voice or data at a speed of 64 kbps.

Bell Operating Company (BOC) - One of the 22 local telephone companies formed after the divestiture of AT&T (e.g., Illinois Bell, Ohio Bell).

Bisync (BSC) or Binary Synchronous Communications Protocol - An IBM proprietary bit-oriented protocol.

bridge - A LAN/WAN device operating at layers 1 (physical) and 2 (data link) of the OSIRM.

broadband - While broadband once represented bandwidths in excess of the voice channel (3 kHz), or in basic data communications using analog, modulated signals, it now refers to channels supporting rates in excess of DS3 (45 Mbps) or E3 (34 Mbps).

Broadband ISDN (B-ISDN) - A set of services, capabilities, and interfaces supporting an integrated network and user interface at speeds greater than that of ISDN. The ITU-T initially decided to develop B-ISDN using ATM in 1988.

broadcast - A transmission to all addresses on the network or subnetwork.

broadcast address - A predefined network address that indicates all possible receivers on a network.

brouter - A device that combines some elements of both bridging and routing.

busy slot - A DQDB slot which is "in use" and not available for access by the QA access functions.

cell - A fixed-length 53-octet packet, or Protocol Data Unit (PDU) used in ATM. The ATM cell has a 5-octet header and a 48-octet payload.

cell header - A 5-octet header that defines control information used in processing, multiplexing, and switching cells.

Central Office (CO) - Telephone company switching office providing local user access to the local switched telephone network and its services; often the first interface to interexchange carriers.

Central Office vendors - A reference to vendors who provide switching equipment conforming to central office standards, such as DQDB switch vendors Siemens and Alcatel.

circuit switching - A connection-oriented technique based on either time- or space-division multiplexing and switching providing minimal delay. Bandwidth is dedicated to the connection.

client-server architecture - The distribution of network control across many computing elements within the network. Thus, some elements act as servers, controlling the transfer, and some as clients which transmit and receive the information. Servers can do all three functions, and are often the workhorse computing elements (multi-MIP machines), while the clients are typically workstations and terminals.

colocated - Devices near one another at the same site.

Committed Information Rate (CIR) - A term defined for frame relay service that defines the average rate at which a user can send frames and be guaranteed delivery by the network. Transmissions exceeding the CIR are subject to lower-priority treatment or discard.

Concatenated Virtual Tributary (VT*x*-*Nc*) - A combination of VTs where the VT envelope capacities from *N* VT*x*'s have been combined to carry a VT*x*-*Nc* that must be transported as a single entity (as opposed to transport as separate signals).

concentrator - A device providing a single network access for multiple user devices. In FDDI, a device which has additional ports beyond what is required for its own attachment to the ring.

congestion - The condition where network resources (bandwidth) are exceeded by an accumulation of demand.

Consolidated Link Layer Management (CLLM) - In frame relay, an ANSI-defined method of sending link layer management messages over the last DLCI (1023). These messages are used to identify the exact cause of congestion and modify transmissions based on each DLCI.

convergence function - A DQDB protocol layer that interfaces service-specific interfaces to higher-layer protocol functions.

countdown counter (CD) - A queued, arbitrated access method for determining how many empty slots must pass before a node has access to the DQDB bus.

customer premises equipment (CPE) - Equipment that resides and is operated at a customer site.

cycle - The Protocol Data Unit (PDU) used in FDDI-II.

Cyclic Redundancy Check (CRC) - An algorithm that detects bit errors caused in data transmission.

D4 - AT&T-defined framing and synchronization format for T1 transmission facilities.

Data Communications (or Circuit Termination) Equipment (DCE) - Data communications equipment defined by the standards as a modem or network communications interface device.

datagram - A packet mode of transmitting data where there is no guaranteed sequential delivery (connectionless service).

Data Link Connection Identifier (DLCI) - A frame relay address designator for each virtual circuit termination point.

data link layer (OSI) - Layer 2 of the OSIRM. Provides for the error-free communications between adjacent network devices over a physical interface. Examples include the LLC and MAC layers which manage LAN and MAN operation.

Data Terminal Equipment (DTE) - Data-processing equipment defined by the standards as interfacing to the communications network (DCE).

D-channel - The ISDN out-of-band (16 kbps or 64 kbps, depending on BRI or PRI, respectively) signaling channel which carries the ISDN user signals or can be used to carry packet-mode data.

default slot generator function - In DQDB, the function defining the identity for each bus in the dual bus network. In the looped bus topology, this function also provides the head of bus function for both buses.

delay-insensitive - *see time- insensitive.*

delay-sensitive - *see time-sensitive.*

derived MAC protocol data unit (MAC-PDU or DMPDU) - In DQDB, single 44-octet portion of the original IMPDU, composed of 4 overhead octets and a 44-octet segmentation unit.

digital - Signals that have discrete values, such as binary bit streams of 0s and 1s.

digital cross-connect system (DXC) - Breaks down a T1 into individual DS0s for testing and reconfiguration.

digital signal 0 (DS0) - One 56 kbps framed channel out of the 24 contained in a DS1 channel.

Digital Signal 1 (DS1) - The North American standard 1.544 Mbps digital channel.

Digital Signal 3 (DS3) - The North American standard 44.736 Mbps digital channel.

Discard Eligibility (DE) bit - Used in frame relay, this bit signals (when set to 1) that the particular frame is eligible for discard during congestion conditions.

distributed processing - Sharing of applications, data, and the tasks operating among several small or midrange processing devices, as opposed to a single mainframe in centralized processing.

distributed queue - The operation of the DQDB Queued Arbitration MAC scheme, where all nodes keep track of the number of stations queued for access in their request counter; when a station queues itself for access, it keeps track of its position in the queue using its countdown counter and it counts the number of stations behind it in the queue in the request counter.

Distributed Queue Dual Bus (DQDB) - The IEEE 802.6 MAN architecture standard for providing both circuit-switched (isochronous) and packet-switched services.

DQDB layer - The lower portion of the DQDB link layer which provides the connectionless MAC data service, connection-oriented data service, and an isochronous service with the help of physical layer services.

dual-attachment station (DAS) - A workstation that attaches to both primary and secondary FDDI MAN rings which enables the capability for network self-healing.

dual bus - Bus A and bus B, dual DQDB bus structure. The dual bus supports both the open dual bus and the looped dual bus.

E1 - The European T1 CEPT standard digital channel operating at 2.048 Mbps.

E1 carrier - Part of the European and Asian (excluding Japan) digital TDM hierarchy: a single multiplexed 2.048 Mbps channel.

E.164 - A CCITT Recommendation for defining addresses in a public data international network, varying in size up to 15 digits (carried as 60-bit addresses in DQDB).

empty slot - In DQDB, a Queued Arbitrated slot not currently in use that may be seized by a node queried for QA access.

enterprise network - A network that spans an entire organization.

entity - In the OSIRM, a service of management element between peers and within a sublayer or layer.

Ethernet - A LAN that uses CSAM/CD media access method and operates at 10 Mbps, usually over coax medium.

Explicit Congestion Notification (ECN) - In frame relay, the use of either FECN and BECN or CLLM messages to notify the source and destination of network congestion (as opposed to implicit congestion notification).

fast packet - The generic term used for advanced packet technologies such as frame relay, DQDB, and ATM.

FastPacket™ - StrataCom Corporation's trademark for its proprietary switching technique, which uses 192-bit packets and packetized voice.

Fiber Distributed Data Interface (FDDI) - Fiber-optic LAN operating at 100 Mbps.

FDDI-II - FDDI standard with the additional capability to carry isochronous traffic (voice/video).

FDDI Follow-On (FDDI-FO) - Future ANSI standards for extending the speed of FDDI up to 600 Mbps.

fiber optics - Plastic or glass fibers which transmit high data rates through optical signals.

filtering - The selection of frames not to remain at the local LAN but to be forwarded to another network by a network device (e.g., router).

flag - Character that signals a beginning or end of a frame.

Forward Explicit Congestion Notification (FECN) - Convention in frame relay for a network device to notify the user (destination) device that network congestion is occurring.

fractional T1 (FT1) - The transmission of a fraction of a T1 channel, usually based on 64 kbps increments but not less than 64 kbps total.

frame - An OSI data-link layer unit of transmission whose length is defined by flags at the beginning and end.

Frame Check Sequence (FCS) - A field in an X.25, SDLC, or HDLC frame which contains the result of a CRC error-checking algorithm.

frame relay - An ANSI and CCITT LAN/WAN networking standard for switching frames in a packet mode similar to X.25, but at higher speeds and with less nodal processing (assuming digital transmission).

frame relay assembler/disassembler (FRAD) - A device which acts as a concentrator and protocol translator from non-frame relay protocols (e.g., SDLC, SNA) to a standard frame relay transmission.

frequency division multiplexing (FDM) - The method of aggregating multiple simultaneous transmissions (circuits) over a single high-speed channel by using individual frequency passbands for each circuit (for example, RF Broadband LANs).

full-duplex - The simultaneous bidirectional transmission of information over a common medium.

gateway - A network device that interconnects dissimilar types of network elements through all seven layers of the OSIRM.

global addressing - A frame relay addressing convention where a single, unique DLCI value is given to each user device on the network.

half-duplex - The bidirectional transmission of information over a common medium, but where information may only travel in one direction at any one time.

head of bus (HOB_A and HOB_B) - In DQDB, the node responsible for generating empty slots and management information octets.

host - An end-communicating station in a network; also an IP address.

implicit congestion notification - A congestion indication which is performed by upper-layer protocols (e.g., TCP) rather than network or data-link layer protocol conventions.

individual address - The address of a specific network station or node. In IP, the format is XXXX.XXXX.XXXX.XXXX.

Initial MAC Protocol Data Unit (IMPDU) - In DQDB, the PDU formed by the DQDB layer providing a connectionless MAC service to the LLC.

Integrated Services Digital Network (ISDN) - CCITT I-series Recommendation defining the digital network standard for integrated voice and data-network access and services and user-network messages.

integrated switching - The method of performing multiple switching techniques with one device or within a single hardware architecture, including consolidated configuration and network management.

IntereXchange Carrier (IXC) - The provider of long distance (inter-LATA) service in the United States; also the provider of worldwide switched voice and data services.

interface - In OSI, the boundary between two adjacent protocol layers (i.e., network to transport).

Interim Local Management Interface (ILMI) - An SNMP-based management protocol for an ATM UNI defined by the ATM Forum.

Internetwork - A master network made up of multiple smaller networks, or the concept of bridging, routing, switching, or gateway between homogeneous network devices, protocols, and standards.

interoperability - The ability of multiple, dissimilar vendor devices and protocols to operate and communicate using a standard set of rules and protocols.

intra-LATA - LEC-defined geographic areas (Local Access Transport Area). LEC must pass cells to IXC to go inter-LATA.

isochronous - The circuit-switched transmission service offered in DQDB and FDDI-II. This allows a consistent timed access of network bandwidth for time-sensitive transmission of voice and video traffic.

latency - The minimum amount of time it takes for a token to circulate around the LAN Token Ring or FDDI ring in the absence of a data transmission.

layer management - Network management functions which provide information about the operations of a given OSI protocol layer.

Layer Management Entity (LME) - In DQDB, the entity within the protocol layer responsible for performing local management of the layer.

Layer Management Interface (LMI) - In DQDB, the interface between the LME and network management systems.

Line-Terminating Equipment (LTE) - A device which either originates or terminates an OC-*N* signal and which may originate, access, modify, and terminate the transport overhead.

Link Access Protocol on the D-channel (LAPD) - CCITT Recommendations Q.920 (I.440) and Q.921 (I.441) defining standards for the data-link layer operation of ISDN D and frame relay channel.

local area network (LAN) - A MAC-level data and computer communications network confined to short geographic distances.

local bridge - A high-throughput, collocated LAN-to-LAN interconnectivity device.

local exchange carrier (LEC) - In the United States, traditionally a local phone service provider, that now can compete in inter-LATA service.

Local Management Interface (LMI) - A set of user device-to-network communications standards used in ATM DXI and frame relay.

Logical Link Control (LLC) - The upper half of the OSIRM data-link layer, layer 2, as defined by the IEEE 802.2 standard. This layer provides a common LAN platform for all IEEE 802.X protocols.

logical ring - The circular closed set of point-to-point links among network stations on a Token Ring and FDDI network.

looped dual bus - A DQDB bus configuration where the head of bus functions for both A and B buses are contained within the same node.

MAN Switching System (SS) - A single metropolitan area network composed of many MAN switches, usually linked by a common DQDB bus.

media - The plural form of medium, or multiple mediums (twisted-pair wire, coax cable, fiber, etc.).

medium - The single common access platform, such as a copper wire, fiber, or free space.

Medium Access Control (MAC) - IEEE 802 protocol defining media-specific access control.

message identifier (MID) - In DQDB, a value used to identify all DMPDUs that together make up the same IMPDU.

metropolitan area network (MAN) - A MAC-level data and computer communications network which operates over metropolitan or campus areas, and recently has been expanded to nationwide and even worldwide connectivity of high-speed data networks. A MAN can carry voice, video, and data, and has been defined as both the DQDB and FDDI standards set.

multicast - A connection type with the capability to broadcast to multiple destinations on the network.

multimode fiber (MMF) - 50- to 100-μm core diameter optical fiber with many propagation paths for light, typically used for lower speed or shorter distances (as compared to single-mode optical fiber).

multiplexing - The technique of combining multiple single channels onto a single aggregate channel for sharing facilities and bandwidth.

network - A system of autonomous devices, links, and subsystems which provide a platform for communications.

Network Layer (OSI) - Layer 3 of the OSIRM. Provides the end-to-end routing and switching of data units (packets), as well as managing congestion control.

network management - The process of managing the operation and status of network resources (e.g., devices, protocols).

node - A device that interfaces with the transmission medium through the physical layer (and often the data-link layer) of the OSIRM. This device is sometimes called an access unit in DQDB.

octet - An 8-bit transmission unit of measure.

open dual bus - In DQDB, a non-fault-tolerant subnetwork configuration where the head of bus functions for bus A and bus B are in different nodes (can also be the configuration after a failure and subsequent network self-healing).

Open Systems Interconnection Reference Model (OSIRM) - A seven-layer model defining the international protocol standards for data communications in a multiple architecture and vendor environment. Both the OSI and CCITT define standards based on the OSIRM.

Optical Carrier level *N* (OC-*N*) - The optical carrier level signal in SONET which results from an STS-*N* signal conversion. In SONET, the basic transmission speed unit is 58.34 Mbps.

Packet Assembler/Disassembler (PAD) - A concentration and network-access device which provides protocol conversion into X.25 packet format.

Packet Switch Public Data Network (PSPDN) - A public data network utilizing packet-switching technology (X.25, SMDS, ATM).

packet switching - A method of switching that segments the data into fixed or variable units of maximum size called packets. These packets then pass the user information (addressing, sequencing, error control, and user-controlled options) in a store-and-forward manner across the network.

packet type - Identifies the type of packet and its use, such as for user data, call establishment and termination, and routing information.

path overhead (POH) - Overhead transported with the SONET payload and used for payload transport functions.

payload pointer - Indicates the starting point of a SONET synchronous payload envelope.

permanent virtual circuit (PVC) - A logical dedicated circuit between two user ports in a point-to-point configuration.

Physical Layer (OSI) - Layer 1 of the OSIRM. Provides the electrical and mechanical interface and signaling of bits over the communications medium.

Physical Layer Convergence Protocol (PLCP) - The IEEE 802.6 standard defining the physical layer that adapts the actual capabilities of the underlying physical network to provide the services required by the DQDB or ATM layer.

Physical Layer Medium Dependent (PMD) - In FDDI, the medium-specific layer corresponding to the lower sublayer of the OSIRM physical layer.

Physical Layer Protocol (PHY) - In FDDI, the medium-independent layer corresponding to the upper sublayer of the OSIRM physical layer.

plastic optical fiber (POF) - A low-cost, low-distance plastic alternative to glass fiber.

Presentation Layer (OSI) - Layer 6 of the OSIRM. Identifies the syntax of the user data being transmitted and provides user service functions such as encryption, file-transfer protocols, and terminal emulation.

Primary Rate Interface (PRI) - An ISDN T1 access interface type comprising 23 B-channels each at 64 kbps and one D-channel at 64 kbps (23B+D). The European version will operate at 2.048 Mbps (30B+D).

primary ring - The main ring for PDU transmission in FDDI, and the only attachment for SAS FDDI stations.

private network - A network providing interorganizational connectivity only.

private [automatic] branch exchange (PBX/PABX) - An [automatic] customer-site telephone switch, with some capability to integrate data.

protocol - The rules and guidelines by which information is exchanged and understood between two devices.

protocol data unit (PDU) - The unit of information transferred between communicating peer layer processes.

public data network (PDN) - A network designed to provide data transmission value-added services to the public.

queued arbitrated access - In DQDB, packet-data users contend for access to the bus by queuing their requests; since all of the nodes know the length of the queue and their position in the queue, the access scheme is referred to as distributed queue.

Regional Bell Operating [or Holding] Company (RBOC or RBHC) - One of seven U.S. regional holding companies formed after the divestiture of AT&T (e.g., Ameritech, Southwestern Bell). The RBOCs also manage the 22 BOCs.

remote bridge - A high-throughput bridge which provides remote LAN-WAN connectivity.

ring - A closed-loop, common bus network topology.

router - A LAN/WAN device operating at layers 1 (physical), 2 (data link), and 3 (network) of the OSIRM. Distinguished from a bridge by its capability to switch and route data based upon network protocols such as IP.

secondary ring - In FDDI, the ring that carries data in the opposite direction as the primary ring; primarily used for backup to the primary ring.

section - A transmission facility between a SONET Network Element and regenerator.

segment - In DQDB, the payload (user data) portion of the slot.

segmentation unit - The 44-octet unit of data transfer in DQDB.

self-healing - The ability for a LAN/MAN to reroute traffic around a failed link or network element to provide uninterrupted service.

service - The relationship between protocol entities in the OSIRM, where the service provider (lower-layer protocol) and the service user (higher-layer protocol) communicate through a *data service*.

service access point (SAP) - The access point at a network node or station where the service users access the services offered by the service providers.

service data unit (SDU) - Unit of information transferred across the OSI interface between service provider and service user.

Session Layer (OSI) - Layer 5 of the OSIRM. Provides the establishment and control of user dialogues between adjacent network devices.

shielded twisted pair (STP) - A twisted-pair wire with jacket shielding, used for long distances and less subject to electrical noise and interference than UTP.

simplex - One-way transmission of information on a medium.

single-attachment stations (SAS) - In FDDI, stations which are attached only to a single ring (primary ring).

single-mode fiber (SMF) - 8- to 10-μm core diameter optical fiber with a single propagation path for light; typically used for higher speeds or longer distances (as compared to multimode optical fiber).

slot - The basic unit of transmission on a DQDB bus.

SMDS Interface Protocol (SIP) - The three layers of protocol (similar to the first three layers of the OSIRM) which define the SMDS SNI user information frame structuring, addressing, error control, and overall transport.

SNA - IBM's communications networking architecture.

source routing - A routing scheme where the routing of packets is determined by the source address and route to the destination in the packet header.

station - An addressable logical or physical network entity, capable of transmitting, receiving, or repeating information.

Station Management (SMT) - FDDI station management entity.

Subnetwork - The smaller units of LANs (called LAN segments) which can be more easily managed than the entire LAN/MAN/WAN.

Subscriber-Network Interface (SNI) - A DQDB user access point into the network or MAN switch.

Switched Multimegabit Data Service (SMDS) - A MAN service offered at present over the IEEE DQDB bus.

switched virtual circuit (SVC) - Virtual circuits similar to PVCs, but established on a call-by-call basis.

Synchronous Digital Hierarchy (SDH) - The CCITT original version of a synchronous digital hierarchy; based on optical fiber; called SONET in ANSI parlance.

Synchronous Optical Network (SONET) - A U.S. high-speed, fiber-optic transport standard for a fiber-optic digital hierarchy (speeds range from 51.84 Mbps to 2.4 Gbps).

synchronous transmission - The transmission of frames which are managed through a common clock between transmitter and receiver.

Synchronous Transfer Mode (STM) - The T1 carrier method of assigning time slots as channels within a T1 or E1 circuit.

Synchronous Transport Module level *N* (STM-*N*) -The SDH line rate of *N* STM-1 signals.

Synchronous Transport Signal level *N* (STS-*N*) - SONET transmission signal created with byte interleaving of *N* STS-1 (51.84 Mbps) signals.

Synchronous Transport Signal level *Nc* (STS-*Nc*) - Concatenated SONET synchronous payload envelope.

T1 - A four-wire repeater system; commonly used to refer to a DS1 signal.

T1 carrier - The TDM digital T1 hierarchy used in North America and Japan, with 24 voice channels constituting a single 1.544 Mbps T1 trunk.

T3 - Commonly used to refer to a DS3 signal.

telecommunications - The transmission of voice, video, data, and images through the use of both computers and a communications medium.

Time-division multiplexing (TDM) - The method of aggregating multiple simultaneous transmissions (circuits) over a single high-speed channel by using individual time slots (periods) for each circuit.

time-insensitive - Traffic types whose data is not affected by small delays during transmission. This is also referred to as delay-insensitive.

time-sensitive - Traffic types whose data is affected by small delays during transmission and cannot tolerate this delay (e.g., voice, video, real-time data).

token - A marker that can be held by a station on a Token Ring or bus indicating the station's right to transmit.

Token Ring - A LAN that uses a token-passing access method for bus access and traffic transport between network elements, where bus speeds operate at either 4 or 16 Mbps.

Transmission Control Protocol/Internet Protocol (TCP/IP) - The combination of a network and transport protocol developed by ARPANET for internetworking IP-based networks.

Transport Layer (OSI) - Layer 4 of the OSIRM. Provides for error-free, end-to-end communications between two "host" users across a network.

transport overhead - In SONET, the line and section overhead elements combined.

twisted pair - The basic transmission medium consisting of 22 to 26 American Wire Gauge (AWG) insulated copper wire. TP can be either shielded (STP) or unshielded (UTP).

unshielded twisted pair (UTP) - A twisted-pair wire without the jacket shielding, used for short distances but subject to electrical noise and interference.

user channel - Portion of the SONET channel allocated to the user for maintenance functions.

User-to-Network Interface (UNI) - The point where the user accesses the network.

user-to-user protocols - Protocols that operate between users and are typically transparent to the network, such as file transfer protocols (e.g., FTP).

virtual channel identifier (VCI) - In DQDB, a field within the segment header which determines whether a node is to read, write, or copy the segment payload. In ATM, a field within the cell header that is used to switch virtual channels.

virtual circuit - A virtual connection established through the network from origination to destination, where packets, frames, or cells are routed over the same path for the duration of the call. These connections seem like dedicated paths to the users, but are actually network resources shared by all users. Bandwidth on a virtual circuit is not allocated until it is used.

Virtual Path Identifier (VPI) - In ATM, a field within the cell header that is used to switch virtual paths, defined as groups of virtual channels.

virtual tributary (VT) - An element that transports and switches sub-STS-1 payloads or VT*x* (VT1.5, VT2, VT3, or VT6).

wide area network (WAN) - A network that operates over a large region and commonly uses carrier facilities and services.

window - The concept of establishing an optimum number of frames or packets that can be outstanding (unacknowledged) before more are transmitted. Window protocols include X.25, LAP, TCP/IP, and SDLC.

X.25 - CCITT recommendation of the interface between packet-switched DTE and DCE equipment.

Parts of this glossary were taken from Gary Kessler's book *Metropolitan Area Networks* with the author's permission.

Bibliography

ATM Forum UNI V3.1

Bertsekas, Dmitri, and Gallager, Robert, *Data Networks*, 2nd Ed., Prentice-Hall, Englewood Cliffs, NJ, 1991.

Black, Uyless, *Computer Networks – Protocols, Standards, and Interfaces*, Prentice-Hall, Englewood Cliffs, NJ, 1987.

Black, Uyless, *Data Communications & Distributed Networks*, Reston Publishing Co., Reston, VA, 1987.

Black, Uyless, *Network Management Standards,* 2nd Ed., McGraw-Hill, New York, 1995.

Blyth, W. John, and Blyth, Mary M., *Telecommunications, Concepts, Development, and Management*, Glencoe Publishing Co., Mission Hills, Ca., 1985.

Bracker, Sarch, *Cases in Network Implementation*, Van Nostrand Reinhold, New York, 1995.

Bryce, James Y., *Using ISDN*, QUE Corporation, Indianapolis, IN, 1995.

Chorafas, Dimitris N., *TRP, Handbook on Data Communications & Computer Networks,* 2nd Ed., 1991.

Comer, Douglas E., *Internetworking with TCP/IP,* 2nd Ed. Vol. I-III, Prentice-Hall, Englewood Cliffs, NJ, 1991.

Computer Communications Review, articles, 1990 – 1996.

Coulouris, George F., and Dollimore, Jean, *Distributed Systems*, International Computer Science Series, Addison-Wesley, Reading, MA, 1991.

Data Communications Magazine, articles, 1990 – 1996.

Datapro Information Services Group, *Data Pro Reports on Communications*, McGraw-Hill, New York, 1996.

Dayton, Robert L., *Guide to Integrating Digital Services*, McGraw-Hill, New York, 1989.

Dayton, Robert L., *Telecommunications, The Transmission of Information*, McGraw-Hill, New York, 1991.

Dickie, Mark, *Internetworks*, Van Nostrand Reinhold, New York, 1994.

Dromard, Horlait, and Pujolle, Seret, *Integrated Digital Communications Networks,* Vol. 1, John Wiley & Sons, New York, 1988.

Evans, Washburn, *TCP/IP*, Addison-Wesley, New York, 1993.

Feit, Sidnie, *TCP/IP*, McGraw-Hill, New York, 1993.

Freeman, Roger L., *Telecommunications Systems Engineering,* 2nd Ed., John Wiley & Sons, New York, 1989.

Frieden, Rob, *International Telecommunications Handbook*, Artech House, Norwood, MA, 1996.

Heckard, Christine, *Guide to Frame Relay Networking*, Flatiron Publishing, New York, 1994.

Held, Gilbert, *Digital Networking*, John Wiley & Sons, New York, 1990.

Held, Sarch, *Data Communications,* 3rd Ed., McGraw-Hill, New York, 1995.

Helmers, Scott A., *Data Communications*, Prentice-Hall, Englewood Cliffs, NJ, 1989.

IEEE Communications Magazine, articles 1990 – 1996.

IEEE Std 802.6-1990, *Local and Metropolitan Area Networks – 802.6*, IEEE, New York, 1991.

Kessler, Gary C., *ISDN*, McGraw-Hill, New York, 1990.

Kessler, Gary C., and Train, David A., *Metropolitan Area Networks, Concepts, Standards, & Services*, McGraw-Hill, Inc., New York, 1992.

Kim, B. G., *LANs, MANs, & ISDN*, Artech House, Norwood, MA, 1989.

Klessig, Tesink, *SMDS*, Prentice-Hall, Englewood Cliffs, NJ, 1995.

Knightson, Keith G., Knowles, Terry, and Larmouth, John, *Standards for Open Systems Interconnection*, McGraw-Hill, New York, 1988.

LAN Magazine, articles 1990-1996.

LAN Times, articles, 1990-1996.

McClimans, Fred J., *Communications Wiring and Interconnection*, McGraw-Hill, New York, 1992.

McDysan, David E., Spohn, Darren L., *ATM Theory and Application*, McGraw-Hill, New York, 1995.

Metropolitan Area Networks, Siemens Stromberg- Carlson, Boca Raton, FL, 1991.

Minoli, Daniel, *Telecommunications Technology Handbook*, Artech House, Norwood, MA, 1991.

Netrix books

Network World, articles, 1990 – 1996.

Potts, William F., *McGraw-Hill Data Communications Dictionary*, McGraw-Hill, New York, 1993.

Powers, John T., and Stair II, Henry H., *Megabit Data Communications, A Guide for Professionals*, Prentice-Hall, Englewood Cliffs, NJ, 1990.

Ranade, Jay, and Sackett, George C., *Introduction to SNA Networking,* 2nd Ed., McGraw-Hill, New York, 1995.

Rose, M. T., *The Simple Book: An Introduction to Management of TCP/IP-based Internets*, Prentice-Hall, Englewood Cliffs, NJ, 1991.

Rosner, Roy D., *Packet Switching*, Van Nostrand Reinhold, New York, 1982.

Schwartz, Mischa, *Computer-Communications Network Design and Analysis*, Prentice-Hall, Englewood Cliffs, NJ, 1977.

Schwartz, Mischa, *Telecommunications Networks*, Addison-Wesley, Reading, MA, 1987.

Sherman, Kenneth, *Data Communications,* 2nd Ed., Reston Publishing Co., Reston, VA, 1985.

Spragins, John D., *Telecommunications: Protocols and Design*, Addison-Wesley, New York, 1991.

Stallings, William, *Data and Computer Communications,* 3rd Ed., Macmillan, New York, 1991.

Stallings, William, *Handbook of Computer Communications Standards,* Vols. 1 and 2, Howard W. Sams & Company, Indianapolis, IN, 1987.

Tannenbaum, A. S., *Computer Networks,* 2nd Ed., Prentice-Hall, Englewood Cliffs, NJ, 1988.

Telecommunications Magazine, articles, 1993 – 1996.

Tittel, Robbins, *Network Design Essentials*, Academic Press, Cambridge, MA, 1994.

US Sprint, *US Sprint Frame Relay Service Interface Specification,* Document No. 5136.03, July 12, 1991.

Williams, Gerald E., *Digital Technology*, Science Research Assoc., Inc., Chicago, 1982.

Index

ABOUT THE AUTHOR

Darren L. Spohn is Chief Technology Officer at NetSolve Inc. in Austin, Texas, where he manages engineering, operations, and product development. Mr. Spohn formerly held engineering and marketing management positions with MCI, and is coauthor (with David E. McDysan) of the best-selling *ATM: Theory and Application*, published by McGraw-Hill.